The Good Food Guide 2001

WHICH? BOOKS

Which? Books is the book publishing arm of Consumers' Association, which was set up in 1957 to improve the standards of goods and services available to the public. Everything Which? publishes aims to help consumers, by giving them the independent information they need to make informed decisions. These publications, known throughout Britain for their quality, integrity and impartiality, have been held in high regard for four decades.

Independence does not come cheap: the guides carry no advertising, and no restaurant or hotel can buy an entry in our guides, or treat our inspectors to free meals or accommodation. This policy, and our practice of rigorously re-researching our guides for each edition, helps us to provide our readers with information of a standard and quality that cannot be surpassed.

The Good Food Guide 2001

Edited by

Jim Ainsworth

CONSUMERS' ASSOCIATION

Which? Books are commissioned and researched by
Consumers' Association and published by
Which? Ltd, 2 Marylebone Road,
London NW1 4DF

Distributed by The Penguin Group:
Penguin Books Ltd, 27 Wrights Lane,
London W8 5TZ

British Library Cataloguing in Publication Data
A catalogue record for this book is
available from the British Library

ISBN 0 85202 820 2

For a full list of Which? books, please write to:
Which? Books, Castlemead, Gascoyne Way,
Hertford X, SG14 1LH
or access our web site at http://www.which.net

Photoset by Tradespools Ltd, Frome, Somerset
Printed in England by Clays Ltd, St Ives plc

Cover design by Price Watkins Design Limited

Contents

Maps centre of book
How to use the Guide 7
Lists
The top-rated restaurants 11
Restaurants with outstanding wine cellars 12
Restaurants of the year 13
The Guide's longest-serving restaurants 14
New entries 15
London restaurants by cuisine 16
London party bookings 17
London restaurants with no-smoking rooms 17
Budget eating 18
Restaurants charging 15 per cent for service 19
Introduction 21

Features

Pardon my French David Wolfe 27
Glossary 29
A beautiful friendship Fergus Henderson 33
Your rights in restaurants 36

Main entries

London 39
England 217
Scotland 527
Wales 593
Channel Islands 629
Northern Ireland 633
Republic of Ireland 641

Round-ups
London 197
England 665
Scotland 693
Wales 698
Channel Islands 701
Northern Ireland 701

The Good Food Club 2000 703
Index 711
Report forms 729

The *Good Food Guide* voucher scheme (£5)

Again this year the Guide includes three £5 vouchers that readers will be able to redeem against the price of meals taken in participating restaurants. (Look for the (£5) symbol at the very end of entries to locate those participating.) Only one voucher may be used per booked table, for a minimum of two people. Remember that your intention to use the voucher MUST be mentioned at the time of booking. Some restaurants may restrict use of the voucher at some sessions or for some menus (usually 'special offer' or lower-cost set meals); it is best to ask when booking. Actual vouchers (not photocopies) must be presented. The vouchers will be valid from 1 October 2000 to 30 September 2001, and may not be used in conjunction with any other offers.

The Guide online

Internet users can find *The Good Food Guide* online at the Which? Online web site http://www.which.net. (You will need to be a Which? Online subscriber to make full use of the Guide online.) For a free CD that will give you more details about Which? Online and how to be connected to the Internet, phone 0645 830254.

Update service

Written details of restaurant sales, closures, chef changes and so on since this edition of the Guide was published will be available free of charge from 1 December 2000 to 1 May 2001. Readers should write to: FREEPOST, Update, *The Good Food Guide*, 2 Marylebone Road, London NW1 4DF (no stamp is required if you post your request in the UK). Alternatively, you may email *goodfoodguide@which.net* (remember to include your full name and address when you email), or phone 020-7770 7551. As always, readers who send in reports on meals will automatically be sent an Update Sheet.

How to use the Guide

FINDING A RESTAURANT

If you are seeking a restaurant in a particular area: *first go to the maps* at the centre of the book. Once you know the locality (or, for London, the restaurant name), go to the relevant section of the book to find the entry for the restaurant. The Guide's main entries are divided into seven sections: London, England, Scotland, Wales, Channel Islands, Northern Ireland, and Republic of Ireland. In the London section, restaurants are listed alphabetically by name; in all other sections, they are listed by locality (usually the name of the town or village).

In addition to the main entries are the Round-ups (a range of restaurants, cafés, bistros and pubs that are worth a visit but do not merit a full entry): those for London can be found just after the London main-entry section, and those for everywhere else are towards the back of the book just after the Republic of Ireland main-entry section.

If you know the name of the restaurant: *go to the index* at the back of the book, which lists both main and Round-up entries.

If you are seeking award-winning restaurants, those offering a particular cuisine, etc.: *make use of the lists* starting on page 11, which feature the top-rated restaurants, restaurants with outstanding wine cellars, restaurants of the year, new entries in the Guide, London restaurants by cuisine, budget eating and other helpful groupings.

HOW TO READ A GUIDE *ENTRY*

A sample entry is set out overleaf. At the top of the entry you will find the restaurant's name, map number, address, telephone and fax numbers, its email address and web site address if it has these, as well as any symbols that may apply to the establishment, (see inside front cover for what the symbols stand for). New this year is a brief description of the style of cuisine offered; this is not meant to be a comprehensive assessment of cooking style, but rather to act as a helpful pointer and in many cases has been suggested by the restaurant itself. At the top of entries you will also find the mark, from 1 to 10, awarded by the editor for cooking (see next page for a full explanation of marks), and the cost range for one person having a three-course meal including wine (see page 9 for how that is worked out). The middle part of the entry describes food, wines, atmosphere and so on, while the final section gives a wealth of additional information (explained in greater detail on pages 9-10).

LOCALITY County map 4

▲ Restaurant Name  £ **NEW ENTRY**

Address
TEL: (01234) 111111 FAX: (01234) 222222 COOKING **6**
EMAIL: restaurant@place.co.uk MODERN BRITISH
WEB SITE: www.restaurant.co.uk £15 to £100

This is where you will find information about the restaurant – cuisine, service, décor, wine list, and any other points of interest not covered by the details at the foot of the entry. Each entry in the Guide has been re-researched from scratch, and is based on information taken from readers' reports received over the past year, confirmed where necessary by anonymous inspection. In every case, readers and inspectors have been prepared to endorse the quality of the cooking. The text usually concludes with a description of the wines offered.

CHEFS: : John and Mary Smith PROPRIETOR: : Mary Smith OPEN: : Mon to Fri L 12 to 2, Mon to Sat D 7 to 10 CLOSED: : 25 and 26 Dec, Easter, 2 weeks July, bank hols MEALS: : alc (main courses £9 to £15). Set D £16 (2 courses) to £20. Cover £1.50. Light L available. SERVICE: : not inc, card slips closed; 10% for parties of 6 or more CARDS: : Amex, Delta, Diners, MasterCard, Switch, Visa DETAILS: : 50 seats. 15 seats outside. Private parties: 25 main room, 15 private room. Car park. Vegetarian meals. Children's helpings. No children under 7. Jacket and tie. No smoking in dining-room. Wheelchair access (also WC). No music. Air-conditioned ACCOMMODATION: : 5 rooms, all with bath/shower. TV. Phone. B&B £35 to £80. Rooms for disabled. Baby facilities. Swimming pool. (*The Which? Hotel Guide*) ⊖ (£5)

• For an explanation of symbols, see inside front cover.

Cooking mark

Marks are given out of 10, and are for cooking only, as perceived by the *Guide* and its readers. They signify the following:

1–2 COMPETENT COOKING Cafés, pubs, bistros and restaurants which offer sound, basic, capable cooking. Those scoring 2 use better ingredients, take fewer short-cuts, please more reporters, and make good neighbourhood restaurants.

3–4 COMPETENT TO GOOD COOKING These restaurants use fine ingredients and cook them appropriately, although some inconsistencies may be noted. They please reporters most of the time. Those scoring 4 show greater skill in handling materials, and are worthy of special note in the locality.

5–6 GOOD TO VERY GOOD COOKING These restaurants use high-quality ingredients, achieve consistently good results, and are enthusiastically reported. Those scoring 6 show a degree of flair, and are among the best in the region.

7–8 VERY GOOD TO EXCELLENT COOKING A high level of ambition and achievement means that the finest ingredients are consistently treated with skill and imagination. Those scoring 8 are worth a special effort to visit.

9–10 THE BEST These are the top restaurants in the country. They are few in number, and can be expensive, but are highly individual and display impressive artistry. Those scoring 10 are the A-team, and can comfortably stand comparison with the stiffest international competition.

Cost

The price range given is based on the cost of a three-course meal (lunch and/or dinner) for one person, including coffee, house wine, service and cover charge where applicable, according to information supplied by the restaurant. The lower figure is the least you are likely to pay, from either à la carte or set-price menus, and may apply only to lunch. The higher figure indicates a probable maximum cost, sometimes based on a set-price meal of more than three courses, if that is what is offered. This figure is inflated by 20 per cent to reflect the fact that some people may order more expensive wine, extra drinks and some higher-priced 'special' dishes, and that price rises may come into effect during the life-time of this edition of the Guide.

Meals

At the bottom of entries information on the types of meals offered is given, with any variations for lunch (L) and dinner (D), and details of availability. An à la carte menu is signified by the letters *alc*. This is followed by a range of prices for main courses, rounded up to the nearest 50p. *Set L* denotes a set-price lunch; *Set D* means set-price dinner. Set meals usually consist of three courses, but can include many more. If a set meal has fewer than three courses, this is stated. If there is a cover charge, this is also indicated. Brief details of other menus, such as light lunch or bar snacks, are also given. If there is a cover charge, that is also mentioned here.

Service

Net prices means that prices of food and wine are inclusive of service charge, and this is indicated clearly on the menu and bill; *not inc*, that service is not included and is left to the discretion of the customer; *10%*, that a fixed service charge of 10 per cent is automatically added to the bill; *10% (optional)*, that 10 per cent is added to the bill along with the word 'optional' or similar qualifier; and *none*, that no service charge is made or expected and that any money offered is refused. *Card slips closed* indicates that the total on the slips of credit cards is closed when handed over for signature.

Other details

Information is also given on *seating, outside seating* and *private parties*. We say *car park* if the restaurant provides free parking facilities for patrons (*small car park* if it has only a few spaces), and say *vegetarian meals* only if menus list at least one vegetarian option as a starter and one as a main course (if this is not noted, a restaurant may still be able to offer vegetarian options with prior notice – it is worth phoning to check). Any restrictions on children are given, such as *no children* or *no children under 6 after 8pm;* otherwise, it can be assumed that children are welcome. In addition, *children's helpings* are noted if smaller portions are available at a reduced price; *jacket and tie* if it is compulsory for men to wear a jacket and tie to the restaurant; *wheelchair access* if the proprietor has confirmed that the entrance is at least 80cm wide and passages at least 120cm wide in accordance with the Royal Association for Disability and Rehabilitation (RADAR) recommendations, and *also WC* if the proprietor has assured us that toilet facilities are suitable for disabled people (*not WC* means these are not available or the proprietor is not sure). *Music* indicates that live or recorded music is usually played in the dining-room; *occasional music* that it sometimes is; *no music* that it never is.

Accommodation

For establishments offering overnight accommodation, the number of rooms, along with facilities provided in the rooms (e.g. bath/shower, TV, phone), is set out. Prices are given usually for bed and breakfast (*B&B*). *D,B&B* indicates that the price also includes dinner. The first figure given is the lowest price for one person in a single room, or single occupancy of a double, the second is the most expensive price for two people in a double room or suite. *Rooms for disabled* means the establishment has stated that its accommodation is suitable for wheelchair-users. Restrictions on children, and facilities for guests with babies, are indicated. *The Which? Hotel Guide* means the establishment is also listed in the 2001 edition of our sister guide to over 1,000 hotels in Britain.

Miscellaneous information

At the end of London entries, the nearest Underground station is given after the symbol ⊖. For restaurants that have elected to participate in the *Good Food Guide* £5 voucher scheme, a (£5) symbol appears at the very end of entries (see page 6 for further details).

The top-rated restaurants

(See pages 8–9 for explanation of marking system.)

Mark **9** for cooking

London

Gordon Ramsay, SW3

England

Le Manoir aux Quat' Saisons, Great Milton
Winteringham Fields, Winteringham

Scotland

Altnaharrie Inn, Ullapool

Mark **8** for cooking

London

cheznico, W1
John Burton-Race at the Landmark, NW1
Pied-à-Terre, W1
The Square, W1
La Tante Claire, SW1

England

Box Tree, Ilkley
Croque-en-Bouche, Malvern Wells
Fat Duck, Bray
Fischer's Baslow Hall, Baslow
Gidleigh Park, Chagford
Hambleton Hall, Hambleton
Merchant House, Ludlow
Waterside Inn, Bray

Restaurants with outstanding wine cellars

marked in the text with a 🍷

London

Bibendum, SW3
Bleeding Heart, EC1
Cambio de Tercio, SW5
Chez Bruce, SW17
Clarke's, W8
Fifth Floor, SW1
John Burton-Race at the Landmark, NW1
Odette's, NW1
Oxo Tower Restaurant, SE1
Pied-à-Terre, W1
Ransome's Dock, SW11
RSJ, SE1
The Square, W1
Tate Gallery Restaurant, SW1

England

Bowness-on-Windermere, Porthole Eating House
Bray, Fat Duck
Bristol, Hotel du Vin & Bistro
Bristol, Markwicks
Chagford, Gidleigh Park
Chinnor, Sir Charles Napier
Corse Lawn, Corse Lawn House
Dedham, Le Talbooth
East Grinstead, Gravetye Manor
Epworth, Epworth Tap
Evershot, Summer Lodge
Faversham, Read's
Grasmere, Michael's Nook
Grasmere, White Moss House
Great Milton, Le Manoir aux Quat' Saisons
Hambleton, Hambleton Hall
Hastings, Röser's
Hetton, Angel Inn
Horton, French Partridge
Huntingdon, Old Bridge Hotel
Ilkley, Box Tree
Keyston, Pheasant Inn
Leeds, Leodis
Leeds, Sous le Nez en Ville
Lewdown, Lewtrenchard Manor
Little Shelford, Sycamore House
Lyndhurst, Le Poussin at Parkhill
Madingley, Three Horseshoes
Malvern Wells, Croque-en-Bouche
Middleham, Waterford House
Moulton, Black Bull Inn
Newton Longville, Crooked Billet
Norwich, Adlard's
Oxford, Cherwell Boathouse
Padstow, Seafood Restaurant
Ramsbottom, Ramsons Restaurant and Café Bar
Romsey, Old Manor House
Ross-on-Wye, Le Faisan Doré (and Pheasants Too)
Shepton Mallet, Bowlish House
Southwold, Crown Hotel
Stockcross, Vineyard at Stockcross
Tunbridge Wells, Hotel du Vin & Bistro
Ullswater, Sharrow Bay
Wareham, Priory Hotel
Waterhouses, Old Beams
Williton, White House
Winchester, Hotel du Vin & Bistro
Worfield, Old Vicarage Hotel

Scotland

Achiltibuie, Summer Isles Hotel
Anstruther, Cellar
Dunkeld, Kinnaird
Edinburgh, Valvona & Crolla Caffè Bar
Fort William, Inverlochy Castle
Glasgow, Ubiquitous Chip
Gullane, Greywalls
Kingussie, The Cross
Linlithgow, Champany Inn
Nairn, Clifton House
Peat Inn, Peat Inn
Port Appin, Airds Hotel
Ullapool, Altnaharrie Inn

Wales

Aberdovey, Penhelig Arms Hotel
Llandewi Skirrid, Walnut Tree Inn
Llandudno, St Tudno Hotel
Llansanffraid Glan Conwy, Old Rectory
Portmeirion, Hotel Portmeirion
Pwllheli, Plas Bodegroes
Reynoldston, Fairyhill
Talsarnau, Maes-y-Neuadd

Republic of Ireland

Dublin, Le Coq Hardi
Dublin, Thornton's
Howth, King Sitric
Kenmare, Park Hotel Kenmare
Kenmare, Sheen Falls Lodge, La Cascade
Newport, Newport House

Restaurants of the year

This award does not necessarily go to the restaurants with the highest mark for cooking, but rather to ones which have shown particular merit or achievement during the year. It may go to an old favourite or to a new entry, but in either case the places listed below are worth visiting in their own right, and have enhanced the eating-out experience in some way. The listings have been simplified this year to overall Chef of the year; Restaurants of the year; Newcomers of the year; and Commended. Although we have looked at all geographical areas, not all have been lucky enough to have such special achievers.

CHEF OF THE YEAR

Heston Blumenthal at the Fat Duck, Bray, England

RESTAURANTS OF THE YEAR

England

Lords of the Manor, Upper Slaughter
Yorke Arms, Ramsgill

Scotland

Restaurant Martin Wishart, Edinburgh

Wales

Carlton House, Llanwrtyd Wells

NEWCOMERS OF THE YEAR

England

Castle House, Hereford
Magenta's, Carlisle
Michael Caines at Royal Clarence, Exeter
60 Hope Street, Liverpool

Wales

Le Gallois, Cardiff

COMMENDED

London

Anglesea Arms House
Mandarin Oriental, Foliage
National Gallery, Crivelli's Garden
Ozer
Real Greek
Sheekey's
Time

England

Brasserie Forty Four, Leeds
Castle, Hurst
Chavignol, Chipping Norton
Churchill Arms, Paxford
Devonshire Arms, Burlington Restaurant, Bolton Abbey
Glass House, Ambleside
Hart's, Nottingham
Horton Grange, Seaton Burn
Howard's House, Teffont Evias
Lemon Tree, Oxford
Little Barwick House, Barwick
Sandgate, Sandgate Hotel
Simpson's, Kenilworth
Three Lions, Stuckton
Yang Sing, Manchester

Scotland

Airds Hotel, Port Appin
Darroch Learg, Ballater
Kilcamb Lodge, Strontian
Three Chimneys, Colbost

Wales

Tyddyn Llan, Llandrillo
Ye Olde Bulls Head, Beaumaris

The *Guide's* longest-serving restaurants

The Guide has seen many restaurants come and go. Some, however, have stayed the course with tenacity. (Qualification for this list is that the restaurant has been in each edition of the Guide subsequent to its first entry.)

Connaught, W1	48 years
Gay Hussar, W1	44 years
Gravetye Manor, East Grinstead	44 years
Porth Tocyn Hotel, Abersoch	44 years
Sharrow Bay, Ullswater	40 years
French Partridge, Horton	36 years
Walnut Tree Inn, Llandewi Skirrid	36 years
Black Bull Inn, Moulton	34 years
Chez Moi, W11	32 years
Rothay Manor, Ambleside	32 years
Sundial, Herstmonceux	32 years
Le Gavroche, W1	31 years
Sumer Isles Hotel, Achiltibuie	31 years
The Capital, SW3	30 years
Miller Howe, Windermere	30 years
Cringletie House, Peebles	29 years
Old Fire Engine House, Ely	29 years
Ubiquitous Chip, Glasgow	29 years
Druidstone, Broad Haven	28 years
Peat Inn, Peat Inn	28 years
Plumber Manor, Sturminster Newton	28 years
Waterside Inn, Bray	28 years
White Moss House, Grasmere	28 years
Carved Angel, Dartmouth	27 years
Isle of Eriska, Eriska	27 years
Airds, Port Appin	25 years
Farlam Hall, Brampton	24 years
Langan's Brasserie, W1	24 years
Corse Lawn House, Corse Lawn	23 years
Croque-en-Bouche, Malvern Wells	23 years
Gidleigh Park, Chagford	23 years
White House, Williton	23 years
Food for Thought, Fowey	22 years
Hambleton Hall, Hambleton	22 years
Hunstrete House, Hunstrete	22 years
Priory Hotel, Wareham	22 years
Sabras, NW10	22 years
The Pier at Harwich, Harwich	22 years
Brown's, Worcester	21 years
Cherwell Boathouse, Oxford	21 years
Grafton Manor, Bromsgrove	21 years
Harveys, Bristol	21 years
Langley House Hotel, Langley Marsh	21 years
Magpie Café, Whitby	21 years

New entries

These restaurants are new main entries in the Guide this year, although some may have appeared in previous years, or in the Round-ups last year.

London

Admiral Codrington, SW3
Admiralty, WC2
a.k.a., WC1
Al Duca, SW1
Azou, W6
Belvedere, W8
Bleeding Heart, EC1
Cantina Vinopolis, SE1
China House, Orient, W1
Clock, W7
Le Colombier, SW3
Cotto, W14
Cow Dining Room, W2
Creelers, SW3
Depot, SW14
Ditto, SW18
English Garden, SW3
Il Forno, W1
Great Eastern Hotel, Aurora, EC2
Holly, SE15
House, SW3
Incognico, WC2
Isola, SW1
JaK's, SW1
John Burton-Race at the Landmark, NW1
Justin de Blank, SW1
Kennington Lane, SE11
Kiku, W1
K10, EC2
Lavender, SW11 and SW9
Light House, SW19
Little Georgia, E8
Mela, WC2
Metrogusto, SW8
National Gallery, Crivelli's Garden, WC2
National Portrait Gallery, Portrait, WC2
New End, NW3
Noble Rot, W1
Ozer, W1
Parade, W5
Popeseye, W14
Porte des Indes, W1
Prospect Grill, WC2
Radha Krishna Bhavan, SW17
Real Greek, N1
Riso, W4
Ritz, W1
Rosmarino, NW8
Salisbury Tavern, SW6
Salusbury, NW6
Schnecke, W1
Soviet Canteen, SW10
Tas, SE1
Time, SE10
Utah, SW19
Waterloo Bar and Kitchen, SE1
William IV, NW10

England

Ashford, Riverside House
Beer, Old Steam Bakery
Beeston, La Toque
Birmingham, Bank
Birmingham, Le Petit Blanc
Birmingham, Swallow Hotel, Sir Edward Elgar
Boston Spa, Spice Box
Brighton & Hove, La Fourchette
Bristol, Hotel du Vin & Bistro
Bristol, Severnshed
Burnham Market, Hoste Arms
Burnsall, Devonshire Fell
Bushey, St James
Campsea Ashe, Old Rectory
Carlisle, Magenta's
Dartmouth, Gunfield
Eaton Bishop, Ancient Camp Inn
Elland, Bertie's Supper Rooms
Exeter, Brazz
Exeter, Michael Caines at Royal Clarence
Funtington, Hallidays
Gateforth, Restaurant Martel
Gittisham, Combe House
Hereford, Castle House
Holt, Tollgate Inn
Huntingdon, Old Bridge
Hurst, Castle
Kendal, Georgian House
Leverton, Old Barn
Liverpool, Shangri La
Liverpool, 60 Hope Street
Llanfair Waterdine, Waterdine
Looe, Trawlers
Ludlow, Hibiscus
Lyndhurst, Le Poussin at Parkhill
Maidstone, Le Soufflé
Manchester, Greens
Manchester, Ocean Treasure
Manchester, Pacific
Manchester, Steven Saunders at the Lowry
Matfen, Matfen Hall
Midhurst, Angel Hotel
Milford on Sea, Rouille
Nantwich, Peppers
Nayland, White Hart
Nether Alderley, The Wizard
Newbury, Newbury Manor, Sharlands
Newton Longville, Crooked Billet
Nottingham, Sonny's
Orford, Crown and Castle, Trinity
Padstow, No. 6 Art & Seafood Café
Painswick, Painswick Hotel
Petworth, Soanes Restaurant
St Ives, Porthminster Beach Café
St Mawes, Rising Sun
Stoke Bruerne, Bruerne's Lock
Stratford-upon-Avon, Boathouse
Stratford-upon-Avon, Desport's
Surbiton, Luca
Todmorden, Old Hall
Waldley, Beeches
Warwick, Cellar
Welwyn Garden City, Auberge du Lac

Scotland

Achnasheen, Loch Torridon
Clachan-Seil, Willowburn
Edinburgh, Rhodes & Co
Fairlie, Fins
Glasgow, Arthouse Hotel, Arthouse Grill
Glasgow, Eurasia
Glasgow, Number Sixteen
Inverkeilor, Gordon's
Kilchrenan, Taychreggan
St Andrews, West Port

Wales

Cardiff, Le Gallois
Hawarden, The Brasserie

Northern Ireland

Belfast, Cayenne

Republic of Ireland

Dublin, Jacob's Ladder
Lisdoonvarna, Ballinalacken Castle

London restaurants by cuisine

Boundaries between some national cuisines – British, French and Italian particularly – are not as marked as they used to be. Therefore, the restaurants listed below are classified by the predominant influence, although there may be some crossover.(These headings are in many cases more generalised than the brief cuisine descriptions given in the entries themselves.)

American
Bradleys, NW3
Cactus Blue, SW3
Christopher's, WC2
Dakota, W11
Montana, SW6
Prospect Grill, WC2
Utah, SW19

Belgian
Belgo Noord, NW1

British
City Rhodes, EC4
Connaught, W1
French House Dining Room, W1
Greenhouse, W1
JaK's, SW1
Justin de Blank, SW1
Popeseye, W14
Quality Chop House, EC1
Rhodes in the Square, SW1
Rules, WC2
St John, EC1
Tate Gallery Restaurant, SW1
Wilsons, W14
Wiltons, SW1

Chinese
Aroma II, W1
Cheng-Du, NW1
China House, Orient, W1
Four Seasons, W2
Fung Shing, WC2
Golden Dragon, W1
Mandarin Kitchen, W2
Mr Kong, WC2
Royal China, W1, W2 and NW8

Danish
Lundum's, SW7

Fish
Back to Basics, W1
Brady's, SW18
Fish!, SE1
Livebait, SE1
Livebait's Café Fish, SW1
Lobster Pot, SE11
Lou Pescadou, SW5
Offshore, W11
One-O-One, SW1
Sheekey's, WC2
Two Brothers, N3

French
Admiralty, WC2
Amandier, W2
Aubergine, SW10
Bleeding Heart, EC1
Brasserie St Quentin, SW3
Le Chardon, SE22
cheznico, W1
Club Gascon, EC1
Le Colombier, SW3
Le Coq d'Argent, EC2
Criterion Brasserie MPW, W1
L'Estaminet, WC2
Le Gavroche, W1
Gordon Ramsay, SW3
Inter-Continental Hotel, Le Soufflé, W1
John Burton-Race at the Landmark, NW1
Mirabelle, W1
Mon Plaisir, WC2
Oak Room Marco Pierre White, W1
L'Oranger, SW1
Pétrus, SW1
Pied-à-Terre, W1
Ritz, W1
Roussillon, SW1
Spread Eagle, SE10
La Tante Claire, SW1

Greek
Real Greek, N1

Hungarian
Gay Hussar, W1

Indian/Pakistani
Babur Brasserie, SE23
Café Spice Namaste, E1 and SW11
Chor Bizarre, W1
Chutney Mary, SW10
Mela, WC2
Mem Saheb, E14
New Tayyabs, E1
Old Delhi, W2
Porte des Indes, W1
Radha Krishna Bhavan, SW17
Sarkhel's, SW18
Salloos, SW1
Soho Spice, W1
Tamarind, W1
Zaika, SW3

Indian vegetarian
Kastoori, SW17
Rani, N3
Rasa, N16 and Rasa W1
Sabras, NW10

Indonesian/ Straits
Gourmet Garden, NW4
Singapore Garden, NW6

Italian
Al Duca, SW1
Al San Vincenzo, W2
Arancia, SE16
Assaggi, W2
Del Buongustaio, SW15
Il Forno, W1
Great Eastern Dining Room, EC2
Green Olive, W9
Halkin Hotel, SW1
Ibla, W1
Isola, SW1
Metrogusto, SW8
Neal Street Restaurant, WC2
Olivo, SW11
Osteria Antica Bologna, SW11
Passione, W1
Purple Sage, W1
Red Pepper, W9
Riso, W4
Riva, SW13
River Café, W6
Rosmarino, NW8
Salusbury, NW6
Sartoria, W1
Spiga, W1
Teca, W1
Zafferano, SW1

Japanese/sushi bars
Asakusa, NW1
Café Japan, NW11
Kiku, W1
K10, EC2
Kulu Kulu Sushi, W1
Matsuri, SW1
Miyama, W1
Moshi Moshi Sushi, EC2, EC4 and E14
Nobu, W1
Sushi-Say, NW2
Wagamama, WC1

Mauritian
Chez Liline, N4

North African/ Middle Eastern
Adams Café, W12
Al Bustan, SW1
Al Hamra, W1
Azou, W6
Istanbul Iskembecisi, N16
Iznik, N5
Laurent, NW2
Tajine, W1
Tas, SE1

Peruvian
Fina Estampa, SE1

Russian/Eurasian
Little Georgia, E8
Soviet Canteen, SW10

Spanish
Cambio de Tercio, SW5
Gaudí, EC1
Lomo, SW10
Moro, EC1

Thai
Blue Elephant, SW6
Mantanah, SE25
Sri Siam Soho, W1
Thai Garden, E2

London party bookings for 25 or more in private rooms

Alastair Little, W1
Aroma II, W1
Asakusa, NW1
Bali Sugar, W11
Bleeding Heart, EC1
Bluebird, SW3
Cactus Blue, SW3
Café Spice Namaste (Prescot Street), E1
Cantina Vinopolis, SE1
Chinon, W14
Chor Bizarre, W1
Chutney Mary, SW10
Le Colombier, SW3
Cotto, W14
Delfina Studio Café, SE1
Del Buongustaio, SW15
Depot, SW14
L'Escargot, W1
First Floor, W11
Fung Shing, WC2
Gaudí, EC1
Globe Restaurant, SE1
Golden Dragon, W1
Grano, W4
Great Eastern Dining Room, EC2
Halkin Hotel, SW1
Ivy, WC2
Kensington Place, W8
Lanesborough, The Conservatory, SW1
Launceston Place, W8
Lavender (Clapham Road), SW11
Lindsay House, W1
Lobster Pot, SE11
Maison Novelli, EC1
Mandarin Oriental Hyde Park, Foliage, SW1
Mela, WC2
Mem Saheb, E14
Mezzo, W1
Mirabelle, W1
Montcalm Hotel, Crescent, W1
Oak Room Marco Pierre White, W1
Odette's, NW1
Offshore, W11
1 Lombard Street, EC3
Parade, W5
Prism, EC3
Purple Sage, W1
Quo Vadis, W1
Ritz, W1
Roussillon, SW1
RSJ, SE1
Salt House, NW8
Schnecke, W1
Searcy's, EC2
Soho Soho, W1
Soho Spice, W1
Spread Eagle, SE10
Sri Siam Soho, W1
Tentazioni, SE1
William IV, NW10

London restaurants with a no-smoking policy

Admiralty, WC2
Babur Brasserie, SE23
Bali Sugar, W11
Cactus Blue, SW3
Cantina Vinopolis, SE1
cheznico, W1
Clarke's, W8
Creelers, SW3
Depot, SW14
L'Estaminet, WC2
Gaudī, EC1
Gresslin's, NW3
Itsu, SW3
JaK's, SW1
K10, EC2
Kulu Kulu Sushi, W1
Light House, SW19
Lindsay House, W1
Livebait, SE1
Livebait's Café Fish, W1
Mem Saheb, E14
Moshi Moshi Sushi, EC2, EC4 and E14
National Gallery, Crivelli's Garden, WC2
National Portrait Gallery, Portrait, WC2
Nobu, W1
Offshore, W11
Rasa/Rasa W1, N16 and W1
Rosmarino, NW8
Rules, WC2
Sarkhel's, SW18
Sugar Club, W1
Tajine, W1
Thai Garden, E2
Villandry, W1
Wagamama, WC1

Budget eating £

At the restaurants below, it is possible to have a three-course meal, including coffee, half a bottle of wine and service, for £25 or less per person, at any time the restaurant is open, i.e. at dinner as well as lunch. It may be possible to spend considerably more than this, but by choosing carefully you should find £25 or less achievable.

London

Adams Café, W12
Anglesea Arms, W6
Arancia, SE16
Aroma II, W1
Asakusa, NW1
Azou, W6
Back to Basics, W1
Brady's, SW18
Café Japan, NW11
Eagle, EC1
Il Forno, W1
Four Seasons, W2
Gourmet Garden, NW4
Istanbul Iskembecisi, N16
Itsu, SW3
Kastoori, SW17
Kiku, W1
Kulu Kulu Sushi, W1
Laurent, NW2
Lavender, SW11 and SW9
Little Georgia, E8
Lomo, SW10
Mantanah, SE25
Mem Saheb, E14
Mesclun, N16
Mr Kong, WC2
Moshi Moshi Sushi, EC2, EC4 and E14
New Tayyabs, E1
Osteria Antica Bologna, SW11
Radha Krishna Bhavan, SW17
Rani, N3
Rasa/Rasa W1, N16 and W1
Red Pepper, W9
Saigon Thuy, SW18
Soviet Canteen, SW10
Sri Siam Soho, W1
Tas, SE1
Thai Garden, E2
Wagamama, WC1

England

Aldeburgh, Lighthouse
Aldeburgh, Regatta
Bath, Richmond Arms
Beverley, Wednesdays
Bishop's Waltham, Wine Bar
Boston Spa, Spice Box
Buckland, Lamb at Buckland
Burnham Market, Hoste Arms
Carterway Heads, Manor House Inn
Cockermouth, Quince & Medlar
Corscombe, Fox Inn
Dargate, Dove
Dartmouth, Carved Angel Café
Elland, Bertie's Supper Rooms
Exeter, Brazz
Foss Cross, Hare & Hounds
Foulsham, The Gamp
Great Yeldham, White Hart
Harrogate, Drum and Monkey
Hexham, Hexham Royal Hotel
Huddersfield, Bradley's
Ilkley, Farsyde
Lavenham, Angel
Leeds, Salvo's
Liverpool, Far East
Liverpool, Shangri La
Liverpool, Tai Pan
Liverpool, Ziba
Ludlow, Courtyard
Manchester, Chiang Rai
Manchester, Greens
Manchester, Koreana
Manchester, Kosmos Taverna
Manchester, Ocean Treasure
Manchester, Tai Pan
Manchester, Yang Sing
Manningtree, Stour Bay Café
Masham, Floodlite
Nantwich, Peppers
Newcastle upon Tyne, Metropolitan
Orford, Crown and Castle, Trinity
Oxford, Al-Shami
Paxford, Churchill Arms
Ponteland, Café 21
Ramsbottom, Ramsons Restaurant and Café Bar
Richmond, Chez Lindsay
Rye, Landgate Bistro
Shelf, Bentley's
Sudbury, Brasserie Four Seven
Sudbury, Red Onion Bistro
Taunton, Brazz
Titley, Stagg Inn
Whitby, Magpie Café
Whitchurch, Red House
Woodbridge, Captain's Table

Scotland

Alyth, Drumnacree House
Auchmithie, But 'n' Ben
Cairndow, Loch Fyne Oyster Bar
Edinburgh, Fishers
Edinburgh, Kalpna
Fairlie, Fins
Glasgow, Café Gandolfi
Glasgow, Number Sixteen
Port Appin, Pierhouse
Stein, Loch Bay
Stonehaven, Tolbooth

Wales

Broad Haven, Druidstone
Colwyn Bay, Café Niçoise
Llanarmon Dyffryn Ceiriog, West Arms
Llanfihangel Nant Melan, Red Lion Inn
Swansea, La Braseria

Northern Ireland

Belfast, La Belle Epoque
Holywood, Fontana
Limavady, The Lime Tree

Republic of Ireland

Cork, Crawford Gallery Café

Service charges

Restaurants still charging 15% for service (sometimes 'optional')

England

Belgo Noord, NW1
Café du Jardin, WC2
The Connaught, W1
Lou Pescadou, SW5
Miyama, W1
Neal Street Restaurant, WC2
Old Delhi, W2

England

Warminster, Bishopstrow House

Introduction

Everybody has to eat. Beyond that doesn't-take-a-rocket-scientist observation lies the endless diversity of what we choose to eat, the myriad ways we prepare, combine and cook ingredients, and the circumstances under which we consume them, a good cross-section of which are represented in this book.

The variety is endless because (except in a small handful of households and restaurants) food is always changing. Think back to what you were eating ten years ago, or if that doesn't work try twenty, or better still childhood, and compare notes. Were you routinely consuming burghul, ceviche, chorizo, bruschetta, polenta, risotto and merguez? Did restaurants shave bottarga or white truffle over things, or froth anything that wasn't coffee into a cappuccino?

The excitement of many of these flavours and ingredients is matched only by their potential for confusion. Do you know your chimichanga from your jambalaya, your fabada from your fajita, harrira from harissa, and mole from mooli? And if not, could you rely on a waiter or waitress to explain and interpret them to your satisfaction? In case you cannot, we have asked the food and wine writer, and former restaurateur, David Wolfe to provide a glossary of some of the more head-scratching examples. David, who used to advertise his own business as 'the long thin restaurant with the short fat proprietor', knows his way round the remotest corners of the culinary world, and is so eager to share his knowledge that he is already compiling another list for when next we need it (suggestions for widely used yet obscure terms that need light throwing on them would be most welcome).

Given the dramatic increase in the range of ingredients, tastes and dishes available from around the world, it seems that we are all being terribly adventurous in our eating. And to a degree we are. Ostrich and kangaroo are now commonplace, surely a sign of our willingness to explore anything out of the ordinary. But that is only part of the story.

When it comes to pigs, sheep and cows, we tend to eat the so-called prime cuts, the meaty (but not too strenuously exerted) muscles that convert into chops, fillet, rump, leg and shoulder. With honourable exceptions such as oxtail, calf's liver, the occasional stuffed pig's trotter, and of course foie gras, we tend to ignore what are in the view of many people the most interesting parts of these animals. Not all cultures are so narrow-minded – look at duck webs in China, or sheep's trotters in Turkey and India – but native British chefs mostly ignore a resource that is on their own doorstep, and yet is as exciting to eat as anything from North Africa, Mexico or the Far East. So we asked the London chef/proprietor Fergus Henderson to put the case for these under-rated treasures. His passion for insides and extremities, combined with a direct and unaffected style of cooking, make his restaurant St John (a sort of 'trottoria', if you will) such a refreshing and satisfying place to eat.

Like many restaurants in the Guide, St John is owned and run by an enthusiast, someone whose primary interest is in food and cooking. A lot of high-profile restaurants, however, seem to be owned by a corporation or a millionaire anxious to satisfy shareholders or accountants. This kind of restaurant is typically designed around a 'concept', with a flashy and expensive cocktail bar, a few global snacks tossed in to soak up the booze, and loud music to keep out the over-40s. When all is ready for opening, somebody remembers they will probably need a chef, to carry out the instructions and replicate the menus of the household-name consultant the PR company has chosen. Sometimes these chefs will stay on for weeks after the rave newspaper reviews are history, but many just up-sticks and move on to the next job. When times are good, these places rake in the money, exploiting the gullibility of those who are drawn to eat where celebrities hang out, or who believe that standards of cooking are directly related to the difficulty of getting a table.

Cheer up?

Recently, there are signs that customer numbers have been dropping, and some of the big names in London have seen their profits start to fall. It is now becoming possible for non-celebrities to book tables in fashionable restaurants at a reasonable hour, only a week or so ahead. One cheer for that.

The expansion of restaurants over the past few years, particularly in London, but also in other metropolitan centres around Britain, has generally been a boon to customers, bringing all kinds of excitement and unprecedented choice. This year, we are pleased to see, it is the long overdue turn of Liverpool and Birmingham to hit the culinary limelight, each fielding in some exciting new entries. Given the size of their populations, they have always seemed to lag behind other cities, but these signs of burgeoning gastronomic life may herald sturdier economic times for them.

The contraction of restaurants in London, on the other hand (if that is what this turns out to be), could in fact produce benefits. When restaurants were on the up, there was a scrabble for talented chefs and front-of-house staff. Unfortunately, demand has always outstripped supply; for many staff, training appears to have been non-existent. And because customers were begging to be let in, there were no restraints on practice.

We have all suffered at the hands of brutal wine mark-ups, all railed against the weaselly 'optional 12.5 per cent' service charge. We have struggled to make ourselves heard against the tyranny of noise bouncing off bare walls (above 85 decibels, a conversation begins to break down and hearing can be impaired; according to *New Scientist*, modern concrete-and-chrome restaurants regularly exceed this). We have all suffered the kind of service that makes us blush and fume with incredulity. Every restaurant has to make money, of course, but some have taken this to extremes in the most high-handed manner imaginable. Those who have been motivated by greed are now reaping the consequences, as even well-off customers find these prices unacceptable. If circumstances now turn in favour of the customer, what are we going to do but offer up a second cheer?

This reversal may mean that, when we telephone to make a booking, we shall not get the automatic and rhetorical 'Can you hold?' without so much as a pause for an answer, but a civilised response. It may mean that when we arrive, we are not greeted by a blank look and a gruff 'Have you booked?', but by somebody who is expecting us, and who seems pleased that we are there.

It may also mean:

- that restaurants will start to listen to appeals and entreaties for at least part of the establishment to be turned over to non-smokers;
- that we are no longer expected to be grateful for a two-hour slot at a time when we don't want to eat;
- that a couple of tables can be removed, to give us a bit of elbow room instead of being jammed in like sardines;
- that the host of extra charges that have crept in – for bread, vegetables, petits fours in some cases, water nearly everywhere – in an effort to squeeze a few more pounds out of us, will be dropped;
- that the more arrogant staff are given their marching orders, so that customers are no longer treated as just fodder for the cash register; and
- that the standards of food will improve, as the more incompetent chefs are weeded out.

It may also mean that kitchens will field their A-teams at all times, not just occasionally; absentee chefs have been responsible for some very poor meals over the past year. The experience of one of our inspectors is typical: 'I did not recall, on making a reservation, nor on entry to the dining room, seeing the message: "The chef cannot be bothered to attend, though a few partly trained assistants will do their best to knock up some food in his absence; we will, however, charge you the same money as if he were here."' Chefs reading this year's Guide may be surprised to find that their cooking mark falls way below what they know they are capable of, and this may be partly because they do not see what goes on when they are not there.

Over to you

Some or all of these reversals may happen, but applause could be premature. Too many restaurateurs, sadly, are unable to put themselves in the shoes of their customers. Many have no idea what it is like for a disinterested party to eat in their restaurant, because they are too involved in running it, and from their perspective everything is going just fine. The only way they can be jolted out of complacency is if somebody tells them that all is not well. That is where we – the Guide and its readers – come in. *The Good Food Guide* is a unique forum for reporters to express their views. There is no need to apologise for not being a 'food professional'; if a restaurant has taken your money in exchange for food and drink, you have an inalienable right to express your view. And without your input, the Guide would not have the depth and scope that it has.

You could, of course, rely on newspaper and magazine reviews to find somewhere to eat, although, with some notable and honourable exceptions, too many small-time reviewers seem wrapped up in their own ramblings to have time for the real world. Why, some of them wonder aloud, should anybody want to use the meticulously researched *Good Food Guide*, based on the experiences of thousands of reporters, backed up by hundreds of commissioned inspections, incorporating information from a detailed questionnaire, confirmed by last-minute phone checks to each of the 1,300 restaurants in the Guide, all of which (along with hundreds of other aspirants) have been re-assessed from scratch annually; why should anyone bother with this when instead they can simply read one person's ego-driven account, gushing or vituperative, depending on which side they got out of bed, about one restaurant that opened last week?

Your reports matter because, taken all together, they give an accurate account of a restaurant's strengths and weaknesses. If your experience of a restaurant differs from the impression given in this edition of the Guide, don't forget that your fellow readers have contributed significantly to the picture we present. If you don't like it, you can influence it, by writing to us and telling us about your meals, so that others will be better informed. If you think a restaurant is accurately described, and it lives up to or exceeds your expectations, then please write to us just the same. Chefs come and go, some get steadily better, others quietly lose interest, so the picture is always changing.

As an illustration, we calculate that around half of this year's main entries score the same as they did last year, while the other half have been sold, closed, transferred to the Round-up sections, raised or lowered their cooking mark, or are appearing as new entries in this edition. The change is most marked in London, but is echoed throughout the UK and Republic of Ireland. That is why the Guide is published every year, why it is updated and completely rewritten for each edition. We want you to have the latest and best information available to us. And we can only get the latest picture if you write to us.

Search me

The Guide aims to be useful, and we hope that a few small changes this year will increase its practicability. Cosmetic amendments to the presentation of entries will, it is hoped, make it easier to read. You will also notice that we have added to main entries a brief description of cooking style. These encapsulations are not intended to pigeonhole restaurants – the last thing we wish to do is erect fences and boundaries – but merely to be just another tool that may prove helpful. Of course, It is only by reading the entry through that you will be able to find out in more detail what is on offer.

The cooking-style descriptions have in most cases been checked with restaurateurs, although we have edited some for appropriateness. You will find considerable overlap: what may be, for example, one chef's Modern British is another's Modern European and yet another's Global or Fusion. There are no hard edges, no easy definitions, and the descriptions are just a pointer.

They will also prove useful to online readers (the Guide can be accessed on the Internet by subscribers to Which? Online) who wish to search for a restaurant on the basis of style or cuisine. (We were initally prompted to insert the descriptions, in fact, by the need of the online Guide for sensible search fields.) Also new this year are web site addresses in the main entries; online users will be able to link directly to them. Such web sites are proliferating, and their quality varies immensely: some helpfully give menus with current prices and a pictorial view of dining rooms, while others provide out-of-date information or advance little more than advertorial hype and a quick 'contact me' email link for booking.

Information technology, certainly, has become increasingly a part of the eating-out experience, whether we like it or not. For some people, booking a table by email – either directly with the restaurant, or through one of the many online booking services that have sprung up – has become standard procedure, while others feel that arranging a meal at a good restaurant should begin with the sound of a human voice at the other end of the phone.

Nobody can say where all this technology will lead. In two years' time it may be the norm to have a device in your car to indicate how far you are from the nearest restaurant in the Guide. A click might display the menu, another might get you a table, while yet another might place your order so that it is ready when you arrive. But the underlying aims of the Guide remain constant: to find the best cooking, regardless of style or category, throughout the UK and Republic of Ireland. There are no electronic short cuts to this – it still takes effort for those who write to the Guide (even for emailers) to compose a few notes while everything is fresh in their minds – but I hope you agree it is well worth it. Everybody has to eat, and with your help we aim to make it as pleasurable as possible.

Pardon my French

David Wolfe, wine and food writer, casts light on some of the obscure, garbled, hybrid and fantastical terms appearing on British restaurant menus

The Ivy has 'recovered a good deal of its glory'. So said *The Good Food Guide* in its 1955-6 edition. The Italian chef was an excellent cook, but his command of menu French (as exemplified by 'chop de Veau à la Sassi') was minimal. Even now, 45 years on, the situation in many restaurants throughout Britain has not improved; in fact, there is now more to criticise than ever. Although menus are supposed to aid diners, not confuse them, here are some of the common problems that restaurant-goers might come across.

Far too many restaurants still cling to the outmoded view that menus with pretensions to quality must be written in French (note the common 'jus' in place of the desperately unfashionable 'gravy'). Mercifully, for the non-French-speaking majority of British diners, untranslated French is nowadays rare, though bilingual descriptions often produce conflicting versions. This inconsistency has been around since the thirteenth century, when words such as beef, veal and mutton entered the English language. No one today would challenge these replacements for ox, calf and sheep, and juggling three eggs in the air we happily accept omelettes, soufflés and sauce béarnaise as naturalised. The heart of the confusion today lies in more recent additions to our culinary vocabulary, largely arising from the globalisation of menus and the blurring of national culinary boundaries. Menu writers these days are like lost map-makers, unsure where to draw the lines.

The mother of invention

Risotto, carpaccio and confit are common sights on the modern British menu, but while risotto used to be (and in Italy still is) a rice dish, it may now be made of anything from barley to buckwheat. The extension to grains other than rice is defensible on the grounds that there is no other concise description of such a preparation. Indeed, this form of menu shorthand may be considered helpful, but not all extended meanings can be justified. The shape of a monkfish's tail suggested to someone's imaginative eye a small leg of lamb, so we have 'gigot de lotte'. But 'osso buco of monkfish' is ridiculous to anyone who knows that osso buco means shin. Yet fantasy is certainly admissible in describing food. The popular Italian name for little balls of fried rice with a blob of cheese at the centre is supplì al telefono. Why? For the answer, bite into one and see the 'wires' of cheese extending from your teeth to the remainder of the sphere.

Far from being revealing, modern interpretations of words such as cappuccino and mille-feuille, or such inventions as Japanese-German wasabislaw, often serve only to perplex. Indeed, some of today's menus would challenge a cryptic crossword solver. One menu was said in *The Good Food Guide 2000* to be 'so wildly inventive that it is quite possible to find nothing immediately recognisable'. Even *Larousse Gastronomique* cannot help with 'scorched rice paper lumpia pot-sticker'. Four lines on the menu specify what it is filled with, surrounded by, and topped with, but there is no clue to what *it* is.

It's all Greek-Thai fusion to me

As for spellings, they are notoriously variable. We can only speculate on the sub-conscious reasons for fois gras ('fat times') in place of foie gras, while Italian ingredients are often cursed with tautology: as in biscotti biscuits and cipollini onions. There are special problems with menus and dishes adopted from cultures that do not use the Western alphabet, where transliteration can produce many spellings for just one dish or ingredient. Take, for example, the Indian name for a puffed-up fried bread, which appears on British menus as puri, poori or even puree.

Misunderstanding can also arise when a familiar ingredient is listed by an unfamiliar name. In Britain's Chinese restaurants the little meat-stuffed dumplings, guo-tieh, are Peking dumplings. In Japanese restaurants they are gyoza, while Americans and Australians know them as pot-stickers. Americans use the Italian word zucchini to describe what we generally refer to by their French name, courgettes, or (still, occasionally) baby marrows.

The glossary that follows is not divided into sections by ethnic origin. This is not least because the boundaries between different cuisines are so vague these days. Consider one menu which, despite being entirely in English, includes aïoli, brandade, porchetta, raita and tapénade (all listed in the glossary). Nor does the glossary attempt to include *all* menu terms that the British restaurant-goer might encounter. Its aim is to be helpful in terms of general usefulness, with the focus on words which are being borrowed from one culinary tradition and squeezed into another, or whose meaning is being changed by use. It omits, for example, Japanese terms on menus in Japanese restaurants, as these almost always have translations. Feedback from readers, however, on anything they feel should have been included but was missed – or just on menus generally – would be most welcome.

Glossary

Abbreviations

E = English *Fr* = French *Gr* = Greek *In* = Indian (and all the Sub-Continent) *It* = Italian *J* = Japanese *M* = Maghreb *ME* = Middle Eastern including Lebanon, Egypt and sometimes also the Maghreb *Mex* = Mexican *P* = Portuguese *R* = Russian *T* = Turkish *Sc* = Scottish *Sp* = Spanish *USA* = United States of America

achar *In* pickled vegetables
agrumes *Fr* citrus fruits
aïoli/alioli *Fr/Sp* garlic mayonnaise
ajillo *Sp (S. American)* tender young garlic
baba/papa ghanoush/ganoush/ ganouge *ME* creamy aubergine purée
ballottine *Fr* meat loaf, similar to galantine [*qv*] but less richly stuffed
bastorma *Balkans* see pastrami
blette *Fr* chard
blini *R* small pancakes entirely or mainly of buckwheat flour
bocconcini *It* fried morsels of mortadella, meatball, pancetta, cheese etc.
borlotti *It* dried (haricot) beans; see *cannellini*
botargo/boutargue *Fr* salted, sun-dried, pressed eggs of grey mullet or tuna, shaved from a block
bourride *Fr* Provençal fish soup with aïoli [*qv*]
brandade *Fr* was Provençal purée of poached salt cod with garlic; now any smoked or salted fish can be used
bresaola *It* air-dried, salted beef, cut very thin
brik *M* envelope of fried filo pastry stuffed with a soft egg and tuna, potato etc.
briouat/briwatte *M* fried filo roll stuffed with minced meat, fish etc.
b'stilla *M* a pie, originally of pigeon, but now often chicken; sweet, salty and spicy (not hot); arguably the crown of Moroccan gastronomy
burghul *ME* cracked wheat
cannon *Fr* fillet of lamb, usually sliced
cannellini *It* beans; cannellini and borlotti (see above) are both types of haricot bean; both are usually bought dried, but either can be eaten fresh in season
caponata *It* Sicilian cold ratatouille with aubergine
cappuccino *It* was milk coffee with a frothed top; now soup, sauce or any liquid which is made frothy
carpaccio *It* was very thin slices of raw beef; now may be other meat or fish, typically tuna
cassoulet *Fr* a rich stew of haricot beans and meat: cassolette is a cocotte, or small, single-portion dish of china glass or metal
ceviche *Sp* marinated raw fish; see also escabèche
charlotte *Fr* dessert of fruit or cream (charlotte russe) in a mould lined with buttered bread or small biscuits or ladies' fingers
chermoula *M* garlic, herb and spice marinade, usually for fish
Chiboust *Fr* confectioners' custard flavoured with vanilla and blended with stiffly beaten egg whites

chimichanga *Mex* fried wheat-flour tortilla-wrapped parcels
chipotle *Mex* smoked jalapeño chilli (hot)
chorizo *Sp* **chouriço** P spicy sausage usually made with garlic and chilli
choy *Ch* bok choy, ung choy and many others are Chinese green vegetables, now often imported from Holland
cioppino *USA* shellfish and fish soup
confit *Fr* meat or poultry cooked in, and preserved in, its own fat; also fruit and vegetables preserved in syrup, alcohol or vinegar
cotechino *It* large sausage of pork including rind
crespelline *It* small pancakes
crostini *It* was toasted slices of bread, canapé bases; now the complete canapés with tomatoes, pancetta, olives etc.
daikon *J* giant white radish a.k.a. mooli
enchilada *Mex* maize tortilla, sauced, stuffed and rolled
escabèche *Fr/Sp* marinated fried fish served cold; see also ceviche
fabada *Sp* rich bean stew, cassoulet
fajita *Mex* was marinated, grilled, beef; now might be grilled anything
feuilleté *Fr* was puff pastry, now anything presented therein
focaccia *It* a flattish bread often enriched with oil
galantine *Fr* brawn or boned meat or poultry, with its jelly, stuffed and pressed into a loaf shape
galette *Fr* small round flat 'cake' of potato, pancake, pastry etc. and especially the Breton wheat or buckwheat pancakes
gazpacho *Sp* this liquid salad was a cold soup, but may now be a sauce
gremolata/gremolada *It* garnish for osso buco including herbs, lemon peel and garlic
gribiche *Fr* a variation of sauce tartare with hard-boiled egg yolks
guacamole *Mex* avocado dip
haleem *I & ME* grain and meat 'porridge'
harira *M* rich vegetable soup sometimes with meat
harissa *M* red chilli paste; also a Tunisian 'ratatouille' and a Middle Eastern version of haleem [*qv*]
hoi-sin *Ch* a thick Chinese sauce made with soya beans, flour, salt, sugar, vinegar, garlic, chilli and sesame oil. Possibly the Chinese equivalent of Worcester sauce, except that Worcester sauce is now a luxury item on Chinese menus; see also *plum sauce*
involtini *It* stuffed rolls of thinly sliced meat or vegetable
jalapeño *Mex* hot green chilli
jambalaya *USA* Louisiana Creole-Cajun version of Spanish paella
jus *Fr* similar to gravy, usually unthickened, although now often applied indiscriminately; or the juice of fruits
kim-chee *Korean* the national dish, a relish of Chinese leaves, or other vegetables pickled with garlic, ginger, chilli etc.
laksa *Singaporean/Malaysian* fish soup with coconut milk and noodles
merguez *M* spicy lamb sausage
mesclun *Fr* salad of mixed leaves
mille-feuille *Fr* was a dessert of 'a thousand leaves', thin puff pastry layers, sandwiching fruit, cream etc., or sometimes savoury things; now anything composed

of any number of layers, however few, of anything
mole *Mex* sauce or broth
mooli *In* giant white radish a.k.a. daikon
mostarda *It* literally mustard, often short for mostarda di frutta, fruit pickled in honey and mustard sauce
mouclade *Fr* mussels in creamy white wine sauce; moules marinières does not include cream
moutabel/moutabal *ME* see *baba ganoush*
mujadarrah *ME* rice and lentils cooked together, often with fried onion on top
pain perdu *Fr* sliced egg-and-milk-dipped bread fried and served with sweetenings
panaché *Fr* mixed
pannacotta, panna cotta *It* literally 'cooked cream', an eggless crème made with gelatine, served cold
pancetta *It* cured, spiced 'bacon', or belly pork; not smoked
paneer/panir *In* curd cheese
panettone *It* rich Christmas cake
partan bree *Sc* crab soup
pastilla *M & ME* see *b'stilla*
pastrami *T, ME & Eastern Europe* spiced salt beef; many variations of recipe and spelling
pavé *Fr* a cold dish of a mixture, often a mousse, in a square or oblong mould; also a cake of the same shape; pavé de boeuf is a steak
peperonata *It* a ratatouille, not necessarily including tomato
pepperoni *It* peppers: green, red and yellow ; also spicy Italian sausage
pipérade *Fr* a Basque ratatouille with scrambled eggs
pizza bianca *It* (erroneously pizzetta) a very thin Roman bread, like a thin pizza base
plum sauce *Ch* a variation on hoisin [*qv*] based on that fruit
polenta *It* a solid or semi-solid 'porridge' made of various grains, although traditionally of corn meal or maize flour
porchetta *It* roast suckling pig
poutargue *Fr* see *boutargue*
prosciutto *It* ham; but outside Italy it is raw, spiced Italian ham, cut very thin
puntarella *It* Roman salad leaf with garlic, anchovy and vinegar dressing
quesadilla *Mex* stuffed, folded, usually maize tortillas either fried or griddled
raita *In* yoghurt relish, often incorporating cucumber, onion, chilli, mint, tomato, etc.
ravigote *Fr* vinaigrette plus herbs, onions, capers etc.
rémoulade *Fr* mayonnaise strongly flavoured with mustard, gherkins, capers and herbs, normally used to accompany celeriac; not a synonym for celeriac
rillettes *Fr* potted fatty pork, duck, goose not chopped or minced but shredded with forks, now used of fish too
risotto *It* rice cooked in stock to a produce a semi-liquid consistency; may include any of a wide variety of meat, fish, vegetables and herbs
romesco *Sp* Catalan sauce typically using fried bread, tomato, nuts, garlic and wine in a smooth paste
sambal *Indonesian* sauce or relish always including chillis
sambar, sambhar *In* a thin mixed vegetable concoction in which tamarind is a main flavour; often used as an accompaniment for dosai or other south Indian snacks
samosa *In* crisp fried triangular

pastry parcel stuffed with meat or vegetables
salsa verde *Fr* sharp green 'vinaigrette' of parsley, capers, anchovy, garlic and mustard, but open to wider interpretation
sauce verte *Fr* mayonnaise with herbs or salsa verde
savarin *Fr* mega rum baba, a large ring of pastry or cake
seviche *Sp* see *ceviche* and *escabèche*
skirlie *Sc* Scottish polenta, a fat and oatmeal cake eaten at breakfast or with game or poultry
smatna/smetana/smitane *Fr/R* sour cream sauce
squab *E* young pigeon
squat lobster/squattie *Sc* flat or slipper lobster (French cigale)
stinco *It* shank of ham, pork or lamb; more appetising than it sounds
stracciatella *It* meat or chicken broth with beaten egg and Parmesan strands
subric *Fr* like a croquette but not deep-fried
sumac *ME* a spice made from purple 'berries'; sprinkled on kebabs and pilaff
tabbouleh *ME & M* a salad of parsley and mint with tomato and a small proportion (5–10%) of cracked wheat or couscous; a common error is to reverse the proportions, making it a cold couscous lightly flavoured with salad ingredients
tahini/tahina *ME, Gr & T* paste of sesame seeds
tajine/tagine *M* a casserole with a curved high conical lid; the meat, poultry or vegetables stewed in it
tartare *Fr* was only applied to steak; now also used of chopped seasoned fish, raw or cooked, especially salmon or tuna
tartare sauce *E* mayonnaise with chopped gherkins, capers and other ingredients
tapénade *Fr* olive paste
tarte Tatin *Fr* the (theoretically) essential feature is that the fruit or vegetable content is cooked with a lid of pastry, and the dish is inverted so it arrives with a pastry base
tempura *J* lightly battered, deep-fried seafood and vegetables
tea-smoked *Ch* hot smoked, over tea leaves
tian *Fr* was a Provençal earthenware pot which gave its name to the contents, a gratin of vegetables; now any circular arrangement of any ingredients
tikka *In* chunks of meat, poultry or fish for cooking in tandoor; not the blend of spices used as flavouring
tortilla *Sp* omelette; *Mex* griddled flat-bread
vacherin *Fr* a pot made of meringue often filled with cream, ice cream or fruit; also a type of Swiss cheese
velouté *Fr* basic white sauce, or soup, smoothed with egg-yolk
ventrêche *Fr* salted or smoked breast of pork
vierge *Fr* gently warmed (not cooked) sauce of olive oil, lemon juice and tomato flesh with herbs
wasabi *J* Japanese green herb resembling horseradish in flavour, the seasoning for sushi and sashimi
zampone *It* large pig's trotter stuffed with meat and offal

A beautiful friendship

Fergus Henderson, chef/proprietor of St John in London, and enthusiastic proponent of 'nose to tail eating', celebrates the delights of offal, and laments its decline in Britain

Soothing, subtle, sophisticated, textural, beautiful, steadying and silky. That is just a plate of tripe and onions – a world away from the cold, chewy, slippery image of the word tripe. Tripe is not alone in being misunderstood: nowadays many people relegate most animal extremities and innards to a gastronomic wilderness of blood and guts, belonging either to the domain of the testosterone-fuelled, macho hard-core foodie or to the cloth-capped world of tripe chomping and jellied calf's foot-noshing. As a nation that prefers its meat to be anonymous, pink and wrapped in plastic, what else can we expect?

There have always been exceptions: London restaurateur Pierre Koffman's trotter, devilled kidneys on toast, calf's liver and sweetbreads, and haggis somehow have slipped through the net. (Haggis is an interesting case, its acceptance no doubt having much to do with its roundness and the British love-affair with anything resembling a sausage; the fact that it is minced-up lambs' liver, lung and heart cooked in a stomach gets forgotten owing to its reassuring geometry.)

Gastronomic possibilities

What the British diner is missing are the incredible gastronomic possibilities of offal. Let's have a quick nose-to-tail moment. The snout is full of lip-sticking possibilities, boiled and eaten hot, dressed with vinaigrette. Cheeks are muscles which have done just the right amount of exercise; braised, they are a joy. Pig's ears crisp up to make the perfect pork-scratching topping for a bowl of split-pea soup. The heart captures the very essence of the creature it comes from: duck's fried in a pan; lamb's stuffed with sage, bread and red onion; ox's sliced, marinated and chargrilled. Tongue offers its own intriguing possibilities: perhaps brined then gently boiled and eaten hot, and I would make a case for the delights of thinly sliced cold tongue eaten with horseradish or green sauce. Tripe can be set in a blushing jelly of calf's hoof and cider – the perfect summer dish. What could be more beautiful than a plate of chitterlings (pigs' intestines) tossed in mustard and grilled?

Now that brains (at least in the culinary sense) are illegal, nothing can produce that 'crunch-then-give' moment like a deep-fried testicle, which is crisp on the outside and softly grainy inside. Pig's spleen is a very neatly formed organ, not dissimilar in flavour and texture to calf's liver – roll it with bacon and sage, then braise, producing a 'spleen Swiss roll'. The trotter brings unctuousness to any dish, and finally, the tail crisped up offers perhaps the best example you will find of not-quite-flesh, not-quite-fat.

Disappearing animal parts

Like the oyster, which was once a staple of the poor but is now definitely a luxury food, offal nowadays may be found on the menus of some smart restaurants, though it hardly features in butchers' windows or on supermarket shelves. Some say the origins of its near-disappearance lie in the post-war period when a general reaction to rationing resulted in a soaring demand for prime cuts of meat such as fillet steak, chicken breast and leg of lamb. That cannot be the whole story, however. The French, for example, who surely experienced even worse wartime hardships, never lost their offal appetite. But then, in France regional cuisine is alive and well, while in Britain to a large extent it has petered out. Regional cooking has always championed offal: witness, for example, 'Bath Chaps' (brined pig's head from the West Country), and the aforementioned Lancastrian dish of tripe and onions. This 'centralisation' of cooking in Britain escalated in the decades that followed with the arrival of fads and fashions – from the influx of 'Continental' dishes such as spaghetti bolognese and chicken Kiev to the rise (and fall) of nouvelle cuisine – not to mention the inroads made into traditional cooking by the advent of fast-food chains, and the general decline of cooking skills.

But it is not just changing tastes that have contributed to offal's decline; it is also a sad sign of the times that over the past few years many animal ingredients have become largely unavailable. I thought pigs were still considered a safe animal to eat, but can you find fresh pig's blood anywhere? No. In Scotland it is still possible to obtain stomachs to wrap haggis in, although they are often replaced by artificial casings (just like sausages). As last year's *Good Food Guide* pointed out, a major reason for the dearth of many animal parts is the closing of small abattoirs. Unlike large abattoirs – which because of commercial constraints tend to concentrate on volume, with production lines geared to feeding the public's desire for legs and loins – small slaughterhouses have traditionally kept alive the skills of innards butchery. Their closure, as the Guide says, is the result of pressure from 'out-of-touch legislators, regulators and agribusiness' in the wake of various food scares. Of course, it goes without saying that strict hygiene practices and good sourcing of materials are essential wherever offal, or any other kind of food, is handled, and my lament is that legal and economic pressures have closed so many of the good along with the bad.

As many animal parts become rarer, the public becomes less and less aware that they exist, and so demand shrinks further: a vicious circle. This seems to me to show a remarkable lack of respect for the animal, let alone the dinner table. Nowadays, meat has become so 'tidied up' that even chickens come without their giblets. The next generation could be forgiven for thinking animals had no innards, just useful cavities for sage and onion stuffing.

A glimmer of hope

Maybe I paint a gloomy picture for those of us who disdain waste, and who have known (or would like to know) the pure delight of eating offal that has been skilfully prepared. But I believe there is room for hope. There are a few great chefs who are expert at preparing offal (among other things), so the opportunity for trying out these wonderful dishes is still out there for those who would seek it.

I take heart (if you don't mind the pun), too, from the way customers at St John attack marrowbones, are happy to experiment with spleens, and relish a plate of tongue. In time, with the percentage of the population going out to eat in restaurants growing, let's hope this enthusiasm will rub off on the collective foodie thoughts of the nation, so that more people can enjoy the elegant, sexy and seductive qualities of offal that the so-called 'prime cuts' lack.

When talking to people about offal I have often heard them say 'yes, that's my kind of food'. So why is it not on more menus? And why does it rarely feature on television food programmes? Surely someone could make tripe the star of the small screen and bring some well-deserved glamour to innards.

Don't let's despair. Enjoy a gastronomic romance and, rather than steak or roast leg of lamb, the next time you eat out order perhaps a plate of devilled lambs' kidneys, or maybe a dish of stuffed pig's trotter. It could be, as Claude Rains says to Humphrey Bogart at the end of *Casablanca*, 'the beginning of a beautiful friendship'.

Your rights in restaurants

Whether it is a celebration at a high-class restaurant, or an informal supper at your neighbourhood bistro, eating out should be a pleasurable experience. When it is not, and it is the restaurant's fault, many of us avoid complaining because we do not wish to create a scene, or risk spoiling a special occasion. However, restaurants provide a service for which we, the customers, pay good money, and we should be able to expect certain standards.

Booking

A booking is a contract between you and the restaurant. This means you have certain rights, but it also means you have certain responsibilities. If you cancel the booking or fail to turn up, you are in breach of contract, and if your table cannot be re-let then you may be held liable for the restaurant's loss of profit (though any charge made by the restaurant in this instance must be reasonable). If you are unavoidably held up, notify the restaurant as soon as possible, but remember that the restaurant may not be able to re-arrange the time of your booking and is not obliged to do so. If you do arrive at the appointed time and find that the restaurant has no record of your booking, or has double-booked the table, then it is in breach of contract and you can claim a reasonable sum to cover any expenses you incur as a result: e.g. travel costs. Since most bookings are made over the telephone, it can be difficult to prove that a booking was ever made, so keep a record of when you made the booking and to whom you spoke. Alternatively, ask the restaurant to write to you (or send a fax or email) to confirm your reservation. Many restaurants, especially in London, impose a time limit on the use of the table, but if they do this they should inform you when you make the booking.

It is commonplace nowadays for restaurants to ask for credit card details to secure a booking. You are not obliged to give them, but if you do not the restaurant is entitled to refuse your booking. In fact, the restaurant may refuse to accept any booking for whatever reason it chooses, as long as it is not on the grounds of race, gender or disability.

Setting and food

While you may not like the colour of the restaurant's walls, the design of the tableware, or the music played, the restaurant is under no legal obligation to compensate; equipment and furniture provided by the restaurant, however, must be at least safe. A menu must be displayed at or near the entrance of the restaurant. It must indicate prices (inclusive of VAT) clearly, including any 'extras' such as a minimum charge, cover charge, a charge for incidentals (such as bread), and any compulsory service charge. Since September 1999, the law has required restaurants to tell customers which dishes contain genetically modified soya or maize.

Unless the menu specifically states otherwise you are not obliged to order a specific number of dishes or eat dishes in a set order. You may, for example, order two starters instead of a starter and main course, a main course only, or even a meal consisting of five desserts.

The food served must be prepared with reasonable skill and care, in a way that does not endanger health, and should conform to generally accepted standards – lamb, for example, is usually served pink nowadays, so that is what you should expect, unless you have asked for it well done. If a dish does not fit the description on the menu (e.g. it arrives cold but was advertised as 'warm') then it is a case of misdescription and you may request a replacement. Quality of ingredients, on the other hand, is largely a matter of opinion, but if you suspect any ingredient of being off, the simple rule is not to eat it. Should you later suffer from a stomach upset, you would find it extremely difficult to prove the source of a case of food poisoning.

You are entitled to refuse to pay for any dishes that are not what you ordered or that you consider to be not of a reasonable standard. Alternatively, if you wish to avoid a fracas, pay under protest and seek to recover the money later through appropriate channels (see below).

Drink

Generally, the same rules apply to wine as to food. This means the restaurant may charge what it likes for wine, as long as the prices are clearly indicated (though it need not display the entire wine list by the entrance, only a representative selection). If you think the price of the wine you want is too high, choose something cheaper.

Waiting staff must take care to serve the correct wine (the producer and vintage must be as advertised on the wine list) and to serve the wine in a good condition. If the wine is 'off' (corked or oxidised), you are entitled to demand a replacement, though disputes about a wine's condition are difficult to resolve. If the sommelier insists that there is nothing wrong with the wine, you should pay for it under protest, take it home with you and seek an expert opinion.

Contrary to what many believe, restaurants and pubs are not required by law to serve tap water free of charge. Licensing regulations state that restaurants must offer suitable drinks (including water) as well as alcohol to accompany food. This might mean bottled water or tap water, for which the restaurant can charge (though in practice most do not for the latter). Pubs are under no obligation to offer any kind of non-alcoholic drink – even water.

Service

Anything that detracts from your enjoyment of the meal counts as bad service, though the type of restaurant and the prices it charges must be taken into consideration. Certain situations may be thought unreasonable in any context. If, for example, a waiter spills wine over your clothes, you may claim the cost of cleaning. Where other aspects of bad service are concerned – rude staff, long waits between courses, waiters getting the order wrong – you should let the restaurant staff know there and then that you are unhappy and give them a chance to rectify the situation. If they cannot, then you are entitled to refuse to pay all or part of any service charge. When service is included in the cost of the meal, you may deduct some of the bill.

How to complain

It is always better to complain at the time, rather than in a letter after the event. Always maintain a civil tone, and explain clearly what you are unhappy about. You are more likely to achieve a satisfactory outcome this way, though you should be prepared to compromise. If, however, you do prefer to complain later and claim a refund, you should first write to the restaurant, stating your reasons. Don't be fobbed off if this fails to produce a satisfactory result. Perseverance can pay off. If not, you may have to take action by issuing legal proceedings in the county court. In any case, seek advice from a solicitor or from a Citizens Advice Bureau, Law Centre or Consumer Advice Centre. Your local council's trading standards department or environmental health officer may also be able to help. Alternatively, join Which? Legal Service (call freephone 0800 252100), which offers legal help to individuals.

London

Adams Café £ — map 12

77 Askew Road, W12 9AH
TEL/FAX: (020) 8743 0572

COOKING **3**
NORTH AFRICAN
£22–£31

The warm hospitality of Abdel and Frances Boukraa is one reason for this restaurant's popularity. Another is knowing exactly what you are going to spend: £9.95 for a main course only, £12.95 for two courses, £14.95 for three. There are a few other items but, apart from the unmissable mint tea, you probably won't need them. Choose a starter from the short list: perhaps ojja (a sort of ratatouille with egg and either shrimps or merguez), doigts de Fatima (beef-stuffed Tunisian spring rolls), or beautifully presented brik (filo pastry with a soft egg and other fillings).

Main dishes offer a selection of six kinds of couscous, a similar number of Moroccan tajines – perhaps chicken with pickled lemons, green olives and potatoes – and a choice of 'grillades' (kebabs), served with rice and vegetables. Desserts include Moroccan pancakes with honey, and North African pastries of the baklava family. The short wine list starts at £8 and keeps below £11.50 for most French and North African bottles. As a digestif, you might try Boukha, a Tunisian eau de vie made from figs. It can be drunk straight or as Boukha Coca.

CHEF: Abdel Boukraa PROPRIETORS: Abdel and Frances Boukraa OPEN: Mon to Sat D only 7 to 10.30 CLOSED: Christmas to New year and bank hols MEALS: Set D £9.95 (1 course) to £14.95 SERVICE: not inc CARDS: Amex, Diners, MasterCard, Switch, Visa DETAILS: 60 seats. Private parties: 36 main room, 24 private room. Vegetarian meals. Wheelchair access (not WC). Music ⊖ Ravenscourt Park (£5)

Admiral Codrington — NEW ENTRY — map 14

17 Mossop Street, SW3 2LY
TEL: (020) 7581 0005 FAX: (020) 7589 2452

COOKING **4**
MODERN BRITISH
£27–£49

Walk past the bar of this quiet, unassuming pub in a Chelsea backwater, to find a long, thin dining room stretching away to the rear. A ship's wheel mounted on a lobster-hued wall, and elegantly framed prints of fish and crustacea, combine to give a heavy hint about what might be on the menu. Without making too much play of the Cod in Codrington (it comes with tomato, mushrooms and a soft herb crust), the kitchen delivers salmon fishcake with sorrel sauce, and an expertly trimmed and pan-fried lemon sole with spinach and tomato butter.

There is more to the cosmopolitan food however, as the menu takes in crispy duck salad with lashings of coriander, Cumberland sausage with sage and onion mash, and a fine, creamy, deep-flavoured porcini risotto infused with truffle oil. Banana Tatin with vanilla ice cream is a crowd-pleaser, vying for attention with treacle tart and cappuccino crème brûlée. White-aproned staff are both professional and helfpul. Wines, supplied by Berry Bros & Rudd, are an intelligent, safe and well-priced collection, concentrating on French staples with a few New World diversions. Good Ordinary Claret and Sauvignon Sec are both £10 a bottle, and a decent number are sold by the glass.

CHEFS: Daniel Pederson and Charlie Rushton PROPRIETOR: Longshot Estates Ltd OPEN: all week 12 to 2.30 (3.30 Sat and Sun), 7 to 11 (10.30 Sun) CLOSED: 24, 25 and 26 Dec MEALS: alc (main courses £8.50 to £13). Cover 50p at D. Bar L available SERVICE: 12.5% (optional), card slips closed CARDS: Amex, Delta, MasterCard, Switch, Visa DETAILS: 56 seats. Private parties: 16 main room. Vegetarian meals. Wheelchair access (not WC). No music ⊖ South Kensington, Sloane Square

Admiralty

NEW ENTRY **map 13**

Somerset House, WC2R 1LA
TEL: (020) 7845 4646 FAX: (020) 7845 4647

COOKING **2**
FRENCH
£39–£63

Centred on an imposing courtyard, Somerset House has been turned once more into a public space. Oliver Peyton has the franchise for a restaurant of three interconnecting rooms, whose atmosphere runs counter to the grandeur of the building, with a child-friendly approach, informal service and a background of pounding heavy rock. Bilingual menus point to their French inspiration, dealing in cuisine du terroir typified by 'terrines of the day', brought to table in their dishes, sliced and served by the waiter, and left with a jar each of gherkins and silverskin onions.

Early chef changes produced varied results, but the robust style of country cooking has extended to roast rabbit with mustard sauce, and chicken legs with a minuscule showing of morel sauce. If light desserts are called for, try Breton sablé of lemon cream and raspberries, or a fruit soup made with sweet Monbazillac and garnished with apricot sorbet. With the exception of champagnes, the French wines are drawn entirely from the northern Rhône downwards, an enterprising approach that takes in many and varied styles, although heavy mark-ups will deter thorough exploration. House wines are £12.90.

CHEF: Darren Templeman PROPRIETOR: Oliver Peyton OPEN: all week 12 to 2.45, 6 to 10.45 CLOSED: 25 and 26 Dec, 1 Jan, Easter Sun and Mon MEALS: alc (main courses £15 to £18) SERVICE: 12.5% (optional), card slips closed CARDS: Amex, Delta, Diners, MasterCard, Switch, Visa DETAILS: 64 seats. Vegetarian meals. No smoking in dining room. Music. Air-conditioned ⊖ Embankment, Temple

London Round-ups listing additional restaurants that may be worth a visit can be found after the main London section.

a.k.a.

NEW ENTRY **map 15**

18 West Central Street, WC1A 1JJ
TEL: (020) 7836 0110 FAX: (020) 7836 1771
EMAIL: info@akalondon.com

COOKING **4**
MODERN EUROPEAN
£31–£55

a.k.a. is a mezzanine restaurant in a bar that is part of a club rather ominously called The End. Bright lights and pounding music dominate an interior of exposed heating ducts, while a gigantic video screen may show sport or clips from 1950s films. Hard to believe it was once part of a Post Office, but easy to understand a menu format that encourages light snacking as much as full meals. Bar selections, for example, can be assembled into platters for multiples of two people, while starters take in anything from spicy duck confit pancakes to asparagus with poached egg and béarnaise.

The house special is a steak sandwich, combining a good piece of fillet with a firm slice of foie gras on focaccia, the rich sauce soaking pleasingly into the bread, or you might opt for a spicy fishcake on stir-fried vegetables, seasoned with sesame oil and soy. Highly commended desserts have included Charentais melon sorbet, and burnt cream with morello cherries. Service from pierced staff is friendly enough, although the ambient noise may reduce you to semaphore. An extensive cocktail list heads up the drinking business, and there is a short list of good modern wines, with house French £11.

CHEF: Paul Holmes PROPRIETOR: Heathcote Advisors OPEN: Tue to Sat D only 6 to 11.30 (1am Thur to Sat) CLOSED: bank hols MEALS: alc (main courses £9 to £14.50) SERVICE: 12.5% (optional), card slips closed CARDS: Amex, Delta, Diners, MasterCard, Switch, Visa DETAILS: 62 seats. Private parties: 15 main room. Vegetarian meals. No children. Music. Air-conditioned ⊖ Holborn, Tottenham Court Road

Alastair Little

map 15

49 Frith Street, W1V 5TE
TEL: (020) 7734 5183 FAX: (020) 7734 5206

COOKING **4**
MODERN EUROPEAN
£37–£55

The style is so unaffected, with white crockery on white tablecloths, it still reminds visitors how pioneering the small dining room was when it opened in 1985. The atmosphere is relaxed, low-key, and 'if one did not know that the head chef was quite famous, one would not have guessed'. In fact James Rix is in charge of day-to-day cooking, and the emphasis remains convincingly and commendably on simply presented ideas, from chicken liver salad with a soft-boiled egg and balsamic dressing, to a buffalo mozzarella and tomato salad with grilled flat bread.

The Italian thrust of the menu is apparent in a wholesome and satisfying Tuscan bean soup, and in sea bass with an Umbrian lentil salad, but there is more besides, not least among fish, from grilled squid chermoula, via bourride, to a plain old-fashioned whole grilled Dover sole with Jersey Royals and parsley butter. Desserts might include a highly charged chocolate tart with espresso ice cream, although the Venetian rice pudding (served with plum compote) seems little different from a conventional British one. It is both welcome and rare to see a West End wine list with bottles under £20, but those with an extra tenner to spend will widen their choice considerably on the short, round-the-world list. House Italian is £14.

CHEFS: Alastair Little and James Rix PROPRIETORS: Alastair Little, Kirsten Tormod Pedersen and Mercedes André-Vega OPEN: Mon to Fri L 12 to 3, Mon to Sat D 6 to 11 CLOSED: bank hols MEALS: Set L £25, Set D £33 SERVICE: not inc CARDS: Amex, Delta, Diners, MasterCard, Switch, Visa DETAILS: 67 seats. Private parties: 25 private room. Vegetarian meals. Children's helpings. Wheelchair access (not WC). No music. Air-conditioned ⊖ Tottenham Court Road

Alastair Little Lancaster Road

map 12

136A Lancaster Road, W11 1TP
TEL: (020) 7243 2220 FAX: (020) 7229 2991

COOKING **3**
MODERN EUROPEAN
£29–£50

The link in both style and tone with Little's sister restaurant in Soho (see entry above) is clear enough, and yet one reporter with experience of both finds this cream-coloured, small but elegant west London venue the more relaxing. Informal service contributes hugely to that, and the laid-back feel seems to suit the sunny Mediterranean food. Fish fares well. Thick, saffron-tinged bourride has come replete with squid, cod and prawns, while brill has been roasted on the bone and served with olive oil mash, rocket and roast tomatoes. At its best the modern food is delivered with some style and can even be exhilarating, although the striving for rustic honesty can occasionally bring it closer to trattoria level. Pear tarte Tatin has received plaudits in more than one report, while a bowl of summer sorbets sent an inspector into orbit, the vivid red version turning out to be 'iced essence of very fresh strawberry'. The same wine list, opening at £14, serves both outlets.

CHEFS: Alastair Little, Tony Abarno and Luigi del Giudice PROPRIETORS: Kirsten Tormod Pedersen, Mercedes André-Vega and Alastair Little OPEN: Mon to Sat 12 to 2.30 (3 Sat), 6.30 to 11 CLOSED: bank hols MEALS: alc L (main courses £8 to £12). Set D £27.50 SERVICE: not inc CARDS: Amex, Delta, Diners, MasterCard, Switch, Visa DETAILS: 40 seats. 10 seats outside. Private parties: 14 main room. Vegetarian meals. Children's helpings. Wheelchair access (not WC). No music. Air-conditioned ⊖ Ladbroke Grove

Al Bustan

map 14

27 Motcomb Street, SW1X 8JU
TEL: (020) 7235 8277 FAX: (020) 7235 1668

COOKING **1**
LEBANESE
£26–£64

This Lebanese restaurant is as comfortable as one might expect in this well-off area. It even has a few tables outside on a tiny terrace. Most meze are vegetarian, among them goats'-cheese salad, hummus, and mouhamara (a paste of nuts and spices in olive oil), while meat options run to lambs' tongue salad, grilled chicken wings with garlic sauce, and kibbeh maklieh (crushed wheat balls stuffed with meat, onion and nuts). Main courses are the usual grills, from marinated chicken with garlic sauce to sea bass with oil and lemon, with some raw lamb items: minced with onions and spices, for instance. Puddings, dispensed from a trolley, run to different types of baklava, and perhaps semolina cake with dates and pistachios. House wines are £12, and a few Lebanese bottles add variety to an otherwise French list.

CHEF: Inam Atalla PROPRIETORS: Mr and Mrs Atalla OPEN: all week noon to 10.45 CLOSED: last two weeks Dec MEALS: alc (main courses £12 to £16). Set L £13, Set D £25. Cover £2 SERVICE: not inc CARDS: Amex, Diners, MasterCard, Switch DETAILS: 70 seats. 20 seats outside. Private parties: 10 main room, 6 to 12 private rooms. Vegetarian meals. Music. Air-conditioned ⊖ Sloane Square, Knightsbridge

Al Duca

NEW ENTRY **map 15**

4–5 Duke of York Street, SW1Y 6LA
TEL: (020) 7839 3090 FAX: (020) 7839 4050

COOKING **4**
ITALIAN
£30–£60

The welcome aim, at Claudio Pulze's venture in a swanky part of town just off Jermyn Street, is to offer reasonably priced Italian food without frills; reporters hope the good value will last. Tans, browns and beige (or terracotta, olive and stone as the PR version has it) combine with bare wooden tables and etched glass to give the oddly shaped room a clean, uncluttered, newly minted look. All this is well matched by Michele Franzolin's capable and unshowy food. He has worked at Zafferano (see entry, London), among other places, and deploys good materials – including his own wide-ribboned pasta with peas and pancetta – to produce a menu of straightforward and approachable dishes.

These are no less successful for using humble ingredients: in a flavourful braised rabbit leg on a pool of creamy polenta with roast endive, or in a tranche of prime, accurately timed roast cod with haricot beans and spring onions. Seasoning has been uneven, and standards might be more consistent, but the simplicity is appreciated, not least in desserts of coconut sorbet with chocolate sauce, or a slice of brownie-like chocolate and almond cake with a fine vanilla ice cream. Friendly, on-the-ball service has a light touch, and the all-Italian wine list combines well- and lesser-known names at largely believable prices that start at £12.50 for Veneto house wine.

CHEF: Michele Franzolin PROPRIETOR: Cuisine Collections OPEN: Mon to Sat 12 to 2.30 (3 Sat), 6 to 10.30 (11 Thur to Sat) CLOSED: bank hols MEALS: Set L £15.50 (2 courses) to £21.50, Set D £18 (2 courses) to £24 SERVICE: 12.5%, card slips closed CARDS: Amex, Delta, MasterCard, Switch, Visa DETAILS: 58 seats. 4 seats outside. Private parties: 11 main room. Vegetarian meals. Wheelchair access (not WC). No music. Air-conditioned ⊖ Piccadilly Circus, Green Park

Al Hamra

map 15

31–33 Shepherd Market, W1Y 7HR
TEL: (020) 7493 1954/1044 FAX: (020) 7493 1044

COOKING **5**
LEBANESE
£35–£58

A rock set in the shifting sea of Shepherd's Market, Al Hamra survives with its unchanging menu, mirror-bright décor and tightly packed tables. The full Lebanese repertoire of more than 40 hot and cold hors d'oeuvres satisfies vegetarians and carnivores alike. Permutations of any two, three or four ingredients from aubergines, leeks, chickpeas, cheese, crushed wheat and couscous, plus a variety of beans and nuts, make up most of the vegetarian dishes. Chicken livers and wings, lambs' kidneys and testicles are among possibilities for meat eaters. Equally adventurous are three versions of raw lamb, with or without parsley and crushed wheat, and there is even raw lamb's liver. By comparison a delicate lambs' tongue salad seems quite conventional.

Chicken and lamb are minced, cut into dice or larger pieces and charcoal-grilled as main courses, and there are a few fish too. Service can seem stern, but with children in the party they will bring out he high chairs and the warmest of welcomes to a new generation of customers. A few outside tables afford a good view of developments carrying on in this carefully preserved, once quiet corner of Mayfair. French house wines are £12.75, Lebanese from the Bekaa valley £16.50.

CHEFS: Mahir Abboud and Ahmad Batah PROPRIETOR: Hassan Fansa OPEN: all week 12 to 11.30 CLOSED: 25 Dec to 1 Jan MEALS: alc (main courses £10 to £13). Cover £2.50 SERVICE: not inc CARDS: Amex, Delta, Diners, MasterCard, Switch, Visa DETAILS: 80 seats. 16 seats outside. Private parties: 80 main room. Vegetarian meals. Children's helpings. Wheelchair access (not WC). Music. Air-conditioned ⊖ Green Park

Al San Vincenzo

map 13

30 Connaught Street, W2 2AF — COOKING **3**
TEL: (020) 7262 9623 — ITALIAN
£37–£58

In a smart street just off the multi-racial, economically diverse Edgware Road, the Borgonzolos' small, quiet, neatly attired restaurant is now a decade old. The menu reads well, its appealing country dishes indicating the deliberately modest ambition in a thin, clear yet robust vegetable soup, and in a generous plateful of mussels, clams and thinly sliced courgette in a slightly salty broth of wine and juices spiked with chilli. Although by current London Italian standards the cooking may seem somewhat old-fashioned, it succeeds within its own terms, producing thinly sliced veal kidney in a mustard sauce, and braised leg of lamb with peas and Parmesan. Desserts were a highlight at inspection: light, moist, carefully flavoured bread-and-butter pudding, and dates stuffed with marzipan and rolled in crushed pistachios, served with vanilla ice cream and chocolate sauce. Puglian red and white house wines at £14 head up a short, all-Italian list.

CHEF: Vincenzo Borgonzolo PROPRIETORS: Elaine and Vincenzo Borgonzolo OPEN: Mon to Fri L 12 to 1.45, Mon to Sat D 7 to 9.45 MEALS: alc L (main courses £12.50 to £21). Set L and D £25 (2 courses) to £31 SERVICE: not inc CARDS: Delta, MasterCard, Visa DETAILS: 24 seats. Private parties: 8 main room. No children under 12. No cigars/pipes in dining room. Music ⊖ Marble Arch

Amandier

map 13

26 Sussex Place, W2 2TH — COOKING **3**
TEL: (020) 7262 6073 FAX: (020) 7723 8395 — FRENCH/PROVENÇALE
£25–£69

Beyond the green awning is a small, narrow dining room with tables down either side, subdued lighting, and a menu with its feet planted in French soil. Tatin of shallot confit takes its place beside baby squid with ratatouille and tomato pistou, followed perhaps by boneless quail stuffed with foie gras on a bed of haricot beans. Some ideas can seem quite strange – langoustine and mandarin orange soup, for example – but execution is generally sound, producing a nicely textured haddock and white kidney bean soup with truffle oil, carefully cooked guinea fowl with root vegetables, and accurately timed sea bass with an aubergine mousse.

Variations on themes among desserts have included vanilla-flavoured goats' milk crème brûlée, and mango bread-and-butter pudding. In-house breads are first-rate. A few wines from around the world (and a dozen or so by the glass) offer some relief from the otherwise aristocratic French collection. Prices start at £12.95 (£3.50 a glass). Bistro Daniel, down a flight of steps, offers less expensive French fare, including snails in garlic and parsley butter, steak frites, and profiteroles with vanilla ice cream.

CHEF/PROPRIETOR: Daniel Gobet OPEN: Mon to Fri L 12 to 2.30, Mon to Sat D 7 to 10.30 MEALS: Set L £9.95 (2 courses) to £18, Set D £25.50 to £37 SERVICE: 12.5% (optional) CARDS: Amex, Delta, Diners, MasterCard, Switch, Visa DETAILS: 25 seats. Private parties: 27 main room, 10 to 24 private rooms. Vegetarian meals. Children's helpings. Wheelchair access (not WC). Music. Air-conditioned ⊖ Lancaster Gate (£5)

Anglesea Arms £

LONDON GFG 2001 COMMENDED

map 12

35 Wingate Road, W6 0UR
TEL: (020) 8749 1291 FAX: (020) 8749 1254

COOKING 4
MODERN EUROPEAN
£22–£35

Gastro-pubs have never developed into a large-scale populist movement, because they rely so much on the talents of the individuals who run them. Dan and Fiona Evans make one of the more effective teams, and their appealing and manifestly popular neighbourhood pub – go early to get a table, or try lunch – combines exciting and original food with commendable value. Ideas are sourced from a seemingly bottomless barrel, taking in cockle, bacon, leek and parsley soup, a Catalan-style gratin of chorizo and eel with garlic, and deep-fried stuffed courgette flowers in beer batter. Dishes are based on sound materials, from line-caught tuna served sashimi-style, to dived scallops with minted split peas.

Sometimes combinations positively crackle with the promise of bright, fresh flavours (perhaps a lobster and mango salad with coriander, lime and salsa), at other times they calm down into a whole roast John Dory with Jersey Royals, spinach and cep butter, but confident execution is the common denominator. Desserts aim to soothe, with toasted banana bread and banana ice cream, or white peach Knockerbocker Glory. Service is bright and friendly, but can also be slow. An ungrasping wine list from all corners has 15 wines by the glass from £2.40; prices start at £9.25 for house Sicilian.

CHEFS: Dan Evans and Jamie Thomas PROPRIETORS: Dan and Fiona Evans OPEN: all week L 12.30 (1 Sun) to 2.45 (3.30 Sun), D 7.30 to 10.30 (10 Sun) CLOSED: 1 week Christmas MEALS: alc (main courses £7 to £10) SERVICE: not inc CARDS: Delta, MasterCard, Switch, Visa DETAILS: 55 seats. 20 seats outside. Private parties: 12 main room. Vegetarian meals. Children's helpings. No cigars/pipes in dining room. Wheelchair access (not WC). No music ⊖ Ravenscourt Park, Goldhawk Road

See inside the front cover for an explanation of the symbols used at the tops of entries.

Arancia £

map 12

52 Southwark Park Road, SE16 3RS
TEL: (020) 7394 1751 FAX: (020) 7394 1044

COOKING **1**
MODERN ITALIAN
£22–£31

A boon to this under-served neighbourhood, Arancia is an Italian restaurant that has been fashioned out of a corner shop and painted orange, as befits the name. From the start it gained plaudits – and crowds of diners – for its 'cool, stylish, restrained' menu, its well-thought-out and well-presented food, and its low prices. A meal might start with pumpkin and mascarpone risotto, or king prawn fritters with fennel, mint and coriander (spot on for both taste and texture), and continue with moderately portioned main courses such as braised cabbage stuffed with couscous and pine nuts in a roast pepper sauce, or pork and tomato ragù on gnocchi. Praise has been lavished on puddings, including chocolate semifreddo. The young, friendly waiters squeeze round the tables with consummate skill, uncorking bottles from the 'fantastically cheap' Italian wine list; house wine is £8.

CHEF: Catherine O'Sullivan PROPRIETOR: A. Rossi OPEN: all week D only 7 to 11 CLOSED: 25 and 26 Dec, Easter MEALS: alc (main courses £9 to £9.50) SERVICE: not inc, card slips closed CARDS: MasterCard, Switch, Visa DETAILS: 40 seats. Private parties: 40 main room. Vegetarian meals. Music (£5)

Aroma II £

map 15

118–120 Shaftesbury Avenue, W1V 7DJ
TEL/FAX: (020) 7437 0377

COOKING **2**
CHINESE
£23–£67

There is no doubting Aroma looks the part, sited between two Chinese herbal medicine shops, and with a window display of roast meats. Two quite small dining areas are decked out in primary colours (yellow walls, deep-blue vinyl tablecloths, red-cushioned chairs) with large fish tanks. The menu is wide-ranging, encompassing undemanding stir-fries of the 'chicken with cashew nuts' ilk (no doubt geared to passing tourists); and luxury seafood such as crab, Dover sole and sea bass. A fascinating specials selection, aimed at keeping Chinese regulars happy, offers pork dumplings fragrant with ginger and coriander, and an adventurous casserole of braised sea cucumber with fish and duck web, although not all dishes taste as fresh as they might. Service is often efficient, but non-Chinese diners might be steered away from ordering the more esoteric dishes. France takes the leading role in a short wine list that starts with house vin de table at £8.20.

CHEF: David Tam PROPRIETOR: Restaurant Aroma London Ltd OPEN: all week 12 to 11.30 (10.30 Sun) MEALS: alc (main courses £6 to £14). Set D from £15 (usually min 2) SERVICE: 12.5% (optional) CARDS: Amex, Delta, Diners, MasterCard, Switch, Visa DETAILS: 120 seats. Private parties: 80 main room, 40 private room. Vegetarian meals. Wheelchair access. Music. Air-conditioned ⊖ Leicester Square, Piccadilly Circus (£5)

indicates that there has been a change of chef since last year's Guide, and the Editor has judged that the change is of sufficient interest to merit the reader's attention.

Asakusa £

map 13

265 Eversholt Street, NW1 1BA
TEL: (020) 7388 8399 FAX: (020) 7388 7589

COOKING **1**
JAPANESE
£16–£35

The printed menu in this charming, pixilated eating house is not just long, but wide-ranging, covering all areas of Japanese cooking from sushi and sashimi to combinations of vegetables, meat or fish, which may be fried, boiled, grilled, or served in soup. Plenty of 'set' dishes for one person make ordering easy (shogayaki, teriyaki and tempura versions come with ginger and soy sauce, rice, soup and pickles), and a nine-course tasting menu includes saké and dessert. Handwritten posters display daily, weekly and seasonal specials. Service is very friendly, so ask for assistance ordering something 'off the wall' if you don't read Japanese. Prices throughout are low. Drink carafes of saké from £2.50, Japanese beer or something from the tiny wine list. House wine is £8.80.

CHEFS: Mr Ishida and Mr Deguchi PROPRIETOR: Mr Hirayama OPEN: Mon to Sat D only 6 to 11.30 (11 Sat) CLOSED: Christmas, New Year, bank hols MEALS: alc (sushi £1 to £3, main courses £4.50 to £12). Set D £9.60 to £18 SERVICE: 12% (optional) CARDS: Amex, Delta, Diners, MasterCard, Switch, Visa DETAILS: 40 seats. Private parties: 40 main room, 30 private room. Vegetarian meals. Wheelchair access (not WC). Occasional music ⊖ Mornington Crescent

Assaggi

map 13

The Chepstow, 39 Chepstow Place, W2 4TS
TEL: (020) 7792 5501

COOKING **3**
ITALIAN
£43–£64

Oddly situated above a perfectly ordinary pub, in a row of large white terraced houses in an affluent part of town, Assaggi appeals for its unaffected down-to-earth style. Tall windows allow plenty of daylight into a room whose plain wooden furniture contrasts agreeably with bright orange walls covered with large, vividly painted canvases. The menu may not change much, but materials are sound as a bell, and the food is perfectly attuned to the times. It is centred around the option to make a meal of starters such as asparagus with poached egg and pancetta, monkfish and squid salad, and beef carpaccio with olive oil, lemon and Parmesan. More substantial but essentially simple main courses are there for the asking too: calf's liver, rack of new-season lamb, or a fillet of turbot or brill served with saffron-flavoured semolina dumplings. Desserts might include fig and almond tart with vanilla ice cream, or fresh poached peaches with meringue and ice cream. A short Italian wine list favours a few expensive bottles, but house Sardinian is £11.95.

CHEF: Nino Sassu PROPRIETORS: Pietro Fraccari and Nino Sassu OPEN: Mon to Sat 12.30 (1 Sat) to 2.30, 7.30 to 11 CLOSED: 2 weeks Christmas, bank hols MEALS: alc (main courses £15.50 to £18.50) SERVICE: not inc, card slips closed CARDS: Amex, Delta, Diners, MasterCard, Switch, Visa DETAILS: 35 seats. Private parties: 6 main room. Vegetarian meals. Children's helpings. No cigars/pipes in dining room. No music. Air-conditioned ⊖ Notting Hill Gate

Atlantic Bar and Grill 🍷

map 15

20 Glasshouse Street, W1R 5RQ
TEL: (020) 7734 4888 FAX: (020) 7734 3609

COOKING **1**
MODERN ENGLISH-PLUS
£27–£78

Cocktails and star-spotting are two of the attractions at this particular Peyton place (he also owns Admiralty, Isola, and Mash – all London, see entries – and Mash, Manchester, see entry). It is a huge underground space with a bouncer at the door, an enormous chandelier in the vast bar, and a high-ceilinged dining room decorated with art installations and covered with acres of tables. A modern menu bristles with up-to-the-minute ideas, alternately precise – specifying Swedish tarragon with cappuccino of crab and langoustines – and vague when it neglects to mention whether the skillet-seared dill-infused mullet is red or grey. Although results can be hit and miss, Thai-flavoured chicken noodle soup, and roast Gressingham duck breast with foie gras have been approved, as have lemon tart and a white chocolate box filled with dark chocolate and raspberry. Prices are on the high side, and those on the wine list rise steeply, with only a few bottles under £20. Carefully chosen from around the world, wines include many great bottles from France, California, Australia and Italy. Fourteen are available by the glass, but the cheapest is £4.60.

CHEF: Richard Sawyer PROPRIETOR: Oliver Peyton OPEN: Mon to Fri L 12 to 3, all week D 6 to 11.30 (7 to 10.30 Sun) CLOSED: 25 and 26 Dec, 1 Jan, Easter Sun and Mon MEALS: alc (main courses £9.50 to £19.50). Set L £14.50, Set D Mon to Fri 6 to 6.30 £14.50 (2 courses) to £16.50. Cover £1 SERVICE: 12.5% (optional), card slips closed CARDS: Amex, Delta, Diners, MasterCard, Switch, Visa DETAILS: 180 seats. Private parties: 70 main room. Music. Air-conditioned ⊖ Piccadilly Circus

Aubergine

map 14

11 Park Walk, SW10 0AJ
TEL: (020) 7352 3449 FAX: (020) 7351 1770

COOKING **7**
FRENCH
£34–£102

Just about the only adult restaurant in an area packed with bars and eateries for the younger set, Aubergine offers distinctly pleasurable food in convivial surroundings. Gold-framed oil paintings of desolate landscapes hang on brushed saffron- and ochre-coloured walls, contributing to the 'understated elegance' of the dining room, whose serious wattage lights make it possible to read menus on other tables. The contemporary French approach incorporates a lot of duck liver, shellfish and other expensive materials, and although dishes are hardly original or innovative, tasting them brings an appreciation of the light touch, technical skill, and refined flavours that characterise William Drabble's style. Try making these at home, suggested one visitor, to discover just how difficult they are to reproduce successfully.

Given the modest price differential, the seven-course menu gourmand is worth a punt, judging by one visitor's meal of herb-enhanced game soup, fine-textured foie gras mousse topped with grilled girolles, first-rate scallops with a central pool of intense pea purée (a trademark dish), red mullet with tomato confit, fillet of beef surrounded by concentric circles of celeriac purée and Madeira jus, French cheeses in tiptop condition (one of London's better examples), and caramelised pineapple with coconut ice cream and vanilla butter sauce. The last is a fine balance of restrained sweetness and a proper understanding of how flavours work together, and most of these dishes succeed because of first-class ingredients and relatively straightforward combinations which produce clear and well-defined outcomes.

Such harmony has shown itself in, for example, a first course combining tender, crisp-skinned quail with crunchy sweetbreads, enriched by foie gras and a truffle dressing. Other successes have included immaculately fresh and accurately timed John Dory, sitting on crushed potatoes with a fine shellfish sauce, while desserts run to poached figs with fromage blanc mousse and sorbet, and lemon Chiboust with passion-fruit sauce. Service is leisurely and just about proficient, although it needs to be much sharper to match the food. Wines from Bordeaux, Burgundy and the Rhône make up the bulk of this classy list, although an effort has been made to include top wines from other countries. Prices, however, take away all the enjoyment. The Sommelier's selection starts at £21.

CHEF: William Drabble PROPRIETOR: A to Z Restaurants Ltd OPEN: Mon to Fri L 12 to 2.30, Mon to Sat D 7 to 11.15 CLOSED: Christmas, 2 weeks Aug, bank hols MEALS: Set L £16 (2 courses) to £19.50, Set D £42 to £80 SERVICE: 12.5% (optional), card slips closed CARDS: Amex, Delta, Diners, MasterCard, Switch, Visa DETAILS: 55 seats. Private parties: 55 main room. Children's helpings. Wheelchair access (not WC). No music. Air-conditioned ⊖ Gloucester Road

Avenue

map 15

7–9 St James's Street, SW1A 1EE
TEL: (020) 7321 2111 FAX: (020) 7321 2500
EMAIL: avenue@egami.co.uk
WEB SITE: www.theavenue.co.uk

COOKING **5**
MODERN EUROPEAN
£33–£65

Some might bemoan the lack of pictures and clutter, and while one reporter likens it to an aircraft hangar, another considers it one of London's 'great eating spaces', thanks to its openness and light, helped by a big window giving on to the street. Dean Carr's menu plays to the gallery with Caesar salad, fish fingers and sticky toffee pudding, but if it opts for comfort over adventure, then at least the results are well controlled and standards pretty well maintained. Menu descriptions tend to be brief – stuffed rabbit saddle with roast venison, or 'vegetarian special' – but then dishes often have a lightness of touch too.

Starters seem to favour southern Europe in the shape of gnocchi with roast red peppers, or leek and truffle cheese tortellini, while mains are more, well, mainstream: seared cod with soft onions and crunchy lentils, or duck breast with caramelised onions. Among desserts, steamed treacle pudding is highly praised, and service is 'attentive without getting in the way'. Anyone counting the pennies may like to note that the comparatively good-value fixed-price lunch is not just an also-ran, but comes with ten or more choices per course. Wines can push the bill up, but they are sharply chosen, and over 20 are available by the glass.

Subscribers to Which? Online can access The Good Food Guide *on www.which.net.*

CHEF: Dean Carr PROPRIETORS: Christopher Bodker and Marian Scrutton OPEN: Mon to Sat 12 to 3, 5.45 to 12 (12.30 Fri and Sat), Sun 12 to 3.30, 7 to 10 CLOSED: 25 and 26 Dec, 1 Jan MEALS: alc D (main courses £12 to £17.50). Set L £17.50 (2 courses) to £19.50, Set D before 7.30 and after 10.15 £14.50 (2 courses) to £16.50 SERVICE: 12.5% (optional), card slips closed CARDS: Amex, Delta, Diners, MasterCard, Switch, Visa DETAILS: 180 seats. Private parties: 180 main room. Vegetarian meals. Wheelchair access (also WC). No music. Air-conditioned ⊖ Green Park

Azou £

NEW ENTRY map 12

375 King Street, W6 9NJ
TEL: (020) 8563 7266 FAX: (020) 8748 1009

COOKING **2**
NORTH AFRICAN
£21–£42

Simple, unpretentious and restrained decor forms the backdrop to a slightly unusual set-up, where the warmly welcoming Algerian owner lists main courses by their country of origin, from Algeria, Morocco or Tunisia. He says the differences are largely in the vegetables and spices in a tajine or couscous. Algerian couscous royale is gargantuan, consisting of accurately cooked lamb shank, crisp-skinned, moist chicken breast, and subtly spiced but not chilli-hot merguez; accompanying vegetables include leeks and courgettes as well as carrot and chickpeas. Moroccan chicken tajine with seafood (mussels, squid and prawns) is equally successful. Brik – ultra-crisp pastry stuffed with tuna, potato and egg – makes a fine starter, puddings include traditional North African pastries, and dates come with the bill. Cineastes can drink Casablanca lager with tagine Casablanca, or enjoy house wines at £9.70.

CHEF/PROPRIETOR: Azou Benarab OPEN: Mon to Fri L 12 to 2.30, all week D 6 to 11 MEALS: alc (main courses £6.50 to £14). Set D £13.50 to £16 (min 2) SERVICE: 12.5% (optional) CARDS: Delta, Diners, MasterCard, Switch, Visa DETAILS: 36 seats. Private parties: 40 main room. Vegetarian meals. Occasional music. Air-conditioned ⊖ Stamford Brook (£5)

Babur Brasserie

map 12

119 Brockley Rise, SE23 1JP
TEL: (020) 8291 2400 and 4881
FAX: (020) 8291 4881
EMAIL: babur-brasserie@compuserve.com

COOKING **2**
INDIAN
£25–£47

The owners say the restaurant is unchanged since last year. True, the white, tiger-topped fascia and the bright interior are as before, but the enlarged menu offers new dishes, and some prices are slightly reduced. Starters now include Goan prawn balchao with red chillies served with mini naan, deep-fried chicken slivers studded with sesame seeds, and tandoori-baked paneer with tomatoes, onions and peppers in a rich makhani sauce. Among new main courses are raan gulnar (pot-roast shank of lamb), caldine, which the menu describes as 'an aristocratic maritime dish' of monkfish in tamarind- and coriander-spiced coconut milk, and salmon au Babur, consisting of a poached cutlet with spicy mashed potatoes, onions and caramelised baby tomatoes. Expect to find chocolate among the desserts. House wines are £7.95.

The nearest underground station is indicated at the end of London entries.

CHEF: Enam Rahman PROPRIETOR: Babur 1998 Ltd OPEN: Sat to Thur L 12.15 to 2.15, all week D 6.15 to 11.15 CLOSED: 25 and 26 Dec MEALS: alc (main courses £7 to £12) SERVICE: not inc CARDS: Amex, Delta, Diners, MasterCard, Switch, Visa DETAILS: 56 seats. Private parties: 20 main room. Vegetarian meals. Children's helpings. No smoking in 1 dining room. Music. Air-conditioned (£5)

Back to Basics £ map 15

21A Foley Street, W1P 7LA COOKING **3**
TEL: (020) 7436 2181 FAX: (020) 7436 2180 SEAFOOD
WEB SITE: www.backtobasics.uk.com £22–£48

It is not just the décor that is basic in this small restaurant on a corner site not far from Oxford Street, where bare bulbs in strong colours hang from metal shades, and there is little space between tables. Exceedingly fresh fish is the main business, and dishes are crossed off the 12-item, daily-changing blackboard menu as supplies run out. Expect to find anything from wing of skate with brown butter and capers, to a large fillet of well-timed sea trout with samphire and watercress mayonnaise, or perhaps monkfish accompanied by spicy, garlicky prawn couscous.

Starters include marinated herring fillet with beetroot and sour cream (an object lesson in assembling and presenting a harmonious dish), and meat eaters get a look-in with sausages and steaks. Side dishes include potatoes most ways except – odd for a fish restaurant, perhaps – chipped. Finish with a deep apple pie with crisp pastry and spicy fruit, or go for bananas baked with rum. Service is skilful and friendly, and house wines are £9.95 and £10.95, with some interesting bottles (and halves) on the 'alternative cellar' list.

CHEFS: Stefan Pflaumer and Philip Banks PROPRIETOR: Stefan Pflaumer OPEN: Mon to Fri 12 to 3, 6 to 10 CLOSED: Christmas, first 3 weeks Sept, bank hols MEALS: alc (main courses £8 to £14.50) SERVICE: 10% (optional), card slips closed CARDS: Amex, Delta, Diners, MasterCard, Switch, Visa DETAILS: 40 seats. 50 seats outside. Private parties: 40 main room. Vegetarian meals. Children's helpings. Wheelchair access (not WC). Occasional music ⊖ Oxford Circus (£5)

Bali Sugar map 13

33A All Saints Road, W11 1HE NEW CHEF
TEL: (020) 7221 4477 FAX: (020) 7221 9955 FUSION
WEB SITE: www.thesugarclub.com £37–£70

As the Guide went to press, David Selex was about to assume overall responsibility for the cooking both here and at Sugar Club (see entry), assisted in this case by Simon Fenwick. Menus fizz and pop with bright ideas, some needing a bit of code-cracking to decipher, but underneath it all is an enthusiastic and effective approach informed by taste and imagination, respecting no culinary boundaries. Among dishes that might (or equally, might not, given the pace of invention) turn up are spicy peanut roast crab and fish mash with cucumber, chicken breast served on an egg noodle 'pancake' with vegetables, and Egyptian boiled orange cake with candied lemon and clotted cream. Reports on progress are welcome. Only a handful of bottles on the equally resourceful wine list is under £20. Vins de Pays d'Oc is the cheapest at £10.95.

CHEFS: David Selex and Simon Fenwick PROPRIETORS: Ashley Sumner and Vivienne Hayman OPEN: Tue to Sun L 12.30 to 3, all week D 6.30 to 11 CLOSED: 24 Dec to 3 Jan, Easter Mon MEALS: alc (main courses £14 to £19). Set L £12.50 (2 courses) SERVICE: 12.5% (optional), card slips closed CARDS: Amex, Delta, Diners, MasterCard, Switch, Visa DETAILS: 70 seats. 20 seats outside. Private parties: 40 main room, 40 private room. Vegetarian meals. No smoking in 1 dining room. Wheelchair access (not WC). No music ⊖ Westbourne Park

Bank

map 13

1 Kingsway, WC2B 6XF
TEL: (020) 7234 3344 FAX: (020) 7234 3343
EMAIL: bank@bgr.plc.uk
WEB SITE: www.bankrestaurant.co.uk

COOKING **4**
MODERN FRENCH
£28–£91

On a prominent corner site between theatre-land and the law courts, Bank obliges all comers with long opening hours, a busy bar, and a brightly coloured and often noisy dining room. Chefs work feverishly in the open-plan kitchen, glass shards hang apparently precariously from the ceiling, and a diverse menu caters equally for shellfish lovers, fish addicts and the steak and chips brigade. Choice is extremely generous, ranging from hot buttered lobster to sausage and mash, and pasta is one of several recurring constituents: perhaps an open ravioli of asparagus with white onion and truffle cream, or thick linguine packed with fresh crab and red chillies.

Given the scale of the operation, it may not be surprising that standards fluctuate, but materials impress and notable desserts have included a refreshing rhubarb soup, and a chocolate and coffee extravaganza called Gâteau Opera. Brunch gets favourable reviews, and seamless service is friendly, helpful and professional. A well-thought-out selection of wines, combining Old and New Worlds, is grouped according to fruit and weight: the range of whites includes 'light crisp', 'juicy aromatic', 'smooth oaky'. House French starts at £12.50, and there are 18 wines by the glass. While prices on the main list are fair, the Bank Cellar selection is there to tempt the expense-account diner. A sister restaurant, also called Bank, has opened in Birmingham (see entry).

CHEF: Julian O'Neill PROPRIETOR: BGR plc OPEN: all week 12 (11.30 Sat and Sun) to 3, 5.30 to 11.15 (9.30 Sun) CLOSED: bank hols MEALS: alc (main courses £7.50 to £28). Set L and D 5.30 to 7 and 10 to 11.15 £13.90 (2 courses) to £17.50 SERVICE: 12.5% CARDS: Amex, Delta, Diners, MasterCard, Switch, Visa DETAILS: 220 seats. Private parties: 20 main room. Vegetarian meals. Children's helpings. Wheelchair access (also WC). Music. Air-conditioned ⊖ Holborn

Belair House

map 12

Gallery Road, SE21 7AB
TEL: (020) 8299 9788 FAX: (020) 8299 6793
WEB SITE: www.belairhouse.co.uk

COOKING **3**
MODERN EUROPEAN
£30–£49

The elegant Georgian-style house, rebuilt after the war, is handy for the art gallery. Its modern interior is quite a contrast to the façade (floodlit at night), with hard surfaces in the bar, and a smart minimalist dining room: all the better, perhaps, to match a menu that deals in blackened cod with butter beans, crispy marinated pork salad, and veal with a snail and parsley sauce. Colin Barnett is a 'dab hand with the blender', puréeing red peppers to accompany an underwhelming prawn starter, and creaming salsify to go with successful rare beef sirloin. Results have been rather hit and miss but have included an impressive chocolate and cherry fondant with Kirsch ice cream. Staff are friendly, and some 80 sharply chosen wines start at £15 and soon rise above the £20 barrier.

CHEF: Colin Barnett PROPRIETORS: Gary and Jayne Cady OPEN: all week 12 to 2.30, 7 to 10.30 CLOSED: Sun D in winter MEALS: Set L Mon to Sat £14.50 (2 courses) to £17.50, Set L and D £25.95 SERVICE: 12.5% (optional), card slips closed CARDS: Amex, Delta, Diners, MasterCard, Switch, Visa DETAILS: 100 seats. 30 seats outside. Private parties: 85 main room, 14 private room. Car park. Vegetarian meals. Children's helpings. No cigars/pipes in dining room. Wheelchair access (also WC). Music (£5)

Belgo Noord

map 13

72 Chalk Farm Road, NW1 8AN — NEW CHEF
TEL: (020) 7267 0718 FAX: (020) 7284 4842 — BELGIAN
WEB SITE: www.belgo-restaurants.co.uk — £25–£59

Although the ambience resembles that of a noisy submarine, it suits a lively clientele of all ages. This strand of Belgian cuisine offers unfussy 'urban peasant food', delivered in satisfyingly substantial quantities by efficient and friendly staff. Derek Smith, who previously worked at the Ladbroke Grove branch, arrived just as the Guide was going to press. Mussels are set to continue as the mainstay (all the way up to a Rabelaisian one kilo pot), supported by anything from crab fritters to Chimay sausages with stoemp, not to mention waffles and pancakes. House wines are £9.95 but beer – about 100 are listed – rules the roost. A two-hour time limit applies, and 'optional' service is 15 per cent.

CHEF: Derek Smith PROPRIETOR: Belgo Group plc OPEN: Mon to Fri 12 to 3, 6 to 11.15, Sat and Sun 12 to 11.15 CLOSED: 24 and 25 Dec MEALS: alc (main courses £8 to £20). Set L £5 (1 course), Set D £17.95 (2 courses); set meals include wine or beer SERVICE: 15% (optional), card slips closed CARDS: Amex, Delta, Diners, MasterCard, Switch, Visa DETAILS: 160 seats. Private parties: 160 main room. Vegetarian meals. Children's helpings. Wheelchair access (not WC). No music. Air-conditioned ⊖ Chalk Farm

Belvedere

NEW ENTRY **map 13**

off Abbotsbury Road, Holland Park, W8 6LU — COOKING **5**
TEL: (020) 7602 1238 FAX: (020) 7610 4382 — MODERN BRITISH/MEDITERRANEAN
WEB SITE: www.whitestarline.org.uk — £31–£78

Located in one of London's best parks, the Belvedere has had several owners over the years, but Jimmy Lahoud's involvement points to a new seriousness of purpose; he has, in his time, set up numerous successful ventures with Marco Pierre White. Visitors can pop into the Japanese garden for a few moments of peace, or spend hours at the opera in summer, before making for the well-designed and convivial space, variously filled with huge black lanterns and big vases of fresh flowers, and lightened by plenty of large windows and glass screens.

Marco Pierre White's imprint is all over the menu, which stays with classical brasserie favourites, many tried and tested at the Mirabelle (see entry, London): a smooth terrine of foie gras is a case in point, surrounded by Sauternes jelly. Seafood is typically well handled, from tagliatelle with half a dozen langoustines in a creamy and flavourful bisque, to a simply and accurately grilled lobster with béarnaise mousseline and crunchy green broccoli. Perhaps because dishes plough a familiar furrow they tend to appear workmanlike rather than exciting, but at least the kitchen gets things right, turning out commendable braised oxtail encased in caul fat, caramelised apple tart, and a delicate and beautifully made champagne jelly set with mixed fruit. Male French staff are chirpy enough, even if some are rather inexperienced, while wine lovers are treated with hauteur, being offered little under £20 but lots in three figures.

CHEF: Tim Payne PROPRIETOR: Jimmy Lahoud OPEN: all week 12 to 2.30 (3.30 Sun), 6 (5.30 during Holland Park opera season) to 11 (10.30 Sun) MEALS: alc (main courses £11.50 to £22.50). Set L Mon to Sat and D 5.30 to 6.30 during opera season £14.95 (2 courses) to £17.95, Set L Sun £19.50 SERVICE: 12.5%, card slips closed CARDS: Amex, Diners, MasterCard, Switch, Visa DETAILS: 100 seats. 24 seats outside. Private parties: 130 main room. No music. Air-conditioned ⊖ Holland Park, High Street Kensington

Bibendum **map 14**

Michelin House, 81 Fulham Road, SW3 6RD
TEL: (020) 7581 5817 FAX: (020) 7823 7148 — COOKING **5**
EMAIL: manager@bibendum.co.uk — MODERN BRITISH
WEB SITE: www.bibendum.co.uk — £42–£105

Bibendum's evocative conversion from a 1905 garage does for dining rooms what the Orient Express has done for trains. It excites a period feel, yet is timeless and impervious to fashion; it delights with countless variations on the Michelin tyre theme, and persuades you that this is the only place to be. No wonder it has a lively atmosphere and a firm following. The menu offers a seductive array of dishes in broadly European mould, from salt-cod salad with niçoise relish to rabbit with beetroot, polenta and horseradish cream. It combines all-time favourites that are unlikely to disappear (Burgundian snails, deep-fried fillet of plaice with chips and tartare sauce, chocolate pithiviers), with more seasonal items on a monthly-changing carte: perhaps risotto with white truffle, or English asparagus with morels and poached egg.

While results do not always match expectations, the kitchen has charmed reporters with cold summery soups of celeriac and curried apple, a warm salad of lambs' tongues, and a redoubtable dish of veal sweetbreads with beurre noisette and French fries. Desserts of hot chocolate fondant with coffee ice cream, or cold rice pudding with mango and cardamom are no less indulgent. Service achieves the right balance between formality and familiarity. Mature wines are a feature of the impeccable French selection, which has eight vintages of Ch. d'Yquem going back to 1945, although the vast list offers an international range littered with star producers. House French is a refreshing £12. A licensed coffee bar has opened in the forecourt (Monday to Sat 8.30 to 5), selling drinks and sandwiches.

CHEF: Matthew Harris PROPRIETORS: Graham Williams, Sir Terence Conran, Lord Hamlyn and Simon Hopkinson OPEN: all week 12 to 2.30 (12.30 to 3 Sat and Sun), 7 to 11.30 (10.30 Sun) MEALS: alc D (main courses £16.50 to £23). Set L £23 (2 courses) to £27.50 SERVICE: 12.5% (optional), card slips closed CARDS: Amex, Delta, Diners, MasterCard, Switch, Visa DETAILS: 72 seats. Private parties: 100 main room. Children's helpings. Wheelchair access (not WC). No music. Air-conditioned ⊖ South Kensington

Birdcage

map 15

110 Whitfield Street, W1P 5RU
TEL: (020) 7323 9655 FAX: (020) 7323 9616

COOKING **3**
FUSION-PLUS
£39–£63

Bland, conformist and big are three words nobody would ever apply to the Birdcage. Indeed, its mission is to kick against such trends in the restaurant world, and size is the first indication of how seriously it means business. Cramped to start with, it shrinks further thanks to the clutter of artefacts from a Tibetan prayer wheel to a display of peacock feathers. 'As you enter and leave you walk through a patch of gravel where a doormat would normally be.' Menus are taped inside old books, the wine list is folded up origami style, the waitress may be wearing face paint and glitter, and instead of butter with the bread, you get a dish of pumpkin purée flavoured with green tea and wasabi. And scorpion ('vaguely nutty in taste') appears as both a canapé and, chocolate covered, for dessert.

Obviously, 'weird' doesn't even begin to describe it, any more than 'fertile' comes close to summing up the kitchen's imaginative approach. Make what you will of black-ink hen terrine with white truffles, goat consommé with Irish moss and wakame tartlet, or cactus rice knapsacks in a pan-leaf canvas wrap. Among the more impressive dishes at inspection were a starter of pine-smoked reindeer carpaccio with anchovy, wasabi and tomato chutney, and a main-course risotto of seaweed, porcini and hemp with coriander mascarpone. If the scorpion doesn't appeal, finish with tagine-steamed cinnamon and quark jaggery, or gum leaf and wheatgrass brûlée. A bell on each table eventually attracts the attention of a server. Please allow four hours for dinner. Wines include one from Eritrea (where else), an Israeli rosé, and one costing over £7,000. Prices start at £17.50.

CHEF: Michael von Hruschka PROPRIETOR: Caroline Faulkner OPEN: Mon to Fri L 12 to 2.30, Mon to Sat D 6 to 11.30 MEALS: Set L £19.50 (2 courses) to £26.50, Set D before 8.15 £25 (2 courses), Set D £32.50 (2 courses) to £38.50 SERVICE: not inc CARDS: Amex, Delta, Diners, MasterCard, Switch, Visa DETAILS: 35 seats. 6 seats outside. Vegetarian meals. Children's helpings. No smoking area. Wheelchair access (not WC). Music ⊖ Goodge St (£5)

Bleeding Heart

NEW ENTRY **map 13**

Bleeding Heart Yard, Greville Street, EC1N 8SJ
TEL: (020) 7242 8238 FAX: (020) 7831 1402
EMAIL: bookings@bleedingheart.co.uk
WEB SITE: www.bleedingheart.co.uk

COOKING **3**
FRENCH
£34–£63

First, get your bearings. The business consists of a basement restaurant with a Bistro above and Terrace next door, plus the Tavern, reached across the cobbled courtyard. The warren-like restaurant has a formal air, with wood-panelling, dim lighting, starched linen and French-speaking waiters. What comes from the kitchen is traditional French cooking plus a few global concessions to modern tastes, yielding dishes from sweet-tasting seared scallops with fennel and ginger, to sauté sea bass on a lobster brandade with provençale sauce. Raw materials are impressive, for example in lean, intensely flavoured roast cutlets of Welsh lamb with rosemary sauce, and in rack of young New Zealand venison with roasted vegetables and wild mushrooms.

Technical accomplishment shines through in desserts too: a fine pear and pineapple parfait with ginger-infused custard for one visitor, and a blueberry and blackberry mousse that pleased for its colours and flavours. Robyn Wilson's New Zealand roots show up throughout the wine list, and house wines come from Trinity Hill, a vineyard she and her husband own in Hawkes Bay. Although New World wines are reasonably priced, French bottles seem to command a premium. Nine house wines are available by the glass, from £3.25 (£14.95 a bottle), and a number of 50-centilitre bottles and halves are on offer.

CHEF: Mickael Weiss PROPRIETORS: Robert and Robyn Wilson OPEN: Mon to Fri 12 to 2.30, 6 to 10.30 CLOSED: 10 days from 24 Dec, bank hols MEALS: alc (main courses £10 to £17) SERVICE: 12.5% (optional), card slips closed CARDS: Amex, Delta, Diners, MasterCard, Switch, Visa DETAILS: 120 seats. 30 seats outside. Private parties: 65 main room, 40 to 150 private rooms. Car park at D. Vegetarian meals. No music. Air-conditioned ⊖ Farringdon, Chancery Lane

Bluebird

map 14

350 King's Road, SW3 5UU — COOKING **3**
TEL: (020) 7559 1000 FAX: (020) 7559 1111 — MODERN EUROPEAN
WEB SITE: www.bluebird-store.co.uk — £27–£81

Bright, airy, casual and comfortable, Bluebird has broad appeal. A stroll around the deli-supermarket is recommended, the bar offers a good perch from which to scan the crowd, and the simply presented menu is generous in scope. In common with other Conran restaurants, seafood is given prominence, from oysters to caviar to a seafood platter (£84 for two including a lobster). At the more affordable end of the scale, consider the set-lunch and early-evening deal. Elsewhere, choice ranges from above-average Caesar salad, via gnocchi, risotto and pizza (with ratte potatoes, fontina and thyme), to rabbit with parsley mash. Roasting and grilling are the main treatments, helped by a wood-fired oven from which might emerge tomatoes (with pesto and rocket), sardines (with olives and capers), and organic pork loin (with bean ragoût). Finish with pavlova and sour cherries, or chocolate tart. Service is brisk enough to get everybody through – in the allotted one and three-quarter hours during busy periods – without being pushy. Liquid refreshment helps the bill to escalate rapidly, although wines are well chosen and there are 18 house selections by the glass.

CHEF: Andrew Sargent PROPRIETOR: Conran Restaurants Ltd OPEN: all week 12 (11 Sat and Sun) to 3.30, 6 to 11 CLOSED: 25 and 26 Dec MEALS: alc (main courses £9.50 to £29.50). Set L and D 6 to 7.30 £12.75 (2 courses) to £15.75 SERVICE: 12.5% (optional), card slips closed CARDS: Amex, Delta, Diners, MasterCard, Switch, Visa DETAILS: 240 seats. Private parties: 30 private room. Vegetarian meals. Children's helpings. Wheelchair access (also WC). Music. Air-conditioned ⊖ Sloane Square

Blue Elephant

map 12

4–6 Fulham Broadway, SW6 1AA
TEL: (020) 7385 6595 FAX: (020) 7386 7665
EMAIL: london@blueelephant.com
WEB SITE: www.blueelephant.com

COOKING **1**
THAI
£26–£79

In an effort to become a blue mammoth, a long-promised enlargement was scheduled for just after the Guide went to press. It will provide a bigger kitchen, extra restaurant tables, and a spacious bar designed in the style of a royal barge in Bangkok. Overall refurbishment will leave the luxuriant jungle décor intact, and the colourful national costumes of the staff. The menu offers two multi-course banquets, and vegetarian options supplement the long carte. Starters include familiar fishcakes, satay, and various crisp-fried delicacies such as prawn and sweetcorn sarika. Among main dishes are many curries, but it is wise to order one, or two at most, and to add stir-fries and grilled or braised dishes for contrast. Thai salads make for variety, but note that they are usually chilli-hot. House wines are £10.50.

CHEFS: Rungsan Mulijan and Sri-Eim Surapol PROPRIETOR: Blue Elephant International plc OPEN: Sun to Fri L 12 to 2.30 (3 Sun), all week D 7 (6.30 Sat) to 12.30 (10.30 Sun) CLOSED: 4 days Christmas MEALS: alc (main courses £7.50 to £19.50). Set L £10 (2 courses) to £15, Set D £29 to £34. Cover £1.50 SERVICE: not inc CARDS: Amex, Delta, Diners, MasterCard, Switch, Visa DETAILS: 250 seats. Private parties: 100 main room. Vegetarian meals. Children's helpings. Wheelchair access (also WC). Music. Air-conditioned ⊖ Fulham Broadway

Blue Print Café

map 13

Design Museum, Butlers Wharf, SE1 2YD
TEL: (020) 7378 7031 FAX: (020) 7357 8810
WEB SITE: www.conran.co.uk

COOKING **5**
MODERN EUROPEAN
£34–£66

The modern white building may be at variance with its neighbouring Victorian warehouses along the river front, but it chimes in well with its own white Formica tables, and black and white photographs. And the view is hard to beat. If Jeremy Lee's cooking has a centre of gravity it is probably in the Mediterranean, although his net extends from northern European herrings (served with cucumber and potato salads) to Arab salads with flat bread. The well-balanced menu is pleasingly 'free of bizarre fusion experiments', and dishes are well conceived, taking in a starter of sea kale with mustard, black truffle and poached egg, followed by rabbit leg with chanterelles, garlic and polenta.

Vegetarians might be offered a main-course tart of ewes'-milk cheese with potatoes and baby artichoke, and fish options have included brill with braised lettuce and carrots in beurre blanc. The range of desserts is equally enticing, from simple Greek yoghurt with blackberry compote and shortcake to an orange curd steamed pudding with custard. Staff go efficiently about their business, but the cost remains a bone of contention for reporters. This is not helped by high wine prices, appealing though the varietally arranged list is. House Merlot and Marsanne are £14.50.

CHEF: Jeremy Lee PROPRIETOR: Conran Restaurants Ltd OPEN: all week L 12 to 2.45, Mon to Sat D 6 to 10.45 CLOSED: Christmas bank hols MEALS: alc (main courses £11 to £20) SERVICE: 12.5% (optional), card slips closed CARDS: Amex, Delta, Diners, MasterCard, Switch, Visa DETAILS: 120 seats. Private parties: 120 main room. Vegetarian meals. Wheelchair access (not WC). No music. Air-conditioned ⊖ Tower Hill, London Bridge

Brackenbury

map 12

129–131 Brackenbury Road, W6 0BQ
TEL: (020) 8748 0107 FAX: (020) 8741 0905

COOKING **4**
MODERN BRITISH
£21–£45

Things don't stand still at this popular Hammersmith spot. The ambience is famously direct and unadorned – four-square wooden tables and flimsy chairs in two split-level rooms – while menus change daily, not once but twice, and sometimes metamorphose during the same service. Scallop salad has offered well-timed shellfish with crunchy leaves and a subtle lacing of ginger in the dressing, while roast vegetable salad with goats' cheese has also scored highly for simplicity. Main-course omelettes have become a feature, perhaps made with goose eggs and filled with sorrel, or enriched with Gruyère.

Italian-inspired dishes are typically done well, be it Piedmontese pepper with rocket and balsamic as an accompaniment to plaice, or rack of lamb with grilled aubergine, courgette and pesto. Stay Italian for pannacotta with strawberry sauce, or go for the visual dazzle of peaches with meringue and a blood-red coulis. Service is variable: one reader found it faultless, another got tired of waving her hand in the air. The conscientiously chosen wines are fairly priced, and span a range from house Languedoc at £9.75 to Chateau Sociando-Mallet 1989 at £55.

CHEF: Marcia Chang Hong PROPRIETOR: Christopher Bodker OPEN: Sun to Fri L 12.30 to 2.45, Mon to Sat D 7 to 10.45 CLOSED: Christmas and New year MEALS: alc (main courses £8.50 to £15). Set L £10.50 (2 courses) to £12.50 SERVICE: not inc CARDS: Amex, Delta, MasterCard, Switch, Visa DETAILS: 60 seats. 20 seats outside. Private parties: 30 main room. Vegetarian meals. Children's helpings. No cigars/pipes in dining room. No music ⊖ Hammersmith

Bradleys

map 13

25 Winchester Road, NW3 3NR
TEL: (020) 7722 3457 FAX: (020) 7435 1392

COOKING **4**
MODERN EUROPEAN
£27–£56

Everything seems understated at the Bradleys' neighbourhood restaurant in a Swiss Cottage side-street. The low-key frontage, minimally decorated interior, and soberly attired staff moving about among large iron urns, combine to give an impression of elegant restraint. Simon Bradley also keeps the cooking simple, concentrating on sound Mediterranean techniques and bright flavours to make an impact. Cheese adds depth to first courses: soft peppered goats' in watercress soup; shavings of Parmesan adorning beef carpaccio; and ravioli of Taleggio and basil accompanying simply grilled seasonal asparagus.

Fish shows up well in main courses of tuna au poivre with frîtes, and sautéed scallops with a leek tart and sweet pea sauce, while an inventive twist on an old theme has produced Gressingham duck with orange-glazed chicory and spinach. Desserts hark back to schooldays in the shape of marmalade ice cream to accompany chocolate pudding, jelly alongside a raspberry mille-feuille, and custard with a rhubarb and orange soufflé. With the exception of champagne, wines are entirely from the southern hemisphere and the USA: look to Chile and Australia for bottles under £20. Seven wines are available by the glass for less than £5.

CHEF: Simon Bradley PROPRIETORS: Simon and Jolanta Bradley OPEN: Sun to Fri L 12 to 3, all week D 6 to 11 MEALS: alc D (main courses £10.50 to £16.50). Set L Mon to Fri £14 (2 courses) to £17, Set L Sun £15 (2 courses) to £18 SERVICE: 12% (optional), card slips closed CARDS: Amex, Delta, MasterCard, Switch, Visa DETAILS: 63 seats. Private parties: 63 main room. Vegetarian meals. Children's helpings. No cigars/pipes in dining-room. Wheelchair access (not WC). Music. Air-conditioned ⊖ Swiss Cottage (£5)

Brady's £ — map 12

513 Old York Road, SW18 1TF — COOKING 1
TEL: (020) 8877 9599 — FISH 'N' CHIPS
£18–£25

Simplicity is the hallmark of this fish 'n' chip shop and restaurant. Wooden tables and a no-nonsense listing of reasonably priced dishes are key to Luke Brady's operation. Starters may take in cod's roe, cockles, potted shrimps, or anchovies and sweet herrings, while mains are helped out by battered or grilled skate, sea bass, or haddock among the dozen or so options. Mushy peas and chips are natural partners, while uncomplicated desserts include unchanging apple crumble, or treacle tart. Ten wines are available from £7.95.

CHEF: Luke Brady PROPRIETORS: Luke and Amelia Brady OPEN: Thur to Sun L 12 to 2.45, Mon to Sat D 6.30 to 10.30 (10.45 Thurs and Fri) CLOSED: Christmas, Easter, bank hols MEALS: alc (main courses £6 to £8) SERVICE: 10% (optional) CARDS: none DETAILS: 50 seats. Children's helpings. Music

Brasserie St Quentin  — map 14

243 Brompton Road, SW3 2EP — COOKING 2
TEL: (020) 7589 8005 FAX: (020) 7584 6064 — FRENCH
£26–£45

The Parisian feel of this Brompton brasserie is reflected in mirrors along either side of a room in which chandeliers twinkle appealingly, and tables feel tiny. Terrine de foie gras gelée au Sauternes and sole de Douvres grillé au beurre maître d'hôtel represent a fast-vanishing species of cooking in the capital. A warm salad of pinkish, tender chicken livers with raspberry vinegar dressing has made a satisfactory starter, as has a straightforward serving of smoked halibut and salmon with warm blinis and herbed crème fraîche. Parsley-crusted rack of tender, young lamb with dauphinoise and a sauce containing roast garlic cloves and rosemary has also been rendered well. Tarte au citron and nougat glacé have passed muster at dessert stage. Wines, like the food, are mainly French. Prices reflect the location, but there is a decent range by the glass; house vin de pays is £10.25.

CHEF: Lionel Lemaitre PROPRIETOR: Groupe Chez Gérard OPEN: Mon to Sat 12 to 3, 6.30 to 11, Sun and bank hols 12 to 3.30, 6.30 to 10.30 MEALS: alc (main courses £12 to £19.50). Set L and D before 7.30 £12.50 (2 courses) SERVICE: 12.5% (optional), card slips closed CARDS: Amex, Delta, Diners, MasterCard, Switch, Visa DETAILS: 70 seats. Private parties: 20 private room. Wheelchair access (not WC). No music. Air-conditioned ⊖ Knightsbridge, South Kensington

Cactus Blue

map 14

86 Fulham Road, SW3 6HR
TEL: (020) 7823 7858 FAX: (020) 7823 8577

COOKING **2**
SOUTH-WEST AMERICAN
£28–£56

A glass-enclosed staircase, a marble bar dramatically lit from below, Native American artefacts, and tables inlaid with copper panels: this is Central America – Mexico specifically – come to the Fulham Road. Making the most of an intriguingly restricted range of principal ingredients, the kitchen offers up crab cakes with cilantro (coriander) pesto, skewered pecan chicken fillets, and quesadillas filled with tuna, avocado and red onion with sweetcorn relish. Chilli fire makes its presence felt in a number of preparations, including cured duck breast with spiced plum chutney, and seafood gumbo with tiger prawns. Sauté pork with chorizo and bourbon apples presents an enlivening twist on a familiar combination of ingredients. There are tequilas and mescals on the drinks list, as well as an inspiring cocktail menu, and wines include plenty of sunny Stateside flavours. House wines at £11.95, however, are French.

CHEF: Ivan Butera PROPRIETOR: Maxwell's Restaurants Ltd OPEN: Sat and Sun 12 to 11.45 (10.45 Sun), all week D 5.30 to 11.45 CLOSED: 24, 25 and 26 Dec MEALS: alc (main courses £9 to £15) SERVICE: 12.5% (optional), card slips closed CARDS: Amex, Delta, Diners, MasterCard, Switch, Visa DETAILS: 140 seats. 24 seats outside. Private parties: 60 main room, 60 private room. Vegetarian meals. Children's helpings. No smoking in 1 dining room. No pipes in dining room. Wheelchair access (not WC). Music ⊖ South Kensington (£5)

Café du Jardin

map 15

28 Wellington Street, WC2E 7BD
TEL: (020) 7836 8769 and 8760
FAX: (020) 7836 4123

COOKING **3**
MODERN BRITISH
£21–£56

There are two levels at the Café: a basement, and a ground floor for those who want to keep tabs on the hurly-burly of Covent Garden. Although this is a popular spot for both pre- and post-theatre eating, it is Tony Howorth's lively cooking rather than mere convenience that pulls in customers. Expect basil aïoli (with salmon), pink turnip pickle (with calf's liver), and split pea dhal (with hot-and-sour shank of lamb). Dishes may not always get the balance right – flavoured oils add weight, and some items can be chilli-hot – but minute steak with spot-on chips has been enjoyed, and there is usually something comforting such as potato and sage dumplings with mascarpone, or grilled sole with spinach and oyster mushrooms. Desserts can be filling, taking in banana parfait with Creole sauce, and a rich dark and white chocolate mousse. Service has ranged from patchy to impeccable. Care has been taken to ensure that the odd bottle under £15 appears on the punchy wine list, which covers the world. A selection of fine wines is available on request, but prices here are seldom competitive. House French is £9.75 a bottle.

CHEF: Tony Howorth PROPRIETORS: Robert Seigler and Tony Howorth OPEN: Mon to Sat 12 to 3, 5.30 to 12, Sun 12 to 11 CLOSED: 24 and 25 Dec MEALS: alc (main courses £9.50 to £14.50). Set L and D 5.30 to 7 and 10 to 12 £9.95 (2 courses) to £13.50 SERVICE: 15% (optional), card slips closed CARDS: Amex, Delta, Diners, MasterCard, Switch, Visa DETAILS: 100 seats. 18 seats outside. Private parties: 70 main room. Vegetarian meals. Wheelchair access (not WC). Music. Air-conditioned ⊖ Covent Garden

Café Japan £

map 13

626 Finchley Road, NW11 7RR
TEL: (020) 8455 6854

COOKING **5**
JAPANESE
£20–£48

'A place for real sushi fans,' says a reporter, impressed by the quality of salmon, sea bass, fatty tuna, sea bream, flounder, flying-fish roll, and salmon roe with seaweed. Lower down the luxury scale he also enjoyed the tonkatsu set lunch in a bento box, comprising miso soup, deep-fried bean curd, and perfectly cooked golden-brown breadcrumbed pork. Another aficionado praised rarities from the chef's weekly specials, such as marinated fried horse mackerel, and fried plaice served with ponzu sauce garnished with crisply fried glass noodles and spring onions. There is also enthusiasm for homely yakitori chicken wing tips grilled on a skewer.

Desserts include fine Japanese ice creams, made from chestnuts, green tea, or red beans, the last also appearing as the filling of dorayaki (pancakes). Set meals range from salt-grilled mackerel with rice, pickles and miso soup, to a choice of sukiyaki with appetisers, soya bean soup, sashimi and deep-fried prawns and vegetables. Such skilful execution of a wide-ranging menu might suggest a de luxe restaurant, but in fact the café is just that, a modest, informal suburban place. Quite how the friendly, smiling waitresses manage to cook sukiyaki so deftly on the small, closely packed tables is a mystery. Japanese plum wine is £11, and house red or white is £8.50. Alternatively, go for Japanese beer or green tea.

CHEF: Masaru Okayama PROPRIETOR: Koichi Konnai OPEN: Wed to Sun L 12 to 2, Tue to Sun D 5.30 to 10.30 MEALS: alc (main courses £7 to £14). Set L £3.90 to £5.90 (both 2 courses), Set D £18.50 to £19.50 SERVICE: not inc CARDS: MasterCard, Switch, Visa DETAILS: 38 seats. Private parties: 6 main room. Vegetarian meals. Music. Air-conditioned ⊖ Golders Green

Café Spice Namaste

maps 12 and 13

16 Prescot Street, E1 8AZ
TEL: (020) 7488 9242 FAX: (020) 7481 0508
247 Lavender Hill, SW11 1JW
TEL: (020) 7738 1717 FAX: (020) 7738 1666

COOKING **4**
INDIAN
£33–£58

Describing the décor of these two branches as a riot of colour suggests lack of control, which is unfair to Cyrus Todiwala's sense of style and to his equally vivacious cooking. To the dishes influenced by the varied regions of the Subcontinent he injects elements of other cuisines on his quarterly-changing menus, to which are added weekly specialities. There might be Goan wild boar sausages, or potato cakes stuffed with curried lamb, followed by organic Devon pork in a red-hot masala, or a southern Indian vegetarian dry stir-fry.

Thoughtful combinations and accurate timing have produced notable successes, particularly with seafood. King prawns and scallops have been stir-fried with baby vegetables, grated coconut and coriander, accompanied by a rich tomato-based fish sauce; and swordfish chutneywala has been marinated in coriander, chilli, garlic and mint: 'chargrilling doesn't come much better than this'. Good breads and rice, plus large portions, mean that few need even the ice creams 'made for Café Spice Namaste under supervision'. Service is plentiful and efficient. Wines on the short list have been well chosen to match the food. House wines are £10.90, and only two bottles are over £20.

CHEFS: Cyrus Todiwala and Angelo Collaco (both alternate between the branches) PROPRIETOR: Café Spice Ltd OPEN: Prescot Street Mon to Fri L 12 to 3, Mon to Sat D 6.15 to 10.30 (6.30 to 10 Sat); Lavender Hill Sun L 12 to 3, Tue to Sun D 6 to 11.30 (10.30 Sun) CLOSED: 1 week Christmas, bank hols (Prescot Street) MEALS: alc (main courses £10.50 to £15.50). Set D Prescot Street from £28, Set D Lavender Hill from £18 (2 courses) to £25 SERVICE: 12.5% (optional), card slips closed CARDS: Amex, Delta, Diners, MasterCard, Switch, Visa DETAILS: Prescot Street 110 seats, Lavender Hill 80 seats. Private parties: Prescot Street 90 main room, 40 private room; Lavender Hill 50 main room, 10 to 20 private room. 8 seats outside (Lavender Hill). Vegetarian meals. Children's helpings. Music. Air-conditioned ⊖ Aldgate (Prescot Street), Clapham Common (Lavender Hill) (£5)

Cambio de Tercio

map 14

163 Old Brompton Road, SW5 0LJ
TEL: (020) 7244 8970

COOKING **3**
MODERN SPANISH
£29–£61

As far as the ochre yellow and sanguine red colour scheme is concerned, this could be a little corner of Spain, its party atmosphere helped along by 'cheerful, cheeky' but knowledgeable service. The carte offers more fish than meat main dishes, all the more reason to order nutty flavoured Jabugo ham as a starter, made from acorn-fed Iberian black pigs. Variety is pleasingly wide, running from octopus Galician style (with potato, paprika and olive oil), to cod confit in Jabugo fat, from kid roasted with lavender, to quails in red wine, served with a cheese and bone marrow risotto.

Portions are large. Nevertheless there are Spanish cheeses with quince marmalade, and refreshing desserts such as a slightly thickened grapefruit juice served with lemon sorbet and vanilla cream. Apart from a token champagne, wines are resolutely Spanish. Well priced and enthusiastically annotated, the list kicks off with seven sherries by the glass (from £3) and shows how diverse the wines of one country can be, from the aromatic whites of Galicia to up-and-coming reds from Priorato and Penedès. House wines start at £12.25.

CHEF: Diego Ferrer PROPRIETORS: Abel Lusa and David Rivero OPEN: all week 12.15 to 2.30, 7 to 11.30 CLOSED: 10 days Christmas MEALS: alc (main courses £9.50 to £15) SERVICE: not inc, 12.5% for parties of 6 or more CARDS: Amex, Delta, MasterCard, Switch, Visa DETAILS: 50 seats. 9 seats outside. Private parties: 80 main room, 17 private room. Wheelchair access (not WC). Music ⊖ Gloucester Road

Use the lists towards the front of the book to find suitable restaurants for special occasions.

Cantaloupe

map 13

35 Charlotte Road, EC2A 3PD
TEL: (020) 7729 5566 FAX: (020) 7613 4411
WEB SITE: www.cantaloupe.co.uk

COOKING **2**
MEDITERRANEAN
£26–£41

When Richard Bigg started up in 1995 there wasn't much else to speak of in the neighbourhood, apart from a few pubs and sandwich shops. Now new openings are commonplace, so that as the Guide went to press he was about to launch another of his own (to be called Cargo, in nearby Rivington Street). In all this, the bar-restaurant has maintained its casual feel, helped by a mix of industrial style fittings, homely wooden tables and the odd comfy chair. Chargrilling is a favoured technique, applied to squid (with sweet and sour caponata), and Aberdeen Angus steak (with an anchovy, caper and rosemary butter). The Mediterranean coast is varied enough to take in fried halloumi with olive salsa, and warm chocolate pudding or banana crème brûlée. Music is loud, and service is likely to be well informed and efficient. A reasonably priced, globally sourced wine list suits the circumstances well: ten or more wines are available by the glass, starting with house French at £8.95 (£2.35).

CHEF: Henry Brereton PROPRIETORS: Richard Bigg and Nigel Foster OPEN: Mon to Fri L 12 to 3, Mon to Sat D 6 (7 Sat) to 11.30 CLOSED: Christmas and bank holiday Mondays MEALS: alc (main courses £7.50 to £13). Tapas served in bar L and 4 to 12 Sun SERVICE: 12.5% (optional), card slips closed CARDS: Delta, MasterCard, Switch, Visa DETAILS: 50 seats. Private parties: 50 main room. Vegetarian meals. Children's helpings. Music. Air-conditioned ⊖ Old Street

Cantina Vinopolis

NEW ENTRY **map 13**

1 Bank End, SE1 9BU
TEL: (020) 7940 8333 FAX: (020) 7940 8334

COOKING **1**
FRENCH/MEDITERRANEAN
£27–£47

In a rejuvenated area of the South Bank not far from the Globe Theatre, Tate Modern, and the wobbly Millennium Bridge, Vinopolis is a contemporary museum, an interactive wine joyride, a 'walk-through Wine Atlas', as Hugh Johnson has called it. A huge, brick-walled, high, vaulted, refectory-style brasserie has been converted from Victorian railway arches, and wines, not surprisingly, constitute a significant part of the attraction. But the food makes a good effort, casting its net wide for deep-fried, crisply battered squid with wasabi-slaw, tender rump of lamb with polenta cake and lots of girolles, and simple desserts of vanilla pannacotta with a mango and strawberry 'minestrone'.

Bread, coffee and service are not strengths, but the wine list – arranged by grape variety and country – makes all 200-plus bottles available by the glass, and most of these (apart from sparkling, fortified and dessert wines) in both large and small sizes. The selection is not as enterprising as it might be, given the aspirations of the site, but prices are fair; the inclusion of Romania, plus some old-fashioned French négociants (Piat d'Or anyone?), ensure that there are even a few below £12.

To find a restaurant in a particular area use the maps at the centre of the book.

CHEF: Jason Whitelock PROPRIETORS: Claudio Pulze and Trevor Gulliver OPEN: all week L 12 to 2.45, Mon to Sat D 6 to 10.15 MEALS: alc (main courses £8 to £13.50) SERVICE: 12.5% (optional), card slips closed CARDS: Amex, Delta, Diners, MasterCard, Switch, Visa DETAILS: 200 seats. Private parties: 100 main room, 100 private room. Vegetarian meals. Children's helpings. No smoking in 1 dining room. Wheelchair access (not WC). No music

▲ The Capital

map 14

22–24 Basil Street, SW3 1AT
TEL: (020) 7589 5171 FAX: (020) 7225 0011
EMAIL: reservations@capitalhotel.co.uk
WEB SITE: www.capitalhotel.co.uk

COOKING **7**
FRENCH
£36–£91

Although the neighbourhood is the haunt of serious shoppers, this small luxury hotel close to the big Knightsbridge stores does not take cynical advantage of its situation. Indeed, the set-price lunch remains 'one of the classy-eating bargains in London'. A small, elegant dining room, beyond a tiny *fin de siècle* bar, sets out its stall with comfortably upholstered chairs, heavy tablecloths and gleaming glassware.

While the high French style of cooking rarely ventures far from familiar ideas – rabbit fricassee with rosemary and mushrooms, or roast scallops with caramelised endive – it is by no means hidebound. The ability to combine indulgence and lightness is a particular strength, for example in a chicken and foie gras boudin accompanied by barley risotto and ceps, and in pan-fried sea bass served in a light bouillon containing pasta, tiny vegetables and cannellini beans. The quality of materials is not in question, judging by a rich dish of whole grilled lobster, its flesh loosened and returned to the shell, along with shrimps, potato, asparagus, and a tarragon-loaded béarnaise sauce. Strong, earthy flavours are handled with equal skill, as in a parcel of pink roast wood pigeon breasts, wrapped in caul and Savoy cabbage, halved and arranged on a truffle consommé scattered with peas and tiny mushrooms.

Presentation is vivid, and dishes are generally well conceived, not least when it comes to desserts of lightly stewed cherries, served with a lemon thyme ice cream squeezed between two thin pastry discs, or a papillote of prunes and figs served with yoghurt ice cream. Extras, from appetiser soup to bread to petits fours, are flawless, and staff are among the best in London. The predominantly French wine list is a humdinger, and while some relative bargains are to be found among more mature classics, prices are high. There is little under under £20 apart from Levin house wine at £14.50.

CHEF: Eric Crouillère-Chavot PROPRIETOR: David Levin OPEN: all week 12.30 to 2.15, 7 to 11.15 MEALS: alc (main courses £22). Set L £24.50, Set D £60 SERVICE: 12.5% (optional), card slips closed CARDS: Amex, Delta, Diners, MasterCard, Switch, Visa DETAILS: 36 seats. Private parties: 8 main room, 10 and 24 private rooms. Jacket and tie. No cigars/pipes in dining room. No music. Air-conditioned ACCOMMODATION: 48 rooms, all with bath/shower. TV. Phone. Room only £180 to £350. Baby facilities *(The Which? Hotel Guide)* ⊖ Knightsbridge

Occasional music *in the details at the end of an entry means live or recorded music is played in the dining room only rarely or for special events.* No music *means it is never played.*

Le Caprice

map 15

Arlington House, Arlington Street, SW1A 1RT
TEL: (020) 7629 2239 FAX: (020) 7493 9040

COOKING **4**
MODERN BRITISH
£33–£79

Sharply attired in black and cream, Caprice seems thoroughly modern, yet is celebrating its twentieth birthday. It is not open all day, so it's hardly a brasserie (although it resembles one for well-heeled customers) and you can eat at the bar. Although the menu deals in familiar staples, from Caesar salad and eggs Benedict to salmon fishcake, it also leaves room for more interesting materials such as River Wye elvers with wild garlic, or herb-baked razor clams with creamed salt cod. And it is sufficiently innovative to produce a remarkably successful combination of sauté baby squid with chorizo and port-roasted figs.

Mash is given an intelligent supporting role, flavoured with mustard to partner carefully cooked lambs' kidneys, and combined with crayfish to accompany wild sea trout with samphire. A strong seasonal sense has brought simple but star-quality fresh peas, and ripe, sweet wild strawberries to a July dinner. Among other desserts, cappuccino brûlée is well rendered. Sunday brunch runs the gamut from bagels with cream cheese to lobster and tarragon risotto, and service is typically pleasant and efficient. Wine prices start at £11.25, and the list features a number of half-bottles plus a dozen by the glass.

CHEFS: Mark Hix and Elliot Ketley PROPRIETORS: Belgo Group plc OPEN: all week 12 to 3 (3.30 Sun), 5.30 (6 Sun) to 12 CLOSED: 25 and 26 Dec, 1 Jan, Aug bank hol MEALS: alc (main courses £10 to £23.50). Cover £1.50 SERVICE: not inc CARDS: Amex, Delta, Diners, MasterCard, Switch, Visa DETAILS: 80 seats. Private parties: 8 main room. Vegetarian meals. Wheelchair access (not WC). Music. Air-conditioned ⊖ Green Park

Le Chardon

map 12

65 Lordship Lane, SE22 8EP
TEL: (020) 8299 1921

COOKING **3**
FRENCH
£24–£43

With drippy candles in bottles on the oilcloth-covered tables and a bilingual menu containing many standards of the genre, the atmosphere could hardly be more convincingly authentic in this French bistro. Escargots with garlic butter, sole meunière, and marinated pork shank with Puy lentils will soon waft you across la Manche, in spirit at least, as might the extra charges levied for vegetables and even bread and butter. Rabbit leg stuffed with mushroom duxelles and sauced with moutarde de Meaux has been highly praised, as have dauphinois potatoes and crème brûlée. Wines are arranged by style and are exclusively French. Prices open at £9.60. Although a service charge is added, credit card totals are left open.

CHEF: Patrick Thomas PROPRIETOR: Robert Benayer OPEN: all week 12 to 11 CLOSED: 26 Dec, bank hols MEALS: alc (main courses £9 to £11). Set L £6.95 to £9.95 (both 2 courses) SERVICE: 10% (optional) CARDS: Amex, Delta, Diners, MasterCard, Switch, Visa DETAILS: 50 seats. 25 seats outside. Private parties: 100 main room. Vegetarian meals. Children's helpings. Wheelchair access (not WC). Music (£5)

Cheng-du

map 13

9 Parkway, NW1 7PG
TEL: (020) 7485 8058 FAX: (020) 7794 5522

COOKING 1
CHINESE
£26–£52

It may be bustling Camden Town outside, but inside, this is a calm, soothing place with some surprising features. Service is usually friendly, and the décor, unlike that of most Chinese restaurants, pleases the eye with its prints, collages and fabric hangings, without a single dragon breathing down diners' necks. The cooking is designed to please Western tastes with few challenging ingredients in a comparatively short menu. Starters include dim sum in an unusual combination of flavours, and breast of chicken dusted with crushed walnuts. In one of two set menus, 'Yin' and 'Yang', crispy aromatic duck precedes scallops and prawns, sizzling lamb slices, and chicken and almonds in yellow bean sauce. Colourful 'special selections' offered à la carte include steamed chicken with red dates, black fungi and golden lilies, and red braised monkfish fillet with Chinese mushrooms. House wine is £9.80, and the list includes some acceptable, mostly Old World bottles. Note that credit card slips are left open although service is included on the bill.

CHEF: Mr Deng PROPRIETOR: Gingerflower Ltd OPEN: all week L 12 to 2.30, D 6.30 to 11.30 CLOSED: 24 to 26 Dec MEALS: alc (main dishes £5.50 to £16). Set L and D £20.90 (min 2) SERVICE: 12.5% CARDS: Delta, MasterCard, Switch, Visa DETAILS: 80 seats. Private parties: 80 main room. Vegetarian meals. Wheelchair access (not WC). Occasional music ⊖ Camden Town

Chez Bruce

map 12

2 Bellevue Road, SW17 7EG
TEL: (020) 8672 0114 FAX: (020) 8767 6648

COOKING 6
MODERN BRITISH
£34–£68

Something has been happening at Chez Bruce. Not perhaps to the décor, a fetching shade of crimson outside, light and appealing inside, with spindly wrought-iron chandeliers, and walls covered in art posters. But to the cooking. Since last year the kitchen seems to have moved up a gear, displaying confidence and flair, and yet remaining unshowy, light and satisfying. The food may not be the last word in novelty, but dishes, even apparently simple ones, involve skill, planning and attention to detail, so that it is possible to taste familiar ingredients and combinations 'as if for the first time all over again'.

Seasonal items have included asparagus in early June, notably appearing as a vertically and artfully arranged cold frittata, served on a base of Serrano ham and scattered with shavings of aged Manchego cheese. The highlight of an inspector's dinner was a tower of well-flavoured, fiercely grilled, crisp-skinned red mullet sitting on fruity sliced tomato and chargrilled courgette, in turn resting on a slab of crumbly buttery puff pastry ('looking like a giant Ryvita'): together with bittersweet black olive paste, it all added up to a rich yet easily digestible Mediterranean triumph.

Desserts, meanwhile, take in a top-notch slightly warm chocolate sponge with a scoop of crunchy hazelnut parfait, and a moist, layered cherry and almond tart with feather-light pastry, accompanied by glossy vanilla custard. Good bread is offered ad libitum, value is unimpeachable, and the place is plentifully supplied with knowledgeable, charming and admirably efficient staff. Wines are catholic and impeccably chosen, filed in ascending order according to price and starting at a competitive £12.95. This means skipping between grape varieties, styles and countries but makes some comparisons easier: choose between Grant Burge Old Vine Semillon from Australia, and Ca' del Solo Malvasia Bianca from California, both 1998, both £22.50. Around 20 wines by the glass and half-bottle make for flexibility.

CHEF: Bruce Poole PROPRIETORS: Bruce Poole, Nigel Platts-Martin and Richard Carr OPEN: all week L 12 to 2 (12.30 to 2.30 Sat, 12.30 to 3.30 Sun), Mon to Sat D 7 (6.30 Fri and Sat) to 10.30 CLOSED: 24 to 30 Dec, bank hols MEALS: Set L Mon to Sat £21.50, Set L Sun £23.50, Set D £27.50 SERVICE: 12.5% (optional), card slips closed CARDS: Amex, Delta, Diners, MasterCard, Switch, Visa DETAILS: 75 seats. Private parties: 70 main room, 18 private room. Children's helpings. No children at D. No cigars/pipes in dining room. No music. Air-conditioned ⊖ Clapham South, Balham

Chez Liline

map 12

25101 Stroud Green Road, N4 3PX
TEL: (020) 7263 6550 FAX: (020) 7272 9717

COOKING **4**
MAURITIAN SEAFOOD
£25–£50

French-speaking waiters emphasise the exotic ambience of this simple restaurant, reflecting its Mauritian origin. The cooking combines subtle spicing with what one reporter called an 'eye-watering wham of chilli', as in a distinctively flavoured starter of mussels and clams with galangal and aniseed. Another successful first course has been delicately smoked halibut with a light vinaigrette and slices of ripe mango.

Main dishes are equally divided between fish and shellfish. Choose perhaps between a plateau Sétoise (including half a lobster); large tiger prawns with tomatoes, chilli and thyme; and accurately cooked sea-bass with ginger and spring onion. Other fishy possibilities are sea-bream provençale, and bourgeois façon Mr Robert (red snapper with a spicy pickled lime sauce). Among mainly conventional side dishes, sweet potatoes with thyme and chilli stands out. A footnote on the menu offers meat or vegetarian options on request. Highly recommended desserts include tarte Tatin and chocolate mousse. House wines are £10.25, 20 French wines stay mostly under £20, while New World prices rarely exceed £16.

CHEFS: Pascal Doudrich and Sylvain Ho-Wing-Chong PROPRIETOR: Thierry Doudrich OPEN: Mon to Sat 12.30 to 2, 6.30 to 10 CLOSED: 2 weeks Aug/Sep, bank hols MEALS: alc (main courses £10 to £17). Set L and D Mon to Thurs £12.75 (2 courses) SERVICE: not inc CARDS: Amex, Delta, MasterCard, Switch, Visa DETAILS: 40 seats. Private parties: 35 main room. Vegetarian meals on request only. Children's helpings. Music ⊖ Finsbury Park (£5)

Although the cuisine style noted at the top of entries has in most cases been suggested to the Guide by the restaurants, some have been edited for brevity or appropriateness.

The Guide's top-rated restaurants are listed near the front of the book.

Chezmax

map 13

168 Ifield Road, SW10 9AF
TEL: (020) 7835 0874 FAX: (020) 7244 0618
WEB SITE: www.chezmax.co.uk

COOKING **1**
FRENCH
£43–£76

Descend a spiral staircase into what seems like an unreconstructed French café with frosted wall-lights, a cabinet of digestifs, and displays of historical menus. Although the kitchen offers a few traditional items such as duck leg confit with pommes sarladaise, its thrust is more ambitious. Lightly roasted saddle of rabbit has come with a slice of prawn, tomato and mushroom tart for example, while monkfish has been stuffed with foie gras, placed on a bed of cabbage soused in anchovy and orange sauce, and given a spiced red wine sauce. Understandably it is the less fiddly stuff that works best: a sausage of salmon mousse on a disc of bubble and squeak with vanilla cream sauce, and intensely flavoured mushroom risotto. Desserts might offer pistachio soufflé, or a rich and smooth mocha crème brûlée. Service can take its time. Wines are predominantly French, with decent choice under £20 and a daily-changing selection available by 25- or 50-centilitre carafe.

CHEF: Nick Reeves PROPRIETORS: Graham Thomson and Stephen Smith OPEN: Tue to Sat L 12 to 3, Mon to Sat D 7 to 11 CLOSED: Chrismas, bank hols MEALS: alc L (prices n.a. as Guide went to press), Set D £25.50 (2 courses) to £35. Bar menu available 12 to 6 SERVICE: 12.5% (optional), card slips closed CARDS: Amex, Delta, Diners, MasterCard, Switch, Visa DETAILS: 46 seats. Private parties: 60 main room, 14 private room. Children's helpings. No cigars/cigars in dining room. No music ⊖ West Brompton

Chez Moi

map 12

1 Addison Avenue, W11 4QS
TEL: (020) 7603 8267 FAX: (020) 7603 3898

COOKING **4**
FRENCH-PLUS
£25–£56

Dusky pink walls and deep green fabrics mingle with imitation zebra skin upholstery and gilt mirrors in this west London fixture. Traditional French dishes mix with occasional ideas from elsewhere: spicy Thai prawn noodle soup and chicken teriyaki among them. Indeed, strong spices and mustards are a feature, with horseradish, ginger, coriander, garlic, chilli, curry, oyster sauce and onions much in evidence. If Chez Moi feels dated, that may be because the repertoire includes several core dishes that don't change from one year (or indeed decade) to the next: one visitor saw little point in describing his rack of lamb à la diable since it 'looked and tasted identical to the ones I had here two years ago, five years ago, seven years ago'. A few worrying lapses have marred the cooking over the past year, from a lack of freshness in materials to several poorly executed dishes, but bortsch has been a success: 'even my Russian mother would have conceded that this was as near perfect as one is likely to find.' Service is singled out for praise as experienced, deft, smooth, and 'especially fast'. Wines are predominantly French, with house red and white at £10.75.

All entries in the Guide are re-researched and rewritten every year, not least because restaurant standards fluctuate. Don't rely on an out-of-date Guide.

CHEF: Richard Walton PROPRIETORS: Richard Walton and Colin Smith OPEN: Mon to Fri L 12.30 to 2, Mon to Sat D 7 to 11 CLOSED: bank hols MEALS: alc (main courses £12.50 to £17). Set L £15 SERVICE: not inc CARDS: Amex, Delta, Diners, MasterCard, Switch, Visa DETAILS: 45 seats. 12 seats outside. Private parties: 16 main room. Vegetarian meals. Children's helpings. No babies. No cigars/pipes in dining room. Wheelchair access (not WC). No music. Air-conditioned ⊖ Holland Park

cheznico map 15

Grosvenor House, 90 Park Lane, W1A 3AA COOKING **8**
TEL: (020) 7409 1290 FAX: (020) 7355 4877 FRENCH
EMAIL: cheznico@globalnet.co.uk £43–£118

As the millennium turned, Nico sent shock waves through the restaurant world when he abdicated from his patriarchal position as elder statesman of haute cuisine. By modernising the dining room, simplifying the cooking, slashing prices, and handing over day-to-day running to his daughters, it seemed as if some of the country's best cooking might at last be accessible to the masses. That was the plan, and in part it has worked. Waiters are less formally dressed, the large rectangular dining room has lost its heavy starched linen, and – although the gastronomic menu for two is still available at last year's price of £75 a head – other prices have come down: the set dinner (formerly £53 for two courses) is now £52 for three, while the cheapest set lunch has dropped to £25 for three courses (from that amount for two). All this, presumably, to tempt in a different sort of customer to whom a few pounds make a difference.

Although many dishes are superficially unaltered, some economies have been made: the 'wild' mushrooms in the risotto are no longer ceps but (at inspection) cultivated varieties like oysters and shiitakes; the sesame-crusted scallop with chive velouté and shredded leek, which used to be a highlight, has become more mundane scallops in garlic butter, and so on. Dishes may not pack quite the same punch as before, but the good news is that the brigade is still overseen by Paul Rhodes, and the food remains largely well (that is to say simply) conceived and properly executed.

Ideas rarely break new ground. The kitchen's strength is to cook classic dishes well: a seasonal plate of accurately timed asparagus with poached egg and hollandaise, veal kidney with mustard sauce, or pink pigeon and foie gras mousse wrapped in a bright green cabbage leaf, appealing not least for its sensuous textures. Lemon tart is still a winner, as is a rich-tasting chocolate mousse. Wines come from all corners of the globe and include some fine old vintage clarets and Burgundies. But prices rise quickly and steeply, there is very little under £20, and only three wines are available by the glass. House wines are £17.

CHEF: Paul Rhodes PROPRIETORS: Nico and Dinah-Jane Ladenis OPEN: Mon to Fri L 12 to 2, Mon to Sat D 7 to 11 CLOSED: 10 days Christmas, bank hols MEALS: alc L (main courses £11 to £26). Set L £25 to £75, Set D £52 to £75 SERVICE: 12.5% (optional), card slips closed CARDS: Amex, Delta, Diners, MasterCard, Switch, Visa DETAILS: 85 seats. Private parties: 20 private room. Children's helpings. No smoking in 1 dining room. No pipes in dining room. Wheelchair access (also WC). No music. Air-conditioned ⊖ Marble Arch

The Guide's longest-serving restaurants are listed near the front of the book.

China House, Orient

NEW ENTRY **map 15**

160 Piccadilly, W1V 9DF
TEL: (020) 7499 6888 FAX: (020) 7659 9300
WEB SITE: www.chinahouse.co.uk

COOKING **4**
CHINESE
£38–£66

Beside the main entrance leading only to the noodle bar, a small door takes you to the lift for the first-floor Orient restaurant. In the opulent listed building, once a car showroom, later a bank, the modish dining room has good feng shui, acres of elbow room, and a feeling of uncluttered calm. The carte offers mostly classical Chinese dishes, with a few pan-Asian touches, and presentation of modestly sized portions is both faultless and attractive. Textures are well rendered – in a heavily garlicked appetiser of spiced soy imperial prawn and pork dumpling with black fungus – and a degree of harmony and refinement is evident, for example in ginger lobster on a crispy noodle base.

Other successes have included braised bean curd with black mushrooms, and stir-fried pork with red bean curd, while crossover desserts run to tamarind toffee pudding, and a Tatin of lightly crunchy Chinese pears. Smartly dressed waiting staff might be more efficient. The wine list is fairly evenly split between France and the New World, although Italy and Spain are both represented and Lebanon makes a brief appearance. Prices start at £14 a bottle, £3.75 a glass, but soon jump over £20.

CHEF: Chris Kwan PROPRIETORS: Eddie Wat and Saeb Eigner OPEN: Mon to Fri L 12 to 2.30, Mon to Sat D 6 to 11.30 (11 Sun) MEALS: alc (main courses £8 to £16). Set L £19.50 (2 courses), Set pre-theatre D £19.50 (2 courses) to £21 SERVICE: 12.5% (optional), card slips closed CARDS: Amex, Delta, MasterCard, Switch, Visa DETAILS: 170 seats. Private parties: 180 main room, 16 private room. Vegetarian meals. No music. Air-conditioned ⊖ Green Park

Chinon

map 12

23 Richmond Way, W14 0AS
TEL: (020) 7602 5968 FAX: (020) 7602 4082

COOKING **5**
FRENCH-PLUS
£29–£62

Set in a parade of shops on a quiet road not far from Shepherd's Bush Green, Chinon's burgundy and beige colours, bare wooden tables and subdued lighting give it a gently reflective atmosphere. It stands out as pleasingly eccentric and old-fashioned. Front-of-house is capably led by owner Barbara Deane, who seems to do an awful lot with very limited resources. The food is hardly modern, but the kitchen applies a light touch to fine ingredients. A single large raviolo packed with crab comes with two accompanying pots, one of crab bisque, the other of aïoli, with everything, including pasta, top-notch.

Flavours and seasonings are properly thought through, producing for example an island of wild salmon fillet on a mound of spinach surrounded by a rich lake of Puy lentils in a lightly creamy sauce, and rack of lamb with sweet-and-sour aubergine and a garlic cream sauce. A keen sense of balance distinguishes desserts such as caramelised pineapple with vanilla butter, and proficiently crisped crème brûlée with passion-fruit sorbet. Wines focus mainly on France, although the New World and other European countries get a look-in too. House wine is £14, and a few are sold by the glass. The owner's antipathy towards filling in our questionnaire means, sadly, that the information below may once again only be approximate.

CHEF: Jonathon Hayes PROPRIETORS: Barbara Deane and Jonathon Hayes OPEN: Mon to Sat D only 7 to 10.45 MEALS: alc (main courses £8 to £17.50). Set D £16.50 SERVICE: 12.5% (optional), card slips closed CARDS: Amex, Delta, MasterCard, Switch, Visa DETAILS: 60 seats. 6 seats outside. Private parties: 30 main room, 30 private room. No children under 10. No cigars/pipes in dining room. Music.

Chiswick  map 12

131 Chiswick High Road, W4 2ED
TEL: (020) 8994 6887 FAX: (020) 8994 5504

COOKING **3**
MODERN EUROPEAN
£20–£50

A café-style restaurant with bare wooden tables and 'designer' chairs (i.e. designed for short occupancy) is brightened by a few paintings and a colourful menu that knocks on more than one European country's door. Expect soused mackerel with beetroot salad, smoked haddock kedgeree, and a warm breakfast-style salad of black pudding with crisp bacon and soft-boiled egg. Materials are fresh, and variety extends from a 'build-your-own' bruschetta of thickly sliced buffalo mozzarella, juicy plum tomatoes and purple basil on crusty bread soaked in fruity olive oil, to flavourful roast shoulder of pork (one of the better cuts for a balance between lean meat and fat) with good crackling, served in a rich gravy with creamy butter beans and spicy chorizo.

A combination of hot chocolate pudding and crème fraîche ice cream has been judged 'a little power-house of taste' and worth the 20-minute wait. Sunday brunch pleases with Caesar salad, steamed beef and Guinness pudding, and rhubarb tart. Service can be haphazard. The well-assorted wine list offers around 40 bins, but more than half are over £20. Plenty come by the glass and half-litre jug, and house red is £11.50, white £10.50.

CHEF: Jim Garvan PROPRIETORS: Kate and Adam Robinson OPEN: Sun to Fri L 12.30 to 2.45 (12 to 3 Sun), Mon to Sat D 7 to 11 CLOSED: Christmas, bank hols MEALS: alc (main courses £6.50 to £16). Set L and D 7 to 8 £9.50 (2 courses) to £12.95, Set D Mon to Thur 8 to 11 £12.95 (2 courses) to £15.50 SERVICE: 12.5% (optional), card slips closed CARDS: Amex, Delta, MasterCard, Switch, Visa DETAILS: 76 seats. 10 seats outside. Private parties: 35 main room. Vegetarian meals. Children's helpings. No-smoking area. No music. Air-conditioned ⊖ Turnham Green (£5)

Chor Bizarre map 15

16 Albemarle Street, W1X 3HA
TEL: (020) 7629 9802 FAX: (020) 7493 7756
EMAIL: cblondon@aol.com
WEB SITE: www.chorbizarre.net

COOKING **1**
INDIAN
£31–£58

Bizarre in name and décor, this interpretation of a thieves' market is stuffed with furniture and artefacts, both genuine and kitsch. No two tables are alike: one is a marble balustrade, another a four-poster bedstead, and chairs are elaborately carved or inlaid. The menu takes inspiration from all over India, ranging from Delhi street food to a Maharaja thali. Opinions on the cooking are divided, but an inspector enjoyed aloo tikki chat, and deep-fried scallops with a salad lifted by curry leaves and fried coconut. Chettinad chicken, a peppery curry, comes freshly spiced, and first-class dal makhani (black lentils simmered overnight with tomatoes and cream) is garnished with shreds of fresh ginger. Smartly dressed waiters are friendly and capable, when you can attract their attention. The wine list, chosen by Charles Metcalfe, includes a chart to aid food matching. Prices start at £13.

CHEF: Deepinder Singh Sondhi PROPRIETOR: India's Restaurant Ltd OPEN: Mon to Sat 12 to 3, 6 to 11.30, Sun 12 to 2.30, 6 to 10.30 MEALS: alc (main courses £7.50 to £14). Set L and D £24 SERVICE: 12.5% (optional), card slips closed CARDS: Amex, Delta, Diners, MasterCard, Switch, Visa DETAILS: 87 seats. Private parties: 80 main room, 30 private room. Vegetarian meals. Music. Air-conditioned ⊖ Green Park (£5)

Christopher's

map 15

18 Wellington Street, WC2E 7DD
TEL: (020) 7240 4222 FAX: (020) 7836 3506
EMAIL: bookings@christophers.uk.net
WEB SITE: www.christophersgrill.co.uk

COOKING **1**
CONTEMPORARY AMERICAN
£29–£77

Huge doors on the corner lead to the three parts of Christopher's: a basement bar, a ground-floor dining room, and, up a grand circular stairway, the main first-floor dining room, whose large windows let in plenty of daylight. Specials such as 'New York City Gorgonzola ribeye steak (10ozs)' point to Christopher Gilmour's source of inspiration: the American grill. To this he adds Maryland crab cake, Maine lobster, and corn chowder with foie gras, though when it comes to a simple Caesar salad, more than one reporter has been disappointed. Vegetables include 'frozen peas' and tobacco onions, and desserts favour chocolate, as in a rich and dense sunken chocolate soufflé cake. A brunch menu replaces the regular carte on Saturday and Sunday lunchtimes. Nobody has a good word to say about service, but hardly anyone could complain about the 50 wines by the glass (in two sizes), nor the list's extensive coverage. Prices start at £12.50.

CHEF: Adrian Searing PROPRIETOR: Christopher Gilmour OPEN: Mon to Sat 12 to 3.30, 5 to 11.45, Sun 11.30 to 4.30 CLOSED: 25 and 26 Dec, 1 Jan MEALS: alc (main courses £11.50 to £28). Set D before 7 and after 10 £14.50 (2 courses) to £17.50. Bar meals available Mon to Sat L, Mon to Sat D. Cover 50p SERVICE: 12.5% (optional), card slips closed CARDS: Amex, Delta, Diners, MasterCard, Switch, Visa DETAILS: 160 seats. Private parties: 120 main room, 50 private room. Vegetarian meals. Children's helpings. No music. Air-conditioned ⊖ Covent Garden

Chutney Mary

map 12

535 King's Road, SW10 0SZ
TEL: (020) 7351 3113 FAX: (020) 7351 7694
EMAIL: action@realindianfood.com
WEB SITE: www.realindianfood.com

COOKING **1**
INDIAN
£26–£68

'Posh Spice' is how one visitor summed up this regionally specialised Indian restaurant on a corner site near the entrance to Chelsea Harbour. Entering the reception area is like walking into a five-star hotel in India, but the kitchen aims to reproduce the domestic cooking of the Subcontinent. Tender and aromatic seekh kebab is a recommended way to start, while a starter selection has included a fine delicately spiced crabcake with mint and coriander dip. Main dishes take in prawn malai curry, and Goan pot-roasted pork knuckle served with tomato pulao rice and apple chutney. Mango sorbet uses the highly prized Alphonso variety, and the floral infusions are a refreshing way to finish. Manager Eddie Khoo is informative when it comes to choosing wines to match the food. The list is stylistically arranged with the cooking in mind, but prices are undoubtedly Chelsea. House Languedoc is £11.50.

CHEF: Murali Dharan PROPRIETORS: Namita Panjabi and Ranjit Mathrani OPEN: all week 12.30 to 2.30, 7 to 11.30 (10.30 Sun) MEALS: alc (main courses £9.50 to £19). Set L and D £12.50 (2 courses) to £15. Cover £1.50 SERVICE: 12.5% (optional) CARDS: Amex, Diners, MasterCard, Switch, Visa DETAILS: 150 seats. Private parties: L 120/D 36 main room, 36 private room. Vegetarian meals. Children's helpings. No cigars/pipes in dining room. Wheelchair access (not WC). Music. Air-conditioned ⊖ Fulham Broadway

Circus

map 15

1 Upper James Street, W1R 4BP
TEL: (020) 7534 4000 FAX: (020) 7534 4010
EMAIL: circus@egami.co.uk
WEB SITE: www.circusbar.co.uk

COOKING **4**
MODERN EUROPEAN/MEDITERRANEAN
£24–£60

Big picture windows take up two sides of this square-shaped ground-floor dining room on a prime corner site in one of the smarter bits of Soho. Its frosted glass, back-lit walls and lights that dim in the evening seem more relaxing and less self-conscious of late, just as the food appears more consistent and mature. Ambition is sensibly tailored in favour of fresh, strong flavours and appealing presentation. Materials are as up-to-date as one might wish. Feta cheese, for example, is oak-aged; less salty than usual, it comes with a fresh-tasting red pepper and aubergine terrine. Other ideas range from crab spring roll with pickled vegetables to a main course of roast ostrich with red curry.

Fish is a strong point: seared tuna arrives in a bowl with wakame seaweed and cucumber in an understated soy dressing, while a fillet of halibut comes with a richly soft champ of spring onion mash, and deep-fried, smoky-flavoured enoki mushrooms. Traditional British steamed sponge pud is reinvented in a zesty lime version, with orange and lime sauce and coconut ice cream. Service bustles along efficiently, while the drinking is as trendy as the surroundings suggest, and as expensive as the West End dictates. Prices start at £14.50 for a Loire Chardonnay or a red Vin de Pays de l'Hérault.

CHEF: Richard Lee PROPRIETORS: Christopher Bodker and Marian Scrutton OPEN: Mon to Fri L 12 to 3, Mon to Sat D 5.45 to 12 CLOSED: Christmas, bank hols MEALS: alc D (main courses £10.50 to £17.50). Set L £10.50 (2 courses) to £19.50, Set D 5.45 to 7.15 and 10.45 to 12 £10.50 (2 courses) to £12.50 SERVICE: 12.5% (optional), card slips closed CARDS: Amex, Delta, Diners, MasterCard, Switch, Visa DETAILS: 130 seats. Private parties: 130 main room, 16 private room. Vegetarian meals. Wheelchair access (not WC). No music. Air-conditioned ⊖ Piccadilly Circus

Restaurateurs justifiably resent no-shows. If you quote a credit card number when booking, you may be liable for the restaurant's lost profit margin if you don't turn up. Always phone to cancel.

City Rhodes

map 13

1 New Street Square, EC4A 3BF
TEL: (020) 7583 1313 FAX: (020) 7353 1662

COOKING **6**
MODERN BRITISH
£50–£85

Proximity to the City and the law courts accounts for the typically blue and grey suitscape in this cool, contemporary first-floor dining room. The spiky-haired impresario's imprint is evident not just in the 'Rhodes Gallery' of cookbooks and publicity by the entrance, but also in a menu that embraces luxury items – foie gras lends its comforting richness to a few dishes, and a twice-baked truffle soufflé is added to celeriac soup – as well as more 'humble' materials, including offal. Braised tournedos of oxtail has come with creamed Savoy cabbage, and roast veal sweetbreads with cep-flavoured mash, for example. Some dishes – pressed tomato cake with peppered goats' cheese – may be familiar from the cookbooks, and a strong link remains with classical British favourites, from smoked haddock kedgeree to bread-and-butter pudding or rhubarb tart. There is even a British pudding plate to emphasise the point. The only quibble may be with cost, which applies to wines as well as food, although sommelier Yves Desmaris has been singled out for praise. Quality is high, and although prices start at £16.50, sanctuary under £20 is very limited.

CHEFS: Michael Bedford and Gary Rhodes PROPRIETOR: Sodexho OPEN: Mon to Fri 12 to 2.30, 6 to 9 CLOSED: Christmas to New Year, bank hols MEALS: alc (main courses £16 to £24) SERVICE: 12.5% (optional) CARDS: Amex, Delta, Diners, MasterCard, Switch, Visa DETAILS: 85 seats. Private parties: 24 main room, 12 private room. Vegetarian meals. No children under 10. No cigars/pipes in dining room. Music. Air-conditioned ⊖ Chancery Lane

Clarke's

map 13

124 Kensington Church Street, W8 4BH
TEL: (020) 7221 9225 FAX: (020) 7229 4564
EMAIL: restaurant@sallyclarke.com
WEB SITE: www.sallyclarke.com

COOKING **6**
MODERN BRITISH
£36–£59

Smokers eat on the ground floor, non-smokers downstairs amid low lighting, fresh flowers and plain glassware and napery, where an open-to-view kitchen confirms the candid nature of the operation. The format – plenty of choice at lunch, but a set meal in the evening – is more or less the opposite of given restaurant wisdom. Ingredients are of prime quality, many from British growers and organic producers, and reporters are struck in different ways by the simplicity of the approach. If goats' cheese on crostini with quartered figs and honey-dressed rocket leaves sounds like something you might throw together at home, it is worth noting that the mark of a professional is often to make things appear easier than they are.

Centrepieces range from West Country roe deer to a skewer of Scottish scallops, and chargrilling and roasting are the preferred cooking methods, applied respectively to tuna with tapénade, and halibut with red wine and capers. One of the four courses at dinner is cheese – perhaps a couple of kinds served with oatmeal biscuits and a choice of radishes, apples, dates or quince – and cheese might even crop up in a first course as well. Among desserts, Yorkshire rhubarb has appeared with almond cake, and lemon tart with crème fraîche and vanilla syrup. Californian wines are the mainstay of an elegant list, which also features France and Italy, and fine producers and vintages abound. A few bottles come in under £15, ten wines are available by the glass, and there are some 40 half-bottles.

CHEFS: Sally Clarke and Elizabeth Payne PROPRIETOR: Sally Clarke OPEN: Mon to Fri 12.30 to 2, 7 to 10 CLOSED: 10 days Christmas, 2 weeks Aug, bank hols MEALS: alc L (main courses £14), Set D £44 SERVICE: net prices, card slips closed CARDS: Amex, Diners, MasterCard, Switch, Visa DETAILS: 90 seats. Private parties: 14 main room. Vegetarian meals. No smoking in 1 dining room. Wheelchair access (not WC). No music. Air-conditioned ⊖ Notting Hill Gate

Clock

NEW ENTRY **map 12**

130–132 Uxbridge Road, W7 3SL
TEL: (020) 8810 1011
EMAIL: clocktickto‌ck@aol.com
WEB SITE: www.clock-restaurant.co.uk

COOKING **2**
MODERN BRITISH
£26–£50

Opposite Hanwell's clock tower, this new venture occupies a split-level dining area and bar, decorated with Belgian chandeliers, large mirrors, cream walls, simple wooden chairs, and a fish tank. Mark Williamson casts his net wide, bringing in chorizo and rocket risotto, fresh crab sushi roll with water chestnut salad, and a thick-textured, pleasingly tasty white bean and garlic soup laced with truffle oil. Disparate ingredients and ideas might fuse in a starter of tiger prawns served with stuffed vine leaves and spicy wasabe dressing, and while not all combinations work equally well, timing is accurate, producing just-cooked loin of pork, and properly textured monkfish on a bed of Puy lentils. Desserts have included sharp lemon tart, and banana spring roll with caramel sauce. Most wines are less than £20, with around a dozen by the glass from £2.75. House wines, from Italy and Australia, are £9.50.

CHEF: Mark Williamson PROPRIETORS: Tim Williams and Kerry Ann Hirst OPEN: Tue to Fri and Sun L 12 to 2.30, Tue to Sun D 6 to 10.30 CLOSED: 25 and 26 Dec, 1 Jan, 7 to 21 Aug MEALS: alc Tue to Fri L and Tue to Sat D (main courses £9 to £14). Set L Tue to Fri £12.50 (2 courses), Set L and D Sun £14.50 (2 courses) to £17 SERVICE: 12.5% (optional), card slips closed CARDS: Delta, MasterCard, Switch, Visa DETAILS: 65 seats. 20 seats outside. Private parties: 12 main room. Vegetarian meals. Children's helpings. No cigars before 10.30. Wheelchair access (also WC). Music. Air-conditioned ⊖ Boston Manor (£5)

Club Gascon

map 13

57 West Smithfield, EC1A 9DS
TEL: (020) 7796 0600 FAX: (020) 7796 0601

COOKING **4**
FRENCH
£32–£72

Making the most of its small, humble, wood-floored premises – exotic flower displays enliven the characterful marble walls and close-together tables – Club Gascon is one of the capital's more unusual restaurants. Booking can be a nightmare, but those who make it find a friendly atmosphere and impeccable service. Even those with high expectations find them fulfilled by the innovative style: no starters and main courses, just a grouping of taster-sized dishes into 'la route du sel', 'le potager', 'les pâturages' and so on, with centre stage reserved for ten or more items based on foie gras. Choose half a dozen between two, which are then served two at a time: perhaps steamed zander with caramelised chorizo, or haddock leaves and aubergine with whipped violet mustard, followed by foie gras consommé with broad beans and grilled oysters, and accurately grilled scallops with potato galette and caviar. A menu at £50 a head includes a glass of wine with each of the five courses. The list covers south-west France admirably, although, given the amount of foie gras, it seems perverse not to offer any sweet wines by the glass. Bottle prices start at £10.50.

CHEF: Pascal Aussignac PROPRIETORS: Vincent Labeyrie and Pascal Aussignac OPEN: Mon to Fri L 12 to 2, Mon to Sat D 7 to 10 (10.30 Sat) CLOSED: Christmas to New Year, bank hols MEALS: alc (main courses £3.50 to £24). Set L and D £30 to £50 (inc wine) SERVICE: 12.5% (optional) CARDS: Delta, MasterCard, Switch, Visa DETAILS: 55 seats. Private parties: 55 main room. Vegetarian meals. Wheelchair access (not WC). Music. Air-conditioned ⊖ Barbican, Farringdon

Le Colombier

NEW ENTRY map 14

145 Dovehouse Street, SW3 6LB
TEL: (020) 7351 1155 FAX: (020) 7351 0077

COOKING **3**
FRENCH
£29–£61

A textbook French bistro on a corner site near Chelsea Square, Le Colombier (the Dovecote, named in honour of the address) impresses for the genuine warmth of the welcome led by Didier Garnier. Its cultural identity is reflected as much in the slightly shoehorned feel of the tables as in the traditional fare on its bilingual menus. Oeufs pochés meurette is a well-rendered starter – two lightly poached eggs in a Burgundian red wine sauce with tiny onions and mushrooms – or there may be a choice of oyster species offered in multiples of three, or snails in puff pastry with garlic cream. Jointed rabbit with thin pasta and apple in a cider sauce pleased one visitor, not least for the timing of the pasta. Entrecôte comes with béarnaise, although grilled calf's liver, in a concession to Anglo tastes, is paired with bacon. Tarte Tatin and crème brûlée keep the end up at dessert stage. Wine glasses are topped up eagerly with French wine by largely French staff. Prices are nearly all on the wrong side of £20, although they start at £11.50.

CHEF: Olivier Galeran PROPRIETOR: Didier Garnier OPEN: all week 12 to 3, 6.30 to 11 MEALS: alc (main courses £10 to £20). Set L Mon to Sat £13 (2 courses), Set L Sun £15, Set D 6.30 to 7.30 £13 (2 courses) SERVICE: 12.5% (optional), card slips closed CARDS: Amex, Delta, Diners, MasterCard, Switch, Visa DETAILS: 75 seats. 35 seats outside. Private parties: 45 private room. No music. Air-conditioned ⊖ South Kensington

▲ The Connaught

map 15

16 Carlos Place, W1Y 6AL
TEL: (020) 7499 7070 FAX: (020) 7495 3262
EMAIL: info@the-connaught.co.uk
WEB SITE: www.savoy-group.co.uk

COOKING **6**
ANGLO-FRENCH
£51–£153

This Edwardian hotel is perfect for people who feel at home in gentlemen's clubs and like to wallow in a few luxuries while keeping a safe distance from fashionable food. Chandeliers and polished mahogany panelling make it feel like walking into a 'living stately home', and the menu itself is a collector's item, expressed in an introverted florid style which even those with a working knowledge of French culinary terms (and Franglais) might struggle with: consommé en surprise 'Prince of Wales', salmi de canard du Norfolk garniture d'un soir, or demoiselle d'Aberdeen à la nage Moscovite.

Underneath all this is a convoluted mixture of French cooking and posh nursery food, ranging from an elaborately decorated and beautifully fresh fish terrine set in a sea of aspic, to grouse 'with all the trimmings', by way of first-class scallops and langoustines served with podded broad beans, young asparagus, baby carrots and cherry tomatoes. Savouries are a welcome idea, although desserts seem to produce better results: light and 'faultless' crêpe soufflés Belle Epoque with a lemony filling, for example. Apparently effortless, friendly service is dispensed by an army of staff who attend to every need, although a lady who considered them arrogant and complacent summed the place up as ideal 'if you're a chap. With a large wallet'. Wines are cynically priced (forget your £20 budget), their service by the glass (for an inspector) not much better, and a 15 per cent service charge is added to everything.

CHEF: Michel Bourdin PROPRIETOR: The Blackstone Group OPEN: all week 12.30 to 2.30, 6 to 10.45 MEALS: alc (main courses £13.50 to £39.50). Set L £28.50, Set D £58 SERVICE: 15% (optional) CARDS: Amex, Delta, Diners, MasterCard, Switch, Visa DETAILS: 100 seats. Private parties: 10 main room, 12 and 22 private rooms. Vegetarian meals. Children's helpings. Jacket and tie. Wheelchair access (also WC). No music. Air-conditioned ACCOMMODATION: 90 rooms, all with bath/shower. TV. Phone. Room only £280 to £370. Rooms for disabled. Baby facilities *(The Which? Hotel Guide)* ⊖ Bond Street, Green Park

Coq d'Argent 🍷 — map 13

1 Poultry, EC2R 8EJ — COOKING **4**
TEL: (020) 7395 5000 FAX: (020) 7395 5050 — FRENCH
WEB SITE: www.conran.co.uk — £30–£87

The rooftop vista may be hemmed in by mundane office blocks, but being whisked above the hoi polloi to a terrace in the sky doubtless has its appeal for the City suits who pop in for lunch. The design is stylish (what else from Sir T?), with curved stone walls, light wood, and leather chairs. Trade-mark seafood plays a prominent role in the shape of oysters, caviar, lobsters, or a tian of crab mixed with chopped avocado and tomato. The cooking is competent if understandably rather conservative, ranging from demonstrably fresh steamed brill garnished with tiny girolles and a shallot vinaigrette (served with buttery mashed potatoes), to accurately grilled calf's liver with sage leaves and crispy bacon.

Desserts are equally reassuring: perhaps a 'skilfully under-roasted', firm-textured peach arranged on pain perdu, or pear Tatin served with caramel sauce, crème anglaise and good-quality vanilla ice cream. Service is efficient. Wine regions of France are thoroughly indulged on this long and pricey list, which includes many de luxe champagnes and fine dessert wines for the expense-account diner. The sommelier's selection recommends choice bottles from around the world for those seeking a short cut. A dozen wines by the glass start at £3.50.

Not inc *in the details at the end of an entry indicates that no service charge is made and any tipping is at the discretion of the customer.*

CHEF: Stephen Goodlad PROPRIETOR: Conran Restaurants Ltd OPEN: Sun to Fri L 11.30 (12 Sun) to 3, Mon to Sat D 6 (6.30 Sat) to 10 CLOSED: bank hols MEALS: alc Mon to Sat (main courses £10.50 to £25). Set L Sun £17.50 (2 courses) to £20 SERVICE: 12.5% (optional), card slips closed CARDS: Amex, Delta, Diners, MasterCard, Switch, Visa DETAILS: 148 seats. 250 seats outside. Private parties: 300 main room. Vegetarian meals. Wheelchair access (also WC). No music. Air-conditioned ⊖ Bank

Cotto

NEW ENTRY **map 12**

44 Blythe Road, W14 0HA
TEL: (020) 7602 9333 FAX: (020) 7602 5003

COOKING **4**
MODERN EUROPEAN
£27–£51

Although the name is Italian for 'cooked', it would be too much to expect an Italian restaurant, and sure enough this new Hammersmith venue is more about the kind of free-ranging food that London feels at home with. Eating takes place in a minimally spare dining room (white walls with colourful geometrical abstracts, and chrome chairs upholstered in black) against background music that ranges from salsa to old-time crooning. This is clearly a capable kitchen where technique is assured, taking in its stride lightly seared, Szechuan pepper-crusted tuna, served cold as a starter, resting in a pool of bouillon; and a clearly flavoured, smooth-textured red pepper and artichoke terrine topped with fried squid and dribbled with basil sauce.

Five choices per course deliver some pretty racy ideas, although not all the speculative combinations are well judged. The more conventional partnerships, from broad bean soup with summer savoury, to baked gurnard with bouillabaisse sauce, may prove their worth. To finish, there is an Anglo-French cheese selection, blueberry pavlova, or light chocolate soufflé with malt chocolate ice-cream. The four-page wine list is helpfully organised according to grape variety, and engineers a clever balance between New and Old World styles. A handful is available by the glass, and house vin de pays is £12.50.

CHEF: James Kirby PROPRIETORS: James and Jane Kirby OPEN: Mon to Fri L 12 to 2.30, Mon to Sat D 7 to 10.30 CLOSED: Christmas MEALS: alc D (main courses £10 to £14.50). Set L £12.50 (2 courses) to £15.50 SERVICE: 12.5% (optional), card slips closed CARDS: Delta, MasterCard, Switch, Visa DETAILS: 70 seats. 8 seats outside. Private parties: 40 main room, 35 private room. Vegetarian meals. No pipes in dining room. Wheelchair access (not WC). Music. Air-conditioned ⊖ Kensington Olympia

Cow Dining Room

NEW ENTRY **map 13**

89 Westbourne Park Road, W2 5QH
TEL: (020) 7221 0021 FAX: (020) 7727 8687

COOKING **3**
MODERN EUROPEAN
£27–£56

This Notting Hill pub, its first-floor dining room adorned by one of Francis Bacon's milder-mannered triptychs, tends to be full to bursting even on weekday nights. Juliet Peston arrived here from Lola's (see entry, London) to oversee things while the day-to-day operation is run by Sue Lewis. All the right components seem to be in place, evidenced in clean-flavoured chilled pea and mint soup, and 'a pleasant compilation' of roast head of garlic, goats' cheese, cherry tomatoes and basil. Lamb cutlets with good merguez, mild hummus and

Greek salad is a satisfying main-course assemblage, while the well-hung, flavourful Angus fillet for two with chips, béarnaise and Caesar salad is a mammoth helping. Finish with raspberry and chocolate tart, or go the whole southern European hog and dip cantuccini biscuits in vin santo. 'Efficient, unrushed, human' service is just what's needed. The short wine list suits the simplicity of the cooking, and a handful is available by the glass. Prices open at £12.50 for a bottle of Italian.

CHEFS: Juliet Peston and Sue Lewis PROPRIETOR: Tom Conran OPEN: Sun L 12.30 TO 3.30, all week D 7 (7.30 Sun) to 11 (10.30 Sun) CLOSED: Christmas MEALS: alc (main courses £8 to £15) SERVICE: not inc, 12.5% for parties of 5 or more CARDS: Amex, Delta, MasterCard, Switch, Visa DETAILS: 35 seats. Private parties: 30 main room. No babies. No music ⊖ Westbourne Park, Royal Oak

Creelers

NEW ENTRY map 14

3 Bray Place, SW3 3LL
TEL/FAX: (020) 7838 0788

COOKING **2**
MODERN BRITISH
£24–£55

Home to several restaurants over the years, this corner site near the King's Road end of Draycott Avenue is now an 'opulent dining room on a tiny scale'. It could hardly be called a chain restaurant, although it does have two links, one on the Isle of Arran, the other in Edinburgh. All three are outlets for fresh seafood, game, and products from the owners' smokehouse, and a long list of dishes centres around these core materials: cold- and hot-smoked salmon, fresh and clean-tasting oysters served with a sweet shallot vinegar, and queen scallops with garlic and parsley butter.

The cooking commendably ventures only as far as it need, turning out ochre-coloured fish soup with a mild-flavoured rouille and crisp croûtons, well-timed roast monkfish tail accompanied by salt-cod ravioli, and haunch of Arran venison, properly rested and sliced into juicy collops, enriched with a game sauce. Pain perdu and a layered chocolate amaretti terrine are among desserts. Prices are a little high, even for Chelsea, although the 30-strong wine list offers some choice under £20, including five house wines.

CHEF: Vicky Hemming PROPRIETORS: Tim and Fran James, and Robert Clayton OPEN: Tue to Sun 12 to 2.30, 6 to 10.30 CLOSED: 25 and 26 Dec MEALS: alc (main courses £12 to £19). Set L £12 (2 courses) to £15 SERVICE: not inc CARDS: Amex, Delta, MasterCard, Switch, Visa DETAILS: 55 seats. Private parties: 30 main room. Vegetarian meals. Children's helpings. No smoking in 1 dining room. Music ⊖ Sloane Square, South Kensington

Criterion Brasserie MPW

map 15

224 Piccadilly, W1V 9LB
TEL: (020) 7930 0488 FAX: (020) 7930 8380

COOKING **5**
FRENCH/MEDITERRANEAN
£31–£81

'Est. 1874' says the sign above the entrance on the south side of Piccadilly Circus, and the dazzling interior, with its high Byzantine ceiling, marble columns and raised stage-like area towards the rear, is one of London's most self-consciously fabulous restaurant settings. Darren Bunn offers the sorts of brasserie dishes that have become the stock in trade of the Marco Pierre White empire, plus a few more besides. Vichyssoise with smoked haddock, and roast suckling pig on a bed of herbed mash have come in for praise from reporters, and nerveless timing has been appreciated in roast pheasant served on unsweetened quince purée in a wine gravy with a few tiny roasted new potatoes.

The famous lemon tart – unadorned save for a light dredging of icing sugar – seems as reliable here as at other Marco addresses. Fixed-price lunch is thought exemplary value, especially when it includes desserts of brioche-and-butter pudding, or caramel parfait with raspberry sorbet. Several readers have found service to be seriously in need of improvement. Wines are a compendious selection from the world's cellars, but mark-ups are such that £20 is soon a distant memory. The list kicks off with vins de pays at £15.

CHEF: Darren Bunn PROPRIETOR: Marco Pierre White OPEN: Mon to Sat L 12 to 2.30, all week D 5.30 to 11.30 (10.30 Sun) CLOSED: 25 and 26 Dec MEALS: alc (main courses £13 to £25). Set L £14.95 (2 courses) to £17.95, Set D Mon to Sat 5.30 to 6.30 £14.95 (2 courses) to £17.95 SERVICE: 12.5% (optional), card slips closed CARDS: Amex, Delta, Diners, MasterCard, Switch, Visa DETAILS: 180 seats. Wheelchair access (also WC). No music. Air-conditioned ⊖ Piccadilly Circus

Crowthers

map 12

481 Upper Richmond Rd West, SW14 7PU
TEL/FAX: (020) 8876 6372

COOKING **3**
MODERN BRITISH/FRENCH
£36–£45

Crowthers' strong local reputation has been built up over the years, based on its honest cooking and sensible prices. It is a small, unpretentious place, with dark-red and cream décor and, at the back, a wooden cabinet stuffed with bottles of spirits. Food on the fixed-price menu is French-based, offering a peppery Mediterranean fish soup with croûtons covered in a punchy, garlicky rouille, and top-quality best end of lamb crusted with mustard, herbs and breadcrumbs, served with a garlic and rosemary sauce.

Philip Crowther keeps abreast of global trends as well, however, producing seared scallops with spiced basmati rice and a light curry dressing, and grilled aubergine with tomato, feta and pesto. A pudding of pineapple spiked with black pepper has arrived with a gooey caramel sauce, vanilla ice cream and kahlua cream. Service, usually from Shirley Crowther, adds to the homely atmosphere. A drinks list with a rich seam of aperitifs contains a varied and reasonably priced choice of 40 or so wines. House wine is £11.50.

CHEF: Philip Crowther PROPRIETORS: Philip and Shirley Crowther OPEN: Tue to Sat D 7 to 10.30 (L by prior arrangement only) CLOSED: 1 week at Christmas, 2 weeks in August MEALS: Set D 19.50 (2 courses) to £24.50 SERVICE: not inc CARDS: Delta, MasterCard, Switch, Visa DETAILS: 30 seats. Private parties: 35 main room. Children's helpings. Wheelchair access (not WC). No music. Air-conditioned ⊖ Richmond (£5)

NEW CHEF *is shown instead of a cooking mark where a change of chef occurred too late for a new assessment of the cooking.*

New main entries and restaurant closures are listed near the front of the book.

Cucina

map 13

45A South End Road, NW3 2QB
TEL: (020) 7435 7814 FAX: (020) 7435 7815
EMAIL: cucinarestaurant@hotmail.com

COOKING **3**
MODERN EUROPEAN
£26–£53

Eating here is an appealing – and evidently popular – option, given the bright, spacious dining room and friendly, efficient service. An enterprising new deli at the front makes some of the kitchen's more unusual ingredients available for customers to experiment with at home. While the roots of the cooking are in Italy, its branches spread out across the world to produce a menu as appealing as it is exotic and varied.

For starters, home-made sage fettucine comes with confit rabbit, sweet potato and spring onions, while sardines in beer batter are served with a tomato, fennel and caper chutney. Mains range from straightforward chargrilled rib of beef with frites to oriental-influenced pan-fried duck breast with potato rendang and sesame-fried bok choy. Vegetarians, meanwhile, are given the option of roast butternut squash and ricotta in a filo parcel, with a pecan, apple and celery salad. Portions are large, so a dessert of Belgian waffles with banana and peanut butter ice cream may have to be shared. Wines are a suitably varied bunch arranged by price, opening at £10.95.

CHEF: Andrew Poole PROPRIETORS: Vernon Mascarenhas and Andrew Poole OPEN: all week L 12 to 2.30, Mon to Sat D 7 to 10.30 (11 Fri and Sat) CLOSED: 3 days Christmas MEALS: alc (main courses £8 to £17). Set L Mon to Sat £7.95 (1 course), Set L Sun £12.95 (2 courses) to £15.95 SERVICE: not inc, 12.5% for parties of 8 or more CARDS: Amex, Delta, MasterCard, Switch, Visa DETAILS: 96 seats. Private parties: 70 main room. Vegetarian meals. Children's helpings. No cigars/pipes in dining room. Occasional music. Air-conditioned ⊖ Belsize Park

Dakota 🍷

map 13

127 Ledbury Road, W11 2AQ
TEL: (020) 7792 9191 FAX: (020) 7792 9090
EMAIL: dakota@montana.plc.uk
WEB SITE: www.hartfordgroup.co.uk

NEW CHEF
CONTEMPORARY AMERICAN/MEXICAN
£29–£52

Despite the movement of chefs – Terence Williamson came from Globe in Swiss Cottage, too late for us to receive any feedback on performance – this small group of restaurants (see entries for Montana and Utah, all in London, as well as Canyon in Richmond) continues to offer a flexible and loosely interpreted version of south-west US food. Weekday lunch and weekend brunch are likely to major on straightforward eggs Benedict or chargrilled tuna, while dinner deals in grilled squid and chorizo salad, tea-smoked chicken breast, and ginger and macadamia sopapillas with roast peaches and ice cream. Drinks run to all manner of juices, smoothies, coffees, cocktails, beers, and a lively list of wines split into 'light', 'medium' and 'full'. Arranged in price order, with most Californians over £20, it starts with vin de pays at £12 and offers around ten wines by the glass.

Dining rooms where music, either live or recorded, is never played are signalled by No music *in the details at the end of an entry.*

CHEF: Terry Williamson PROPRIETOR: Hartford Group OPEN: all week 12 to 3.30, 6.30 to 11 CLOSED: 25 Dec MEALS: alc (main courses £9 to £15). Set L Mon to Fri £14 (2 courses). Brunch menu Sat and Sun SERVICE: 12.5%, card slips closed CARDS: Amex, MasterCard, Visa DETAILS: 70 seats. 30 seats outside. Private parties: 24 main room. Vegetarian meals. Children's helpings. Wheelchair access (not WC). Music. Air-conditioned ⊖ Ladbroke Grove

Del Buongustaio

map 12

283–285 Putney Bridge Road, SW15 2PT
TEL/FAX: (020) 8780 9361

COOKING **2**
ITALIAN
£21–£48

A welcoming ambience is generated partly by pink-washed fresco-style walls, and partly by pleasant staff who, though few in number, cope well with a busy restaurant. Although some ideas on the monthly-changing menu continue to reflect those of its former owner Aurelio Spagnuolo (of Osteria Antica Bologna, see entry, London), taking in dishes from Italy's Renaissance and Roman periods, there is much that is modern too: tartare of salmon on spinach, or cold roast beef with salsa verde.

Varied main courses – encompassing lamb, duck, veal, quail, trout and monkfish – are substantial, but it is worth trying to find room for commendable pasta as well, which might come with prawns, scallops, garlic and lemon. The green olive paste served with bread is highly rated. The lunch menu is much shorter but still tempting. Italian wines dominate on a cheerful list that offers four by the 50-centilitre jug. Further in, more serious wines can be found from producers such as Antinori and Conterno, but they don't come cheap. A few New World bins provide alternatives. House wines are £9.90.

CHEF: Giovanni Di Novella PROPRIETORS: Del Buongustaio Ltd OPEN: all week L 12 (12.30 Sun) to 3 (3.30 Sun), Mon to Sat D 6.30 to 11 CLOSED: Christmas MEALS: alc (main courses £9 to £16.50). Set L £9.75 (2 courses) to £12.75, Set D £26.95. Cover £0.90 SERVICE: not inc, 10% for parties of 5 or more, card slips closed CARDS: Amex, Delta, MasterCard, Switch, Visa DETAILS: 120 seats. Private parties: 50 main room, 50 private room. Vegetarian meals. Children's helpings. No cigars/pipes in dining room. Wheelchair access (also WC). Music. Air-conditioned ⊖ East Putney (£5)

Delfina Studio Café

map 13

50 Bermondsey Street, SE1 3UD
TEL: (020) 7357 0244 FAX: (020) 7357 0250
EMAIL: events@delfina.org.uk
WEB SITE: www.delfina.org.uk

COOKING **4**
GLOBAL
£31–£48

A converted chocolate factory not far from London Bridge station, Deflina combines an art gallery with a large, white, noisy restaurant offering an ostentatiously modern menu. Maria Elia cooks weekday lunch menus for the style-hungry, mobilising unusual techniques for dishes that make the most of today's favoured ingredients. Balls of fried aubergine in spicy batter with beetroot salad and walnut sauce makes an arresting way to start, and sesame prawn toast has appeared as a substantial wedge served with a slice of admirably fresh seared tuna and threads of Szechuan cucumber.

Ask for details of the day's chargrilled fish, or opt for rich, meaty roast duck with lychees and coconut curry. Side orders include potatoes with Thai basil and chilli. To finish, there may be apple 'pizza' (actually a puff-pastry tart) or vanilla and coffee-bean crème caramel with biscotti. The crème fraîche ice cream that comes with chocolate and lime pudding is of star quality. Service is smart and efficient. Wine prices may feel higher than the surroundings warrant, but choice is mostly very sound. A pair of Spanish wines opens the bidding at £12.50.

CHEF: Maria Elia PROPRIETORS: Digby Squires and Delfina Entrecanales OPEN: Mon to Fri L 12 to 3 CLOSED: 23 Dec to 2 Jan MEALS: alc (main courses £9 to £14) SERVICE: 12.5% (optional), card slips closed CARDS: Amex, Delta, Diners, MasterCard, Switch, Visa DETAILS: 70 seats. Private parties: 300 main room, 5 to 600 private rooms. Vegetarian meals. Wheelchair access (also WC). No music ⊖ London Bridge

Depot

NEW ENTRY map 12

Tideway Yard, Mortlake High Street, SW14 8SN
TEL: (020) 8878 9462 FAX: (020) 8392 1361

COOKING **1**
MODERN BRITISH
£23–£44

From a long, narrow conservatory, diners enjoy 'the finest vista of the Thames imaginable', and there is a terrace (without the view) for al fresco eating and drinking. Inside, the fresh, clean, minimalist look is relieved by abstract paintings, and a contemporary menu offers starters of goats' cheese roulade with herb pesto, or chargrilled baby squid in a vibrant, rustic salsa of tomato, chilli and red pepper. Main courses range from smoked haddock fishcakes with avocado salad, or grilled lamb rump with spinach, feta and olives, to richly flavoured, crisp-skinned tamarind-glazed duck with sesame seeds and refreshingly sappy bok choy. Commendable desserts have included baked vanilla and lemon cheesecake, and a fresh-tasting summer-fruit sorbet. House wines are £10.50, with six more by the glass on a short, fairly priced list.

CHEFS: Robert Veint and Karen Pedder PROPRIETOR: Tideway Restaurant Ltd OPEN: Mon to Sat 12 to 3, 6 to 11, Sun noon to 10.30 CLOSED: 25 and 26 Dec MEALS: alc (main courses £7.50 to £12.50). Set L Mon to Fri £9.95 (2 courses), Set D Sun to Thur £13.50 (2 courses) SERVICE: 12.5% (optional), card slips closed CARDS: Amex, Delta, Diners, MasterCard, Switch, Visa DETAILS: 120 seats. 40 seats outside. Private parties: 120 main room, 40 private room. Car park. Vegetarian meals. Children's helpings. No smoking in 1 dining room. Wheelchair access (not WC). Music

Ditto

NEW ENTRY map 12

55–57 East Hill, SW18 2QE
TEL: (020) 8877 0110 FAX: (020) 8875 0110
WEB SITE: www.doditto.com

COOKING **4**
MODERN EUROPEAN
£28–£53

This double-fronted shop conversion, done in blue and white with windows opening on to the pavement, features a bar and function room to one side, and a dining room to the other. Colourful abstract paintings contribute to an impression of contemporary cool, well suited to the menu's up-to-date approach. There are no prissy presentations, just forthright flavours, for example in a hefty and earthily satisfying lamb shank with 'scorched roots' (caramelised vegetables including celery, carrots and turnips).

Calum Watson's confident and technically sound cooking is evident in a crisp, sweet-tasting skate wing with spinach and caper butter, and familiarity with oriental technique (an essential nowadays) has produced a vibrant and colourful crab and vegetable spring roll with oyster sauce. To finish, there may be honey parfait with fig purée, pannacotta with berries, or alcoholic tiramisù given extra dimension by white and dark chocolate sauces. Service is smart in every sense of the word. France and the southern hemisphere account for most of the wines, which are at commendably restrained prices. House French is £10.95.

CHEF: Calum Watson PROPRIETORS: Giles Cooper and Christian Duffell OPEN: Sun to Fri L 12 to 3, all week D 7 to 11, Sat and Sun breakfast 10 to 12 MEALS: alc (main courses £10 to £14.50). Set L £10 (2 courses) to £18.50 (inc wine), Set D £14.50 (2 courses) to £18.50. Breakfast available Sat and Sun SERVICE: not inc, 12.5% for parties of 6 or more CARDS: Delta, MasterCard, Switch, Visa DETAILS: 75 seats. Private parties: 24 main room, 24 private room. Vegetarian meals. Children's helpings. Wheelchair access (not WC). No music (£5)

Eagle £ — map 13

159 Farringdon Road, EC1R 3AL — COOKING **2**
TEL: (020) 7837 1353 — MEDITERRANEAN
£20–£37

This lively old pub, always packed, is a fashionable, noisy haunt with a food counter and kitchen in full view, where chefs can be seen chargrilling, simmering and assembling dishes at full throttle. Those who don't mind being deafened can pull up a mismatched chair, others might head outside to the picnic-table sets on busy Farringdon Road. Simplicity reigns, good-value one-course meals are the norm, and Iberia exerts a big influence on the cooking. A Basque sauce of pine nuts, butter, raisins and fish stock has accompanied first-rate chargrilled halibut, and other options have included chorizo and potato soup with spring greens, and grilled marinated leg of lamb served with the Catalan equivalent of ratatouille. Finish with Portuguese custard tarts, or Spanish goats' and ewes' milk cheeses. How staff manage to survive the noise is a mystery, but they remain friendly and obliging. Moderate prices distinguish the chalked-up wine list, with house Italian £9.50 a bottle, £2.20 a glass.

CHEF: Tom Norrington-Davies PROPRIETOR: Michael Belben OPEN: all week L 12 to 2.30 (3.30 Sat and Sun), Mon to Sat D 6.30 to 10.30 CLOSED: Christmas, bank hols MEALS: alc (main courses £4.50 to £12) SERVICE: none CARDS: none DETAILS: 60 seats. 20 seats outside. Vegetarian meals. Music ⊖ Farringdon

English Garden — NEW ENTRY — map 14

10 Lincoln Street, SW3 2TS — COOKING **5**
TEL: (020) 7584 7272 FAX: (020) 7584 1961 — ANGLO-FRENCH
£32–£62

The name may evoke some vision of Home Counties pastoral, but the restaurant is a mere jog from the King's Road. A recent makeover has pared down the décor, and the conservatory at the back has lost its greenery and is now panelled and adorned with an abstract representation of a mountain range. Into this remodelled Garden in December 1999 stepped Malcolm Starmer, bringing with him a refined Anglo-French style that works well. A starter of baked egg with two brioche 'sandwiches' of Serrano ham, for example, is a novel take on ham and eggs with fried bread.

Presentations can be quite complicated, as when a long piece of smoked eel is encased in red cabbage and served alongside a trio of roast scallops, but the kitchen can handle this level of technicality. Proudly risen blackcurrant soufflé comes with its own sorbet and a tiny glass of lemon cream, and, in a nod to the garden idea, herbs play their part in sweet things, basil going into a syrup for lemon tart, sorrel appearing with poached pears. Efficient and courteous service adds to the pleasure. Great care has gone into sourcing wines, and there is just enough choice below £20 to cater for those on a budget. House wines start at £12.50.

CHEF: Malcom Starmer PROPRIETOR: Searcy Corrigan Ltd OPEN: all week 12 to 3, 6 to 11 (10.30 Sun) CLOSED: 25 Dec MEALS: alc D (main courses £15 to £20). Set L £19.50 SERVICE: 12.5% CARDS: Amex, Delta, Diners, MasterCard, Switch, Visa DETAILS: 50 seats. Private parties: 8 to 32 private rooms. Vegetarian meals. No music. Air-conditioned ⊖ Sloane Square (£5)

L'Escargot

map 15

48 Greek Street, W1V 5LQ — COOKING **5**
TEL: (020) 7439 7474 FAX: (020) 7437 0790 — MODERN FRENCH
EMAIL: l'escargot@whitestarline.org.uk — £30–£57

Paintings abound. Apart from what you would expect in the Picasso Room, the ground floor displays works by Hockney, Miró, Chagall and Matisse, although there is no suggestion that the artists actually paid for dinner with canvas. Main courses can be quite involved: an assiette of lamb incorporating best end, neck and tongue (Picasso Room), or red mullet and John Dory served with a tart of tomato, red onion and tiger prawns in a shellfish dressing (ground floor). And the range is ambitious too, from roast cod saltimbocca, via choucroute with Toulouse sausage, to a vegetarian plate of wild mushrooms, globe artichokes, creamed lentils and thyme-flavoured potatoes.

The lengthy ground-floor menu imposes a few supplements – for foie gras, scallops, brill and sea bass – but there is no shortage of other options, from starters of watercress and horseradish soup, or skate and potato salad, to blueberry cheesecake or a panettone, banana and chocolate pudding. Each dessert is offered with a complementary (but not complimentary) glass of sweet wine. There is a pre-theatre option, although it may need more effort to lift it above the local competition. And more effort could be made to accommodate ordinary drinkers on the prestige-hungry list, which features more bottles over £1,000 than under £20. House vin de pays is £14.

CHEF: Andrew Thompson PROPRIETOR: Jimmy Lahoud OPEN: Mon to Fri L 12.15 to 2.15, Mon to Sat D 6 to 11.30 CLOSED: 25 and 26 Dec, 1 Jan, bank hols MEALS: alc (main courses £13). Set L and D before 7pm £14.95 (2 courses) to £17.95 SERVICE: 12.5% (optional), card slips closed CARDS: Amex, Delta, Diners, MasterCard, Switch, Visa DETAILS: 80 seats. Private parties: 26 and 60 private rooms. Vegetarian meals. No cigars/pipes in dining room. Wheelchair access (also men's WC). Occasional music. Air-conditioned ⊖ Leicester Square, Tottenham Court Road

London restaurants by cuisine are listed near the front of the book.

L'Estaminet

map 15

14 Garrick Street, WC2E 9BJ
TEL: (020) 7379 1432 FAX: (020) 7379 1530

COOKING **1**
FRENCH
£22–£52

'We said we'd have to leave for the theatre at a particular time and they met it without rush or compromising quality,' enthused one party, happy with their fish on the good-value early-evening menu. Others have found the pre-theatre choice limited and a bit uninspiring. Still, the place leaves a 'good feeling', whether you dine early or late: is it the easy-on-the-eye candlelit décor, or the even-handed service, or the reliable French bourgeois cuisine? Here you can find all those bistro classics like crème vichyssoise, friture de fruits de mer and pâté en croûte; then to follow, Saint-Jacques grillés, suprême de volaille à l'estragon, or chateaubriand with itsy-bitsy vegetables. Commendable cheeses come in 30 different guises, 'all flagged with illegible names', while ever-so-traditional desserts run to crème brûlée, or one tarte aux fruits or another. Wines are fine French, *tout court*.

CHEF: Philippe Tamet PROPRIETOR: Christian Bellone OPEN: Mon to Sat 12 to 2.30, 5.45 to 11.15 CLOSED: bank hols MEALS: alc (main courses £12.50 to £16.50). Set D Mon to Fri before 7.30 £11.99, Set D Sat before 7.30 £14.50. Bar meals available Mon to Fri SERVICE: 12.5%, card slips closed CARDS: Amex, Delta, MasterCard, Switch, Visa DETAILS: 60 seats. Private parties: 12 main room, 22 private room. Children's helpings. No smoking in 1 dining room. No pipes in dining room. Wheelchair access (not WC). Music. Air-conditioned ⊖ Leicester Square, Covent Garden

Euphorium

map 13

203 Upper Street, N1 1RQ
TEL: (020) 7704 6909
EMAIL: bookings@euphorium.fsnet.co.uk

COOKING **2**
MODERN BRITISH/MEDITERRANEAN
£30–£64

Euphorium is a stylish and contemporary cocktail bar and restaurant (with bakery attached). A huge tree at the back offers shade for Sunday brunchers, and a change from the rather stark interior. Bold, punchy flavours and a constantly changing menu chime well with the feel of the place, from soft but crisply-fried baby globe artichokes, to roast pork stuffed with a summery Mediterranean mix of tapénade, peppers and pine nuts. There is plenty for vegetarians to choose from, including pappardelle with coriander pesto and grilled asparagus (as a starter or main course), and roast mushroom and goats' cheese tart. A few Middle Eastern influences are at work, for example in a fig and pistachio tart, and crème brûlée has come in a Cape gooseberry version. Incidentals are well executed, and staff friendly and efficient. Like the menu, the wine list is a short and evenly balanced collection from around the world, with only a handful over £20. Prices start at £11.75.

CHEF/PROPRIETOR: Marwan Badran OPEN: all week L 12 to 2.30 (3.30 Sun), Mon to Sat D 6 to 10.30 CLOSED: Christmas to New Year, Easter, bank hols MEALS: alc (main courses £9 to £17). Set L and D 6 to 7.30 £12.50 (2 courses) SERVICE: 12.5% (optional), card slips closed CARDS: Amex, Delta, MasterCard, Switch, Visa DETAILS: 60 seats. 40 seats outside. Private parties: 80 main room. Vegetarian meals. Children's helpings. Wheelchair access (not WC). No music. Air-conditioned ⊖ Highbury & Islington, Angel

Fifth Floor 🍷

map 14

Harvey Nichols, 109-125
Knightsbridge, SW1X 7RJ
TEL: (020) 7235 5250 FAX: (020) 7823 2207

COOKING **4**
MODERN BRITISH
£36–£78

The busy fifth floor is shared by a sushi bar, café, drinks bar, deli and wine shop, but the culinary centre of gravity remains with the restaurant. Bemusing Grandma Moses-type murals and strangely low-slung armchairs at the tables create their own singular impressions, while the kitchen's global approach is handled authoritatively. Henry Harris's extensive menus exude bold cutting-edge confidence, pairing deep-fried oysters with belly pork in a soy and yuzu dressing, and offering organically farmed salmon, cured with rosemary and Lagavulin malt whisky, accompanied by turnip pickle.

Materials extend from Lincolnshire duck (served with smoked eel), via roast Dorset lobster, to Yorkshire's Black Sheep ale, used as the cooking liquor for pot-roast rabbit with herb dumplings. Simple Mediterranean ideas have their place too: reporters have enjoyed grilled sardines on provençale vegetables, and lamb steak with an aubergine mousse. A tempting plate of chocolate and orange puddings combines a mousse with a hot soufflé and Cointreau ice cream. Prices have crept up on the wine list, which nevertheless includes a fascinating mix, ranging from fine clarets and Burgundies to inspiring selections of Italian and Californian reds. Own label house wines are £12.50 and 11 wines are available by the glass.

CHEF: Henry Harris PROPRIETOR: Harvey Nichols & Co Ltd OPEN: all week L 12 to 3 (3.30 Sat and Sun), Mon to Sat D 6.30 to 11.30 CLOSED: 25 and 26 Dec MEALS: alc D (main courses £11 to £20). Set L £24 SERVICE: 12.5% CARDS: Amex, Delta, Diners, MasterCard, Switch, Visa DETAILS: 110 seats. Vegetarian meals. No pipes in dining room; non-smoking area. Wheelchair access (also WC). Air-conditioned ⊖ Knightsbridge

Fina Estampa

map 13

152 Tooley Street, SE1 2TU
TEL/FAX: (020) 7403 1342

COOKING **2**
PERUVIAN
£27–£50

Peruvian plates, mirrors, photographs and other artefacts decorate the cream, gold and burgundy dining room. Bianca, originally from Lima, cooks the food of her homeland, while amiable Richard serves it. Starters include cebiche (raw white fish marinated in red onions, chillies and coriander) served with a sweet potato mash and chilli sauce, and ocopa (new potatoes covered in peanut and walnut sauce). Main courses – likely to come with both rice and potatoes – range from simple baked salmon with a tomato sauce to pollo almendrado (chicken in a slightly sweet almond and pecan sauce). Desserts (passion-fruit ice cream, for instance) are bought in. Be aware that an 'optional' 10 per cent cover charge is added to the bill 'to cover extra charges on the table' and service is not included. All bottles on the short wine list hail from South America. House Peruvian is £10.50.

The Guide always appreciates hearing about changes of chef or owner.

CHEF: Bianca Jones PROPRIETORS: Richard and Bianca Jones OPEN: Mon to Fri L 12 to 2.30, Mon to Sat D 6.30 to 10.30 CLOSED: Chrismas, bank hols MEALS: alc (main courses £8 to £15). Cover 10% SERVICE: not inc CARDS: Amex, Delta, Diners, MasterCard, Switch, Visa DETAILS: 100 seats. Private parties: 60 main room, 30 and 50 private rooms. Children's helpings. Music ⊖ London Bridge (£5)

First Floor **map 13**

186 Portobello Road, W11 1LA
TEL: (020) 7243 0072 FAX: (020) 7221 9440

COOKING **4**
MODERN ENGLISH
£25–£49

'Pleasingly extraordinary' was one reporter's first impression of this singular dining room over a pub. Linen-covered tables sit among what appears to be 'faux classical debris', making it feel like the set of a Fellini movie. The kitchen borrows ideas from all over, turning up anything from zucchini flowers stuffed with Taleggio, to braised rabbit with guajillo quesadilla accompanied by a papaya and habañero salsa. At the same time it keeps its feet on the ground, pleasing reporters with, for example, a starter of tuna carpaccio with deep-fried, salted capers and masses of rocket.

Flavours can be bold and yet complement each other well, as in show-stopping pistachio- and herb-crusted lamb, piled neatly on sweet potato gratin with gently sweet jalapeño jelly. Warm dark chocolate tart with white chocolate ice cream has been agreeably oozy and rich, and alternatives might include passion-fruit bavarois with macadamia nut tuile. Service can be unco-ordinated. France and the southern hemisphere provide most of the wines, of which ten are sold by the glass. House French is £10.50 a bottle, £2.50 a glass.

CHEF: Andy Appleton PROPRIETOR: Antony Harris OPEN: all week L 12 to 3 (4 Sat and Sun), Mon to Sat D 7 to 11 (11.30 Fri and Sat) MEALS: alc Sat and Sun L and Mon to Sat D (main courses L £5.50 to £15, D £9.50 to £15). Set L Mon to Fri £11.50 (2 courses) to £16 SERVICE: 12.5% (optional) CARDS: Amex, Delta, Diners, MasterCard, Switch, Visa DETAILS: 100 seats. Private parties: 80 main room, 30 and 50 private rooms. Vegetarian meals. Music ⊖ Ladbroke Grove (£5)

Fish! **map 13**

Cathedral Street, SE1 9AL
TEL: (020) 7234 3333 FAX: (020) 7234 3343
EMAIL: fish@bgr.plc.uk
WEB SITE: www.fishdiner.co.uk

COOKING **2**
SEAFOOD
£27–£57

Sandwiched between a railway bridge and Southwark Cathedral, the glass and metal structure (a converted Victorian pavilion) is furnished as a diner, with brightly coloured table tops, paper serviettes and a menu that doubles as a place mat. The format is straightforward. Tick-boxes indicate which fish are available: maybe tuna, monk, John Dory, and squid. You choose whether to have it steamed or grilled, and which sauce to add: salsa, hollandaise or olive oil dressing, perhaps. If it doesn't work, who's to blame? Conventional starters take in prawn cocktail, fish soup, and smoked salmon, while desserts run the gamut from A to B (sticky toffee to commended bread-and-butter pudding). The place mat also lists around a dozen wines, mostly under £20, half of them available by the glass. Branches are at 41a Queenstown Rd, SW8 3RE; Hanover House, 33 Westferry Circus, E14 8RR; and County Hall, 3b Belvedere Rd, SE1 7GP. Telephone bookings can be made for any branch at the telephone number given above. Further outlets are planned for Guildford and Birmingham.

CHEF: Claire Rankin PROPRIETORS: Tony Allan and Ronnie Truss OPEN: Mon to Sat 11.30 to 3, 5.30 to 11 CLOSED: bank hols MEALS: alc (main courses £10 to £17). Set L and D £25 to £35 SERVICE: 12.5% (optional), card slips closed CARDS: Amex, Delta, Diners, MasterCard, Switch, Visa DETAILS: 90 seats. 30 seats outside. Private parties: 8 main room. Vegetarian meals. Children's helpings. Wheelchair access (also WC). Music. Air-conditioned ⊖ London Bridge

Il Forno £

NEW ENTRY **map 15**

63–64 Frith Street, W1V 5TA
TEL: (020) 7734 4545 FAX: (020) 7287 8624

COOKING **2**
MODERN ITALIAN
£23–£34

'Each time I come here it's a different chef or restaurant,' remarked one bemused visitor. The successor to Claudio Pulze's Frith Street Restaurant (which formerly occupied the site) builds on the success of Al Duca in St James's (see entry). It is a jolly place with youthful, friendly and professional service, where the food is 'fresh, beautifully presented, healthy and cheap'. Bright, buzzy and not too minimalist, it focuses on pasta and pizza, the latter including an enormous fluffy yet crisp calzone, filled with mozzarella, artichoke, ham and mushrooms. If you are going to eat polenta, it might as well be organic (here served five ways). If not, the pasta section offers reginette with peas and pancetta, and linguine with clams and sweet chilli. Half a dozen starters and main courses extend the options with pan-fried salmon and green beans, or chargrilled leg of lamb with ratatouille, while desserts take in fresh fruit with good sorbets. The food is 'excellent value for the West End', although wine from the lively Italian list can soon bump up the total. Prices start at £11.50.

CHEF: Marco Stucchi PROPRIETOR: Claudio Pulze OPEN: Mon to Fri L 12 to 2.45, Mon to Sat D 6 to 10.45 CLOSED: bank hols MEALS: alc (main courses £6.50 to £9.50) SERVICE: 12.5% (optional), card slips closed CARDS: Amex, Delta, MasterCard, Switch, Visa DETAILS: 70 seats. Vegetarian meals. Music. Air-conditioned ⊖ Tottenham Court Road

Four Seasons £

map 13

84 Queensway, W2 3RL
TEL: (020) 7229 4320

COOKING **3**
CHINESE
£22–£44

Hopes aroused by appetising barbecued meats in the window are fully realised in large portions of first-rate, unpretentious Cantonese fare at modest prices. The restaurant combines the best aspects of a Chinatown establishment with brisk yet friendly service, and appeals equally to Westerners and Chinese customers. A long carte, plus nearly 40 'chef's special recommended' dishes, delivers solid cooking without aspirations to delicacy, producing for example steamed chicken with masses of savoury sausages and good-quality mushrooms in lotus leaf. Also pleasing have been more mundane yet tender and meaty Peking-style spare ribs, and Singapore-style fried noodles hinting of curry. Mixed seafood satay

Malaysian-style consists of skewers of prawn, squid and monkfish with a pale brown sauce that turns out to be a cross between classic satay and a Chinese curry, with enough chilli to bite back. Hotpots run from stewed lamb brisket with dried bean curd, to braised aubergine with fish and pork. House vins de pays are £8.50.

CHEF: Norman Lo PROPRIETOR: Rosegate Trading Ltd OPEN: all week noon to 11.15 (10.45 Sun) MEALS: alc (main courses £4.50 to £17.50). Set D £11 to £17 SERVICE: 12.5% CARDS: Amex, Delta, MasterCard, Switch, Visa DETAILS: 70 seats. Private parties: 70 main room. Vegetarian meals. Music. Air-conditioned ⊖ Bayswater, Queensway

French House Dining Room

map 15

49 Dean Street, W1V 5HL
TEL: (020) 7437 2477 FAX: (020) 7287 9109

COOKING **3**
MODERN EUROPEAN
£31–£52

There is something reassuringly 'old Soho' about eating in a room above a pub, thought one visitor, given the smart, expensive mega-restaurants that have sprouted nearby. It is a relaxed, unassuming place, with a dark-wood floor and mottled walls adorned with old photographs. Dishes are given short, sharp descriptions and, like its sister restaurant St John (see entry), the kitchen makes a virtue of humble ingredients, including some that other chefs pass by: ox tongue and green sauce maybe, or a pile of sweetbreads and caramelised shallots on chargrilled bread with chopped mint. Accurate timing is a feature, applied to crisp-skinned, spatchcocked quail beside a pile of rough textured chickpea purée, and to plump breast of flavourful duck, served with a mix of beetroot and watercress. Desserts are equally simple, from a slice of lemon tart on thin crisp pastry with a small scoop of clotted cream, to clove-infused poached pear with vanilla ice cream. Thirty plus wines are mostly French, starting with house vin de table at £11.

CHEF: Margot Henderson PROPRIETORS: Melanie Arnold and Margot Henderson OPEN: Mon to Sat 12 to 3, 6 to 11.15 CLOSED: Christmas, bank hols MEALS: alc (main courses £8.50 to £15) SERVICE: not inc CARDS: Amex, Delta, Diners, MasterCard, Switch, Visa DETAILS: 32 seats. Private parties: 32 main room. Vegetarian meals. No music ⊖ Piccadilly Circus, Leicester Square

Fung Shing

map 15

15 Lisle Street, WC2H 7BE
TEL: (020) 7437 1539 FAX: (020) 7734 0284

COOKING **4**
CHINESE
£29–£75

Long held in high regard both inside and outside London's Chinese community (despite several changes of chef), Fung Shing was due for refurbishment as the Guide went to press, so a short closure may be on the cards. The menu is long and wide-ranging, incorporating standard Cantonese stir-fries, quite a few satisfyingly homely dishes, and luxury ingredients prepared in classical Chinese style. There are novelties, too, including tender ostrich ('like gamey beef') with ginger and spring onion.

Starters vary from crisp appetisers such as soft-shell crab with chilli and garlic, to textural pairings such as jellyfish with shredded chicken. Steamed eel with black bean sauce might follow, otherwise there is a variety of more domestic dishes, including spicy aubergine with minced meat in a pot. Scrutinise the list of chef's specials for some of the most challenging and enticing flavours: wind-dried oyster with preserved pork, for instance. Service can be efficient and quite pleasant, but staff might try to steer non-Chinese away from authentic delicacies. The wine list contains some choice bottles among a selection of over 50. House wine is £12.

CHEF: Fook-On Chung PROPRIETOR: Forum Restaurant Ltd OPEN: all week 12 (6.30 bank hols) to 11.15 CLOSED: 24 to 26 Dec MEALS: alc (main courses £7.50 to £16). Set L and D £32 (for 2 people) to £80 (for 5 people) SERVICE: 10%, card slips closed CARDS: Amex, Delta, Diners, MasterCard, Switch, Visa DETAILS: 120 seats. Private parties: 50 main room, 25 to 50 private rooms. Vegetarian meals. Music. Air-conditioned ⊖ Leicester Square

Gaudí **map 13**

63 Clerkenwell Road, EC1M 5PT
TEL: (020) 7608 3220 FAX: (020) 7250 1057 COOKING **4**
EMAIL: gaudi@turnmills.co.uk MODERN SPANISH
WEB SITE: www.turnmills.co.uk/turnmills £40–£56

Gaudí's influence is more general inspiration than direct model, judging by the tile-covered walls and a massive wooden ram's horn winding round the bar. The food, though, is distinctly modern Spanish, involving native ingredients such as Jabugo ham, piquillo peppers, swordfish and roast suckling lamb. Many dishes are quite involved, for example loin of boar larded with thyme and garlic, served with wild mushrooms in a crisp potato nest and accompanied by small glazed onions filled with aubergine paste. Foie de pato en escabèche templado de verduras is another impressive combination: of melting foie gras served with a warm vegetable salad incorporating four kinds of onion, all complemented by a sharp, clean dressing.

Desserts are equally resourceful, taking in deep-fried cream ('like Chinese fried milk but firmer') served with a basket of glazed berries and warm walnut sauce. 'If there is anything more sensual than Pedro Ximénez ice cream I have yet to meet it,' drooled one visitor who enjoyed it with rosemary syrup alongside a nougat soufflé. An all-Spanish list brings together some high-quality wines along with more affordable bottles: house red and white (two of each) are £11.50.

CHEF: Nacho Martinez PROPRIETOR: John Newman OPEN: Mon to Fri 12 to 2.30, 7 to 10 MEALS: alc (main courses £14 to £16). Set L £10 (2 courses) SERVICE: 12.5% (optional), card slips closed CARDS: Amex, Delta, Diners, MasterCard, Switch, Visa DETAILS: 60 seats. Private parties: 400 main room, 100 and 300 private rooms. Vegetarian meals. Children's helpings. No children under 4. No smoking in 1 dining room. Wheelchair access (not WC). No music. Air-conditioned ⊖ Farringdon (£5)

The Guide relies on feedback from its readers. Especially welcome are reports on new restaurants appearing in the book for the first time. All letters to the Guide are acknowledged.

Le Gavroche 🍷

map 15

43 Upper Brook Street, W1Y 1PF
TEL: (020) 7408 0881 FAX: (020) 7491 4387
EMAIL: gavroche@cwcom.net

COOKING **6**
FRENCH
£43–£141

Le Gavroche remains barely touched by fashion. The basement dining room in the heart of Mayfair feels much as it did 20 or more years ago. People come for classical French food, some of it based on original Roux recipes: soufflé suissesse, for example, has been mentioned in the Guide on and off since the early 1970s. Ingredients are of outstanding quality – an inspector's exemplary rib of real came with a light Mediterranean touch that included herbs, tomato and olive oil – and daily options make good use of seasonal supplies: the finest roast grouse one reporter had ever eaten, carved at table and served with bread sauce.

Technique is generally sound, although standards, even at a single meal, can fluctuate considerably, producing bland flavours in poached lobster with asparagus, and chicken in brioche, but also a fine artichoke heart covered with foie gras and smooth chicken mousse, served with a matchless truffle sauce. Omelette Rothschild (an airy pan-cooked soufflé with a sweet apricot sauce) is another survivor from the old days, sorbets from the trolley are first-rate, and a flaky puff pastry feuillantine of summer fruits has come with a faultless mascarpone ice cream and a light mango sauce.

Cheeses are as good as you will find. Service has varied from clumsy and unhelpful at lunch (though lunch itself is a comparative bargain) to immensely professional and smooth as velvet at dinner, when the pleasant and charming Michel Roux does a tour of the tables. If money is no object, indulge in one of the best wine lists for miles around. The finest bottles, predominantly French, are offered in numerous prime vintages with many prices heading into four-figure sums. However, there are now substantial numbers priced between £17 and £30, which is an effort worth acknowledging.

CHEF: Michel Roux PROPRIETOR: Le Gavroche Ltd OPEN: Mon to Fri 12 to 2, 7 to 11 CLOSED: Christmas to New Year, bank hols MEALS: alc (main courses £28 to £34.50). Set L £38.50, Set D £78 SERVICE: 12.5% (optional), card slips closed CARDS: Amex, Delta, Diners, MasterCard, Switch, Visa DETAILS: 60 seats. Private parties: 80 main room, 8 to 20 private room. Jacket. No cigars/pipes in dining room. Occasional music. Air-conditioned ⊖ Marble Arch

Gay Hussar

map 15

2 Greek Street, W1V 6NB
TEL: (020) 7437 0973 FAX: (020) 7437 4631
EMAIL: gayhussar@gayhussar.fsnet.co.uk
WEB SITE: www.gayhussar.co.uk

COOKING **1**
HUNGARIAN
£28–£53

The Hussar has hardly changed in its nearly five decades at this site, so regulars can be forgiven for not warming immediately to the unexciting brown replacement of its atmospheric old red décor. Pretty well everything else, though, is as it was, including such traditional items as pressed boar's head, wild cherry soup, and smoked Hungarian sausage. Fish turns up in a number of guises, in a terrine with a beetroot-spiked mayonnaise, and in rough-textured quenelles with a creamy dill and mushroom sauce, but this is above all a place for the hungry to go in winter to stock up on 'huge portions of heavy food':

perhaps roast duck with red cabbage, apple sauce and epic caraway-flavoured potatoes cooked in goose fat, or a rich dessert of sweet cheese pancakes. 'Friendly, happy service' may not be the sharpest in London, but it gets by, as does the 30-strong wine list, starting with house Hungarian at £10.50.

CHEF: Laszlo Holecz PROPRIETOR: Restaurant Partnership plc OPEN: Mon to Sat 12.15 to 2.30, 5.30 to 10.45 CLOSED: bank hols MEALS: alc (main courses £10.50 to £16.50). Set L £15 (2 courses) to £18 SERVICE: 12.5% (optional), card slips closed CARDS: Amex, Delta, Diners, MasterCard, Switch, Visa DETAILS: 70 seats. Private parties: 40 main room, 12 and 20 private rooms. Vegetarian meals. Children's helpings. No pipes in dining room. Wheelchair access (not WC). No music. Air-conditioned ⊖ Tottenham Court Road (£5)

Globe Restaurant

map 13

New Globe Walk, SE1 9DR
TEL: (020) 7928 9444 FAX: (020) 7902 1574
EMAIL: globe@milburn.co.uk

COOKING **1**
MODERN BRITISH
£31–50

At the heart of Bankside's redevelopment, near Vinopolis and Tate Modern, with fine views of St Paul's and the Thames, the restaurant's primary mission may be to serve pilgrims to the Bard's theatre (it is particularly useful before and after performances), but it also caters for those after a more leisurely meal. Contemporary credentials are evident in home-cured salt cod with gremolata and beetroot, and in cardamom and orange cheesecake with a cinnamon crust. Main courses are all 'grills', ranging from sirloin with chilli-roast shallots and deep-fried cabbage, to bass fillet with leeks, butter beans and hollandaise. Vegetarians might be tempted by roast butternut squash and sage ravioli with a walnut sauce. A couple of dozen wines constitute a serviceable list, starting with house wine at £11.95.

CHEF: Eddie Grimes PROPRIETOR: Milburns Restaurants Ltd OPEN: all week L 12 to 2.30, Mon to Sat D 6 to 10.30 CLOSED: 24 to 26 Dec, 1 Jan MEALS: alc (main courses £11.50 to £16.50). Set L and D £17 (2 courses) to £21 SERVICE: not inc CARDS: Amex, Delta, Diners, MasterCard, Switch, Visa DETAILS: 90 seats. Private parties: 40 main room, 90 to 500 private rooms. Vegetarian meals. Children's helpings. Wheelchair access (also WC). Music ⊖ London Bridge, Mansion House, Southwark

Golden Dragon

map 15

28–29 Gerrard Street, W1V 7LP
TEL: (020) 7734 2763 FAX: (020) 7734 1073

COOKING **2**
CHINESE
£25–£56

This large red and gold Chinese eating house has been improved by a changed layout, eliminating a side room where customers often felt a bit neglected. Now pleasant, helpful service reaches everyone. Portions are so large that single diners should heed a waitress's advice not to over-order. An even better idea at lunchtime is to enjoy the wide range of dim sum. The typically Cantonese menu offers a long list of seafood dishes, from stir-fries of squid or prawns to grilled marinated fish, steamed eel fillet with garlic, and crab and lobster prepared in several ways. Recommended dishes have included hot and sour soup, crispy fried smoked chicken, shredded beef, and the intriguingly named mixed seafood tart: actually leaves of iceberg lettuce wrapped around chopped shrimps, squid and scallops, with bamboo shoots, water chestnuts and some carrot. House wines are £8.50.

CHEF: Y.C. Man PROPRIETOR: Evernell Ltd OPEN: all week 12 (11 Sun) to 11.15 (11.45 Fri and Sat, 10.45 Sun) SERVICE: 10% CARDS: Amex, Delta, Diners, MasterCard, Switch, Visa DETAILS: 220 seats. Private parties: 300 main room, 10 and 40 private rooms. Vegetarian meals. Music. Air-conditioned ⊖ Leicester Square

Gordon Ramsay 🍷 map 14

68 Royal Hospital Road, SW3 4HP
TEL: (020) 7352 4441 FAX: (020) 7352 3334

COOKING **9**
FRENCH
£46–£121

The smart, sophisticated, square room is cheerful, pretty and bright at lunchtime, more serious and intimate at dinner, with an aubergine leitmotif to the colour scheme, prominent glass sculptures not to everyone's taste, and a classy and confident air. With Nico Ladenis and Marco Pierre White out of the picture, Gordon Ramsay has taken on the mantle of London's number one chef, and while those who eat regularly at fine restaurants may find the food a trifle short on mould-breaking innovation or excitement, it is among the most technically accomplished on the circuit.

Although menus change every few months, and some dishes demonstrate tremendous flair, the impression is of a kitchen that likes to perfect a small repertoire and strive laudably for consistency. The soft, buttery tranche of hot foie gras on a bed of earthy lentils is one such dish, 'made in heaven', according to a regular. Apart from that, offal may feature only as a bit player, perhaps in a starter salad of crispy pig's trotter and calves' sweetbreads, while shellfish options might take in tortellini filled with chunky lobster and langoustine in a resonant shellfish bisque, or four thick slices of uniformly grilled, fresh-tasting scallop, given lift from a line of sweet, sour and vinous Barolo vinaigrette.

This is a French restaurant, and it sources accordingly. Bresse poultry has appeared in the form of poached and grilled chicken with an old-fashioned farmyard flavour, and a triumphant, lightly gamey pigeon in a clear vegetable broth with wild mushrooms, a dish notable for its delicacy. While desserts may not be the highlight, they have produced an unbeatable crème brûlée, unmoulded on to the plate, and a tangy, sweet-sharp blood orange pudding, its segments set in a 'fabulous' jelly. The brightly coloured macaroon accompaniments to coffee are overshadowed by a box of dark, smoky chocolates, while the appetiser soup – roast pumpkin with wild mushrooms and truffle oil, or a startling chilled tomato consommé – is a stunning way to tease the palate and set up expectations. Consensus relegates the set lunch to the second division.

Service is very proper, and there is lots of it. Maître d' Jean-Claude Breton acts the irrepressible Frenchman, freely dispensing over-the-top Franglais chitchat and old jokes. He is always happy to see you again, even if it is your first visit. But the humour is infectious, and even if menu, appetisers and wine list all tend to arrive at once, staff are friendly, helpful and attentive, and attention to detail is meticulous. A stunning range of predominantly French wines includes 15 vintages of Ch. Pétrus and several pages of grand cru Burgundies. Astronomical bills tend to be blamed on the wine list, although there are a few bottles under

£30 (prices start at £18), and several customers have praised the sommelier's skills.

CHEF/PROPRIETOR: Gordon Ramsay OPEN: Mon to Fri 12 to 2.15, 6.45 to 11 CLOSED: 2 weeks Christmas, bank hols MEALS: Set L £28, Set D £55 to £70 SERVICE: not inc CARDS: Amex, Delta, Diners, MasterCard, Switch, Visa DETAILS: 45 seats. Private parties: 45 main room. No cigars/pipes in dining room. No music. Air-conditioned ⊖ Sloane Square

Gourmet Garden £

map 12

59 Watford Way, NW4 3AX COOKING **1**

TEL: (020) 8202 9639 FAX: (020) 8203 5229 CHINESE/MALAYSIAN/SINGAPOREAN

£11–£49

Now redecorated, this restaurant's menu supports the theory that fusion cooking was a Singaporean invention. Unusual Chinese dishes on the main list include steamed king prawns with garlicky plum sauce and egg white, boiled Hainanese chicken, and pork ribs in preserved red bean curd sauce. Also on the menu are Thai fishcakes and tom yum soup among starters, with main courses of Malaysian nonya chicken curry, dry beef rendang curry, and Singaporean kweh pi tee (pastry cups filled with prawns and vegetables). Still greater choice obtains on the menu's 'Malaysian and Singaporean food corner': choose perhaps laksa, hokkien fried noodles in soya sauce with seafood and chicken, or Indonesian nasi lemak (coconut rice with chicken curry, sambal prawns, peanut, egg, ikan bilis, achar and cucumber). Finish perhaps with chendol (green jelly strips with palm sugar syrup and coconut milk). House wines are £7.80.

CHEF: Kia Lian Tan PROPRIETORS: Annie and Kia Lian Tan OPEN: Wed to Mon 12 to 2.15 (2.45 Sun and bank hols), 6 to 11.15 (10.45 Sun and bank hols) CLOSED: 25 and 26 Dec, 2 weeks July to Aug MEALS: alc (main courses £5 to £17). Set L £5.50, Set D £11.80 to £15.80 SERVICE: 10% CARDS: Amex, Delta, Diners, MasterCard, Switch, Visa DETAILS: 70 seats. Private parties: 70 main room. Vegetarian meals. Children's helpings. Music. Air-conditioned ⊖ Hendon Central

Granita

map 13

127 Upper Street, N1 1QP COOKING **4**

TEL: (020) 7226 3222 MODERN EUROPEAN

£23–£43

If it's frills you're after, look elsewhere. Starkly minimal décor pits wooden furniture against washes of turquoise, lilac and indigo, and it can be noisy when busy, although one visitor found it all 'rather energising'. The food makes a similar impression, with fish and vegetables to the fore, and grilling a favoured technique: asparagus with sliced Manchego and balsamic vinegar, or sardines with olives, orange zest and parsley. Partnerships tend to be light and aromatic throughout – perhaps a blend of lemon, garlic, rosemary, sage and olive oil to accompany grey mullet and butter beans – while the kitchen's performance is relaxed and generally successful: four who lunched 'very agreeably' found everything imaginatively and skilfully cooked. Desserts have paired Seville orange tart with vanilla ice cream, and Lancashire and Garrotxa cheeses. Some two dozen wines, mostly under £20, successfully combine interest and variety. House Vin de Pays d'Oc is £10.50.

CHEF: Ahmed Kharshoum PROPRIETORS: Vikki Leffman and Ahmed Kharshoum OPEN: Wed to Sun L 12.30 to 2.30 (3 Sun), Tue to Sun D 6.30 to 10.30 (10 Sun) CLOSED: 10 days Christmas, 5 days Easter, 2 weeks Aug MEALS: alc D (main courses £10.50 to £14). Set L £11.95 (2 courses) to £13.95 SERVICE: not inc CARDS: MasterCard, Switch, Visa DETAILS: 72 seats. Private parties: 72 main room. Vegetarian meals. No cigars/pipes in dining room. Wheelchair access (not WC). No music. Air-conditioned ⊖ Angel, Highbury & Islington

Great Eastern Dining Room  map 13

54–56 Great Eastern Street, EC2A 3QR
TEL: (020) 7613 4545 FAX: (020) 7613 4137

COOKING **3**
MODERN ITALIAN
£27–£47

Great Eastern Street is a busy and noisy thoroughfare, but there is little relief inside this popular venue. The hubbub reverberates off minimally decorated walls although, in contrast to the spartan bar, tables in the dining room are elegantly set with white linen and heavyweight cutlery. A sharp version of modern Italian cooking takes in seared tuna carpaccio, and orecchiette with spring greens, peas, goats' cheese and mint. Robust flavours are apparent, for example in a light puff pastry tart of tomato, olives and anchovies, and in a salad of bresaola, beetroot, endive and horseradish.

Impressive main courses have included rump of lamb with aubergines, borlotti beans and lavender sauce, and chicken breast accompanied by cotechino, lentils and a punchy salsa verde, although occasional lapses in timing can lessen the impact of some dishes. Finish perhaps with affogato – vanilla ice cream pepped up with a shot of espresso and a measure of liqueur. Service is charming and enthusiastic but can be slow at busy times. The compact but varied wine list opens with six house wines from £10, also available by the large or small glass.

CHEF: Steve Pooley PROPRIETOR: Will Ricker OPEN: Mon to Fri L 12 to 3, Mon to Sat D 6.30 to 11 CLOSED: 24 Dec to 5 Jan MEALS: alc (main courses £8.50 to £10) SERVICE: 12.5% (optional), card slips closed CARDS: Amex, Delta, Diners, MasterCard, Switch, Visa DETAILS: 65 seats. Private parties: 12 main room, 200 private room. Vegetarian meals. Wheelchair access (not WC). No music ⊖ Old Street

▲ Great Eastern Hotel, Aurora 🍷 NEW ENTRY map 13

Great Eastern Hotel, Liverpool Street, EC2M 7QN
TEL: (020) 7618 7000 FAX: (020) 7618 7001
EMAIL: restaurantres@great-eastern-hotel.co.uk
WEB SITE: www.great-eastern-hotel.co.uk

COOKING **5**
MODERN EUROPEAN-PLUS
£46–£76

When complete, the hotel's refurbishment will incorporate an oyster bar, fish restaurant and Japanese restaurant as well as the Terminus bar and grill and several private dining rooms. Aurora itself, huge and classically proportioned, complete with domed skylight, is intended to evoke an era of grand dining. The menu by contrast bobs along on the current that sweeps through many a modern kitchen, taking in caramelised scallops on a mound of aubergine relish, steamed saddle of rabbit, and a layering of vegetables with fresh, well-timed red mullet in pastry. The ambitious and largely accomplished kitchen employs fine materials, including rare roast loin of venison sandwiched between celeriac purée and roast endive, and turns out flavourful food with a deft juxtaposition of textures: a crunchy potato lattice accompanies a starter of expertly pan-fried foie gras and boudin blanc.

Summer berries with basil sorbet indicate seasonal input, while chocolate Aurora sounds like a year-round winner: a tripartite collection of well-executed fondant, a wedge of tart and firm-textured mousse, accompanied by a small scoop of orange sorbet. The lengthy and impressive wine list takes in fine bottles from Bordeaux and Burgundy as well as high-calibre New World options, although prices throughout are as hefty as the list itself. The keen and well-informed sommelier has been singled out for praise, his short selection including a few bottles below £20. Twelve wines are available by the glass from £3.50.

CHEF: Robert Stirrup PROPRIETOR: Great Eastern Hotel OPEN: Mon to Fri 12 to 2.45, 6.45 to 10.45 MEALS: alc (main courses £16.50 to £24). Set D 6.45 to 8 £28 (2 courses) to £34 SERVICE: 12.5% (optional), card slips closed CARDS: Amex, Delta, Diners, MasterCard, Switch, Visa DETAILS: 170 seats. Private parties: 12 main room. Vegetarian meals. Wheelchair access (also WC). Occasional music. Air-conditioned ACCOMMODATION: 267 rooms, all with bath/shower. TV. Phone. Room only £195 to £515. Rooms for disabled. Baby facilities ⊖ Liverpool Street

Greenhouse **map 15**

27A Hays Mews, W1X 7RJ COOKING **5**
TEL: (020) 7499 3314 and 3331 GLOBAL
FAX: (020) 7499 5368 £32–£66

'Another year, another chef' began one report, noting that Paul Merrett brings with him high expectations from his time at the former Interlude in Charlotte Street. The setting, at the end of a short canopied walkway, is 'like an outpost of British Indian colonial clubbery', an impression strengthened by a few of the dishes, among them pan-fried sea bass on sag aloo with a 'splattered fritter' of onion bhajia and a 'sweet, jammy' tomato pickle. Paul Merrett's strength is bold and innovative spicing, and given the Anglo-Indian tenor of some dishes it came as no surprise to one visitor 'to find that he grew up in Zanzibar'.

First courses stand out among the variable results, from a first-rate creamy-textured Thai soup generously filled with squid rings, mussels and monkfish, to a thin lobe of sweetly caramelised foie gras in a 'stewy essence of smoke and pulses' made from Puy lentils and strong-cure bacon. Vertical assemblies (and tepid temperatures at inspection) are the norm, while commendable desserts have included a warm fig and port broth with goats' cheese ice cream, and an espresso custard with a warm maple and banana compote, accompanied by white coffee ice cream. High-pressure salesmanship and some long waits have taken the edge off otherwise professional service. With only five wines under £20 (but David Levin's own house Touraine is £13.25) on an uninviting list, there is plenty of room for improvement.

Net prices *in the details at the end of an entry indicates that the prices given on a menu and on a bill are inclusive of VAT and service charge, and that this practice is clearly stated on menu and bill.*

CHEF: Paul Merrett PROPRIETORS: David and Joseph Levin OPEN: Sun to Fri L 12 to 2.30, all week D 6.30 to 11 CLOSED: 25 and 26 Dec, bank hols MEALS: alc (main courses £12.50 to £19.50). Set L Mon to Fri £10.50 (2 courses) to £14.50, Set L Sun £22.50 SERVICE: 12.5% (optional), card slips closed CARDS: Amex, Delta, Diners, MasterCard, Switch, Visa DETAILS: 90 seats. Private parties: 100 main room. Vegetarian meals. Children's helpings. No pipes in dining room. Wheelchair access (not WC). No music. Air-conditioned ⊖ Green Park

Green Olive

map 13

5 Warwick Place, W9 2PX
TEL/FAX: (020) 7289 2469

NEW CHEF
ITALIAN
£36–£54

The various branches of Bijan Behzadi's London restaurant group are named after a positive store cupboard of Mediterranean ingredients (see also entries for Purple Sage, Red Pepper and White Onion). This one, situated just off Warwick Avenue in Maida Vale, plays its part as an attractive neighbourhood restaurant, benefiting from obvious local popularity. Maurizio Morelli (who used to work at Ibla and the Lanesborough, see entries) arrived just as the Guide went to press, to oversee a set menu (with a few price supplements) that deals in updated Italian ideas such as marinated red mullet with orange, mango and chilli; roast breast of duck with prickly pear and limoncello sauce; and warm chocolate sponge with coconut ice cream. Delightful, voluble service is of the old school. The mostly Italian wines are not cheap, but there are many good producers on the list. Prices start at £12.50.

CHEF: Maurizio Morelli PROPRIETOR: Red Pepper Group OPEN: Sun L 12.30 to 2.30, all week D 7 to 10.30 CLOSED: Christmas and Easter MEALS: alc L (main courses £7 to £14.50). Set D £22 (2 courses) to £28 SERVICE: 12.5% (optional), card slips closed CARDS: Amex, Delta, MasterCard, Switch, Visa DETAILS: 60 seats. Private parties: 16 main room. Vegetarian meals. No pipes/cigars in dining room. Wheelchair access (not WC). Music. Air-conditioned ⊖ Warwick Avenue

Gresslin's

map 13

13 Heath Street, NW3 6TP
TEL: (020) 7794 8386 FAX: (020) 7433 3282
EMAIL: restaurant@gresslins.co.uk
WEB SITE: www.gresslins.co.uk

COOKING **5**
MODERN EUROPEAN-PLUS
£28–£58

Formerly hard-edged and rather noisy, Gresslin's underwent major refurbishment just as the last edition of the Guide appeared. The bar is now downstairs, and the new low-ceilinged dining room features dramatic black leather banquette seating to set against walls of glass, stainless steel and a giant photograph of bicycle wheels (Margaret Gresslin is a photographer). The cooking remains much the same, however: an inventive mix of European and oriental ideas in which fish and vegetables play a more central role than red meats.

Ideas are up to date but are not designed to impress merely by being fashionable, rather they stem from Michael Gresslin's experience of cooking in Sri Lanka. While there are relatively straightforward dishes to choose from (Jerusalem artichoke soup with Stilton and truffle oil, or spicy tiger prawns with noodle salad) the fun generally lies elsewhere, for example in a dish of monkfish cheeks with green butter gratin, steamed bok choy, ka chay couscous and orange Puy lentils; or in banana, walnut and chocolate strudel with coconut custard. A short wine list offers around 10 by the glass and starts with house Chenin Blanc and Cabernet-Syrah at £10.50.

CHEF: Michael Gresslin PROPRIETORS: Michael and Margaret Gresslin, and Sir Harold Hood and Gervase Hood OPEN: Tue to Sun L 12 to 2.30, Mon to Sat D 7 to 10.30 CLOSED: bank hols exc 25 Dec MEALS: alc (main courses £12.50 to £18.50). Set L Sun £14.95 (2 courses) to £17.95, Set D Mon to Thur £14.95 (2 courses) to £17.95 SERVICE: 12.5% (optional), card slips closed CARDS: Amex, MasterCard, Switch, Visa DETAILS: 44 seats. Private parties: 50 main room. Vegetarian meals. Children's helpings. No smoking in dining room. Music. Air-conditioned ⊖ Hampstead

▲ Halkin Hotel — map 14

Halkin Street, SW1X 7DJ
TEL: (020) 7333 1234 FAX: (020) 7333 1100 — COOKING **4**
EMAIL: res@halkin.co.uk — ITALIAN
WEB SITE: www.halkin.co.uk — £39–£93

Marble, candles and subtle lighting – all 'very Milan' – provide an appropriately swish background to Stefano Cavallini's restaurant in the heart of Belgravia. The food is refined too, calling on foie gras with Castelluccio lentils, deep-fried oysters with ceps, and an unusual pairing of pigeon with lobster ravioli, served with black truffle sauce. Yet it manages to achieve sufficient variety within the scope of nearly two dozen savoury items on the carte: from a light, spring-like starter of sole topped with pickled ginger, to a main course of venison wrapped around venison mousse, served with pumpkin and Savoy cabbage.

Likewise, to balance the langoustines, sea bass and veal fillet, there are likely to be potato gnocchi, a hare sauce for pappardelle, and stuffed saddle of rabbit with polenta. Cheeses are mostly Italian, although when one reporter wished to know what all nine of them were, the waiter 'simply asked which ones I wanted to know about'. If prices seem high, don't forget the 'classic example of a lunchtime bargain' where three courses are cheaper than most of the main courses on the carte. Wines are well chosen but prices, sadly, remain daunting.

CHEF: Stefano Cavallini PROPRIETOR: Christina Ong OPEN: Mon to Fri L 12.30 to 2.30, all week D 7.30 to 11.30 (7 to 10 Sun) MEALS: alc (main courses £18.50 to £28). Set L £25, Set D £55 SERVICE: 12.5%, card slips closed CARDS: Amex, Delta, Diners, MasterCard, Switch, Visa DETAILS: 45 seats. Private parties: 60 main room, 30 private room. Vegetarian meals. No children under 7. No cigars/pipes in dining room. Wheelchair access (also WC). Music. Air-conditioned ACCOMMODATION: 41 rooms, all with bath/shower. TV. Phone. Room only £265 to £575. Baby facilities *(The Which? Hotel Guide)* ⊖ Hyde Park Corner

Report forms are at the back of the book; write a letter if you prefer; or email us at goodfoodguide@which.net

The Guide is totally independent, accepts no free hospitality, and survives on the number of copies sold each year.

Helter Skelter  map 12

50 Atlantic Road, SW9 8JN
TEL/FAX: (020) 7274 8600

COOKING **1**
MODERN BRITISH
£28–£46

Plaster walls, polished café tables, an open-to-view kitchen and large flower displays combine with relaxed and friendly service to make this an enjoyable neighbourhood restaurant that delivers 'the best food in Brixton'. Daily blackboard specials supplement a menu that zips through a contemporary roll call of ingredients, including ceviche of whiting with chilli croûton and lime leaf oil, tea-smoked quail with sweet miso aubergine, and a stargazy fritter of salt-cod and whitebait (their heads looking out from the purée of salt-cod) with anchovy mayo. Although handling can be variable, fine materials have included quickly seared blue-fin tuna in a Japanese-style broth, an attractively presented pink rack of lamb, and Valrhona chocolate in a tart accompanied by a chilli and chocolate ice cream. Forty mostly affordable wines start with house Chilean Merlot and Sauvignon Blanc at £12.

CHEFS: Malachi O'Gallagher and John Swerdlow PROPRIETOR: John Swerdlow OPEN: all week D only 6.30 (7 Thur to Sat) to 11 (11.30 Fri and Sat) CLOSED: Christmas MEALS: alc (main courses £9.50 to £13). Set D Sun to Wed before 7.30 £10 (2 courses) SERVICE: 10% (optional) CARDS: Amex, Delta, Diners, MasterCard, Switch, Visa DETAILS: 70 seats. Private parties: 30 main room. Vegetarian meals. Music. Air-conditioned ⊖ Brixton (£5)

Hilaire 🍷 map 14

68 Old Brompton Road, SW7 3LQ
TEL: (020) 7584 8993 FAX: (020) 7581 2949

COOKING **7**
MODERN BRITISH
£35–£64

'I am pleased to say that we are still here after 14 years,' writes Bryan Webb, sounding somewhat surprised. Given the PR blizzards and column inches devoted to new openings of large restaurants, this is no mean achievement. Hilaire is small and seems self-effacing in its role as an intermediary between a network of small producers and a loyal following of regular customers. Not all reporters have come away happy, but Hilaire certainly pleases our more long-standing contributors, and it is one of a handful of places strongly favoured by off-duty inspectors, who agree that the rating is well justified.

The appeal lies not in fashionable ingredients, global dishes and in-your-face flavours, but rather in materials that are well sourced, intelligently handled, and sometimes simply presented: buffalo mozzarella with tapénade crostini, oysters au gratin with laverbread and Stilton, or commendable tagliatelle with tender broad beans and bacon, suffused with a well-balanced mustard sauce. Materials cover a wide spread, from a humble dish of rabbit and black pudding, via crisp goujons of plaice with a Thai dip, to well-timed sea bass on a bed of first-rate leek risotto in a pool of reduced red wine sauce. Seasonality, so often absent from London menus, is important too, producing for one visitor an ace dish of tender roast Norfolk partridge, served with cabbage, bread sauce, game chips and a 'lovely sauce/gravy'.

Although officially a set price, the menu's flexibility is much appreciated, offering the chance to eat anything from a couple of starters, via main course only, to main course and dessert (perhaps chocolate cheesecake, or rhubarb crumble and custard), all priced accordingly. Service is 'friendly and capable', and an intelligent selection of Old and New World wines is arranged according to style rather than by country. Prices are reasonable by London standards, and the wine waiter's advice has proved reliable. Duck Pond Columbia Valley Merlot, from Oregon, comes highly recommended at £25. Fourteen house wines range between £14 and £19.

CHEF/PROPRIETOR: Bryan Webb OPEN: Mon to Fri L 12.15 to 2.30, Mon to Sat D 6.30 to 11 CLOSED: 10 days Christmas, 2 weeks Aug, bank hols MEALS: Set L £21.50, Set D before 7.30 and after 10 £18.50 (2 courses), Set D £37.50 SERVICE: 12.5% (optional), card slips closed CARDS: Amex, Delta, Diners, MasterCard, Switch, Visa DETAILS: 55 seats. Private parties: 40 main room, 20 private room. Children's helpings. No cigars/pipes in dining room. Wheelchair access (not WC). No music. Air-conditioned ⊖ South Kensington (£5)

Holly

NEW ENTRY map 12

38 Holly Grove, SE15 5DF
TEL: (020) 7277 2928

COOKING **3**
FRENCH/DUTCH
£27–£40

Occupying an old corner shop, Holly is something of an unexpected find on the Peckham-Dulwich border. Artwork is for sale, and the gift shop décor is of the 'stylish on a budget' school. The scale is small. With only six tables, and open just five sessions a week, it offers three main courses: a choice between fish, meat and vegetarian, the last perhaps a well-made quiche filled with creamy blue Fourme d'Ambert cheese and artichoke hearts. Herb-crusted grey mullet has come enterprisingly with samphire, and organic materials include finely minced chicken in a terrine, and commendable ribeye steak with horseradish onion chutney. Portions are generous, and the cooking is unusual for its Dutch input, which might take in white asparagus with egg and beurre blanc, and a rather solid Dutch apple tart like a raised pie, served with whipped cream; alternatively, finish with orange sorbet with a custardy coriander sauce. Service is charming and attentive, and house wine, at £9.75, starts off a small list.

CHEF/PROPRIETOR: Norbert van Hest OPEN: Tue to Sat D only 6 to 11 CLOSED: 24 Dec to 7 Jan, Aug MEALS: alc (main courses £9.50 to £15) SERVICE: not inc CARDS: MasterCard, Switch, Visa DETAILS: 35 seats. 10 seats outside. Vegetarian meals. Wheelchair access (not WC). Music (£5)

House

LONDON GFG 2001 COMMENDED

NEW ENTRY map 14

3 Milner St, SW3 2QA
TEL: (020) 7584 3002
FAX: (020) 7581 2848

COOKING **5**
MODERN EUROPEAN
£29–£44

The makeover of what was the English House has given it something of a country house feel. Opting for antique chairs, autumnal berry fabrics, crisp white tablecloths, and napkins starched like a nun's coif, it has a calmingly chintzy effect on its well-heeled and casually smart customers. The contemporary menu, with input from Richard Corrigan (see Lindsay House,

London), tends towards earthiness. A sophisticated version of grandmotherly cooking, it has turned out a substantial hot-water crust pie, packed tight with stock absorbers of neatly diced pork and chopped herbs, served with crunchy, bright yellow piccalilli; and a crisp-skinned roast breast and tasty confit leg of Norfolk chicken, with diced liver and nuggets of smoked bacon stirred into the cooking juices.

Other dishes aim for the comfort zone in the shape of a thoroughbred asparagus risotto, its poached egg 'done to a turn'. Meats tend to predominate over fish (although crispy, creamy fritters of salt-cod and potato have been a hit), and less expensive cuts are a feature: you pay for skill rather than posh ingredients here. Graham Garrett seems to relish robust, sustaining dishes and knows how to make them sing: for example, tender, slow-cooked belly pork with five-star crackling, served with braised lentils and sage oil. Desserts lag behind a little, although rhubarb trifle, and Sauternes and almond cake with marinated prunes have been recommended. Reserved but efficient management ensures that meals are pleasingly paced, and a concise, well-composed wine list starts with a trio of French house wines under £14.

CHEF: Graham Garrett PROPRIETOR: Searcy-Corrigan Restaurants OPEN: Mon to Fri L 12 to 2.30, Mon to Sat D 6 to 11 CLOSED: 26 Dec to 4 Jan, last 2 weeks Aug MEALS: Set L £16.50, Set D £23 SERVICE: 12.5% (optional), card slips closed CARDS: Amex, Delta, Diners, MasterCard, Switch, Visa DETAILS: 55 seats. Private parties: 25 main room, 6 to 14 private rooms. Vegetarian meals. Children's helpings. No cigars/pipes in dining room. Occasional music ⊖ Sloane Square, South Kensington

Ibla

map 15

89 Marylebone High Street, W1M 3DE — COOKING **4**
TEL: (020) 7224 3799 FAX: (020) 7486 1370 — ITALIAN
EMAIL: ibla@ibla.co.uk — £30–£56

Behind the shopfront façade two dining rooms here have been made over dramatically, the front one a shade of olive green, the back glossy damson. A warmly enthusiastic greeting indicates that this is an Italian restaurant dedicated to the old-fashioned virtue of hospitality. Stefano Frigerio, who arrived in June 2000, oversees a menu that combines humble materials with a few more luxuries than before, taking in a salad of asparagus and poached quails' eggs with pickled black truffle, and offering main courses of sea bass (one of a few dishes to attract a price supplement), and crisp-skinned sea bream with a lemon-thyme dressing.

Pasta variations ring the changes from clams in spaghetti to rabbit with tagliolini, while one of the more novel combinations has been pigeon with cod brandade and figs in a red wine sauce. Meals might end with pleasantly gooey chocolate sponge timbale with strawberry sauce and coconut ice cream, or perhaps a grappa-flavoured mousse with apple in a coffee sauce. The Italian-led wine list has sourced some interesting bottles, but mark-ups are fairly severe. The base price is £14 for a blended Greco-Malvasia white.

Card slips closed *in the details at the end of an entry indicates that the total on the slips of credit cards is closed when handed over for signature.*

CHEF: Stefano Frigerio PROPRIETOR: Luciano Pellicano OPEN: Mon to Fri L 12 to 2.30, Mon to Sat D 7 to 10.30 CLOSED: 1 week Christmas, bank hols MEALS: Set L £15 (2 courses) to £18, Set D £23 (2 courses) to £27 SERVICE: not inc CARDS: Amex, Delta, MasterCard, Switch, Visa DETAILS: 45 seats. Private parties: 22 main room. Vegetarian meals. Children's helpings. Wheelchair access (not WC). No music. Air-conditioned ⊖ Baker Street, Bond Street

Incognico

NEW ENTRY **map 15**

117 Shaftesbury Avenue, WC2H 8AD — COOKING **5**
TEL: (020) 7836 8866 FAX: (020) 7240 9525 — FRENCH
EMAIL: cheznico@globalnet.co.uk — £24–£66

Nico Ladenis's avowed aim, to serve his style of food at prices that ordinary customers can afford, was behind the revamp of Cheznico (see entry, London), although, thanks to more realistic pricing, the idea arguably works better here. Nobody could accuse the dining room of being colourful, given its two tones of buff and boardroom brown, but it is handily placed for those seeking just one or two courses before or after the theatre. The menu is not an exact replica of the Park Lane original but has some dishes in common: grilled baby Dover sole is among the starters, although there is no lemon tart.

The style is rich and comforting, more sustaining than summery; indeed, seasons are probably the last thing on the menu's mind, as it deals in perennials such as escalope of foie gras (two thick tranches with a sweet-bitter orange counterpoint), rich and creamy Parmesan risotto with button mushrooms, and crisp, lightly battered, deep-fried flakes of salt-cod with aïoli. The food aims for consistency rather than originality, taking in plump, fresh, expertly cooked skate with capers, and nuggets of pink veal kidney on a pool of creamy, whole-grain mustard sauce. Dishes come as described, without additions or garnishes, and vegetables are charged extra. Salting tends to be heavy-handed.

Desserts may not be up to the same standard but have included citrus fruits tightly packed in champagne jelly, and a fine version of apple tart on thin pastry, served with vanilla ice cream. Service is friendly and businesslike, and a few wines manage to squeeze in under £20 on the compact yet varied list. Over a dozen wines 'worth a second glance' are also available by the glass.

CHEF: Richard Hugill PROPRIETORS: Nico and Dinah-Jane Ladenis OPEN: Mon to Sat 12 to 3, 5.30 to 12 CLOSED: 10 days Christmas MEALS: alc (main courses £8.50 to £15). Set L and D 5.30 to 7 £12.50 SERVICE: 12.5% (optional), card slips closed CARDS: Amex, Diners, MasterCard, Switch, Visa DETAILS: 85 seats. Private parties: 10 main room. Vegetarian meals. Wheelchair access (not WC). Music. Air-conditioned ⊖ Leicester Square, Tottenham Court Road

▲ Inter-Continental, Le Soufflé 🍷

map 14

1 Hamilton Place, W1V 0QY
TEL: (020) 7318 8577 FAX: (020) 7491 0926 — COOKING **5**
EMAIL: london@interconti.com — MODERN EUROPEAN
WEB SITE: www.interconti.com — £41–£89

'It is hard to imagine a more splendid location,' observed one visitor to this big hotel just off Park Lane. A large white piano 'resembling the one Liberace played on' is used every evening, and there is a dinner-dance on Saturdays, but despite such old-fashioned pursuits the restaurant keeps abreast of developments. A tartlet of goats' cheese is served with onion jam, red pepper bavarois and asparagus tempura, and roast cod comes on a pea purée. In case the bias towards fish and vegetables, and a reduction in the use of cream, butter and animal fats, strikes fear into the heart of any hedonist, do not panic.

There is still foie gras (in a terrine, or seared with spiced figs), and numerous other comforts in the shape of sauté lobster and monkfish with mango and vanilla, grilled beef fillet with rösti and wild mushrooms, and the inevitable soufflés to follow: Grand Marnier with orange truffle, or raspberry with a crème brûlée tart. Organic food plays a part, in every dish of one particular three-course menu at £39, with organic and biodynamic wines to match. Service is 'exemplary', and wines are predominantly French and include many fine vintages from Bordeaux and Burgundy. Brief homage is paid to California, Australia and New Zealand, and a good selection of half-bottles and wines by the glass makes for plenty of flexibility. House wines start at £16.

CHEF: Peter Kromberg PROPRIETOR: Bass Hotels & Resorts OPEN: Tue to Fri and Sun L 12.30 to 3, Tue to Sat D 7 to 10.30 (11.15 Sat) CLOSED: 2 weeks after Christmas, L Aug, bank hols MEALS: alc D (main courses £15 to £28.50). Set L £19.50 (2 courses) to £33.50, Set D £39 to £46 SERVICE: not inc CARDS: Amex, Delta, Diners, MasterCard, Switch, Visa DETAILS: 80 seats. Vegetarian meals. Children's helpings. No-smoking area. No pipes in dining room. Music. Air-conditioned ACCOMMODATION: 458 rooms, all with bath/shower. TV. Phone. Room only £341 to £441. Rooms for disabled ⊖ Hyde Park Corner (£5)

Isola 🍷

NEW ENTRY **map 14**

145 Knightsbridge, SW1 7PA
TEL: (020) 7838 1044 FAX: (020) 7838 1099

COOKING **4**
ITALIAN
£33–£83

This is a restaurant of two halves, both visible from the pavement. The downstairs casual bistro, Osteria, is quicker, noisier and cheaper than the high-ceilinged Isola restaurant, and one visitor thought it 'best to treat it as a wine bar' and enjoy a selection of wines by the glass along with a single dish. Isola itself is a huge clean-lined space full of designer chrome and glass. On the face of it, Oliver Peyton and Bruno Loubet make a formidable team, even though the operation does involve a French chef cooking Italian food. What this may lack in sheer authenticity is made up for in a number of successful renderings, from beetroot ravioli with chargrilled duck, via fish soup Livornese style (like a rich-tasting bouillabaisse) to a meat-laden plate of bollito misto in a 'lip-smacking' stock.

Among desserts, 'an excellent tart filled with zabaglione' sounds like a good Franco-Italian compromise, while a pot of chocolate blancmange topped with a layer of unctuous dark runny chocolate would be 'first rate' in any country. Bread, which arrives in a box with a bowl of olive oil for dipping, can't be faulted for variety. Staff are friendly, informative and patient, and an extremely generous number of wines by the glass – around 60 – kick off a vast and exclusively Italian list. Those curious to expand their Chianti/Frascati repertoire can submit to the 'taster' experience and sample five small glasses from ranges such as Native Italian Varieties, Supertuscans or Aromatic Whites. The inspiring concept and flawless selection are marred only by inflated prices. There are no house wines as such, although a few bins can be found under £20.

CHEF: Bruno Loubet PROPRIETOR: Oliver Peyton OPEN: Isola Mon to Fri L 12 to 2.30, Mon to Sat D 6 to 10.30; Osteria d'Isola all week 12 to 2.30 (3.30 Sat and Sun), 6 to 10.30 (9.30 Sun) MEALS: Isola alc D (main courses £8 to £20). Set L £19 (2 courses) to £24, Set D £50; Osteria d'Isola alc (main courses £7 to £19.50). Set L Mon to Fri £15, Set L Sat and Sun £20 SERVICE: 12.5% (optional) CARDS: Amex, Delta, Diners, MasterCard, Switch, Visa DETAILS: 100 seats (Isola), 129 (Osteria d'Isola). Private parties: 100 main room (Isola), 130 (Osteria d'Isola). Vegetarian meals. Wheelchair access (Isola only; also WC). Music. Air-conditioned ⊖ Knightsbridge

Istanbul Iskembecisi £ map 12

9 Stoke Newington Road, N16 8BH
TEL/FAX: (020) 7254 7291

COOKING **2**
TURKISH
£17–£28

Homely décor and notably friendly staff draw a faithful following to this restaurant in a string of shops, especially from the local Turkish population, who throng here until the early hours. The food satisfies most appetites: a simple kebab or grill, or a massive portion of firin kofta (baked meatballs with potatoes, green peppers, tomatoes and onions) served with rice and salad, might be preceded by falafel or Albanian-style liver. A highly successful main course is etli biber dolma, green peppers baked to a silky softness and stuffed with minced lamb, rice, onion, parsley, mint and dill, accompanied by garlicky yoghurt and salad. Many prefer a meal of meze, although the list is not very long. Armut tatlisi – poached pear stuffed with nuts and covered in a chocolate overcoat – is 'just what a pud should be'. House wines, plus a few Turkish bottles, are all £7.95.

CHEF: Ahmet Poyraz PROPRIETORS: Ahmet Poyraz and Ali Demir OPEN: all week noon to 5am MEALS: alc (main courses £6 to £10). Set L Mon to Sat and D Mon to Thur £15 SERVICE: not inc, 10% for parties of 10 or more CARDS: none DETAILS: 90 seats. Private parties: 100 main room. Vegetarian meals. Music. Air-conditioned ⊖ Highbury & Islington (£5)

Itsu £ map 14

118 Draycott Avenue, SW3 3AE
TEL: (020) 7584 5522 FAX: (020) 7582 8716
EMAIL: gavin@itsu.co.uk
WEB SITE: www.itsu.co.uk

COOKING **3**
JAPANESE
£21–£36

Itsu could hardly have a a more visible location: on a corner site with glass all round. The food is largely self-service – from three conveyor belts – so staff have little to do except show people to their seats, explain what's going on to newcomers, and bring wine, but they do it with outstanding courtesy and friendliness. This is a particularly relaxing way to eat, as reporters are entertained by an endless succession of enticing dishes from beetroot cured salmon, via eel fillets on a mound of sticky rice, to tender nuggets of beef on skewers with a chillied mango sauce. Don't be surprised to end up eating more than you planned. The fact that it is not authentic Japanese can be considered a strength, allowing it to serve hot dishes (bonito duck broth, prawn satay) as well as grilled pineapple with butterscotch sauce, and tirami-itsu. A tiny wine list (starting at £11.95) is supplemented by a few beers and juices.

CHEF: Clive Fretwell PROPRIETORS: Clive Schlee and Julian Metcalfe OPEN: all week 12 to 11 (10 Sun) MEALS: alc (plate prices £2.50 to £3.50) SERVICE: not inc CARDS: Amex, Delta, MasterCard, Switch, Visa DETAILS: 70 seats. Private parties: 70 main room. Vegetarian meals. Children's helpings. No smoking in dining room. Wheelchair access (not WC). Music. Air-conditioned ⊖ South Kensington

Ivy

map 15

1–5 West Street, WC2N 9NE
TEL: (020) 7836 4751 FAX: (020) 7240 9333

COOKING **5**
MODERN BRITISH
£29–£81

The wedge-shaped dining room's formal disposition, with wood panelling and stained glass reminiscent of a French restaurant, is a comforting place to be, especially after the struggle some reporters go through to secure a booking. Fancy a table at either 5.30 or 11? That's fine if a theatre visit is planned, but hardly otherwise. And it is not because the waiters dawdle, indeed they positively scoot around. But they are polite and friendly with it, and the place is busy not just because of its celebrity count, but because the food is genuinely good.

The straightforward, no-nonsense modern British cooking is polished and confident, with a solid foundation in high-quality ingredients. Reporters are enthusiastic about most things on the menu, from eggs Benedict and 'memorable' foie gras, to cold poached salmon with mayonnaise on a hot summer's day, and a Mexican salad with convincingly authoritative guacamole. Leek and wild mushroom tart is a favourite too, and this is one place that can chargrill calf's liver successfully. The kitchen goes out of its way to please, with a vegan menu as well as a vegetarian one, and it delights with simple desserts of English berries with vanilla ice cream, or roast plums with almond polenta. The weekend set lunch is considered a steal, but the cover charge doesn't go down well with everybody. With a budget of £25 it is possible to drink reasonably well, and 17 wines by the glass help.

CHEFS: Alan Bird and Des McDonald PROPRIETOR: Caprice Holdings OPEN: all week 12 to 3 (3.30 Sun), 5.30 to 12 CLOSED: 25 and 26 Dec, 1 Jan, Aug bank hol MEALS: alc (main courses £9.50 to £23.50). Set L Sat and Sun £16.50. Cover £1.50 SERVICE: not inc CARDS: Amex, Delta, Diners, MasterCard, Switch, Visa DETAILS: 100 seats. Private parties: 6 main room, 60 private room. Vegetarian meals. Wheelchair access (not WC). No music. Air-conditioned ⊖ Leicester Square

Iznik

map 13

19 Highbury Park, N5 1QJ
TEL: (020) 7704 8099 FAX: (020) 7354 5697

COOKING **2**
TURKISH
£17–£30

The 'cosmetic improvements' mentioned in the last edition of the Guide have now come to fruition. They include laminated wood-effect flooring, solid wooden tables and chairs, and a more polished look generally. 'Charming and oddly enthusiastic' was one impression of the service, some of it by members of the Oner family. Meze can constitute an entire meal, but a couple of reporters shared just three: imam bayaldi, mücver (courgette and feta fritters), and kisir (cracked wheat with tomatoes, peppers and lemon juice), which was bright, fresh and well seasoned. Aubergines appear in many dishes, stuffed or as a creamy sauce with chicken and lamb. Pastries are sweet and 'well made without being greasy'. Turkish house wines are £8.95, and the rest of the list is reasonably priced.

CHEF: Adem Oner and B. Pehlivan PROPRIETORS: Adem and Pirlanta Oner OPEN: all week 10 to 3, 6.30 to 11 CLOSED: Christmas MEALS: alc (main courses £5.50 to £9.50) SERVICE: 10% CARDS: Delta, Diners, MasterCard, Switch, Visa DETAILS: 76 seats. Vegetarian meals. Music ⊖ Highbury & Islington

JaK's

NEW ENTRY map 14

77 Lower Sloane Street, SW1W 8DA
TEL: (020) 7730 9476 FAX: (020) 7823 5040
EMAIL: info@jaksclub.com
WEB SITE: www.jaksclub.com

COOKING **2**
ENGLISH
£25–£37

English cooking, New World wines, a fuss-free approach and suburban prices are the aims in this basement restaurant. Its wooden flooring, linen tablecloths and minimally adorned walls reinforce the philosophy, and the cooking is appreciably direct as well. The kitchen works securely within its limits, and is hearteningly free of pretension, offering lamb sweetbreads with salt beef and gnocchi, and a main course of grilled smoked haddock and deep-fried whitebait. Distinctive flavours are evident in an attractively presented salad of sardine (just the one) with broad beans and shredded shallots, and fine roast poussin (with peas, morels and asparagus) points to the calibre of main ingredients. Iced desserts – passion-fruit sorbet and pistachio ice cream – show up reasonably well, although cheeses might be improved. Some southern European interlopers have got in among the New World wines, but choices are sound, although prices are by no means giveaway. House Australian is £13.50.

CHEF: Adrian Jones PROPRIETOR: Justin Wheeler OPEN: Mon to Fri 12 to 2.15, 6.30 to 10 CLOSED: Christmas MEALS: Set L £12.50 (2 courses) to £15, Set D £17.50 (2 courses) to £20 SERVICE: 6.5% (optional) CARDS: Delta, MasterCard, Switch, Visa DETAILS: 60 seats. 4 seats outside. Private parties: 60 main room. Children's helpings. No smoking in 1 dining room. No cigars/pipes in dining room. Music. Air-conditioned ⊖ Sloane Square

John Burton-Race at the Landmark

NEW ENTRY map 13

222 Marylebone Road, NW1 6JQ
TEL: (020) 7723 7800 FAX: (020) 7723 4700
EMAIL: jbrthelandmark@btinternet.co.uk

COOKING **8**
FRENCH
£44–£115

John Burton-Race is not the first chef to leave Shinfield (where he ran L'Ortolan) and head for the bright lights. Nico Ladenis did the same some years ago, also moving to a hotel dining room. This one is rather short on character; indeed, the tall atrium of the hotel with its giant palm trees and airy disposition would be a worthier setting for the kitchen's talents. On offer is a daily menu, a seven-course taster version for two, and a carte written in French with a detailed translation.

Although some dishes bear a family resemblance to those at L'Ortolan (and have not lost their taste for luxury ingredients) the style now is less elaborate.

Classy materials and accurate timing can be taken as read, and saucing is highly accomplished: a sticky glaze clinging to quail breasts, served as a starter with fine green beans dressed in truffle oil. Sole bonne femme seems old-fashioned on an aspiring menu, but this is a fine version in which a light, bouncy mousse squats in a filleted Dover sole surrounded by indulgently fat ceps, all in a creamy truffle-infused sauce. Not all dishes make the right sort of impact – a starter combining langoustine tails with foie gras is no more than the sum of its parts – but signs of Burton-Race at his best do surface, for example in a dish of veal: soft and lightly crisp sweetbread on a truffley creamy sauce; just-pink fillet; and a chunk of deep-flavoured kidney on a dark stock reduction.

Desserts can be a bit of a letdown. The food has to struggle against some hefty prices – no desserts in single figures, no starters under £20 – and service that varies from friendly to linguistically challenged, although the set lunch is considered good value and the sommelier is tiptop. Fixed mark-ups means that it pays to drink extravagantly from the extensive, though selective, wine list. Fine clarets are a highlight, with 13 vintages of Chateau Lafite, for example, the majority under £200. For mere mortals, decent drinking below £30 is plentiful, with 'special selection' wines starting at £18.

CHEF/PROPRIETOR: John Burton-Race OPEN: Sun to Fri L 12 to 2.15, Mon to Sat D 7 to 10.30 MEALS: alc (main courses £30 to £35). Set L £28, Set D £45 SERVICE: not inc CARDS: Amex, Delta, Diners, MasterCard, Switch, Visa DETAILS: 75 seats. Private parties: 75 main room. Vegetarian meals. Children's helpings. Wheelchair access (also WC). No music. Air-conditioned ⊖ Marylebone (£5)

Justin de Blank

NEW ENTRY **map 13**

50–52 Buckingham Palace Road, SW1W 0RN
TEL: (020) 7828 4111 FAX: (020) 7828 3666

COOKING **2**
BRITISH
£24–£56

The location near Victoria Station was perfect for a bank and remains very useful for the bar/brasserie it has now become. The dining room is simply decorated, with standard pine flooring and white paper covers over tablecloths. British food, neither old-fashioned nor modern, is both decent and unfussy. Daily specials might include well-timed English asparagus with simple melted butter, or al dente ribbon noodles with black truffle. The carte might take in main courses of calf's liver with bacon, cabbage and mash, or a vast, 'sweetly fresh' lemon sole, impeccably cooked, with an unusual mayonnaise containing peas and shredded lettuce. Intense, dark, fudgy chocolate tart with marinated cherries is one way to finish, poached peach with brioche another. Service is charming and efficient, and the short, skilfully chosen wine list is fairly priced, with house wines £9.90, and nine more by the glass.

CHEF: Dorothy Harrison PROPRIETOR: Jonathan Choat OPEN: Mon to Fri 11.30 to 3, 6 to 10.30 CLOSED: Christmas, bank hols MEALS: alc (main courses £8.50 to £17.50). Set L £12.50 (2 courses) to £15.50, Set D £18.50 (2 courses) to £22.50 SERVICE: 12.5% (optional) CARDS: Amex, Delta, MasterCard, Switch, Visa DETAILS: 60 seats. Vegetarian meals. Children's helpings. Music. Air- conditioned ⊖ Victoria

Kastoori £

map 12

188 Upper Tooting Road, SW17 7EJ
TEL/FAX: (020) 8767 7027

COOKING 1
GUJARATI
£20–£31

'In keeping with the Thanki family's roots, the Kastoori menu comprises Indo-African and pan-Indian vegetarian recipes,' writes the manager. The dining room is light and spacious, with reproductions of Hindu sculpture, and a menu that starts with crisp puri snacks (light, piping hot, hollow dough balls), mogo bhajia (cassava fritters), and samosas. To follow, a reporter advocates palak panir (spinach and cheese), and the spring onion curry (which includes tomato, as do many dishes). The latter is on the enticing specials list, but only one of these dishes is available at any given time. It pays to order widely as portions are not huge; perhaps augment a thali set meal with a dosa pancake. The adequate wine list contains a batch of bottles selected to suit the cuisine. House wine is £7.50.

CHEF: Manoj Thanki PROPRIETOR: Dinesh Thanki OPEN: Wed to Sun L 12.30 to 2.30, all week D 6 to 10.30 CLOSED: 25 Dec, 1 week mid-Jan MEALS: alc (main courses £3.50 to £5.50) SERVICE: not inc, card slips closed CARDS: MasterCard, Visa DETAILS: 82 seats. Private parties: 20 main room. Children's helpings. Wheelchair access (not WC). Music. Air-conditioned ⊖ Tooting Broadway

Kennington Lane

NEW ENTRY map 13

205–209 Kennington Lane, SE11 5QS
TEL: (020) 7793 8313 FAX: (020) 7793 8323

COOKING 4
MODERN EUROPEAN
£27–£49

White awnings and a green frontage strike a fresh note at this corner site, where light plank flooring, and white walls studded with stained-glass panels create a light and airy effect. A varied menu immediately arouses interest, touching base with a range of European cuisines and styles, taking in pizzetta bianca, bourride, and lomo Iberico with goat's cheese, tapénade and socca. It also takes a balanced approach to main courses, ensuring a fair supply of fish and vegetables, from wild mushroom tagliarini to crisply seared fillets of red mullet accompanied by braised fennel and vibrantly flavoured saffron potatoes.

Frances McKellar (who has worked at Alastair Little and Le Manoir aux Quat' Saisons, see entries, London and Great Milton) deals in precise cooking, attractive presentation, and positive flavours, including a harmonious tataki of beef, and a twist on saltimbocca: a fine, juicy rump of veal wrapped in Parma ham and sage. Desserts run to rich torta Caprese with pistachio ice cream, and panettone bread-and-butter pudding. Smart staff contribute to the confident feel established by the kitchen, and the globally sourced wine list, arranged by style, is packed with value. Prices start at £11.50 for vins de pays, and around ten are sold by the glass.

CHEF: Frances McKellar PROPRIETOR: Charles Hill OPEN: all week L 12 to 2.30, Mon to Sat D 6 to 10.30 MEALS: alc (main courses £9.50 to £15). Set L and D 6 to 7.30 £14.50 (2 courses) to £16.75 SERVICE: 12.5% (optional), card slips closed CARDS: Amex, Delta, Diners, MasterCard, Switch, Visa DETAILS: 42 seats. 40 seats outside. Private parties: 10 main room. Vegetarian meals. No cigars in dining room. Music. Air-conditioned ⊖ Kennington (£5)

Kensington Place 🍷 map 13

201 Kensington Church Street, W8 7LX
TEL: (020) 7727 3184 FAX: (020) 7229 2025

COOKING **6**
MODERN BRITISH
£24–£72

Bustle and noise come with the territory at this glass-fronted old stager. That it has survived fads and fashions in the robust way that it has is a tribute to its no-nonsense approach and to Rowley Leigh's universally appealing style of food. The place seems designed for fast eating – and service has been known to reinforce this impression – but the cooking is serious. Choice on the carte is extensive enough to please traditionalists – with omelette fines herbes, fish soup with rouille, or steak béarnaise – and up to date enough for fried squid to come with crème fraîche and chilli jam. Variety derives less from exotic ingredients than from a sensible mix of roasting (squab pigeon with rhubarb), steaming (sea bass with leeks, chilli and dill), and griddling (chicken livers with celeriac purée).

Much to their credit, dishes don't get too complicated, opting for simple saucing – beurre rouge with wood pigeon, or chive butter with sole – and finding room for seasonal items such as English asparagus with pea leaves. Desserts, too, can be as everyday as lemon tart or hot chocolate pudding with custard. The wine list kicks off with four sherries by the glass, then a few reasonably priced champagnes, increasingly a rarity in London. Wines are arranged by style – 'Alsace and Similar', 'Burgundy and Other Pinot Noir', for instance – which simplifies selection and allows for pointed price comparisons. House wines start at £11 for Chardonnay Vin de Pays d'Oc.

CHEF: Rowley Leigh PROPRIETOR: Moving Image Restaurants OPEN: all week 12 to 3 (3.30 Sat and Sun), 6.30 to 11.45 (10.15 Sun) MEALS: alc (main courses £11 to £18.50). Set L Mon to Sat £14.50, Set L Sun £16.50 SERVICE: not inc CARDS: Amex, Delta, MasterCard, Switch, Visa DETAILS: 190 seats. Private parties: 20 main room, 40 private room. Vegetarian meals. Children's helpings. Wheelchair access (also WC). No music. Air-conditioned ⊖ Notting Hill Gate

Kiku £ NEW ENTRY map 15

17 Half Moon Street, W1Y 7RB
TEL: (020) 7499 4208 FAX: (0200 7409 3259

COOKING **3**
JAPANESE
£24–£74

An extended frontage of tall windows discreetly covered with bamboo blinds gives way to a surprisingly long and narrow dining room with clean, crisp décor of beech panelled walls, grey slate floor and rattan chairs at black lacquered tables. A few steps up from the entrance, on a mezzanine floor, is the traditional sushi bar, which claims to be London's largest. Its long menu offers a wide range of nigiri, such as saketoro (salmon belly), colourful, crunchy kazunoko (herring roe) and tobiko (flying fish roe), as well as rolled sushi and assortments.

In the main room, the whole Japanese repertoire is offered à la carte or in various kaseiki (set meals). Stimulate the appetite with nameko oroshi (small mushrooms with shredded mooli) or itawasa (fishcake garnished with salmon caviar) before moving on to ishiyaki (well-flavoured grilled marinated beef on a bed of onion and sweet pumpkin), or a good version of agedashi dofu (deep-fried beancurd). Saké sorbet is a fun and unusual way to finish. Pricing generally is restrained for the restaurant's location and style. This is a family business and service is charmingly overseen by Mariko Taoka. House wine is £10.50 and most others below £20

CHEFS: Hattori, Yamauchi and Kamei PROPRIETORS: Hishashi and Mariko Taoka OPEN: Mon to Sat 12 to 2.30, 6 to 10.15 MEALS: alc (main courses £5.50 to £27). Set L £9.80 to £21, Set D £34 to £51. Sushi £1.50 to £4.50. Light meals available SERVICE: 12.5%, card slips closed CARDS: Amex, Delta, Diners, MasterCard, Switch, Visa DETAILS: 95 seats. Private parties: 60 main room, 10 private room. Vegetarian meals. Wheelchair access (also WC). Music. Air-conditioned
⊖ Green Park (£5)

K10

NEW ENTRY map 13

20 Copthall Avenue, EC2R 7DN
TEL: (020) 7562 8510 FAX: (020) 7562 8515
EMAIL: copthall@k10.net
WEB SITE: www.k10.net

COOKING 2
JAPANESE
£10–£32

The atmosphere in this basement Japanese restaurant is lively, with conversation just possible against the music, and bare white walls given a lilac tinge by blue lighting. The main feature is the kaiten, or conveyor belt, which gives the place its pun of a name, bearing tempting little dishes. You sit facing it, or at a table jutting out from it, which is more convivial for groups of three or four. A variety of classical sushi and other delicacies come on colour-coded plates. Modern fusions include a spectacular large roll of avocado and tuna coated with bright green, wasabi-marinated flying-fish roe. A treat, not just for vegetarians, is an assembly of cold soba noodles with mushroom and asparagus, while other dishes range from tuna and salmon sashimi to tempura fishcake. For pudding, play safe with fresh fruit, or go for something like a pastry, or a sweet omelette topped with sugar leaves. House wine is £12.50 a bottle, £2.90 a glass, or drink saké.

CHEF: Miguel Choy PROPRIETOR: K10 Ltd OPEN: Mon to Fri 11.30 to 3, 5 to 10 CLOSED: 24 to 26 Dec, bank hols MEALS: alc (plate prices £1 to £3.50) SERVICE: not inc CARDS: Amex, Delta, Diners, MasterCard, Switch, Visa DETAILS: 70 seats. Private parties: 100 main room. Vegetarian meals. No smoking in dining room. Wheelchair access (also WC). Music. Air-conditioned ⊖ Moorgate, Liverpool Street

Kulu Kulu Sushi £

map 15

76 Brewer Street, W1R 3PH
TEL: (020) 7734 7316 FAX: (020) 7734 6507

COOKING 2
JAPANESE
£18–£27

Simplicity is the key to the success of this unadorned sushi café. That doesn't imply an absence of skill in the kitchen, as can be seen from watching the talented sushi chef as he prepares the snacks before placing them on the kaiten (conveyor belt) to circulate at eye level in front of diners sitting at the low counter (get there early to guarantee a seat). Manifestly fresh fish is the highlight, including glistening scallop nigiri, the raw shellfish placed atop a rectangle of rice. Other memorable items have included robust, meaty mackerel nigiri, salmon and avocado maki roll 'stuffed with good ingredients', and fried aubergine served warm with a coating of teriyaki sauce. Pickled ginger and wasabi are provided on the counter. To drink, help yourself to green tea (free); otherwise there are Japanese beers, saké, and house wine at £12 a bottle.

CHEF: Mr Y. Hashiramoto PROPRIETOR: Mr K. Toyama OPEN: Mon to Sat 12 to 2.30 (4 Sat), 5 to 10 CLOSED: bank hols MEALS: alc (sushi £1.20 to £3, main courses £4.80 to £10) SERVICE: not inc CARDS: Delta, MasterCard, Switch, Visa DETAILS: 30 seats. Private parties: 4 main room. No smoking in dining room. Music. Air-conditioned ⊖ Piccadilly Circus

▲ Lanesborough, The Conservatory **map 14**

1 Lanesborough Place, Hyde Park Corner, SW1X 7TA
TEL: (020) 7259 5599 FAX: (020) 7259 5606
EMAIL: info@lanesborough.co.uk
WEB SITE: www.lanesborough.com

COOKING **4**
MODERN EUROPEAN/ASIAN
£36–£80

Rich fabrics and vibrant colours match the prestigious location, and the Chinoiserie-themed Conservatory dining room is pure theatre with its oriental chandeliers, amphorae and palm trees. The grand hotel atmosphere is generally restful and welcoming, although there is a dinner dance on Fridays and Saturdays. A bright, look-at-me menu deals broadly in Mediterranean and Pacific Rim ideas, from falafel to lettuce and crab spring rolls with soy and ginger.

Paul Gayler's vegetarian leanings still leave room for plenty of meat and fish options, from foie gras terrine with dates and duck ham to spiced barbecued salmon with coconut rice and Thai vegetables. In this context, lemon grass can turn up almost anywhere: for example, in a crème brûlée with ginger-roasted plums. Service – as charming as it is professional – comes in for high praise. Visiting chefs, a children's menu, Sunday brunch, and 'designer afternoon teas' with a samovar trolley add to the options available. The wine list is designed for deep pockets, with only two humble French wines coming in under £20.

CHEF: Paul Gayler PROPRIETOR: Rosewood Hotels OPEN: all week 12 to 2.30, 6.30 to 11.30 (12 Fri and Sat) MEALS: alc Mon to Sat L, all week D (main courses £13.50 to £27.50). Set L Mon to Sat £15 (1 course) to £26.50, Set L Sun £29.50, Set D Sun to Thur £32, Set D Fri £39, Set D Sat £44 SERVICE: net prices, card slips closed CARDS: Amex, Diners, MasterCard, Switch, Visa DETAILS: 120 seats. Private parties: 40 main room, 12 to 100 private rooms. Vegetarian meals. Children's helpings. Wheelchair access (also WC). Music. Air-conditioned ACCOMMODATION: 95 rooms, all with bath/shower. TV. Phone. Room only £255 to £4,000. Rooms for disabled. Baby facilities ⊖ Hyde Park Corner

Langan's Brasserie **map 15**

Stratton Street, W1X 5FD
TEL: (020) 7491 8822 FAX: (020) 7493 8309

COOKING **1**
ANGLO-FRENCH
£31–£62

A heady, starry atmosphere has kept Langan's popular for years. 'Even at 10.45 when we arrived,' observed one visitor, 'the place was jumping'. Tables are turned round ruthlessly to keep the numbers flowing, and service usually has its ups and downs; the first-floor room, with its murals of Venice, is a little more laid back. The classical Anglo-French bistro cooking, still overseen by Richard Shepherd, remains as dependable as ever. Line up for croustade d'oeufs de caille, monkfish with bacon and leeks, and escalope of veal cordon bleu. Wallow in unreconstructed Englishry at the end with rice pudding, spotted dick, or Manchester tart. Budget for a cover charge as well as service, and be aware that the credit card slips are still left open, but wine prices may come as a pleasant surprise. House French is £12.

CHEF: Ken Whitehead PROPRIETOR: Richard Shepherd CBE OPEN: Mon to Fri 12.15 to 11.45, Sat 7 to 12 MEALS: alc (main courses £9.50 to £15). Cover £1.50 SERVICE: 12.5% (optional) CARDS: Amex, Delta, Diners, MasterCard, Switch, Visa DETAILS: 200 seats. Vegetarian meals. Music. Air-conditioned ⊖ Green Park

Lansdowne

map 13

90 Gloucester Avenue, NW1 8HX
TEL: (020) 7483 0409 FAX: (020) 7586 1723

COOKING **2**
MODERN BRITISH
£24–£45

One of London's first gastro-pubs, the Lansdowne has added a restaurant for more formal dining, thereby perhaps ceding some of its spontaneity: tables here can be booked, and there is no need to queue at the bar. The style of food remains the same, however, with carefully sourced seasonal ingredients the norm. A simple, no-nonsense carte doesn't waste words, offering roasted peppers with capers, anchovies and egg; seared scallops; or pâté with onion relish to start. Main courses are equally uncluttered, featuring poached wild salmon with chives, new potatoes and mayonnaise, or, in winter, roast partridge with bacon and celery sauce. Cheeses are from Neal's Yard, and strawberries with Muscat-soaked cake and cream may be among desserts. Seven wines by the glass find their way on to an unpretentious list, with the majority of bottles under £20. Prices start at £10 for vin de pays.

CHEFS: Mark Watkins and James Knight PROPRIETOR: Amanda Pritchett OPEN: Sat and Sun L 1 to 2.30, Tue to Sat D 7 to 10 CLOSED: Christmas, 1 Jan MEALS: alc (main courses £8.50 to £14.50). Set L Sun £15 SERVICE: 12.5% (optional), card slips closed CARDS: Delta, MasterCard, Switch, Visa DETAILS: 60 seats. 30 seats outside. Private parties: 70 main room. Vegetarian meals. No music ⊖ Chalk Farm

Launceston Place 🍷

map 14

1A Launceston Place, W8 5RL
TEL: (020) 7937 6912 FAX: (020) 7938 2412

COOKING **3**
MODERN BRITISH
£31–£63

Although not far from bustle and activity, Launceston Place manages to feel decidedly rural, helped by country-house furnishings and still-life prints. This sense of a gentler pace is echoed in a style of food that comforts with many familiar ingredients prepared in sympathetic fashion: a delicate cauliflower and Stilton soup, deep-fried oysters with tartare sauce, or a simple but well-prepared Caesar salad. Alongside main courses of John Dory (with rhubarb and ginger) and grilled sirloin steak (with béarnaise) appear veal sweetbreads, or perhaps a hearty oxtail stew with root vegetables in winter. Herb butters are a preferred accompaniment to fish – flavoured with dill for salmon, with parsley for Dover sole – and puddings might run to Bakewell tart or apple pie soufflé. In one visitor's view 'staff have a bistro attitude and dress accordingly'. House wines start at £12.50, but most of the interesting drinking is over £20 a bottle. Wines are helpfully arranged by grape variety and style, a trend that encourages experimentation.

CHEF: Phil Reed PROPRIETOR: Moving Image Ltd OPEN: Sun to Fri L 12.30 to 2.30 (3 Sun), Mon to Sat D 7 to 11.30 CLOSED: bank hols MEALS: alc (main courses £14 to £17.50). Set L Sun to Fri and D Mon to Fri 7 to 8 £15.50 (2 courses) to £18.50 SERVICE: not inc CARDS: Amex, Delta, MasterCard, Switch, Visa DETAILS: 90 seats. Private parties: 60 main room, 14 and 30 private rooms. Vegetarian meals. No pipes in dining room. Wheelchair access (not WC). No music. Air-conditioned ⊖ Gloucester Road

Laurent £

map 13

428 Finchley Road, NW2 2HY
TEL: (020) 7794 3603

COOKING **2**
NORTH AFRICAN
£21–£32

'You wouldn't eat here for the ambience, and certainly not for the décor,' confides a reporter, 'but if you want couscous, this is the place to come.' Indeed, the sign above the door says as much. Lamb, fish and vegetarian couscous there may be, but it's all couscous: this is no-frills cooking done with single-minded commitment. Help yourself from large pots of North African stew containing substantial chunks of meat in 'loads of beautiful rich brown gravy'. Merguez sausages are succulent, blackened lamb chops irresistibly pink inside, while the grains themselves are suitably light and fluffy. Harissa is home made and red hot. Brique à l'oeuf remains the only starter, but you will need it only 'if you are planning on not eating again for a week'. By the same token, if the cold desserts are too much to contemplate, finish with a digestive glass of mint tea. North African wines from £9.50 suit the mood.

CHEF/PROPRIETOR: Laurent Farrugia OPEN: Mon to Sat 12 to 2, 6 to 11 CLOSED: Christmas, New Year, last 3 weeks Aug, bank hols MEALS: alc (main courses £7 to £11.50) SERVICE: not inc CARDS: Amex, Delta, MasterCard, Visa DETAILS: 36 seats. Private parties: 50 main room. Vegetarian meals. Children's helpings. No cigars/pipes in dining room. Wheelchair access (not WC). No music ⊖ Golders Green

Lavender £

NEW ENTRY **map 12**

171 Lavender Hill, SW11 5TE
TEL: (020) 7978 5242
24 Clapham Road, SW9 0JG
TEL: (020) 7793 0770

COOKING **2**
MEDITERRANEAN
£22–£36

The Clapham branch of this mini-chain has a pavement terrace, popular with early-evening drinkers, as well as a colourful patio at the back. Inside, a bar dominates the small room, which is furnished with old rustic tables and chairs, and church pews. The lively Battersea branch creates a similar impression, and each offers the same menu, chalked up on blackboards, of well-conceived and generally well-executed modern dishes: perhaps charcoal grilled halloumi cheese salad, followed by rare seared tuna steak with charred courgettes and a tomato spring onion salsa, or brightly flavoured lamb cutlets with flageolet mash, crunchy sautéed leeks and mint pesto. Desserts might be rich, moist

Tunisian orange cake or chocolate tart with crisp pastry and creamy filling. A short, decently priced wine list opens with house French at £8.95. Other branches are at 193 Lower Richmond Road, SW15 (tel (020) 8785 6004), and 112 Vauxhall Walk, SE1 (tel (020) 7735 4440).

CHEF: Jim Brown (Lavender Hill), Simone Zacton (Clapham Road) PROPRIETORS: Erdal Niyazoglu and Trevor Young OPEN: all week; 12 to 3, 7 to 11 (10.30 Sun Clapham Road) CLOSED: 25 Dec MEALS: alc (main courses £6.50 to £10.50). Set L and D £18.95 (2 courses) to £19.95 SERVICE: 12.5% (optional) CARDS: Amex, Delta, MasterCard, Switch, Visa DETAILS: 70 seats (Lavender Hill), 45 seats (Clapham Road). 25 seats outside (Lavender Hill), 20 seats outside (Clapham Road). Private parties: 20 main room, 25 private room (Clapham Road). Vegetarian meals. Children's helpings. Wheelchair access (Lavender Hill only, not WC). Occasional music ⊖ Oval (Clapham Road)

Light House

NEW ENTRY map 12

75–77 Ridgway, SW19 4ST
TEL: (020) 8944 6338 FAX: (020) 8946 4440

COOKING 3
FUSION
£29–£53

The appearance is stark, with no pictures, soft furnishings or plants to relieve the effects of stone, blond wood, white paint and hard chairs; and acoustics were predictably the last thing on the designer's mind. But windows and doors allow in enough natural daylight to make the name credible. Whether the food is considered Italian fusion or pan-Asian (it owes inspiration mostly to Peter Gordon and the Sugar Club, see entry, London), it is not something that Wimbledon has seen much of. The menu is arranged in Italian format, ingredients come from all over the place, and dishes are imaginatively conceived.

Skilful execution has produced a refreshing cold starter of braised cuttlefish with feta, rocket, red onions and deep-fried artichoke, and while not all combinations work equally well, individual components are fresh and generally well handled. Some, such as coriander pappardelle with yellow beans and shiitake, show what fusion cooking can deliver when all cylinders are firing. A fine example of vanilla pannacotta makes the point that desserts owe more to Italy than anywhere, and smiling staff in grey tunics contribute to a relaxed atmosphere. Around 40 wines are nearly as diverse as the food, with a dozen available by the glass. Prices start at £10.50.

CHEF: Gianni Vatteroni PROPRIETORS: Ian Taylor, Bob Finch and Kate Sim OPEN: all week 12 to 2.45 (3.15 Sun), 6.30 to 10.45 (9.30 Sun) MEALS: alc (main courses £10 to £14.50). Set L Mon to Sat £12.50 (2 courses) SERVICE: 12.5% (optional), card slips closed CARDS: Amex, Delta, MasterCard, Switch, Visa DETAILS: 75 seats. 10 seats outside. Private parties: 14 main room. Vegetarian meals. No smoking in 1 dining room. Wheelchair access (also WC). No music ⊖ Wimbledon (£5)

The 2002 Guide will be published before Christmas 2001. Reports on meals are most welcome at any time of the year, but are particularly valuable in the spring (no later than June). Send them to The Good Food Guide, *FREEPOST, 2 Marylebone Road, London NW1 4DF. Or email your report to goodfoodguide@which.net*

Lindsay House 🍷 ✱

map 15

21 Romilly Street, W1V 5TG
TEL: (020) 7439 0450 FAX: (020) 7437 7349

COOKING **7**
MODERN BRITISH
£38–£99

Beyond the dark-red door (ring to get in) of this tall, white-painted town house, the scraped white walls, bare floorboards and rough textures hint at a rustic edge in some of the dishes to come. The food is exciting, right from the 'amusette' (of perhaps lentil soup with juniper cream and chopped chestnuts), and ideas are strong: from jellied skate with fennel bavarois and aubergine compote, to pheasant boudin with white bean cassoulet. The best dishes tend to be sharp and spare, saucing is kept to a minimum, and yet there is refinement too: in a superlative starter of five warm, poached, caviar-topped oysters for example, laid on batons of salsify and surrounded by a herb-strewn pool of creamy, foamy sauce tasting of oyster liquor.

In a city where everything is always available, it is refreshing to find the seasons observed. January, for example, has seen poached and grilled pink partridge breast, served with a sticky raviolo of roughly minced pig's trotter, buttery shredded Savoy cabbage and a scattering of the tiniest girolles. Trotter also appears in the form of a crubeen, alongside spicy black pudding to accompany suckling pig (a favourite among reporters). Although savoury courses radiate the greatest energy, colourful desserts are not without appeal, from a 'spectacular selection of bite-size raspberry confections' (including single berries in jelly, and a small hot tart), to a slice of layered white chocolate terrine studded with griottine cherries, and topped with a scoop of intense chocolate sorbet.

Service – 'French to the fingertips' – has been courteous, attentive and professional, but not without long waits for several reporters: lunch can easily take two hours or more. The food may not be cheap, but most reporters consider the cost justified. An impressive range of wines from some enticing areas and producers, most notably south-west France, are grouped according to style and grape variety, with pithy tasting notes: 'weirdly nice' describes a Côtes du Jura white. Although quality is not in dispute, prices are unkind to ordinary drinkers. House white begins at £18.50 and ten are available by the glass, prices starting at £3.50.

CHEF: Richard Corrigan PROPRIETOR: Searcy Corrigan Ltd OPEN: Mon to Fri L 12 to 2.30, Mon to Sat D 6 to 11 CLOSED: 2 weeks Christmas, 2 weeks Aug MEALS: alc L (main courses £15 to £20). Set L £23, Set D £43 to £62 SERVICE: 12.5% (optional), card slips closed CARDS: Amex, Delta, Diners, MasterCard, Switch, Visa DETAILS: 48 seats. Private parties: 8 to 35 private rooms. Vegetarian meals. Children's helpings. No smoking in 1 dining room. No music. Air-conditioned ⊖ Leicester Square, Piccadilly Circus

All details are as accurate as possible at the time of going to press, but chefs and owners often change, and it is wise to check by telephone before making a special journey. Many readers have been disappointed when set-price bargain meals are no longer available. Ask when booking.

Little Georgia £

NEW ENTRY **map 12**

2 Broadway Market, E8 4QJ
TEL: (020) 7249 9070 FAX: (020) 7275 0208

COOKING **1**
GEORGIAN/RUSSIAN
£21–£33

Named not after Georgia in the southern USA but the one bordering Russia and Turkey, this former pub is pleasantly decorated with dark red walls and scenes of rural life. The décor also takes in bowls of dried pomegranates and walnuts, key ingredients in a cuisine influenced by Turkey, Iran and the Middle East. Among cold starters are three pâtés – walnuts with spinach, with beetroot, and with leeks – while hot starters take in kachapuri, a crumbly, cakey flat bread, made with yoghurt, eggs, and flour, stuffed with molten cheese: every bit as appetising as it sounds. Influence from the north appears in Ukrainian bortsch, which adds bacon, sausage and black olives to the usual cabbage and beetroot. Satsivi, a strongly aromatic sauce of walnuts and a tang of coriander, is used for both pan-fried trout fillet and roast poussin, and other main courses include gupta (beef and pork meatballs in spicy red pepper sauce). There are a few Georgian wines, but house wines, at £9.50, are French.

CHEF: Elena Gambashidze PROPRIETOR: Antony Jones OPEN: Sun L 1 to 3, Tue to Sat D 6.30 to 10 (10.30 Fri and Sat) CLOSED: 25 Dec MEALS: alc (main courses £7.50 to £10) SERVICE: not inc CARDS: Delta, MasterCard, Switch, Visa DETAILS: 45 seats. 10 seats outside. Private parties: 45 main room. Vegetarian meals. Children's helpings. Wheelchair access (not WC). Music. Air-conditioned ⊖ Bethnal Green

Livebait 

map 13

43–45 The Cut, SE1 8LF
TEL: (020) 7928 7211 FAX: (020) 7928 2279
EMAIL: livebaitwaterloo@groupechezgerard.co.uk
WEB SITE: www.santeonline.co.uk

COOKING **3**
SEAFOOD
£26–£75

Whether they strike you as 'tiled and spacious as a Victorian public lavatory' or like a 'converted pie-and-mash shop', branches of Livebait are typically as busy and noisy as they are immaculately clean, and serve up a varied menu of fish and shellfish. The range includes three or four kinds of oyster, Dorset crab, cockles and whelks, seafood platters, and anything from kipper fishcakes with red cabbage and lobster oil (which works well in case you were wondering) to Moroccan tempura lemon sole with tomato chutney. High-quality supplies – perhaps two huge, briefly seared scallops as fresh as sea air – are augmented by the kitchen's confident timing, producing crisp-skinned, moist-fleshed sea bream, smokily chargrilled sardines, and hunks of pink pepper-crusted tuna in a fishy broth with bok choy. Daily arrivals such as sea bass, skate or Dover sole are simply prepared: choose grilling or pan-roasting, then a sauce to go with it, and perhaps a side order of notably good spinach. Crisp, fluffy chips warrant special mention. Predominantly white wines are arranged by style. Although prices tend to be high, many are available by the glass, starting with house Muscadet at £3.25, £11.95 a bottle.

Branches at 175 Westbourne Grove, W11 (tel (020) 7727 4321), and 21 Wellington Street, WC2 (tel (020) 7836 7161), follow the same formula as the Waterloo original in terms of both décor and menu.

CHEF: Stephen Parkinson PROPRIETOR: Groupe Chez Gérard OPEN: Mon to Sat 12 to 3, 5.30 to 11.30 MEALS: alc (main courses £13.50 to £25.50). Set L and D 5.30 to 7 and 10 to 11.30 £12.50 (2 courses) to £15.50 SERVICE: 12.5% (optional), card slips closed CARDS: Amex, Delta, Diners, MasterCard, Switch, Visa DETAILS: 90 seats. 10 seats outside. Private parties: 30 main room. Children's helpings. No smoking in 1 dining room. No cigars/ pipes in dining-room. Wheelchair access (also WC). Music ⊖ Waterloo

Livebait's Café Fish

map 15

36–40 Rupert Street, W1V 7FR
TEL: (020) 7287 8989 FAX: (020) 7287 8400

COOKING **2**
SEAFOOD
£30–£59

Despite a name change, the erstwhile Café Fish has not altered in any material respect. It does a highly professional job, serving fresh seafood to an appreciated formula in the heart of Soho. Listed fish (priced daily) are either chargrilled or pan-fried as a main course, and served with a choice of dressing from lemon oil to béarnaise; alternatives might include smoked haddock kedgeree. Start maybe with a bowl of cockles or whelks, chargrilled squid, or steamed mussels. One couple enjoyed queen scallops in garlic and herb butter followed by Dover sole with crisp chips, another praised fresh, accurately timed, flavourful sea bream. Finish perhaps with warm chocolate brownie, or generously served mango sorbet. Service is commended as uniformly on the ball, catering efficiently for theatre-goers along the way. Wines do a good job too: mostly white of course, arranged by style. Prices open at £10.35.

CHEF: Andrew Magson PROPRIETOR: Groupe Chez Gérard OPEN: Mon to Fri 12 to 3, 5.30 to 11.30, Sat noon to 11.30, Sun noon to 10.30 CLOSED: Christmas MEALS: alc (main courses £9 to £20.50). Set D 7 to 11.30 £18.50. Bar meals available. Cover £1.50 SERVICE: 12.5% (optional) CARDS: Amex, Delta, Diners, MasterCard, Switch, Visa DETAILS: 150 seats. Private parties: 40 main room. Vegetarian meals. Children's helpings. No smoking in 1 dining room. No cigars/pipes in dining room. Wheelchair access (also WC). Music. Air-conditioned ⊖ Piccadilly Circus, Leicester Square

Lobster Pot

map 13

3 Kennington Lane, SE11 4RG
TEL: (020) 7582 5556

COOKING **3**
FRENCH SEAFOOD
£23–£61

The Régents' ten-year old enterprise is as resolutely and evocatively French as a 1960s quayside restaurant in Brittany, and as fishy as the inside of a trawler, with cabin seating, brass lamps, a ship-to-shore radio, fish swimming behind portholes, and any amount of nets, corks and shells, not to mention the sound of seagulls and sea shanties. The mustachioed skipper, meanwhile, takes a hands-on approach to his first-rate ingredients, offering a version of bouillabaisse, and a seafood platter (in two sizes) of impeccably fresh oysters, crab, clams, crevettes, pink and brown shrimps and winkles, any of which can be taken separately.

Main courses take in traditional pan-fried skate wing with brown butter and capers, as well as monkfish with Cajun spices, although it is difficult to resist the appeal of a mixed chargrill of plaice, monk, grouper, hake, squid, sardine and chunks of sweet lobster in finger-licking garlicky butter. There are hearty meat dishes too, and desserts of crêpes and profiteroles. The captain's mate is in charge of service, helped by a couple of deckhands in blue and white T-shirts. It is easy to run up a hefty bill, although the short wine list doesn't make it inevitable. House wine is £10.50 (£3 a glass).

CHEF: Hervé Régent PROPRIETORS: Hervé and Nathalie Régent OPEN: Tue to Sat 12 to 2.30, 7 to 10.45 CLOSED: 24 Dec to early Jan MEALS: alc (main courses £14.50 to £25.50). Set L £10 (2 courses) to £13.50, Set D £19.50 to £39.50 SERVICE: 12.5% (optional), card slips closed CARDS: Amex, Delta, Diners, MasterCard, Switch, Visa DETAILS: 44 seats. Private parties: 30 main room, 14 and 30 private rooms. Children's helpings. No cigars/pipes in dining room. Wheelchair access (not WC). Music. Air-conditioned ⊖ Kennington (£5)

Lola's

map 13

The Mall Building, 359 Upper Street, N1 0PD
TEL: (020) 7359 1932 FAX: (020) 7359 2209

COOKING **2**
MODERN EUROPEAN
£25–£47

As Juliet Peston left late in 1999 to oversee the cooking at Cow Dining Room (see entry), Gary Lee, late of Le Caprice (see entry) took over at this bright and airy first-floor restaurant at the pulsing heart of Upper Street. The style remains minimal, light and Mediterranean, including a starkly simple starter of Cantabrian anchovies with chopped shallots and olive-oiled toast, and cumin-scented chicken with hummus, harissa, tabbouleh and flat bread. There are plenty of meatless options, from Roquefort pizza to red mullet with olive oil mash, and desserts take in an outstanding Vin Santo syllabub with biscotti and dried apricots. Look out for the good-value set-price lunches and Sunday dinner menu. Wines are an eclectic bunch from all corners of the globe, and a suitably titled 'Offbeat' selection includes enticing and unusual bottles such as the increasingly fashionable Marcillac from south-west France. Sixteen wines are available by the glass, and bottle prices start at £10.50.

CHEF: Gary Lee PROPRIETORS: Carol George and Morfudd Richards OPEN: all week 12 to 2.30 (3 Sat and Sun), 6 to 11 (7 to 10 Sun) CLOSED: some bank hols MEALS: alc exc Sun D (main courses £11 to £15). Set L Mon to Fri £15, Set D Mon to Fri 6 to 7.15 £10 (2 courses), Set D Sun £15. Cover £1 SERVICE: not inc CARDS: Amex, Delta, Diners, MasterCard, Switch, Visa DETAILS: 80 seats. Private parties: 9 main room. Vegetarian meals. Children's helpings. Music. Air-conditioned ⊖ Angel (£5)

Lomo £

map 14

222 Fulham Road, SW10 9NB
TEL/FAX: (020) 7349 8848

COOKING **2**
SPANISH
£19–£35

Opposite the Chelsea and Westminster Hospital, and more a bar-café than a restaurant, Lomo offers fast food Spanish-style. Raciones (little tapas dishes) are the main business, eaten off high tables, or sitting on tall pillar stools at the small bar. The list runs from tortilla to hot chorizo, from salt codfish cakes to skewered spiced lamb with herb salad and flatbread. Additional blackboard specials might offer Cantabrian anchovies with shallots and thick toast, or tender fried squid rings and tentacles with muted aïoli. Lomo itself (cured pork loin) comes with goat's cheese, roast peppers, top-notch tapénade and socca (a thin rolled pancake). With sharply flavoured sorbets or crema Catalana to finish, friendly service, and a fine list of sherries in all styles, this is a reliable operation all round. There is also a short, workaday wine list (starting at £9.75 a bottle) and a rather longer, more inventive list of cocktails.

CHEFS: Halim Izghouti PROPRIETORS: Lomo Limited OPEN: all week noon to 11.30 MEALS: alc (main courses £2.50 to £7.50) SERVICE: not inc, 12.5% for parties of 6 or more CARDS: Amex, Delta, Diners, MasterCard, Switch, Visa DETAILS: 60 seats. Vegetarian meals. Wheelchair access (not WC). Music. Air-conditioned ⊖ Fulham Broadway (£5)

▲ London Marriott, County Hall Restaurant map 13

County Hall, SE1 7PB COOKING **4**
TEL: (020) 7902 8000 FAX: (020) 7928 5300 MODERN BRITISH
£31–£69

This may be only a refurbished municipal building, but appropriately grand restoration has added a degree of opulence and even elegance to the former corridors of power. Generously proportioned rooms with high ceilings, oak panelling and huge modern paintings provide a rich background for David Ali's straightforward yet imaginative dishes. Seafood – as fresh as can be – is a strong suit, and subject to a wide variety of techniques and treatments, including seared scallops with caramelised pineapple, cod brandade with lobster salad, and roast curried haddock with smoked salmon bubble and squeak.

Among highlights have been a dramatic starter of white crabmeat served with two shiny black-bean pancakes and chilli oil, and tender, well-flavoured roast wood pigeon in a 'masterly combination' with red cabbage, rösti and a liver-enriched sauce. Desserts are equally well rendered, judging by a sticky tarte Tatin of figs with cinnamon ice cream. Service is well trained and attentive, and around 80 cannily chosen wines are helpfully grouped by style. House Vaucluse is £13.50.

CHEF: David Ali PROPRIETOR: Whitbread plc OPEN: all week 12 to 2.30, 5.30 to 11 (10.30 Sun) MEALS: alc D (main courses £12.50 to £21). Set L and D 5.30 to 7 £16.50 (2 courses) to £19.50 SERVICE: not inc CARDS: Amex, Delta, Diners, MasterCard, Switch, Visa DETAILS: 90 seats. Private parties: 120 main room. Vegetarian meals. Children's helpings. Music. Air-conditioned ACCOMMODATION: 200 rooms, all with bath/shower. TV. Phone. Prices on application. Rooms for disabled. Swimming pool *(The Which? Hotel Guide)* ⊖ Westminster

Lou Pescadou map 13

241 Old Brompton Road, SW5 9HP COOKING **2**
TEL: (020) 7370 1057 FAX: (020) 7244 7545 SEAFOOD
£21–£52

Continuing stolidly to resist fashion, with its blue and white décor, nautical prints and menu of fishy French classics that would not have sounded too outlandish 50 years ago, Lou Pescadou none the less succeeds in pleasing with its relaxed atmosphere, fresh materials, and dependable kitchen. Try the plate of whelks, winkles and prawns with aïoli, or the Plateau Pescadou, which also includes oysters, crab and clams. Otherwise, king prawns with fennel and garlic, or ravioli of crab and scallops, might precede roast monkfish à la niçoise, smoked haddock with juniper butter, or pan-fried salmon with bordelaise sauce, all served with boiled potatoes or commendable frites. To finish, there may be tarte au chocolat. Unsurprisingly, wines are all French; prices start at £10.50 (£2.50 a glass). The cover charge and 'optional' 15 per cent for service help to augment the bill.

CHEF: Laurent David PROPRIETORS: Daniel Chobert and Laurent David OPEN: all week 12 to 3, 6.30 to 12 CLOSED: 10 days Christmas MEALS: alc (main courses £6.50 to £14). Set L £9.90, Set D weekends £13.50. Cover £1.50 SERVICE: 15% (optional), card slips closed CARDS: Amex, Delta, Diners, MasterCard, Switch, Visa DETAILS: 62 seats. 20 seats outside. Private parties: 50 main room. Vegetarian meals. Children's helpings. Wheelchair access (not WC). No music. Air-conditioned ⊖ Earls Court (£5)

Lundum's

map 14

119 Old Brompton Road, SW7 3RN
TEL: (020) 7373 7774 FAX: (020) 7373 4472

COOKING **3**
DANISH
£24–£52

Lundum's bills itself as The (not 'A') Danish Restaurant, and for the time being at least seems to have this corner of the market to itself. The formula is traditional dishes at lunch – platters of herrings, meatballs, prawns, chicken salad and so forth – with a more experimental style the proprietors describe as 'Danish nouvelle cuisine' in the evenings. Several ways with salmon are offered, including an inventive and attractively presented smoked salmon 'cannelloni' with dill pesto.

The house special of cured duck served with radishes and carrots in honey sauce and mashed potato has again been favourably reported, as has poached guinea fowl with corn pancakes, baby corn and a creamy sweetcorn sauce. Chocolate features prominently in desserts – warm chocolate cake with chocolate and orange sorbet has been praised – or you might prefer to finish with gamle ole, 18-month-old Danish cheese with rye bread and lard, served with 'onions, aspic and rum dripping'. House Vin de Pays d'Oc is £11.50, and there is of course akvavit for purists.

CHEFS: Frank Dietrich and Kay Lundum PROPRIETORS: the Lundum family OPEN: all week L 12 to 3 (4 Sun), Mon to Sat D 6 to 10.30 CLOSED: Christmas, 2 weeks end Aug MEALS: alc (main courses L £6.50 to £14.50, D £10 to £15.50). Set L Mon to Sat £12.50 (2 courses) to £15.50, Set brunch Sun £15.50 (buffet), Set D £17.25 (2 courses) to £21.50 SERVICE: 12.5% (optional), card slips closed CARDS: Amex, Delta, MasterCard, Switch, Visa DETAILS: 40 seats. 15 seats outside. Children's helpings. Wheelchair access (not WC). Music. Air-conditioned ⊖ Gloucester Road, South Kensington

Maison Novelli 

map 13

29 Clerkenwell Green, EC1R 0DU
TEL: (020) 7251 6606 FAX: (020) 7490 1083

COOKING **4**
MODERN EUROPEAN
£40–£77

After spending several years in a business suit, diversifying around London and overseas, Jean-Christophe Novelli has gone back to cooking: for an enlarged restaurant that now includes what used to be Novelli EC1. In the interim, his distinctive Northern French input has been replaced by more universal ideas and materials: pig's trotter has gone, and dishes typically contain lots of ingredients, keeping up to date with the help of cardamom salsa, coriander risotto, chorizo oil and the like.

Early results yielded a simple, effective and refreshing starter of red pepper and tomato gazpacho with lobster, and while the food may lack focus, and standards have see-sawed, the kitchen has turned out successes. Well-timed halibut has come on roughly bashed potatoes with splashes of spring onion oil and red pepper coulis, and a characteristic robustness is evident in meat dishes such as beef fillet with mustard polenta, and in lightly peppered venison sliced over butternut squash Tatin. Desserts seem heavily dependent on chocolate and caramel – a rich and fine chocolate fondant with white chocolate ice cream for example – and while service is well meaning, it can be over-attentive. Four French varietal house wines from the Languedoc are £14.95. Otherwise, there is next to nothing under £20.

CHEF: Jean-Christophe Novelli PROPRIETOR: J.J. Restaurants OPEN: Mon to Fri L 12 to 3, Mon to Sat D 6 to 11 MEALS: alc (main courses £13.50 to £23.50) SERVICE: 12.5% (optional), card slips closed CARDS: Amex, Delta, Diners, MasterCard, Switch, Visa DETAILS: 110 seats. 20 seats outside. Private parties: 110 main room, 30 to 85 private rooms. Vegetarian meals. Music. Air-conditioned ⊖ Farringdon

Mandarin Kitchen

map 13

14–16 Queensway, W2 3RX
TEL: (020) 7727 9012 FAX: (020) 7727 9468

COOKING **3**
CHINESE
£26–£77

A mini Chinatown has grown up around this large, frantically busy eating house, with tables close enough for aromas to float from one to another, and for new acquaintances to be made. Its menu is renowned for running the gamut of seafood, from fish – Dover sole, sea bass, and eel, prepared in various ways – to molluscs: mussels, scallops and razor clams. Crustacean stars include what the menu calls 'gigantic' king prawns as well as the grand specialities of crab and Scottish lobster, the menu recommending a bed of soft noodles for the latter. There are many pork, beef and poultry dishes, with whole or half- chickens roasted Cantonese style, or with ginger and spring onions, or even, as a starter, drunken. Vegetarian dishes are few, but off-menu items were provided to a reporter who, unlike some, has always enjoyed excellent service. House wines are £10.90.

CHEF: K.W. Man PROPRIETOR: Steven Cheung OPEN: all week noon to 11.30 CLOSED: 25 and 26 Dec MEALS: alc (main courses £5 to £25) SERVICE: not inc CARDS: Amex, Delta, Diners, MasterCard, Switch, Visa DETAILS: 110 seats. Private parties: 110 main room. Vegetarian meals. Music. Air-conditioned ⊖ Queensway

Although the cuisine style noted at the top of entries has in most cases been suggested to the Guide by the restaurants, some have been edited for brevity or appropriateness.

🍾 *denotes an outstanding wine cellar;* 🍷 *denotes a good wine list, worth travelling for.*

▲ Mandarin Oriental Hyde Park, Foliage 🍷

LONDON GFG 2001 COMMENDED

map 14

66 Knightsbridge, SW1X 7LA
TEL: (0171) 235 2000 FAX: (0171) 235 4552
WEB SITE: mandarin-oriental.com

COOKING **7**
MODERN EUROPEAN
£40–£60

Just occasionally, a restaurant manages to pull a rabbit out of a hat by offering top quality at an extremely reasonable price. Such is the case with Foliage, its theme inspired by the park visible through double-glazed windows, and emphasised here and there by a leaf motif. While the dining room may not win prizes for décor, its lofty ceiling, comfortable seating, and fine tableware all seem in keeping with the high style to which it aspires. The format is straightforward: three courses for a set price with no supplements, but with a generous eight or nine choices per course at dinner (three at lunch), and everything begging to be tried.

Ingredients are of prime quality, some quite luxurious, for example a ring of warm collops of Scottish lobster, alternating with blobs of dressed caviar, around a small tower of cold crab meat and dark red, smoky-tasting tomato confit. Precise timing is another welcome asset, producing a crisp-skinned fillet of sea bass, accompanied by small pasta cups filled with chopped lobster, and a smooth raisin and caper vinaigrette.

The cooking is sharply honed and provides 'surprises but no shocks'. Scallops have been partnered by creamy turnip purée, plus a couple of large snails and ceps in a refined creamy sauce. Despite the apparent complexity, dishes are harmonious, not least when the foundations are quite classical: two large breasts of fine-flavoured, tender, pot-roast Bresse pigeon, evenly dark red, are served beside a ball of foie gras-enriched green cabbage, with a full-flavoured bouillon brought separately in a small sauce boat.

Delicacy is a feature throughout, for example in a whisky ice cream to accompany hot Cuban chocolate fondant, while the simple skill of turning out a first-rate ice cream is rehearsed in a pain d'épices version, served with a baked apple and calvados soufflé. Service is friendly, helpful and solicitous, and the roll call of fine wines on the French-dominated list is generous to a fault. Mark-ups are not always high, although there is little under £20. House wines at £18 are worth serious consideration.

CHEF: Hywel Jones PROPRIETOR: Mandarin Oriental Hotels OPEN: Mon to Fri L 12 to 2.30, Mon to Sat D 7 to 10.30 MEALS: Set L £19 (2 courses) to £23.50, Set D £32. Bar meals and all-day menu available SERVICE: not inc CARDS: Amex, Delta, Diners, MasterCard, Switch, Visa DETAILS: 50 seats. Private parties: 8 main room, 20 to 200 private rooms. Children's helpings. Wheelchair access (not WC). Music. Air-conditioned ACCOMMODATION: 200 rooms, all with bath/shower. TV. Phone. Room only £295 to £450 (prices exc VAT). Rooms for disabled ⊖ Knightsbridge

---

Restaurateurs justifiably resent no-shows. If you quote a credit card number when booking, you may be liable for the restaurant's lost profit margin if you don't turn up. Always phone to cancel.

Mantanah £

map 12

2 Orton Building, Portland Road, SE25 4UD
TEL: (020) 8771 1148 FAX: (020) 8771 2341
WEB SITE: www.mantanah.co.uk

COOKING **4**
THAI
£22–£42

A fresh coat of powder-blue paint outside, and a reduction in the number of artefacts in the dining room, have improved the appearance of this unpretentious family-run restaurant, where the cooking shows a flair for subtlety and for spice combinations that lift it above the chilli-hot simplicity of much Thai food. All regions of Thailand are covered on the extensive menu, and vegetarians are well-provided for, with nearly a third of the menu given over to meat-free dishes, such as a version of pad Thai noodles with small cubes of tender fried tofu.

Ungreasy and well-flavoured fishcakes come with a sweet-and-sour chilli sauce, and classic tom yum soup has authentically rich and complex flavours. Traditional dishes such as moo pad king (thinly sliced pork with oyster mushrooms, spring onions, garlic and ginger) have also impressed, while innovations include 'Old Fashion', a curry of banana blossom with sweet potato, oyster mushrooms and sweet basil, steamed and served in a container of banana leaves. Fresh fruit may be a better choice than desserts. Service is polite, welcoming and efficient even at busy times, and prices on the brief wine list start at £8.50.

CHEF: Tym Srisawatt PROPRIETOR: Mantanah Ltd OPEN: Tue to Sun D only 6.30 to 11 CLOSED: 25 and 26 Dec, 1 Jan MEALS: alc (main courses £5.50 to £8.50). Set D £16 to £20 SERVICE: 10% (optional), card slips closed CARDS: Amex, Delta, Diners, MasterCard, Switch, Visa DETAILS: 40 seats. Private parties: 40 main room. Vegetarian meals. Children's helpings. No cigars in dining room. Wheelchair access (not WC). Music. Air-conditioned (£5)

Mash

map 15

19–21 Great Portland Street, W1N 5DB
TEL: (020) 7637 5555 FAX: (020) 7637 7333

COOKING **3**
MODERN BRITISH
£29–£57

First-timers might be surprised at what there is to see in this well-designed multi-purpose outlet, from the ground-floor shop and bar, with its huge brewing-vats, to the upstairs dining room, where chrome-supported tables with green glass vases look like a 1950s sci-fi writer's vision of the future. Maddalena Bonino, ex-Bertorelli's (see entry, London Round-ups), now heads the kitchen, and the menus plough a fairly constant furrow. Salmon ceviche with tomato salsa, perky avocado dressing and an unexpected pile of prawn crackers is a lively enough starter, and a well-constructed main course of grilled halibut with garlic courgettes and a dressing of sun-dried peppers and tomatoes suggests that fish might be a smart option.

A wood-fired oven delivers pizzas with toppings ranging from smoked haddock to duck confit, while rich and moist chocolate brownie rounds things off in populist fashion. Grilled pineapple pavlova comes with coconut sorbet, and good cheeses are partnered with pickled things. Wines are arranged by style and offer a cosmopolitan range of Old and New World success stories. Although house wines start at £13, prices are quick to rise above the £30 mark. Around a dozen by the glass offer good variety but are likewise pricey.

CHEF: Maddalena Bonino PROPRIETOR: Oliver Peyton OPEN: all week L 12 to 3 (11 to 4 Sat and Sun), Mon to Sat D 6 to 11.30 CLOSED: 25 and 26 Dec, 1 Jan, Easter Sun and Mon MEALS: alc (main courses £9 to £15.50). Set L £16.50 SERVICE: 12.5% (optional), card slips closed CARDS: Amex, Delta, Diners, MasterCard, Switch, Visa DETAILS: 140 seats. 16 seats outside. Private parties: 28 private room. Vegetarian meals. Children's helpings. Music. Air-conditioned ⊖ Oxford Circus

Matsuri

map 15

15 Bury Street, SW1Y 6AL — COOKING **4**
TEL: (020) 7839 1101 FAX: (020) 7930 7010 — JAPANESE
EMAIL: matsuri@japanglobe.net — £40–£98

Any restaurant located behind Fortnum & Mason must bring expectations of high prices and a certain well-groomed charm. Despite its office-block exterior, Matsuri doesn't disappoint on either count: the cost of an evening meal makes the large choice of set lunches (starting with a cold noodle lunch for £10) seem a bargain. The L-shaped basement dining room's walls are decorated with Japanese fans and lanterns, and large tables are grouped around stainless-steel teppanyaki hotplates. The menu incorporates all the mainstays of Japanese cuisine. Ox tongue with vinegared vegetables, or soft-shelled crab, might appeal from the specialities section, while the range of sushi runs from salmon skin to 'London roll' (with prawns, fish eggs and salmon). Japan meets France in a teppanyaki dish of duck with teriyaki orange sauce, and 'modern Japanese' starters feature tuna with caviar. Service, from waitresses in kimonos, is impeccable, and the wine list concentrates on France, with prices starting at £18. Saké is a recommended alternative.

CHEF: Kanehiro Takase PROPRIETOR: Central Japan Railway Co OPEN: Mon to Sat 12 to 2.30, 6 to 10.30 CLOSED: Christmas, bank hols MEALS: alc (main courses £11 to £30). Set L £10 to £40, Set D £35 to £55 SERVICE: 12.5% (optional), card slips closed CARDS: Amex, Diners, MasterCard, Visa DETAILS: 133 seats. Private parties: 18 main room, 9 private room. Wheelchair access (also WC). Music. Air-conditioned ⊖ Green Park, Piccadilly Circus

Mela

NEW ENTRY **map 15**

152–156 Shaftesbury Avenue, WC2H 8HL — COOKING **2**
TEL: (020) 7836 8635 FAX: (020) 7379 0527 — INDIAN
WEB SITE: www.melarestaurant.co.uk — £16–£46

Soho's vitality now extends to this stretch of Shaftesbury Avenue in the shape of a lively Indian brasserie. A single peacock-blue wall, deep-red fabrics, and colourful artefacts stand out, and the glass-enclosed kitchen is by the entrance. The clientele is a happy mixture of families and young people, and the light, ungreasy food is varied enough to please all. Dinner offers original starters: guinea-fowl samosas, and bhalla papri chaat (mini puris of lentils), calling for spoons to scrape up the sweet-and-sour yoghurt and tamarind sauce. Main courses are listed as 'tandoori' (among them moist chicken leg marinated in beetroot juice and chillies), 'tawa' (hotplate), 'vegetarian' and 'traditional'; curries in the last group include accurately cooked saffron-flavoured lamb with almonds. For dessert, briefly roasted fruit kebab is a possibility. One-course bread-based snacks with various toppings and fillings are the norm at lunchtimes. House wines on the short, modestly priced wine list are £8.90.

CHEF: Kuldeep Singh PROPRIETOR: Chandan Ltd OPEN: all week 12 to 11.45 MEALS: alc D (main courses £7 to £12). Set L £4.95 (1 course), Set D 5.30 to 7 £9.95 to £29.95 (for 2 people) SERVICE: 12.5% (optional), card slips closed CARDS: Amex, Delta, MasterCard, Switch, Visa DETAILS: 85 seats. 10 seats outside. Private parties: 27 main room, 45 private room. Vegetarian meals. Wheelchair access (not WC). Music. Air-conditioned ⊖ Leicester Square, Tottenham Court Road

Mem Saheb £ map 15

65–67 Amsterdam Road, E14 3UU
TEL/FAX: (020) 7538 3008
EMAIL: memsabeb@memsaheb.demon.co.uk
WEB SITE: www.memsaheb.demon.co.uk

COOKING 1
INDIAN
£23–£37

Neither the exterior of this bar and restaurant, nor its river view, has benefited greatly from the Docklands revival, but the inside is pleasantly and simply decorated: one of the two rooms with wooden flooring, the other carpeted, with white tablecloths and napkins in both. The menu draws inspiration from Goa for chicken cafrael and lamb xacuti, Bangladesh for fillets of boal (giant catfish), and southern India for konju papas (prawns with tamarind, mustard seeds, and coconut, giving a nice balance of hot and sour). There are no thalis, but for single diners, or couples, combination dishes make for interesting eating, including chicken jalfrezi with bhuna lamb, and king prawn bhuna with fish masala. House wines are £7.95.

CHEF: Anwar Hussain PROPRIETORS: Mridul Kanti Das, Rabiul Hoque and Iuliana Kadir OPEN: Mon to Fri L 12 to 2.30, all week D 6 to 11.30 CLOSED: 25 and 26 Dec MEALS: alc (main courses £6 to £10) SERVICE: not inc CARDS: Amex, Delta, Diners, MasterCard, Switch, Visa DETAILS: 80 seats. 12 seats outside. Private parties: 40 main room, 40 private room. Car park. Vegetarian meals. Children's helpings. No smoking in 1 dining room. Wheelchair access (not WC). Music. Air-conditioned ⊖ Canary Wharf (£5)

Mesclun £ map 12

24 Stoke Newington Church Street, N16 0LU
TEL: (020) 7249 5029 FAX: (020) 7275 8448

COOKING 3
MODERN EUROPEAN
£23–£38

A high-ceilinged but intimate place in the heart of Stoke Newington, Mesclun specialises in what might be described as modern bistro food. In the low-lit and engagingly cramped room, meals begin with home-baked bread with a dish of green tapénade before going on to such well-rendered standards as intensely flavoured carrot and coriander soup, or salmon fishcakes with tsatsiki. Aubergine, the vegetable of the moment, appears deep-fried as a starter with Bayonne ham and buffalo mozzarella.

Daily fish specials are nearly always good, and may include red snapper, or properly cooked cod falling in glistening flakes into a well-judged red wine sauce. Meats include duck confit with rösti, and calf's liver with smoked bacon, onion gravy and a mound of mash. Finish with lemon tart that arrives under a hat of caramelised zest, a rich, gooey and satisfying chocolate tart with coffee syrup, or crème brûlée. Service has been described as 'chaotic but charming'. Nearly everything on the short wine list is under £20, with house French and Italian £9.95.

CHEF: Dirceu Pozzebon PROPRIETORS: Dirceu Pozzebon and Salih Çiçek OPEN: Mon to Sat D only 6 to 11 CLOSED: 1 week Christmas MEALS: alc (main courses £8 to £13). Set D 6 to 7.30 £10.95 (2 courses) to £12.95 SERVICE: 10% (optional), card slips closed CARDS: Delta, MasterCard, Switch, Visa DETAILS: 34 seats. Private parties: 14 main room. Vegetarian meals. No cigars/pipes in dining room. Wheelchair access (not WC). Music. Air-conditioned (£5)

Metrogusto

NEW ENTRY **map 12**

153 Battersea Park Road, SW8 4BX
TEL: (020) 7720 0204 FAX: (020) 7720 0888

COOKING **3**
MODERN ITALIAN
£24–£46

A plainly decorated room with wooden tables and white walls is the setting for Ambro and Susi Ianeselli's mission to serve a contemporary version of Italian food in an English context. By the time the Guide appears, they should also be doing it at a second branch in Islington (11 Theberton Street, N1). Menus point to the crossover, with a linguistic mix that produces 'timballino di grano and sun-dried cherry tomatoes con funghi', and 'polletto in umido con mash di patate'. Indeed unusual combinations are one of the kitchen's hallmarks.

A salad of buffalo mozzarella and segments of blood orange opened one spring dinner, and a main course of duck has been served divertingly like a tall hamburger layered between Jerusalem artichokes with a beetroot ketchup relish. Finish with pear and almond tart accompanied by a highly acclaimed Pecorino ice cream, or perhaps a sweet red-bean cream flavoured with Earl Grey. Front-of-house is run with great warmth and charm. The Italian wine list is a pedigree collection, but most bottles are well over £20. House wines from the Piedmont house of Bava, a Chardonnay and a Barbera d'Asti, are £11.50.

CHEF: Antonello Serra PROPRIETORS: Ambro and Susi Ianeselli OPEN: all week L 12 to 2.45 (3.30 Sat and Sun), Mon to Sat D 6.30 to 10.45 MEALS: alc (main courses £8.50 to £14.50) SERVICE: 10% (optional), card slips closed CARDS: Delta, MasterCard, Switch, Visa DETAILS: 48 seats. Private parties: 50 main room. Vegetarian meals. Children's helpings. No-smoking area. Wheelchair access (not WC). Music

Mezzo

map 15

100 Wardour Street, W1 3LE
TEL: (020) 7314 4000 FAX: (020) 7314 4040
WEB SITE: www.mezzo.co.uk

COOKING **3**
MODERN EUROPEAN
£22–£73

A wide, curving staircase leads down to a huge, bright basement with ceramic masks of heavily made-up women on the walls, and plastic M-shaped ashtrays on tables. Smoking is positively encouraged, as is the consumption of seafood, which shares the wide-ranging carte with a few grills and roasts, alongside modern British plates of braised rabbit leg with cumin-spiced aubergine, or rump of lamb with chickpeas, chorizo and sour cream. Timings are sound, seasonings fine and ingredients fresh. First-course salads have included deep-pink, gamey pigeon breast on a pile of richly dressed leaves, while 'nicely chargrilled' baby chicken is typical of straightforward, well-executed main courses. Cheeses may be a better bet than dessert.

Beyond its superficial sophistication, service is deemed unprofessional and careless, and prices are considered high. Wines are well chosen but have been poorly handled; house Vin de Pays d'Oc is £12.75. Mezzonine on the ground floor has switched allegiance from Asian food to Middle Eastern, and now serves 'skewers' of, for example, chicken with lemon and garlic, lamb kofte with pine nuts and cumin, and Moroccan-spiced salmon, all at £4.95 (including salad and pitta bread).

CHEF: David Laris PROPRIETOR: Conran Restaurants Ltd OPEN: Mezzo all week 12 to 3, 6 to 12 (1 Fri and Sat, 11 Sun); Mezzonine Mon to Sat 12 to 3, 5.30 to 1 (3 Fri and Sat) CLOSED: 25 Dec, 1 Jan MEALS: Mezzo alc (main courses £11.50 to £16.50). Set L and D before 7 £12.50 (2 courses) to £15.50. Cover £5 after 10pm. Mezzonine alc (main courses £6.50 to £11). Set L and D before 7 £8.90 (2 courses) to £11.90 SERVICE: 12.5% (optional), card slips closed CARDS: Amex, Delta, Diners, MasterCard, Switch, Visa DETAILS: Mezzo 350 seats, Mezzonine 130 seats. Private parties: 500 main room, 44 private room. Vegetarian meals. Wheelchair access (also WC). Music. Air-conditioned ⊖ Piccadilly Circus

Mirabelle **map 15**

56 Curzon Street, W1Y 8DL — COOKING **6**
TEL: (020) 7499 4636 FAX: (020) 7499 5449 — FRENCH
WEB SITE: www.whitestarline.org.uk — £31–£88

Apart from fine food at reasonable prices, an exciting interior, professional service, a phenomenal wine list, a worthy history, grade-A location and real buzz, what has Mirabelle got to offer? A new chef for a start, who supervises the production of Marco Pierre White's repertoire of dishes, many with a classical French bias. This is up-market brasserie food, served in the glamorous surroundings of a basement with enough daylight not to feel like one, trompe l'oeil wall paintings, and four long uncluttered rows of tables occupied by a colourful cross-section of the beau monde. The long and relatively unchanging menu of some 30 savoury items may seem like a production line, but the selling point is good renditions of generally comforting dishes that soothe rather than challenge.

'You feel in capable hands,' summed up one visitor, sharing a meal of pretty unbeatable foie gras parfait, nuggets of pot-roast pork strewn with springtime vegetables, and first-rate crisp-skinned sea bass in a light brown reduction. Some of the food may appear to have lost a little of its edge in terms of materials and workmanship, and not all menu terminology retains its original meaning, but the general level of consistency remains high, from a big disc of nicely judged omelette Arnold Bennett to simple but accomplished fresh fruits in champagne jelly, and voluptuous chocolate fondant with milk ice cream. Staff are numerous and unflappable, and wines are an impressive collection of fine bottles from around the world, although French classics dominate. There is little under £20, but the sommelier's selection charts some interesting possibilities under £30 and is a good place to begin. Around a dozen wines by the glass start at £3.75.

All entries, including Round-ups, are fully indexed at the back of the Guide.

CHEF: Martin Caws PROPRIETOR: Marco Pierre White OPEN: all week 12 to 2.30 (3 Sat and Sun), 6 to 11.30 MEALS: alc (main courses £13.50 to £26). Set L £14.95 (2 courses) to £17.95 SERVICE: 12.5% (optional), card slips closed CARDS: Amex, Delta, Diners, MasterCard, Switch, Visa DETAILS: 110 seats. Private parties: 120 main room, 36 and 48 private rooms. Music. Air-conditioned ⊖ Green Park

Mr Kong £

map 15

21 Lisle Street, WC2H 7BA
TEL: (020) 7437 7341 FAX: (020) 7437 7923

COOKING **3**
CHINESE
£21–£39

In a long-running Cantonese restaurant such as this, where little changes, it takes a sharp-eyed regular to note that its famous speciality, paper-wrapped chicken (previously available only on request), is now actually listed beside the 20 other chicken dishes. Also on the menu are old-time stalwarts from won ton soup, to spring rolls and sweet-and-sour pork, as well as less familiar dishes, such as stewed oysters with roasted pork and mushrooms, steamed minced pork with salted egg, and sauté vegetables with dried scallop.

Under 'miscellaneous dishes', temptations for the adventurous include Mr Kong's special stuffed aubergine with green peppers and bean curd, fried scallop with minced prawn rolls, and boiled ox tripe. The even more enticing specials of the day might include such delicacies as boiled cuttlefish with jellyfish, deep-fried crispy aubergine with yam paste and sweet-and-sour sauce, or braised goose web with fish lips and sea cucumber. The unchanging décor and sometimes brusque service might not be attractions, but the cooking certainly is. House wines are £7.50.

CHEF/PROPRIETOR: Mr K. Kong OPEN: all week noon to 2.45am CLOSED: 24 to 26 Dec MEALS: alc (main courses £5 to £12). Set D £9.30 to £22 SERVICE: not inc CARDS: Amex, Delta, Diners, MasterCard, Switch, Visa DETAILS: 110 seats. Private parties: 50 main room. Vegetarian meals. Music. Air-conditioned ⊖ Leicester Square

Miyama

map 15

38 Clarges Street, W1Y 7PJ
TEL: (020) 7499 2443 FAX: (020) 7493 1573

COOKING **3**
JAPANESE
£24–£90

Dating from a time (nearly 20 years ago) when a cheap Japanese meal was still an impossibility in London, Miyama is a select Mayfair restaurant that does not try to compete with the value-conscious sushi and noodle bars currently in vogue throughout the capital. Bright lighting, largely monochrome furnishings and courteous, kimono-clad waitresses lend an authentic feel to the place. Most customers are Japanese, many of them on business. The menu is wide-ranging, covering everything from teriyaki to tempura, sashimi to sushi. Set meals provide an easy way of ordering a balanced selection, and high-quality ingredients and attractive presentation characterise the food. Dinner might begin with a complimentary appetiser of pickled cold meat cubes, followed by starters of tuna sashimi or soft-shell crab. Teppanyaki beef fillet as a main course comes as fine bite-sized seared chunks. An old-fashioned, limited wine list (house wine £10) is supplemented by Japanese beers and saké.

CHEF/PROPRIETOR: Mr F. Miyama OPEN: Mon to Fri L 12 to 2.30, all week D 6 to 10.30 CLOSED: 25 Dec, 1 Jan, L bank hols MEALS: alc (main courses £10 to £24). Set L £12 to £18, Set D £34 to £42 SERVICE: 15%, card slips closed CARDS: Amex, Delta, Diners, MasterCard, Switch, Visa DETAILS: 64 seats. Private parties: 26 main room, 4 and 8 private rooms. Wheelchair access (not WC). Music. Air-conditioned ⊖ Green Park

Mon Plaisir

map 15

21 Monmouth Street, WC2H 9DD
TEL: (020) 7836 7243 FAX: (020) 7240 4774

COOKING **2**
FRENCH
£25–£57

Despite a more up-to-date menu, this half-century-old fixture still offers a good deal. Tablecloths, now cloth instead of paper, plus bright lighting and colourful pictures suit a twenty-first-century bistro. The short carte and blackboard specials typically offer a modern salad of duck confit with celery and pear rémoulade and lentils, or roast sea bass on crushed potatoes with glazed shallots and red wine reduction. The menu Parisienne includes a glass of wine to wash down escargots or black pudding, followed by grilled rib of beef, and home-made tart of the day. Nostalgia rules in the 'classiques', such as onion soup, coquilles Saint-Jacques meunières, steak tartare, and coq au vin. Comments on service are mixed. Some have found it charming, even when trying to deal with the non-arrival of various items, from bread to vegetables to water. House wine on the almost entirely French list is £10.50.

CHEF: Richard Sawyer PROPRIETOR: Alain Lhermitte OPEN: Mon to Fri L 12 to 2.15, Mon to Sat D 5.50 to 11.15 MEALS: alc (main courses £9.50 to £16). Set L £14.95, Set D before 8 £14.95 (inc wine), Set D £23.50 (min 2, inc wine) SERVICE: 12.5% (optional), card slips closed CARDS: Amex, Delta, Diners, MasterCard, Switch, Visa DETAILS: 96 seats. Private parties: 30 main room. Vegetarian meals. Children's helpings. Wheelchair access (not WC). Music. Air-conditioned ⊖ Covent Garden, Leicester Square

Montana

map 12

125–129 Dawes Road, SW6 7EA
TEL: (020) 7385 9500 FAX: (020) 7386 0337
EMAIL: congress@montana.plc.uk
WEB SITE: www.hartfordgroup.co.uk

COOKING **2**
CONTEMPORARY AMERICAN
£30–£55

This is the original branch of the little restaurant empire that devotes itself to bringing the fiery cuisine of the southwest USA (not in fact Montana at all) to London. A different musician struts his or her stuff every night, and the broad and expansive welcome is unmistakably Stateside in style. A corn blini topped with tequila-cured salmon with cucumber salsa and horseradish cream sets the tastebuds up for what's to come, which might be a portion of roast halibut with a pleasant and unusual accompaniment of citrus bean stew. This is hearty stuff – there are 10oz steaks and braised lamb shank to contend with too – and the kitchen evidently feels at home with it. Most desserts seem to be partnered with an ice cream or sorbet, raspberry and melon sorbets getting the vote at inspection. A trend-conscious wine list includes Californian versions of Viognier, Gewürztraminer and Sangiovese. Prices go from £12.

CHEF: Cynthia Mascarenhas PROPRIETOR: Hartford Group OPEN: Mon to Thur D only 6.30 to 11, Fri 12 to 4, 6.30 to 11, Sat 12 to 11, Sun 12 to 5, 6.30 to 11 CLOSED: 25 Dec MEALS: alc (main courses £9 to £15). Set L £14 (2 courses). Brunch Sat and Sun 12 to 5 SERVICE: 12.5%, card slips closed CARDS: Amex, MasterCard, Visa DETAILS: 80 seats. Vegetarian meals. Children's helpings. Wheelchair access (not WC). Music. Air-conditioned ⊖ Fulham Broadway

▲ Montcalm Hotel, Crescent

map 15

Great Cumberland Place, W1A 2LF
TEL: (020) 7402 4288 FAX: (020) 7724 9180
EMAIL: montcalm@montcalm.co.uk

COOKING **4**
MODERN BRITISH
£22–£33

'This must be the best value in London,' enthused one visitor, while another felt able to entertain the 'humblest and snootiest' here with equal assurance. Money lavished on décor has been well spent, producing lots of space, big tables, rich furnishings, expensive flowers and a tasteful line in artefacts. Although there are one or two supplements (for foie gras and lobster), prices include coffee with good petits fours, and half a bottle of Chilean Cabernet-Merlot or Vin de Pays d'Oc Chardonnay.

The kitchen is an enthusiastic one, with seafood a strong suit judging by hot and cold oysters (three grilled with pancetta, three in champagne jelly), scallop ravioli, and roast salmon with crab and sweetcorn chowder. Dishes are self-contained, and their components impress: creamy potato purée with a large rare steak, or faultless risotto with crispy sea bass. Among dramatically decorative desserts might be a nougatine and raspberry compote, or a white chocolate box of tiramisù with cappuccino ice cream. For those who prefer to splash out on wine, a short but varied list is on hand.

CHEF: Stephen Whitney PROPRIETOR: The Montcalm – Hotel Nikko OPEN: Mon to Fri L 12.30 to 2.30, all week D 6.30 to 10.30 MEALS: Set L and D £20 (2 courses) to £25 (inc wine). Bar menu available all week. Supper menu available Sun SERVICE: not inc CARDS: Amex, Diners, MasterCard, Switch, Visa DETAILS: 60 seats. Private parties: 80 main room, 20 to 60 private rooms. Vegetarian meals. Children's helpings. No-smoking area. Wheelchair access (not WC). Occasional music. Air-conditioned ACCOMMODATION: 120 rooms, all with bath/shower. TV. Phone. Room only £220 to £600. Rooms for disabled. Baby facilities ⊖ Marble Arch (£5)

Moro

map 13

34–36 Exmouth Market, EC1R 4QE
TEL: (020) 7833 8336 FAX: (020) 7833 9338
WEB SITE: www.moro-restaurant.com

COOKING **6**
SPANISH/NORTH AFRICAN
£26–£43

Even without the range of sherries, this is an intoxicating place for relaxed enjoyment of distinctive food which has its roots in Spain, North Africa and the Middle East. The lack of pretence is signalled by a long zinc bar, wooden floor, bare tables and an open-to-view kitchen. A wood-fired oven produces, among other things, splendid springy bread, which comes with olive oil for dunking.

Tapas, available all day, run to baba ghanoush, Spanish omelette, roasted almonds, marinated anchovies, and piquillo peppers, some assisted by a liberal application of garlic, all full of flavour. Chickpeas, pomegranate molasses, sumac, tahini and judion beans are just some of the evocative ingredients, and results range from a satisfying white bean, nettle and paprika soup to a crisp, deep-fried brik, filled with chopped egg, anchovy, and a whole egg, its yolk still runny, accompanied by fierce harissa sauce.

The oven is applied to cod, pork belly, chicken and duck, while the charcoal grill has turned out well-flavoured lamb – black outside, pink within – served with beetroot and a yoghurt and garlic sauce. Still popular among desserts are the orange tart with thin crisp pastry, and Malaga raisin ice cream with a slug of Pedro Ximénez. Staff are young, relaxed and pleasant, and a short but sharply chosen wine list adds to the appeal. House French is £9.75, but consider Albariño Valminor and Rioja Amezola for more characterful drinking.

CHEFS: Mr and Mrs Sam Clark PROPRIETORS: Sam Clark and Mark Sainsbury OPEN: Mon to Fri L 12.30 to 2.30, Mon to Sat D 7 to 10.30 CLOSED: Christmas to New Year, bank hols MEALS: alc (main courses £9.50 to £14.50). Tapas menu available SERVICE: not inc CARDS: Amex, Delta, Diners, MasterCard, Switch, Visa DETAILS: 75 seats. 16 seats outside. Private parties: 14 main room, 12 private room. Vegetarian meals. Wheelchair access (also WC). No music. Air-conditioned ⊖ Farringdon

Moshi Moshi Sushi £ map 13

24 Upper Level, Liverpool Street Station, EC2M 7QH
TEL/FAX: (020) 7247 3227
7–8 Limeburner Lane, EC4M 7HY
TEL: (020) 7248 1808 FAX: (020) 7248 1807
Level 2, Cabot Place East, Canary Wharf, E14 4QT
TEL: (020) 7512 9911 FAX: (020) 7512 9201
WEB SITE: www.moshimoshi.co.uk

COOKING **2**
JAPANESE
£12–£26

The conveyor belt, with its colour-coded plates of sushi, is the centrepiece at all three branches, with chefs preparing dishes in front of you. The technological service is modern, but the only non-classic thing on the menu is the phrase 'Japanese tapas' heading a list of small dishes, some available only in the evening. Among them are aji no tataki (marinated horse mackerel with ginger and spring onions), and usuzukuri (thinly sliced sashimi of red snapper). Hot dishes include gyoza (deep-fried pork and vegetable dumplings), prawn and vegetable tempura, and various donburi (bowls of rice) topped with eel, salmon, chicken, or assorted fish and vegetables. Temaki, hand-rolled sushi, are made to order at the counter. Finish with fruit salad, or a sweet pancake filled with custard, and drink green tea, saké, or house white at £8.80, red at £12.80. Details below are based on Liverpool Street and may vary at the other two branches. A new branch was due to open in Brighton as the Guide went to press.

CHEF: Sui Hong PROPRIETOR: Caroline Bennett OPEN: Mon to Fri 11.30 to 9 CLOSED: Christmas, Easter, bank hols MEALS: alc (plate prices £1.50 to £3). Set L and D £5.90 to £11.50. Cover 50p SERVICE: none, card slips closed CARDS: Delta, MasterCard, Switch, Visa DETAILS: 82 seats. Private parties: 100 main room. Vegetarian meals. No smoking in dining room. Wheelchair access (not WC). Music. Air-conditioned ⊖ Liverpool Street

Card slips closed *in the details at the end of an entry indicates that the total on the slips of credit cards is closed when handed over for signature.*

National Gallery, Crivelli's Garden

LONDON GFG 2001 COMMENDED

map 15

NEW ENTRY

Trafalgar Square, WC2N 5DN
TEL: (020) 7747 2869 FAX: (020) 7747 2438

COOKING 4
FRENCH/MEDITERRANEAN
£27–£40

The location over the foyer of the National Gallery's Sainsbury Wing provides views of Trafalgar Square from tables near the high windows. They are reserved for the restaurant, which is beyond a Tuscan bar section offering a range of the pizzas applauded in other Red Pepper Group of restaurants (see Red Pepper, Green Olive, Purple Sage, White Onion, all in London), plus salads, bruschette and panini. Afternoon tea is also served, with or without a smoked salmon sandwich and a glass of champagne. The whole area is carpeted, resulting in a contented hum.

In the restaurant, charming and helpful service brings interesting breads in a dim sum basket as part of one-, two- or three-course set-price menus. Starters range from straightforward salade niçoise, via gnocchi with wild mushrooms and rocket, to a salad of tender marinated beef with carrots and caramelised onion. Among the three meat and three fish main dishes have been crisp, lightly battered deep-fried sole with sauce gribiche, and grilled marinated rib of pork with lemon mash and baby artichoke; a vegetarian option has offered mille-feuille of polenta and grilled vegetables with tomato coulis. Cheeses come with bread, biscuits, grapes and walnuts, while a strawberry sablé sandwiches the fruit between discs of flawlessly soft yet crisp shortbread. The wine list, mostly Italian, and mainly under £20, offers house wines from £9.75, with 12 by the glass.

CHEFS: Eric Guignard and Pasquale Manni PROPRIETOR: Red Pepper Group OPEN: all week L 12 to 3, Wed D 6 to 8 CLOSED: 25 and 26 Dec, Easter MEALS: Set L and Wed D £13.50 (1 course) to £17.50 SERVICE: 12.5% (optional), card slips closed CARDS: Amex, Delta, MasterCard, Switch, Visa DETAILS: 120 seats. Vegetarian meals. No smoking in dining room. Wheelchair access (also WC). No music ⊖ Charing Cross

National Portrait Gallery, Portrait

NEW ENTRY map 15

Trafalgar Square, WC2 0HE
TEL: (020) 7312 2490 FAX: (020) 7925 0244
EMAIL: portrait.restaurant@talk21.com

COOKING 3
MODERN BRITISH
£30–£50

The view from the restaurant at the revamped National Portrait Gallery can lay just claim to being one of the best in London. One whole wall is given over to picture windows, the vista taking in Nelson's Column, Big Ben and the London Eye, and Kerwin Browne's cooking is just as appealing as the view. Indeed this is exactly the sort of restaurant one ought to find in a gallery or museum. Dishes are deftly handled yet sturdily built and boldly flavoured, from a generous starter of ham knuckle with green beans and shallots, to mains of salt-cod fishcake with artichoke salad and aïoli, and well-hung, flavourful, grilled ribeye steak with new season's garlic, all distinguished by fine raw materials.

A few organic ingredients turn up, along with sensible notions such as Lancashire cheese tartlet with poached egg, and roast rabbit with black olives and tomatoes. Desserts put new spins on old ideas, producing doughnuts with coffee cream, or roast peaches with punch sorbet and lavender shortbread. Friendly and helpful service adds to the pleasure. A compact but impressive range of globally sourced wines includes some organic bottles. Prices are refreshingly low for London, with house French starting at £11.95, plenty around the £20 mark, and 18 by the glass.

CHEF: Kerwin Browne PROPRIETOR: Searcy's OPEN: all week L 11.45 to 2.45, Thur and Fri D 5.30 to 8.30 MEALS: alc (main courses £11 to £15) SERVICE: 10% (optional), card slips closed CARDS: Amex, Delta, MasterCard, Switch, Visa DETAILS: 100 seats. Private parties: 60 main room. Vegetarian meals. No smoking in dining room. Wheelchair access (also WC). No music. Air-conditioned ⊖ Leicester Square

Neal Street Restaurant

map 15

26 Neal Street, WC2H 9PS
TEL: (020) 7836 8368 FAX: (020) 7240 3964

COOKING **4**
ITALIAN
£44–£77

After 16 years, the handsome dark blue frontage of Antonio Carluccio's thorough-going Italian restaurant still looks discreetly expensive, while bright geometric paintings and a collection of hand-carved walking sticks divert attention from the fact that tables are sardined together. The menu is classic Carluccio, and likely to remain so when Kirk Vincent leaves during the currency of this edition. Materials are persuasive, with mushrooms to the fore: a mixed sauté of what is available on the day, or a thick, rich and satisfying soup garnished with fried porcini, for example.

Dishes can be as straightforward as a plate of San Leo prosciutto, and as accomplished as butter-soft chunks of calfs liver bound in a thin but rich sauce sharpened with vinegar. Successful fish options have included sea bass with braised fennel, although cold and overcooked halibut was a disappointment at inspection. Desserts take in tiramisù, and a huge, crumbly wedge of ricotta tart with a craggy, fluffy filling enlivened with orange zest and raisins. A 15 per cent service charge, and the absence of a fixed-price lunch menu, can result in large-ish bills. Prices on the Italy-centred wine list are not exactly competitive either, starting at £14 and rising quickly, but there are plenty of pedigree bottles.

CHEF: Kirk Vincent PROPRIETOR: Antonio Carluccio OPEN: Mon to Sat 12.30 to 2.30, 6 to 11 CLOSED: Christmas to New year MEALS: alc (main courses £10 to £19.50) SERVICE: 15% (optional), card slips closed CARDS: Amex, Delta, Diners, MasterCard, Switch, Visa DETAILS: 65 seats. Private parties: 24 main room, 24 private room. Vegetarian meals. No pipes in dining-room. Wheelchair access (not WC). No music. Air-conditioned ⊖ Covent Garden

---

£ *means that it is possible to have a three-course meal, including coffee, half a bottle of house wine and service for £25 or less per person, at any time the restaurant is open, i.e. at dinner as well as lunch. It may be possible to spend considerably more than this, but by choosing carefully you should find £25 or less achievable.*

New End

NEW ENTRY **map 13**

102 Heath Street, NW3 1DR
TEL: (020) 7431 4423 FAX: (020) 7794 7508

COOKING **4**
EUROPEAN
£29–£59

Tom Ilic, formerly at Searcy's in the Barbican (see entry), moved to Hampstead in early 2000, giving the already thriving local restaurant scene a bit of a lift. The venue is a bright, modern corner site, with windows opening on to the pavement, and dramatic flower photographs against exposed brick aiming for the high class look. Robust European flavours characterise the cooking: for example in a large slice of foie gras and ox tongue terrine edged with compressed dried fig and served with brioche; thick, creamy white-bean soup has also been praised.

Fish is well handled, including roast fillets of John Dory with baby fennel and a red pepper vinaigrette, and a variation on surf and turf in which turbot has been unusually but successfully partnered with braised rabbit, accompanied by an impeccable truffled velouté containing peas, broad beans and tomato. For dessert there may be rich yet zingy lemon syllabub, or a warm compote of berries with Granny Smith sorbet. Wines are divided into two short lists: one a broad range with lots from the New World (prices starting at £13.95), the other a sheet of fine wines, concentrating on Bordeaux and Burgundies.

CHEF: Tom Ilic PROPRIETOR: Charles Elliot OPEN: Wed to Sun L 12 to 2.45, Tue to Sun D 6 to 10.45 MEALS: alc D (main courses £10.50 to £18.50). Set L £15 (2 courses) to £17.80 SERVICE: not inc CARDS: Amex, Delta, MasterCard, Switch, Visa DETAILS: 50 seats. Vegetarian meals. No cigars/pipes in dining room. Wheelchair access (not WC). Occasional music ⊖ Hampstead

New Tayyabs £

map 12

83 Fieldgate Street, E1 1JU
TEL/FAX: (020) 7247 9543
EMAIL: tayyab@lineone.net
WEB SITE: www.tayyabs.co.uk

COOKING **3**
PAKISTANI
£13–£30

This Pakistani café might be a little rudimentary in design – plastic-topped tables, an L-shaped counter, and bright lighting are features – but its exemplary cooking attracts devotees from both within and outside the local Pakistani and Bangladeshi community. Tandoori food is especially accomplished (witness well-marinated and subtly spiced mutton tikka), and vegetarian dishes are also enthusiastically received, including a notable pumpkin curry (a daily special cooked with pulses and plenty of spices). For dessert, kulfi can be supplemented with takeaways from Tayyabs' sweet centre next door. Waiters are genuinely friendly, but service is sometimes a mite haphazard (starters and main courses turning up together, for instance). 'The trick is to go early,' according to one reader keen to avoid the crowds. The restaurant is unlicensed, although diners can bring their own alcohol. New Tayyabs is closed at lunchtime, when its next-but-one neighbour Tayyabs is open.

CHEF/PROPRIETOR: M. Tayyab OPEN: all week D only 5 to 11.30 MEALS: alc (main courses £4 to £10) SERVICE: not inc CARDS: none DETAILS: 80 seats. 8 seats outside. Vegetarian meals. Children's helpings. Music ⊖ Whitechapel

Nico Central

map 15

35 Great Portland Street, W1N 5DD
TEL: (020) 7436 8846 FAX: (020) 7436 3455

NEW CHEF
FRENCH
£28–£62

Nigel Trebble arrived just as the Guide went to press, too late for us to award a cooking mark, but he is expected to continue producing the same modern brasserie fare that has always been the restaurant's stock in trade. That might include salmon ballottine wrapped in endive with a herb salad, roast duck breast with lentils and a foie gras sauce, and maybe frangipane pear tart, or crème brûlée with raspberry sorbet to finish. A good international wine list is offered at prices that are reasonable for the area. Southern French house wines, a Grenache Blanc and a Merlot, are £12.

CHEF: Nigel Trebble PROPRIETOR: Restaurant Partnership OPEN: Mon to Fri L 12 to 2.20, Mon to Sat D 6.30 to 11 CLOSED: bank hols MEALS: alc (main courses £14 to £18.50). Set L £14.50 (2 courses) to £18.50 SERVICE: 12.5% (optional) CARDS: Amex, Delta, Diners, MasterCard, Switch, Visa DETAILS: 50 seats. Private parties: 50 main room, 10 private room. Vegetarian meals. Music. Air-conditioned ⊖ Oxford Circus

Nicole's

map 15

158 New Bond Street, W1Y 9PA
TEL: (020) 7499 8408 FAX: (020) 7409 0381

COOKING **4**
MODERN EUROPEAN
£42–£66

The restaurant operation of Nicole Farhi's designer boutique is as studiedly chic as her couture. Natural materials such as limestone, oak and leather have been used to fit it all out, and the sense of understatement is reflected in the raised stainless-steel bar area. Casually dressed, seamlessly professional staff reinforce the tone. Not that there is anything pallid or minimal about Annie Wayte's cooking style. This is global larder stuff, with the emphasis on bold, vivid flavours.

Seafood is treated robustly, producing grilled squid with chilli and lime-marinated black beans, and a pairing of baked sea bream and monkfish accompanied by Moroccan spiced couscous and harissa. Grilled veal chop, meanwhile, comes with braised white beans, garlic, tomato and rosemary. Fine British and Irish cheeses make a sound alternative to puddings such as baked vanilla cheesecake with sun-dried cherries, or rhubarb and custard tart. Breakfasts and afternoon teas are also served. The wine list motors around to pick up some tempting bottles, but prices (which start at £12.50) soon rise to New Bond Street levels.

CHEF: Annie Wayte PROPRIETOR: Stephen Marks OPEN: Mon to Sat L 11.30 to 5.30, Mon to Fri D 6.30 to 10.45 CLOSED: bank hols MEALS: alc (main courses £16 to £19.50). Breakfast, afternoon tea and bar meals available. Cover £1 (12 to 4, 6 to 11) SERVICE: 12.5% (optional), card slips closed CARDS: Amex, Delta, Diners, MasterCard, Switch, Visa DETAILS: 90 seats. Private parties: 90 main room. Vegetarian meals. No-smoking area. Music. Air-conditioned ⊖ Green Park, Bond Street

The Guide's longest-serving restaurants are listed near the front of the book.

Noble Rot

NEW ENTRY **map 15**

3–5 Mill Street, W1R 9TF
TEL: (020) 7629 8877 FAX: (020) 7629 8878
WEB SITE: www.noblerot.com

COOKING **5**
MODERN EUROPEAN
£43–£83

Under the same ownership as 1 Lombard Street (see entry), Noble Rot is a long, thin restaurant with large windows and a few old-fashioned 'psychedelic and groovy' paintings. Matthew Owsley-Brown's CV includes stints with Rick Stein (see Seafood Restaurant, Padstow) and Henry Harris at Harvey Nichols (see Fifth Floor, London), so he is no stranger to modern European ideas, which here include more or less straight renditions of regional specialities, such as Alsatian choucroute, périgourdine gizzard salad, and lobster armoricaine. Luxuries abound, from truffled chicken breast to foie gras several ways: an impeccably prepared terrine served with noble rot jelly, and a spicier version with oily piquillo pepper and chilli salt.

As well as turning out straightforward but skilfully prepared dishes such as fresh and well-timed sea bass with lemon-flavoured couscous, the kitchen demonstrates a bit of flair and imagination with its lobster and snow crab gazpacho, tea-smoked halibut, and an unusual terrine combining powerful Valrhona chocolate with a central kernel of foie gras, served with a slick of caramel sauce made from Pineau des Charentes. Sweet wine recommendations come into their own with foie gras and desserts: Noble One Botrytis with the chocolate and foie gras terrine, for example; there is also a list of 26 botrytised wines and a dozen other assorted sweet wines, nearly all available by the glass (but no half-bottles) at prices ranging from £4.50 for Miranda Estate Golden Botrytis 1995 to £33 for Ch. D'Yquem 1990. The rest of the wine list offers just two bottles under £20, plus six house wines which are also available by the glass.

CHEF: Matthew Owsley-Brown PROPRIETOR: Soren Jessen OPEN: Mon to Sat 12 to 4, 6 to 11 MEALS: alc (main courses £11 to £25). Bar L available SERVICE: 12.5% (optional), card slips closed CARDS: Amex, Delta, Diners, MasterCard, Switch, Visa DETAILS: 60 seats. 28 seats outside. Private parties: 45 main room. Vegetarian meals. Children's helpings. Wheelchair access (not WC). Music. Air-conditioned ⊖ Oxford Circus

Nobu

map 15

Metropolitan Hotel, 19 Old Park Lane, W1Y 4LB
TEL: (020) 7447 4747 FAX: (020) 7447 4749

COOKING **5**
JAPANESE/SOUTH AMERICAN
£35–£105

Here at the very sharpest end of plutocratic West End fashion, black-clad staff are both alert and charming, clientele are smartly turned out, and banquette seating affords eyrie-like views of Park Lane. A distinctive take on fusion food deftly links the Orient with Latin America, and if the menu appears to confuse by the sheer number of choices it offers, take a leaf out of one visitor's book: choose about three dishes per head and let them come as staff think best.

Raw or nearly raw items, including various types of sashimi and ceviche, are given the spotlight, in, say, sashimi salad of seared tuna in a soy-based Matsuhisa dressing, and raw tuna dressed in Japanese citrus and slivers of jalapeño chilli. Rock shrimp tempura is tossed in a sparse creamy sauce, the top-notch beef version of sashimi is seared so lightly as to remain red-raw within, while Peruvian spiced chicken skewer is rubbed with smouldering chilli marinade. Artfully presented desserts have included chocolate cake with green tea ice cream, and orange charlotte dressed up to look like the Millennium Dome. Fine wines and creative cocktails, share the drinks list with a selection of sakés, but prices tend to be high. Languedoc varietals, a Marsanne and a Merlot, open the bidding at £15.

CHEF: Mark Edwards PROPRIETORS: Nobuyuki Matsuhisa, Robert De Niro and Drew Nieporent OPEN: Mon to Fri L 12 to 2.15, all week D 6 to 10.15 (11 Fri and Sat, 9.30 Sun) CLOSED: public hols MEALS: alc (main courses £8.50 to £22.50). Set L £24 to £50, Set D £70 SERVICE: 12.5%, card slips closed CARDS: Amex, Delta, Diners, MasterCard, Switch, Visa DETAILS: 150 seats. Private parties: 120 main room. Vegetarian meals. No smoking in 1 dining room. No cigars or pipes. Wheelchair access (not WC). Occasional music. Air-conditioned ⊖ Hyde Park Corner

Oak Room Marco Pierre White

map 15

21 Piccadilly, W1V 0BH
TEL: (020) 7437 0202 FAX: (020) 7851 3141

COOKING **6**
FRENCH
£52–£82

Although it still bears his name, the Oak Room has lost some of its magic since Marco Pierre White retired from active service. It is still a grand setting. Drinks are sipped in the antechamber, and meals eaten in the massively proportioned dining room, where male business groups predominate, and a massive display gobbles up the flower budget. The MPW repertoire (which surfaces at several restaurants, including Mirabelle and Belvedere; see entries) takes in, for example, foie gras parfait scattered with crushed peppercorns sitting in a pool of Sauternes jelly, an aspic of oysters and watercress, and grilled lobster with béarnaise mousseline. Prices, thankfully, have been reduced to rather more realistic levels.

Timing has varied from a very bloody, gamey, tender Bresse pigeon wrapped in a cabbage leaf with equally rare foie gras, to slices of Pauillac lamb, brown rather than pink, with a strewing of sweetbreads and vegetables. Fish is sensitively handled: for example a roundel of silky raw salmon, vivid and clean-flavoured, with dill, chervil and spinach pressed round the edge, attended by caviar and nuggets of crayfish. Desserts may struggle to reach the same heights, but a crème caramel Box Tree friandises, to give it its full name, has provided a slippery treat. Service is deferential and obliging; the maître d' is enthusiastic, other staff less so. Prices on the biblically proportioned wine list are written in pencil, though that doesn't lessen their impact. Ordinary mortals would appreciate more help under £20 rather than 64 vintages of Ch. D'Yquem, most in four figures. House wine is £18.

CHEF: Robert Reid PROPRIETOR: Marco Pierre White OPEN: Mon to Fri L 12 to 2.30, Mon to Sat D 7 to 11.15 CLOSED: bank hols MEALS: Set L £20 (2 courses) to £30, Set D £38 to £48 SERVICE: not inc CARDS: Amex, Delta, Diners, MasterCard, Switch, Visa DETAILS: 80 seats. Private parties: 120 main room, 70 to 100 private rooms. Vegetarian meals. No cigars/pipes in dining room. Wheelchair access (also WC). No music. Air-conditioned ⊖ Piccadilly Circus

The nearest underground station is indicated at the end of London entries.

L'Odéon

map 15

65 Regent Street, W1R 7HH
TEL: (020) 7287 1400 FAX: (020) 7287 1300

COOKING **4**
MODERN FRENCH
£31–£73

With Piccadilly Circus just round the corner, this is as central a location as one could wish for; and since it is on the first floor, customers with window seats can find themselves eyeballing passengers on double decker buses that stop outside. Considered rather smart and formal for a large brasserie, it offers a wide-ranging carte in full blown contemporary mode, starting with simple rock oysters and shallot vinegar, seared foie gras with a prune and cinnamon tarte Tatin, and pea risotto with Parma ham and a poached egg. No culinary stone is left unturned, it would seem, judging by sesame-crusted tuna, grilled chicken served with spicy couscous and a dressing of preserved lemon and coriander, and desserts such as chocolate cappuccino or peach tart with basil and mascarpone ice cream. Reports of dryness and lack of flavour have taken the shine off a couple of meals during the year, however. 'Native regional grape varieties' lend colour to a sound wine list that makes few concessions on price, although a dozen or more house recommendations (from £13.50) are also offered by the glass.

CHEF: Colin Layfield PROPRIETORS: Pierre and Kathy Condou OPEN: Mon to Sat 12 to 2.45, 5 to 10.45 CLOSED: bank hols MEALS: alc (main courses £14.50 to £22). Set L and D before 7 £14.50 (2 courses) to £19.50. Cover £1.50 SERVICE: 12.5% (optional) CARDS: Amex, Delta, Diners, MasterCard, Switch, Visa DETAILS: 220 seats. Private parties: 20 main room, 20 private room. Vegetarian meals. Children's helpings. No-smoking area. Wheelchair access (also WC). Music. Air-conditioned ⊖ Piccadilly Circus

Odette's

map 13

130 Regents Park Road, NW1 8XL
TEL: (020) 7586 5486 FAX: (020) 7586 2575
EMAIL: odettes@aol.com

COOKING **5**
MODERN BRITISH
£20–£58

Odette's is a 'great local restaurant'. More up-market than many, its broad appeal is carefully nurtured and sensitively managed, offering the choice between a bright garden room at the back and a genteel mirrored front dining room whose French doors open to the street in fine weather. Simon Bradley favours a predominantly European approach and has the good sense to keep things simple, be it roast root vegetable terrine with horseradish dressing, or grilled halibut with stir-fried greens. Although results may look straightforward, that does not prevent him producing a starter of pig's head with mustard and poached egg, or a dessert of pears in walnut shortcake with nutmeg ice cream and espresso butterscotch.

The set lunch offers no choice, but its value remains astonishingly good. Typical of the output has been shellfish bisque followed by chargrilled leg of lamb with sauce paloise, and rhubarb and blood orange fool with pistachio nut shortbread. Downstairs, the wine bar conveys no sense of being a poor relation, having its own less formal, less expensive but equally appealing menu of smoked haddock and mozzarella risotto, roast neck of lamb with greens and gratin dauphinoise, and warm baked chocolate truffle. Service has varied from slow to prompt but is generally attentive and friendly. Stylistically arranged, the wine list is a joy to read and includes the great and the good from around the world. Virtually all palates and prices are catered for, and tasting notes are helpful. Thirty wines by the glass (including seven sweet ones) increase the chance of a perfect food/wine combination.

CHEF: Simon Bradley PROPRIETOR: Simone Green OPEN: Sun to Fri L 12.30 to 2.30, Mon to Sat D 7 to 11 CLOSED: 1 week Christmas, bank hols MEALS: alc (main courses £10.50 to £17.50). Set L £10 SERVICE: not inc CARDS: Amex, Delta, Diners, MasterCard, Switch, Visa DETAILS: 60 seats. 10 seats outside. Private parties: 30 main room, 8 and 30 private rooms. Vegetarian meals. Children's helpings. No music ⊖ Chalk Farm

Offshore

map 13

148 Holland Park Avenue, W11 4UE
TEL: (020) 7221 6090 FAX: (020) 7313 9700
EMAIL: reservations@offshore.uk.com
WEB SITE: www.offshore.uk.com

COOKING **1**
SEAFOOD
£23–£63

After its refurbishment, this place looks handsome enough, with South Seas paintings and artefacts standing out against cream walls, and well-spaced, neatly set tables. There is a bar menu at lunchtimes and in the early evening, with a set-price lunch too, but the main event is a carte, with just two main dishes for carnivores (perhaps including a flavourful pan-fried fillet of lamb). The rest is seafood, with starters of fish carpaccio (with scallop as an optional extra), or a fresh and piquant white gazpacho with smoked mussels and black radish. Main courses have taken in grilled snapper with a ginger and chilli tomato sauce, tiger prawns with pumpkin fritters, and grilled fillet of sea bass with caraway rice and asparagus. Wine prices start at £14.50 for a Loire Sauvignon Blanc, but soon ascend beyond £20, with some extraordinary bottles among the 'private cellar and bin-ends'.

CHEF: Pascal Boursier PROPRIETORS: Philippe Cohen and Lina Haggar OPEN: Mon to Fri L 12 to 3, Mon to Sat D 6.30 to 11.30 CLOSED: bank hols MEALS: alc (main courses £11.50 to £19.50). Set L £12.95 (2 courses) to £15.50 SERVICE: 12.5% (optional), card slips closed CARDS: Amex, Delta, Diners, MasterCard, Switch, Visa DETAILS: 65 seats. 10 seats outside. Private parties: 40 main room, 15 and 25 private rooms. Vegetarian meals. Children's helpings. No smoking in 1 dining room. Wheelchair access (not WC). Music. Air-conditioned ⊖ Holland Park, Shepherd's Bush (£5)

Old Delhi

map 13

48 Kendal Street, W2 2BP
TEL: (020) 7723 3335

COOKING **2**
INDIAN/IRANIAN
£37–£84

The imperial crown of Persia on the menu is a sure enough sign that there is more to Old Delhi than the name alone might suggest. In a sophisticated and comfortable setting, it offers on the one hand a familiar list of Indian dishes and, on the other, an insight into Iranian cuisine. Specialities include kebabs, gormeh sabsi (lamb stewed with herbs and vegetables), gaimeh (lamb with split peas and dried lime), and, under the heading 'special lamb or chicken dish', those meats cooked with aubergines, fried onions and garlic. Among Persian starters are savoury meatballs, and combinations of aubergine with yoghurt and sometimes egg. Monkfish tikka is an innovative Indian dish, but more conventional dhal soup, chicken vindaloo with saffron rice, and the usual accompaniments of raita and poppadoms have all been endorsed. House wines are £11.50, and Ch. Margaux 1982 is £1,195. Other good bottles bridge the gap.

CHEFS: Mr Bhatti and Mr H. Jalalrand PROPRIETOR: Oldelms Ltd OPEN: all week 12.30 to 3.30 (1 to 4 Sat, Sun and bank hols), 6.30 (7 Sat, Sun and bank hols) to 11 CLOSED: 24 to 31 Dec MEALS: alc (main courses £8.50 to £26) SERVICE: 15% (optional) CARDS: Amex, Delta, Diners, MasterCard, Switch, Visa DETAILS: 54 seats. Private parties: 20 main room. Vegetarian meals. No children under 10 after 8pm. Wheelchair access (not WC). Music Wed and Sat D (£2 cover). Air-conditioned ⊖ Marble Arch

Olivo

map 13

21 Eccleston Street, SW1W 9LX
TEL: (020) 7730 2505 FAX: (020) 7824 8190

COOKING **2**
ITALIAN/SARDINIAN
£29–£50

Self-confident, upbeat and invariably crowded, Olivo, with its blue and gold colour scheme, can be counted on to produce some convincingly characterful Sardinian food. One reporter greatly enjoyed the whole show, from the 'really green virgin olive oil for us to dunk our great country bread chunks in' to a creamy and sharp lemon tart for pudding. In between, there is much char-grilling: of stuffed baby squid, vegetables from peppers to courgettes, as well as veal escalope, and marinated lamb with rosemary. Otherwise, a Pecorino-dressed salad might be followed by sauté lambs' kidneys with lentils and artichokes from the set-price lunch menu. The simplicity is welcome, for example in a plate of grilled calf's liver with spinach, and desserts can be rather rich: perhaps sebada, a deep-fried pastry shell filled with cheese and dressed with honey. All wines are from Italy, starting off with Sardinian house wines at £11.

CHEF: Marco Mellis PROPRIETORS: Jean-Lousi Journade and Mauro Sanna OPEN: Mon to Fri L 12 to 2.30, all week D 7 to 11 CLOSED: Christmas, Easter, bank hols MEALS: alc D (main courses £11 to £14). Set L £15 (2 courses) to £17.50. Cover £1.50 SERVICE: not inc, card slips closed CARDS: Amex, Delta, MasterCard, Switch, Visa DETAILS: 45 seats. Private parties: 6 main room. Vegetarian meals. No cigars/pipes in dining room. No music. Air-conditioned ⊖ Victoria

1 Lombard Street

map 13

1 Lombard Street, EC3V 9AA
TEL: (020) 7929 6611 FAX: (020) 7929 6622
EMAIL: lombard@1lombardstreet.com
WEB SITE: www.1lombardstreet.com

COOKING **4**
MODERN EUROPEAN
£41–£91

A large brasserie with a circular bar under its cupola represents the informal half of this City restaurant. It plays to the gallery with adult nursery food, from prawn and crab cocktail, via wild mushrooms on toast, to chicken Kiev, and Cumberland sausage and mash. Beyond this is a smaller and quieter dining room with more serious purpose, where starters cost as much as main courses in the brasserie. Here the tone is more classical. Barigoule artichokes come with a liquorice, fennel and olive oil infusion, fillet of lamb (poached, not roasted) comes in a mint broth, and black-leg chicken is served with morels and vin jaune.

Seafood embraces the posh end of the spectrum – lobsters, langoustines, scallops, sea bass and turbot – and other luxuries are neatly sewn into the tapestry: fillet of Angus beef with seared foie gras and white truffle oil mash. 'Specialities' for two include sea bass baked in salt with a ginger and wasabi beurre blanc, while puddings range from a feuillantine of caramelised Granny Smith with Guinness ice cream to a bitter Ecuadorian chocolate pyramid with almond milk granité. Few wines on the well-chosen list make it under the £20 barrier, among them eight house wines all available by the glass.

CHEF: Herbert Berger PROPRIETOR: Soren Jessen OPEN: Mon to Fri 11.30 to 3, 6 to 10 CLOSED: bank hols MEALS: alc (main courses £24.50 to £29.50). Set L £32 (2 courses) to £39, Set D £22 (2 courses) to £28. Brasserie menu also available SERVICE: 12.5% (optional) CARDS: Amex, Delta, Diners, MasterCard, Switch, Visa DETAILS: 210 seats. Private parties: 250 main room, 32 private room. Music. Air-conditioned ⊖ Bank

192

map 13

192 Kensington Park Road, W11 2ES
TEL: (020) 7229 0482 FAX: (020) 7229 3300

COOKING **1**
MODERN BRITISH
£25–£51

Don't think of this place as a 'regular' restaurant, advised one visitor, who felt it seemed more like a club for well-heeled thirty-somethings and Gallagher brothers lookalikes. Arrive early and it will just be gearing up; get there at 10pm and it should be approaching full swing. Starters outnumber mains on the short carte, and might take in a leek, broccoli and Cheddar tart, half a dozen small seared scallops arranged around a pile of lentils, or a salad of kumquats, chicory, beetroot and parsnips that impressed for its interesting textures. Sound materials have included good-quality rack of lamb cooked as requested, and moist, fresh and flavoursome baked cod on a potato cake with fennel and green beans. Finish perhaps with smooth and well-flavoured sorbets under a dribble of chocolate sauce, or banoffi tart made with firm, sweet pastry. Service is good-natured rather than sharp, and wines are varied and full of interest, with fair choice under £20. House vin de pays is £10.50.

CHEF: Mark Parry PROPRIETOR: The Groucho Club plc OPEN: all week 12.30 to 3 (3.30 Sat and Sun), 6.30 to 11.30 (11 Sun) CLOSED: 25 and 26 Dec, 1 Jan, Aug bank hol MEALS: alc (main courses £7.50 to £13.50). Set L Mon to Fri £11.50 (2 courses), Set L Sun £12.50 (2 courses) SERVICE: not inc, 12.5% for parties of 6 or more CARDS: Amex, Diners, MasterCard, Switch, Visa DETAILS: 96 seats. 16 seats outside. Private parties: 12 main room. Vegetarian meals. Children's helpings. No-smoking area. Wheelchair access (not WC). Occasional music. Air-conditioned ⊖ Notting Hill Gate

The cuisine styles noted at the tops of entries are only an approximation, often suggested to us by the restaurants themselves. Please read the entry itself to find out more about the cooking style.

▲ One-O-One

map 14

101 William Street, SW1X 7RN
TEL: (020) 7290 7101 FAX: (020) 7235 6196

COOKING **5**
SEAFOOD
£43–£99

Part of the Sheraton Hotel, this brightly decorated, glassed-in restaurant is one of the best fish specialists in town. Pascal Proyart is a particular whiz when it comes to sea bass, which might appear caked in rock salt (for two), or pan-roasted and surrounded by a truffled salad and jus. Given the location, luxuries are to be expected, although their manifestation may be unusual: for example, a terrine combining foie gras and langoustine, accompanied by a light truffle cream. Other treatments span the range from familiar Dover sole with langoustine and asparagus, to rather more adventurous brill with mango-apple fondant, ginger mash and a coconut and curry emulsion.

Shellfish offerings might include Maine lobster salad, dived scallops with candied tomato, and a creature they reckon is exclusive to them, at least in the UK: royal king crab (a type of snow crab) from the Barents Sea, its legs served either with parsley butter and sauce vierge, or else on black truffle risotto. Among other options, crispy duck with Chinese cabbage has been 'delicate, delightful and memorable'. Desserts are well thought out, combining, for example, a mini chocolate soufflé with banana sorbet and a pool of piña colada sauce, or else an apple and goats' cheese honey-crusted parcel with ginger ice cream. Service is so professional and friendly it is considered 'exemplary', and wines are so heavily marked up that even Mouton-Cadet is £27. Perhaps better stick to an abstemious wine by the glass (there are 16).

CHEF: Pascal Proyart PROPRIETOR: Starwood Hotels and Resorts OPEN: all week 12 to 2.30, 7 to 10.30 MEALS: alc (main courses £15.50 to £32). Set L £21 (2 courses) to £25 SERVICE: not inc, card slips closed CARDS: Amex, Delta, Diners, MasterCard, Switch, Visa DETAILS: 86 seats. Private parties: 120 main room. Children's helpings. Wheelchair access (also WC). Music. Air-conditioned ACCOMMODATION: 289 rooms, all with bath/shower. TV. Phone. Room only £219 to £319. Rooms for disabled. Baby facilities ⊖ Knightsbridge (£5)

L'Oranger

map 15

5 St James's Street, SW1A 1EF
TEL: (020) 7839 3774 FAX: (020) 7839 4330

COOKING **6**
FRENCH/MEDITERRANEAN
£41–£78

In the most indelibly old-English quarter of London, surrounded by gentlemen's outfitters, hatters, shoemakers and suchlike, and with leather sofas and wood panelling of its own, L'Oranger makes its French presence felt discreetly. A generous carte (with a few supplements) doesn't let the grass grow under its feet, as it combines prime fish and meat with such ideas as provençale chickpea soup, and braised Swiss chard in veal broth with bone marrow and herbs. Although details (such as seasoning) can sometimes throw dishes off balance, they are generally well constructed, highlighting for example the potent contrast between crisp smoky bacon and sweet seared scallops, or combining fiercely pan-fried, but just cooked, turbot with peas à la française.

Such combinations are hardly ground-breaking, but timing, materials, judgement, and the welcome absence of gimmicks lift them above the norm: roast breast of corn-fed chicken makes a fine main course, for example, generously accompanied by honey-coloured girolles. Caraib chocolate fondant with nougat and vanilla ice-cream is still mentioned in dispatches, while a tartlet of summer berries with a haunting violet aroma and a sorbet of fromage blanc made a lasting impression on one diner. Other desserts have been under par, incidentals vary in quality, and determinedly French service ranges from polished to unco-ordinated. The wine list picks its way meticulously through the crus and communes of Burgundy and Bordeaux before gesturing perfunctorily elsewhere. Mark-ups are fierce and there is no house wine; the opening price is £19.

CHEF: Kamel Benamar PROPRIETOR: A to Z Restaurants OPEN: Mon to Fri L 12 to 2.30, Mon to Sat D 6 to 11 MEALS: Set L £20 (2 courses) to £24.50, Set D £35 (2 courses) to £39.50 SERVICE: 12.5% (optional), card slips closed CARDS: Amex, Delta, Diners, MasterCard, Switch, Visa DETAILS: 55 seats. 12 seats outside. Private parties: 8 main room, 20 private room. Children's helpings. Wheelchair access (not WC). No music. Air-conditioned ⊖ Green Park

Orrery

map 15

55 Marylebone High Street, W1M 3AE
TEL: (020) 7616 8000 FAX: (020) 7616 8080
EMAIL: patrickf@conran-restaurants.co.uk
WEB SITE: www.orrery.co.uk

COOKING **6**
CLASSIC FRENCH
£37–£101

No one is left in any doubt that this is a Conran restaurant, of which there are now 16, counting overseas branches. Occupying a long, narrow, first-floor room (above a Conran food shop), with windows down one side, a mirror along the other, it lays out Conran-branded mineral water, butter dishes, ashtrays and matches: smoking is positively encouraged. The food is smooth, slick, and 'safe' in the sense that what it lacks in thrills it makes up for in proper handling of first-class raw materials, with many items beyond criticism: a 'modern, clean, spare version of Elizabeth David', one visitor suggested. Jarret de veau is pure French provincial, as is boeuf bourguignon, and breast of duck with sarladaise potatoes.

Seafood is well handled, judging by impeccably fresh scallops turned into a thin pancake of overlapping slices, then roasted, served on a mound of leeks, surrounded by a thin, creamy sauce. Timing is generally accurate, making the most of roast pigeon breasts served on a mound of roughly chopped Savoy cabbage and mushrooms, followed a short while later by the braised legs; accompaniments have included 'unctuous' olive oil mash. Textural contrasts show to good effect in a pineapple dessert combining caramelised fruit, crisps and fresh pineapple with a shyly flavoured ice cream. Cheeses (English and French) and bread are also singled out for praise. Service is smart, formal and polished – 'nothing goes unnoticed' – without being overbearing. Prices, already on the high side, are not helped by a wine list (admittedly top quality) that all too rarely dips below £20, plus of course the 'optional' service charge on everything.

The Guide always appreciates hearing about changes of chef or owner.

CHEF: Chris Galvin PROPRIETOR: Conran Restaurants Ltd OPEN: all week 12 to 2.45, 7 to 10.45 (10.30 Sun) CLOSED: 25 and 26 Dec, Good Fri MEALS: alc (main courses £14.50 to £23.50). Set L £23.50, Set D Mon to Sat £45 to £75, Set D Sun £28.50 to £75 SERVICE: 12.5% (optional), card slips closed CARDS: Amex, Delta, Diners, MasterCard, Switch, Visa DETAILS: 80 seats. Private parties: 80 main room. Vegetarian meals. No pipes in dining room. Wheelchair access (also WC). No music ⊖ Baker Street, Regent's Park

Osteria Antica Bologna 🍷 £ map 12

23 Northcote Road, SW11 1NG
TEL/FAX: (020) 7978 4771

COOKING **3**
ITALIAN
£23–£49

An Australian-Italian partnership running a rustic Italian eating house near Clapham Junction seems as improbable as some of the menu. Ancient Roman cuisine is a closed book to most people, but here you might find epytirium (herbed ricotta with olives, cumin, coriander, broad beans, chicory and a garlic crostino) or haedum sive agnum particum (lamb cooked with prunes, thyme, onion and garum with herbed barley). Most assaggi (tasters) come in starter or main-course sizes, as do pasta dishes such as ravioli with aubergine and smoked cheese, but it is worth remembering that portions tend to be large.

Some details epitomise the best of Italian cooking: grilled polenta, for example, is crisp outside, feather-light inside, and also unexpectedly light is rich chocolate and date tart with cream and vanilla ice cream. Service sometimes comes under pressure from sheer numbers. Jugs of Sicilian house wine at £8.90 offer good-value, uncomplicated drinking, while the full list reveals plenty of stylish bottles from the length and breadth of Italy. Tasting notes are helpful and straightforward: Vinnae, made from the native Ribolla Gialla grape, is described as 'the boss's favourite' and costs £23.50.

CHEF: Aurelio Spagnuolo PROPRIETORS: Rochelle Porteous and Aurelio Spagnuolo OPEN: Mon to Thur 12 to 3, 6 to 11, Fri 12 to 3, 6 to 11.30, Sat noon to 11.30, Sun noon to 10.30 CLOSED: Christmas to New Year MEALS: alc (main courses £7 to £16). Set L Mon to Sat £8.50 (2 courses). Cover 80p SERVICE: 10% (optional), card slips closed CARDS: Amex, Delta, MasterCard, Switch, Visa DETAILS: 70 seats. 12 seats outside. Private parties: 20 main room. Vegetarian meals. Music. Air-conditioned (£5)

Oxo Tower 🍾 map 13

Oxo Tower Wharf, Barge House Street, SE1 9PH
TEL: (020) 7803 3888 FAX: (020) 7803 3838
EMAIL: marc.whitley@harveynichols.co.uk

COOKING **5**
MODERN BRITISH
£40–£78

In the few years it has been operating, Oxo Tower has itself become a landmark nearly as famous as some of the ones it overlooks. Spectacular views alone are a good enough reason to make the trip to the eighth floor, and it is possible to get a table by the window in the restaurant without being a celebrity: simply arrive early, suggests one reporter. Choice is generous on a modern British menu that makes good use of the global larder, whether at the luxury level – ravioli of lobster and black truffle – or at the artisanal, represented by Spanish charcuterie from acorn-fed pigs.

Clean flavours are exemplified by tuna and crab sashimi roll with wasabi mayonnaise, and risotto is well reported: asparagus with smoked Alsace bacon has been first class. Among more resourceful and successful ideas might be steamed brill fillet with a prawn and lemon mousse, accompanied by cauliflower cream and a shellfish jus. Portion sizes vary but tend to be large, so extra vegetables may not be necessary, and in any case it is well worth leaving room for desserts such as pain perdu with caramelised pineapple, or lemon parfait with poached rhubarb.

Service at its best has been attentive and efficient, making for a comfortable and enjoyable time. A 25-strong selection of house wines, opening at £12.50, provides plenty of choice for those put off by the bulk of 'the Big list'. It deserves the title, combining classic French hits with many impressive New World wines. Prices remain reasonable with plenty of interesting wines under £20 a bottle.

CHEFS: Simon Arkless and Mitchel Hill PROPRIETOR: Harvey Nichols Restaurant Ltd OPEN: Sun to Fri L 12 to 3 (3.30 Sun), all week D 6 to 11.30 (10.30 to 6.30 Sun) MEALS: alc D (main courses £13 to £25). Set L £27.50 SERVICE: 12.5% CARDS: Amex, Delta, Diners, MasterCard, Switch, Visa DETAILS: 130 seats. 80 seats outside. Private parties: 130 main room. Vegetarian meals. Children's helpings. Wheelchair access (also WC). No music. Air-conditioned ⊖ Blackfriars

Ozer

LONDON GFG 2001 COMMENDED

NEW ENTRY **map 15**

4–5 Langham Place, W1N 7DD
TEL: (020) 7323 0505
FAX: (020) 7323 0111

COOKING **5**
MODERN OTTOMAN
£29–£64

Huseyin Ozer founded the Sofra chain, a restaurant group that did much to bring Turkish cooking to a wide audience. His new richly appointed restaurant aims to raise the culinary stakes in an idiom now described as 'modern Ottoman'. Menus are full of Eastern enticements, starting with the touchstone dish, imam bayaldi, the aubergine cooked to oily softness, the pungently tomatoey topping stewed long and slow, an object lesson in how to achieve power and depth of flavour. Fish is good all round, from seared tuna in a spiced filo crust (served with a fragrant, gently spicy chutney of ginger, fig and lime), to a lightly grilled sea bream fillet accompanied by a caraway-seeded cake of chickpeas and a vivid saffron sauce.

Shoulder of lamb, meanwhile, is roasted and basted kleftiko-fashion and given added tang with a marmalade of kumquats and limequats. The must-have dessert would appear to be baby aubergines that are cooked, filled with a cumin-scented sorbet of the flesh, and served with red wine ice cream. Rose-water, pistachios and melissa tea also add convincing aromatic character to desserts. Staff are friendly and efficient but can be over-zealous. 'France' and 'Worldwide' are the geographical indicators on the wine list, the latter providing interest in the shape of Greece, Morocco, Lebanon and Turkey, but not much in the way of price relief. House Chardonnay and Cabernet Sauvignon are £13.50.

All entries in the Guide are re-researched and rewritten every year, not least because restaurant standards fluctuate. Don't rely on an out-of-date Guide.

CHEF: Jérome Tauvron PROPRIETOR: Huseyin Ozer OPEN: Sun to Fri L 12 to 2.30, all week D 6 to 11 MEALS: alc D (main courses £12 to £19.50). Set L and D 6 to 7.30 £14.95 (2 courses) to £17.95 SERVICE: 12.5% (optional), card slips closed CARDS: Amex, Delta, Diners, MasterCard, Switch, Visa DETAILS: 90 seats. Private parties: 110 main room. No cigars/pipes in dining room. Wheelchair access (also WC). Occasional music. Air-conditioned ⊖ Oxford Circus

Palais du Jardin

map 15

136 Long Acre, WC2E 9AD
TEL: (020) 7379 5353 FAX: (020) 7379 1846

COOKING **2**
FRENCH
£24–£60

Reporters always seem to find the Palais crammed – the bar in particular is very popular – and a certain amount of judicious elbowing may be necessary to reach the dining area. Amid the flamboyant flower displays and party atmosphere you may dine fairly classically on dressed crab, generous platters of fruits de mer, or finely rendered, moist lobster thermidor. Seafood seems to be the key, but don't overlook sauté lamb with button onions and mushrooms in mustard sauce, with a plate of the well-reported dauphinois (charged separately). Desserts might include crème brûlée with rhubarb and custard sorbet, or roast peaches with champagne and strawberry ice cream. Service can suffer lapses, what with the press of custom, but people seem to emerge happy. France dominates the wine list, with white Burgundy fans particularly well looked after. House wines from Bouchard Aîné are £11.50, or £3.50 for a 200ml glass.

CHEF: Winston Matthews PROPRIETOR: Le Palais du Jardin Ltd OPEN: all week 12 to 3.30, 5.30 to 11.45 CLOSED: 25 and 26 Dec, half-day 1 Jan MEALS: alc (main courses £8.50 to £21.50) SERVICE: 12.5% (optional), card slips closed CARDS: Amex, Delta, Diners, MasterCard, Switch, Visa DETAILS: 250 seats. 20 seats outside. Private parties: 150 main room. Vegetarian meals. Wheelchair access (not WC). Music. Air-conditioned ⊖ Covent Garden, Leicester Square

Parade

NEW ENTRY **map 12**

18–19 The Mall, W5 2PJ
TEL: (020) 8810 0202 FAX: (020) 8810 0303

COOKING **5**
MODERN EUROPEAN
£29–£49

By comparison with central London, the suburbs tend to get neglected, but Rebecca Mascarenhas and James Harris have made them something of a speciality, bringing Sonny's to Barnes, Phoenix to Putney (see entries, London), and now Robert Jones to Ealing. Despite a large glass frontage, Parade looks positively discreet amid the flurry of coloured awnings round about; it combines a long zinc bar with a stark yet welcoming white dining room decorated with fine modern paintings and photographs.

The menu may look like just another magpie collection of modern British dishes featuring ideas from Italy and the Orient, but it is worth remembering that Robert Jones has worked with both Stephen Bull and Philip Howard (see Stephen Bull and the Square, both London). He is a talented chef who brings a keen sense of culinary intelligence to bear, for example in a complex starter featuring a crispy fritter of gelatinous pig's trotter, beside a fine, flavourful cube of belly pork with 'exquisite' crackling, all offset by a lightly acidic rocket and araccina bean salad.

Notably fresh seafood has included crab cannelloni, while pink roast duck breast has come with first-class frites. Although not all flavours have been equally well balanced, those in a Thai salad – hot, sweet chilli and herby coriander with crisp noodles and firm squid – demonstrate the essence of good judgement. Anglo-French desserts run from apple and prune clafoutis to summer pudding with a strident berry sauce and clotted cream. Olive bread is a bonus, and the friendly service is considered exemplary. A short, effective wine list starts with house vins de pays at £10.50.

CHEF: Robert Jones PROPRIETORS: Rebecca Mascarenhas and James Harris OPEN: all week L 12.30 to 3.30 (3 Sun), Mon to Sat D 6.30 to 11 CLOSED: 25 Dec, bank hols MEALS: alc L (main courses £12.50). Set L £15 (2 courses) to £18.50, Set D £19.50 (2 courses) to £23.50 SERVICE: 12.5% (optional), card slips closed CARDS: Amex, Delta, MasterCard, Switch, Visa DETAILS: 100 seats. Private parties: 100 main room, 40 private room. Vegetarian meals. Children's helpings. No cigars/pipes in dining room. Wheelchair access (also WC). No music. Air-conditioned ⊖ Ealing Broadway

Passione

map 15

10 Charlotte Street, W1P 1HE
TEL: (020) 7636 2833 FAX: (020) 7636 2889
EMAIL: liz.przybylskie@lineone.net

COOKING **4**
MODERN ITALIAN
£33–£54

If Charlotte Street appears to be thriving, it is due in no small measure to restaurants such as Passione. Its bright, clean, modern space is both airy and intimate, while the cooking is modern Italian; or perhaps modern London-Italian might be nearer. The menu is a sensible length, with a balance between meat, fish and vegetables, ingredients are fresh, and dishes look good. Starters invariably include a few salads: honey fungus with olives, garlic and chilli for example, or smoked duck with artichokes, rocket and parmesan.

Wild sorrel risotto is something of a fixture, and seafood runs from squid ink tagliatelle with scallops, to griddled swordfish spiked with capers, anchovies and mint. Along with such agreeable diversity goes an equally welcome traditional strain producing a winning calf's liver and onions for one reporter. As for dessert, enthusiasm for the limoncello and wild strawberry ice cream continues virtually unabated. Expect a warm welcome, and courteous, efficient and unobtrusive service. 'Bravo!' exclaimed one enthusiast for the 30-strong, carefully chosen and sympathetically priced Italian wine list. House Puglian red and Verdicchio white are £10.50.

CHEF: Gennaro Contaldo PROPRIETORS: Gennaro Contaldo, Gennaro D'Urso and Liz Przybylski OPEN: Mon to Fri L 12.30 to 2.30, Mon to Sat D 7 to 10.30 CLOSED: 1 week Christmas, bank hols MEALS: alc (main courses £10 to £16) SERVICE: 10% (optional), card slips closed CARDS: Amex, Delta, Diners, MasterCard, Switch, Visa DETAILS: 40 seats. 8 seats outside. Private parties: 18 main room, 12 private room. Vegetarian meals. Wheelchair access (not WC). No music ⊖ Goodge Street

If a restaurant is new to the Guide this year (did not appear as a main entry in the last edition), NEW ENTRY *appears opposite its name.*

Pétrus

map 14

33 St James's Street, SW1A 1HD
TEL: (020) 7930 4272 FAX: (020) 7930 9702

COOKING 7
FRENCH
£38–£88

Pétrus is a serious and 'stonkingly good' restaurant with a high comfort level and businesslike atmosphere. It is plush and discreet, with well-spaced tables and white napery, and feels classy without being intimidating. Although luxuries play a part, Marcus Wareing's high French style of cooking gratifies partly because it is not too complicated and partly because he combines a true understanding of flavours and textures with the ability to balance the composition of a dish.

Among many reported successes are a chunk of super-fresh braised halibut (materials are beyond reproach) with baby leeks and black truffle, accompanied by a delicate horseradish sabayon; and foie gras (a menu staple), typically roasted, perhaps served with caramelised Cox's apple and a Banyuls wine reduction. Pasta, often in the form of ravioli, is a favoured vehicle for pairing flavours: perhaps filled with leek and onion confit as a partner for sauté scallops, or given centre stage when stuffed with sweetbreads in a well-judged combination with braised salsify and a sherry vinegar jus.

A sense of lightness also adds to the appeal, even with red meats such as tender venison on rösti with a fricassee of peas and girolles, or well-sourced and accurately timed cannon of lamb, served simply but effectively with artichokes and braised shallots in a rosemary jus. Presentation is a strength too, not least among desserts of exemplary caramelised lemon tart, a caramel and praline mousse sandwiched between chocolate wafers, and a prune and armagnac parfait that came with a winter fruit compote and mascarpone ice cream.

Plentiful staff, many French, deliver formal but generally unobtrusive service. Prices have crept up since last year, but meals come complete with appetisers, a pre-dessert and petits fours, and value is considered fair given the quality and location. Wines are a different matter, with a heavy emphasis on aristocratic and expensive bottles, most of them French. Only 10 wines (out of 250) make it under the £20 barrier.

CHEF: Marcus Wareing PROPRIETORS: Marcus Wareing and Gordon Ramsay OPEN: Mon to Fri L 12 to 2.45, Mon to Sat D 6.45 to 11 MEALS: Set L £24 to £40, Set D £40 to £50 SERVICE: not inc CARDS: Amex, Delta, Diners, MasterCard, Switch, Visa DETAILS: 45 seats. No children under 10. No cigars in dining room. Wheelchair access (not WC). No music. Air-conditioned ⊖ Green Park

Pharmacy Restaurant and Bar

map 13

150 Notting Hill Gate, W11 3QG
TEL: (020) 7221 2442 FAX: (020) 7243 2345
WEB SITE: pharmacylondon.com

COOKING 4
MODERN EUROPEAN
£28–£73

The ambience at Pharmacy is what you might call clinical, with bar stools designed to resemble giant aspirins, vitrines containing surgical gloves, and the window of the first-floor restaurant overlooking Notting Hill Gate dominated by a large molecular model by Damien Hirst. Mediterranean cooking is what's on offer, some of it quite straightforward – gazpacho, or pea and artichoke risotto with lemon oil – and some of it requiring explication: maybe Joselito gran reserva pata negra with melon, or tripe 'in the Roman style'.

There is also a hint of the East in a starter of white fish carpaccio dressed with ginger, soy and sesame oil, or seared tuna with Chinese-spiced aubergines and coriander. Intensely flavoured accompaniments give depth to the range: bottarga with poached salmon and carrots, for example, or salsa verde with baked sea bass. Finish with chocolate Florentine torte, buttermilk pannacotta with stewed plums or British and Irish cheeses. Service does its job well, and so does the wine list, although mark-ups are pretty merciless. A Languedoc Merlot and Chardonnay start the ball rolling at £14.

CHEF: Michael McEnearney PROPRIETOR: Hartford plc OPEN: all week 12 to 3, 6.45 to 10.45 CLOSED: Christmas and New Year MEALS: alc (main courses £11.50 to £23). Set L Mon to Fri £15.50 (2 courses) to £17.50 SERVICE: 12.5% (optional), card slips closed CARDS: Amex, Delta, Diners, MasterCard, Switch, Visa DETAILS: 110 seats. Private parties: 110 main room. Vegetarian meals. Children's helpings. No music. Air-conditioned ⊖ Notting Hill Gate

Phoenix

map 12

162–164 Lower Richmond Road, SW15 1LY
TEL: (020) 8780 3131 FAX: (020) 8780 1114

COOKING **3**
MODERN BRITISH
£22–£53

Those who know Sonny's (see entries, London and Nottingham) will recognise the style. A big, white-walled interior hung with modern watercolours, cleverly staged mirrors and old photographs provides the backdrop for a far-reaching menu. France is represented by seared foie gras with caramelised apple purée, while Italy weighs in with peperonata, creamed goats' cheese and focaccia, and the Far East is not left out either: a starter of roast duck comes with spring onion nori rolls and plum sauce.

Regardless of where they originate, the best dishes are well judged for timing and texture, delivering crisp breadcrumbed strips of deep-fried artichoke and avocado with a well-balanced salsa, and flavourful juniper-infused grilled quail with runny polenta. Puddings echo the global approach, from English strawberries with clotted cream, through admirable passion-fruit parfait with mango salad, to pannacotta with cranberries. Service, by a bevy of apron-clad waiters sporting pagers, is 'willing and interested'. A to-the-point wine list climbs above the £20 mark around halfway through, although house Vins de Pays d'Oc are £9.75.

CHEF: Carol Craddock PROPRIETORS: Rebecca Mascarenhas and James Harris OPEN: all week 12.30 to 2.30 (3.30 Sun), 7 to 11 (11.30 Fri and Sat, 10 Sun) CLOSED: Sat L mid-Sept to mid-May, bank hols MEALS: alc (main courses £9.50 to £14). Set L Mon to Fri and D 7 to 7.45 Sun to Thur £12 (2 courses) to £15 SERVICE: 12.5% (optional), card slips closed CARDS: Amex, Delta, Diners, MasterCard, Switch, Visa DETAILS: 100 seats. 40 seats outside. Private parties: 100 main room. Vegetarian meals. Children's helpings. No-smoking area. Wheelchair access (also WC). No music. Air-conditioned ⊖ Putney Bridge (£5)

London Round-ups listing additional restaurants that may be worth a visit can be found after the main London section.

Pied-à-Terre  map 15

34 Charlotte Street, W1P 1HJ
TEL: (020) 7636 1178 FAX: (020) 7916 1171
EMAIL: p-a-t@dircon.co.uk
WEB SITE: www.pied.a.terre.co.uk

COOKING **8**
FRENCH
£42–£106

Dramatic pop art pictures of Chairman Mao and President Johnson have been replaced by more subdued prints; otherwise the dark floor and mushroom-coloured canvases remain, and on the face of it little seems to have changed since Tom Aikens left at the end of 1999 in controversial circumstances. That former sous-chef Shane Osborn has maintained such an impeccably high standard and made a virtually seamless transition is a remarkable accomplishment.

His food is a modern interpretation of high French, but some of the flourishes and more elaborately worked dishes of his predecessor have been tempered by a greater sense of balance. Appetisers offer an insight into the fine craftsmanship: a smear of salt-cod brandade sandwiched between crisp potato wafers, a deep-fried breadcrumbed blob of liquid foie gras, and what looks like a tiny pint of lager but is in fact carrot purée topped with tarragon-flavoured froth are all harbingers of good things.

What is striking about the best dishes is that they explore similarities and contrasts in a way that gives them cohesion and integrity. At a summer meal, for example, an upright triangle of foie gras terrine ('like a slice from a large Toblerone') sat beside a warm Tatin of slightly bitter endive topped with contrastingly sweet pear and sensuous, melting foie gras; beside this, a light frisée salad strewn with crunchy hazelnuts and black truffle added yet more depth of flavour. The food's voluptuous side often gives dishes a boost: a generous knobbly nugget of well-browned calf's sweetbread, for example, surrounded by spinach and flaked toasted almonds echoing the sweetbread's nuttily roasted exterior.

Presentation is a strong point, sauces are fine reductions, and flavours are vivid where they need to be, delicate where they need to be supportive, for example in a 'magic' fig and almond tart accompanied by gently flavoured cinnamon ice cream and a sticky, jam-like dribble of sauce. Service is expertly overseen by David Moore, whose advice on wines is well worth taking, although a dilemma is caused by an exquisite range of top-class wines from around the world subjected to some staggering mark-ups. Fifteen wines by the glass are chosen to complement dishes, and a few bottles under £20 can be found. House wines start at £18.

CHEF: Shane Osborn PROPRIETOR: David Moore OPEN: Mon to Fri L 12.15 to 2.15, Mon to Sat D 7 to 10.45 CLOSED: 2 weeks Christmas and New Year, last 2 weeks Aug MEALS: Set L £19.50 (2 courses) to £50, Set D £39.50 (2 courses) to £65 SERVICE: 12.5% (optional), card slips closed CARDS: Amex, Delta, Diners, MasterCard, Switch, Visa DETAILS: 40 seats. Private parties: 7 main room, 14 private room. Children's helpings. Wheelchair access (not WC). No music. Air-conditioned ⊖ Goodge Street

---

Net prices *in the details at the end of an entry indicates that the prices given on a menu and on a bill are inclusive of VAT and service charge, and that this practice is clearly stated on menu and bill.*

Le Pont de la Tour 🍷  map 13

36D Shad Thames, Butlers Wharf, SE1 2YE
TEL: (020) 7403 8403 FAX: (020) 7403 0267
WEB SITE: www.conran.com

COOKING 4
FRENCH/MEDITERRANEAN
£42–£86

One side of the long dining room is covered in Edwardian prints; the other opens on to a terrace with a splendid view of the river, Tower Bridge and the City. A brasserie-length carte dispenses plain, classically oriented food, from simple fish and shellfish – lobster mayonnaise, or grilled Dover sole – to ballottine of foie gras, and chateaubriand with béarnaise. If it feels unadventurous, then at least good materials are generally well handled: deep-coloured, tasty veal tournedos with a clear stock reduction, properly seared pink calf's liver, or steamed wild sea bass with lentils.

While the cooking may miss a few opportunities to make something of crisp textures, it deals in well-constructed dishes, be it a Dorset crab salad with a tomato, chilli and coriander salsa, or salt-cod fishcake with scallops and a shellfish sauce. It also deploys a range of skills, from accurate timing to pasta-making: for example, in a tarragon- and truffle-infused mushroom raviolo served with breast of wood pigeon. Vegetables are charged extra, and desserts have included iced Amaretto soufflé, and a light pastry tart laid with thin apple slices served with caramel ice cream. Service has varied from otherwise occupied to warmly professional. Classical French wines dominate the 40-page list, though there are many adventurous alternatives from Italy, Australia and California. Quality is high all round but so, unfortunately, are prices. House French is £12.95, and around ten wines are served by the glass.

CHEFS: Earl Cameron, Tim Powell and John Nolan PROPRIETOR: Conran Restaurants Ltd OPEN: Sun to Fri L 12 to 3, all week D 6 to 11.30 (11 Sun) MEALS: alc (main courses £17.50 to £25). Set L £28.50, Set D 6 to 6.45 and 10.30 to 11.30 £19.50 SERVICE: 12.5% (optional), card slips closed CARDS: Amex, Delta, Diners, MasterCard, Switch, Visa DETAILS: 105 seats. 102 seats outside. Private parties: 20 private room. Vegetarian meals. Wheelchair access (also WC). Music ⊖ Tower Hill, London Bridge

Popeseye NEW ENTRY map 12

108 Blythe Road, W14 0HD
TEL: (020) 7610 4578

COOKING 2
STEAK AND CHIPS
£23–£60

Bright pictures on white walls, simple furnishings, paper-clothed tables, and knowledgeable and charming staff mark out this former shop near Olympia. It takes its name from the Scottish word for rump steak, although chargrilled sirloin and fillet are also from grass-fed Aberdeen Angus, hung for at least two weeks, and delivered daily from Scotland. Crisp, tasty chips are the accompaniments, along with a simple garnish of tomato and watercress, and a variety of mustards, ketchup, and first-class béarnaise. For anyone wanting more there is salad. With weights ranging from six to twenty ounces, starters are clearly redundant, although farmhouse cheeses, ice creams and sorbets, or home-made puddings, among which an inspector found a 'classic' crème brûlée, bring things to a happy conclusion. The wine list is virtually monochrome red, with clarets celebrating the 'Auld Alliance' and some interesting Spanish and New World bottles. House red is £11.50. An almost identical sibling, with the benefit of a garden for warm-weather eating, is at 277 Upper Richmond Road, Putney (tel (020) 8788 7733).

CHEF/PROPRIETOR: Ian Hutchison OPEN: Mon to Sat D only 6.45 to 10.30 CLOSED: Aug MEALS: alc (main courses £9.50 to £30) SERVICE: 12.5% (optional) CARDS: none DETAILS: 34 seats. Wheelchair access (not WC). No music ⊖ Olympia (£5)

Porte des Indes

NEW ENTRY **map 13**

32 Bryanston Street, W1H 7AE — COOKING **2**
TEL: (020) 7224 0055 FAX: (020) 7224 1144 — INDIAN
WEB SITE: www.la-porte-des-indes.com — £42–£74

Nothing outside prepares you for the spectacular display of dark red wooden floors, colourful draped fabrics, murals of jungle scenes, spectacular flower arrangements, enormous palm trees, and a 'wall of water' beside the marble staircase. Exotic and evocative, it is perhaps the grandest setting of all London's Indian restaurants. Compared with the carte, thalis offer a reasonably priced way to sample the goods, which are a mix of commonplace curries and some more unusual items. Rasoul (lamb samosa) is exemplary, and Parsee sole steamed in a banana leaf with mint and coriander is a fragrant success. Main courses might include expertly marinated tandoori lamb chop, tender rogan josh, and, from the French-Creole cuisine of Pondichéry, the speciality of the house, cassoulet de fruits de mer in a curried coconut sauce. Service might be sharpened up. House wines are £10.50.

CHEF: Mehernosh Mody PROPRIETOR: Blue Elephant International plc OPEN: Sun to Fri L 12 to 2.30 (3 Sun), all week D 7 to 12 (6 to 10.30 Sun) CLOSED: 25 and 26 Dec MEALS: alc (main courses £10 to £19.50). Set L and D £29 to £41.50. Cover £1.50 SERVICE: not inc CARDS: Amex, Delta, Diners, MasterCard, Switch, Visa DETAILS: 300 seats. Vegetarian meals. Children's helpings. Wheelchair access (not WC). Music. Air-conditioned ⊖ Marble Arch

Prism 🍷

map 13

147 Leadenhall Street, EC3V 4QT — COOKING **4**
TEL: (020) 7256 3888 FAX: (020) 7256 3876 — MODERN BRITISH
WEB SITE: www.prismrestaurant.co.uk — £45–£75

No longer needed as marble temples to Mammon, many of London's old bank buildings have been transformed into large-scale restaurants; this one, not far from the old Leadenhall market, used to house the Bank of America. Decibel levels in city eateries seem to be at an all-time high, and the dining room's large size and reflective surfaces make the acoustics predictably dramatic; try the covered courtyard for a quieter spot.

Menus rove the world for inspiration, drawing on influences from Thailand for a pork and crab salad, Greece for a 'moussaka' of wild mushrooms with mint and cucumber dressing, and Whitby for the cod that comes with puréed (i.e. mushy) peas. No less exotic, at least mid-week, is a generous and commendable special of roast beef and Yorkshire pudding. Homely desserts run from fresh fruit salad to pear and custard tart, by wayof Dime-bar cheesecake. The wine list favours France, though choice bottles from Italy and America are noteworthy.

Quality is high but so are mark-ups. For bottles under £20 look to Chile and regional France. Six wines are available by the glass.

CHEF: Simon Shaw PROPRIETOR: Harvey Nichols Restaurants Ltd OPEN: Mon to Fri L 11.30 to 3, Mon and Wed to Fri D 6 to 10. Bar meals 11 to 10 CLOSED: bank hols MEALS: alc (main courses £12 to £21) SERVICE: 12.5% (optional), card slips closed CARDS: Amex, Diners, MasterCard, Switch, Visa DETAILS: 130 seats. 30 seats outside. Private parties: 130 main room, 30 to 50 private rooms. Vegetarian meals. Children's helpings. Wheelchair access (also WC). Occasional music. Air-conditioned ⊖ Bank, Monument

Prospect Grill

NEW ENTRY **map 15**

4–6 Garrick Street, WC2E 9BH
TEL: (020) 7379 0412 FAX: (020) 7836 3936
WEB SITE: www.prospectgrill.com

COOKING **1**
AMERICAN GRILL
£28–£50

Although the décor is a modern take on 'English clubby', the owners see this more as a New York/Manhattan kind of place, relying on Pussy Galore and James Bond cocktails for a touch of glamour. The kitchen, meanwhile, is sensibly modest in its ambitions, ranging prawn cocktail and warm Morecambe Bay potted shrimps against the anticipated grills. It is also serious about materials, procuring organic beef, occasionally from rare Longhorn or Sussex breeds, pork chops from Tamworths or Gloucester Old Spots, and free-range chicken, perhaps breast and thigh roasted with lemon and rosemary. Portions are large – try the 10-ounce hamburger with thick-cut chips for size – and non-meat dishes are equally successful, judging by baked leek and tarragon tart. Ice creams and sorbets come either with a chocolate shortbread biscuit or as a partner for baked egg custard, or chocolate brownie. Service takes care over details, and a sharply chosen wine list starts at £11.50 and offers eight by the glass. Note the late closing time to accommodate post-theatre bookings.

CHEF/PROPRIETOR: Shelly Fowler OPEN: Mon to Fri 11.45 to 3.30, 5.30 to 12, Sat 11.45am to 12 CLOSED: 24 Dec to 1 Jan MEALS: alc (main courses £10 to £16) SERVICE: not inc CARDS: Amex, Delta, MasterCard, Switch, Visa DETAILS: 74 seats. Private parties: 8 main room. Vegetarian meals. Wheelchair access (not WC). Music. Air-conditioned ⊖ Covent Garden, Leicester Square

Purple Sage

map 15

90-92 Wigmore Street, W1H 9DR
TEL: (020) 7486 1912 FAX: (020) 7486 1913

COOKING **3**
ITALIAN
£27–£49

'Every high street should have one,' concluded a visitor to this member of Bijan Behzadi's small group (see Red Pepper, Green Olive, the National Gallery's Crivelli's Garden, and White Onion, all London). It is a double-fronted building with huge windows, a high ceiling supported by fat pillars, one brick wall and wooden furniture, and looks at the world through Italian eyes. This takes in broad bean salad, home-made tagliatelle with scallops, and risotto with red mullet, asparagus and saffron.

Sadly, the wood-burning oven, which provided an opportunity to make cracking pizzas, is no longer in use, but the draw is good ingredients given simple treatment. Chargrilling and roasting are the cooking methods of choice:

tuna (rare as requested) pleased one reporter, as did a skewer of chicken, turkey and peppers. Finish with a white chocolate version of profiteroles, or tiramisù. Slow service is the weak link, and the place can get noisy when busy. Around 30 well-chosen wines start with the house offering at £9.75.

CHEF: Paolo Zanca PROPRIETOR: Red Pepper Group OPEN: Mon to Sat 12 to 2.30, 6 to 10.30 CLOSED: 25 and 26 Dec MEALS: alc (main courses £9 to £14) SERVICE: 12.5% (optional), card slips closed CARDS: Amex, Delta, MasterCard, Switch, Visa DETAILS: 85 seats. Private parties: 110 main room, 35 private room. Vegetarian meals. Wheelchair access (not WC). Music. Air-conditioned ⊖ Bond Street

Putney Bridge

map 12

Embankment, SW15 1LB
TEL: (020) 8780 1811 FAX: (020) 8780 2011
EMAIL: demetre@globalnet.co.uk
WEB SITE: www.putneybridgerestaurant.com

COOKING **7**
MODERN FRENCH
£33–£115

Set at 90 degrees to the real bridge (where the Oxford and Cambridge boat race starts), this purpose-built downstairs bar and first-floor restaurant – in pink granite, hardwood, steel and glass – makes the best of river views. Concentration nowadays, however, is less on the spectacle than on a new dynamism in the kitchen. Anthony Demetre seems at last to have found his métier. He is a talented chef, now aspiring to greater heights than when he first arrived from L'Odéon (see entry, London) a year or two back.

Simplicity is part of the key to success, providing an inspector with one of his best dishes of the year: a first-course ragoût of well-timed summer vegetables, their sweetness and freshness emphasised by a thyme-scented vinaigrette and pungent shavings of summer truffle. Equally straightforward has been a mound of fresh Dorset crabmeat set beside one of pea and pistachio mousse. There are some fancy visual effects, and a little bit of overworking, but consistent technique sees everything through, as in a two-stage dish of brill: first the flesh, just-cooked and firm, with a sweet-edged Gewürztraminer sauce, then the fiercely grilled skin set on a pile of mainly rocket leaves.

The kitchen's take on chocolate fondant is impressive, combining a dense but soft sponge with a thick, dark, oozing sauce, served with a vanilla cappuccino, while the simplicity principle has also produced a dish of wild strawberries with just a berry juice and well-matched basil mascarpone ice cream. In addition to all this, a new management team is in place, the atmosphere is more formal, the menu more elaborate, and prices have been jacked up, while service varies from high-handed to smiling and enthusiastic, depending who you get. The sommelier is a star, overseeing an extensive range of wines, including some fine bottles from Bordeaux, Burgundy and the Rhône, plus many interesting bins from further afield. Prices remain a stumbling block, with greedy mark-ups all round. Look to Argentina for sub-£20 respite.

CHEF: Anthony Demetre PROPRIETOR: Gerald Davidson OPEN: Tue to Sun L 12 to 2.30 (12.30 to 3 Sun), Tue to Sat D 7 to 10.30 (6.30 to 11 Fri and Sat) CLOSED: 25 and 26 Dec MEALS: Set L Tue to Sat £19.50, Set L Sun £25.50, Set D £32 (2 courses) to £85 (inc wine) SERVICE: 12.5% (optional), card slips closed CARDS: Amex, Delta, Diners, MasterCard, Switch, Visa DETAILS: 100 seats. Vegetarian meals. No children under 10. No cigar smoking before 10. Wheelchair access (also WC). No music. Air-conditioned ⊖ Putney Bridge

Quality Chop House

map 13

94 Farringdon Road, EC1R 3EA
TEL: (020) 7837 5093 FAX: (020) 7833 8748

COOKING **3**
BRITISH
£24–£68

The Chop House doesn't change much. Its cream walls, dark wooden booths and marked absence of pampering herald a no-nonsense approach to the food. The 'working-class caterer' peg is a handy one on which to hang a range of humble dishes, from jellied eels to steak and kidney pie, from corned beef hash to a plate of bacon, egg and chips; but that doesn't preclude the incorporation of caviar and grilled lobster, and a spot of rocket and Parmesan along the way.

Simple warmed potted shrimps are thankfully left unadorned, apart from slices of toasted walnut bread, and the anchovies in a salad are fresh, glistening and full of flavour. If the aim is satisfying, well-handled and unfussy food, then it is achieved handsomely in, for example, a large bowl of saffron broth piled high with plump scallops, loads of clams and sliced potato. Caramel cheesecake has been pretty good too, creamy yet light and not over-sweetened. Well-paced service does its job proficiently. Wine prices are where the working-class credentials get lost a bit, but this is central London. House French is £11.

CHEF/PROPRIETOR: Charles Fontaine OPEN: Sun to Fri L 12 to 3.30 (4 Sun), all week D 6.30 (7 Sun) to 11.30 CLOSED: 24 Dec to 3 Jan MEALS: alc (main courses £7 to £22) SERVICE: not inc CARDS: Delta, MasterCard, Switch, Visa DETAILS: 65 seats. Private parties: 12 main room. Vegetarian meals. Children's helpings. No-smoking area. No music. Air-conditioned ⊖ Farringdon (£5)

Quo Vadis 

map 15

26–29 Dean Street, W1V 6LL
TEL: (020) 7437 9585 FAX: (020) 7434 9972
WEB SITE: www.whitestarline.org.uk

COOKING **5**
MODERN EUROPEAN
£31–£71

Quo Vadis radiates a very Soho kind of glamour, with geometrically designed stained-glass windows and a neon sign along its expansive façade. As to its artwork, Marco's offerings are surprisingly gentle displays of butterflies and such, though the odd dangling lizard skeleton maintains the erstwhile cabinet-of-curiosities approach. Spencer Patrick took over the kitchen in late 1999, to consolidate a move towards traditional brasserie fare, doing so with the panache that the best Marco-trained chefs invariably seem to exhibit. Even fresh English asparagus (in November too) with hollandaise can win plaudits, while foie gras parfait, properly rich and moreish, comes with sweet fig jam.

Top-quality lemon sole, filleted at table, is served simply with parsley butter, while a more intricate option might be 'duck Marco Polo', a pink-cooked, tender breast with fondant potato, fried apple and a butter sauce containing foie gras and green peppercorns. Clever dessert ideas have included a jelly of summer fruits with a sauce of pink champagne (complete with the prickle of fresh bubbly), and pineapple tarte Tatin discreetly seasoned with black pepper. Service is usually – but not always – professional. Wines come from France, southern Europe and the New World, but mark-ups don't allow much room for manoeuvre. The opening price is £13.50.

CHEF: Spencer Patrick PROPRIETORS: Jimmy Lahoud, Fernando Peire and Marco Pierre White OPEN: Mon to Fri L 12 to 2.45, Mon to Sat D 5.30 to 11.45 CLOSED: 25 and 26 Dec, 1 Jan, L bank hols MEALS: alc (main courses £9.50 to £18.50). Set L and D 5.30 to 6.45 £14.50 (2 courses) to £17.50 SERVICE: 12.5% (optional), card slips closed CARDS: Amex, Delta, Diners, MasterCard, Switch, Visa DETAILS: 90 seats. Private parties: 8 main room, 14 and 38 private rooms. Wheelchair access (not WC) ⊖ Tottenham Court Road

Radha Krishna Bhavan £

NEW ENTRY map 12

86 Tooting High Street, SW17 0RN
TEL: (020) 8682 0969 and 8767 3462
EMAIL: tharidas@aol.com
WEB SITE: www.haridas.co.uk

COOKING **3**
SOUTH INDIAN
£17–£36

This house (bhavan) of Krishna and his consort, Radha, was founded by migrants from the nearby Sree Krishna. The large, rectangular room dominated by floor-to-ceiling colour photographs of beaches, palms and flowers displays attractive artefacts, including a statuette of Krishna. The largely Keralan menu takes in a number of standard curry-house dishes, but the main attractions are the mostly vegetarian southern Indian specialities and a few meat and fish dishes from Cochin. Paper dosai, the thin, crisp, unstuffed version of the rice and lentil flour rolled pancake, comes with coconut-based chutneys, one mild with red chillies, the other slightly hotter with green.

Good ingredients are cooked with skill and understanding, producing an impressive Mysore bonda, a fried lentil ball laced with black pepper, curry leaves and green chillies. Subtly balanced flavours characterise a richly sauced Cochin prawn curry, and kalan, a simple, not over-sweet mango curry. Incidentals such as chapati, rice and kulfi have won praise, and service is warm, welcoming, informed and helpful. Lassi is well made, and house wines, on the short, uninformative list, are £8.

CHEFS: T. Ali and Mr Madhu PROPRIETORS: T. Haridas and family OPEN: all week 12 to 3, 6 to 11 (12 Fri and Sat) CLOSED: 25 and 26 Dec MEALS: alc (main courses £2 to £7). Set L Sun £4.95 to £6.95 SERVICE: 10%, card slips closed CARDS: Amex, Delta, Diners, MasterCard, Switch, Visa DETAILS: 50 seats. 9 seats outside. Private parties: 60 main room. Vegetarian meals. Children's helpings. Occasional music. Air-conditioned ⊖ Tooting Broadway (£5)

Rani £

map 12

7 Long Lane, N3 2PR
TEL/FAX: (020) 8349 4386
EMAIL: ranivegetarian@aol.com
WEB SITE: www.rani.uk.com

COOKING **1**
GUJARATI VEGETARIAN
£20–£32

Rani's décor of red and white, with blue paper napkins, hasn't changed, but an alteration to the menu, doubtless welcomed by seekers after authenticity, is the dropping of Italian pizzas due to lack of demand. The menu is now almost entirely devoted to what Jyotindra Pattni calls home-style vegetarian cooking based on the region of Kathiawar in Gujarat. Freshly made poppadoms with 'terrific' home-made chutneys raise great expectations sometimes only partly fulfilled.

Starters include variations on bhel puri and an unusual hot bhakervelli (spiced vegetables rolled and fried in pastry), served with date chutney. Masala dosai, with sambhar, dhal, and notable coconut chutney, is offered as a South Indian meal, while Gujarati sak (pronounced 'shak') are vegetable curries, some dry, some with a sauce. Home-made desserts include a recommended carrot halva, and there are fine ice creams from Marine Ices. Wines are limited to one bottle of red, one of white, at £9.70, but Cobra beer comes in two sizes.

CHEF: Sheila Pattni PROPRIETOR: Mr and Mrs J. Pattni OPEN: Sun L 12.30 to 2.30, all week D 6 to 10 CLOSED: 25 Dec MEALS: alc (main courses £4.50 to £6). Set L and D £12.45 (2 courses) SERVICE: 10% (optional), card slips closed CARDS: Amex, Delta, MasterCard, Switch, Visa DETAILS: 70 seats. Private parties: 40 main room. Vegetarian meals. Children's helpings. No-smoking area. Wheelchair access (not WC). Music ⊖ Finchley Central (£5)

Ransome's Dock

map 12

35–37 Parkgate Road, SW11 4NP
TEL: (020) 7223 1611 and 7924 2462
FAX: (020) 7924 2614
EMAIL: martinlam@compuserve.com
WEB SITE: ransomesdock.co.uk

COOKING 5
MODERN EUROPEAN
£29–£63

A little inlet from the Thames, not far from Battersea Park, helps to seal off Martin Lam's restaurant and generate an intimate feel. Tables are put outside in summer, although the dining room's bright blue walls and Matisse posters make it pleasant enough indoors. A preoccupation with British produce takes in Morecambe Bay potted shrimps, Craster kippers, and Norfolk smoked eel served with buckwheat pancake and crème fraîche. The food lives up to its promise. Fine materials are cooked simply, sometimes with striking accompaniments, and deliver strong flavours, as in main courses of Guernsey veal with morels and Parmesan polenta, or shorthorn sirloin steak with a mustard and tarragon sauce and big chips.

A sense of what works well, no matter where it originates, keeps the cooking vibrant, be it a straightforward rustic bruschetta of buffalo mozzarella with grilled pepper and tapénade, or free-range chicken with oloroso sherry and ground almonds. Desserts might include Bramley apple and quince tart, or waffles with blueberries. Service is informal and friendly, and an enthusiastically diverse collection of wines makes this list a delightful read. They are grouped by style and peppered with pithy and knowledgeable tasting notes. The emphasis is on Californian, Australian, Spanish and Italian super-stars, although a few good French bottles sneak in. Prices are very fair, and house wines start at £13.50.

CHEFS/PROPRIETORS: Martin and Vanessa Lam OPEN: all week noon to 11 (3.30 Sun) CLOSED: Christmas, Aug bank hol MEALS: alc (main courses £9.50 to £17.50). Set L Mon to Fri £12.50 (2 courses) SERVICE: 12.5% (optional), card slips closed CARDS: Amex, Delta, Diners, MasterCard, Switch, Visa DETAILS: 55 seats. 20 seats outside. Private parties: 14 main room. Car park D and weekends. Vegetarian meals. Children's helpings. No pipes in dining room. Wheelchair access (also WC). Music. Air-conditioned

Rasa/Rasa W1 £

maps 12 and 15

55 Stoke Newington Church Street, N16 0AR
TEL: (020) 7249 0344
6 Dering Street, W1R 9AB
TEL: (020) 7629 1346 FAX: (020) 7491 9540
WEB SITE: www.rasa.com

COOKING **2**
INDIAN VEGETARIAN
£22–£42

Das Sreedharan has done much to bring Keralan cooking, and more especially that of the country's Nair community, to London, allowing diners to explore the cuisine for a fraction of the cost of a trip to India (the fraction being smallest at the original branch in Stoke Newington). The entirely meat-free menus are similar, with cashew nuts, coconuts, green bananas and yoghurt being key ingredients. Among the better dishes at recent meals have been starters of cashew-nut pakoda, and light, fluffy, crispy Mysore bonda (deep-fried spicy potato balls with coconut chutney).

Subtle spicing and rounded flavours have characterised Rasa ka (a mixed vegetable curry), while pal payasam (rice pudding with cashews and raisins) makes for a comforting end to a meal. Pre-meal nibbles of poppadom-like snacks and chutneys (all made in-house) are a revelation. Rasa's choice of teas, its own imported Indian lager, lassi and fruit juices are alternatives to a short wine list tailored to spicy flavours. House wine is £7.95. A third branch, Rasa Samudra, at 5 Charlotte Street, W1P 1HD (tel: (020) 7637 0222), has a menu devoted exclusively to fish and seafood.

CHEF: Sivaprasad Mahade Van Nair (Rasa), Rajan Karattil (Rasa W1) PROPRIETOR: Das Sreedharan OPEN: Rasa Thur to Sun L 12 to 2.45, all week D 6 to 10.45 (11.45 Fri and Sat); Rasa W1 Mon to Sat L 12 to 2.30, all week D 6 to 10.30 CLOSED: Christmas MEALS: Rasa alc (main courses £3 to £5.50). Set L £5.95, Set D £15. Light L available; Rasa W1 alc (main courses £6.50 to £11) SERVICE: 12.5% (optional), card slips closed CARDS: Amex, Delta, Diners, MasterCard, Switch, Visa DETAILS: 45 seats (Rasa), 120 seats (Rasa W1). Private parties: 25 main room (Rasa), 100 main room (Rasa W1). Vegetarian meals. No smoking in dining room. Music. Air-conditioned ⊖ Oxford Circus (Rasa W1)

Real Greek

LONDON GFG 2001 COMMENDED

NEW ENTRY **map 13**

15 Hoxton Market, N1 6HG
TEL: (020) 7739 8212
FAX: (020) 7739 4910
WEB SITE: www.therealgreek.co.uk

COOKING **4**
GREEK
£35–£52

Many other cuisines have had makeovers in recent years, and now it looks as if it might be Greece's turn. Those who know the country are aware that there is more to its food than commercial taramasalata and tough kebabs. Hinting at what that might encompass, Theodore Kyriakou adopts an individual, imaginative and unfussy approach, serving up fresh clean flavours with lots of pizazz, and conveying enthusiasm and zest.

Meze typically come as taster plates containing three or four items, employing anything from grilled lambs' tongue to yellow split pea purée. One offers variations on a roe theme (grey mullet, lumpfish and smoked cod); others go in for more of a contrast, perhaps featuring roast salt-cod with caper leaves, savoury octopus in red wine and cumin, 'fresh as a daisy' razor clam with garlic, and potato and garlic aïoli with roast beetroot. Small dishes, the next rung up the ladder, are individual plates, perhaps calf's liver with peas cooked with dill. Then come main courses for those who like to eat conventionally: perhaps Cretan-style chicken baked with yoghurt, served with okra and dried apricots. Inspired juxtapositions are nowhere more apparent than in desserts: crunchy honeycomb ice cream with a dribble of dark red, syrupy balsamic sauce, or a Cézanne-like palette of bright saffron-yellow brioche, beetroot ice cream, pungent feta lemon curd and a piece of honey-roast fig.

All this takes place amid unaffected décor, with plain wooden tables and chairs, and lots of cheffy action behind the counter, helped by delightful service from 'abnormally tolerant' staff; the lady in charge is smart, witty and welcoming. An all-Greek wine list may not sound the most enticing prospect, but it is full of interest, bottles are grouped according to their suitability for poultry, fish etc., and ten are available by the glass. Prices start at £10.95 (£2.85 a glass).

CHEF: Theodore Kyriakou PROPRIETORS: Theodore Kyriakou and Paloma Campbell OPEN: Mon to Sat 12 to 3, 5.30 to 10.30 CLOSED: 1 week Christmas, bank hols MEALS: alc (main courses £15). Set L £10 (2 courses) SERVICE: not inc, 12.5% for parties of 7 or more CARDS: Amex, Delta, MasterCard, Switch, Visa DETAILS: 65 seats. 12 seats outside. Private parties: 15 main room, 8 private room. Vegetarian meals. No cigars/pipes in dining room. No music ⊖ Old Street

Redmond's 🍷 map 12

170 Upper Richmond Road West, SW14 8AW COOKING **5**
TEL: (020) 8878 1922 FAX: (020) 8878 1133 MODERN BRITISH
£23–£49

Recent redecoration has endowed the dining room of this popular neighbourhood restaurant with warmer tones, and readers continue to sing its praises for food, wine, ambience and charming service overseen by Pippa Hayward. The style is a lively one, turning to tapènade oil, annato dressing and mint tabbouleh to throw main ingredients into relief. A stacked tartare of smoked haddock and trout, for example, is spiked with ginger and served with a lemon and saffron mayonnaise.

Dishes are well judged, taking care with both taste and texture – in a smooth, concentrated celeriac and spinach soup – as well as composition: roast pheasant breast has been served with a cabbage-leaf parcel of black pudding and chestnut, dauphinois potato, and a flavourful red wine sauce. Rump of lamb with Puy lentils and cep jus has been recommended by more than one reporter.

Among desserts to get the thumbs-up are a prune and armagnac parfait with poached figs and blackcurrant sauce, and a pear and chocolate tart. Neal's Yard cheeses offer a savoury alternative. The short wine list manages to be both diverse and characterful, with cleverly chosen bottles from around the world. Empreinte du Temps (£17) from the Catalan region of Spain impressed one reporter so much that he subsequently ordered a case. House Chilean starts at £12.95.

indicates that there has been a change of chef since last year's Guide, and the Editor has judged that the change is of sufficient interest to merit the reader's attention.

CHEF: Redmond Hayward PROPRIETORS: Redmond and Pippa Hayward OPEN: Sun to Fri L 12 to 2 (2.30 Sun), Mon to Sat D 7 to 10.30 CLOSED: 4 days Christmas, bank hols exc Good Fri MEALS: Set L Mon to Fri £10 (2 courses) to £21.50, Set L Sun £15.50 (2 courses) to £18.50, Set D £22 (2 courses) to £28.50 SERVICE: not inc, 10% for parties of 6 or more CARDS: Delta, MasterCard, Switch, Visa DETAILS: 54 seats. Private parties: 50 main room. Vegetarian meals. Children's helpings. No cigars/pipes in dining room. Wheelchair access (not WC). No music. Air-conditioned

Red Pepper £ map 13

8 Formosa Street, W9 1EE
TEL: (020) 7266 2708

COOKING **4**
ITALIAN
£25–£51

The décor in this cousin of Green Olive, National Gallery's Crivelli's Garden, Purple Sage and White Onion (see entries, all London) is minimal, but no matter: customers provide all the noise and colour necessary. Fine weather might bring tables outside; otherwise expect close-together tables and a view of the wood-fired oven in the basement. This is what produces first class, thin, crisp pizza bases with a dozen or more toppings, from basic margherita via calzone to porro, with lots of melted mozzarella, masses of thin-cut ham, and tiny leeks.

The other strengths are fine, fresh raw materials – tuna tartare scattered with capers, or well-flavoured marinated octopus with new potatoes – and generally accurate timing: grilled sea bass has come with samphire, and tender roast duck breast with courgette salsa. Pasta is another option, while desserts take in almond and lemon tart, and delicate tiramisù in a crisp filo cup. Staff work hard and fast and know their stuff: 'they made a sensible suggestion of a wine by the glass which did not appear on the list, a good Pinot Grigio'. The all-Italian list is short but interesting, with prices starting at £9.

CHEF: Santino Busciglio PROPRIETORS: Red Pepper Group OPEN: Sat and Sun L 12.30 to 2.30, all week D 6.30 to 10.45 (10.30 Sun) MEALS: alc (main courses £6 to £18) SERVICE: not inc, 12.5% for parties of 5 or more CARDS: Delta, MasterCard, Switch, Visa DETAILS: 70 seats. 10 seats outside. Private parties: 30 main room. No music. Air-conditioned ⊖ Warwick Avenue (£5)

Rhodes in the Square map 13

Dolphin Square, Chichester Street, SW1V 3LX
TEL: (020) 7798 6767

COOKING **6**
MODERN BRITISH
£33–£59

This is a smooth, slick operation, everything about it smart and professional, from the sweeping chrome-railed staircase and dark blue colour scheme to well-trained staff (service is plentiful, friendly and 'pretty sharp') and the serious tone of the menu. Compared with the live-wire owner, it may all seem rather sober and restrained, but this is a posh address. With one or two exceptions, the discreetly British food lacks the playfulness of Gary Rhodes at his best – no Jaffa Cakes or Wagon Wheel puddings here – though it does deliver generally polished cooking, from a first-class lobster thermidor omelette, to a logical development of classic eggs Benedict, where a piece of moist, salty tuna replaces the traditional ham, the whole coated in lemony, herby hollandaise of 'just the right consistency'.

Dishes have a high comfort rating, using top-quality ingredients that are accurately timed and served with entirely appropriate accompaniments. A plate of two salmons – one thickly cut and lightly smoked, the other thin, accurately timed escalopes of fresh fish – have come on their respective beds of squeaky leeks and creamy potato purée, while 'butter-soft' roast loin of lamb has been enriched with bone marrow and subtly seasoned with anchovy and mushroom. Trade-mark bread-and-butter pudding, spooned out of a large dish, is 'a masterpiece', and its tall, dome-shaped, sticky toffee cousin is predictably smooth and rich. A rather conservative list of wines, at prices to reflect the surroundings (a bare handful under £20), starts with a dozen or so by the glass.

CHEFS: Gary Rhodes and Michael James PROPRIETOR: Gary Rhodes OPEN: Tue to Fri L 12 to 2.30, Tue to Sat D 7 to 10 MEALS: Set L £16.50 (2 courses) to £19.50, Set D £25.50 (2 courses) to £31 SERVICE: 12.5% CARDS: Amex, Delta, Diners, MasterCard, Switch, Visa DETAILS: 70 seats. Private parties: 100 main room. Vegetarian meals. Children's helpings. No cigars/pipes in dining room. No music. Air-conditioned ⊖ Pimlico

Riso

NEW ENTRY map 12

76 South Parade, W4 5LF
TEL/FAX: (020) 8742 2121

COOKING **3**
ITALIAN
£30–£48

A tiny green and an expanse of park are visible across the busy road from the wide windows of this cheerfully decorated modern restaurant. Hard-working, friendly and efficient staff create a relaxed style that customers enjoy, and the place might be considered an excellent 'trattoria', without the mundane connotations this term has historically acquired. The flexible menu offers both starters and pasta dishes in two sizes, and pizzas as a main or single course: eight of them offering varying combinations of buffalo mozzarella, tomatoes, peppers, Parma ham and artichokes.

Fine materials are evident in dish of bresaola and rocket with a dressing of crumbled goats' cheese, and sound technique has produced light and soft gnocchi coated in richly flavoured pesto, with a few French beans for crunch. A blackboard lists daily specials of perhaps grilled swordfish with cannellini beans, or calf's liver with roasted shallots and mash. Coffee pannacotta with chocolate sauce makes a fitting conclusion. Prices on the exclusively Italian wine list rise gently, starting at £11.50 for Merlot and Chardonnay.

CHEF: Sandro Medda PROPRIETORS: Mauro Santoliquido, Sandro Medda and Maurizio Rimerici OPEN: Sun L 12 to 2.30, all week D 7 to 11 (10.30 Sun) CLOSED: Christmas MEALS: Set L and D £12 (1 course) to £23.50. Pizzas £4.50 to £8 SERVICE: 12.5%, card slips closed CARDS: Delta, MasterCard, Switch, Visa DETAILS: 70 seats. Private parties: 50 main room. Vegetarian meals. No cigars in dining room. Music ⊖ Chiswick Park

indicates that smoking is either banned altogether or that a dining-room is maintained for non-smokers. The symbol does not apply to restaurants that simply have no-smoking areas.

▲ Ritz

NEW ENTRY **map 15**

150 Piccadilly, W1V 9DG
TEL: (020) 7300 2370 FAX: (020) 7493 2687
EMAIL: ritzfandb@aol.com
WEB SITE: www.theritzhotel.co.uk

COOKING **4**
FRENCH/ENGLISH
£46–£166

The elegant Louis XIV-style dining room, just across the park from Buckingham Palace, is equally geared to business or romance. Its ornate painted ceiling and wall panels, chandeliers, gilded statues, swagged curtains and pink reproduction chairs are matched by morning-suited service that is professional, attentive, fast and discreet. While starry guest chefs fly in to be let loose in the kitchen from time to time, the normal preoccupation is a handful of menus including pre- and post-theatre, dinner-dance, and a seriously expensive carte that deals in as many luxuries as it can lay its hands on.

Its business ranges from crab cake, topped with lobster and served with nantaise sauce, to moist chicken breast with a slice of black truffle inserted under the skin, in a vegetable-strewn truffle consommé. Old-fashioned menuspeak – omelette Marie Antoinette, sauce Matignon – indicates a preference for traditional treatments, and the comfort level is high. There is little to shock the system, and timing is conservative, producing monkfish on a cake of potato and pancetta in a tasty Fleurie wine sauce for one visitor, but desserts tend to reach for bolder flavours: perhaps prune and armagnac parfait glacé wrapped in a thin chocolate casing. Wines cover a broad spectrum, with little below £30, although there is a decent choice by the glass from £6.

CHEF: Giles Thompson PROPRIETOR: Ellerman Investments OPEN: all week 12 to 2.30, 6 to 11 (6.30 to 10.30 Sun) MEALS: alc (main courses £22.50 to £63). Set L £35, Set pre- and post-theatre D £43, Set D £51, Set dinner-dance D Fri and Sat £59 SERVICE: net prices, card slips closed CARDS: Amex, Delta, Diners, MasterCard, Switch, Visa DETAILS: 120 seats. 30 seats outside. Private parties: 28 main room, 20 to 55 private rooms. Vegetarian meals. Children's helpings. Jacket and tie. Wheelchair access (also WC). Occasional music. Air-conditioned ACCOMMODATION: 133 rooms, all with bath/shower. TV. Phone. Room only £335 to £1,750. Rooms for disabled. Baby facilities ⊖ Green Park

Riva

map 12

169 Church Road, SW13 9HR
TEL/FAX: (020) 8748 0434

COOKING **4**
NORTHERN ITALIAN
£30–£58

Andrea Riva and Francesco Zanchetta have been making their case for simple northern Italian cooking for a decade. The long, narrow dining room, behind a green and white awning in a parade of shops, is simply decorated in cream and grey, with a mirror down one side, wooden chairs, paper-covered cloths and fresh flowers. Small-scale, and impervious to fashion, it takes a low-key approach, aiming for modest home cooking rather than sophisticated urban chic. This produces simple plates of grilled seasonal vegetables, cold meats such as San Daniele or Culatello ham, perhaps paired with fruit or cheese, and something deep-fried to start, maybe lightly battered Mediterranean prawn with salt-cod, calamari, artichokes and a well-judged balsamic dip.

Pasta can be taken as a starter or main course – perfectly textured linguine with fresh-tasting mussels, clams and bottarga for one visitor – while mains culminate in a piatto nobile such as a robust country-style version of osso buco combining shins of veal and pork. Cheeses at inspection were not up to snuff, nor was the pannacotta, but pancakes of prune and blueberries stewed in grappa fared better, served with a nutmeg ice cream. It may help to be a familiar face to get the best out of service. Thirty-plus Italian wines are well chosen, and start with Pinot Bianco and Merlot from Veneto at £10.50.

CHEF: Francesco Zanchetta PROPRIETOR: Andrea Riva OPEN: Sun to Fri L 12 to 2.30, all week D 7 to 11 (9.30 Sun) CLOSED: Christmas, Easter, last 2 weeks Aug, bank hols MEALS: alc (main courses £9 to £16) SERVICE: 10%, card slips closed CARDS: Amex, MasterCard, Switch, Visa DETAILS: 45 seats. 8 seats outside. Private parties: 40 main room. Vegetarian meals. Children's helpings. No cigars/pipes in dining room. Wheelchair access (not WC). No music. Air-conditioned ⊖ Hammersmith

River Café 🍷

map 12

Thames Wharf Studios, Rainville Road, W6 9HA — COOKING **6**
TEL: (020) 7381 8824 FAX: (020) 7381 6217 — ITALIAN
WEB SITE: www.rivercafe.co.uk — £45–£73

Despite the drawbacks that have been chronicled over the years, this remains a favourite destination for some. Its uncluttered décor combines informality with designer looks, as do the customers. The food may lack a little refinement, but that directness is part of its appeal. It is essentially uncomplicated, although, as many readers and reporters know from experience, it takes skill to bring this off successfully, demanding both fine ingredients and careful handling. Wood-roasting is not the easiest way of controlling cooking temperature, but when it works (and they have had a lot of practice) it can produce crisp exteriors and moist interiors like nothing else, be it Bresse pigeon, or Dover sole with a scattering of fresh oregano.

Expect a soup (maybe salt-cod) to start, or a properly cooked risotto (seafood, perhaps, or asparagus), or else a colourful assembly of buffalo mozzarella, grilled polenta, black olives, sun-dried tomatoes and celery leaves. To finish, chocolate nemesis is as rich and intense as ever, and cheeses (individually priced) are worth considering seriously. Nobody pretends that the food is cheap (one visitor's main course consisted of just two scallops, with Tuscan tomato bread sauce), which may not make it everybody's cup of tea. The wine list is exclusively Italian, except for a short run of Billecart-Salmon champagnes. An authoritative selection includes impressive wines and producers, although prices rise fairly quickly above the £20 mark. A laudable 12 table wines and 16 dessert wines are available by the glass, with house wine £9.50.

CHEFS: Rose Gray, Ruth Rogers and Theo Randall PROPRIETORS: Rose Gray and Ruth Rogers OPEN: all week L 12.30 to 2.45 (3 Sat and Sun), Mon to Sat D 7 to 9.30 CLOSED: Christmas, New Year, Easter MEALS: alc (main courses £19 to £28) SERVICE: 12.5% (optional), card slips closed CARDS: Amex, Delta, Diners, MasterCard, Switch, Visa DETAILS: 108 seats. 56 seats outside. Car park at D. Vegetarian meals. Children's helpings. No cigars/pipes in dining room. Wheelchair access (also WC). No music ⊖ Hammersmith

Rosmarino 🍷 $*

NEW ENTRY map 13

1 Blenheim Terrace, NW8 0EH
TEL: (020) 7328 5014 FAX: (020) 7625 2639

COOKING **3**
MODERN ITALIAN
£30–£64

The A To Z group, which also owns Zafferano (see entry), acquired this site in 1999. It was already an Italian restaurant but Marzio Zacchi has brought it bang up to date. Sicilian olive oil in a bright green enamelled bottle is left on the table for dunking the rustic focaccia in, setting the tone for a fixed-price menu (with supplements) that has turned up a thick, herby velouté soup of king prawns and chickpeas, and inventive pasta dishes such as chicken and duck ravioli in shellfish stock.

Among main courses, calf's liver is precisely timed and served on spinach with a balsamic-scented sauce, while sauté beef fillet comes with polenta and a porcini sauce. Meals might end with 'soaked Neapolitan baba' (a cake, not a drenched Italian infant) with limoncello sauce. Service for one visitor was rather unco-ordinated, though a regular finds it 'splendidly professional'. A diverse bunch of Italian wines dominates the intelligent list. Mark-ups are reasonable, with A Mano Primitivo, from Puglia, well recommended at £19.

CHEF: Marzio Zacchi PROPRIETOR: A To Z Restaurants OPEN: Mon to Sat 12 to 2.30, 7 to 10.30, Sun 12 to 3, 7 to 10 CLOSED: 1 week Christmas/New Year, bank hols MEALS: Set L £16 (2 courses) to £19, Set D £19.50 (2 courses) to £26.50 SERVICE: 12.5% (optional) CARDS: Amex, Delta, MasterCard, Switch, Visa DETAILS: 50 seats. 15 seats outside. Private parties: 8 main room. Vegetarian meals. Children's helpings. No smoking in 1 dining room. Music. Air-conditioned ⊖ St John's Wood (£5)

Roussillon 🍷

map 14

16 St Barnabas Street, SW1W 8PB
TEL: (020) 7730 5550 FAX: (020) 7824 8617
EMAIL: info@roussillon.co.uk
WEB SITE: www.roussillon.co.uk

COOKING **3**
MODERN FRENCH
£30–£65

Considered an innovative neighbourhood restaurant, with a huge bay window that accentuates the feeling of being in a tea room, Roussillon achieves a generally sound level of cooking. Vegetarians are not neglected: a 'garden menu' might include Jerusalem artichoke soup, risotto, and poached egg in a cream of wild leek. At their best, dishes are simple but well prepared, although reporters remain divided about value for money. The quality and sourcing of materials, however, is not in question, with 'biodynamic' lamb from Dorset, and organic chickens and eggs.

Accurate timing has produced tender, tasty meats including lamb fillet, and slices of venison with pumpkin and chestnut, but be prepared for an unusual mix of ingredients in some dishes: perhaps braised monkfish with caramelised figs. Chocolate features prominently in desserts – a warm, gooey fondant cake with cinnamon ice cream for one reporter – or there may be chrysanthemum soufflé with roasted leaves. Roussillon (and the south generally) is well represented on a French-dominated list that offers 25 wines by the glass, which include wines from Italy and California as well. House Roussillon starts at £13 a bottle, but there is little else under £20.

CHEF: Alexis Gauthier PROPRIETORS: James and Andrew Palmer, and Alexis Gauthier OPEN: Sun to Fri L 12 to 2.15, all week D 6.30 to 11 (10 Sun) CLOSED: Christmas, 13 to 27 Aug, bank hols MEALS: Set L £13.50 (2 courses) to £16, Set D £25 (2 courses) to £28.50, Set L and D £29 to £38 SERVICE: 12.5% (optional), card slips closed CARDS: Amex, Delta, Diners, MasterCard, Switch, Visa DETAILS: 43 seats. Private parties: 58 main room, 30 private room. Vegetarian meals. Children's helpings. No music. Air-conditioned ⊖ Sloane Square

Royal China

maps 13 and 15

40–42 Baker Street, W1M 1DA
TEL/FAX: (020) 7487 4688
13 Queensway, W2 4QJ
TEL: (020) 7221 2535 FAX: (020) 7792 5752
68 Queens Grove, NW8 6ER
TEL: (020) 7586 4280 FAX: (020) 7722 2681

COOKING **4**
CHINESE
£28–£85

The newest branch of Royal China in St John's Wood in is in a low, windowless building, whose lacquered panels, patterned carpet and mirrored ceiling – not to say menus – are similar to those in the other two branches. Despite the ambitious haute cuisine style, service is friendly and helpful in guiding Westerners through the options. They include such delicacies as what the menu calls 'superior' abalone, or braised 'superior' shark's fin, at very superior prices.

Less expensive but still intriguing dishes are listed under 'chef's favourites', running from seafood hotpot to pan-fried minced pork with salted fish. Lunchtime dim sum are considered remarkable; among them may be prawn and coriander dumplings, baby bok choy with garlic and ginger, and 'heavenly' lotus leaf-wrapped rice enlivened by little pieces of duck, mushrooms and prawns. For dim sum, early arrival is suggested at Sunday lunchtime as you can't book. Nearly 60 wines rise from house at £9.50 via some big names to first-growth clarets priced in three figures. Unless otherwise specified, details below are for the Baker Street branch.

CHEF: David Pang (Baker Street), Mr Long (Queensway), Mr Hy (Queens Grove) PROPRIETOR: Royal China Restaurant Group OPEN: Mon to Sat 12 to 11 (11.30 Fri and Sat), Sun 11 to midnight CLOSED: Christmas MEALS: alc (main courses £6 to £20). Set L £8 (2 courses) to £25, Set D £25 to £32 SERVICE: 12.5%, card slips closed CARDS: Amex, Delta, MasterCard, Switch, Visa DETAILS: 80 seats (Baker Street), 160 seats (Queensway), 100 seats (Queens Grove). Private parties: 80 main room, 10 private room (Baker Street), 40 main rooms (Queensway), 90 main rooms (Queen's Grove). Vegetarian meals. Music. Air-conditioned ⊖ Baker Street, Queensway, St John's Wood

RSJ

map 13

13A Coin Street, SE1 8YQ
TEL: (020) 7928 4554 FAX: (020) 7401 2455
EMAIL: info@rsj.uk.com
WEB SITE: www.rsj.uk.com

COOKING **3**
MODERN FRENCH
£28–£54

'This remains our favourite place in London for quality of food, service and price,' recounts one reporter of this noisy two-tiered restaurant handy for the South Bank's expanding cultural complex. The kitchen puts on a show of some lively contemporary cooking, and the carte's ideas are engaging, taking in wild boar rillettes with apple chutney, a warm smoked eel and bacon salad, and fried duck egg with foie gras. A combination of fresh materials and careful handling has turned up moist crab in crisp pancakes, daube of beef with roast vegetables, and grilled lemon sole with highly rated chips.

Desserts may not always hit the bulls' eye, though banana crème brûlée and pecan tart both come recommended. An impressive wine list celebrates the oft-overlooked region of the Loire, offering the best producers and very good value for money: dessert wines remain a highlight from this region. An introduction to grapes and vintages, and careful tasting notes throughout, ensure that beginners will not feel daunted. A smattering of bottles from the rest of France and the New World appear at the end. Six house wines start at £10.95 and include Saumur red and white at £12.75.

CHEFS: Ian Stabler and Sean Thompson PROPRIETOR: Nigel Wilkinson OPEN: Mon to Fri L 12 to 2, Mon to Sat D 5.30 to 11 CLOSED: 4 days at Christmas MEALS: Set L and D £15.95 (2 courses) to £16.95 SERVICE: 12.5% (optional), card slips closed CARDS: Amex, Diners, MasterCard, Switch, Visa DETAILS: 90 seats. 15 seats outside. Private parties: 8 main room, 24 and 30 private rooms. Vegetarian meals. Children's helpings. No cigars/pipes in dining room. Occasional music. Air-conditioned ⊖ Waterloo, Southwark (£5)

Rules

map 15

35 Maiden Lane, WC2E 7LB
TEL: (020) 7379 0258 FAX: (020) 7497 1081
EMAIL: info@rules.co.uk
WEB SITE: www.rules.co.uk

COOKING **4**
TRADITIONAL BRITISH
£42–£66

Now into its third century, Rules is a West End institution. Hidden down an unlikely back street, it retains the power to strike a first-time visitor with its period feel, the walls adorned with theatrical memorabilia, the menu with meticulously itemised furred and feathered game. Everybody should eat here at least once, and perhaps more often: many have stayed loyal over a lifetime. David Chambers is a fine practitioner of the traditional British cookery in which Rules specialises. Pheasant casserole with creamed leeks and braised lentils, and steak and kidney pudding with mash pleased one pair mightily, not least for the trencherman portions in which they were served.

The more unusual game offerings in season extend to snipe, widgeon and teal, the last braised and served with chicken mousse in a crayfish and brandy cream sauce. The simpler starters tend to be best – Morecambe Bay potted shrimps, perhaps, or scrambled eggs and smoked salmon – and the prospect of a savoury might just tempt some away from Olde English puddings such as raspberry syllabub trifle. A short wine selection does sturdy service to the food. House French is £13.95.

CHEF: David Chambers PROPRIETOR: John Mayhew OPEN: all week 12 to 11.15 CLOSED: 4 days Christmas MEALS: alc (main courses £16 to £20). Set pre-theatre D Mon to Fri 3 to 5 £19.95 (2 courses) SERVICE: not inc CARDS: Amex, Delta, Diners, MasterCard, Switch, Visa DETAILS: 130 seats. Private parties: 6 main room, 12 to 24 private rooms. No smoking in dining room. Wheelchair access (not WC). No music. Air-conditioned ⊖ Charing Cross, Covent Garden (£5)

Subscribers to Which? Online can access The Good Food Guide *on www.which.net.*

Sabras

map 12

263 High Road, NW10 2RX
TEL/FAX: (020) 8459 0340

COOKING **4**
INDIAN VEGETARIAN
£30–£39

This unassuming eating house has been tidied up. The many press cuttings have been neatly framed, wooden chairs with velvet seats have been installed, and a counter has been removed to create more space between tables. Newcomers to Indian vegetarian cooking may find the menu bewildering, as it is divided partly by regions, partly by ingredients. An easy way in is a thali, a set meal for one, although this is available only until 8pm and not at all on Friday and Saturday. And there are mixed plates of starters, two specially recommended by a reporter being patra (yam leaves spread with spiced batter then rolled, steamed, sliced and fried), and kachori, a fried dumpling of mushy peas.

Southern Indian dosai – ground rice and lentil pancakes – include some stuffed with potatoes and onions, making satisfying main courses, with ravaiya (slow-cooked stuffed baby aubergine and banana, a subtle blend of flavours) among alternatives. Instead of plain or fried rice, try Kashmiri pilau, garnished with flaked almonds, steamed vegetables, and colourful, crunchy pomegranate pearls. House wines are £11.95, or go for organic juices or unusual variations on lassi, including khari, with salt and cumin, or mithi, with sugar and ground pistachios.

CHEFS/PROPRIETORS: Hemant and Nalinee Desai OPEN: Tue to Sun D only 6.30 to 10.30 MEALS: alc (main courses £6 to £7). Set D 6.30 to 8 Tue to Thur and Sun £10.30 to £15.50 SERVICE: 12.5%, card slips closed CARDS: Amex, Delta, Diners, MasterCard, Switch, Visa DETAILS: 32 seats. Private parties: 16 main room. Vegetarian meals. Wheelchair access (not WC). Music ⊖ Dollis Hill (£5)

Saigon Thuy £

map 12

189 Garratt Lane, SW18 4DR
TEL: (020) 8871 9464

COOKING **1**
VIETNAMESE
£23–£33

'Authentic Vietnamese' is how Mrs Nguyen describes her restaurant, although the menu also includes a few Chinese dishes. The long list of starters features various Vietnamese spring rolls, such as hand-rolled crystal roll with pork; or with noodles, coriander and mint accompanied by chicken. Spicy salads may incorporate chicken, beef, prawns or crab, and among the satays, served with noodles, is goat. Special Vietnamese fondue, a complete meal cooked at the table, contains prawns, scallops, squid, chicken, and prawn dumplings plus vegetables and inevitably noodles. There is pho bo, the national dish of beef noodle soup, as well as stir-fries, curries and sizzling platters. This little eating house, typically decorated with simple pine furniture, offers charming and relaxed service in an ambience as convincingly Vietnamese as the cuisine. House wine is £8.75.

CHEF/PROPRIETOR: Mrs T. Nguyen OPEN: all week D only 6 to 11 (10 Sun) CLOSED: 2 weeks from 23 Dec MEALS: alc (main courses £5 to £6.50) SERVICE: not inc CARDS: Delta, MasterCard, Switch, Visa DETAILS: 50 seats. Private parties: 30 main room, 30 private room. Vegetarian meals. Children's helpings. Wheelchair access (not WC). Music ⊖ East Putney

St John

map 13

26 St John Street, EC1M 4AY
TEL: (020) 7251 0848 FAX: (020) 7251 4090
EMAIL: tg@stjohnrestaurant.co.uk
WEB SITE: www.stjohnrestaurant.co.uk

COOKING **5**
BRITISH
£28–£56

Given the enthusiasm among reporters for this restaurant – 'a delight from beginning to end' is typical – it is a surprise there are not more like it. Fergus Henderson's style is relaxed, confident and unassuming; the best ingredients are carefully cooked and prices are ungreedy. The underlying principle seems to be: don't waste anything. That certainly applies to the décor – stark, white-painted walls, wooden floor, plainly set tables – and the food is often completely unadorned.

Starters may be simply described items such as sea kale, or razor clams, and dishes often use the parts other chefs might throw away: skate cheeks with tartare sauce, or chitterlings and chips. 'Any place that does andouillettes in a bun as a bar snack has got some bottle.' The famous roasted bone marrow never fails to arouse interest: a phalanx of four slim pieces, fiercely crisp and brown from the oven, on a salad of flat leaf parsley with shallots and capers in an oil and lemon juice dressing; a lobster pick helps to excavate the rich, seductive, molten marrow.

While the menu may not always be as 'nose to tail' as some would like, it certainly offers an escape route for those who find standard menus rather monotonous, producing main courses of Stinking Bishop and potatoes, smoked Gloucester Old Spot and parsnip, and breast of veal with trotter. Desserts range from Eccles cake with Lancashire cheese to a large and concentrated chocolate custard. Staff are young, cheerful and efficient, and some two dozen wines are available by the glass on a largely French list that starts at £11 for vin de pays.

CHEF: Fergus Henderson PROPRIETORS: Fergus Henderson and Trevor Gulliver OPEN: restaurant Mon to Fri L 12 to 3, Mon to Sat D; bar Mon to Sat 11 to 11 CLOSED: Christmas and New Year MEALS: alc (main courses £6.50 to £16). Bar menu available SERVICE: not inc CARDS: Amex, Delta, Diners, MasterCard, Switch, Visa DETAILS: 100 seats. Private parties: 150 main room, 18 private room. Vegetarian meals. No music. Air-conditioned ⊖ Farringdon

Salisbury Tavern

NEW ENTRY **map 12**

21 Sherbrooke Road, SW6 2HX
TEL: (020) 7381 4005 FAX: (020) 7381 1002

COOKING **5**
MODERN BRITISH
£26–£52

Under the same go-ahead ownership as Admiral Codrington (see entry), the Salisbury is a rather grand, yellow-fronted corner building, with stately double-door entrances on two sides. Beneath a skylight roof, the restaurant section has a bare wood floor, crimson walls and banquettes with a striking flower motif. Head chef Charlie Rushton, ex-Mirabelle (see entry), brings with him all the authority of experience in the Marco Pierre White group. It is a measure of the success of this style of cooking in the capital that many dishes now sound like old favourites: truffled parsley soup, foie gras and chicken liver parfait, and salmon fishcake with spinach and sorrel sauce are all here.

Performance is of a generally high order, demonstrated by tagliolini with mussels, prawns and fresh herbs, and one reporter's (though not another's) starter of onion and goats'-cheese tarte Tatin, with a thin trickle of caramel-sweet sauce. Also endorsed has been rump of lamb, cooked pink and tender, on truffled celeriac and artichoke, discreetly supported by a wine-based, herb-infused sauce. Puddings include crème brûlée with ginger and lemon grass, and chocolate orgasm. Lashings of service help to keep things moving smoothly. The short wine list is commendably imaginative, but prices soon hop over £20. House Bordeaux is £10.

CHEF: Charlie Rushton PROPRIETOR: Longshot Estates Ltd OPEN: all week 12 to 2.30 (3.30 Sat and Sun), 7 to 11 (10.30 Sun) CLOSED: Christmas, Easter MEALS: alc (main courses £8.50 to £15.50). Cover 50p at D SERVICE: 12.5% (optional), card slips closed CARDS: Amex, Delta, MasterCard, Switch, Visa DETAILS: 70 seats. Private parties: 70 main room. Wheelchair access (also WC). Music. Air-conditioned ⊖ Fulham Broadway

Salloos

map 14

62–64 Kinnerton Street, SW1X 8ER
TEL: (020) 7235 4444 FAX: (020) 7259 5703

COOKING **4**
PAKISTANI
£25–£63

Unchanged for years except for prices, Salloos makes a virtue of tradition. Appetisers consist of no more than soups and stuffed breads, but charcoal tandoori grills are one of the highlights. Cooked to order (expect to wait 25 minutes) without colourings, they are recommended as a separate course with naan, roti or paratha breads. Among specialities are lamb, chicken or prawns served sizzling on iron karahis. Saalan, otherwise known as curries, include palak gosht (lamb with spinach), shahi kofta (chicken balls), and nargisi kofta (a nineteenth-century fusion of curried Scotch eggs). Only a few vegetable dishes are offered.

Desserts are lychees, halva, or kulfi flavoured with cardamom. The décor suggests rich austerity with its paintings, dried flower arrangements against a cream and red background, and the curious layered ceiling like an inverted staircase. Beige linen tablecloths and napkins reinforce a luxurious feeling appropriate to the Knightsbridge village location. Fully priced wines are undistinguished except for Corney & Barrow's French and New World bottles. House wines £12.50.

CHEF: Abdul Aziz PROPRIETOR: Muhammad Salahuddin OPEN: Mon to Sat L 12 to 2.30, D 7 to 11.15 CLOSED: 25 and 26 Dec, bank hols MEALS: alc (main courses £11 to £15). Set L £16. Cover £1.50 SERVICE: 12.5% (optional), card slips closed CARDS: Amex, Delta, Diners, MasterCard, Switch, Visa DETAILS: 65 seats. Private parties: 65 main room. Vegetarian meals. No children under 6 at D. No cigars/pipes in dining room. No music. Air-conditioned ⊖ Hyde Park Corner, Knightsbridge

Occasional music *in the details at the end of an entry means live or recorded music is played in the dining room only rarely or for special events.* No music *means it is never played.*

Salt House

map 13

63 Abbey Road, NW8 0AE
TEL: (020) 7328 6626 FAX: (020) 7625 9168

COOKING **1**
MODERN EUROPEAN
£22–£44

A dazzlingly white-painted pub on the corner of Abbey Road and Belgrave Gardens, Salt House aims to provide essentially simple, domestic cooking a cut above the usual city pub standard. The restaurant is a high-ceilinged area with comfortable sofa-type banquette seating and a skylight. In it, you may eat good fish (perhaps roast cod with tomato, saffron and mint), lamb shank 'with a stonking gravy', or something as arresting as rabbit stuffed with black pudding. Homely desserts include pear and almond tart, and perhaps apple fritters with vanilla ice cream, and there may well be Manchego cheese with quince. Friendly and civilised staff add to the appeal, and the wine list is a carefully chosen, short selection with nearly everything under £20, including south-west French house wines at £9.75 (white) and £10 (red).

CHEF: Andrew Green PROPRIETOR: Robinson's Restaurants OPEN: Tue to Fri L 12.30 to 3, Mon to Fri D 6.30 to 10.30, Sat 12.30 to 4, 7 to 10.30, Sun 12.30 to 4, 7 to 10 CLOSED: Christmas MEALS: alc (main courses L £6 to £11, D £7 to £14). Set L Tue to Fri £9.50 (2 courses) to £12.50 SERVICE: 12.5% (optional), card slips closed CARDS: Amex, Delta, MasterCard, Switch, Visa DETAILS: 50 seats. 50 seats outside. Private parties: 8 main room, 10 to 25 private room. Vegetarian meals. Wheelchair access (not WC). No music. Air-conditioned ⊖ St John's Wood

Salusbury

NEW ENTRY map 13

50–52 Salusbury Road, NW6 6NN
TEL/FAX: (020) 7328 3286

COOKING **3**
MODERN ITALIAN
£22–£42

Upwardly mobile Queen's Park now has a restaurant it can be proud of. New owners took over this old pub late in 1999 and installed Enrico Sartor in the kitchen. He is a Venetian with a fondness for the robust flavours of northern Italian cooking, a sophisticated and inventive version of which he serves up in the plainly decorated dining room that merges seamlessly with the bar and shares its typically pubby atmosphere. Fish and seafood feature prominently, starters taking in tuna carpaccio with celeriac, pan-fried sardines stuffed with parsley and rocket, or whole crab with chilli mayonnaise. Main courses run to grilled sea bass with samphire.

Game has produced rabbit with spicy sausage in a rich Neapolitan-style tomato sauce, a winner at inspection, and impressive ways with pasta have included two large ravioli filled with a pumpkin paste and garnished with fried sage leaves. Vanilla-flecked pannacotta containing strawberries has figured among tempting dessert options. Service is casual. The wine list offers varied global bottles at very reasonable prices, bolstered occasionally with additions from the owner's private cellar. Prices start at £9.75.

(£5) *indicates that the restaurant has elected to participate in the* Good Food Guide *voucher scheme. For full details, see page 6.*

CHEF: Enrico Sartor PROPRIETORS: Nicholas Mash and Robert Claassen OPEN: Tue to Sun L 12.30 to 3.30, all week D 7 to 10.30 CLOSED: 25 Dec MEALS: alc (main courses £8.50 to £13). Set L Sun £15 SERVICE: not inc, 12.5% for parties of 7 or more CARDS: Delta, MasterCard, Switch, Visa DETAILS: 50 seats. 16 seats outside. Private parties: 20 main room. Vegetarian meals. Children's helpings. No children at D. No cigars/pipes in dining room. No music ⊖ Queen's Park

Sarkhel's

map 12

199 Replingham Road, SW18 5LY — COOKING **2**
TEL: (020) 8870 1483 FAX: (020) 8874 6603 — INDIAN
WEB SITE: www.sarkhels.com — £27–£50

Service in these enlarged premises is in the best tradition of Indian attentiveness and hospitality, and the food is real Indian, not curry-house stuff. Udit Sarkhel offers dishes from a number of regions, including Goan galinha cafreal (pan-fried marinated chicken served with potatoes), and a mild lamb curry flavoured with coriander and pepper from the Nilgiri hills. Starters are largely vegetarian, ranging from spinach and yoghurt soup to roast chickpeas tossed with onion, coriander, tomatoes and spices.

Meat and fish eaters might opt for lambs' liver and kidneys cooked with onions, tomatoes, pepper and lemon, the tandoor is used for chicken, quail and pomfret, and a few specials such as red snapper piri-piri supplement the printed menu. Desserts are limited to gulab jamun and commendable kulfis of mango, or cardamom-flavoured malai. Only a couple of bottles on the short, helpfully annotated wine list are above £20. Around a dozen are sold by the glass, from £2.75 for house French (£10.90 a bottle).

CHEF: Udit Sarkhel PROPRIETORS: Udit and Veronica Sarkhel OPEN: Fri to Sun L 12 to 2.30, Tue to Sun D 6 to 10.30 (11 Fri and Sat) CLOSED: 25 and 26 Dec, 2 weeks Aug MEALS: alc (main courses £4.50 to £12). Set L £9.95, Set D before 8 £10 (2 courses) to £12 SERVICE: not inc CARDS: Amex, Delta, MasterCard, Switch, Visa DETAILS: 88 seats. Private parties: 93 main room. Vegetarian meals. Children's helpings. No smoking in 1 dining room. Wheelchair access (also women's WC). Music. Air-conditioned ⊖ Southfields

Sartoria

map 15

20 Savile Row, W1X 1AE — COOKING **2**
TEL: (020) 7534 7000 FAX: (020) 7534 7070 — ITALIAN
£33–£90

Tailoring puns are everywhere in this smartly themed Italian restaurant, from framed shirts, tape measures, buttons, bow ties and pincushions, to two portly tailors' dummies ('I like to think they are Ann Widdecombe and Roy Hattersley'). The smooth operation, which has something of the production line about it, turns out antipasti of mixed vegetables or cured meats, a few pasta dishes, fish such as grilled sea trout with broad beans, and light meat dishes, for example rabbit combined with waxy potatoes and girolles.

Simple techniques are responsible for much of the output, including pink grilled young Dorset lamb at inspection, although what appears on the plate may not always correspond to its menu description. Well-rendered pannacotta has come with first-rate raspberries, and cheeses are well selected. Service is generally polite, willing and professional, although it has lapses. Those who can afford Savile Row suits will presumably not be daunted by high prices on the all-Italian wine list, which includes many fashionable producers and an impressive range of Super-Tuscans. House wines start at £14, although there is not much else under £20.

CHEF: Piero Boi PROPRIETOR: Conran Restaurants OPEN: Mon to Sat L 12 to 3, all week D 6.30 to 11 (6 to 10 Sun) CLOSED: Christmas, Easter MEALS: alc (main courses £15 to £30). Set bar L and D £15 (2 courses) to £20 SERVICE: 12.5% CARDS: Amex, Delta, Diners, MasterCard, Switch, Visa DETAILS: 120 seats. Private parties: 12 main room, 16 private room. Vegetarian meals. Wheelchair access (also WC). No music. Air-conditioned ⊖ Oxford Circus, Piccadilly Circus

Schnecke

NEW ENTRY **map 15**

58–59 Poland Street, W1V 3DF
TEL: (020) 7287 6666 FAX: (020) 7287 3636
EMAIL: soho@schnecke-restaurants.com
WEB SITE: www.schnecke-restaurants.com

COOKING **1**
ALSATIAN
£26–£50

The creators and former owners of Belgo (see Belgo Noord, London) have gone Alsatian, aiming to popularise the hearty food of this region in a bierkeller ambience, with rough wooden walls, red gingham paper cloths, and young, friendly staff. The jokiness apparent in cross-sections of cabbages in Damien Hirst-style formaldehyde tanks does not extend to the kitchen, which works seriously. Geared up for informal group eating, the menu opens with tartes flambées (ultra-thin Alsace 'pizzas') with toppings from Munster cheese to smoked trout and asparagus, meant to be shared and eaten with fingers. 'Sides' are salads and, curiously, escargots (at £23.99 for 48, although there are smaller portions), while 'Alsace traditionals' include coq-au-Riesling, six sorts of sausage, and choucroute. Tartes reappear in sweet versions with fruit, flambéed at table with eau-de-vie. A list of exclusively Alsatian wines (champagne apart) opens at £13, otherwise drink German beers. A second branch is at 80–82 Upper Street, London N1 (tel (020) 7226 6800).

CHEFS: Kwame Boaten and Philippe Blaise PROPRIETOR: André Plisnier OPEN: all week noon to 11.30 (10.30 Sun) CLOSED: 25 Dec MEALS: alc (main courses £6 to £16) SERVICE: 12.5%, card slips closed CARDS: Amex, Delta, Diners, MasterCard, Switch, Visa DETAILS: 170 seats. Private parties: 80 main room, 40 private room. Vegetarian meals. Children's helpings. Wheelchair access (also WC). Music. Air-conditioned ⊖ Oxford Circus

Searcy's

map 13

Level 2, Barbican Centre, Silk Street, EC2Y 8DS
TEL: (020) 7588 3008 FAX: (020) 7382 7247

COOKING **2**
MODERN BRITISH
£33–£61

Searcy's is a long, narrow room in the Barbican complex overlooking a patio and concrete fountain, and facing St Giles Cripplegate church. Catering to theatre- and concert-goers, it keeps an eye on London fashion, although the cooking can be inconsistent. A menu du jour of three choices at each course supplements the short carte, and the repertoire takes in a tiny but well-balanced serving of Devon crab with mint in a globe artichoke base, and roast duck breast with lentils. At its best, careful timing has produced roast cod in a light broth accompanied by white beans, carrot and pancetta, and an apposite serving of buttery mash. Earl Grey ice cream may accompany rhubarb and strawberry crumble. Wines are French-led and prices are ambitious, although house wine is £12.95.

CHEF: Richard Brookes PROPRIETOR: Searcy's OPEN: Sun to Fri L 12 to 2.45, all week D 5 to 10.45 (7.30 Sun) CLOSED: 24 and 25 Dec, weekends and D in Aug MEALS: alc (main courses £17.50 to £20). Set L and D £18.50 (2 courses) to £21.50 SERVICE: not inc CARDS: Amex, Delta, Diners, MasterCard, Switch, Visa DETAILS: 130 seats. Private parties: 30 main room, 30 to 300 private rooms. Vegetarian meals. Children's helpings. No-smoking area. Wheelchair access (also WC). Occasional music. Air-conditioned ⊖ Barbican, Moorgate (£5)

Sheekey's

map 15

28–32 St Martin's Court, WC2N 4AL
TEL: (020) 7240 2565 FAX: (020) 7240 8114

COOKING **5**
BRITISH SEAFOOD
£26–£87

Founded in 1890, and now technically into its third century, Sheekey's is reminiscent of the Ivy (under the same ownership, see entry, London), with old photographs, recent paintings, tables in alcoves, and a lot of male businessmen sitting at them. Exceptionally well run, it specialises in first-class fish and seafood, from lobster mayonnaise, and caviar with blinis, to jellied eels, and moist fresh haddock in a thick, rich batter, with minted pea purée and chips. The strong-on-comfort menu also includes a tip-top version of fish pie, and impeccable crab bisque. For every dish with traditional leanings (such as Morecambe Bay potted shrimps with toast and land-cress), there is another with a modern slant: perhaps roast artichoke soup with queen scallops, poured 'hot and creamy' from a copper pan at table.

Desserts might run to a light, refreshing and fragrant jelly of pink grapefruit and rosemary, or rice pudding with prunes in armagnac worthy of 'special mention'. This being a popular theatreland address, there is more than one sitting, and the reason for a cover charge in the main restaurant but not the bar is apparently to 'differentiate between the two' for those who are unable otherwise to tell the difference. Nevertheless, the food is considered good value (note the weekend set-price lunch), helped by seamless, prompt and courteous service. In place of half-bottles, the wine list offers 20 or more decanted into half-litre carafes; there are more wines over £20 than under, but prices start at £11.25.

CHEF: Tim Hughes PROPRIETORS: Caprice Holdings OPEN: all week 12 to 3 (3.30 Sun), 5.30 to 12 CLOSED: 25 and 26 Dec, 1 Jan, bank hols MEALS: alc (main courses £9.50 to £27). Set L Sat and Sun £9.75 (2 courses) to £13.50. Cover £1.50 (main restaurant) SERVICE: not inc CARDS: Amex, Delta, Diners, MasterCard, Switch, Visa DETAILS: 105 seats. Vegetarian meals. No cigars in dining room. Wheelchair access (not WC). No music. Air-conditioned ⊖ Leicester Square

The Guide office can quickly spot when a restaurateur is encouraging customers to write recommending inclusion. Such reports do not further a restaurant's cause. Please tell us if a restaurateur invites you to write to the Guide.

Singapore Garden

map 13

83–83A Fairfax Road, NW6 4DY
TEL: (020) 7328 5314 FAX: (020) 7624 0656

COOKING **2**
SINGAPOREAN
£18–£66

Light, airy and businesslike, Singapore Garden's two rooms are decorated with orchids and pictures of old Singapore. Chinese-style Straits cooking is the mainstay of an impressively long menu, so roast duck, various stir-fries and sweet-and-sour chicken can all be ordered. However, Singaporean and Malaysian hawker-style dishes are one of the main attractions. Laksa soup with notably fresh prawns and a thick coconut sauce got one reporter's meal off to a flying start, followed by soft-textured tauhu goreng (fried bean curd served cold with mild peanut sauce). Nonya bean sprouts come with pungent dried salt-fish: relished by some, too strong for others. Authentic desserts, such as Indonesian chendol (red beans, pandan jellies and palm sugar in coconut milk) keep up the consistently high standards, as does well-paced, amenable and informative service. A varied wine list of 50 reasonably priced bottles is augmented by cocktails and Singaporean Tiger beer. Four house wines are £11.50 and £12.50.

CHEF: Mrs Siam Kiang Lim PROPRIETORS: the Lim family OPEN: all week 12 to 2.45, 6 to 10.45 (11.15 Fri and Sat) CLOSED: 1 week Christmas MEALS: alc (main courses £5.50 to £20). Set L £7 (2 courses) to £8.50, Set D £18.50 to £30 SERVICE: 12.5% (optional), card slips closed CARDS: Amex, Delta, Diners, MasterCard, Switch, Visa DETAILS: 100 seats. 12 seats outside. Private parties: 50 main room, 8 private room. Vegetarian meals. No cigars in dining room. Music. Air-conditioned ⊖ Swiss Cottage

Snows on the Green

map 12

166 Shepherd's Bush Road, W6 7PB
TEL: (020) 7603 2142 FAX: (020) 7602 7553

COOKING **2**
MODERN BRITISH/MEDITERRANEAN
£29–£52

It may be situated on a busy arterial road, but, inside, Snows is all bright relaxation. A provençale colour scheme predominates, with walls in muted citrus shades, primary-coloured chairs and pictures of lavender fields hung about. Sebastian Snow's food is Mediterranean-led with the odd pan-Asian note, and many dishes have pleased. Chicken liver and foie gras parfait is obligingly smooth and rich, and a main course of scallops with buckwheat noodles in a sauce of ginger, coconut and spring onions has been 'vivid, well-seasoned, successful stuff'. The long menus might also offer roast veal rump with Piedmontese pepper and anchovy juices, poached duck with cotechino sausage and marrow toasts, and desserts such as black and white chocolate cheesecake. The lemon tart is appropriately sharp, as is the friendly service. House French at £10.95 leads a concise, but inspiring, wine list that stays mostly below £20.

CHEF/PROPRIETOR: Sebastian Snow OPEN: Mon to Fri L 12 to 3, Mon to Sat D 6 to 11 CLOSED: 4 days Christmas, bank hol Mons MEALS: alc (main courses £10 to £14). Set L and D 6 to 8 £13.50 (2 courses) to £16.50 SERVICE: not inc, 12.5% for parties of 6 or more CARDS: Amex, Delta, Diners, MasterCard, Switch, Visa DETAILS: 80 seats. 10 seats outside. Private parties: 75 main room, 15 and 20 private rooms. Vegetarian meals. Children's helpings. Wheelchair access (not WC). Occasional music. Air-conditioned

Soho Soho

map 15

11–13 Frith Street, W1V 5TS
TEL: (020) 7494 3491
WEB SITE: www.sante-gcg.com

COOKING **2**
FRENCH/MEDITERRANEAN
£27–£59

Street views of the heart of Soho justify the name as well as allowing diners to keep an eye on what is going on. Andrew Parkinson's cooking, shown to best effect in the first-floor dining-room, mobilises sound Anglo-French technique to deliver the likes of pigeon suprême with Puy lentils, the meat rare, smoked and deeply flavoured, a pâté of its liver appearing as an unexpected extra spread on toast. An intense stuffing of leek and bacon lends depth to a leg of rabbit, the mild mustard sauce providing discreet support, while sea bass comes with lemon and parsley oil on a bed of Jerusalem artichokes. Warm apple compote also receives plaudits, not least for its excellent honey and ginger ice cream, as does the passion-fruit crème brûlée. Service is friendly, but takes its time. Wines are listed by style, starting at £10.50, and stopping at £44 for Cuilleron's brilliant Côte-Rôtie.

CHEF: Andrew Parkinson PROPRIETOR: Groupe Chez Gérard OPEN: Mon to Fri L 12 to 3, Mon to Sat D 5.30 to 11.30 MEALS: alc (main courses £9.50 to £17.50). Set D before 7.30 and after 10 £12.50 (2 courses) to £15.50. Cover £1.50 SERVICE: 12.5% (optional), card slips closed CARDS: Amex, Delta, Diners, MasterCard, Switch, Visa DETAILS: 65 seats. Private parties: 120 main room, 60 private room. Vegetarian meals. Music. Air-conditioned ⊖ Leicester Square, Tottenham Court Road

Soho Spice

map 15

124–126 Wardour Street, W1V 3LA
TEL: (020) 7434 0808 FAX: (020) 7434 0799
EMAIL: info@sohospice.co.uk
WEB SITE: www.sohospice.co.uk

COOKING **1**
INDIAN
£24–£44

This lively Soho bar-restaurant pleases young people who appreciate vibrant colours and vibrating music. Main courses, served on a thali dish, come with rice, naan, dhal and vegetables. Most are old friends, with both chicken tikka masala and its hotter cousin murgh jalfrezi. A less obvious choice is chukandari champ (spicy lamb chops marinated with beetroot, black pepper and ginger), and among vegetarian options is kadai paneer (cubes of home-made cottage cheese with pepper and ginger in a tomato and onion sauce). Varied starters take in minced lamb patties, and spinach and onion bhaji. A frequently changing three-course menu offers regional specialities – from Bengal to Uttar Pradesh – and modest two-course lunch and pre-theatre menus provide further choice. Finish with rasmalai or kulfi. House Vin de Pays d'Oc is £12.50 on the short, well-described wine list.

CHEF: S.S. Rana PROPRIETOR: Amin Ali OPEN: all week noon to midnight (3am Fri and Sat) CLOSED: 25 Dec MEALS: alc (main courses £8.50 to £15.50). Set L £7.50 (2 courses), Set D Mon to Sat 5 to 7 £7.50 (2 courses), Set D £15.95 SERVICE: not inc CARDS: Amex, Delta, Diners, MasterCard, Switch, Visa DETAILS: 140 seats. Private parties: 100 main room, 45 private room. Vegetarian meals. Wheelchair access (also WC). Music. Air-conditioned ⊖ Tottenham Court Road, Piccadilly Circus (£5)

Sonny's

map 12

94 Church Road, SW13 0DQ
TEL: (020) 8748 0393 FAX: (020) 8748 2698

COOKING **5**
MODERN EUROPEAN
£26–£51

Managing to appear both stylish and suburban, this long, narrow dining room is the setting for an individual style of cooking: 'traditional combinations with mildly exotic variations' is how one visitor summed it up. At one end of the spectrum is an appealingly earthy inclination, represented by pig's trotter and ox tongue with onion and chicory salad, or a tartlet of deep-fried sweetbreads with onion sauce and liquorice glaze. At the other is an enterprising way with fish, partnering steamed brill with horseradish velouté, and roast fillet of eel with beetroot chutney.

Diners can opt for a small glass of Sauternes (for a supplement) to accompany their boudin of foie gras with quince and rosemary compote, while an interesting line in soups takes in garlic and thyme with Swiss chard, and Jerusalem artichoke with chanterelle ravioli. Although extra vegetables can be ordered separately, dishes are usually complete in themselves: pan-fried scallops for example come with a carrot and Parmesan risotto. Desserts may not be as exciting as the rest, but have included mango tarte Tatin with fromage frais sorbet, and rhubarb and almond tart. A short contemporary wine list starts with house vin de pays at £9.50, and a café menu serves late and light lunches until 4pm.

CHEF: Leigh Diggins PROPRIETOR: Rebecca Mascarenhas OPEN: all week L 12.30 to 2.30 (3 Sun), Mon to Sat D 7.30 to 11 CLOSED: bank hols MEALS: alc (main courses £10.50 to £14.50). Set L £12 (2 courses). Café menu available 12 to 4 SERVICE: 12.5% (optional), card slips closed CARDS: Amex, Delta, Diners, MasterCard, Switch, Visa DETAILS: 100 seats. Private parties: 80 main room, 20 private room. Vegetarian meals. Children's helpings. Wheelchair access (not WC). No music. Air-conditioned ⊖ Hammersmith (£5)

Soviet Canteen £

NEW ENTRY **map 13**

430 King's Road, SW10 0LJ
TEL: (020) 7795 1556 FAX: (020) 7795 1562
EMAIL: food@sovietcanteen.com
WEB SITE: www.sovietcanteen.com

COOKING **3**
FRENCH/RUSSIAN
£22–£45

The theme is highlighted by stainless-steel tables, splashes of colour (generally red) on white walls, and pictures of Lenin. Authenticity happily does not apply to chatty and informative service, nor to a menu that embraces bits of the old USSR, from Estonia and Georgia to south-eastern Siberia, extending in time from before the Revolution to the present day. While techniques may be Western, ingredients run to rye bread, beetroot, mushrooms and sour cream. Traditional openers (zakuski) take in garlicky aubergine and mushroom 'caviars', served with pickled vegetables marinated with dill and caraway, as well as the real thing (oscietra or sevruga with blinis and sour cream).

Despite tongue-in-cheek side dishes of 'mashski' and 'chipski', the cooking is both thoughtful and convincing, from a starter of pirozhki (little deep-fried goat's cheese pies) to a main course of Kamchatka manti (steamed crab and oyster mushroom parcels on vegetable ribbons and tarragon cream). Tvorozhniki (sour-sweet pancakes with strawberries and cinnamon sour cream) is a reasonable approximation of a traditional dish. House wines are £10.75 on a short, reasonably priced list, but a collection of around 100 vodkas is the main attraction.

CHEF: Michael Soutar PROPRIETOR: Peoples Pleasure Limited OPEN: all week D only 6.30 to 11 (10 Sun) MEALS: alc (main courses £8 to £14). Set D £9.95 (2 courses) to £12.95 SERVICE: 12.5% (optional), card slips closed CARDS: Amex, Delta, Diners, MasterCard, Switch, Visa DETAILS: 40 seats. Private parties: 30 main room, 2 to 8 private rooms. Vegetarian meals. Children's helpings. Music. Air-conditioned ⊖ Sloane Square (£5)

Spiga

map 15

84–86 Wardour Street, W1V 3LF
TEL: (020) 7734 3444 FAX: (020) 7734 3332

COOKING **2**
ITALIAN
£30–£44

Spiga may be ultra-modern in its cool décor, with efficient and stylishly uniformed waiters, but the cooking is much more a blend of old and new. Home-smoked mussels make an original starter, while pasta might come with shiitake mushrooms, leeks and fontina, but pizzas from a wood-fired oven are the heart of the menu. They range from simple Margherita to a less usual one of swordfish with capers and shallots. The few main dishes are equally varied, offering perhaps chargrilled ribeye with grilled raddicchio and potatoes, guinea-fowl breast wrapped in smoked ham accompanied by turnip tops, and fried cod with black olives. Desserts take in lemon and mascarpone tart, pannacotta with rhubarb, and, of course, tiramisù. Wines on the short, sharp Italian list are decently priced, from £12, with four half-bottles and the same number sold by the glass.

CHEF: Nick Melmoth-Coombs PROPRIETOR: A To Z Restaurants OPEN: all week 12 to 3, 6 to 12 (11 Sun to Tue) CLOSED: 25 and 26 Dec MEALS: alc (main courses £8.50 to £13.50) SERVICE: 12.5% (optional), card slips closed CARDS: Amex, Delta, Diners, MasterCard, Switch, Visa DETAILS: 125 seats. Private parties: 135 main room. Vegetarian meals. Children's helpings. No cigars/pipes in dining room. Wheelchair access (also WC). Music. Air-conditioned ⊖ Piccadilly Circus, Leicester Square

Spread Eagle

map 12

1–2 Stockwell Street, SE10 9JN
TEL: (020) 8853 2333 FAX: (020) 8305 0447
EMAIL: bookings@spreadeagle.org

COOKING **2**
FRENCH
£24–£51

History permeates every inch of this listed seventeenth-century coaching inn. It became a restaurant more than 30 years ago, though the décor still has a pubby feel, with artefacts and old pictures adorning the walls. The emphasis is firmly on traditional French cuisine, though some concessions to new ideas are allowed, producing a warm salad of pigeon with quails' eggs and tapénade, and pan-fried sea bass with creamed polenta and a ginger and pepper coulis. Reporters occasionally find the various elements of a dish mismatched, but sound materials are at the core of things, from smoked salmon in orange with blinis and sour cream, to grilled red snapper with aubergine. Red wine and pear tart with crisp pastry has been a successful dessert. French house wines at £9.75 (£2.75 a glass) head up a list that dips into the major regions.

CHEF: Bernard Brique PROPRIETOR: Richard Moy OPEN: all week L 12 to 3, Mon to Sat D 6.30 to 10.30 CLOSED: Christmas to New Year MEALS: alc exc Sun L (main courses £10.50 to £14.50). Set L £12.50 (2 courses) to £15.50, Set D Mon to Thur £15.50 SERVICE: 12.5% (optional), card slips closed CARDS: Amex, Delta, Diners, MasterCard, Switch, Visa DETAILS: 80 seats. 25 seats outside. Private parties: 40 main room, 16 to 42 private rooms. Vegetarian meals. No-smoking area. Children's helpings. Wheelchair access (also WC). Music. Air-conditioned (£5)

The Square

map 15

6–10 Bruton Street, W1X 7AG
TEL: (020) 7495 7100 FAX: (020) 7495 7150

COOKING **8**
MODERN FRENCH
£43–£106

The large, airy dining room, with well-spaced tables and strikingly colourful modern canvases, can get a little noisy: rare for such a fine restaurant, but preferable to the whispering mausoleum alternative. Dinner offers not just a generous choice but lots of appealing ideas as well, from jelly of oysters and langoustines with sour cream, to pea and ham soup with pig's trotter and morels. Riches, luxury and soft textures abound, and while not all the truffles and foie gras may be strictly necessary they can produce sensuous results, for example in a white, frothy, truffle-infused velouté containing mushroom duxelles wrapped in expertly made pasta.

Sound materials, unquestionable technical skill and safe handling are the watchwords, giving rise to many a fish and shellfish delight, from splendid sea bass with risotto, to a salmon and herb fishcake like no other. The food can be dazzlingly good, only let down by an occasional glitch, plus generally salty seasoning on more than one occasion. Among highlights have been a revelatory goose sausage – moist, gamey, intense – served with a goose liver salad, and Bresse pigeon accompanied by a small jacket potato stuffed with mushrooms and topped with foie gras.

Soufflés are a fine way to finish – perhaps a creamy, zestful blood orange version, with a scoop of not too sweet chocolate ice cream inserted by the waiter – or there may be a refreshing citrus fruit terrine in champagne jelly to counteract all the richness. Incidentals are first-class, from carefully crafted amuse-gueules and an intensely flavoured appetiser soup, via bread and a fine pre-dessert beignet with yoghurt and raspberry coulis, to impeccable petits fours. Lunch is a steal.

While the business of asking for a signed contract for parties of six or more did not endear itself to one group, service from mainly French staff has varied from very poor to well paced and 'among the best in London'. A hefty wine list concentrates on French classics at up-market prices, although Australia, California and Italy are also well represented. The sommelier is notably helpful, regardless of price bracket. House wines are £17.50, and seven table wines are served by the glass.

The Guide is totally independent, accepts no free hospitality, and survives on the number of copies sold each year.

CHEF: Philip Howard PROPRIETORS: Philip Howard and Nigel Platts-Martin OPEN: Mon to Fri L 12 to 2.45, all week D 6.30 to 11 (10.30 Sun) CLOSED: L bank hols MEALS: Set L £20 (2 courses) to £25, Set D £50 to £65 SERVICE: 12.5% (optional), card slips closed CARDS: Amex, Delta, Diners, MasterCard, Switch, Visa DETAILS: 75 seats. Private parties: 85 main room, 18 private room. Vegetarian meals. No cigars/pipes in dining room. Wheelchair access (also WC). No music. Air-conditioned ⊖ Green Park

Sri Siam Soho

map 15

16 Old Compton Street, W1V 5PE — COOKING **2**
TEL: (020) 7434 3544 FAX: (020) 7287 1311 — THAI
£24–£51

Painted palm and banana trees on pastel-coloured walls are reminders of tropical Thailand in this cheerful, trendy Soho long-runner. The vegetarian list is comparatively short, but an adequate choice includes mixed starters, satay, and deep-fried 'golden bags', as well as tom yum soup and green curry. There is more than a touch of authentic Thai fire in koong pao (grilled marinated king prawns with tamarind and chilli sauces), hot and sour mixed vegetable casserole, and papaya pok pok, a hot and sour salad. For a refreshing change, try ba chore, a light cucumber soup, as a palate-cleanser before the main course. Finish with something like fruit salad, or banana fritters with ice cream. Staff are unobtrusive and efficient, and an interesting wine list is arranged by style, with house wines £11.95.

CHEF: Nico Thongsumrit PROPRIETOR: Oriental Restaurant Group plc OPEN: Mon to Sat L 12 to 3, all week D 6 to 11.15 (10.30 Sun) CLOSED: 25 and 26 Dec, 1 Jan MEALS: alc (main courses £7 to £10.50). Set L £14, Set D £17 to £28 SERVICE: 12.5% (optional) CARDS: Amex, Delta, Diners, Mastercard, Switch, Visa DETAILS: 150 seats. Private parties: 30 main room, 30 private room. Vegetarian meals. Wheelchair access (not WC). Music. Air-conditioned ⊖ Leicester Square, Tottenham Court Road (£5)

Stephen Bull

map 15

5–7 Blandford Street, W1H 3AA — COOKING **6**
TEL: (020) 7486 9696 FAX: (020) 7224 0324 — MODERN BRITISH
£29–£51

Stephen Bull has disposed of his other two restaurants, in Smithfield and St Martin's Lane, since the last edition of the Guide, and there was even some uncertainty in the air as we went to press about this, the first-born of his progeny. There may or may not be a revamp, but if not expect cool, minimally adorned décor and modern paintings, and a continuation of the confidently handled, earthy European cooking that originally made the proprietor's name. The kitchen baton has passed to Roger Gorman, but assured technique and culinary understanding remain the same. Twice-baked goats'-cheese soufflé is a positively flavoured regular that impresses, whether accompanied by beetroot confit, or a salad of olive, parsley and coriander.

Moist and impeccably timed fillet of mackerel served on minted tabbouleh has been another highly satisfying starter, and more than one reporter has praised a main-course of calf's liver and kidney with creamed potato and mustard sauce. Desserts show the same panache, in a brown-sugar meringue with bananas and hot butterscotch, and a properly made English suet pudding flavoured with ginger and served with golden syrup sauce. Service can be a bit distant. Great consideration has gone into the stylistically arranged and usefully annotated wine list, which picks up pedigree Australians, top-notch Burgundies and good southern French wines, among others, at generally fair prices, starting at £12.50.

CHEF: Roger Gorman PROPRIETOR: Stephen Bull OPEN: Mon to Fri L 12 to 2.30, Mon to Sat D 6 to 10.30 CLOSED: 1 week Christmas, bank hols MEALS: alc (main courses £8 to £15) SERVICE: not inc, card slips closed CARDS: Amex, Delta, Diners, MasterCard, Switch, Visa DETAILS: 55 seats. Private parties: 55 main room. Vegetarian meals. Children's helpings. No cigars/pipes in dining room. Wheelchair access (not WC). No music. Air-conditioned ⊖ Bond Street

Sugar Club £✱ **map 13**

21 Warwick Street, W1R 5RB — COOKING **5**
TEL: (020) 7437 7776 FAX: (020) 7437 7778 — FUSION
WEB SITE: thesugarclub.co.uk — £42–£70

Two rather ordinary dining rooms (the cramped basement reserved for non-smokers), in a quiet spot near Regent Street, are the venue for some of the most inventive fusion cooking in the capital. Although Peter Gordon left in 1999, his culinary fingerprints are all over the menus. Some dishes are played fairly straight – fat, fresh, accurately grilled scallops with sweet chilli sauce and crème fraîche for example – while others verge on the wacky: spicy kangaroo salad with lime-chilli dressing, or duck confit falafel with pickled red cabbage and guindilla chilli. In the seemingly endless quest for novelty, not all combinations work equally well. For loud, clear and harmonious flavours, look to some of the more straightforward dishes such as rose-pink rack of lamb with herbed couscous, roast cherry tomatoes and mint harissa.

Technique throughout is impeccable, while portions vary from the supermodel's option of brightly flavoured, wafer-thin salmon sashimi scattered with coriander leaves and mujjol (fish roe) in a lemon-yuzu dressing, to substantial main courses. Fruity and refreshing puddings provide a welcome break after all the excitement, ranging from summer berries with an aromatic orange flower custard, to an expertly made and intensely flavoured cherry tart with clotted cream. Service is alert and responsive. Much care and effort has gone into the wine list, with New World choices standing out, although there is also a strong showing of classed-growth clarets. Unfortunately, mark-ups are high. House French wines, a Marsanne and a Merlot, are £12.50.

CHEF: David Selex PROPRIETORS: Ashley Sumner and Vivienne Hayman OPEN: all week 12 to 3, 6 to 11 CLOSED: 24 to 26 Dec; Good Fri to Easter Mon MEALS: alc (main courses £14 to £21.50) SERVICE: 12.5% (optional), card slips closed CARDS: Amex, Delta, Diners, MasterCard, Switch, Visa DETAILS: 150 seats. Private parties: 80 main room, 50 private room. Vegetarian meals. No smoking in 1 dining room. Wheelchair access (not WC). No music. Air-conditioned ⊖ Oxford Circus, Piccadilly Circus

Card slips closed *in the details at the end of an entry indicates that the total on the slips of credit cards is closed when handed over for signature.*

Sushi-Say

map 12

33B Walm Lane, NW2 5SH
TEL: (020) 8459 2971 and 7512
FAX: (020) 8907 3229

COOKING **3**
JAPANESE
£27–£67

'Even the soy sauce is specially prepared in a traditional way here,' writes Mrs Yuko Shimizu, who runs this informal restaurant with her bandana-wearing husband Katsuharu. The Japanese feel is further enhanced by monochrome pictures, a ledge of knick-knacks, and bare wooden tables set close together. Eating options on a long, user-friendly menu range widely from plates of mixed sushi, and set dinners based on tempura, teriyaki and sashimi, to noodle and rice dishes, by way of grills and fries: horse mackerel with salt perhaps, or crispy battered soft shell crabs. Lunch plates (with miso soup) look good value, while à la carte starters take in dumplings (of minced pork, or scallop and squid) alongside grilled salted chicken gizzard, and grilled aubergine with bonito flakes. House wine is £9.80, though the well-annotated choice of sakés is worth exploring.

CHEF: Katsuharu Shimizu PROPRIETORS: Katsuharu and Yuko Shimizu OPEN: Sat and Sun L 12 to 2.30, Tue to Sun D 6.30 to 10.30 CLOSED: 25 and 26 Dec, 1 Jan, 1 week summer MEALS: alc (main courses £6 to £19). Set L £6.90 (2 courses) to £12.40, Set D £17.70 to £28 SERVICE: not inc CARDS: Amex, Delta, MasterCard, Switch, Visa DETAILS: 36 seats. Private parties: 15 main room. Vegetarian meals. No-smoking area. Wheelchair access (also WC). No music. Air-conditioned ⊖ Willesden Green

Tajine

map 15

7A Dorset Street, W1H 3FE
TEL/FAX: (020) 7935 1545

COOKING **1**
MOROCCAN
£21–£46

The cheerful ambience of this busy restaurant owes much to attractive artefacts and prints on its terracotta walls, even more to amiable service led by owner Mehdi Barradi. Vegetarian starters include harira soup, tabbouleh, and fried aubergines with yoghurt and harissa, while pastry dishes (briouattes or b'stilla) might be filled with cheese, chicken or seafood. Grills, tajines and couscous are the main business, typically centred around chicken or lamb. Couscous Imperial combines both meats with merguez, vegetables and 'kedera', a garnish of caramelised onion and raisins. Other appealing variations include lamb with black pepper sauce and caramelised pear. Non-carnivores will appreciate tajine Berber, its vegetables cooked in paprika, cumin and herbs. Desserts are now mainly Moroccan too, from rice pudding with orange blossom to the ubiquitous pastries. Ten red wines and five white are Moroccan, with the house selection £10.50.

CHEF: Gonul Ozturk PROPRIETOR: Mehdi Barradi OPEN: Mon to Fri L 12.30 to 3, Mon to Sat D 6 to 11 CLOSED: Christmas, some bank hols MEALS: alc (main courses £8.50 to £13.50). Set L £7.50 (2 courses) SERVICE: not inc CARDS: Delta, MasterCard, Switch, Visa DETAILS: 36 seats. 8 seats outside. Private parties: 46 main room. Vegetarian meals. Children's helpings. No smoking in 1 dining room. No cigars/pipes in dining room. Wheelchair access (not WC). No music ⊖ Baker Street (£5)

Tamarind

map 15

20 Queen Street, W1X 7PJ
TEL: (020) 7629 3561 FAX: (020) 7499 3561
EMAIL: tamarind.restaurant@virgin.net

COOKING **2**
INDIAN
£27–£68

Set in a quiet Mayfair side street, this Indian restaurant befits its location with opulent decorative touches that include gold-painted pillars and sari silks. Curry-house aficionados will not find many familiar items on the menu. Among starters may be a salad of tandoori prawns and scallops with sour grapes and mint, a Bombay-style 'snack' of lentil dumplings with tamarind and yoghurt sauce, or fried chicken livers and mushrooms in a poppadum basket. Curried lamb shank on the bone with bags of flavour impressed at inspection, as did John Dory with unusual, seaweed-like crispy spinach. Commendable breads include skilfully prepared roomali roti and flaky pudhina paratha, while lassi comes in a salt version flavoured with cumin, and a fruity mango alternative. Service is abundant and solicitous, perhaps to a fault. The mainly French wine list, with interesting New World interpolations, suits the food reasonably well. House wines start at £14.50

CHEF: Atul Kochhar PROPRIETOR: Indian Cuisine Ltd OPEN: Sun to Fri L 12 to 2.45, all week D 6 to 11.30 (10.30 Sun) CLOSED: 25 and 26 Dec, 1 Jan MEALS: alc (main courses £10 to £17). Set L £10 (2 courses) to £14.95, Set D before 7 and after 10.30 £22.50, Set D £28.50 to £40 SERVICE: 12.5% (optional) CARDS: Amex, Delta, Diners, MasterCard, Switch, Visa DETAILS: 100 seats. Private parties: 100 main room. Vegetarian meals. Music. Air-conditioned ⊖ Green Park (£5)

La Tante Claire 🍷

map 14

Wilton Place, SW1X 7RL
TEL: (020) 7823 2003 FAX: (020) 7823 2001
EMAIL: tanteclaire@relaischateaux.fr

COOKING **8**
FRENCH
£43–£124

As hotel dining rooms go, this one (attached to the Beverley Hotel) feels opulent enough for the talents of Pierre Koffmann. Walls change colour smoothly from mint green to lilac, while large and generously spaced tables sport trendy pieces of ornamental fruit, all seemingly part of an effort to combine modernity with quiet restraint. The operation is uncompromisingly French, and while the generous menu follows classic lines – first courses of foie gras and shellfish helped out by snails and frogs' legs, for example – and embraces luxury ingredients with a will, it also expresses an individual style. An important element of this is the balance that dishes achieve, combining flavour, texture and colour in one harmonious whole, perhaps exemplified by grilled red mullet garnished with black truffle on pea risotto.

Reports of the food, however, continue to be mixed, inconsistencies occurring during the course of a single meal. The cooking mark is thus a bit of a compromise between some ordinary dishes and some dazzling ones, such as the benchmark tian of crab laced with avocado mayonnaise, layered with cucumber and topped with finely diced red pepper. Ideas may not always be original, but polished execution makes some of them stand out: at inspection a fan of pink venison slices with a red wine and bitter chocolate sauce, accompanied by a little pile of root vegetables.

French cheeses are kept in fine condition, and desserts have produced a copybook assiette of chocolate featuring a first-rate chocolate tart (pastry work is a strength), a velvety mousse, and a 'completely perfect' dark chocolate sorbet. Battalions of waiters deliver a variable standard of service, and improvable bread comes round at intervals on an old-fashioned trolley. High prices foster high expectations, and the 'discretionary' service charge can seem like rubbing salt in the wound. The wine list is no longer exclusively French, with the introduction of a smattering of New World bottles and rather more reverential Italian and Spanish sections. This is good news, although the bulk of the list remains overpriced for ordinary drinkers. The odd bottle from regional France and Argentina comes in under £20.

CHEF/PROPRIETOR: Pierre Koffmann OPEN: Mon to Fri L 12.30 to 2, Mon to Sat D 7 to 11 CLOSED: Christmas, Easter, bank hols MEALS: alc (main courses £26 to £35). Set L £28 SERVICE: 12.5% (optional), card slips closed CARDS: Amex, Delta, Diners, MasterCard, Switch, Visa DETAILS: 60 seats. Private parties: 60 main room, 14 private room. Vegetarian meals. No cigars/pipes in dining room. No music. Air-conditioned ⊖ Hyde Park Corner

Tas £

NEW ENTRY **map 13**

33 The Cut, SE1 8LF
TEL: (020) 7928 1444 FAX: (020) 7633 9686

COOKING **2**
MEDITERRANEAN
£18–£40

The long open kitchen at the back of this bustling modern brasserie makes its presence felt by flares from the chargrills and appetising aromas that waft through the room. A generous, good-value menu includes a familiar run of meze, grills, casseroles (Tas refers to the Anatolian pot in which they are cooked), vegetarian and seafood dishes. The cooking veers towards a sophisticated, rather than earthy or peasanty, approach, yet offers some vibrant flavours, particularly among meze: tasty kisir – crushed walnuts and hazelnuts with bulgur wheat and a herby tomato sauce – is one of the more unusual options. An inspector enjoyed karisik izgara – a mixed grill of lamb, meatballs and chicken with couscous – while a dessert that takes time, but is worth the wait, is kunefe: shredded wheat with unsalted white cheese and honey syrup. Turkish house wines, at £8.90, don't please everyone, but the short, diverse and modestly priced list offers enough variety.

CHEFS: Onder Sahan and Erdal Tilki PROPRIETOR: Two Men and a Lady Ltd OPEN: all week noon to 11.30 (10.30 Sun) MEALS: alc (main courses £6 to £14.50). Set L and D £6.45 to £17.95 SERVICE: 10% CARDS: Amex, MasterCard, Switch, Visa DETAILS: 150 seats. 4 seats outside. Private parties: 40 main room. Vegetarian meals. Wheelchair access (also WC). Music. Air-conditioned ⊖ Southwark

Dining rooms where music, either live or recorded, is never played are signalled by No music *in the details at the end of an entry.*

Not inc *in the details at the end of an entry indicates that no service charge is made and any tipping is at the discretion of the customer.*

Tate Gallery Restaurant 🍷 map 13

Millbank, SW1P 4RG
TEL: (020) 7887 8825 FAX: (020) 7887 8902
EMAIL: email@tate.org.uk
WEB SITE: www.tate.org.uk

COOKING **3**
MODERN BRITISH
£32–£62

Long considered to hold the title of 'best restaurant in any museum or gallery in the UK', the Tate now has a bit of competition from elsewhere (see also National Gallery and National Portrait Gallery). The 1926 Rex Whistler mural remains an impressive background to a lunchtime menu that offers the chance of seasonally adjusted light meals – asparagus with hollandaise, spring risotto with grilled buffalo mozzarella – and a monthly-changing set-price deal that has taken in onion and goats'-cheese tart, and cold poached cod.

Meatier roast rack of lamb, or grilled beef fillet with chunky chips and béarnaise, may be on hand for larger appetites, and desserts have pursued a vinous theme in the form of sparkling Shiraz jelly, and raspberries in Cabernet Sauvignon. Service has been found wanting but, as art forms go, the wine list excels in what it sets out to do. Its simple presentation belies an impressive range of great wines at seductive prices, and, bearing in mind this is a lunchtime-only restaurant, there are plenty of half-bottles, plus 13 wines by the glass. But this is one venue where it would be well worth writing off the afternoon and spending that bit more on a truly memorable bottle. A few wines come in under £20, and the Pinot Grigio 1998 from Sergio and Mauro Drius in Friuli, is particularly recommended at £19.

CHEF: Richard Zuber PROPRIETOR: Tate Gallery Restaurant Ltd OPEN: all week L only 12 to 3 (4 Sun) CLOSED: 24 to 26 Dec MEALS: alc (main courses £9.50 to £17.50). Set L £16.75 (2 courses) to £19.50 SERVICE: not inc, card slips closed CARDS: Amex, Delta, Diners, MasterCard, Switch, Visa DETAILS: 96 seats. Private parties: 30 main room. Vegetarian meals. Children's helpings. No-smoking area. Wheelchair access (also WC). No music. Air-conditioned ⊖ Pimlico

Teatro map 15

93–107 Shaftesbury Avenue, W1V 8BT
TEL: (020) 7494 3040 FAX: (020) 7494 3050
EMAIL: teatroclub@btconnect.com

COOKING **4**
MODERN EUROPEAN
£31–£74

The entrance, up a flight of stairs and along a corridor, may not look particularly inviting, but the bar and white-walled restaurant are pleasant spaces, with windows overlooking Romilly Street adding to the sense of lightness. An appealing mix of modern ideas is served up with commendable restraint and economy, taking in risotto (a theme with many variations), potato gnocchi with cherry tomatoes and diced olives, and lambs' sweetbreads with pappardelle and wild mushrooms.

The carte changes every couple of months, although many dishes return as the cycle spins round again: salade niçoise, a light dish of pig's trotter well balanced by a sharp salad, and bitter chocolate tart with milk ice cream. Staff are helpful and efficient, and lunch is considered good value, especially when compared with the carte. Wines can add a significant wodge to the bill, although the small selection of mature clarets is fairly priced. To offset the paucity of half-bottles, more than a dozen are available by the large glass from £3.25 to £10.50. A second branch opened in Leeds just before the Guide went to press, at Quays, Concordia Street, Leeds LS1 4BJ (tel (0113) 243 2244).

CHEF: Stuart Gillies PROPRIETORS: Lee Chapman and Leslie Ash OPEN: Mon to Fri L 12 to 3, Mon to Sat D 6 to 11.45 CLOSED: Christmas to New Year, bank hol Mons MEALS: alc D (main courses £13 to £20). Set L £15.50 (2 courses) to £18, Set pre-theatre D £15 (2 courses) to £18. Cover £1.50 SERVICE: 12.5% (optional), card slips closed CARDS: Amex, Delta, Diners, MasterCard, Switch, Visa DETAILS: 100 seats. Private parties: 200 main room. Vegetarian meals. Children's helpings. Wheelchair access (also WC). No music. Air-conditioned ⊖ Leicester Square

Teca 🍷 — map 15

54 Brooks Mews, W1Y 2NY — COOKING **4**
TEL: (020) 7495 4774 FAX: (020) 7491 3545 — MODERN ITALIAN
£34–£67

Even if the glass, wood, and steel-framed chairs had not already proclaimed Teca's modern credentials, the menu would leave no doubt as to where it stands. The idea behind an enoteca is to sample a few wines, and accompany these with simple dishes that won't interfere with the main business. The food is more ambitious than that might suggest, but hats off to Marco Torri for keeping the menu appropriately straightforward and yet full of interest. The repertoire ranges from dishes obviously designed with one eye on the national flag – chilled tomato soup with peas and sour cream – to simple adaptations such as beef carpaccio with shiitakes, celery and truffle oil.

Items are clearly conceived and lucidly presented, taking in sliced salmon with a basil and goats' cheese dressing, and potato gnocchi stuffed with artichoke purée in a ginger and white wine sauce. Uncomplicated fish dishes are brightly turned out – fillet of sea bass with sauté potatoes, black olives, capers and basil – while desserts such as tiramisù or chocolate and carrot cake give the wine list a chance to show what it is made of: seven sweet wines are available by the glass. The all-Italian list is a showcase of quality and diversity, stretching the length and breadth of the country. Many of the great names are here – Gaja, Conterno, Allegrini – though prices are not cheap, with little under £20. Eleven wines are sold by the glass, from £4, with bottle prices opening at £15.

CHEF: Marco Torri PROPRIETOR: A To Z Restaurants OPEN: Mon to Fri L 12 to 2.30, Mon to Sat D 7 to 10.30 MEALS: Set L £18 (2 courses) to £21, Set D £19 (2 courses) to £27 SERVICE: 12.5% (optional), card slips closed CARDS: Amex, Delta, MasterCard, Switch, Visa DETAILS: 60 seats. Private parties: 40 main room. Vegetarian meals. Children's helpings. Cigars/pipes at manager's discretion. Wheelchair access (not WC). Music ⊖ Bond Street

The text of entries is based on unsolicited reports sent in by readers, backed up by inspections conducted anonymously. The factual details under the text are from questionnaires the Guide sends to all restaurants that feature in the book.

NEW CHEF *is shown instead of a cooking mark where a change of chef occurred too late for a new assessment of the cooking.*

Tentazioni

map 13

2 Mill Street, SE1 2BD
TEL/FAX: (020) 7237 1100
EMAIL: tentazioni@aol.com
WEB SITE: www.tentazioni.freeserve.co.uk

COOKING **4**
MODERN ITALIAN
£30–£58

A few alterations to this former warehouse have turned it into more of a restaurant than a bar-restaurant, its yellow walls replaced by peach, and its large, well-spaced tables served by anxious-to-please staff. The disappearance of guiding light Alessio Brusadin has left the quality of cooking virtually unaltered, as a bilingual menu continues to avoid clichés and deal in simple but interesting ideas, from truffled cheese ravioli with asparagus to thinly sliced calf's tongue and roast beetroot with salsa verde.

Some humble materials help to give the food its identity: perhaps mackerel with sweet-and-sour onions, or moist, aubergine-stuffed saddle of rabbit. Combinations are handled well, including a creamy dish of chickpeas with first-rate crab tortelli; and red mullet accompanied by quartered artichokes and light, crisp, well-flavoured polenta. Desserts run from delicate pannacotta with grappa and ripe fruits to ricotta and morello cherry tart, by way of chocolate 'salami'. The all-Italian list (apart from champagne) doesn't offer much under £20, preferring to head for the finer end of the market, but wines are well chosen, and house red and white are £12.50.

CHEF: Nicola Ducceschi PROPRIETORS: Christian di Pierro, Mauro Santoliquido and Maurizio Rimerici OPEN: Tue to Fri L 12 to 2.30, Mon to Sat D 7 to 11 CLOSED: 24 Dec to 5 Jan, bank hols MEALS: alc (main courses £14 to £17.50). Set L £15 (2 courses) to £19, Set D £35 SERVICE: 12.5% (optional), card slips closed CARDS: Amex, Delta, Diners, MasterCard, Switch, Visa DETAILS: 50 seats. Private parties: 40 main room, 30 private room. Vegetarian meals. Children's helpings. Wheelchair access (not WC). Music ⊖ London Bridge (£5)

Terrace

map 13

33C Holland Street, W8 4LX
TEL: (020) 7937 3224 FAX: (020) 7937 3323

COOKING **4**
MODERN BRITISH
£25–£70

Simple, seasonal English food, with a few diversions to France and Italy, is the draw at this small Kensington restaurant. A warm welcome is extended both in the modern but far from bleak dining room and, in summer, outside on the terrace, where a gas heater supplements (or counters) the weather. On a menu of five or six choices per course, starters range from lightly curried smoked haddock soup, via sauté potato gnocchi, to luxurious options such as foie gras with caramelised blood oranges, and warm lobster salad (also available as a main course).

Typical of the meatier side of things might be steak, kidney, mushroom and Guinness pie, and grilled pork chop served with buttered leeks and an apple and date chutney. Puddings run to rhubarb bavarois, and chocolate soufflé with pistachio ice cream. Weekend set lunches offer classic brunch-style dishes such as toasted muffin with spinach, ham, egg and hollandaise sauce. A maximum mark-up of £15 makes the pricier end of the mainly French wine list particularly attractive, while a small selection of impeccable New World bottles offer viable alternatives. House wines are £11.50 and six are available by the glass.

CHEF: Sam Metcalfe PROPRIETOR: Steven Loverage OPEN: Mon to Sat 12 to 2.30, 7 (5.45 summer) to 10.30, Sun L 12.30 to 3 CLOSED: 24 Dec to 3 Jan MEALS: alc (main courses £10.50 to £23). Set L Mon to Fri £12.50 (2 courses) to £14.50, Set L Sat and Sun £16.50 (2 courses) to £19.50, Set D summer before 7 £14.50 (2 courses) SERVICE: 12.5% (optional), card slips closed CARDS: Amex, Delta, Diners, MasterCard, Switch, Visa DETAILS: 27 seats. 14 seats outside. Private parties: 28 main room. Vegetarian meals. No music. Air-conditioned ⊖ High Street Kensington (£5)

Thai Garden £

map 12

249 Globe Road, E2 0JD
TEL: (020) 8981 5748

COOKING **1**
THAI
£22–£35

Serving substantial portions of prettily presented meat-free Thai food at affordable prices, this restaurant maintains its popularity, even if the modest shop premises stand in need of some refreshment. Both vegetarian and seafood menus divide into appetisers, soups, mains, and rice and noodle dishes. Praise comes for tom yum goong (hot-and-sour prawn soup) and appealingly spicy tom khar (crisp cauliflower in thick coconut soup), the latter big enough for a main course. Seafood includes fried pomfret with a choice between mushrooms and vegetables, hot chilli sauce, dry curry, or sweet-and-sour vegetables, while the generally serviceable nature of the cooking is apparent in a red curry of aubergines with fried gluten, pineapple, tomato, grapes and bamboo shoots. House wine is £7.50.

CHEF: Naphaphorn Duff PROPRIETORS: Jack and Suthinee Hufton OPEN: Mon to Fri L 12 to 2.45, all week D 6 to 10.45 CLOSED: bank hols MEALS: alc (main courses £4.50 to £7). Set L £7.50 (2 courses), Set D £16 to £21 SERVICE: 10%, card slips closed CARDS: Amex, Delta, Diners, MasterCard, Switch, Visa DETAILS: 32 seats. Private parties: 20 main room, 12 and 14 private rooms. Vegetarian meals. No smoking in 1 dining room. Wheelchair access (not WC). Music ⊖ Bethnal Green (£5)

Time

LONDON GFG 2001 COMMENDED

NEW ENTRY map 12

7A College Approach, SE10 9HY
TEL: (020) 8305 9767
FAX: (020) 8293 0267
EMAIL: enquiries@timerestaurant.com
WEB SITE: www.timerestaurant.com

COOKING **3**
MODERN EUROPEAN-PLUS
£34–£47

Britain's first purpose-built music hall, dating from 1831, is now a restaurant, bar and gallery. The last two, sharing the first floor, exhibit monochrome photographs of pop icons, while the restaurant is another flight up, on a glassed-in balcony. Clearly, a young and decibel-resistant crowd is aimed at, and the food is offbeat and diverting: one visitor's dish of ostrich with sweet potato mash, garnished with plantain crisps, brought together ingredients native to Asia, Africa and South America. Judging by the enthusiasm for crisps, textures are something of a priority: shredded, deep-fried crunchy duck has come mixed with salad leaves and celeriac crisps, with a jelly-like chilli plum sauce.

Flavour combinations are well judged too, the star turn at inspection being a main course of lightly poached halibut with cauliflower and parsley purée and a vanilla velouté sprinkled with chives. Desserts are a little more workaday, encompassing rhubarb tart with stewed berries, and lemon cheesecake with raspberry coulis. Service makes up in enthusiasm what it lacks in panache. The short, serviceable wine list doesn't offer the same interest as the menu, but opens with house French at £12.

CHEF: Adrian McLeod PROPRIETOR: Pascal Dowers OPEN: Tue to Fri and Sun L 12 to 2.15 (3.15 Sun), 7 to 10.15 CLOSED: 25 Dec, 1 Jan MEALS: Set L £14.50 (2 courses, inc wine), Set D £19.50 (2 courses) to £23.50 SERVICE: not inc, 10% for parties of 6 or more CARDS: Amex, MasterCard, Switch, Visa DETAILS: 100 seats. Private parties: 250 main room. Vegetarian meals. Children's helpings. No cigars/pipes in dining room. Music. Air-conditioned

Titanic

map 15

81 Brewer Street, W1R 3FH
TEL: (020) 7437 1912 FAX: (020) 7439 4747

COOKING **3**
MODERN BRITISH
£35–£67

Since opening in 1998, this particular Titanic has survived its maiden voyage without sinking into the Atlantic (see entry) below. Passengers may experience serious interrogation before embarkation but, once aboard, all is plain sailing. The art deco feel of the ocean liner is convincing, and shipboard pursuits include as much drinking as eating, but the galley earnestly maintains its line in unashamedly British cooking and, considering the scale of the operation, turns out surprisingly consistent results. Alongside such stalwarts as fish and chips with pea purée, eggs Benedict with hollandaise, and smoked haddock kedgeree, are slightly less usual but equally comforting wild mushrooms on toast, Spanish omelette with fresh crab, and roast suckling pig. Anyone whose appetite for nursery nostalgia is still not satisfied will be able to assuage it with knickerbocker glory or Black Forest gâteau. Service is 'good and quick', and a long list of wines arranged by style includes a few under £20. House vin de pays is £15.

CHEF: Peter Reffell PROPRIETOR: Marco Pierre White OPEN: Mon to Sat D only 5.30 to 12 MEALS: alc (main courses £9.50 to £25) SERVICE: 12.5% (optional), card slips closed CARDS: Amex, Delta, Diners, MasterCard, Switch, Visa DETAILS: 360 seats. Private parties: 610 main room. No children in bar area. Wheelchair access (also WC). Music. Air-conditioned ⊖ Piccadilly Circus

Turner's

map 14

87–89 Walton Street, SW3 2HP
TEL: (020) 7584 6711 FAX: (020) 7584 4441

COOKING **4**
MODERN EUROPEAN
£31–£73

The square room with its blue and yellow décor and smart napery helps to make reporters feel comfortable and properly looked after. Service is both friendly and attentive, adding to the civilised air that media chef Brian Turner has built up over the years. The food's French roots are never far away, as the carte deals in chicken liver and foie gras pâté, or an artichoke heart filled with smoked haddock brandade and served with a tarragon butter sauce, although pasta makes an appearance now and again, and a lemon and chilli glaze has perked up a dish of baked salmon. Indeed, seafood is generally well treated, yielding accurately timed pan-fried sea bass (to start), and moist, crisp-skinned red mullet fillet accompanied by lightly sauté scallops.

Soft textures permeate desserts such as a rich chocolate and hazelnut silk, or blueberry and fromage frais mousse, and if the food is soothing rather than cutting edge, that suits reporters fine. The set lunch (with a choice of three options per course) has sent more than one away happy: a turbot starter, loin of veal, and chocolate marquise is the sort of straightforward yet effectively cooked food that can make a mockery of the competition. Prices on the wine list reflect its blue-blooded nature, as it concentrates on champagnes, Burgundies and clarets, though there are some respectable New World and regional French offerings. There is a page each of half-bottles and desert wines, and cognac and armagnac are also well represented. House selections start at £15.50.

CHEF: Jon Jon Lucas PROPRIETOR: Brian Turner OPEN: Mon to Sat 12.30 to 2.30, 7.30 to 11 CLOSED: Christmas, 13 to 27 Aug, bank hols MEALS: Set L £15 (2 courses) to £44.50, Set D £26.50 (2 courses) to £44.50 SERVICE: not inc, 10% for parties of 8 or more CARDS: Amex, Delta, Diners, MasterCard, Switch, Visa DETAILS: 52 seats. Private parties: 52 main room. Vegetarian meals. Children's helpings. Wheelchair access (not WC). Music. Air-conditioned ⊖ South Kensington

Two Brothers

map 12

297–303 Regents Park Road, N3 1DP
TEL: (020) 8346 0469

COOKING **2**
SEAFOOD
£19–£45

Maritime blue paintwork and brassy lettering announce an old-style chippie, confirmed by piscine prints lining the walls, although heavy white linen points to something a bit smarter than average. Blackboard specials bolster the carte, widening the scope to take in anything from jellied eels to rock oysters, from Arbroath smokies to avocado with prawns. Freshness and accurate timing are never in question, producing fat, juicy, pan-fried mackerel, served laudably plain as a starter. Main courses of cod and haddock are crisply deep-fried in light batter, with grilling, steaming or frying in matzo meal also on offer. Tartare sauce and mushy peas are the real thing, although chips can be mundane, and desserts of apple pie or ice cream are hardly a strength. Service is capable and efficient, and the short wine list kicks off with a Côtes de Duras, at £9.85, unique to the restaurant.

CHEFS/PROPRIETORS: Leon and Tony Manzi OPEN: Tue to Sat 12.30 to 2.30, 5.30 to 10.15 CLOSED: Christmas, last 2 weeks Aug, bank hol Mon and following Tue MEALS: alc (main courses £7.50 to £17.50) SERVICE: not inc, card slips closed, 10% for parties of 6 or more CARDS: Amex, Delta, MasterCard, Switch, Visa DETAILS: 90 seats. Children's helpings. No-smoking area. Music. Air-conditioned ⊖ Finchley Central

Several sharp operators have tried to extort money from restaurateurs on the promise of an entry in a guidebook that has never appeared. The Good Food Guide *makes no charge for inclusion.*

▲ *means accommodation is available.*

Utah 🍷

NEW ENTRY **map 12**

18 High Street, SW19 5DX
TEL: (020) 8944 1909 FAX: (020) 8944 1890
EMAIL: mail@utahfood.co.uk
WEB SITE: www.utahfood.co.uk

COOKING **4**
CONTEMPORARY AMERICAN
£28–£57

The Hartford group, which has dotted London and the suburbs with restaurants named after American states (see Dakota and Montana), opened Utah in Wimbledon early in 2000. A large, exotic flower display draws attention to the bar, and colossal wine glasses suggest that drinking is taken seriously. Format and menu echo those of other branches, and Gavin Houghton (who has done stints at Le Caprice and Putney Bridge, see entries) seems to have slipped easily into the idiom here. Chargrilled Iowa ribeye is a steak for an ample appetite, served with hand-cut fries and barbecue sauce, while cross-hatch stripes are also branded on to meaty blue-fin tuna, served with anchovy and cilantro (coriander) sauce.

The theme also takes in roasted corn fritters with a sweet pasilla chilli dipping sauce to start, and chimichanga (sweet spring roll) of rhubarb and cheese to finish; alternatively, try a motherly slice of maple-glazed apple pie with vanilla ice cream. Slick yet unobtrusive service is typical. A global list of wines divided by style is accompanied by succinct, enticing tasting notes. The range is diverse and impressive, a handful singled out for their sustainable agriculture credentials. House wines are £12, and 11 wines are available by the glass.

CHEF: Gavin Houghton PROPRIETOR: The Hartford Group OPEN: Mon to Fri 12 to 2.30, 6.30 to 11, Sat 12 to 4, 6.30 to 11, Sun 12 to 4, 6.30 to 9 MEALS: alc (main courses £10 to £16). Set L Mon to Fri £12.95 (2 courses inc wine) SERVICE: 12.5% (optional), card slips closed CARDS: Amex, Delta, MasterCard, Switch, Visa DETAILS: 80 seats. 25 seats outside. Private parties: 100 main room. Vegetarian meals. Children's helpings. Wheelchair access (also WC). Music. Air-conditioned ⊖ Wimbledon

Villandry

map 15

170 Great Portland Street, W1N 5TB
TEL: (020) 7631 3131 FAX: (020) 7631 3030

COOKING **3**
MODERN EUROPEAN
£30–£49

Villandry has expanded, with a bar now augmenting the food store and florist. As far as the restaurant is concerned, a saunter through the enticing deli on the way there is about the best appetiser they have, followed perhaps by a slice of savoury tart such as loose-textured courgette with leek and ricotta on light, crisp and buttery shortcrust. Better still may be a salad of calf's liver and black pudding with a poached egg. The kitchen turns out some impressive modern dishes, notable for the freshness of materials; fish options combine accurate timing with characterful flavouring in pink-cooked seared tuna with Caesar salad and anchovies, and skate wing with lyonnaise potatoes and capers.

Dense, dark chocolate cake comes with a jug of superb thick cream ('I would imagine cream used to taste like this before the war,' commented one too young to know), or there may be exotic fruit pavlova with passion-fruit syrup. France dominates the wine list in surprisingly old-fangled fashion, with a few from

Italy, Spain, Australia and New Zealand bringing up the rear. House Languedoc is £11, and there are about a dozen wines by the glass.

CHEF: Steven Evennett-Watts PROPRIETORS: Martha Greene and Jeremy Sinclair OPEN: Mon to Sat noon to 10, Sun noon to 3 CLOSED: Christmas, New Year MEALS: alc (main courses £10 to £15) SERVICE: 12.5% (optional), card slips closed CARDS: Amex, Diners, MasterCard, Switch, Visa DETAILS: 100 seats. 20 seats outside. Private parties: 10 to 20 private rooms. Vegetarian meals. No smoking in dining room. Wheelchair access (not WC). No music. Air-conditioned ⊖ Great Portland Street

Wagamama £ map 15

4A Streatham Street, WC1A 1JB
TEL: (020) 7323 9223 FAX: (020) 7323 9224
EMAIL: mail@wagamama.com
WEB SITE: www.wagamama.com

COOKING **1**
JAPANESE-STYLE
£14–£25

'A noodle canteen, not a conventional restaurant' is Wagamama's own definition of this cavernous, minimally designed space where tables are shared and no bookings are taken. No smoking is part of the healthy-eating policy, and the lack of both starters and desserts would seem to be part of the policy of encouraging customers to eat fast and leave. Side dishes, which may arrive before, with or after main courses, include chicken or vegetable yakitori, and various gyoza dumplings. Main dishes are three sorts of noodles – soba, udon, and ramen – which come teppan-fried or in a variety of soups, with accompaniments ranging from grilled pork escalope to chargrilled salmon fillet. There are a few rice dishes too. House wines are £9.50, with a further four also sold by the glass, or drink saké, Japanese beers or one of the raw fruit or vegetable juices; green tea is free on request. This is the flagship of a growing chain with London branches at 10A Lexington Street, W1R 3HS, 101A Wigmore Street, W1H 9LA, 26 Kensington High Street, W8 4PF, and 11 Jamestown Road, NW1 7BW, and another in South King Street, Dublin 2.

CHEF: Jason Petit PROPRIETOR: Wagamama Ltd OPEN: Mon to Sat noon to 11, Sun (and bank hols) 12.30 to 10.30 CLOSED: 25 and 26 Dec MEALS: alc (main courses £5 to £10) SERVICE: not inc CARDS: Amex, Delta, Diners, MasterCard, Switch, Visa DETAILS: Private parties: 20 main room. Vegetarian meals. No smoking in dining room. No music. Air-conditioned ⊖ Tottenham Court Road

Waterloo Bar and Kitchen NEW ENTRY map 13

131 Waterloo Road, SE1 8UR
TEL: (020) 7928 5086 FAX: (020) 7928 1880

COOKING **3**
GLOBAL
£21–£46

Conveniently located just behind the Old Vic and close to Waterloo Station, this cream-painted bar/restaurant is a lively (and often noisy) new addition to the thriving local scene. Its imaginative, modern cooking takes inspiration from just about everywhere, producing oriental duck with spiced pecan salad, and braised oxtail with horseradish and parsley-flavoured mash. Despite the informal feel, the kitchen has turned out some classy dishes, including an up-market risotto laden with ceps and anointed with truffle oil. Skilful fish cookery has also been demonstrated in light, crisp tempura of brill with tartare sauce, and well-timed seared tuna with wilted bok choy. Homely puddings might run to pear and blackberry crumble, or dark chocolate truffle torte. A short wine list rattles through samples from most major wine-producing countries or regions. Prices are very fair, with plenty under £15 and house vins de pays at £10.25.

CHEF: Christian Hodgskin PROPRIETOR: Clive Watson OPEN: Mon to Sat 12 to 2.45, 5.30 to 10.30 CLOSED: 22 Dec to 2 Jan MEALS: alc D from 7 (main courses £10 to £14). Set L and D 5.30 to 7 £10 (2 courses) to £13 SERVICE: not inc, 10% for parties of 6 or more CARDS: Amex, Delta, Diners, MasterCard, Switch, Visa DETAILS: 50 seats. 6 seats outside. Private parties: 50 main room. Vegetarian meals. No pipes in dining room. Music ⊖ Waterloo

White Onion 

map 13

297 Upper Street, N1 2TU
TEL/FAX: (020) 7359 3533

COOKING **5**
MODERN EUROPEAN
£31–£46

The Islington branch of Bijan Behzadi's ingredient-named restaurant group (see Red Pepper, Green Olive, the National Gallery's Crivelli's Garden and Purple Sage, all London) is only a short trot from the Almeida Theatre, with dinner service helpfully opening at 6.30. The place is neither large nor cramped, and modern, stylishly spare design creates a good visual impression. Menus have never stuck exclusively to the Mediterranean repertoire, but Pasquale Amico, who arrived in May 2000, appears to have extended them still further: Italian sushi with sweet grape dressing is nothing if not fusion food. Some of the combinations may be unusual, but they are intelligently put together: a tranche of well-timed, lightly caramelised foie gras has been satisfyingly paired with a slice of mozzarella, the two well balanced by the bitter tang of rocket leaves.

Those who reckon it is difficult to beat slow cooked meat on the bone will relish sweet, tender lamb shank, served with a cake of earthy aubergine caviar, garlic gnocchi and an aromatic tomato and rosemary jus. Desserts also take a shrewd approach, producing a variation on crêpes suzette by partnering the pancake with Grand Marnier ice cream and a sauce combining confit orange and shredded mint. French cheeses are a good bet: a well-kept selection served with quince preserve. Service is normally smart and agreeable. There are few bargains to be had on the predominantly French wine list. A couple are offered by the glass, and house wines start at £14.50.

CHEF: Pasquale Amico PROPRIETOR: Red Pepper Group OPEN: Sat and Sun L 12.30 to 3, all week D 6.30 to 10.45 (10.30 Sun) MEALS: alc L (main courses £9 to £11). Set D £21.50 (2 courses) to £24.50 SERVICE: 12.5% (optional), card slips closed CARDS: Amex, MasterCard, Switch, Visa DETAILS: 65 seats. Private parties: 50 main room, 15 private room. Vegetarian meals. No cigars/pipes in dining room. Music. Air-conditioned ⊖ Angel, Highbury & Islington

The 2002 Guide will be published before Christmas 2001. Reports on meals are most welcome at any time of the year, but are particularly valuable in the spring (no later than June). Send them to The Good Food Guide, *FREEPOST, 2 Marylebone Road, London NW1 4DF. Or email your report to goodfoodguide@which.net*

William IV £

NEW ENTRY map 12

786 Harrow Road, NW10 5JX — COOKING **3**
TEL: (020) 8969 5944 FAX: (020) 8964 9218 — MODERN EUROPEAN
WEB SITE: www.williamiv.co.uk — £23–£47

Distancing themselves from a gastro-pub, the owners note that bar and restaurant are separate, although both are housed in a large Victorian pub. The division has produced a big, airy dining room with well-spaced tables, quiet enough for diners to enjoy a conversation. Charming and friendly waitresses serve amid the stylish retro décor, and there are more tables in the heated garden. A modern British menu, changed daily, borrows ideas from the Mediterranean and executes them well. Asparagus comes pleasingly chargrilled with roast peppers and mozzarella, and pan-fried chicken legs are partnered with chorizo, purple-sprouting broccoli and a light chilli sauce. Inspirations from further afield include hoisin roast belly of pork with rocket and yellow mustard. Portions are generous.

A star among desserts has been a velvety, crisp-topped mascarpone brûlée with a fruity mix of strawberry, raspberry and blueberry, while fruit salad is enterprisingly composed of lychees, passion fruit, pineapple, blueberries and melon. Bread is charged for, and £1.30 brings a basket of two Italian varieties. At Sunday lunch there are various roasts plus fish and vegetarian alternatives. House wines are £10.50, the rest mostly under £20, with more than a dozen by the glass.

CHEF: Rufus Deakin PROPRIETOR: Megamade Ltd OPEN: Mon to Wed 12 to 3, 6 to 10.30, Thur and Fri 12 to 3, 6 to 11, Sat 12 to 3, 7 to 11, Sun 12 to 4, 7 to 10 CLOSED: 24 to 26 Dec, 1 Jan MEALS: alc (main courses £7 to £15). Set L Mon to Fri £7.50 (1 course), Set L Sun £12 (2 courses) to £15 SERVICE: not inc, card slips closed, 10% for parties of 5 or more CARDS: Amex, Delta, Diners, MasterCard, Switch, Visa DETAILS: 70 seats. 60 seats outside. Private parties: 40 main room, 12 and 40 private rooms. Vegetarian meals. Music ⊖ Kensal Green (£5)

Wilsons

map 12

236 Blythe Road, W14 0HJ
TEL: (020) 7603 7267 FAX: (020) 7602 9018 — COOKING **2**
EMAIL: bob@wilsons-restaurant.co.uk — SCOTTISH-PLUS
WEB SITE: www.wilsons-restaurant.co.uk — £27–£51

On the face of it this is a fiercely Scottish outpost, where Robert Wilson greets visitors in a kilt, where the Edwardian style dining room is hung with Scottish paintings, and where the air is thick with Scottish folk-songs and bagpipe music. Haggis comes with mashed potato, swede and a dram. On the other hand there are some Buddhist artefacts, the tape veers occasionally towards Thai music, the bottled water is from Devon, bread comes from France (no bannocks or oatcakes), and the cheese is Stilton rather than Dunsyre Blue. Think of it perhaps as a successful neighbourhood restaurant, serving anything from first-class salmon fishcakes with parsley sauce to moist, crisp-skinned confit of duckling with apple and calvados sauce. Vegetables and chips are also commended. Desserts include intensely flavoured lemon posset, and Atholl brose, accurately described by Mr Wilson as 'swimming in booze'. House wines are £10.50, and whiskies include distinguished single malts and double-matured bottlings dating back to 1979.

CHEF: Robert Hilton PROPRIETORS: Bob Wilson and Robert Hilton OPEN: all week 12 to 2.30, 7 to 10.30 MEALS: alc (main courses £11 to £16.50) SERVICE: 12.5% (optional), card slips closed CARDS: Delta, MasterCard, Switch, Visa DETAILS: 44 seats. Private parties: 35 main room. Vegetarian meals. Children's helpings. Wheelchair access (not WC). Music. Air-conditioned ⊖ Hammersmith

Wiltons

map 15

55 Jermyn Street, SW1Y 6LX
TEL: (020) 7629 9955 FAX: (020) 7495 6233
EMAIL: wiltons@wiltons.co.uk
WEB SITE: www.wiltons.co.uk

COOKING **2**
TRADITIONAL ENGLISH
£36–£98

This is an old-established, discreetly opulent restaurant serving fresh, well-prepared traditional English food: at a price. As a refuge from the modern world it could hardly be bettered, offering a clubby Edwardian ambience and old-fashioned solicitous service. The food is so traditional it might be labelled 'heritage', taking in luxurious lobster and caviar, rich omelette Arnold Bennett, and simple grills from sirloin steak to lamb cutlets. Ingredients are typically first rate, although standards of cooking have varied, yielding poor whitebait and grouse, as well as expertly prepared English asparagus with hollandaise, prime Dover sole meunière, and equally impressive grilled halibut. Desserts are not a highlight, apart perhaps from a superlative crème brûlée. Wine is impeccably served from a mainly French list, with house wines £17.25 for white, £17.50 for red, and only three others below £25.

CHEF: Ross Hayden PROPRIETOR: J.O. Hambro Ltd OPEN: Sun to Fri 12 to 2.30, 6 to 10.30 CLOSED: bank hols MEALS: alc (main courses £14 to £29). Set L Sun £19.75. Cover £1.50 SERVICE: not inc CARDS: Amex, Diners, MasterCard, Switch, Visa DETAILS: 80 seats. Private parties: 80 main room, 20 private room. Jacket and tie. Wheelchair access (not WC). No music. Air-conditioned ⊖ Green Park

Zafferano

map 14

15 Lowndes Street, SW1X 9EY
TEL: (020) 7235 5800 FAX: (020) 7235 1971

COOKING **7**
ITALIAN
£33–£77

If tables are hard to come by, it is because this is rather a special place. It has the disarming air of an up-market neighbourhood restaurant, where food is meant to be enjoyed, yet delivers it with a skill and integrity that few local haunts can hope to match. Above all it captures the spirit of Italian cooking, which involves much ingenuity with often humble materials, and much culinary rejoicing when something out of the ordinary comes along. Salads offer an opportunity for resourcefulness, delighting not least for their simple treatment of seasonal ingredients: chargrilled asparagus with Parmesan, or early peas and broad beans with Pecorino, both from a spring menu. Pasta takes many forms too, from simple trenette al pesto, via tagliolini with zucchini and bottarga, to ravioli: perhaps filled with oxtail, or, less usually, with borage. And when it comes to risotto, the langoustine version is 'as stunning as ever'.

Simple roasting and chargrilling are typically applied to main courses – of duck, tuna, and perhaps pork stuffed with herbs and fried zucchini – and greens often accompany: veal chop with garlic and cavolo nero stew, or robustly seasoned pot-roast lamb shank with spinach and potato purée. Desserts are usually paired with an ice cream for contrast: polenta cake with cooked wine ice cream, chocolate soufflé torte with a liquorice ice, or orange and pine nut tart with a Cointreau version. The food is considered good value, and while there has been a quibble about wine prices there can be no questioning the quality and variety on the proudly Italian list. House wines from Marche are £12.50.

CHEF/PROPRIETOR: Giorgio Locatelli OPEN: all week 12 to 2.30, 7 to 11 (10.30 Sun) CLOSED: 2 weeks Christmas to New Year MEALS: Set L £18.50 (2 courses) to £21.50, Set D £29.50 (2 courses) to £39.50 SERVICE: not inc CARDS: Amex, Delta, Diners, MasterCard, Switch, Visa DETAILS: 55 seats. Private parties: 6 main room. Vegetarian meals. Children's helpings. Wheelchair access (not WC). Music. Air-conditioned ⊖ Knightsbridge

Zaika

map 14

257–259 Fulham Road, SW3 6HY
TEL: (020) 7351 7823 FAX: (020) 7376 4971

COOKING **5**
MODERN INDIAN
£26–£53

Vineet Bhatia has succeeded in breaking the mould of Indian restaurants. The décor inhabits the contemporary brown, grey and purple end of the spectrum, with lighting to please the eye, and the food wows all comers with its particular approach to fusion. Chief among the examples of Indo-European co-operation must be tandoori smoked salmon, but there are plenty of others, including risotto made with basmati rice: this dish – topped with two king prawns dipped in batter and deep-fried – flouts all convention and reason about the best kind of rice to use for risotto, yet works splendidly. It is not easy to push back the boundaries of Indian cooking while still retaining the basic premises, yet that is just what this food does.

Spicing throughout is spot on, and the essence is never obscured by crude heat: for example, a lightly battered mixed vegetable patty on a bed of chickpeas with a zigzag of tamarind sauce, or a generous crab masala of 'tremendous flavour', served with garlic naan. It is possible, though not necessarily advisable, to eat three courses in which rice features. Chilled mango rice pudding is flavoured with cardamom and roast pine nuts, but there may also be cardamom kulfi to rank with the best, or skewers of tandoor-baked fruit. Service is chatty, helpful, efficient and knowledgeable, and 50-plus wines are well chosen and fairly priced. House wine is from £13.

CHEF: Vineet Bhatia PROPRIETOR: Cuisine Collection OPEN: Sun to Fri L 12 to 2.30, all week D 6.30 to 10.45 MEALS: alc (main courses £9.50 to £14.50). Set L £12.95 (2 courses) to £22, Set D £22 SERVICE: 12.5% (optional), card slips closed CARDS: Amex, Delta, MasterCard, Switch, Visa DETAILS: 65 seats. Private parties: 14 private room. Vegetarian meals. No cigars/pipes in dining room. Wheelchair access (not WC). No music. Air-conditioned ⊖ South Kensington

London round-ups

With so many venues vying for attention, finding a place to eat out in London that offers the right blend of food, location, style and price to suit the occasion can often be very much down to pot luck. This section aims to make choosing easier by providing details of a broad range of restaurants, bistros, cafés, hotel dining rooms, and so on, that are deserving of attention, though they do not merit a full entry. There are also one or two rising stars, well worth keeping an eye on, and in some cases establishments have been included here rather than in the main entries because of significant late changes or a lack of positive feedback. Reports on these places are particularly welcome. Brief details of opening times are given in each entry where available.

Apprentice SE1
Butlers Wharf Chef School, map 13
31 Shad Thames
(020) 7234 0254
The set lunch menu at £10.50 for two courses and £13.50 for three may be reasonable value, but levels of skill in a chefs' school are inevitably going to vary. A reporter felt that such basic skills as the placing of cutlery, and not over-filling wine glasses should be taught early on in the training. The short, well-balanced menu with four choices at each stage might include crab and asparagus risotto, or seared red mullet with baby fennel as starters, and main courses of salmon on samphire and artichokes, or roast marinated guinea fowl on sweet-and-sour leeks. Desserts run to minted charlottes with bitter chocolate sorbet, and passion fruit pavlova with blueberries. Open Mon to Fri.

Aurora W1
49 Lexington Street map 15
(020) 7494 0514
This relaxed place in an eighteenth-century artisan's house is dimly lit and 'nicely unmodern', with a tiny walled garden for al fresco eating. The short menu might include Thai beef salad or confit of tuna, followed by roast pork with sweet potato, bean purée and caramelised apples. Lunchtime specials include a soup, pasta, fish dish and dessert, perhaps sticky-toffee pudding with ice cream. Now licensed, it offers house wines at £11.90 on a short, modestly priced globe-trotting list. Closed Sun.

L'Aventure NW8
3 Blenheim Terrace map 11
(020) 7624 6232
Located just off Abbey Road, this small neighbourhood restaurant has a cheerful buzz, courteous and efficient service, and offers traditional French cooking. Reporters have enjoyed artichoke salad with wild mushroom risotto, followed by wild duck stuffed with foie gras, or poached monkfish with provençale herbs. Tarte aux poires, or île flottante might finish a meal. Mostly French wines are reasonably priced. Closed Sat L.

Balzac Bistro W12
4 Wood Lane map 12
(020) 8743 6787
French bistro at the Shepherds Bush end of Wood Lane, with eccentric décor. Set menus are supplemented by blackboard specials, and the 'promotional menu' at £8.90 is worth considering. This year visitors have enjoyed roast goats' cheese with figs, and an assiette de trois saumons (smoked, marinated, roe) for starters, and main courses of steak frites and tender côtelettes d'agneau, which are typically accompanied by red cabbage and herby baked potato chunks. Finish with crème brûlée or apple tart. Service is polite and

attentive. A predominantly French wine list opens at £9.60 (£2.50 a glass). Closed Sat L and Sun.

Belgo Centraal WC2
50 Earlham Street map 15
(020) 7813 2233
Service in this 'pleasantly noisy' subterranean branch of the moules-frites chain appears to be by Trappist monks pretending to be waiters. The toiling cooks, seen from the bridge by which you enter, continue to serve up mussels by the kilo. These have been disappointing on occasion, but the menu also offers fish soup, stuffed chicken, and a highly rated carbonade of beef, with crème brulée to finish. Belgian beers are recommended to accompany; waiters can advise which go best with your meal. The few determined wine-drinkers will find a reasonable selection. Open all week.

Belle Epoque SW3
151 Draycott Avenue map 14
(020) 7460 5000
The South Kensington sibling of Palais du Jardin (see main entry, London) now offers a very similar menu to its relative. Among fruits de mer, generous platters comprise ten different crustaceans and molluscs, but lobster is the star turn, served thermidor, grilled with king prawns, or cold with asparagus or oysters. Aside from seafood, the typical brasserie fare takes in starters of carpaccio, baked goats' cheese, or pan-fried foie gras with apple galette, while the range of meat and fish main dishes run from simple grilled steaks to more elaborate fillet of venison with a herb mousse and pink peppercorn sauce. Closed Sun.

Beotys WC2
79 St Martin's Lane map 15
(020) 7836 8768/8548
Better preserved than the Elgin Marbles, the 'French' menu with full English explanations at this family-run restaurant in theatreland encapsulates all that was most popular in the 1950s. Start with prawn cocktail or, more adventurously, avocado and prawns in cocktail sauce, or for the utterly fearless les Escargots de Bourgogne. Continue with sole Bonne Femme, chicken Kiev, caneton à l'orange, or entrecôte Diane flambéed at your table. Greek Cypriot specialities include stuffed vine leaves, and taramasalata, followed perhaps by moussaka, or beef stifado. Friendly service is a plus. Closed Sun.

Bertorelli's WC2
44A Floral Street map 15
(020) 7836 3969
Wavy-patterned dark blue carpets, blue tiling and huge mirrors give this traditional Italian restaurant something of a nautical feel. Fish seems an appropriately good bet, approval coming in for marinated squid with aïoli, grilled monkfish with lime and ginger butter, and a brochette of king prawns with stir-fried Mediterranean vegetables. Desserts have included crème caramel and blueberry cheesecake. A cover charge pays for bread, olives, gherkins and olive oil; vegetables are also charged extra. Service is pleasant but can be slow. Fifty wines are exclusively Italian. Lighter meals are offered in the café downstairs, and another branch is at 19–23 Charlotte Street, W1, tel (020) 7636 4174. Closed Sun.

Boisdale SW1
15 Eccleston Street map 13
(020) 7730 6922
You get the full Belgravia clubby works here: dark panelling, comfortably worn leather armchairs, a vast choice of whiskies, classic wines and cigars, and jazz. On the plate in the restaurant is the finest Scots produce that the heir to the Clanranald chiefdom can supply. This means Shetland crab; Crannoch Moor hot smoked wild venison; Angus steaks with a choice of sauces; haggis, of course; and lobster, salmon and Orkney king scallops. It is no surprise to find savouries on the menu – Scotch woodcock, or its cousin that calls on black truffle instead of anchovies and capers – and desserts

include traditional Scottish tart and raspberry cranachan. Closed Sat L and Sun.

Books for Cooks W11
4 Blenheim Crescent map 13
(020) 7221 1992
This small shop off Ladbroke Grove, crammed full of cookery books, is a wonderful place to while away some time browsing for inspiration, while a miniature kitchen at the back tests recipes from the books and offers up the results for lunch. Go early because lunch starts at noon (with a second sitting at 1.45 on Saturdays) and finishes when the food runs out. The menu is always interesting, perhaps starting with Mexican gazpacho, followed by tomato and saffron tartlet with fennel and potato salad, and finishing with blueberry and poppy seed muffins. Unlicensed. Booking advised. Closed Sun.

Bu-San N7
41–43 Holloway Road map 13
(020) 7607 8264
Long-established, friendly, family-run eating house using home-grown organic vegetables in much of the long menu. There are Japanese dishes and some chef-patron's inventions among the classic Korean repertoire, which takes in mixed seafood in soup; bulgogi (marinated sirloin steak cooked at the table); stir-fried pork with pickled Chinese cabbage; and Korean-style 'tortilla' with oysters and shrimp; as well as rice and noodle assemblies and, of course, kim-chee. Reasonably priced wines start with house French at £9.45. Closed Sat and Sun L.

Butlers Wharf Chop House SE1
36E Shad Thames map 13
(020) 7403 3403
A branch of the Conran empire with views of the Thames and Tower Bridge, the Chop House has a home-grown feel to its menu with prawn cocktail, warm Scotch egg and piccalilli, steak and kidney pudding, fish and chips with mushy peas, and beef and horseradish sausages with parsley mash and gravy. Finish with rhubarb trifle or bread-and-butter pudding with custard. Next door is a bar serving light meals and snacks. The wine list is impressive, but so are the prices. Closed Sat L and Sun D.

Le Cadre N8
10 Priory Road map 12
(020) 8348 0606
Art nouveau pictures and posters adorn the walls of this engaging blue and cream restaurant in Crouch End, near Alexandra Palace. Diverse set or à la carte menus are mostly French, perhaps incorporating foie gras parfait and wild mushroom brioche, followed by game pie or provençale fish casserole with saffron couscous. Finish with île flottante or tarte Tatin. The wine list has a remarkable selection of classic Burgundies at a price, and plenty of New and Old World bottles under £20. Closed Sat L and Sun.

Café du Marché EC1
22 Charterhouse Square map 13
(020) 7608 1609
Down an alleyway off Charterhouse Square, Café du Marché offers traditional French cooking, including splendid fish soup, grilled sardines with fennel, beef with béarnaise, and pork knuckle with broad beans and parsley sauce. Desserts might include tarte aux fruits or glace et sorbet. The mostly French wine list includes half a dozen under £20. Closed Sat L and Sun.

Café Portugal SW8
5A & 6A Victoria House, map 13
South Lambeth Road
(020) 7587 1962
New owners took over as the Guide went to press, bringing with them a new chef, but it seems homely Portuguese cooking will continue to be the mainstay. Portugal has a legendary 365 recipes for salt cod, of which there are three on offer, along with crab Portuguese style, espetada mista (mixed meat cubes an a skewer), and paella. The tapas bar continues too, producing garnished pig's trotters,

Portuguese sausage in red wine, and seafood salad. Portuguese wines start at £8.50. Open all week.

Carluccio's Caffè W1
8 Market Place map 15
(020) 7636 2228
Planned to be the first of many, the caffè has an Italian deli at the front selling breads and snacks, as well as olive oils, rice, pasta, wine, and other essentials. Wooden flooring, plain white walls, some communal tables and some smaller ones, make it functional without being hard-edged. The menu of mainly light dishes is designed more for snacking than full three-course meals. Sicilian arancini, and vegetable antipasto have been pleasing starters, while 'main' dishes run to focaccia sandwiches, semolina gnocchi alla Romana, calzone, or grilled swordfish with Parmesan. Espresso is notably good, and the short Italian wine list rises gently from £9.95. Open all week, from 8 weekdays. Bookings D only.

Cassia Oriental W1
12 Berkeley Square map 15
(020) 7629 8886
Here be no dragons, but an elegant, luxurious Mayfair restaurant, serving oriental food below Mayfair prices. A large, relaxing bar leads to the deep-carpeted dining room, where set-price menus range from £12 for two-course lunches, to £22 for three-course dinners. The food is mainly Chinese, but extends to Vietnamese spring rolls, Burmese pho (beef soup), and Japanese yakitori. Good fried rice, and Peking bread in dim sum steamers, are included. Service is friendly and helpful. Diverse wines start at £15.50. Open Mon to Fri L and D.

Chapel NW1
48 Chapel Street map 13
(020) 7402 9220
Don't be surprised if even the most traditional and British sounding dishes have a Moorish twist at this pub-restaurant just off the Edgware Road. It's the influence of the Moroccan chef. Mostly the menu goes in for Mediterranean-style dishes such as leek and Provolone cheese tart with vine tomato salad, or a pancetta and chorizo salad with gherkin, potatoes and aubergine allumettes. Praise has come in for tender guinea fowl in a rich, creamy mushroom sauce with a tian of vegetables and roast potatoes, and interesting dressings on the salads. Summer fruit Pimms cheesecake is a typical dessert. Open all week.

Chapter Two SE3
Montpelier Vale map 12
(020) 8333 2666
Strong colours in a contemporary building announce a modern restaurant, and the menu confirms it with up-to-date British cooking. Largely carnivorean, it offers such original starters as salad of roast rabbit, salt beef and French beans, and grilled sole with lentil and coriander broth, followed by deep-fried salt cod, or perhaps a fricassee of chicken with peas and morels. Recommendations have included slow-cooked lamb shank with ratatouille of vegetables; and a trio of pork, comprising loin, chop and a succulent sausage. Service might be warmer and more efficient. House wines at £13.50 head a fully priced list. Open all week.

Che SW1
23 St James's Street map 14
(020) 7747 9380
Housed in a former bank, Che's ground-floor contains a bar and cigar lounge, while the comfortable first-floor dining room is reached by the original (now non-functioning) escalators. Reporters have enjoyed Egyptian lentil soup, French onion tart, and seared tuna, and the menu extends to salmon tatare, roast Barbary duck or Thai red chicken curry. The large choice of desserts might include honey roasted purple figs with Amaretto ice cream, or crème brûlée. Service has been highly praised. Closed Sat L and Sun.

Chez Gérard W1
8 Charlotte Street map 15
(020) 7636 4975
The flagship of this long-standing chain of steak and chip eateries offers bargain pre- and post-theatre meals, a set dinner, Sunday lunch and a carte. Steaks come in all shapes and sizes, though not always cooked as requested; otherwise try confit de canard or délice de saumon. Puddings typically include tarte au citron or crème brûlée. Vegetarian choices available; cover charge includes bread, anchovy butter, olives and nuts. Branches are spread throughout central London, plus one at Heathrow Airport, and more are due to open in Manchester and Birmingham (see the web site at www.sante-gcg.com for details). Closed Sat L.

Chuen Cheng Ku W1
17 Wardour Street map 15
(020) 7734 3281 and 3509
This cavernous Chinatown restaurant is one of a few serving dim sum from heated trolleys; flag them down as they weave around tables, expertly guided by staff. Expect the usual array of staples: har gau, cheung fun and char sui bao among them. They also offer a standard Cantonese menu, including plenty of set meals, and Chinese-style afternoon tea is a popular option. Service has been praised and children are made to feel at home. Open all week, dim sum served from 11 to 5.30.

Como Lario SW1
22 Holbein Place map 14
(020) 7730 2954
Tables are tightly packed in this busy, boisterous Italian restaurant near Sloane Square. The wide-ranging Northern Italian menu offers a blend of old and new in starters, bresaola with Pecorino appearing next to deep-fried smoked mozzarella with spicy tomato sauce. Pasta dishes take in tagliolini with spider crab, while mostly traditional mains run from simply grilled Dover sole or calf's liver to lamb chops with basil and pine nuts. A two-sittings policy operates at busy times. Closed Sun.

Corney & Barrow WC2
116 St Martin's Lane map 15
(020) 7655 9800
The food at this West End wine bar merits attention, though the emphasis is on wine; indeed, the menu suggests a wine to accompany each dish and 38 of the 50 wines are available by the glass. The menu in the ground-floor wine bar features light snacks and platters for sharing, while the modern European cooking in the restaurant might offer scallop and prawn kebab on a sweetcorn and spring onion pancake with rosemary dressing, followed by herb-crusted rack of lamb with a gratin of Scamorza cheese and bacon and a mint jus. Set lunch and pre-theatre menus offer good value. Closed Sun and bank hols. There are 12 branches throughout London.

Daphne NW1
83 Bayham Street map 13
(020) 7267 7322
This Greek Cypriot restaurant has friendly, obliging owners and an interior bedecked with pictures of home. Well-known dishes – taramasalata, kalamari, moussaka, dolmades and a range of charcoal grilled meats – are joined by a speciality of the day: marinated tuna, charcoal grilled octopus or artichokes cooked with fennel. Meze are £10.75 for the meat selection and £15.50 for fish. Greek wines predominate. Closed Sun.

Daphne's SW3
112 Draycott Avenue map 14
(020) 7589 4257
Part of the Belgo group, with a new chef appointed as the Guide went to press, Daphne's produces an Italian menu with salads (spinach, avocado and crispy bacon), pastas (ravioli with pumpkin, sage and Pecorino cheese) and risottos (wild mushroom) starting things off. Roasts (corn-fed chicken or rack of lamb) and grills, plus a selection of fish (salmon, sea bass or Dover sole) are likely main

courses, while desserts might include pannacotta. The extensive wine list offers plenty by the glass. There is a time limit on tables, and the garden room roof opens for al fresco eating. Open all week.

Daquise SW7
20 Thurloe Street map 14
(020) 7589 6117
This long-standing Polish restaurant has evolved over the years, with a range of East European dishes on the printed menu. Golonka is pork knuckle with cabbage, peas, mashed potatoes and horseradish sauce; available in the Polish version (the meat is boiled) or Bavarian (using marinated pork). Old favourites include barszcz, salted herring, chlodnik, stuffed cabbage, Russian zrazy – stuffed meat roll – and various pancakes and continental pâtisseries. Set lunch is two-courses plus a glass of wine and tea or coffee. House wine is £8.50 but Polish beers and vodkas are tempting. Open all week.

Diwana Bhel Poori NW1
121 Drummond Street map 13
(020) 7387 5556
Drummond Street is a lively thoroughfare full of Indian supermarkets, sweet shops and restaurants, and definitely the place to go for authentic South Indian food. At this particular outlet, the laminated menus, basic décor and wooden benches are signs that the focus is on the food rather than the incidentals. Buffet lunch is excellent value, but crisp bhel poori is the real star, with various dosas and the substantial thali also receiving praise. Drink lassi, salted or sweetened. Open all week; note bookings not accepted Fri to Sun unless for six or more people.

Ebury Wine Bar SW1
139 Ebury St map 13
(020) 7730 5447
This popular wine bar, with an upstairs panelled dining room, offers much more than the run-of-the-mill cooking often associated with the genre. Typical of the style might be seared salmon with a smoked oyster chowder, pan-fried halibut with tomato and basil risotto, and loin of pork with ceps (the latter accompanied by crisp chips). Excellent apple crumble, and poached pear with honey and cardamom ice cream, have also been approved. Chef Josh Hampton was due to leave as we went to press, so reports please. Open all week.

Efes Kebab House W1
80 Great Titchfield Street map 15
(020) 7636 1953
Reports suggest that, after 25 years, Efes is still as popular as ever. The format has not changed over time and owners Kazim Akkus and Ibrahim Akbas are still very much in evidence. Start with hot and cold meze, then move on to the meats: shish kofta and chicken kebab have been praised this year; try the grilled trout for something lighter. Desserts include fresh fruit – the pineapple is topped with a sparkler – or pastries. Coffee is good and the whole deal represents good value. Closed Sun. Kebabs are also available to take away, and a sister restaurant is just around the corner, at 175–177 Great Portland Street, W1 (tel (020) 7436 0600).

Fish Central EC1
149–151 King's Square map 13
(020) 7253 4970
As far as traditional fish and chip shops are concerned, this one improves on the formula by offering a choice of matzo meal or 'our special' batter on fried cod, haddock, plaice, skate or rock salmon. The menu's 'gourmet's choice' lists halibut steak, scampi, and Dover sole fried or meunière with oyster mushrooms. Starters are as old-fashioned as (English) fish soup, as modern as grilled goats' cheese with tomato and basil dressing. Carnivores can choose steak, lamb, Cumberland sausage, liver and bacon or steak and kidney pie. A short wine list is modestly priced from £7.50. Closed Sun.

Formula Veneta SW10
14 Hollywood Road map 14
(020) 7352 7612
Hollywood Road is not quite Chelsea, although this modish restaurant, with its little courtyard, is. Nor is its menu the usual Italian formula. Bresaola with flakes of goat's cheese is venison, not beef; artichoke comes with cooked, not raw, ham in a salad; while timbale of courgettes in basil coulis is another offbeat starter. Pasta might include green gnochetti in tomato and soft-cheese sauce; or noodles with crab and shrimp. Risotti for two need 20 minutes to cook. A fish of the day supplements sea bass, scallops, squid and monkfish, while duck with honey and cloves is a rare bird. Closed Sun.

Frederick's N1
Camden Passage map 13
(020) 7359 2888
The stylish dining rooms (including a conservatory-style Garden Room) are light, bright and covered with abstract paintings, and there are tables outside for al fresco eating in summer. Set-price lunches and an evening carte demonstrate a modern approach, taking in a crispy parcel of goats' cheese, or spicy salt cod and crayfish crêpe to start, followed by confit of lamb with a herb crust, and lightly smoked haddock with duck egg tortilla. Finish with lemon tart and blackberry compote. Portions are described as generous, and service as friendly and professional. Closed Sun.

Gate W6
Temple Lodge map 12
(020) 8748 6932
The world is combed for inspiration in this stylish, Hammersmith vegetarian restaurant; Japan, Spain, Italy and Mexico are just some of the stopovers on the whistle-stop tour. A selection of sushi rolls, or noodle salad with crispy onions and deep-fried tofu, can start the ball rolling, followed by tortilla filled with baby corn, peppers, and fine beans; or ravioli stuffed with Gorgonzola and shallot confit. Puddings – elderflower pavlova, blueberry brûlée and sweet chimichanga – are equally global. Closed Sat L and all day Sun.

Gilbeys W5
77 The Grove map 12
(020) 8840 7568
As at the branches in Amersham (see entry, England round-ups) and Eton, the main attraction of this light and airy shop conversion, apart from its floodlit garden dining area, is an excellent list of mainly French wines with low mark-ups. A simple menu offers straightforward dishes such as soft poached egg on a salmon fishcake, followed by braised lamb shank with parsnip and potato mash, or pan-fried calf's liver with Puy lentils in red wine sauce. Desserts might include apricot, cognac and almond brûlée. Service is efficient and helpful. Open Tue to Sun L, Tue to Sat D.

Le Gothique SW18
Royal Victoria Patriotic map 12
Building, Fitzhugh Grove
(020) 8870 6567
This strange Gothic building started as an orphanage and has also been a hospital, a school, and even a detention centre for such notable prisoners as Rudolph Hess. The dining room may seem dark, but there is also a large outdoor dining area. Recommended dishes from the French menu have included fish soup with strong rouille, goats' cheese salad with croûtons and walnuts, and quail in a port sauce (two small birds per serving). Desserts such as banana bavarois and chocolate parfait have also been approved, and there is a short, well-priced wine list. It may be difficult to find, so ask for directions when booking. Open Mon to Fri L, Mon to Sat D.

Great Nepalese NW1
48 Eversholt Street map 13
(020) 7388 6737
Gopal Manandhar proudly names his sons as chefs in the family restaurant, and while India is the main influence there is

Tibetan input too: in meat-filled momocha, or vegetarian momo, which resemble Chinese dumplings. Among special Nepalese vegetarian dishes is gundruk ko tarkari (a dry curry). Achar (pickle) appears with mixed vegetables and in dhaniya achar (coriander pickle). A three-course set lunch at £5.95 changes weekly and might offer chicken ra piaj with naan, rice and a vegetable. Open all week.

Greek Valley NW8
130 Boundary Road map 13
(020) 7624 3217
Half this taverna's 40 wines, starting with the house offering at £7.50, come from born-again Greek vineyards. Variety is what meze are all about and there is plenty of choice among the cold dips and salads, as well as hot starters of sausages and smoked ham. Mixed dips – hummus, tzatziki, taramasalata and melitzanosalata (aubergine) – are £6.50, while meze supreme at £15 per person includes grilled chicken and lamb souvlaki. New to the menu is a fish meze featuring cold dips, seafood salad, kalamari, prawns and salmon. Open Mon to Sat D only, with live music on Fridays.

House E14
27 Ropemaker's Field map 12
(020) 7538 3818
Formerly The House They Left Behind, this old pub on a quiet residential street has been reinvented as a laid-back, contemporary pub-restaurant with bare wooden floorboards and a chunky stainless steel bar counter. Eat in the bar area at the front, or in the smartly turned-out dining area at the back, from a cosmopolitan menu that takes in mozzarella, avocado and tomato salad, followed by herb-crusted salmon with garlic and sweet potato mash, or braised shank of lamb in a red wine jus. Finish perhaps with profiteroles or fruit salad. Wines offer good value. Weather permitting, barbecues are held outside on the green on Sundays. Open Sat and Sun L, all week D.

ICA Café SW1
12 Carlton House Terrace map 15
(020) 7930 8619
Menus at the Institute of Contemporary Arts live up to the name with lunchtime 'modern Italian' dishes including chilled spinach and sorrel soup, skewers of ham-wrapped pork, and a Sicilian pasta dish echoing moussaka. The evening 'streetwise' menu might offer a choice between Japanese or Brazilian, with gyoza dumplings or yakitori skewered chicken representing one hemisphere, and black-eye pea fritters or salt-cod croquettes the other. Bar food is even more diverse, with Lebanese falafel, or Alamo chilli beans to accompany international cocktails such as the rum trinity of Brazilian Caipirinha, Cuban Mojito or oriental Mai Tai. Open all week.

Ichi-Riki SW1
17 Strutton Ground map 13
(020) 7233 1701
Simple pine furniture, wall posters depicting menu specials, and a tiny kitchen all contribute to the sushi bar atmosphere, while sushi itself comes as 'sets' including miso soup, and in a variety of à la carte nigiri and maki rolls. Side dishes (or 'starters') include teriyaki salmon, yakitori chicken, and interesting vegetarian dishes of variously cooked tofu, spinach with sesame, and nimono (mixed vegetables cooked in soy sauce). Drink Japanese beer or saké, hot or cold, or house wine at £10.90 per litre. Open Mon to Fri.

Idaho N6
13 North Hill map 12
(020) 8341 6633
Potatoes are not the only item on the menu at the restaurant named after a state famous for its tubers. They do, however, appear as chunky fries to accompany chargrilled Iowa ribeye steak on the main carte, or as hash browns on the weekend brunch menu. As at sister establishments (see Montana and Dakota, London main entries), the cooking covers a broad contemporary American range,

producing prawn and sweet potato chowder, and roast chicken breast with mushroom ragoût and garlic mash. Prices may seem high for the hit-and-miss cooking, and service has few fans, but when it hits the mark, Idaho has been impressive, not least in the wine department. Open all week.

Inaho W2
4 Hereford Road map 13
(020) 7221 0754
It is perhaps surprising that this tiny restaurant seats as many as twenty. Also surprising is the Swiss cuckoo-clock that takes pride of place among a collection of Japanese artefacts. The menu lists much of the Japanese repertoire, though no sukiyaki cooked at table due to the limited space. Among sushi are hand-rolled tuna, salmon skin, fresh water prawns, salmon roe, and cuttlefish with natto (strongly-flavoured fermented soya paste, an acquired taste). House wine is £7.50 but fine saké (£11.50 to £18 per half-litre), served chilled, is more exciting. Closed Sat L and Sun.

L'Incontro SW1
87 Pimlico Road map 14
(020) 7730 3663/6327
In among Pimlico's array of antique shops, L'Incontro, with its glass frontage shedding light into the dining room, specialises in Venetian dishes. The set two- or three-course lunch is a good introduction: dry-cured beef, roast pork with fennel, lemon tart, for instance. The evening carte extends to red mullet in a mussel and mushroom broth, scallops with saffron risotto or a selection of home-made pasta. The wine list is all big Italian names and prices, except for a few French and New World bottles. Closed L Sat and Sun.

Joe Allen WC2
13 Exeter Street map 15
(020) 7836 0651
A reporter returning ten years since a previous visit found little other than minor cosmetic details had changed at this buzzing venue just off the Strand. Dining options run to set-price pre-theatre and lunch menus, a carte and brunch (including a glass of Buck's fizz) at weekends. The lunch menu has produced 'the best Caesar salad this side of the pond', followed by lightly cooked cod steak. Other offerings might be beef and Guinness sausages with red cabbage, or grilled marlin with Cajun vegetables in puff pastry. Finish with 'glorious' pecan pie. Nine wines by the glass. Open all week.

Konditor & Cook SE1
The Young Vic Theatre map 13
(020) 7620 2700
The small theatre restaurant is open for breakfast from 8.30am and for lunch and dinner from noon to 8pm. Salad niçoise, Toulouse sausages, and risotto of smoked haddock and oyster mushrooms indicate the level of ambition, and the relative simplicity of dishes puts the spotlight on good-quality ingredients (the sausages *really* come from Toulouse). Finish with warm dark chocolate cake with crème fraîche and raspberries, or one of the excellent home-made cakes and pastries, which can also be purchased at their shops at 22 Cornwall Road and 10 Stoney Street (both SE1). Closed Sun.

Lahore Kebab House E1
2 Umberston Street map 13
(020) 7488 2551
The palace shown on the on the back of the business card may be in Lahore, but it is a far cry from this very basic eating house. The menu, on a board on the wall, is short and basic too and prices are rock bottom. Start with vegetable samosa, seekh kebab, chicken or mutton tikka, or grilled lamb chops, then choose from a small range of curries, karahi dishes and biryanis. Only offered on Fridays are lamb chop curry and paya (lamb's trotters), but every day there are specials of fish or prawn karahi. Unlicensed, so BYO. Open all week.

Leith's at Dartmouth House W1
37 Charles Street map 15
(020) 7493 3328
Open to non-members for weekday lunches, the Revelstoke room is the ornately decorated members' dining room of the English Speaking Union. It overlooks a fine courtyard, which is also used in summer. The wide-ranging modern menu might offer starters of chilled watercress and chive soup, or the splendidly Anglo-Thai smoked haddock lemon-grass and chilli fishcakes with coriander tartare, followed by roast cod, lamb kofte brochettes, or honey and ginger pork with wild rice, bok choy and mango salsa. Finish with strawberry and passion fruit pavlova, or peach tarte Tatin with almond mascarpone. Service is generally friendly.

Lemonia NW1
89 Regents Park Road map 13
(020) 7586 7454
At first glance the Greek-Cypriot menu contains all the standard stuff, but look more closely and you will find some more unusual dishes: Trahana, for example, is a Cypriot winter soup of yoghurt and wheat. 'Today's specials' might include hare stifado, grilled bream, halibut, tuna or scallops, and kolokithakia avgolemono are stuffed courgettes with egg and lemon sauce. Finish with rizogalo (rice pudding) or ricotta parcels. French House wine is £11 per litre, and there are 18 Greek wines from £12. Closed Sat L and Sun D.

London Hilton, Windows Rooftop Restaurant W1
22 Park Lane map 15
(020) 7208 4021
Superb views of London appear not to attract many Guide readers to Jacques Rolancy's well-groomed restaurant. Perhaps it is the Park Lane prices that put them off. Those who come will be treated to elaborate, upmarket French cooking: perhaps smoked salmon 'frivolity' with lobster tartare, fresh salmon and shellfish jus, followed by roast fillet of veal served with both parsley mash and a soubise-stuffed potato galette, and an anchovy-scented jus. To finish there may be chocolate délice with five-spiced pear and red wine sauce. Closed Sat L and Sun D. Meals and, to some extent, prices are lighter in the adjacent Park Brasserie.

Love Café W1
62–64 Weymouth Street map 15
(020) 7487 5683
High-quality ingredients and robust flavours characterise the food at the café in the Aveda cosmetics store. The mostly vegetarian (and mostly organic) menu has Mediterranean leanings, with pistachio-rolled goats'-cheese salad, and Tuscan bean salad with tuna setting the tone for starters. Pies, quiches and pasta form the bulk of main-course options, perhaps including gnocchi with basil pesto, or asparagus and ricotta ravioli with butter and sage. Puddings take in wheat-free cakes and ice creams. Two large Japanese tables are the focus of the dining room, where communal eating adds to the relaxed and friendly atmosphere. Breakfast all day from 8am. Open Mon to Sat L..

Magno's WC2
65A Long Acre map 15
(020) 7836 6077
This is a useful brasserie for pre-theatre suppers (5.30 to 7.15) in a prime Covent Garden site. The menu turns up plenty of salady starters (Caesar, mozzarella and avocado) among its repertoire of French classics (coq au vin, calf's liver with bacon), plus a few surprises: perhaps kangaroo fillet 'Rossini' with foie gras-stuffed potatoes. For those not rushing off for curtain-up there might be Cointreau rice pudding with chocolate ice cream. Wines start at £11.95. Closed Sat L and Sun (except for large parties).

Mandalay W2
444 Edgware Road map 13
(020) 7258 3696
Colourful, busy, inexpensive and run by a charming Burmese family who cook the food of their country. The style relates to

Indian, Chinese and Thai in spring roll and samosa starters, but only to itself in fritters of shrimp and bean sprouts, calabash or chicken and vegetable. Curries and stir-fries of prawns and off-the-bone chicken or lamb make up much of the menu, but garnished noodles or rice can make a light meal, perhaps with a salad. Order balachaung (dried prawn pickle) to go with everything, for an extra kick. House wine is £7.50 but green tea is a good bet. Closed Sun.

Manzi's WC2
1–2 Leicester Street map 15
(020) 7734 0224
This old campaigner, no more than a stone's throw from Leicester Square, is a useful venue for meals before or after the theatre. Whenever you visit, seafood is the order of the day. A typical starter might be plump, well-cooked grilled sardines, while successful main courses have included grilled plaice on the bone; generally it seems best to stick to the simpler treatments. Chips have also been hit and miss, at their best well cooked, brown and crisp. House wine is £10.50. Closed Sun L.

Marquis W1
121A Mount Street map 15
(020) 7499 1256/7493 9382
Menus at this Italian long-stayer in the heart of Mayfair add modern touches to an otherwise classic repertoire. Two courses at £14.50 might include cabbage leaves enclosing chicken livers and foie gras, and then courgette and hazelnut polpette with grilled poussin. Choice widens on the carte, to perhaps fried calamari with ruby chard salad, then osso buco with saffron risotto. Grilling is a favoured technique: for breast of chicken wrapped in pancetta with mozzarella and porcini stuffing, and fillet of beef with rucola, for example. Open Mon to Fri.

Mezzanine SE1
National Theatre map 13
(020) 7452 3600
Two courses and coffee served in under an hour make this a good bet for a meal before the show, or a late supper afterwards. Only a few tables enjoy a view over the Thames, but the ambience is warm throughout, helped by unobtrusive but attentive service. Wide choice is offered on the menu, taking in spinach mould, fishcakes, marinated halloumi cheese, eggs Benedict, and focaccia to start, perhaps followed by a thick chunk of accurately cooked liver, or spicy, meaty sausages with mash. Closed Sun.

Mirch Masala SW16
1416 London Road map 12
(020) 8679 1828
Friendly staff who prepare the food in view of customers will happily explain the menu. Headed 'food extraordinaire', it is divided into 'warmers' (starters) and 'steamers' (mains), each section further split into vegetarian and non-vegetarian. Tandoori-cooked options from the non-vegetarian warmers are a good bet: lamb tikka, or chicken wings, for example. Mains include the eponymous chilli and potato dish, plus a range of karahi and deigi ('on-the-bone') options. 'Coolers' are rice dishes, 16 breads (mostly naans and parathas), flavoured lassi and sweets. Prices are good, with only prawn dishes costing more than £6. Unlicensed, so BYO. Open all week.

Mitsukoshi SW1
Dorland House, 14–20 Lower Regent Street map 15
(020) 7930 0317
Set in the basement of a Harrods-style Japanese department store, Mitsukoshi provides authentic Japanese cooking for a largely Japanese clientele. Set menus start at £35 and might include una-ju (grilled eel on rice), miyabi zen (tempura, grilled beef with teriyaki sauce and salad), or sushi options. On the carte are ten varieties of nigiri sushi, from fatty tuna to sea urchin (or choose the 'best selection' for £22), as well as grilled, steamed and deep-fried versions. In addition, 'vinegar dishes' might take

in sliced octopus salad, or salted jellyfish. A range of sakés is available, and house wines are £17. Service is 15 per cent. Closed Sun.

Momo W1
25 Heddon Street map 15
(020) 7434 4040
A Moroccan mystery is why this luxuriously furnished place calls itself a 'restaurant familial' when its hugely successful downstairs club-bar is not for the very young, nor for their grandparents. Menus offer fried panissa (chickpea polenta, the national dish of Gibraltar) to accompany seared tuna, while stevia leaves, a natural sweetener, turn up in the lamb burek. Or find carpaccio of marinated cod with alfalfa and caviar; fillet of sea bass cooked and served in semolina pastry; and crème brûlée with fennel confit and caramelised tomatoes. Open all week.

Moxon's SW4
14 Clapham Park Road map 12
(020) 7627 2468
Apart from one vegetarian and two meat dishes, the rest is fish, fish, fish. Expect seared scallops in a coconut and lemongrass broth, or skate and leek terrine with parsley jelly to start, and hefty main courses of roast cod with cassoulet and Toulouse sausage, or roast monkfish with oxtail ravioli. Fruity puddings might include banana tarte Tatin or pineapple fritter with honey crème fraiche. The Clapham Common setting is one of wooden boards, pale walls and 'music played for the benefit of the staff'. Set meals are available Monday to Thursday, with whatever caught the chef's eye at the market. Open Mon to Sat D.

New World W1
1 Gerrard Place map 15
(020) 7434 2508
This vast 700-seater eating house is always busy, particularly for lunchtime dim sum from perambulating trolleys. The cooking is Cantonese plus the usual Peking duck, and in a short list of house specialities you will find Szechuan pork with bamboo shoots. One page of the menu is dedicated to lamb prepared nine ways, including sliced with snow peas in yellow bean sauce, and grilled cutlets coated in black pepper, or seasoned with chilli and salt. Open all week.

Nosh Brothers W11
12 All Saints Road map 13
(020) 7243 2808
That modern, minimalist restaurants need not be noisy is proved by this one. New chef Brian Danclair from Trinidad arrived shortly before the Guide went to press, too late for inspection. The cooking is set to take a regional European direction, an early menu offering codfish fritters with ginger and lime sauce, and omelette de Provence with mushrooms, tomato and parsley purée. Follow this with grilled salmon on lentils, guinea fowl with saffron potatoes and juniper jus, or pot-au-feu of calf's tongue with root vegetables. Staff are 'exceptionally pleasant and know the food and wines'. House wines are £12; after that prices rise steeply. Closed Mon L and Sun D.

Orsino W11
119 Portland Road map 12
(020) 7221 3299
Neighbourhood restaurant in a high-ceilinged room with a lively atmosphere, where Holland Park residents go for traditional Italian cooking with some modern twists. Pizzas might be topped with salami, courgette and Gorgonzola; pasta dishes encompass saffron taglierini with shrimps, mussels, rocket and tomato; and main courses take in swordfish with courgette, rocket and herb mayonnaise, as well as veal escalopes with Parma ham, Fontina and sage. Flexible eating options run to a good-value set lunch, early dinner and late supper, while all-day opening (noon to 11.45) seven days a week makes for added convenience. Wines are wall-to-wall Italian at accessible prices.

Patio W12
5 Goldhawk Road map 12
(020) 8743 5194
It's Polish, old-fashioned enough to have strips of carpet on the floor, old reviews on the walls and samovars on sideboards. It is open every day, late diners are welcomed, and owner Ewa Michalik and her waitresses are very friendly. The food is said to be 'filling, filling, filling'. Bigos is a thick, country vegetable soup, while tasty pirogi (Polish ravioli) are stuffed with either vegetables or meat. There is fresh fruit or pudding to finish; but not quite, for three courses at £10.90 includes 'vodka on the house'. House wine is £8.50. Open Mon to Fri L and all week D.

Philpotts Mezzaluna NW2
424 Finchley Road map 13
(020) 7794 0455/0452
David Philpott obviously likes this part of the Finchley Road; having spent the '90s cooking at Quincy's he has now opened this restaurant close to his old work place (now under new ownership). The Italian menu might start with a salad of chicken livers, avocado and balsamic, and carpaccio of tuna with lime and sweet potato salsa. A range of pastas (crespolini with beef and porcini) and risottos (prawn and saffron) precede main courses such as lemon sole with stuffed peppers and olives. Choose two courses for £14 at lunch, or anything from the pasta section with a glass of wine and coffee for £10. Reports please. Closed all day Mon and Sat L.

Pizzeria Castello SE1
20 Walworth Road map 13
(020) 7703 2556
Pick your pizza from more than 20 listed and add your own variations with extras such as cheese, mushrooms, onions, salami, tuna, rocket or king prawns. Or choose a pasta and one of a dozen sauces: perhaps vulcano (chicken, peppers, courgettes and tomato) or arrabbiata (spicy chilli and tomato). This pizzeria proves its independence with a long list of house specials, from king prawns to halibut steak, or veal with fresh peperonata. Wines are nearly all Italian, with house Montepulciano d'Abruzzo or Trebbiano at £8.50. Closed Sat L and all day Sun.

The Poet EC3
20 Creechurch Lane map 13
(020) 7623 3999
Overhead TVs show sport and add to the lively atmosphere at this busy bar-cum-restaurant. The menu is an enterprising mix of traditional – fish and chips, burgers and chicken tikka masala (they have their own tandoori oven) – and more imaginative dishes including chickpea tagine, risotto primavera, and home-cured herrings with crispy Parma ham and caper mayonnaise. Desserts are on the imaginative side too, and might include lemon scented buttermilk pudding with summer berries, or home-made ice creams, perhaps cinnamon and honeycomb. Closed Sat and Sun.

Pomegranates SW1
94 Grosvenor Road map 13
(020) 7828 6560
When hands-on chef-patron Patrick Gwynn-Jones opened his clubby, basement restaurant 25 years ago, its menu gave a whole new meaning to the word 'eclectic': before 'fusion' became the buzz term. Mauritian spicy raçon soup, Danish pickled herrings, Welsh salt duck, and West Indian curried goat give an idea of the flavour spectrum. But a traditional side, doubtless part of the restaurant's appeal to politicians, appears in Aberdeen Angus steaks, including properly made-to-order steak tartare. Finish with English farmhouse cheese or retro treacle tart. Well-chosen eclectic wine list too. Open Mon to Fri L, Mon to Sat D.

Poons WC2
4 Leicester Street map 15
(020) 7437 1528
A short dim sum menu is available until 4pm, with every item priced at £1.80. Among the long list of dishes on the main menu are noodle- or rice-based plate

meals: spicy soup noodles with minced pork; Shanghai style wheat noodles with shredded pork and preserved cabbage; steamed rice with eel or scallops; and fried glutinous rice with wind-dried food. 'Exotic casseroles' include wind-dried duck with yam, fishcake and turnip, and original braised lamb with bean sticks. A non-smoking area in a Chinese restaurant is rare, so their basement one is welcome. Open all week.

Poons WC2
27 Lisle Street map 15
(020) 7437 4549
Amiable service is led by owner Shirley Chiu at 'little Poons', a tiny eating house, now expanded to four simply decorated rooms. Its long-standing wind-dried foods and Cantonese hot-pots are combined in a hotpot of duck, two sorts of sausage, and Chinese bacon on rice. A party menu, arranged in advance (a good way to appreciate the cooking), might include braised leg of pork with bok choy, or drunken chicken in a pot with wine sauce. At the other extreme, 'plate meals' for one are rice or noodles with a wide choice of fish or meat toppings. Open all week.

Poons W2
Unit 205, Whiteleys, map 13
151 Queensway
(020) 7792 2884
Friendly staff and a lively clientele help to brighten the ambience of this black, gold, beige and mirrored room. The menu is not as encyclopaedic as some, but is adequately long with a wide choice of Cantonese stalwarts and a few less familiar dishes. Among these are Vietnamese spring rolls, fried rice with seafood steamed in lotus leaf, and stir-fried chicken with white fungi (aka wood ears, which are more familiar in the black variety). Vegetarians might have the choice of mange-tout, asparagus, aubergines, French beans and spinach, as well as mixed vegetables and tofu dishes. Open all week.

Quaglino's SW1
16 Bury Street map 15
(020) 7930 6767
In the eight years since this 1930s favourite was resurrected, Quaglino's has become an institution, a destination on the tourist map; 'you always feel a million dollars when you walk down the fabulous staircase.' The departure of chef Henrik Iverson just as the Guide went to press has resulted in its placement in the Round-up section. A new chef had not yet been appointed, although the style of the kitchen that has turned out parsley-crusted seared tuna with salsa, braised lamb shank with beetroot and spring onion, and Bramley apple bread-and-butter pudding, is unlikely to change. Open all week.

Ragam W1
57 Cleveland Street map 15
(020) 7636 9098
This modest but bright eating house was among the first to bring south Indian vegetarian cooking to London, but it also offers conventional curry house dishes. Meals could easily include dishes from both styles, starting with a vegetarian speciality such as masala vadai (spicy lentil-flour 'doughnut'), or masala dosai (thin rice and lentil flour pancake stuffed with potatoes), followed by lamb dopiaza, or hot-sour chicken dansak from the notable range of curries. Among recommended vegetable options are various bhajis, while rice comes flavoured with lemon or coconut, or as vegetable pilau. Closed Sun.

Randall & Aubin W1
16 Brewer Street map 15
(020) 7287 4447
The eponymous butchers may not have survived into the twenty-first century, but their spirit lives on in Ed Baines's and Jamie Poulton's champagne and oyster bar. They very sensibly kept the best elements of the décor – including original tiles, marble and stone – and have produced one of the most atmospheric

rooms in Soho. A good choice of shellfish extends beyond excellent oysters, taking in lobster, langoustine, whelks and crab, with a full *plateau de fruits de mer* for the ultimate fix. Meat is not forgotten, with a rôtisserie providing herb chicken, and a roast of the day. Filled baguettes – salt beef, for example – come with chips and offer a cheaper alternative to caviar.

R.K. Stanleys W1
6 Little Portland Street map 15
(020) 7462 0099
This sausage diner two blocks north of Oxford Circus serves all manner of bangers made on the premises: coarse-textured bratwurst, Caribbean-style jerk sausage, or plain ones with onion gravy and champ. Helpings are large so think twice before ordering a starter of whitebait, or smoked haddock with poached egg, and leave room for sticky toffee pudding. 'Exciting' beers and organic cider complement the food, as does Wild Pig Shiraz at £11.95. All sausage dishes cost £6 between 5.30 and 7 every night. Closed Sat L and Sun.

Royal Opera House, Amphitheatre Restaurant WC2
Covent Garden map 15
(020) 7212 9254
There is no doubting the splendour of the new Opera House, although the restaurant, with its low ceiling, minimalist décor, and lack of a view is not so inspiring. The short menu might start with Italian meat terrine with olive salsa and rocket, and pea soup with Parmesan, while main courses have included roasted sea bass with fondant potato, and beef medallions with parsley mash and horseradish beignet. Finish with tarte Tatin or Neal's Yard cheeses. Eight wines by the glass are available from a worldwide list not offering much under £20. Open Mon to Sat L only when there is no matinee (phone to be sure); open D for ticket holders only.

Saga W1
43–44 South Molton Street map 15
(020) 7629 3931
Changes to this Japanese restaurant since the last edition include a new chef and lighter, more modern décor, though it hasn't lost the rustic appeal. Successful dishes are characterised by strong flavours, for example herring marinated in rice vinegar oil with a seaweed garnish, and tender grilled fillet of beef (with an onion and carrot marinade) served with miso paste. The wine list is limited but there is a superb collection of sakés, including some of the best warm saké ever tasted by an experienced inspector. Closed Sun L.

Selasih W1
114 Seymour Place map 13
(020) 7724 4454
A Malaysian inspector was reminded of a 'typical small café in Kuala Lumpur' by the colourful, simple décor of this eating house. He was pleased to find not the Chinese-influenced food of many London places, but real Malay Muslim cuisine. In fried kway teow, recommended by the helpful, knowledgeable owner, he appreciated authentically tasty soft noodles and prawns 'cooked just right'. Tea or beer is a good choice to accompany the food. Closed Sun L.

Simply Nico SW1
48A Rochester Row map 13
(020) 7630 8061
Originally Nico Ladenis's main restaurant, this pleasantly relaxed narrow shop conversion, is now owned by the Restaurant Partnership. Set-price menus offer the likes of 'good, flavoursome' salade niçoise, best end of lamb with ratatouille, or pan-fried sea bream with escabèche; 'great' summer pudding and a 'delicious' chocolate mousse finished off the meal for one reporter. The wine list is short and expensive, with eight by the glass. Closed Sat L and Sun. Branches are at 7 Goswell Road, EC1, (020) 7336 7677; 10 London Bridge Street, SE1, (020) 7407 4536; 12 Sloane Square, SW1, (020) 7896

9909; and Crowne Plaza Hotel, Stockley Road, West Drayton, (01895) 437564.

62 Restaurant & Theatre Bar SE1
62 Southwark Bridge Road map 13
(020) 7633 0831
At the centre of London's new fine arts complex, this lively place sells modern pictures off its walls and modern cooking from a short carte, changed monthly. Starters might include home-cured gravadlax, caramelised red onion tart, or Parma ham with polenta and herb sauce. Among main dishes are lemon and fennel risotto with queen scallops, mussels and tiger prawns; seared salmon with a warm salad of chargrilled chicory; roast lamb with cumin spiced chickpeas and sweet potato; and duck confit with dauphinoise potatoes and roasted plums. Closed Sat L and all day Sun.

Sofra WC2
36 Tavistock Street map 15
(020) 7240 3773
A wide choice of traditional Turkish food is available on three central London Sofra sites. Guvech are casseroles served in covered pots, including lamb, chicken, liver or kidney, and the charcoal grill produces shish kebabs (request them rare, medium or well-done), kofte, and the Adana special (kofte spiced with chillies). The meze of 11 different hot and cold dishes includes imam bayaldi, kisir salad (bulghar wheat, nuts, vegetables and spices) and börek, and is available all day until midnight, handy for the post-theatre crowd. The other branches with the same menu are at 18 Shepherd Market (tel (020) 7493 3320) and 1 St Christopher Place (tel (020) 7224 4080), both in W1. Open all week.

Sotheby's Café W1
34–35 New Bond Street map 15
(020) 7293 5077
The Café provides a posh venue for breakfast, lunch or afternoon tea in between shopping on Bond Street. Lobster club sandwich is a firm favourite, and gazpacho has been well received. Otherwise, the simple cooking runs to twice-baked spinach and goats'-cheese soufflé; chargrilled swordfish with bok choy and broccoli; and chicken salad with artichokes, broad beans and bitter leaves. To finish, there might be a tart of bitter chocolate, almond and orange served with cappuccino ice cream. All the wines on the impeccable list can be had by the glass, including Sotheby's champagne at £6.50. Open Mon to Fri.

La Spighetta W1
43 Blandford Street map 15
(020) 7486 7340
This is a member of the A to Z restaurant group (alongside Aubergine, L'Oranger, Spiga and Zafferano, see main entries), and specialises in pizzas from a wood-fired oven, served in a bright and cheerful basement. Toppings include roast suckling pig, mushrooms and rocket; spicy salami; or buffalo mozzarella, cherry tomatoes and basil dressing. The menu also extends to rocket and Parmesan salad to start, or 'very fresh' scallops with saffron, and main courses of pasta or sea bream with potatoes and olives. Tiramisù and cherry tart with sorbet are typical desserts. Closed Sun L.

Stafford Hotel SW1
16–18 St James's Place map 15
(020) 7493 0111
This upmarket hotel in the heart of St James's lives up to all expectations of grandeur and opulence, not least in the highly polished but friendly service and the immense historical wine cellars. Chris Oakes's cooking appropriately follows luxurious and mainly traditional lines, with some modern ideas thrown in, producing the likes of sauté langoustines with mascarpone tortellini and red pepper sauce, followed perhaps by pan-fried foie gras with tarte Tatin and a sultana and calvados sauce. English desserts typically include custard tart or sherry trifle. Prices befit the location. Closed Sat L.

Star of India SW5
154 Old Brompton Road map 14
(020) 7373 2901
This star has shone apparently for light years, its popularity with local residents ensured by amazing Italianate decor, the hospitality of the Mahammad family, and distinctive cuisine. The new chef's cooking, lighter than before, emphasises tandooris with half a chicken on the bone, and lamb cutlets marinated in cream cheese, black pepper and ginger juice. Vegetarians (and others) appreciate okra (fried in batter until crisp, or crunchy in yoghurt spiced with mustard seeds), asafoetida and curry leaves. House wines at £9.75 and eight more by the glass match the food. Open all week.

Tate Modern SE1
Bankside map 13
(020) 7373 2901
Hungry visitors to the Tate Modern can choose either the much-hyped seventh-floor restaurant with spectacular views, frequently changing digital murals on two walls and long queues for a table; or the more informal café on 'level 2' with its sometimes even longer queues. Either way, menus are the same, and might offer Chinese duck and bok choy salad, followed by chargrilled chicken, then rhubarb and ginger crumble. Sandwiches and savouries are also available, and those arriving before lunch revs up can choose pain au chocolat or blueberry muffin to accompany teas, infusions or coffees. A short wine list also covers both venues, and offers ten by the glass. Open all week from 10am to 5.30pm (9.30pm Fri and Sat). More reports please.

Tatsuso EC2
32 Broadgate Circle map 13
(020) 7638 5863
This smart Japanese restaurant has a teppanyaki bar on one floor and a restaurant with sushi bar on another. It is not cheap, but the food is of a consistently high standard. Set meals are a good bet, comprising an appetiser of the day, followed by Japanese clear soup and various sushi, sashimi or grilled dishes, plus rice, pickles, dessert and coffee. The carte also merits exploration, with kazunoko shoyu-zuke (marinated herring roe in soy sauce), buia kakuni (sweetened pork loaf), and single-pot dishes (dinner only) such as sukiyaki (beef, vegetables and tofu in soy sauce and saké). Closed Sat and Sun.

Tbilisi N7
91 Holloway Road map 13
(020) 7607 2436
The location seems appropriate for this very affordable if unexcitingly decorated restaurant devoted to the cuisine of what was an outlying Soviet republic bordering Turkey. Helpful Georgian waiters explain gastronomic discoveries such as phali (beetroot purée with walnuts and herbs), fried liver and heart, or socko (fried mushrooms and vegetables). These come in starter combinations for two with Georgian bread, while main courses include chakapuli (lamb in tarragon sauce) and khinkhali (large dumplings filled with minced beef and pork). The wine list features some Georgian examples. Open all week D only.

Ten EC2
10 Cutlers Garden Arcade map 13
(020) 7283 7888
This large, brightly decorated basement dining room in a smart new mall off Houndsditch is a favoured lunch venue for City business folk. Smoked salmon and scrambled eggs from the bar menu is one possibility, otherwise choose the two- or three-course set menu (Greek-style salad with fried feta, braised lamb with aubergine and celery confit, raspberry Pavlova), or go for the carte, which simply offers more choice in the same vein: tomato and black olive ravioli, or roast monkfish with green banana and sweet potato. Wines are listed by price, opening at £13.50. Open Mon to Fri L only.

Thai Bistro W4
99 Chiswick High Road map 12
(020) 8995 5774
Lively, cheerful and relaxed are some of the words used to describe this small Thai restaurant in Chiswick High Road. The bright, modern décor and large communal tables add to the sense of informality, and create a refreshingly different environment to sample the likes of chicken satay, pork toasts, tom ka gai soup (hot-and-sour chicken with coconut milk), red curries and pad Thai noodles. A large vegetarian section and regional specialities are available for those wishing to try something different. Children are welcome. Closed Tue and Thur L.

3 Monkeys SE24
136–140 Herne Hill map 12
(020) 7738 5500
This stylish, modern place in former bank premises has a bridge over the bar, leading to a fashionably bare dining area with views of the kitchen below, and of the tandoor where naan is baked. Service is pleasant and good at explaining unusual regional dishes, such as chicken malwani from Maharashtra. Presentation of food is attractive, but high prices are noted, especially for such usually unconsidered trifles as poppadums, rice, water and beer. Superb lassi, either a sweetish mango version or the refreshing, brightly flavoured savoury one, is recommended. Open Sun L and all week D.

Tokyo Diner WC2
2 Newport Place map 15
(020) 7287 8777
This unpretentious place is open noon to 11.30pm (last orders) 365 days a year, and you can't book or pay by cheque: but credit cards are now accepted. Perched on cushioned stools at small tables, customers admire delightfully kitsch Japanese artefacts, and are served by friendly young people who in admirable Japanese style politely refuse tips if offered. They bring free tea and a range of sushi, sashimi, noodles, and curries (very mild), or donburi (bowls of rice with various toppings) and bento boxes (salmon teriyaki, perhaps, with rice, salad, sashimi and pickled radish). Open all week.

The Vale W9
99 Chippenham Road map 13
(020) 7266 0990
West London neighbourhood restaurant with daily-changing menus offering traditional English and Mediterranean cooking with modern influences. The repertoire runs from deep-fried skate with chips and aïoli through to lamb kofta with couscous and raita, with smoked haddock and leek pasty, and calf's liver with sage mash somewhere between those extremes. Sunday brunch brings on eggs Benedict and roast beef with Yorkshire pudding, while weekday lunches focus on fishcakes and pies. A good selection of wines start at £10. Closed L Mon and Sat.

Vama – The Indian Room SW10
438 Kings Road map 14
(020) 7351 4118
Well suited to its World's End location, this smart restaurant offers a short à la carte menu mainly drawn from the north-west of the Sub-Continent. There are equal numbers of vegetarian and non-vegetarian dishes, and few have familiar names. Many items are finished in the tandoor, besides those with 'tandoori' in the name, such as phool (cauliflower and broccoli), jhinga (prawns), and bater (quail). The game section of the menu includes braised Barbary duck, venison and smoked partridge. Open all week.

Vasco & Piero's Pavilion W1
15 Poland Street map 15
(020) 7437 8774
Long-standing favourite dishes at this ever-popular Italian include scaloppine of pork milanese, and strips of fried calf's liver, but new ideas appear regularly on the lunchtime carte and set-price dinner menus: rare tuna with fresh chilli and

cannellini beans, for example, or tagliata of Angus beef. Desserts are on the lines of a sweet tart of pine nuts and crème fraîche, or fresh pineapple with ice cream. The good-value, mainly Italian wine list includes plenty under £20. Open Mon to Fri L, Mon to Sat D. A sister restaurant, Caffè Umbria, at 108 Heath Street, NW3, tel (020) 7431 4949, offers a shorter menu and also serves breakfast.

Village Bistro N6
38 Highgate High Street map 12
(020) 8340 5165
This pleasant neighbourhood restaurant with a regularly changing menu is appreciated for its ample portions, consistent standards, good value for money and friendly service. The best market produce might appear as daily specials, and one reporter enjoyed warm chicken liver salad, Barbary duck with mash, and an accomplished rhubarb fool. A short wine list offers a good choice of half-bottles. Open all week.

Vrisaki N22
73 Myddleton Road map 12
(020) 8889 8760
Yes, it's the Greek-Cypriot kebab house, exactly as we know it (takeaway counter at the front, busy dining room beyond), but it's a lot larger inside than the exterior suggests. The menu offers a wide choice of fish including sea bass, grey bream and Dover sole; and as starters, smoked trout or dressed crab. As well as lamb, chicken and pork kebabs there are charcoal-grilled steaks, veal chops, lamb cutlets, grilled poussin and sheftalia (rough-cut pork sausages wrapped in caul). The house meze selection – a generous meal in itself – is a popular option. House wines are £8.50.

Wiz W11
123A Clarendon Road map 13
(020) 7229 1500
This relaxed bar-restaurant, with young staff and clientele, mirrors Antony Worral Thompson's perpetual motion. The menu of tapas-style dishes (mostly between £4 and £6) is divided into sections by country of origin: representing the Americas may be guacamole, or southern fried chicken nuggets, while the UK and Eire list takes in Cumberland chipolatas, and salmon and haddock fishcakes. Northern Europe offers chicken liver parfait and North Atlantic goujons, while buratta cheese and roast garlic spread, and beef carpaccio, are Southern European. North Africa, the Subcontinent and the Orient are there too. It's not 'fusion' but a multi-ethnic jamboree. Brunch is available at weekends. House wines are £10.95; others as eclectic as the food. Closed Sun D.

Wodka W8
12 St Albans Grove map 14
(020) 7937 6513
Modern decoration blends well with old-fashioned Polish strong vodka and mainly traditional dishes. Start with a wild mushroom soup called grzybowa (easier done than said), or zur (sour rye and sausage soup), or with smoked eel, celeriac rémoulade and cwikla (a combination of beetroot and horseradish probably better known as Jewish chrane). Lots of main dishes are something inside something else: salmon coulibiac in pastry, zrazy (stuffed beef olives), and golabki (cabbage leaves stuffed with pork, wild rice and cranberry sauce). Continuing this theme, salesniki are pancakes filled with sweet cheese, nuts and raisins, and racuchy are fried apple pancakes. Closed Sat and Sun L.

Yoshino W1
3 Piccadilly Place map 15
(020) 7287 6622
In this modern, but not austere, restaurant the clientele and staff are mainly Japanese, though it has also been appreciated by non-Japanese reporters. Sushi was not on the menu as the Guide went to press, apparently because the perfectionist owner had been unable to find a specialist sushi chef from Japan. However, assorted sashimi can be

exceptional in quality and unusual in content. Reports have also praised tofu with ginger, spring onion and soy sauce, and tempura prawns, served with three salt dips, flavoured with chilli, wasabi, and dried shiso herb. Closed Sun.

Zen Central W1
20 Queen Street Mayfair map 15
(020) 7629 8089/8103
Set in the heart of Mayfair, with chic, minimalist black and white décor, Zen Central has a simple credo: to offer modern Chinese food, combining dishes from Szechuan, Pekinese and Cantonese cuisines, using first-class ingredients. Start perhaps with steamed prawns with crushed garlic in lotus leaves before moving on to a braised mixed seafood in clay pot or, if you are feeling particularly flush (and hungry), a Canton-style roasted whole suckling pig. Service is friendly and professional; valet parking is available. House wines start at £16. Open all week.

Zen Chelsea SW3
Chelsea Cloisters map 14
(020) 7589 1781
Offering upmarket Chinese cooking for the comfortable denizens of Chelsea at prices that seem to relate to the local property market, Zen is appropriately decked out with gold silk curtains, and staffed by exemplary waiters in bow-ties. The lengthy menu covers the Cantonese repertoire and beyond, producing tender soft-shell crabs crusted with pepper, garlic and chilli; delicate chive and shrimp dumplings; steamed chicken with water mushroom and Yunnak ham; and stewed whole eel with garlic and preserved cabbage. A tendency to under-season has been noted, occasionally resulting in blandness. House French wines are £13.80. Open all week.

Zinc Bar & Grill W1
21 Heddon Street map 15
(020) 7255 8899
In a side street off Regent Street, this attractive Conran restaurant declares itself a bar-grill, and has a suitably vibrant and informal atmosphere. The £11.50 two-course set lunch might be homely roast chicken sitting on garlic mash, followed by nectarines in a toffee nut sauce. 'Light meals' include chicken Caesar salad, and enticing sandwiches such as roast beef on onion and bacon bread with creamed horseradish. The carte offers bistro food – duck liver parfait, Toulouse sausage, wing of skate – and there is a rôtisserie too. Eight wines are sold by the glass. Closed Sun.

England

ALDEBURGH Suffolk map 6

Lighthouse 🍷 £

77 High Street, Aldeburgh IP15 5AU
TEL/FAX: (01728) 453377

COOKING **4**
MODERN BRITISH-PLUS
£21–£44

The Lighthouse shines as brightly as ever, according to reports. Tables are small and rather close, but the bistro ambience extends to seating outside on a patio and even the pavement (Suffolk weather permitting). Both the upstairs non-smoking and ground-floor dining room are unpretentiously furnished and decorated with posters. Fish may not have the menu entirely to itself, but Aldeburgh cod comes heartily approved: perhaps roast with a tapénade crust, or fried in beer batter with chips, mushy peas and tartare sauce. A combination of straightforward ideas and varied ingredients provides another part of the attraction, from local asparagus with shaved Parmesan, via roast duck breast with apple and ginger relish, to passion fruit mascarpone with coconut tart.

Lunch, meanwhile, has provided simple luxuries of potted Norfolk shrimps, dressed local crab with herb mayonnaise, and calf's liver with bacon. Service is keen, knowledgeable, cheerful and competent. The down-to-earth wine list is not without flair and manages to combine safe staples (Forrest Estate Sauvignon from New Zealand, £15.75) with more imaginative selections (Murphy Goode Zinfandel from California, £18.95). Nine house wines all hover around the £10 mark, and mark-ups throughout are fair.

CHEFS: Sara E. Fox and Guy Welsh PROPRIETORS: Sara E. Fox and Peter G.R. Hill OPEN: all week 12 to 2.30, 7 to 10 CLOSED: 2 weeks Jan, 1 week Oct MEALS: alc L (main courses £6 to £10.50). Set D £13.50 (2 courses) to £15.75 SERVICE: not inc, card slips closed CARDS: Delta, MasterCard, Switch, Visa DETAILS: 95 seats. 25 seats outside. Private parties: 45 main room, 20 and 25 private rooms. Vegetarian meals. No smoking in 1 dining room. Wheelchair access (also WC). No music. Air-conditioned (£5)

All entries in the Guide are re-researched and rewritten every year, not least because restaurant standards fluctuate. Don't rely on an out-of-date Guide.

Dining rooms where music, either live or recorded, is never played are signalled by No music *in the details at the end of an entry.*

Regatta £

171–173 High Street, Aldeburgh IP15 5AN — COOKING **4**
TEL: (01728) 452011 — SEAFOOD/EUROPEAN
£18–£39

There is something for everyone at this smart and popular seaside restaurant, whose cheerful atmosphere owes much to its blue and yellow décor and enthusiastic staff. Robert Mabey prides himself on using as much local produce as possible, offering plenty of fish from April to September, with local game coming into force in winter. Daily specials listed on blackboards have produced fine fresh cod in batter with good chips and tartare sauce, and grilled scallops with ratatouille, while fixtures on the carte include potted crayfish with coriander, oriental-style squid with ginger and noodles, and home-cured gravad lax. Fishcakes also 'deserve a mention'. For meat eaters there may be sirloin steak with garlic butter or Thai green chicken curry. Puddings range from a novelty fudge and Malteser ice cream to lemon syllabub with 'boudoir' biscuits. Prices generally are reasonable, but the early-evening menu is particularly good value. A succinct wine list kicks off in France with house wines at £9.50 and picks up other countries, including Chile and New Zealand, along the way.

CHEF: Robert Mabey PROPRIETORS: Robert and Johanna Mabey OPEN: Nov to Easter Thur to Sun L 12 to 2, Thur to Sat D 6 to 10; Easter to August all week 12 to 2, 6 to 10 (last orders later in summer and during Aldeburgh festival); open 6 days a week in Sept and Oct (phone for details) MEALS: alc (main courses £7.50 to £14). Set D Sun to Fri (exc bank hols and Aug) before 7 £8 (2 courses) to £10. Light L available summer SERVICE: not inc CARDS: Amex, Delta, MasterCard, Switch, Visa DETAILS: 100 seats. Private parties: 50 main room, 20 to 40 private rooms. Vegetarian meals. Children's helpings exc Sat D. Wheelchair access (also WC). Occasional music. Air-conditioned (£5)

ALTRINCHAM Greater Manchester — **map 8**

Juniper

21 The Downs, Altrincham WA14 2QD — COOKING **7**
TEL: (0161) 929 4008 FAX: (0161) 929 4009 — MODERN FRENCH
£37–£64

The white-walled dining room, with bare floorboards and simple tables set with gleaming glassware, has survived without refurbishment for the five years Paul Kitching has been here. Although it has not pleased all reporters equally, it is generally considered 'head and shoulders above anything in the north west'. The focus remains on a carte that offers around five or six choices per course at dinner (lunch is more like three), with a series of themed evenings (one majoring on cheese, another on French peasant food for example) adding interest for regulars.

Seafood is a particularly strong suit, perhaps taking in a 'masterful' dish of Dover sole fillets partnered by preserved lemon and flat parsley in a creamy broth, or a generous plateful of accurately timed grilled scallop slices, swimming in a thin, sharp beurre blanc scattered with sweetcorn, carrot, peas and spinach. Scallops have also appeared unusually with apricots and mustard. This reflects an innovative streak that has also produced a starter of poached egg and cheese beignet with bacon and sage butter, and a terrine in which pieces of chicken, mushroom, red pepper and carrot are bound together in a light jelly, and topped with an intense 'tomato custard'.

Classical simplicity is backed up by attractive presentation, from roast lamb with ratatouille to the highly rated lemon tart, perhaps served with a rosemary sorbet. Other desserts have included a tribute to Sharrow Bay's (see entry, Ullswater) famous sticky toffee pudding, which has been turned into a soufflé. Value for money is considered good, bread and the pre-meal soup are first class, and service is both 'slick and informative'. Four house wines start the ball rolling at a whisker under £20.

CHEF: Paul Kitching PROPRIETORS: Nora and Peter Miles OPEN: Tue to Fri L 12 to 2, Mon to Sat D 7 to 9.30 (10 Fri and Sat) CLOSED: bank hols MEALS: alc (main courses L £13 to £16, D £16 to £21) SERVICE: not inc, card slips closed CARDS: Amex, Delta, MasterCard, Switch, Visa DETAILS: 45 seats. Private parties: 30 main room. Children's helpings. Music. Air-conditioned (£5)

ALVECHURCH Worcestershire **map 5**

Mill

Radford Road, Alvechurch B48 7LD
TEL: (0121) 447 7005 FAX: (0121) 447 8001

COOKING **3**
MODERN BRITISH
£27–£41

The Mill's stately three storeys of red brick make it one of the most attractive buildings in the village; inside, beams and rough-plastered white walls set the tone. The friendly McKernon family and chef Carl Timms know their customers, and have found that adopting the tried-and-tested approach is the better part of valour, offering a monthly-changing set-price menu that deals mainly in familiar modern themes. Favoured ingredients have included chicken livers, used in a parfait or with bacon in a risotto; salmon, which might come with a chervil and spinach sauce; and smoked haddock, perhaps in a soup with potatoes and crispy leeks, or together with crab in a warm tart. Heartier main courses might include rack of lamb with onion and fennel purée. Flavours are clear, combinations balanced, the cooking more than competent. Puddings are fruity, boozy or traditional (ranging from bread-and-butter pudding with lemon curd to Tia Maria slice with coffee crème anglaise). Prices are attractive on the global wine list and a smattering of interesting bin-ends and clearance sale wines are worth scanning. Devotees of Lebanon's flagship Ch. Musar will be pleased to find a run of vintages going back to 1964. House wines start at £9.25

CHEF: Carl Timms PROPRIETORS: Stefan, Vivienne and Geoffrey McKernon OPEN: Tue to Sat D only 7 to 8.30 (9.15 Sat) CLOSED: first week Jan, first two weeks Aug MEALS: Set D Tue to Fri £17.50 (2 courses) to £19.50, Set D Sat £26.50 SERVICE: not inc CARDS: Amex, Delta, MasterCard, Switch, Visa DETAILS: 28 seats. Private parties: 28 main room. Car park. Vegetarian meals. No children under 5. No smoking in dining room. Music (£5)

The text of entries is based on unsolicited reports sent in by readers, backed up by inspections conducted anonymously. The factual details under the text are from questionnaires the Guide sends to all restaurants that feature in the book.

AMBERLEY West Sussex — map 3

▲ Amberley Castle, Queen's Room

Amberley BN18 9ND
TEL: (01798) 831992 FAX: (01798) 831998
EMAIL: info@amberleycastle.co.uk
WEB SITE: www.amberleycastle.co.uk
on B2139, between Storrington and Bury Hill

NEW CHEF
ANGLO-FRENCH
£38–£94

Given a 900-year-old castle with a grassy moat and gatehouse, the setting could hardly fail to impress. The portcullis is lowered each night to keep out marauders, and a first-floor, barrel-vaulted, tapestried dining room contributes to the unique atmosphere. As the Guide went to press Billy Butcher left for Summer Lodge (see entry, Evershot) and his sous-chef Nick Craft (who had previously cooked at Gravetye Manor, see entry, East Grinstead) took over the stoves. No change to the country-house style was planned immediately, so the menu may still offer roast loin of local rabbit in a cumin-scented broth (a first course, incidentally), and lemon- and tarragon-crusted halibut in a sauce of mustard, white wine and cream, followed by a variation on the crème brûlée theme. Staff are formally dressed but friendly and welcoming, and the mostly French wine list is dominated by big names and high prices, although there are a few bottles under £20. Four house wines, for example, are £17.50.

CHEF: Nick Craft PROPRIETORS: Martin and Joy Cummings OPEN: all week 12.30 to 2, 7 to 9.30 MEALS: alc (main courses £21 to £29). Set L Mon to Sat £12.50 (2 courses), Set L Sun £25.50, Set D £35 SERVICE: not inc CARDS: Amex, Delta, Diners, MasterCard, Switch, Visa DETAILS: 48 seats. Private parties: 55 main room, 12 and 48 private rooms. Car park. Vegetarian meals. No children under 12. Jacket and tie. No smoking in dining room. No music ACCOMMODATION: 20 rooms, all with bath/shower. TV. Phone. Room only £145 to £300. No children under 12 (*The Which? Hotel Guide*) (£5)

AMBLESIDE Cumbria — map 8

Glass House

CUMBRIA GFG 2001 COMMENDED

Rydal Road, Ambleside LA22 9AN
TEL: (015394) 32137 FAX: (015394) 33384
WEB SITE: www.theglasshouserestaurant.co.uk

COOKING 3
MODERN EUROPEAN
£20–£48

'An extremely interesting place to eat,' summed up one visitor to this restored fifteenth-century Grade II listed mill. Next door to the owner's glass studio and workshop, it deals well with light and space (there are four levels), is friendly and informal, and serves imaginative food at fair prices. 'There should be more places like this.' The set lunch and early-doors options tend to be simpler and lighter, along the lines of rollmop and rocket salad, soup (perhaps a bright blend of pumpkin, coconut, chilli, coriander and pesto) or chicken suprême with mushroom risotto, while the carte is more ambitious. Here, grilled scallops might be served on a potato pancake with sour cream and sweet chilli, alongside more traditional partnerships such as calf's liver with mash and onion gravy, or steamed strawberry jam sponge with custard. Results are tasty and well executed, 'especially fish' for a regular, and children get their own small menu.

Pleasant and thoughtful service has had the occasional glitch. Around 50 well-chosen wines stay mostly under £20, starting with house Duboeuf at £9.75.

CHEF: Stuart Birket PROPRIETOR: Adrian Sankey OPEN: all week 12 to 3, 6 to 10 CLOSED: 25 Dec MEALS: alc (main courses L £5 to £10.50, D £9 to £15). Set L £9 (2 courses), Set D 6 to 7.30 Sun to Fri £9.95 (2 courses) SERVICE: not inc CARDS: Delta, MasterCard, Switch, Visa DETAILS: 80 seats. 20 seats outside. Private parties: 100 main room, 40 private room. Car park. Vegetarian meals. Children's helpings. No smoking in dining room. Wheelchair access (not WC). Music (£5)

▲ Rothay Manor

Rothay Bridge, Ambleside LA22 0EH
TEL: (015394) 33605 FAX: (015394) 33607
EMAIL: hotel@rothaymanor.co.uk
WEB SITE: www.rothaymanor.co.uk
off A593 to Coniston, ¼m W of Ambleside

COOKING 3
MODERN BRITISH
£21–£48

The white house, its flower-bordered lawn stretching down to the River Rothay, offers a warm welcome from relaxed but efficient staff for whom nothing appears to be too much trouble. Sparkling cutlery and heavy glassware set the tone for a dinner menu of three to five courses that combines both traditional and contemporary ideas. Caponata of tuna, capers and olives in 'a little pie' was an impressive starter for one reporter; otherwise there may be truffle-dressed scallops on celeriac and saffron purée, or a tarte Tatin of onion and goats' cheese, before main courses of tender chicken breast in a mild curry sauce, or braised lamb shank with root vegetables.

Lighter lunch options might take in salmon fillet on a potato pancake, while Sunday offers a traditional roast beef and Yorkshire pudding. Finish perhaps with flavourful pannacotta with raspberries, or bread-and-butter pudding. Wines offer a thorough selection incorporating old and new. Although half-bottles are limited, the management is happy to serve half a whole bottle for three fifths of the price, or let you take home what you don't drink. House wines start at £12 for South African Sauvignon or Chilean Cabernet Sauvignon/Malbec.

CHEFS: Jane Binns and Colette Nixon PROPRIETORS: Nigel and Stephen Nixon OPEN: all week 12.30 to 2 (12.45 to 1.30 Sun), 7.45 to 9 CLOSED: 3 Jan to 9 Feb MEALS: Set L Mon to Sat £13.50, Set L Sun £16.50, Set D £24 (2 courses) to £30 SERVICE: not inc, card slips closed CARDS: Amex, Delta, Diners, MasterCard, Switch, Visa DETAILS: 70 seats. Private parties: 34 private room. Car park. Vegetarian meals. Children's helpings. No children under 8 at D. No smoking in dining room. Wheelchair access (also WC). No music. Air-conditioned ACCOMMODATION: 18 rooms, all with bath/shower. TV. Phone. B&B £65 to £130. Rooms for disabled. Baby facilities (*The Which? Hotel Guide*)

The Guide always appreciates hearing about changes of chef or owner.

The Guide relies on feedback from its readers. Especially welcome are reports on new restaurants appearing in the book for the first time. All letters to the Guide are acknowledged.

AMERSHAM Buckinghamshire map 3

Kings Arms

30 High Street, Old Amersham HP7 0DJ
TEL: (01494) 726333 FAX: (01494) 433480
WEB SITE: www.kingsarmsamersham.co.uk

COOKING 1
MODERN BRITISH
£22–£44

Old Amersham is not short of antique shops, nor of venerable beams, and plenty of the latter are incorporated into the pleasingly intimate, salmon-pink restaurant of this old inn. The menu shows a few Mediterranean influences, turning up red mullet with roast red pepper salsa, and chicken breast stuffed with feta and sun-dried tomatoes. Reports are mixed, though one visitor enthused about a main course of lamb's liver with thyme gravy, and another enjoyed a large portion of pan-fried strips of ultra-fresh cod in a pimento and basil sauce. Brown-bread ice cream, served in a brandy-snap basket, has won plaudits, too. The wine list is grouped by style and includes a 13-strong 'cellar selection'. Prices start at £9.75 for house Chilean.

CHEF: Simon Harbour PROPRIETOR: John Jennison OPEN: Tue to Sun L 12 to 2, Tue to Sat D 7 to 9.30 CLOSED: 26 to 30 Dec MEALS: alc (main courses £13 to £16). Set L Tue to Sat £10.50 (2 courses) to £13.50, Set L Sun £15, Set D Tue to Fri £17, Set D Sat £25 SERVICE: not inc CARDS: Amex, Delta, Diners, MasterCard, Switch, Visa DETAILS: 57 seats. 12 seats outside. Private parties: 50 main room, 12 to 50 private rooms. Car park. Vegetarian meals. Children's helpings. No cigars/pipes in dining room. Wheelchair access (not WC). No music (£5)

APPLETHWAITE Cumbria map 10

▲ Underscar Manor

Applethwaite CA12 4PH
TEL: (017687) 75000 FAX: (017687) 74904
off A66, ½m N of Keswick

COOKING 6
ANGLO-FRENCH
£36–£78

Set high above Keswick, looking across to Derwent Water and the hills beyond (binoculars are provided), Underscar is considered 'very impressive in all ways'. It deals in luxury and comfort, with thick-pile carpets, deep settees, and stuffed animals 'on every chair, table and sofa within sight'. Robert Thornton treats the modern classical repertoire with a degree of imagination as well as skill, using fine ingredients along the way, from seared scallops with spiced cabbage to roast saddle of rabbit with a carrot and potato hotpot. Meals are characterised by 'plenty of taste and texture', from the 'delightful decadence' of pan-fried foie gras served with a soft, warm, partly set grape jelly and a Sauternes sauce, to smoked haddock on spinach with a well-timed poached egg.

Sauces are balanced and presentation is impressive, judging by an attractively set-out ragoût of chunky lobster tail and claw, with dinky little carrots and turnips. 'Lunchers may have to persevere if they wish to choose from the à la carte menu.' Our inspector did and found it well worth doing so, ending with a steamed whisky sponge and custard, and a tasting plate of seven small desserts. Breads are first-rate, as are appetisers and petits fours, and domes are lifted, but service is friendly. Two pages of wines from around the world add interest to a conventionally French list which starts with house Côtes du Rhône and Chardonnay at £15.

CHEF: Robert Thornton PROPRIETORS: Pauline and Derek Harrison, and Gordon Evans OPEN: all week 12 to 1, 7 to 8.30 (9 Sat) MEALS: alc (main courses £19 to £28). Set L £25, Set D £30 SERVICE: not inc, card slips closed CARDS: Amex, MasterCard, Switch, Visa DETAILS: 55 seats. 12 seats outside. Private parties: 30 main room. Car park. Vegetarian meals. No children under 12. Jacket (not tie). No smoking in dining room. No music ACCOMMODATION: 11 rooms, all with bath/shower. TV. Phone. D,B&B £95 to £250. No children under 12. Swimming pool (*The Which? Hotel Guide*)

ARNCLIFFE North Yorkshire **map 8**

▲ Amerdale House

Arncliffe, Littondale BD23 5QE COOKING **4**
TEL: (01756) 770250 FAX: (01756) 770266 MODERN EUROPEAN
£40–£48

Way up the Dales in remote limestone country (ten miles from Malham), Amerdale is a roomy house in a small village (pop. 60) where the vicarage is bigger than the church. As local materials are used for building, so they are for cooking, among them beef and lamb from the family farm of a butcher in Grassington. He also makes his own 'charcuterie', which might turn up in first-course salads of minted new potato and Cumberland sausage, or black pudding and dry-cure bacon (derived from old breeds of pig). The five-course format is not too daunting, and Nigel Crapper's cooking stays mercifully simple, producing perhaps a tomato and basil tart for course two, followed by baked haddock fillet in lemon butter sauce, or roast leg of Dales lamb stuffed with garlic and rosemary. Results at inspection ranged from 'ordinary' to a first-class shellfish bisque, by way of an unusual dessert of wattle seed ice cream that melted obligingly over a puff pastry fig tart. Cheeses typically include Wensleydale, Swaledale and Coverdale. Service tends to be 'one thing at a time' (dinner can take all evening), but is smiling and obliging. Sensibly chosen wines from around the world offer good choice under £20, with house selections at £12.95.

CHEFS: Nigel Crapper and Anthony Chamley PROPRIETORS: Paula and Nigel Crapper OPEN: all week D only 7.30 to 8.30 CLOSED: mid-Nov to mid-Mar MEALS: Set D £30 SERVICE: none, card slips closed CARDS: MasterCard, Switch, Visa DETAILS: 22 seats. Car park. Vegetarian meals. Children's helpings. No children under 8. No smoking in dining room. No music ACCOMMODATION: 11 rooms, all with bath/shower. TV. Phone. D,B&B £80 to £143. Baby facilities (*The Which? Hotel Guide*)

'The head waitress [is] the woman I am going to nominate for restaurant personality of the year. I happened to say "ah, a new face" when she first appeared. Huge hilarity. "I wish it were, darling."' (On eating in Warwickshire)

The Guide's top-rated restaurants are listed near the front of the book.

ASENBY North Yorkshire map 9

▲ Crab & Lobster

Dishforth Road, Asenby YO7 3QL
TEL: (01845) 577286 FAX: (01845) 577109
EMAIL: reservations@crabandlobster.co.uk
WEB SITE: www.crabandlobster.co.uk
off A168, between A19 and A1

COOKING **2**
FISH/MODERN EUROPEAN
£23–£73

What appears to be a charming, well-kept, thatched country inn turns out to be an 'eccentric Aladdin's cave' of curiosities and themed bric-à-brac; it is 'like sitting in a bazaar'. Rooms in the adjacent Crab Manor are unusual too, echoing famous hotels from Marrakesh to Singapore and New York. Seafood is not the only choice – duck confit with toffee apples, and sausage with bubble and squeak have impressed – but it does offer the most options, from classic cod and chips with minted mushy peas, and skate wing with brown butter and capers, to more exotic sea bass with a tropical fruit salsa, or baked crab with Indian spices and coconut crust. Desserts take in steamed lemon sponge with rhubarb, and chocolate and banana pancakes with cardamom ice cream. Staff might be more helpful (you may need to request the set-price menu), and 50-plus wines are as varied as they are interesting. Six of the eight house selections cost around £15.

CHEFS: David Barnard and Steven Dean PROPRIETORS: David and Jackie Barnard OPEN: all week 12 to 2.30, 7 to 10 MEALS: alc (main courses £9.50 to £27.50). Set L £11.50 (2 courses) to £14.50, Set D £25 SERVICE: not inc, card slips closed CARDS: Amex, Delta, MasterCard, Switch, Visa DETAILS: 150 seats. 150 seats outside. Private parties: 100 main room, 100 private room. Car park. Vegetarian meals. Children's helpings. No smoking in dining room. Occasional music. Air-conditioned ACCOMMODATION: 12 rooms, all with bath/shower. TV. Phone. B&B £55 to £75. Rooms for disabled

ASHBOURNE Derbyshire map 8

▲ Callow Hall

Mappleton Road, Ashbourne DE6 2AA
TEL: (01335) 300900 FAX: (01335) 300512
EMAIL: enquiries@callowhall.co.uk
WEB SITE: www.callowhall.co.uk
¾m NW of Ashbourne, turn left off A515 at crossroads with Bowling Green pub on left; Mappleton Road first on right

COOKING **4**
MODERN BRITISH-PLUS
£29–£62

The Spencers take the hotel business as seriously as anybody. Some members of the family have degrees in it, several generations have dedicated their lives to it, and their imposing Victorian house set in 40 acres is a hive of industry. The kitchen takes a pride in seafood: seared scallops and grilled red mullet might come with tomato and basil oil, and their own smoked salmon might be served with a warm potato cake and dill butter sauce. Both the monthly-changing carte and the four-course set dinner are broadly based, dishes ranging from asparagus spears with a white port and lime butter sauce, to breast and confit leg of squab pigeon with chanterelles in a rich game sauce. Choice at any one time is generous, and might take in desserts of mango tarte Tatin, or a hot chocolate fondant with Grand Marnier sauce and a kirsch and raspberry coulis. A global wine list includes choice bottles from as far afield as Canada and Tasmania, although classic France regions contribute the bulk of the cellar. House wines start at £11.75 and half bottles are plentiful, if a little pricey.

CHEFS: David and Anthony Spencer PROPRIETORS: David, Dorothy and Anthony Spencer OPEN: Sun L 12.30 to 1.30, Mon to Sat D 7.30 to 9.30 (residents only Sun D) MEALS: alc D (main courses £19.50 to £20). Set L £20.50, Set D £38 SERVICE: not inc CARDS: Amex, Delta, Diners, MasterCard, Switch, Visa DETAILS: 80 seats. Private parties: 40 main room. Car park. Vegetarian meals. Children's helpings. No smoking in dining room. No music ACCOMMODATION: 18 rooms, all with bath/shower. TV. Phone. B&B £85 to £190 (double room). Rooms for disabled. Baby facilities. Fishing (*The Which? Hotel Guide*) (£5)

ASHFORD Derbyshire — map 9

▲ Riverside House — NEW ENTRY

Fennell Street, Ashford DE45 1QF
TEL: (01629) 814275 FAX: (01629) 812873
EMAIL: riversidehouse@enta.net

COOKING **4**
ANGLO-FRENCH
£34–£56

Set in the heart of the Peak District, its extensive gardens running down to the River Wye, this stone-built country-house hotel offers two dining rooms, each elegantly furnished with walnut tables, flowers and polished silverware. The atmosphere is warm, the comfort factor high, and prime produce – from Cornish sea bass and organic pork to local beef and lamb – is delivered with some imagination. Classic dishes are typically given a modern twist: partridge and veal terrine with red onion and sultana chutney, for example, or braised spiced pork with black pudding and foie gras sauce.

An inspection meal impressed with a 'brilliant' chowder of seared scallops sitting in a ham-flavoured sauce with cubed potato, and a gamey flavoured wild mushroom risotto doused with truffle oil. Although puddings and cheeses may not always be up to scratch, a tart summer fruit jelly with sweet cicely ice cream is one that has pleased. Staff are friendly, knowledgeable and accommodating, and the French-dominated wine list starts off with house vin de pays at £14.75 a bottle, £3.70 a glass.

CHEF: John Whelan PROPRIETOR: Penelope Thornton OPEN: all week 12 to 2, 7 to 9.30 MEALS: Set L £23.95, Set D £34.95 SERVICE: not inc CARDS: Amex, Delta, Diners, MasterCard, Switch, Visa DETAILS: 40 seats. 20 seats outside. Private parties: 30 main room, 24 and 27 private rooms. Car park. Vegetarian meals. No children under 12. No smoking in dining room. No music ACCOMMODATION: 15 rooms, all with bath/shower. TV. Phone. B&B £95 to £155. Rooms for disabled. No children under 12 (£5)

▲ means accommodation is available.

Prices quoted in the Guide are based on information supplied by restaurateurs. The prices quoted at the top of each entry represent a range, from the lowest meal price to the highest; the latter is inflated by 20 per cent to take account of likely price rises during the year of the Guide.

AYLESBURY Buckinghamshire map 3

▲ Hartwell House 

Oxford Road, Aylesbury HP17 8NL
TEL: (01296) 747444 FAX: (01296) 747450
EMAIL: info@hartwell-house.com
WEB SITE: www.hartwell-house.com
on A418, 2m from Aylesbury towards Oxford

COOKING **3**
BRITISH
£36–£62

Country-house hotels could hardly come much grander than this if they tried. The Grade I listed stately home, set in 90 landscaped acres, has been sympathetically restored with busts, plinths, gilt-framed portraits and all the paraphernalia to be expected of a place with links to Louis XVIII, who held court here in exile. There are, for example, four elegant lounges just for taking coffee. New (formerly sous) chef Daniel Richardson continues the up-market style, using foie gras (in a starter with spiced apples) and truffle (in a celeriac purée to accompany pot-roast fillet of beef), alongside more modest materials such as saddle of rabbit. The quality is high – good-quality pan-fried brill with pickled celery, and three small lamb cutlets on a thin circle of crushed potato – although portion control is not considered generous. Among desserts that have pleased is a marbled chocolate cheesecake with an enjoyably sharp apricot sauce. Service is formal (assuming you call full morning dress formal) but has also been 'forgetful', while wines (and prices) are geared to the surroundings. That said, the five house wines cost less than £20.

CHEF: Daniel Richardson PROPRIETOR: Historic House Hotels Ltd OPEN: all week 12.30 to 1.45, 7.30 to 9.45 CLOSED: dining room closed to non-residents Christmas to New Year MEALS: Set L £22 (2 courses) to £29, Set D £45 SERVICE: net prices, card slips closed CARDS: Delta, MasterCard, Switch, Visa DETAILS: 60 seats. 20 seats outside. Private parties: 60 main room, 18 to 60 private rooms. Car park. Vegetarian meals. No children under 8. Jacket and tie at D. No smoking in dining room. Wheelchair access (also WC). Occasional music ACCOMMODATION: 46 rooms, all with bath/shower. TV. Phone. Room only £135 to £400. Rooms for disabled. No children under 8. Swimming pool. Fishing (*The Which? Hotel Guide*)

BAKEWELL Derbyshire map 8

Renaissance

Bath Street, Bakewell DE45 1BX
TEL: (01629) 812687

COOKING **4**
FRENCH
£20–£34

'I do not believe in frozen, powder, or tins,' proclaims Eric Piedaniel from his French stronghold in a side street set back from the town's main shopping area. Instead, local produce and essential French imports are transformed into 'glamorous bistro' set meals (particularly good-value mid-week) that present some hard choices made no easier by their English translations. Visitors have reported favourably on starters – 'none of them overfacing' – of Camembert profiteroles with spinach sauce, crayfish salad, and poached egg in filo pastry, followed by a calvados and apple sorbet. Lightly sauced main courses of pheasant breast with chicken mousseline, or wine-braised lamb shank, come with a variety of pleasing vegetables. A few dishes, such as a starter casserole of cidery artichokes and asparagus, attract a supplement. There's no tailing off at dessert stage, to judge by chocolate caramelised gâteau in a white chocolate sauce, or well executed iced nougatine with a pineapple coulis, two among several rich, well-presented and flavourful alternatives to French cheeses. 'It would have felt treacherous to order anything other than a French bottle', but nevertheless the 15 or so traitors would make attractive drinking; house wines are £10.99. Service is down-to-earth and charming.

CHEF: Eric Piedaniel PROPRIETORS: E. and C. Piedaniel, and D. Béraud OPEN: Tue to Sun L 12 to 1.30, Tue to Sat D 7 to 9.30 CLOSED: 25 Dec to third week Jan, first two weeks Aug MEALS: Set L and D £12.95 (exc Fri to Sun) to £19.95. Light L available Tue to Sat SERVICE: not inc CARDS: MasterCard, Switch, Visa DETAILS: 75 seats. Private parties: 50 main room, 25 private room. Vegetarian meals. Children's helpings. No smoking in dining room. Wheelchair access (also women's WC). Music

BARNET Hertfordshire map 3

Mims

63 East Barnet Road, Barnet EN4 8RN
TEL/FAX: (020) 8449 2974

COOKING **6**
MEDITERRANEAN
£23–£32

Changes are afoot at Mims. A real maître-d' has been appointed, and interior refurbishment had begun shortly before the Guide went to press, which will be welcome news to local supporters who have wished the place would make a little more effort in those departments. Ali Al-Sersy has never been one to make a show of himself, at least in culinary terms. His terse, hand-scrawled menus do nothing to signal the quality and artistry that may turn up on the plate. One reporter's 'roast quail, herbed noodles' presented the moistly cooked bird sitting in a nest of strongly seasoned noodles with a couple of its eggs added to complete the scene.

Following this might be grilled black bream with a sliced and graded 'drystone wall' of courgettes and tomatoes, or sauté guinea fowl with mashed potatoes and a foie gras sauce. 'Cornucopia looks like this,' reckoned one reporter of his tropical fruit sorbet in a brandy-snap pannier furnished with strawberries, raspberries, redcurrants, lychees and mango sauce. 'Bread and butter' might sound a little plain as a dessert, until you realise you have to fill in the missing word. The wine list is far less economical with its descriptions but is limited in scope, though prices are commendably restrained. House Bordeaux is £9.50.

CHEF: A. Al-Sersy PROPRIETORS: A. Al-Sersy and F. Falcone OPEN: Tue to Fri 12.30 to 2.30, 6.30 to 10.30, Sat and Sun 12.30 to 10.30 MEALS: Set L £10.50 (2 courses) to £16.25, Set D £14 (2 courses) to £19.75. Light L available SERVICE: 10%, card slips closed CARDS: Delta, MasterCard, Visa DETAILS: 45 seats. Private parties: 50 main room. No children under 7. No smoking in 1 dining room. Wheelchair access (not WC). Music (£5)

The 2002 Guide will be published before Christmas 2001. Reports on meals are most welcome at any time of the year, but are particularly valuable in the spring (no later than June). Send them to The Good Food Guide, *FREEPOST, 2 Marylebone Road, London NW1 4DF. Or email your report to goodfoodguide@which.net*

BARNSLEY South Yorkshire map 9

Armstrongs

102 Dodworth Road, Barnsley S70 6HL
TEL/FAX: (01226) 240113

COOKING **4**
MODERN BRITISH
£37–£50

Shortly after the last edition of the *Guide* appeared, the Crookes took over this large, detached Victorian house on the edge of town, with its upstairs lounge, ground-floor dining room and discreet yet fashionable colour scheme. They run it as a family operation, serving dinner only, four nights a week. Despite the old-fashioned gesture of a mid-meal sorbet, dishes cover the spectrum from loin of lamb with rosemary sauce to more modern seared tuna with black olive couscous and sauce vierge.

Presentation is a strong point, quality ingredients are evident, and materials are well handled. Partnerships are carefully considered too, from a wide, thin slab of smooth, pink duck liver parfait, served with a first-rate kumquat and pear chutney, to haunch of venison, cooked rare and sliced, in a sauce combining juniper berries and liquorice. Among more unusual ideas, a purée of butter beans and black pudding served with roast pork fillet has proved a success. 'Properly cooked' vegetables are served separately but are included in the price, and desserts might take in warm Black Forest pudding with clotted cream, or pannacotta topped with a pale green ball of smooth, well-judged rhubarb sorbet. The cost is on the high side, but a short wine list which starts out in France but then takes a very brisk trot further afield, stays mainly under £20, starting with house French at £12.50. For those who wish to spash out, however, a page of fine wines offers just over a dozen.

CHEF: Robert Crookes PROPRIETORS: Robert and Elizabeth Crookes OPEN: Wed to Sat D only 7 to 9.30 CLOSED: 2 weeks Christmas, 2 weeks summer MEALS: Set D Wed and Thur £25, Set D Fri and Sat £30 SERVICE: not inc, card slips closed CARDS: Delta, MasterCard, Switch, Visa DETAILS: 44 seats. Private parties: 50 main room. Car park. Vegetarian meals. No smoking in dining room. Music

BARWICK Somerset map 2

▲ Little Barwick House

SOMERSET GFG 2001 COMMENDED

Barwick BA22 9TD
TEL: (01935) 423902 FAX: (01935) 420908
take first exit off A37 roundabout 1m S of Yeovil;
Little Barwick House ¼m on left

COOKING **6**
MODERN ENGLISH
£23–£48

Tim and Emma Ford acquired this restaurant-with-rooms at the beginning of 2000, Tim having previously been head chef at Summer Lodge in Evershot (see entry). They oversee a listed Georgian dower house in three acres of wooded garden, with views from the dining room and conservatory extension, and quietly understated décor: a few botanical prints in gold frames serve as wall adornment. The culinary style is oriented towards luxurious flavours and textures, but with a keen eye to the quality of raw materials, producing for example well-handled starters of lobster bisque, boned quail stuffed with a mousse of wild mushrooms, and chicken liver parfait with apple and plum chutney. Full flavoured, well-timed grilled Cornish red mullet has benefited from the minimal accompaniment of a few salad leaves, tomatoes and basil oil.

Timing has also contributed to the success of a tender main-course venison fillet, roasted to a dark outer crust but pink inside, served with mushrooms and a sweet sauce of poached blueberries. Lighter options might include sea bream with courgettes and pesto potatoes, or simply grilled Dover sole with lemon butter. Fruit is enthusiastically used at dessert stage: perhaps passion-fruit délices with lime syrup, or a glazed poached pear with chocolate ice cream. Service has struggled with the language on some nights. Wines are stylistically grouped and well chosen, and come at prices that feel surprisingly comfortable in the surroundings. House wines from France, Chile and Australia are all £11.50.

CHEFS: Tim Ford, Maxine Perrier and Stuart Judge PROPRIETOR: Emma and Tim Ford OPEN: Tue to Sun L 12 to 2, Tue to Sat D 7 to 9.30 MEALS: Set L Tue to Sat £10.50 (2 courses) to £12.95, Set L Sun £15.95, Set D £19.95 (2 courses) to £25.95 SERVICE: not inc, card slips closed CARDS: Amex, Diners, MasterCard, Switch, Visa DETAILS: 40 seats. 20 seats outside. Private parties: 60 main room. Car park. Vegetarian meals. Children's helpings. No smoking in dining room. No music. Air-conditioned ACCOMMODATION: 6 rooms, all with bath/shower. TV. Phone. D,B&B £43.50 to £133 (*The Which? Hotel Guide*) (£5)

BASLOW Derbyshire **map 9**

▲ Fischer's Baslow Hall

Calver Road, Baslow DE45 1RR
TEL: (01246) 583259 FAX: (01246) 583818

COOKING **8**
MODERN EUROPEAN
£37–£76

On the edge of the village, in the middle of the Peak District close to Chatsworth House, Baslow Hall could hardly have a more propitious location, which it combines with a happily relaxed atmosphere. An open fire in the comfortably upholstered lounge leaks woody smells, while colourful fabrics and oak furniture give the place a sense of individuality and warmth. Sourcing is a strength, with named breeds and traceable animals providing a secure foundation, and a small, frequently changing four-course dinner menu makes an enticing read. It might feature anything from flavourful crispy roast scallops with a delicate balsamic and truffle vinaigrette, to pig's trotter stuffed with chicken and morel mushrooms.

Balance between delicacy and richness is a mark of the style, for example in an 'out-this-world' chargrilled duck sausage (incorporating gizzard and ceps, among other things), served with cannellini beans and an apple reduction, in a convincingly sticky, caramelly sauce, accompanied by a generous portion of foie gras that wasn't even mentioned on the menu. This is not fussy cooking; rather it makes an impact for that much sought after yet all too rarely encountered combination of simplicity and intensity: for example, in 'as good as you can get' fillet of Derbyshire beef, on a rösti cake surrounded by vegetables in a light yet richly flavoured red wine sauce. Saddle of Forest of Dean venison has come in a similarly intense and sticky reduction based on port.

Straightforward as they are, taste combinations are well considered, not least among desserts of chocolate and raspberry soufflé, or rhubarb tartlet and sorbet with prune fritter. Incidentals include first-rate appetisers, and chocolate truffles that alone are 'reason enough to return'. Minimalist tasting notes accompany a precise and fine range of wines sourced from around the world. A sound list of clarets and Burgundies is worth paying more for, although there is much elsewhere on the list under £15. House Primitivo di Puglia 1999 is £14 (£3.50 per glass).

CHEF: Max Fischer PROPRIETORS: Max and Susan Fischer OPEN: Mon to Fri and Sun L 12 to 1.30, Mon to Sat D 7 to 9.30 (Sun D residents only) CLOSED: 25 and 26 Dec MEALS: Set L Mon to Fri £20 (2 courses) to £24, Set L Sun £24, Set D £48 SERVICE: not inc CARDS: Amex, Delta, Diners, MasterCard, Switch, Visa DETAILS: 76 seats. 16 seats outside. Private parties: 40 main room, 12 and 24 private rooms. Car park. No children in dining room after 7pm. No smoking in dining room. Wheelchair access (not WC). No music ACCOMMODATION: 6 rooms, all with bath/shower. TV. Phone. Room only £80 to £130. Baby facilities (*The Which? Hotel Guide*)

BATH Bath & N.E. Somerset **map 2**

▲ Bath Priory

Weston Road, Bath BA1 2XT
TEL: (01225) 331922 FAX: (01225) 448276 COOKING **6**
EMAIL: bathprioryhotel@compuserve.com MODERN EUROPEAN
WEB SITE: www.slh.com/theprior £35–£69

This well-ordered, smart, stone-fronted restaurant brings a note of country-house opulence to the edge of town with its standard lamps, generous display of paintings, and monumental French windows leading to the garden. The food is as comforting as the surroundings – ravioli of smoked haddock with shellfish sauce, and corn-fed chicken breast with sarladaise potatoes – but it also has the ability to excite, when prime materials are treated accurately and sympathetically. Presentation is good and, despite a degree of 'showing off', Robert Clayton is undoubtedly a talented chef, able to produce 'fish as it should be' from scallops with mushroom risotto to turbot on a bed of spinach.

Although there are exceptions, such as roast chicken and goats'-cheese sausage with a lemon dressing, dishes tend to be organised around traditional ideas: squab pigeon with foie gras and apple chutney, or roast loin of venison with braised red cabbage. Likewise among desserts, raspberry and coconut muffin (with cinnamon ice cream) shares the billing with more familiar partnerships such as a warm chocolate and Kirsch cherry fondant. While there may be little under £20 on it, the wine list makes a genuine effort to find interesting bottles from both hemispheres (have a look at Italy). Nine house recommendations, starting at £17.50, include Viognier and Primitivo varietals.

CHEF: Robert Clayton PROPRIETOR: Andrew Brownsword OPEN: all week 12 to 1.45, 7 to 9.45 MEALS: Set L £22, Set D £42.50 SERVICE: not inc, card slips closed CARDS: Amex, Delta, Diners, MasterCard, Switch, Visa DETAILS: 50 seats. 16 seats outside. Private parties: 60 main room, 20 private room. Car park. Children's helpings. No children under 7 in dining room. No smoking in dining room. Wheelchair access (also WC). Occasional music ACCOMMODATION: 28 rooms, all with bath/shower. TV. Phone. D,B&B £140 to £340. Rooms for disabled. Swimming pool

Clos du Roy

1 Seven Dials, Saw Close, Bath BA1 1EN
TEL: (01225) 444450 FAX: (01225) 404044

NEW CHEF
FRENCH/EUROPEAN
£22–£49

The centrally situated and musically themed restaurant has a distinct Gallic feel, with a relaxed ambience, a French proprietor, and attentive service from staff 'fresh from across the Channel'. As the Guide went to press, and too late for us to make an assessment, a new chef arrived to continue the cosmopolitan style of cooking, with salmon and spinach tartlet, duck breast with honey and soy on Chinese noodles, and an orange and Drambuie variation on bread-and-butter pudding. Reports are welcome. Wines are grouped by style, offer fair choice under £20, and start with house vin de pays at £9.95.

CHEF: Adrian Couzens PROPRIETOR: Philippe Roy OPEN: all week 12 to 2.30, 6 (7 Sun) to 9.30 (10.30 Fri and Sat) MEALS: alc (main courses £13 to £18.50). Set L and pre-theatre D before 7 £9.95 (2 courses) to £13.95, Set D from 7 £16.50 (2 courses) to £19.50 SERVICE: not inc, 10% for parties of 6 or more, card slips closed CARDS: Amex, Delta, Diners, MasterCard, Switch, Visa DETAILS: 100 seats. 10 seats outside. Private parties: 100 main room. Vegetarian meals. Children's helpings. No cigars/pipes in dining room. Wheelchair access (not WC). Music (£5)

Green Street Seafood Café

6 Green Street, Bath BA1 2JY
TEL: (01225) 448707

COOKING **3**
FISH
£30–£53

The combination of tiptop seafood and casual café-style surroundings is hard to resist. Supply lines are well established and effective (there is a wet fish shop below), turning up Newlyn crab, diver-caught scallops and Cornish-landed fish from bream to hake. Harmonious accompaniments don't overwhelm – 'sweet, tender squid' with chilli, coriander and lime, or grilled tuna on slabs of roasted aubergine with a heap of straw potatoes – and vegetables impress: from a plate of buttered spinach to spring onion mash. Portion sizes have varied from 'a few forkfuls and it had gone', to fish soup that was 'a meal in itself', while incidentals include good bread, grassy olive oil for dipping, and perhaps a small plate of marinated anchovies to start. Pear tart with cinnamon ice cream, and a sharp and creamy lemon tart have both drawn applause, while service has ranged from 'chaotic' to 'on the ball and keen to please'. The wine list was under revision as the Guide went to press; house wines were set to start at £9.90.

CHEFS: Mitchell Tonks and Andy Bird PROPRIETOR: Mitchell Tonks OPEN: Tue to Sat 12 to 3, 6 to 10 CLOSED: 25 and 26 Dec, 1 Jan, bank hols MEALS: alc (main courses £9.50 to £16.50) SERVICE: not inc, card slips closed CARDS: Amex, Delta, Diners, MasterCard, Switch, Visa DETAILS: 38 seats. Private parties: 25 main room. Vegetarian meals. Children's helpings. No cigars in dining room. Music (£5)

The Guide is totally independent, accepts no free hospitality, and survives on the number of copies sold each year.

▲ Lettonie

35 Kelston Road, Bath BA1 3QH
TEL: (01225) 446676 FAX: (01225) 447541
WEB SITE: www.bath.co.uk/lettonie

COOKING **7**
MODERN EUROPEAN
£43–£82

As befits a grand, immaculately restored eighteenth-century mansion on the outskirts of Bath, décor is formal, with swags and drapes at the windows, portraits of the owners and their family, and a dining room – with views through French windows over the Kelston Valley – that goes in for mirrors and chandeliers. By contrast, the cooking avoids country house clichés, thanks to Martin Blunos's original approach. The most notable thing about it is the blend of craftsmanship, quiet good taste, and irrepressible wit, typified for example by the 'signature' starter of scrambled duck egg with caviar and a glass of vodka, and its echo in a surreal pre-dessert of 'boiled egg and soldiers' made from vanilla cream and mango purée with a biscuit for dipping.

Dishes typically require a lot of workmanship, but nothing is done simply for effect: most are models of balance and restraint. Rosy pink lamb cutlets might be served with a jaunty shepherd's pie set in a thin, crisp pastry case; mint in the gravy and a garnish of roast red peppers and garlic combine to produce a harmonious marriage of English and provençale flavours. The food combines a real sense of generosity with a good cook's natural frugality and love of honest yet humble ingredients: pig's trotter stuffed with chicken mousse, mushrooms and sweetbreads ('or shortbread, as the young French waiter said endearingly before correcting himself'). This sophisticated mix of textures is served simply with mashed potatoes, and garnished with what can only be described as 'pork scratchings': a crunchy supplement that prevented the whole thing from appearing too solemn.

Skilled pastrywork is apparent at all stages, not least in a chocolate tart accompanied by banana ice cream in a tiny tartlet case, while a sharp ginger and cardamom sauce has proved a choice partner for a perfectly risen, frothily sweet rhubarb soufflé. A global wine list includes many fine bottles. However, with house wines starting at £28.50 a bottle, prices will suit only those with deep pockets. A few half-bottles provide drinking opportunities under £20.

CHEF: Martin Blunos PROPRIETORS: Siân and Martin Blunos OPEN: Tue to Sat 12.30 to 2, 7 to 9.30 MEALS: Set L £25 to £47.50, Set D £47.50 SERVICE: not inc CARDS: Amex, Delta, Diners, MasterCard, Switch, Visa DETAILS: 38 seats. Private parties: 38 main room, 8 private room. Car park. Children's helpings. No smoking in dining room. Wheelchair access (not WC). Music ACCOMMODATION: 4 rooms. TV. Phone. Room only £75 to £150 (*The Which? Hotel Guide*) (£5)

Moody Goose

7A Kingsmead Square, Bath BA1 2AB
TEL/FAX: (01225) 466688

COOKING **5**
ENGLISH
£28–£53

The bar and two small dining rooms, in a quiet, pretty square, are 'light, clean, crisp, pleasant', according to one who obviously found the large blue pottery goose in a good mood. Apart from beef, which comes from Scotland, and fish from Devon and Cornwall (maybe baked bream with rosemary beurre blanc), the Shores get most of their produce from within a 50-mile radius of Bath: a large enough area to go hunting for rabbit (turned into a consommé, perhaps, with herb dumplings), or calf's liver (served with Stilton butter and braised lentils). Menus change every six weeks and, despite one or two supplements, prices are considered fair: the lunch and pre-theatre menu might run to a drizzle of truffle oil over the haricot bean soup, or to a crépinette of braised lamb shank with buttered spring greens. Glazed lemon tart is a recommended way to finish, or there might be a warm chocolate and pear pithiviers. Wines are sensibly chosen, with fair choice under £20. House wines start at £12.50 (£2.80 a glass).

CHEF: Stephen Shore PROPRIETORS: Stephen and Victoria Shore OPEN: Mon to Sat 12 to 2, 6 to 9.30 (10 Sat) CLOSED: 2 weeks Jan, bank hols exc Good Friday MEALS: alc D (main courses £16 to £18). Set L and D before 7pm £12 (2 courses), Set D £23 SERVICE: not inc CARDS: Amex, Delta, Diners, MasterCard, Switch, Visa DETAILS: 30 seats. Private parties: 23 main room, 8 private room. Vegetarian meals. No children under 7. No smoking in dining room. Music

▲ Queensberry Hotel, Olive Tree 🍷

Russel Street, Bath BA1 2QF
TEL: (01225) 447928 FAX: (01225) 446065 — COOKING **6**
EMAIL: enquiries@batholivetree.com — MODERN BRITISH-PLUS
WEB SITE: www.batholivetree.com — £25–£56

Part of a long row of terraced Georgian houses in a quiet part of the city, the hotel draws attention to itself with a bright façade, but exudes a homely English atmosphere inside. The cooking stays laudably simple, guided by forthright ideas and well-sourced ingredients, which include organic beef and rare-breed pork (Gloucester Old Spot). Dishes look attractive without being arty, and commendably avoid unnecessary garnishing: perhaps a pile of diced fir apple potato and fennel, topped with three fat and impeccably timed scallops. A rather old-fashioned touch – typified by chicken liver parfait with Cumberland sauce, or provençale fish soup – can equally be construed as 'good, solid, honest cooking'.

Despite the practice of serving both dauphinoise and well-flavoured new potatoes with all main courses – even with lamb and couscous, or red mullet and risotto – combinations are generally carefully considered, including an inspector's roast duck breast on a mound of roughly textured parsnip purée, surrounded by a well-seasoned stock sauce flavoured with apple and rosemary. Desserts may not be quite on a par with the rest, but have included 'squidgy' pear tart with a red berry sorbet, and light, wobbly lemon mousse with vanilla-poached raspberries. Top-drawer extras include bread and pre-meal nibbles, and prices are considered reasonable, while responsive and well-informed staff make sure that customers feel 'comfortable and happy'. A stylish selection of mainly French wines, with interesting alternatives from Italy and the New World, is well priced and accessible. Seven wines by the glass are £3.75 and house Chilean Chardonnay and Merlot are £12.50.

CHEF: Matthew Prowse PROPRIETORS: Stephen and Penny Ross OPEN: Mon to Sat L 12 to 2, all week D 7 to 10 CLOSED: 1 week Christmas/New year, L bank hol Mons MEALS: alc (main courses £11.50 to £20). Set L £12.50 to £14.50, Set D Mon to Fri £24 SERVICE: not inc, card slips closed CARDS: Delta, MasterCard, Switch, Visa DETAILS: 70 seats. Private parties: 30 main room, 30 private room. Vegetarian meals. Children's helpings. No smoking in dining room. Wheelchair access (also WC). Occasional music. Air-conditioned ACCOMMODATION: 29 rooms, all with bath/shower. TV. Phone. B&B £90 to £210. Rooms for disabled. Baby facilities (*The Which? Hotel Guide*)

Richmond Arms £

7 Richmond Place, Lansdown, Bath BA1 5PZ
TEL: (01225) 316725

COOKING **2**
FUSION
£22–£31

The Cunninghams have been running this quirky pub about a mile out of Bath city centre since the 1960s. One of their strengths has been a willingness to move with the times, since there cannot have been much call 30 years ago for wok-fried squid with chorizo on salad leaves dressed with lemon, ginger and coriander, or a main course of kangaroo steak with wasabi and pickled ginger 'aïoli'. Praise has come in for 'interesting and crunchy' sesame-crusted chicken-burgers, and a light and garlicky houmous to accompany artichoke. Finish with iced pear terrine with blackberry and sambuca coulis. Lunch (except on Sunday) tends to be a lighter affair, drawing heavily on evening-meal first courses. Wines from Australia and New Zealand dominate the small selection listed on blackboards behind the bar (even the solitary sparkling wine is Australian), though house red and white at £7.50 are French.

CHEF: Marney Cunningham PROPRIETORS: John and Marney Cunningham OPEN: Tue to Sun L 12 to 2, Tue to Sat D 6 to 8.30 (9 Fri and Sat) CLOSED: no food 25 and 26 Dec, 1 Jan, most bank hols MEALS: alc (main courses L around £5.50 or less, D £7 to £9.50) SERVICE: not inc CARDS: none DETAILS: 30 seats. 20 seats outside. Private parties: 20 main room. Vegetarian meals. No children under 14. Music

▲ Royal Crescent, Pimpernel's

16 Royal Crescent, Bath BA1 2LS
TEL: (01225) 823333 FAX: (01225) 339401
EMAIL: reservations@royalcrescent.co.uk
WEB SITE: www.royalcrescent.co.uk

COOKING **4**
FUSION
£37–£83

Pimpernel's has moved from its cramped quarters in the main building to take up more roomy residence in the Dower House (replacing the Brasserie, which has closed) at the back of the hotel. The repertoire not only combines European and Far Eastern influences, but does so in a particular way. Starters tend to have a predominantly oriental flavour, perhaps tiger prawns in Thai curry cream, or glazed cod with wakami salad and miso sauce; even foie gras is given a spicy Szechuan lift.

Main courses on the other hand tend to favour a more European approach, taking in roast monkfish with truffle risotto and celeriac emulsion, and roast rack of lamb with dauphinois aubergine gâteau. The rule is not universal, given a main course of seared scallop with Bombay potato and onion bhaji, but it does lend a structure to meals, which typically finish in more crossover mode, offering lime brûlée with coconut ice cream, or rice pudding with baked pineapple. France dominates a wine list led by an impressive range of clarets, although bottles from the New World provide quality alternatives. Mark-ups, however, are steep, with little to be found under £20. House wines start at £16.

CHEF: Steven Blake PROPRIETOR: Cliveden Limited OPEN: all week 12.30 to 2, 7 to 10 CLOSED: Christmas exc residents MEALS: alc D (main courses £18 to £26). Set L £15 (2 courses) to £22 SERVICE: not inc CARDS: Diners, MasterCard, Switch, Visa DETAILS: 70 seats. 45 seats outside. Private parties: 90 main room. Car park. Vegetarian meals. No smoking in dining room. Occasional music. Air-conditioned ACCOMMODATION: 45 rooms, all with bath/shower. TV. Phone. Room only £195 to £750. Rooms for disabled. Baby facilities. Swimming pool (*The Which? Hotel Guide*)

BEAMINSTER Dorset **map 2**

▲ Bridge House

Prout Bridge, Beaminster DT8 3AY
TEL: (01308) 862200 FAX: (01308) 863700
EMAIL: enquiries@bridge-house.co.uk
WEB SITE: www.bridge-house.co.uk

COOKING **1**
MODERN BRITISH
£22–£43

The ancient building has been added to over the years, latterly acquiring a pretty conservatory. Big, old stone fireplaces are a feature: one in the small sitting room, another in the light dining room with its wood panelling, floral curtains and well-spaced tables. Local meats and fish contribute to a short lunch and longer dinner menu that might offer baked cod with a cheese and herb crust, or roast rack of lamb with redcurrant sauce.

Not all dishes lived up to expectation at inspection, but one that did was fresh and accurately timed Dover sole with lemon butter. Another was a moist chocolate truffle tart made with good short pastry and topped with almond and chocolate cream. Regional cheeses in prime condition come with fine oatcakes, good canapés get things off to a rolling start, and wines are left on the table for guests to pour: they come from a reasonably priced list that starts with around ten house recommendations at £9.95.

CHEF: Linda Paget PROPRIETOR: Peter Pinkster OPEN: all week 12 to 2, 7 to 9 MEALS: Set L £9.50 (2 courses) to £12.75, Set D £23.50 (2 courses) to £27.50 SERVICE: not inc CARDS: Amex, Delta, Diners, MasterCard, Switch, Visa DETAILS: 36 seats. 16 seats outside. Private parties: 40 main room, 16 private room. Car park. Vegetarian meals. Children's helpings. No smoking in dining room. No music ACCOMMODATION: 14 rooms, all with bath/shower. TV. Phone. B&B £68 to £124. Rooms for disabled. Baby facilities (*The Which? Hotel Guide*)

'It is hard to recommend it when one of your party says that by far the best thing about the meal was her After Eight mint'. (On eating in Suffolk)

The Guide office can quickly spot when a restaurateur is encouraging customers to write recommending inclusion. Such reports do not further a restaurant's cause. Please tell us if a restaurateur invites you to write to the Guide.

BEER Devon **map 2**

Old Steam Bakery

NEW ENTRY

Fore Street, Beer EX12 3JJ
TEL: (01297) 22040 FAX: (01297) 625886

COOKING **4**
PACIFIC RIM
£29–£52

The Strides are an Anglo-New Zealand partnership. They met in Australia, and have brought a breath of the Pacific Rim to a tiny Devon village. Their corner site with large shop-front windows is on the steep and narrow main street, its uncluttered interior kitted out with stripped wood, warm colours and white table linen. Michael Stride's cooking can impose considerable artistry on dishes that in essence are quite simple: at inspection, rare pigeon breast on chargrilled artichoke hearts with a fine balsamic dressing given power by white truffle oil. Japanese spices have been used to marinate chicken breast, which is wrapped in spring roll pastry and served with rice wine and plum sauce, while a clever take on the fish-and-chip theme is to serve tempura-battered sweet potato with fried brill fillet.

Accompaniments are well handled too, judging by loose-textured and buttery rösti, balanced on silky, nutmeg-flavoured spinach, that have come with herb-crusted pork. Although puddings have elicited less enthusiasm, they are well presented and may take in lemon tart with mango coulis, or chocolate and coconut bavarois with coffee anglaise. Sarah Doak-Stride runs a warm and friendly front-of-house. The wine list requires a bit of hopping about for those choosing by price, but the effort is rewarded with some good producers. France leads the way, but southern-hemisphere house wines begin at £10.50.

CHEF: Michael Stride PROPRIETORS: Michael Stride and Sarah Doak-Stride OPEN: Sun L 12 to 2, Wed to Mon D 7 to 10 (may vary in winter) MEALS: Set L £16.50 (2 courses) to £19.50, Set D £23.50 (2 courses) to £27.50 SERVICE: not inc, card slips closed CARDS: Delta, MasterCard, Switch, Visa DETAILS: 40 seats. Private parties: 40 main room. No smoking before 10.30. Wheelchair access (also WC). Music (£5)

BEESTON Nottinghamshire **map 5**

La Toque

NEW ENTRY

61 Wollaton Road, Beeston NG9 2NG
TEL: (0115) 922 2268 FAX: (0115) 922 7979
EMAIL: mattias@latoque.fs.net.co.uk

COOKING **3**
FRENCH
£36–£48

Mattias Karlsson's relaxed restaurant has a distinctly Gallic ambience thanks to posters from the celebrated Restaurant Bocuse on its predominantly blue walls, a soundtrack of chansons, and simple, domestic cooking predicated on conscientiously sourced materials. The boundaries may be extended by an impressive starter of prawn and Thai vegetable pasties, but chicken livers appear conventionally in a salad with roast tomatoes and French beans, while a main course of moist guinea fowl has been served with roast vegetables and tagliatelle in a pesto bouillon. While there may be a tendency for main ingredients to disappear under a blanket of sauce, there have been no grumbles about the chocolate cappuccino dessert, a rich mousse served in a cup topped with warm, frothed cream and orange segments. Service does its best to make everybody feel at home. The wine list works methodically through the French regions, adding a couple of pages of others at the end. Choices are sound, mark-ups reasonably friendly. House wines start from £11.50.

CHEFS: Mattias Karlsson and Johan Wiklund PROPRIETOR: Mattias Karlsson OPEN: Sun L 12 to 3.30, Mon to Sat D 7 to 10.30 CLOSED: 25 to 30 Dec, bank hols MEALS: alc (main courses £13 to £15) SERVICE: net prices CARDS: Amex, Delta, Diners, MasterCard, Switch, Visa DETAILS: 52 seats. Private parties: 40 main room, 20 to 40 private rooms. Car park. Vegetarian meals. Children's helpings. No children under 6 at D. No smoking in 1 dining room. Wheelchair access (not WC). Music (£5)

BEVERLEY East Riding of Yorkshire **map 9**

Wednesdays 🍷 £

8 Wednesday Market, Beverley HU17 0DG — COOKING **2**
TEL/FAX: (01482) 869727 — ANGLO-MEDITERRANEAN
EMAIL: bobathove@aol.com — £20–£43

Located in the market square near the minster, Wednesdays is a handy venue for an 'outstanding-value' lunch in a cheery atmosphere set by bistro chairs and gingham-clothed tables on quarry tiles (though refurbishment was due as the Guide went to press). Robert Griffin makes a special effort for vegetarians, with starters of field mushrooms in a puff pastry strudel, or a plate of hummus, tzatziki and baba ghanoush, vying for attention with Scarborough crab, and crispy duck salad.

Main courses might turn up chilli-battered cod with spiced potato wedges, or fillet steak with borlotti beans and anchovy mayonnaise, while recommended desserts have included chocolate bread-and-butter pudding, and pear and almond tart made with light, crisp pastry. Service has veered from 'unhelpful' to 'charming and informed'. Wines are carefully chosen and arranged according to style, with a selection of finer wines at the end of each colour section. Mark-ups are fair, with four house wines from France, Spain and Australia at £9.75 (£2.95 a glass).

CHEFS: Wendy Rowley and Alan Chamberlain PROPRIETORS: Matthew and Wendy Rowley, and Robert Griffin OPEN: Mon to Sat 12 to 2, 7 to 9.30 CLOSED: 31 Dec MEALS: alc (main courses £7.50 to £15). Set L £7.50 (2 courses) SERVICE: not inc CARDS: Delta, MasterCard, Switch, Visa DETAILS: 70 seats. 15 seats outside. Private parties: 40 main room, 20 private room. Vegetarian meals. Children's helpings. Wheelchair access (not WC). Music (£5)

BIDDENDEN Kent **map 3**

West House

28 High Street, Biddenden TN27 8AH — COOKING **4**
TEL/FAX: (01580) 291341 — MODERN BRITISH-PLUS
£40–£57

Occupying a heavily beamed, sixteenth-century former weaver's cottage in the centre of this Weald village, West House is a small operation serving no more than 20 covers, and open only four sessions a week. This gives the Cunninghams ample opportunity to attend to detail, and their care is considered 'quite exceptional'. Dishes cover a familiar range of flavours, and their simplicity is to be applauded: home-cured gravlax comes with pickled cucumber and mustard dressing, and game terrine with a home-made chutney.

Main courses tend to incorporate a plain centrepiece along the lines of grilled sea bass or pork loin chop, and although results may not always hit the button, accompaniments are well suited: perhaps a version of shepherd's pie with lamb cutlets, or barley risotto with roast quail. The same 'unrevolutionary' approach extends to desserts of pannacotta with fresh mango, and apple crumble with cinnamon ice cream, and to a tolerably priced wine list which offers half a dozen by the glass. House French red and white are £10.50 and £13 respectively.

CHEF: Susan Cunningham PROPRIETORS: Susan and David Cunningham OPEN: Wed to Sat D only 7 to 9 CLOSED: 25 and 26 Dec, 1 Jan, 3 weeks Jan, 1 week autumn MEALS: Set D £27.50 SERVICE: not inc, card slips closed CARDS: Delta, MasterCard, Switch, Visa DETAILS: 20 seats. Private parties: 20 main room. Car park. No pipes/cigars in dining room. Music (£5)

BIRCH VALE Derbyshire — map 8

▲ Waltzing Weasel

New Mills Road, Birch Vale SK22 1BT
TEL/FAX: (01663) 743402 — COOKING **3**
WEB SITE: www.w-weasel.co.uk — ANGLO-EUROPEAN
on A6015, ½m W of Hayfield — £24–£42

Choose a table by the log fire in the bar for a drink while perusing the menu, which offers predominantly English and European 'peasant' cooking, to use the restaurant's own description. Then move to the tapestried dining room with its polished oak tables and views of Kinder Scout (the highest point in the Peak District). Mushroom soufflé or bradan rost (Loch Fyne's hot smoked salmon) are possible temptations among starters, while the casserole, stew or ragoût of the day (made with peppered beef or wild boar perhaps) might fit the bill for a main course. Otherwise options run to praiseworthy halibut in a lemon sauce, beef in whisky, roast duck with plum sauce, or osso buco. Summer pudding was 'the best we had ever eaten', according to a reporter who also found the service exceptional. A mainly French wine list touches base with the New World; house wines are £10.50.

CHEF: George Benham PROPRIETORS: Michael and Linda Atkinson OPEN: all week 12 to 2, 7 to 9 MEALS: alc L (main courses £8.50 to £13.50). Set D £22.50 (2 courses) to £26.50 SERVICE: not inc, card slips closed CARDS: Amex, Delta, MasterCard, Switch, Visa DETAILS: 60 seats. 20 seats outside. Private parties: 36 main room. Car park. Vegetarian meals. Children's helpings. No children under 8 at D. No smoking in dining room. Wheelchair access (not WC). No music. Air-conditioned ACCOMMODATION: 8 rooms, all with bath/shower. TV. Phone. B&B £39 to £99 (*The Which? Hotel Guide*)

Several sharp operators have tried to extort money from restaurateurs on the promise of an entry in a guidebook that has never appeared. The Good Food Guide *makes no charge for inclusion.*

BIRKENHEAD Merseyside map 8

Beadles

15 Rose Mount, Oxton, Birkenhead CH43 5SG
TEL: (0151) 653 9010

COOKING **3**
MODERN EUROPEAN
£24–£45

Right in the heart of Oxton, a village-like suburb of Birkenhead, Richard and Mellanie Peel's intimate restaurant has much to offer, starting with Richard's enthusiasm and genuine hospitality. A good-value set-price menu is supplemented at dinner by a carte of about half a dozen choices per course. The cooking shows an inclination for strong, rich flavours and a dash of fruit in the saucing for meat: a warm starter salad of venison sausage with wild mushrooms and raspberry vinaigrette may be followed by guinea-fowl casserole with smoked bacon and a creamy red wine and Cassis sauce, for example. On a lighter note, there may be a filo tartlet of smoked salmon with sour cream and dill, and an intriguing combination of pan-fried calf's liver with fresh lime juice and rosemary. Fruit might also feature in desserts, as in crystallised orange frangipane tart with Grand Marnier crème anglaise. Nearly everything on the short wine list is under £20, with house French £9.25.

CHEF: Mellanie Dixon-Peel PROPRIETORS: Mellanie Dixon-Peel and Richard Peel OPEN: Tue to Fri L 12 to 2, Tue to Sat D 7 to 9.30 MEALS: alc D (main courses £14 to £16.50). Set L and D (exc Sat) £13.75 (2 courses) to £15.95. Light L menu available SERVICE: not inc; 10% for parties of 8 or more CARDS: Delta, MasterCard, Switch, Visa DETAILS: 32 seats. Private parties: 35 main room. Vegetarian meals. No children under 7. No smoking before coffee. Wheelchair access (not WC). Music (£5)

BIRMINGHAM West Midlands map 5

Bank

NEW ENTRY

4 Brindley Place, Birmingham B1 2JB
TEL: (0121) 633 7001 FAX: (0121) 633 4465

COOKING **3**
FRENCH-PLUS
£24–£70

Why it took smart out-of-town operators so long to discover Birmingham is anybody's guess, but after a long wait suddenly three new restaurants come along at once. Sister to the original Bank (see entry, London), this new venture follows the same design trail: a revolving door in the discreet, dark glass frontage leads to the first of a capable team of greeting and waiting staff, kitted out in Mao-style grey trouser suits. Walk through the bar past an army of chefs, wonder anxiously at the sheets of glass hanging from the ceiling, and sit in a dining room amid blocks of colour, giant polystyrene tiles, and a beach scene mural that reinforces the airy ambience. Eating options in the 'food factory' are many and varied, from breakfast through to late supper, and the carte is as big on choice as it is cryptic in style: 'macaroni, wild mushroom and pesto' turns out to be a huge crisp-crumbed pasta dumpling topped with shiitake and oyster mushrooms.

The self-styled 'liberated French' food may be better described as 'anything goes', given that it takes in simple British fish and chips alongside rump of lamb with brinjal potatoes and minted yoghurt dressing. Fish offers much of interest, from bite-sized chunks of lightly seared tuna with a flutter of green salad garnish and a bowl of Thai dipping sauce, to the 'Spanish rusticity' of baked hake on broad beans and clams with olive oil and tomato. Timing is impressive, quality ingredients are the bedrock, and desserts have included a 'textbook' dense, bitter chocolate tart, and a finely judged blackcurrant sorbet in an overcoat of lemon and vodka parfait. Up-to-the-minute user-friendly wines are arranged by style and span a good range of prices, starting with house vin de pays at £9.90.

CHEFS: Idris Caldora and David Colcombe PROPRIETOR: BGR plc OPEN: all week L 12 (11 Sat and Sun) to 3 (5.30 Sun), Mon to Sat D 5.30 to 11 (11.30 Sat) MEALS: alc (main courses £8.50 to £28). Set L and D 5.30 to 7.30 and 10 to 11 £12.50 (2 courses) to £15.50 SERVICE: not inc, card slips closed, 10% for parties of 8 or more CARDS: Amex, Delta, Diners, MasterCard, Switch, Visa DETAILS: 150 seats. 60 seats outside. Private parties: 100 main room, 100 private room. Vegetarian meals. Children's helpings. No-smoking area. Wheelchair access (also WC). No music. Air-conditioned (£5)

Chung Ying

16–18 Wrottesley Street, Birmingham B5 4RT
TEL: (0121) 622 5669 FAX: (0121) 666 7051

COOKING **1**
CHINESE
£28–£61

Number 1 on the menu of this long-established Cantonese restaurant in the heart of Chinatown is deep-fried seafood rolls, while number 308 is boiled rice, and there are still 30 un-numbered vegetarian dishes to add to the 306 choices in between. Among dim sum (over 50 of them), prawns have been praised for their fresh taste whether baked with chilli and salt or fried in rice-paper, while 'better than satisfactory' starters have produced deep-fried cuttlefish cakes, and salt and pepper spare ribs wrapped in a paper bag. 'Special dishes' include stuffed bean curd, fried or steamed, and frogs' legs with bitter melon. Most of the wide variety of rice or noodle one-plate meals is as easy to enjoy as beef and scrambled egg with rice, or shredded pork chow mein; rather more challenging is assorted ox tripe chow mein. Forty-plus wines start with house French at £11.

CHEF: T.C. Tsang PROPRIETOR: Siu Chung Wong OPEN: all week 12 to 11.30 (10.30 Sun) CLOSED: 25 Dec MEALS: alc (main courses £6.50 to £17.50). Set L and D £28 for 2 people to £108 for 6 people SERVICE: 10% (optional) CARDS: Amex, Delta, Diners, MasterCard, Switch, Visa DETAILS: 250 seats. Private parties: 250 main room, 120 private rooms. Vegetarian meals. Wheelchair access (not WC). Music. Air-conditioned

▲ Hyatt Regency, Number 282

2 Bridge Street, Birmingham B1 2JZ
TEL: (0121) 643 1234 FAX: (0121) 616 2323
WEB SITE: www.birmingham.hyatt.com

COOKING **5**
GLOBAL FUSION
£28–£69

This neat, modern hotel dining room would be rather impersonal were it not for charming service to counter the professional formality. Roger Narbett, now in his second year at the helm, produces ambitious, complex cooking and has impressed for his ability to successfully combine ideas from around the world. A three-course menu rapide with two choices per course is available alongside the carte, where starters may include a ballottine of guinea fowl with foie gras, or seared sea bass with a soy and sweet chilli dressing.

Culinary boundaries are crossed at a stroke in a main course dish of Gressingham duck accompanied by couscous and mustard mash, or a vegetarian option of mushroom and spiced potato with Stilton rarebit and tomato chilli salsa. A mini-rack of Cornish lamb with fondant potatoes and tarragon risotto has come with an intensely flavoured tomato sauce, and Szechuan-peppered chicken with Chinese greens has also impressed. Mille-feuille of yoghurt and orange parfait with a Drambuie sauce made a successful finish to one reporter's meal; for those who can't choose, 'Wait 'n' See' offers a good-value selection. An accessible global wine list, arranged by style, offers plenty under £20, with prices starting at £14.75.

CHEF: Roger Narbett PROPRIETOR: Clifford Grauers OPEN: Mon to Fri L 12 to 2, Mon to Sat D 7 to 10 MEALS: alc (main courses £13 to £18.50). Set L and D £14.50 (2 courses) to £16.50 SERVICE: not inc CARDS: Amex, Delta, Diners, MasterCard, Switch, Visa DETAILS: 76 seats. Private parties: 76 main room. Vegetarian meals. Children's helpings. Wheelchair access (not WC). Music. Air-conditioned ACCOMMODATION: 319 rooms, all with bath/shower. TV. Phone. Room only £85 to £160. Rooms for disabled. Baby facilities. Swimming pool (£5)

Leftbank

79 Broad Street, Birmingham B15 1QA
TEL: (0121) 643 4464 FAX: (0121) 643 5793

COOKING **2**
MODERN EUROPEAN
£30–£49

The door opens straight into a large and opulent room with stripped pine floors and an old grille serving as a room divider. Since this was a Victorian bank, the construction is solid; painting the old vault door silver was obviously easier than trying to move it. While the name may have Parisian overtones, the food takes inspiration from further afield: buffalo mozzarella is combined in a salad with chorizo, chicken boudin comes with mango and apple chutney, and a main course parcel of rabbit and foie gras wrapped in mash is something of a novelty.

Ribeye of beef may be a regular item, but a good showing of fish and vegetables helps to keep things light, producing thyme-roast cod with couscous, tuna with Thai spices, and a main-course salad of tabbouleh and chickpeas. English cheeses offer an alternative to desserts of ginger and praline parfait, or coffee torte with shortbread, and a short global wine list starts with house French at £10.95.

CHEF: Bill Marmion PROPRIETORS: Bobby Browns Ltd, Caroline Furby and Chris Benbrook OPEN: Mon to Fri L 12 to 2, Mon to Sat D 7 to 10 CLOSED: 25 Dec to 2 Jan, bank hols MEALS: alc (main courses £10 to £13.50). Set L and D £24.50 (2 courses) to £29.50 SERVICE: not inc, 10% for parties of 6 or more CARDS: Amex, Delta, Diners, MasterCard, Switch, Visa DETAILS: 75 seats. Private parties: 70 main room, 16 private room. Vegetarian meals. Children's helpings. No cigars in dining-room. Wheelchair access (also WC). Music. Air-conditioned (£5)

If a restaurant is new to the Guide this year (did not appear as a main entry in the last edition), NEW ENTRY *appears opposite its name.*

Le Petit Blanc

NEW ENTRY

9 Brindley Place, Birmingham B1 2HS — COOKING **4**
TEL: (0121) 633 7333 FAX: (0121) 633 7444 — MODERN FRENCH
WEB SITE: www.petit-blanc.com — £24–£52

Raymond Blanc's mini chain is expanding northwards (another branch is scheduled to open in Manchester shortly after the Guide's publication) and not before time, judging by the volume of reports. It is an airy and spacious development – clean, efficient and user-friendly – in the revamped heart of the city centre's eating, drinking and entertainment quarter. Step into a serene world of professional greeters, smiling and helpful staff, and the sort of relaxed yet stylish environment that 'makes you feel better just for being there'. The format is tried and tested, with a rustic French bias that takes in sticky braises of pig's cheek with girolles and glazed onions, or fat shank of lamb with a rosemary flavoured reduction, alongside pistou soup, and duck confit with a butter-bean broth.

Dishes requiring fast cooking are also successful, judging by a starter of chargrilled scallops with mashed potato (the kitchen gets through a lot of mash) and grilled tuna loin with boldly spiced lentils. Seasonal items are woven into the fabric, from a homely Jerusalem artichoke soup to a summer pumpkin risotto, its comfort rating jacked up by a well-judged combination of creaminess, cheesiness and sweetness. Indulgent chocolate desserts – classic fondant, or a sensuous feuillantine with hazelnut sauce – are balanced by lighter passion fruit sorbet in mango soup. A short selection of up-to-date wines starts with five house wines under £15, all available by the glass.

CHEF: Walter Blakemore PROPRIETOR: Raymond Blanc OPEN: all week 12 to 3, 5.30 to 11.30 (open for all-day menu 11am to 11.30pm (10.30 Sun) CLOSED: 25 Dec MEALS: alc (main courses £8.50 to £14.50). Set L and D before 7 £12.50 (2 courses) to £15. All-day menu available SERVICE: not inc, 10% for parties of 8 or more CARDS: Amex, Delta, Diners, MasterCard, Switch, Visa DETAILS: 182 seats. 70 seats outside. Private parties: 20 main room, 25 to 50 private rooms. Vegetarian meals. Children's helpings. No smoking in 1 dining room. No cigars in dining room. Wheelchair access (also WC). Music. Air-conditioned (£5)

Restaurant Gilmore

27 Warstone Lane, Hockley, Birmingham B18 6JQ — COOKING **3**
TEL: (0121) 233 3655 FAX: (01543) 415511 — MODERN BRITISH
WEB SITE: www.restaurantgilmore.com — £26–£55

Paul Gilmore's premises in Birmingham's upwardly mobile Jewellery Quarter do not conceal their industrial origin, although the effect of high, angled ceilings and heavy girder beams is softened by warm brick walls, stained glass windows and swathes of red velvet drapes. The set menu offers a simple cooking style that brings forth starters of full-flavoured asparagus with poached egg and Parmesan, or terrine of duck confit with Agen prunes, while main courses might involve breast of Deben duckling with honey-roast parsnip mash, or pan-fried loin of pork with spiced apple couscous.

It may all sound robust, but an inspector was won over by the delicacy of a Cornish crab and cucumber terrine, and the lightness of a main course bouillabaisse supporting succulent, crisp-skinned fish. A blackboard offers additional main courses, such as fillet of turbot on soft, creamy asparagus with saffron risotto and a red wine jus. For dessert, glazed apple on crisp pastry with cinnamon ice cream has met with approval. Service is polished and professional. A short, varied wine list opens with house white Bergerac and red Côtes du Ventoux at £13, plus a pair of wines of the month.

CHEF: Paul Gilmore PROPRIETORS: Paul and Dee Gilmore OPEN: Tue to Fri L 12.30 to 2, Tue to Sat D 7.30 to 9.30 CLOSED: 25 Dec to 2nd week Jan, 1 week Easter, 2 weeks Aug, Tue after bank hols MEALS: Set L £13.50 (2 courses) to £24, Set D £24 SERVICE: not inc CARDS: Amex, Delta, Diners, MasterCard, Switch, Visa DETAILS: 36 seats. Private parties: 42 main room. Vegetarian meals. Children's helpings. No-smoking area. Wheelchair access (also WC). Music. Air-conditioned (£5)

▲ Swallow Hotel, Sir Edward Elgar

NEW ENTRY

12 Hagley Road, Five Ways, Birmingham B16 8SJ | COOKING **5**
TEL: (0121) 452 1144 FAX: (0121) 456 3442 | FRENCH/MEDITERRANEAN
EMAIL: birmingham@swallow-hotels.co.uk | £45–£79

Despite the unprepossessing location on a major intersection, the Swallow is a plush, flawlessly professional, modern grand hotel, with acres of marble and glitter and 'flower arrangements the size of telephone kiosks'. The Sir Edward Elgar restaurant, an L-shaped room complete with pianist, is now under the guidance of Ian Mansfield, formerly of Eastwell Manor (see entry, Boughton Lees). His cooking employs enough luxury ingredients to justify the bill, though the menu is not just a stiff roll-call of classics, instead offering thoughtful interpretations of old favourites, often bringing them right down to earth, as in seared foie gras with boiled bacon, split peas and truffle.

Presentation is a strong point. A starter of cannelloni filled with crab and Swiss chard is attractively served with a subtly flavoured cardamom jus, while a light and technically accomplished warm terrine of goats' cheese, studded with potato to cut the richness, has come with a poached fig and bright purple damson dressing. Main courses range from earthy treatments of fish, such as John Dory with chorizo, to a complex but well-balanced dish of gamey-tasting pink roast squab pigeon with celeriac choucroute, harmoniously accompanied by a rich and sensuous liquorice sauce. Pineapple croustade with coconut ice-cream is 'heaven' for those with a sweet tooth. Service echoes the high-toned accomplishment of it all. The wine list pays more attention to France than anywhere else. Australia is fairly well represented, but prices, which start at £17, are no kinder than would be expected in such a context.

CHEF: Ian Mansfield PROPRIETOR: Whitbread Hotel Co OPEN: Sun to Fri L 12.30 to 2.30, all week D 7.30 to 10.30 (10 Sun) CLOSED: bank hols MEALS: alc (main courses £18.50 to £28). Set L £18.50 (2 courses) to £21.50, Set D £32 to £36.50. Brasserie meals also available SERVICE: not inc, card slips closed CARDS: Amex, Delta, Diners, MasterCard, Switch, Visa DETAILS: 60 seats. Private parties: 70 main room, 20 private room. Car park. Vegetarian meals. Children's helpings. Wheelchair access (also WC). Music. Air-conditioned ACCOMMODATION: 98 rooms, all with bath/shower. TV. Phone. Room only £120 to £250. Rooms for disabled. Swimming pool (*The Which? Hotel Guide*)

BISHOP'S WALTHAM Hampshire **map 2**

Wine Bar £

6–8 High Street, Bishop's Waltham SO32 1AA
TEL: (01489) 894476

COOKING **2**
GLOBAL FUSION
£20–£41

Despite the bricks, beams and wooden floor, this converted cellar bar manages to convey a contemporary feel. Lunch operates more in snack mode, with open sandwiches and a few cooked items such as grilled sardines or omelette with French fries, while dinner broadens to include seared tuna with spiced guacamole, and grilled sea bass with crushed potatoes and aïoli. The blackboard menu changes from meal to meal depending on what is available: one reporter's salmon and deep-fried rocket was supposed to be served with vegetables 'but came with new potatoes and the comment "we haven't got anything else"'. Apart from fish, there may also be chargrilled ribeye steak or Cajun-spiced chicken breast, followed by dark chocolate mousse or peppered pineapple with toffee sauce. A short, roving wine list starts with house Duboeuf at £9.95.

CHEFS: Paul Waite and Russell Parker PROPRIETORS: Mr and Mrs Peter J. Hughes OPEN: Mon to Sat 12 to 2.30, 7 to 9.30 CLOSED: Christmas, bank hols MEALS: alc (main courses £5 to £14) SERVICE: not inc CARDS: Delta, MasterCard, Switch, Visa DETAILS: 100 seats. Private parties: 50 main room. Vegetarian meals. Children's helpings. No smoking in dining room. Music. Air-conditioned (£5)

BLACKPOOL Lancashire **map 8**

September Brasserie

15–17 Queen Street, Blackpool FY1 1PU
TEL: (01253) 623282 FAX: (01253) 299455

COOKING **3**
MODERN BRITISH
£21–£43

Michael Golowicz almost single-handedly runs this first-floor kitchen, situated above his wife's hairdressing business in a closed-off street near the prom. Reporters have been pleased by pale, peaceful décor, and accomplished cooking that has produced chicken livers in a creamy mustard-edged sauce, and soft potted shrimps with crunchy chopped red cabbage. For a main course you may land fillets of brill strewn with shrimps in a rich buttery sauce, or pigeon breasts on polenta with an oniony jus. Soft, grainy brown bread is good for mopping up, but separate vegetables may be no more than a couple of roast potato cakes. Good-value set-price menus offer less choice but are equally imaginative: goose and duck rillettes with gooseberry chutney, or Dover sole fillets stuffed with nori, wasabi and scampi. Save room for apple strudel in a creamy vanilla custard or crème brûlée 'the size of a 45rpm record'. The score of attractively described and well-priced wines comes from all over, starting at £12.50.

CHEF/PROPRIETOR: Michael Golowicz OPEN: Tue to Sat 12 to 2, 7 to 10 (pre- and post-theatre D by arrangement) CLOSED: 2 weeks summer, 2 weeks winter MEALS: alc (main courses L £6 to £10, D £10.50 to £14.50). Set L £8 (2 courses), Set D £16.95 (2 courses) to £18.95 SERVICE: not inc CARDS: Amex, Delta, Diners, MasterCard, Switch, Visa DETAILS: 45 seats. Private parties: 30 main room. Vegetarian meals. Children's helpings. Music (£5)

BLAKENEY Norfolk **map 6**

▲ White Horse Hotel

4 High Street, Blakeney NR25 7AL
TEL: (01263) 740574 FAX: (01263) 741303
off A149 between Cley and Morston

COOKING **2**
GLOBAL FUSION
£24–£44

The White Horse's setting, just a few strides from the water, is immediately alluring. Bar lunches and suppers may be all that's required (cockle chowder is recommended), but those who go for dinner in the old stables that overlook a walled garden and courtyard can expect generous helpings of meat and game. These have come in the form of lamb tagine with couscous, and beef medallions with either a mustardy crust or an anchovy and caper one, accompanied by simple buttered vegetables in a big white bowl. Hot asparagus with Parmesan shavings, or a well-flavoured terrine (venison, juniper and pistachio) might start things off, and rich chocolate mousse with a crisp brandy-snap basket, or baked pear in Marsala may be good ways to finish. Service is 'friendly and unrushed'. Draught Adnams will draw many, while 40-odd wines grouped by colour within country are virtually all under £20. Australian and Spanish house wines are £10.95.

CHEF: Christopher Hyde PROPRIETOR: Daniel Rees OPEN: Tue to Sat and bank hol Sun D only 7 to 9 CLOSED: first 2 weeks Jan MEALS: alc (main courses £9 to £17). Bar food available SERVICE: not inc CARDS: Amex, Delta, MasterCard, Switch, Visa DETAILS: 100 seats. 60 seats outside. Private parties: 40 main room. Car park. Vegetarian meals. Children's helpings. Wheelchair access (not WC). Occasional music ACCOMMODATION: 10 rooms, all with bath/shower. TV. Phone. B&B £40 to £90 (*The Which? Hotel Guide*)

BOLTON ABBEY North Yorkshire **map 9**

NORTH YORKS GFG 2001 COMMENDED

▲ Devonshire Arms, Burlington Restaurant 

Bolton Abbey BD23 6AJ
TEL: (01756) 710441 FAX: (01756) 710564
WEB SITE: www.thedevonshirearms.co.uk
at junction of A59 and B6160, 5m NW of Ilkley

COOKING **7**
MODERN BRITISH
£30–£65

Built from the same stone as nearby Bolton Abbey, the Devonshire Arms started life as a coaching inn in the seventeenth century. Old architectural drawings combine with forest-green colours to lend an air of serenity to the two small dining rooms, and although the cooking has had its ups and downs over the years, an inspection meal confirmed that, with the arrival of Steve Williams in February 2000, it is now back on rattling fine form. Dinner is the main event, with around six options per course, and although the cooking is characterised by complexity and a few luxuries, it has a sense of purpose, smacks of honest workmanship, and manages to be subtle and gutsy by turns.

Fresh ingredients contribute significantly to success, for example in a sophisticated layered salad of octopus with celery, herbs and a squid ink dressing. Materials don't come much better than local Loddesdale lamb (the best ever, according to an inspector who has eaten her way through whole flocks of sheep over the years) with crisp fat, served on minted tagliatelle, surrounded by assorted top-class vegetables and a few blobs of pea froth. A good stock-based sauce added a silky yet restrained counterpoint to this variation on a classic British lamb-mint-and-pea combination.

Clear, well-balanced flavours and interesting contrasts are part of the appeal: for example in small chunks of stewed spiced rhubarb, its pronounced, clear flavour enhanced with orange juice, lodged in a biscuit cage and topped with chiboust cream. Extras may not be in quite the same league, but bread is 'hugely enjoyable' and the cheeseboard is 'worth a mention'. Service at a single meal has varied from 'oafish to seriously well informed and charming', and the wine list aims for big hitters, many in three figures. There is little under £20, although house Spanish is £15. An informal brasserie with a separate kitchen serves up sausage and mash, haddock fishcakes, and a few grills and roasts at much lower prices than the main restaurant.

CHEF: Steve Williams PROPRIETORS: The Duke and Duchess Of Devonshire OPEN: Sun L 12 to 2, all week D 7 to 10 MEALS: Set L £19.50, Set D £42 SERVICE: not inc, card slips closed CARDS: Amex, Delta, Diners, MasterCard, Switch, Visa DETAILS: 65 seats. Private parties: 12 main room, 12 to 100 private rooms. Car park. Vegetarian meals. Children's helpings. Jacket and tie. No smoking in dining room. Wheelchair access (also WC). No music ACCOMMODATION: 41 rooms, all with bath/shower. TV. Phone. B&B £115 to £325. Rooms for disabled. Baby facilities. Swimming pool. Fishing (*The Which? Hotel Guide*) (£5)

BOSTON SPA West Yorkshire **map 9**

Spice Box £

NEW ENTRY

152 High Street, Boston Spa LS23 6BW
TEL: (01937) 842558 FAX: (01937) 849955

COOKING **4**
MODERN BRITISH-PLUS
£19–£41

Old storage boxes and drawers for potions remain from former times at this restored pharmacy, while pictures of mussels and garlic point to its new incarnation. Painted red and brown, with candlelight and a buzzing atmosphere, it makes fish the centrepoint of its closely handwritten menus, with a few daily specials chalked on the wall by reception. Expect to find lobsters, oysters, potted shrimps and razor clams, alongside well-rendered fishcakes with Thai peanut sauce, or crisp baby squid surrounding a field mushroom topped with risotto.

Dishes are interestingly but not fussily presented, using good-quality ingredients, and timing is accurate enough. At an inspection meal this produced pink lamb's liver with a couple of rashers of good bacon, served on creamy mash infused with thyme and rosemary, and thick chunks of mature-tasting ribeye of beef, cooked as requested, served with polenta as well as sauté oyster mushrooms and Yorkshire pudding. A long list of cheeses provides a viable alternative to desserts such as banana crumble, or a wedge of rich and highly recommended chocolate tart with mascarpone ice cream. Service is 'polite, unrushed and helpful'. Wines, arranged by style, rarely stray above £20, with house French £9.50, Chilean £11.95.

CHEF: Karl Mainey PROPRIETORS: Karl and Amanda Mainey OPEN: Tue to Sun L 12 to 2, Mon to Sat D 7 to 9.30 (10 Fri and Sat) MEALS: alc (main courses L £5.50 to £11, D £10.50 to £13.50). Set D £14.95. Light L cheese menu SERVICE: not inc, card slips closed CARDS: Amex, Delta, MasterCard, Switch, Visa DETAILS: 57 seats. Private parties: 57 main room. Vegetarian meals. Children's helpings. No smoking in dining room. No music (£5)

BOUGHTON LEES Kent **map 3**

▲ Eastwell Manor

Eastwell Park, Boughton Lees TN25 4HR
TEL: (01233) 213000 FAX: (01233) 635530 COOKING **5**
EMAIL: eastwell@btinternet.com ANGLO-FRENCH
on A251, 3m N of Ashford £32–£85

The sprawling, grey-stone manor house sits in the middle of a 3,000-acre estate, its mullioned windows and exuberant brick chimneys testifying to a colourful 1,000-year history: a queen of Romania, when Romania had such things, was born here. Dark wood predominates inside, where Steven Black turns out a selection of well-heeled dishes, from seared foie gras with Sauternes syrup to grilled Dover sole, filleted at table, with parsley butter. It may all seem rather conventional, but ingredients are sound and the cooking is 'slick' in its handling of materials.

Menus are attractively balanced, taking in starters of scallops (with a lemon grass and tomato dressing), and offal (calves' sweetbreads on a champagne sauce), followed by fish (John Dory with mussel beignets) and game (venison with caramelised onions). These are all beside more mainstream items such as loin of lamb with a light curry froth, and Aberdeen Angus fillet with braised oxtail and Savoy cabbage. Desserts have a fondness for the familiar, in the shape of tiramisù, chocolate marquise, and pineapple tarte Tatin, and wines an affection for classy bottles, mostly French. A few make it under the £20 barrier, including a Gros Manseng white and Tannat red from Alain Brumont at £14.

CHEF: Steven Black PROPRIETORS: Mr and Mrs T.F. Parrett OPEN: all week 12 to 2.30 (3.30 Sun), 7 to 10 MEALS: alc (main courses £15.50 to £24.50). Set L Mon to Sat £16.50 (2 courses) to £19.50, Set L Sun £24.50, Set D £30 to £55. Bar snacks 10am to 10pm SERVICE: not inc, card slips closed CARDS: Amex, Delta, Diners, MasterCard, Switch, Visa DETAILS: 70 seats. 30 seats outside. Private parties: 140 main room, 12 to 140 private rooms. Car park. Vegetarian meals. Children's helpings. No smoking in dining room. Wheelchair access (also WC). Music ACCOMMODATION: 62 rooms, all with bath/shower. TV. Phone. B&B £150 to £340. Rooms for disabled. Baby facilities. Swimming pool (*The Which? Hotel Guide*) (£5)

£ *means that it is possible to have a three-course meal, including coffee, half a bottle of house wine and service for £25 or less per person, at any time the restaurant is open, i.e. at dinner as well as lunch. It may be possible to spend considerably more than this, but by choosing carefully you should find £25 or less achievable.*

Occasional music *in the details at the end of an entry means live or recorded music is played in the dining room only rarely or for special events.* No music *means it is never played.*

BOWNESS-ON-WINDERMERE Cumbria **map 8**

▲ Linthwaite House

Crook Road, Bowness-on-Windermere LA23 3JA
TEL: (015394) 88600 FAX: (015394) 88601 COOKING **5**
EMAIL: admin@linthwaite.com MODERN BRITISH
WEB SITE: www.linthwaite.com £24–£56

Set high above Lake Windermere in 15 acres of grounds, with its own small tarn 'the size of a municipal boating lake', Linthwaite House lays claim to a slice of the peace and quiet that draws visitors to the Lake District. Decorated in 'modern colonial' style, and feeling small and intimate, it sports a conservatory with a view, and two dining rooms, one covered in gilt-framed mirrors. Ian Bravey's wide-ranging and approachable style takes in curried sweetcorn soup, sea bass with a soy, ginger and spring onion glaze, and smoked and roasted pork loin in a port and maple syrup sauce.

At lunch the kitchen has also turned out exemplary Caesar salad, a torpedo of smooth chicken liver parfait with tomato and chilli chutney, and a generous helping of seafood ragoût incorporating salmon, sea bass and scallop corals in an intensely fishy sauce. Although desserts may not be quite on a par with the rest, they have produced a light sticky toffee pudding with a sauce of 'cloying sweetness', plus a number based on chocolate, from bread-and-butter pudding via fondant to a white chocolate brûlée. A global selection of wines is arranged by grape variety in the case of Chardonnays and Sauvignons, and according to style for the rest, including a page of fine clarets. House wines from £15.20 are also available by the half-carafe and glass.

CHEF: Ian Bravey PROPRIETOR: Mike Bevans OPEN: Sun L 12.30 to 1.30, all week D 7.15 to 8.45 MEALS: alc Sun L (main courses £8 to £13). Set Sun L £15.95, Set D £39. Bar L available Mon to Sat SERVICE: net prices, card slips closed CARDS: Amex, Delta, Diners, MasterCard, Switch, Visa DETAILS: 60 seats. Private parties: 45 main room, 16 to 45 private rooms. Car park. Vegetarian meals. Children's helpings. No children under 7. No smoking in dining room. Wheelchair access (also WC). Music ACCOMMODATION: 26 rooms, all with bath/shower. TV. Phone. D,B&B £77 to £252. Rooms for disabled. Baby facilities. Fishing (*The Which? Hotel Guide*) (£5)

Porthole Eating House

3 Ash Street, Bowness-on-Windermere LA23 3EB
TEL: (015394) 42793 FAX: (015394) 88675 COOKING **4**
EMAIL: gianni.berton@which.net ITALIAN/FRENCH/ENGLISH
WEB SITE: homepages.which.net7gianni.berton £21–£53

Bare wooden tables and a flagstone floor contribute to a relaxed and convivial atmosphere at this Bowness stalwart. Dating from the seventeenth-century, the cottage now finds itself in a pedestrianised street and has to use its small space carefully. Despite Gianni Berton's Italian credentials, its culinary passport also carries French and English visas, producing a range of dishes spanning everything from bacon and black pudding salad via lasagne to raspberry pavlova.

Old-fashioned prawn cocktail and Dover sole meunière rub shoulders with Thai beef stir fry, and there is usually charcoal-grilled beef fillet with a choice of parsley butter or red wine and peppercorn sauce. The kitchen makes its own beef and horseradish sausages, and given that it refers to scallops wrapped in bacon as a 'new dish', it may come as no surprise to find tiramisù, orange positano and even rumtopf among desserts. Over 350 bottles from around the world make up a catholic wine list, which has particularly strong German and Australian sections. Mark-ups are reasonable but a tendency for P.O.A. to accompany the finer bottles makes for all-round tedium. House wines are £11.50, and only two wines are available by the glass.

CHEF: Andrew Fairchild PROPRIETORS: Judy and Gianni Berton OPEN: Mon, Wed to Fri and Sun L 12 to 2.30, Wed to Mon D 6.30 to 10.30 CLOSED: mid-Dec to mid-Feb MEALS: alc (main courses L £7 to £11, D £10 to £18). Set L £11.50 (2 courses) to £12.50 SERVICE: not inc, card slips closed CARDS: Amex, Delta, Diners, MasterCard, Switch, Visa DETAILS: 40 seats. Private parties: 40 main room, 40 private room. Vegetarian meals. Children's helpings. Wheelchair access (not WC). Music

BRAITHWAITE Cumbria **map 10**

▲ Ivy House

Braithwaite CA12 5SY
TEL: (017687) 78338 FAX: (017687) 78113
EMAIL: stay@ivy-house.co.uk
WEB SITE: www.ivy-house.co.uk
just off B5292 Keswick to Braithwaite road

COOKING **2**
MODERN BRITISH
£31–£40

Nick Shill does the greeting, and looks after everything front-of-house with an easy and friendly manner, serving drinks in the beamed bar before taking up waiting duties at 7 for four-course dinners in the spacious first-floor dining room. The kitchen borrows widely, producing starters of Stilton and walnut pâté alongside chicken satay with guacamole. A choice between soup (perhaps cream of onion and coriander) and sorbet (wild strawberry) precedes main courses that have included tender steak au poivre with mustard sauce, and lemon sole with prawn, tomato and dill sauce. An over-generous hand with seasoning and spicing was evident at inspection, but a luxurious dessert of clotted cream with strawberries and a brûlée topping ended the meal on a high note. Enthusiasm runs through a lively, fairly priced and heftily annotated wine list, which brings together new offerings and old favourites. It is arranged by style – Simon Hackett's Old Vine Grenache from McLaren Vale is worth a punt in the Red Blockbusters section – and eight wines are available by the glass. House French is £11.95.

CHEFS: Peter Holten and Lee Scrimgeour PROPRIETORS: Nick and Wendy Shill OPEN: all week D only 7 to 8 (1 sitting) MEALS: Set D £21.95 SERVICE: not inc CARDS: Delta, Diners, MasterCard, Switch, Visa DETAILS: 30 seats. Private parties: 10 main room. Car park. Vegetarian meals. Children's helpings. No children under 6. No smoking in dining room. Music ACCOMMODATION: 12 rooms, all with bath/shower. TV. Phone. D,B&B £56 to £100. Rooms for disabled. Baby facilities

BRAMPTON Cumbria map 10

▲ Farlam Hall

Brampton CA8 2NG
TEL: (016977) 46234 FAX: (016977) 46683
EMAIL: farlamhall@dial.pipex.com
WEB SITE: www.farlamhall.co.uk
on A689, 2½m SE of Brampton (not at Farlam village)

COOKING **3**
ENGLISH COUNTRY HOUSE
£42–£50

Run by the same families for over a quarter of a century, Farlam Hall doesn't try to be up to date. Rather it embraces the English country-house tradition of a single sitting for dinner, in a generously spaced dining room decorated in blue and faded gold; the ladies who serve do so graciously in what appear to be ball gowns. The simply conceived food achieves its modest aims well, dealing in twice-baked Stilton soufflé, roast monkfish, and boned stuffed quail. Sound materials and sensitive handling have produced a creamily fishy lobster mousse with cucumber salad, and a fine piece of best end of local lamb with minted mash and a first-rate rosemary-infused sauce. English cheeses come with lots of extras, and desserts have included almond meringue gâteau, and a layered raspberry and oatmeal terrine. For interest and value, look outside the traditional French offerings on a 40-strong wine list that starts with a quartet of southern hemisphere house wines at £13.50.

CHEFS: Barry Quinion and Martin Langford PROPRIETORS: the Quinion family and the Stevenson family OPEN: all week D only 8 to 8.30 CLOSED: 25 to 30 Dec MEALS: Set D £31 SERVICE: not inc, card slips closed CARDS: MasterCard, Switch, Visa DETAILS: 40 seats. Private parties: 45 main room. Car park. No children under 5. No cigars/pipes in dining room. Wheelchair access (not WC). No music ACCOMMODATION: 12 rooms, all with bath/shower. TV. Phone. D,B&B £110 to £250. No children under 5 (*The Which? Hotel Guide*)

BRAY Berkshire map 3

Fat Duck

CHEF OF THE YEAR GFG 2001

1 High Street, Bray SL6 2AQ
TEL: (01628) 580333 FAX: (01628) 776188

COOKING **8**
MODERN EUROPEAN
£41–£93

Behind the simple white building on the main street of this picturesque village works a chef of true creativity, which tends to make visits both special and memorable. 'I would trade all the inspections so far this year simply to have a meal here,' wrote a seasoned member of our team. Don't expect the usual indulgent trappings of a fine restaurant; this informal, rustic dining room has a 'village pub-like atmosphere', outside lavatories and no tablecloths, although some improvements may have taken place by the time the Guide appears.

It is pioneering food that never stops developing. Heston Blumenthal is moving away from the idea of a large central main course towards a succession of smaller ones, for example wafer-thin pasta enclosing three langoustines, served with thin slices of gelatinous pig's trotter, piled high with black truffles; or two fat juicy scallops accompanied by caramelised cauliflower purée, marinated cep, and an oloroso jelly. This is one of the few restaurants where complex cooking and elaborate preparation pay off: as in a filo parcel containing shredded pigeon breast and dark cherries, served with two pink flavourful thighs, plus a thin shaving of chocolate and a fine watercress velouté.

The laboratory is never far away. Blumenthal has reduced the calcium content of the water used for cooking vegetables, the better to preserve their colour, and has developed some innovative ice creams: made from crab (to serve with crab risotto), and from smoked bacon (as a dessert). Alternatively, there may be a plate combining smooth rice pudding, intense apricot purée, melting chocolate fondant, and a coconut sorbet. The kitchen puts as much effort into incidentals as some chefs put into entire menus: jelly of pigeon with cream of langoustine uses whole pigeons to produce an essence, and is only an amuse-bouche. Do not be fooled by the casually dressed staff: they are highly professional.

Beyond the rather ornate script and slightly confusing layout, the wine list yields some pleasant discoveries. It shows an intelligent juxtaposition of old and new, and the whole page devoted to up-and-coming wines from south-west France is encouraging, Prices can be high, but wines under £20 are interesting, and around 20 (plus 30 sherries) are sold by the glass. House wines start at £18.

CHEF: Heston Blumenthal PROPRIETORS: Heston and Susanna Blumenthal OPEN: Tue to Sun L 12 to 2 (2.30 Sun), Tue to Sat D 7 to 9.30 (10 Fri and Sat) MEALS: alc (main courses £23.50 to £28). Set L Tue to Sat £23.50 SERVICE: 12.5%, card slips closed CARDS: Amex, Delta, Diners, MasterCard, Switch, Visa DETAILS: 45 seats. Private parties: 45 main room. Children's helpings. No cigars/pipes in dining room. Wheelchair access (not WC). Music

▲ Waterside Inn

Ferry Road, Bray SL6 2AT
TEL: (01628) 620691 FAX: (01628) 784710 — COOKING **8**
EMAIL: waterinn@aol.com — FRENCH
WEB SITE: www.waterside-inn.co.uk — £50–£187

The white-painted building is at the end of a cul de sac where Ferry Road meets the Thames, and where the door is only unlocked at the appointed hour. The terrace, at least in summer, is a tranquil delight, with swans and oarsmen to divert and entertain, while aperitifs and canapés are delivered with elaborate care. One half of the dining room, with panelled mirrors, feels cocooning, the other, a square conservatory with sliding doors, is light and expansive. Both seem a long way from the real world, and the recommended approach is to surrender to a realm where life is regulated by a small army of ministering French waiters, and where money seems no longer tied to its customary moorings: a green side salad, for example, is £15.

Menus (unpriced for ladies) include an 'exceptionnel' that combines first-rate cooking with well-paced delivery, leaving one couple 'contentedly full but not bloated'. The carte, meanwhile, sets a course between old-fashioned standards, such as poached eggs in a pastry case with sauce mousseline, and more than a few luxuries: three enormous, meaty, just-cooked scallops, for example, served with summer truffles and a strewing of wild mushrooms. Materials range from roast Challandais duck (carved at table), to five lightly battered, deep-fried, saffron-infused langoustines sitting beside a rustic pile of parsley and tarragon tossed with squid rings.

Seasons are respected, producing for example a salad of St Enodoc asparagus in spring to accompany a ballottine of foie gras and duck confit, and the cooking is generally considered exemplary but safe. Results range from poorly executed sea bass at inspection, to a harmonious dish of veal: a thin escalope wrapped round a triumphant mushroom duxelles, served with pink kidney and a puff pastry parcel stuffed with gamy-tasting minced sweetbread. Cheeses arrive on a large 'beautifully smelly trolley' in fine condition, though served with commercial water biscuits, and desserts, though perfectly decent, are not the most inspired. The wine list trumpets the glories of France at prices that bring tears to the eyes. Does it have to be so cynical? Only one wine (a rosé) comes in under £20.

CHEFS: Michel Roux and Mark Dodson PROPRIETOR: Michel Roux OPEN: Wed to Sun L 12 to 2 (2.30 Sun), Tue to Sun D 7 to 10 CLOSED: 26 Dec to 1 Feb, Tue D Sept to May MEALS: alc (main courses £34 to £49.50). Set L Wed to Sat £32 to £71.50, Set L Sun £48 to £71.50, Set D £71.50 SERVICE: 12.5% (optional), card slips closed CARDS: Amex, Delta, Diners, MasterCard, Switch, Visa DETAILS: 75 seats. Private parties: 80 main room, 8 private room. Small car park. Vegetarian meals. Children's helpings. No children under 12. No cigars in dining room. Wheelchair access (not WC). Occasional music ACCOMMODATION: 9 rooms, all with bath/shower. TV. Phone. B&B £150 to £275. No children under 12

BRIGHTON & HOVE East Sussex **map 3**

Black Chapati

12 Circus Parade, New England Road, Brighton BN1 4GW
TEL: (01273) 699011

COOKING **4**
GLOBAL
£29–£42

Despite the acclaim they have received over 12 years, Stephen Funnell and Lauren Alker seem happy to remain in this unremarkable location beneath a block of flats and offices just off London Road. Their modestly furnished restaurant has black Formica tables, blond wood chairs, and yellow walls hung with pictures of South East Asia, while the menu deals in innovatively treated pan-Asian ingredients. Balance and flavours are spot on, as evidenced by starters of unctuous potted duck with Chinese spices, pickled cucumber and toast, or Sri Lankan lamb patties with two chutneys (fiery chilli, and cool coconut and coriander).

Main courses continue the theme, partnering roast cod with a shrimp and lime leaf sauce and a sweet-and-sour salad; while grilled chicken ('moist, tender, full of flavour') might come with lemon grass and coconut. Puddings alone betray a European ancestry: witness an impressive lemon polenta cake served with lemon and sultana sauce and white chocolate ice-cream. Food can take a while to arrive, but serving staff are willing and pleasant. The wine list is concise and without annotation, but includes a decent choice of varietals. Vin de pays costs £10.

CHEFS/PROPRIETORS: Stephen Funnell and Lauren Alker OPEN: Tue to Sat D only 7 (6.30 Sat) to 10 CLOSED: 2 weeks Christmas, 2 weeks July MEALS: alc (main courses £10.50 to £13.50) SERVICE: 10%, card slips closed CARDS: Amex, Delta, MasterCard, Switch, Visa DETAILS: 32 seats. Private parties: 9 main room. Vegetarian meals. No children under 6. No cigars/pipes in dining room. Wheelchair access (not WC). Music

La Fourchette

NEW ENTRY

101 Western Road, Brighton BN1 2AA
TEL: (01273) 722556

COOKING **4**
FRENCH
£24–£48

Close to the border of Brighton and Hove, on a busy main shopping street, La Fourchette has brought a dash of Gallic flair to a crowded restaurant scene. The small room with its plywood tables and 'ethnic peasant' artefacts may be short on visual style, but the good news is that Pascal Madjoudj is an exciting chef who takes great care in sourcing raw materials, and whose cooking is technically accurate and totally assured. First-course salads are carefully composed assemblies, perhaps of warm shredded duck confit with apple, or lightly grilled smoked haddock with tomato and avocado.

The unmistakably French style demonstrates a passion for clear and robust flavours, producing thick-cut rack of lamb with plenty of garlic in a light reduction, while fish of the day has included a pairing of monkfish and red mullet with potato and spinach in a lightly creamy sauce. An unusual red wine parfait in a lake of dark, foamy chocolate sabayon is a grown-up dessert, while pastrywork comes to the fore in a flavourful lemon tart. Several reports have criticised the music, and service can be a little chaotic, but the cooking is worth being patient for. The wine list won't set the pulse racing, although prices are fair enough. House French is £9.75.

CHEF/PROPRIETOR: Pascal Madjoudj OPEN: Tue to Sat L 12 to 2.30, Mon to Sat D 6.30 to 10.30 CLOSED: first 2 weeks Jan MEALS: alc (main courses L £7 to £10, D £12 to £15) SERVICE: 10%, card slips closed CARDS: Amex, Delta, Diners, MasterCard, Switch, Visa DETAILS: 37 seats. Private parties: 40 main room. Vegetarian meals. Children's helpings. No music (£5)

Gingerman 🍷

21A Norfolk Square, Brighton BN1 2PD
TEL/FAX: (01273) 326688

COOKING **3**
MODERN EUROPEAN
£22–£37

There are no gingerbread men on the menu; the name refers to Ben McKellar's hair colour. This is a small, unpretentious place just off the square, decorated in muted autumnal tones with modern foodie pictures on the walls. Modern food is on the menu too, and is presented with skill and assurance. Robust flavours are evident in dishes such as pea soup with poached ham hock, scallop and merguez salad with lemon and coriander dressing, and veal kidneys and sweetbreads with black pudding and a serving of garlic mash. The same description applied to a reporter's lunch of 'confident, generous and brilliantly handled' fillet steak with a piece of oxtail, followed by moist, rich, dark chocolate soufflé with a salad of peppered strawberries. Other desserts have included caramelised banana tart with rum and raisin ice-cream, and steamed treacle pudding. Short and pithy, the wine list nevertheless contains a clever and thorough selection from around the world, the majority under £20. House French is £9.25 and five dessert wines are all available by the glass.

CHEF: Ben McKellar PROPRIETORS: Ben and Neil McKellar, and Pamela Abbott OPEN: Tue to Sat 12.30 to 2, 7 to 10 CLOSED: 2 weeks summer, 2 weeks winter MEALS: Set L £9.95 (1 course) to £14.95, Set D £18.95 (2 courses) to £21.50 SERVICE: not inc CARDS: Amex, Delta, Diners, MasterCard, Switch, Visa DETAILS: 32 seats. Private parties: 32 main room. Children's helpings. Music

One Paston Place

1 Paston Place, Brighton BN2 1HA
TEL: (01273) 606933 FAX: (01273) 675686

COOKING **6**
MODERN EUROPEAN
£27–£60

'Eating at One Paston Place is pure pleasure,' enthused one visitor, while a local wondered where Brighton would be without it. Décor is agreeable without appearing to contribute to the cost of the meal, tables are well spaced and neatly set, and Mark Emmerson's cooking stands out from the crowd not least because he starts with high-quality raw materials, from wild salmon to 'the finest lamb'. His style is at once classical yet contemporary, embracing game terrine with fig compote, alongside a less usual partnership of pan-fried foie gras with rhubarb, Szechuan pepper and crispy beetroot. Luxuries, of which there are quite a few, are properly deployed. Dishes are integrated, and don't appear cluttered even when they involve several components: for example roast leg and confit shoulder of rabbit with fennel, foie gras and potato galette. As for timing, one couple considered the cooking of scallops here to be the 'gold standard' by which others should be judged.

A sense of balance also applies to the well-kept selection of cheeses, and to desserts such as iced coconut parfait with pineapple confit, and chocolate macaroon with pistachio ice cream and griottine cherries. Properly trained staff, who are 'professional but not starchy', deliver 'impeccable' service, and the mostly traditional French list starts with four house wines, including Tannat and Gros Manseng, at £12.50.

CHEF: Mark Emmerson PROPRIETORS: Mark and Nicole Emmerson OPEN: Tue to Sat 12.30 to 2, 7 to 10 CLOSED: first 2 weeks Jan, first two weeks Aug MEALS: alc (main courses £19 to £21). Set L £16.50 (2 courses) to £19 SERVICE: net prices, card slips closed CARDS: Amex, Delta, Diners, MasterCard, Switch, Visa DETAILS: 45 seats. No cigars/pipes in dining room. Music. Air-conditioned

Quentin's

42 Western Road, Hove BN3 1JD
TEL/FAX: (01273) 822734

COOKING **2**
MODERN BRITISH
£30–£36

Behind an unprepossessing bottle-green frontage lurks a small, intimate dining room with heavy country-kitchen tables and mismatched chairs. Quentin Fitch looks after his customers, offering them the full deal from olives, nibbles and bread at the outset to petits fours with coffee, and his cooking has gathered confidence over the last seven years. An inspector was impressed by the timing and quality of chargrilled breast and confit leg of guinea-fowl on tarragon mash, and by fillet of tender Scotch beef that came with a luxuriously pungent ragout of its kidneys and button mushrooms. Fish is well-sourced too, perhaps turning up as sea bass with an accompaniment of spiced lentils, or in a first-course turban of lemon sole and fresh crab with tomato sauce. Finish with the likes of fine dark chocolate tart or fresh fruit jelly. The short, adequate wine list opens with house French at £9.95 (white) or £10.95 (red).

CHEF: Quentin Fitch PROPRIETORS: Quentin and Candy Fitch OPEN: Tue to Fri L 12 to 2, Tue to Sat D 7 to 9.30 CLOSED: 1 week from 25 Dec, 2 weeks Aug MEALS: Set L and D £17.95 (2 courses) to £19.95 SERVICE: not inc CARDS: Amex, Delta, Diners, MasterCard, Switch, Visa DETAILS: 28 seats. Private parties: 35 main room, 20 private room. Vegetarian meals. No cigars/pipes in dining room. Wheelchair access (not WC). Music. Air-conditioned

Terre à Terre

71 East Street, Brighton BN1 3HQ
TEL: (01273) 729051 FAX: (01273) 327561

COOKING **4**
MODERN GLOBAL VEGETARIAN
£28–£41

'Evening excitement' is promised on the cover of the dinner menu at this town-centre restaurant just off the seafront. It is a commodity in no short supply in Brighton, but here it translates into extravagantly wide-reaching cooking that deals in unusual ingredients, vivid colours and flavours, and large portions. The strengthening confidence that the kitchen has demonstrated over the last few years is testimony to the fact that vegetarian cookery need not be dull.

Punning neologisms are the menu's lingua franca. 'Zhuganoush' turns out to be chargrilled aubergine with griddled minted halloumi, roasted red pepper and a poached egg, while 'Chianti pomodoro bolla' are balls of ricotta, mozzarella and oregano, coated in polenta and served on pappardelle pasta with a slow-cooked, tomato-based Chianti sauce. Various ways with rösti are offered – perhaps topped with aubergine, chipotle and tamarillo salsa – while desserts bring on 'blasted bananas and passion colada', a dish of sugar-scorched bananas with toffee and banana ice cream and a passion-fruit and coconut sauce. Service is young and cool, and the list of organic, vegetarian and vegan drinks furnishes plenty of choice, from French house wine at £10.25 to cannabis beer at £3.10 a bottle.

CHEFS: Paul Morgan and Rickie Hodgson PROPRIETORS: Philip Taylor and Amanda Powley OPEN: Tue to Sat L 12 (11 Sat and Sun) to 5.30, all week D 6 to 10.30 CLOSED: 25 and 26 Dec, 1 Jan MEALS: alc (main courses £8 to £10.50) SERVICE: not inc CARDS: Amex, Delta, Diners, MasterCard, Switch, Visa DETAILS: 70 seats. Private parties: 20 main room. Vegetarian meals. Children's helpings. No-smoking area. No cigars/pipes in dining room. Wheelchair access (also WC). Music. Air-conditioned

Restaurateurs justifiably resent no-shows. If you quote a credit card number when booking, you may be liable for the restaurant's lost profit margin if you don't turn up. Always phone to cancel.

All details are as accurate as possible at the time of going to press, but chefs and owners often change, and it is wise to check by telephone before making a special journey. Many readers have been disappointed when set-price bargain meals are no longer available. Ask when booking.

Whytes

33 Western Street, Brighton BN1 2PG
TEL: (01273) 776618 FAX: (01444) 410822 COOKING **3**
EMAIL: janthony@lineone.net MODERN EUROPEAN
WEB SITE: www.whytesrestaurant.com £33–£41

The décor at this tiny restaurant on two floors is spare and elegant, with modern art on plain cream walls, minimalist flower arrangements, and comfortable red chairs and banquettes adding a dash of colour. The short menu, far-reaching but thoughtful, has offered diverse starters from a generous heap of crab risotto, fragrant with lemon grass and lime leaves, to a muscular pigeon breast with lentils and a nutty, minty salsa verde. Raw materials are first rate and timing impressive, for example in a well flavoured pork fillet served with a sweet potato version of bubble and squeak, and in a rather hefty dish of polenta-crusted, cumin-spiced lamb that came with couscous and grilled vegetables.

Among successful desserts have been an emphatically sticky banana and ginger pudding with caramel ice cream, and chocolate pot with raspberry sorbet. Good breads are brought with olive oil for dipping, and a flute of grapefruit and vodka sorbet may be offered between courses. Service is brisk but friendly. Wines range from a Romanian Pinot Noir at £11 to Ch. Latour 1983 at £110, with the house selection, from France, Australia and England, starting at £9.95.

CHEF: Paul Gunn PROPRIETOR: John Anthony OPEN: Tue to Sun D only 7 to 9.30 CLOSED: 25 Dec to New Year, last 2 weeks Feb MEALS: alc (main courses £14) SERVICE: not inc, card slips closed CARDS: Amex, Delta, MasterCard, Switch, Visa DETAILS: 36 seats. Private parties: 28 main room, 18 private room. Vegetarian meals. No smoking in 1 dining room. Music. Air-conditioned (£5)

BRIMFIELD Herefordshire **map 5**

▲ Roebuck

Brimfield SY8 4NE
TEL: (01584) 711230 FAX: (01584) 711654
EMAIL: dave@roebuckinn.demon.co.uk
WEB SITE: www.roebuckinn.demon.co.uk COOKING **3**
just off A49 Leominster to Ludlow road, 4m W of Tenbury Wells MODERN BRITISH
£20–£49

Orders are taken in the old-fashioned bar lounge at this pleasantly friendly pub, and meals are eaten in a bright conservatory-style dining room amid wicker chairs, chintzy curtains and well-spaced tables. The menu – supplemented by a blackboard of extras – is rather long for the circumstances, offering upwards of two dozen savoury items in a try-and-please-everybody effort. Choices might range from crab filo parcels to wild mushroom risotto, from a properly made steamed steak and mushroom suet pudding to half a grilled Cornish lobster with orange and coriander butter.

Some starters are more like small main courses – rare pigeon breasts on pearl barley risotto with a chocolate and red pepper sauce, for example – but high-quality raw materials and accurate timing are among the kitchen's strengths, producing translucent scallops, chicken breast from a well-chosen bird, and moist wild venison fillet. Sauces and accompaniments may not always be in the same class, but portions are generous, and desserts favour time-honoured ideas such as bread-and-butter pudding and rhubarb crumble tart with custard. Service is cheerful and well organised, and the stylistically arranged wine list does an exemplary job under £20, starting at £9.95.

CHEFS: Jonathan Waters and David Willson-Lloyd PROPRIETORS: David and Susan Willson-Lloyd OPEN: all week 12 to 2.30, 7 to 9.30 CLOSED: 25 Dec MEALS: alc (main courses £9 to £20). Set L £9.95 (2 courses) to £12.95. Light L menu available SERVICE: not inc, card slips closed CARDS: Delta, MasterCard, Switch, Visa DETAILS: 70 seats. 14 seats outside. Private parties: 50 main room, 16 private room. Car park. Vegetarian meals. Children's helpings. No smoking in dining room. Wheelchair access (not WC). Occasional music ACCOMMODATION: 3 rooms, all with bath/shower. TV. Phone. B&B £45 to £60. Baby facilities (*The Which? Hotel Guide*) (£5)

BRISTOL Bristol **map 2**

Bell's Diner

1–3 York Street, Montpelier, Bristol BS6 5QB
TEL: (0117) 924 0357 FAX: (0117) 924 4280
take Picton Street off Cheltenham Road (A38) – runs into York Road

COOKING **5**
MODERN BRITISH
£25–£45

Christopher Wicks believes in the virtues of self-sufficiency, as far as is practically possible. To that end, he employs a picker to go out and gather wild herbs and garlic, wood sorrel and nettles. For a city brasserie, this represents some commitment. It is a fairly small place consisting of three interconnecting rooms with a real log fire on chilly days, and with dark blue woodwork and a grey slate floor that contribute to a period feel.

Those nettles and wild garlic may well turn up in a soup, thickened with potato, enriched with crème fraîche and served with Parmesan biscuits. Aubergine has muscled its way to the forefront of many a modern menu, and here it appears sliced and spiced in a salad with yoghurt dressing. A certain earthiness is pervasive of the style, meaning that cep and pea risotto may accompany a piece of seared foie gras, while cannellini beans, baby leeks and romesco sauce are the supports for a main course of roasted black bream. Lamb is organic, the rack roasted and served with spinach and salsa verde. Finish with something like pedigree Valrhona chocolate tart with chocolate ice cream. A relatively compact wine list opens with ten house wines from £10.

CHEFS: Christopher Wicks and Steven Plaister PROPRIETOR: Christopher Wicks OPEN: Tue to Sat L 12 to 2.15, Mon to Sat D 7 to 10.30 CLOSED: 23 to 31 Dec MEALS: alc (main courses £8.50 to £15) SERVICE: not inc, 10% for parties of 8 or more CARDS: Amex, Delta, MasterCard, Switch, Visa DETAILS: 50 seats. Private parties: 30 main room. Vegetarian meals. Children's helpings. No smoking in dining room. Music (£5)

indicates that smoking is either banned altogether or that a dining-room is maintained for non-smokers. The symbol does not apply to restaurants that simply have no-smoking areas.

Glass Boat

Welsh Back, Bristol BS1 4SB
TEL: (0117) 929 0704 FAX: (0117) 929 7338 NEW CHEF
EMAIL: ellie@glassboat.co.uk MODERN EUROPEAN
WEB SITE: www.glassboat.co.uk £27–£58

Although built of timber, this smart, well run affair – on an attractively converted barge moored on the river – earns its 'glass' handle from the huge windows allowing views of traffic, pedestrians, workers, boatmen and swans by day, and colourful reflections at night. As the Guide went to press, Gary Rosser arrived from the Blue Goose (see Round-up entry, Bristol) to take over the kitchen, bringing a few bright ideas with him, from a terrine of asparagus with spring onions and saffron potatoes, via oxtail and pig's trotter braised in red wine, to a Pimms and fruit jelly served with green tea sorbet. Reports on progress are particularly welcome. Wines include some interesting choices, and manage to stay reasonably priced without sacrificing quality. Prices start at £11.

CHEF: Gary Rosser PROPRIETOR: Arne Ringner OPEN: Mon to Fri L 12 to 2, Mon to Sat D 6 to 10.30 CLOSED: 25 and 26 Dec, 1 Jan MEALS: alc (main courses L £9 to £10.50, D £13 to £16). Set D £17.50 SERVICE: 10% (optional), card slips closed CARDS: Amex, Delta, Diners, MasterCard, Switch, Visa DETAILS: 130 seats. Private parties: 130 main room, 20 to 40 private rooms. Vegetarian meals. Children's helpings. Wheelchair access (not WC). Occasional music. Air-conditioned (£5)

Harveys

12 Denmark Street, Bristol BS1 5DQ COOKING **5**
TEL: (0117) 927 5034 FAX: (0117) 927 5001 MODERN EUROPEAN
WEB SITE: j-harvey.co.uk £28–£72

The wine cellars are centuries old, their timeless business recalled by vaulted ceilings, sherry casks and stained glass celebrating Bristol's famous blue glass. Attired in mid-nineties shades of blue and sand, with colourful paintings on white walls, the room appeals with warm acoustics and jolly staff, not the least of whom is an enthusiastic sommelier. Although there may be a tussle between its reputation as a businessman's lunchtime haunt and the desire to innovate – the battleground drawn around such items as sweetbreads and frogs' legs, with cockscombs no more than a twinkle in the chef's eye – luxuries seem to please all parties. Foie gras appears in a terrine of duck, and truffles in a warm potato salad with fat roast scallops.

The carte seems to favour fish over meat, subjecting springy fresh materials to rather cautious timing, as in a piece of turbot with tagliatelle in a creamy mushroom and truffle sauce, and crisp monkfish tail with an enterprising crab and guinea fowl jus, sticky and earthy at the same time. Meat eaters might be offered loin of lamb with herbed risotto and butter beans, and meals end with a large and complex list of desserts, perhaps including a spiced crème brûlée served with pear cake and a fruit coulis, although roast figs in spring have fallen rather short of their full, oozing maturity. The restaurant has chosen not to furnish the Guide with any menus, a wine list, opening times or other details, so the information below cannot be confirmed.

CHEF: Daniel Galmiche PROPRIETORS: John Harvey and Sons OPEN: Mon to Fri L 12 to 2, Mon to Sat D 7 to 10.45 CLOSED: bank hols MEALS: Set L £14.95 (2 courses) to £17.95, Set D £34.95 (2 courses) to £39.95 SERVICE: net prices CARDS: Amex, Delta, Diners, MasterCard, Switch, Visa DETAILS: 120 seats. Private parties: 120 main room, 50 private room. Music. Air-conditioned

▲ Hotel du Vin & Bistro

NEW ENTRY

Narrow Lewins Mead, Bristol BS1 2NU
TEL: (0117) 925 5577 FAX: (0117) 925 1199
EMAIL: admin@bristol.hotelduvin.co.uk
WEB SITE: www.hotelduvin.co.uk

COOKING **4**
MODERN EUROPEAN
£35–£50

The city's former Sugar House has been imaginatively converted into a third outlet for this tiny chain (see entries, Tunbridge Wells and Winchester). Thick walls, big pillars and arched cellars indicate a sturdy frame, but the courtyard has a lighter provençale feel to it, and the décor is a trade-mark mix of huge armchairs, aged walls, wine prints, posters, empty bottles, a corkscrew collection and other ephemera. The dining room, a mass of glasses and white napkins, tends to be noisy. Twenty or so savoury items run from a large cod fillet on butter bean purée, livened up with cockles and squid, to tender, rare roast pigeon served with creamed cabbage and an intense and sticky red wine reduction.

Poached smoked haddock has appeared conventionally and successfully with a poached egg, and less so in its uncooked form accompanied by a blob of walnut cream. Vegetables are charged extra. Generally sound raw materials incorporate seasonal ingredients such as Jersey Royals, asparagus, samphire, and gooseberries in a tart with rhubarb sorbet, although dishes tend to lack the gutsiness that this kind of food seems to require, and results at inspection were more variable than the wines demand. An elegant, global list judiciously combines classical favourites with up-and-coming stars. South-west France offers affordable alternatives to clarets and Burgundies, and there are bottles from Switzerland, Greece and Canada. Prices are reasonable, but only six wines are offered by the glass.

CHEF: Eddie Grey PROPRIETOR: Alternative Hotel Co OPEN: all week 12 to 2, 6 to 9.45 MEALS: alc (main courses £10.50 to £14.50) SERVICE: not inc, card slips closed CARDS: Amex, Delta, Diners, MasterCard, Switch, Visa DETAILS: 85 seats. 25 seats outside. Private parties: 72 main room, 36 to 72 private rooms. Car park. Vegetarian meals. Children's helpings. No cigars/pipes in dining room. Wheelchair access (also WC). No music ACCOMMODATION: 40 rooms, all with bath/shower. TV. Phone. Room only £99 to £195. Rooms for disabled. Baby facilities (*The Which? Hotel Guide*)

'The fifty-plus bloke at the next table, who was seducing a girl half his age at most, had the foie (gras), which he pronounced to rhyme with hoi (polloi). He did this frequently, as he was doing his utmost to impress, and went out of his way to describe his fondness for "foi" and his huge experience of it.' (On eating in Devon)

Markwicks

43 Corn Street, Bristol BS1 1HT — COOKING **5**
TEL/FAX: (0117) 926 2658 — MODERN BRITISH
£27–£56

By night, this part of the city centre comes alive with restaurants, cafés and noisy bars, but all is peace and quiet down the steps in the former bank vaults. It feels like a cross between Regency and art deco, perked up with pristine white napery and sparkling glassware. Judy Markwick's unfussy but professional approach ensures that diners are warmly welcomed and put instantly at ease. The repertoire doesn't appear to change much, still offering provençale fish soup, and roast squab pigeon, but the kitchen takes advantage of the best that markets and local suppliers can come up with. Ingredients (some organic) are of the highest quality, from a thick fillet of baked turbot to a pink, juicy rack of lamb divided into chops.

Although reports tell us that incongruous accompaniments and heavy-handed seasoning have taken the shine off some meals, successes have included risotto (of wild mushrooms, and of mussel and saffron), pan-fried calf's liver, and beef fillet with black peppercorn sauce. Desserts run to rhubarb trifle with elderflower sorbet, and a warm ginger and molasses spice cake with mascarpone cream. The admirable wine policy keeps prices low to encourage experimentation. An appealing selection of house wines, mostly under £15, kicks off a global list that includes great wines and famous producers. Bin-ends are well worth leafing through at the end.

CHEF: Stephen Markwick PROPRIETORS: Stephen and Judy Markwick OPEN: Mon to Fri L 12 to 2, Mon to Sat D 7 to 10 CLOSED: 1 week Christmas, 1 week Easter, 2 weeks Aug, bank hols MEALS: alc (main courses £15.50 to £17.50). Set L £14.50 (2 courses) to £17.50, Set D £25 SERVICE: not inc, card slips closed CARDS: Amex, Delta, Diners, MasterCard, Switch, Visa DETAILS: 45 seats. Private parties: 10 main room, 4 to 20 private rooms. Children's helpings. No pipes in dining room. No music

Quartier Vert

85 Whiteladies Road, Bristol BS8 2NT — COOKING **4**
TEL: (0117) 973 4482 FAX: (0117) 974 3913 — MEDITERRANEAN
£25–£47

It is at the same location as Rocinantes (in last year's Guide), and with the same owners, though there has been a change of name, perhaps more accurately reflecting the organic credentials and neighbourhood appeal, as well as a new direction. Expanded and renovated premises are now also home to a bar and café, as well as a bakery, cookery school and outside catering business. In the restaurant, meanwhile, the Mediterranean and provincial European style of food continues. Regular items such as provençale fish soup, and paella for two (when available), share the billing with supplì and pesto, Cornish crab bruschetta, and sausages (Toulouse or wild boar) with cabbage and gravy.

Balanced menus tend to favour fish and vegetables – tomato and bread soup, or brill with oyster mushrooms, broad beans and tarragon – while desserts run from raspberry crème brûlée to an armagnac parfait with prunes in an Earl Grey tea syrup. Six organic wines feature among the 18-strong house selection, which includes stylish bottles from France, Italy, Spain and California, all available by the glass, 50cl carafe or bottle (prices starting at £2.15, £8 and £10.25 respectively). The rest of the list is equally varied: try Spain's fashionable Albariño from Martin Codax at £17.95.

CHEF/PROPRIETOR: Barny Haughton OPEN: restaurant all week L 12 to 3, Mon to Sat D 6 to 10.30; bar/café Mon to Sat 9.30am to 11pm, Sun 10 to 4 CLOSED: 1 week Christmas MEALS: alc (main courses £10 to £16.50). Set L £11.50 (2 courses) to £13.95. Bar/café meals available SERVICE: not inc, 10% for parties of 5 or more CARDS: Amex, Delta, MasterCard, Switch, Visa DETAILS: 80 seats. 25 seats outside. Private parties: 50 main room, 25 private room. Vegetarian meals. Children's helpings. Music

River Station

The Grove, Bristol BS1 4RB — COOKING **4**
TEL: (0117) 914 4434 FAX: (0117) 934 9990 — MODERN BRITISH-PLUS
WEB SITE: www.riverstation.co.uk — £22–£47

The dockside setting may be reminiscent of riverside renovations in London, but cosmopolitan River Station has its own pace and style. A downstairs café and deli opens early for coffee and cake, while the upstairs dining room, with a big glass frontage and few straight lines, closes late. Whatever the option – set lunch, early-evening one-plate meals with a drink, weekend brunch or the carte – the food goes in for modern ideas that are skilfully interpreted: scallops with coriander noodles and black bean dressing, goats' cheese and marjoram soufflé with aubergine confit, or dandelion and smoked eel salad with lardons and poached egg.

Dishes are kept simple, and fashionable ingredients used wisely – truffle oil drizzled on sage polenta with stickily roasted butternut squash – while refreshingly plain presentation takes in a wedge of Parmesan and onion tart, served with a handful of well-dressed salad leaves. Desserts have a penchant for gooey things: for example maple and pecan pudding with butterscotch sauce. Service has varied between 'apathetic' and 'genuinely interested', while wines are on the ball and fairly priced: ten house wines start at £9.75.

CHEFS: Peter Taylor and Simon Green PROPRIETORS: Shirley-Anne Bell, Mark Hall, John Payne and Peter Taylor OPEN: all week 12 (10.30 Sat) to 2.30, 6 to 10.30 (11 Fri and Sat, 9 Sun) CLOSED: Christmas MEALS: alc (main courses £9.50 to £14). Set L Mon to Sat £11.50 (2 courses) to £15, Set L Sun £12.95 (2 courses) to £15, Set D Fri to Sun before 7.15 £7 (1 course inc wine) SERVICE: not inc, 10% for parties of 8 or more CARDS: Delta, Diners, MasterCard, Switch, Visa DETAILS: 120 seats. 32 seats outside. Private parties: 120 main room. Vegetarian meals. Children's helpings. No-smoking area. No music

denotes an outstanding wine cellar; *denotes a good wine list, worth travelling for.*

Not inc *in the details at the end of an entry indicates that no service charge is made and any tipping is at the discretion of the customer.*

Severnshed

NEW ENTRY

The Grove, Harbourside, Bristol BS1 4RB
TEL: (0117) 925 1212 FAX: (0117) 925 1214
EMAIL: info@severnshed.co.uk
WEB SITE: www.severnshed.co.uk

COOKING **3**
MODERN MIDDLE EASTERN
£20–£38

Formerly a boathouse, once the river police's HQ, this aptly named huge barn of a building is bang up to date in terms of décor, style and cuisine. A stone floor, timbered roof, much chrome and stainless steel, and blue-grey-green colours set the tone, while a central bar separates café from restaurant. A sign outside proclaims 'modern middle eastern organic food' to be the kitchen's business, confirmed by a menu that takes in salads (including cracked wheat and flatbread variations), grilled vegetables, wood-roast cod, partridge or duck, sliced tongue with Judion beans, and organic lamb tajine.

The cooking divides reporters. Even at a single inspection meal standards varied widely, the high points being a skewer of tender marinated monkfish and giant prawns on a refreshing salad with a mint and yoghurt sauce, and a thick, grilled, flavour-packed organic pork chop, served with olive oil mash and bright green spicy zhug relish. Some desserts can also be first rate, judging by a mocha and cinnamon ice cream, and a crumbly pastry tart of juicy figs with flaked almonds and rum. Service is willing and friendly, and as well as beers and cocktails there is a short, appealing selection of wines – some organic, some available in several sizes – starting with house Vin de Pays du Gers at £8.95.

CHEF: Raviv Hadad PROPRIETORS: Matthew Pruen, Peter Meacock and Patrick Dempsey OPEN: restaurant Mon to Sat breakfast 8 to 11 (10 to 12 Sat), L 12.30 to 2.30, D 7 to 10.30, Sun brunch 10am to 10.30pm; café Mon to Sat noon (10 Sat) to 1am, Sun 10am to 10.30pm CLOSED: 24 to 26 Dec MEALS: alc (main courses £8.50 to £15). Set L £10.50 (2 courses) to £12.50. Café menu available SERVICE: not inc, 10% for parties of 6 or more CARDS: Amex, Delta, MasterCard, Switch, Visa DETAILS: 180 seats. 70 seats outside. Car park. Vegetarian meals. No smoking in dining room. Wheelchair access (also WC). No music. Air-conditioned

BRITWELL SALOME Oxfordshire **map 2**

The Goose

Britwell Salome OX9 5LG
TEL: (01491) 612304 FAX: (01491) 614822
on the B4009, just outside Watlington, 5 minutes drive from M40 junction 6

COOKING **4**
ENGLISH
£31–£49

Locals treat this pub restaurant sensibly, popping in for a quick two courses mid week, without feeling the need to dress up for the occasion. Walls are hung with enough locally produced pictures to sink an art gallery, and extras are conspicuous by their absence, helping to keep prices down and focus the kitchen's attention on essentials. Indeed, simplicity is a feature: three items per course on both the lunchtime carte and the set-price dinner, perhaps starting with parsnip soup, or a lightly grilled goats'-cheese salad (with a rasher of burnt bacon at one meal) on a bed of interesting leaves with a subtle vinaigrette.

Local materials (including garden produce) feature prominently, in flavourful roast lamb, for example, served with a cake of roast vegetables and morel sauce. Combinations may not always be well judged, but when technical skills and sound ideas come together they can produce excellence, as in an inspector's fresh and warm rhubarb cake with 'silkily creamy' rhubarb ice cream. At its best, service is characterised by 'lots of smiles, help and cheerfulness', and a short wine list offers fair choice under £20 plus around ten wines by the glass.

CHEFS: Chris Barber and Michael North PROPRIETORS: Chris and Kate Barber OPEN: Tue to Sun L 12 to 2, Tue to Sat D 7 to 9 CLOSED: first 2 weeks Jan MEALS: alc L Tue to Sat (main courses £12 to £17). Set L Tue to Sat £10, Set L Sun and Set D £20 (2 courses) to £25. Bar snacks available Tue to Sat L SERVICE: not inc CARDS: Delta, MasterCard, Switch, Visa DETAILS: 42 seats. 20 seats outside. Private parties: 32 main room. Car park. Children's helpings. No smoking in dining room. Wheelchair access (not WC). Music (£5)

BROADHEMBURY Devon **map 2**

Drewe Arms

Broadhembury EX14 0NF — COOKING **3**
TEL: (01404) 841267 FAX: (01404) 841765 — SEAFOOD
off A373, between Cullompton and Honiton — £33–£50

This prosperous-looking fifteenth-century pub with 'loads of atmosphere' carefully avoids the horse brasses and beer mats image, although food is still ordered off blackboards. It specialises in seafood, briefly described, and much of it – crab, langoustines, red mullet, sea bass – comes straightforwardly with pesto, hollandaise or herb butter, served thermidor-style, in a salad, or 'just plain plain'. Indeed, the simplicity of treatments is a positive bonus, helped by often admirable raw materials and generally accurate timing: an inspector's warm salmon salad, for example, coated in thin, creamy, home-made mayonnaise.

A few open sandwiches (gravlax or marinated herring) and token meat dishes (venison tenderloin or beef fillet) extend the choice, and desserts spring few surprises: bread-and-butter pudding comes with whisky sauce, and hazelnut parfait is richly creamy and generous in quantity. Nigel Burge runs a tight ship and keeps a keen eye on proceedings. Wines are mostly under £30, including five house wines under £12.

CHEFS: Nigel, Andrew and Kerstin Burge PROPRIETORS: Nigel and Kerstin Burge OPEN: all week L 12 to 2, Mon to Sat D 7 to 9.30 CLOSED: 25 and 31 Dec, Mon D Oct to Mar MEALS: alc (main courses £15.50). Set L and D £23 SERVICE: not inc CARDS: none DETAILS: 40 seats. 40 seats outside. Private parties: 22 main room. Car park. Children's helpings. No smoking in dining room. Wheelchair access (also WC). No music

'A disturbing smell of burnt bread wafts up from the kitchen at regular intervals, and when our bread eventually arrived we saw why. . . . When I pointed this out to the waiter he said, "Ah, the bread is crispy; if it is burnt then it is not a great tragedy," and flounced off.' (On eating in London)

BROADWAY Worcestershire **map 5**

▲ Dormy House

Willersey Hill, Broadway WR12 7LF
TEL: (01386) 852711 FAX: (01386) 858636 COOKING **5**
EMAIL: reservations@dormyhouse.co.uk MODERN EUROPEAN-PLUS
just off A44, 1m NW of Broadway £29–£65

On a steep wooded hillside above Broadway, overlooking the Vale of Evesham, this seventeenth-century farmhouse is not short of twenty-first-century appointments. As well as oak beams and mellow stone walls, there are conference facilities, and a large mock-medieval wall-hanging in the comfortable conservatory dining room that calls itself the Tapestries Restaurant. Despite country-house gestures, from mid-meal sorbet to lengthy menus (there are three separate ones at dinner: set-price, carte and 'gourmet' option), Alan Cutler's smooth-running kitchen is a cut above the norm.

Upmarket materials lay the foundation – scallops, Cornish turbot, loin of English lamb – but dishes rely as much on ingenuity as on luxuries, as individual variations are applied to tried and trusted themes. Smoked Barbary duckling, for example, comes with an apple and blackberry compote, and chicken breast (paired with tiger prawns) is served on cardamom rice with a spring onion sauce. The food's aim is to soothe, not challenge; a goal that desserts take particularly seriously, with caramelised lemon curd, chestnut mousse on dark chocolate wafers, and a trio of crème brûlée (vanilla, apple and cinnamon). Service can be a little sleepy. The extensive wine list has considerably more to offer above the £20 mark than below. French wines dominate, though there are some interesting New World alternatives. House vin de pays is £12.50 for white, £14.50 for red.

CHEF: Alan Cutler PROPRIETOR: Jorgen Philip-Sorensen OPEN: Sun to Fri L 12.30 to 2, all week D 7 to 9.30 (9 Sun) CLOSED: 24 to 26 Dec MEALS: alc (main courses L £8 to £11.50, D £16.50 to £21). Set L Sun £19.50, Set D £31.50 to £35 SERVICE: not inc CARDS: Amex, Delta, Diners, MasterCard, Switch, Visa DETAILS: 80 seats. Private parties: 40 main room, 8, 14 private rooms. Car park. Vegetarian meals. Children's helpings. No children under 6 at D. No smoking in 1 dining room. Occasional music. Air-conditioned ACCOMMODATION: 48 rooms, all with bath/shower. TV. Phone. B&B £73 to £174. Rooms for disabled. Baby facilities (*The Which? Hotel Guide*)

▲ Lygon Arms

Broadway WR12 7DU
TEL: (01386) 852255 FAX: (01386) 854470 COOKING **5**
EMAIL: info@the-lygon-arms.co.uk MODERN BRITISH
WEB SITE: www.savoy-group.co.uk £37–£82

If the Cotswolds represent an idealised view of the English countryside, and Broadway is a rose-tinted spectacle of a village, then the romantic stone-built Lygon Arms, with its barrel-vaulted dining room and minstrels' gallery, is ideally placed at the heart of all this. Since 1999 the carte has disappeared, leaving just a set-price menu at lunch and dinner. The former tends towards a brasserie style, taking in vegetable spring rolls, crab and coriander cakes, and red mullet with saffron mash and salsa, while dinner is where the kitchen's energy and resources are concentrated. Among the offerings might be braised sea bass served in a coriander and lemon grass broth with spinach dumplings, or cannon of Cotswold venison with aubergine caviar and plum chutney mille-feuille.

This being part of the Savoy Group, a few luxuries are to be expected – perhaps wild mushroom risotto with sauté foie gras and asparagus, or seared scallops with langoustine tortellini – but these are well complemented by a few plainly prepared traditional items, such as fillet steak, calf's liver and bacon, or grilled Dover sole. Most desserts aim straight for the comfort zone, with a version of Black Forest gâteau, or hot treacle soufflé with chocolate sauce. Rooted in classical French regions, the extensive wine list includes many impressive bottles, but there is little under £20, and hefty mark-ups appear across the spectrum. House wines from the south of France are £15.50 a bottle.

CHEF: Graeme Nesbitt PROPRIETOR: Savoy Group OPEN: all week 12.30 to 2.15, 7.30 to 9.15 (10 Fri and Sat) MEALS: Set L Mon to Sat £22.50, Set L Sun £25, Set D £39.50 SERVICE: not inc, card slips closed CARDS: Amex, Delta, Diners, MasterCard, Switch, Visa DETAILS: 90 seats. 40 seats outside. Private parties: 90 main room, 12 to 70 private rooms. Car park. Vegetarian meals. Children's helpings. No children under 8. No smoking in dining room. Wheelchair access (also WC). No music ACCOMMODATION: 65 rooms, all with bath/shower. TV. Phone. B&B £110 to £250. Rooms for disabled. Baby facilities. Swimming pool (*The Which? Hotel Guide*)

BROCKENHURST Hampshire **map 2**

Simply Poussin 

The Courtyard, Brookley Road,
Brockenhurst SO42 7RB
TEL: (01590) 623063 FAX: (01590) 623144
EMAIL: sales@simplypoussin.co.uk
WEB SITE: www.simplypoussin.co.uk

COOKING **3**
MODERN BRITISH
£28–£46

Alex and Caroline Aitken have moved to Parkhill Hotel (see entry, Lyndhurst), leaving the running of the re-named, new-look premises to son Justin, and the cooking to former sous chef Angus Hyne. Bare wooden tables help to make it feel more casual, and the menu is lighter, briefer, and less expensive. Among dishes that have survived the change are well-executed soufflés from twice-baked cheese to passion fruit, and a main course of three meats (beef, lamb and pork) in a red wine sauce.

Fish options have included a generous starter of five grilled species served with salsa, and well-timed brill with crisply fried wild mushrooms and truffled butter. Slow-cooked dishes generally benefit from their dose of alcohol – boneless saddle of rabbit braised in port-like Banyuls, and ham hock poached in cider, served with mustard mash – although over-seasoning has upset the balance of some dishes. If the soufflé doesn't appeal for dessert, try the banana brûlée with matching parfait, or perhaps a warm tutti frutti tart. A short list of fair value wines under £20, supplemented by a few posher ones on a separate sheet, starts with house Spanish white at £11.50 and Italian red at £12.50.

CHEF: Angus Hyne PROPRIETOR: Le Poussin Ltd OPEN: Tue to Sat 12 to 2, 7 to 10 CLOSED: 25 to 26 Dec, 1 Jan MEALS: Set L £10.50 (2 courses) to £16, Set D £19.50 (2 courses) to £25 SERVICE: not inc CARDS: Amex, Delta, MasterCard, Switch, Visa DETAILS: 35 seats. 6 seats outside. Private parties: 30 main room. Car park. No smoking in dining room. Music

BROMSGROVE Worcestershire map 5

▲ Grafton Manor

Grafton Lane, Bromsgrove B61 7HA
TEL: (01527) 579007 FAX: (01527) 575221
EMAIL: steven@grafman.u-net.com
WEB SITE: www.graftonmanorhotel.co.uk
off B4091, 1½m SW of Bromsgrove

COOKING **4**
MODERN INDIAN/EUROPEAN
£31–£53

Commissioned by the Earl of Shrewsbury in 1567 and largely rebuilt in the early eighteenth century, the distinctive L-shaped red-brick building sports Elizabethan-style chimneys, a private sandstone chapel (wedding parties are not uncommon), and tall mullioned windows. An Indian theme runs gently through the menu, with Bombay prawns, or lamb cooked in yoghurt and roast spices, bringing variety to meals that largely deal in more European dishes, such as goats'-cheese mousse with confit tomatoes, or sea bass with caponata.

The food can appear 'routine country house' in style, with more ingredients than are strictly necessary in a dish, but impressive technical skills are brought to bear: in a butter sauce to accompany three big seared scallops sitting on soft leek purée, and in a 'positively huge' quantity of well-timed, crisp-skinned, roast Barbary duck breast with a host of accompanying vegetables. The more confident Indian approach has produced a simple and effective dessert: two flat, round, salty, deep-fried poori, making the best of the textural contrast with their subtly spiced filling of apple, sultanas and raisins. Service has left something to be desired on more than one occasion, including an inspection. Eight house wines under £15 head up a sound list.

CHEFS: Simon Morris and William Henderson PROPRIETORS: the Morris family OPEN: Mon to Fri and Sun L 12 to 1.30, all week D 7 to 9.30 CLOSED: bank hols MEALS: Set L Mon to Fri £20.50, Set L Sun £18.50, Set D £27.85 to £32.95 SERVICE: not inc, card slips closed CARDS: Amex, Delta, Diners, MasterCard, Switch, Visa DETAILS: 60 seats. Private parties: 60 main room, 60 private room. Car park. Children's helpings. No smoking in dining room. Wheelchair access (also male WC). No music ACCOMMODATION: 9 rooms, all with bath/shower. TV. Phone. B&B £85 to £150. Rooms for disabled. Fishing (*The Which? Hotel Guide*)

BRUTON Somerset map 2

Truffles

95 High Street, Bruton BA10 0AR
TEL/FAX: (01749) 812255

COOKING **5**
MODERN BRITISH
£24–£40

After a brief closure for refurbishment, Truffles has emerged in new garb. The dark green décor has been replaced by navy blue, terracotta and cream in what is now an open-plan interior over two levels. The food remains consistently good, according to reporters, who appreciate Martin Bottrill's flair, imagination and confident handling of prime materials, much of it British, some of it organic. A global approach takes in anything from black bean salsa (with duck rillettes) via lemon-grass sauce (with a mille-feuille of king prawns and asparagus) to a composite dish of pigeon breast served with ceps, apple, spicy chorizo and red cabbage.

The kitchen's accomplishments include 'crunchy, creamy, zingy' spring rolls filled with feta, spinach and pine nuts, and a 'visually enchanting' lemon parfait with a winter fruit compote. Otherwise there might be pear and almond tart with a chocolate and armagnac ice cream, or hot ginger pudding with a spicy red wine sauce. Service is charming, and Denise Bottrill is singled out for her help with wines. A house selection of seven keenly priced bottles, from £10.95, kicks off the list, which has a good selection of halves.

CHEF: Martin Bottrill PROPRIETORS: Denise and Martin Bottrill OPEN: Sun L 12 to 2, Tue to Sat D 7 to 10 CLOSED: 2 weeks Feb, 1 week Oct MEALS: Set L £13.95, Set D Tue to Thur £13.95 (2 courses) to £22.95, Set D Fri and Sat £22.95 SERVICE: not inc, card slips closed CARDS: Delta, MasterCard, Switch, Visa DETAILS: 28 seats. Private parties: 22 main room. Vegetarian meals. Children's helpings. No children under 8. No smoking while others eat. Wheelchair access (not WC). No music. Air-conditioned (£5)

BUCKLAND Gloucestershire **map 5**

▲ Buckland Manor

Buckland WR12 7LY
TEL: (01386) 852626 FAX: (01386) 853557
EMAIL: buckland-manor-uk@msn.com
WEB SITE: www.relaischateaux.fr/buckland
off B4632, 2m SW of Broadway

COOKING **5**
MODERN EUROPEAN
£40–£83

A short distance from the thirteenth-century church, this honey-coloured stone manor house feels quite intimate for its size. White-painted wooden panelling, polished floors, tapestries and rugs set the tone, along with plenty of easy chairs, and log fires that are replenished as regularly as the mineral water. A lot of work goes on in the kitchen, and results can appear rather fussy: there is a mid-meal sorbet in addition to nibbles, appetisers and petits fours, and main courses can be complex assemblies involving stuffings and layerings. But prime materials are at the heart of it, and the cooking is technically sound. Indeed, the food impresses mostly for its sheer competence, as in a starter of smooth, poached seafood boudin on a potato salad, topped with impeccably fresh scallops and langoustine, surrounded by a trickle of sharp vinaigrette.

Thought is given to the composition of each dish, and vegetables are an integral part of main courses, just as ice creams are of desserts: a honey-flavoured malted version has accompanied a fine, wobbling banana soufflé. The numerous staff are well-trained, courteous and professional. While reporters generally find it expensive (at these prices, service could easily be included), most are happy to pay up in view of the quality. More than 600 bottles and 173 halves constitute a hefty list, featuring quality wines from France, the rest of Europe and the New World. Were money no object, this list would be a dream. As it is, careful scouring reveals only a handful under £20. House wines start at £14.90.

CHEF: Kenneth Wilson PROPRIETORS: Roy and Daphne Vaughan OPEN: all week 12.30 to 1.45, 7.30 to 9 MEALS: alc D (main courses £22.50 to £28.50). Set L £28.50. Light L available Mon to Sat SERVICE: not inc CARDS: Amex, Delta, Diners, MasterCard, Switch, Visa DETAILS: 40 seats. 20 seats outside. Private parties: 40 main room. Car park. Vegetarian meals. No children under 8. Jacket and tie. No smoking in dining room. Wheelchair access (not WC). No music ACCOMMODATION: 13 rooms, all with bath/shower. TV. Phone. B&B £205 to £355. Rooms for disabled. No children under 12. Swimming pool (*The Which? Hotel Guide*)

BUCKLAND Oxfordshire map 2

▲ Lamb at Buckland £

Lamb Lane, Buckland SN7 8QN COOKING **2**
TEL: (01367) 870484 FAX: (01367) 870675 BRITISH
£23–£55

At his golden-stone Cotswolds pub, Paul Barnard never veers from his philosophy of combining high-quality raw materials with spot-on timing, to produce generous servings of simple, traditional dishes. Whether in the civilised, uncluttered bar, with its sheep theme, or the classy, low-ceilinged dining room, the menu is identical. Home in on kedgeree, or half a dozen fat scallops on a crisp salad as a prelude to baked lemon sole stuffed with crab, or roast rack of lamb with sorrel, mint and a well-made stock-based sauce. Well-timed vegetables are fresh, copious and plainly cooked. The nursery dominates the pudding stage, with junket, meringues, various rice puddings and ices, even warm poached dates. Service is pleasant and relaxed 'without being in the least familiar', and half a dozen decent house wines, from £9.95 a bottle, £1.85 a glass, are worth a look before you turn back to the main list.

CHEF: Paul Barnard PROPRIETORS: Paul and Peta Barnard OPEN: all week 12 to 2 (3 Sun), 6.30 to 9.30 MEALS: alc (main courses £6.50 to £18). Set L Sun £20.50 SERVICE: not inc, card slips closed CARDS: Amex, Delta, MasterCard, Switch, Visa DETAILS: 65 seats. 45 seats outside. Private parties: 18 private room. Car park. Vegetarian meals. Children's helpings. No smoking in dining room. Music ACCOMMODATION: 4 rooms, all with bath/shower. TV. Phone. B&B £40 to £56 (£5)

BURNHAM MARKET Norfolk map 6

Fishes'

Market Place, Burnham Market PE31 8HE COOKING **3**
TEL: (01328) 738588 FAX: (01328) 730534 SEAFOOD
£21–£46

Set in a north Norfolk village that draws the tourists, Fishes' is easily picked out by its blue and white frontage. There are newspapers, books and magazines in the sitting room, and cork-topped tables in the dining room, where Brancaster oysters and mussels share the billing with dressed local crab and potted brown shrimps. Ray Maddox joined the kitchen early in 2000, in order to do 'the majority of the cooking under my interference', according to Gillian Cape, who started here herself in 1973.

But 'nothing much changes', according to a recent visitor, confirming the continuation of a simple, informal and straightforward style with a classic take on most seafood dishes: skate wing with capers and black butter, or halibut with hollandaise, for example. An invitation to order multiple starters, or larger portions as a main course, is both welcome and sensible. Desserts are as simply conceived as the rest, with iced nougat terrine or rhubarb meringue pie among them. Children are welcome, particularly if they are prepared to eat small portions of what is on the menu and are happy to do it sitting down. A good-value wine list features a quintet from the Chablisienne Co-op and starts with house Côtes de Duras white at £9.

CHEF/PROPRIETOR: Gillian Cape OPEN: Tue to Sun L 12 to 2 (2.15 Sun), Tue to Sat D 6.45 to 9.30 (9 weekdays in winter) CLOSED: 4 days Christmas, 3 weeks Jan MEALS: alc (main courses £8 to £13.50). Set L weekdays £13.50, Set L weekends £15 SERVICE: not inc, card slips closed CARDS: Amex, Delta, Diners, MasterCard, Switch, Visa DETAILS: 42 seats. Private parties: 14 main room. Children's helpings. No children under 5 after 8.30. No smoking in dining room. Wheelchair access (not WC). No music (£5)

▲ Hoste Arms £ **NEW ENTRY**

The Green, Burnham Market PE31 8HD
TEL: (01328) 738777 FAX: (01328) 730103
EMAIL: thehostearms@compuserve.com — COOKING **3**
WEB SITE: www.hostearms.co.uk — MODERN EUROPEAN/PACIFIC RIM
on B1155, 5m W of Wells — £23–£48

Despite its three dining areas, this refurbished seventeenth-century inn is often heaving with customers. Local and North Sea ingredients constitute the kitchen's bedrock, taking in dressed Cromer crab, steamed mussels with white wine and cream, and oysters with shallot red wine vinegar. The varied style of cooking derives in part from Andrew McPherson's training in Australia, where Chinese, Thai and Japanese flavours find a second home: tempura king prawns, a fricassee of mixed seafood (including well-timed queen scallops, halibut, tuna and salmon) in a Thai-style coconut curry, or salmon and chilli fishcakes served with sweet-salt spinach, lemon and keta.

Other cultures are not ignored, nor is meat. One meal, for example, turned up accurately timed beef fillet with horseradish cream, and pink best-end of tasty lamb with minted mash. Desserts may be less exciting, but have included perfectly good cinnamon poached pear with vanilla-flavoured rice pudding, and triangles of 'squidgy dark chocolate' embedded with pistachios, almonds and walnuts. Staff cope well with numbers, and a varied selection of wines, from humble to blue-blooded, starts with a user-friendly short list that includes southern French house wine at £9.75.

CHEF: Andrew McPherson PROPRIETOR: Paul Whittome OPEN: all week 12 to 2, 7 to 9 (9.30 Fri) MEALS: alc (main courses £7 to £15) SERVICE: not inc CARDS: Delta, MasterCard, Switch, Visa DETAILS: 140 seats. 65 seats outside. Private parties: 50 main room, 16 to 20 private rooms. Car park. Vegetarian meals. No smoking in 1 dining room. Wheelchair access (also WC). Occasional music. Air-conditioned ACCOMMODATION: 28 rooms, all with bath/shower. TV. Phone. B&B £64 to £120. Rooms for disabled (*The Which? Hotel Guide*)

BURNSALL North Yorkshire map 8

▲ Devonshire Fell

NEW ENTRY

Burnsall BD23 6BT
TEL: (01756) 729000 FAX: (01756) 729009
EMAIL: reservations@thedevonshirefell.co.uk
WEB SITE: www.devonshirefell.co.uk
on B6160, 4m N of Skipton

COOKING **3**
MODERN BRITISH
£29–£45

This classy Dales hotel was originally built as a club for gentlemen mill owners, and is now under the same ownership as the Devonshire Arms in nearby Bolton Abbey (see entry). Behind the grey façade, cool blues and greens set a bright fresh tone, and meals can be eaten in either the bistro or conservatory. Michael Ward cooks modern English food, using touchstone ingredients of smoked haddock, goats' cheese, wild boar sausage, even pickled pear. Grills include fine ribeye steak, gammon loin and lamb rump, and there are fresh fish and crustacea of the day. A large free-range pork chop with a thick, crisp layer of crackling, served with sweetish apple purée, was a success at inspection. To finish there may be sponge pudding with custard, or white chocolate tart with raspberry coulis and raspberry sorbet. Service is willing but formal, with wine being whisked away as soon as a glass is poured. A global, 90-strong wine list opens with a selection of 12, all at £15.95 (or £2.80 a glass). The rest of the list is a quality collection, but offers little under £20 and plenty above £30. House Spanish is £10.95.

CHEF: Michael Ward PROPRIETORS: The Duke and Duchess of Devonshire OPEN: all week 12 to 2.30, 6.30 to 10 MEALS: alc (main courses £9.50 to £13). L snacks available SERVICE: not inc, card slips closed CARDS: Amex, Delta, Diners, MasterCard, Switch, Visa DETAILS: 65 seats. Private parties: 80 main room, 80 private room. Car park. Vegetarian meals. No smoking in dining room. Wheelchair access (also WC). Music ACCOMMODATION: 41 rooms, all with bath/shower. TV. Phone. B&B £115 to £350. Baby facilities (*The Which? Hotel Guide*)

BURRINGTON Devon map 1

▲ Northcote Manor

Burrington EX37 9LZ
TEL: (01769) 560501 FAX: (01769) 560770
EMAIL: rest@northcotemanor.co.uk
WEB SITE: www.northcotemanor.co.uk
on A377 between Umberleigh and Crediton, 4m NW of Chulmleigh

COOKING **3**
MODERN BRITISH
£35–£54

'This is a place to come to unwind,' concluded one visitor, and indeed the attractive old hall, built in 1716, prides itself on peace and quiet. High-backed chairs and bold, historically themed murals (in which the present owners appear in period costume) decorate the dining room, and service is provided by a small, friendly and dedicated team. Dinner is set-price only, with around four choices per course, and Chris Dawson's country-house style of food embraces truffled parsley soup, goujons of Dover sole with a cauliflower fondue, and roast rump of West Country lamb with Puy lentils, Savoy cabbage and rösti potato. Scallops and red mullet are also likely to turn up, showing a penchant for top-of-the-range materials, as well as a tartlet of veal sweetbreads with baby vegetables and mushroom duxelles in a Sauternes sauce. Finish maybe with hot chocolate fondant, and drink from a wide-ranging wine list with plenty on offer under £20. Half a dozen house wines are around £12 to £14.

CHEF: Chris Dawson PROPRIETOR: David Boddy OPEN: all week L (by arrangement only) 12 to 1.30, D 7 to 9 MEALS: Set L £25.50, Set D £32.50. Light L available SERVICE: not inc, card slips closed CARDS: Amex, Delta, Diners, MasterCard, Switch, Visa DETAILS: 40 seats. Private parties: 40 main room, 12 private room. Car park. Vegetarian meals. Children's helpings. No smoking in dining room. Music ACCOMMODATION: 11 rooms, all with bath/shower. TV. Phone. D,B&B £80 to £250. Baby facilities (*The Which? Hotel Guide*) (£5)

BURTON ON THE WOLDS Leicestershire **map 5**

Langs

Horse Leys Farm, 147 Melton Road, COOKING **3**
Burton on the Wolds LE12 5TQ MODERN EUROPEAN
TEL/FAX: (01509) 880980 £22–£45

Just outside the village, Langs inhabits a comfortably converted typical Wolds farm building. The lounge and dining room have been extended, the latter now sporting rag-rolled yellow walls, starched linen cloths, and a manageable menu that roams from cream of mushroom soup with sorrel and chicken to Cajun-spiced tiger prawns. Successful salads have included one of smoked salmon and caper berries, and one of kidneys and sweetbreads. Saucing tends to be as straightforward as it is effective: Madeira glaze with beef fillet, and highly-rated lobster sauce with halibut. Lunchers get a good deal: typically lamb noisettes with sauté potatoes followed by nutmeggy crème brûlée or peach in a lime sabayon. Service is informed and efficient. French house wines on the mainly French list are £11.95.

CHEF: Gordon Lang PROPRIETORS: Gordon Lang and Paul Simms OPEN: Tue to Fri and Sun L 12.15 to 2.15 (3 Sun), Tue to Sat D 7.25 to 9.30 (10 Sat) CLOSED: 2 weeks in winter MEALS: alc Tue to Fri L, Tue to Sat D (main courses £12 to £15.50). Set L Tue to Fri £12 (2 courses), Set L Sun £13 SERVICE: not inc, card slips closed CARDS: Delta, MasterCard, Switch, Visa DETAILS: 50 seats. 8 seats outside. Private parties: 60 main room, 12 private room. Car park. Vegetarian meals. Children's helpings. No smoking in dining room. Wheelchair access (also WC)

BURY ST EDMUNDS Suffolk **map 6**

Maison Bleue at Mortimer's

30/31 Churchgate Street, COOKING **2**
Bury St Edmunds IP33 1RG FRENCH
TEL: (01284) 760623 FAX: (01284) 761611 £24–£50

Fulfilling a need in these parts, Maison Bleue was compared by one reader to the sorts of places he enjoys finding in Paris. Indeed, the tone is as French as the name, from 'splendidly professional service' to the 'glorious fish soup' praised by another. Fixed-price menus are reckoned seriously good value for their respectful approach to fish dishes such as grilled tuna with béarnaise, salmon with tagliatelle carbonara, or fillet of lemon sole on a curry sauce. Fried sardines might start a meal, accompanied by a tomato and shallot salad dressed with thyme. Puddings tend not to be mentioned in despatches, but there may be chocolate mousse or lemon tart. Well-chosen wines open with a French house selection from £9.50 (£1.70 a glass).

CHEF: Pascal Canevet PROPRIETOR: Régis Crepy OPEN: Mon to Sat 12 to 2.30, 6.30 to 9.30 (10 Fri and Sat) CLOSED: 3 weeks Jan MEALS: alc (main courses £9 to £17.50). Set L £6.95 (1 course) to £14.95, Set D Mon to Fri £18.95. Snack L available SERVICE: not inc CARDS: Amex, Delta, MasterCard, Switch, Visa DETAILS: 75 seats. Private parties: 36 main room, 16 to 36 private rooms. Vegetarian meals. Children's helpings. No smoking in dining room. Wheelchair access (not WC). Music

BUSHEY Hertfordshire **map 3**

St James

NEW ENTRY

30 High Street, Bushey WD2 3DN
TEL: (020) 8950 2480

COOKING **2**
MODERN EUROPEAN
£28–£58

The ecclesiastical theme extends beyond the name (the parish church is visible through the big picture window) to halos on plates and menus. But this is neither twee nor quirky, rather a welcome find on London's northern fringe, a thoroughly modern, light, airy and well-designed restaurant deploying wood and rustic brick to good effect, giving it a bistro-like feel, but with tablecloths. Printed menus supplemented by blackboard specials offer standards of the repertoire – chicken liver parfait with red onion marmalade, or salmon fishcakes with lemon butter sauce – alongside a modern version of fish and chips: squid and plaice in a crispy beer batter, with a fresh salsa and punchy tartare sauce.

Other successes have included a starter of warm goats' cheese melting over soft red peppers, aubergines and courgettes, sandwiched between two light, crisp layers of pastry. Desserts are not a highlight, although Toblerone cheesecake sounds worth a punt. Staff are young, friendly, helpful and prompt. While the wine list includes some reasonably priced and well-annotated bottles from around the world, the layout puts the more expensive bottles up front. House Italian, however, is an affordable £11.95.

CHEF: Simon Trussel PROPRIETORS: Alfonso La Cava and Simon Trussel OPEN: Mon to Sat 12 to 2, 6.30 to 9.30 CLOSED: bank hols MEALS: alc (main courses £14 to £17). Set L £12.95 (2 courses), Set D Mon to Fri £13.50 (2 courses) to £17.95 SERVICE: 10%, card slips closed CARDS: Amex, Delta, MasterCard, Switch, Visa DETAILS: 96 seats. Private parties: 60 main room, 45 private room. Vegetarian meals. Children's helpings. No smoking in dining room. Wheelchair access (also WC). Music. Air-conditioned

'For this price [£1.95 for a cup of tea-bag tea] I would have expected the finest rare tea, rushed daily from the foothills of their own plantation, the tea lovingly stripped from the bush in a ceremony at the table.' (On eating in London)

Although the cuisine style noted at the top of entries has in most cases been suggested to the Guide by the restaurants, some have been edited for brevity or appropriateness.

CAMBRIDGE Cambridgeshire **map 6**

Midsummer House

Midsummer Common, Cambridge CB4 1HA
TEL: (01223) 369299 FAX: (01223) 302672

COOKING **5**
FRENCH/MEDITERRANEAN
£32–£76

Ring for directions or a map to save time hunting for this detached grey-stone Victorian villa located between the Cam and the common (complete with grazing cows). A conservatory dining room 'the size of an average house' overlooks a small garden, and the pastel fabrics, bright, modern paintings and crisp white linen strike reporters as stylish. The food is ambitious and sophisticated, as the menuspeak makes clear with 'roast saddle of French rabbit, risotto of tarragon, baby artichokes, étuvée of celery, jus of moutarde de Meaux'. Such complexity is not always easy to handle, and although the cooking can achieve greater heights than the score would suggest, it does not do so consistently, having disappointed some reporters.

When it works, however, it delivers some fine dishes: discs of seared scallop arranged in a circle, each topped with a thin slice of black truffle and drizzled with truffle vinaigrette, and roast rump of spring lamb accompanied by a colourful array of Mediterranean vegetables. Desserts proved the highlight of an inspection meal, producing a feather-light pistachio soufflé with matching ice cream, dark chocolate fondant with cardamom ice cream, and an intensely flavoured caramelised lemon tart with lime sorbet and honey sauce. Presentation is attractive, extras are impressive, and the set lunch is fairly priced. Service is professional, smart, formal and attentive, and the heftily priced wines are rescued for ordinary mortals by the inclusion of a house selection under £20 and over a dozen wines by the glass.

CHEF: Daniel Clifford PROPRIETOR: Russell Morgan OPEN: Tue to Fri and Sun L 12 to 2, Tue to Sat D 7 to 10 MEALS: Set L Tue to Fri £14.50 (2 courses) to £18.50, Set L Sun £27.50, Set D £39.50 SERVICE: not inc CARDS: Amex, Delta, MasterCard, Switch, Visa DETAILS: 50 seats. 10 seats outside. Private parties: 50 main room, 6 to 16 private rooms. Vegetarian meals. Children's helpings. Wheelchair access (not WC). No music (£5)

22 Chesterton Road 🍷

22 Chesterton Road, Cambridge CB4 3AX
TEL: (01223) 351880 FAX: (01223) 323814

COOKING **4**
MODERN EUROPEAN
£33–£48

Part of an unremarkable Victorian terrace not far from the Cam and city centre, 22 is small and intimate, with a pink and green dining room that is tasteful in a 'safe' kind of way. Open just five sessions a week, it operates a monthly-changing, three-course set-price menu, with an optional extra fish course for a £6 supplement: crab and salmon raviolo, perhaps, or steamed mussels with coconut juice, ginger and lemon grass. Borrowing freely from Italy, menus seek to entice rather than challenge, offering rabbit and mushroom tortellini, sardine bruschetta, and spinach gnocchi with tomato sauce.

Presentation and flavours live up to expectation: one reporter's cannon of lamb with couscous, in a truffle-scented stock packed with peas, broad beans and tomato, 'tasted every bit as good as it looked'. Puddings – chocolate and Grand Marnier parfait, or strawberry tart and ice cream – appear not to be the strongest suit. Good-value drinking is a priority, and a balanced selection of wines includes sound offerings from France and some fine pickings from Spain, Italy and the New World. Adventurous palates are rewarded with a separate list of bin-ends. House wines start at £9.75.

CHEFS: Ian Reinhardt and Martin Cullum PROPRIETOR: David Carter OPEN: Tue to Sat D only 7 to 9.45 CLOSED: 1 week Christmas MEALS: Set D £23.50 SERVICE: not inc CARDS: Amex, Delta, Diners, MasterCard, Switch, Visa DETAILS: 40 seats. Private parties: 26 main room, 12 private room. Vegetarian meals. No children under 10. No smoking while others eat. Occasional music. Air-conditioned

CAMPSEA ASHE Suffolk **map 6**

▲ Old Rectory

NEW ENTRY

Campsea Ashe IP13 0PU
TEL/FAX: (01728) 746524
on B1078, 1½m E of A12

COOKING **2**
ANGLO-FRENCH
£27–£38

This creeper-clad former rectory became a restaurant in the early 1980s and is still run by Stewart Bassett to the same formula as ever of a no-choice dinner menu. Standards appear to have wavered in recent years, but an inspector found the place back on song, commending a fillet of sea bass sandwiched between two discs of feather-light puff pastry with creamy spinach mousse, followed by a North African-style stew of spiced lamb with apricots, dates and almonds. Others have praised lobster bisque, lamb en croûte, and chicken in a creamy mushroom sauce. Dessert may be raspberry shortcake, and good English and French cheeses are an optional extra. Mr Bassett has acquired a lot of wine over the years, and the burgeoning list of mature clarets and Burgundies will provide happy hunting for high rollers, though prices start at a modest £9.50.

CHEF/PROPRIETOR: Stewart Bassett OPEN: Mon to Sat D only 7.30 to 8.45 CLOSED: 1 week Christmas, 3 weeks March MEALS: Set D £19.80 SERVICE: not inc CARDS: Amex, Diners, MasterCard, Visa DETAILS: 50 seats. Private parties: 36 main room, 18 to 30 private rooms. Car park. Vegetarian meals. Children's helpings. No smoking in dining room. Wheelchair access (not WC). No music. Air-conditioned ACCOMMODATION: 7 rooms, all with bath/shower. B&B £40 to £75 (*The Which? Hotel Guide*)

CARLISLE Cumbria **map 10**

Magenta's

CUMBRIA NEWCOMER OF THE YEAR

NEW ENTRY

18 Fisher Street, Carlisle CA3 8RH
TEL/FAX: (01228) 546363

COOKING **4**
MODERN ENGLISH/MEDITERRANEAN
£29–£43

Down an alley off a cobbled street, Magenta's is part of a renaissance taking place in the cathedral and castle area of Carlisle. Dark wooden herringbone floor tiles, pink-upholstered chairs, and the eponymous colour itself in a stencilled diamond motif on lime-green walls provide an attractive setting for brothers

Paul and Chris Taylor's modern menu. This has brought starters of tasty pea soup with mint oil and Greek yoghurt, and a moist filo pastry sandwich layered with smoked trout, tomato salsa and sour cream. Accurate timing and dramatic colours characterised an inspector's main course of pan-fried salmon with peas and green beans.

'Boy, are they keen on puddings!' commented a reporter who enjoyed an assiette of five, including a 'light and melty' chocolate sponge tower, and an intensely flavoured glazed apple tart made with fine pastry. Incidentals run from stimulating appetiser soups to fine petits fours. Service is 'attentive but never fussy'. Wines (red and white) are listed by weight, the reasonable choice covering a global range, and mark-ups are fixed, not a percentage, so 'you do not have to be a lottery winner to get a decent bottle of wine'. Four house selections are £12.95.

CHEFS: Paul and Chris Taylor PROPRIETORS: Alison Watkin, and Paul and Chris Taylor OPEN: Mon to Sat D only 7 to 9.30 CLOSED: bank hols MEALS: alc (main courses £12.50 to £14). Set D £18 SERVICE: not inc CARDS: Delta, MasterCard, Switch, Visa DETAILS: 32 seats. Private parties: 16 main room. No smoking in dining room. Music (£5)

CARLTON-IN-COVERDALE North Yorkshire **map 9**

▲ Foresters Arms

Carlton-in-Coverdale DL8 4BB — COOKING **3**
TEL/FAX: (01969) 640272 — SEAFOOD
off A684, 5m SW of Leyburn — £29–£62

The setting of this stone-built Dales pub is apparently 'everything anyone could wish for', with fine views, a small river running 'just where it should', flagstone floors, beams, log fires and lots of old wood. The bar deals in cask-conditioned ales and a blackboard menu, and although the comfortable dining room is marginally more formal, this does seem an odd place to find domes being lifted. Fish is the forte on a long menu that necessarily changes with supplies, taking in smoked haddock and mussel chowder, monkfish cheeks on lemon risotto, and sole fillets with a wild mushroom tart.

What the cooking may lack in accuracy (of timing, for example) it makes up for in generosity and enthusiasm – demonstrated in an inspector's sea bass with chargrilled king prawns and herb tagliatelle – while desserts have included lemon and almond tart, and firm crème brûlée. Cheeses sometimes include local Coverdale. Wines include a useful choice from Old and New Worlds, with most under £20 and a good selection by the glass; house wines start at £10.50.

CHEF/PROPRIETOR: B.K. Higginbotham OPEN: Wed to Sun L 12 to 2, Tue to Sat D 7 to 9.30 CLOSED: 3 weeks Jan MEALS: alc (main courses L £6 to £10.50, D £10 to £18; prices on menus exclude VAT) SERVICE: not inc, card slips closed CARDS: Delta, MasterCard, Switch, Visa DETAILS: 30 seats. 20 seats outside. Private parties: 30 main room, 12 to 20 private rooms. Car park. Children's helpings. No children under 12 at D. No smoking in 1 dining room. Occasional music ACCOMMODATION: 3 rooms, all with bath/shower. TV. B&B £40 to £75 plus VAT (*The Which? Hotel Guide*)

CARTERWAY HEADS Northumberland map 10

▲ Manor House Inn £

Carterway Heads, Shotley Bridge DH8 9LX
TEL/FAX: (01207) 255268
on A68, 3m W of Consett

COOKING 1
MODERN BRITISH
£18–£30

Damaged by fire as the last edition of the Guide was in preparation, this old stone farmhouse near the Derwent Reservoir with Pennine views has been tastefully refurbished. Considered an 'eater's pub', it serves the same extensive blackboard menu in both bar and dining room (where a vast array of jugs hangs from the ceiling), offering anything from marinated mushroom tikka masala to locally smoked kippers, from 'juicy' king prawns in Szechuan sauce to Cumberland sausage and mash with mustard sauce. Finish with a slice of soft chocolate truffle cake or bread-and-butter pudding, and drink from a chatty list of around 50 wines. House wine is £8.65.

CHEF: Peter Tiplady PROPRIETORS: Chris and Moira Brown OPEN: all week 12 to 2.30, 7 to 9.30 CLOSED: D 25 Dec MEALS: alc (main courses £6 to £11) SERVICE: not inc, card slips closed CARDS: Amex, MasterCard, Switch, Visa DETAILS: 58 seats. 24 seats outside. Private parties: 50 main room. Car park. Vegetarian meals. Children's helpings. No smoking in dining room. Wheelchair access (not WC). No music ACCOMMODATION: 4 rooms, all with bath/shower. TV. B&B £33 to £55 (£5)

CARTMEL Cumbria map 8

▲ Aynsome Manor

Cartmel LA11 6HH
TEL: (015395) 36653 FAX: (015395) 36016
EMAIL: info@aynsomemanor.co.uk
off A590, ½m N of village

NEW CHEF
ENGLISH COUNTRY HOUSE
£20–£36

In 2001 the Varleys clock up 20 years at their elegant Georgian 'all-round' hotel and restaurant, and apart from a bit of redecoration here and there things continue pretty much as before. Except for one thing: two new chefs arrived just as the Guide was going to press. Nicholas Stopford and Andy Duff (who has worked at Borrowdale Gates, see entry, Grange in Borrowdale) look set to continue the format, however. Dinner can be anything from three to five courses: perhaps starting with smoked venison and wild mushroom risotto, followed by wild seabass in shellfish velouté. The sweets trolley remains a fixture, and a rejigged wine list contains just short of 100 bottles from all over, many under £20. Reports particularly welcome.

CHEFS: Nicholas Stopford and Andy Duff PROPRIETORS: Tony and Margaret Varley, and Chris and Andrea Varley OPEN: Sun L 1 (1 sitting), Mon to Sat D 7 to 8.30 (residents only Sun D) CLOSED: 2 to 26 Jan MEALS: Set L £12.75, Set D £17 to £21 SERVICE: not inc, card slips closed CARDS: Amex, Delta, MasterCard, Switch, Visa DETAILS: 30 seats. Private parties: 30 main room. Car park. Vegetarian meals. Children's helpings. No children under 5 at dinner. No smoking in dining room. No music ACCOMMODATION: 12 rooms, all with bath/shower. TV. Phone. D,B&B £58 to £120. Baby facilities (£5)

▲ Uplands

Haggs Lane, Cartmel LA11 6HD
TEL: (015395) 36248 FAX: (015395) 36848
EMAIL: uplands@kencomp.net
2½m SW of A590, 1m up road opposite Pig and Whistle

COOKING **4**
BRITISH
£23–£44

Little changes at this smart cream and brown house to the north of Morecambe Bay. The lounge is bright and fresh, with a forest of identical table lamps, the dining room small enough to feel intimate yet big enough not to feel cramped. The hot malty loaf with a tureen of soup (Jerusalem artichoke, perhaps, or broccoli and Stilton) is an institution, and the alternative starter is generous enough to be a meal on its own: maybe a simple salad of white and brown crabmeat, or shelled Morecambe Bay shrimps tossed in lightly curried mayonnaise with avocado, mango, melon and lime.

The style is not slick or cosmopolitan, more 'a simple country affair' using some fine ingredients (game from Holker Estate, for example) often presented traditionally: three thick medallions of venison with redcurrant and juniper sauce for one visitor. Fish, the other main-course choice, has ranged from Windermere brown trout to baked lemon sole fillet with lemon chive butter. Desserts can be as straightforward as slices of fig doused in Pernod on a mound of crème fraîche, or a raspberry, strawberry and passion-fruit pavlova. Around 40 fairly priced wines start with five house wines at £10.70.

CHEF: Tom Peter PROPRIETORS: Tom and Diana Peter OPEN: Thur to Sun L 12.30 for 1 (1 sitting), Tue to Sun D 7.30 for 8 (1 sitting) MEALS: Set L £15.50, Set D £28 SERVICE: not inc, card slips closed CARDS: Amex, Delta, MasterCard, Switch, Visa DETAILS: 28 seats. Private parties: 20 main room. Car park. No children under 8. No smoking in dining room. Wheelchair access (also WC). No music ACCOMMODATION: 5 rooms, all with bath/shower. TV. Phone. D,B&B £66 to £152. No children under 8 (*The Which? Hotel Guide*) (£5)

CASTLE COMBE Wiltshire **map 2**

▲ Manor House, Bybrook Restaurant

Castle Combe SN14 7HR
TEL: (01249) 782206 FAX: (01249) 782159
EMAIL: enquiries@manor-house.co.uk
WEB SITE: www.manor-house.co.uk
on B4039, 3M NW of junction with A420

COOKING **4**
ENGLISH
£31–£71

With its mullioned windows and formal Italianate gardens, one might be forgiven for mistaking this fourteenth-century Cotswold-stone house for a National Trust property. It is the same story inside, with wood panelling and carving, a ceiling frieze and a great stone fireplace, although obliging, courteous and relaxed staff dispel the formal feel. An ambitious kitchen goes through all the country-house gestures, including a sorbet between courses, but generally avoids excessive complexity. Instead it impresses with skilful technique, producing for example a starter of scallops, spinach and smoked salmon, fashioned into a sausage and served on a bed of mash in a pool of lemon oil.

Prime raw materials have included a saddle of rabbit whose flavour stood up to its robust accompaniments of pancetta and creamy wild mushroom risotto. The menu's 'classical section' perennially includes chateaubriand and crêpes suzette. British and Irish cheeses are available as an extra course, or instead of desserts such as banana parfait served with lightly battered banana fritters, roasted nuts and chocolate sauce. Wines, with a heavy leaning towards France, are numerous and pricey. A dozen house selections start with white Bergerac and a red Vin de Pays d'Oc at £17.95.

CHEF: Mark Taylor PROPRIETOR: Manor House Hotel Ltd OPEN: all week 12 to 2, 7 to 9 (9.30 weekends) MEALS: Set L £16.95 (2 courses) to £18.95, Set D Sun to Thur £35, Set D Fri and Sat £45. Light meals available SERVICE: not inc, card slips closed CARDS: Amex, Diners, MasterCard, Switch, Visa DETAILS: 105 seats. 20 seats outside. Private parties: 105 main room, 12 to 30 private rooms. Car park. Vegetarian meals. Children's helpings. No smoking in dining room. Wheelchair access (also WC). No music ACCOMMODATION: 45 rooms, all with bath/shower. TV. Phone. Room only £120 to £350. Rooms for disabled. Baby facilities. Swimming pool. Fishing (*The Which? Hotel Guide*)

CHADDESLEY CORBETT Worcestershire **map 5**

▲ Brockencote Hall

Chaddesley Corbett DY10 4PY
TEL: (01562) 777876 FAX: (01562) 777872
EMAIL: info@brockencotehall.com
WEB SITE: www.brockencotehall.com
on A448, Kidderminster to Bromsgrove road, just outside village

COOKING **4**
FRENCH
£32–£71

Sweeping up the long, imposing drive through open parkland to the Hall transported one visitor into a BBC period drama; perhaps something by Flaubert, since the building itself looks rather like a French château. The conservatory dining room is draped in tented fabric, 'giving the impression of sitting inside a huge turban', but despite the unusual look of the place, front-of-house operations are attentive to a fault and old-school formal. Didier Philipot cooks a defiantly Gallic menu (using fine English produce), including a signature starter of Hereford snails and frogs' legs with a potato and garlic pancake and parsley cream.

Artichoke mousse served with a roughly chopped mix of feta and black olives offered one diner a successful blend of contrasting flavours, while a main course of tuna – seared with a sesame-seed crust on one side, almost raw on the other – was well partnered with a light, carefully seasoned lemon risotto. Alcohol features in several dishes, including Izarra (a Basque herbal liqueur) used to flavour an ice cream to partner chocolate pastilla. An extensive wine list caters well for those who don't mind paying three-figure sums for mature claret, though seven house selections start at £12.80.

Restaurateurs justifiably resent no-shows. If you quote a credit card number when booking, you may be liable for the restaurant's lost profit margin if you don't turn up. Always phone to cancel.

CHEF: Didier Philipot PROPRIETORS: Joseph and Alison Petitjean OPEN: Sun to Fri L 12 to 1.30, all week D 7 to 9.30 CLOSED: 1 Jan MEALS: alc (main courses £13.50 to £22.50). Set L £22.50, Set D £27.50. Light L available SERVICE: not inc, card slips closed CARDS: Amex, Delta, Diners, MasterCard, Switch, Visa DETAILS: 50 seats. Private parties: 48 main room, 12 to 32 private rooms. Car park. Vegetarian meals. Children's helpings. No smoking in dining room. Wheelchair access (also WC). No music ACCOMMODATION: 17 rooms, all with bath/shower. TV. Phone. B&B £110 to £170. Rooms for disabled. Baby facilities (*The Which? Hotel Guide*) (£5)

CHAGFORD Devon **map 1**

▲ Gidleigh Park

Chagford TQ13 8HH
TEL: (01647) 432367 FAX: (01647) 432574
EMAIL: gidleighpark@gidleigh.co.uk
WEB SITE: www.gidleigh.com
from Chagford Square turn right at Lloyds Bank into Mill Street, take right fork after 150 yards, follow lane for 1½m

COOKING **8**
MODERN EUROPEAN
£45–£96

Gidleigh's lush country-house look is built around fine antiques, oak panelling and skilfully colour-co-ordinated fabrics, the whole infused with the soothing smell of wood smoke and the sound of ticking clocks. Although Michael Caines has taken time out to set up his own restaurant (Royal Clarence, Exeter; see entry), consistent standards point to solid teamwork in the kitchen. He is a confident, ambitious chef who excels at complex and intricate dishes that are rehearsed to near perfection. Soups are a good barometer, the balance between lightness of texture and intensity of flavour carefully handled: in a simple but meaty and powerful crab bisque, or in a Jerusalem artichoke and truffle soup that was 'like drinking satin'.

Many flavour combinations are unsurprising – a fennel purée to accompany red mullet with olives and tomato – although multiple flavours in a single dish are the norm: saddle of venison, for example, is served with braised pork belly and lettuce, roast figs and chestnut purée. Pigeon appears to be a favourite with reporters, whether in an expertly executed first-course pithiviers, accompanied by a truffle and wild mushroom mousse, or as pink slices arranged in a tight sphere ('rather like a Terry's chocolate orange') on a potato galette, a little pan-fried foie gras crowning the pigeon, all resting in a pool of rich Madeira sauce.

Regional cheeses are kept in good condition, though it is difficult to resist the appeal of hot pistachio soufflé with matching ice cream, mille-feuille of crème brûlée with caramelised pears, or hot apple tart with vanilla ice cream. This is one of a small handful of country-house hotels where all departments work together agreeably and effectively, the food matched by first-rate service under the management of Catherine Endacott. Wine is one of Paul Henderson's great enthusiasms, and the list encourages diners to pay for quality by ensuring that the more expensive the wine, the lower the mark-up as a proportion of the price. France is honoured thoroughly, although excellent Italian and Californian sections exert a strong pull. If in doubt, starred recommendations are worth heeding. Eight wines are available by the glass, ranging from £5 to £11.

CHEF: Michael Caines PROPRIETORS: Kay and Paul Henderson OPEN: all week 12.30 to 2, 7 to 9 MEALS: Set L Mon to Thur £24 (2 courses) to £32, Set L Fri to Sun £30 (2 courses) to £38, Set D £62.50 to £67.50. Light L available SERVICE: net prices, card slips closed CARDS: Delta, Diners, MasterCard, Switch, Visa DETAILS: 40 seats. Private parties: 30 main room. Car park. Children's helpings. No children under 7. No smoking in dining room. Wheelchair access (not WC). No music ACCOMMODATION: 15 rooms, all with bath/shower. TV. Phone. D,B&B £250 to £500. Baby facilities. Fishing

▲ 22 Mill Street

22 Mill Street, Chagford TQ13 8AW
TEL: (01647) 432244 FAX: (01647) 433101

COOKING **6**
MODERN EUROPEAN
£29–£54

Looking a bit like a tea room, just off the village square, the compact restaurant consists of a small reception area housing a tiny bar and a large golden retriever, and two dining rooms: one with big windows looking out on to the street, the other a back room next to the wine store. It runs on dedication, charm and integrity: 'most villages in England would kill for a place of this standard'. Duncan Walker's relatively short menus seem to evolve slowly, typically taking in prime ingredients such as sauté scallops in a consommé flavoured with coriander and ginger, but he is not averse to grilled saddle of rabbit either. Classical techniques and European flavourings are the foundation, often given an individual identity: in pea and mint soup with sauté foie gras for example.

While some reports indicate that flavours may not thrill quite so much as they did, Duncan Walker can still turn out some fine dishes, from an intense appetiser soup of parsnip with truffle oil, to top-quality pink grilled venison with béarnaise, from a warm lemon-grass-infused salad of lobster sandwiched between two small poppadoms, to a light and beautifully balanced prune and armagnac soufflé. Service from Amanda Leaman is highly professional as well as being friendly and helpful, and all-round good value is helped by an intelligently chosen, 40-plus wine list. House Italian white is £14.50, Californian red £14.25.

CHEF: Duncan Walker PROPRIETORS: Amanda Leaman and Duncan Walker OPEN: Wed to Sat L 12.30 to 1.45, Mon to Sat D 7.30 to 9 CLOSED: 2 weeks Jan MEALS: Set L £14.95 (2 courses) to £16.95, Set D £24.50 (2 courses) to £30 SERVICE: not inc, card slips closed CARDS: Delta, MasterCard, Switch, Visa DETAILS: 30 seats. Private parties: 10 main room, 10 private room. No children under 14. No smoking in dining room. Wheelchair access (not WC). No music ACCOMMODATION: 2 rooms, both with bath/shower. TV. B&B £35 to £45

CHEESDEN Greater Manchester **map 8**

Nutters

Edenfield Road, Cheesden OL12 7TY
TEL/FAX: (01706) 650167
WEB SITE: www.biteit.net/nutter

COOKING **6**
MODERN BRITISH
£27–£47

'Not just a meal but an adventure' promises the menu, and followers of *Ready Steady Cook* will certainly not have missed the thrill-a-minute antics of Andrew Nutter. His restaurant now has a conservatory extension, which adds an airier feel to what was previously a rather pubby atmosphere, and the polished service has much improved of late. Furthermore, if you were expecting food that startles for the sake of it, think again. There is a real sense of culinary intelligence at work here, so that even the more novel pairings seem to come off. A starter of warm pheasant salad with Puy lentils and a sweet ginger dressing is a clever composition of textures and flavours, and a crust of dill and Parmesan on a fillet of undyed smoked haddock also works well, as does its accompanying chilled spring onion 'sabayon'.

Coating fish is clearly a favoured procedure, working equally well in sesame-crusted salmon with couscous and coriander butter sauce. Imaginative technique is also evident with meats: stir-fried lettuce is used to top a fillet of beef that comes with a smoked bacon and blue cheese gratin. Re-inventions continue into desserts of banana tarte Tatin with honey and mascarpone cream, or lemon curd cheesecake with crisp baklava fritters. Australian house wines, at £10.80, head up a list that majors on clarets and Burgundies at fairly reasonable prices, especially in Spain and the New World.

CHEF: Andrew Nutter PROPRIETORS: Rodney, Jean and Andrew Nutter OPEN: Wed to Mon 12 to 2 (4.30 Sun), 7 (6.45 Fri, 6.30 Sat and Sun) to 9.30 CLOSED: first 2 weeks Aug MEALS: alc (main courses £10 to £16.50). Set L Sun £19.95, Set D £29.95 SERVICE: not inc CARDS: Amex, Delta, MasterCard, Switch, Visa DETAILS: 82 seats. Private parties: 50 main room, 40 private room. Car park. Children's helpings. No smoking in dining room. Wheelchair access (also WC). Music

CHELTENHAM Gloucestershire **map 5**

Le Champignon Sauvage 🍷

24–26 Suffolk Road, Cheltenham GL50 2AQ
TEL: (01242) 573449 FAX: (01242) 254365

COOKING **7**
FRENCH
£29–£69

Everything runs smoothly in this small, smart restaurant offering 'surely one of the greatest bargains in fine dining to be had the in the country': given the set-price menus there is no excuse for anybody not to visit. Examine one of these on a big sofa in the comfortable bar lounge, then transfer to a fresh and relaxing dining room done in buttercup yellow and royal blue, with bright, lively paintings and immaculately laid tables. David Everitt-Matthias cooks an imaginative and personal version of modern European food, ranging from a pressed terrine of guinea fowl and pear with a dollop of rich quince chutney, via eel tortellini with watercress cream, to skate wing with a pearl barley and squid risotto.

The food is characterised by vivid and intense flavours, and freshness can be 'startling', be it a piece of roast cod, or three small, thick, rare lamb steaks inspiringly paired with a macaroni and cauliflower dumpling. A starter of braised shredded beef stuffed into paper-thin cylinders of white radish, accompanied by choucroute and caramelised carrots in a sweetish jus, was so original and successful that it kept an inspector busy thinking about it for days afterwards. Desserts, meanwhile, run the gamut from a feuillantine of mango with Thai-spiced cream, to a slice of nearly black, powerful-tasting, thick-textured chocolate tart on thin pastry, accompanied by a scoop of coriander and sultana ice cream: 'another great dish'.

Service from Helen Everitt-Matthias is warm, personal, friendly, cheerful and 'absolutely correct in every detail'. Wines on the compact list hail mainly from France and include some fine clarets and Burgundies, though a few New World bottles are slipped in towards the end. Mark-ups are fair, with house wines starting at £10.50.

CHEF: David Everitt-Matthias PROPRIETORS: David and Helen Everitt-Matthias OPEN: Tue to Sat 12.30 to 1.30, 7.30 to 9 MEALS: Set L Tue to Fri £14.50 (2 courses, inc wine), Set L Tue to Sat £16.50 (2 courses) to £18.50, Set D Tue to Fri £19.95, Set D Tue to Sat £32 to £44 SERVICE: not inc CARDS: Amex, Diners, MasterCard, Switch, Visa DETAILS: 28 seats. Private parties: 24 main room. No smoking at D before 10. Wheelchair access (not WC). No music (£5)

Mayflower

32–34 Clarence Street, Cheltenham GL50 3NX
TEL: (01242) 522426 FAX: (01242) 251667

COOKING **1**
CHINESE
£15–£62

Caring service, and a décor of dusky pinks and blues with Chinese wallpaper, paintings and scrolls, combine to create a warm, welcoming ambience at this long-established restaurant. Over 200 à la carte dishes steer clear of the more outlandish (for most Western tastes) ingredients found in metropolitan Chinatowns. Supplementing the Cantonese repertoire are some Szechuan dishes, such as deep-fried crispy lamb, accompanied, like the more usual aromatic duck, by thin rice-flour pancakes, cucumber, spring onions and hoisin sauce. Flavours are well judged – in tender Szechuan squid, or stir-fried sliced roast duck with vegetables – while set menus rise to a seafood feast, with Cantonese lobster and noodles preceding main dishes of fish, scallops and prawn. A list of around 60 wines opens with house vins de pays at £9.50 and features a good selection of reasonably priced champagne and other sparkling wines.

CHEFS: C.F. Kong and M.M. Kong PROPRIETORS: the Kong family OPEN: Mon to Sat L 12 to 1.45, all week D 6 to 10 (10.30 Fri and Sat, 9 Sun) CLOSED: 24 to 26 Dec MEALS: alc (main courses £5.50 to £12). Set L £6.95, Set D £19.50 SERVICE: not inc CARDS: Amex, Delta, Diners, MasterCard, Switch, Visa DETAILS: 120 seats. Private parties: 80 main room, 40 private room. Vegetarian meals. Music. Air-conditioned (£5)

Le Petit Blanc

The Queens Hotel, The Promenade,
Cheltenham GL50 1NN
TEL: (01242) 266800 FAX: (01242) 266801

COOKING **4**
MODERN EUROPEAN
£24–£46

Occupying the ground floor of a grand hotel, Petit Blanc is smart, bold and colourful, with mirrors, brushed steel-topped tables, and a clientele that runs from businessmen to babies. The style of food, as at branches in Oxford and Birmingham (see entries), is centrally determined – orthodox French provincial with modern British input – and the menu sticks to what it knows well: only the set price menus change with any regularity. Fine raw materials have made a success of, for example, salmon confit on cauliflower purée, and a deep-fried filo pillow of goats' cheese and tapénade, sitting on green beans and tomato chutney.

Accurate timing and accomplished stock-based sauces are applied to main courses such as gamey braised guinea-fowl legs, and a plate of breadcrumbed calf's liver topped with onions in a well-judged lime-flavoured sauce. Desserts may not be quite as interesting as savoury courses, but feature quite a few ice creams: vanilla accompanies a wedge of dense chocolate feuillantine. Prices are generally fair, although bread (which comes with olive oil and tapénade for dipping) and vegetables are charged extra. Dapper young staff keep everything under control, and three dozen wines are more or less evenly balanced around the £20 fulcrum.

CHEF: Phillip Alcock PROPRIETOR: Blanc Restaurants Ltd OPEN: all week 12 to 3, 6 to 10.30 (10 Sun) CLOSED: 25 Dec, 1 Jan MEALS: alc (main courses £8 to £14.50). Set L and D £12.50 (2 courses) to £15 SERVICE: not inc, 10% for parties of 8 or more CARDS: Amex, Delta, Diners, MasterCard, Switch, Visa DETAILS: 155 seats. 25 seats outside. Private parties: 80 private room. Vegetarian meals. Children's helpings. No smoking in dining room. Wheelchair access (not WC). Music. Air-conditioned (£5)

CHESTER Cheshire map 7

▲ Chester Grosvenor Hotel, Arkle 🍷

Eastgate, Chester CH1 1LT
TEL: (01244) 324024 FAX: (01244) 313246 COOKING **6**
EMAIL: marketing@chestergrosvenor.co.uk TRADITIONAL EUROPEAN
WEB SITE: www.chestergrosvenor.co.uk £35–£72

The posh setting is very 'gentleman's club', with a book-lined lounge (referred to as the Library), and a dining room whose large skylight brightens the dark red and green fabrics. It is a place to come not so much for warmth and informality as for 'routine extravagance and luxury'. The food certainly piles them on, whether as raw material – a meal might start with a pavé of foie gras and progress to John Dory with poached oysters and caviar – or in the form of strenuously worked extras. A fish saveloy thus becomes a bit player in a starter of grilled Scottish lobster with a cassoulet of cannellini beans, for example, and pasta features in a few dishes, perhaps as mushroom tortellini to partner turbot.

The cooking is skilful, accomplished and clever, and as complex as one might expect in a swish hotel: a 'composition' of beef, for example, combining a crépinette of oxtail, plus braised shin, and fillet, accompanied by a cep purée. The busy kitchen takes a similar approach to desserts, producing three tastings of bitter chocolate, and a chilled mandarin curd served with granita and a hot soufflé. Professionally baked bread typically appears in a dozen guises, and although service may not live up to the food, a serious wine list includes top names from Burgundy and Bordeaux plus many New World legends, including 18 vintages of the Mondavi-Rothschild co-operative venture, Opus One. There is good drinking to be had under £20, though this is mainly in the half-bottle section. Two house wines – a French Sauvignon Blanc and a Chilean Cabernet Sauvignon – cost £12.75.

(£5) *indicates that the restaurant has elected to participate in the* Good Food Guide *voucher scheme. For full details, see page 6.*

CHEF: Simon Radley PROPRIETOR: Grosvenor Estate Holdings OPEN: Tue to Sat 12 to 2.30, 7 to 9.30 CLOSED: 25 Dec to 22 Jan (exc 31 Dec), 3rd week Aug MEALS: Set L £25, Set D £45, Set L and D £40 (2 courses) to £48. Bar menu available SERVICE: not inc CARDS: Amex, Delta, Diners, MasterCard, Switch, Visa DETAILS: 40 seats. Private parties: 22 main room. Vegetarian meals. Children's helpings. No smoking while others eat. No cigars/pipes in dining room. Wheelchair access (also WC). Music. Air-conditioned ACCOMMODATION: 85 rooms, all with bath/shower. TV. Phone. Room only £130 to £230 (exc VAT). Rooms for disabled. Baby facilities

CHINNOR Oxfordshire **map 2**

Sir Charles Napier

Sprigg's Alley, nr Chinnor OX9 4BX
TEL: (01494) 483011 FAX: (01494) 485311
exit 6 from M40; at Chinnor roundabout turn right, continue straight up hill; Sprigg's Alley signposted after 1m

COOKING **4**
MODERN ANGLO-FRENCH
£37–£56

A single track with passing places leads to Julie Griffiths's restaurant, set in a large garden with huge terracotta pots and sculptures. Its leisurely 'down-at-heel' charm derives from unmatched tables and chairs, a log fire, and a host of quirky oddments and accessories, while a patio and garden offer the chance of al fresco eating. Bright-sounding handwritten menus deliver coconut and lime soup, or scallops with truffle polenta to start, while a combination of notably fresh materials and accurate timing have made the best of crispy oriental salmon with mildly spiced noodles, and a thick slice of pink rump of lamb in a tasty rosemary jus.

Generous portions may put a stop on desserts for some, but light date pudding with a toffee sauce delighted one visitor, or there might be caramel soufflé. Staff are 'pleasant, relaxed and smiley'. An unpretentious though extensive wine list offers an intelligent selection of some of the finest wines and producers from around the world, at reasonable prices. First-growth clarets are absent 'because of the price they command' (says the wine list), although the restaurant is happy to source them for a special occasion. House wines start at £12.50.

CHEF: José Cau PROPRIETOR: Julie Griffiths OPEN: Tue to Sun L 12 to 2.30 (3.30 Sun), Tue to Sat D 7 to 10 CLOSED: 25 and 26 Dec MEALS: alc (main courses £13.50 to £17). Set L Tue to Sat £15.50 (2 courses), Set D Tue to Fri £15.50 (2 courses) SERVICE: 12.5% (optional), card slips closed CARDS: Amex, Delta, Diners, MasterCard, Switch, Visa DETAILS: 70 seats. 70 seats outside. Private parties: 40 main room. Car park. Vegetarian meals. No children under 7 at D. No smoking in 1 dining room. Wheelchair access (not WC). Music. Air-conditioned

Subscribers to Which? Online can access The Good Food Guide *on www.which.net.*

The Good Food Guide *is a registered trade mark of Which? Ltd.*

The cuisine styles noted at the tops of entries are only an approximation, often suggested to us by the restaurants themselves. Please read the entry itself to find out more about the cooking style.

CHIPPING NORTON Oxfordshire map 2

Chavignol 🍷 ✱

7 Horsefair, Chipping Norton OX7 5AL
TEL: (01608) 644490 FAX: (01608) 646794
EMAIL: chavignol@virginbiz.com
WEB SITE: www.chavignol.co.uk

COOKING **7**
MODERN EUROPEAN
£35–£72

Natural stone, brick and stripped wood combine with muslin drapes and good lighting to produce a bright, uncomplicated effect at this Cotswold hot spot. Small, higgledy-piggledy rooms and low ceilings give away the building's age, while pale lemon walls and dark blue tablecloths confirm its serious orientation. The menu appears not to change much but deals in stimulating and original ideas – some modern, some classic – that are 'well-nigh perfectly executed'. Its complexity has a point, and everything is artistically presented. One starter, for example, combines roughly shredded skate with ratatouille and grain mustard in a layered timbale, which is topped with a skate beignet and surrounded by a fine vinaigrette containing chopped herbs and fresh young capers.

Quality and freshness of raw materials are a match for any, although richness and portion size make this no place for the faint-hearted: as an inspector discovered with a pink roast, crisp-skinned, beautifully textured Barbary duck breast. What made this interesting as well as good to eat were the well-tuned accompaniments: a tower of celeriac fondant surmounted by pea purée and a slice of foie gras; first-class rösti potato; and a big pool of well-reduced sauce incorporating lentils and bacon. Texture combinations constitute a significant part of the delight, evident for example in a tall, fat cylinder of iced banana and pistachio parfait coated in glassy praline, wreathed in poached plum slices spiced with cinnamon, in turn surrounded by groups of walnuts, almonds and pistachios.

Incidentals – and there are many – merely serve to confirm the kitchen's talents, while smooth, professional yet relaxed service is welcoming, affable and contributes to a sense of occasion. A flowery wine list strewn with vinous poems and quotes fails to disguise some hefty mark-ups, but with careful selection there are several good bottles to be had for around £20. Classical French regions predominate, although European and New World wines are of a high standard. There are plenty of half-bottles, and 20 wines are available by the glass, priced between £4.50 and £9.50.

CHEF: Marcus Ashenford PROPRIETORS: Mark and Donna Maguire OPEN: Tue to Sat 12 to 2, 7 to 10 MEALS: Set L £25, Set D £30 (2 courses) to £48 SERVICE: not inc CARDS: Amex, Delta, MasterCard, Switch, Visa DETAILS: 28 seats. Private parties: 24 main room, 8 private room. Vegetarian meals. Children's helpings. No smoking in dining room. No music (£5)

Several sharp operators have tried to extort money from restaurateurs on the promise of an entry in a guidebook that has never appeared. The Good Food Guide *makes no charge for inclusion.*

All entries, including Round-ups, are fully indexed at the back of the Guide.

CHOBHAM Surrey — map 3

Quails

1 Bagshot Road, Chobham GU24 8BP
TEL/FAX: (01276) 858491

COOKING **3**
MODERN BRITISH-PLUS
£20–£50

Subdued décor which 'probably looks better at night' did not restrain the enthusiasm of a pair of lunchers who were charmingly served with grilled sardines, and crab and goats'-cheese tart, followed by marinated fillet steak with ginger and shallots, and quails wrapped in ham with wild mushrooms. The fixed price deal offers three balanced choices per course. This modern British cooking exhibits striking French, Italian and Asian influences in such starters as wild mushroom spring roll with sweet chilli and wasabi; and dolcelatte and pancetta risotto. Equally appealing main dishes might include sea bass steamed over pastis with another risotto and bouillabaisse sauce. Desserts, on the other hand, embrace more mainstream ideas, from a chunky marmalade bread-and-butter pudding to fig and almond tart with mascarpone. Cheeses hail from England, Scotland and France. Wines are a compact international selection arranged by style, prices starting at £10.95 (£2.95 a glass).

CHEFS: Christopher and Robert Wale PROPRIETORS: the Wale family OPEN: Tue to Sat L 12 to 2, Tue to Fri D 7 to 9.30 MEALS: alc (main courses £14 to £16.50). Set L £9.95 (1 course) to £16.95, Set D (inc wine) £16.95 (2 courses) to £19.95 SERVICE: not inc CARDS: Amex, Delta, Diners, MasterCard, Switch, Visa DETAILS: 50 seats. Private parties: 50 main room. Car park. Vegetarian meals. No cigars/pipes in dining room. Wheelchair access (not WC). Music. Air-conditioned (£5)

CHRISTCHURCH Dorset — map 2

Splinters

12 Church Street, Christchurch BH23 1BW
TEL: (01202) 483454 FAX: (01202) 588011
WEB SITE: www.splinters.co.uk

COOKING **5**
FRENCH/INTERNATIONAL
£31–£55

An enviable location on a cobbled street near the eleventh-century priory gives Splinters a head start in attracting diners, but Jason Davenport's forthright flavours and modern fusion cooking have ensured its success. There is a confidence about the place, manifest in both presentation of the food and the efficient, courteous service from owners Robert Wilson and Timothy Lloyd. The restaurant occupies several rooms of an old cottage, one with a small, split-level bar, another with a large dining table for parties, a third with varnished wooden walls and high-backed pine booths, and a fourth, the more modishly attired 'blue room'. Next door is a related bistro and coffee bar.

Set-price menus offer ample choice, with plenty of trendy combinations from a vibrant dish of fresh, crisp-skinned bass fillet topped with crab ravioli and tomato and chilli jam, to equally well-handled novelties such as a scallop omelette with Thai dressing and enokitake mushroom salad. A main course of roasted pigeon with foie gras has also impressed, not least for its harmonious accompaniments of sappy asparagus, puréed swede, black pudding, foie gras and braised potato. Nor are puddings a let-down: a light, fluffy but sharp apple crumble soufflé has combined surprisingly well with its Lancashire cheese ice-cream. The wine list offers adequate choice, starting with house Gamay and Australian Semillon Chardonnay at £12.95.

CHEF: Jason Davenport PROPRIETORS: Robert Wilson and Timothy Lloyd OPEN: Tue to Sat 12 to 2.30, 7 to 10 CLOSED: 26 Dec MEALS: Set L £16 (2 courses) to £20, Set D Tue to Fri £22.50, Set D Tue to Sat £27 (2 courses) to £32 SERVICE: not inc CARDS: Amex, Delta, Diners, MasterCard, Switch, Visa DETAILS: 45 seats. 6 seats outside. Private parties: 24 main room, 8 to 24 private rooms. Vegetarian meals. Children's helpings. No smoking in dining room. Music (£5)

CLAYGATE Surrey map 3

Le Petit Pierrot

4 The Parade, Claygate KT10 0NU COOKING **2**
TEL: (01372) 465105 FAX: (01372) 467642 MODERN FRENCH
£22–£49

The Brichots' pint-sized bistro in a parade of shops on the high street offers the sorts of dishes that have always found favour along Surrey's highways and byways. Potage of cabbage and bacon might be followed by gigot d'agneau grillé with olives and thyme, and then bavarois à la vanille to finish. That is not to say that more novel preparations are not regularly tried: star anise and onion marmalade accompanying braised pork belly, perhaps, or sesame-seeded halibut with a celeriac quenelle; however, dishes such as mussel soup and tournedos Rossini have been singled out as 'worthy of special note', which might be a pointer to where the real strengths lie. Wines work through the major French regions, with clarets and Burgundies inevitably leading the charge. House wines, a Sémillon and a Grenache, are £11.25.

CHEF: Jean-Pierre Brichot PROPRIETORS: Jean-Pierre and Annie Brichot OPEN: Mon to Fri L 12.15 to 2, Mon to Sat D 7.15 to 9.30 CLOSED: 1 week Christmas, 2 weeks summer, bank hols MEALS: Set L £12.25 (2 courses) to £20.25, Set D £23.50 SERVICE: not inc CARDS: Amex, Diners, MasterCard, Visa DETAILS: 32 seats. Vegetarian meals. No children under 8. Occasional music. Air-conditioned

CLITHEROE Lancashire map 8

Auctioneer

New Market Street, Clitheroe BB7 2JW COOKING **4**
TEL: (01200) 427153 FAX: (01200) 444518 MODERN EUROPEAN
£29–£37

Although its atmosphere may evoke the '60s, the food at this Ribble Valley stalwart – in the Guide for a decade now – is lively enough. Excursions into regional European cuisines are at the heart of dinner: perhaps featuring bagna cauda from Piedmont in January, or albondigas (chicken and smoked ham meatballs) from Spain's Ribera del Duero in March. A more permanent mainstream carte might offer scallops and bacon with tarragon cream sauce, as well as generous-sounding entrecôte double and king-sized Dover sole.

This is confident cooking, working within its capacity and not striving too hard for effect, producing well-timed chicken livers in a red wine sauce on roast polenta, and fillet of lamb – three thick nuggets, pink as ordered – served with light basil gnocchi. The set lunch menu dips into a Europe-wide pot, bringing out maize-fed chicken breast with Parma ham and mozzarella, perhaps followed by baked peaches or creamy tiramisù. Service is polite and knowledgeable, though one reporter felt greater warmth and energy might not go amiss. Ten house wines (£12, or £2.40 a glass) head up a resourceful list that covers similar territory to the food.

CHEF: Henk Van Heumen PROPRIETORS: Henk and Frances Van Heumen OPEN: Thur to Sun L 12 to 1.30, Wed to Sat D 7 to 8.30 (9.30 Sat) MEALS: alc (main courses £14 to £18.50). Set L £9.95 (2 courses) to £11.95, Set D £19.75 SERVICE: not inc CARDS: Amex, Delta, MasterCard, Switch, Visa DETAILS: 48 seats. Private parties: 24 main room, 24 private room. Vegetarian meals. No babies. Children's helpings. No smoking in dining room. Music. Air-conditioned

COCKERMOUTH Cumbria **map 10**

Quince & Medlar £

13 Castlegate, Cockermouth CA13 9EU
TEL: (01900) 823579

COOKING **2**
MODERN EUROPEAN/VEGETARIAN
£23–£30

A vegetarian restaurant may not need the endorsements of omnivores, but the phrase 'We are not vegetarians but . . .' does tend to crop up in readers' reports with impressive frequency. Located in the centre of town near the castle, its broad appeal ranges from a light onion tart, via courgette and coconut soup, to a Mediterranean vegetable bake with saffron couscous. Dishes can be quite robust as well, judging by roast red onions filled with bulgur wheat, mung beans and asparagus, and served with mustard sauce. Iced mango soufflé is a good bet for dessert, or there are British cheeses with celery, fruit and biscuits. Coffee comes with home-made chocolates. The short wine list is exclusively organic, and prices are gentle, starting with house wines at £7.80.

CHEFS/PROPRIETORS: Colin and Louisa Le Voi OPEN: Tue to Sat D only 7 to 9.30 CLOSED: 1 week mid-Nov, 24 Dec to 26 Dec, 2 weeks mid-Jan MEALS: alc (main courses £9) SERVICE: not inc, card slips closed CARDS: MasterCard, Visa DETAILS: 26 seats. Private parties: 14 main room. Vegetarian meals. No children under 5. No smoking in dining room. Music

COLERNE Wiltshire **map 2**

▲ Lucknam Park

Colerne SN14 8AZ
TEL: (01225) 742777 FAX: (01225) 743536
EMAIL: reservations@lucknampark.co.uk
WEB SITE: www.lucknampark.co.uk
off A420 at Ford, 6m W of Chippenham

COOKING **6**
MODERN BRITISH
£42–£104

Lucknam Park aims for 'the elegance and style of a past era', with the help of meticulously manicured lawns, oceans of chintz, old oil portraits and cake-stands with paper doilies. The comfortable dining-room with its well-spaced tables, high-backed chairs and muted pinkish-brown tones makes a suitably elegant setting for new chef Robin Zavou's grand country-house style of cooking.

Elaborate presentation works with the food rather than against it, as demonstrated by a starter of roast quail salad with green beans, pancetta and truffle oil, built around a top-hat-shaped pasta parcel of spinach and truffle, which 'felt as if there were lots of little treats on the plate'. While many dishes may sound creamy and refined, gutsy flavours have characterised an immaculately timed, crisp-skinned salmon on provençale vegetables with olive-roasted potatoes and pesto, and a loin of lamb stuffed with sweetbreads and a courgette mousse, served with an earthy boiled onion in white sauce.

Although prices are high they pay for a lot of workmanship, for example in an exquisitely presented three-tiered cone of dark, milk and white chocolate mousses, served with quenelles of chocolate ices, while 'oozingly ripe' French and British cheeses are paraded on a trolley and served in generous wedges. Service throughout is near to flawless, successfully diffusing the formal atmosphere and attending to every need without being in any way servile. Don't expect any financial favours from the exhaustive wine list. With a bottle of non-vintage Bollinger costing £85, few will feel in the mood to celebrate. Prices start at £17.50.

CHEF: Robin Zavou PROPRIETOR: Lucknam Park Hotels Ltd OPEN: Sun L 12.30 to 2.30, all week D 7.30 to 9.30 (10 Fri and Sat) MEALS: alc (main courses £26 to £30). Set L Sun £25, Set D £40. Light meals available all day SERVICE: not inc, card slips closed CARDS: Amex, Delta, Diners, MasterCard, Switch, Visa DETAILS: 80 seats. Private parties: 64 main room, 10 to 24 private rooms. Car park. Vegetarian meals. No children under 12. Jacket and tie. No smoking in dining room. Wheelchair access (also WC). Occasional music ACCOMMODATION: 41 rooms, all with bath/shower. TV. Phone. Room only £140 to £390. Rooms for disabled. Baby facilities. Swimming pool (*The Which? Hotel Guide*) (£5)

COLN ST ALDWYNS Gloucestershire map 2

▲ New Inn

Coln St Aldwyns GL7 5AN
TEL: (01285) 750651 FAX: (01285) 750657
EMAIL: stay@new-inn.co.uk
WEB SITE: www.new-inn.co.uk
off B4425, Cirencester to Burford road, 2m SW of Bibury

COOKING **2**
MODERN BRITISH/ MEDITERRANEAN
£27–£46

Reporters reckon that despite appearances – a rustic red-tiled bar and printed menu – this is a Cotswold pub that delivers the goods. It serves set meals in the dining room and individually priced dishes in the Courtyard Bar, where first courses come in two sizes: perhaps a well-dressed Caesar salad, or fishcakes encouragingly 'full of fish'. The range takes in squid tempura with noodles and coconut sauce, rhubarb and ginger brûlée, and a 'just right' summer pudding. Vegetarians do well with parallel menus that might include bean sprout and pepper spring roll, or chestnut and cabbage cakes with cranberry sauce. Service is courteous and efficient, and wines – starting with house French at £10.75 and staying mostly under £20 – hail from some good-value regions.

CHEF: Stephen Morey PROPRIETOR: Brian Evans OPEN: all week 12 to 2 (2.30 Sun), 7 to 9 (9.30 Fri and Sat) MEALS: Set L Mon to Sat £16.75 (2 courses) to £21.50, Set L Sun £16.75, Set D £22.50 (2 courses) to £26.50. Bar meals available all week L and D (main courses £9 to £14) SERVICE: not inc CARDS: Amex, Delta, MasterCard, Switch, Visa DETAILS: 32 seats. 50 seats outside. Private parties: 20 main room. Car park. Vegetarian meals. Children's helpings. No children under 10 in dining room. No smoking in dining room. Wheelchair access (also WC). No music ACCOMMODATION: 14 rooms, all with bath/shower. TV. Phone. B&B £68 to £115. No children under 10 (*The Which? Hotel Guide*)

COOKHAM Berkshire **map 3**

Alfonso's

19–21 Station Hill Parade, Cookham SL6 9BR COOKING **4**
TEL: (01628) 525775 MEDITERRANEAN
£15–£43

Alfonso's is the very model of a neighbourhood restaurant; many among the loyal local following have been supporters since it opened in the mid-1980s. The homely, welcoming atmosphere is very much the achievement of Alfonso Baena himself, and may well be reinforced by strains of José Carreras in the background. A Spanish flavour runs through the menus too, with substantial openers including a terrine of suckling pig and chorizo wrapped in Serrano ham, or fabada asturiana: bean casserole with cured sausage and black pudding.

The accent changes a little for main courses, which may take in halibut fillet wrapped in filo with soy- and saké-dressed noodles, but returns with a first-class crema catalana, a kind of Spanish brûlée aromatised with cinnamon and lemon. Alternatively, end with hot cherry and almond tart, or English and Continental cheeses. Wines have been chosen with a keen eye for value, with hardly anything over £20. House French is £9.80.

CHEFS: Mr and Mrs Richard Manzano PROPRIETORS: Mr and Mrs Alfonso Baena OPEN: Mon to Fri L 12.30 to 2, Mon to Sat D 7 to 10 CLOSED: 2 weeks Aug; bank hols MEALS: Set L £5 (2 courses) to £7.50, Set D £19.50 (2 courses) to £23 SERVICE: not inc CARDS: Amex, Diners, MasterCard, Visa DETAILS: 34 seats. 16 seats outside. Private parties: 34 main room. Car park. Vegetarian meals. Children's helpings. Wheelchair access (not WC). Occasional music. Air-conditioned (£5)

Report forms are at the back of the book; write a letter if you prefer; or email us at goodfoodguide@which.net

indicates that there has been a change of chef since last year's Guide, and the Editor has judged that the change is of sufficient interest to merit the reader's attention.

'[Customer to waiter:] "Can you do the salade niçoise without anchovies? If you can, my wife will have the tuna. If not, she'll have the cod. If you can't do the tuna without the anchovies and my wife is *having the cod, I'll have the tuna. If she* is *having the tuna, then I'll have the halibut."'* (On eating in Scotland)

CORSCOMBE Dorset map 2

▲ Fox Inn  £

Corscombe DT2 0NS
TEL/FAX: (01935) 891330
EMAIL: dine@fox-inn.co.uk
WEB SITE: www.fox-inn.co.uk
off A356, 6m SE of Crewkerne

COOKING **2**
MODERN BRITISH
£22–£41

The Inn is a low, rambling, thatched building at the crossroads which, to one couple at least, presented 'the perfect English country-garden experience': flowering plants, creepers and climbing roses are a tribute to somebody's green fingers. Inside, a huge menu incorporates blackboard specials, of which there may be no fewer than 20. Fish is a strong point: tender squid stir-fried with a stab of Szechuan pepper, or a whole John Dory for main course, roasted in garlic and sea salt.

As to meat, there were no complaints from one reporter who ate a pink, aromatic rack of lamb that came with a smoky gravy of meat juices, garlic and rosemary. Gaze at a smaller blackboard of desserts to choose between treacle tart, perhaps, or vanilla cream terrine with a redcurrant coulis. Service is willing and amiable, and the short main wine list is bolstered by a decent showing of halves, as well as a slate of fine wines. House Spanish is £9.50.

CHEFS: George Marsh and Dan Clarke PROPRIETORS: Martyn and Susie Lee OPEN: all week 12 to 2, 7 to 9 (9.30 Fri and Sat) CLOSED: 25 Dec MEALS: alc (main courses £7.50 to £16) SERVICE: not inc, card slips closed CARDS: Amex, Delta, MasterCard, Switch, Visa DETAILS: 90 seats. 40 seats outside. Private parties: 32 main room, 20 to 32 private rooms. Car park. Vegetarian meals. Children's helpings. No smoking in 1 dining room. Wheelchair access (not WC). No music ACCOMMODATION: 3 rooms. TV. B&B £50 to £80 (*The Which? Hotel Guide*)

CORSE LAWN Gloucestershire map 2

▲ Corse Lawn House 

Corse Lawn GL19 4LZ
TEL: (01452) 780771 FAX: (01452) 780840
EMAIL: hotel@corselawnhouse.u-net.com
WEB SITE: www.corselawnhousehotel.co.uk
on B4211, 5m SW of Tewkesbury

COOKING **3**
ANGLO-FRENCH
£27–£59

The group of red-brick buildings with an ancient 'coach wash' out front constitutes a very English hotel. Refurbishment over recent years has produced an elegant, airy dining room, and one regular visitor reckons that service and general easy-going comfort remain 'exceptionally high'. Given the number of menus (there's a bistro too), and the generous choice on some of them, the kitchen is a busy one. Baba Hine's Anglo-French style is typified by pork terrine with apple chutney, stuffed rabbit saddle with mustard sauce, and roast rump of lamb provençale. Well-rendered soups might run to celeriac, Mediterranean fish, or rich and creamy tomato and basil.

One visitor recommended 'any pudding in a shortcrust case' – lemon tart with lemon ice cream is a good example – while another praised 'the lightest ever' syrup sponge and a well-executed assiette of chocolate desserts. A wide range of house wines, starting at £10.50 and featuring two shipped personally by Denis Hine, introduce a lengthy list that concentrates predominantly on classic French regions. Half-bottles are numerous though a touch pricey.

CHEFS: Baba Hine and Andrew Poole PROPRIETORS: the Hine family OPEN: all week 12 to 2, 7 to 9.30 CLOSED: 25 and 26 Dec MEALS: alc (exc Sun D; main courses £16 to £20). Set L £14.95 (2 courses) to £16.95, Set D £25 SERVICE: not inc, card slips closed CARDS: Amex, Delta, Diners, MasterCard, Switch, Visa DETAILS: 90 seats. 40 seats outside. Private parties: 80 main room, 18 and 35 private rooms. Car park. Vegetarian meals. Children's helpings. No smoking in dining room. Wheelchair access (also WC). No music ACCOMMODATION: 19 rooms, all with bath/shower. TV. Phone. B&B £75 to £120. Rooms for disabled. Baby facilities. Swimming pool (*The Which? Hotel Guide*)

CRANBROOK Kent **map 3**

▲ Kennel Holt Hotel

Goudhurst Road, Cranbrook TN17 2PT
TEL: (01580) 712032 FAX: (01580) 715495 — COOKING **3**
EMAIL: hotel@kennelholt.demon.co.uk — MODERN EUROPEAN
WEB SITE: www.kennelholt.co.uk — £32–£54

Set back from the road in five well-kept acres, this Elizabethan manor house with Edwardian additions betokens 'individuality and artistic taste', with books on art and music to prove it. Neil Chalmers's menus are not too ambitious, and dishes are well composed, managing to explore a good range of flavours without getting lost in wild fancy: confit loin of pork with rosemary risotto, perhaps, or roast cod with spring onion mash and red wine sauce. Local ingredients help things along too: roast loin of Mrs Harrison's lamb with a herb crust, and salad leaves from Frances Smith at Appledore, perhaps served with goats' cheese and a pecan dressing. Finish with iced pear parfait or orange and ginger cheesecake. Incidentals include good bread, service is cheerful, knowledgeable and friendly, and France is the major player on the annotated wine list, where house red and white are £13.50 and £12.50 respectively.

CHEFS: Neil Chalmers and Audrey Ratcliffe PROPRIETORS: Neil and Sally Chalmers OPEN: Wed to Fri L, and Sun L Oct to Apr, 12.30 to 1.15, Tue to Sat D 7.30 to 8.45 (residents only Sun D) CLOSED: 1 week Jan MEALS: Set L £17.50 (2 courses) to £21, Set D £27.50 to £32.50 SERVICE: 10% (optional), card slips closed CARDS: Delta, MasterCard, Switch, Visa DETAILS: 44 seats. 12 seats outside. Private parties: 25 main room, 16 private room. Car park. Vegetarian meals. Children's helpings. No children under 10 at D. No smoking in dining room. Occasional music ACCOMMODATION: 10 rooms, all with bath/shower. TV. Phone. B&B £90 to £175. Baby facilities

---

Prices quoted in the Guide are based on information supplied by restaurateurs. The prices quoted at the top of each entry represent a range, from the lowest meal price to the highest; the latter is inflated by 20 per cent to take account of likely price rises during the year of the Guide.

CROSTHWAITE Cumbria map 8

▲ Punch Bowl Inn

Crosthwaite LA8 8HR
TEL: (015395) 68237 FAX: (015395) 68875
EMAIL: enquiries@punchbowl.fsnet.co.uk
WEB SITE: www.punchbowl.fsnet.co.uk
off A5074, 3m S of Windermere

COOKING **4**
MODERN EUROPEAN
£19–£41

Despite outward appearances, this is one country pub where food definitely takes precedence over pints of beer, just as at Spread Eagle (see entry, Sawley) under the same ownership. Set in the Lyth Valley, and sharing a car park with the church, the Doherty's operation exudes a feeling of 'sincerity and goodwill', which counts for a lot. Occasional sightings of the food's classical background – rabbit and foie gras terrine with a truffle oil dressing – are more than offset by contemporary borrowings, not least from the Far East: roast cod fillet has come with prawn beignets and a Thai dipping sauce, for example.

Given a good solid British dimension in the shape of braised oxtail with herb dumplings, and an Italian slant in semolina gnocchi served with a gorgonzola and tomato sauce, it is clear that most appetites will be whetted by this direct style of cooking. Lunch is particularly good value, perhaps offering cream of vegetable soup, braised shank of lamb, and Greek honey syrup cake. A short global list offers twelve wines by the glass and ten half-bottles, and if wines were not already opened before being brought to table, reporters would be even happier. House Argentinian is £10.25.

CHEFS: Steven Doherty and Paul Harris PROPRIETORS: Steven and Marjorie Doherty OPEN: Tue to Sun L 12 to 2, Tue to Sat D 6 to 9 (9.30 Sat) CLOSED: 3 weeks Nov and 25 Dec MEALS: alc (main courses £9 to £13). Set L Tue to Sat £8 (2 courses) to £10.95, Set L Sun £10.95 (2 courses) to £12.95 SERVICE: not inc, card slips closed CARDS: MasterCard, Switch, Visa DETAILS: 60 seats. 20 seats outside. Private parties: 40 main room. Car park. Vegetarian meals. Children's helpings. No smoking in dining room. No music ACCOMMODATION: 3 rooms, all with bath/shower. TV. B&B £37.50 to £55 (*The Which? Hotel Guide*)

DARGATE Kent map 3

Dove £

Plum Pudding Lane, Dargate ME13 9HB
TEL: (01227) 751360

COOKING **3**
FRENCH
£24–£42

'What you'd like to find in France, but nowadays find much less often' is one impression of the Dove's bare-boarded and pine charms, half of it primarily a bar, the other half mostly given over to food. This French overlay to the Garden of England has produced pan-fried crevettes with pickled ginger and herbs, and a full-flavoured warm chicken salad in a fine spicy stew of olives, peppers and onions. Garlicky, herby sea bass and plenty of other fish (marlin, mackerel, red mullet, sardines) frequently appear in appetising guises, as do vegetables such as fennel and salsify. To finish, consider baked chocolate pudding with crème anglaise or a plate of English cheeses. Other pluses for Nigel and Bridget Morris's Victorian pub are a beer garden full of nooks and crannies, an open wood fire, good wine prices for the score of bottles (all but three under £20), and courteous and efficient service.

CHEF: Nigel Morris PROPRIETORS: Nigel and Bridget Morris OPEN: Tue to Sun L 12 to 2, Wed to Sat D 7 to 9 MEALS: alc (main courses £9 to £15) SERVICE: not inc, card slips closed CARDS: Delta, MasterCard, Switch, Visa DETAILS: 22 seats. 10 seats outside. Car park. Music

DARTMOUTH Devon **map 1**

Carved Angel

2 South Embankment, Dartmouth TQ6 9BH
TEL: (01803) 832465 FAX: (01803) 835141

COOKING **5**
MODERN BRITISH-PLUS
£40–£60

When the team at Horn of Plenty (see entry, Tavistock) took over this light, airy, uncluttered restaurant in February 2000, it marked a significant shift. As one of the country's seminal post-war chefs, previous owner Joyce Molyneux played her part in revolutionising the way we eat out, by the simple expedient of tracking down first-rate ingredients and cooking them with skill and intelligence. Like many of his contemporaries, David Jones, who has stayed on as chef, doubtless takes such an approach for granted.

Fresh flavours are evident at every turn, from pressed crab with shellfish gazpacho to roast cod with parchment-crisp skin. Timing is spot on, in just-cooked turbot with green bean fritters and morel cream, or *à point* roast salmon on a well-made risotto incorporating cockles, mussels and a richly flavoured crustacean stock. Such accuracy also produces crusty outsides and soft insides in, for example, impeccably sourced Devon beef fillet and its accompanying rösti. Silky, stock-based sauces also add to the appeal, and while seasoning may sometimes appear over-generous, and ideas can be a bit routine, a sound technical grasp underpins the whole show.

Desserts range from the 'ideal way' of treating strawberries – roasted, with clotted cream ice cream – to an enterprising warm elderflower and polenta cake with greengage compote. Well-paced service functions smoothly, and the practice of including water and service in the price is appreciated, not least by those up from London. The wine list offers a cannily selected range from around the world, although prices have increased quite a bit under the new ownership; but tasting notes are helpful and quality is consistent. Eight recommended wines (including two dessert wines) from £17 are also available by the glass (from £4).

CHEF: David Jones PROPRIETORS: Paul and Andie Roston, and Peter Gorton OPEN: Tue to Sun L 12 to 2, Mon to Sat D 7 to 9 CLOSED: 3 days Christmas MEALS: Set L £24.50 (2 courses) to £29.50, Set D £39.50 SERVICE: net prices CARDS: Amex, Delta, MasterCard, Switch, Visa DETAILS: 55 seats. Private parties: 35 main room, 15 to 20 private rooms. Vegetarian meals. Children's helpings. No children under 14 at D. No smoking in dining room. Music (£5)

'Pub regulars were downing pints and holding up the bar, bright young slender things in designer dresses looked like they were stoking up for a night's clubbing, and one man sat at a table alone, eating his dinner with a copy of Balzac's Cousin Bette *propped against his bottle of wine.'* (On eating in Dorset)

Carved Angel Café £

7 Foss Street, Dartmouth TQ6 9DW
TEL: (01803) 834842

COOKING **2**
GLOBAL
£21–£30

Taken over by the same team who now own the Carved Angel itself (see previous entry), the café continues its round of all-day eating, with morning coffee and afternoon tea filling the gaps outside lunch and dinner. Light meals are the stock in trade, from soups of basil and tomato, or beef and vegetable, to open sandwiches (ham with tomato chutney, perhaps) or maybe a dish of ratatouille with pasta. More substantial offerings include deep-fried Glamorgan cheese sausages with a pair of dipping sauces, and grilled salmon with Thai barbecue sauce and stir-fried vegetables. Equally uncomplicated desserts run to sticky toffee pudding with clotted cream, and meringue with fruit compote. Service is speedy and friendly, and six of the seven bottles on the wine list cost £12 (£2.10 a small glass).

CHEFS: Helen Farmer and Tim Hoban PROPRIETORS: Peter and Karen Gorton, and Paul and Andie Roston OPEN: Tue to Sun L 11 to 4, Fri and Sat D 6 to 9 (morning coffee 10 to 11, afternoon tea 4 to 6) CLOSED: 3 days Christmas MEALS: alc (main courses £4 to £7). Cover £1.25 SERVICE: not inc CARDS: Amex, Delta, MasterCard, Switch, Visa DETAILS: 30 seats. Private parties: 30 main room. Vegetarian meals. Children's helpings. No smoking in dining room. Wheelchair access (also WC). No music

▲ Gunfield

NEW ENTRY

Castle Road, Dartmouth TQ6 0JN
TEL: (01803) 834571 FAX: (01803) 834772
EMAIL: enquiry@gunfield.co.uk
WEB SITE: www.gunfield.co.uk

COOKING **1**
MODERN EUROPEAN
£26–£41

Big windows and a spacious terrace make the most of Gunfield's unrivalled location overlooking the Dart estuary, the lights of Kingswear an entertaining diversion on the opposite bank at night. Against a backdrop of stone floors, contemporary prints and starched napkins, the wide-ranging contemporary menu delivers wholesome and tasty food along the lines of brill with a coriander-flavoured sauce, and chicken breast beefed up with a salty jacket of Serrano ham, in a wine-sharpened mushroom sauce. The food scores for 'fresh ingredients simply presented' – four juicy fillets of smoked trout draped over a cucumber and crème fraîche salad with chives – but the kitchen has also turned out a fine raspberry crème brûlée with crisp, thin caramel, and bananas encased in filo pastry with caramel sauce. Service at inspection could hardly have been improved upon for expertise and professionalism, and a short, affordable wine list adds to the appeal. House Californian is £9.50.

£ *means that it is possible to have a three-course meal, including coffee, half a bottle of house wine and service for £25 or less per person, at any time the restaurant is open, i.e. at dinner as well as lunch. It may be possible to spend considerably more than this, but by choosing carefully you should find £25 or less achievable.*

CHEF: Chloë Wreford-Brown PROPRIETORS: Mike and Lucy Swash OPEN: Mon to Sat D only 7.30 to 9.30; also Sat and Sun L 12.30 to 3 in summer for barbecues, Sun L 12.30 to 3 in winter; opening hours may be restricted out of season MEALS: alc (main courses £10 to £15) SERVICE: not inc, card slips closed CARDS: Amex, Delta, MasterCard, Switch, Visa DETAILS: 40 seats. 60 seats outside. Private parties: 50 main room, 18 and 30 private rooms. Car park. Vegetarian meals. Children's helpings. No children under 5. Music ACCOMMODATION: 10 rooms, all with bath/shower. TV. B&B £45 to £120. Baby facilities. Fishing (*The Which? Hotel Guide*)

DEDDINGTON Oxfordshire map 5

Dexter's

Market Place, Deddington OX15 0SA
TEL: (01869) 338813 COOKING **3**
EMAIL: dexteruk@globalnet.co.uk MODERN BRITISH
WEB SITE: www.dextersuk.com £29–£56

The ancient, somewhat eccentric, half-timbered building with its contemporary lighting and artworks provides a refreshing blend of old and new. The same could be said of Jamie Dexter Harrison's confident, self-assured cooking, which has a high success rate 'even on the wilder shores of flavour and combinations'. Field mushrooms with artichokes on lemony linguini, and Thai fishcakes fired up by chilli have been pleasing starters, while a direct approach has characterised main courses of slow-roast lamb shank with Cumberland sauce, and grilled sea bass counterpointed with pungent mushrooms and salty bacon in a rich red wine sauce.

Classic desserts range from a powerful St Emilion au chocolat, to a crisp tarte Tatin with delicate ginger ice cream, or creamy pear parfait with marinated fruits. Service has varied from 'effusively friendly' to 'amateur'. A short, unusual selection of wines from around the world is mostly under £20, with house vins de pays at £11.50 (£2.50 a glass).

CHEF: Jamie Dexter Harrison PROPRIETORS: Jamie Dexter Harrison and Roger Blackburn OPEN: Tue to Sat 12 to 2.15, 7 to 9.15 MEALS: alc (main courses £9 to £17). Set L Tue to Sat and D Tue to Thur £15.50 (2 courses) to £19.50. Light L available SERVICE: 10% (optional) CARDS: Delta, MasterCard, Switch, Visa DETAILS: 60 seats. Private parties: 70 main room. Vegetarian meals. Children's helpings. Wheelchair access (not WC). Occasional music

DEDHAM Essex map 6

▲ Le Talbooth

Gun Hill, Dedham CO7 6HP
TEL: (01206) 323150 FAX: (01206) 322309 COOKING **4**
EMAIL: ltreception@talbooth.co.uk MODERN EUROPEAN
WEB SITE: www.talbooth.com £29–£70

The setting – with climbing plants, hanging baskets, swans, and a bridge over the Stour – could be from a tourist poster, making fair-weather lunches under large umbrellas an 'idyllic' way to pass the time. Terry Barber is now executive chef in charge of banqueting and outside catering, while Daniel Clarke takes command of the restaurant kitchen; given materials in typically peak condition, little appears to have changed as far as reporters are concerned. Set-price meals (lunch incorporates a roast of the day) run to home-smoked salmon (hardly improved by mayonnaise and couscous), perhaps a beetroot risotto, and pink, tender roast lamb, served with the meat juices and mint sauce. The carte, meanwhile, is more adventurous, offering a trio of pancake rolls, ravioli of shellfish, or guinea fowl stuffed with wild mushrooms and foie gras mousse.

Desserts might range from bread-and-butter pudding to an iced raspberry soufflé with marinated raspberries that was ideal for a summer's day. Service is 'attentive and pleasant,' and wines are attractively priced. Traditionalists will revel in the choice of classed-growth clarets, while modernists will enjoy a dizzying selection of South African wines, many under £20. New Zealand's Allan Scott Sauvignon is hard to come by and is particularly recommended. Eight house wines are served by the glass, from £3.

CHEFS: Terry Barber and Daniel Clarke PROPRIETORS: Gerald and Paul Milsom OPEN: Mon to Sat 12 to 2, 7 to 9.30, Sun Sept to May 12 to 4 only, Sun June to Sept 12 to 2, 7 to 9 MEALS: alc (main courses £15.50 to £22). Set L £17 (2 courses) to £19.50, Set D £22 (2 courses) to £27 SERVICE: 10%, card slips closed CARDS: Amex, Delta, Diners, MasterCard, Switch, Visa DETAILS: 75 seats. 50 seats outside. Private parties: 80 main room, 34 private room. Car park. Vegetarian meals. No smoking while others eat. No music ACCOMMODATION: 10 rooms, all with bath/shower. TV. Phone. B&B £120 to £195. Rooms for disabled (*The Which? Hotel Guide*)

DENMEAD Hampshire map 2

Barnard's

Hambledon Road, Denmead PO7 6NU — COOKING **1**
TEL/FAX: (01705) 257788 — MODERN BRITISH
on B2150, 2m NW of Waterlooville — £21–£49

Flowers appear in various guises behind the green-striped awning of this chalet-style building – fresh, dried, as big prints, and on the curtains – and service from Sandie Barnard is 'very smiley and helpful'. Among praiseworthy ingredients are smoked salmon enveloping a generous chilli-spiced crab mix, and cutlets of well-flavoured pink lamb liberally infused with rosemary on a bed of grilled red peppers. Results are variable but have included side plates of 'perfectly good' vegetables, and a creamy iced parfait of aniseed and Pernod, cleverly contrasted with caramelised oranges. Wines offer a fairly priced if predictable global selection. House wines are £10.

CHEFS: Brian Wright and David Barnard PROPRIETORS: David and Sandie Barnard OPEN: Tue to Fri L 12 to 1.45, Tue to Sat D 7 to 9.30 CLOSED: Christmas to New Year MEALS: alc (main courses £11.50 to £17.50). Set L £10 (2 courses) to £12.50. Light L available SERVICE: not inc, card slips closed CARDS: Amex, Delta, MasterCard, Switch, Visa DETAILS: 46 seats. 20 seats outside. Private parties: 34 main room, 22 and 34 private rooms. Car park. Vegetarian meals. Children's helpings. No smoking in dining room Sat D only. Music (£5)

(£5) *indicates that the restaurant has elected to participate in the* Good Food Guide *voucher scheme. For full details, see page 6.*

DERBY Derbyshire map 5

Darleys

Darley Abbey Mill, Darley Abbey, Derby DE22 1DZ
TEL: (01332) 364987 FAX: (01332) 541356 COOKING **4**
WEB SITE: www.darleys.com MODERN BRITISH
off A6, 2m N of city centre £26–£59

Part of an old mill beside a fast-flowing weir, Darleys leaves the nineteenth century behind not only with its airy, well-designed interior of pastels, mirror and carpet but also by dint of a busy-sounding menu laced with contemporary ideas and materials. Meals might start with an assiette of salmon (tartare, smoked, roe and mousseline) served with horseradish crème fraîche and a caper and citrus salsa, or else a roast plum tomato and mozzarella tartlet with tapénade. Meatless mains have included a steamed wild mushroom pudding with mustard beurre blanc, and reporters have approved sirloin tournedos with a crust of melted goats' cheese, accompanied by buttery spinach and shallot confit. Iced banana parfait with coconut sorbet has gone down well too, as has an individual apple pie with toffee ice cream. Service has ranged from 'very slow' to 'pleasant, friendly and professional'. An 11-page list of carefully chosen and well annotated wines starts at £14.

CHEF: Ian Wilson PROPRIETOR: David Pinchbeck OPEN: all week L 12 to 2.30, Mon to Sat D 7 to 10 (10.30 Fri and Sat) CLOSED: bank hols MEALS: alc (main courses £13 to £19). Set L £12.50 (2 courses) to £14.50, Set D Mon to Fri £22 SERVICE: not inc CARDS: Amex, Delta, Diners, MasterCard, Switch, Visa DETAILS: 70 seats. Private parties: 70 main room. Car park. Vegetarian meals. Children's helpings. No smoking in dining room. Wheelchair access (not WC). Music. Air-conditioned (£5)

DINTON Buckinghamshire map 3

La Chouette

Westlington Green, Dinton HP17 8UW
TEL/FAX: (01296) 747422 COOKING **3**
off A418, following signs to Westlington and Ford, BELGIAN
4m SW of Aylesbury £21–£61

Reached along twisting country roads, this timbered and gabled former pub is distinguished by pictures of owls, background jazz, and a line of Belgian beers along the windowsill pointing to the owner's national and culinary heritage. Expect to find goose rillettes, veal kidneys in mustard sauce, and a range of fish dishes from red mullet salad to grilled sea bass with beurre blanc. There is no doubt that Frédéric Desmette can cook, producing successful pigeon with red cabbage and lyonnaise potatoes at inspection, and well-flavoured crêpe suzette, although he doesn't always take the trouble to do it well. The place can be 'good fun', although eccentricities in service – this is a one-man band – have left one or two reporters with the feeling that they are there as much for the owner's entertainment as to have a good time themselves. Two Italian wines infiltrate an otherwise exclusively French list, which offers fantastic range and a choice of highly regarded producers, whether you are seeking a first-growth claret or a bottle from Aix-en-Provence. Prices are fair and house wine is £11.

CHEF/PROPRIETOR: Frédéric Desmette OPEN: Mon to Fri L 12 to 2, Mon to Sat D 7 to 9 MEALS: alc (main courses £10 to £16). Set L £11, Set L and D £27.50 to £36.50 SERVICE: 12.5% (optional), card slips closed CARDS: Delta, MasterCard, Visa DETAILS: 40 seats. 16 seats outside. Private parties: 40 main room. Car park. Children's helpings. No cigars/pipes in dining-room. Music

DONCASTER South Yorkshire **map 9**

▲ Hamilton's

Carr House Road, Doncaster DN4 5HP
TEL: (01302) 760770 FAX: (01302) 768101
EMAIL: ham760770@aol.com
WEB SITE: www.hamiltonshotel.com

COOKING **5**
MODERN EUROPEAN
£24–£59

Built for the Hamiltons (Lord and Lady, not Neil and Christine) in the mid-nineteenth century, this sumptuously decorated manor house may seem rather out of place in modern Doncaster. Everything that can be polished has been, from floors to glassware, and although it may impress more for style than comfort there is no quibbling with the opulence and visual impact. Thanks to Christopher Randle-Bissell, it has brought serious cooking to Doncaster (go for lunch to avoid serious prices) in the shape of a modern European menu that might include black pudding tortellini in a powerful-tasting broth, roast pork fillet with pease pudding, or halibut wrapped in pancetta with a shrimp and caper butter.

There is clearly talent in the kitchen, though ambition can outstrip achievement: whether scallops on mash with foie gras is more than just a way of combining two luxury ingredients is an open question. Cheeses are praised, and desserts have included passion-fruit curd tart, and chocolate and orange arctic roll. Front of house, eager though it is, does not yet match the cooking. More than 50 briefly annotated wines are arranged by style, starting with house French at £10.50.

CHEF: Christopher Randle-Bissell PROPRIETORS: Hamilton's Ltd and Andrew Roberts OPEN: Tue to Fri and Sun L 11.30 to 3, Tue to Sat D 6 to 10 CLOSED: 26 to 28 Dec MEALS: alc (main courses £13 to £20). Set L £10.95 (2 courses) to £14.95, Set D £22.95 (2 courses) to £25.95 SERVICE: not inc CARDS: Amex, Delta, MasterCard, Switch, Visa DETAILS: 80 seats. Private parties: 50 main room, 40 to 250 private rooms. Car park. Vegetarian meals. Children's helpings. No smoking in dining room. Wheelchair access (not WC). Music ACCOMMODATION: 4 rooms, all with bath/shower. TV. Phone. B&B £70 to £150. Baby facilities (£5)

'Later in my meal I asked about the cheese. The waitress didn't know anything about them but shortly afterwards the owner arrived to invite us to look at the cheese selection in the kitchen and consult his cheese expert. We followed him into the kitchen and found a young chef standing by the cheese board. We were handed over to him, so I asked what the various cheeses were. He obviously didn't have the faintest idea about any of them, except a Lancashire, so I took pity on the poor wretch and pointed to four, saying that I'd like to try some of each.' (On eating in Yorkshire)

DORRINGTON Shropshire map 5

▲ Country Friends

Dorrington SY5 7JD
TEL: (01743) 718707
EMAIL: whittaker@countryfriends.demon.co.uk
on A49, 5m S of Shrewsbury

COOKING **5**
ANGLO-EUROPEAN
£40–£53

The unprepossessing black and white timbered building beside the A49 represents Middle England at its most tweedily respectable, with painted Anaglypta walls, little pictures haphazardly displayed, and beams ranging from genuinely gnarled to gloss-painted brown. The food is equally unshowy, giving fine-quality ingredients a gentle European treatment. Graig Farm organic chicken breast, for example, is stuffed with goats' cheese and served with red onion and beetroot, while confit duck leg comes with braised butter beans and sausage. Otherwise there is a concentration on homespun ideas, such as a damson sauce to accompany venison, and a starter of twice-baked leek and Llanboidy soufflé (the Welsh border isn't far away). Speaking of which, Welsh rarebit makes a savoury appearance as an alternative to desserts of lemon flan, or summer pudding with elderflower ice cream. A short yet global wine list combines French classics with fashionable bins from the New World. Cloudy Bay Sauvignon Blanc is reasonably priced at £25.95, and house wines are £12.50.

CHEF: Charles Whittaker PROPRIETORS: Charles and Pauline Whittaker OPEN: Tue to Sat 12 to 2, 7 to 9 (9.30 Sat) MEALS: Set L and D £27.50 (2 courses) to £33.90. Light L available SERVICE: not inc CARDS: MasterCard, Switch, Visa DETAILS: 40 seats. Private parties: 40 main room. Car park. Vegetarian meals. No smoking in dining room. Wheelchair access (not WC). No music ACCOMMODATION: 1 room, with bath/shower. D,B&B £75 to £130. No children

DRYBROOK Gloucestershire map 5

Cider Press

The Cross, Drybrook GL17 9EB
TEL/FAX: (01594) 544472
EMAIL: cider.press@virgin.net
WEB SITE: freespace.virgin.net/christopher.challener/index.htm

COOKING **4**
MODERN BRITISH/SEAFOOD
£32–£45

The lounge bar of this homely yet smart restaurant has been refurbished to include sofas for 'schmoozing and general pre-dinner relaxation', which should give an idea of the unstuffy atmosphere. Christopher Challener takes fierce pride in the sourcing of organic and wild raw materials. 'Fish and shellfish continue to be our mainstay,' he reports, which may mean spicy grilled squid and scallops, salt-baked bream with green mayonnaise and salpicon, or simply grilled Cornish lobster with garlic butter. Monkfish escabèche is a permanent fixture.

These are backed up by seasonal organic meats: in spring, cider-roast loin of Cotswold lamb is stuffed with apples, sage, cloves, ginger and garlic, and served with a ragoût of aubergine and tomato, while winter brings a hearty dish of woodcock stuffed with prunes, sage and walnuts and served with chestnut sauce. Finish with fresh fruit roulade or home-made ice cream, or opt for the cheeseboard. Service can be leisurely. English wines play a part in the short, well-rounded list; seven house wines are available from £7.95. There is a chance that the restaurant may move or be sold during the currency of the Guide.

CHEF: Christopher Challener PROPRIETOR: Bernadette Fitzpatrick OPEN: Wed to Sat D only 7 to 11 (L Wed to Sun and D Sun and Mon by arrangement) CLOSED: mid-Jan MEALS: alc (main courses £14.50 to £16.50) SERVICE: not inc, card slips closed CARDS: Delta, MasterCard, Switch, Visa DETAILS: 22 seats. Private parties: 28 main room. No smoking in dining room. Wheelchair access (also WC)

DURHAM Co Durham **map 10**

Bistro 21

Aykley Heads House, Aykley Heads, Durham DH1 5TS
TEL: (0191) 384 4354 FAX: (0191) 384 1149

COOKING **2**
MEDITERRANEAN
£24–£51

With an ochre and eau de nil colour scheme, and sacking for curtains, the converted farmhouse adopts a relaxed, informal air, where customers might turn up equally happily in sequins or jeans. It conveys a pleasing Mediterranean feel, helped by a menu that includes fish soup with rouille and trimmings, or lightly battered field mushroom fritters with buffalo mozzarella and basil oil. The net spreads wider, however, to cover bang bang chicken salad, and fishcakes with parsley cream and chips. Good-quality materials lay the foundation – veal fillet cooked saltimbocca style, or scallops from the daily specials blackboard for one visitor – although it is worth noting that vegetables are charged extra. Finish with a refreshing lime mousse, a more-indulgent baked Alaska with hot cherries, or perhaps apple tart paired with Lancashire cheese. Around 40 wines are sensibly priced, starting with house French at £12.50.

CHEF: Adrian Watson PROPRIETORS: Terence and Susan Laybourne OPEN: Mon to Sat 12 to 2, 6 to 10.30 CLOSED: bank hols MEALS: alc (main courses £9.50 to £13.50). Set L £12 (2 courses) to £14.50, Set D £23.50 SERVICE: not inc CARDS: Amex, Delta, Diners, MasterCard, Switch, Visa DETAILS: 55 seats. 20 seats outside. Private parties: 55 main room, 10 to 20 private rooms. Car park. Vegetarian meals. Children's helpings. No smoking in dining room. Music

EASTBOURNE East Sussex **map 3**

▲ Grand Hotel, Mirabelle

King Edwards Parade, Eastbourne BN21 4EQ
TEL: (01323) 435066 FAX: (01323) 412233
EMAIL: reservations@grandeastbourne.co.uk
WEB SITE: www.grandeastbourne.co.uk

COOKING **6**
MODERN EUROPEAN
£28–£68

The wedding-cake exterior remains unchanged, but the inside of this grand Victorian seaside hotel has undergone much alteration. With the bar shifted downstairs, and the draped curtains gone, the no-smoking dining room is now 'safer and softer' in its muted creamy colours. Marc Wilkinson's menu is not without its jargon de cuisine (and its rather unnecessary price supplements) but the kitchen buys well, and dishes are well conceived. This is classic modern cooking mercifully free of gimmicks, but by no means boring or complacent, as is apparent in a fine terrine of chunky pieces of duck confit, accompanied by a pile of diced marinated pear well balanced for sweetness and acidity.

A high level of technical skill is evident throughout: in baked monkfish with a properly made and forceful risotto of lemon and herbs, and in chunks of moist chicken breast on a bed of creamy leeks, with morels and broad beans in a clear, rich-flavoured Madeira jus. The kitchen also takes a lively interest in contrasts of taste, texture and colour: for example, in a small pile of soft sweetbreads sandwiched between spinach and filo, scattered with salted almonds. Presentation is not overdone, although eye-catching dishes have included a crisp hazelnut 'cigar' filled with pistachio ice cream, sitting on a firm-textured praline mousse. Poor coffee contrasts absurdly with everything else. Staff, many of them French, are charming and efficient, and the set-price lunch is worthy of consideration. Grand names and high prices are the wine list's stock in trade, although a few concessions are made to ordinary drinkers, including house Vin de Pays d'Oc at £12.95.

CHEF: Marc Wilkinson PROPRIETOR: Elite Hotels OPEN: Tue to Sat 12.30 to 2, 7 to 10 CLOSED: first two weeks Jan MEALS: Set L £21.50, Set D £34 SERVICE: net prices, card slips closed CARDS: Amex, Delta, Diners, MasterCard, Switch, Visa DETAILS: 50 seats. Private parties: 55 main room. Car park. Vegetarian meals. No children under 12. Jacket and tie. No smoking in dining room. Wheelchair access (also WC). Music. Air-conditioned ACCOMMODATION: 152 rooms, all with bath/shower. TV. Phone. B&B £152 to £400. Rooms for disabled. Swimming pool (£5)

EAST CHILTINGTON East Sussex — map 3

Jolly Sportsman

Chapel Lane, East Chiltington BN7 3BA
TEL: (01273) 890400
EMAIL: jollysportsman@mistral.co.uk
off Novington Lane between B2116 and Plumpton Green

COOKING **1**
MODERN EUROPEAN
£23–£49

Located down a leafy Sussex lane, the Jolly Sportsman is owned by Bruce Wass, whose other operation, Thackeray House in Tunbridge Wells, was on the market as the Guide went to press, which means he could be spending more time here in the near future. In a simple, small dining room with brick walls and thick warped wooden tables, Richard Willis's cooking shows ambition. A lively starter salad of smoked anchovies, capers, artichokes and olives might be followed by a whole gilt-head bream, grilled and served with Jersey Royals in season, or braised lamb shank with butter-beans and chorizo. Finish with a sweet steamed pudding containing apricot, walnut, ginger and toffee. A wide-ranging wine list motors gently up to £50, and the seven house wines come in three sizes of glass from £1.85 to £5.50, or by the bottle at £9.45.

CHEF: Richard Willis PROPRIETORS: Bruce and Gwyneth Wass OPEN: Tue to Sun L 12.30 to 2 (3 Sun), Tue to Sat D 7 to 10 CLOSED: 4 days Christmas MEALS: alc Tue to Sat (main courses £8 to £18.50). Set L Tue to Sat £10 (2 courses), Set L Sun £19.50. Bar menu available SERVICE: restaurant: 10%, bar: not inc CARDS: Delta, MasterCard, Switch, Visa DETAILS: 50 seats. 100 seats outside. Private parties: 40 main room, 16 to 40 private rooms. Car park. Vegetarian meals. Children's helpings. Wheelchair access (also WC). No music

EAST END Hampshire map 2

East End Arms

East End SO41 5SY
TEL/FAX: (01590) 626223
EMAIL: jennie@eastendarms.co.uk
off B3054, 2m E of Lymington; follow signs for Isle of Wight ferry and continue 2m

COOKING **4**
MODERN BRITISH/SEAFOOD
£22–£41

John Illsley, a founder member of rock group Dire Straits, has discovered a new métier running country inns (see also George Hotel, Yarmouth), acquiring this one about a decade ago to prevent it from being turned into a theme pub. Spared that indignity, East End Arms still boasts its open fireplace and stone floors, and Paul Sykes cooks a short menu of high-class comfort food in keeping with the tone. Cheese adds richness to both a starter of asparagus risotto with melting Brie and a roast chicken main course with fennel, grilled peppers and Port-Salut. Fish dishes chalked on the blackboard are always worth a look – skewered salmon, monkfish and scallops on a salad of artichokes and samphire, for example – while meats include favourites such as chunky pork, sage and garlic sausages with thick lentil gravy, or steak and kidney pie. Finish with rhubarb crumble, or apple and honey ice cream. Jenny Sykes 'whizzes about' at front-of-house with friendliness and efficiency. The short, serviceable wine list offers everything bar champagne under £20 (and even that's only £26 for Taittinger). House wines, an Australian Chardonnay and a Chilean Merlot, are £10.

CHEF: Paul Sykes PROPRIETOR: John Illsley OPEN: Tue to Sun L 12 to 2, Tue to Sat D 7 to 9 CLOSED: 25 and 26 Dec, 1 Jan, Tue after bank hols MEALS: alc (main courses L £4 to £12, D £8 to £15) SERVICE: not inc, card slips closed CARDS: Delta, MasterCard, Switch, Visa DETAILS: 34 seats. 60 seats outside. Private parties: 25 main room. Car park. Children's helpings. Wheelchair access (not WC). Music

EAST GRINSTEAD West Sussex map 3

▲ Gravetye Manor

Vowels Lane, East Grinstead RH19 4LJ
TEL: (01342) 810567 FAX: (01342) 810080
EMAIL: gravetye@relaischateaux.fr
off B2110, 2 miles SW of East Grinstead

COOKING **7**
TRADITIONAL ENGLISH
£39–£75

'It's always grand at Gravetye,' summed up a regular visitor to this delightful stone-built Elizabethan mansion only 30 miles from central London. The tall-chimneyed house itself dates from 1598, William Robinson's natural garden from some three centuries later. Stroll round it in summer, or sit in front of a log fire in the lounge in winter, before making for the dark-oak-panelled dining room, where two levels of set-price menu await. The more expensive typically offers five choices per course, the other two choices, and while the latter might rely on more everyday materials – cod instead of sea bass, for example – there is no sense of its being a poor relation.

On the main menu, prime materials feature in abundance: pan-fried foie gras, roast Bresse chicken with Perigord truffles, and grilled Dover sole (opened and filled with a ragoût of mussels, langoustine, tomato and basil). The skill level is high, the cooking sure-footed, and nothing is left to chance. Lightness and delicacy are features of the style, particularly among first courses of goats'-cheese ravioli, a light and creamy cappuccino of ceps, or lobster encased in pasta.

Although the food exhibits a strong traditional vein, in provençale fish soup with rouille and croûtons, for example, or in skate wing with anchovies and caper sauce, the kitchen is equally happy to deliver roast West Coast scallops with coriander purée and a port and sesame reduction. Meat is equally well handled – moist breast of pheasant, or crisp, pink roast medallions of venison – and portions tend to be generous. Cheeses, a choice of around 30, are kept in fine condition, and desserts run from pannacotta with poached rhubarb to rich chocolate tart with vanilla ice cream. Service from young staff can be 'quite chatty and jolly'.

Alphabetically arranged, the vast, global wine list kicks off with a 1976 Gewurztraminer, Sélection de Grains Nobles, from Alsace for £176, an intimidating introductory bottle. There is very little under £20 but house recommendations (under 'A Few Ideas', listed between Champagne and Hock) show that there is plenty of good drinking to be had around the £30 mark. Those with a fine palate, and the pocket to support it, will be overwhelmed by the plethora of rare and exquisite bottles. House wines start at £19.50.

CHEF: Mark Raffan PROPRIETORS: Peter Herbert and family OPEN: all week 12.30 to 1.45, 7.30 to 9.30 (9.45 Sat, 9 Sun) CLOSED: D 25 Dec exc residents MEALS: Set L £23 (2 courses) to £52, Set L Sun £35, Set D £37 to £52 SERVICE: net prices, card slips closed CARDS: MasterCard, Switch, Visa DETAILS: 55 seats. Private parties: 8 main room, 16 private room. Car park. Vegetarian meals. No children under 7 in dining room. Jacket and tie preferred. No smoking in dining room. Wheelchair access (not WC). No music ACCOMMODATION: 18 rooms, all with bath/shower. TV. Phone. Room only £90 to £300. No children under 7 exc babies in hotel. Baby facilities. Fishing (*The Which? Hotel Guide*)

EAST WITTON North Yorkshire **map 8**

▲ Blue Lion

East Witton DL8 4SN
TEL: (01969) 624273 FAX: (01969) 624189 COOKING **3**
EMAIL: bluelion@breathemail.net MODERN BRITISH
on A6108 between Masham and Leyburn £28–£46

Log fires, stone floors, wooden bench seats and meat hooks on the ceiling help to maintain the feel of a relaxed, characterful and traditional village pub. Polite, attentive and knowledgeable staff bustle about serving dishes from an ambitiously long bar menu of some three dozen savoury items on top of the restaurant's carte. Naturally, the spread is wide, from Thai-style fishcakes with chilli jam, via onion and blue Wensleydale tart, to pork fillet rolled in ceps. Seafood is well handled – perhaps a trio of sea bass, cod and salmon with star anise sauce, or seared scallops with a tangy but creamy lemon risotto – and game makes appearances in the shape of a flavoursome daube of wild boar with garlic mash, roast saddle of hare, and richly flavoured loin of rare-cooked roe deer.

Vegetarians are well looked after with eggs Florentine and home-made tagliatelle with broad beans, while desserts might include a fresh-sounding summer fruit and champagne jelly as well as traditional sticky toffee pudding. A compact, well-chosen wine list, with good choice under £20, offers a dozen by the glass, including Anselmi Soave and Norton Estate Barbera from Argentina.

CHEF: John Dalby PROPRIETORS: Paul and Helen Klein OPEN: Sun L 12 to 2.30, all week D 7 to 9.30 CLOSED: 25 Dec MEALS: alc (main courses £11 to £17). Bar food available SERVICE: not inc CARDS: Delta, MasterCard, Switch, Visa DETAILS: 80 seats. 30 seats outside. Private parties: 40 main room, 16 private room. Car park. Vegetarian meals. Children's helpings. No music ACCOMMODATION: 12 rooms, all with bath/shower. TV. Phone. B&B £53.50 to £89. Rooms for disabled. Baby facilities (*The Which? Hotel Guide*)

EATON BISHOP Herefordshire map 5

▲ Ancient Camp Inn

NEW ENTRY

Ruckhall, Eaton Bishop HR2 9QX — COOKING **2**
TEL: (01981) 250449 FAX: (01981) 251581 — MODERN BRITISH-PLUS
off A465 at Belmont Abbey, 4m W of Hereford — £21–£45

At the end of a narrow, winding road, a stunning vantage point high above the river gives a wonderful vista of a stretch of the Wye. The long, white-painted old inn derives its character from stone walls, flagstone floors and log fires, and feels well cared for. The kitchen scores for sourcing fine ingredients, and dishes are simply and well conceived, as well as attractively presented. A pastry case filled with oyster and shiitake mushrooms plus a few strands of leek, all splashed with a frothy sauce began one meal, followed by a chunky roast loin of pork laid over mushroom risotto.

A couple of the six main courses usually involve fish, perhaps pan-fried sea bass or herb-crusted cod. Underseasoning and the absence of some advertised flavours took the edge off an inspection meal, but technical competence holds everything together, and desserts are a strong suit: apple and raspberry crumble with a crunchy, sugary oatmeal topping, and thin slivers of pineapple spread out like a carpet, served with two scoops of white chocolate ice cream. Service is cheerful, and around 50 appealing and reasonably priced wines start with house Côtes du Roussillon at £9.50.

CHEF: Jason Eland PROPRIETORS: Jason and Lisa Eland OPEN: Tue to Sun L 12 to 2, Tue to Sat D 7 to 9 CLOSED: 1st 2 weeks Jan MEALS: alc (main courses L £6 to £11, D £10 to £16). Set D £19.95 SERVICE: not inc CARDS: Delta, MasterCard, Switch, Visa DETAILS: 24 seats. 20 seats outside. Private parties: 24 main room, 20 private room. Car park. Vegetarian meals. No children under 12 in dining room. No smoking in dining room. Wheelchair access (not WC). Music ACCOMMODATION: 5 rooms, all with bath/shower. TV. Phone. B&B £45 to £70. No children under 12 in accommodation. Fishing (*The Which? Hotel Guide*)

---

indicates that smoking is either banned altogether or that a dining-room is maintained for non-smokers. The symbol does not apply to restaurants that simply have no-smoking areas.

Not inc *in the details at the end of an entry indicates that no service charge is made and any tipping is at the discretion of the customer.*

ELLAND West Yorkshire **map 8**

Bertie's Supper Rooms £ NEW ENTRY

Brook Street, Elland HX5 9AW COOKING **2**
TEL: (01422) 371724 FAX: (01422) 372830 BRASSERIE
EMAIL: info@berties-catering.co.uk £21–£37

Bertie's is a multifaceted operation. Occupying the ground floor of a stolid civic building, it acts as pub, wine merchant and brasserie, with function rooms available too. Eating is as informal as it gets, with banquettes in a raised area and seats at the bar. A short brasserie-style menu offers the likes of seafood bisque with good shellfish flavour and all the trimmings, tender lamb shank on a bed of olive-oiled mash, and calf's liver and bacon. More urbane dishes have included tempura of Scarborough woof with chilli and sesame coleslaw, or seared tuna with bok choy, chilli, honey and soy. Potted Stilton and Guinness cake makes an unusual way to finish. Service is rapid to a fault. The walk-in wine cellar is stocked with 250 bottles, mostly from the Old World, though a short list of 30 bottles is provided in the dining room. House wines are £10 and six are available by the glass.

CHEF: Richard Wood PROPRIETOR: Brett Woodward OPEN: Tue to Fri L 12 to 3, Mon to Fri D 5.30 to 10.30 CLOSED: bank hols MEALS: alc (main courses £6 to £9.50) SERVICE: not inc, card slips closed CARDS: MasterCard, Switch, Visa DETAILS: 90 seats. Private parties: 70 main room, 80 to 250 private rooms. Car park. Vegetarian meals. Children's helpings. Wheelchair access (not WC). Music. Air-conditioned (£5)

ELSTREE Hertfordshire **map 3**

▲ Edgwarebury Hotel, Beaufort Restaurant

Barnet Lane, Elstree WD6 3RE COOKING **3**
TEL: (020) 8953 8227 FAX: (020) 8207 3668 FRENCH
EMAIL: edgwarebury@corushotels.com £33–£62

The neo-Tudor mansion, with ten acres of woodland and views over London (it is about half an hour from Islington), sets about the historical theme with a will, sporting paintings of the Spanish Armada, a front door that used to guard Lewes prison, much dark wood, mullioned windows, and heraldic printed fabrics. Chris Fisher's food, however, hardly ever looks back, preferring a contemporary approach that takes in red mullet with squid ink risotto, and a Madeira-sauced variation on pigeon pastilla.

The style is attractive, materials varied and dishes interesting: chargrilled skate wing comes with preserved artichokes and laverbread, and lambs' kidneys are served with pea purée and a root vegetable broth. Desserts ('please allow 30 minutes') arouse as much curiosity as anything, given prune stew Bramley ragoût custard crumble splash, a butterscotch leche-frita with cardamom custard, and tequila-soaked brioche with vanilla and chilli fruit salad, accompanied by crème fraîche and spearmint dust. A short, global wine list offers a fair proportion under £20, including house vin de pays at £13.50.

CHEF: Chris Fisher PROPRIETOR: Corus and Regal Hotels OPEN: Sun to Fri L 12.30 to 2.15, all week D 7 to 9.30 MEALS: alc (main courses £11 to £20). Bar menu available SERVICE: not inc CARDS: Amex, Diners, MasterCard, Switch, Visa DETAILS: 60 seats. Private parties: 84 main room, 18 and 40 private rooms. Car park. Children's helpings. No smoking in dining room. Wheelchair access (not WC). Music ACCOMMODATION: 47 rooms, all with bath/shower. TV. Phone. Room only £70 to £195. Rooms for disabled (£5)

ELY Cambridgeshire **map 6**

Old Fire Engine House

25 St Mary's Street, Ely CB7 4ER COOKING **2**
TEL: (01353) 662582 FAX: (01353) 668364 TRADITIONAL ENGLISH FARMHOUSE
£29–£44

Once a fire station, now partly an art gallery, this long-standing restaurant (opened in 1968) derives its character from a blend of informality and simplicity. As the owners concede, the lack of sophistication might be viewed as basic to the point of crudity by those to whom food is now a branch of the fashion industry, but the style, based on farmhouse cookery of the late nineteenth/early twentieth century is to be cherished for more than just its rarity value.

Local and seasonal materials – including game and Fens fish – help to give the food its particular identity, from lovage soup through Norfolk samphire to pike mayonnaise and Brancaster mussels in white wine. Braises (beef and mushrooms in beer), and casseroles (pigeon with bacon and black olives) appear regularly, followed perhaps by syllabub, lemon meringue pie, or apple Betty. France dominates the rather traditional wine list, which starts with house Liebfraumilch at £7.50 and Chilean Cabernet Sauvignon at £9.

CHEF: Terri Kindred PROPRIETORS: Ann Ford and Michael Jarman OPEN: all week L 12.15 to 2, Mon to Sat D 7.15 to 9 (morning coffee Mon to Sat 10.30 to 11.30, afternoon tea all week 3.30 to 5.30) CLOSED: 24 Dec to 6 Jan, bank hols MEALS: alc (main courses £13 to £15) SERVICE: not inc CARDS: Delta, MasterCard, Switch, Visa DETAILS: 58 seats. 24 seats outside. Private parties: 36 main room, 22 private room. Small car park. Vegetarian meals. Children's helpings. No smoking in 1 dining room. No music

EMSWORTH Hampshire **map 2**

Spencers

36 North Street, Emsworth PO10 7DG COOKING **3**
TEL/FAX: (01243) 372744 MODERN BRITISH
£19–£41

The Spencers run two operations – a ground-floor brasserie with marble-topped tables, and a slightly more formal upstairs restaurant, with booth seating, flickering gas fire and laden bookshelves – but the same menu is offered in each (with a cheaper, set-price version available in the brasserie before 7pm). The style is modern and robust, with substantial salads and pasta dishes, and an additional fish menu bulking the core starters and mains: perhaps seared scallops dressed with chilli, mango and papaya, or a hefty portion of 'patently fresh' anchovy-crusted roast cod on a bed of Puy lentils with wasabi mustard.

Bold flavours also crop up in a crisp cake of salmon and crab with a sweetly contrasting plum and hoisin sauce, and in highly spiced onion soup, while praise has been heaped on tender braised shank of lamb, served with rich, garlic-infused gravy. Side-orders of veg can be a touch disappointing, but tangy glazed lemon tart has been an impressive dessert. Service is commended for swiftness and efficiency. A concise, well-selected wine list keeps nearly everything under £20, with French and Australian house wines at £10.50.

CHEF: Denis Spencer PROPRIETORS: Denis and Lesley Spencer OPEN: brasserie Mon to Sat 12 to 2, 6 to 10.30, restaurant D only 7 to 10.30 MEALS: alc (main courses £8 to £13.50). Set L and D before 7 brasserie only £6.95 (2 courses) SERVICE: not inc CARDS: Amex, Delta, Diners, MasterCard, Switch, Visa DETAILS: 64 seats. Private parties: 30 main room, 10 private room. Vegetarian meals. No smoking in 1 dining room. Music. Air-conditioned (£5)

36 on the Quay

47 South Street, Emsworth PO10 7EG
TEL: (01243) 375592 and 372257 — COOKING **6**
FAX: (01243) 375593 — MODERN BRITISH/FRENCH
WEB SITE: www.36onthequay.co.uk — £33–£68

The smart, whitewashed cottage has bagged itself a prime spot down by the bobbing boats, where the cumulative effect of its designer curtains, upholstered chairs, warm yellow walls and top-of-the-range table appointments is one of luxury and comfort. Fish understandably figures prominently, not least among starters: meaty sea bass has come in a puff pastry box, its glazed lid raised at a jaunty angle, with asparagus and fennel in attendance, all surrounded by a light rosemary butter sauce. 'Ramon is a stacker,' according to one visitor who ate a tower of red mullet fillets interleaved with potato and sweet onion.

Embellishment is a feature of the cooking style: dishes can reach great heights, although a large number of intricate elements offer plenty of opportunity for things to go wrong with peripherals. The essentials, however, are sound, consisting of prime materials accurately timed: for example, four fat medallions of well-seasoned, pink Welsh lamb, served with a wedge of liver on a colourful mound of spaghetti vegetables, all in a light thyme gravy.

Equally labour-intensive desserts might feature a plate of themed miniatures, and there is usually a hot soufflé: a rich but light orange one, accompanied by poached kumquats and vanilla ice for one visitor. The menu's hint that meals may take a long time is no idle boast, and Karen Farthing's friendly and direct presence is appreciated. Classy French wines are the mainstay of the lengthy list, although a careful selection of New World stars provides plenty of diversion. However, quality comes at a price, and those seeking a bottle below £20 had best stick to the house wine selections, which kick off at £13.50

CHEF: Ramon Farthing PROPRIETORS: Ramon and Karen Farthing OPEN: Tue to Fri L 12 to 1.45, Mon to Sat D 7 to 9.45 CLOSED: 25 Dec, bank hols exc Good Fri MEALS: Set L £16.95 (2 courses) to £19.95, Set D £34.50, gourmet menu L and D £42.50 SERVICE: not inc CARDS: Amex, Delta, Diners, MasterCard, Switch, Visa DETAILS: 38 seats. Private parties: 35 main room, 10 private room. Car park. Children's helpings. No smoking in dining room. Wheelchair access (not WC). Occasional music

EPWORTH North Lincolnshire map 9

Epworth Tap

9–11 Market Place, Epworth DN9 1EU
TEL: (01427) 873333 FAX: (01427) 875020
3m S of M180 junction 2

COOKING **4**
MODERN EUROPEAN
£25–£42

Thoughts of retirement have been put to one side for at least another year, as a new range has been installed in the kitchen, and Helen Wynne continues tirelessly to make her own bread and ice cream, and produce dependable cooking in the unchanging, unpretentious wine bar-cum-bistro setting. Sensibly, for a single-handed operation, the menu includes a few dishes that can be prepared in advance – maybe pear and parsnip soup, ham set in a Riesling jelly, or a casserole of locally farmed venison in red wine with thyme – the better to concentrate on last-minute timing where it matters.

Fish from Cornwall or Scotland might appear as fillet of salmon and scallops with a fresh sorrel sauce, while roast loin of Tamworth pork from a specialist supplier is stuffed with Agen prunes and sage. Finish with a selection of cheeses from Neal's Yard, or panettone bread-and-butter pudding. John Wynne ensures his extensive cellar moves with the times and has updated his Portuguese and New World sections. However, mature clarets and Burgundies are the mainstay of a largely traditional list. While there are many good wines under £20, this is one of the times where it pays to spend a little more.

CHEF/PROPRIETOR: Helen Wynne OPEN: Wed to Sat D 7.30 to 9.15 MEALS: alc (main courses £9.50 to £14.50). Set D Sat £22.50 SERVICE: not inc, card slips closed CARDS: Amex, Delta, MasterCard, Switch, Visa DETAILS: 30 seats. Private parties: 22 main room, 22 private room. No children under 4. Children's helpings. Vegetarian meals if pre-booked. Smoking restrictions if pre-booked. Music

ERPINGHAM Norfolk map 6

▲ Ark

The Street, Erpingham NR11 7QB
TEL: (01263) 761535
3m off A140 Cromer road, 4m N of Aylsham

COOKING **4**
ENGLISH COUNTRY COOKING
£23–£48

Far away from the bright lights, indeed well out in the country a few miles inland from Cromer, Mike and Sheila Kidd run the kind of unpretentious restaurant that has been the backbone of rural eating for decades. They shop and cook with integrity, using local suppliers for beef, lamb, fish and shellfish, producing mussel soup, sea bass with sorrel sauce, and roast loin of spring lamb with a gratin of aubergine, tomato and cream. Organic chicken might be roasted with honey, coarse salt and peppercorns, and loin of Gloucester Old Spot pork, one of a number of rare-breed meats, has been braised with Marsala and red wine. Home-grown vegetables, herbs and fruit add their own vitality.

There is little in the way of trimming or embellishment, just straightforward cooking and a sensible respect for the seasons: expect perhaps a simple wild mushroom feuilleté to start, and venison with pepper ragoût and herb butter to follow. British and Irish cheeses are from Neal's Yard, and desserts have included lemon tart, raspberry syllabub, and poached figs. Wines are chosen with an eye for both interest and value. Around twenty half-bottles extend the options, and eight house wines start the ball rolling at £10.50 (£2.50 a glass).

CHEF: Sheila Kidd PROPRIETORS: Michael and Sheila Kidd OPEN: Sun L 12.30 to 2, Tue to Sat D 7 to 9.30 (may also open Sun and Mon D in high season) CLOSED: Tue D in winter MEALS: Set L £15.25, Set D £21.25 (2 courses) to £28 SERVICE: not inc CARDS: none DETAILS: 28 seats. 16 seats outside. Private parties: 30 main room, 8 private room. Car park. Vegetarian meals. Children's helpings. No smoking in dining room. Wheelchair access (also WC). No music ACCOMMODATION: 3 rooms, 2 with bath/shower. TV. D,B&B £70 to £135. Rooms for disabled. Baby facilities

EVERSHOT Dorset — map 2

▲ Summer Lodge

Summer Lane, Evershot DT2 0JR — NEW CHEF
TEL: (01935) 83424 FAX: (01935) 83005 — MODERN EUROPEAN
WEB SITE: www.summerlodgehotel.com — £44–£72

The secluded eighteenth-century dower house, in a tiny time-warped rural village, is a tall, rambling, cream-coloured building clothed in wisteria, its floor-to-ceiling dining room windows giving views over its walled garden. The cooking has traditionally taken advantage of high-quality produce and adopted a soothing country-house approach, offering perhaps lobster ravioli, roast breast of Gressingham duck with foie gras, and warm chocolate mousse with praline ice cream. Whether the style will remain the same under Billy Butcher, newly arrived from Amberley Castle in Sussex as the Guide went to press, remains to be seen, but we welcome reports on the new regime. Mature bins from Bordeaux and Burgundy stand out on the impressive wine list, which also covers the rest of Europe and the New World with assurance and skill. The cost of keeping such an extensive cellar does not come cheap, although care has been taken to provide numerous bottles under £20. Half-bottles are plentiful too. House wines start at £12.50.

CHEF: Billy Butcher PROPRIETORS: Nigel and Margaret Corbett OPEN: all week 12 to 2, 7 to 9.30 MEALS: alc (main courses £15 to £24) SERVICE: not inc, card slips closed CARDS: Amex, Delta, Diners, MasterCard, Switch, Visa DETAILS: 50 seats. 20 seats outside. Private parties: 40 main room, 40 private room. Car park. Vegetarian meals. No smoking in dining room. Wheelchair access (not WC). Occasional music ACCOMMODATION: 17 rooms, all with bath/shower. TV. Phone. Room only £85 to £285. Rooms for disabled. Baby facilities. Swimming pool (*The Which? Hotel Guide*)

EXETER Devon — map 1

Brazz £ — NEW ENTRY

10–12 Palace Gate, Exeter EX1 1JA — COOKING **3**
TEL: (01392) 252525 FAX: (01392) 253045 — BRITISH BRASSERIE
£22–£55

Building on the success of the pioneer in Taunton (see entry), Kit Chapman formed the English Brasserie Company to manage this emerging mini-chain. As an alternative to burger joints and bistros, Brazz shows what can be done when a serious outfit gets its teeth into the business of providing informal food in clean, smart and stylish surroundings. The door handles are ten feet high, the tropical fish tank is even bigger than the one in Taunton, and the half-dome is carefully mirrored to look like a whole one (this is 'millennium modernism' for those who follow such things). A sense of purpose runs through everything, including a clearly set out menu that allows for all-day grazing as well as more substantial appetites.

The focus throughout is on simple, honest cooking, from fat, accurately timed scallops encased in a light, crisp batter with an aromatic dressing, to 'dreamy' pan-fried foie gras with an unctuous lentil purée. Classics are well handled – admirable ribeye steak with proper béarnaise and crisp, thin frites – and puddings tend to be indulgent, taking in strawberry and scone mousse, sticky toffee, and a chocolate extravaganza called cathedral pudding, part of whose proceeds are donated to the Exeter Cathedral Music Foundation. The PDQ lunch looks inviting, service is friendly, and the wine list aims for drinkability without frills, starting with house French at £9.95. Local cider is £3.

CHEF: Nick Fisher PROPRIETOR: The English Brasserie Company OPEN: all week 11.30 (12 Sun and Mon) to 3, 6 to 10.30 (11 Fri and Sat) CLOSED: 25 Dec MEALS: alc (main courses £7 to £15). Set L Mon to Fri £8.95 (2 courses) SERVICE: not inc CARDS: Amex, Delta, Diners, MasterCard, Switch, Visa DETAILS: 200 seats. Private parties: 100 main room. Vegetarian meals. Children's helpings. Wheelchair access (also WC). Music. Air-conditioned

Michael Caines at Royal Clarence

DEVON NEWCOMER OF THE YEAR

NEW ENTRY

Cathedral Yard, Exeter EX1 1HD
TEL: (01392) 310031 FAX: (01392) 310032
EMAIL: tables@michaelcaines.com
WEB SITE: www.michaelcaines.com

COOKING **5**
FRENCH
£28–£48

With the arrival of two new pedigree restaurants, Exeter seems to be taking off. Michael Caines (who continues to cook at Gidleigh Park: see entry, Chagford) sees this as the first of a small chain of restaurants within the Corus and Regal Hotels group. A modern, stylish refit takes the cathedral as its theme – those with a view through the large glass frontage will not be disappointed – and small, tightly packed tables are likely to be occupied by a wide spread of ages.

While it may owe inspiration to Gidleigh, it doesn't deal in the same luxury ingredients, time-consuming procedures, busy incidentals, or highly skilled dishes: the trade off is a lower bill. All the same, it is a notch or two above brasserie food, subjecting fine raw materials to accurate timing: for example, in a starter of five scallops, each on a mound of tasty diced tomato flesh, encircling a tiny slab of layered aubergine and pepper terrine, the plate first streaked with tapénade, tomato and aubergine splashes.

Such complex cooking is rare for the price, and while there may be weak spots (saucing at inspection) it still pleases and impresses with, for example, a tightly packed grilled brochette of flavourful lamb saddle and kidney (pink as ordered), served on finely diced and subtly creamed root vegetables. Colourful and artistic presentation extends to desserts such as a chocolate-covered banana parfait on pale green lime coulis. Although side dishes are charged extra (small quantities of vegetables are first rate), overall value is good, helped by 80-plus wines arranged by varietal, the majority below £25. House Chilean is £13.

CHEF: Jean-Marc Zanetti PROPRIETOR: Michael Caines OPEN: all week 12 to 2.30, 7 to 10 (open 6 for pre-concert D) MEALS: alc (main courses £12.50 to £15). Set L £14 (2 courses) to £17 SERVICE: not inc CARDS: Amex, Delta, Diners, MasterCard, Switch, Visa DETAILS: 76 seats. Private parties: 76 main room, 30 to 90 private rooms. Vegetarian meals. Children's helpings. No smoking in dining room. Wheelchair access (also WC). No music. Air-conditioned

FARNBOROUGH Kent **map 3**

Chapter One

Farnborough Common, Locksbottom,
Farnborough BR6 8NF
TEL: (01689) 854848 FAX: (01689) 858439 COOKING **4**
EMAIL: pennyatch1@aol.com MODERN EUROPEAN
WEB SITE: www.chapter-1.co.uk £34–£54

The white, mock-Tudor building, near a junction of the A21, is easily picked out by its blue neon sign. Inside, cool contemporary décor features cream walls with splashes of colour, and stained glass in art deco style. Andrew McLeish, who has previously worked at Chez Nico (before it became Cheznico) and the Ritz (see entries, London), arrived in March 2000 to head up the kitchen. Sound technique and a willingness to experiment are evident in, for example, a starter of roast gnocchi with braised chestnut, pumpkin and lobster, and a North African inspired rump of lamb with aubergine, chickpeas and couscous spiked with preserved lemon and parsley.

Balancing this, a classical rendition of beef bourguignon has come with parsnip mash, and fish options have taken in baked brill with spinach and a reduction of red wine and ceps. Desserts are often accompanied by a sorbet: crème fraîche for mango and papaya spring rolls, or bitter chocolate with hot chocolate fondant. Service is informed and attentive. The wine list is classified into France and everywhere-else sections; choices are good, but the base price is high. House wines, identified only by their nationality, start at £11.

CHEF: Andrew McLeish PROPRIETOR: Selective Restaurants Group OPEN: all week 12 to 2.30 (3 Sun), 6.30 to 10.30 (11 Fri and Sat, 9.30 Sun) MEALS: alc (main courses £13.50). Set L £16 (2 courses) to £19.50. Brasserie menu available SERVICE: 12.5% (optional), card slips closed CARDS: Amex, Delta, Diners, MasterCard, Switch, Visa DETAILS: 120 seats. Private parties: 55 private room. Car park. Vegetarian meals. Children's helpings. No cigars/pipes in dining room. Wheelchair access (also WC). Music. Air-conditioned (£5)

FAVERSHAM Kent **map 3**

Read's

Painter's Forstal, Faversham ME13 0EE
TEL: (01795) 535344 FAX: (01795) 591200 COOKING **7**
WEB SITE: www.reads.com MODERN BRITISH
on Eastling road, 2m S of Faversham £31–£63

It was a relief, felt one visitor, not to be overwhelmed by décor. Read's has the solid appeal of a country restaurant, with muted cream and beige colours, discreet and tasteful pictures, and candles on white-clothed tables. David Pitchford uses some classical French techniques in his firmly modern British approach, and their effects on texture and flavour contribute in large measure to the operation's success. They also help to keep output consistent. The kitchen works with good supplies from Whitstable fish to tender and flavourful roast Kentish lamb, by way of Brogdale apples and pears. And it keeps pace with the seasons: local asparagus with a trembling seafood mousse and a rich beurre blanc was an evocative summer dish for one visitor.

All the elements in dishes work both individually and collectively, and there are no superfluous gestures, frills or trimmings. A three-way starter of smoked haddock – vichyssoise, a mini fishcake, and a rich, creamy brandade – managed to coax a wide range of flavours out of one everyday ingredient. This may not be pushing back the culinary boundaries, but the ability to keep things focused produces food that is simply enjoyable to eat, as in a bouillabaisse of exactly cooked local lobster in a deeply flavoured bisque, served with garlicky rouille, croûtons and a few simple boiled potatoes.

Desserts are equally well thought out and executed, judging by a combination of iced banana soufflé, banana tarte Tatin and rum and raisin ice cream that rated highly at inspection. Threaded through meals are hot canapés, an appetiser soup, a pre-dessert (perhaps a creamy lemon posset), and the presence of Rona Pitchford, who presides over service by a mix of French and local youngsters. Those without time to peruse the extensive and knowledgeable wine list will welcome the distillation of 60 bottles under £20 which appears at the front. Those who do have time will be delighted by a selection of the world's greatest wines at affordable prices. Ten wines are available by the glass and a fine selection of half-bottles ensure plenty of flexibility.

CHEF: David Pitchford PROPRIETORS: David and Rona Pitchford OPEN: Tue to Sat 12 to 2, 7 to 9.30 MEALS: Set L £18.50, Set D Tue to Fri £24 to £38, Set D Sat £36 to £38 SERVICE: not inc, card slips closed CARDS: Amex, Delta, Diners, MasterCard, Switch, Visa DETAILS: 40 seats. 12 seats outside. Private parties: 65 main room, 20 private room. Car park. Vegetarian meals. Children's helpings. No cigars/pipes in dining-room. Wheelchair access (not WC). No music

(£5)

FERNHURST West Sussex **map 3**

Kings Arms

Midhurst Road, Fernhurst GU27 3HA COOKING **2**
TEL: (01428) 652005 MODERN BRITISH
on A286, 1m S of Fernhurst £23–£38

The Hirsts' seventeenth-century pub, set in Sussex farmland near Haslemere, certainly looks the part: hanging baskets give the right bucolic impression outside, and low-slung beams within mean much ducking of heads. Pew seating and plenty of horse brasses complete the picture. The menu, chalked up on boards, mostly conforms to what would be expected in this setting: that is, as long as you expect beef carpaccio with truffle-oiled salad, or seafood and saffron soup from a country pub these days. Among main courses, rack of lamb with cranberry sauce, poached salmon on a bed of spinach, and pork with apricots have all been praised, while desserts are somewhat more exuberant concoctions, maybe banana tarte Tatin with toffee cream, or rhubarb and white chocolate in a trifle, which won over an inspector. Wines have been chosen with care, and prices are fair throughout. House French is £9.65.

CHEF: Michael Hirst PROPRIETORS: Michael and Annabel Hirst OPEN: all week L 12 to 2.30, Mon to Sat D 7 to 9.30 CLOSED: 25 Dec, first 2 weeks Jan MEALS: alc (main courses £6.50 to £12) SERVICE: not inc CARDS: Delta, MasterCard, Switch, Visa DETAILS: 46 seats. 70 seats outside. Private parties: 28 main room, 12 to 50 private rooms. Car park. Vegetarian meals. Children's helpings No children under 14 after 7. No smoking in 1 dining room. Wheelchair access (not WC). No music

FERRENSBY North Yorkshire **map 9**

▲ General Tarleton

Boroughbridge Road, Ferrensby HG5 0QB
TEL: (01423) 340284 FAX: (01423) 340288 COOKING **5**
EMAIL: gti@generaltarleton.co.uk MODERN BRITISH
off A6065, 3m N of Knaresborough £25–£40

The conversion of this eighteenth-century pub into a bar/brasserie and more-formal dining-room has not obscured its original function. Well-kept hand-pumped beers, such as Black Sheep, are still served for those who only want to pop in for a pint. Once ensconced, however, your attention may well be drawn to the blackboard menu with its offers of seafood and items such as slow-cooked lamb with mash.

In the dining-room, properly spaced tables laid with expensive napery form the setting for John Topham's assured, modern cooking. Chilli salt squid, or corn-fed chicken breast wrapped in Parma ham and cabbage, sound a more metropolitan note than may be expected in a Yorkshire village with a duck pond. More traditional preparations have also drawn praise, including chicken liver and foie gras parfait, and top-drawer grilled pork sausages from Ilkley, served with red onion gravy. To finish there might be an agreeably light tiramisù, or toffee pudding, commended by one reader for being 'as rich and sticky as you could hope for'. Courteous and efficient staff add to the sense of well-being. France dominates the down-to-earth, well-priced wine list, which includes many bottles under £15. Eighteen wines are offered by the glass.

CHEF: John Topham PROPRIETORS: John Topham, and Denis and Juliet Watkins OPEN: all week 12 to 2.15 (2.30 Sun), 6 to 9 (8.30 Sun all year, 9.30 Mon to Fri summer, 10 Sat summer) CLOSED: 25 Dec MEALS: Set L £17.50, Set D £25. Bar/brasserie meals available (main courses £7.50 to £14) SERVICE: not inc CARDS: Amex, Delta, MasterCard, Switch, Visa DETAILS: 60 seats. 40 seats outside. Private parties: 36 main room, 36 private room. Car park. Vegetarian meals. Children's helpings. No smoking in dining room. Wheelchair access (also WC). No music ACCOMMODATION: 14 rooms, all with bath/shower. TV. Phone. Room only £60 to £100. Rooms for disabled (£5)

Dining rooms where music, either live or recorded, is never played are signalled by No music *in the details at the end of an entry.*

All entries in the Guide are re-researched and rewritten every year, not least because restaurant standards fluctuate. Don't rely on an out-of-date Guide.

FLETCHING East Sussex map 3

▲ Griffin Inn

Fletching TN22 3SS
TEL: (01825) 722890
WEB SITE: www.thegriffininn.co.uk
off A272, between Maresfield and Newick, 3m NW of Uckfield

COOKING **2**
MODERN EUROPEAN
£26–£48

For four centuries now, the Griffin has been the focal point of this unmarred Sussex village. Local lamb, organic pork, game birds in season and fish from Cornwall testify to the owners' commitment to real food, which is given decidedly contemporary treatment by Jason Williams. Lentils with star-anise accompany sauté scallops in a starter, while for main courses a broad world view is evidenced in salmon with harissa, spring onions and red pepper 'aïoli'; pumpkin gnocchi with basil, garlic and Parmesan; and spiced duck with stir-fried vegetables, noodles and ginger. Spices find their way into desserts, too: cardamom and saffron in the lemon posset, for example. Thursdays are devoted to fish. A resourceful wine list makes real efforts to provide a good range of flavours; a dozen house selections start at £9.80.

CHEF: Jason Williams PROPRIETORS: Nigel and Bridget Pullan OPEN: all week 12 to 2.30, 7 to 9.30 CLOSED: Sun D in winter, 25 Dec MEALS: alc exc Sun L (main courses £8.50 to £17.50). Set L Sun £18.50. Bar menu available all week L and D SERVICE: not inc CARDS: Amex, Delta, Diners, MasterCard, Switch, Visa DETAILS: 60 seats. 30 seats outside. Private parties: 35 main room. Car park. Vegetarian meals. Children's helpings. No music ACCOMMODATION: 8 rooms, all with bath/shower. TV. B&B £50 to £85. Rooms for disabled. Baby facilities (*The Which? Hotel Guide*) (£5)

FOSS CROSS Gloucestershire map 2

Hare and Hounds £

Foss Cross GL54 4NN
TEL/FAX: (01285) 720288
on A429, just S of Fossebridge, 6m N of Cirencester

NEW CHEF
MODERN BRITISH
£21–£41

'Everything one could want from a pub with food – a roaring log fire on a freezing day and an equally warm welcome.' Well-heeled locals also appreciate the value and informal atmosphere that prevails at one of a threesome of Gloucestershire pubs run by Sonya Kidney and Leo Brooke-Little (see also Marsh Goose at Moreton-in-Marsh and Churchill Arms at Paxford), here in partnership with Emma and Shaun Davis.

Guy Simpson arrived just as the Guide was going to press, too late for us to receive any reports or send an inspector, but the daily menu is likely to continue steering its clever course between run-of-the-mill and more outlandish ideas: perhaps taking in mackerel with lemon and coriander mayonnaise, rare breed meat from nearby Chesterton Farm (Old Spot belly pork with sauerkraut maybe), and plum and berry crumble. Ten house wines beckon at under £10, with nothing more than £30.

CHEF: Guy Simpson PROPRIETORS: Emma and Shaun Davis, and Leo and Sonya Brooke-Little OPEN: all week 12 to 2, 7 to 9 CLOSED: 25 Dec MEALS: alc (main courses £7 to £12.50) SERVICE: not inc CARDS: Delta, MasterCard, Switch, Visa DETAILS: 90 seats. 90 seats outside. Private parties: 20 main room. Car park. Vegetarian meals. Children's helpings. Wheelchair access (also WC).No music

FOULSHAM Norfolk **map 6**

The Gamp £ ✱

Claypit Lane, Foulsham NR20 5RW
TEL: (01362) 684114

COOKING **2**
MODERN BRITISH
£19–£39

Not much in the way of passing trade troubles the secluded village of Foulsham, home to this 200-year-old, creeper-covered building. A bar with copper-topped tables and a cottagey dining room overlooking the garden are the setting for simple, old-fashioned, homely cooking: locally smoked eel with horseradish and dill relish might be followed by roast Norfolk duckling with tangy orange sauce, or something from the grill: whole Dover sole, or a 12oz rump steak. Vegetarian choices might include a sauté of fennel, kohlrabi, leeks and almonds in a puff pastry case, while baked lemon and lime cream with honey and oatmeal biscuit is a typical sweet ending. The weekday set menu offers a good-value alternative to the carte. An enthusiastically annotated wine list affords reasonable breadth of choice (although no vintages are listed), with nearly all bottles under £20. House wines are £7.95.

CHEFS: Simon Nobbs and Andy Bush PROPRIETORS: Daphne and Andy Bush OPEN: Wed to Sun L12 to 1.30, Tue to Fri D 7 to 9.30 CLOSED: first 2 weeks Jan MEALS: alc exc Sun L (main courses £9.50 to £16.50). Set L £11.95, Set Tue to Fri D £11.95 SERVICE: not inc, card slips closed CARDS: MasterCard, Switch, Visa DETAILS: 40 seats. Private parties: 40 main room. Car park. Vegetarian meals. Children's helpings. No smoking in dining room. Wheelchair access (also WC). No music

FOWEY Cornwall **map 1**

Food for Thought

4 Town Quay, Fowey PL23 1AT
TEL: (01726) 832221 FAX: (01726) 832077

COOKING **3**
MODERN EUROPEAN/SEAFOOD
£31–£62

The converted customs house on the quay, just a few yards from the water's edge, makes an appropriate setting for the modern seafood cookery offered by the Billingsleys, now into their third decade here, and chef Glynn Wellington, who has clocked up two years. A long dining-room with beams and exposed shale walls is the setting for River Fowey oysters dressed in red wine and shallot vinegar, or squid sautéed with chilli, mint, coriander and pine nuts. Main courses offer a varied choice, ranging from grilled sole with sun-dried tomatoes, chorizo, chillies and garlic, to sea bass with beurre blanc, while crisp-skinned cod comes with spring onion mash and a lightly curried dressing. For meat-eaters, it might be best end of lamb with rosemary risotto and red wine sauce, and to finish there may be sticky date pudding with toffee sauce, or West

Country cheeses with oatcakes. The compact wine list opens with a house selection of French wines from £9.75.

CHEF: Glynn Wellington PROPRIETORS: Martin and Caroline Billingsley OPEN: Mon to Sat D only 7 to 9.30 CLOSED: 1 Jan to Easter MEALS: alc (main courses £12 to £22). Set D £19.95 SERVICE: not inc CARDS: Delta, Diners, MasterCard, Switch, Visa DETAILS: 45 seats. Vegetarian meals. Children's helpings. Wheelchair access (not WC). Music

FUNTINGTON West Sussex map 3

Hallidays

NEW ENTRY

Watery Lane, Funtington PO18 9LF
TEL: (01243) 575331

COOKING **3**
MODERN BRITISH
£22–£45

A sign with 'Hallidays' writ large guides visitors to this attractive thirteenth-century thatched cottage in a pretty village near Chichester. Once past the heavy oak door, they will find a beamed interior of muted green and cream, where helpful and efficient Peter Creech greets, and son-in-law Andy Stephenson mans the stoves. His careful, unpretentious cooking is enlivened by notably fresh and often seasonal ingredients. Griddled asparagus ('picked that day from just down the road') has come well dressed with herb-flecked olive oil and generously shaved Parmesan, and line-caught sea bass from a local fisherman has arrived on fresh tagliatelle with a delicate saffron sauce.

Quality ingredients are matched by attractive presentation: thick sliced gravad lax well partnered by its potato blini, and tender medallions of new season's lamb with local baby broad beans. Puddings maintain momentum with 'feather-light' lemon flummery on a crisp shortbread base, partnered by English strawberries in caramel sauce, and an 'immaculate' crème brûlée. Half a dozen house wines, from £9.75, open the list, which covers both Old and New Worlds and has a 'premier selection' of around a dozen bins.

CHEF: Andy Stephenson PROPRIETORS: A.M. Stephenson and P.R. Creech OPEN: Tue to Fri and Sun L 12.30 (12 Sun) to 1.30, Tue to Sat D 7.30 to 9.30 CLOSED: 2 weeks Mar, 1 week Sept MEALS: alc (main courses £12.50 to £15). Set L Tue to Fri £10.50 (2 courses) to £12.50, Set L Sun £14.95 SERVICE: not inc CARDS: Delta, MasterCard, Switch, Visa DETAILS: 30 seats. Private parties: 30 main room. Car park. No smoking in dining room. Wheelchair access (also women's WC). No music

GATEFORTH North Yorkshire map 9

Restaurant Martel

NEW ENTRY

Gateforth Hall, Gateforth YO8 9LJ
TEL: (01757) 228225 FAX: (01757) 228189
just off A63, 2½m E of Monk Fryston

COOKING **4**
MODERN BRITISH
£30–£61

Yorkshireman Martel Smith, after a spell with Marco Pierre White in London, has returned to his roots, choosing an elegant out-of-the-way Georgian hunting lodge in which to display his talent. A spacious, high-ceilinged dining room comes suitably attired with polished wood, modern art, upholstered chairs and smart linen, while a short menu ably combines modish and classical ideas. It is helped by a few luxuries – confit of duck and foie gras in Sauternes jelly, lobster ravioli, and veal fillet with girolles and truffles – and by a confident line in seafood: four notably fresh, skilfully seared scallops with a moist provençale risotto, or a main course of thick, firm fillet of roast sea bass with anchovy beignets and mushroom sauce.

Accurate timing and attention to detail are also evident in meat dishes, for example two towers of lamb fillet cooked pink, with a sweet, herby crust and a minty couscous. Proficiency reaches across the board, judging by an intensely flavoured banana and passion-fruit pyramid, and gooey, spicy pear tarte Tatin. Service at inspection was knowledgeable and professional, and the 80-plus global wine list has a healthy number of bottles under £20, with house vins de pays at £12.75.

CHEF/PROPRIETOR: Martel Smith OPEN: Tue to Fri and Sun L 12 to 2 (3 Sun), Tue to Sat D 7 to 10 MEALS: alc (main courses £16.50 to £19.50). Set L £14.50 (2 courses) to £17 SERVICE: not inc, card slips closed CARDS: Delta, MasterCard, Switch, Visa DETAILS: 45 seats. Private parties: 55 main room. Car park. Vegetarian meals. No smoking in 1 dining room. Music

GATESHEAD Tyne & Wear — map 10

▲ Eslington Villa

8 Station Road, Low Fell, Gateshead NE9 6DR
TEL: (0191) 487 6017 FAX: (0191) 420 0667
leave A1(M) at Team Valley Trading Estate, approach Gateshead along Team Valley; at top of Eastern Avenue, turn left into Station Road

COOKING **3**
ENGLISH/FRENCH
£25–£43

After the last edition of the Guide appeared, Barry Forster sold his own restaurant, Forsters in East Boldon, and took over the kitchens of this expanded and refurbished Edwardian hotel. The internal transformation – sandy-ochre walls, modern pictures, big settees – has produced more space and brought a new freshness and feeling of purpose. Rather than striking out into the wild blue yonder, Barry Forster prefers familiar but cosmopolitan ideas, such as black pudding and sausage cake with mushy peas, belly pork with wasabi mash and chilli tomato relish, and spicy pieces of cold chicken breast on well-flavoured couscous mixed with vegetables and coriander.

Dishes are generally well rendered: tender sirloin steak with a pepper sauce and decent chips, and a classic combination of smoked haddock with poached egg, spinach and beurre blanc. Portions are on the large side, but a traditional dessert awaits those with room: perhaps chocolate truffle cake, or sticky toffee pudding. Beer is a popular drink, although most of the 40 wines stay below £20. House wines – two French, two Australian and two Chilean – are £11.50.

CHEF: Barry Forster PROPRIETORS: Nick and Melanie Tulip OPEN: Sun to Fri L 12 to 2, Mon to Sat D 7 to 9.45 CLOSED: Christmas MEALS: alc (main courses £9 to £13). Set L Mon to Fri £11.50 to £15.50 (2 courses), Set L Sun £16.95 SERVICE: not inc CARDS: Amex, Delta, MasterCard, Switch, Visa DETAILS: 86 seats. 20 seats outside. Private parties: 55 main room, 36 private room. Car park. Vegetarian meals. Children's helpings. No smoking in dining room. Wheelchair access (not WC). Music ACCOMMODATION: 18 rooms, all with bath/shower. TV. Phone. B&B £45 to £75. Baby facilities (*The Which? Hotel Guide*)

GILLINGHAM Dorset **map 2**

▲ Stock Hill House

Stock Hill, Gillingham SP8 5NR
TEL: (01747) 823626 FAX: (01747) 825628
EMAIL: reception@stockhill.net
WEB SITE: www.stockhill.net
off B3081, 1m W of Gillingham

COOKING **5**
EUROPEAN/AUSTRIAN
£29–£51

Stock Hill's rural situation is highlighted by its duck pond and the woods that surround the grey stone Victorian house. But it is no rustic backwater. Housekeeping is immaculate, and the draped and mirrored lounge and tasteful dining room are cared for to a fault. There are not many Austrian restaurants in the British Isles, and while Peter Hauser doesn't ram his native food down people's throats, so to speak, he does indulge in a few excursions that add colour and distinctiveness to his otherwise Anglo-French menus, from spätzli, Wiener schnitzel, and pork tenderloin with Tyrolean bread dumpling, to the inevitable Salzburger nockerl (for two).

Among such regularly occurring items as home-cured herring fillet with white wine and onion cream, or grilled Somerset goats' cheese on Dutch cabbage vinaigrette, might be ox tongue salad, or a gamey-tasting partridge, roasted in the Aga and served with Madeira jus. If the nockerl's eggy richness sounds too much at the end of a meal, consider cinnamon parfait with mulled dates. Staff, who are 'nice as pie', deliver meticulous service: crumbs are swept, glasses removed and bread dispensed with practised precision. A weighty collection of French wines is supplemented by a few others from around the world, including Austria, of course, and South Africa, each of which provides a house wine at £14.95.

CHEF: Peter Hauser PROPRIETORS: Peter and Nita Hauser OPEN: Tue to Fri and Sun L 12.30 to 1.45, all week D 7.30 to 8.45 (8.15 Sun) MEALS: Set L £22, Set D £32 to £35 SERVICE: not inc, card slips closed CARDS: MasterCard, Switch, Visa DETAILS: 36 seats. 8 seats outside. Private parties: 22 main room, 36 private room. Car park. Vegetarian meals. Children's helpings. No children under 7. Jacket and tie. No smoking in dining room ACCOMMODATION: 8 rooms, all with bath/shower. TV. Phone. D,B&B £145 to £300. No children under 7 (*The Which? Hotel Guide*)

GITTISHAM Devon **map 2**

▲ Combe House

NEW ENTRY

Gittisham EX14 0AD
TEL: (01404) 540400 FAX: (01404) 46004
EMAIL: stay@thishotel.com
WEB SITE: www.thishotel.com
1½m off A30, 2m W of Honiton

COOKING **4**
MODERN BRITISH
£24–£47

Gittisham is a pretty village of thatched cottages, Combe House a grey-stone Elizabethan manor in three and a half thousand acres, with additions and out-houses, as well as serious herb and vegetable gardens. Oak panels and huge paintings in its lofty rooms are balanced by modern furniture and some high-powered flower arranging. The welcome is friendly, and staff and owners are keen to ensure enjoyment: this place is about 'total experience' rather than just eating.

The kitchen aims to integrate English, Mediterranean and Asian ideas, along the lines of duck confit spring roll with sweet chilli sauce, or guinea fowl marinated in cumin and lime. Although a little more care with marrying flavours would not go amiss, and some timings might be improved, materials are fine, and individual components well rendered: in a starter of three fat, juicy, accurately seared scallops for instance, or tender roast boneless quail on a huge bed of red and yellow peppers. British puddings take in steamed sponge with clotted cream, and a glazed rhubarb and lemon tart. A selection of mature Australian reds is scheduled to be added to the safe and sensible wine list, which starts at £15.50 and offers relatively little under £20.

CHEF: Philip Leach PROPRIETORS: Ken and Ruth Hunt OPEN: all week 12 to 2, 7 to 9.30 MEALS: Set L Mon to Sat £10, Set L Sun £18.50, Set D £28.50 SERVICE: not inc, card slips closed CARDS: Amex, Diners, MasterCard, Switch, Visa DETAILS: 50 seats. 20 seats outside. Private parties: 30 main room, 50 private room. Car park. Vegetarian meals. Children's helpings. No smoking in dining room. Wheelchair access (also men's WC). No music ACCOMMODATION: 15 rooms, all with bath/shower. TV. Phone. DB&B £75 to £225. Baby facilities. Fishing (*The Which? Hotel Guide*) (£5)

GOLCAR West Yorkshire **map 8**

▲ Weavers Shed

Knowl Road, Golcar HD7 4AN
TEL: (01484) 654284 FAX: (01484) 650980 COOKING **5**
EMAIL: info@weavers-shed.demon.co.uk MODERN BRITISH
on B6111, 2m W of Huddersfield from A62 £22–£52

The Colne Valley was once the centre of the Yorkshire wool trade, and the name of this restaurant-with-rooms acknowledges the part it once played in that industry. Over the last seven years or so Stephen Jackson has turned the place into a little industry all of its own, with a working kitchen garden prolifically yielding everything from chilli peppers to Cox's Pippins. Opening the dinner menu might at first induce a glance at your watch. Egg and soldiers has not escaped from the breakfast menu, but combines a crisp-coated soft-boiled egg with toast fingers flavoured with mushroom and truffle.

Fish of the day may be taken in any of three ways – grilled, steamed or pan-seared – and is served comfortingly with crushed new potatoes and lemon and parsley butter. While Lunesdale duckling is given an Anglo-French treatment (confit leg with hotpot vegetables and French beans), a firm sense of regionality informs the serving of Yorkshire puddings in the old way, as a lunch starter with onion gravy. In a cross-border nod, Mrs Kirkham's benchmark Lancashire cheese appears with a warm Eccles cake as one possible dessert, while the wilder shores are represented by pannacotta of Tahitian vanilla with figs roasted in port and muscovado sugar. A fine, compendious wine list is well annotated, but prices will annoy thrifty folk. House wines are £12.95.

'We offer home-made canopies.' (From a West Country restaurateur)

CHEFS: Ian McGunnigle, Stephen Jackson, Robert Jones and Cath Sill PROPRIETORS: Mr and Mrs S.D. Jackson OPEN: Tue to Fri L 12 to 2, Tue to Sat D 7 to 10 CLOSED: 25, 26 and 31 Dec, 1 Jan, L Good Fri MEALS: alc (main courses £9 to £16). Set L £13.95 SERVICE: not inc CARDS: Amex, Delta, Diners, MasterCard, Switch, Visa DETAILS: 60 seats. Private parties: 38 main room, 32 private room. Car park. Vegetarian meals. No cigars/pipes in dining room. Music ACCOMMODATION: 5 rooms, all with bath/shower. TV. Phone. B&B £40 to £65. Rooms for disabled. Baby facilities (*The Which? Hotel Guide*) (£5)

GORING Oxfordshire **map 2**

Leatherne Bottel

Goring RG8 0HS
TEL: (01491) 872667 FAX: (01491) 875308
EMAIL: leathernebottel@aol.com
WEB SITE: www.leathernebottel.co.uk
on B4009 out of Goring, 5m S of Wallingford

COOKING **4**
MODERN EUROPEAN
£29–£58

Outside all is spaciousness, flowers and vistas, while inside is rather more confined, with a smouldering fire, exposed brick, strong blues and ragged apricot walls. Keith Read ran the Leatherne Bottel for 11 years until, after a long illness, he finally succumbed to cancer in March 2000 at the early age of 44. Now run by his former partner Annie Bonnet, it remains true to his spirit, offering imaginative dishes full of refreshingly novel ideas and culinary quirks. While the Mediterranean may be its centre of gravity, the repertoire also takes in nori-wrapped marinated monkfish, and crisp-skinned, jasmine-tea-smoked duck breast glazed the colour of old wood.

Fresh herbs, spices and salad leaves are used in profusion, many grown in the garden: nasturtiums and flowering rocket spiked with lemon balm, for example, to accompany a piece of rare seared tuna on cannellini beans in a light anchovy dressing. Freshness of materials is impressive – huge, meaty, dark-gilled field mushrooms on black olive toast – as is timing and the simplicity of many dishes: spatchcocked baby chicken, for example, flavoured with lemon and tarragon.

Desserts appear to be the weak link, and if à la carte prices raise an eyebrow, remember that light lunches are cheaper, and the set-price option at dinner is considered reasonable. Flavoured bread is so good, it is a shame it has to be rationed. Service has had its ups and downs but at inspection was both informal and efficient. The wine list seems to have been put together by e e cummings, and although french and italian house wines are 14.50, prices soon escalate.

CHEF: Julia Storey PROPRIETOR: Annie Bonnet OPEN: all week L 12 to 2 (2.30 Sat, 3.30 Sun), Mon to Sat D 7 to 9 (9.30 Sat) CLOSED: 25 Dec MEALS: alc (main courses £16.50 to £20). Set D £19.50. Light L available Mon to Fri SERVICE: 10%, card slips closed CARDS: Amex, Delta, MasterCard, Switch, Visa DETAILS: 45 seats. 80 seats outside. Private parties: 36 main room. Car park. Vegetarian meals. No children. No pipes in dining room. Wheelchair access (also WC). No music (£5)

'I was intrigued by the menu referring under (very expensive) vegetables to something called "frozen peas". Thinking of some new delicacy, I asked what they were. "Peas that have been frozen," I was cheerfully told.' (On eating in London)

GRANGE IN BORROWDALE Cumbria map 10

▲ Borrowdale Gates Hotel

Grange in Borrowdale CA12 5UQ
TEL: (017687) 77204 FAX: (017687) 77254
EMAIL: hotel@borrowdale-gates.com
WEB SITE: www.borrowdale-gates.com
off B5289, about 3m S of Keswick, ¼m N of Grange

COOKING **4**
ANGLO-FRENCH
£23–£64

Big windows in the plush dining room of this comfortable, 'glitzier than I expected' hotel maximise views of the rugged valley outside. Its maze of rooms is geared to pampering, and welcoming, well-oiled service makes visitors feel in safe hands: 'quite a few pairs of them'. Michael Heathcote, after a two-year absence, returned as last year's Guide went to press to oversee a country-style Anglo-French menu that takes in chicken liver parfait, Lakeland game terrine, and Dover sole meunière. First courses have produced a flavoursome Easter bonnet-like ravioli of chicken livers, and well-timed scallops topped with crispy bacon in a creamy sauce.

This being a country-house hotel, a choice of sorbet or soup precedes main courses of perhaps best end of local lamb paired with a croquette of lamb shank, and if Cumberland farmhouse or Wensleydale cheeses don't appeal, a parfait of strawberry ice cream, or one of prune and armagnac, may complete the picture. A canny global selection of wines suits most palates and pockets, offering fine French wines at fair mark-ups, and tempting the more adventurous further afield with helpful tasting notes. House wines start at £12.75, around 50 or so half-bottles are offered, and five wines are available by the glass.

CHEF: Michael Heathcote PROPRIETORS: Terry and Christine Parkinson OPEN: all week 12.15 to 1.30, 7 to 8.45 CLOSED: Jan MEALS: alc L Mon to Sat (main courses £8 to £10.50). Set L Sun £14.50, Set D £29.50 SERVICE: not inc CARDS: Amex, Delta, MasterCard, Switch, Visa DETAILS: 60 seats. 15 seats outside. Car park. Vegetarian meals. No children under 7 at D. Children's portions at L. No smoking in dining room. Wheelchair access (not WC). No music ACCOMMODATION: 29 rooms, all with bath/shower. TV. Phone. D,B&B £73 to £158. Rooms for disabled. Baby facilities (*The Which? Hotel Guide*)

GRASMERE Cumbria map 8

▲ Michael's Nook

Grasmere LA22 9RP
TEL: (015394) 35496 FAX: (015394) 35645
EMAIL: m-nook@wordsworth-grasmere.co.uk
WEB SITE: www.grasmere-hotels.co.uk/
off A591, just N of Grasmere village, turn off between Swan Hotel and its car park

COOKING **6**
ENGLISH/FRENCH
£51–£75

Furnished with covetable antiques, this stone-built Victorian house has been likened to an upper-class English country home. Appropriately, it has two dining rooms – one deep red the other oak panelled – where Michael Wignall's accomplished food makes quite a splash. The format follows archetypal French lines, with starters of seafood and offal, some of which can sound more like main courses: roast veal kidney with thyme and garlic mash, for example. But despite that, and the number of courses, meals do not become an endurance test, thanks to the food's lightness and delicacy. Saucing, for example, is often in the form of a jus: truffled for veal sweetbreads, or squeezed from morels to accompany a main-course combination of pork fillet and braised oxtail.

Partnerships are deftly managed – herb dumplings with roast quail, or seared foie gras and white bean velouté to accompany poached turbot – and bring a degree of individuality to the classical framework. Second-course soups are not without interest either, and successes have included a refreshing chilled tomato essence with basil and truffle oil. Well-chosen Anglo-Irish cheeses come with their own menu, and desserts span the range from lemon mille-feuille with raspberries, to hot chocolate soufflé with coffee ice cream. Service has been friendly, relaxed and efficient, and the degree of cosseting is 'just what you want after a day's walking'. The wine list features serious bottles from Bordeaux, Burgundy and the Rhône, as well as some older vintages from South Africa and California. They don't come cheap, indeed the list as a whole is pricey, although there are a few wines under £20 plus a good range of half-bottles.

CHEF: Michael Wignall PROPRIETOR: R.S.E Gifford OPEN: all week 12.30 to 1, 7.30 to 8.30 MEALS: Set L £37.50, Set D £48 SERVICE: not inc CARDS: Amex, Delta, Diners, MasterCard, Switch, Visa DETAILS: 50 seats. Private parties: 40 main room, 40 private room. Car park. No children under 7. Jacket and tie. No smoking in dining room. No music ACCOMMODATION: 14 rooms, all with bath/shower. TV. Phone. D,B&B £148 to £280 (*The Which? Hotel Guide*) (£5)

▲ White Moss House

Rydal Water, Grasmere LA22 9SE
TEL: (015394) 35295 FAX: (015394) 35516
EMAIL: sue@whitemoss.com
WEB SITE: www.whitemoss.com
on A591, at N end of Rydal Water

COOKING **6**
TRADITIONAL BRITISH
£38–£46

There is no attempt to 'glitzify' the ancient timbers of this small country house once owned by Wordsworth. After a brief aperitif, diners transfer simultaneously to an unassuming, low-ceilinged dining room with a Lakeland slate fireplace and polished wood tables. Regular visitors tend to think of their annual return as a pilgrimage. 'It has now become something of a ritual,' confesses one of them, 'and it is probably fair to say so has the menu.' Many items seem to appear regularly, among them grainy-textured carrot and coriander soup flavoured with lentils and orange, or roast mallard with sage and onion stuffing and a sauce combining Lyth Valley damsons, port and Pinot Noir.

The fish course might involve a soufflé (perhaps of smoked haddock and halibut) or a 'compare and contrast' plate of poached Shetland salmon and oak-smoked River Eden salmon with a mustard-dressed salad. Lakeland char appears from time to time, too, fished by an enterprising team of miners who put their redundancy money to good use, and an indication of the Dixons' willingness to seek out small independent producers and suppliers. Traditional British puddings constitute the fourth course, including Eton mess and steamed huntsman's pudding (a sort of plum duff), followed by cheeses (many unpasteurised) that are always worth exploring. The fairly priced, wide-ranging and intelligently ordered wine list (Pinot Noirs from around the world follow the red Burgundy section, for instance) is a textbook example of how stylish and simple a list can be. Highlights include both rare, mature clarets (going back to 1945 and 1961) and adventurous New World choices. House wines start around £10.95. At the time of going to press, the wine list was being updated, with plans to increase the Italian section substantially.

CHEFS: Peter Dixon and Robert Simpson PROPRIETORS: Sue and Peter Dixon OPEN: Mon to Sat D only 8 (1 sitting) CLOSED: Dec to early Feb MEALS: Set D £29 SERVICE: not inc, card slips closed CARDS: MasterCard, Visa DETAILS: 18 seats. Private parties: 18 main room. Car park. No smoking in dining room. Wheelchair access (not WC). No music. Air-conditioned ACCOMMODATION: 8 rooms, all with bath/shower. TV. Phone. D,B&B £65 to £89. No very young children. Fishing (*The Which? Hotel Guide*) (£5)

GREAT GONERBY Lincolnshire **map 6**

Harry's Place

17 High Street, Great Gonerby NG31 8JS — COOKING **7**
TEL: (01476) 561780 — MODERN FRENCH
on B1174, 1m N of Grantham — £56–£87

An understated atmosphere pervades the single family-sized dining room in this attractive Georgian house. With a pine floor, large oak sideboard, walls 'the colour of Heinz tomato soup', and a warm welcome from Caroline Hallam, the scene is set for a high-quality performance. In the dozen or so years the Hallams have been here they have made the search for good ingredients something of a mission. Their sources include French poultry, British game (Yorkshire grouse, Lincolnshire partridge), and Scottish seafood: seared Orkney scallops with a coral and prawn sauce, and Esk wild salmon with a champagne and chive beurre blanc.

Harry Hallam aims to provide a balanced meal from start to finish, which is easier to control with only two choices per course. One party, for example, followed their satiny soup of chicken and celeriac with rare fillet of Devon beef, cut into chunky slices and served with wild mushrooms on a sauce of red wine, shallots, Madeira and tarragon. Then came a creamy textured prune ice cream with a hefty tot of armagnac, accompanied by crisp and buttery shortbread biscuits. A long-standing classic among desserts is the light frothy caramel mousse served with a crisp, thin brûlée topping and fresh raspberries. The only major drawback is that when high wine prices (not one of the 15 bottles is under £20) are added to main courses costing up to £30, bills can soon mount.

CHEF: Harry Hallam PROPRIETORS: Harry and Caroline Hallam OPEN: Tue to Sat 12.30 to 2, 7 to 9.30 CLOSED: 25 and 26 Dec, bank hols MEALS: alc (main courses £22.50 to £30) SERVICE: not inc CARDS: MasterCard, Visa DETAILS: 10 seats. Private parties: 10 main room. Car park. Children's helpings. No children under 5. No smoking in dining room. Wheelchair access (not WC). No music (£5)

All details are as accurate as possible at the time of going to press, but chefs and owners often change, and it is wise to check by telephone before making a special journey. Many readers have been disappointed when set-price bargain meals are no longer available. Ask when booking.

Subscribers to Which? Online can access The Good Food Guide *on www.which.net.*

GREAT MILTON Oxfordshire **map 2**

▲ Le Manoir aux Quat' Saisons

Church Road, Great Milton OX44 7PD
TEL: (01844) 278881 FAX: (01844) 278847
EMAIL: lemanoir@blanc.co.uk
WEB SITE: www.manoir.co.uk
off A329, 1m from M40 junction 7

COOKING **9**
MODERN FRENCH
£56–£134

The scale of the undertaking may have increased in recent years, but the Manoir still runs like a well-oiled machine, producing top-notch food in a fine setting, all delivered with exemplary service. It is worth choosing a sunny day just to wander round the immaculate gardens, but equally pleasant to sit amid the plants and cream-coloured napery of the conservatory, munching on an appetiser tartlet of crab, an intense gazpacho, or a sliver of suckling pig terrine. The attention devoted to these and other incidentals (including bread and unbeatable petits fours) indicates a restaurant that is striving for the best.

To call the cooking merely 'French' is to underestimate the personal vision of Raymond Blanc, who invokes other ideas whenever it suits. A parcel of wild salmon confit sitting on flakes of salted cod has been partnered by a layer of mooli and cucumber, the balance of piquancy adjusted by a smear of horseradish sauce; and three 'beautifully cooked' langoustines have been joined by a heap of macaroni topped with generous shavings of black truffle. Impeccable sourcing can be taken for granted, producing among other things that elusive grail in the poultry world, chicken that is full of flavour. At one meal the poached breast of a Landais bird sat on a striking nage of vegetables – this is where the garden comes into its own – accompanied by a sliver of truffle and a slice of flawless pan-fried foie gras.

Picturesque delivery has always been a hallmark of the Blanc style, although this is never at the expense of composition or flavour. Roast monkfish, for example, has appeared in two pieces on a rectangular plate, framed at each end by a perfectly timed sweet scallop sitting on a ring of courgette; accompanying vegetables, roasting juices and watercress sauce added not merely their colour, but combined to produce a harmonious dish of the highest calibre. Sometimes the artistic element is tongue in cheek. Nobody could pick holes in the ice creams and sorbets – intense passion fruit and velvety rich chocolate among them – even if they were just thrown on to a plate, but given the edible biscuit 'palette' and spun sugar 'brush' they make a dazzling dessert.

All this does not come cheap – indeed, this is inevitably one of the most expensive restaurants in the country – and 38 pages of impeccably sourced wines, including the best that France and the rest of the wine-producing world have to offer, delivers no bargains. Those seeking something under £30 should look towards south-west France and South America. Given the staggering range, it seems churlish that only two wines are available by the glass.

'The asparagus, in answer to a question, was Spanish. It had obviously been grown in sand, some of which was retained to greet the teeth.' (On eating in Scotland)

CHEFS: Raymond Blanc and Gary Jones PROPRIETOR: Raymond Blanc OPEN: all week 12.15 to 2.45, 7.15 to 9.45 MEALS: alc (main courses £30 to £36). Set L £35 to £84, Set D £84 SERVICE: not inc CARDS: Amex, Delta, Diners, MasterCard, Switch, Visa DETAILS: 120 seats. Private parties: 8 main room, 55 private room. Car park. Vegetarian meals. Children's helpings. No smoking in dining room. Wheelchair access (also WC). No music. Air-conditioned ACCOMMODATION: 32 rooms, all with bath/shower. TV. Phone. B&B £230 to £550. Rooms for disabled. Baby facilities (*The Which? Hotel Guide*)

GREAT MISSENDEN Buckinghamshire map 3

La Petite Auberge

107 High Street, Great Missenden HP16 0BB — COOKING **4**
TEL: (01494) 865370 — FRENCH
£36–£50

For a dozen years the Martels have run the sort of place that most Brits love to find on holiday in France. The long front room of an ordinary house is decorated with a few evocative posters, Mrs Martel finds time to chat without being in the least intrusive, and the kitchen (visible at the far end) doesn't go out of its way to catch up with trends; indeed, the style barely alters at all. Expect to find terrine of duck foie gras, and fish soup with rouille and croûtons among the starters, followed by guinea fowl with cider sauce, and veal entrecôte with herb butter. Results please regulars for both consistency and value, judging by John Dory 'as fresh as could be', and tender grouse in September, simply and effectively cooked with capers. Among desserts, caramelised lemon tart, and hot apple with cinnamon ice cream have gone down particularly well. A short French wine list offers fair choice under £20.

CHEF: Hubert Martel PROPRIETORS: Mr and Mrs Hubert Martel OPEN: Mon to Sat D only 7.30 to 10.30 CLOSED: 2 weeks Christmas MEALS: alc (main courses £15 to £16) SERVICE: not inc CARDS: Delta, MasterCard, Switch, Visa DETAILS: 30 seats. Private parties: 36 main room. Children's helpings. Wheelchair access (also WC). No music

GREAT YELDHAM Essex map 3

White Hart £

Poole Street, Great Yeldham CO9 4HJ
TEL: (01787) 237250 FAX: (01787) 238044 — COOKING **4**
on A604, between Haverhill and Halstead, 6m NW of Halstead — MODERN BRITISH
£22–£51

This sixteenth-century inn was acquired by John Dicken early in 2000, to add to his eponymous restaurant in Wethersfield (see entry), and he has installed himself as chef. A period feel is set by beams, wood panelling and huge original fireplaces, and wide-ranging menus offer plenty of choice, covering everything from bar snacks to an à la carte dinner. The enterprising cooking turns up crispy ocean tempura with spicy chilli dip alongside a salad of pigeon breast with mushrooms and onion marmalade.

Fresh-tasting materials are treated to accurate timing, producing for example cod on creamy mash speckled with spring onions and parsley, accompanied by a sharp-tasting beurre blanc; and pink rack of lamb grand-mère, complete with button mushrooms, onions and bacon. A rich, chocolatey bread-and-butter pudding cooked in a copper pan might be offered for dessert, or perhaps a Normandy apple tart with layer upon layer of thin apple slices, served with gently spicy cinnamon ice cream. Service in the restaurant is formal, while the bar is more laid-back: the same menu is offered, along with a selection of real ales. An inspiring modern wine list, grouped by style, is full of interesting flavours. Mark-ups are on the high side, though a dozen house wines open at £9.95 (£1.95 a glass).

CHEF/PROPRIETOR: John Dicken OPEN: restaurant all week 12 to 2, 7 to 9.30 (9 Sun); bar all week 12 to 2, 6.30 to 9.30 MEALS: alc (main courses £6 to £15.50) SERVICE: not inc CARDS: Amex, Delta, Diners, MasterCard, Switch, Visa DETAILS: 120 seats. 40 seats outside. Private parties: 80 main room, 30 private room. Car park. Vegetarian meals. Children's helpings. No smoking in dining room. Wheelchair access (also men's WC). Occasional music (£5)

HALIFAX West Yorkshire **map 9**

Design House

Dean Clough Mills, North Bridge, Halifax HX3 5AX
TEL: (01422) 383242 FAX: (01422) 322732

COOKING **3**
ITALIAN/MODERN BRITISH
£25–£50

Set in an imposing Victorian mill building, the Design House comes in three parts: restaurant, café bar and delicatessen. The boldly austere décor of the restaurant (bare flagstone floor, plain painted brick walls) makes for poor acoustics, but reporters have found Michael Ricci's modern cooking deserving of praise. Starters run from a sophisticated parfait of foie gras and chicken livers with Sauternes, to rustic peperonata with chargrilled olive ciabatta and Pecorino. Whitby is a handy source for scallops (with spaghetti), and steamed halibut (with saffron potatoes), while local suckling pig might come in a broth of butter beans and cabbage. Desserts have featured chocolate and macadamia nut brownie, and pannacotta with figs and almonds in a honey sauce. Service has been found wanting on occasion, at other times friendly and helpful. Wines come from all corners of the globe, and an impressive selection of half-bottles is offered. House wines are £9.95.

CHEF: Michael Ricci PROPRIETOR: Christian Rooney OPEN: Mon to Fri L 12 to 2, Tue to Sat D 6 to 10 CLOSED: 25 and 26 Dec, 1 Jan MEALS: alc (main courses £8 to £16). Set L Mon to Fri and D Tue to Fri before 7 £11.95 (2 courses) to £15.95. Café bar menu available SERVICE: not inc CARDS: Amex, Delta, Diners, MasterCard, Switch, Visa DETAILS: 70 seats. Private parties: 80 main room. Car park (D only). Vegetarian meals. Wheelchair access (not WC). Music. Air-conditioned

---

'Tomato and orange soup topped with croûtons and confit orange zest . . . the description was a little misleading. This was soup with soggy bread drifting about in it like socks in a washing machine.' (On eating in Suffolk)

'Our server executed her routines with all the charm of a constipated rattlesnake'. (On eating in Suffolk)

HAMBLETON Rutland map 6

▲ Hambleton Hall

Hambleton LE15 8TH
TEL: (01572) 756991 FAX: (01572) 724721
EMAIL: hotel@hambletonhall.com
WEB SITE: www.hambletonhall.com
off A606, 3m SE of Oakham

COOKING **8**
MODERN BRITISH
£33–£103

Hambleton welcomes with a smile and whisks visitors through to a lounge (or terrace in fine weather) within sight of Rutland Water, and then to a dining room where dusky pinks, heavy drapes and a high standard of housekeeping contribute to a sense of indulgence. Tiny, delicate canapés, from a tartlet of scrambled egg with spinach and salmon, to a deep-fried pea and goats'-cheese fritter, indicate a more than usually industrious kitchen, a notion confirmed by the length and intricacy of the seasonally changing menu. It toys with a few luxuries, is not without whimsy (truffled eggs with brioche soldiers), and selects high-quality materials, from Dexter beef to Bresse pigeon. Encouragingly, it also takes on board a range of other meats, including loin of hare, and braised pig's trotter stuffed with sweetbreads and morels.

Results are of a consistently high standard, and meals delight at every stage. Three lightly crisp, stickily fresh roasted Arran scallops might be surrounded by a basil-strewn sauce vierge, for example, while crab tortellini rests on a frothy, creamy, buttery nage containing baby squid, clams, shelled langoustine and a tranche each of turbot and sea bream. Accompaniments play an integral role: for example, crisp-skinned honey-roast breast of Goosnargh duck, next to a tartlet of shredded duck, on soy-roasted baby leeks; or loin of Dorset lamb on spinach and rösti, beside a tower of aubergine, tomato, courgette and peppers, surrounded by garlic cloves in a rosemary-infused brown jus. Regular visitors also note small changes that indicate a wide-awake kitchen, ever alive to improvements.

The food looks dazzling, be it a well-risen chocolate and pistachio soufflé with a pool of dark chocolate sauce in the bottom, and a pistachio ice cream by the side, or a 'Hambleton classic' of caramelised apple tart with a compote of blackberries, vanilla ice cream and a trickle of caramel sauce. This is not a place for those on a budget, although the food is generally considered to justify the expense. An extensive but manageable wine list pays homage to France in great detail but also finds time for detailed Californian, Italian and Spanish listings. 'Wines of the moment' include fairly priced, fashionable bottles drinking particularly well. Although there are only around six wines by the glass, half-bottles are numerous and skilfully chosen.

CHEF: Aaron Patterson PROPRIETORS: Tim and Stefa Hart OPEN: all week 12 to 1.30, 7 to 9.30 MEALS: alc (main courses £20 to £32). Set L Mon to Sat £16.50 (2 courses) to £21.50, Set D £35 SERVICE: net prices, card slips closed CARDS: Delta, Diners, MasterCard, Switch, Visa DETAILS: 60 seats. Private parties: 40 main room, 14 and 20 private rooms. Car park. Vegetarian meals. Children's helpings. No babies in dining room. No smoking in dining room. Wheelchair access (also WC). No music ACCOMMODATION: 17 rooms, all with bath/shower. TV. Phone. B&B £130 to £305. Rooms for disabled. Baby facilities. Swimming pool (*The Which? Hotel Guide*)

HAMPTON HILL Greater London map 3

Monsieur Max

133 High Street, Hampton Hill TW12 1NJ
TEL: (020) 8979 5546 FAX: (020) 8979 3747

COOKING **5**
FRENCH
£27–£67

'Cuisine bourgeoise' is how Max Renzland styles the cooking on offer at his popular neighbourhood restaurant, though there is a bit more class in the operation than that implies. The tone is set by art deco styling, plenty of flowers, crisp linen and sparkling glassware, making it a pleasant place to dine. Alex Bentley's cooking employs classical techniques, and dishes can be rather complex and labour-intensive, perhaps goats'-cheese beignets with red pepper mousse and a spiced tabbouleh salad, followed by grilled loin of rabbit with a cannelloni of pine nuts, sweetbreads and lardons served on Puy lentils and chestnuts, with a peppercorn and port sauce. Simpler options have included half a dozen Irish oysters with shallot vinegar, and shrimp cocktail on crisp cos lettuce.

To finish, there may be rice pudding with Agen prune and cognac caramel, or rum baba with crème Chantilly. Service has not always been on the ball, but at best the mostly young and French staff have been 'friendly and professional'. Service, a cover charge, and a plethora of supplements on the fixed-price menu help push the bill up. Wines are a tour de force, mainly French though by no means neglectful of other areas, but mark-ups weigh heavy. The base price is £13.50 for Côtes du Roussillon or white Bergerac.

CHEF: Alex Bentley PROPRIETOR: Max Renzland OPEN: Sun to Fri L 12 to 2.30, all week D 7 to 10.30 MEALS: Set L Mon to Fri £14 (2 courses) to £17, Set L Sun and Set D £24.50. Cover £1.50 SERVICE: 12.5%, card slips closed CARDS: Amex, Delta, Diners, MasterCard, Switch, Visa DETAILS: 75 seats. Vegetarian meals. No children under 8. No cigars/pipes in dining room. Wheelchair access (not WC). No music. Air-conditioned (£5)

HAROME North Yorkshire map 9

Star Inn

Harome YO62 5JE
TEL: (01439) 770397 FAX: (01439) 771833
off A170, 3m SE of Helmsley

COOKING **4**
MODERN BRITISH
£25–£52

This charmingly part-thatched old pub in a small village attracts its share of switched-on custom (the bar fills up quickly) and projects a cottagey feel in the quieter restaurant, with beams, bare wooden tables and spindleback chairs. The kitchen deals in 'modernised old favourites', as Andrew Pern has it, such as foie gras 'toad-in-the-hole' with candied onions. The style is appealing not least for its comforting treatment of rustic materials: steamed venison pudding, braised saddle of rabbit, and roast loin of suckling pig with black pudding risotto.

Local resources (Harome honey, hen and duck eggs) and seasonal ingredients both play a role, perhaps in a risotto of blue leg mushrooms (with a bowl of grated Lancashire cheese by the side), or roast Ampleforth partridge served with chestnuts and bacon in a well-reduced sauce. Vegetables come in generous quantity, and while timings and flavours may not always hit the button, meals end well with, for example, first-rate bramble roly-poly with Granny Smith sorbet and apple sauce. Service is 'full of smiles, politeness and charm', and a globetrotting wine list is broadly but usefully tailored to food compatibility. South African house wine is £11.

CHEF: Andrew Pern PROPRIETORS: Andrew and Jacquie Pern OPEN: Tue to Sat 1.30 to 2, 6.30 to 10, Sun 12 to 6 CLOSED: 1 week Nov, 25 Dec, 3 weeks Jan MEALS: alc (main courses £8 to £16) SERVICE: not inc, card slips closed CARDS: Delta, MasterCard, Switch, Visa DETAILS: 60 seats. 40 seats outside. Private parties: 34 main room, 10 private room. Car park. Vegetarian meals. Children's helpings. No smoking in 1 dining room. Music

HARROGATE North Yorkshire **map 8**

Drum and Monkey £

5 Montpellier Gardens, Harrogate HG1 2TF
TEL: (01423) 502650 FAX: (01423) 522469

COOKING **4**
SEAFOOD
£17–£46

If you don't have a booking, be sure to arrive early, especially at lunchtime when queues are ample testament to the popularity of this long-running seafood restaurant and bar. One menu serves both the bookable upstairs dining room and the bar downstairs, where stools at the counter make the most of available space. Top-quality supplies arrive daily from Fleetwood, Brixham and Whitby and are typically turned into salmon and watercress mousse, hot or cold seafood platters (available with or without lobster), Malaysian-style spicy grilled scallops, seafood pie, or medallions of monkfish, trout, tuna and scallops with béarnaise. Relaxed and friendly service, overseen by the proprietor, encourages diners to linger. Just as the menu makes no concessions to carnivores or vegetarians, the wine list offers little for red wine drinkers, though the varied selection of around 30 whites is reasonable value. House selections are £8.05 (£1.85 a glass).

CHEFS: Keith Penny and Tina Nuttall PROPRIETOR: William Fuller OPEN: Mon to Sat 12 to 2.30, 6.30 to 10.15 CLOSED: 24 Dec to 2 Jan MEALS: alc (main courses £5.50 to £15.50) SERVICE: not inc CARDS: Delta, MasterCard, Switch, Visa DETAILS: 58 seats. Private parties: 10 main room. Children's helpings. No music

HARWICH Essex **map 6**

▲ The Pier at Harwich 🍷

The Quay, Harwich CO12 3HH
TEL: (01255) 241212 FAX: (01255) 551922
EMAIL: lesley@thepieratharwich.co.uk

COOKING **2**
SEAFOOD/ENGLISH
£27–£63

The Pier is divided into two distinct restaurants: the two-tiered, tableclothed, nautically themed Harbourside, with a fishy menu to match, and the Ha'Penny Pier, with simpler décor and fare. Both have views of the sea, and the outfit now has moorings for yachts. The Harbourside's flexible carte changes according to on-the-doorstep fish supplies but always includes lobster, crab, oysters and home-smoked salmon. The set-lunch menu provides good choice, from dressed local crab, or praiseworthy smoked haddock with poached egg and hollandaise, to battered plaice with chips, or salmon fillet in a pesto crust. Nor is the kitchen averse to cooking meat, turning out venison medallions and sausage with chestnuts and braised red cabbage. Commendable hot chocolate sauce with vanilla ice cream, and an 'absolutely top-hole' lemon cheesecake end things on a high note. Colchester-based wine merchants Lay & Wheeler are responsible for the seafood-friendly wine list, which is particularly strong in France and South Africa. Vergelegen Chardonnay 1998 is recommended at £15.25. House wines start at £9.95.

CHEF: C.E. Oakley PROPRIETOR: G. Milsom OPEN: all week 12 to 2, 6 to 9.30 MEALS: alc (main courses £8.50 to £26). Set L £17.50 (2 courses Mon to Sat, 3 courses Sun), Set D £19.50 SERVICE: 10%, card slips closed CARDS: Amex, Delta, Diners, MasterCard, Switch, Visa DETAILS: 80 seats. Private parties: 80 main room, 40 and 60 private rooms. Car park. Children's helpings. Music ACCOMMODATION: 14 rooms, all with bath/shower. TV. Phone. B&B £67.50 to £150. Rooms for disabled (*The Which? Hotel Guide*)

HASTINGS East Sussex map 3

Röser's

64 Eversfield Place, St Leonards,
Hastings TN37 6DB
TEL/FAX: (01424) 712218
EMAIL: gerald@rosers.co.uk
WEB SITE: www.rosers.co.uk

COOKING **7**
MODERN EUROPEAN
£29–£65

Set between karaoke pubs and much fish and chippery on the seafront (albeit at the posh St Leonards end), this is 'the last place you'd expect to find a restaurant of this quality'. Behind the dimple-glass bow window and net curtain the interior is hardly likely to set the pulse racing either: 'comfortable and quiet is the best you can say of it.' Give the Rösers smarter premises and a slick front-of-house operation, with access to a cosmopolitan clientele, and they would doubtless be lauded in the press and full all week.

The core repertoire may not change much, but there are daily specials to consider, and in any case every dish is tempting, not least because it explores beyond the customary shopping list, where it finds razor-shells (served with garlic butter and Parmesan), oak-smoked wild boar ham (with mango), line-caught sea bass (with chanterelles), and roast saddle and braised haunch of hare. The cocktail of excitement, skill and integrity has produced generous dollops of crab on crisp leaves with a truffle dressing: not a meagre slick of oil, as is now customary, but several slices of real black truffle ranged around the plate. Gently flavoured, freestanding pike soufflé – 'poised miraculously between wobbly collapse and solidity' – is served engagingly with a creamy pool of dill-flavoured sauce full of finely chopped smoked salmon.

Sound judgement is another characteristic of this 'grown-up cooking', evident in pink, best end of Romney Marsh milk-fed lamb flavoured with ginger, rosemary and coriander; and in a dish of fat, juicy, seared Rye Bay scallops in a sensibly restrained saffron cream sauce, accompanied by a bittersweet combination of lightly caramelised aubergine, courgette, red pepper and fennel. Desserts exploit some interesting contrasts too: for example caramelised pineapple, served with black pepper ice cream and a lemon grass and apricot sauce.

Incidentals are tiptop, service is unhurried, and the predominantly French wine list excels in its range of clarets and Burgundies but also finds time for some choice Californians and Super-Tuscans. There are few bottles under £15, though house wines start at £11.50. Lovers of cognac, vintage armagnac and vintage port will enjoy the final few pages.

CHEF: Gerald Röser PROPRIETORS: Mr and Mrs Gerald Röser OPEN: Tue to Fri L 12 to 2, Tue to Sat D 7 to 10 CLOSED: first 2 weeks Jan, last 2 weeks June MEALS: alc (main courses £16 to £24.50). Set L £20.95, Set D Tue to Fri £23.95 SERVICE: net prices, card slips closed CARDS: Amex, Delta, Diners, MasterCard, Switch, Visa DETAILS: 30 seats. Private parties: 16 main room, 30 private room. Vegetarian meals. No cigars/pipes in dining room. Wheelchair access (not WC). No music (£5)

HAWORTH West Yorkshire map 8

▲ Weavers

13–17 West Lane, Haworth BD22 8DU
TEL: (01535) 643822 FAX: (01535) 644832
EMAIL: colinjane@aol.com

COOKING **3**
MODERN BRITISH
£22–£46

If you are tramping the heritage trail and have come to see where the Brontës lived, be sure to make a booking at Weavers. The Rushworths (Colin was born here) have not gone for wholesale commercialism, despite the milling tourist hordes, but run their restaurant-with-rooms in a style that retains genuine regional identity. Their leaflet cheerfully describes the place as 'informal, eccentric, cluttered'. As for evidence of culinary cosmopolitanism, forget Thailand or Tuscany. What could be more foreign in these parts than Lancashire cheese fritters with apple and grape chutney? Smoked haddock soup with bacon and potato is another way to start, then it's on to salmon with spinach and prawns in pastry, or a steak and kidney pie with shortcrust pastry and 'lashings of gravy'. Expect lashings of cream or custard at the end of a meal too, where the choice embraces 'old school pud', and 'Nannie's meringue' with brown-bread ice cream and apricot sauce. A broad-minded international wine selection is offered at reasonable prices, opening at £9.95 for Paul Boutinot house wines.

CHEFS/PROPRIETORS: Colin and Jane Rushworth OPEN: Tue to Sat D only 6.30 to 9 CLOSED: 1 week Christmas, 1 week end June MEALS: alc (main courses £9.50 to £16.50). Set D Tue to Fri 6.30 to 7.30 £13.50 SERVICE: not inc, 10% for parties of 6 or more CARDS: Amex, Delta, Diners, MasterCard, Switch, Visa DETAILS: 60 seats. Private parties: 16 main room. Vegetarian meals. Children's helpings. No smoking in dining room. Music. Air-conditioned ACCOMMODATION: 3 rooms, all with bath/shower. TV. Phone. B&B £50 to £75 (*The Which? Hotel Guide*) (£5)

The 2002 Guide will be published before Christmas 2001. Reports on meals are most welcome at any time of the year, but are particularly valuable in the spring (no later than June). Send them to The Good Food Guide, *FREEPOST, 2 Marylebone Road, London NW1 4DF. Or email your report to goodfoodguide@which.net*

The Guide always appreciates hearing about changes of chef or owner.

HAYDON BRIDGE Northumberland **map 10**

General Havelock Inn  

9 Ratcliffe Road, Haydon Bridge NE47 6ER
TEL: (01434) 684376 FAX: (01434) 684283
EMAIL: generalhavelock@aol.com
WEB SITE: www.haydonbridge.org
on A69, 8m W of Hexham, 100yds from junction with B6319

COOKING **2**
MODERN EUROPEAN
£21–£38

There is a cheerful, cottage-like feel to this unimposing roadside inn, which, at the back, has a dining room with stone walls, pink banquettes and an enviable riverside view. New owners Gary and Joanna Thompson run kitchen and front-of-house respectively. The fixed-price menu provides a soup of the day – flavourful fresh tomato and basil at one meal – then four starters, perhaps including a professionally made and well-presented smoked chicken and leek terrine with grain mustard yoghurt, followed by half a dozen uncomplicated, but well-judged main courses. Salmon has come with leek confit, and grilled chicken breast on Italian bean broth. The lunchtime bar menu has provided beef and Guinness stew, a 'slow-cooked farmhouse dish that could hardly be bettered'. There has been praise, too, for accompanying vegetables, and home-made ice cream. A simple, inexpensive wine list has the New World well represented. Duboeuf house wine is £8.95.

CHEF: Gary Thompson PROPRIETORS: Gary and Joanna Thompson OPEN: Tue to Sun L 12 to 2, Tue to Sat D 7 to 9 MEALS: Set L £12.75, Set D £14.50 (2 courses) to £19.50. Light L and bar meals available SERVICE: not inc, card slips closed CARDS: Delta, Diners, MasterCard, Switch, Visa DETAILS: 30 seats. 20 seats outside. Private parties: 40 main room. Vegetarian meals. Children's helpings. No smoking in dining room. Wheelchair access (also WC). No music (£5)

HAYWARDS HEATH West Sussex **map 3**

Jeremy's at Borde Hill

Balcombe Road, Haywards Heath RH16 1XP
TEL: (01444) 441102 FAX: (01444) 443936
EMAIL: jeremys.bordehill@btinternet.com
WEB SITE: www.bordehill.co.uk/jeremys

COOKING **5**
MODERN EUROPEAN
£30–£54

The low brick building, arranged around a courtyard at the entrance to Borde Hill Gardens just outside Haywards Heath, welcomes with a bright dining room decorated with colourful paintings and elongated sculptures. Having relinquished the Crabtree in Lower Beeding, Jeremy Ashpool now concentrates his energies here, adopting a predominantly European style of cooking. While it embraces tapénade, couscous, balsamic vinegar and many other commonly available materials, it makes an effort to avoid too many clichés, serving up a starter of pressed duck liver and potato terrine with dry-cure bacon, and breast of guinea fowl served with a julienne of vegetables braised in lemon and cumin. Materials, timing and generally appropriate handling are all in its favour, producing a varied choice that runs from red mullet with courgette fritters to slow-roast belly of pork with sage and onion. Desserts tend to favour more traditional ideas, such as apple and almond tart, or sticky toffee pudding. Service, though polite, might be sharper. A wide-ranging list of around 40 attractive wines starts with house Italian white (£10.65) and red (£11.75).

CHEF: Jeremy Ashpool PROPRIETORS: Jeremy and Vera Ashpool OPEN: Tue to Sun L 12.15 (12 Sat) to 2.30, Tue to Sat D 7.15 to 9.30 MEALS: alc (main courses £11 to £20). Set L Tue to Sat and Set D Tue to Fri £15 (2 courses) to £19.50, Set L Sun £19.50 (2 courses) to £24 SERVICE: not inc, card slips closed, 10% for parties of 8 or more CARDS: Amex, Diners, MasterCard, Switch, Visa DETAILS: 55 seats. 34 seats outside. Private parties: 55 main room. Car park. Vegetarian meals. Children's helpings. No smoking in dining room. Wheelchair access (not WC). Music (£5)

HEREFORD Herefordshire **map 5**

▲ Castle House

NEW ENTRY

Castle Street, Hereford HR1 2NW
TEL: (01432) 356321 FAX: (01432) 365909
EMAIL: info@castlehse.co.uk

COOKING **7**
ANGLO-FRENCH
£28–£62

'What a find,' observed an early visitor. Close to the cathedral in the city's quiet Central Conservation Area, recently renovated Castle House is under the same ownership as the shops and restaurants at Left Bank Village, about half a mile away. 'It seems to have had a small fortune thrown at it, plus a lot of yellow paint.' The transformation may be swish rather than personal, but the appointment of Stuart McLeod has set the kitchen off to a rollicking start.

He oversees a short, monthly-changing menu in which technical challenges are met with ease, which is a good job because much of the food is subject to a high degree of workmanship, as if the kitchen feels it has something to prove. Skills, however, are set in the context of intelligent flavour combinations and appropriate textures. Three tiny frogs' legs, for example, are neatly encased in a thin crisp batter ('all puffed and golden') and set on a small mound of indulgently rich, orientally flavoured risotto to produce a refined and enjoyable starter.

Trios are a feature, evident in a 'study of foie gras', as the menu has it: a thin raviolo containing a mousse, a jellied terrine, and a tranche of fresh foie gras supporting a seared scallop, the latter combination working better than anticipated. Hereford duckling also comes as a threesome, with rare breast on rhubarb compote, a crisp-skinned leg, and a hollowed-out courgette filled with shredded, spicy, well-cooked flesh. By the time the Guide appears, they hope to be using beef, pork and poultry from their own 500-acre farm.

Desserts are done with equal care and presentational agility, from variations on a pineapple theme to a quartet of Valrhona chocolate incorporating an ice cream, fondant sponge, orange-flavoured jelly, and a white chocolate cream. Service comes with rather more flourish and formality than substance, while wines aim for prestige: there are not many bottles under £20, but four house wines are among them.

CHEF: Stuart McLeod PROPRIETOR: Dr A. Heijn OPEN: all week 12.30 to 2, 7 to 10 MEALS: Set L £16.95, Set D £27.95 to £39.95. Bar menu available SERVICE: not inc, card slips closed CARDS: Amex, Delta, MasterCard, Switch, Visa DETAILS: 36 seats. 30 seats outside. Private parties: 30 main room. Car park. Vegetarian meals. Children's helpings. Wheelchair access (also WC). No music. Air-conditioned ACCOMMODATION: 15 rooms, all with bath/shower. TV. Phone. B&B £90 to £210. Rooms for disabled. Baby facilities (£5)

HERSTMONCEUX East Sussex **map 3**

Sundial

Gardner Street, Herstmonceux BN27 4LA
TEL: (01323) 832217 FAX: (01323) 832909

COOKING **4**
FRENCH-PLUS
£31–£76

The Bertolis are now into their fourth decade at this red-brick building decorated in old-fashioned style, with landscapes on the dining room walls and tiny-paned windows adding period atmosphere. Time has not stood still in the kitchen, however, and new dishes are constantly being tried out. Crab roulade with smoked salmon and basil has made a recent appearance, as have main courses of sea bass with celeriac, and a robust pairing of ostrich and venison medallions with green peppercorn sauce. The fixed-price lunch menu offers a handsome range of choice, from mussels in pastis to lamb in port. It is all served with panache and charm, and meals end with either a cheese selection or perhaps a slice of home-made gâteau. The approach to wines is deeply traditional. It takes the list several pages to get out of Bordeaux and Burgundy, but there are a few good Italian choices. House wines from south-west France are £13.25.

CHEF: G. Bertoli PROPRIETORS: Mr G. and Mrs L. Bertoli OPEN: Tue to Sun L 12 to 2 (2.30 Sun), Tue to Sat D 7 to 9 (9.30 Sat) CLOSED: Christmas to 20 Jan, 8 Aug to early Sept MEALS: alc (main courses £15.50 to £27.50). Set L £15.50 (2 courses) to £19.50, Set D £27.50 SERVICE: 10%, card slips closed CARDS: Amex, Delta, Diners, MasterCard, Switch, Visa DETAILS: 60 seats. 20 seats outside. Private parties: 60 main room, 23 private room. Car park. Vegetarian meals. Children's helpings. No smoking in dining room. Wheelchair access (also WC). Music (£5)

HETTON North Yorkshire **map 8**

Angel Inn

Hetton BD23 6LT
TEL: (01756) 730263 FAX: (01756) 730363
EMAIL: info@angelhetton.co.uk
WEB SITE: www.angelhetton.co.uk
off B6265, 5m N of Skipton

COOKING **5**
MODERN BRITISH
£23–£51

In its 18 years under Denis Watkins, the Angel has become an institution: an archetypal pub, in a quiet grey-stone village off the main road, that successfully caters to all comers. To eat in the bar, which doesn't take bookings, or from the early-bird menu in the dining room, needs careful timing to beat the queues that can form at busy times. The reward is a good-value meal that might take in chicken and foie gras parfait, the 'very '70s' little moneybags of seafood in filo pastry, sausage and mash, and chocolate marquise or crème brûlée.

New in 2000 was a North Country menu, priced to fill a gap between early-bird and other options. It concentrates on regionally produced foods, including first-rate lamb from Fleets Farm (young loin, cooked just right for one visitor), and home-made black pudding with lentils, as well as locally cured hams and bacon, and local cheeses (Shepherd's Purse Yorkshire Blue, perhaps). Elsewhere, the repertoire runs from oft-reported tomato tart to Goosnargh duckling, and from a huge wedge of thick Yorkshire curd tart with cinnamon ice cream to chocolate melting pudding. Service is attentive, while fine wines from Bordeaux and Burgundy are offered at irresistible prices on a list that includes stylish bottles from the rest of Europe and the New World. Twenty-six wines by the glass and an impressive range of half-bottles encourage experimentation. Ten house wines start at £10.50.

CHEFS: Denis Watkins, Bruce Elsworth and John Topham PROPRIETORS: Denis and Juliet Watkins, and John Topham OPEN: Sun L 12 to 2.45, Mon to Sat D 6 to 9.30 CLOSED: 25 Dec, 2 weeks Jan MEALS: alc D Mon to Fri (main courses £9.50 to £15.50). Set L Sun £20.50, Set D 6 to 7 Mon to Fri £11 (2 courses) to £16.50 (inc wine), Set D Mon to Fri £20, Set D Sat £29.50. Bar food available SERVICE: not inc CARDS: Amex, MasterCard, Switch, Visa DETAILS: 56 seats. 40 seats outside. Private parties: 40 main room. Car park. Vegetarian meals. Children's helpings. No smoking in 1 dining room. Wheelchair access (not WC). No music. Air-conditioned

HEXHAM Northumberland **map 10**

▲ Hexham Royal Hotel £

Priestpopple, Hexham NE46 1PQ
TEL: (01434) 602270 FAX: (01434) 604084 — COOKING **2**
EMAIL: service@hexham-royal-hotel.co.uk — MODERN EUROPEAN
WEB SITE: www.hexham-royal-hotel.co.uk — £14–£41

The menu is the same in both the ground-floor brasserie and the high-ceilinged first-floor dining room at this three-storey Georgian coaching inn: a short carte that deals in Chinese smoked duck salad with spiced plum dressing, as well as Dover sole terrine with pear and ginger marmalade. About half the items can be taken as either first or main courses, from warm asparagus salad with lemon butter to cold rare beef fillet with chilli and ginger, and Tuesday is fish night: perhaps seared scallops with wild mushrooms, or baked sea bream with orange butter sauce. Not all dishes are equally successful, but the roll call of achievement includes provençale fish soup, pink calf's liver, almond tart, and sweet sticky toffee pudding. Service is quietly attentive, and all but a couple of the three dozen wines stay under £20, including four house wines under £10.

CHEF: Michael Scott PROPRIETORS: Anthony and Jane Pelly OPEN: all week L 12 to 2.30, Mon to Sat D 5.30 to 9.30 MEALS: alc (main courses £7 to £16). Set L and D 5.30 to 6.30 £6.99 (2 courses) to £7.99, Set D 6.30 to 9.30 £10 (2 courses) SERVICE: not inc, card slips closed CARDS: Amex, Delta, MasterCard, Switch, Visa DETAILS: 40 seats. Private parties: 20 main room, 20 to 100 private rooms. Car park. Vegetarian meals. Children's helpings. No smoking in 1 dining room. Music ACCOMMODATION: 10 rooms, all with bath/shower. TV. Phone. B&B £35 to £70 (*The Which? Hotel Guide*) (£5)

HINDON Wiltshire map 2

▲ Grosvenor Arms

High Street, Hindon SP3 6DJ
TEL: (01747) 820696 FAX: (01747) 820869

COOKING **2**
MODERN EUROPEAN
£29–£58

The welcome is 'large and gruff', the service 'efficient, charming, enthusiastic and willing' at this informal Georgian inn with flagstone floor and wooden furniture. The dining room looks out on a pretty garden and into a spotlessly clean kitchen, which was taken over by Chris Lee at the beginning of 2000. Evening menus offer half a dozen dishes in two sizes (scallops with lemon and herb risotto, for example), plus a range of main courses proper: calf's liver with pancetta and thyme gravy, or roast sea bass on an aubergine and garlic compote. Although a few corners appear to be cut, the kitchen has turned out perfectly cooked rare beef and full-flavoured lamb, followed by steamed ginger pudding with orange sauce, and well-judged lemon tart with crisp pastry. Six wines at £10.75 head up a fairly priced, predominantly French list.

CHEF: Chris Lee PROPRIETOR: West Country Village Inns OPEN: all week 12 to 2.30, 7 to 10 MEALS: alc (main courses L £7 to £16, D £10 to £19) SERVICE: not inc CARDS: Amex, Delta, MasterCard, Switch, Visa DETAILS: 70 seats. 40 seats outside. Private parties: 45 main room, 20 private room. Car park. Vegetarian meals. Children's helpings. No smoking in dining room. No music ACCOMMODATION: 10 rooms, all with bath/shower. TV. Phone. B&B £45 to £95. No children under 5 (*The Which? Hotel Guide*) (£5)

HINTON CHARTERHOUSE Bath & N.E. Somerset map 2

▲ Homewood Park

Hinton Charterhouse BA3 6BB
TEL: (01225) 723731 FAX: (01225) 723820
WEB SITE: www.homewoodpark.com
off A36, 6m SE of Bath

COOKING **4**
MODERN ENGLISH
£35–£71

Large and rambly from outside, the mellow-stone building is divided into several small rooms, where wing chairs and stripy Regency wallpaper contribute to a Georgian ambience. Nigel Godwin, sous-chef for two years before taking over the kitchens in spring 2000, operates a two- or three-course format with a hefty price tag and a modern outlook: scallops are served with discs of black pudding, minted peas and lemon vinaigrette, and duck breast comes with fennel praline and a ginger sauce. A combination of 'sweet and earthy' elements is not unusual: for example, pan-fried langoustines with crunchy hazelnuts and morels.

Although luxuries are kept under control, extra items such as sabayons (sometimes unannounced) can add richness to a meal, for example with a sizeable chunk of sauté sea bass on squid ink risotto. Ideas are fine on paper, although quite a few flavours at inspection lacked the necessary punch. Desserts, like everything else, tend to incorporate several components, perhaps combining pannacotta with a roast pear and vanilla ice cream, or pineapple confit with chocolate sorbet and an orange caramel sauce. Service is 'efficient and charming', and although wines balance the security of classic French regions with some good New World bottles, prices take much of the fun out of it. House Bordeaux, red and white, is £16.

CHEF: Nigel Godwin PROPRIETOR: Carmox Ltd OPEN: all week 12 to 1.45, 7 to 9.30 MEALS: alc (main courses £23). Set L £19.50, Set D £37 (2 courses) to £46 SERVICE: not inc CARDS: Amex, Diners, MasterCard, Visa DETAILS: 80 seats. Private parties: 40 main room, 18 to 40 private rooms. Car park. Children's helpings. No smoking in dining room. Wheelchair access (also WC). Occasional music ACCOMMODATION: 19 rooms, all with bath/shower. TV. Phone. B&B £109 to £249. Rooms for disabled. Baby facilities. Swimming pool (*The Which? Hotel Guide*) (£5)

HOLT Norfolk **map 6**

Yetman's

37 Norwich Road, Holt NR25 6SA
TEL: (01263) 713320

COOKING **4**
MODERN BRITISH
£46–£61

Inside this crisp yellow and white converted house just off the high street is a flower-filled interior with a laid-back atmosphere. Alison Yetman's daily-changing menu offers a varied range of dishes based on sound ingredients treated with imagination and skill, producing satisfying food at good-value prices. Clear and expert technique is at the heart of it: chargrilling of Cornish squid with sweet red chilli jam, poaching for a fine fillet of turbot with a champagne and potted shrimp sauce, and roasting of local goose stuffed with Agen prunes.

Desserts, too, come in for praise: toasted apricot pancakes, for example, and wild strawberry brûlée. Efficient service is provided by Peter Yetman, whose passion spills over into wine: a colourful, eclectic and global list steers clear of the phrase 'house wines', 'as the expression for us has connotations of cheap bulk buys'. Instead a few current favourites are listed, all available by the glass. Prices start at £15.50 and are mostly fair, though there are few bargains to be had.

CHEF: Alison Yetman PROPRIETORS: Alison and Peter Yetman OPEN: Sun L 12.30 to 2, Wed to Sat (Wed to Mon in summer) D 7.30 to 9.30 CLOSED: 25 and 26 Dec, 31 Dec, 3 weeks Oct/Nov MEALS: Set L and D £23.75 (2 courses) to £32.50 SERVICE: not inc CARDS: Amex, Delta, MasterCard, Switch, Visa DETAILS: 30 seats. Private parties: 20 main room, 12 and 20 private rooms. Vegetarian meals. No smoking in dining room. Wheelchair access (not WC). No music

HOLT Wiltshire **map 2**

Tollgate Inn

NEW ENTRY

Ham Green, Holt BA14 6PX
TEL: (01225) 782326

COOKING **2**
MODERN BRITISH
£22–£40

The Tollgate is an unpretentious old stone village inn where Alexander Venables has forsaken his grander culinary past – he used to be at the Savoy and at Lucknam Park (see entry, Colerne) – in favour of what he calls 'forgotten English cuisine'. The same menu is served both in the upstairs restaurant and in the bar, with its comfortable sofas and log fire. Uncomplicated dishes, such as salade niçoise, omelette Arnold Bennett, or devilled kidneys, demonstrate the simpler route taken. Main courses might run to locally sourced good-quality fillet of beef served rare with a wild mushroom sabayon, or salmon in filo pastry with a lime sauce. Sticky toffee pudding with vanilla ice cream, or syllabub, may round off a meal. Service is 'attentive if a little naive', while the wine list, short and suitable for the food, is reasonably priced, starting at £9.50 for house Australian.

CHEF: Alexander Venables PROPRIETORS: Alexander Venables and Alison Ward-Baptiste OPEN: Tue to Sun L 12 to 2, Tue to Sat D 7 to 9.30 CLOSED: bank hols MEALS: alc (main courses L £7 to £10, D £8.50 to £13) SERVICE: not inc, card slips closed CARDS: Delta, MasterCard, Switch, Visa DETAILS: 68 seats. 32 seats outside. Private parties: 68 main room. Car park. Vegetarian meals. No children under 12. No smoking in 1 dining room. Occasional music

HONLEY West Yorkshire **map 8**

Mustard and Punch

6 Westgate, Honley HD7 2AA
TEL: (01484) 662066

COOKING **3**
MODERN EUROPEAN
£19–£43

A brightly painted sign depicting Mr Punch's hat identifies this former shop, located on Honley's steep main street. Inside, cartoons and more hats embody the theme in both the ochre-walled basement and wood-panelled ground-floor dining room, where tightly packed tables are covered with green-checked cloths. The menu offers a familiar range of British brasserie staples, enlivened by oriental and Mediterranean influences, starting with tomato and herb breads accompanied by aïoli and olives.

Among first courses, a well-crafted terrine of guinea fowl layered with mushrooms, shallots and bacon in a light jelly has shared the honours with a successful saffron-infused fish soup containing a generous selection of 'spanking fresh' clams, prawns and monkfish. Typical of main courses are a huge chargrilled duck breast with an intense red pepper coulis, sweetly flavoured rack of lamb with spiced aubergine and sweetbreads, and a ballottine of chicken in a stew of tomato, broad beans and chorizo. Finish with lemon and lime tart, pistachio brûlée or local cheeses served at room temperature. Service is relaxed and friendly. A short, global wine list opens with house Chilean at £10.50.

CHEFS: Christopher Dunn and Matthew Evans PROPRIETORS: Christopher Dunn and Dorota Pencak OPEN: Tue to Fri L 12 to 2, Tue to Sat D 7 to 10 CLOSED: bank hols MEALS: alc D (main courses £8 to £13.50). Set L £6.50 (2 courses), Set D Tue to Thur £15.95 (2 courses inc wine) SERVICE: not inc CARDS: Delta, MasterCard, Switch, Visa DETAILS: 60 seats. Private parties: 34 main room. Car park. Vegetarian meals. No cigars/pipes in dining room. Wheelchair access (also women's WC). Music

The text of entries is based on unsolicited reports sent in by readers, backed up by inspections conducted anonymously. The factual details under the text are from questionnaires the Guide sends to all restaurants that feature in the book.

HORNCASTLE Lincolnshire map 9

Magpies

71–75 East Street, Horncastle LN9 6AA
TEL: (01507) 527004 FAX: (01507) 524064
EMAIL: magpies@fsbdial.co.uk

COOKING **4**
MODERN BRITISH
£16–£40

The continued popularity of this family-run restaurant, set in a cottagey building on the main coast road, can be put down to an interesting wine list, some accomplished cooking from brothers Matthew and Simon Lee, and not least value for money. Sunday lunch in particular seems a bargain. While the style is unlikely to set the pulse racing, the set-price dinner menu of half a dozen choices per course offers variety enough to satisfy most tastes, and some rare-breed meats add interest. Roast loin of British Lop pork comes with apple sauce, while Lincoln Red beef might appear as steak béarnaise. Roast Gressingham duck with creamed leeks, honey and five-spice caters for the more adventurous.

Fish and seafood also show up well (smoked haddock risotto, herb-crusted cod), timing and seasoning are generally spot on, and accompanying vegetables are not merely an afterthought. Finish with a traditional dessert (pear and apple crumble, perhaps) or a plate of English and Irish cheeses. A well-balanced collection from around the world includes some fine wines at reasonable prices. Bin ends and specials are particularly starry, and include Spain's prestigious Vega Sicilia. House South African is £10 a bottle.

CHEFS: Matthew and Simon Lee PROPRIETORS: the Lee family OPEN: Sun L 12.30 to 2, Wed to Sat D 7.15 to 10 CLOSED: 3 weeks Aug MEALS: Set L Sun £10, Set D £20 SERVICE: not inc CARDS: Delta, MasterCard, Switch, Visa DETAILS: 40 seats. Private parties: 40 main room, 8 private room. No smoking in dining room. Occasional music

HORNDON ON THE HILL Essex map 3

▲ Bell Inn

High Road, Horndon on the Hill SS17 8LD
TEL: (01375) 642463 FAX: (01375) 361611
EMAIL: bell-inn@fdn.co.uk
WEB SITE: www.bell-inn.co.uk
off M25 at junction 30/31, signposted Thurrock, Lakeside; take A13, then B1007 to Horndon

COOKING **2**
MODERN EUROPEAN
£24–£45

Green and lemon-yellow paintwork and brightly coloured flowers make it easy to spot this picturesque 500-year-old inn, while thick beams and a bustling, friendly atmosphere give it 'oodles of charm'. Eat in the bar or the quirkily decorated dining room from a contemporary-sounding menu that shows no fear of bold flavours. For starters, a caul-wrapped parcel of shredded braised pork knuckle comes with roasted pineapple and tapénade, while smoked eel is partnered by oxtail ravioli and apple and celeriac rémoulade. Complex layering of ingredients continues with main courses of rabbit confit with black pudding, chorizo, roast salsify and broad beans, and unusual combinations are met in desserts too: Parmesan and caramel with red wine poached pear a case in point.

A hundred keenly priced wines, including 20 available by the glass, span the globe, starting with house French white and Australian red at £9.75.

CHEF: Finlay Logan PROPRIETORS: John and Christine Vereker OPEN: all week 12 to 1.45, 7 to 9.45 CLOSED: 25 and 26 Dec MEALS: alc (main courses £8.50 to £14.50). Set L Mon to Fri £15.95 (2 courses) to £17.95. Bar and sandwich menus available SERVICE: not inc, card slips closed CARDS: Amex, Delta, MasterCard, Switch, Visa DETAILS: 80 seats. 36 seats outside. Private parties: 10 main room, 26 to 36 private rooms. Car park. Vegetarian meals. Children's helpings. No smoking in dining room. No music ACCOMMODATION: 15 rooms, all with bath/shower. TV. Phone. Room only £40 to £85. Rooms for disabled. Baby facilities (*The Which? Hotel Guide*)

HORTON Northamptonshire **map 5**

French Partridge

Horton NN7 2AP — COOKING **6**
TEL: (01604) 870033 — FRENCH
on B526, 6m SE of Northampton — £36–£44

The small bar and two linked dining rooms can hardly have changed much since the Partridges opened here in 1963: old prints and bright lamps struggle to enliven the greens and blacks of walls and seating, but the place exudes an atmosphere of honesty, decency and industry, and in any case all eyes are on the food. Few would describe smoked salmon parcels with cucumber salad, or melon with port, as exciting starters, but the Partridge kitchen doesn't go in for showbiz flannel: just quiet dedication to sound principles of good cooking – 'sophisticated but orthodox' – wrapped up in a good value and largely French-inspired menu of four courses.

Dishes are plucked from a revolving repertoire that takes in coarse pork pâté with Cumberland sauce, well-executed grilled marlin steak with ginger, soy and chilli sauce, and ox tongue with Madeira sauce. Meals have a shape, and the main course typically impresses most. Fine raw materials and impressive technical skills are behind such successes as intensely flavoured braised young rabbit in tomato sauce with cheesy polenta. Vegetables may not be geared to the food they accompany, but the professionalism doesn't falter at dessert stage, where six options might include oeufs à la neige, iced orange soufflé, or traditional summer pudding.

Fine wines from all round France are temptingly priced and accompanied by helpful, unpretentious tasting notes. Contrasts and comparisons are invited with an impeccable selection of bottles from the New World, with New Zealand's Cloudy Bay Pelorus a great alternative to champagne, at £19. With such a good range it is a shame to find only two wines by the glass. Eleven house selections start at £10.

CHEFS: David and Justin Partridge PROPRIETORS: David and Mary Partridge OPEN: Tue to Sat D only 7.30 to 9 CLOSED: 2 weeks Christmas, 2 weeks Easter, 3 weeks July/Aug MEALS: Set D £28 SERVICE: net prices CARDS: none DETAILS: 45 seats. Private parties: 20 main room. Car park. Vegetarian meals. No smoking in dining room. No music (£5)

To find a restaurant in a particular area use the maps at the centre of the book.

HUDDERSFIELD West Yorkshire **map 9**

Bradley's £

84 Fitzwilliam Street, Huddersfield HD1 5BB
TEL: (01484) 516773 FAX: (01484) 538386

COOKING **2**
MEDITERRANEAN/MODERN BRITISH
£17–£44

Informal decor sets the right tone at this lively bistro. Not that there is anything slapdash about it: service does everything properly and efficiently, and the appealing Mediterranean/British style takes in black pudding fritters with beetroot salsa, a chorizo and herb risotto, and calf's liver with pancetta and mash. The three-course lunch (with three choices at each stage) is a 'terrific bargain', showing what can be done when imagination and sound technique are brought to bear on budget ingredients: one luncher enjoyed a thick and satisfying tomato soup, coral trout (a grouper 'reminiscent of whiting') with a first-rate basil dressing, and a rich chocolate and walnut tart with crème anglaise. There are ten house wines to choose from on the short serviceable list. Bottle prices start at £9.50.

CHEFS: Jonathan Nichols and Eric Paxman PROPRIETORS: Jonathan Nichols and Andrew Bradley OPEN: Mon to Fri L 12 to 2, Mon to Sat D 6 to 10 (10.30 Fri and Sat) CLOSED: bank hols (exc 25 and 26 Dec) MEALS: alc (main courses £8 to £15.50). Set L £6.25, Set D £14.50 inc wine (Set D not available after 7 Sat) SERVICE: not inc CARDS: MasterCard, Switch, Visa DETAILS: 130 seats. Private parties: 130 main room, 55 and 75 private rooms. Car park (D only). Vegetarian meals. Children's helpings. No smoking in 1 dining room. Wheelchair access (also WC). Music. Air-conditioned

▲ Lodge Hotel

48 Birkby Lodge Road, Birkby,
Huddersfield HD2 2BG
TEL: (01484) 431001 FAX: (01484) 421590

COOKING **3**
MODERN EUROPEAN
£22–£39

The Lodge is a handsome, ivy-covered Victorian building in a suburb. Its decorative tone is set by oak panelling, a real fire and ornate chandeliers, though the atmosphere is very much that of a friendly family-run hotel. Menus change seasonally and increasingly rely on locally produced organic ingredients, which are subjected to an uncomplicated, broadly European treatment. Among starters on a typical winter menu might be a warm salad of snails with bacon, or a 'confusion of seafood' in a champagne and seaweed broth, perhaps followed by saddle of roe deer with a port and sultana sauce, or Parmesan-crusted lemon sole and salmon in a lobster bisque. Vegetarian choices have included a tart of caramelised red onion and goats' cheese, and desserts might take in strawberry brûlée with minted pears, or egg custard tart with nutmeg ice cream and blackcurrant sauce. Wines come from all corners of the globe, with strong French, Australasian and American sections and customers have a choice between the full 18-page wine list, or a summary condensed on to one sheet. Mark-ups are very reasonable, with house wines starting at £10.95, but only three wines are available by the glass.

CHEF: Richard Hanson PROPRIETORS: Kevin and Garry Birley OPEN: Sun to Fri L 12 to 1.45, Mon to Sat D 7.30 to 9.45 CLOSED: bank hol Mons MEALS: Set L £10.95 (2 courses) to £14.95, Set D £23.95. Light L available Mon to Fri SERVICE: not inc, card slips closed CARDS: Amex, Delta, Diners, MasterCard, Switch, Visa DETAILS: 80 seats. Private parties: 60 main room, 6 to 22 private rooms. Car park. Vegetarian meals. Children's helpings. No children under 5 at D. No smoking in dining room. Wheelchair access (also WC). Music ACCOMMODATION: 12 rooms, all with bath/shower. TV. Phone. B&B £60 to £80. Baby facilities (*The Which? Hotel Guide*)

Thorpe Grange Manor

Thorpe Lane, Almondbury, Huddersfield HD5 8TA — COOKING **5**
TEL/FAX: (01484) 425115 — ANGLO-FRENCH
off A629, 2m E of Huddersfield — £22–£49

Despite the crunchy gravel and two and a half acres of secluded lawns, this eighteenth-century manor house is not at all intimidating. In place of the usual country-house atmosphere it presents more of a Scandinavian feel, with a relaxing bar (note the draught beers) and light, airy dining areas. Jason Neilson's culinary ambition is at least as high as the towers he builds on plates: 'little cigars' of langoustine wrapped in spinach and filo pastry, for example, set on tangy sun-dried tomatoes with a thatch of fried onion bits. Choice is plentiful, and the food is creative, good value and well executed. Even elaborate dishes seem to work: one reporter's starter of sea bass fillet, with baby squid and focaccia croûtons in a cherry tomato and saffron sauce was 'a revelation'.

Luxuries are competently handled too, judging by a morel and truffle accompaniment to first-rate beef fillet in Madeira sauce, and some vegetables work well, although the ubiquitous chopped mixed ones don't seem to add much to enjoyment. Desserts are a real treat, however. When a cannelloni of crisp dark chocolate filled with light coffee mousse, served on sambuca cream with toasted marshmallows, appeared from the kitchen it justifiably 'caused many pairs of envious eyes to follow it across the dining room'. Bread comes highly praised (try the focaccia). Although service may lack a professional edge, it is friendly and helpful, and wines run the gamut from enviable to affordable, starting with six house wines under £12.

CHEF: Jason Neilson PROPRIETORS: Ronald, Gillian, Jason and Ruth Neilson OPEN: Tue to Fri and Sun L 12 to 2, Tue to Sat D 6 (7 Fri and Sat) to 9.30 CLOSED: 28 July to 13 Aug MEALS: alc (main courses £13.50 to £17). Set L Tue to Fri £12.50 (2 courses) to £14.95, Set L Sun £14.95, Set D Tue to Thur before 7.30 £14.95, Set D £19.95 SERVICE: not inc CARDS: Delta, MasterCard, Switch, Visa DETAILS: 60 seats. 20 seats outside. Private parties: 85 main room, 40 private room. Car park. Vegetarian meals. Children's helpings. Children welcome before 7.30. No cigars/pipes in dining room. Wheelchair access (also WC). Music. Air-conditioned

(£5)

'The atmosphere was so hushed that when plates of petits fours were delivered to three tables at once you could hear the steady munching of biscuits throughout the dining room.' (On eating in the West Country)

Card slips closed *in the details at the end of an entry indicates that the total on the slips of credit cards is closed when handed over for signature.*

HUNSTRETE Bath & N.E. Somerset **map 2**

▲ Hunstrete House

Hunstrete BS39 4NS
TEL: (01761) 490490 FAX: (01761) 490732
EMAIL: info@hunstretehouse.co.uk
WEB SITE: www.hunstretehouse.co.uk
off A368, 4m S of Keynsham

NEW CHEF
COOKING **4**
ENGLISH COUNTRY HOUSE
£29–£81

Hunstrete is understated, low key, mellow and relaxing: 'a very English experience', according to one visitor. Philip Hobson, who worked here in the mid-'90s, and more recently at Bath Priory (see entry, Bath), took over the kitchen just as the Guide went to press, but given the setting – extensive grounds, and a high-ceilinged, pink-washed dining room with trompe l'oeil pillars – it is likely that the typical country-house combination of luxury materials (foie gras, truffle and oysters for example) and hard labour will continue. Reports are particularly welcome. Although pricey, the wine list has some impeccable choices, including fine wines from Bordeaux and Burgundy plus many innovative ones from California. Financial relief can be found in the South of France; house wines start at £13.

CHEF: Philip Hobson PROPRIETOR: Hunstrete House Ltd OPEN: all week 12 to 2, 7 to 9.30 MEALS: alc (main courses £24 to £25). Set L £14.95 (2 courses) to £19.95, Set D Sun to Thur £35, Set D all week £55 SERVICE: not inc, card slips closed CARDS: Amex, Delta, Diners, MasterCard, Switch, Visa DETAILS: 50 seats. 20 seats outside. Private parties: 50 main room, 14 and 30 private rooms. Car park. Vegetarian meals. Children's helpings. Jacket and tie. No smoking in dining room. Wheelchair access (not WC). Occasional music ACCOMMODATION: 23 rooms, all with bath/shower. TV. Phone. B&B £80 to £240. Baby facilities. Swimming pool (*The Which? Hotel Guide*)

HUNTINGDON Cambridgeshire **map 6**

▲ Old Bridge Hotel

NEW ENTRY

1 High Street, Huntingdon PE18 6TQ
TEL: (01480) 424300 FAX: (01480) 411017
EMAIL: oldbridge@huntsbridge.co.uk

COOKING **4**
MODERN BRITISH
£27–£52

This handsome ivy-clad eighteenth-century building overlooking the River Ouse, on the edge of the town that was Oliver Cromwell's birthplace, had a change of gear in January 2000 with the arrival of Martin Lee from sister establishment the Pheasant Inn (see entry, Keyston). A lavish kitchen refurbishment can't have done any harm either. As is customary with other members of the Huntsbridge group (see also Three Horseshoes, Madingley), the same menu is available throughout: in a garden-like indoor 'terrace' or a more formal-looking dining room.

Menus are built around sensibly sourced rather than exotic materials: asparagus from Abbey Parks Farm with hollandaise, or fine breast of Goosnargh chicken with a stickily reduced cep sauce. Even relatively humble items get a look-in, generally jazzed up a bit, as in a hot salad of chickpeas and spinach with green chilli salsa. Fish is well judged – brill and scallops in a convincing broth graced with spring greens, skinned broad beans and potato cubes – and while desserts are less well reported, cheeses are admirable in terms of both selection and handling. Service, though it might be more efficient, is perfectly willing.

The wine list offers a wide range of styles and prices. Twenty house wines from £9.95 (none more than £20) are available by the glass from £2.50, and set the tone for good-value, innovative drinking. Top-class traditional wines from Bordeaux, Burgundy, California and Italy share level-headed mark-ups and succinct write-ups.

CHEF: Martin Lee PROPRIETORS: John Hoskins and Martin Lee OPEN: all week 12 to 2.30, 6 to 10 MEALS: alc (main courses £9 to £17.50). Set L £14.95 (2 courses) SERVICE: not inc CARDS: Amex, Delta, Diners, MasterCard, Switch, Visa DETAILS: 110 seats. 20 seats outside. Private parties: 100 main room, 25 private room. Car park. Vegetarian meals. Children's helpings. No smoking in dining room. Wheelchair access (not WC). No music. Air-conditioned ACCOMMODATION: 24 rooms, all with bath/shower. TV. Phone. B&B £80 to £140. Rooms for disabled. Fishing

HURST Berkshire map 2

Castle

BERKSHIRE GFG 2001 COMMENDED

NEW ENTRY

Church Hill, Hurst RG10 0SJ
TEL: (0118) 934 0034 FAX: (0118) 934 0334
EMAIL: info@castlerestaurant.co.uk
WEB SITE: www.castlerestaurant.co.uk
off A321, just N of M4 junction 10

COOKING **5**
MODERN EUROPEAN
£27–£64

Opposite the church, the inn is of uncertain age but probably has at least five centuries under its belt. A bread oven (still there, next to a fireplace) was installed during the eighteenth century, and rifle racks hang from the ceiling, all adding character to an ambitious new restaurant. The menu (which changes every eight weeks or so) offers an intriguing array of dishes, from a spiced endive tart with goats' cheese, via ravioli of salt-pork with a reduction of chicken and morels, to roast cod cheeks with cured mackerel and potato vinaigrette.

Damian Broom, who has worked with a couple of noted chefs, turns out some fine and original cooking, with a proper appreciation of the importance of flavour: the marine component of 'foie gras from the land and sea', for example, turned out to be delicate monkfish liver, successfully accompanied by small cubes of apple in caramel sauce. Freshness of materials is apparent in a tartare of kingfish topped with a cold poached quail's egg and a substantial garnish of salmon roe, and maturity is characteristic of meats: well-hung roast rib and fillet of Scottish beef, with a flavourful wild mushroom raviolo, and two cylinders of dark lamb fillet, sitting on a spinach cushion in a lamb consommé filled with an assortment of vegetables.

Desserts, no less inventive, have a habit of introducing unexpected items, adding beetroot to a rhubarb dessert (served with a goats'-cheese sabayon), and parsnip to a version of summer pudding (using a hollowed-out baked apple instead of bread) filled with dark, flavourful fruit. Service is friendly, and some 50 wines are a cogent mix of styles and prices, starting with a handful of house wines under £12.50.

CHEF: Damian Broom PROPRIETORS: Anthony Edwards and Amanda Hill OPEN: all week 12 to 2.30 (3 Sun), 7 to 10 (9 Sun) MEALS: Set L £12.95 (2 courses) to £17.95, Set D £26 (2 courses) to £33 SERVICE: 10% (optional), card slips closed CARDS: Amex, Delta, Diners, MasterCard, Switch, Visa DETAILS: 75 seats. 70 seats outside. Private parties: 36 main room, 10 to 36 private rooms. Car park. Vegetarian meals. Children's helpings. No smoking in 1 dining room. Music

HURSTBOURNE TARRANT Hampshire **map 2**

▲ Esseborne Manor

Hurstbourne Tarrant SP11 0ER
TEL: (01264) 736444 FAX: (01264) 736725 — COOKING **3**
EMAIL: esseborne-manor@compuserve.com — TRADITIONAL ENGLISH
on A343, 1½m N of Hurstbourne Tarrant — £26–£56

Extensive and sympathetic renovation has been carried out at this isolated old manor house deep in the Hampshire countryside. It is small and unpretentious – a china collection adds a personal touch – and meals are taken in an elegant, warmly attractive dining room. Fixed-price menus suffer an outbreak of the usual disease – supplements – but convey no sense of being in any way inferior to the carte, either in materials or workmanship.

Lunch might offer warm pigeon salad, grilled mackerel with pesto dressing, and apple and quince crumble tart, while the set-price dinner weighs in with toasted scallops, calf's liver with horseradish stovies, and hot chocolate soufflé. Ideas are generally restrained, and dishes seem less elaborate than previously, which is to be commended. Service is attentive, friendly and cheerful, and six cleverly chosen wines are available by the glass, encompassing a range of countries and styles, although an exclusively French selection of halves confirms the balance of the list as a whole. House Australian starts at £13.50, and it is in the New World sections that bottles under £20 can most easily be found.

CHEF: Ben Tunnicliffe PROPRIETOR: Ian Hamilton OPEN: all week 12 to 2, 7 to 9.30 MEALS: alc Fri and Sat D (main courses £12 to £20). Set L £12 (2 courses) to £15, Set D Sun to Thur £15 (2 courses) to £18 SERVICE: not inc, card slips closed CARDS: Amex, Delta, Diners, MasterCard, Switch, Visa DETAILS: 70 seats. 30 seats outside. Private parties: 30 main room, 40 private room. Car park. Vegetarian meals. Children's helpings. No smoking in dining room. Wheelchair access (also women's WC). Occasional music ACCOMMODATION: 14 rooms, all with bath/shower. TV. Phone. B&B £95 to £160. Rooms for disabled (*The Which? Hotel Guide*) (£5)

HUXHAM Devon **map 1**

▲ Barton Cross

Huxham, Stoke Canon EX5 4EJ — COOKING **3**
TEL: (01392) 841245 FAX: (01392) 841942 — ANGLO-FRENCH
on A396 to Tiverton, 4m N of Exeter — £33–£44

The hotel, housed in three seventeenth-century cottages, attracts quite an international clientele, doubtless drawn by the friendly atmosphere, and by Brian Hamilton's use of both local and more exotic ingredients. These might translate into locally dived scallops (pan-fried with bacon and citrus fruit), free-range poultry from a Cullompton breeder (in a chicken, mango and pesto salad), or Dorset ham hock (glazed with honey and served on sage and onion mash with braised vegetables).

Seafood has impressed, from a smooth and intensely flavoured lobster bisque to a simply pan-fried fillet of sea bass, served on scrambled egg with smoked salmon and a creamy chive sauce. Meat alternatives have included an elaborate but nevertheless well-balanced brace of quail stuffed with wild mushrooms and wrapped in Parma ham, set on a pithiviers of beetroot, in turn on a little bed of spinach, with a Madeira sauce.

Puddings tend to be fruity: a filo bag of exotic fruits, or passion-fruit parfait with Cointreau sauce. Service is eager to please but can be stretched. The wine list, helpfully annotated, runs to around a hundred bins. Prices only occasionally creep above £20, and ten house wines start at £9.25.

CHEF: Paul George Bending PROPRIETOR: B.A. Hamilton OPEN: Mon to Sat D only 6.45 to 9.30 MEALS: alc (main courses £12.50 to £16.50). Set D £16.50 (2 courses) to £25 SERVICE: not inc, card slips closed CARDS: Amex, Delta, MasterCard, Switch, Visa DETAILS: 50 seats. 12 seats outside. Private parties: 50 main room. Car park. Vegetarian meals. Children's helpings. No smoking in dining room. Wheelchair access (also WC). Occasional music ACCOMMODATION: 9 rooms, all with bath/shower. TV. Phone. B&B £65.50 to £120. Rooms for disabled (£5)

ILKLEY West Yorkshire **map 8**

Box Tree

37 Church Street, Ilkley LS29 9DR
TEL: (01943) 608484 FAX: (01943) 607186 COOKING **8**
EMAIL: info@theboxtree.co.uk MODERN EUROPEAN
WEB SITE: www.theboxtree.co.uk £46–£67

There is much to keep the eye occupied and entertained at this 'red grotto', with its porcelain animal figures, and Eastern face masks guarding the entrance to the dining room. But the whole lot, including masses of pictures and stacks of plates in glass cases, has the welcome stamp of a personal and tasteful collection rather than being merely a decorative gesture. A sense of individuality and purpose also pervades the food, which has a strong French presence and a contemporary slant. The five or six choices per course (three on the set-price menu) are all worth considering, from a terrine of white haricot beans with smoked pork and sausage, to crisp-skinned, well-flavoured roast sea bass with wild mushrooms and new potatoes.

Technical accomplishment and clean, clear flavours, can be taken for granted, and contrasts are well handled: for example, between sweet, crunchy, sharp and juicy in a dish of roast scallops with a fruit chutney incorporating pineapple, red pepper and a lemon-grass sauce. Presentation may be simple, but flavours are sophisticated and well integrated: a bowl of velvety mushroom soup, for example, containing half a dozen ultra-light, herb-studded gnocchi overlaid with a few strands of melting Parmesan. Ideas may be traditional rather than innovative, but the food certainly packs a punch. Poached pigeon breast has appeared as four roundels wrapped in a little livery pâté and a Savoy cabbage leaf, with an unfussy accompaniment of 'sensible and flavourful' vegetables in a well-reduced fowl-based stock: nothing explosive, but a simple success.

It is not unusual ingredients or elaborate gestures that produce match-winning form, rather consideration and thoughtfulness that convince, for example in the contrasts of flavour and texture in an ordinary-sounding plum clafoutis with chocolate and vanilla ice creams in filo baskets. Service is well organised, professional and friendly. The hefty wine list, a pleasure to read, is dominated by a classic French selection where quality is undisputed, though mark-ups are a little high. Other areas get a look-in, with Italy, Australia and California at the forefront. A bit of ferreting reveals plenty of wines under £20. House Burgundy is £14 and there is a good selection of wines by the glass. Lovers of vintage port will not be disappointed.

CHEF: Thierry LePrêtre-Granet PROPRIETOR: The Box Tree Restaurant (Ilkley) Ltd OPEN: Tue to Sun L 12 to 2.30, Tue to Sat D 7 to 9.30 CLOSED: Christmas to New Year, last two weeks Jan MEALS: alc (main courses £16.50 to £20). Set L and D £19.50 (2 courses) SERVICE: not inc, card slips closed CARDS: Amex, Delta, MasterCard, Switch, Visa DETAILS: 50 seats. Private parties: 25 main room, 15 to 25 private rooms. Vegetarian meals. No smoking in dining room. Wheelchair access (not WC). Occasional music

Farsyde £

38A The Back Grove, Ilkley LS29 9EE
TEL: (01943) 602030 FAX: (01943) 435334

COOKING **4**
MODERN BRITISH
£16–£37

Despite an inconspicuous location behind Betty's tea rooms (see Round-ups, Ilkley), the split-level dining area is a bright, airy space with yellow walls and wooden flooring. It frequently fills to capacity with a friendly, vibrant crowd keen on sampling Gavin Beedham's accomplished modern cooking. Mediterranean flavours are to the fore, though an enjoyable dinner for one visitor started with crab spring roll (with a salad of water chestnuts, mango and bok choy), followed by roast rump of lamb with a pine nut and herb crust, in port sauce.

The choice widens for lunch, which could be simply a filled bagel, or a full-blown affair with salmon on prawn and pesto couscous as a centrepiece. Desserts, too, range from traditional (sticky toffee pudding) to imaginative (deep-fried pineapple and Malibu ravioli). A brunch menu is offered on Sundays. Staff are helpful and 'appear to enjoy serving'. The well-priced wine list offers plenty of choice by the glass, and has witty notes to boot. House wine is £7.75. As the Guide went to press, there were plans to open a branch in Leeds during 2001, with Gavin Beedham moving to the new site and installing another chef here.

CHEF/PROPRIETOR: Gavin Beedham OPEN: Tue to Sun L 11.30 to 2 (2.30 Sat, 3.30 Sun), Tue to Sat D 6 to 10 CLOSED: Sun L May to Sept MEALS: alc (main courses L £4.50 to £7, D £9 to £14). Set L Tue to Sat £11, Set D before 7.25 £10.50 (2 courses). Light L and snacks available SERVICE: not inc CARDS: Delta, MasterCard, Switch, Visa DETAILS: 55 seats. Vegetarian meals. Children's helpings. No-smoking area; no cigars/pipes in dining room. Wheelchair access (not WC). Music

Dining rooms where music, either live or recorded, is never played are signalled by No music *in the details at the end of an entry.*

IPSWICH Suffolk map 6

Mortimer's Seafood Restaurant

Wherry Quay, Ipswich IP4 1AS
TEL/FAX: (01473) 230225

COOKING **1**
SEAFOOD
£21–£54

'Good ingredients with minimal interference' is what Mortimer's does best, and it is Grimsby fish market that provides much of the fresh seafood prepared at this bustling, bistro-style restaurant overlooking Neptune marina. The large dining room has a fittingly piscine theme, decorated with lobster creels, fish posters and copper ship's lanterns. No fewer than 17 fishy starters have included smoked trout and salmon from Loch Fyne, and a generous platter of big, fresh oysters, 'sweet-tasting' crevettes, languoustines, crab claw and shell-on prawns. Though fish is invariably well cooked, sauces can let the side down, but reporters have praised chargrilled black bream, and steamed fillet of lemon sole. Desserts have failed to impress. Service is quiet and unobtrusive but can be slow, while the reasonably priced, mainly French wine list also extends to a smattering of New World offerings, plus around ten half-bottles. House wines start at £9.95.

CHEFS: Kenneth Ambler, Alison Mott and Reda A. Irain PROPRIETORS: Kenneth and Elizabeth Ambler OPEN: Mon to Fri L 12 to 2, Tue to Sat D 6.30 to 9 (8.30 Mon) CLOSED: 24 Dec to 5 Jan MEALS: alc (main courses £5.50 to £18) SERVICE: not inc CARDS: Amex, Delta, Diners, MasterCard, Switch, Visa DETAILS: 85 seats. Private parties: 16 main room, 30 private room. Vegetarian meals. Children's helpings. No smoking in 1 dining room. Wheelchair access (not WC). Occasional music (£5)

IXWORTH Suffolk map 6

Theobalds

68 High Street, Ixworth IP31 2HJ
TEL/FAX: (01359) 231707

COOKING **4**
ANGLO-FRENCH
£29–£57

Occupying a charming timbered building dating from 1650, on the main street of a village rendered quiet by a bypass, Theobalds is a comfortably furnished house, with a large inglenook fireplace, paintings for sale, and simple table settings. Part of the appeal of Simon Theobald's contemporary Anglo-French style is that he presents dishes straightforwardly without fussy garnishes or decoration: a golden dome of twice-baked mature Cheddar cheese soufflé with a soft, airy texture and crisp skin, or fresh-tasting fillets of seared turbot on a mound of creamy wild mushroom risotto. The impression is of interesting food, mainly prepared with skill and care, although not without its weak points: 'could do better' summed up an inspector who ate roast Barbary duck breast of 'indeterminate flavour'. Desserts are competently done: for example, a cylinder of rich, dark chocolate and walnut mousse with candied orange peel and crème anglaise. Bread is good, and service 'mumsy'. Wines are mainly French, though they are bulked together according to colour without regional or stylistic groupings. Succinct tasting notes accompany recommended bottles. House wines start at £14.60, and there are numerous halves.

CHEF: Simon Theobald PROPRIETORS: Simon and Geraldine Theobald OPEN: Tue to Fri and Sun L 12.15 to 1.30, Tue to Sat D 7.15 to 9.15 CLOSED: 2 weeks Aug, bank hols MEALS: alc Tue to Sat (main courses £10 to £19). Set L Sun £18.95 SERVICE: not inc, card slips closed CARDS: Delta, MasterCard, Switch, Visa DETAILS: 50 seats. 8 seats outside. Private parties: 30 main room, 20 private room. Vegetarian meals. Children's helpings. No children under 8 at D. No smoking in dining room. No music

JEVINGTON East Sussex **map 3**

Hungry Monk

Jevington BN26 5QF
TEL/FAX: (01323) 482178 COOKING **3**
WEB SITE: www.hungrymonk.co.uk ENGLISH/FRENCH COUNTRY COOKING
off A22 between Polegate and Friston £36–£59

Walkers on the South Downs Way might consider dropping down from the rolling grasslands to this long-standing favourite in the flint-built village of Jevington. Guests may take pre-dinner drinks in one of the pretty sitting rooms in front of an open fire, before proceeding to the small beamed dining room with its assorted polished wooden tables. The menu might offer anything from a straightforward smoked salmon omelette with asparagus to, more trendily, a crab fishcake with red pepper and chilli relish.

Meats are well sourced, typically served as several small slices, perhaps prosciutto-fringed best end of lamb in a sauce that uses aubergine, raisins and cumin. Creamy dauphinoise is highly recommended. The Monk is where banoffi pie was invented (in 1972), and this rendition – coffee-flavoured cream on a layer of banana on an inch-thick layer of toffee – made one visitor realise 'how awful most other versions are'. Women in maroon kilts deliver warm and purposeful service. Classed-growth claret may be had seemingly by the yard, although the list is sparser in other areas. The house selection starts at £11.

CHEFS: Sharon Poulton and Gary Fisher PROPRIETORS: Nigel and Sue Mackenzie OPEN: Sun L 12 to 2.30, all week D 6.45 to 10.15 CLOSED: 24 to 26 Dec, bank hols MEALS: Set L £24.95, Set D £26.50 SERVICE: not inc, card slips closed, 12.5% for parties of 8 or more CARDS: Amex, MasterCard, Switch, Visa DETAILS: 40 seats. 8 seats outside. Private parties: 16 main room, 6 to 16 private rooms. Car park. Vegetarian meals. Children's helpings. No children under 5. Jacket and tie. No smoking in dining room. Occasional music. Air-conditioned (£5)

KENDAL Cumbria **map 8**

Georgian House

NEW ENTRY

99 Highgate, Kendal LA9 4EN COOKING **3**
TEL: (015397) 22123 FAX: (015397) 21223 MODERN BRITISH/MEDITERRANEAN
£27–£43

Don't be fooled by the name or the period façade: inside, the décor is relentlessly austere with bare wood floors and plain white walls hung with contemporary artworks. Whatever your aesthetic taste, there is much to admire in what the kitchen produces for both the ground-floor bar-café (from sandwiches to confit duck with Cumberland sauce) and the second-floor restaurant. Robust meat dishes have included a starter of lambs' kidneys and bacon on herb brioche with an onion sauce, and roast lamb shank with olive oil mash, minted pesto and plenty of green vegetables.

A varied output takes in traditional rump steak with a cognac and green peppercorn sauce, served with rustic chunky potato wedges, and more up-to-date marinated salmon on pickled vegetables with coriander-flavoured crème fraîche. Finish perhaps with a warm frangipane tart of apricots and dates, served with thick pouring cream, or hot apple fritters with butterscotch sauce. Reports have commended friendly, helpful and efficient service. A compact list of 30 wines opens at around £12 and stays mostly under £20. Eight wines are available by the glass from £2.35.

CHEF: C.G. Davies PROPRIETOR: J. Kennedy OPEN: Tue to Sat D only 6.30 to 9.30 (10 Sat) MEALS: alc (main courses £6.50 to £13.50). Bar meals available Tue to Sat L and D SERVICE: not inc, card slips closed CARDS: Delta, Diners, MasterCard, Switch, Visa DETAILS: 72 seats. Private parties: 72 main room. Vegetarian meals. Children's helpings. No smoking in dining room. Music (£5)

KENILWORTH Warwickshire **map 5**

Restaurant Bosquet 🍷

97A Warwick Road, Kenilworth CV8 1HP COOKING **5**
TEL: (01926) 852463 FRENCH
£34–£53

The front-parlour dining room of this unremarkable house on the main road is very domestic, with pinstripe wallpaper and heavily fringed curtains. After 20 years (they set up here in 1981) the Ligniers don't feel the need to inject new life into either décor or menu, which is firmly committed to a circumscribed repertoire in classical French style. Many dishes have a south-western provenance, where appetites take some satisfying: hence chips cooked in goose fat to accompany beef fillet, and a plate combining venison, pigeon and partridge in a game sauce.

Luxuries are integral to the style, from asparagus with truffle dressing to pan-fried foie gras with a spicy fig sauce, and everything is carefully and professionally turned out: a generous, notably fresh fillet of turbot for instance, surrounded by a fry-up of shallots, morels and shiitakes, simply rendered with cream and pan juices. Vegetables include an old-fashioned, hollowed-out and spinach-filled tomato, and marble-sized new Jersey potatoes in spring that were 'roasted, buttery, and seriously herbed'.

Desserts extend to lemon tart, intensely flavoured passion-fruit and mango sorbets, and a rough-textured prune and armagnac ice cream. Jane Lignier handles front-of-house in a bright and friendly manner without being too familiar: a natural, in other words. Exclusively French, the wine list nevertheless combines tradition with innovation and includes first-rate wines from up-and-coming producers of southwest France alongside more-established names from Burgundy and Bordeaux. Mark-ups are very fair and encourage splashing out. House wines start at £12.50, though it is surprising to find only two wines by the glass.

Use the lists towards the front of the book to find suitable restaurants for special occasions.

CHEF: Bernard Lignier PROPRIETORS: Bernard and Jane Lignier OPEN: Sat and Sun L 12 to 1.15 (booking essential), Tue to Fri D 7 to 9.15 MEALS: alc (main courses £16 to £17). Set L Sun and D Tue to Fri £25 SERVICE: not inc CARDS: Amex, Delta, MasterCard, Switch, Visa DETAILS: 30 seats. Private parties: 30 main room. Vegetarian meals. Children's helpings. Wheelchair access (not WC). No music

Simpson's

101–103 Warwick Road, Kenilworth CV8 2SY
TEL: (01926) 864567 FAX: (01926) 864510

COOKING **5**
MODERN EUROEAN
£31–£51

The main road through Kenilworth is liberally supplied with restaurants, including this former shop with large plate-glass windows, colourful Mediterranean landscapes, and table settings enhanced by crisp napkins folded to resemble shirt fronts. Andreas Antona cooks in a modern style that runs from crab and avocado torte to squab pigeon feuilleté with cabbage and garlic confit. He takes risotto-making in his stride – a well-made creamy pea version at inspection, topped with slices of nutty sauté scallops – and uses good materials sensibly. A first rate specimen of Gressingham duck for example, contrives a purposeful contrast between its supple, well timed breast and large, crisp-skinned, melting drumstick, and comes with chunky mashed potatoes mixed with streaky bacon, and unctuous truffled celeriac. Vegetarians should note that some dishes marked with a 'v' may contain seafood, apparently on the grounds that 'most vegetarians will eat fish'.

Presentation is appealing. For dessert, there might be an 'attractive and fun' banana-shaped puff-pastry sandwich filled with chunks of roast banana in custard, and served with walnut ice-cream and caramel sauce, or perhaps Valrhona chocolate fondant with orange sorbet. Smartly dressed waiting staff are well trained. An enterprising global collection of wines offers plenty of variety for those on a relatively modest budget, and also obliges those with more extravagant tastes. Ten house wines come in under £20.

CHEFS: Andreas Antona and Luke Tipping PROPRIETORS: Andreas and Alison Antona OPEN: Mon to Fri L 12.30 to 2, Mon to Sat D 7 to 10 MEALS: Set L £15 (2 courses) to £20, Set D £22.95 (2 courses) to £29.95 SERVICE: not inc, 10% for parties of 6 or more, card slips closed CARDS: Amex, Delta, Diners, MasterCard, Switch, Visa DETAILS: 70 seats. Private parties: 10 main room, 40 private room. Small car park. Children's helpings. Music. Air-conditioned

KEW Greater London **map 3**

The Glasshouse

14 Station Parade, Kew TW9 3PZ
TEL: (020) 8940 6777 FAX: (020) 8940 3833

COOKING **6**
MODERN BRITISH
£32–£61

A few yards from the tube station, in a villagey arrangement of shops and leafy pavements, the Glasshouse is 'just what affluent suburbs like this are looking for'. Its parquet floor, white walls and wide expanses of glass ensure a constant background buzz when busy, and when it is quiet it feels sedate. Staff run a tight ship, with staggered bookings and sharp, attentive service which earns its 12.5

per cent. The confident style has proved popular with reporters, not least because the generous menu's well-conceived modern dishes use fine materials, among them firm, fresh, crisp-skinned red mullet, and a dish of scallops served three ways: a smooth dark bisque, a ceviche with avocado, tomato and onion, and a single grilled queen scallop wrapped in Alsace bacon.

Accurate timing and some unusual but successful partnerships have produced a poached egg dipped in truffle-oiled breadcrumbs and deep-fried, served with a salad of duck confit, and a hearty, flavourful dish of pink lambs' kidneys with merguez sausage. Five sweet wines are available by the glass to accompany desserts such as hot chocolate mousse with orange ice cream, and banana Tatin with clotted cream. The rest of the engaging, versatile wine list is full of interest, even if most bottles cost over £20.

CHEF: Anthony Boyd PROPRIETOR: Larkbrace Ltd OPEN: Mon to Sat L 12 to 2.30, Sun L 12.30 to 3, Mon to Sat D 7 (6.30 Fri and Sat) to 10.30 CLOSED: bank hols MEALS: Set L £19.50, Set D £25 SERVICE: 12.5% (optional), card slips closed CARDS: Amex, Delta, MasterCard, Switch, Visa DETAILS: 65 seats. Private parties: 8 main room. Vegetarian meals. Children's helpings. No cigars/pipes in dining room. No music. Air-conditioned TUBE: Kew Gardens

KEYSTON Cambridgeshire — map 6

Pheasant Inn

Keyston PE18 0RE — COOKING **5**
TEL: (01832) 710241 FAX: (01832) 710464 — MODERN EUROPEAN/BRITISH
on B663, 1m S of junction with A14 — £27–£51

After a brief stint at Merchants in Nottingham (see entry), Clive Dixon joined the Huntsbridge Group (see Three Horseshoes, Madingley; Old Bridge, Huntingdon) as chef/patron of this old thatched and beamed inn. While members of the group share a free-ranging philosophy – eat just one or two courses off solid wood tables, anywhere you like – each is in full charge of their own patch. Although supplemented by snacks and blackboard specials, the main carte is self-sufficient in terms of interest and variety, offering starters such as pan-fried ox tongue with polenta and ceps, or a single raviolo filled with shredded casseroled beef, served with truffled spring cabbage. A similarly wide spectrum produces main courses of braised lamb shank on spiced couscous with preserved lemon, and fresh, carefully timed brill fillet with oyster mushrooms and chicken juices.

Materials take in Goosnargh chicken with trompettes, and Aberdeen Angus beef: for one visitor a large, top-quality chargrilled sirloin steak served with roast flat cap mushrooms, plum tomatoes and a bowl of crisp chunky chips sprinkled with sea salt. Not all reporters have come away happy, but an inspection meal found most of the food on form, not least a well-risen chocolate soufflé and matching sorbet. The wine list concentrates on sourcing 'interesting' wines, 'by which we mean characterful individual and intriguing – not necessarily classic': so trying something new will most likely be a rewarding experience. A choice of 16 house wines (from £9.75), all available by the glass (from £1.90), encourage experimentation, and mark-ups are fair.

'The salmon was accurately timed, the sauce zingy, and the garnishing of slices of lime kept me clear of scurvy for days.' (On eating in Yorkshire)

CHEF: Clive Dixon PROPRIETOR: Huntsbridge Ltd OPEN: all week 12 to 2, 6.30 (6 Sat) to 10 (7 to 9.30 Sun) CLOSED: D 25 and 26 Dec, D 1 Jan MEALS: alc (main courses £9 to £16). Snack menu available Mon to Sat L, Sun to Thur D SERVICE: not inc CARDS: Amex, Delta, Diners, MasterCard, Switch, Visa DETAILS: 100 seats. 30 seats outside. Private parties: 30 main room. Car park. Vegetarian meals. Children's helpings. No smoking in 1 dining room. No music

KING'S CLIFFE Northamptonshire **map 6**

King's Cliffe House

31 West Street, King's Cliffe PE8 6XB COOKING **4**
TEL: (01780) 470172 FAX: Same MODERN EUROPEAN
EMAIL: kchr@ukgateway.net £28–£47

The big old house has nearly two acres of garden and orchard, where herbs and vegetables point to the owners' motivation: theirs is a cottage industry with an eye on local resources. Although open only four sessions a week, they track down free-range chickens, ducks, guinea fowl and eggs, while a local butcher and small abattoir supply Dexter and Longhorn beef and Gloucester Old Spot pork. They take advantage of a farmers' market, and customers sometimes bring in offerings of mulberries, medlars, pears, quince, vine leaves or puffballs.

All this is reflected in a style of English cooking that links traditional techniques with contemporary ideas. A combination of home-smoking and curing has produced salt beef with guacamole and horseradish, and a starter plate of goose including rillettes, confit and smoked breast. Fish comes from Devon (maybe skate goujons in a spiced chickpea batter with a salsa) and desserts range from rum and raisin ice cream to poached William pear with ginger pannacotta. The pace is gentle, and wines – divided by colour and arranged in ascending order of price – are opened and left for customers to pour. Pithy annotations and intelligent, global selections can make choosing tricky. Prices are fair, with plenty under £20, house white at £9.95 and a long list of half-bottles.

CHEFS/PROPRIETORS: Emma Jessop and Andrew Wilshaw OPEN: Wed to Sat D only 7 to 9.15 CLOSED: 25 Dec, 1 Jan, 2 weeks spring, 2 weeks autumn, bank hols exc Good Fri MEALS: alc (main courses £11 to £14.50) SERVICE: net prices CARDS: none DETAILS: 20 seats. Private parties: 20 main room. Car park. Vegetarian meals. Children's helpings. No smoking in dining room. No music

KING'S LYNN Norfolk **map 6**

Rococo

11 Saturday Market Place, King's Lynn PE30 5DQ
TEL: (01553) 771483 and (07000) 762626 COOKING **6**
FAX: (01553) 771483 MODERN BRITISH
EMAIL: rococorest@aol.com £25–£58

In keeping with its seemly surroundings – near the church and museum, a stone's throw from the River Ouse – this seventeenth-century town house lives up to its name the instant you step through the door. A dark green lounge sports cream and turquoise sofas, a fuchsia-coloured dresser and colourful modern art, although the blond wood and mustard-coloured walls of the L-shaped dining room are more restrained. Local materials feature prominently, including Cromer crab, locally cured bresaola, and pigeon salad with quince crisps and chutney, while a well-balanced, modern British menu brims with bright ideas: warm Finnan haddie sausage, or fillet of Norfolk lamb bound in couscous and served with cumin-scented jus and Jerusalem artichoke.

Fish is well handled – a chunk of hot-smoked salmon with dabs of mussel purée in a summer herb salad – and saucing is a strong suit: creamy but powerfully flavoured with Norfolk brown shrimps to accompany poached turbot, or a first-rate raspberry vinegar version for crisp-skinned, tender-fleshed duck confit. Desserts have included an enjoyable construction of iced sloe gin and roast almond parfait with dark chocolate mousse, and lemon tart (with 'little to fault in the pastry') accompanied by a very sweet citrus caramel sauce. Well-trained service now leaves wine bottles within diners' reach. Carefully chosen wines hail mainly from France and the New World. A personal selection highlights innovative, bold producers. French and South American house wines start at £12.75.

CHEFS: Nick Anderson and Alex Howard PROPRIETORS: Nick and Anne Anderson OPEN: Tue to Sat L 12 to 2, Mon to Sat D 7 (6.30 if pre-booked) to 10 CLOSED: 24 to 31 Dec MEALS: alc L (main courses £7 to £10). Set D £24.50 (2 courses) to £34.50 SERVICE: not inc, card slips closed, 10% for parties of 6 or more CARDS: Amex, Delta, Diners, MasterCard, Switch, Visa DETAILS: 40 seats. Private parties: 40 main room. Vegetarian meals. Children's helpings. No smoking while others eat. Wheelchair access (also WC). Music (£5)

KINGTON Herefordshire **map 5**

▲ Penrhos Court

Kington HR5 3LH
TEL: (01544) 230720 FAX: (01544) 230754 COOKING **3**
WEB SITE: www.penrhos.co.uk MEDITERRANEAN
on A44, ½m E of Kington £42–£50

The fact that 'you could be in a different century' is a testament to the owners' years of hard work spent sympathetically restoring the collection of ancient stone and timber buildings. Four-course dinners are eaten off bare wooden tables in a high-ceilinged hall, although any medieval impression is dispelled by the fact that no red meat is served: this is not a Soil Association requirement (the restaurant is certified organic) but a personal preference. Instead, meals are built around vegetables, grains, pulses, seeds and fruit, usually with a fish and poultry main-course option: perhaps a bowl of thick black-bean soup spiked with coriander, followed by grilled monkfish and salad.

Ideas tend to be spare – roast red pepper sauce accompanying chicken breast on one occasion, John Dory on another – and Daphne Lambert is concerned that the natural balance of minerals and vitamins should be 'as undisturbed as possible' when the food is served. This can have the effect of reducing cooking to a minimum. Indeed there appears to be more advance preparation than cooking on the spot: a simple plate of cold mixed roast vegetables (some tastier than others), followed by straightforward mushroom and feta frittata, and either a plain fresh fruit salad, or a standard tiramisù. Bread is first rate, and most of the wines are organic, the majority under £20.

CHEF: Daphne Lambert PROPRIETORS: Daphne Lambert and Martin Griffiths OPEN: all week D only 7 to 10 (8.30 Sun) CLOSED: Jan MEALS: Set D £31.50 SERVICE: not inc, card slips closed CARDS: Amex, MasterCard, Switch, Visa DETAILS: 80 seats. 200 seats outside. Private parties: 80 main room, 20 to 100 private rooms. Car park. Vegetarian meals. Children's helpings. No smoking in dining room. Occasional music ACCOMMODATION: 15 rooms, all with bath/shower. TV. Phone. B&B £55 to £105. Rooms for disabled. Baby facilities (*The Which? Hotel Guide*) (£5)

KIRKHAM Lancashire **map 8**

Cromwellian

16 Poulton Street, Kirkham PR4 2AB
TEL: (01772) 685680 FAX: (01772) 684381

COOKING **3**
MODERN BRITISH
£28–£43

Peter Fawcett is a welcoming and friendly host, setting an informal tone to this 15-year-old family enterprise. Frills and fancy touches are conspicuous by their absence, and rather than trying to dazzle, Josie Fawcett adopts a straightforward approach to the food. Standard main-course meats and fish are subject to a range of treatments, from chicken breast in Mediterranean mode to salmon fillet with sweet chilli sauce. Starters, meanwhile, have delivered regionally inspired items such as filo pastry parcels of Lancashire cheese and apple, and black pudding on mushy peas. Morecambe Bay shrimps have appeared too, followed by large and well-timed fillet steaks (a regular fixture, with a £5 supplement), accompanied by the dauphinoise-like potato speciality of the house. Upside-down apple sponge pleased one visitor, and the impression of a domestically oriented kitchen is confirmed by profiteroles with vanilla ice cream, and mincemeat and apricot crumble. Wines touch on many countries and are attuned to modest pockets, starting with house French at £10.50.

CHEF: Josie Fawcett PROPRIETORS: Peter and Josie Fawcett OPEN: Tue to Sat D only 7 to 9 CLOSED: 1 week spring, 1 week autumn MEALS: Set D £18 SERVICE: not inc, card slips closed CARDS: Amex, Delta, MasterCard, Switch, Visa DETAILS: 28 seats. Private parties: 10 main room, 10 private room. Vegetarian meals. No music

LANGAR Nottinghamshire **map 5**

▲ Langar Hall

Langar NG13 9HG
TEL: (01949) 860559 FAX: (01949) 861045
EMAIL: langarhall-hotel@ndirect.co.uk
between A46 and A52, 4m S of Bingham
WEB SITE: www.langarhall.com

COOKING **4**
ENGLISH
£19–£58

Inhabiting a world of its own, overlooking acres of gardens and medieval moats stocked with carp, historic Langar Hall is a mildly eccentric place with crystal chandeliers, gilt mirrors, statues and marble pillars. It still feels like a family home, largely thanks to the efforts of Imogen Skirving, who manages to be everywhere at once and whose presence adds enormously to the atmosphere. 'Natural, organic and wild' ingredients dictated by the seasons are to the fore on Toby Garratt's menus, which have a predominantly traditional feel.

Pink, tender chargrilled fillet of Langar lamb is served with a minted gravy, while local game has produced a generous salad of Belvoir rabbit with black pudding and bacon, and juicy roast partridge with a fat slice of crisply fried foie gras. Brixham seafood has also shown up well in the form of escabèche of red mullet on crisp rösti, and simply grilled lobster with lemon butter, while desserts have ranged from a light and creamy panettone bread-and-butter pudding to hot chocolate fondant with caramel ice cream. Stilton, a local cheese, is offered as an alternative. A varied, good-value wine list opens with 20 house selections from £10.50, five of which are available by the glass from £2.50.

CHEFS: Toby Garratt and Chris Ansell PROPRIETOR: Imogen Skirving OPEN: all week 12 to 1.45, 7 to 9.30 (10 Fri and Sat, 8 Sun) MEALS: alc D (main courses £10 to £20). Set L £8 (2 courses) to £11.50, Set D Sun to Fri £17.50, Set D Sat £20.25 SERVICE: 5% (optional), card slips closed CARDS: Amex, Diners, MasterCard, Switch, Visa DETAILS: 60 seats. 10 seats outside. Private parties: 42 main room, 10 to 22 private rooms. Car park. Vegetarian meals. Children's helpings. No smoking in dining room. Wheelchair access (also WC). Occasional music ACCOMMODATION: 10 rooms, all with bath/shower. TV. Phone. B&B £75 to £150. Baby facilities. Fishing (*The Which? Hotel Guide*) (£5)

LANGFORD BUDVILLE Somerset **map 2**

▲ Bindon Country House, Wellesley Restaurant

Langford Budville TA21 0RU — COOKING **2**
TEL: (01823) 400070 FAX: (01823) 400071 — ENGLISH COUNTRY-HOUSE
EMAIL: bindonhouse@msn.com — £29–£69

It may look a bit like a wedding cake, but this tranquil, peaceful and comfortable seventeenth-century house is a gem of a place. The traditional style of cooking – grilled Dover sole, beef Wellington, orange and Grand Marnier soufflé – is arranged around set menus with a few supplements. It deals in upmarket ingredients such as scallops (on broccoli purée), sea bass (with saffron sauce), and foie gras (sharing a terrine with duck confit and poached pear). Meals favour lots of protein, in the shape of roast rack of lamb, or loin of pork with apple and mustard sauce, and end on a high with desserts such as crème brûlée with blood orange sorbet, or chocolate fondant. Friendly staff deliver 'great service', and the wine list's dizzy heights are balanced by more down-to-earth selections at not unreasonable prices. House wines start at £13.50.

CHEF: Patrick Roberts PROPRIETORS: Lynn and Mark Jaffa OPEN: all week 12 to 1.45, 7 to 9.30 MEALS: alc L Tue to Sat (main courses £14 to £15). Set L £12.95 (2 courses) to £16.95, Set D £29.50 SERVICE: not inc, card slips closed CARDS: Amex, Delta, Diners, MasterCard, Switch, Visa DETAILS: 50 seats. 30 seats outside. Private parties: 50 main room, 20 private rooms. Car park. Vegetarian meals. No children under 10. No smoking in dining room. Music ACCOMMODATION: 12 rooms, all with bath/shower. TV. Phone. B&B £85 to £185. Baby facilities. Swimming pool (*The Which? Hotel Guide*) (£5)

'We were told we had the best table in the house. Unfortunately, in order for us to have this table, a local regular was rushed through his pudding by the owner and moved to the bar for coffee. I felt a bit bad about this but the regular didn't seem to mind. It had obviously happened before.' (On eating in Cornwall)

LANGHO Lancashire **map 8**

▲ Northcote Manor

Northcote Road, Langho BB6 8BE
TEL: (01254) 240555 FAX: (01254) 246568
EMAIL: admin@ncotemanor.demon.co.uk
WEB SITE: www.ncotemanor.demon.co.uk
on A59, 8½m E of M6 exit 31

COOKING **6**
MODERN BRITISH
£26–£72

The setting is a reassuring, comfortable nineteenth-century building with a lot of late-Victorian 'twiddly bits', much self-promotional material on the walls, and a light and airy, sunny yellow dining room. Since last year a less expensive, no-choice, three-course dinner has joined the carte and set-price menu, the latter offering half-bottle wine suggestions with each course. Although rather static (black pudding with buttered trout has been a fixture for many years), the repertoire has a regional feel, and the cooking is founded on first-rate, well-sourced raw materials. These have shown to good effect in, for example, a simple starter of sliced cold beef, cured in-house, served with a stack of well-timed asparagus spears and a salad of rocket and frisée leaves in prime condition.

The cooking is technically sound rather than exciting, producing thick slices of succulent Middle White pork fillet rolled in thin smoky bacon, accompanied by a large squat round of unremarkable couscous layered with spinach. Saucing is highly rated – for example, a properly reduced and 'aromatically lickable' one to partner pigeon and foie gras – and vegetables have included triumphantly 'big, square Stonehenges of chips' to partner fillet steak. Finish perhaps with pear Tatin and ginger cream, a 'routine' raspberry soufflé with sarsaparilla ice cream, or apple and rhubarb crumble with juniper custard. Craig Bancroft 'works the room like Laurence Olivier worked the Old Vic audience', although his Mechanicals could do with livening up. A lengthy wine list gives equal weight to bottles from the Old and New Worlds. Mark-ups are fair, plenty of sparkling wines provide champagne alternatives, and the half-bottle list is impressive. House wines, from France, Spain and Italy, are £14.50.

CHEF: Nigel Haworth PROPRIETORS: Craig Bancroft and Nigel Haworth OPEN: Sun to Fri L 12 to 1.30 (2 Sun), all week D 7 to 9.30 (9 Sun) CLOSED: 25 Dec, 1 Jan MEALS: alc (main courses £18 to £23.50). Set L £16, Set D £25 to £40 SERVICE: 10% (optional) CARDS: Amex, Delta, MasterCard, Switch, Visa DETAILS: 90 seats. Private parties: 90 main room, 35 private room. Car park. Children's helpings. No smoking in dining room. Wheelchair access (not WC). Music ACCOMMODATION: 14 rooms, all with bath/shower. TV. Phone. B&B £80 to £130. Rooms for disabled. Baby facilities (*The Which? Hotel Guide*)

The 2002 Guide will be published before Christmas 2001. Reports on meals are most welcome at any time of the year, but are particularly valuable in the spring (no later than June). Send them to The Good Food Guide, *FREEPOST, 2 Marylebone Road, London NW1 4DF. Or email your report to goodfoodguide@which.net*

LANGLEY MARSH Somerset map 2

▲ Langley House Hotel

Langley Marsh, Wiveliscombe TA4 2UF
TEL: (01984) 623318 FAX: (01984) 624573
EMAIL: user@langley.in2home.co.uk
½m N of Wiveliscombe

COOKING **5**
MODERN BRITISH
£40–£54

After 15 years the Wilsons are still doling out old-fashioned English hospitality in a sedate, genteel and polite atmosphere: one visitor found that 'it exceeded my hopes by several orders of magnitude'. The setting is ideal for anybody who wants to slow down and enjoy tranquil surroundings, with the bonus of a 'friendly and cheerful hostess' in the form of Anne Wilson. Everybody gathers at the same time for drinks in the lounge, followed by four courses with no choice before dessert. Such a simple format helps to ensure optimal treatment of materials, and if the style is more accomplished than challenging then it suits its purpose well.

One meal began with a warm scallop and bacon salad, followed by roast fillet of Somerset lamb with a mint crust; vegetables sometimes come from the kitchen's own walled garden. After a British cheese, Peter Wilson puts on as many as five puddings, from icky sticky pudding with toffee sauce to an elderflower and elderberry syllabub. In spite of its confusing layout, the wine list contains plenty for lovers of mature wines. Bordeaux and Burgundy figure, although there are some fine, and considerably cheaper, Australian reds. House wines start at £12.50, but there is very little to be had under £20.

CHEF: Peter Wilson PROPRIETORS: Peter and Anne Wilson OPEN: all week D only 7.30 to 8.30 MEALS: Set D £27.50 to £32.50 SERVICE: not inc, card slips closed CARDS: Amex, Delta, MasterCard, Switch, Visa DETAILS: 18 seats. Private parties: 18 main room. Car park. Children's helpings. No children under 7. No smoking in dining room. Wheelchair access (not WC). No music ACCOMMODATION: 8 rooms, all with bath/shower. TV. Phone. B&B £77.50 to £127.50. Baby facilities (*The Which? Hotel Guide*) (£5)

LAVENHAM Suffolk map 6

▲ Angel £

Market Place, Lavenham CO10 9QZ
TEL: (01787) 247388 FAX: (01787) 248344
EMAIL: angellav@aol.com
WEB SITE: www.lavenham.co.uk/angel
on A1141, 6m NE of Sudbury

COOKING **1**
MODERN BRITISH
£19–£34

Lavenham's well-kept timbered Medieval houses date from the time this was a prosperous wool town. Although the Angel looks more modern, it was first licensed in 1420, and serves above-average pub food at reasonable prices, from homely casseroles, via steak and ale pie with suet crust pastry, to barramundi with mango and red onion salsa. The span is broad enough to suit most tastes, making it 'a safe choice for granny and the kids', and often includes a game dish such as braised rabbit or seared venison steak. Standards appear to shift up and down – some reporters are disappointed, others well pleased – and service is likewise variable: 'an element of luck seems to be involved here.' A short wine list stays mostly below £20, and the eight house wines are all under £10.

CHEF: Mike Pursell PROPRIETORS: Roy and Anne Whitworth, and John Barry OPEN: all week 12 to 2.15, 6.45 to 9.15 CLOSED: 25 and 26 Dec MEALS: alc (main courses £5.50 to £11) SERVICE: not inc, card slips closed CARDS: Amex, Delta, MasterCard, Switch, Visa DETAILS: 100 seats. 60 seats outside. Private parties: 50 main room, 15 private room. Car park. Vegetarian meals. Children's helpings. No smoking in 1 dining room. Wheelchair access (not WC). Occasional music ACCOMMODATION: 8 rooms, all with bath/shower. TV. Phone. B&B £45 to £70. Rooms for disabled. Baby facilities (*The Which? Hotel Guide*) (£5)

▲ Great House

Market Place, Lavenham CO10 9QZ
TEL: (01787) 247431 FAX: (01787) 248007 — COOKING **2**
EMAIL: info@greathouse.co.uk — FRENCH
WEB SITE: www.greathouse.co.uk — £22–£56

A little tranche of France on a quintessentially English square, the Great House is a beautiful old building that was converted into a restaurant-with-rooms in the mid-1980s. Bare floorboards and exposed beams characterise the small, formal dining room. Both lunch and evening set menus offer an ample choice of French-inspired dishes, perhaps starting with a cassolette of scallops and mushrooms in Noilly Prat sauce, then tender, well-cooked shark steak with béarnaise. Dinner à la carte might have grilled saddle of venison with poached pear and spicy red wine sauce as its main course, while pudding could be crème brûlée with rum, or cheeses in first-class condition. French staff occasionally brush against tables in the confined space, but they 'know and care about food'. The lengthy, mostly French wine list has useful descriptions and plenty of choice by the glass and half-bottle. House wines cost from £10.20.

CHEF: Régis Crépy PROPRIETORS: Régis and Martine Crépy OPEN: Tue to Sun L 12 to 2.30, Tue to Sat D 7 to 9.30 (10 Sat) CLOSED: 3 weeks Jan MEALS: alc (main courses L £6 to £11, D £14 to £18). Set L £9.95 (2 courses) to £15.95, Set D £19.95 SERVICE: not inc CARDS: Amex, Delta, MasterCard, Switch, Visa DETAILS: 45 seats. 30 seats outside. Private parties: 60 main room. Children's helpings. No smoking in dining room. Music ACCOMMODATION: 5 rooms, all with bath/shower. TV. Phone. B&B £55 to £140. Baby facilities (*The Which? Hotel Guide*)

LEEDS West Yorkshire — **map 8**

Brasserie Forty Four

44 The Calls, Leeds LS2 7EW — COOKING **5**
TEL: (0113) 234 3232 FAX: (0113) 234 3332 — MODERN EUROPEAN
£22–£49

Mirrors help to prevent the long, narrow brick building from feeling too tunnel-like, and dangling 'harem-like' silver tassels complement the black lacquered floor and tables of this relaxing brasserie. The cosmopolitan style of food is immediately appealing, offering a blend of comfort and innovation which sets it apart from the brasserie norm: ham hock terrine with pease pudding, a 'posh pastie' made with potted duck and foie gras, and Whitby cod with a crab sauce tartare.

'Simple but well executed' sums up the style – for example, a first-course pastry tartlet with a soft and creamy Roquefort cheese filling – while accurate timing, sound judgement and well-balanced flavours make the best of sometimes humble materials, as in a tightly wrapped Catherine wheel of salt-beef brisket with lentils and spinach. Textures are well considered too, from the indulgence of treacle tart and clotted cream to the gentle contrasts in a winter fruit jelly with ice cream and shortbread. The combination of professional polish and lack of pretension make the lunchtime and early-evening deals particularly good value. Fifty-plus wines are sensibly chosen, with bags of choice under £20.

CHEF: Jeff Baker PROPRIETOR: Michael Gill OPEN: Mon to Fri L 12 to 2, Mon to Sat D 6.30 to 10.30 (11 Fri and Sat) CLOSED: bank hols MEALS: alc (main courses £9.50 to £13.50). Set L and D 6.30 to 7.15 £9.75 (2 courses) to £12.95 SERVICE: 10% (optional), card slips closed CARDS: Amex, Delta, Diners, MasterCard, Switch, Visa DETAILS: 90 seats. Private parties: 90 main room, 50 private room. Vegetarian meals. Children's helpings. No cigars/pipes in dining room. Music. Air-conditioned (£5)

Fourth Floor

Harvey Nichols, 107–111 Briggate, Leeds LS1 6AZ — COOKING **4**
TEL: (0113) 204 8000 FAX: (0113) 204 8080 — MODERN BRITISH
£26–£54

With a cocktail bar down one side, a view of the kitchen on the other, and big windows to let in daylight, this is a place for informal yet reliable eating – 'just what shoppers need' – which looks more like a restaurant in the evening when the white tablecloths come out. A short businesslike carte of attractive-sounding, modern dishes might take in deeply savoury chicken liver parfait (a match for the best), a simple but effective three-allium tart using onion, shallots and chives, and flavourful pork cutlet, timed to be 'just cooked inside', on apple mash.

Supplies are not all shipped up from London – many come from the region – and flavours are typically fresh and distinct, as in roast breast of chicken with braised cabbage and haricot beans, or a square of lasagne in which smoked cod, prosciutto and crème fraîche came together to make 'one of the best and most creative dishes' one visitor had eaten in a long time. Chocolate desserts are generally well reported – fluffy chocolate sponge with marshmallow ice cream, and dense, smooth chocolate tart with strawberry sorbet – and service is welcoming, professional, polite and smiling. A fervently up-to-date wine list spans a good range and includes 18 by the glass; bottle prices start at £12.25.

CHEF: Richard Allen PROPRIETOR: Harvey Nichols & Co OPEN: all week L 12 to 3 (4 Sun), Thur to Sat D 6 (7 Sat) to 10.30 CLOSED: 25 and 26 Dec, 1 Jan MEALS: alc (main courses £9.50 to £16). Set L £13 (2 courses) to £16, Set D Thur and Fri £15 (2 courses) to £18. Bar menu available afternoons, some early evenings SERVICE: 10% (optional) CARDS: Amex, Delta, Diners, MasterCard, Switch, Visa DETAILS: 75 seats. 12 seats outside. Vegetarian meals. No-smoking area. Wheelchair access (also WC). Music. Air-conditioned

(£5) *indicates that the restaurant has elected to participate in the* Good Food Guide *voucher scheme. For full details,* *see page 6.*

Leodis

Victoria Mill, Sovereign Street, Leeds LS1 4BJ
TEL: (0113) 242 1010 FAX: (0113) 243 0432
WEB SITE: www.leodis.co.uk

COOKING **4**
BRASSERIE/MODERN BRITISH
£25–£62

This cavernous warehouse overlooking the canal is well located for a daytime business clientele who come in their droves, although the bustling, lively brasserie atmosphere is equally popular in the evening. The name of the game is to combine good-quality ingredients with uncomplicated modern cooking to produce a menu with broad appeal. Comfort food comes in the form of wild boar sausages with leek and bacon mash, steak pudding, and well-timed calf's liver with bacon and rösti.

Fish lovers can indulge in Rossmore oysters, tender monkfish wrapped in Parma ham with a piquant caper salsa, or squid risotto. Expensive ingredients plus side orders can bump up the prices. Pannacotta, and a light, fresh raspberry parfait are recommended puddings. Those who tackle the long wine list are rewarded with an international selection arranged by price, supplemented by personal choices and fine wines. Mark-ups are very fair, with the more expensive wines heading up sections on their own. Six house bottles of varying styles are £11.95.

CHEF: Steve Kendell and John Wilks PROPRIETORS: Martin Spalding, Steve Kendell and Phil Richardson OPEN: Mon to Fri L 12 to 2, Mon to Sat D 6 to 10 (11 Fri and Sat) CLOSED: 26 and 31 Dec, L bank hols MEALS: alc (main courses £9.50 to £15). Set L and D exc Sat after 7.15 £14.95 SERVICE: 10% (optional), card slips closed CARDS: Amex, Delta, Diners, MasterCard, Switch, Visa DETAILS: 180 seats. 60 seats outside. Private parties: 180 main room. Vegetarian meals. Children's helpings. Wheelchair access (also WC). Music

Pool Court at 42

44 The Calls, Leeds LS2 7EW
TEL: (0113) 244 4242 FAX: (0113) 234 3332
EMAIL: poolcourt@aol.com

COOKING **7**
ANGLO-FRENCH
£32–£76

The tranquil oval dining room beside the water, quietly but stylishly decorated in restful colours, exudes a feeling of discreet luxury, its closely set tables formally laid with gleaming glassware and heavy napery. A savvy menu deploys a few luxuries (to be expected at these prices), such as terrine of duck foie gras, or a substantial slice of black truffle parked on a perfectly timed poached egg set in a frothy creamy purée of white beans. Vegetarians and fish eaters do well, perhaps majoring on a summer salad of lobster, crab and green beans ('a dish of great freshness and colour') or a cheese soufflé with mushrooms and vegetables.

Saucing is a strong suit – a rich thyme-infused jus for grilled duck on a cake of celeriac and potato – and the kitchen has the knack of delivering dishes which epitomise the best of whatever season it happens to be: English partridge on creamed cabbage, with a stock reduction incorporating aged sherry, for one October visitor. As well as 'visual treats', such as a light wobbly pannacotta centred in a fruit soup, the food delights with proper textures: crisp-surfaced crème brûlée, for example, that is 'unctuous and creamy within'. Pastry work is impressive, and extras and incidentals from appetisers to bread and butter are 'impeccable'. Bookings may be staggered, but this seems designed to set an even pace rather than squeeze in a second sitting. Service is knowledgeable, experienced and 'friendly in a very professional way', while a varietally organised wine list offers limited choice under £20 and some fine wines above.

CHEF: Jeff Baker PROPRIETORS: Michael and Hanni Gill OPEN: Mon to Fri L 12 to 2, Mon to Sat D 7 to 10 (10.30 Fri and Sat) CLOSED: bank hols MEALS: Set L £14.50 (2 courses) to £29.50, Set D £29.50 (2 courses) to £50 SERVICE: 10%, card slips closed CARDS: Amex, Delta, Diners, MasterCard, Switch, Visa DETAILS: 38 seats. 20 seats outside. Private parties: 38 main room. Vegetarian meals. Children's helpings. No smoking in dining room. Wheelchair access (also WC). Music. Air-conditioned (£5)

Rascasse

Canal Wharf, Water Lane, Leeds LS11 5BB — COOKING **4**
TEL: (0113) 244 6611 FAX: (0113) 244 0736 — MODERN ANGLO-FRENCH
WEB SITE: www.rascasse-leeds.co.uk — £28–£62

The salient features of this converted warehouse are a grand entrance through big glass doors, a small bar up a flight of stairs where, for reasons best known to the management, nobody is permitted to read a menu, and an open-plan dining room with stainless steel, polished wood, and plain lemon walls with not a picture in sight. After a successful five-year stint as chef, Simon Gueller left to open his own restaurant as the Guide went to press, and John Lyons moved from the rural tranquility of Well House at St Keyne, where he was listed in the Guide last year, to head up a busy cosmopolitan operation.

The generous, contemporary, French-oriented menu remains full of interest, taking in bouillabaisse terrine, John Dory with a cassoulet of cockles and bacon, and saddle of hare with marrow bone and braised cabbage. Elaborate presentation includes some elements that may well be considered superfluous, while a few misjudgements took the shine off an inspection meal. But prime fish and shellfish are among the notably first-class ingredients: a chunky ravioli of lobster in a foamy, flavourful, truffle-doused asparagus 'soup' for one visitor.

Desserts run from peach Melba to a trio of apple (a dark and syrupy Tatin, a jelly and a sorbet). Staff are friendly, bright, attentive, knowledgeable and professional. Unpretentious and helpful, the wine list combines the French classics with rising stars from the New World, and includes brief and knowledgeable tasting notes. Prices are fair, starting at £12, and ten wines are available in large glasses (175ml).

CHEF: John Lyons PROPRIETOR: Nigel Jolliffe OPEN: Mon to Fri L 12 to 2, Mon to Sat D 6.30 to 10 (10.30 Fri and Sat) CLOSED: 1 week after Christmas, bank hol Mons MEALS: alc (main courses £12 to £18.50). Set L Mon to Fri and Set D Mon to Sat before 7.30 £14 (2 courses) to £18 SERVICE: not inc CARDS: Amex, Delta, Diners, MasterCard, Switch, Visa DETAILS: 100 seats. 25 seats outside. Private parties: 50 main room. Car park. Vegetarian meals. No pipes in dining room; cigars only after coffee. Wheelchair access (also WC). Music. Air-conditioned

'They could make lots of money by selling the recipe for the sauce as a strong rival to epoxy resin.' **(On eating in London)**

Salvo's £

115 Otley Road, Headingley, Leeds LS6 3PX
TEL: (0113) 275 5017 FAX: (0113) 278 9452 COOKING **2**
EMAIL: bookings@salvos.co.uk MODERN MEDITERRANEAN/ITALIAN
WEB SITE: www.salvos.co.uk £17–£43

The pale wooden floor, cream walls with a 'wave' of metal, and colourful food paintings are defining features of this long-running restaurant. Staff remain calm no matter how crowded and noisy it gets, and menu and ingredients are authentically Italian with pasta and pizza as mainstays: del golfo among the latter, topped with scampi tails, scallops, prawns and spring onions. Rich, creamy duck liver pâté has come with whisky marmalade, devilled chicken breast with lime butter sauce, and incontro orientale is an appropriately named stir-fry of king prawns, beef, lamb and chicken with asparagus and noodles. Desserts have included Mars Bar fondue with chunks of fruit and marshmallow to dip into the molten delicacy. House wines at £9.90 are Italian, otherwise the list is an international selection with 20 bottles under £15. Note that bookings are not taken for dinner, so arrive early or join the queue.

CHEFS: Michael Leggiero and Pam Nelson PROPRIETORS: the Dammone family OPEN: all week 12 to 2, 6 to 10.45 (5.30 to 11 Fri and Sat, 12 to 9 Sun) MEALS: alc (main courses £6 to £13). Set L £6 (2 courses) SERVICE: not inc CARDS: Amex, Delta, Diners, MasterCard, Switch, Visa DETAILS: 65 seats. Private parties: 65 main room. Vegetarian meals. Children's helpings. No-smoking area. Music. Air-conditioned (£5)

Sous le Nez en Ville

The Basement, Quebec House, Quebec Street, Leeds LS1 2HA COOKING **4**
MODERN EUROPEAN
TEL: (0113) 244 0108 FAX: (0113) 245 0240 £19–£52

In a wood-panelled basement setting, Andrew Carter offers simple, direct cooking, turning his hand well to such crowd-pleasing items as rare-cooked steak frîtes with pungent aïoli, and well-timed whole grilled lemon sole sprinkled with chives. 'For simple cooking with good ingredients, this is about as good as it gets,' thought an aficionado. More cosmopolitan tastes are catered for with spiced marinated chicken fillets with mango and papaya salsa, or Thai-style swordfish in coconut, lime and coriander with a chillied spinach salad. Although not all dishes have pleased, vegetarians get a fair look-in, and meals end on a lively note, perhaps with toasted Jamaican ginger cake with ginger custard and glazed pear. The hefty wine list, compiled with intelligence and enthusiasm, takes in sensible house wines, innovative personal recommendations, fairly priced champagnes and bottles from star producers around the world. House wines start at £9.50 and mark-ups are fair throughout.

CHEF: Andrew Carter PROPRIETORS: Andrew Carter and Robert Chamberlain OPEN: Mon to Sat 12 to 2.30, 6 to 10 (11 Fri and Sat) CLOSED: 25 and 26 Dec, bank hols exc Good Friday MEALS: alc (main courses £8 to £14.50). Set D before 7.30 (7 Sat) £15.95 (inc wine). Bar meals, tapas and sandwiches available SERVICE: not inc CARDS: Amex, Delta, Diners, MasterCard, Switch, Visa DETAILS: 85 seats. Private parties: 70 main room, 20 private room. Vegetarian meals. Music

LEVERTON Lincolnshire **map 6**

Old Barn

NEW ENTRY

Leverton PE22 9AZ
TEL: (01205) 870215
EMAIL: elaine@oldbarn.co.uk
WEB SITE: www.oldbarn.co.uk
on A52 Boston to Skegness road, 6m NE of Boston

COOKING **2**
SEAFOOD
£26–£53

The fish that can be seen swimming happily in tanks set into the walls of this cottagey, low-ceilinged dining room are pets, though they do give a clue as to what is going on in the kitchen. The set-price menu, with supplements for specials, deals almost exclusively in fish and seafood done up in a range of traditional and modern treatments, from moules marinière, bouillabaisse, and lobster thermidor to Chinese-style salmon with noodles, chilli and coriander. A tendency to list every last ingredient can lead to disappointment when advertised flavours fail to make their presence felt, but good-quality raw materials are generally well handled, an inspector praising well-timed monkfish medallions with a red pepper vinaigrette, and meurette of sea bass and bream liberally garnished with prawns and mussels. Crème brûlée with caramelised berries proved a fine dessert for one reporter. A short, serviceable wine list starts with eight house recommendations under £10.

CHEF: Tony Coates PROPRIETORS: Tony Coates and Elaine Martin OPEN: Wed to Fri and Sun L 12 to 2, Tue to Sun D 6.30 to 9.30 MEALS: Set L and D £16.75 (2 courses) to £18.95 SERVICE: not inc CARDS: Delta, Diners, MasterCard, Switch, Visa DETAILS: 40 seats. Private parties: 25 main room, 10 private room. Car park. No children under 12. No smoking in 1 dining room. Wheelchair access (not WC). Music

LEWDOWN Devon **map 1**

▲ Lewtrenchard Manor  

Lewdown EX20 4PN
TEL: (01566) 783256 FAX: (01566) 783332
EMAIL: s&j@lewmenchard.co.uk
off old A30 Okehampton to Launceston road, turn left at Lewdown

COOKING **4**
MODERN BRITISH
£28–£50

The house looks convincingly old, but according to Pevsner it is 'an intriguing confection by Sabine Baring Gould' (collector of folk songs and writer of hymns) who transformed a plain rectangular house into an E-shaped 'Jacobethan' one. The combined effect of its dark wood, copper warming pans, and soft lighting is a feeling of pleasurable warmth and relaxation, with the Murrays themselves much in evidence as welcoming hosts, supported by an amiable maitre d' and impeccably trained staff. David Swade's modern cooking is ambitious and largely successful, taking in some unusual yet soundly based ideas such as artichoke and oyster soup with deep-fried rocket, chargrilled smoked fillet steak served with crushed truffle mash, and parfait of chicken livers in port jelly with a beetroot and black pudding salad.

As so often, it is the simpler dishes that give rise to most enjoyment: for example a raviolo of chargrilled cod and tomato, surrounded by three lightly seared scallops in a well-judged buttery sauce, and a light vanilla mousse with champagne-marinated strawberries. Pear Tatin with a strongly caramelised sauce also comes recommended. Vegetables are appropriately chosen and imaginatively cooked, and top-notch incidentals include appetiser, bread and petits fours. New sommelier Roger Hamley has worked wonders with a wine list that already boasted a fine South African selection. It has filled out globally and mark-ups remain on the whole very reasonable, though clarets disappoint slightly with some indifferent years. House South African starts at £11, and 14 wines are available by the glass.

CHEF: David Swade PROPRIETORS: James and Sue Murray OPEN: Tue to Sun L 12 to 1.30 (booking essential L), all week D 7 to 9 MEALS: Set L £19.50, Set D £32 SERVICE: not inc, card slips closed CARDS: Amex, Delta, Diners, MasterCard, Switch, Visa DETAILS: 35 seats. 12 seats outside. Private parties: 26 main room, 16 to 60 private rooms. Car park. Children's helpings. No children under 8 exc by arrangement. No smoking in dining room. Wheelchair access (not WC). Music ACCOMMODATION: 9 rooms, all with bath/shower. TV. Phone. B&B £85 to £170. No children under 8 exc by arrangement. Fishing (*The Which? Hotel Guide*) (£5)

LIDGATE Suffolk **map 6**

Star Inn

The Street, Lidgate CB8 9PP COOKING **1**
TEL: (01638) 500275 FAX: (01799) 524805 MEDITERRANEAN
on B1063, 6m SE of Newmarket £22–£40

While retaining its country pub looks – chunky wooden furniture, seats at the bar, open fireplaces and olde-worlde photographs – and serving fine Greene King ales, the emphasis is none the less on food. Influences from the Catalan owner's homeland are evident on the lengthy blackboard menus, incoporating fish dishes and authentic paella. The style also takes in wider Mediterranean and English modes, producing carpaccio of venison, monkfish marinière, scampi provençale, and tasty and accurately cooked wild boar with a sweet cranberry sauce. Interesting vegetables are a bonus, and puddings might take in banoffi pie or apricot and almond tart. Friendly and willing service copes well even on busy days. Criticism is mostly aimed at prices, which are more restaurant than pub. Wines are mostly Spanish and start at £11.

CHEF/PROPRIETOR: Maria Teresa Axon OPEN: all week L 12 to 2 (2.30 Sun), Mon to Sat D 7 to 10 CLOSED: 25 and 26 Dec, 1 Jan MEALS: alc Mon to Sat (main courses £9.50 to £13.50). Set L Mon to Sat £9.50 (2 courses), Set L Sun £13.50 SERVICE: not inc, card slips closed CARDS: Amex, Delta, Diners, MasterCard, Switch, Visa DETAILS: 55 seats. 20 seats outside. Private parties: 24 main room, 24 private room. Car park. Children's helpings. No smoking in dining room. Music (£5)

All details are as accurate as possible at the time of going to press, but chefs and owners often change, and it is wise to check by telephone before making a special journey. Many readers have been disappointed when set-price bargain meals are no longer available. Ask when booking.

LIFTON Devon map 1

▲ Arundell Arms

Lifton PL16 0AA
TEL: (01566) 784666 FAX: (01566) 784494
EMAIL: arundellarms@btinternet.com
just off A30, 3m E of Launceston

COOKING **5**
MODERN BRITISH/FRENCH
£30–£56

The rambling old creeper-clad coaching-inn, set in a grey-stone Devon village amid largely untouched countryside, functions on several levels: as a pub offering good bar food, a comfortable hotel, and an ambitious restaurant, as well as catering for sporting types, with facilities for anglers that include a trout lake. Philip Burgess has headed the kitchen for nearly 20 years, producing a highly refined version of traditional English food, counterpointed with the odd Mediterranean touch. Materials run to griddled Cornish scallops, and rack of lamb with rhubarb compote, while sympathetic treatment of fish has included lemon sole and mullet fried in light, crisp, ungreasy saffron and beer batter, served with green mayonnaise.

A sharp sense of timing has yielded pink Gressingham duck served with hot asparagus vinaigrette and peppercorn sauce, while a well-conceived gratin of exotic fruits has featured passion fruit, mango and pineapple drizzled with sabayon and topped with a scoop of passion-fruit sorbet. Cheeses are properly kept, and everything is competently and amiably served in a grand golden-yellow dining room. There is a certain grandeur to the wine list too, which plies a mostly French trade at fairly unforgiving prices. Six house wines start at £11.

CHEFS: Philip Burgess and Nick Shopland PROPRIETOR: Anne Voss-Bark OPEN: all week 12.30 to 2, 7.30 to 9.30 CLOSED: 24 and 25 Dec, D 26 Dec MEALS: Set L £17 (2 courses) to £36.50, Set D £29.50 to £36.50. Afternoon teas and bar meals available SERVICE: not inc CARDS: Amex, Diners, MasterCard, Switch, Visa DETAILS: 70 seats. 35 seats outside. Private parties: 80 main room, 36 private room. Car park. Vegetarian meals. Children's helpings. No very young children at D. No smoking in dining room. Wheelchair access (not WC). Music ACCOMMODATION: 28 rooms, all with bath/shower. TV. Phone. B&B £45 to £113. Baby facilities. Fishing (*The Which? Hotel Guide*) (£5)

LINCOLN Lincolnshire map 9

Jew's House

15 The Strait, Lincoln LN2 1JD
TEL: (01522) 524851 FAX: (01522) 520084

COOKING **3**
ANGLO-FRENCH
£20–£59

After a decade in one of the oldest inhabited houses in Britain (it dates from the twelfth century) at the bottom of a steep hill leading to the castle and cathedral, Richard and Sally Gibbs were planning a major refurbishment as the Guide went to press. A short, well-thought-out menu, allied to an uncomplicated style of cooking, produces a range of mainly traditional Anglo-French dishes, from cream of mushroom soup with red peppers, via chicken supreme with a hazelnut mousseline, to a soufflé Grand Marnier. Choice is extended with blackboard specials, and dishes have been rated highly for depth of flavour (fish soup with a spicy rouille) and for texture (sticky roasted lamb shank). Desserts, which have a French bias, may include an assiette of chocolate, incorporating a parfait and cheesecake. Service is friendly, welcoming, and attentive without being fussy. House wines on the approachable, mainly French wine list start at £10.95.

CHEF: Richard Gibbs PROPRIETORS: Richard and Sally Gibbs OPEN: Tue to Sat 12 to 2, 7 to 9 MEALS: alc (main courses £12.50 to £18). Set L £9, Set D £25 SERVICE: not inc CARDS: Amex, Delta, MasterCard, Switch, Visa DETAILS: 40 seats. Private parties: 26 main room, 6 to 10 private rooms. Vegetarian meals. Children's helpings. No smoking in dining room. Music

Wig & Mitre

30 Steep Hill, Lincoln LN2 1TL — COOKING **3**
TEL: (01522) 535190 FAX: (01522) 532402 — MODERN BRITISH
EMAIL: reservations@wigandmitre.co.uk — £19–£47

This 'haven of peace' is an intriguing old building centrally situated near the cathedral, but despite the jumble of rooms of varying sizes, and dark-green walls decorated with prints, cigarette card collections and fleur-de-lis motifs, it manages to feel light and airy. A variety of all-day eating options runs from breakfast through an 'express' lunch to a carte that changes twice daily and offers bang up-to-date dishes such as squid in beer batter with guacamole, and Malaysian seafood laksa.

While the seasonal menu may not show much evidence of seasonality, and standards of cooking can vary, the kitchen has turned out successful roast guinea fowl stuffed with spinach and served with a puff-pastry tart of mushrooms, and a smooth, tangy lemon tart with crunchy brûlée topping and rich, crumbly pastry. The wine list is arranged by style from 'dry crisper whites' to 'bigger reds' and covers most regions, with a preference for France. House red and white Burgundy are keenly priced at £10.45 a bottle.

CHEFS: Paul Vidic and Peter Dodd PROPRIETORS: Valerie and Michael Hope, and Paul Vidic OPEN: all week 8 to 11 MEALS: alc (main courses £7.50 to £17.50). Set L 12 to 4 £8 (2 courses) to £11. Breakfast, sandwiches and light meals also available SERVICE: not inc CARDS: Amex, Delta, Diners, MasterCard, Switch, Visa DETAILS: 135 seats. Private parties: 65 main room, 20 private room. Vegetarian meals. Children's helpings. No smoking in dining room. No music
(£5)

indicates that smoking is either banned altogether or that a dining-room is maintained for non-smokers. The symbol does not apply to restaurants that simply have no-smoking areas.

The Guide office can quickly spot when a restaurateur is encouraging customers to write recommending inclusion. Such reports do not further a restaurant's cause. Please tell us if a restaurateur invites you to write to the Guide.

Prices quoted in the Guide are based on information supplied by restaurateurs. The prices quoted at the top of each entry represent a range, from the lowest meal price to the highest; the latter is inflated by 20 per cent to take account of likely price rises during the year of the Guide.

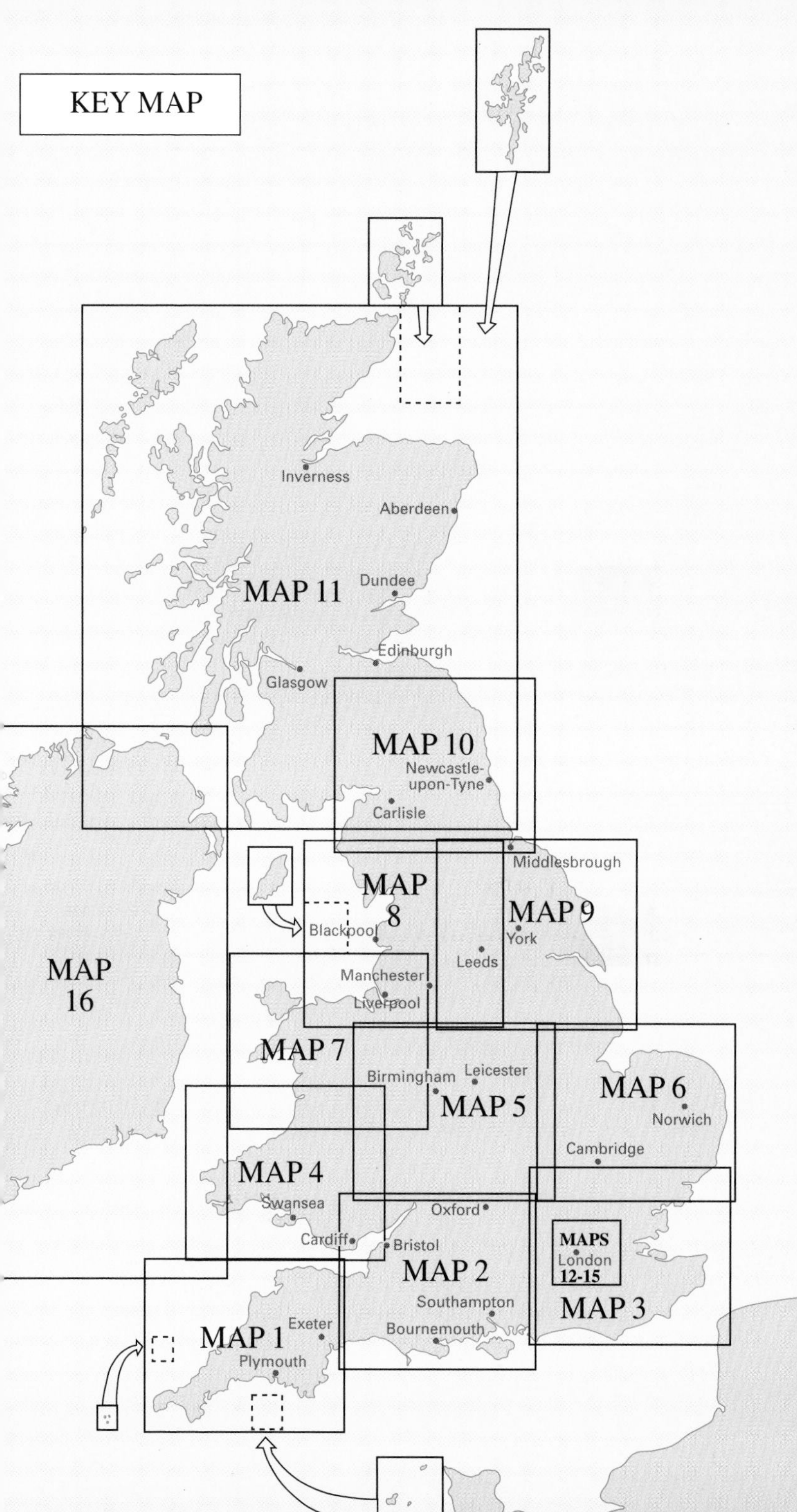

KEY MAP
MAP 11
Inverness
Aberdeen
Dundee
Edinburgh
Glasgow
MAP 10
Newcastle-upon-Tyne
Carlisle
Middlesbrough
MAP 8
Blackpool
MAP 9
York
Leeds
Manchester
Liverpool
MAP 16
MAP 7
Birmingham
Leicester
MAP 5
MAP 6
Norwich
Cambridge
MAP 4
Swansea
Cardiff
Oxford
Bristol
MAPS
London
12-15
MAP 2
Southampton
Bournemouth
MAP 3
MAP 1
Exeter
Plymouth

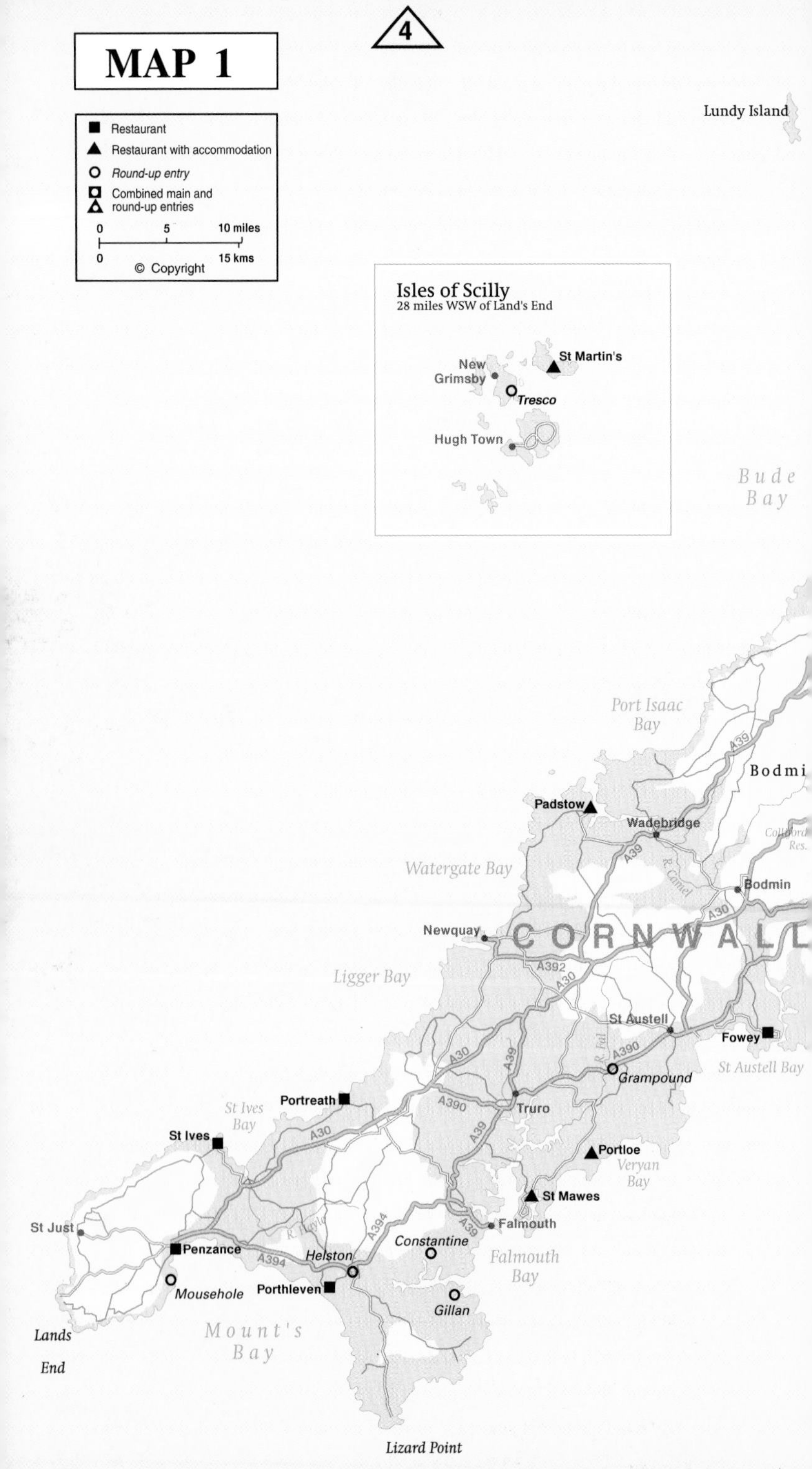

MAP 1

4

■ Restaurant
▲ Restaurant with accommodation
○ *Round-up entry*
Combined main and round-up entries

0 5 10 miles
0 15 kms
© Copyright

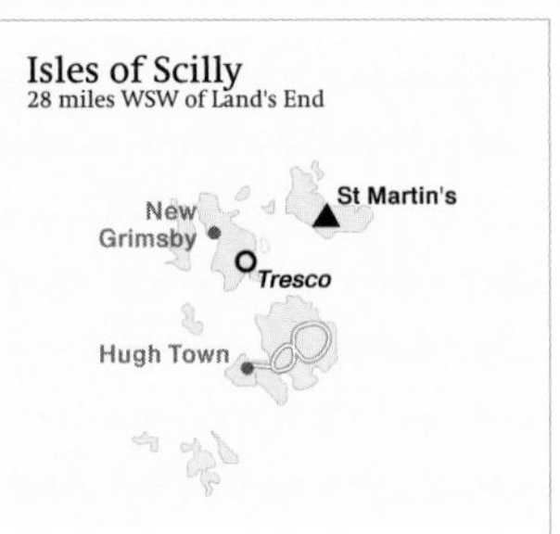

Lundy Island

Bude Bay

Port Isaac Bay

Bodmi

Padstow

Wadebridge

Watergate Bay

Bodmin

Newquay

CORNWALL

Ligger Bay

St Austell

Fowey

St Austell Bay

Grampound

Portreath

St Ives Bay

Truro

St Ives

Portloe

Veryan Bay

St Mawes

Falmouth

St Just

Penzance

Helston

Constantine

Falmouth Bay

Mousehole

Porthleven

Gillan

Lands End

Mount's Bay

Lizard Point

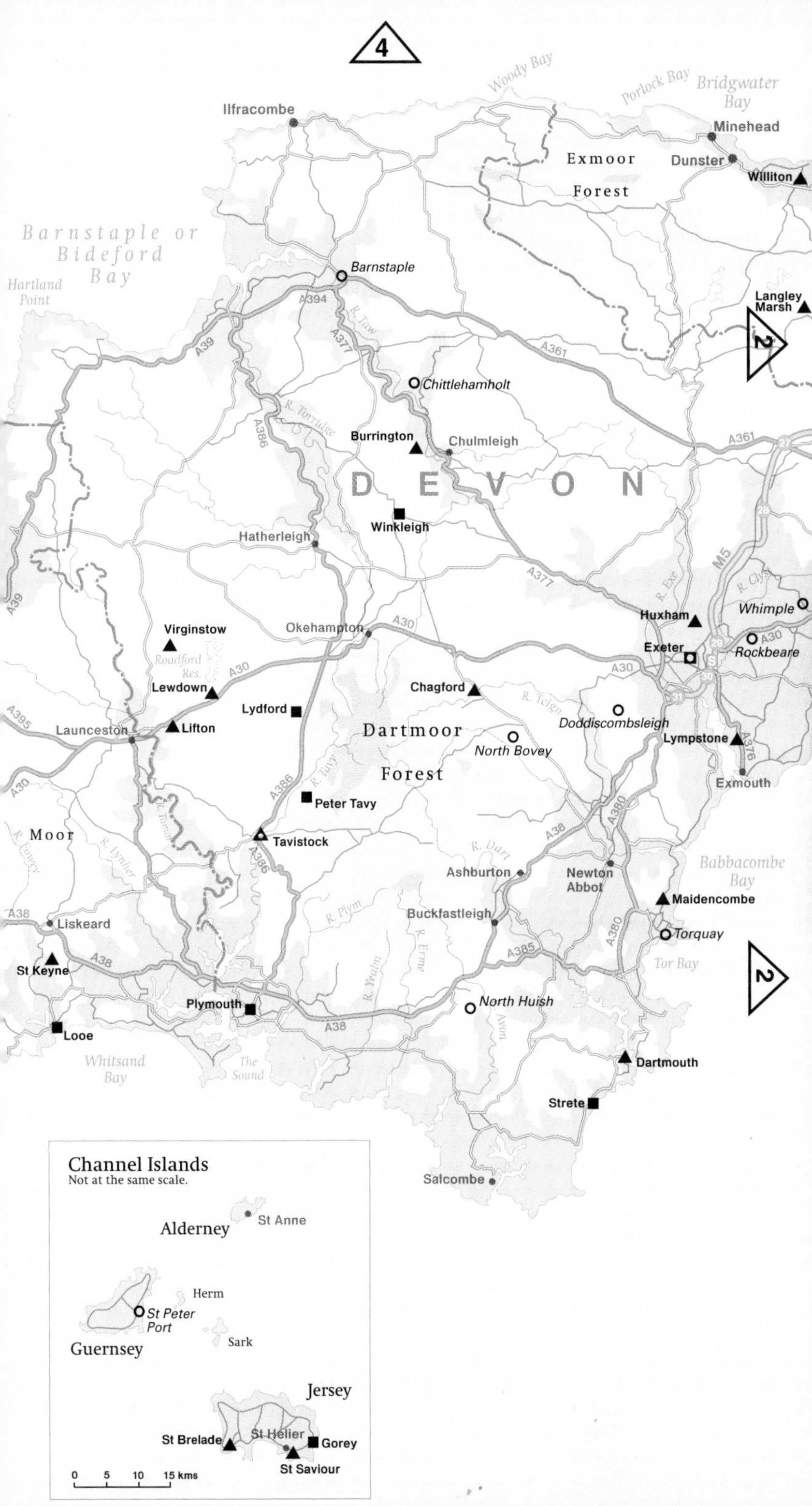

4
Woody Bay
Porlock Bay
Bridgwater Bay
Ilfracombe
Minehead
Exmoor
Dunster
Williton
Forest
Barnstaple or Bideford Bay
Hartland Point
Barnstaple
A394
R. Taw
A377
Langley Marsh
2
A39
A361
Chittlehamholt
R. Torridge
A386
Burrington
Chulmleigh
A361
27
DEVON
Winkleigh
28
Hatherleigh
A377
M5
R. Exe
R. Clyst
A39
Whimple
Huxham
Virginstow
Okehampton
A30
Rockbeare
A30
29
Exeter
Roadford Res.
S
A30
A30
Lewdown
Chagford
30
A395
R. Teign
31
Lydford
Doddiscombsleigh
Launceston
Lifton
Dartmoor
North Bovey
Lympstone
A376
A30
Forest
Exmouth
A386
R. Tavy
Peter Tavy
A380
Moor
Tavistock
A38
R. Fowey
R. Lynher
R. Tamar
A386
R. Dart
Babbacombe Bay
Ashburton
Newton Abbot
Maidencombe
A38
R. Plym
Buckfastleigh
Liskeard
R. Erme
A380
Torquay
St Keyne
A38
A385
Tor Bay
R. Yealm
2
Plymouth
North Huish
A38
Avon
Looe
Whitsand Bay
The Sound
Dartmouth
Strete
Salcombe
Channel Islands
Not at the same scale.
St Anne
Alderney
Herm
St Peter Port
Sark
Guernsey
Jersey
St Brelade
St Helier
Gorey
St Saviour
0 5 10 15 kms

4
5
1
Crickhowell
Llandewi Skirrid
Drybrook
Monmouth
GLOUCESTER
SHIRE
Painswick
BLAENAU GWENT
Merthyr Tydfil
TORFAEN
Clytha
Whitebrook
Usk
Pontypool
MONMOUTHSHIRE
Tredunnock
CAERPHILLY
Chepstow
Cotswolds
Tetbury
Bassaleg
NEWPORT
New Severn Crossing
SOUTH GLOUCESTERSHIRE
Creigiau
CARDIFF
Cardiff
Mouth of the Severn
Portishead
Castle Combe
BRISTOL
Bristol
Chippenham
VALE OF GLAMORGAN
Colerne
N.W. SOMERSET
Bath
Hunstrete
Weston-Super-Mare
Holt
Hinton Charterhouse
BATH & N.E. SOMERSET
Shipham
Mendip Hills
Burnham-on-Sea
Frome
Bridgwater Bay
Wells
Williton
Shepton Mallet
Glastonbury
Bruton
Bridgwater
SOMERSET
Langley Marsh
Gillingham
Taunton
Langford Budville
Yeovil
Sturminster Newton
Barwick
Chard
DEVON
Evershot
Blandford Forum
Broadhembury
Stockland
Corscombe
N. Dorset Downs
Honiton
Beaminster
DORSET
Whimple
Gittisham
Maiden Newton
West Bay
Dorchester
Beer
Lyme Bay
Sidmouth
Restaurant
Restaurant with accommodation
Round-up entry
Combined main and round-up entries
0 5 10 miles
0 15 kms
© Copyright
Weymouth
Weymouth Bay
Babbacombe Bay
Bill of Portland

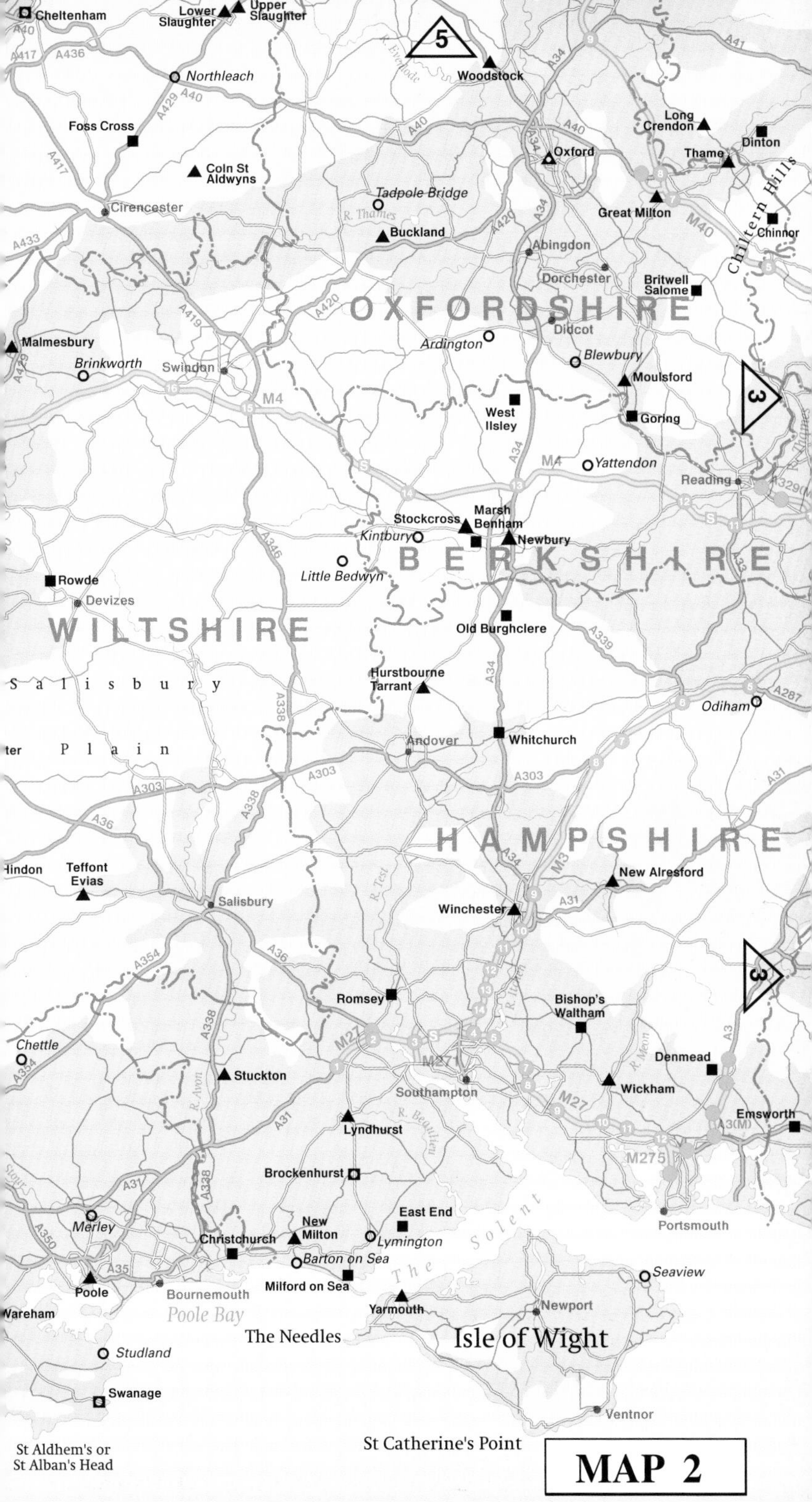
Cheltenham
Lower Slaughter
Upper Slaughter
5
Northleach
Woodstock
Foss Cross
Coln St Aldwyns
Long Crendon
Dinton
Oxford
Thame
Cirencester
Tadpole Bridge
Buckland
Great Milton
Chiltern Hills
Chinnor
Abingdon
Dorchester
Britwell Salome
OXFORDSHIRE
Didcot
Malmesbury
Ardington
Blewbury
Brinkworth
Swindon
Moulsford
3
West Ilsley
Goring
Yattendon
Reading
Stockcross
Marsh Benham
Kintbury
Newbury
BERKSHIRE
Little Bedwyn
Rowde
Devizes
WILTSHIRE
Old Burghclere
Salisbury Plain
Hurstbourne Tarrant
Odiham
Whitchurch
Andover
HAMPSHIRE
Hindon
Teffont Evias
New Alresford
Salisbury
Winchester
3
Romsey
Bishop's Waltham
Chettle
Denmead
Stuckton
Southampton
Wickham
Emsworth
Lyndhurst
Brockenhurst
Portsmouth
East End
Merley
New Milton
Lymington
Christchurch
Barton on Sea
Seaview
Poole
Bournemouth
Milford on Sea
Yarmouth
Newport
Wareham
Poole Bay
The Solent
The Needles
Isle of Wight
Studland
Swanage
Ventnor
St Aldhem's or St Alban's Head
St Catherine's Point
MAP 2

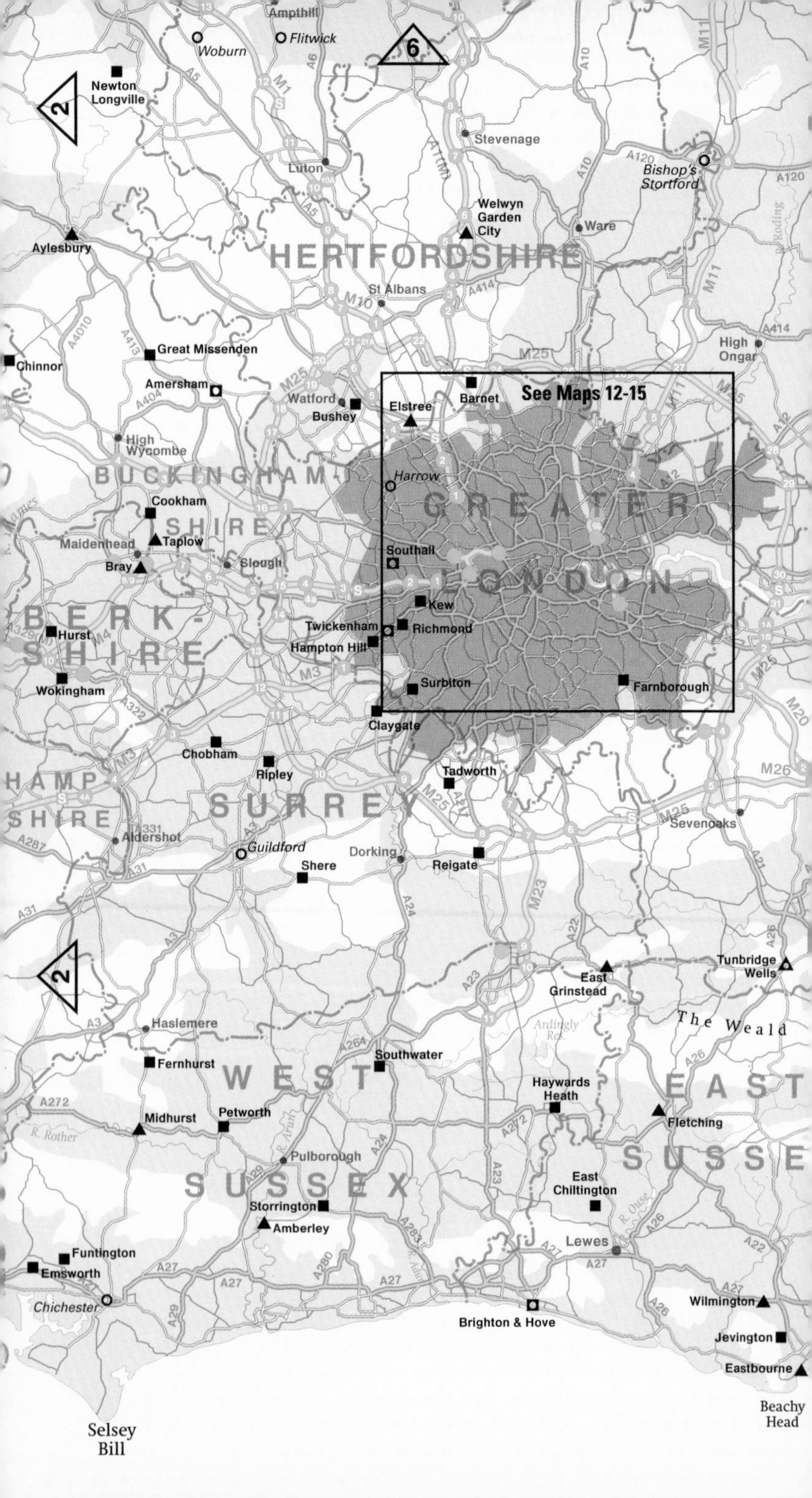

Ampthill
Flitwick
Woburn
6
Newton Longville
2
Stevenage
Luton
Bishop's Stortford
Welwyn Garden City
Ware
Aylesbury
HERTFORDSHIRE
St Albans
High Ongar
Chinnor
Great Missenden
Amersham
Watford
Bushey
Elstree
Barnet
See Maps 12-15
High Wycombe
BUCKINGHAM-SHIRE
Harrow
GREATER LONDON
Cookham
Taplow
Maidenhead
Bray
Slough
Southall
Kew
BERK-SHIRE
Hurst
Twickenham
Richmond
Hampton Hill
Wokingham
Surbiton
Farnborough
Claygate
Chobham
Ripley
Tadworth
HAMP-SHIRE
SURREY
Sevenoaks
Aldershot
Guildford
Dorking
Reigate
Shere
2
Tunbridge Wells
East Grinstead
The Weald
Ardingly Res.
Haslemere
Southwater
Fernhurst
WEST
Haywards Heath
EAST
Midhurst
Petworth
Fletching
R. Rother
Pulborough
SUSSEX
SUSSE
East Chiltington
Storrington
Amberley
Lewes
Funtington
Emsworth
Chichester
Wilmington
Brighton & Hove
Jevington
Eastbourne
Beachy Head
Selsey Bill

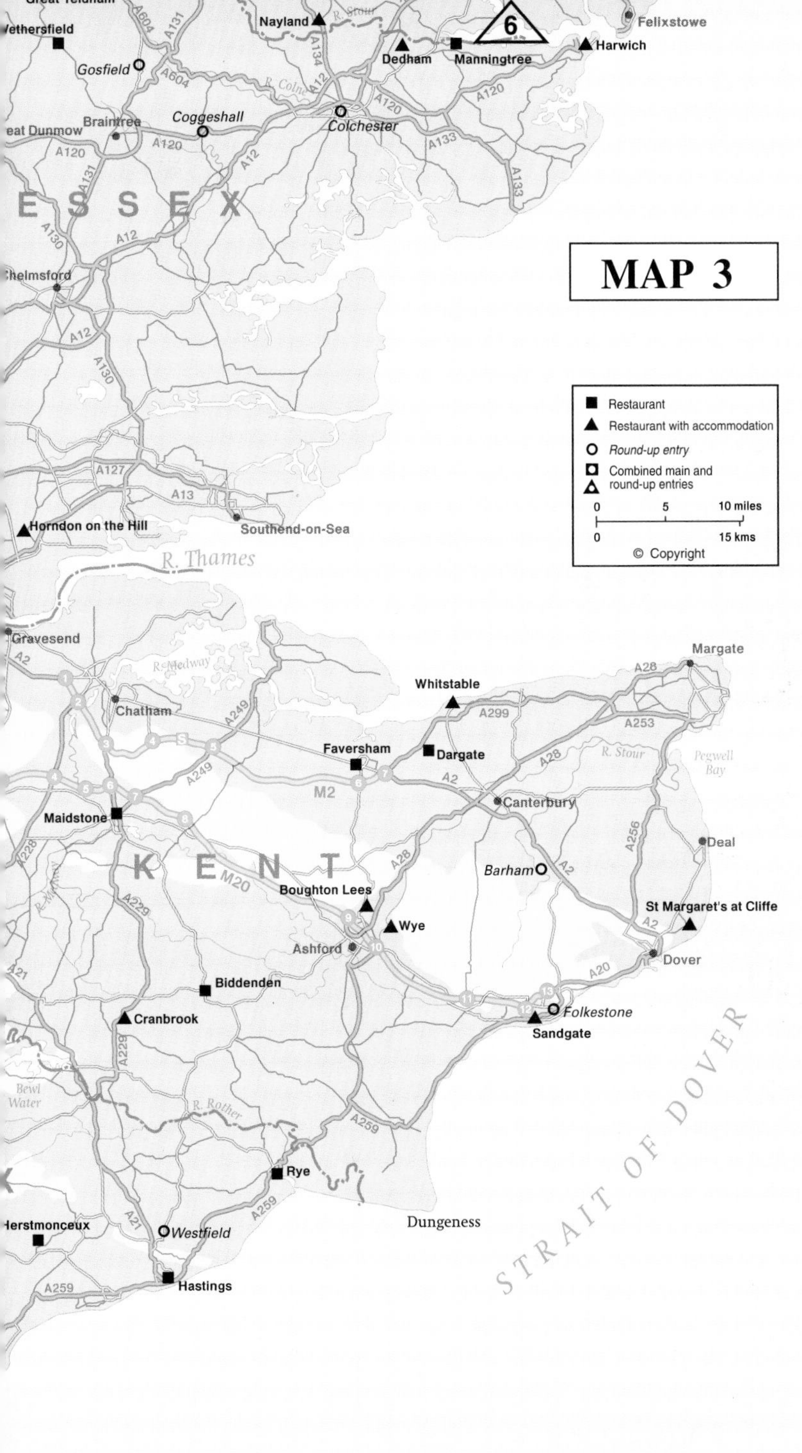

MAP 3
6
Restaurant
Restaurant with accommodation
Round-up entry
Combined main and round-up entries
0 5 10 miles
0 15 kms
© Copyright
Great Yeldham
Wethersfield
Gosfield
Nayland
Dedham
Manningtree
Harwich
Felixstowe
Braintree
Coggeshall
Colchester
ESSEX
Chelmsford
Horndon on the Hill
Southend-on-Sea
R. Thames
Gravesend
Chatham
Maidstone
KENT
Whitstable
Margate
Faversham
Dargate
Canterbury
Pegwell Bay
Deal
Barham
Boughton Lees
Wye
Ashford
St Margaret's at Cliffe
Dover
Biddenden
Cranbrook
Folkestone
Sandgate
Bewl Water
R. Rother
Rye
Dungeness
Herstmonceux
Westfield
Hastings
STRAIT OF DOVER

MAP 4

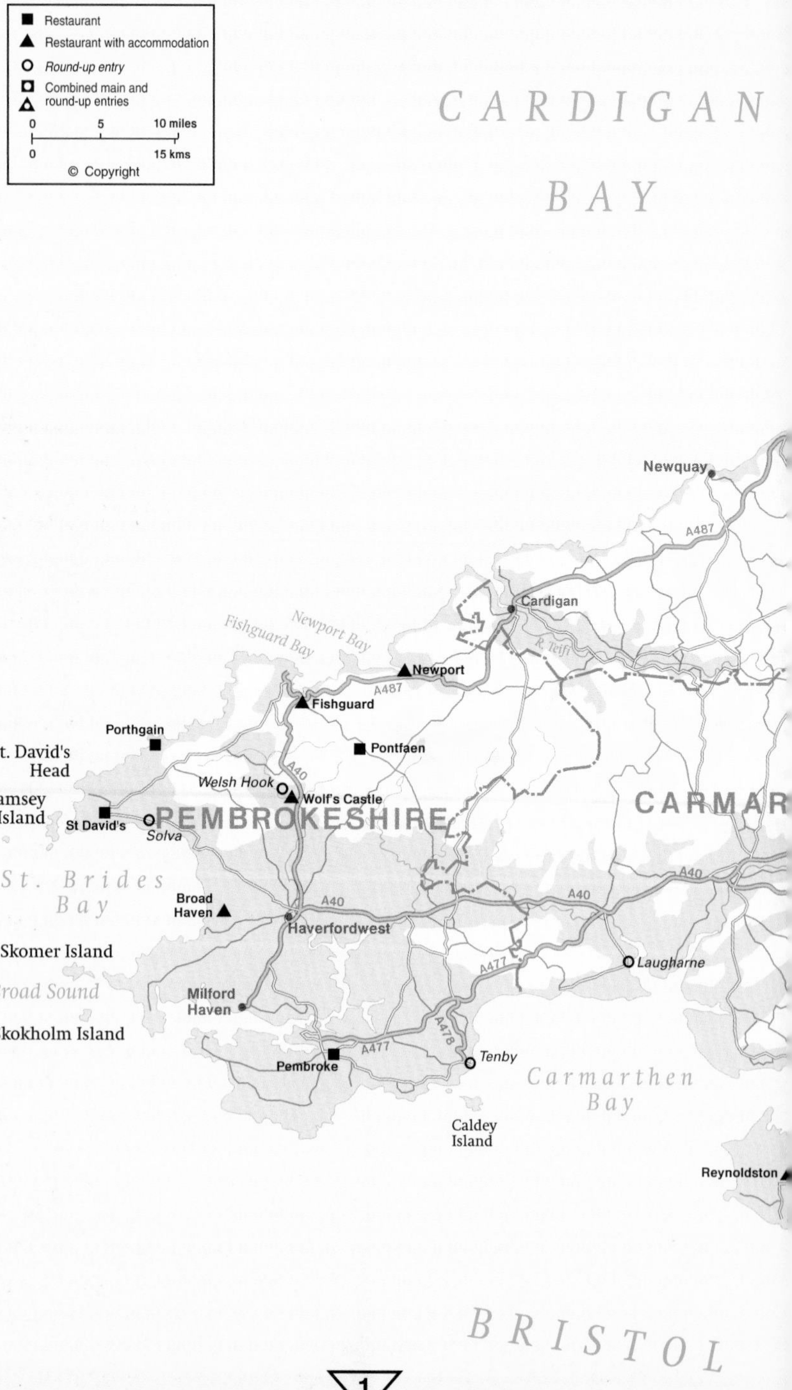

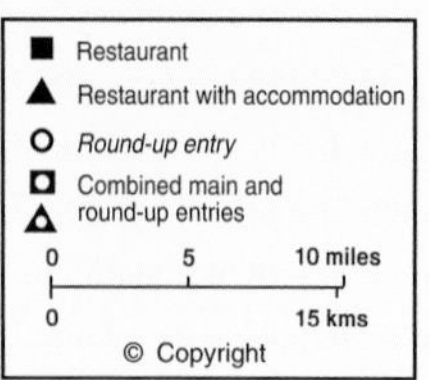

CARDIGAN BAY

Newquay
A487
Cardigan
Newport Bay
Fishguard Bay
R. Teifi
Newport
A487
Fishguard
Porthgain
St. David's Head
Pontfaen
A40
Welsh Hook
Wolf's Castle
Ramsey Island
St David's
Solva
PEMBROKESHIRE
CARMAR
A40
St. Brides Bay
Broad Haven
A40
A40
Haverfordwest
Skomer Island
A477
Laugharne
Broad Sound
Milford Haven
A478
Skokholm Island
A477
Pembroke
Tenby
Carmarthen Bay
Caldey Island
Reynoldston

BRISTOL

Llanaber
Penmaenpool
Dolgellau
Barmouth
Cader Idris
893
L. Vyrnwy
7
Llanwddyn
Llanfyllin
SHROPSHIRE
Aberdovey
Eglwysfach
Cambrian Mountains
Montgomery
Newtown
Aberystwyth
5
Llangurig
POWYS
Presteigne
CEREDIGION
Llandrindod Wells
Llanfihangel nant Melan
Kington
Builth Wells
Lampeter
Llanwrtyd Wells
Llangammarch Wells
Llyswen
Llandovery
R. Usk
R. Monnow
THENSHIRE
Brecon
R. Tywi
Nantgaredig
Llandeilo
Brecon Beacons
Crickhowell
Llandewi Skirrid
BLAENAU GWENT
Merthyr Tydfil
NEATH PORT TALBOT
RHONDDA CYNON TAFF
MERTHYR TYDFIL
CAERPHILLY
TORFAEN
SWANSEA
Swansea
Llanrhidian
Port Talbot
Swansea Bay
BRIDGEND
Bassaleg
NEWPORT
Creigiau
CARDIFF
Cardiff
2
CHANNEL
VALE OF GLAMORGAN
Mouth of the Severn

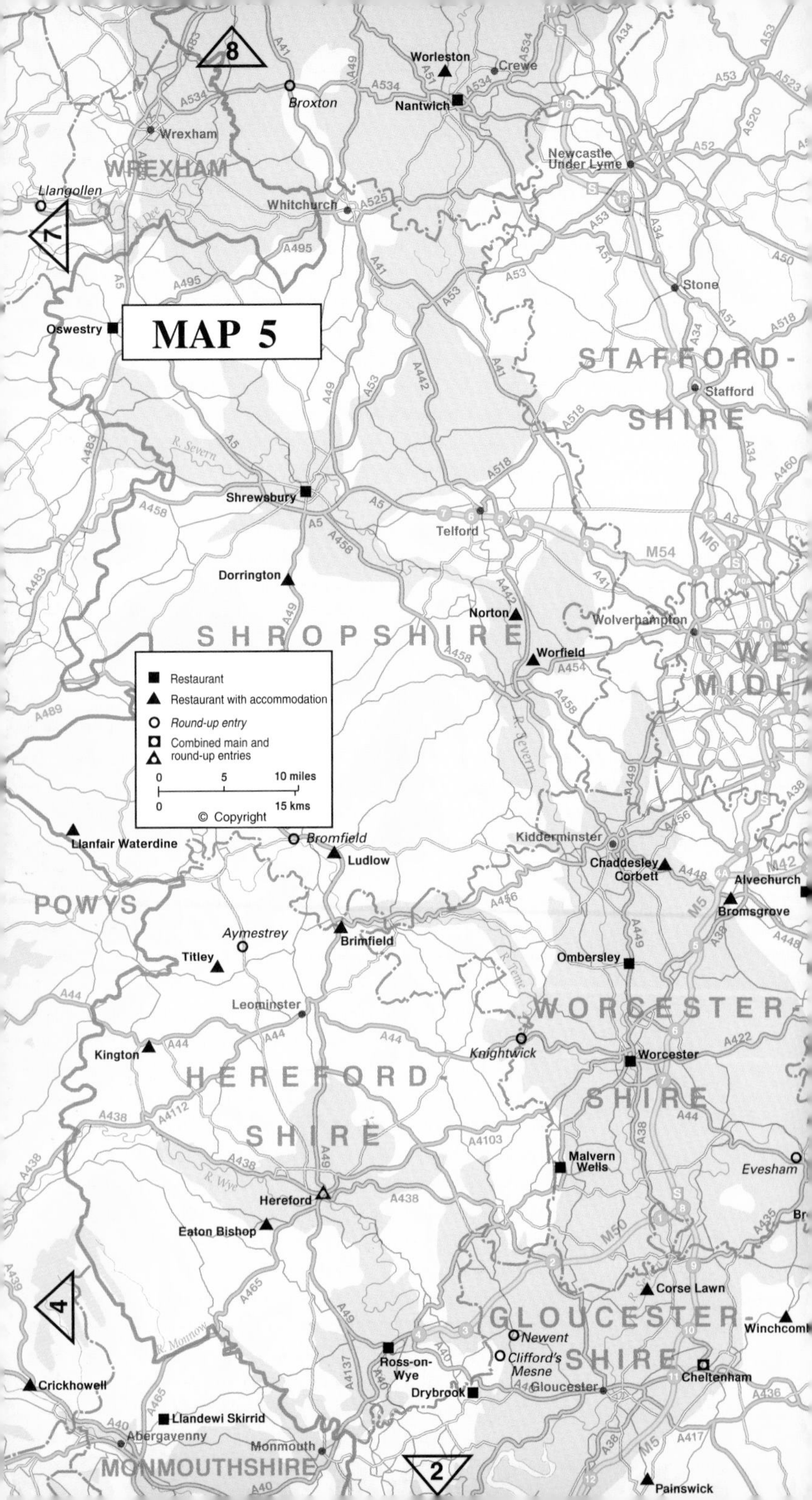

MAP 5
Restaurant
Restaurant with accommodation
Round-up entry
Combined main and round-up entries
0 5 10 miles
0 15 kms
© Copyright
WREXHAM
SHROPSHIRE
STAFFORD-SHIRE
WEST MIDLANDS
POWYS
WORCESTER-SHIRE
HEREFORD-SHIRE
GLOUCESTER-SHIRE
MONMOUTHSHIRE
Worleston
Crewe
Broxton
Nantwich
Wrexham
Newcastle Under Lyme
Llangollen
Whitchurch
Stone
Oswestry
Stafford
Shrewsbury
Telford
Dorrington
Norton
Wolverhampton
Worfield
Llanfair Waterdine
Bromfield
Ludlow
Kidderminster
Chaddesley Corbett
Alvechurch
Bromsgrove
Aymestrey
Brimfield
Titley
Ombersley
Leominster
Knightwick
Kington
Worcester
Malvern Wells
Evesham
Hereford
Eaton Bishop
Corse Lawn
Newent
Winchcomb
Clifford's Mesne
Ross-on-Wye
Cheltenham
Crickhowell
Drybrook
Gloucester
Llandewi Skirrid
Abergavenny
Monmouth
Painswick
R. Dee
R. Severn
R. Teme
R. Wye
R. Monnow

Mansfield
Caunton
Newark
Waterhouses
DERBY-SHIRE
Ashbourne
NOTTINGHAM-SHIRE
Nottingham
Great Gonerby
Waldley
Derby
Beeston
Plumtree
Langar
Grantham
Burton on the Wolds
Loughborough
Longdon Green
Lichfield
LEICESTERSHIRE
Rutland Water
Hambleton
RUTLAND
Leicester
Kibworth Beauchamp
Nuneaton
Market Harborough
Birmingham
Coventry
Kettering
Pitsford Res
Wellingborough
Kenilworth
Warwick
Daventry
Northampton
WARWICKSHIRE
Stratford-upon-Avon
NORTHAMPTON-SHIRE
Horton
Roade
Stoke Bruerne
Paulerspury
Chipping Campden
Banbury
Paxford
Buckland
Buckingham
Deddington
Moreton-in-Marsh
Newton Longville
Chipping Norton
Lower Oddington
Lower Slaughter
Upper Slaughter
Bicester
OXFORDSHIRE
BUCKINGHAMSHIRE
Woodstock
Aylesbury
Northleach
Oxford
9
6
3
2

LINCOLNSHIRE
Lincoln
Horncastle
9
Burgh le Marsh
Skegness
Leverton
Boston
The Wash
Great Gonerby
Grantham
5
Corby Glen
Grimsthorpe
Gedney Dyke
King's Lynn
Grimston
RUTLAND
Hambleton
Rutland Water
Stamford
Wisbech
Peterborough
King's Cliffe
Fotheringhay
Elton
Littleport
Sutton Gault
Ely
Kettering
Keyston
CAMBRIDGESHIRE
Huntingdon
Grafham Water
Wellingborough
Newmarket
Madingley
Cambridge
Lidgate
5
Milton Ernest
Little Shelford
Bedford
BEDFORDSHIRE
Melbourn
Biggleswade
Houghton Conquest
Saffron Walden
ESSEX
Flitwick
Woburn
Wethersfield
Stevenage
3
Luton
Bishop's Stortford

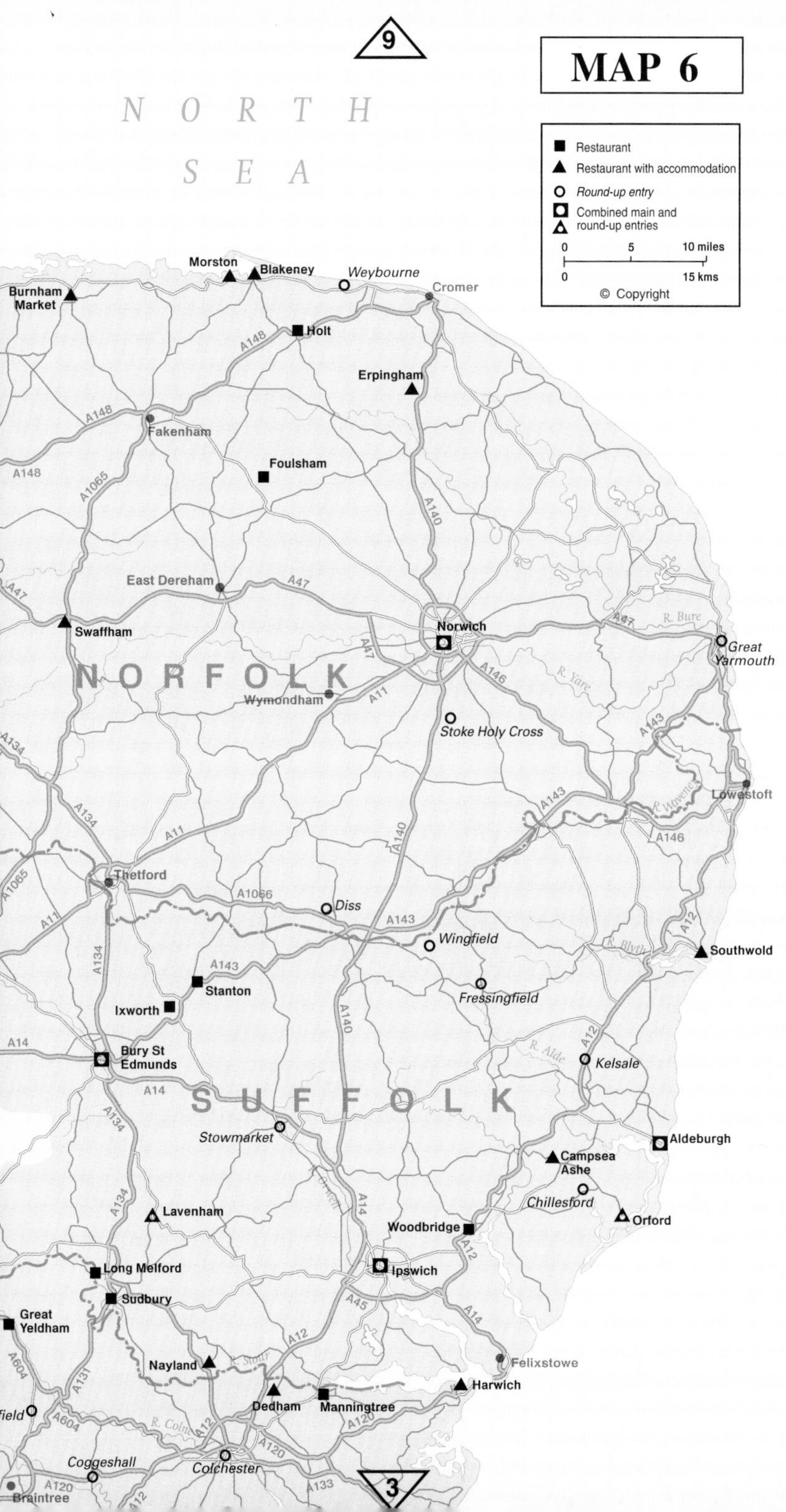

MAP 6
9
NORTH SEA
Restaurant
Restaurant with accommodation
Round-up entry
Combined main and round-up entries
0 5 10 miles
0 15 kms
© Copyright
Morston
Blakeney
Weybourne
Cromer
Burnham Market
Holt
Erpingham
Fakenham
Foulsham
East Dereham
Swaffham
Norwich
Great Yarmouth
NORFOLK
Wymondham
Stoke Holy Cross
Lowestoft
Thetford
Diss
Wingfield
Southwold
Stanton
Ixworth
Fressingfield
Bury St Edmunds
Kelsale
SUFFOLK
Stowmarket
Aldeburgh
Campsea Ashe
Chillesford
Lavenham
Orford
Woodbridge
Ipswich
Long Melford
Sudbury
Great Yeldham
Felixstowe
Nayland
Harwich
Dedham
Manningtree
field
Coggeshall
Colchester
Braintree
3

MAP 7

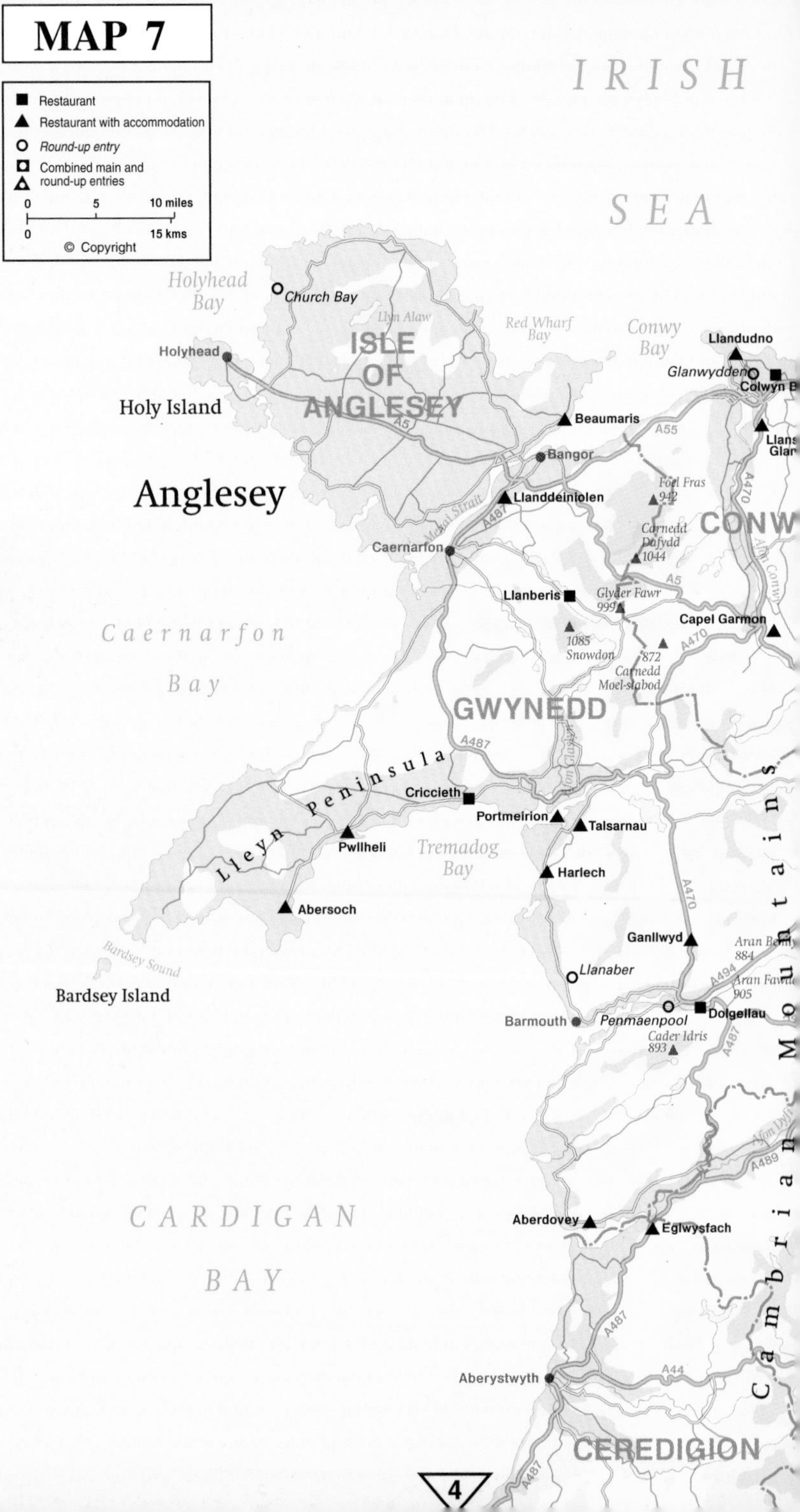

■ Restaurant
▲ Restaurant with accommodation
○ *Round-up entry*
◘ △ Combined main and round-up entries

0 5 10 miles
0 15 kms

© Copyright

IRISH SEA

Holyhead Bay
Church Bay
Llyn Alaw
ISLE OF ANGLESEY
Red Wharf Bay
Conwy Bay
Llandudno
Glanwydden
Colwyn B
Holyhead
Holy Island
A5
Beaumaris
A55
Llans Glan
Bangor
Anglesey
Foel Fras 942
A470
Llanddeiniolen
Menai Strait
A487
Carnedd Dafydd 1044
CONW
Caernarfon
Afon Conwy
A5
Llanberis
Glyder Fawr 999
Capel Garmon
A470
Caernarfon Bay
1085 Snowdon
872 Carnedd Moel-siabod
GWYNEDD
A487
Afon Glaslyn
Lleyn Peninsula
Criccieth
Portmeirion
Talsarnau
Pwllheli
Tremadog Bay
Harlech
A470
Abersoch
Ganllwyd
Aran Benllyn 884
Bardsey Sound
Llanaber
A494
Aran Fawddwy 905
Bardsey Island
Barmouth
Penmaenpool
Dolgellau
Cader Idris 893
A487
Afon Dyfi
A489
Cambrian Mountains
CARDIGAN BAY
Aberdovey
Eglwysfach
A487
Aberystwyth
A44
CEREDIGION
A487

4

8
Southport
Wrightington
Coppull Moor
Bolton
Ormskirk
Skelmersdale
Wigan
GTR MANCHESTER
MERSEYSIDE
St Helens
Wallasey
Liverpool
Birkenhead
Warrington
Colwyn Bay
Prestatyn
Rhyl
R. Mersey
R. Weaver
CHESHIRE
FLINTSHIRE
Hawarden
Chester
Denbigh
DENBIGHSHIRE
Worleston
Crewe
Broxton
Nantwich
Wrexham
WREXHAM
Whitchurch
Llangollen
Llandrillo
Llanarmon Dyffryn Ceiriog
Oswestry
Bala Lake
L. Vyrnwy
Llanfyllin
Llanwddyn
R. Severn
Shrewsbury
Dorrington
SHROPSHIRE
Norton
Newtown
POWYS
Llanfair Waterdine
Bromfield
Ludlow
5

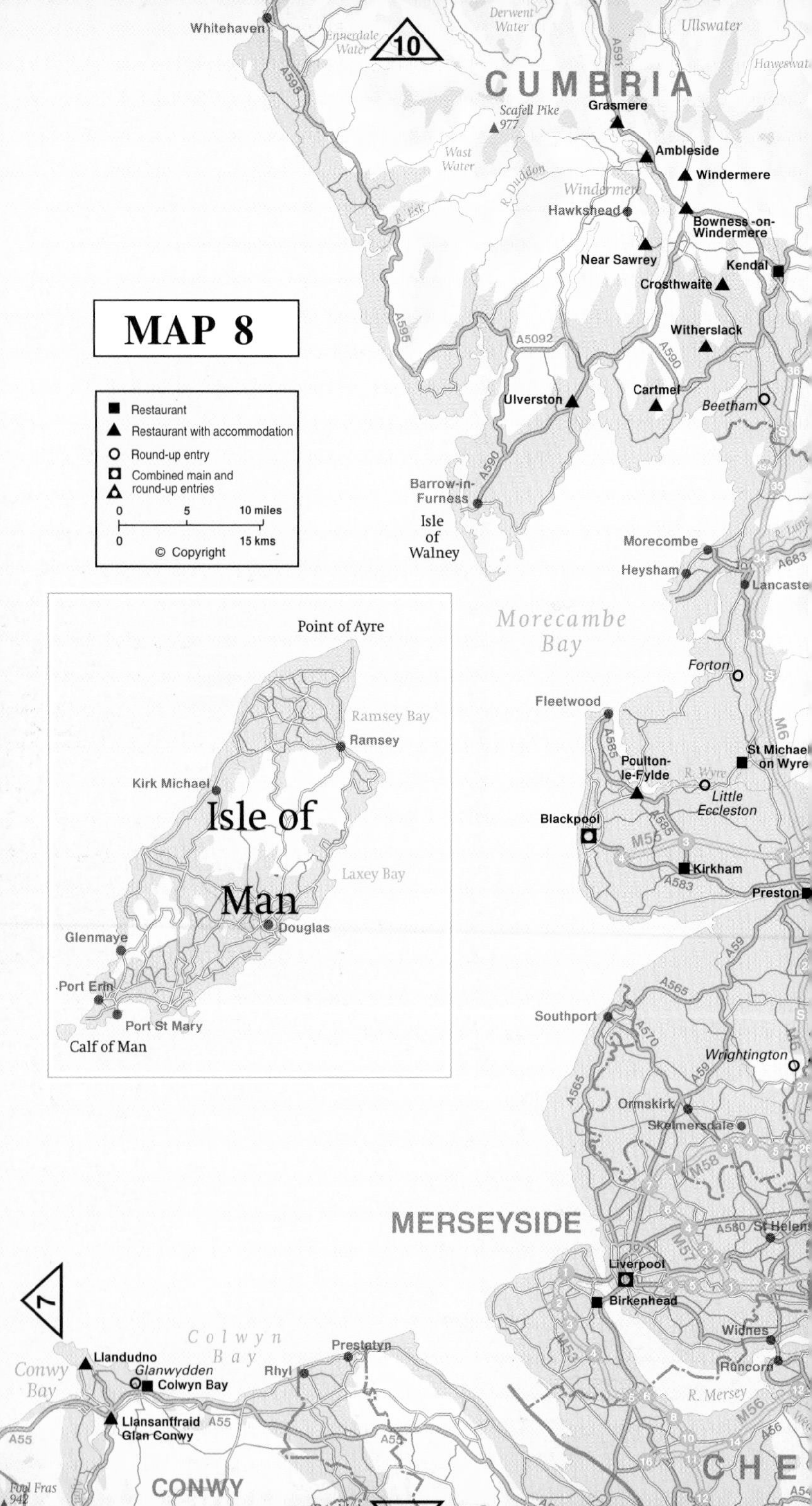

MAP 8
Restaurant
Restaurant with accommodation
Round-up entry
Combined main and round-up entries
0 5 10 miles
0 15 kms
© Copyright
CUMBRIA
Whitehaven
Ennerdale Water
Derwent Water
Ullswater
Scafell Pike 977
Wast Water
Grasmere
Ambleside
Windermere
Hawkshead
Bowness-on-Windermere
Near Sawrey
Kendal
Crosthwaite
Witherslack
Ulverston
Cartmel
Beetham
Barrow-in-Furness
Isle of Walney
Morecambe
Heysham
Lancaster
Morecambe Bay
Forton
Fleetwood
Poulton-le-Fylde
St Michael's on Wyre
Little Eccleston
Blackpool
Kirkham
Preston
Point of Ayre
Ramsey Bay
Ramsey
Kirk Michael
Isle of Man
Laxey Bay
Douglas
Glenmaye
Port Erin
Port St Mary
Calf of Man
Southport
Wrightington
Ormskirk
Skelmersdale
MERSEYSIDE
St Helens
Liverpool
Birkenhead
Widnes
Runcorn
R. Mersey
Colwyn Bay
Conwy Bay
Llandudno
Glanwydden
Colwyn Bay
Llansanffraid Glan Conwy
Prestatyn
Rhyl
CONWY
Denbigh
Hawarden
Chester

10
Barnard Castle
Yarm
Moulton
Richmond
Northallerton
6
Middleham
East Witton
Yorkshire
Carlton-in-Coverdale
Masham
West Tanfield
NORTH
Dales
Arncliffe
Ramsgill
Asenby
YORKSHIRE
Wath-in-Nidderdale
Low Laithe
Ripley
Ferrensby
Burnsall
Hetton
Bolton Abbey
Harrogate
Skipton
Ilkley
Boston Spa
Sawley
Linton
Clitheroe
LANCASHIRE
Longridge
Haworth
Leeds
Langho
Burnley
Bradford
Accrington
Blackburn
WEST
Shelf
Halifax
Todmorden
Brighouse
Elland
Dewsbury
YORKSHIRE
Wakefield
Cheesden
Ramsbottom
Lydgate
Huddersfield
Newmillerdam
Rochdale
Golcar
Heywood
Marsden
Roydhouse
Honley
6
Bolton
Barnsley
GREATER MANCHESTER
SOUTH
Eccles
Manchester
YORKSHIRE
Sale
Rotherham
Derwent Res.
Altrincham
Stockport
Warrington
Birch Vale
Sheffield
Ladybower Res.
Wilmslow
Ridgeway
Knutsford
Prestbury
Nether Alderley
Northwich
Buxton
Baslow
Chesterfield
Ashford
Bakewell
5
DERBYSHIRE

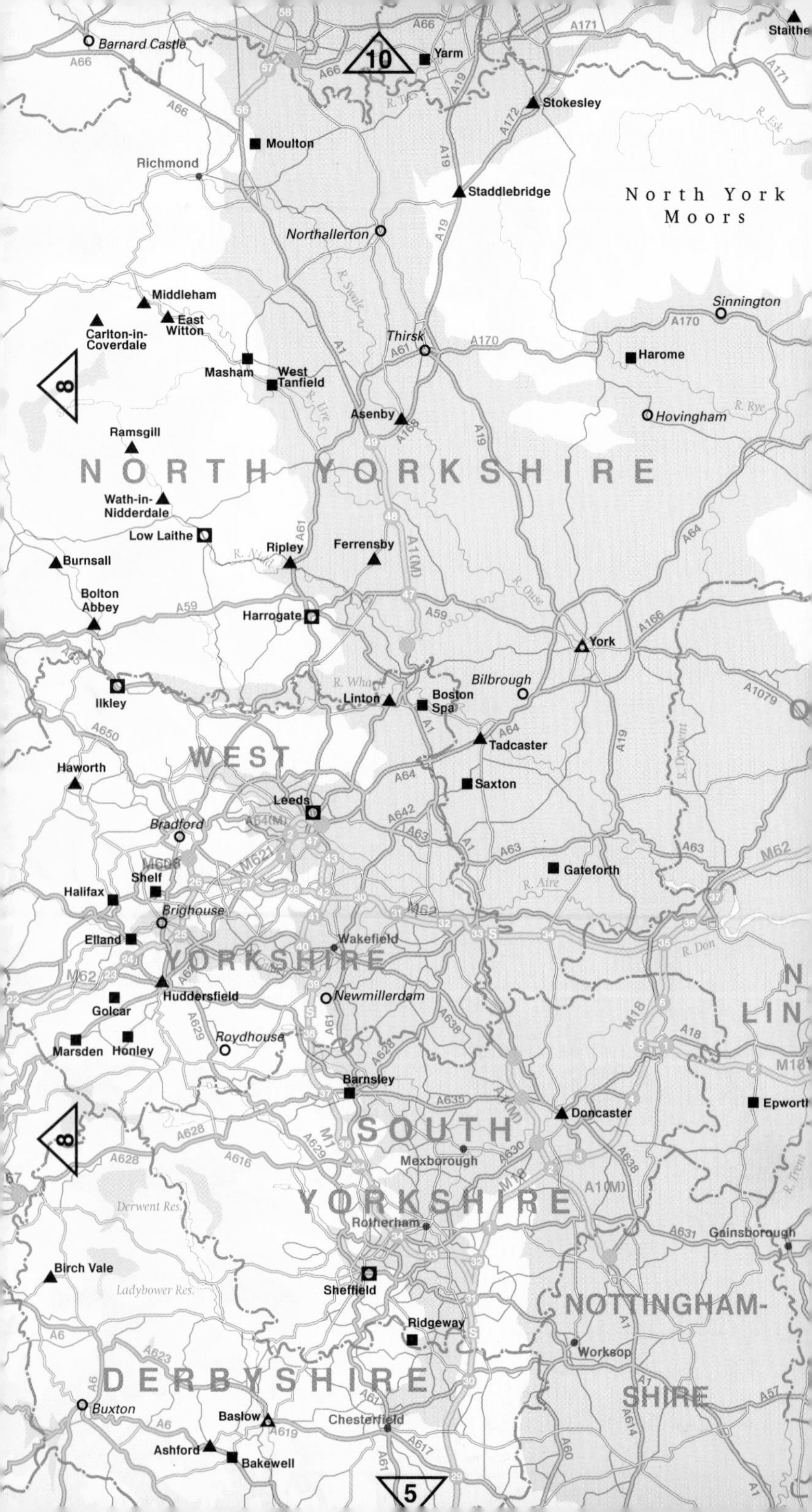

Barnard Castle
10
Yarm
Staithes
Stokesley
Moulton
Richmond
Staddlebridge
North York Moors
Northallerton
Middleham
Carlton-in-Coverdale
East Witton
Sinnington
Thirsk
Harome
Masham
West Tanfield
8
Asenby
Hovingham
Ramsgill
NORTH YORKSHIRE
Wath-in-Nidderdale
Low Laithe
Ripley
Ferrensby
Burnsall
Bolton Abbey
Harrogate
York
Ilkley
Bilbrough
Linton
Boston Spa
Tadcaster
Haworth
WEST
Saxton
Leeds
Bradford
Gateforth
Shelf
Halifax
Brighouse
Wakefield
Elland
YORKSHIRE
Huddersfield
Newmillerdam
Golcar
Marsden
Honley
Roydhouse
Barnsley
Epworth
Doncaster
SOUTH
Mexborough
YORKSHIRE
Rotherham
Gainsborough
Birch Vale
Sheffield
NOTTINGHAM-
Ridgeway
Worksop
DERBYSHIRE
SHIRE
Buxton
Baslow
Chesterfield
Ashford
Bakewell
5

10
MAP 9
Restaurant
Restaurant with accommodation
Round-up entry
Combined main and round-up entries
0 5 10 miles
0 15 kms
© Copyright
Whitby
Scarborough
Flamborough Head
Bridlington
Bridlington Bay
Yorkshire Wolds
EAST RIDING OF YORKSHIRE
Lund
Lockington
Beverley
Walkington
KINGSTON UPON HULL
Kingston upon Hull
R. Humber
Barton-upon-Humber
Winteringham
NORTH LINCOLNSHIRE
Scunthorpe
Spurn Head
Grimsby
Cleethorpes
N.E. LINCOLNSHIRE
Louth
The Wolds
LINCOLNSHIRE
Lincoln
Horncastle
Burgh le Marsh
Skegness
6

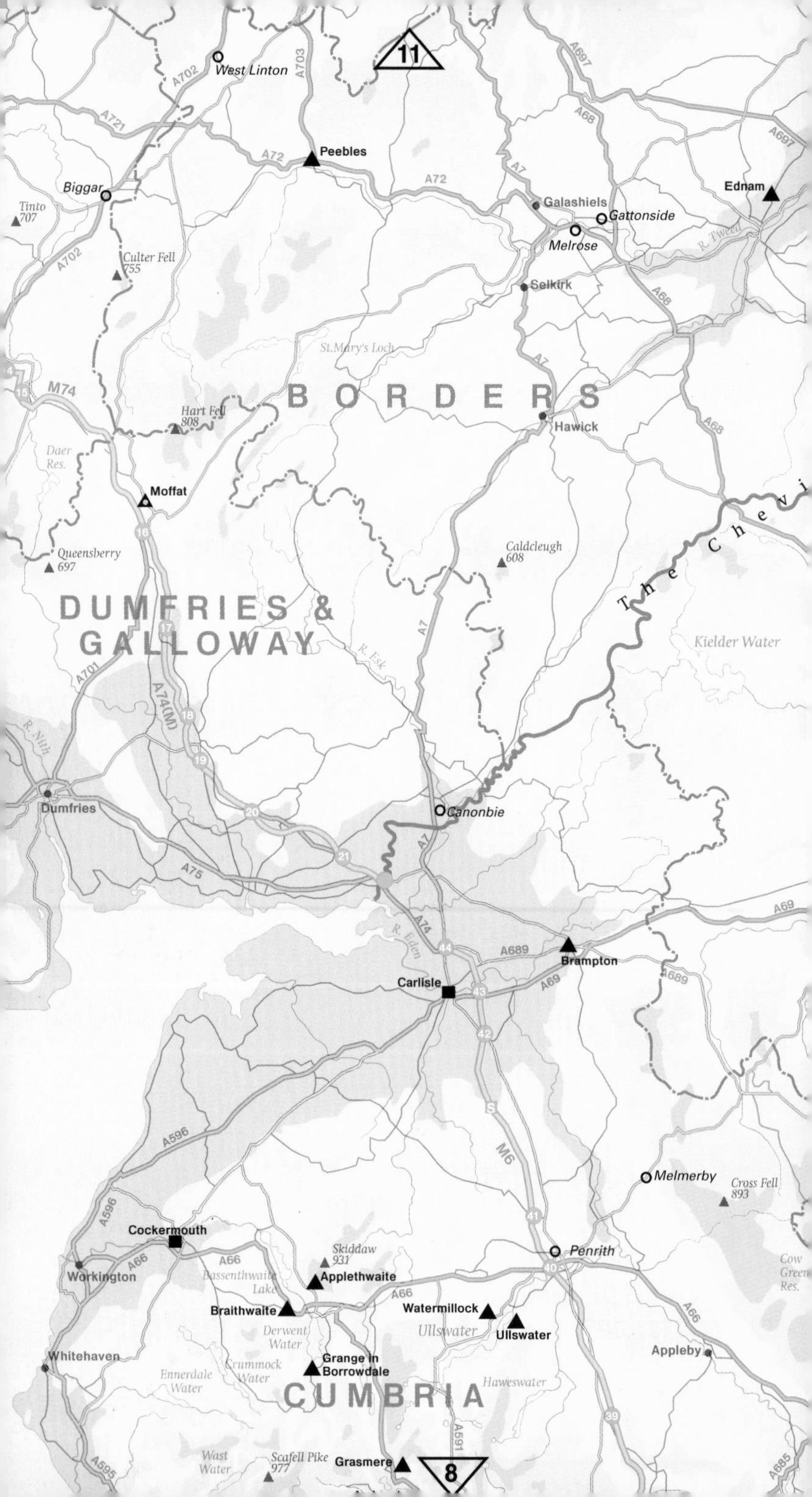
11
West Linton
Peebles
Biggar
Tinto 707
Culter Fell 755
Galashiels
Gattonside
Melrose
Ednam
R. Tweed
Selkirk
St.Mary's Loch
BORDERS
Hawick
Hart Fell 808
Daer Res.
Moffat
Queensberry 697
Caldcleugh 608
The Chevi
Kielder Water
DUMFRIES & GALLOWAY
R. Esk
R. Nith
Dumfries
Canonbie
R. Eden
Brampton
Carlisle
Melmerby
Cross Fell 893
Cockermouth
Workington
Skiddaw 931
Applethwaite
Penrith
Cow Green Res.
Bassenthwaite Lake
Braithwaite
Watermillock
Ullswater
Derwent Water
Whitehaven
Crummock Water
Grange in Borrowdale
Ennerdale Water
Haweswater
Appleby
CUMBRIA
West Water
Scafell Pike 977
Grasmere
8
A702
A703
A697
A68
A721
A72
A7
M74
A701
A74(M)
A75
A74
A689
A69
A596
A595
A66
M6
A591
A685

MAP 10
11
9
Restaurant
Restaurant with accommodation
Round-up entry
Combined main and round-up entries
0 5 10 miles
0 15 kms
© Copyright
Berwick-upon-Tweed
Swinton
Holy Island
Farne Is.
Wark
The Cheviot 815
Hills
Alnwick
Alnmouth
R. Aln
R. Coquet
NORTHUMBERLAND
R. Blyth
Ponteland
Seaton Burn
Great Whittington
Matfen
R. Pont
Tynemouth
Haydon Bridge
Corbridge
Newcastle upon Tyne
TYNE & WEAR
Hexham
R. Tyne
Gateshead
Sunderland
Derwent Res.
Stanley
Carterway Heads
Consett
Chester-le-Street
Durham
Willington
DURHAM
Hartlepool
HARTLEPOOL
Tees Bay
Redcar
STOCKTON-ON-TEES
Middlesbrough
Romaldkirk
REDCAR
MIDDLESBROUGH
Barnard Castle
Yarm
R. Tees
Stokesley
A1
A697
A68
A1068
A696
A189
A19
A69
A692
A194(M)
A690
A167
A688
A1(M)
A179
A689
A66
A171
A172

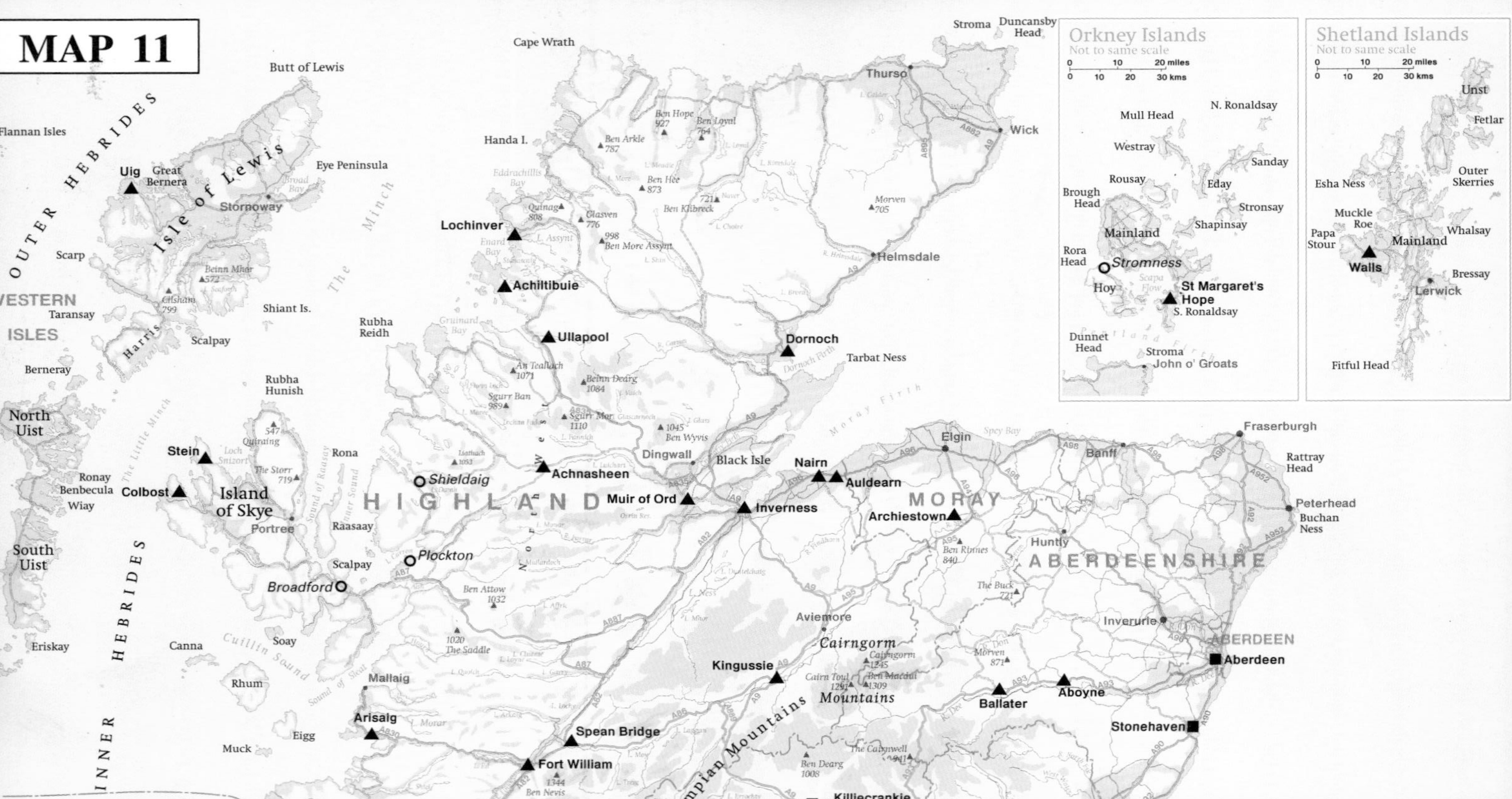
MAP 11
Orkney Islands
Not to same scale
0 10 20 miles
0 10 20 30 kms
Mull Head
N. Ronaldsay
Westray
Sanday
Rousay
Eday
Brough Head
Stronsay
Mainland
Shapinsay
Rora Head
Stromness
Hoy
St Margaret's Hope
S. Ronaldsay
Dunnet Head
Stroma
John o' Groats
Shetland Islands
Not to same scale
0 10 20 miles
0 10 20 30 kms
Unst
Fetlar
Esha Ness
Outer Skerries
Muckle Roe
Whalsay
Papa Stour
Mainland
Walls
Bressay
Lerwick
Fitful Head
Cape Wrath
Stroma
Duncansby Head
Thurso
Wick
Butt of Lewis
Flannan Isles
OUTER HEBRIDES
Uig
Great Bernera
Isle of Lewis
Stornoway
Eye Peninsula
Handa I.
Ben Hope 927
Ben Loyal 764
Ben Arkle 787
Ben Hee 873
Ben Klibreck
Morven 705
Lochinver
Quinag 808
Glasven 776
998 Ben More Assynt
Helmsdale
Scarp
Beinn Mhor 572
Clisham 799
WESTERN ISLES
Taransay
Shiant Is.
The Minch
Achiltibuie
Harris
Scalpay
Rubha Reidh
Ullapool
Dornoch
Tarbat Ness
Dornoch Firth
Berneray
Rubha Hunish
An Teallach 1071
Beinn Dearg 1084
Sgurr Ban 989
Sgurr Mor 1110
1045 Ben Wyvis
Moray Firth
North Uist
547 Quiraing
Stein
Rona
Ronay
Benbecula
Wiay
Colbost
The Storr 719
Island of Skye
Portree
Raasaay
Shieldaig
Achnasheen
Dingwall
Black Isle
Nairn
Auldearn
Elgin
Spey Bay
Banff
Fraserburgh
Rattray Head
HIGHLAND
Muir of Ord
Inverness
MORAY
Archiestown
Peterhead
Buchan Ness
South Uist
Scalpay
Plockton
Broadford
Ben Attow 1032
Ben Rinnes 840
Huntly
ABERDEENSHIRE
The Buck 721
Inverurie
ABERDEEN
Aberdeen
Eriskay
HEBRIDES
Canna
Cuillin Sound
Soay
1020 The Saddle
Aviemore
Cairngorm
Cairngorm 1245
Cairn Toul 1293
Ben Macdui 1309
Mountains
Morven 871
Kingussie
Mallaig
Rhum
Ballater
Aboyne
Arisaig
Stonehaven
Eigg
Spean Bridge
Grampian Mountains
Muck
INNER
Fort William
1344 Ben Nevis
The Cairnwell 941
Ben Dearg 1008
Killiecrankie
Coll
Strontian

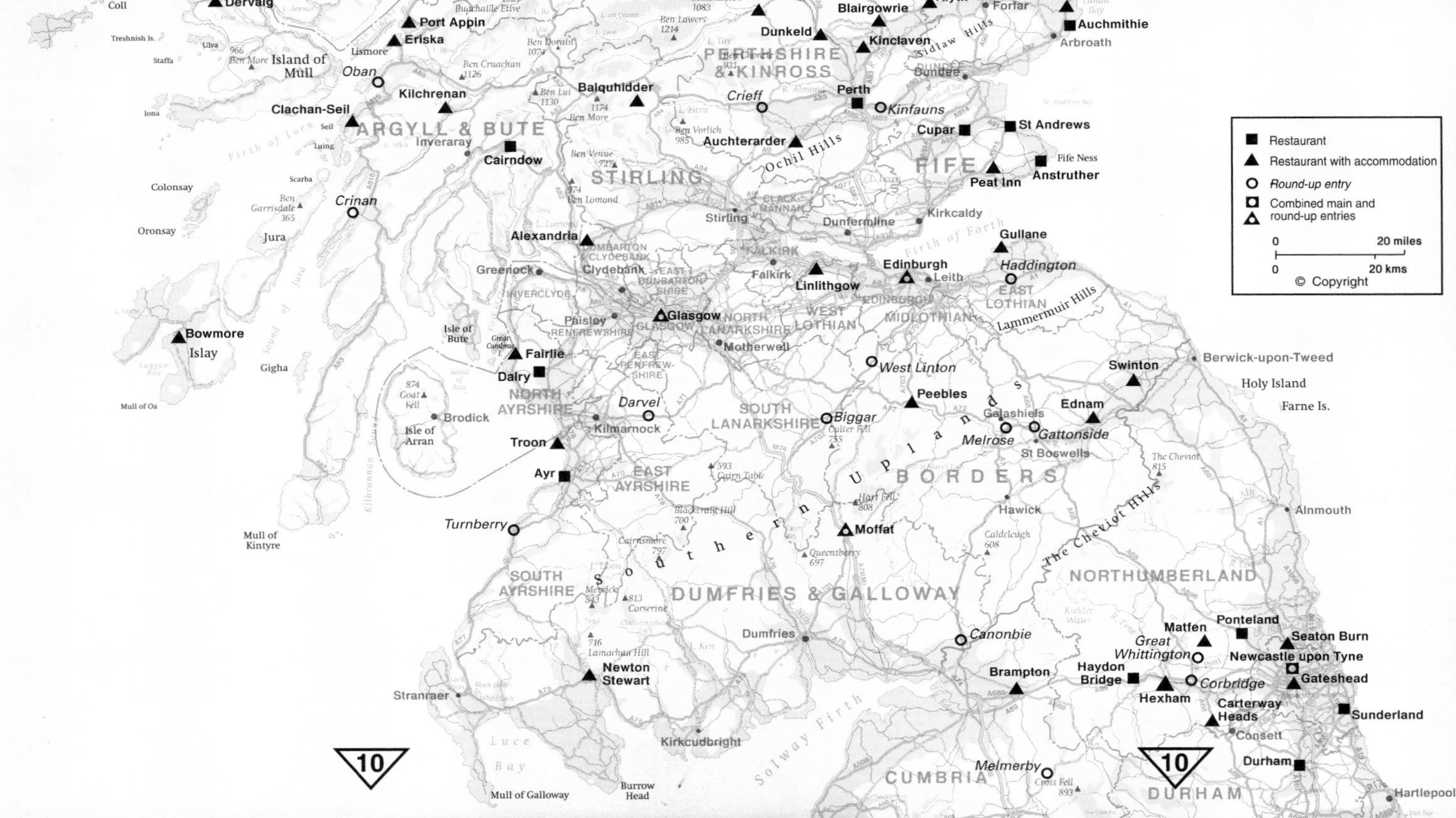
Restaurant
Restaurant with accommodation
Round-up entry
Combined main and round-up entries
0 20 miles
0 20 kms
© Copyright
10
Dervaig
Port Appin
Eriska
Oban
Kilchrenan
Clachan-Seil
Crinan
Bowmore
Cairndow
Balquhidder
Alexandria
Glasgow
Fairlie
Dalry
Troon
Ayr
Turnberry
Darvel
Newton Stewart
Dunkeld
Blairgowrie
Kinclaven
Crieff
Perth
Kinfauns
Auchterarder
Cupar
St Andrews
Peat Inn
Anstruther
Auchmithie
Gullane
Haddington
Edinburgh
Linlithgow
West Linton
Biggar
Peebles
Moffat
Melrose
Gattonside
Ednam
Swinton
Canonbie
Brampton
Melmerby
Haydon Bridge
Hexham
Great Whittington
Corbridge
Matfen
Ponteland
Seaton Burn
Newcastle upon Tyne
Gateshead
Carterway Heads
Sunderland
Durham
ARGYLL & BUTE
STIRLING
PERTHSHIRE & KINROSS
FIFE
EAST LOTHIAN
MIDLOTHIAN
WEST LOTHIAN
SOUTH LANARKSHIRE
NORTH AYRSHIRE
EAST AYRSHIRE
SOUTH AYRSHIRE
DUMFRIES & GALLOWAY
BORDERS
NORTHUMBERLAND
CUMBRIA
DURHAM
Southern Uplands

Greater London
BARNET
Stanmore
HARROW
Finchley
Rani
Two Brothers
Hendon
Gourmet Garden
Wood Green
Vrisaki
Le Cadre
Idaho
Village Bistro
Chez Liline
Cafe Japan
WEMBLEY
Willesden
Sushi-Say
Sabras
Hampstead
See Map 13
CAMDEN
BRENT
William IV
HAMMERSMITH AND FULHAM
See Map 15
Alastair Little Lancaster Road
Orsino
Balzac Bistro
Chez Moi
CITY OF WEST-MINSTER
Ealing
Parade
Acton
Gilbey's
Clock
Anglesea Arms
Patio
Brackenbury
Chinon
Adams Café
Wilsons
Cotto
Riso
Thai Bistro
Snows on the Green
Popeseye
KENSINGTON AND CHELSEA
See Map 14
Chiswick
Azou
HAMMERSMITH
Brentford
Montana
Blue Elephant
Ransome's Dock
Gate
Riva
River Café
Salisbury Tavern
Chutney Mary
Metrogusto
Sonny's
Fulham
Depot
Phoenix
Putney Bridge
Redmonds
Lavender
Café Spice Namaste
Brixton
Crowthers
Del Buongustaio
Brady's
Moxon's
Osteria Antica Bologna
RICHMOND
Wandsworth
Ditto
Le Gothique
WANDSWORTH
Saigon Thuy
3 Monkeys
Twickenham
Sarkhel's
Chez Bruce
Kastoori
Radha Krishna Bhavan
Utah
Light House
Wimbledon
Streatham
Merton
Kingston upon Thames
Morden
Mitcham
Mirch Masala
KINGSTON UPON THAMES
Malden
MERTON
M1
A40(M)

CHIGWELL
EDMONTON
Woodford
Hainault
REDBRIDGE
Walthamstow
WALTHAM FOREST
Mesclun
Rasa
Istanbul Iskembecisi
ILFORD
HACKNEY
Little Georgia
Thai Garden
HACKNEY
A102(M)
NEWHAM
Barking
BARKING & DAGENHAM
East Ham
New Tayyabs
TOWER HAMLETS
R. Thames
Poplar
House
Moshi Moshi Sushi
Mem Saheb
Thamesmead
Woolwich
SOUTHWARK
Time
Greenwich
Spread Eagle
A102(M)
Holly
GREENWICH
Chapter Two
Lewisham
LAMBETH
Le Chardon
Babur Brasserie
Dulwich
Eltham
Catford
LEWISHAM
Sidcup
Crystal Palace
BROMLEY
Beckenham
Mantanah
BROMLEY
MAP 12
Restaurant
Restaurant with accommodation
Round-up entry
0 5km
0 4 miles
© Copyright

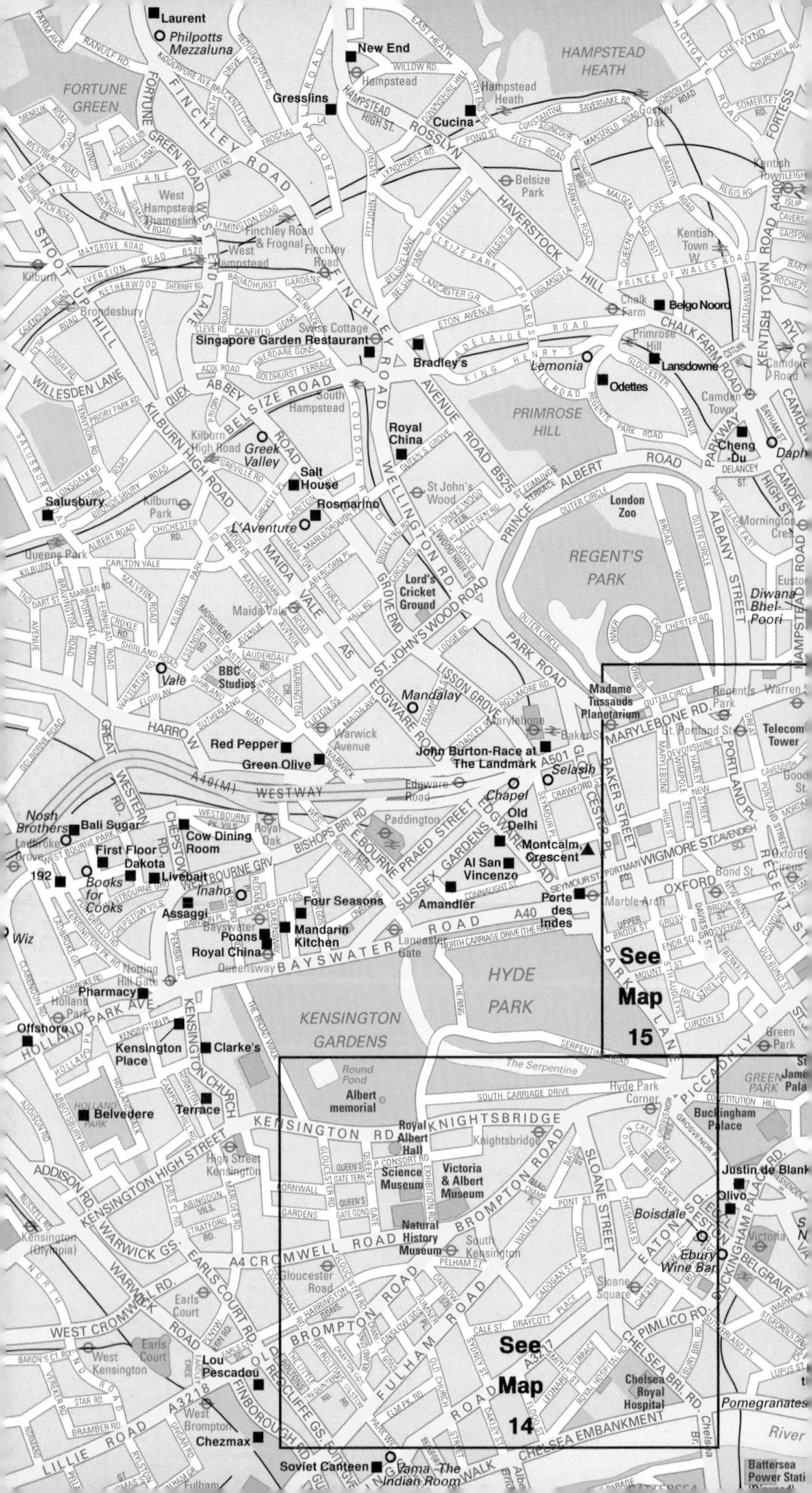

Laurent
Philpotts Mezzaluna
New End
Hampstead
HAMPSTEAD HEATH
FORTUNE GREEN
Gresslins
Cucina
Hampstead Heath
Gospel Oak
FINCHLEY ROAD
HAMPSTEAD HIGH ST.
ROSSLYN
Belsize Park
Kentish Town
West Hampstead Thameslink
Finchley Road & Frognal
West Hampstead
Finchley Road
HAVERSTOCK HILL
Kentish Town W.
Kilburn
SHOOT UP HILL
Brondesbury
Chalk Farm
Belgo Noord
Swiss Cottage
Singapore Garden Restaurant
Bradley's
Primrose Hill
Lemonia
Lansdowne
Odettes
WILLESDEN LANE
KILBURN HIGH ROAD
BELSIZE ROAD
South Hampstead
Camden Town
PRIMROSE HILL
Royal China
Cheng-Du
Daph
Kilburn High Road
Greek Valley
Salt House
Rosmarino
St John's Wood
London Zoo
Salusbury
Kilburn Park
L'Aventure
PRINCE ALBERT ROAD
Mornington Cres.
Queens Park
MAIDA VALE
WELLINGTON RD.
Lord's Cricket Ground
REGENT'S PARK
Euston
Diwana Bhel-Poori
Maida Vale
ST. JOHN'S WOOD ROAD
PARK ROAD
Vale
BBC Studios
EDGWARE ROAD
Mandalay
LISSON GROVE
Madame Tussauds Planetarium
Regent's Park
Warren S
Telecom Tower
HARROW ROAD
Red Pepper
Warwick Avenue
Marylebone
John Burton-Race at The Landmark
Green Olive
A40(M) WESTWAY
Selasih
Edgware Road
Chapel
BAKER STREET
Nosh Brothers
Bali Sugar
Paddington
Old Delhi
Ladbroke Grove
Cow Dining Room
Royal Oak
PRAED STREET
Montcalm Crescent
WIGMORE ST.
First Floor
Dakota
Al San Vincenzo
192
Books for Cooks
Livebait
Inaho
Amandier
Bond St.
Oxford Circus
Marble Arch
Assaggi
Four Seasons
Porte des Indes
OXFORD
Wiz
Bayswater
Poons
Mandarin Kitchen
Royal China
Lancaster Gate
Queensway
BAYSWATER ROAD
HYDE PARK
See Map 15
Notting Hill Gate
Pharmacy
Holland Park
KENSINGTON GARDENS
Offshore
HOLLAND PARK AVE.
Kensington Place
Clarke's
Green Park
The Serpentine
Round Pond
GREEN PARK
Albert memorial
Hyde Park Corner
PICCADILLY
Buckingham Palace
Belvedere
Terrace
KENSINGTON RD
KNIGHTSBRIDGE
Royal Albert Hall
Knightsbridge
High Street Kensington
Science Museum
Victoria & Albert Museum
Justin de Blank
Olivo
KENSINGTON HIGH STREET
BROMPTON ROAD
SLOANE STREET
Boisdale
Kensington (Olympia)
Natural History Museum
South Kensington
Victoria
A4 CROMWELL ROAD
Ebury Wine Bar
Gloucester Road
Sloane Square
Earls Court
WEST CROMWELL RD.
FULHAM ROAD
PIMLICO RD.
See Map 14
West Kensington
Earls Court
Lou Pescadou
Chelsea Royal Hospital
Pomegranates
West Brompton
CHELSEA EMBANKMENT
River
LILLIE ROAD
Chezmax
Soviet Canteen
Vama -The Indian Room
Battersea Power Stati

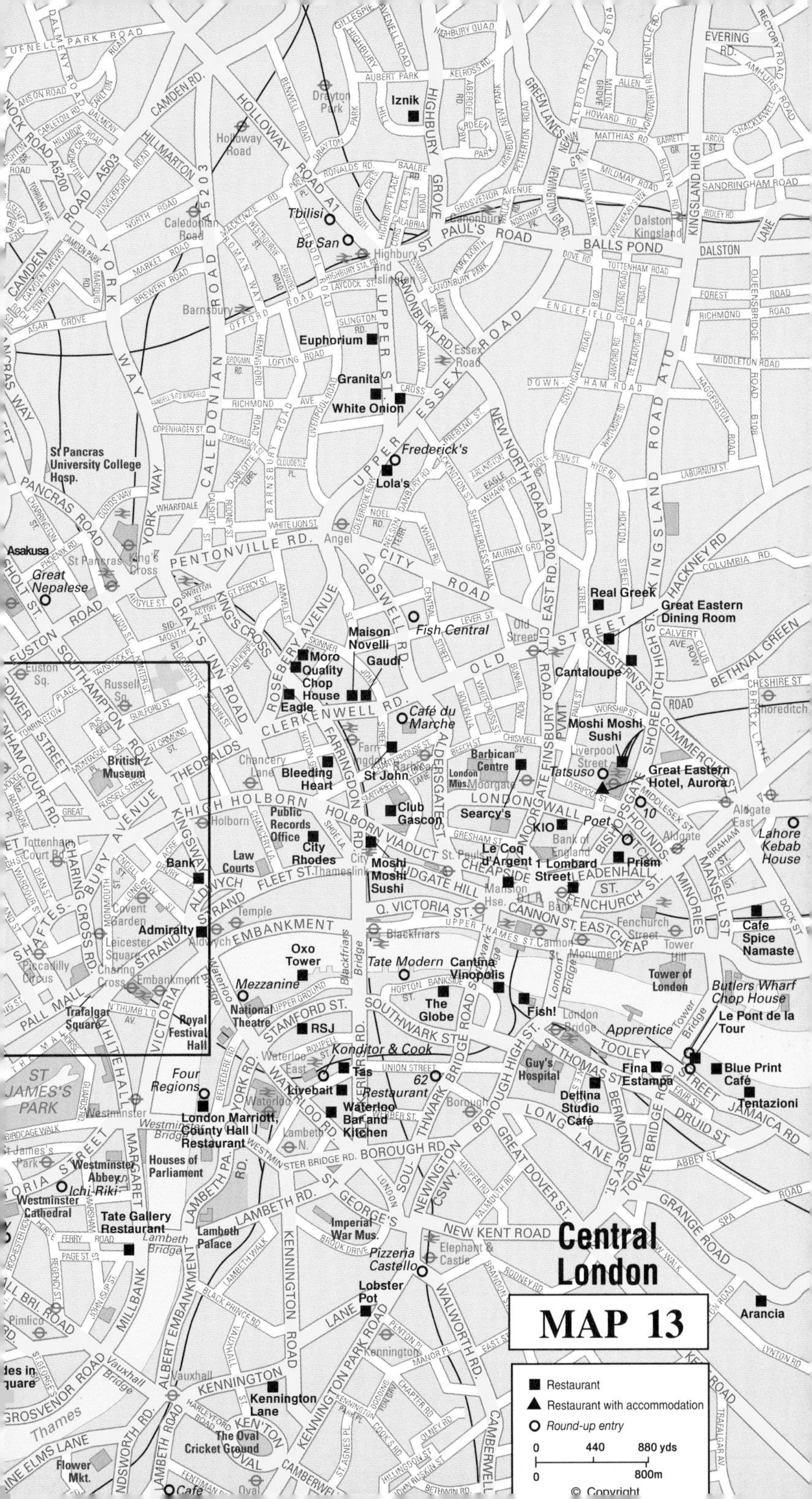
Central London
MAP 13
Restaurant
Restaurant with accommodation
Round-up entry
0
440
880 yds
0
800m
© Copyright
Iznik
Tbilisi
Bu San
Euphorium
Granita
White Onion
Frederick's
Lola's
Asakusa
Great Nepalese
Real Greek
Great Eastern Dining Room
Fish Central
Maison Novelli
Moro
Quality Chop House
Gaudí
Eagle
Cantaloupe
Café du Marche
Moshi Moshi Sushi
Bleeding Heart
St John
Barbican Centre
Tatsuso
Great Eastern Hotel, Aurora
Club Gascon
Searcy's
10
Lahore Kebab House
City Rhodes
Moshi Moshi Sushi
Le Coq d'Argent
KIO
Poet
Prism
1 Lombard Street
Bank
Admiralty
Cafe Spice Namaste
Oxo Tower
Tate Modern
Cantina Vinopolis
Mezzanine
The Globe
Fish!
Butlers Wharf Chop House
Le Pont de la Tour
Apprentice
RSJ
Konditor & Cook
Tas
62 Restaurant
Livebait
Waterloo Bar and Kitchen
Fina Estampa
Blue Print Café
Tentazioni
Delfina Studio Café
Four Regions
London Marriott, County Hall Restaurant
Ichi-Riki
Tate Gallery Restaurant
Pizzeria Castello
Lobster Pot
Arancia
Kennington Lane
Cafe
Drayton Park
Holloway Road
Caledonian Road
Barnsbury
Highbury and Islington
Canonbury
Dalston Kingsland
Essex Road
Angel
St Pancras University College Hosp.
St Pancras
King's Cross
Old Street
Euston Sq.
Russell Sq.
British Museum
Chancery Lane
Farringdon
Barbican
London Mus.
Moorgate
Liverpool Street
Aldgate East
Aldgate
Shoreditch
Holborn
Public Records Office
Law Courts
Tottenham Court Rd.
Covent Garden
Temple
Aldwych
Blackfriars
Mansion Hse.
Bank
Cannon St.
Monument
Fenchurch Street
Tower Hill
Tower of London
Leicester Square
Piccadilly Circus
Charing Cross
Embankment
Trafalgar Square
National Theatre
Royal Festival Hall
London Bridge
Guy's Hospital
Waterloo East
Waterloo
Borough
Westminster
St James's Park
Lambeth N.
Westminster Abbey
Houses of Parliament
Westminster Cathedral
Lambeth Palace
Imperial War Mus.
Elephant & Castle
Kennington
Pimlico
Vauxhall
The Oval Cricket Ground
Flower Mkt.
Thames

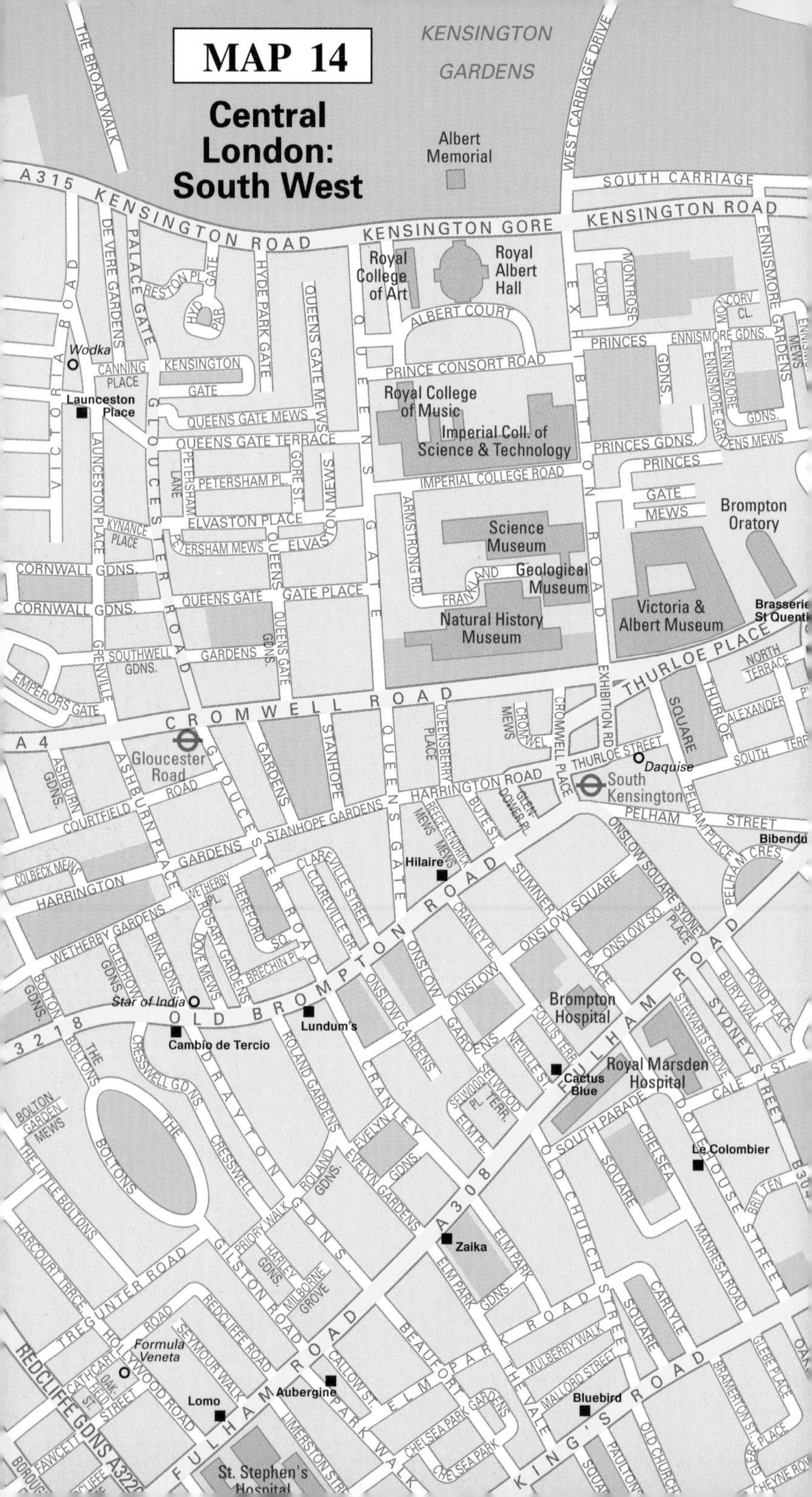

MAP 14
Central London: South West
KENSINGTON GARDENS
Albert Memorial
Royal College of Art
Royal Albert Hall
Royal College of Music
Imperial Coll. of Science & Technology
Science Museum
Geological Museum
Natural History Museum
Victoria & Albert Museum
Brompton Oratory
Brasserie St Quentin
Wodka
Launceston Place
Gloucester Road
South Kensington
Daquise
Bibendum
Hilaire
Star of India
Lundum's
Cambio de Tercio
Brompton Hospital
Royal Marsden Hospital
Cactus Blue
Le Colombier
Zaika
Formula Veneta
Lomo
Aubergine
Bluebird
St. Stephen's Hospital
A315 KENSINGTON ROAD
KENSINGTON GORE
KENSINGTON ROAD
SOUTH CARRIAGE
WEST CARRIAGE DRIVE
THE BROAD WALK
PRINCE CONSORT ROAD
IMPERIAL COLLEGE ROAD
EXHIBITION ROAD
QUEENS GATE
GLOUCESTER ROAD
VICTORIA ROAD
A4 CROMWELL ROAD
THURLOE PLACE
HARRINGTON ROAD
PELHAM STREET
OLD BROMPTON ROAD
A3218
FULHAM ROAD
A308
KING'S ROAD
OLD CHURCH STREET
REDCLIFFE GDNS A3220

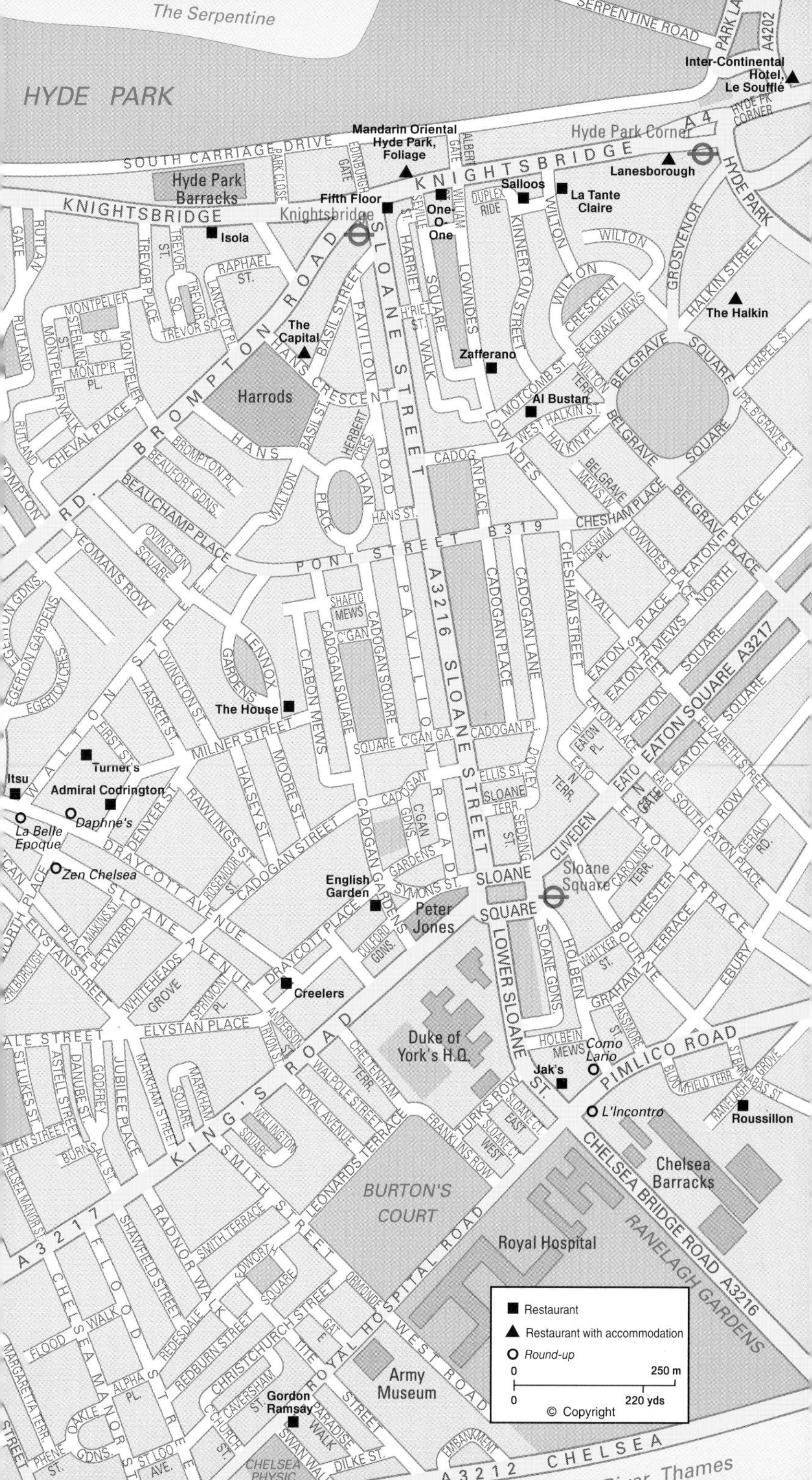
The Serpentine
HYDE PARK
Hyde Park Barracks
Harrods
Peter Jones
Duke of York's H.Q.
BURTON'S COURT
Royal Hospital
Army Museum
Chelsea Barracks
CHELSEA PHYSIC GARDEN
River Thames
Hyde Park Corner
Knightsbridge
Sloane Square
Inter-Continental Hotel, Le Soufflé
Mandarin Oriental Hyde Park, Foliage
Lanesborough
Fifth Floor
One-O-One
Salloos
La Tante Claire
Isola
The Capital
The Halkin
Zafferano
Al Bustan
The House
Turner's
Itsu
Admiral Codrington
Daphne's
La Belle Epoque
Zen Chelsea
English Garden
Creelers
Como Lario
Jak's
L'Incontro
Roussillon
Gordon Ramsay
KNIGHTSBRIDGE
SOUTH CARRIAGE DRIVE
SERPENTINE ROAD
BROMPTON ROAD
SLOANE STREET
A3216
PONT STREET
B319
CADOGAN PLACE
BELGRAVE SQUARE
EATON SQUARE
A3217
KING'S ROAD
LOWER SLOANE ST.
PIMLICO ROAD
CHELSEA BRIDGE ROAD
RANELAGH GARDENS
ROYAL HOSPITAL ROAD
CHELSEA EMBANKMENT
A3212
Restaurant
Restaurant with accommodation
Round-up
0
250 m
0
220 yds
© Copyright

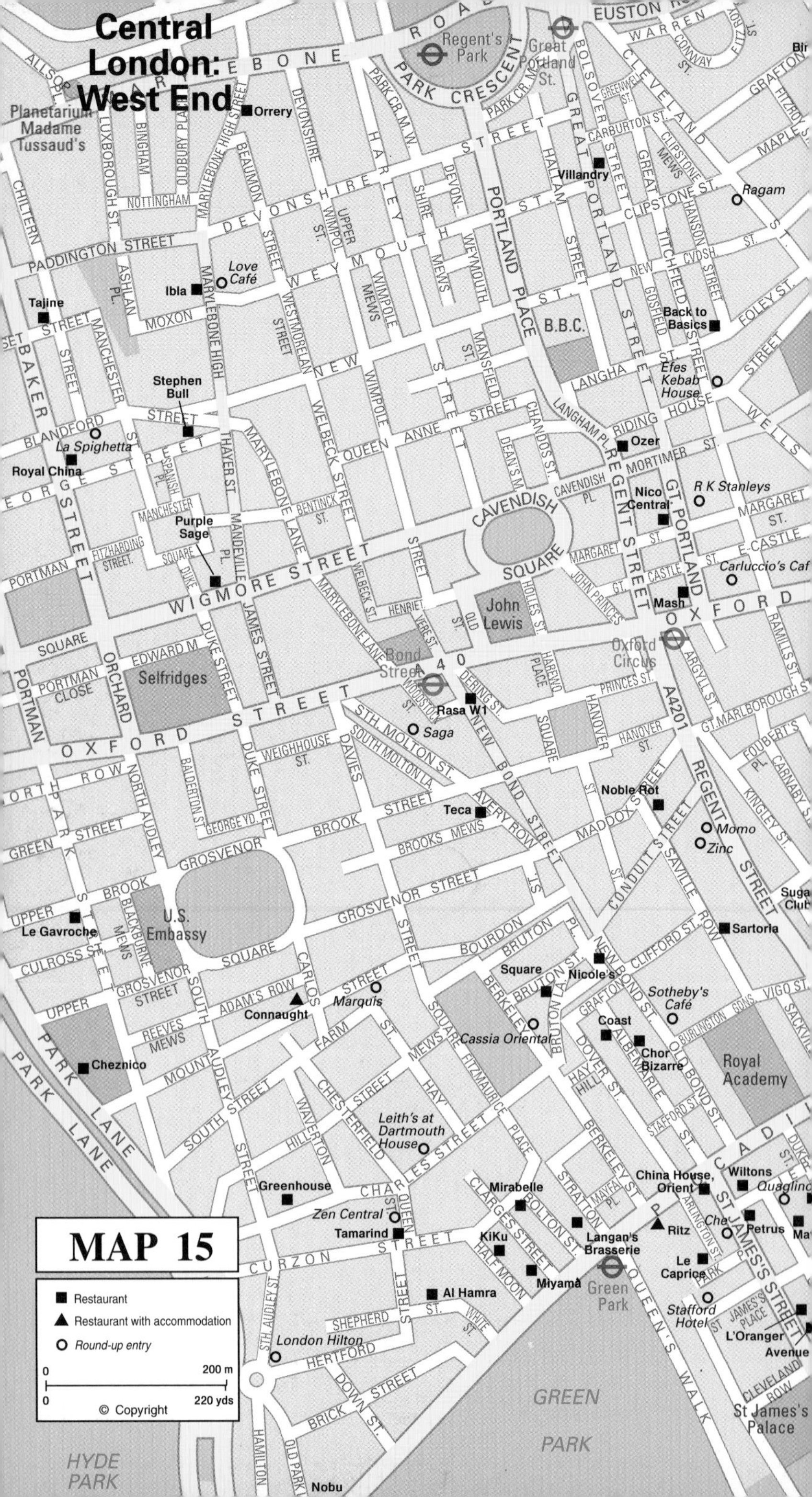

Central London: West End
MAP 15
Restaurant
Restaurant with accommodation
Round-up entry
0
200 m
0
220 yds
© Copyright
Planetarium
Madame Tussaud's
Orrery
Regent's Park
Great Portland St.
Villandry
Ragam
Love Café
Ibla
Tajine
Back to Basics
B.B.C.
Efes Kebab House
Stephen Bull
La Spighetta
Royal China
Ozer
R K Stanleys
Nico Central
Purple Sage
Carluccio's Caf
Mash
John Lewis
Oxford Circus
Selfridges
Bond Street
Rasa W1
Saga
Noble Rot
Teca
Momo
Zinc
Sugar Club
Sartoria
Le Gavroche
U.S. Embassy
Square
Nicole's
Sotheby's Café
Connaught
Marquis
Cassia Oriental
Coast
Chor Bizarre
Royal Academy
Cheznico
Leith's at Dartmouth House
China House, Orient
Wiltons
Quaglino
Greenhouse
Mirabelle
Zen Central
Tamarind
Ritz
Che
Petrus
KiKu
Langan's Brasserie
Le Caprice
Miyama
Green Park
Al Hamra
Stafford Hotel
L'Oranger
London Hilton
GREEN PARK
St James's Palace
HYDE PARK
Nobu
OXFORD STREET
WIGMORE STREET
CAVENDISH SQUARE
GROSVENOR SQUARE
PARK LANE
PICCADILLY
REGENT STREET
PORTLAND PLACE
MARYLEBONE HIGH STREET
NEW BOND STREET

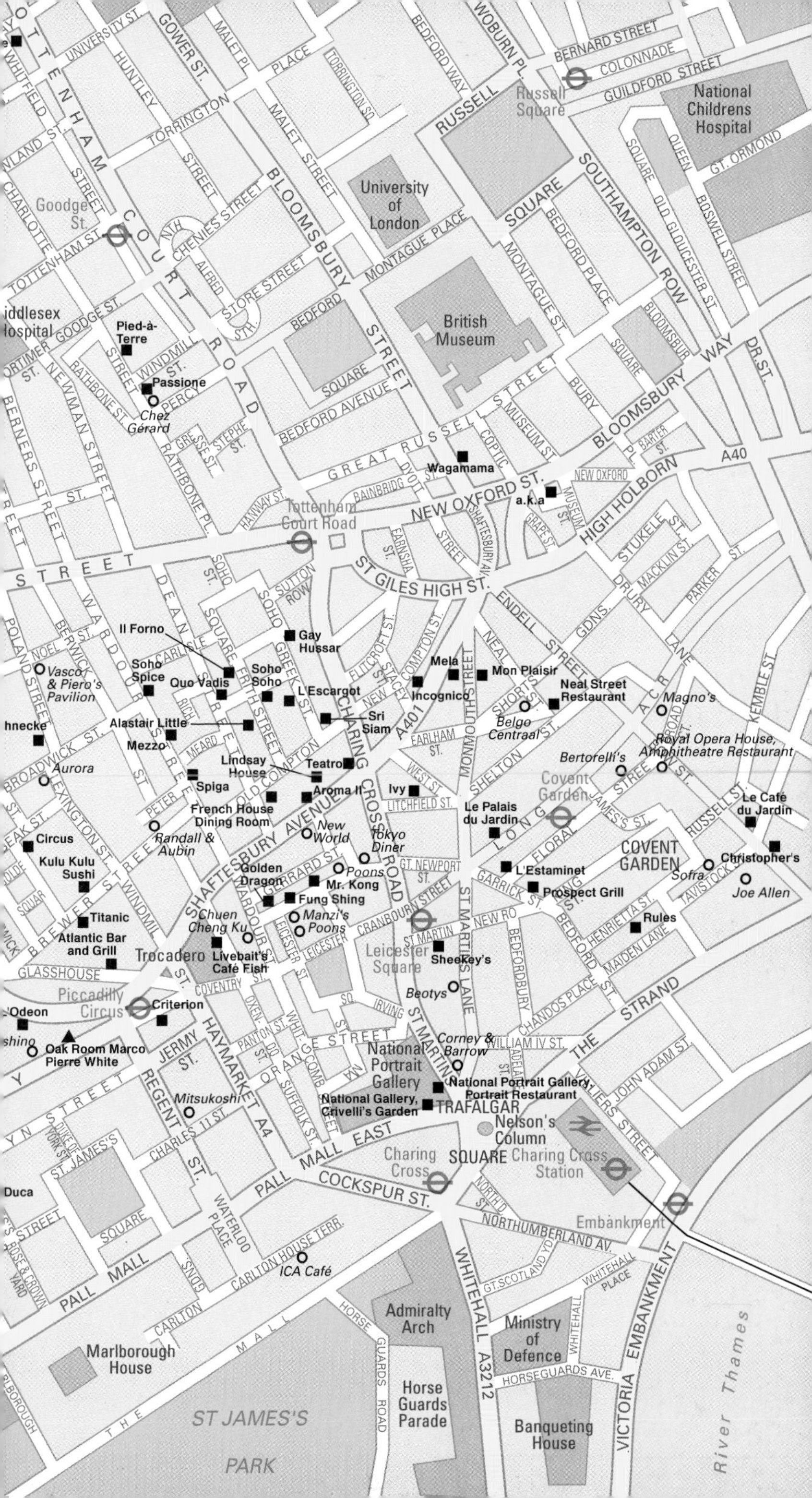

UNIVERSITY ST.
GOWER ST.
MALET PL.
WOBURN PL.
BERNARD STREET
COLONNADE
GUILDFORD STREET
BEDFORD WAY
TORRINGTON SQ.
RUSSELL
Russell Square
National Childrens Hospital
GT. ORMOND
HUNTLEY
TORRINGTON
MALET STREET
University of London
SOUTHAMPTON ROW
QUEEN SQUARE
OLD GLOUCESTER ST.
BOSWELL STREET
Goodge St.
TOTTENHAM ST.
TOTTENHAM COURT ROAD
CHENIES STREET
ALFRED
STORE STREET
BLOOMSBURY
MONTAGUE PLACE
MONTAGUE ST.
BEDFORD PLACE
British Museum
Middlesex Hospital
GOODGE ST.
Pied-à-Terre
WINDMILL ST.
BEDFORD SQUARE
BEDFORD AVENUE
BLOOMSBURY SQUARE
BLOOMSBURY WAY
Passione
PERCY
Chez Gérard
RATHBONE ST.
NEWMAN STREET
BERNERS STREET
GREAT RUSSELL STREET
MUSEUM ST.
COPTIC
BURY
BARTER ST.
A40
Wagamama
NEW OXFORD ST.
a.k.a
HIGH HOLBORN
Tottenham Court Road
SHAFTESBURY AV.
STUKELEY ST.
MACKLIN ST.
PARKER ST.
OXFORD STREET
SOHO SQUARE
SUTTON ROW
ST GILES HIGH ST.
ENDELL STREET
DRURY LANE
DEAN STREET
WARDOUR STREET
POLAND STREET
BERWICK ST.
NOEL ST.
Il Forno
Gay Hussar
Vasco & Piero's Pavilion
Soho Spice
Quo Vadis
Soho Soho
L'Escargot
Mela
Mon Plaisir
Neal Street Restaurant
Magno's
KEMBLE ST.
Incognico
Sri Siam
Belgo Centraal
Alastair Little
Mezzo
FRITH STREET
GREEK ST.
CHARING CROSS ROAD
A401
NEW COMPTON ST.
FLITCROFT ST.
EARLHAM ST.
MONMOUTH STREET
SHORTS GDNS.
NEAL ST.
Royal Opera House, Amphitheatre Restaurant
BROADWICK ST.
Aurora
Lindsay House
Teatro
Bertorelli's
Covent Garden
Spiga
Aroma II
Ivy
WEST ST.
LITCHFIELD ST.
SHELTON
Le Palais du Jardin
LONG ACRE
FLORAL ST.
JAMES'S ST.
RUSSELL ST.
Le Café du Jardin
French House Dining Room
OLD COMPTON
PETER ST.
LEXINGTON ST.
Circus
Randall & Aubin
SHAFTESBURY AVENUE
New World
Tokyo Diner
COVENT GARDEN
Christopher's
Kulu Kulu Sushi
Golden Dragon
GERRARD ST.
Poons
Mr. Kong
GT. NEWPORT ST.
L'Estaminet
Prospect Grill
GARRICK ST.
Sofra
Joe Allen
TAVISTOCK ST.
Fung Shing
Chuen Cheng Ku
Manzi's
Poons
CRANBOURN STREET
NEW ROW
Rules
HENRIETTA ST.
MAIDEN LANE
Titanic
BREWER STREET
Atlantic Bar and Grill
Trocadero
Livebait's Café Fish
LEICESTER SQ.
Leicester Square
ST MARTIN'S LANE
Sheekey's
BEDFORDBURY
BEDFORD ST.
GLASSHOUSE
Piccadilly Circus
Criterion
COVENTRY
Beotys
CHANDOS PLACE
THE STRAND
Odeon
Oak Room Marco Pierre White
JERMYN ST.
HAYMARKET
ORANGE STREET
IRVING
National Portrait Gallery
Corney & Barrow
WILLIAM IV ST.
National Portrait Gallery, Portrait Restaurant
JOHN ADAM ST.
VILLIERS STREET
REGENT ST.
Mitsukoshi
CHARLES II ST.
A4
SUFFOLK ST.
National Gallery, Crivelli's Garden
TRAFALGAR SQUARE
Nelson's Column
Charing Cross Station
PALL MALL EAST
Charing Cross
ST. JAMES'S SQUARE
DUKE OF YORK ST.
Duca
COCKSPUR ST.
Embankment
NORTHUMBERLAND AV.
WATERLOO PLACE
CARLTON HOUSE TERR.
ICA Café
WHITEHALL PLACE
GT. SCOTLAND YD.
PALL MALL
Admiralty Arch
WHITEHALL A3212
VICTORIA EMBANKMENT
River Thames
Ministry of Defence
HORSEGUARDS AVE.
CARLTON
THE MALL
Marlborough House
Horse Guards Parade
HORSE GUARDS ROAD
ST JAMES'S PARK
Banqueting House

MAP 16

■ Restaurant
▲ Restaurant with accommodation
○ *Round-up entry*
Combined main and round-up entries

0 40 80 miles
0 40 80 120 Kms

© Copyright

LINTON West Yorkshire **map 8**

▲ Wood Hall

Trip Lane, Linton LS22 4JA
TEL: (01937) 587271 FAX: (01937) 584353
EMAIL: woodhall@arcadianhotels.co.uk
WEB SITE: www.arcadianhotels.co.uk
from Wetherby take A661 N for ½m, turn left to Sicklinghall and Linton, then left to Linton and Wood Hall, turn right in Linton opposite Windmill pub, continue 2m along single-track road

COOKING **3**
MODERN BRITISH
£24–£56

This Grade II listed Georgian hall, set in 100 acres of parkland, brings together a restaurant, hotel and health club. Dark wood panelling, fleur-de-lis motifs and green and white striped wallpaper create a formal, traditional atmosphere, though menus present classic and modern ideas in equal measure, resulting in dishes such as smoked haddock and Welsh rarebit fishcake with salsa verde, baked guinea-fowl suprême with a sage jus, and roast lamb with herbed Yorkshire pudding. Bubble and squeak with glazed goat's cheese and basil olive oil is marked V for vegetarian, while grilled sea bass with potato and tomato salad and a vanilla cappuccino earns an H for low fat content. Finish perhaps with a light and enjoyable Bakewell tart, or traditional rhubarb crumble (made to a recipe supplied by the chef's grandma). Service has had its off days, but at best has been 'swift and efficient'. Wines run to 140 bottles with many classic French names. Look towards the back of the list for reasonable New World drinking around £20. Eight house selections start at £12.50.

CHEF: Phillip Pomfret PROPRIETOR: Hand Picked Hotels OPEN: Mon to Fri L 12 to 2.30, Sun L 12.30 to 3, all week D 7 to 10 (9.30 Sat and Sun) MEALS: alc (main courses £14.50 to £20). Set L Mon to Fri £15.95, Set L Sun £14.25, Set D £24.95. Light meals and snacks available SERVICE: not inc CARDS: Amex, Delta, Diners, MasterCard, Switch, Visa DETAILS: 60 seats. Private parties: 20 main room, 10 to 100 private rooms. Car park. Vegetarian meals. No children under 5. Children's helpings. No smoking in dining room. Wheelchair access (also WC). Music ACCOMMODATION: 42 rooms, all with bath/shower. TV. Phone. Room only £90 to £125. Rooms for disabled. Baby facilities. Swimming pool. Fishing (£5)

LITTLE SHELFORD Cambridgeshire **map 6**

Sycamore House

1 Church Street, Little Shelford CB2 5HG
TEL: (01223) 843396

COOKING **4**
MODERN BRITISH
£32–£39

All is neat, uncluttered and unshowy in this detached old house in a quiet residential area of the village. Plain wooden chairs and white linen are the backdrop to a daily-changing menu of four starters and four mains, separated by a fresh, colourful salad. Fine-quality raw materials are treated in a straightforward, uncomplicated manner (saucing is minimal) with strong flavours often to the fore: a starter of black pudding fritters with horseradish, or a main course of first-class pan-fried fillet of beef with nothing more than melted Cashel blue and roughly mashed potato for company.

Meals are prepared with a degree of technical proficiency, yet don't attempt anything fancier than the kitchen can comfortably handle: a mix of roughly chopped prawns, cucumber and herbs in a wobbly cream cheese mousse to start, and a brandy-snap basket filled with ice cream (professionally made Grand Marnier for one visitor) to finish. Susan Sharpe shines like a beacon front-of-house, providing observant, sensitive and well-paced service. Fine wines at very fair prices are the province of a compact round-the-world list: Guigal's 1996 Côte-Rôtie for £26.45 and Rockford, Basket Press Shiraz 1996, from Australia at £22, to name but two. French house wines start at £9.95.

CHEF: Michael Sharpe PROPRIETORS: Michael and Susan Sharpe OPEN: Tue to Sat D only 7.30 to 9 CLOSED: Christmas MEALS: Set D £23.50 SERVICE: not inc, card slips closed CARDS: Delta, MasterCard, Switch, Visa DETAILS: 24 seats. Private parties: 24 main room. Car park. Vegetarian meals. No children under 12. No smoking in dining room. No music (£5)

LIVERPOOL Merseyside **map 8**

Becher's Brook

29A Hope Street, L1 9BQ
TEL: (0151) 707 0005 FAX: (0151) 708 7011

COOKING 5
GLOBAL
£25–£90

Hard by the city's two cathedrals and the Everyman Theatre, Becher's Brook takes its name from Aintree's famed Grand National jump. The restaurant is run by a Canadian with a penchant for Inuit art, which hangs liberally on the plain walls, while the kitchen takes a lively interest in whatever's going: from an all-day breakfast terrine on toasted molasses bread (incorporating baked beans, grilled tomato and sweetbreads), to braised veal shank with langoustine gumbo and deep fried okra. Not all dishes make such a dramatically global impact, but there is interest at every turn, in an oriental mushroom consomme with prawn won tons and quail's egg, or in spanakopitta with barley and ratatouille. Desserts pick up the baton, in the shape of apple and Cheddar rissoles, flavoured with tarragon and served with calvados and cinnamon ice cream, but also make room for a more homely vanilla mousse with meringue. Service is friendly and efficient, although it could be more knowledgeable, especially about wines. A 70-plus wine list is arranged by style and character, and offers a fair number of bottles under £20. House wines are £13.75, and six wines are available by the glass.

CHEFS: David Cooke and Gerard Hogan PROPRIETOR: Becher's Brook Ltd OPEN: Mon to Fri L 12 to 2.30, Mon to Sat D 5 to 10 CLOSED: Christmas, 31 Dec, bank hols MEALS: alc (main courses L £6 to £8, D £12.50 to £21). Set L £17.50, Set D 5 to 7 £17.50 to £68 SERVICE: not inc, 10% (optional) for parties of 8 or more CARDS: Amex, Delta, Diners, MasterCard, Switch, Visa DETAILS: 38 seats. Private parties: 38 main room. Vegetarian meals. Children's helpings. No children under 7. No smoking in dining room. Wheelchair access (not WC). Music (£5)

£ means that it is possible to have a three-course meal, including coffee, half a bottle of house wine and service for £25 or less per person, at any time the restaurant is open, i.e. at dinner as well as lunch. It may be possible to spend considerably more than this, but by choosing carefully you should find £25 or less achievable.

Far East £

27–35 Berry Street, Liverpool L1 9DF
TEL: (0151) 709 3141 FAX: (0151) 708 9798

COOKING 1
CHINESE
£14–£47

Old Chinatown customs persist here, including ultra-basic décor. On the other hand, there is also the sensible notion of offering many starters in large or small portions. The menu runs to over 200 numbered dishes, as well as 'today's specials' and vegetarian options. It is short on seafood (only two dozen prawn and squid choices) but long on meat and poultry. Most of it is familiar stuff, but curiosities include flambé satay kebabs, and seafood hotpots incorporating fried rice. Dim sum include a wide choice of dumplings, and seekers after authenticity will relish 'duck's web with four meats wrapped'. House wines are £9.10, and prices throughout the list are low.

CHEF: C.K. Cheung PROPRIETOR: Ma-Sang Ho OPEN: all week 12 to 11.15 (1 Fri and Sat, 11 Sun) CLOSED: 25 and 26 Dec, Good Fri MEALS: alc (main courses £5 to £11). Set L £6 (2 courses) to £6.80, Set D £15.50 to £17.50 SERVICE: not inc CARDS: Amex, Diners, MasterCard, Switch, Visa DETAILS: 240 seats. Private parties: 220 main room. Car park. Vegetarian meals. No smoking in 1 dining room. Wheelchair access (not WC). Music. Air-conditioned

Shangri La £

NEW ENTRY

Ashcroft Buildings, 37 Victoria Street,
Liverpool L1 6BQ
TEL: (0151) 227 2707 FAX: (0151) 236 6560

COOKING 2
CHINESE
£21–£45

Ornamental woodwork and dragons' heads adorn the walls of this huge city-centre restaurant, decorated in reds, greens and golds. The long carte includes authentic hotpots, while set menus offer good value, but dim sum appear to be the forte. Notable successes have included steamed dumplings with thin, light pastry concealing mixture of prawn and scallop, fresh char siu cheung fun, and guo-tieh (Peking dumplings), given a lift with crisp pastry and a good dose of ginger. Steamed whelks come 'as expected, chewy and rubbery', and moreish turnip cake is a distant relation of bubble and squeak. One Sunday lunchtime visitor (the best time to go) found the English version of the menu rather too concise, but was able to order from the full Chinese list with the aid of helpful and caring staff. Out of 40 clearly described wines, only champagne is over £21.50; house wines are £9.80.

CHEF: Mr Huang PROPRIETOR: Mr Ho OPEN: all week 12 to 2.30, 6 to 11.30 (3am Fri and Sat) CLOSED: 25 Dec MEALS: alc (main courses £7 to £10). Set L £5.10, Set D £14 (min 2) to £24 (min 4) SERVICE: not inc CARDS: Amex, Delta, Diners, MasterCard, Switch, Visa DETAILS: 350 seats. Private parties: 100 main room, 90 private room. Vegetarian meals. Music. Air-conditioned

'The waiter recited the contents of the blackboard, although it was fully visible, but he pronounced the asperges hollandaise as "asparagus with Dutch sauce".'
(On eating in London)

60 Hope Street

NEW ENTRY

60 Hope Street, Liverpool L1 9BZ
TEL: (0151) 707 6060 FAX: (0151) 707 6016
EMAIL: hopestreet.60@btinternet.com

COOKING **4**
MODERN EUROPEAN
£29–£55

With Becher's Brook, Ziba (see entries) and this newcomer all within a few hundred yards of each other, plus another new entry (Shangri La), the comparatively barren years of the past decade in Liverpool would seem to be over. The end-of-terrace, double-fronted Georgian house, not far from the Philharmonic Hall, contains a basement café bar and ground-floor restaurant, where deep blues and reds help to create a feeling of warmth and luxury amid stripped floorboards and light wood tables. Husband and wife Colin and Holly Manning oversee service, while brother Gary takes charge of the kitchen, cooking a manageable selection of dishes in modern European brasserie style, with an eye for some interesting juxtapositions: tea-smoked duckling with pear relish, 'treacle beef' with rösti and rocket, and Asian crab omelette with soy dressing.

The concentration on doing simple things well has produced a fine open ravioli of goats' cheese and red pepper, and moist sea bass with Jerusalem artichokes. Well-defined flavours flow from a combination of prime materials and sharp execution: lightly seared scallops have come on a bed of crushed new Jersey Royal potatoes and tabouleh, a blend that worked better than might be expected. The house speciality dessert, worthy of Gary Rhodes, is a very British deep-fried jam sandwich with Carnation milk ice cream. Service is friendly and unobtrusive, yet knowledgeable and professional. House champagne comes recommended on a well-spread list of around 60 wines at par-for-the-course prices, starting around £11.

CHEF: Gary Manning PROPRIETORS: Colin and Holly Manning, and Gary Manning OPEN: Tue to Fri and Sun L 12 to 2.30, Tue to Sat D 7 to 10.30 CLOSED: 25 and 26 Dec MEALS: alc (main courses £10.50 to £17) SERVICE: not inc, 10% for parties of 10 or more CARDS: Delta, MasterCard, Switch, Visa DETAILS: 80 seats. Private parties: 100 main room, 30 private room. Vegetarian meals. Children's helpings. No-smoking area. Music. Air-conditioned

Tai Pan £

W.H. Lung Building, Great Howard Street,
Liverpool L5 9TZ
TEL: (0151) 207 3888 FAX: (0151) 207 0100

COOKING **5**
CHINESE
£15–£44

Some two miles north of the city centre above a large Chinese supermarket, Tai Pan has inherited many features of the Manchester original (see entry), though in the opinion of an inspector, the infant now excels the parent. Food-wise, Tai Pan operates at two levels. It has an English menu, with all the usual suspects from crispy duck pancakes to sweet-and-sour pork, but the best dishes, and the best value, are on the Chinese-only menu.

High points from the latter have included impressively moist and tender whole steamed bass; stewed duck garnished with 'eight treasures', including king prawns, scallops, squid, chicken and liver; pei pa (balls of minced fried beancurd flavoured with Chinese mushroom, spring onions and dried shrimp); and 'wonderfully earthy' crispy pig's intestine. Crispy pigeon with spicy salt 'could have come straight from a Hong Kong kitchen', thought one visitor, though the real star of his meal was succulent beef brisket with soft, gelatinous beef tendon. Dessert might run to sago in coconut milk with diced yams. Highly rated dim sum and one-plate meals are also served. House wines are £8.50, and useful European and New World bottles rarely exceed £20.

CHEF: Garry Wan PROPRIETOR: Mr Chan OPEN: all week 12 to 11 (9.30 Sun and bank hols) MEALS: alc (main courses £6.50 to £8.50). Set L £5.45 to £8.45, Set D £14 to £25 (all min 2) SERVICE: not inc, card slips closed CARDS: Amex, Delta, Diners, MasterCard, Switch, Visa DETAILS: 300 seats. 2 seats outside. Private parties: 250 main room, 70 private room. Car park. Vegetarian meals. Wheelchair access (also WC). Music. Air-conditioned

Ziba £

15–19 Berry Street, Liverpool L1 9DF
TEL: (0151) 708 8870 FAX: (0151) 707 9926

NEW CHEF
MODERN ENGLISH
£22–£50

In the three years since it opened, this up-to-the-minute bar/brasserie in a converted car showroom on the edge of Chinatown has played a full and dynamic part in the gastronomic reinvention of Liverpool. 'Modern food in a modern space' is the chosen tag-line, and nobody familiar with this style of clean, minimal design and simple, direct, open-minded cooking would fail to concur. As the Guide went to press, however, Neil McKevitt joined the management team and his sous-chef took over the reins, continuing to serve up pork rillettes with chorizo and apple jelly, lamb pastrami on red wine risotto, and a new take on an old northern favourite, chocolate egg custard with shortbread. Service is mostly commended, and a cosmopolitan list of wines is arranged stylistically, from 'fruity aromatic white' to 'full-bodied, gutsy red'. House wines from France, Sicily and Australia start at £10 to £10.50, and a separate fine wine list, available on request, includes some impressive clarets and white Burgundy. The same owners run Number Seven Café at 7–15 Falkner Street (tel (0151) 709 9633).

CHEF: Glenn Fritter PROPRIETOR: Bispham Green Brewery Co Ltd OPEN: Mon to Sat 12 to 2, 6 to 10 (10.30 Sat) CLOSED: bank hols MEALS: alc (main courses £11 to £15.50). Set L and D £10.50 (2 courses) to £13.50 SERVICE: not inc, 10% for parties of 8 or more CARDS: Amex, Delta, MasterCard, Switch, Visa DETAILS: 120 seats. 12 seats outside. Private parties: 100 main room, 12 private room. Car park. Vegetarian meals. No smoking in 1 dining room. Wheelchair access (also WC). Music (£5)

LLANFAIR WATERDINE Shropshire map 5

▲ Waterdine

NEW ENTRY

Llanfair Waterdine LD7 1TU
TEL: (01547) 528214 FAX: (01547) 529992

COOKING **2**
MODERN BRITISH
£29–£50

After six years at Oaks in Ludlow (now renamed Hibiscus, see entry), Ken and Isabel Adams moved out to the country: to a sixteenth-century black and white longhouse further up the Teme Valley, on the Welsh border. Two pink lions guard the entrance, a fireplace takes up nearly half the bar (which has its own menu), and the eating area – a small dining room at the back – may soon be enlarged. Simple, decently made dishes are the forte: a single large raviolo, enclosing crab and scallop, in a sauce vierge; and a light yet satisfying, runny goats'-cheese soufflé inverted on to the plate. Main courses were the weaker part of an inspection meal, but desserts have included a dinner-party-style chocolate mousse, and a clear, light, golden, home-made primrose jelly (vintage 1990) served with strawberry sauce. A short, balanced wine list is sensibly priced, starting with southern French house varietals at £10.50.

CHEF: Ken Adams PROPRIETORS: Ken and Isabel Adams OPEN: Tue to Sun 12.15 to 1.45, 7.15 to 9.15 MEALS: alc (main courses £10.50 to £18). Bar meals available SERVICE: not inc, card slips closed CARDS: Delta, MasterCard, Switch, Visa DETAILS: 40 seats. 20 seats outside. Private parties: 8 main room, 8 private room. Car park. Vegetarian meals. No children under 8 in dining room. No smoking in dining room. No music ACCOMMODATION: 3 rooms, all with bath/shower. B&B £25 to £60. No children. Fishing

LOCKINGTON East Riding of Yorkshire **map 9**

▲ Rockingham Arms

52 Front Street, Lockington YO25 9SH — COOKING **4**
TEL: (01430) 810607 FAX: (01430) 810734 — MODERN EUROPEAN-PLUS
off A164, between Beverley and Driffield — £42–£50

Once a village inn, the Rockingham derives its name from a horse that won the 1833 St Leger when its more fancied stablemate was poisoned in mysterious circumstances. Guests are nowadays well-stabled if they stay overnight, for the listed redbrick building is impeccably kept, and attractively decorated with Ralph Lauren prints on curtains, tablemats and napkins. David Barker leads attentive and friendly service, while Sue Barker's simply structured menus offer five or six choices per course, plus a daily special: perhaps locally sourced crab, or confit belly of rare breed pork.

The food works equally well in seasonal mode – an elegantly balanced pea, lettuce and mint soup – as in more exotic. Szechuan spiced duck with seared duck liver on smoked aubergine shows how to spice up a menu with oriental ideas without contrivance. Mediterranean flavours range from cumin spiced lamb meatballs with tzatziki, to roast rump of lamb with charcoal grilled provençale vegetables, while desserts might include caramelised pineapple with coconut ice cream and lime syrup, or crème brûlée. Sixty wines, many below £20, include familiar Old World as well as less familiar but interesting New World names. House wine is £12.95.

CHEFS: Sue Barker and Trajan Drew PROPRIETORS: David and Sue Barker OPEN: Tue to Sat D only 7 to 10 CLOSED: Christmas, New Year, bank holidays MEALS: Set D £24.95 (2 courses) to £28.95 SERVICE: not inc CARDS: MasterCard, Switch, Visa DETAILS: 50 seats. Private parties: 14 main room. Car park. Vegetarian meals. No children. Music ACCOMMODATION: 3 rooms, all with bath/shower. TV. B&B £85 to £110 (£5)

The cuisine styles noted at the tops of entries are only an approximation, often suggested to us by the restaurants themselves. Please read the entry itself to find out more about the cooking style.

LONG CRENDON Buckinghamshire map 2

▲ Angel Inn

47 Bicester Road, Long Crendon HP18 9EE
TEL: (01844) 208268 FAX: (01844) 202497
on B4011, 2m NW of Thame

COOKING 3
SEAFOOD/PACIFIC RIM
£27–£52

Trevor Bosch specialises in fish, sourced from Billingsgate and Scotland, at this sixteenth-century beamed restaurant, which can be served either in the dining room amid fireplaces, a wattle-and-daub wall, wooden floors and tall-backed pews, or in the spacious conservatory. Much of it is given a simple Pacific Rim treatment, producing spicy moules with chillies and garden herbs, or chargrilled squid salad, followed perhaps by red snapper on oriental stir-fry vegetables sauced with spring onion and ginger.

There are enthusiastic nods to the Mediterranean too, in the form of grilled tuna steak with pipérade and basil pesto, as well as a good range of game, meat and vegetarian dishes on the printed menu. Pleasing desserts include 'Fallen Angel' (chocolate cake and coffee cream), or you could try banana tarte Tatin with rosemary ice cream. Service has been deemed 'very attentive'. Plenty of fish-friendly whites can be found on the global wine list, which trawls through France before casting its net further afield. Red wine drinkers are best served by the Californian and Australian sections. House wines start at £12.95.

CHEFS: Trevor Bosch and Donald Joyce PROPRIETOR: Angie Good OPEN: all week L 12 to 2.30 (3 Sun), Mon to Sat D 7 to 10 MEALS: alc Mon to Sat L and D (main courses £10 to £17.50). Set L Sun £13.95 (2 courses) to £15.95. Light L menu available SERVICE: not inc CARDS: Delta, MasterCard, Switch, Visa DETAILS: 75 seats. 25 seats outside. Private parties: 40 main room, 7 to 40 private rooms. Car park. Vegetarian meals. Children's helpings. No smoking in 1 dining room. Music ACCOMMODATION: 3 rooms, all with bath/shower. TV. Phone. B&B £55 to £65. Baby facilities (*The Which? Hotel Guide*) (£5)

LONG MELFORD Suffolk map 6

Scutchers Bistro

Westgate Street, Long Melford CO10 9DP
TEL: (07000) 728824 FAX: (07000) 785443
WEB SITE: www.scutchers.com

COOKING 2
MODERN BRITISH
£26–£46

Scutchers is a bright, modern-feeling, relaxed space created out of an old beamed one, with little alcoves and painted panelling. Nicholas Barrett turns out a mean soufflé – maybe Stilton, served on ratatouille chutney – and it is worth enquiring after the day's soup, which may be creamy cheese and onion with a fine texture and flavour. If sauté foie gras on mushy peas with a shallot Tatin sounds a bit ambitious for a starter, there are plenty of safer yet enticing choices at mains stage – perhaps chicken Kiev, or grilled fillet of lemon sole on parsley mash – and, later, clotted cream brûlée, or steamed marmalade pudding with Grand Marnier custard. Visitors commend the wine list's 20 or so half-bottles; full ones are grouped by grape variety, with patchy vintage information, and the house selection starts at £9.50.

CHEF: Nicholas Barrett PROPRIETORS: Nicholas and Diane Barrett OPEN: Tue to Sat 12 to 2, 7 to 9.30 CLOSED: 4 days Christmas, first week Jan, last week Aug MEALS: alc (main courses £9 to £16) SERVICE: not inc CARDS: Amex, Delta, MasterCard, Switch, Visa DETAILS: 75 seats. 45 seats outside. Private parties: 75 main room. Car park. Vegetarian meals. Children's helpings. No cigars/pipes in dining room. Wheelchair access (also WC). No music. Air-conditioned

LONGRIDGE Lancashire **map 8**

Paul Heathcote's 

104–106 Higher Road, Longridge PR3 3SY
TEL: (01772) 784969 FAX: (01772) 785713
EMAIL: longridge@Heathcotes.co.uk
WEB SITE: www.heathcotes.co.uk
from Preston, follow Town Centre signs, drive uphill through centre of Longridge, then turn left, following signs for Jeffery Hill

COOKING **6**
MODERN BRITISH
£26–£88

Three terraced stone cottages are linked by niches, arches and steps, decorated in dark red wood, with colours from grey-blue to dusky pink. It is a remarkably small scale for one of the county's leading restaurants, where lunch is something of a bargain. One who went for Sunday lunch appreciated the fact that Paul Heathcote himself was cooking; an inspector who went for dinner found Brendan Fyldes in charge and came away well pleased.

Helping to ensure consistency is a sharp modern menu that deals assertiv lely with regional ideas and humble materials. Veal tongue, sweetbreads and braised pig's cheek have been combined in a terrine (served with gribiche dressing and cep oil), while black pudding has turned up in several guises, for example made into a hash brown with Lancashire cheese, to accompany scallops with a pork crackling salad. Salting can be on the generous side, and some combinations work better than others: scallops with cinnamon is not recommended, but creamed white bean soup is, thanks not least to a paste of black pudding in the bottom of the bowl.

Among desserts, hot soufflés are a well-attested strength, a match for any in terms of texture and intensity of flavour: outstanding passion fruit at inspection, with a coconut ice cream. Coffee might be improved, service has its ups and downs, and the quality-conscious wine list is weighted in favour of those with deep pockets. A few bottles under £20 are available, including house French at £13.50.

CHEFS: Paul Heathcote and Brendan Fyldes PROPRIETOR: Paul Heathcote OPEN: Wed to Fri and Sun L 12 to 2, Wed to Sun D 7 to 9 (9.30 Sat) MEALS: alc D (main courses £16 to £28.50). Set L £16.50, Set D £38 to £60, Set D Sun £25 SERVICE: 10% (optional; max £20), card slips closed CARDS: Amex, Delta, Diners, MasterCard, Switch, Visa DETAILS: 65 seats. Private parties: 65 main room, 16 private room. Car park. Vegetarian meals. Children's helpings. No smoking in dining room. Music

Restaurateurs justifiably resent no-shows. If you quote a credit card number when booking, you may be liable for the restaurant's lost profit margin if you don't turn up. Always phone to cancel.

LOOE Cornwall map 1

Trawlers

NEW ENTRY

Buller Quay, East Looe PL13 1AH
TEL: (01503) 263593

COOKING **2**
CAJUN/PROVENÇALE SEAFOOD
£27–£44

Picture windows afford a great view of bobbing boats and seagulls performing aerobatics above this small harbourside restaurant. Both name and location (50 metres from the fish market) hint at priorities, and Todd Varnedoe, a native of Louisiana, applies the cooking style of his homeland to local supplies. Pan-fried Creole crabcakes with tangy rémoulade sauce have received endorsement from more than one reporter, while Cajun seafood gumbo at inspection was a rich spicy stew, and mixed grill of fish à la Louisiane produced a deftly cooked combination of various fish with a light dusting of spices and a delicate lemon dressing. Provençale ideas are also favoured, as in pan-fried prawns and monkfish with tomatoes, capers and herbs. Meat and vegetarian alternatives are offered, and traditional desserts might include classic crème brûlée. Service from the friendly owner is 'swift and efficient', and the short but thoughtfully compiled wine list opens with house Burgundy at £9.25 (£2.30 a glass).

CHEF: Todd Varnedoe PROPRIETORS: Roger Stamp and Cathy Styche OPEN: Tue to Sat (Mon to Sat June to Aug) D only 6.30 to 9.30 CLOSED: Jan to mid-Feb MEALS: alc (main courses £11.50 to £16.50). Set D £15.25 (2 courses) SERVICE: not inc CARDS: Amex, Delta, MasterCard, Switch, Visa DETAILS: 30 seats. Private parties: 30 main room. Vegetarian meals. Children's helpings. No children under 5. Children's helpings. No-smoking area. Wheelchair access (not WC). Occasional music (£5)

LOWER SLAUGHTER Gloucestershire map 5

▲ Lower Slaughter Manor

Lower Slaughter GL54 2HP
TEL: (01451) 820456 FAX: (01451) 822150
EMAIL: lowsmanor@aol.com
WEB SITE: www.lowerslaughter.co.uk
off A429, at sign 'The Slaughters'

COOKING **5**
ANGLO-FRENCH
£35–£75

Settings, even in the Cotswolds, don't come much more appealing than this. Gardens and clipped hedges are kept in apple pie order, the elegantly furnished house (dating from 1658) is maintained to a high standard, and the atmosphere is pleasingly 'smart casual'. Lunch is a comparatively simple affair with three options per course, while dinner extends to seven choices and pulls out all the stops. Anyone wanting to be pampered with culinary luxuries has come to the right place: foie gras usually appears in some form, lightly smoked in a terrine maybe, and a salad of pan-fried scallops has incorporated asparagus and truffle. The kitchen also takes advantage of some unusual items, such as zander, which it roasts and serves with a clam, bacon and parsley nage.

Fine-quality materials are generally subject to European treatments, along the lines of pasta with wild mushrooms, sea bass with pressed tomatoes and white beans, or roast loin of pork with cider potatoes and sage sauce. Desserts likewise put a typically lavish spin on familiar materials, coming up with mint and chocolate soufflé served with pistachio ice cream, or there may be mascarpone and lime tart with poached rhubarb. Extras amount to a meal on their own, staff are 'quiet, unobtrusive and efficient', and the wine list has an eye for the best, although deep pockets or an expense account are required to make the most of it. Half a dozen house wines run from Trimbach Pinot Blanc (£17.50) to Duboeuf Beaujolais (£25.50).

CHEF: Dominic Blake PROPRIETORS: Roy and Daphne Vaughan OPEN: all week 12.30 to 2, 7.30 to 9.30 (10 Sat) MEALS: Set L £12.95 (2 courses) to £16.95, Set D £42. Light L available SERVICE: not inc CARDS: Amex, Delta, Diners, MasterCard, Switch, Visa DETAILS: 30 seats. 15 seats outside. Private parties: 32 main room, 22 private room. Car park. Vegetarian meals. Children's helpings. No children under 8 in dining room. No smoking in dining room. Occasional music ACCOMMODATION: 16 rooms, all with bath/shower. TV. Phone. B&B £175 to £325. No children under 12 in accommodation. Swimming pool (*The Which? Hotel Guide*)

LOW LAITHE North Yorkshire **map 9**

Dusty Miller

Low Laithe, Summerbridge HG3 4BU — COOKING **6**
TEL: (01423) 780837 FAX: (01423) 780065 — ANGLO-FRENCH
on B6165, 2m SE of Pateley Bridge — £33–£57

A scattering of antiques contributes to the classy feel of this roadside restaurant with its warm atmosphere and consistently fine cooking. It typifies many of the things that appeal to reporters about their favourite places, starting with a total lack of pretension: there is 'no arrogance' and the Dennisons are utterly friendly without being familiar. Indeed, service from Elizabeth Dennison is always immaculate, and the whole operation appears totally unflappable. There is no ostentation in the cooking either, which straddles the Anglo-French divide with Beaujolais pâté, a 'rack on black' combination of roast lamb and black pudding, and chicken with chanterelles.

The excellence of raw materials is matched by skilled treatment. This is an assured place that always puts on a high-quality performance, from a fresh, tasty and generous salad of Whitby crab – 'exactly what a starter ought to be' – to rich roast duck with tart apple sauce. The practice of providing extra jus in a little sauce boat is welcomed, and extends to desserts: perhaps a well-judged vanilla sauce with blackberry and apple tart. The short, well-selected wine list fails to mention half-bottles, but around six are available, along with a couple of house wines served by the glass. Bottle prices start around £12.

CHEF: Brian Dennison PROPRIETORS: Brian and Elizabeth Dennison OPEN: Tue to Sat D only 6.30 to 11 (other times by arrangement) CLOSED: 25 and 26 Dec, 1 Jan, 2 weeks Aug/Sept MEALS: alc (main courses £16 to £20). Set D £24 SERVICE: not inc, card slips closed CARDS: Amex, MasterCard, Visa DETAILS: 45 seats. Private parties: 30 main room, 15 private room. Car park. Vegetarian meals. Children's helpings. No children under 9. No smoking in dining room. Wheelchair access (not WC). Occasional music

The text of entries is based on unsolicited reports sent in by readers, backed up by inspections conducted anonymously. The factual details under the text are from questionnaires the Guide sends to all restaurants that feature in the book.

LUDLOW Shropshire **map 5**

Courtyard £

2 Quality Square, Ludlow SY8 1AR
TEL: (01584) 878080

COOKING 1
MODERN BRITISH
£18–£39

Down a quiet cobbled alley off Ludlow's main market square, near the castle, the Courtyard is simply furnished in pink and green with bare wooden tables (sometimes shared), and with a small kitchen open to view. A varied evening carte offers plentiful choice from crab strudel, via spinach and goats'-cheese tart, to fillet of beef with potato and celeriac rösti. Lunch is from a blackboard that might come up with broccoli and Stilton quiche, a couple of soups, and moist, tender salmon fillet with chive mash and hollandaise. The cooking is straightforward, desserts run from steamed puddings to cheesecakes and baked pears, and service is welcoming and efficient. Two dozen wines start with house Australian at £9.50.

CHEF: Philip Woodhall PROPRIETOR: Jane Lloyd OPEN: Mon to Sat L 12 to 2, Thur to Sat D 7 to 9 CLOSED: 25 and 26 Dec, 1 Jan, May bank hol MEALS: alc (main courses L £5 to £7, D £7 to £13.50) SERVICE: not inc CARDS: none DETAILS: 30 seats. 8 seats outside. Private parties: 12 main room. Vegetarian meals. No smoking in dining room. Music. Air-conditioned

Hibiscus

NEW ENTRY

17 Corve Street, Ludlow SY8 1DA
TEL: (01584) 872325 FAX: (01584) 874024

COOKING 5
FRENCH
£37–£67

Ludlow can now add the game of 'musical chefs' to its list of accomplishments. As Ken Adams left to set up Waterdine in Llanfair Waterdine (see entry), Claude Bosi moved from Overton Grange (where Wayne Vicarage now cooks) to take over Oaks and convert it into Hibiscus. A lot of oak panelling remains, and its combination with rough stone walls, white tablecloths and plain glasses makes a rather spartan impression. Lunch is considered great value, and dinners are lengthy four-course affairs, although apparently small portion sizes are well judged, taking account of all the country-house-style extras that are thrown in.

Menus are renewed daily, and dishes typically ring the changes by swapping accompaniments: langoustine tails with a velouté of white beans for one visitor; the same tails with celeriac, Granny Smith and Thai curry paste for another; then the same accessories for yet another reporter's main-course cod. One visitor approved pink spring lamb (seared, sliced and fanned) with a scattering of peas *à la française*, not least because of the pleasure that such simple ingredients afford when handled well; another likewise praised veal sweetbreads with the same accompanying peas as a simply conceived dish, plainly and honestly presented.

Much of the food is inventive and confidently put together, with well-balanced and often subtle flavours, although a few seasoning, flavouring and other shortcomings took the shine off an inspection meal. Sorbets and ice creams provide a star turn, however, for two reasons: first, the sorbets (served as a pre-dessert) are unusually and delicately flavoured with hibiscus and hawthorn; and second, because a smart ice cream machine takes just three minutes to make it fresh to order. Otherwise, warm chocolate tart filled with black, sludgy, semi-runny chocolate is a hit. The pace of meals can be slow, but service from Claire Crosby is friendly, courteous and relaxed. A fair choice of half-bottles adds to the appeal of a 50-plus wine list grouped by style. House wine from Domaine Perrin is £12.50.

CHEF:Claude Bosi PROPRIETORS: Claire Crosby and Claude Bosi OPEN:Tue to Sat L 12.30 to 1.45, Mon to Sat D 7 to 10 CLOSED:Christmas MEALS:Set L £19.50 (2 courses) to £25, Set D £32.50 to £42.50 (7 courses) SERVICE:not inc, card slips closed CARDS:Delta, MasterCard, Switch, Visa DETAILS:28 seats. Private parties: 30 main room. Car park. No smoking in dining room. No music

Merchant House

Lower Corve Street, Ludlow SY8 1DU
TEL: (01584) 875438 FAX: (01584) 876927

COOKING **8**
MODERN BRITISH
£39–£47

Everything about Merchant House is unostentatious. Step straight off the pavement into a plainly decorated room where oak beams, polished wooden tables, and simple cutlery and crockery contribute to a quiet, informal atmosphere. Frills are conspicuous by their absence, to the disappointment of some and the delight of many others. The cooking looks easy, which may be why some reporters seem to find it 'ordinary', but no one should underestimate the skill involved in making a professional job appear effortless. In terms of technique, taste, balance and precision, what Shaun Hill delivers on to the plate is thoroughly accomplished.

He aims for simplicity and transparency, using high-quality ingredients, many of them local, some organic (chicken 'tasting like chickens used to' for example), then timing them accurately and serving them relatively plainly. Main-course plates usually arrive with large servings of meat, a small vegetable garnish and no gimmicks. 'Finesse' perhaps describes the cooking best, in for instance risottos of just the right consistency, made with saffron and artichoke, or with tiny spring broad beans.

Fish has rightly garnered much praise, both for its outstanding freshness and deft, confident handling, typically with a light sauce: John Dory or sea bass with sweet basil and gently acidic crème fraîche to start, and either roast brill or Dover sole with velvety beurre blanc and a scattering of vegetables for main course. Among meats, Aylesbury duck has impressed, first steamed then crisply fried, the meat 'lightly pink, full of flavour, sweet and tender', served with a deeply fungoid morel sauce.

Iced nougat parfait with apricot sauce is a star turn, and pastry is a strength, notably light, crumbly shortcrust for tarts of plum, or rhubarb with a creamy ginger custard. Cheeses (usually a trio) are kept in first-rate condition, and appetisers and 'irresistible' bread (especially the milk roll) are as good as everything else. Quiet service from Anja Hill and a helper is generally efficient and helpful. Value is almost universally considered good (service is included in the price), not least when it comes to a 50-strong, sharply chosen wine list. House Aquilea del Friuli white is £13.50, Ornellaia Le Volte red is £14.50.

CHEF: Shaun Hill PROPRIETORS: Shaun and Anja Hill OPEN: Fri and Sat L 12.30 to 2, Tue to Sat D 7 to 9 CLOSED: 1 week Christmas, 1 week spring MEALS: Set L and D £29.50 SERVICE: net prices, card slips closed CARDS: Delta, MasterCard, Switch, Visa DETAILS: 24 seats. Private parties: 8 main room. No smoking in dining room. Wheelchair access (not WC). No music

▲ Mr Underhill's

Dinham Weir, Ludlow SY8 1EH
TEL: (01584) 874431

COOKING **7**
MODERN EUROPEAN
£37–£44

Below the castle walls, beside the River Teme, Mr Underhill's is considered a 'little gem of a place'. A re-landscaped garden has opened up more river frontage, the atmosphere is relaxed, and the place manages to be comfortable without going in for all the usual country-house trappings. There is no choice before dessert (preferences are checked by phone in advance), but reporters are happy with this arrangement given the quality of the cooking. Meals begin with a small tartlet (perhaps cheese, egg and bacon) which might be followed by an attractively presented warm salad of asparagus with herb risotto pancake, or a tower of moist curds of warm, undyed smoked haddock set on a beurre blanc sauce.

While the tried-and-tested repertoire may not take any risks, it does produce well-executed dishes such as seared salmon with tomato and basil sauce, or slow-cooked shoulder of Welsh lamb, taken off the bone, wrapped in filo pastry, and served with provençale vegetables and lemon-flavoured mash. The star of one meal was Springfield Farm organic chicken – its flavour 'the nearest to childhood memories' – legs marinated first, the breast simply roasted, all set on a risotto of mushrooms 'gathered that morning'.

Choice, when it finally comes, might be between first-rate chocolate mousse cake, rich Italian bread-and-butter pudding with a creamy custardy texture, or an acclaimed winter apple pudding, the warm fruit layered with brioche. Alternatively, an impressive collection of eight or ten different cheeses comes with wholemeal bread. Judy Bradley runs front of house 'with vigour', ably assisted by young helpers, and it is hard to question the value of the operation. Wines successfully achieve the stated aim of combining 'lesser-known wines with the classics, without compromising on quality or value'. A core selection from France, including interesting bottles from Pic St Loup and other up-and-coming regions, is backed up by plenty of New World stars, including a heady range of Australian reds. Prices start at £12 for house French. Half-bottles are plentiful and halving of full-bottles is open to negotiation.

CHEF: Christopher Bradley PROPRIETORS: Christopher and Judy Bradley OPEN: all week D only 7.30 to 8.30 (L by arrangement) CLOSED: some Tues MEALS: Set D £25 SERVICE: not inc CARDS: MasterCard, Visa DETAILS: 24 seats. 36 seats outside. Private parties: 8 main room. Car park. Children's helpings. No smoking in dining room. No music ACCOMMODATION: 6 rooms, all with bath/shower. TV. Phone. B&B £62.50 to £105. Fishing (*The Which? Hotel Guide*)

Restaurateurs justifiably resent no-shows. If you quote a credit card number when booking, you may be liable for the restaurant's lost profit margin if you don't turn up. Always phone to cancel.

▲ Overton Grange

Ludlow SY8 4AD
TEL: (01584) 873500 FAX: (01584) 873524
WEB SITE: www.go2.co.uk/lesmarches

COOKING **5**
ANGLO-FRENCH
£27–£55

A short, narrow drive leads to a solidly comfortable house that looks the better part of a century old. The smart lounge bar, a room to linger in, looks out over green fields, while the dining room is a down-to-earth mix of oak panels and green walls. Wayne Vickerage, who in recent years has worked at Nunsmere Hall in Sandiway and at Pied-à-Terre (see entry, London), took over the kitchen in spring 2000 as Claude Bosi left to open his own restaurant, Hibiscus (see entry, also Ludlow). Two set-price menus operate, one with no choice, the more expensive offering five options per course, but both dedicated to sourcing high-quality materials. French poultry might include Bresse pigeon en vessie, and périgourdine duck served on choucroute with a nugget of foie gras, inside a ring of cassoulet-style baked beans.

Fish runs from Cornish crab and lobster to prime roast scallops on smoked bacon purée, and a fine piece of accurately timed turbot. Although vegetable accompaniments may be shredded so finely that they contribute little in the way of taste or texture, partnerships are often well judged, as in a starter of cannelloni filled with quail and foie gras sitting on broad beans, sprue and morels. A savoury – creamy, melting Pavé d'Affinois baked in filo with summer truffle – offers a reasonable alternative to desserts such as an assiette of plums consisting of soufflé, sorbet, jelly, croquant, Tatin and pannacotta. Service from the personable Igi Gonzalez is full of charm and vitality, and his wine recommendations are well worth taking. The list is a cosmopolitan mix of European classics and New World stars, and the Californian and Spanish selections in particular offer innovative and competitive alternatives to Bordeaux and Burgundy. Prices are fair, with house wines starting at £13.

CHEF: Wayne Vickerage PROPRIETOR: Grange Hotels Ltd OPEN: Tue to Sun L 12.15 to 1.45, Mon to Sat D 7.15 to 9.30 (10 Fri and Sat) CLOSED: last 2 weeks Jan MEALS: Set L Tue to Sat £25, Set L Sun £16.50, Set D £22.50 to £32.50 SERVICE: not inc, card slips closed CARDS: Delta, MasterCard, Switch, Visa DETAILS: 30 seats. 20 seats outside. Private parties: 60 main room, 8 to 60 private rooms. Car park. Children's helpings. No smoking in dining room. Wheelchair access (also women's WC). Occasional music ACCOMMODATION: 14 rooms, all with bath/shower. TV. Phone. B&B £57 to £120. Fishing (*The Which? Hotel Guide*) (£5)

LUND East Riding of Yorkshire **map 9**

Wellington Inn

19 The Green, Lund YO25 9TE
TEL: (01377) 217294 FAX: (01377) 217192
take B1284 out of Beverley towards Driffield and Malton

COOKING **3**
MODERN BRITISH
£29–£42

Sitting at the centre of a well-kept little village next to the church, this successful country pub features a flagstone floor, an open fire, two bars and a smart, compact, two-room restaurant. Its appeal is based on down-to-earth yet accomplished cooking and 'efficient, polite and quick' service. One reader has praised bar lunches, enjoying Madras curried prawns 'with fluffy parsleyed rice and excellent naan bread'. Restaurant meals, too, are notable for high-quality ingredients and attractive presentation. Smoked haddock fishcakes with curried apple sauce is a perennial favourite, and could be followed by loin of lamb with a port and blackcurrant jus, or fillet of sea bream roasted with parsley, oregano, chilli and lime. Desserts might include hazelnut lemon meringue with lemon sauce. The New World plays a starring role in the well-annotated wine list. Chilean house wine is £9.95.

CHEFS: Sarah Jeffery and Toby Greensides PROPRIETORS: Russell and Sarah Jeffery OPEN: Tue to Sat D only 7 to 9.30 MEALS: alc (main courses £12.50 to £15). Bar L available Tue to Sun SERVICE: not inc, card slips closed CARDS: Delta, MasterCard, Switch, Visa DETAILS: 45 seats. Private parties: 30 main room. Car park. No children under 16 in restaurant. No smoking in 1 dining room. Music

LYDFORD Devon **map 1**

Dartmoor Inn

Lydford EX20 4AY COOKING **4**
TEL: (01822) 820221 FAX: (01822) 820494 MODERN BRITISH-PLUS
on A386 Tavistock to Okehampton road £21–£47

This unassuming sixteenth-century coaching inn, with an informally rustic atmosphere, is within the Dartmoor National Park. Organic salad leaves and vegetables from St Giles on the Heath, fish from Looe, and naturally raised lamb and beef from a Launceston master butcher are some of the exemplary materials used by the seasonally led kitchen, finding their way into farmhouse sausages with mash, deep-fried cod fillet with green mayonnaise, braised oxtail with a thyme and Madeira sauce, and organic ice creams. The carte might offer red mullet soup with tapénade toasts, or crisp won tons with smoked chicken and red pepper mayonnaise, followed by marinated loin of rare-breed pork with ratatouille, or roast Cornish scallops in a warm salad with pesto and celeriac. Limited-choice set-menu menus typically run to a plate of salmon (rillettes, smoked and cold poached), followed by Gressingham duck, with maybe lemon meringue tart with clotted cream to finish. Prices on the short wine list are virtually all below £20, starting around £10.

CHEFS: Philip Burgess and Ian Brown PROPRIETORS: Karen and Philip Burgess, and Anne Voss-Bark OPEN: Tue to Sun L 12 to 2.15, Tue to Sat D 6.30 to 10 CLOSED: bank hols exc Easter Mon MEALS: alc (main courses L £6 to £14, D £9.50 to £16.50). Set L £11.75 (2 courses) to £13.75, Set D £15 (2 courses) to £18. Light L available SERVICE: not inc, card slips closed CARDS: Delta, MasterCard, Switch, Visa DETAILS: 65 seats. 25 seats outside. Private parties: 20 main room, 20 private room. Car park. Vegetarian meals. Children's helpings. No children under 5 Fri and Sat D. No smoking in dining room. Music (£5)

Report forms are at the back of the book; write a letter if you prefer; or email us at goodfoodguide@which.net

indicates that smoking is either banned altogether or that a dining-room is maintained for non-smokers. The symbol does not apply to restaurants that simply have no-smoking areas.

LYDGATE Greater Manchester map 8

▲ White Hart

51 Stockport Road, Lydgate OL4 4JJ
TEL: (01457) 872566 FAX: (01457) 875190
EMAIL: charles@thewhitehart.co.uk COOKING **5**
WEB SITE: www.thewhitehart.co.uk ANGLO-FRENCH
on A6050, 3m E of Oldham £22–£45

Expansion and refurbishment have given this old pub more bedrooms and a new kitchen. At the same time, the restaurant was re-styled as a more informal 'contemporary' brasserie to accompany the existing 'rustic, traditional' brasserie. The style of food in the latter remains much the same, with sausages (from the in-house Saddleworth Sausage Company) featuring prominently: anything from pork and leek to a meaty chicken and black pudding, with a choice of mash (well-judged bacon and cheese for one visitor). Other staples include deep-fried cheese soufflé with chilli jam, and slow-roast belly pork with peppered fillet, bok choy and tagliatelle.

The new brasserie's repertoire is in similar vein with a few more elaborate dishes, such as roast Barbary duck studded with langoustines, but John Rudden handles it all equally well, and there is 'no skimping on ingredients', from Loch Fyne salmon to Irish oysters. Rillettes have been 'the embodiment of duck', while flaked crab – bound with cream and piled on slices of smoked salmon – has been served with an oyster and watercress sauce 'tasting powerfully of the sea'. Cheeses are well reported, and are an alternative to blueberry and almond tart or cappuccino crème brûlée. An enterprising wine list digs around for inexpensive bottles (£11 is the starting point) from Italy, the south of France, Iberia and the southern hemisphere; adds a few finer ones; and offers around 30 by the glass, mostly between £2 and £4.

CHEF: John Rudden PROPRIETORS: Charles Brierley and John Rudden OPEN: restaurant Sun L 1 to 3, Tue to Sat D 6:15 to 9.30, brasserie Mon to Sat 12 to 2.30, 6 to 9.30 and Sun L 1 to 8 MEALS: brasserie alc (main courses £9.50 to £15); restaurant Set L Sun £16, Set D £24.75 SERVICE: not inc, card slips closed CARDS: Amex, Delta, MasterCard, Switch, Visa DETAILS: 105 seats. 20 seats outside. Private parties: 70 main room, 14 and 20 private rooms. Car park. Vegetarian meals. Children's helpings. No smoking in 1 dining room. Wheelchair access (also WC). Music. Air-conditioned ACCOMMODATION: 12 rooms, all with bath/shower. TV. Phone. Room only £55 to £90. Baby facilities (£5)

LYMPSTONE Devon map 1

▲ River House

The Strand, Lympstone EX8 5EY COOKING **1**
TEL: (01395) 265147 MODERN EUROPEAN/MEDITERRANEAN
EMAIL: theriverhouse@talk21.com £25–£63

Local produce is used as an article of faith in Shirley Wilkes's kitchen; so local indeed that most of the soft fruits, some vegetables and herbs come from River House's own allotment garden. The cooking blends British, French and Mediterranean modes to produce a first-course tart topped with a 'marmalade' of red onion, red pepper and melted Somerset Brie, followed by roast duck with damsons (if you catch the season). 'Flashy' fillet steak is flamed in brandy, mustard and black pepper. End with ice-cream bombe or lemon roulade. Classed-growth clarets help to push up the base price of the wine list, but the 11 house wines open at £10.75.

CHEF: Shirley Wilkes PROPRIETOR: Michael Wilkes OPEN: Tue to Sat 12 to 1.30, 7 to 9.30 CLOSED: 25 to 27 Dec, 1 and 2 Jan, bank hol Mons MEALS: Set L £15 to £37, Set D £32.50 to £37; brasserie-style menu sometimes available L SERVICE: not inc CARDS: Amex, MasterCard, Visa DETAILS: 30 seats. Private parties: 45 main room, 14 private room. Vegetarian meals. Children's helpings. No children under 6. No smoking in dining room. Wheelchair access (not WC). No music ACCOMMODATION: 3 rooms, all with bath/shower. TV. B&B £62 to £108

LYNDHURST Hampshire **map 2**

▲ Le Poussin at Parkhill

NEW ENTRY

Beaulieu Road, Lyndhurst SO43 7FZ
TEL: (023) 8028 2944 FAX: (023) 8028 3268
EMAIL: sales@lepoussinatparkhill.co.uk
WEB SITE: www.lepoussinatparkhill.co.uk
from Lyndhurst take B3056 towards Beaulieu; Le Poussin is on right after 1m (signposted)

COOKING **5**
MODERN BRITISH
£27–£48

Alex and Caroline Aitken have expanded from their single small dining room at Brockenhurst (now Simply Poussin, see entry) to two comfortably gracious high-ceilinged ones just outside Lyndhurst. Refurbishment in summer 2000 has brought new furniture, linen curtains and off-white walls. The food remains comfortingly familiar to those who knew the previous operation, taking in twice-baked cheese soufflé, smoked salmon wrapped around salmon mousse, and a selection of miniature starters.

The New Forest is a handy source of materials, notably pork (brined in beer, or pot-roasted with honey) and saddle of venison, cooked rare, accompanied by a venison 'haggis' and a red wine sauce. The penchant for fish, poultry and game is also evident in brill topped with crispy fried oyster mushrooms, and squab pigeon served with its kidney and liver. A few errors at inspection (including over-salting to a remarkable degree) indicated that the transition to a larger operation has taken some toll on the kitchen, but the food has also had its highlights, for example chunks of fresh monkfish, bass, brill, scallop, salmon and red mullet poached in a light herb-flavoured fish stock.

Desserts run to dark chocolate marquise, a hot soufflé, and perhaps a pineapple variation on tarte Tatin, while 'buffalo herds' of attentive and conscientious French staff are overseen by Caroline Aitken. The broad wine list offers many fine clarets and Burgundies alongside fashionable New World producers: Bonny Doon, Jade Mountain and Ridge dominate the Californian section. Prices are a little steep, but 30 wines by the glass and a couple of pages of intelligent house selections, mainly under £20, are redeeming features. Wine service has been reported as excellent.

Net prices *in the details at the end of an entry indicates that the prices given on a menu and on a bill are inclusive of VAT and service charge, and that this practice is clearly stated on menu and bill.*

CHEFS: Alex Aitken and Ben Streak PROPRIETOR: Le Poussin Ltd OPEN: all week 12 to 2, 7 to 9.30 MEALS: Set L £15.50, Set D £27.50 SERVICE: not inc CARDS: Amex, Delta, MasterCard, Switch, Visa DETAILS: 70 seats. Private parties: 40 main room, 40 private room. Car park. No smoking in dining room. Wheelchair access (also women's WC). No music ACCOMMODATION: 20 rooms, all with bath/shower. TV. Phone. D,B&B £70 to £150. Rooms for disabled. Swimming pool. Fishing (*The Which? Hotel Guide*)

MADINGLEY Cambridgeshire **map 6**

Three Horseshoes

High Street, Madingley CB3 8AB
TEL: (01954) 210221 FAX: (01954) 212043
of A1303, 2m W of Cambridge, close to M11 junction 13

COOKING **3**
MEDITERRANEAN/GLOBAL
£27–£45

The thatched, white-walled pub, in a pretty and finely manicured village, isn't a pub in the true sense, but more of an informal restaurant, with white damask-clothed tables in the conservatory, and polished wooden ones in the bar-diner. Lots of roasting and chargrilling are on offer, with ideas and ingredients coming from all corners of the globe. A salad of blackened sugar snap, choi sum, rice noodle, aniseed, mint and chilli may precede seared partridge breast, served with black pudding, sweet potato rösti, green bean relish and chutney.

Rosy roast beef fillet has been partnered more conventionally by lentils, white beans and leek purée, and an accomplished lemon verbena and mascarpone tart has come with a punchy, bitter compote of tamarillo and cherries. Helpful service is notably child friendly. 'Please be prepared to try something you've never heard of,' encourages Master of Wine John Hoskins at the beginning of this challenging, good-value list. Twenty wines by the glass support his statement that 'interesting' means characterful, individual, intriguing and not necessarily classic, although some of the latter do slip in. The restaurant takes a lower percentage on the more expensive bottles. House wines start at £9.75.

CHEF: Richard Stokes PROPRIETOR: Huntsbridge Ltd OPEN: all week L 12 to 2, Mon to Sat D 6.30 to 10 MEALS: alc (main courses £9 to £14.50). Set L Sun £22.50 SERVICE: not inc, 10% for parties of 10 or more, card slips closed CARDS: Amex, Delta, Diners, MasterCard, Switch, Visa DETAILS: 110 seats. 50 seats outside. Private parties: 70 main room. Car park. Vegetarian meals. Children's helpings. No smoking in dining room. Wheelchair access (not WC). No music

MAIDENCOMBE Devon **map 1**

▲ Orestone Manor

Rockhouse Lane, Maidencombe TQ1 4SX
TEL: (01803) 328098 FAX: (01803) 328336
EMAIL: manor@orestone.co.uk
WEB SITE: www.orestone.co.uk
On A379 between Torquay and Teignmouth

COOKING **2**
MODERN ENGLISH
£24–£42

Not only has the manor acquired new owners and a new chef, but it has also had a total makeover, at what appears to be no small cost. Now resembling an exotic colonial hideaway – as evocative of the Ganges as the English Riviera, according to one visitor – it boasts a drawing room with carved elephants, an exotic veranda with palms and bamboo, and a dining room where an oil painting takes up nearly a whole wall. The food remains in country-house mode, rather ambitious, and succeeding better with some dishes than others.

Expect a bit of comfort in the shape of a warm salad of bacon with black pudding and poached egg, or summer truffle shaved over wild mushroom risotto, and enjoy some fine materials such as pink and supple Gressingham duck breast sitting on a potato rösti surrounded by young vegetables. Cheeses are local, and desserts aim to soothe with cherry brandy pancakes, or a large slice of apricot and almond puff pastry with amaretto custard. Bread and appetisers are better than coffee and petits fours. A sensibly chosen and ungreedy wine list (prices start at £9.25) includes a red and a white from Devon's Sharpham Vineyard.

CHEF: Anthony Hetherington PROPRIETORS: Peter Morgan and F. Etessami OPEN: all week D only 7 to 9 MEALS: alc (main courses £9 to £18). Set D £30. Light snacks available SERVICE: net prices, card slips closed CARDS: Delta, MasterCard, Switch, Visa DETAILS: 45 seats. 20 seats outside. Private parties: 55 main room. Car park. Vegetarian meals. Children's helpings. No smoking in dining room. Wheelchair access (also WC). Occasional music ACCOMMODATION: 12 rooms, all with bath/shower. TV. Phone. B&B £50 to £160. Rooms for disabled. Baby facilities. Swimming pool

MAIDSTONE Kent map 3

Soufflé

NEW ENTRY

The Green, Bearsted, Maidstone ME14 4DN
TEL/FAX: (01622) 737065

COOKING **3**
ANGLO-FRENCH
£27–£54

Sitting beside the green, in a deeply suburban quarter of Maidstone, this converted sixteenth-century house offers fine-weather eating amid miniature fountains on the front patio, and an expensive-looking cream and burgundy dining room with small bay windows and crisp white napery. When Nick Evenden emerged from the Marco Pierre White empire he brought a few cosmopolitan ideas with him: among them a commendable starter of scallops interleaved with slices of black pudding set in a line of creamy mash.

Eye-catching presentation is a feature, for example in a green and white main course of sweet, firm sea bass, filled with a light tarragon mousse, sitting on a pile of diamond-shaped mange-tout, topped with crossed asparagus spears, in a sauce flecked with leek. Other stimulating ideas have included an offal construction that pairs pig's trotter with veal sweetbreads and morels. Sound technique is also evident in a square slice of chocolate terrine inset with a smaller square of white chocolate mousse. Pleasant and helpful service ensures that meals move at an efficient pace. The wine list doesn't exert itself much outside Bordeaux and Burgundy, so prices on average are fairly high, but house French Sauvignon and Merlot are £10.95.

Several sharp operators have tried to extort money from restaurateurs on the promise of an entry in a guidebook that has never appeared. The Good Food Guide *makes no charge for inclusion.*

CHEF: Nick Evenden PROPRIETORS: Nick and Karen Evenden OPEN: Tue to Fri and Sun L 12 to 2, Tue to Sat D 7 to 9.30 MEALS: alc Tue to Sat (main courses £16 to £17.50). Set L £13.50 (2 courses) to £16.50, Set D Tue to Fri £22.50 SERVICE: 10%, card slips closed CARDS: Amex, Delta, MasterCard, Switch, Visa DETAILS: 40 seats. 25 seats outside. Private parties: 50 main room, 20 private room. Car park. Children's helpings. No children under 7 at D. No cigars/pipes in dining room. Wheelchair access (not WC). Occasional music (£5)

MALMESBURY Wiltshire map 2

▲ Old Bell

Abbey Row, Malmesbury SN16 0AG
TEL: (01666) 822344 FAX: (01666) 825145 COOKING 4
EMAIL: woolley@luxury-hotel.demon.co.uk MODERN BRITISH
WEB SITE: www.luxury-family-hotels.co.uk £25–£44

One who remembered the wisteria-covered inn as 'pleasant, ancient and reliable' returned after an absence to find it transformed with gleaming brass and roaring fires, although the friendly, helpful service turned out to be even more striking: children are made particularly welcome. As we might expect of one of the country's oldest hostelries, there are lots of rooms in which 'to hide away from the outside world', including a relaxing dining room where an antique dresser serves as a cutlery store.

For a supplement, diners can seesaw between the carte and a set-price menu, both of which take an Anglo-Mediterranean view of life: crostini of wood pigeon breast with Italian vegetables, perhaps, or sea bass with herb risotto. Among more unusual ideas might be a starter of calves' kidneys served with a potato, onion and bacon terrine, and crab salad with a carrot and ginger sauce. Desserts inhabit the more traditional territory of glazed lemon tart, or dark chocolate fondant with pistachio ice cream. Bar snacks are available in the Great Hall. Many good bottles can be found on the classy wine list, although there is little to get excited about under £20 a bottle. House wines start at £15.

CHEF: Michael Benjamin PROPRIETORS: Nigel Chapman and Nicholas Dickinson OPEN: all week 12.30 to 7, 2.30 to 9.30; Great Hall 10 to 3, 6 to 10 MEALS: Set L £15, Set D £19.75 to £26. Light meals menu available in Great Hall SERVICE: not inc, card slips closed CARDS: Amex, Delta, Diners, MasterCard, Switch, Visa DETAILS: 60 seats. 20 seats outside. Private parties: 80 main room, 12 to 24 private rooms. Car park. Vegetarian meals. Children's helpings. Older children only at D. No smoking in dining room. No music ACCOMMODATION: 31 rooms, all with bath/shower. TV. Phone. B&B £75 to £170. Rooms for disabled. Baby facilities (*The Which? Hotel Guide*)

'Grilled "baby sea bass" looked like an anaemic farmed trout in need of a good swim at a health club, a rub-down and a meal of confit of worm followed by samphire bavarois.'
(On eating in Suffolk)

(£5) *indicates that the restaurant has elected to participate in the* Good Food Guide *voucher scheme. For full details, see page 6.*

The Guide is totally independent, accepts no free hospitality, and survives on the number of copies sold each year.

MALVERN WELLS Worcestershire **map 5**

Croque-en-Bouche

221 Wells Road, Malvern Wells WR14 4HF
TEL: (01684) 565612 FAX: (0870) 706 6282
EMAIL: mail@croque-en-bouche.co.uk
WEB SITE: www.croque-en-bouche.co.uk
on A449, 2m S of Great Malvern

COOKING **8**
MODERN EUROPEAN-PLUS
£36–£54

Chintzy curtains and potted plants help to give this Victorian former shop an appealing 'bourgeois provincial' feel. Old-fashioned craftsmanship is at the heart of the cooking, and at this level the prices are a real draw; but then this is a two-person operation, scaled down to a manageable three openings a week. The format is unchanging: an obligatory tureen of soup (perhaps thick smoked haddock with tomato and celery), followed by a choice of three fish or vegetable dishes, then three meat mains, a salad, and half a dozen desserts. Many of the dishes are themselves enduring, for example the Japanese selection (although its composition may vary).

Within this framework, however, the cooking renews itself by small degrees, building on materials such as Welsh mountain lamb, grilled Bobbington boar steaks, and Herefordshire Trelough duck. Cornish fish is a strength: skate has come with salsa, and skinless turbot has been partnered by golden yellow beetroot and a matchless orange-flavoured hollandaise. Timing tends to be conservative, while composition achieves a fine balance between interest and complexity, as in a rough-textured, subtly minted pea purée and pesto accompanying sliced honey-glazed duck breast. A light potato gratin is always served with main courses.

To say the salad is intriguing is an understatement, judging by one visitor's mix of cocarde, cerize, fiamma, wild rocket, erba stella and purple basil with a dressing of chopped walnuts, red onions, diced tomatoes and water melon. Puddings (considered 'beyond criticism') might include a thin shortcrust pastry tart, filled with almond frangipane and topped with blistered apricot wedges, in a light custard, accompanied by a gently flavoured cinnamon and praline ice cream. Robin Jones's manner may not endear itself to all, although when he unwinds he can be storyteller, showman, even charmer. His attitude to wines is passionate and unpretentious in equal measure. The shorter version of the list runs to 18 pages, so customers who wish to choose at leisure should request a copy by post (£3) or email (free) in advance. Over a thousand temptingly priced bottles come from all over the globe, and diners are encouraged to ask advice. A short list of house wines starting at £11.50 is one route to easy selection.

CHEF: Marion Jones PROPRIETORS: Robin and Marion Jones OPEN: Thur to Sat D only 7 to 9.30 CLOSED: 25 Dec to 1 Jan, 1 week May, 1 week Sept MEALS: Set D Thur £26.50 to £29, Set D Fri and Sat £33.50 to £37 SERVICE: net prices, card slips closed CARDS: Delta, MasterCard, Switch, Visa DETAILS: 22 seats. Private parties: 6 main room, 6 private room. No smoking in dining room. Wheelchair access (not WC). No music

---

Card slips closed *in the details at the end of an entry indicates that the total on the slips of credit cards is closed when handed over for signature.*

Planters

191–193 Wells Road, Malvern Wells WR14 4HE — COOKING **3**
TEL: (01684) 575065 — SOUTH EAST ASIAN
on A449, 3m S of Great Malvern — £28–£44

Sandra Pegg's thoroughly idiosyncratic Malvern restaurant next door to the post office is a tribute to what can be achieved with a little vision. South East Asian cooking is the order of the day, drawing influences from Sri Lanka, Thailand and Indonesia, the repertoire underpinned by Chandra de Alwis's conscientious approach. (All curry pastes and powders are made in-house from whole roasted spices.) The rijsttafel option is a good bet: for £17.50 a head, you choose from a wide array of dishes, adding tasting portions to a plate with a mound of coconut rice at its centre. Those with a stubbornly Eurocentric sense of gastronomic structure, who prefer to eat in courses, could start with deep-fried king prawns with plum and chilli sauces, before going on to Singapore sweet-and-sour duck breast, lamb cooked in yoghurt, or opar ayam (chicken in a lightly spiced coconut milk sauce). Accompaniments include roti canai (Malaysian unleavened bread), and potatoes with channa dhal, while locally made ice creams are a good way to finish. The thoughtfully annotated wine list is full of apposite flavours, and prices are eminently fair, starting at £9.

CHEF: Chandra de Alwis PROPRIETOR: Sandra Pegg OPEN: Tue to Sat D only 7 (6.30 for theatre bookings) to 9 (9.30 Fri and Sat) CLOSED: Tue Jan to Apr, 25 and 26 Dec, 31 Dec MEALS: alc (main courses £9 to £9.50). Set D £17.50 to £28.50 SERVICE: not inc, card slips closed CARDS: Delta, MasterCard, Switch, Visa DETAILS: 32 seats. Private parties: 26 main room. Vegetarian meals. No cigars/pipes in dining room. Wheelchair access (not WC). No music

MANCHESTER Greater Manchester — **map 8**

Bridgewater Hall, Charles Hallé Restaurant

Lower Mosley Street, Manchester M2 3WS
TEL: (0161) 907 9000 and 950 0000 — COOKING **3**
FAX: (0161) 950 0001 — MODERN EUROPEAN
EMAIL: box@bridgewater-hall.co.uk — £26–£32

The Hallé Orchestra's home is an impressive piece of new British architecture, a soaring glass and steel construction of hard-edged, angular grandeur. Concert-goers can be fed and watered in comfort and style both before and after the performance, and Robert Kisby has come up with some diverting dishes. Game terrine with rose petal jam is a cut above standard concert-hall fare, and may be followed by roast cod with herbed courgettes and paprika cream, or Spanish-style pork medallions with caramelised fennel and spinach. To finish, there might be roast pineapple with chocolate marquise and vanilla ice cream, while a 'gourmet selection' of British, Irish and French cheeses is served with celery, grapes and saffron pear chutney. Service is commended as 'impeccable', the ambience 'quiet and relaxed'. Chilean Cabernet and Spanish Viura-Chardonnay at £11.95 kick off a short and fairly priced wine list.

Dining rooms where music, either live or recorded, is never played are signalled by No music *in the details at the end of an entry.*

CHEF: Robert Kisby PROPRIETORS: Paul Ford and Hallogen Ltd OPEN: all week D only 5.30 to 10.30 CLOSED: Christmas, bank hols MEALS: Set D £14.50 (2 courses) to £17.95 SERVICE: not inc, card slips closed CARDS: Amex, Delta, Diners, MasterCard, Switch, Visa DETAILS: 45 seats. Private parties: 40 main room, 20 private room. Vegetarian meals. No smoking in dining room. Wheelchair access (also WC). Occasional music. Air-conditioned (£5)

Chiang Rai £

1st Floor, 762–766 Wilmslow Road, Manchester M20 2DR
TEL: (0161) 448 2277 FAX: (0161) 438 0695

COOKING **2**
THAI
£24–£38

The white-painted dining room with bare wooden floor may appear fashionably minimal or reminiscent of a staff canteen, depending on your mood, but crowds of diners ensure the atmosphere is never bleak. Successful starters have included thick, moist spicy fishcakes with a sweet dip, and a generous portion of crisp tempura of succulent prawns and vegetables. Among main courses, deep-fried trout with shredded pork and mushrooms has been appreciated, while green chicken curry with aubergines provided 'real flavour impact'. Otherwise the repertoire runs to pla lat prik (deep-fried three-flavoured fish with hot chilli), and poysien (seven meats and vegetables stir-fried with vermicelli noodles). Vegetarians have a separate menu offering interesting dishes ranging from fried potato with mushrooms and ginger to hot jungle curry. Service, overseen by Mrs Parkhouse, compensates with enthusiasm for what it lacks in panache. House wine is £9.50.

CHEF: Andy Parkhouse PROPRIETORS: Mr and Mrs Parkhouse OPEN: Tue to Fri L 12 to 2, Tue to Sat D 6 to 10.30 CLOSED: bank hols MEALS: alc (main courses £7 to £10). Set L £5 to £9, Set D £42.60 (for 2 people) to £88.75 (for 4 people) SERVICE: not inc, 10% for parties of 7 or more; card slips closed CARDS: Amex, Delta, Diners, MasterCard, Switch, Visa DETAILS: 90 seats. Private parties: 100 main room, 80 private room. Vegetarian meals. Children's helpings. Music

▲ Crowne Plaza Midland, French Restaurant 

Peter Street, Manchester M60 2DS
TEL: (0161) 236 3333 FAX: (0161) 932 4100
WEB SITE: www.crowneplaza.co.uk

COOKING **3**
FRENCH
£43–£77

Part of an international hotel catering for the business traveller, the French Restaurant offers a comfortable, ornate, if rather formal dining room replete with chandeliers, pink wallpaper, wood panelling and gilt-framed portraits. Luxuries pepper the menu, from truffles to foie gras by way of lobster and Bresse pigeon, but it is also happy to deal in rabbit (pot-roast saddle and confit leg) and oxtail (in a starter sausage with creamed potato and horseradish).

The cooking aspires to a version of complex, classical French food, which is delivered with due competence rather than passion. Given the skills demonstrated at inspection, the kitchen may be setting its sights rather high, although it did produce tender roast quail with Puy lentils and beetroot crisps, and well-timed halibut with a generous, creamy casserole of shellfish. Among desserts, layers of filo pastry interspersed with pear purée and honey-roast red fruits has impressed. Service goes through the dome-lifting motions, and despite the corporate feel, staff are friendly and make a genuine effort. Wines are a bit ordinary and unfocused for their price: house French is £13.50. The hotel's other dining option, the Trafford Room, is under a different chef and produces more informal, brasserie-style cooking.

CHEF: Simon Holling PROPRIETOR: Bass Hotels and Resorts OPEN: Mon to Sat D only 7.30 to 10.30 MEALS: alc (main courses £20 to £24.50). Set D Mon to Thur £29 SERVICE: not inc, card slips closed CARDS: Amex, Delta, Diners, MasterCard, Switch, Visa DETAILS: 45 seats. Private parties: 450 main room, 450 private room. Vegetarian meals. Children's helpings. Wheelchair access (also WC). Music. Air-conditioned ACCOMMODATION: 303 rooms, all with bath/shower. TV. Phone. Room only £99 to £155. Rooms for disabled. Baby facilities. Swimming pool (*The Which? Hotel Guide*) (£5)

Greens £

NEW ENTRY

43 Lapwing Lane, West Didsbury, Manchester M20 2NT
TEL: (0161) 434 4259 FAX: (0161) 448 2098

COOKING **1**
GLOBAL VEGETARIAN
£13–£31

Seventy-five per cent of his customers are carnivores, according to Simon Rimmer, confirming his philosophy that interesting vegetarian food can appeal across the board. Paintings of elephants decorate the walls of the converted end-of terrace shop, and the kitchen's modern ideas mix styles and ingredients from different countries including Vietnam (for rice-paper rolls served with a hot dipping sauce), and Indonesia (for fried sweet potato, bean sprouts, radish and peanuts layered with crispy won ton papers). A fresh and enticing pea, avocado, mint and rocket salad may precede main courses such as a convincingly spiced green Thai sweet potato curry, accompanied by a mould of jasmine rice, or Santa Fe salad, a variation on the Caesar theme involving avocado, red kidney beans and a chilli-spiked dressing. Desserts are well reported, from lime cheesecake to a 'classic' summer pudding. Service is efficient and pleasant. Greens is unlicensed, but no corkage is charged for BYO.

CHEF: Darren Chapman PROPRIETORS: Simon Connolly and Simon Rimmer OPEN: Tue to Fri and Sun L 12 to 2 (2.30 Sun), all week D 5.30 to 10.30 CLOSED: bank hols MEALS: alc (main courses £5 to £10). Set L Sun £10 (2 courses), Set D Tue to Sat 5.30 to 7 £10 (2 courses), Set D Sun and Mon £10 (2 courses). BYO (no corkage) SERVICE: not inc CARDS: Delta, MasterCard, Switch, Visa DETAILS: 36 seats. 8 seats outside. Private parties: 40 main room. Vegetarian meals. Children's helpings. No cigars/pipes in dining room. Music

Koreana £

Kings House, 40A King Street West, Manchester M3 2WY
TEL: (0161) 832 4330 FAX: (0161) 832 2293

COOKING **2**
KOREAN
£12–£36

Claiming to be the only place for Korean food outside London, this family-run restaurant offers nearly the whole national repertoire, in the form of an extensive carte plus several set menus. Chinese influences also show in stir-fries and hot-pots, and Japanese sushi and cold noodles. Vegetarian dishes include japchae (Korean for chop suey) of stir-fried glass noodles with mixed vegetables. Kim-chee, the great Korean pickle-cum-condiment-cum-vegetable, appears in miniature pancakes made from potato, beef and peas, as well as in various hot-pots, and above all as a side-dish with anything. Galbi (grilled beef-ribs) are another popular speciality, and, for more adventurous tastes, yook hwae is a wonderful version of beef tartare with oriental pear and a subtle sesame dressing. The hospitality of the owners and pleasantly rustic setting add to the enjoyment of the modestly priced food. Korean rice wine, plum wine and beer appear on a short French-dominated list. Prices start at £7.95.

CHEFS: Mrs H. Kim and Cheung Hong PROPRIETOR: Koreana Ltd OPEN: Mon to Fri L 12 to 2.30, Mon to Sat D 6.30 (5.30 Sat) to 10.30 (11 Fri) CLOSED: Christmas, L bank hols MEALS: alc (main courses £6.50 to £8). Set L £4.50 to £9.90 (all 2 courses), Set D £9.90 (2 courses) to £17.50 SERVICE: not inc, card slips closed CARDS: Amex, Delta, Diners, MasterCard, Switch, Visa DETAILS: 60 seats. Private parties: 60 main room. Vegetarian meals. Children's helpings. Music (£5)

Kosmos Taverna £

248 Wilmslow Road, Fallowfield, Manchester M14 6LD
TEL: (0161) 225 9106 FAX: (0161) 256 4442

COOKING 2
GREEK
£18–£40

In its twentieth year in 2001, Kosmos is still very much an authentic no-frills Greek taverna. It bravely tries to evoke the Hellenic countryside and seascape in the Manchester suburbs, both in its decoration (the long, well-worn room is adorned with a hotchpotch of Greek memorabilia) and its food. The lengthy menu incorporates salads, various dips made in-house – skortalia (Greek aïoli), for instance – and 20-plus starters ranging from aubergines filled with tomatoes, peppers and herbs, to grilled sardines wrapped in vine leaves. Main courses include chargrilled meats and fish, melting kleftiko, and weekly specials such as chargrilled marinated quail. Typical Greek desserts populate the sweets trolley, and Greece and Cyprus dominate the wine list, with house wine £12 a litre.

CHEF: Loulla Astin PROPRIETORS: Stewart and Loulla Astin OPEN: Sun L 1 to 5, all week D 6 to 11.30 (12 Fri and Sat) CLOSED: 25 Dec, 1 Jan MEALS: alc (main courses £6.50 to £13.50). Set L Sun £8.95, Set D 6 to 7.30 £8.95, Set D £13 to £15 SERVICE: not inc CARDS: Amex, Delta, MasterCard, Switch, Visa DETAILS: 92 seats. Private parties: 45 main room. Vegetarian meals. Children's helpings. No cigars/pipes in dining room. Wheelchair access (not WC). Music. Air-conditioned (£5)

Lime Tree

8 Lapwing Lane, West Didsbury, Manchester M20 2WS
TEL/FAX: (0161) 445 1217
WEB SITE: www.thelimetree.com

COOKING 2
GLOBAL
£25–£43

Diners get two and a quarter hours in which to eat, drink and pay up, such is the popularity of Patrick Hannity's reliable brasserie near Withington Hospital in this buzzing suburb. Jeans are just as welcome as strappy little numbers, and the mood of 'lively and romantic, modern and intimate' goes down well. Damien Kay's modern British starter repertoire encompasses oxtail soup with herb dumplings, smoked haddock fritters with lime and caper mayonnaise, and roast duck breast with black pudding and lentils. Mediterranean and oriental tendencies at main-course stage might produce Thai chicken breast with wok-fried vegetables, or loin of lamb with roast vegetables and a sun-dried tomato jus. Puddings, listed with recommended dessert wines, range from tarte Tatin to chocolate truffle cake. An affordable range of wines from France, Italy, Spain, and the New World will keep both traditionalists and modernists content. Four wines of the month combine good value and interest, while another four house wines, from France and Chile, are £9.95.

CHEF: Damien Kay PROPRIETOR: Patrick Hannity OPEN: Tue to Fri and Sun L 12 to 2.30, all week D 6 to 10.30 CLOSED: 25 and 26 Dec, 1 Jan, bank hol Mons MEALS: alc (main courses £6.50 to £14.50). Set L Tue to Fri £9.95 (2 courses), Set L Sun £12.95, Set D 6 to 7 £9.95 (2 courses) SERVICE: not inc, 10% for parties of 8 or more CARDS: Amex, Delta, MasterCard, Switch, Visa DETAILS: 85 seats. 20 seats outside. Vegetarian meals. Children's helpings. No smoking in 1 dining room. Wheelchair access (not WC). Music

Lincoln

1 Lincoln Square, Manchester M2 5LN COOKING **2**
TEL: (0161) 834 9000 FAX: (0161) 834 9555 GLOBAL
£26–£72

Centrally situated, in the corner of a quiet square, Lincoln evokes the feel of a 1920s transatlantic liner with its floor-to-ceiling windows, inverted cone-shaped pillars, dark-blue rounded chairs and coloured spotlights. Menus borrow ideas from around the globe, the East particularly, taking in Szechuan-roasted duck breast with pork won tons, and chicken with pumpkin gnocchi. More homespun options range from mixed grill, or cod and chips, to grilled black and white puddings with white bean purée. Fresh and well-timed materials have produced grilled grouper with haddock risotto, and pink slices of roast lamb on a mound of spinach and Mediterranean vegetables with a rosemary-scented stock reduction. Puddings may include 'light, crunchy, buttery' plum and rhubarb crumble, or banana tarte Tatin with nutmeg ice cream. Around half the bottles on the well-put-together wine list are below £20, with prices starting at £11, or £3 a glass.

CHEF: Jem O'Sullivan PROPRIETOR: Nicola Done OPEN: Sun to Fri L 12 to 3 (4 Sun), Mon to Sat D 6 to 10.30 (11 Fri and Sat) CLOSED: Christmas, bank hols MEALS: alc Mon to Sat (main courses £13.50 to £23.50). Set L Mon to Sat £14.50 (2 courses) to £16.50, Set L Sun £16.95 SERVICE: 10% (optional), card slips closed CARDS: Amex, Delta, MasterCard, Switch, Visa DETAILS: 100 seats. Private parties: 100 main room. Vegetarian meals. Wheelchair access (also WC). Music. Air-conditioned

Little Yang Sing

17 George Street, Manchester M1 4HE COOKING **2**
TEL: (0161) 228 7722 FAX: (0161) 237 9257 CHINESE
£18–£57

This is an unconventional Cantonese restaurant in many ways, not least the pleasant setting, and cloth table covers and napkins. Also innovative by Chinese standards are some surprises on the comparatively short menu. Among dim sum, available in the evening too, are chicken in rice paper, samosas of curried minced beef, and curried lamb fillet. Duck features prominently and in many forms, including steamed with dried Chinese vegetables; extra pancakes are offered with aromatic crispy duck. Among vegetarian dishes are Chinese vegetable and bean curd flapjack, and spicy yam twist, while uncommon main courses have included shredded preserved vegetable with dried bean curd, and stir-fried yam with garlic in a spicy sauce. Banquets for parties (from £19.50 to £32 a head) offer variations on popular favourites, such as stuffed savoury pork rasher, and Vietnamese-style prawn-wrapped sugar cane. House wines are £9.95 on the skilfully selected list.

CHEF: T.B. Phuong PROPRIETOR: L.Y.S. Ltd OPEN: all week 12 to 11.30 (12.30 Sat) CLOSED: 25 Dec MEALS: alc (main courses £7 to £12.50). Set L 12 to 5.30 £9.95, Set D £17 to £32 (min 2 to 5 people for some set meals) SERVICE: 10% CARDS: Amex, Delta, MasterCard, Switch, Visa DETAILS: 90 seats. Private parties: 90 main room. Vegetarian meals. Children's helpings. Music. Air-conditioned

Mash

40 Chorlton Street, Manchester M1 3HW
TEL: (0161) 661 6161 FAX: (0161) 661 6060

COOKING **4**
MEDITERRANEAN
£27–£46

The northern outpost of Oliver Peyton's empire has contracted a little. Air, which was the top-floor dining-room of this warehouse conversion on the corner of Canal Street, is no more, and Paul Wadham now concentrates his efforts in the first-floor's glossy green brasserie. A central shaft houses the brewing equipment, for beer is made here too.

Wholesome Mediterranean flavours are the principal feature of the food, with aubergine and mozzarella salads, risottos, sun-dried tomatoes and olive oil much in evidence. Brianzetta, a sweet-cured Italian ham, comes with a corn pancake, capers, rocket and roasted red pepper, while pizzas are unusually topped with such items as confit duck with plum sauce and Chinese greens, or smoked salmon and fromage frais. Main-course meats are big on vivid flavours, as in Goosnargh chicken breast on spinach, shallots, lentils and ginger, with a chillied-up coriander salsa. To finish, try chocolate parfait with crunchy nut brittle, pineapple pavlova with coconut ice cream, or British and Irish cheeses. Relaxed and informal service suits the mood. Wines are varietally arranged, and cover a good spread of styles, but prices are a touch stiff. House Languedoc is £13.

CHEF: Paul Wadham PROPRIETOR: Oliver Peyton OPEN: Mon to Sat 12 to 3, 5 to 11 (12 Thur to Sat) CLOSED: 25 and 26 Dec, 1 Jan, Easter Sun and Mon MEALS: alc (main courses £5.50 to £13) SERVICE: 10% (optional), card slips closed CARDS: Amex, Delta, Diners, MasterCard, Switch, Visa DETAILS: 80 seats. Private parties: 80 main room. Vegetarian meals. Wheelchair access (also WC). Music. Air-conditioned

The Guide relies on feedback from its readers. Especially welcome are reports on new restaurants appearing in the book for the first time. All letters to the Guide are acknowledged.

All entries, including Round-ups, are fully indexed at the back of the Guide.

Moss Nook

Ringway Road, M22 5WD | COOKING **6**
TEL: (0161) 437 4778 FAX: (0161) 498 8089 | CLASSIC ENGLISH
on B5166, 1m from Manchester Airport | £26–£76

In an unlikely spot just a mile from the airport, Moss Nook welcomes with art nouveau-style stained glass, polished wood, plenty of lace, and 'lots of fuss'. Seriousness of purpose, indicated by low comfortable chairs at well-spaced tables, is confirmed by an ambitious menu involving classy materials, from lobster salad, via Welsh lamb and Lunesdale duckling, to turbot: in a twice-baked souffle with asparagus, or accurately timed and simply served with beurre blanc. While a strong traditional vein runs through the kitchen, it is not averse to a coriander and chilli lime dressing for spiced chicken breast, or a well-balanced starter of king prawns in a sweet and sour sauce with basmati rice and almonds.

Presentation is a strong point, all the more effective for its lack of frills, be it a starter of pan-fried foie gras on rösti with morels and Madeira jus, or a main course of tuna, turbot, salmon and scallop with a red pepper sauce. When it comes to desserts, it is difficult to beat the Grand Selection, taking in a tiny syrup pudding, raspberry meringue, chocolate cup, brandy-snap cone, hazelnut and toffee torte, and vanilla ice cream hidden in a spun sugar dome. Alternatively, English and French cheeses are properly served. Unobtrusive and professional service adds to the appeal, and while prices may seem high, they include lots of extras. A commendable French-based wine list makes significant nods to the New World and other parts of the Old. The majority of bottles are over £20, but house wines start at £9.95.

CHEF: Kevin Lofthouse PROPRIETORS: Pauline and Derek Harrison OPEN: Tue to Fri L 12 to 1.30, Tue to Sat D 7 to 9.30 CLOSED: 2 weeks from 24 Dec MEALS: alc (main courses £19.50 to £28). Set L £18.50, Set D £31.50 (whole tables only) SERVICE: not inc, card slips closed CARDS: Amex, Delta, MasterCard, Switch, Visa DETAILS: 65 seats. 20 seats outside. Private parties: 55 main room. Car park. Vegetarian meals. No children under 12. No pipes in dining room. No music

New Emperor

52–56 George Street, Manchester M1 4FH
TEL: (0161) 228 2883 FAX: (0161) 228 6620 | COOKING **1**
EMAIL: reservations@newemperor.co.uk | CHINESE
WEB SITE: www.newemperor.co.uk | £26–£61

Even early evening on a weekday, New Emperor can be busy with mainly Chinese families. The usual encyclopedic carte also offers a short list of dim sum, and at lunchtime there is a buffet. For a more authentic Chinese meal, consider something from the category 'main course noodles in soup': perhaps crabmeat and egg, or roast pork, ginger and spring onion. Those daunted by the vast menu will find banquets rather more adventurous than usual, adding extra dishes for extra diners. The attractions include pan-fried asparagus with garlic, steamed halibut or sea bass, and, on the most expensive, lobster in a spicy sauce preceded by shredded duck soup, and dim sum with seaweed. House wines are £9.90, with some interesting bottles among the other 40 or so.

CHEF: Tommy Chan PROPRIETOR: K.L Lee OPEN: all week 12 to 11.45 (12.45 Sat, 10.45 Sun) MEALS: alc (main courses £5.50 to £15). Set L £5.50 (buffet), Set D £15.50 to £29.50 (min 2 to 6 people) SERVICE: 10% CARDS: Amex, Delta, Diners, MasterCard, Switch, Visa DETAILS: 300 seats. Private parties: 250 main room, 20 private room. Vegetarian meals. Wheelchair access (also WC). Occasional music. Air-conditioned

Nico Central

Mount Street, Manchester M60 2DS — COOKING **3**
TEL: (0161) 236 6488 FAX: (0161) 236 8897 — MODERN EUROPEAN
£26–£61

Lofty rooms with big art deco fittings, smartly set tables and attentive, efficient service bring a sense of occasion to the reasonably priced brasserie food. The accent is on straightforward dishes mostly from France, Italy and Britain. Set-price lunch offers minimal choice, pre-theatre menus marginally more, while the carte is more generous, taking in Roquefort soufflé with pears, chargrilled squid with lemon dressing and tomato salsa (one of a handful of dishes available in two sizes), and duck breast accompanied by an unusual Puy lentil and zampone pie. Capable handling has produced smooth chickpea soup with coriander and cumin, and moist and flaky cod encased in crisp, eggy and ungreasy batter, with fat chips and fresh, strongly minty pea purée. Desserts run from simple, smooth, vanilla-flecked ice cream to a beignet of rice pudding and almond with peach and ginger marmalade. Some 50 wines are evenly balanced around the £20 fulcrum, starting with house vin de pays at £12.50.

CHEF: Steven Dray PROPRIETOR: Restaurant Partnership OPEN: Mon to Fri L 12 to 2.30, all week D 6 (5.30 Sat) to 10.30 (11 Fri and Sat, 10 Sun) CLOSED: bank hols MEALS: alc exc Sun D (main courses £12 to £16.50). Set L £12.50 (2 courses) to £14.95, Set D 6 to 6.30 Mon to Sat £14.95, Set D Sun £22.50 SERVICE: 12.5% (optional), card slips closed CARDS: Amex, Delta, Diners, MasterCard, Switch, Visa DETAILS: 100 seats. Private parties: 100 main room. Vegetarian meals. Wheelchair access (not WC). Music. Air-conditioned (£5)

Ocean Treasure £

NEW ENTRY

Greenside Way, Middleton, Manchester M24 1SW — COOKING **2**
TEL: (0161) 653 6688 FAX: (0161) 653 3388 — CHINESE
EMAIL: paul@oceantreasure.co.uk — £19–£49

This large restaurant above a cash-and-carry is 'reassuringly plush' with decorative features such as fish tanks and mirrors framed in dark wood. Although styling itself as a seafood restaurant, it also lists every sort of meat, poultry and game, a term that here covers venison, ostrich and crocodile. Among a regular customer's recommendations have been Mongolian lamb with pancakes (a variation on the crispy duck theme), vermicelli soup with cuttlefish dumplings, barbecued belly pork, and dim sum, including steamed whelks with satay sauce. 'Seafood live from the sea', seasonally priced, includes turbot, lobster, and chilled drunk crab (which needs 24 hours notice). Otherwise, the long menu runs from baked stuffed tofu, salt and pepper squid, and scallops with ginseng, to cold platters of roast suckling pig and jellyfish, or spicy boneless goose feet. More mysterious items include the exotic-sounding 'Eastern pearl at night'. Wines from around the world are helpfully arranged according to style on the list, which includes useful annotations. Prices are fair, with house French £8.90.

CHEF: Chun Ming Sin PROPRIETORS: Mr Yip and Mr Lui OPEN: all week 12 to 11 (12 Fri and Sat) MEALS: alc D (main courses £6.50 to £10). Set L £3.80 to £11.50, Set D £14 to £28 SERVICE: 10%, card slips closed CARDS: Amex, Delta, Diners, MasterCard, Switch, Visa DETAILS: 250 seats. 50 seats outside. Private parties: 300 main room, 10 private room. Car park. Vegetarian meals. No smoking in dining room. Wheelchair access (also WC). Music. Air-conditioned

Pacific

NEW ENTRY

58–60 George Street, Manchester M1 4HF
TEL: (0161) 228 6668 and 6669
FAX: (0161) 236 0191

COOKING 2
CHINESE AND THAI
£31–£61

A no-smoking room is just one revolutionary feature of this smart Chinese restaurant, with its fresh, modern décor of blond wood floor, white walls and recessed lighting. Above it is a Thai restaurant, similarly attired, with its own kitchen. (A Japanese restaurant in the same building is unconnected.) An extensive dim sum menu, available from noon to 6, contains some unusual items, including har dor se (prawn, water chestnut and egg on toast and rice paper), and chi se coon (shredded tofu, chicken and Chinese mushrooms in cheese sauce wrapped in filo). The chef's specials tempt adventurous eaters with honey-glazed braised eel, prawn-stuffed scallops with chilli pepper, and classic crabmeat and egg white with seasonal vegetable. Customers can choose their own accompaniments, sauces, and even cooking methods, to match other main courses: pork chop stir-fried with either straw mushrooms or seasonal vegetables for example, served with a choice of black-bean or spicy Szechuan-style sauce.

The Thai food is praised for authoritative fieriness in green curry, and in fried soft noodles with lime leaf and chilli incorporating egg and many vegetables. Grilled marinated duck breast with tamarind sauce may provide a gentle contrast. In set banquets, dishes 'may be altered as wished with discretional extra charge if necessary'. Staff are courteous and attentive, and a pithy global wine list includes plenty of decent bottles below £15 as well as a connoisseurs' selection of first-growth clarets and grand cru Burgundies at not unreasonable prices. Four house wines, from £9.90, are also sold by the glass.

CHEF: Tony Cheung PROPRIETOR: Special Charm Co Ltd OPEN: all week, Chinese 12 to 12, Thai 12 to 3, 6 to 12 MEALS: alc (main courses £7.50 to £18). Set L £5.95 to £9.50, Set D £18.50 to £38 (some set D meals 2 people min) SERVICE: 10% CARDS: Amex, Delta, Diners, MasterCard, Switch, Visa DETAILS: 250 seats. Private parties: 120 main room, 40 and 100 private rooms. Vegetarian meals. No smoking in 1 dining room. Wheelchair access (also WC). Music. Air-conditioned

All entries in the Guide are re-researched and rewritten every year, not least because restaurant standards fluctuate. Don't rely on an out-of-date Guide.

Rhodes & Co

Waters Reach, Trafford Park, Manchester M17 1WS
TEL: (0161) 868 1900 FAX: (0161) 868 1901

COOKING **4**
MODERN BRITISH
£25–£50

Ensconced in a new hotel on the edge of Trafford Park, near United's football ground, the odds on this place becoming a runaway success would appear to be low. But successful it is, no doubt partly because of the shock-haired proprietor's popularity, but also because Ian Morgan and his large brigade turn out dishes with ease and confidence. The rectangular room with pine tables, comfortable bench seating and an open-to-view kitchen, has something of the feel of a refectory, while the lengthy carte is a showcase for the Rhodes style, which aims to brings traditional British dishes up to date with a flourish. The core repertoire – represented by poached egg Benedict, smoked haddock topped with Welsh rarebit, and braised shank of lamb with creamed potatoes – is joined by pappardelle with walnuts and Gorgonzola, and fresh, moist roast monkfish with pan-fried Parma ham and a pot of saffron-flavoured aïoli. Praiseworthy desserts have included whisky-infused rice pudding with a compote of strawberries. Well-trained staff are very pleasant and spend time chatting to customers, and around thirty wines (eight of them available by the glass) start with house French at £12.50.

CHEF: Ian Morgan PROPRIETORS: Gary Rhodes and Sodexho OPEN: Mon to Fri L 12 to 2.30, all week D 6.30 to 9.45 (9 Sun); breakfast Mon to Fri 6.30 to 9.30, Sat and Sun 7 to 10, bar snacks all week 10 to 9.45 MEALS: alc (main courses £8 to £15). Set L £11.50 (2 courses). Children's menu £10.50. Bar snack menu available SERVICE: 10% (optional), card slips closed CARDS: Amex, Delta, Diners, MasterCard, Switch, Visa DETAILS: 85 seats. Private parties: 30 main room, 10 to 80 private rooms. Car park. Vegetarian meals. Children's helpings. Wheelchair access (also WC). Music. Air-conditioned (£5)

Simply Heathcotes 

Jackson's Row, Manchester M2 5WD
TEL: (0161) 835 3536 FAX: (0161) 835 3534
EMAIL: simply@heathcotes.co.uk
WEB SITE: www.heathcotes.co.uk

COOKING **2**
MODERN ENGLISH
£24–£54

The large dining room with its hard wooden floor, curtainless windows, primary colours and plastic chairs might be ready for a bit of a spruce-up, but the smart brasserie food makes this a useful local resource. A carte of around 20 savoury dishes includes regular Heathcote favourites from black pudding to breast of Goosnargh duckling (with gnocchi and foie gras butter), but also takes in slightly less usual crab cakes with chilli coleslaw, and well-flavoured tarte Tatin of Mediterranean vegetables with a sharp plum chutney.

Timing is generally accurate – a poached egg between two big pasta tubes filled with marinated cod, and calf's liver on creamy mash – while smears of dark brown sauce seem to figure prominently: a sweet-sour version, for example, to accompany a moist terrine made with ham hock, air-dried ham and Cumberland sausage. Desserts typically aim for comfort: strawberry trifle, maybe, or bread-and-butter pudding. Reception staff are welcoming, waiting staff sometimes a little hesitant, and 40-plus wines include 10 by the glass. House French is £11.50 (£2.75 a glass).

CHEF: Andrew Owen PROPRIETOR: Paul Heathcote OPEN: all week 11.45 to 2.30, 5.30 (6 Sun) to 10 (11 Sat, 9 Sun) CLOSED: 25 and 26 Dec, 1 Jan, bank hol Mons MEALS: alc (main courses £11.50 to £18). Set L £12.50 (2 courses) to £14.50, Set D Mon to Sat 5.30 to 7 £12.50 (2 courses) to £14.50, Set D Sun £12.50 SERVICE: 10% (optional), card slips closed CARDS: Amex, Delta, Diners, MasterCard, Switch, Visa DETAILS: 170 seats. Private parties: 170 main room, 50 and 70 private rooms. Vegetarian meals. Children's helpings. Wheelchair access (also WC). Music. Air-conditioned

Steven Saunders at the Lowry **NEW ENTRY**

Pier 8, Salford Quays, Manchester M5 2AZ
TEL: (0161) 876 2121 FAX: (0161) 876 2021 — COOKING **2**
EMAIL: info@thelowry.com — MODERN BRITISH
WEB SITE: www.thelowry.com — £23–£52

With its metal-clad tower and massive buttress above the entrance, the new Lowry Museum is an impressive example of brave modern architecture. Food in the striking spilt-level dining area, with views over the quay, is also built around contemporary themes, and cooking is overseen by head chef Ian Samson under the direction of Steven Saunders, who divides his time between here and Sheene Mill (see entry, Melbourn). It takes comforting ideas in its stride – braised silverside of beef in red wine with mushrooms and bacon – but also turns out light dishes from a salad of chargrilled Tuscan vegetables to accurately seared cod with a well-judged tomato cream sauce. Textbook summer pudding ended one June dinner, or there may be a refreshing sounding orange Muscat jelly with vanilla froth. Wines are arranged to suit different main-course options, a neat idea that works well, and the choice is limited but sound. Prices start at £11.95.

CHEF: Ian Samson PROPRIETOR: The Lowry Trust OPEN: all week 12 to 3, 7.45 to 11 (5.15 to 7.30 for pre-theatre meals) MEALS: alc D (main courses £10 to £14.50). Set L £10 (2 courses) to £14, Set pre-theatre D 5.15 to 7.30 £12 (2 courses) to £16. Bar-café meals and snacks available SERVICE: 10% CARDS: none DETAILS: 250 seats. 60 seats outside. Private parties: 200 main room, 60 to 200 private rooms. Vegetarian meals. Children's helpings. No smoking in dining room. Wheelchair access (also WC). Music

Tai Pan £

Brunswick House, 81–97 Upper Brook Street, — COOKING **4**
Manchester M13 9TX — CHINESE
TEL: (0161) 273 2798 FAX: (0161) 273 1578 — £16–£48

Like its Liverpool offshoot, this spacious dining room occupies the first floor above a Chinese supermarket a couple of miles outside the town centre. Décor, although quite bright, is of secondary importance to the serious and skilful Chinese cooking. Steamed blocks of bean curd, stuffed with succulent prawns, have been served with black bean and garlic sauce and crisp choy sum, while the ability to blend complex tastes and textures in an apparently simple dish is evident in king prawns stir-fried with Chinese chives and XO sauce.

Stir-fried Dover sole has also been commended, along with shredded beef with chilli and garlic, and sliced chicken with straw mushrooms, while Sunday's dim sum have been rated on a par with Hong Kong. A mid-week set-price deal includes soup and dessert, the former perhaps a clear palate-cleansing broth of pork and dried cabbage, the latter possibly a thick, sweet, milky almond gruel. The English menu offers a decent range of conventional Westernised Chinese dishes, but anyone interested in real Chinese food should insist on the Chinese menu. Forty fairly priced wines are carefully chosen and described; house selections are £8.95.

CHEF: Hon Sun Woo PROPRIETOR: Tai Pan Restaurant Ltd OPEN: all week 12 to 11.30 (9.30 Sun) MEALS: alc (main courses £4.50 to £12). Set L £5.45 (2 courses) to £8.95, Set D £14.95 SERVICE: not inc CARDS: Amex, Delta, Diners, MasterCard, Switch, Visa DETAILS: 300 seats. Private parties: 280 main room, 100 private room. Car park. Vegetarian meals. Wheelchair access (also WC). Music. Air-conditioned

Yang Sing 🍷 £

34 Princess Street, Manchester M1 4JY
TEL: (0161) 236 2200 FAX: (0161) 236 5934
WEB SITE: www.yang-sing.co.uk

COOKING **6**
CANTONESE
£25–£59

Shortly after the last edition of the Guide was published, Yang Sing celebrated its happy return to Princess Street, where rebuilding after the fire has resulted in a place much like the original, but with a smarter bar area, and a ground-floor dining room extending the scope of the basement. Dim sum continue to be favourably reported, from standard items such as yam croquettes, sui mai, and prawn cheung fun, to more unusual large red chillies stuffed with minced prawn and deep-fried in tempura batter, cuttlefish cakes with lemon grass, and chicken and sweetcorn in filo pastry. East amiably meets West in spicy Chinese Cornish pasties with impressive flaky pastry.

The main menu similarly embraces a mix of both conventional and original ideas. Presentation is careful without being fussy, and cooking of seafood and deep-frying are strong points. Recommended dishes have included pan-fried noodles with seafood; stir-fried goujons of grouper with asparagus, mushroom and spring onion; and simple barbecued pork. A perceptible improvement in service has been remarked on by several reporters: under the guidance of Gerry Yeung, staff these days are warm, efficient and knowledgeable about the menu. However, some restriction on smoking in at least part of the premises would be welcome. A catholic range of wines sees first-growth clarets rubbing shoulders with bargain bins from the New World. Prices are fair and there is an impressive selection of liqueurs, brandies and whiskies. House Chilean red and white are £9.95

CHEF: Harry Yeung PROPRIETOR: Yang Sing Ltd OPEN: all week 12 to 11.15 (12.15 Fri and Sat, 10.15 Sun; dim sum all week 12 to 4.30) CLOSED: 25 Dec MEALS: alc (main courses £8 to £11.50). Set menus £33 (for 2 people) to £82.50 (for 5 people). Banquet menus £20 to £24 per head SERVICE: not inc CARDS: Amex, Delta, MasterCard, Switch, Visa DETAILS: 240 seats. Private parties: 240 main room, 36 to 240 private rooms. Vegetarian meals. Wheelchair access (also WC). Music. Air-conditioned

▲ *means accommodation is available.*

MANNINGTREE Essex — map 6

Stour Bay Café £

39–43 High Street, Manningtree CO11 1AH
TEL: (01206) 396687 FAX: (01206) 395462

COOKING 3
MODERN BRITISH-PLUS
£17–£44

Beams, bricks and polished floorboards set the tone in this 400-year-old Grade II listed building in the heart of Manningtree. Walls are decorated with works for sale by local artists, tables are laid with damask cloths, and main courses are served in deep soup plates: 'we are patiently waiting for the craze to die out,' wrote one couple. 'Slightly unorthodox' is how the restaurant describes its own cooking. It is nothing if not lively, helped by a few unusual ingredients, producing slices of tea-smoked pigeon on Caesar leaves to start, followed perhaps by marinated rump of lamb with celeriac skordalia. While some traditional items do feature – chicken breast with sage and onion hash brown, for example – seafood dishes tend to be more animated: perhaps grilled mackerel fillets with green vegetable curry, or marinated tiger prawns with lime, ginger and sweet cucumber pickle. Alongside homely bread-and-butter pudding and banana crème brûlée there may also be baklava. Dinner on Wednesday is sometimes accompanied by live music. A varietally organised wine list takes in some appealing bottles while rarely straying above £25.

CHEF: Stas Anastasiades PROPRIETORS: Mark and Emma Bright OPEN: Tue to Fri L 12 to 2, Tue to Sat D 7 to 9.30 CLOSED: 3 weeks from L 26 Dec MEALS: alc D (main courses £7 to £15). Set L £8.50 (2 courses) to £10, Set D Wed £13.50 (2 courses) to £15 (inc wine) SERVICE: not inc CARDS: Amex, Delta, Diners, MasterCard, Switch, Visa DETAILS: 50 seats. Private parties: 50 main room. Vegetarian meals. Wheelchair access (not WC). Music

MARSDEN West Yorkshire — map 8

▲ Olive Branch

Manchester Road, Marsden HD7 6LU
TEL: (01484) 844487 FAX: (01484) 841549
EMAIL: reservations@olivebranch.uk.com
WEB SITE: www.olivebranch.uk.com
on A62, between Slaithwaite and Marsden

COOKING 3
MODERN ENGLISH
£23–£50

Warm and welcoming, with friendly and helpful young staff, this old stone inn high in the Pennines retains something of a pub atmosphere despite its concentration on food. Meals are served in a series of small, low-ceilinged rooms (would it be too much to ask for one of them to be non-smoking?) and although there is now a written menu, other offerings are chalked on blackboards or posted busily on cards around door frames. The food scores for both quality and originality – in a salad combining Parma ham, carmelised shallots, pine nuts and raisins, all dressed with a champagne sauce – and has a penchant for positive flavours, for example in a fine chicken liver parfait enlivened by pink onion jam and a slick of chilli oil.

The Guide always appreciates hearing about changes of chef or owner.

The kitchen's admirable confidence in its own convictions is shared by visitors. Salmon might come blackened, with a creamy, zingy lime sauce, or grilled with a crab sauce and pesto. Portions tend to be generous, but those who make it to puddings may find an exemplary chocolate and cherry tart, or light and fluffy banana cheesecake. Service is efficient and unobtrusive, and a sharply chosen, global wine list generally keeps below £20 a bottle. House wines are £9.90.

CHEFS: John Lister and Paul Kewley PROPRIETORS: John and Ann Lister OPEN: Wed to Fri L 12 to 1.45, Mon to Sat D 6.30 to 9.30, Sun all day 1 to 8.30 CLOSED: 26 Dec, first 2 weeks Jan, second week Aug MEALS: alc (main courses £9.50 to £17). Set L and D 6.30 to 7.30 £14.95 SERVICE: not inc, card slips closed CARDS: Amex, Delta, MasterCard, Switch, Visa DETAILS: 68 seats. 12 seats outside. Private parties: 40 main room. Car park. Vegetarian meals. No smoking in 1 dining room. Wheelchair access (not WC). Music ACCOMMODATION: 3 rooms, all with bath/shower. TV. Phone. B&B £45 to £60 (*The Which? Hotel Guide*)

MARSH BENHAM Berkshire **map 2**

Red House

Marsh Benham RG20 8LY COOKING **2**
TEL: (01635) 582017 FAX: (01635) 581621 FRENCH
off A4 between Newbury and Hungerford £27–£48

Formerly in the Guide as the Water Rat, this red-brick thatched building on the edge of a Berkshire hamlet has re-emerged with a new name, a new chef and a complete architectural makeover. Cottagey in the bar, and like 'an elegant country-house drawing room' in the new extension, it may not be to everybody's taste, but the menu has certainly struck a few chords. Roast scallops interleaved with sliced potato and sun-dried tomato made an effective and simple starter at inspection. Main courses run the gamut from monkfish with Pommery mustard and green peppercorns to Barbary duck breast marinated in Chinese spices, with vegetables charged extra. Mousses, marshmallow and cheesecake suggest a soft-centred approach to desserts. Service is a little formal by today's standards, but attentive. The wine list is short and to the point, with house wines at £11.95.

CHEF: Rupert Rowley PROPRIETOR: Tricrane Ltd OPEN: Tue to Sun L MEALS: alc (main courses £6.50 to £14.50). Set L and D £11.50 (2 courses) to £19.50. Bar meals available SERVICE: not inc CARDS: Amex, Delta, MasterCard, Switch, Visa DETAILS: 70 seats. 25 seats outside. Private parties: 60 main room. Car park. Vegetarian meals. Children's helpings. No children under 4. No smoking in 1 dining room. No cigars/pipes in dining room. Wheelchair access (also WC). Music (£5)

MASHAM North Yorkshire **map 9**

Floodlite £

7 Silver Street, Masham HG4 4DX COOKING **5**
TEL: (01765) 689000 ENGLISH/FRENCH
off A6108, 9m NW of Ripon £19–£46

The name is etched into a big glass panel in the window of this former shop, behind which is an old-fashioned downstairs bar, and a comparatively light and airy dining room with crystal chandeliers, pink walls, dark blue fabrics, and good-value food offering 'something for all tastes'. The carte is a long one, and although there are regular fixtures – such as a creamy salmon and pike terrine – it is not afraid to take a few chances outside the European theatre of operations: with properly cooked chicken breast for example, enclosing a whole banana, served with a mild, well matched, cumin-flavoured curry sauce.

Charles Flood lays claim to some of the best supplies of game available, which might appear as firm, smooth hare pâté packed with pistachio nuts and served with a powerfully flavoured blackcurrant sauce; or young roast grouse with rösti and wild mushrooms. Although there are minor lapses now and again, the essentials include well-sourced ingredients ably presented and cooked with assurance, including four giant well-timed scallops at inspection, accompanied by a sweet lobster sauce. Desserts, too, come in for praise, from strawberry pavlova with vanilla custard, to well turned-out sorbets. Service is courteous, if reserved, and a broad selection of reasonable-value drinking from around the world starts with half a dozen Australian and French house wines under £10.

CHEF: Charles Flood PROPRIETORS: Charles and Christine Flood OPEN: Fri to Sun L 12 to 2, Tue to Sat D 7 to 9.30 MEALS: alc (main courses £9.50 to £17.50). Set L £10.50 (2 courses) to £12.50, Set D £12.50 (2 courses) to £15 SERVICE: not inc, card slips closed CARDS: Amex, Delta, MasterCard, Visa DETAILS: 36 seats. Private parties: 28 main room. Vegetarian meals. Children's helpings. No music (£5)

MATFEN Northumberland **map 10**

▲ Matfen Hall **NEW ENTRY**

Matfen NE20 0RH
TEL: (01661) 886500 FAX: (01661) 886055
EMAIL: info@matfenhall.com
WEB SITE: www.matfenhall.com

COOKING **2**
MODERN ENGLISH
£26–£54

The estate was turned into a golf course just under a decade ago, while the house – built around 1830, looking Jacobethan outside, more Gothic inside – opened up its library as a restaurant just as the last edition of the Guide went to press. With wood panelling and a huge ornate stone fireplace it can seem rather subdued, but the food is notably fresh, well cooked and fair value. The country style might take in a cauliflower and mustard soup tasting like 'home-made broth' to start, maybe a salad, or perhaps a terrine of roughly chopped pink lamb and flavourful wild mushrooms.

A fish such as roast turbot generally shares the main-course billing with a vegetarian option (sweet pepper and potato tortilla) or perhaps a terrine-like pastry pie of pork with black pudding and apple. A savoury such as toasted goats' cheese with artichokes offers an alternative to desserts of raspberry crème brûlée or dark chocolate torte. Around 60 wines on a standard list begin with house vin de pays at £12.50.

CHEF: Julian Prosser PROPRIETORS: Sir Hugh and Lady Blackett OPEN: Sun L 12 to 2.30, all week D 7 to 9.30 MEALS: Set L £14.95 to £20.15, Set D Sun to Thur £18.50 to £23.50, Set D Fri and Sat £24.95 to £29.95 SERVICE: not inc CARDS: Amex, Delta, MasterCard, Switch, Visa DETAILS: 120 seats. 40 seats outside. Private parties: 120 main room, 20 to 100 private rooms. Car park. Vegetarian meals. Children's helpings. No smoking in dining room. Wheelchair access (also WC). Music ACCOMMODATION: 30 rooms, all with bath/shower. TV. Phone. B&B £80 to £185. Rooms for disabled. Baby facilities (*The Which? Hotel Guide*)

MELBOURN Cambridgeshire **map 6**

Pink Geranium

25 Station Road, Melbourn SG8 6DX COOKING **5**
TEL: (01763) 260215 FAX: (01763) 262110 ENGLISH/FRENCH
just off A10, 2m N of Royston £28–£74

Opposite the church in a quiet village, the pink-painted cottage deploys beams, floral chintz, a log fire and candlelight to cocoon its clientele. When Lawrence Champion, who use to be manager here in the early 1990s, took on the ownership during 2000, he wisely hung on to Mark Jordan, who remains in charge of the kitchen. He services a luxury-strewn menu that might take in a pressing of leeks with red mullet and foie gras, or roast sea bass with fluffy caviar mash and a champagne fish velouté.

A light hand has produced some appealing dressings (pesto with goats'-cheese bruschetta, or sherry and herb with a ballottine of chicken and Toulouse sausage), and while not all dishes fully scale the heights, the combination of simple presentation and strong flavours is successful, judging by one visitor's calf's liver with garlic mash and onion jus, for example. Desserts run to chocolate crème brûlée, and a raspberry ripple soufflé with matching sorbet. Lunch is considered good value, especially in view of the other options, and there is something for most tastes and pockets on the roving wine list, which starts with French red and white varietals at £11.95 and £13.95.

CHEF: Mark Jordan PROPRIETOR: Lawrence Champion OPEN: Tue to Sun L 12 to 2, Tue to Sat D 7 to 9.30 MEALS: alc (main courses £18 to £25). Set L £12 (2 courses) to £16, Set D Tue to Fri £30, Set D £45 SERVICE: 10% (optional), card slips closed CARDS: Amex, Delta, MasterCard, Switch, Visa DETAILS: 60 seats. Private parties: 50 main room, 6 and 14 private rooms. Car park. Vegetarian meals. Children's helpings. No smoking in dining room. No music (£5)

▲ Sheene Mill

Melbourn SG8 6DX
TEL: (01763) 261393 FAX: (01763) 261376 COOKING **2**
EMAIL: mail@stevensaunders.co.uk GLOBAL
WEB SITE: www.stevensaunders.com £22–£55

Although Steven Saunders has moved on to more cosmopolitan things at Steven Saunders at the Lowry in Manchester (see entry), and relinquished control of Pink Geranium (see above), he continues his involvement at this stylish, white-painted hotel and brasserie next to the millpond. A blue and yellow, formally set dining room, with French windows opening on to the patio, provides the backdrop for a wide-ranging menu that might take in a dramatic and colourful bouillabaisse, or a tagine of lemon chicken with a richly aromatic sauce and couscous. Far Eastern pickings have involved a simple but tasty king prawn tempura with two dipping sauces, and spicy duck pancakes packed with tender shredded meat, served with a plum dip. Vegetables are well reported, and desserts have included brioche-and-butter pudding with vanilla ice cream, and strawberry brûlée. Service is friendly, though not always proficient. A roving, briefly annotated wine list is organised into broad food-friendly groups; prices start at £10.95.

CHEFS: Steven Saunders and Craig Rowland PROPRIETORS: Sally and Steven Saunders OPEN: all week L 12 to 2.30 (3.30 Sun), Mon to Sat D 6.30 to 10 (10.30 Sat) CLOSED: 26 Dec MEALS: alc (main courses £10 to £17.50). Set L £10 (2 courses) to £14. Bar food available exc Sat D and Sun L SERVICE: not inc, card slips closed CARDS: Amex, Delta, MasterCard, Switch, Visa DETAILS: 120 seats. 50 seats outside. Private parties: 125 main room. Car park. Vegetarian meals. Children's helpings. No-smoking area. No smoking before 2.30 at L, 9.30 at D. Wheelchair access (not WC). Music. Air-conditioned ACCOMMODATION: 9 rooms, all with bath/shower. TV. Phone. B&B £60 to £110. Baby facilities (*The Which? Hotel Guide*) (£5)

MIDDLEHAM North Yorkshire **map 8**

▲ Waterford House

Kirkgate, Middleham DL8 4PG
TEL: (01969) 622090 FAX: (01969) 624020

COOKING **2**
ANGLO-FRENCH
£31–£56

Set in a small but thriving village, Waterford feels like a country home, its comfortable lounge decorated with fresh flowers, large sofas and a grand piano. The dining room is more cottagey, like a 'clean and tidy antique shop', from where Everyl Madell can be glimpsed in the kitchen cooking a simple but attractive collection of timeless favourites ranging from provençale fish soup, via terrine of chicken livers, to well-hung tournedos Rossini. Fish and game vary according to supplies, and some main courses – rack of lamb, or whole roast duck – are for two people only. Desserts may include banana brûlée and Yorkshire curd tart.

Brian Madell runs everything with 'total enthusiasm', not least the wine list. Covering the length and breadth of the wine-producing world, it demands serious attention, although house wines (starting at £10.50) have been thoughtfully distilled down to a mere three pages. Seventy wines are listed by the glass, but the patron is happy to open any of his 800 bottles and charge by the quarter. Wine lovers should do themselves a favour and stay overnight.

CHEF: Everyl Madell PROPRIETORS: Everyl and Brian Madell OPEN: all week D only 7 to 10 (L by arrangement) MEALS: alc (main courses £14 to £18.50). Set L £19.50, Set D £22.50 SERVICE: not inc, card slips closed CARDS: Delta, MasterCard, Switch, Visa DETAILS: 20 seats. Private parties: 24 main room. Car park. Children's helpings. No smoking in dining room. Occasional music ACCOMMODATION: 5 rooms, all with bath/shower. TV. Phone. B&B £50 to £95. Baby facilities (*The Which? Hotel Guide*) (£5)

MIDDLESBROUGH Middlesbrough **map 10**

Purple Onion

80 Corporation Road, Middlesbrough TS1 2RF
TEL: (01642) 222250 FAX: (01642) 248088
WEB SITE: www.thepurple-onion.co.uk

COOKING **3**
MODERN EUROPEAN
£22–£51

The art nouveau-style brasserie, complete with marble-topped tables, a long bar, a dark-red colour scheme and piped jazz, attracts a lively crowd. Evening menus are particularly wide-ranging, encompassing pastas and risottos, fusion dishes such as grilled duck breast with sun-dried cherries, couscous and pancetta, and a vegetarian list that might include mushroom and spinach cake with sweet potato rösti and roast garlic sauce. Portions can be hefty. Lunch might range from a snack – a sandwich of Yorkshire ham on sour-dough bread, say – to a meal of duck and chicken liver parfait paired with robustly flavoured kumquat marmalade, followed by chargrilled ribeye steak in its own peppered meat juice with chips. Tiramisù makes a creamy and 'highly alcoholic' way to finish. Teatime Specials (prawn and chilli risotto, fish and chips with mushy peas) are served from 5.30 to 7.30 Monday to Friday. The pithily annotated wine list, ordered by price, hops all over the world. House French is £10.95.

CHEF: Tony Chapman PROPRIETORS: John and Bruno McCoy OPEN: all week L 12 to 2.30 (5 Sun), Mon to Sat D 5.30 to 10 (11 Fri and Sat) MEALS: alc (main courses L £6.50 to £11, D £11 to £16.50). Set L Sun £12.50 (2 courses) SERVICE: not inc CARDS: Delta, MasterCard, Switch, Visa DETAILS: 80 seats. Private parties: 70 main room, 180 private room. Vegetarian meals. Children's helpings. Wheelchair access (also WC). Occasional music (£5)

MIDHURST West Sussex **map 3**

▲ Angel Hotel **NEW ENTRY**

North Street, Midhurst GU29 9DN
TEL: (01730) 812421 FAX: (01730) 815928
EMAIL: angel@hshotels.co.uk
WEB SITE: www.hshotels.co.uk

COOKING **3**
MODERN BRITISH/ENGLISH
£22–£48

Under new ownership, this white Georgian-fronted building in the centre of town has taken on a less formal identity. The brasserie's wooden panelling and well-spaced tables induce a feeling of wellbeing, and the simply arranged menu, short for a brasserie perhaps but long enough by restaurant standards, goes in for a typical run of modern British materials and ideas, including mackerel with horseradish mash, cod fillet with pea purée, and chump of lamb with provençale vegetables.

Simon Malin, who has worked at Broadway's Lygon Arms and London's Halcyon Hotel (see entries), puts in a generally consistent performance, producing at inspection an expertly prepared and generously herby risotto, and an earthy, uncomplicated dish of plump, crisp-skinned and flavourful duck confit, served with 'rich and peasanty' lentils and wilted bok choy. The straightforward style is equally welcome at dessert stage, for example in a first-rate sharp rhubarb tart with good crème anglaise. Eager and alert staff are 'real pros', and a short wine list offers a dozen by the glass, including house French Chardonnay and Merlot at £11.60 (£3.15).

CHEF: Simon Malin PROPRIETOR: Mrs A. Goodman OPEN: all week 12 to 2.30, 6.30 to 10 MEALS: alc Mon to Sat L, all week D (main courses £13 to £15). Set L Mon to Fri £9.75 (2 courses) to £12.50, Set L Sun £14.50 SERVICE: not inc CARDS: Amex, Delta, Diners, MasterCard, Switch, Visa DETAILS: 60 seats. 30 seats outside. Private parties: 60 main room, 24 to 120 private rooms. Car park. Vegetarian meals. Children's helpings. No smoking in 1 dining room. Wheelchair access (not WC). Music ACCOMMODATION: 28 rooms, all with bath/shower. TV. Phone. B&B £90 to £125. Rooms for disabled. Baby facilities (£5)

indicates that there has been a change of chef since last year's Guide, and the Editor has judged that the change is of sufficient interest to merit the reader's attention.

Maxine's

Elizabeth House, Red Lion Street,
Midhurst GU29 9PB — COOKING **2**
TEL: (01730) 816271 — EUROPEAN
EMAIL: maxines@lineone.net — £26–£45

The de Jagers have been stalwarts of this South Downs market town's food scene for nearly two decades, and regulars continue to commend it for its consistency and value. The tiny dining room is a haven of old-fashioned values, both in terms of décor – beams, wood panelling and brick fireplace – and Robert de Jager's classical menu. Salmon mousse with cucumber, melon and Ardennes ham, duck with orange sauce, and chicken breast with tarragon are all typical of the retro style, though occasional forays into contemporary modes might produce prawn salad in Thai sauce, crabcakes with tomato and coriander, and crispy duck with five-spice and garlic. Time tends to stand still with desserts, which may include Dutch apple pie, a signature dish for many years, or a lime and lemon brûlée. Service is attentive. Drink from a list of mainly French wines with a good selection of half-bottles. House French is £10.50.

CHEF: Robert de Jager PROPRIETORS: Robert and Marti de Jager OPEN: Wed to Sun L 12 to 1.30, Wed to Sat D 7 to 9.30 CLOSED: 2 weeks Jan MEALS: alc (main courses £11 to £16.50). Set L and D £16.95 SERVICE: net prices, card slips closed CARDS: Amex, Delta, MasterCard, Switch, Visa DETAILS: 24 seats. Private parties: 30 main room. Children's helpings. No smoking in dining room. No music

MILFORD ON SEA Hampshire — **map 2**

Rouille

NEW ENTRY

69–71 High Street, Milford on Sea SO41 0QG
TEL/FAX: (01590) 642340 — COOKING **6**
EMAIL: rouille@ukonline.co.uk — MODERN FRENCH
WEB SITE: www.rouille.co.uk — £25–£43

The Hollombys took over what use to be Rocher's just as the last edition of the Guide went to press. A relaxed atmosphere obtains in the uncluttered dining room, where Nicola Hollomby runs front-of-house in a homely and unpretentious way. Floral curtains and brown walls may not make much of a personal statement, but the food certainly does. One of the lessons Lui Hollomby learned from his mentor, Raymond Blanc, is how to source good materials – asparagus from up the road, chicken and duck from Somerset, live langoustines from Scotland – which shows in the quality and absolute freshness of 'every item on the plate'.

Prices are ungrasping, there is no obligation to eat more than two courses, and dishes can be mixed across menus. Carefully considered contrasts between well-defined tastes and textures give the food its momentum: a well-executed tart featuring a circle of wafer-thin scallop slices laid on chorizo and topped with a lightly dressed salad. Visual appeal is another strength (towers are the preferred assembly method) and although dishes can be complex, all components are there for a purpose, for example in a dish of high quality well-timed lamb combining shoulder (minced, wrapped in caul and sliced), sweetbreads and best end with dauphinois potatoes. Light, flavourful saucing is as professional as everything else.

The combination of intense flavour and subtlety extends to a fat ring of roasted pineapple sitting on a base of rice pudding made with coconut milk, with a scoop of coconut sorbet parked on top. 'They should make service included, and get rid of the Muzak,' suggested one visitor, but otherwise little comes in for criticism: incidentals are the work of a perfectionist, and a short list of wines arranged by style starts with Vin de Pays d'Oc at £12.

CHEF: Lui Hollomby PROPRIETORS: Nicola and Lui Hollomby OPEN: Tue to Sat L 12 to 2.30, 7 to 10.30 (Wed to Sat L Oct to Mar by arrangement) CLOSED: first 2 weeks Jan MEALS: Set L and D Wed to Fri and Sun £9.95 (2 courses) to £24.50, Set D Sat £20.95 (2 courses) to £24.50 SERVICE: not inc, card slips closed CARDS: Amex, Delta, Diners, MasterCard, Switch, Visa DETAILS: 24 seats. Private parties: 30 main room. Vegetarian meals. Children's helpings. No smoking in dining room. No music. Air-conditioned (£5)

MILTON ERNEST Bedfordshire **map 6**

Strawberry Tree

3 Radwell Road, Milton Ernest MK44 1RY — COOKING **6**
TEL: (01234) 823633 — MODERN BRITISH
5 miles north of Bedford on A6 towards Kettering — £27–£58

From its thatched roof and wishing well to its highly decorated interior, the Tree has a well-kept air about it. Neatness extends from plainly set tables to a concise menu (three, three and four choices per course) that makes use of vegetables, herbs and saladings from the garden in season, and seeks out free-range and organically reared meats, including some rare breeds. A cutlet of Gloucester Old Spot pork, for example, comes with a sage and Parmesan crust, broad beans, cider fondant potato and sage jus. That combination illustrates the classically inclined thrust of the repertoire, which might also take in a starter of duck confit served on a caramelised onion tart with a well-judged orange sauce: one of the better examples of a dish on the duck and orange theme.

Fish is treated well, too: perhaps herb-crusted ballottine of salmon with a blob of fromage blanc to start, or fillets of monk, plaice and red mullet in prime condition in a simple nage of tasty asparagus, spinach and green beans. Flavours and seasoning are spot on, indicative of a kitchen that combines skill with restraint. Desserts range from a homely apricot bread-and-butter pudding to a handsomely presented poached William pear with ginger ice cream and caramel sauce. Pre-meal nibbles are not in the same class. Service, otherwise capable and experienced, has produced one disgruntled party. France dominates the concise wine list, which also touches base with the New World. House French is £12.

CHEFS: Jason and Andrew Bona PROPRIETORS: John and Wendy Bona OPEN: Wed to Fri and Sun L 12 to 1.30, Wed to Sat D 7.30 to 8.30 CLOSED: 2 weeks summer, 2 weeks winter, bank hols MEALS: alc L Wed to Fri (main courses £16 to £18). Set L Sun £16, Set D £34 SERVICE: not inc, card slips closed CARDS: Delta, MasterCard, Switch, Visa DETAILS: 22 seats. Private parties: 18 main room, 8 private room. Car park. Children's helpings. No smoking in dining room. Wheelchair access (not WC). Music (£5)

NEW CHEF *is shown instead of a cooking mark where a change of chef occurred too late for a new assessment of the cooking.*

MORETON-IN-MARSH Gloucestershire **map 5**

Annie's

3 Oxford Street, Moreton-in-Marsh GL56 0LA
TEL/FAX: (01608) 651981

COOKING **2**
ANGLO-FRENCH
£35–£55

Husband-and-wife team David and Anne Ellis have created a loyal following for their brand of easy cottage welcome (with no fewer than three fireplaces), local food cooked to order, and a compact, mostly French wine list that does well to complement the food. This could hardly be further from the sea, yet fish is a speciality, perhaps filo-wrapped tiger prawns to start, then first-class, unadorned Dover sole. Given the cross-Channel style, expect steak, kidney and mushroom pie, and treacle tart at the Anglo end, and starters of warm chicken livers, mushrooms and bacon, or herby meat-filled crêpes on salad leaves, with French saucing *de rigueur* for main courses. Service is efficient and attentive, and house wines are £12.50.

CHEF: David Ellis PROPRIETORS: David and Anne Ellis OPEN: Mon to Sat D only 7 to 9.30 (L by arrangement for large parties) CLOSED: early Nov MEALS: alc (main courses £15.50 to £20) SERVICE: none, card slips closed CARDS: Amex, Diners, MasterCard, Visa DETAILS: 30 seats. Private parties: 30 main room. Vegetarian meals. Children's helpings. No smoking while others eat. Music (£5)

Marsh Goose

High Street, Moreton-in-Marsh GL56 0AX
TEL: (01608) 653500 FAX: (01608) 653510

COOKING **6**
MODERN BRITISH
£26–£48

After setting up two food pubs, the Churchill Arms at Paxford and the Hare & Hounds at Foss Cross (see entries), Sonya Kidney has returned to take over direct running of the kitchen. And there have been other changes too. A café now occupies the front part of the restaurant, serving breakfasts, light lunches, and cakes and pastries all day long, while the restaurant itself, with fewer seats, has abandoned the carte in favour of set-price meals. What has not changed, however, is the appealing style and simple yet confident cooking, in which sometimes humble materials are given a chance to shine. Expect to find grilled sardines, a pigeon and rabbit terrine, or braised belly of pork, as well as more mainstream cuts such as roast saddle of lamb with black olive stuffing, and loin of pork on horseradish mash.

Dishes arouse interest with an endlessly inventive stream of judicious accompaniments: calf's liver with Jerusalem artichoke cream and coriander jus, for example, or roast hake with chorizo and caper cream. Desserts, which take a simpler and more predictable route, have included banana fritters with a white chocolate mousse in dark chocolate sauce, a dish that would 'make a dietician's hair stand on end'. Service is generally assiduous and friendly. Wines are grouped stylistically, and quality is high with the emphasis on youthful and lively rather than venerable stock. House wines from France, Spain and Australia are £12.50 a bottle, £3.25 a glass.

CHEF: Sonya Kidney PROPRIETORS: Leo Brooke-Little and Sonya Kidney OPEN: Wed to Sun L 12.30 to 2.30, Tue to Sat D 7.30 to 9.30 MEALS: Set L Wed to Sat £17, Set L Sun £20, Set D £30 SERVICE: not inc CARDS: Amex, Delta, Diners, MasterCard, Switch, Visa DETAILS: 45 seats. Private parties: 20 main room. Children's helpings. No smoking in dining room. Wheelchair access (also WC). No music

MORSTON Norfolk **map 6**

▲ Morston Hall

Morston NR25 7AA
TEL: (01263) 741041 FAX: (01263) 740419
EMAIL: reception@morstonhall.com
WEB SITE: www.morstonhall.com
on A149, 2m W of Blakeney

COOKING **6**
MODERN BRITISH
£29–£55

Despite the tranquil setting – boat trips leave from just over the road to take trippers to the seal colony or ternery – a degree of energy is apparent. The hotel gets a makeover every year, and menus change daily: lack of choice does not imply a lazy kitchen here, rather it is well focused and treats materials with integrity. Fish naturally plays a starring role, typically as the second course: sea bass, and a combination of black bream and sea trout, have been particularly successful. Ideas can often be simple to the point of sounding mundane, yet a starter of ripe goats' cheese and tasty tomatoes in pastry proved a highlight for one visitor, while another praised steamed Roquefort mousse on a watercress sauce with ribbons of courgette.

Consistency is a hallmark, and correct cooking ensures proper textures: knives go through beef fillet as if it were butter. Meat suppliers are generally from Norfolk, providing the raw material for main courses of roast lamb with buttered greens and aubergine caviar, or pot roast duck with orange. Cheeses are properly kept and served, and desserts range from pistachio soufflé to classic lemon tart. Competent staff – 'as nice as you can find anywhere' – deal with everything quietly and efficiently, and Galton Blackiston generally does a tour of the dining room at the end of the evening. Wines are arranged according to grape variety rather than region and include intelligent selections from around the world. Prices are reasonable, with one diner delighted to find a half of Chilean red for as little as £6. House wines start at £10.

CHEFS: Galton Blackiston and Samantha Wegg PROPRIETORS: Tracy and Galton Blackiston OPEN: Sun L 12.30 for 1 (1 sitting), all week D 7.30 for 8 (1 sitting) CLOSED: 25 and 26 Dec, 2 weeks early Jan MEALS: Set L £21, Set D £34 SERVICE: not inc, card slips closed CARDS: Amex, Delta, Diners, MasterCard, Switch, Visa DETAILS: 40 seats. Private parties: 40 main room. Car park. Vegetarian menus on request. Children's helpings. No smoking in dining room. Wheelchair access (also men's WC). No music ACCOMMODATION: 6 rooms, all with bath/shower. TV. Phone. D,B&B £110 to £200. Baby facilities. Garden (*The Which? Hotel Guide*)

London Round-ups listing additional restaurants that may be worth a visit can be found after the main London section.

Report forms are at the back of the book; write a letter if you prefer; or email us at goodfoodguide@which.net

MOULSFORD Oxfordshire map 2

▲ Beetle & Wedge

Ferry Lane, Moulsford OX10 9JF
TEL: (01491) 651381 FAX: (01491) 651376
off A329, down Ferry Lane to river

COOKING **5**
ANGLO-ENGLISH
£42–£68

An enviable setting beside the Thames overlooking water meadows is a plus at this Victorian hotel; both the Dining Room (a formal restaurant in the hotel proper), and the Boat House (a more relaxed, beamed bar-restaurant), share river views and a pretty garden. Boat House visitors have appreciated the range of lighter dishes, which take in soups, casseroles and a good selection from the charcoal grill: crispy duck salad, or sea bass with spinach and bearnaise. But the repertoire also takes in calf's liver and kidneys with black pudding in mustard sauce, and a hearty hare casserole with red wine sauce. Main dishes are accompanied by good rösti and a choice of vegetables – fresh, ratatouille, or salad – and desserts might run from rice pudding with apricot and armagnac compote to hot beignets soufflés with lemon curd.

In the Dining Room the cooking becomes a little more sophisticated while still retaining a clear focus: hand-dived scallops come with chive tomato salsa, and warm onion tart with foie gras, perhaps followed by medallions of English veal with wild mushroom sauce, or roast monkfish with lobster sauce. Fruit figures prominently among desserts: a hot Cointreau soufflé with raspberry coulis, for example, or roast plums with vanilla ice cream and caramel sauce. Service, from mainly young French staff, is attentive. An appealing if pricey range of French wines predominates on the largely traditional list, with a few Italians and 'wines from other areas' thrown in for good luck. Six house wines are £13.50, also available at £3.50 a glass.

CHEFS: Richard Smith and Olivier Bouet PROPRIETORS: Kate and Richard Smith OPEN: Dining Room Tue to Sun L 12 to 1.45, Tue to Sat D 7 to 10; Boat House all week 12 to 1.45, 7 to 10 MEALS: alc (main courses Dining Room £12.50 to £21.50, Boat House £12 to £19.50) SERVICE: not inc CARDS: Amex, Delta, Diners, MasterCard, Switch, Visa DETAILS: Dining Room 30 seats; Boathouse 65 seats. 40 seats outside. Private parties: 64 main room, 64 private room. Car park. Vegetarian meals. No smoking in Dining Room. Wheelchair access (also WC). Occasional music ACCOMMODATION: 10 rooms, all with bath/shower. TV. Phone. B&B £90 to £150. Rooms for disabled. Baby facilities (*The Which? Hotel Guide*)

MOULTON North Yorkshire map 9

Black Bull Inn

Moulton DL10 6QJ
TEL: (01325) 377289 FAX: (01325) 377422
EMAIL: sarah@blackbullinn.demon.co.uk
1m SE of Scotch Corner

COOKING **4**
SEAFOOD
£24–£66

Although it can seat 100, a series of small rooms make this attractive and well-maintained pub feel much more intimate: beyond the bar is a wood-panelled room filled with Victoriana, a conservatory with a flourishing grape-vine, and a 1932 Pullman carriage from the Brighton Belle. Praised equally by those who just call in for a sandwich (from ploughman's to 'sophisticated cosmopolitan concoctions') as by those who eat from the long carte, it specialises in seafood, from dressed crab cake with celeriac mayonnaise, via grilled oysters with pesto, to honey-roast salmon fillet.

The style may be old-fashioned, with cheese sauces and garlic butter to the fore, but this doesn't prevent the kitchen turning out simple grilled Dover sole, lobster salad, and a version of bouillabaisse 'as good as any in France'. Staff – 'the same for 25 years' – are pleasant, charming and helpful. At first glance the wine list seems prosaic, kicking off with Liebfraumilch and a steady French house selection, starting at £9.50. But further analysis reveals a very fine run of champagnes, Bordeaux and Burgundy at knock-down prices. A page devoted to the New World also provides sound drinking.

CHEF: Paul Grundy PROPRIETORS: G.H. and A.M.C. Pagendam OPEN: Mon to Fri L 12 to 2, Mon to Sat D 6.45 to 10.15 CLOSED: 24 to 26 Dec MEALS: alc (main courses £14 to £25). Set L £15.50 SERVICE: not inc CARDS: Amex, Delta, Diners, MasterCard, Switch, Visa DETAILS: 100 seats. 16 seats outside. Private parties: 12 main room, 12 and 30 private rooms. Vegetarian meals. No children under 7. No music

NANTWICH Cheshire map 7

Peppers £ NEW ENTRY

Mill Street, Nantwich CW5 5ST
TEL: (01270) 629100 FAX: (01270) 629688

COOKING **2**
MODERN EUROPEAN
£19–£45

A framed Roll of Honour still hangs on the wall of what is now the dining room of this double-fronted Georgian building, giving it the institutional air of a set of meeting rooms. Its stained wood flooring and bare boardroom-type tables may be low on charisma, but staff inspire confidence with their efficient, watchful and informative service. Light lunches are available throughout the day – baguettes, inventively filled jacket potatoes, and dishes such as stir-fried lemon chicken with vegetable fried rice – while a more substantial carte operates at lunchtime and in the evening.

'Simplified country-house hotel cookery' is how the kitchen sees its role, as it moves easily between omelette Arnold Bennett and a chunky parslied ham and leek terrine. Modern credentials are displayed in a rich and spicy duckling spring roll with a sharply contrasting plum chutney, and accurate timing has yielded crisp-skinned fillet of sea bass on sweet red pepper sauce, and pink rump of lamb on horseradish mash. Puddings run to smooth, well-flavoured ice creams, summer pudding, and apple and sultana cheesecake. Ten wines by the glass, from £1.95 (£9.80 the bottle) form part of a reasonable list.

CHEF: Andrew Hollinshead PROPRIETOR: Mike Williams OPEN: Tue to Sun L 11 to 3, Tue to Sat D 6 to 9.30, light L 11 to 7, afternoon tea 2.30 to 5.30 MEALS: alc (main courses £7 to £16). Set L Sun £12.95. Light L and afternoon tea available SERVICE: not inc, card slips closed CARDS: Amex, Delta, MasterCard, Switch, Visa DETAILS: 90 seats. 65 seats outside. Private parties: 50 main room, 20 and 50 private rooms. Car park. Vegetarian meals. Children's helpings. No smoking in dining room. Wheelchair access (not WC). Music (£5)

If a restaurant is new to the Guide this year (did not appear as a main entry in the last edition), NEW ENTRY *appears opposite its name.*

NAYLAND Suffolk map 6

▲ White Hart **NEW ENTRY**

11 High Street, Nayland CO6 4JF
TEL: (01206) 263382 FAX: (01206) 263638
EMAIL: nayhart@aol.com
WEB SITE: www.whitehart-nayland.co.uk
on A134 between Colchester and Sudbury

COOKING **2**
MODERN EUROPEAN
£29–£52

The transformation from village pub to restaurant-with-rooms (and occasionally grooms, since it has a wedding licence) has been completed. The former coaching inn now has a tiny bar and a smart, rather formal, cream-coloured dining room, having gone 'positively posh'. The menu may have a French starting point – chicken liver and foie gras terrine with fig chutney – but soon branches out into Andalucian gazpacho, or corn-cake blinis with smoked salmon and horseradish cream.

Dishes may sometimes struggle to make their expected impact, but among successes have been grilled rabbit legs with Jerusalem artichoke, and roast duck served in two parts: skinless breast with a sauce of wine and meat juices, then a while later the legs on a salad. Sunday lunch brings a carving trolley – accurately timed roast leg of lamb for one party – and vegetables are commended. Desserts run to a mirabelle version of clafoutis, and chocolate fondant served with marmalade and Grand Marnier custard, while cheeses are kept in good condition. Service is polite, willing and friendly. A mostly French and New World wine list starts with a handful by the glass, including Duboeuf house wine (£11 and £2.50).

CHEF: Neil Bishop PROPRIETOR: Michel Roux OPEN: Tue to Sun 12 to 2.30, 6.30 to 9 (9.30 Sat; also open bank hol Mons) CLOSED: 26 Dec to 4 Jan MEALS: alc (main courses £9 to £16). Light L available in summer SERVICE: 12.5% (optional), card slips closed CARDS: Amex, Delta, Diners, MasterCard, Switch, Visa DETAILS: 50 seats. 40 seats outside. Private parties: 65 main room, 40 private room. Car park. Vegetarian meals. Children's helpings. No pipes in dining room. Wheelchair access (not WC). Music ACCOMMODATION: 6 rooms, all with bath/shower. TV. Phone. B&B £64.50 to £69.50. Baby facilities (*The Which? Hotel Guide*)

NEAR SAWREY Cumbria map 8

▲ Ees Wyke

Near Sawrey LA22 0JZ
TEL/FAX: (015394) 36393
EMAIL: eeswyke@aol.com
on B5286 from Hawkshead

COOKING **2**
BRITISH
£31–£37

The small, friendly, family-run hotel, in which the Williamses appear to do everything themselves, is a square, white-painted Georgian house with views across fields to Esthwaite. It is the sort of hideaway with 'above-average guesthouse cooking' that Lakeland visitors appreciate. Guests congregate for drinks at a rather early 7pm, but there are five courses to go and the evening runs at a relaxing pace. Good sourcing is evident, and the kitchen's solid, classical techniques are not diverted towards an unduly ambitious menu. Meals might begin with asparagus soup, or hot Flookburgh shrimps in spiced butter, before a no-choice item such as seafood parcel with Nantua sauce. After beef Stroganoff, or salmon with watercress sauce, comes a dessert such as bread-and-butter pudding or summer fruit brûlée, and then cheese. Fair prices and a 'successful house-party atmosphere' add value to the enterprise, as does a varied and ungrasping wine list, with a quintet of house wines around £10.50.

CHEF: John Williams PROPRIETORS: Margaret and John Williams OPEN: all week D only 7 to 7.30 MEALS: Set D £23 (£14 for residents) SERVICE: not inc, card slips closed CARDS: Amex DETAILS: 20 seats. Private parties: 35 main room. Car park. Children's helpings. No children under 8. No smoking in dining room. No music ACCOMMODATION: 8 rooms, all with bath/shower. TV. D,B&B £46 to £120. No children under 8 (*The Which? Hotel Guide*)

NETHER ALDERLEY Cheshire **map 8**

The Wizard

NEW ENTRY

Macclesfield Road, Nether Alderley SK10 4UB
TEL: (01625) 584000 FAX: (01625) 585105

COOKING **3**
MODERN BRITISH
£25–£46

Set in a lush, woody part of Cheshire, on the road out of the village, this white-walled pub conversion conveys a rugged impression, but its flagstone floor and simple wooden tables are offset by subtle lighting and handsome framed pictures. Mark Wilkinson offers ambitious modern cooking, his fondness for deep, earthy flavours – evident in wild mushroom risotto, or braised beef brisket with horseradish mash – balanced by a penchant for bright ones in the right context, such as seared tuna on bruschetta with chargrilled baby corn and chilli and ginger oil.

Fine materials are presented with a certain amount of visual flair. Dishes are usually built on or around a central turret: slices of braised shoulder of lamb arranged on a base of olive and pepper couscous, or Goosnargh duck breast around a double-decker mound of creamed sweet potato and celeriac. Most desserts feature chocolate, toffee or caramel: pecan, chocolate and bourbon pie, for example, or sticky toffee pudding with butterscotch sauce. About half the wines are under £20. One or two producers' names are missing, but selections are otherwise sound enough. House wines start at £10.50.

CHEF: Mark Wilkinson PROPRIETOR: Bispham Green Brewery OPEN: Tue to Sun L 12 to 2 (2.30 Sun), Tue to Sat D 7 to 9.30 CLOSED: bank hols D MEALS: alc Tue to Sat (main courses L £6.50 to £12.50, D £8.50 to £15). Set L Sun £9.95 (1 course) to £15.95 SERVICE: not inc, card slips closed CARDS: Amex, Delta, MasterCard, Switch, Visa DETAILS: 90 seats. 20 seats outside. Private parties: 16 main room, 40 private room. Car park. Vegetarian meals. Children's helpings. No smoking in 1 dining room. Wheelchair access (also men's WC). Occasional music

The cuisine styles noted at the tops of entries are only an approximation, often suggested to us by the restaurants themselves. Please read the entry itself to find out more about the cooking style.

Dining rooms where music, either live or recorded, is never played are signalled by No music *in the details at the end of an entry.*

NEW ALRESFORD Hampshire map 2

▲ Hunters

32 Broad Street, New Alresford SO24 9AQ
TEL/FAX: (01962) 732468
EMAIL: debbie@huntersrestaurant.co.uk

COOKING **2**
ENGLISH/FRENCH
£21–£50

Occupying a double-fronted shop in a broad parade, Hunters is the sort of place that constitutes the backbone of informal eating in small country towns, combining a casual atmosphere with unshowy food at fair prices. As the Guide went to press refurbishment was planned, but the essentials look set to remain, including a repertoire that takes in simple classics from light, smooth chicken liver parfait with onion relish, to a friable and flavourful mushroom tart with an accurately poached egg and hollandaise. A few more contemporary-sounding dishes might appear at dinner – seared hand-dived scallops with gazpacho and basil oil, or confit leg and roast breast of guinea fowl with pear barley risotto and tempura of herbs – while desserts have included chocolate and griottine trifle, and prune and custard tart. Service is efficient and friendly. A ten-strong house selection of wines under £12 heads up a short global list that rarely strays above £20 anyway.

CHEF: Nicholas Wentworth PROPRIETOR: Martin Birmingham OPEN: Mon to Sat 12 to 2, 7 to 9.30 CLOSED: 1 week Christmas MEALS: alc (main courses L £5 to £8.50, D £11 to £18). Set D Mon to Thur £12.50 (2 courses) to £15 SERVICE: not inc, 10% for parties of 6 or more CARDS: Amex, Delta, Diners, MasterCard, Switch, Visa DETAILS: 32 seats. 20 seats outside. Private parties: 70 main room. Vegetarian meals. Children's helpings. No smoking in dining room. Wheelchair access (not WC). Music ACCOMMODATION: 3 rooms, all with bath/shower. TV. B&B £40 to £55. Baby facilities (£5)

NEWBURY Berkshire map 2

▲ Newbury Manor, Sharlands **NEW ENTRY**

Sharlands Restaurant, London Road,
Newbury RG14 2BY
TEL: (01635) 528838 FAX: (01635) 523406
WEB SITE: www.sharlands.co.uk

COOKING **6**
MODERN EUROPEAN
£32–£58

Set in nine acres of sumptuous grounds with two rivers flowing through, this Georgian building with modern extensions opened in 1999 as an upmarket hotel. Co-proprietor and executive chef David Sharland was previously at the Vineyard in Stockcross (see entry) and for some years before that head chef of the Savoy Grill in London, but day-to-day charge of the kitchen has been handed to Jason Gladwin. The dining room, decorated in striking turquoise and gold, with an oil-lamp on every table, and full-length windows giving views of the gardens, offers the choice of a fixed-price menu or a more expansive (and expensive) carte, dealing in bold modern ideas such as seared red mullet with sweet pepper risotto and vanilla sauce, and rabbit ragoût with mushrooms and artichokes and a port sauce.

The kitchen's facility across a range of techniques and styles is illustated by its handling of crisp-skinned duck leg confit with honey and ginger sauce, followed at inspection by chunky, flavoursome monkfish in a crisp and crunchy tempura batter, served with braised fennel and potato rösti. Desserts tend to be lighter creations, skilfully done and prettily presented: lemon sponge with summer berries and crème anglaise, or sharply flavoured crêpes suzette. Service is mainly French and highly polished. Two wine lists, one focusing on bottles under £35, the other devoted to fine wines spiralling into three-figure sums, both provide an intelligent and varied global selection, though an ornate flowery script makes reading them difficult. Eleven house recommendations from £11.50 are all available by the glass (from £3), and 16 half-bottles are hidden away at the end of the fine wine section.

CHEF: Jason Gladwin PROPRIETORS: David Sharland, Bob Rae and Adrian Wiley OPEN: Sun to Fri L 12 to 1.45, all week D 7 to 9.45 MEALS: alc (main courses £12 to £20.50). Set L and D £16.50 (2 courses) to £25, Set L Sun £19.50 SERVICE: not inc, card slips closed CARDS: Amex, Delta, MasterCard, Switch, Visa DETAILS: 70 seats. 20 seats outside. Private parties: 100 main room, 8 to 50 private rooms. Car park. Vegetarian meals. Children's helpings. No smoking in dining room. Wheelchair access (also WC). Music. Air-conditioned ACCOMMODATION: 33 rooms, all with bath/shower. TV. Phone. B&B £110 to £250. Rooms for disabled. Baby facilities. Fishing

NEWCASTLE UPON TYNE Tyne & Wear **map 10**

Fisherman's Lodge

Jesmond Dene, Jesmond, NE7 7BQ
TEL: (0191) 281 3281 FAX: (0191) 281 6410

COOKING **5**
SEAFOOD
£30–82

Down a leafy lane just off the dual carriageway to Tynemouth, past a rippling brook, the lodge has been under new ownership since early 2000. Changes so far seem minimal. Service in the modern lounge bar and comfortable dining room is skilled and friendly, and the kitchen team remains in place. Fish is still a strong suit, taking in rich, hot and plentiful crab soup, grilled lobster with garlic butter, and monkfish cheeks with niçoise salad. Materials are notably fresh and of high quality, and timing is all it should be, judging by a large piece of pure white flaky cod, strewn with prawns and served with cooking juices. Success is not confined to seafood, however. One luncher enjoyed the deep savour of a creamy mushroom risotto featuring generous quantities of blewits, trompettes, ceps and chanterelles.

Sound technique extends to desserts, for example a cylindrical coconut mousse sandwiched between layers of rum-soaked sponge and a translucent jelly, served with a delicate coconut ice cream. Main courses are accompanied by a side plate of vegetables, old-fashioned hotel style, and there are 'lots of ancillary bits to eat', from a plate of appetisers to Melba toast, three kinds of butter, and petits fours with coffee. Simply split between Europe and the New World, wines are a classy collection and include a well-priced and helpfully annotated page of recommendations. House wines start at £13.50.

CHEFS: Steven Jobson and Paul Amer PROPRIETORS: Tom and Jocelyn Maxfield OPEN: Mon to Fri L 12 to 2, Mon to Sat D 7 to 11 CLOSED: 25 and 26 Dec, bank holidays MEALS: alc (main courses £19 to £30). Set L £19.50, Set D Mon to Fri £34.50 SERVICE: not inc CARDS: Amex, Delta, MasterCard, Switch, Visa DETAILS: 70 seats. 30 seats outside. Private parties: 70 main room, 14 and 40 private rooms. Car park. Vegetarian meals. No smoking in dining room. Music

Metropolitan £

35 Grey Street, Newcastle upon Tyne NE1 6EE
TEL: (0191) 230 2306 FAX: (0191) 230 2307
EMAIL: info@metropolitanbrasseries.co.uk
WEB SITE: www.themetropolitan.co.uk

COOKING **1**
MODERN BRITISH
£18–£46

Occupying a former bank, in what seems like a whole street of them, this '1930s Odeon-style' eatery is on the go all day from mid-morning, with sandwiches, salads and snacks, throwing in a one-course early-bird supper for good measure. Dishes can be hit and miss, but reporters have enjoyed venison terrine with courgette chutney, gnocchi with cherry tomatoes, and a fresh piece of salmon with pearl barley risotto and apricots. Desserts range from successful apple crumble to chocolate nemesis served with a rather faint-hearted Newcastle Brown ice cream. Service is prompt and polite, and around half the 40-odd wines are available by the glass, starting with house Vin de Pays du Gers at £8.95.

CHEFS: Andrew Weatherill and Kevin Burlison PROPRIETORS: Sean Parkinson and Nick Gardiner OPEN: Mon to Sat 11 to 10.45 CLOSED: 25 Dec MEALS: alc (main courses £6 to £14). Set L £8.95 (2 courses) to £11.95, Set D 5 to 7 £3.50 (1 course) SERVICE: 10% (optional), card slips closed CARDS: Amex, Delta, Diners, MasterCard, Switch, Visa DETAILS: 175 seats. 60 seats outside. Private parties: 120 main room, 35 private room. Vegetarian meals. Children's helpings. No smoking in 1 dining room. Wheelchair access (also WC). Music. Air-conditioned (£5)

NEW MILTON Hampshire **map 2**

▲ Chewton Glen

Christchurch Road, New Milton BH25 6QS
TEL: (01425) 275341 FAX: (01425) 272310
EMAIL: reservations@chewtonglen.com
WEB SITE: www.chewtonglen.com
from A35 follow signs to Walkford and Highcliffe; take second turning on left after Walkford down Chewton Farm road

COOKING **5**
MODERN EUROPEAN
£38–£92

Next time the Olympic Games are held in Britain, the organisers might consider hiring Chewton Glen rather than building a new stadium, given its gymnasium, sauna, nine-hole golf course, croquet lawn, snooker room, swimming pools (two), and tennis courts (three). It would not take long, though, for athletes to get sidetracked by the food and service. To say that the 'seriously wealthy, no-longer-young' guests are pampered is to understate the degree to which they are indulged, mollycoddled, cosseted and made a fuss of. Despite 'wellness choice' menu options, the kitchen plays its part in this, offering starters of foie gras terrine, scallops with ginger butter, and Emmental cheese soufflé with a kirsch-flavoured fondue sauce.

Dover sole meunière, and lobster with béarnaise may not be cutting edge (and, given the price of dinner, supplements seem rather excessive), but a large brigade certainly manages the technical side of things well, even if flavours are sometimes barely more than polite: top quality rare tuna comes on 'wild' rocket leaves with a 'tame' dressing. The kitchen resists the temptation to garnish things unnecessarily, which is a blessing, serving a small pink fillet of lamb coated in herbs, mustard and breadcrumbs on spring vegetables with a silky and subtle stock-based sauce. Desserts do not appear to be the highlight, although they may include rhubarb and cream cheese tart made with fresh and fragile puff pastry, accompanied by a voluptuous strawberry ice cream.

Meticulously trained staff set a personal, welcoming and obliging tone, while an elegant and impressive wine list contains fine bottles from around the world. Bordeaux and Burgundy are well represented, but Italy, California and Australia are strong sections too: and there is even an offering from Ukraine. In spite of the undoubted quality and range, mark-ups are too high for comfort, particularly on wines that are expensive in the first place, although bottles below £20 are scattered throughout. Prices start at £16.25.

CHEF: Pierre Chevillard PROPRIETORS: Martin and Brigitte Skan OPEN: all week 12.30 to 2, 7.30 to 9.30 MEALS: alc L Mon to Sat (main courses £12.50 to £18). Set L Sun £30, Set D £47.50 SERVICE: not inc, card slips closed CARDS: Amex, Delta, Diners, MasterCard, Switch, Visa DETAILS: 110 seats. Private parties: 120 main room, 6 to 120 private rooms. Car park. Vegetarian meals. No children under 6. No smoking in dining room. Wheelchair access (also WC). No music. Air-conditioned ACCOMMODATION: 55 rooms, all with bath/shower. TV. Phone. Room only £235 to £665. Rooms for disabled. No children under 6. Swimming pool (*The Which? Hotel Guide*)

NEWTON LONGVILLE Buckinghamshire **map 3**

Crooked Billet £ **NEW ENTRY**

Newton Longville MK17 0DF
TEL: (01908) 373936 FAX: (01908) 631979 COOKING **3**
EMAIL: booking@the-crooked-billet-pub.co.uk BRITISH
WEB SITE: www.the-crooked-billet-pub.co.uk £17–£42

Still popular with local drinkers, this sixteenth-century, white-painted, timber framed, brick and thatched pub in the middle of the village took on a new lease of life when ownership changed in May 2000. Emma Sexton offers a generous slate of appealing dishes from country-style to cosmopolitan. The cooking is bold, assured and gutsy, taking in beef broth with horseradish croûtons, and slow-cooked ham hock with champ and cabbage, alongside seafood from lobster thermidor to roast skate wing with garlic butter.

Simple grilling has made the most of corn-fed chicken breast with minted peas, onion rice and a tasty gravy, and vegetables are integral to main courses: pork loin at inspection, with lightly roasted celeriac, potato, parsnip and plenty of green beans. Finish with appetisingly tart apple pie, ginger sponge and custard, or a selection of Neal's Yard cheeses.

Youthful but well-drilled service is headed up by John Gilchrist, who also oversees the wine side of the business. Previously sommelier at the 1837 restaurant at Browns Hotel (see entry, London), he is continuing his drinker-friendly policy by making all of the 250 wines on the classy and fairly priced list available by the glass (for about one fifth of the bottle price). Half-bottles are not in short supply either, and a dozen house recommendations start at £9.50.

'Waiting staff are a few plates short of a dinner service.' (On eating in Ireland)

CHEF: Emma Sexton PROPRIETORS: John Gilchrist and Emma Sexton OPEN: Tue to Sun L 12 to 2.30, Mon to Sat D 7 to 10 MEALS: alc (main courses L £5 to £10, D £5 to £15) SERVICE: not inc, card slips closed CARDS: Delta, MasterCard, Switch, Visa DETAILS: 60 seats. 60 seats outside. Private parties: 70 main room, 14 private room. Car park. Vegetarian meals. Children's helpings. No children in bar. No smoking in dining room. Wheelchair access (not WC). Occasional music (£5)

NORTON Shropshire map 5

▲ Hundred House Hotel

Bridgnorth Road, Norton TF11 9EE
TEL: (01952) 730353 FAX: (01952) 730355
EMAIL: hphundredhouse@messages.co.uk
WEB SITE: www.hundredhouse.co.uk
on A442, 6m S of Telford

COOKING **3**
MODERN EUROPEAN
£27–£61

'Inside, it's dark and warm: old bricks, old timber and generous log fires with their own happy smell,' wrote one contented visitor to this roadside pub. It divides itself into several rooms and offers both à la carte and brasserie menus. The former goes in for chargrilled John Dory with chive beurre blanc (fish comes from Devon), and Hereford duck with parsnip rösti and spiced damsons, while the latter spans a range from homely steak and kidney pie to chargrilled chicken with polenta, sage pesto and lemon mayonnaise.

Recommended dishes have included a leafy rocket and potato soup; rack of lamb with enough flavour to stand up to its accompanying garlicky aubergines, courgettes, and chickpeas with yoghurt; and fig tart to finish. Service is friendly and courteous. As well as seeking out Ludlow venison and Staffordshire wild boar, the Phillipses also list an unusual local wine, Staffordshire Halfpenny ('peppery like Syrah'), part of an ambitious list with no fewer than 12 house wines at £12.50, all available by the large or small glass.

CHEF: Stuart Phillips PROPRIETORS: the Phillips family OPEN: all week L 12 to 2.30, Mon to Sat D 6 to 10 MEALS: alc Mon to Sat L and D (main courses £15 to £18). Set L Sun £13.50 (2 courses) to £16.50. Brasserie menu available SERVICE: not inc CARDS: Delta, MasterCard, Switch, Visa DETAILS: 70 seats. Private parties: 35 main room, 35 private room. Car park. Vegetarian meals. Children's helpings. No smoking in dining room. Occasional music ACCOMMODATION: 10 rooms, all with bath/shower. TV. Phone. B&B £69 to £120. Baby facilities (*The Which? Hotel Guide*) (£5)

NORWICH Norfolk map 6

Adlard's

79 Upper St Giles Street, Norwich NR2 1AB
TEL: (01603) 633522 FAX: (01603) 617733

COOKING **5**
MODERN BRITISH
£30–£61

Adlard's is no longer green. Now lighter and more spacious after its very public makeover, it sports a pine floor, rag-rolled walls in beige and cream, cane-backed chairs, and cheesecloth curtains draped over a brass pole. The new look extends to revitalised menus, now a mix of set-price options and a carte with varying degrees of choice: none at all on the £25 dinner, three or four per course on the carte. Supporters maintain that this is still one of the best restaurants in East Anglia, a claim backed up by high-quality ingredients evident in a moist terrine of foie gras and duck confit layered with asparagus, served with celeriac purée, and a prime fillet of roast turbot with a crisp sea salt topping, in a wild mushroom 'casserole' with purée potatoes.

Properly reduced sauces are a feature: to accompany four pink oval fillets of seared lamb, with roast shallots and garlic, at inspection. A few lapses are evident, but successes are plentiful, including treacle tart with crisp pastry and a 'squidgy, fudgy' lemon-flavoured filling, served with crème anglaise and passion-fruit sorbet. Service has varied from 'slow' to 'spot on', but is generally pleasant and helpful, incidentals such as bread and the appetiser soup are top drawer, and if prices at dinner are fair they are a bargain at lunchtime.

'We are not ashamed about our house wines,' states the wine list, which presents only praiseworthy bottles throughout its weighty 28 pages. French wines are refreshingly left until last, allowing New World superstars to shine more brightly. Wines of the month ring fashionable changes, and prices are reasonable, the aforesaid house selection £12.50 a bottle.

CHEF: Roger Hickman PROPRIETOR: David Adlard OPEN: Tue to Sat L 12.30 to 1.45, Mon to Sat D 7.30 to 10.30 MEALS: alc (main courses £16.50 to £18.50). Set L £15 (2 courses) to £19, Set D £25 SERVICE: not inc CARDS: Amex, Delta, Diners, MasterCard, Switch, Visa DETAILS: 40 seats. Private parties: 40 main room. Vegetarian meals. Children's helpings. No music. Air-conditioned (£5)

Marco's

17 Pottergate, Norwich NR2 1DS — COOKING **2**
TEL: (01603) 624044 — ITALIAN
£25–£49

Don't be put off by a closed door at this long-standing town-centre Italian restaurant; just ring the bell and a waitress will come and open it. Inside is a comfortable bar lounge and a small, square, smartly appointed dining room. Marco himself is an 'absolute charmer', dividing his time between kitchen and front-of-house, serving up large fresh sardines with garlic and herb sauce, a huge bowl of pasta with herbs and cream, and home-made potato gnocchi with basil sauce. The strength is simple, honest food, which can take in wild boar bresaola, a brace of large crab cakes, and chicken cooked in a typically Italian blend of olive oil, garlic, basil, white wine and tomatoes. Desserts include classic zabaglione as well as a dish of strawberries with mascarpone and brown sugar flashed under the grill. The wine list takes a tour round Italy, picking up a good range of styles and prices, starting with house Soave and Valpolicella at £12.50.

CHEF/PROPRIETOR: Marco Vessalio OPEN: Tue to Sat 12 to 2, 7 to 10 CLOSED: 25 and 26 Dec, bank hols MEALS: alc (main courses £12.50 to £17). Set L £15 SERVICE: not inc, card slips closed, 10% for parties of 8 or more CARDS: Amex, Diners, MasterCard, Visa DETAILS: 22 seats. Private parties: 12 main room. Vegetarian. Children's helpings. No smoking in dining room. Wheelchair access (not WC)

Although the cuisine style noted at the top of entries has in most cases been suggested to the Guide by the restaurants, some have been edited for brevity or appropriateness.

NOTTINGHAM Nottinghamshire map 5

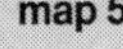

Hart's

1 Standard Court, Park Row,
Nottingham NG1 6GN
TEL: (0115) 911 0666 FAX: (0115) 911 0611

COOKING **6**
MODERN ENGLISH
£23–£63

Occupying part of a former hospital in a quiet Regency quarter of the city, Hart's is cast very much in modern brasserie mould, but with more serious intent than most. Beyond the small bar is a bright, well-regulated dining room with comfortably upholstered chairs and smartly set tables, where service is generally correct, informative and friendly. 'All in all, Hart's does everything well,' summed up one visitor, noting that the short, sensibly priced menu provides relief from the tyranny of current brasserie staples. It knows how to dispense comfort – in the shape of half a lobster, baked and served with baby artichokes and hollandaise, or chicken breast served with foie gras and wild mushroom risotto – and how to play to the gallery, with tiger prawns in a light, crisp tempura batter, accompanied by a thick dipping sauce of chillied tomato.

Seafood appears to be a particular strength, judging by favourable reports of herb-crusted monkfish fillet on linguine with a creamy saffron sauce, and well-timed, assertively flavoured baked brill on the bone, with floury new potatoes and good beurre blanc. Other options range from roast sweetbreads with morels and asparagus, via simply braised shoulder of lamb with Mediterranean vegetables, to a vegetarian main course such as grilled halloumi with roasted aubergine and vegetable fritters. Finish with a creamy raspberry crème brûlée, or hot chocolate pudding with pistachio ice cream. A short, enterprising and businesslike wine list offers commendable choice under £20, plus some finer bottles. Four house wines range from £11.50 to £22.50.

CHEF: Mark Gough PROPRIETOR: Tim Hart OPEN: all week 12 to 2, 7 (6 Sat) to 10.30 CLOSED: 26 Dec, 1 Jan MEALS: alc (main courses £8.50 to £15.50). Set L £9.90 (2 courses) to £13.40. Pre-theatre menu available all week but must be pre-booked SERVICE: 10% (optional), card slips closed CARDS: Amex, Delta, MasterCard, Switch, Visa DETAILS: 80 seats. 20 seats outside. Private parties: 88 main room, 14 private room. Vegetarian meals. Children's helpings. No-smoking area. Wheelchair access (also WC). No music

▲ Merchants

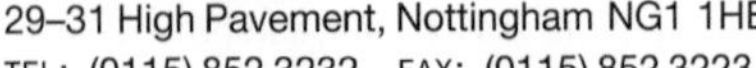

29–31 High Pavement, Nottingham NG1 1HE
TEL: (0115) 852 3232 FAX: (0115) 852 3223
EMAIL: reservations@lacemarkethotel.co.uk
WEB SITE: www.lacemarkethotel.co.uk

COOKING **2**
MODERN BRITISH BRASSERIE
£23–£48

Formerly a stand-alone restaurant, Merchants has become the dining room of a brand-new hotel, the Lace Market. Décor may seem starkly minimal but smartly set tables and sympathetic lighting soften the overall effect. Dean Rogers took over the kitchen in early 2000 and has simplified the menus a great deal. A salad of artichoke and plum tomatoes with herbed vinaigrette pleased one reporter, while another approved thick and comforting tomato, basil and white bean soup with a spicy kick. Cod fillet with cabbage and spinach surrounded by crisp crab won tons has been a successful main course, as has chargrilled rare ribeye steak with chips and béarnaise. Finish perhaps with nougat parfait and raspberry coulis, or Bakewell tart. The short wine list deals in sharp modern flavours such as Chilean Sauvignon Blanc and River Gum Shiraz Cabernet from Australia. Prices start at £10.95.

CHEF: Dean Rogers PROPRIETOR: Lace Market Hotel Ltd. OPEN: Sun to Fri L 12 to 2.30, Mon to Sat D 6.30 to 10.30 (bar meals all week 11 to 11) CLOSED: 25 Dec MEALS: alc D (main courses £9 to £15). Set L Mon to Fri £12.50 (2 courses) to £14.50, Set L Sun £16.50, Set D Mon to Thur £16.50 SERVICE: 10% CARDS: Amex, Delta, MasterCard, Switch, Visa DETAILS: 75 seats. Private parties: 75 main room, 20 private room. Vegetarian meals. Music. Air-conditioned ACCOMMODATION: 29 rooms, all with bath/shower. TV. Phone. Room only £65 to £99

Sonny's

NEW ENTRY

3 Carlton Street, Hockley, Nottingham NG1 1NL
TEL: (0115) 947 3041 FAX: (0115) 950 7776

COOKING **3**
MODERN BRITISH
£22–£48

This large, pale-walled modern brasserie with a hard-edged interior smack in the centre of Nottingham is a cool and trendy place that can attract the crowds. David Hodgins's arrival appears to have arrested a period of decline in the kitchen's performance, and the cooking is once more pursuing the vivid flavours and light textures that have typically featured both here and in the branch in Barnes (see entry, London). Linguine with roast peppers, rocket and pine nuts uses soft-cooked, home-made pasta and pedigree olive oil to make a bright starter, which might be followed by grilled sea bass with broad bean and tarragon risotto, full of appealing, natural flavours.

The emphasis on freshness extends to a red wine jelly of summer fruits with shortbread and raspberry coulis, while the single-cheese course might offer Colston Bassett Stilton with apple chutney and oatcakes. Staff are knowledgeable, friendly and professional. Appetising whites and rich reds form the nucleus of the short, sensibly priced wine list. House vin de pays is £9.50.

CHEF: David Hodgins PROPRIETOR: Rebecca Mascarenhas OPEN: all week 12 to 2.30 (3 Sun), 7 to 10 (11 Fri and Sat) CLOSED: Christmas, bank hols MEALS: alc (main courses £10 to £15). Set L Sun to Fri £13.95 SERVICE: 10% (optional), card slips closed CARDS: Amex, Delta, MasterCard, Switch, Visa DETAILS: 80 seats. Private parties: 80 main room, 30 private room. Vegetarian meals. No cigars/pipes in dining room. Wheelchair access (not WC). Music. Air-conditioned

OLD BURGHCLERE Hampshire **map 2**

Dew Pond

Old Burghclere RG20 9LH
TEL: (01635) 278408 FAX: (01635) 278580
WEB SITE: www.dewpond.co.uk
off old A34, 3m W of Kingsclere

COOKING **6**
ANGLO-FRENCH
£37–£53

The whitewashed building belies its sixteenth-century origins with a couple of domestic-scale lounges and two inter-linked dining rooms. Keith Marshall's nightly set-price menus offer a generous choice of seven items per course, with a supplement here and there for perhaps a scallop starter or main-course beef fillet with béarnaise. Materials are sound, and a high degree of skill is brought to bear, although this is not showy cooking. Rather it is a well-rendered version of Anglo-French provincial, in which roast artichoke heart is filled with shallot purée and given an hollandaise sauce, or calf's liver and bacon are served with a bubble and squeak 'cake' and a sage-infused brown onion sauce.

Centrepieces remain at the centre, with just enough accompaniment to support them without getting in the way, and desserts don't let the side down. Expect tarte Tatin with vanilla ice cream and cinnamon crème anglaise, or a trio of chocolate: warm tart, white parfait, and Baileys milk chocolate mousse. Service is considered 'efficient and correct' rather than warm, and a concise but global list arranges wines according to style and features fashionable regions and producers at fair prices. For a weighty red, try South Africa's Glen Carlou Grande Classique 1997, a blend of Cabernet and Merlot (£18.50). Four house wines are £11.95 a bottle, £3 a glass.

CHEF: Keith Marshall PROPRIETORS: Keith and Julie Marshall OPEN: Tue to Sat D only 7 to 10 CLOSED: last week Dec, first week Jan, 2 weeks Aug MEALS: Set D £25 SERVICE: not inc CARDS: Amex, Delta, Diners, MasterCard, Switch, Visa DETAILS: 50 seats. Private parties: 50 main room, 25 private room. Car park. Vegetarian meals. No children under 5. No smoking in dining room. Wheelchair access (not WC). No music (£5)

OMBERSLEY Worcestershire **map 5**

Venture In

Main Road, Ombersley WR9 0EW
TEL/FAX: (01905) 620552

COOKING **2**
MODERN BRITISH/FRENCH
£25–£43

One of many half-timbered buildings in a village just off the A449, Venture In welcomes with black beams, a large inglenook fireplace, and a partitioned dining room whose old windows overlook the street. A special fish evening every second Wednesday indicates the kitchen's partiality, when it might offer red sea bream with couscous and a Thai-style sauce, or monkfish wrapped in smoked bacon on a roasted vegetable tart. The carte's quota of seafood varies by the day, but there are plenty of meat options as well, from duck leg confit on sage and garlic polenta, to braised pig's cheek with seared foie gras and caramelised apple. Desserts generally aim to soothe, with pear Tatin on cocoa sorbet, or caramelised pineapple pancake with vanilla ice cream. A short roving list starts with French and Chilean house wines at £10.95.

CHEF/PROPRIETOR: Toby William Fletcher OPEN: Tue to Sun L 12 to 2, Tue to Sat D 7 to 9.45 CLOSED: 26 Dec, 2 weeks winter, 2 weeks summer, bank hols MEALS: Set L £13.95 (2 courses) to £16.95, Set D £25.95 SERVICE: not inc, card slips closed CARDS: Delta, MasterCard, Switch, Visa DETAILS: 32 seats. Private parties: 20 main room. Car park. Vegetarian meals. No smoking in dining room. Music. Air-conditioned

Several sharp operators have tried to extort money from restaurateurs on the promise of an entry in a guidebook that has never appeared. The Good Food Guide *makes no charge for inclusion.*

ORFORD Suffolk map 6

▲ Crown and Castle, Trinity £ NEW ENTRY

Orford IP12 2LJ
TEL: (01394) 450205 FAX: (01394) 450176 COOKING 1
EMAIL: info@crownandcastlehotel.co.uk MODERN BRITISH
WEB SITE: www.crownandcastlehotel.co.uk £24–£48

David and Ruth Watson come with a track record – they used to run the Fox & Goose in Fressingfield (see Round-up entry), and Hintlesham Hall before that, and Ruth has also had a career in food journalism – so they knew what they were letting themselves in for when they embarked on a two-year refurbishment of this Tudoresque house in a pretty seaside village between Snape and Aldeburgh. Trinity, the name of the restaurant, apparently symbolises simple hospitality in the form of bread, cheese and wine, although the menu stretches further, into oysters with Vietnamese vinegar, smoked haddock Benedict, and a salty dish (at inspection) of lambs' kidneys on a cake of black pudding bubble and squeak with a mustard sauce. Materials have also included first-rate asparagus wrapped in good-quality ham and lightly grilled. Food is piled into faddish towers or served in big soup plates, cheeses are kept in good order, and desserts run to hot chocolate sponge, or treacle tart. Staff are friendly and 'fairly efficient', and wines are grouped by grape variety and sensibly priced, starting with house Sicilian at £9.50.

CHEF: Brendon Ansbro PROPRIETORS: David and Ruth Watson OPEN: all week 12 to 3, 6.30 to 10 MEALS: alc (main courses £7.50 to £13.50) SERVICE: not inc CARDS: Delta, MasterCard, Switch, Visa DETAILS: 68 seats. 40 seats outside. Private parties: 50 main room, 12 private room. Car park. Vegetarian meals. Children's helpings. No smoking while others eat. Wheelchair access (not WC). No music ACCOMMODATION: 19 rooms, all with bath/shower. TV. Phone. B&B £60 to £100. Rooms for disabled

OSWESTRY Shropshire map 7

▲ Sebastians

45 Willow Street, Oswestry SY11 1AQ
TEL: (01691) 655444 FAX: (01691) 653452 COOKING 3
EMAIL: sebastians.rest@virgin.net FRENCH
WEB SITE: www.virtual-shropshire.co.uk/sebastians £35–£46

Uneven floors hint at the age of the blue-and-white-painted building, French posters in the small drinks area herald a Gallic slant to the food, and sewing machine tables in the dining room point to an informal style. Mark Sebastian Fisher's monthly-changing menus indeed offer an English perspective on French provincial cooking that avoids many of the clichés while still managing to produce a dusky-pink seafood bisque with rouille and croûtons, and duck breast with bacon, cabbage and lentils. Saucing may be the weakest link in the chain, but materials are fine and their treatment sound, be it brief cooking of turbot fillet on ratatouille with hollandaise, or lengthy braising of a sticky and covetable jarret d'agneau: 'a big lump of meat on the bone' served on cannellini beans. Presentational towers prevail – a rough puff pastry tart of aubergine, mozzarella, chorizo and tapénade under a green haystack of salad leaves – and desserts run to strawberry vacherin ('like Eton mess waiting to happen') and crêpe suzette. A largely French wine list doesn't ignore the New World, and keeps prices at a sensible level, starting at £11.50.

CHEF: Mark Sebastian Fisher PROPRIETORS: Michelle and Mark Sebastian Fisher OPEN: Tue to Sat D only 6.30 to 9.45 CLOSED: 25 and 26 Dec, 1 Jan MEALS: Set D £19.95 (2 courses) to £23.95 SERVICE: not inc, card slips closed CARDS: Amex, Delta, MasterCard, Switch, Visa DETAILS: 45 seats. 25 seats outside. Private parties: 60 main room. Vegetarian meals. Children's helpings. No smoking in dining room. Wheelchair access (not WC). Music ACCOMMODATION: 8 rooms, all with bath/shower. TV. Phone. Room only £45 to £55 (£5)

OXFORD Oxfordshire map 2

▲ Al-Shami £

25 Walton Crescent, Oxford OX1 2JG
TEL: (01865) 310066 FAX: (01865) 311241
WEB SITE: www.al-shami.co.uk/oxfordshire/secretgarden/al-shami

COOKING **2**
LEBANESE
£18–£39

It is the meze that attract both townsfolk and gownsfolk to this popular Lebanese restaurant in a quiet Victorian crescent. Once you are seated in the light dining room, with its bright Middle Eastern paintings, chandeliers and potted plants, there's a choice of 39 snacks – both hot and cold – to peruse. Highlights include hummus topped with lamb strips of 'bacon-like crispness', foul medames (brown beans in lemon, garlic and olive oil), and hugely enjoyable Armenian sausages. Main courses are less thrilling, although chargrilled meats such as baby chicken with garlic sauce are generally well executed. The large plateful of raw vegetables included in the cover charge obviates the need to order side dishes, and puddings run to Arabic ice cream. Formally dressed waiters cope efficiently with a full restaurant. Lebanese house wine is available by the half-bottle; alternatively, there's arak, Lebanese beer and various vintages of Ch. Musar.

CHEF: Mimo Mahfouz PROPRIETOR: Al-Shami OPEN: all week noon to midnight MEALS: alc (main courses £6.50 to £12). Cover £1 SERVICE: not inc, card slips closed, 10% for parties of 6 or more CARDS: MasterCard, Switch, Visa DETAILS: 90 seats. Private parties: 45 main room, 45 private room. Vegetarian meals. Wheelchair access (also WC). Music ACCOMMODATION: 12 rooms, all with bath/shower. TV. Phone. B&B £35 to £45 (£5)

Cherwell Boathouse

50 Bardwell Road, Oxford OX2 6ST
TEL: (01865) 552746 FAX: (01865) 553809
WEB SITE: www.cherwellboathouse.co.uk

COOKING **3**
MODERN ENGLISH/FRENCH
£25–£35

Set bucolically down a little-used lane off the Banbury Road, the Boathouse offers light bites in the River Bar (formerly known as the Tea Hut), and more substantial food in the brick-walled, parquet-floored slightly 'makeshift' restaurant overlooking the river. The kitchen focuses on careful sourcing of materials – including organic and free-range – and cooks them accurately and in sensible combinations. Pink, juicy pigeon breast has appeared in a warm salad with smoked bacon, enlivened by dribbles of raspberry dressing, while a thick slice of good-quality pork was well complemented by an apple and prune compote at inspection.

Traditional puddings of treacle tart or lemon cheesecake round things off. Service is informal and 'good-natured'. As the Boathouse is owned by Anthony Verdin (half of London wine merchants Morris & Verdin), it is not surprising that the list offers high quality and good value. Burgundy and Bordeaux feature strongly, although 'The Riesling Page' provides interesting and food-friendly alternatives. House wines start at a cheerful £8.50, and there is plenty of opportunity to splash out: Ch. Margaux 1983 is a find at £150.

CHEFS: Wayne Cullen and Nathan Tuckwell PROPRIETOR: Anthony Verdin OPEN: all week 12 to 2, 6.30 to 10 CLOSED: 24 to 30 Dec MEALS: Set L Mon to Sat £9.75 (2 courses) to £18.50, Set L Sun £19.50, Set D £20.50 SERVICE: not inc, 10% for parties of 6 or more CARDS: Amex, Delta, Diners, MasterCard, Switch, Visa DETAILS: 60 seats. 100 seats outside. Private parties: 50 main room, 80 private room. Car park. Vegetarian meals. Children's helpings. No smoking in dining room. Wheelchair access (also WC). No music (£5)

Lemon Tree 

268 Woodstock Road, Oxford OX2 7NW
TEL: (01865) 311936
FAX: (01865) 310021

COOKING **5**
BRITISH/MEDITERRANEAN
£33–£65

It is hard to miss the brightly coloured building – more 'Dijon mustard' than lemon – set back a little from the road. Inside is equally striking, with a horseshoe-shaped bar, potted palms, huge mirrors, curly metal light fittings, and splashes of cobalt blue glassware. Shaun Mitchell (who has worked for several years at Plas Bodegroes, see entry, Pwllheli) was appointed in May 2000, bringing with him a confident approach to the kitchen's already established take on British and Mediterranean cooking.

Success is founded on sound materials, from chargrilled Welsh Black beef to a generous serving of warm, meaty lobster dressed in coriander, garlic and ginger. Extras are listed on a specials board: lightly grilled hake flamed in Pernod for one visitor, with crisp, salted skin, served on stir-fried fennel and peppers. Technical expertise does not appear to be in question, judging by a spatchcocked poussin served on couscous with a yoghurt-dressed, almond-strewn salad. Vegetables, charged extra, are up to scratch.

Accomplished desserts were the stars of an inspection meal: a light and daringly citric lemon tart, and a superior version of crème brûlée, with cooked banana and pistachios melting into the cream, and an exquisitely thin brittle top. Service is generally polite and charming. The wine list is an inviting selection of bright, interesting flavours, with a reasonable spread of prices starting at £9.95 for white Bordeaux or Chilean Merlot.

CHEF: Shaun Mitchell PROPRIETOR: Clinton Pugh OPEN: all week 12 to 11 CLOSED: 25 and 26 Dec, 1 Jan MEALS: alc (main courses £11 to £21) SERVICE: not inc, 10% (optional) for parties of 5 or more CARDS: Amex, Delta, MasterCard, Switch, Visa DETAILS: 80 seats. 40 seats outside. Private parties: 20 main room. Car park. Vegetarian meals. Children's helpings. Wheelchair access (also WC). Music (£5)

▲ Old Parsonage Hotel, Parsonage Restaurant & Bar

1 Banbury Road, Oxford OX2 6NN
TEL: (01865) 310210 FAX: (01865) 311262 — COOKING **2**
EMAIL: info@oldparsonage-hotel.co.uk — ENGLISH/MEDITERRANEAN
WEB SITE: www.oxford-hotels-restaurants.co.uk — £27–£48

Close-together tables and banquette seating in the bar lounge of this attractive old building, close to the centre of town, make it more of a casual venue than a place for a whole evening out: 'we go before or after the theatre', wrote one couple. The food obliges, offering twice-baked spinach soufflé, or baked pear with Stilton and walnuts, followed by poached smoked haddock, or roast chicken with fennel and tomatoes, although there are more substantial items, such as calf's liver and bacon, or venison steak. A few bright flavours give some dishes a lift – stir-fried prawns with chilli, pesto, coriander and couscous salad – while desserts are cast in more traditional mould, with lemon crème brûlée, or bitter chocolate tart with matching sorbet. Around 40 varied and well-chosen wines are fairly priced, starting at £11.25.

CHEF: Alison Watkins PROPRIETOR: Jeremy Mogford OPEN: Mon to Sat 12 to 3, 6 to 11, Sun 12.30 to 3.30, 6.30 to 11 CLOSED: 24 to 28 Dec MEALS: alc (main courses £10 to £13.50) SERVICE: not inc, 12.5% for parties of 8 or more CARDS: Amex, Delta, Diners, MasterCard, Switch, Visa DETAILS: 36 seats. 48 seats outside. Private parties: 14 main room. Car park. Vegetarian meals. Children's helpings. No cigars/pipes in dining room. Wheelchair access (not WC). Music. Air-conditioned ACCOMMODATION: 30 rooms, all with bath/shower. TV. Phone. B&B £130 to £200. Baby facilities (*The Which? Hotel Guide*)

Le Petit Blanc

71-72 Walton Street, Oxford OX2 6AG — COOKING **4**
TEL: (01865) 510999 FAX: (01865) 510700 — FRENCH
WEB SITE: www.petit-blanc.com — £22–£45

The Petit Blanc brand now extends from Cheltenham to Birmingham (see entries), but without detriment to the original, which serves food most of the day in two rooms: one with a city mural and zinc-topped bar, the other with a view of the kitchen. A busy atmosphere and small, close-together tables are a reminder that, even though newspapers are available, this is not a place to linger and relax; rather it has a sense of vitality quite in keeping with the food (try the Blanc Vite menu if speed is of the essence). The menu's French backbone – crêpes, skate wing with beurre noisette, Toulouse sausage – is fleshed out with a few modern British flourishes along the lines of salmon and haddock fishcakes.

Mr White (as opposed to Monsieur Blanc) does the cooking, treating well-sourced raw materials professionally: for example a smooth foie gras and chicken liver parfait, served with a well made onion marmalade, and pink sliced rump of lamb with creamy shallots and mint oil. Ribeye steak with frites and bearnaise also gets the thumbs-up, as does blackcurrant vacherin. Children (as in all Raymond Blanc's restaurants) are made to feel particularly welcome. Around 30 wines are listed by grape variety, starting with house Chenin Blanc and Merlot at £9.95.

CHEF: Martin White PROPRIETOR: Raymond Blanc/Blanc Restaurants Ltd OPEN: all week 12 to 3 (3.30 Sat and Sun), 6 to 11 (10 Sun) CLOSED: 25 Dec and 1 Jan MEALS: alc (main courses £7.50 to £14). Set L and D £12.50 (2 courses) to £15. Children's menu £5.95 (2 courses) to £7.95. Light meals 12 to 11 (10 Sun) SERVICE: not inc, 10% (optional) for parties of 8 or more CARDS: Amex, Delta, Diners, MasterCard, Switch, Visa DETAILS: 130 seats. Private parties: 50 main room, 20 private room. Vegetarian meals. Children's helpings. No smoking in dining room. Smoking in bar only. Wheelchair access (also WC). Music. Air-conditioned (£5)

White House

2 Botley Road, Oxford OX2 0AB
TEL: (01865) 242823 FAX: (01865) 793331 — COOKING **1**
EMAIL: thewhitehouseoxford@btinternet.com — MODERN BRITISH
WEB SITE: www.oxfordpages.co.uk/thewhitehouse — £28–£52

Whether you're arriving in Oxford by train or boat, the White House – sited between the river and the railway station – will prove handy, and in summer the walled garden makes for pleasant outdoor eating in the shade of a spreading chestnut tree. Originally a toll-house, it became an inn in 1869 and has never looked back. The menu is wide-ranging, majoring in what might be considered modern brasserie food: curried chicken livers in cream-cheese pastry, penne carbonara, and salmon roasted with peppers and herbs, for example. 'You will need a good appetite to manage three courses,' commented one who enjoyed a spring roll, and halibut with stir-fried vegetables. Friendly, interested service helps things go with a swing. Vivid flavours are much in evidence on the wine list, which offers nearly all its choices under £20, and starts at £9.95.

CHEF: Chris Bland PROPRIETORS: Michael White and John Martin OPEN: Mon to Sat 12 to 2.30, 6 to 9.30, Sun 12 to 3, 7 to 9 CLOSED: 25 and 26 Dec MEALS: alc (main courses £9 to £13). Bar menu available Mon to Sat SERVICE: not inc CARDS: Amex, Delta, Diners, MasterCard, Switch, Visa DETAILS: 60 seats. 40 seats outside. Private parties: 100 main room, 40 to 60 private rooms. Car park. Vegetarian meals. Children's helpings. Wheelchair access (also WC). Occasional music (£5)

PADSTOW Cornwall — **map 1**

Brock's  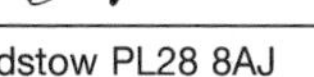

The Strand, Padstow PL28 8AJ — COOKING **3**
TEL: (01841) 532565 FAX: (01841) 533991 — MODERN BRITISH
EMAIL: brocks@compuserve.com — £26–£55

Above an estate agent's, not quite overlooking the harbour, this first-floor dining room combines beams and bright yellow walls with large pot plants and an old-fashioned saloon-style bar. Despite a change in the kitchen (Carl Hamilton has worked at good addresses in London as well as at the Seafood Restaurant; see entry, also Padstow), the same format obtains. A short carte and set-price menu offer simple dishes of asparagus with hollandaise, or seared scallops with spinach, ginger and soy, followed by red mullet with baked fennel, or maybe rump of Cornish lamb with soured aubergine. The Anglo-French style continues with desserts of banana Tatin, or chocolate marquise, and a short wine list stays mostly under £20, starting with house Italian white at £11.95 and Australian red at £12.95.

CHEF: Carl Hamilton PROPRIETORS: Tim and Hazel Brocklebank OPEN: Mon to Sat 12.30 to 2, 7 to 9.30 (10 Fri and Sat) CLOSED: early Jan to early Feb MEALS: alc (main courses L £7 to £12, D £12 to £17). Set D £19.50 (2 courses) to £23.50 SERVICE: not inc CARDS: Delta, MasterCard, Switch, Visa DETAILS: 45 seats. Private parties: 35 main room, 20 private room. Children's helpings. No smoking in dining room. Music

Margot's

11 Duke Street, Padstow PL28 8AB — COOKING **2**
TEL: (01841) 533441 — MODERN BRITISH
WEB SITE: www.margots.co.uk — £26–£37

Jaunty artwork depicting local fishing scenes decorates this small, efficiently run, bright pink and blue restaurant, where chatty, observant and personable staff oversee proceedings. There is no fancy-pants stuff, just straightforward and largely consistent cooking that takes local produce as its starting point: a hotpot of crab and mussels; grilled red mullet with a tomato dressing; or well-timed steamed sea bass with a rich and creamy, chive-flecked butter sauce.

Not everything is fishy, however. One enjoyable meal began with meze-style roast aubergine with artichokes and feta, followed by loin of pork wrapped in Parma ham with a well flavoured mushroom risotto. Crisp and crunchy vegetables plainly served in bamboo steamer baskets are commended, and a light, tangy, properly made lemon tart makes a classy way to finish. Wines from the New World outnumber those from the Old on the short, bright list, although Italy, at £9.95 a bottle, heads up the house selection.

CHEF: Adrian Oliver PROPRIETORS: Adrian and Julie Oliver OPEN: Wed to Sat 12 to 2, 7 to 9 CLOSED: Nov, Jan MEALS: alc L (main courses around £5.50). Set D £18.95 (2 courses) to £22.95 SERVICE: not inc CARDS: Amex, Delta, MasterCard, Switch, Visa DETAILS: 25 seats. Private parties: 25 main room. Children's helpings. No smoking in dining room. Wheelchair access (not WC). Music (£5)

▲ No. 6 Art & Seafood Café — NEW ENTRY

6 Middle Street, Padstow PL28 8AP — COOKING **4**
TEL/FAX: (01841) 532093 — SEAFOOD
£34–£54

No matter how many good restaurants Padstow comes up with, it seems there is always room for one more. Karen Scott's self-styled bistro-with-rooms is a white-fronted eighteenth-century house boasting a pleasantly spacious dining room with a black and white draughtboard floor. The cooking applies a global approach to its impeccably fresh ingredients, producing fat, succulent tiger prawns with a palate-rousing dressing of chilli oil, grated ginger and garlic. Fine local scallops, also chillied, are accompanied by rocket dressed in walnut oil, tempered with a blob of crème fraîche, and tandoori cod has also pleased one reporter.

Not everything is spicy however: monkfish, for example, has been stewed in tomatoes, onions, lentils and oregano, and pork tenderloin (there is usually one meat option for main course) has come with prunes and shiitake mushrooms. A single well-kept cheese (maybe Roquefort with Bath Olivers) offers an alternative to straightforward pear and raspberry crumble, or crème brûlée livened up with a star anise infusion. The wine list, though modestly proportioned, zips hither and yon, collecting Chardonnays and Sauvignons aplenty to go with the fish, plus a few more varied reds. House wines – French white, Australian red – are £11.50.

CHEF/PROPRIETOR: Karen Scott OPEN: Wed to Sun D only 7 to 9.30 (10.30 weekends in summer; phone to check in winter) MEALS: alc (main courses £15). Set D £19.50 (2 courses) to £23.50 SERVICE: not inc CARDS: Switch, Delta DETAILS: 35 seats. 6 seats outside. Private parties: 30 main room. Vegetarian meals only with notice. Children's helpings. No smoking in dining room. Music ACCOMMODATION: 3 rooms, all with bath/shower. TV. B&B £55 to £65 £5

▲ Rick Stein's Café 

10 Middle Street, Padstow PL28 8AP
TEL: (01841) 532700 FAX: (01841) 532942 — COOKING **2**
EMAIL: seafoodpadstow@cs.com — GLOBAL
WEB SITE: www.rickstein.com — £23–£37

Next door to the deli, and recently refurbished with banquettes, blue and white cushions and cheery seaside paintings, the café offers a straightforward and relatively inexpensive shot at the Stein seafood experience. Julian Lloyd spent six years at the Seafood Restaurant (see below) before taking over at the most informal of this stable of eateries. He is in charge of simple dishes, from grilled kipper and moules marinière to cod with noodles, chilli broth and coriander, with an occasional interloper such as chargrilled sirloin steak or chicken breast. As with most seafood cafés, desserts tend to be token offerings – meringues, lemon tart, or locally produced ice cream – while a compact wine list does a good job in the £10 to £20 range. There is live music some evenings, loud recorded music on others.

CHEF: Julian Lloyd PROPRIETORS: Rick and Jill Stein OPEN: Mon to Sat 12 to 2.30, 7 to 9.30; phone to check in winter CLOSED: 25 and 26 Dec, May Day bank hol MEALS: alc (main courses £5 to £10). Set D £18 SERVICE: not inc CARDS: Delta, MasterCard, Switch, Visa DETAILS: 43 seats. 8 seats outside. Private parties: 16 main room. Vegetarian meals. Children's helpings. No smoking in dining room. Music ACCOMMODATION: 3 rooms, all with bath/shower. TV. Phone. B&B £65 to £85. Baby facilities

▲ St Petroc's

4 New Street, Padstow PL28 8EA — *NEW CHEF*
TEL: (01841) 532700 FAX: (01841) 532942 — BISTRO
EMAIL: seafoodpadstow@cs.com — £31–£43

Chefs move about within the Rick Stein group. David Pope, listed last year, is now working at the deli, and Alistair Clive arrived from the Seafood Restaurant (see below) too late for us to receive any feedback. However, it is unlikely that the simple seafood theme will change. Moules marinière, plain roast cod, and grilled lemon sole with lemon grass butter are typical of the offerings, fleshed out so to speak with sirloin steak (with salsa verde and chips), and warm Bakewell tart with clotted cream. Around 30 varied and well-chosen wines start with house French at £12.75.

CHEF: Alistair Clive PROPRIETORS: Rick and Jill Stein OPEN: Tue to Sun 12 to 2, 7 to 9.30 CLOSED: 1 week Christmas, 1 May MEALS: alc (main courses £11.50 to £12.50) SERVICE: not inc CARDS: Delta, MasterCard, Switch, Visa DETAILS: 52 seats. 10 seats outside. Private parties: 34 main room, 6 and 12 private rooms. Children's helpings. No smoking in dining room. Music. Air-conditioned ACCOMMODATION: 13 rooms, all with bath/shower. TV. Phone. B&B £45 to £140. Baby facilities

▲ Seafood Restaurant

Riverside, Padstow PL28 8BY
TEL: (01841) 532700 FAX: (01841) 533574 — COOKING **6**
EMAIL: seafoodpadstow@cs.com — SEAFOOD
WEB SITE: www.rickstein.com — £44–£98

The light and airy dining room near the waterfront is large, yet intimate and relaxing, its white walls covered with paintings in bright seaside colours. Easy-going, lively, committed, professional and efficiently organised, it conveys the well-heeled sophistication of South Kensington-sur-Mer: 'being one-eighth Cornish myself, I was probably the nearest thing to a local that day,' reckoned one visitor. Despite an occasional claim to the contrary, reporters feel they get fair value for money on a wide-ranging menu that runs from Thai seafood broth via bourride to Chinese-style scallops with black beans.

Timing is generally accurate and (with rare exceptions) materials are zingily fresh: a crumb-crusted fillet of plaice, or firm red mullet served with a serious collection of wild mushrooms. Cooking techniques provide plenty of variety, from deep-frying (local cod with chips and tartare sauce) and chargrilling (Dover sole with sea salt and lime) to stir-frying (brill with spinach and coriander). Shellfish includes oysters (local, Scottish or Irish) lobster (grilled or steamed), and a big DIY platter. The results of Rick Stein's world travels are apparent in a number of dishes, including a bold, perky squid salad with chilli, lemon grass, coriander and mint, and porbeagle vindaloo, the fish itself at inspection outclassed by its accompaniments of fragrant onions, basmati rice, hot but subtle lime pickle, mango chutney, unctuous raita, salad and chapati. Homespun desserts take in chocolate cake with candied kumquats, and meringue with banana and custard.

The wine list is friendly, informative and stuffed full of inspirational bottles from around the world, though mark-ups tend to be a little high. Western Australia is the latest bee in Rick Stein's bonnet, represented by a short, top-quality selection. House vin de pays white and Côtes du Rhône red are £14.95 and £18.75 respectively.

'Him: "Try that wine. You'll like that." Her: "Mmmm! Moist."'
(On eating in Scotland)

CHEF: Rick Stein PROPRIETORS: Rick and Jill Stein OPEN: all week 12 to 2, 7 to 10.30 CLOSED: 1 week Christmas, Mayday MEALS: alc (main courses £15 to £38). Set L £30.50, Set D £36 SERVICE: not inc CARDS: Delta, MasterCard, Switch, Visa DETAILS: 104 seats. Private parties: 12 main room. Vegetarian meals. Children's helpings. No children under 3. Occasional music. Air-conditioned ACCOMMODATION: 13 rooms, all with bath/shower. TV. Phone. B&B £90 to £150. Baby facilities

PAINSWICK Gloucestershire **map 2**

▲ Painswick Hotel **NEW ENTRY**

Kemps Lane, Painswick GL6 6YB
TEL: (01452) 812160 FAX: (01452) 814059 COOKING **5**
EMAIL: reservations@painswickhotel.com BRITISH
WEB SITE: www.painswickhotel.com £27–£62

Despite its severely classical appearance, its pillars, pediments and croquet lawn, this grey-stone former rectory, built in 1790 in the Palladian style, is a relaxed place, its sedate English character tempered by small intimate dining rooms and the absence of any jacket and tie nonsense. Kevin Barron, who arrived early in 2000 from Lewtrenchard Manor (see entry, Lewdown), offers a short, fixed-price daily menu, supplemented at dinner by an ambitious carte.

The cooking doesn't aim to be daring or flirt with fusion, but deploys good judgement allied to sound technical skills, producing an appropriately light first course of sauté scallops with roughly mashed aubergine caviar and little samosa parcels of confit tomato. For this to work, materials must be first rate, and the kitchen goes to some lengths to source fine materials. Beef is Angus, fish and cheeses come from the West Country, and duck is Trelough from Herefordshire: its pink, tender flesh and well-browned fat accompanied by confit carrots, fondant potato and a dark reduced sauce.

Presentation is a strength, producing 'three flavours of toffee', served on a plate bought expressly for the purpose: warm sticky pudding, glazed banana with toffee ice cream, and smooth toffee parfait. Incidentals include first-class breads, and good coffee served with plentiful petits fours. Service is knowledgeable and friendly. The wine list has been compiled by an enthusiast. Choices are interesting throughout, from the half-dozen house wines starting at £12.50 to the Haut-Brion 1970 at £250, though the list would benefit from more choice at the lower end of the scale.

CHEF: Kevin Barron PROPRIETORS: Gareth and Helen Pugh OPEN: all week 12.15 to 2, 7 to 9.30 MEALS: alc D (main courses £18 to £22.50). Set L £13 (2 courses) to £16, Set D £23 (2 courses) to £26. Light L available SERVICE: not inc, card slips closed CARDS: Amex, Delta, MasterCard, Switch, Visa DETAILS: 40 seats. 20 seats outside. Private parties: 50 main room, 18 private room. Car park. Vegetarian meals. Children's helpings. No smoking in dining room. Music ACCOMMODATION: 19 rooms, all with bath/shower. TV. Phone. B&B £75 to £175. Baby facilities (£5)

Use the lists towards the front of the book to find suitable restaurants for special occasions.

'The chef put in an appearance at the end of the evening and did the rounds. This didn't take long, as there were just three diners.' (On eating in Wales)

PAULERSPURY Northamptonshire map 5

▲ Vine House

100 High Street, Paulerspury NN12 7NA
TEL: (01327) 811267 FAX: (01327) 811309
off A5, 2m SE of Towcester

COOKING **4**
MODERN BRITISH
£38–£46

Occupying an old building of rough yellow stone on the straggly main road through the village, Vine House welcomes with a pretty garden at the back, a small bar, and a dining room decorated with framed prints and a china collection set against a background of ruched and gathered fabrics. Marcus Springett's menu changes frequently ('take a few moments to enjoy the spelling,' implored one visitor) by reworking pâtés (ham and chorizo, perhaps), jellies (from prawns in gazpacho to summer fruits in apple jelly), and crumbles (apple and greengage). Flavour combinations may not always be wholly successful, but meals are marked by first-rate ingredients and a good grasp of technique – crisp-skinned pink breast and confit leg of Gressingham duck, for example – and come with an impressive vegetable accompaniment: unctuous potato purée is a winner. Orders are taken by an observant Julie Springett, and while information about dishes may not always be at her fingertips, service is pleasant and well paced. Wines cover a fair range, with prices starting at about £15.

CHEF: Marcus Springett PROPRIETORS: Marcus and Julie Springett OPEN: Thur to Fri L 12.15 to 1.45, Mon to Sat D 7.15 to 9.30 MEALS: Set L and D £24.95 SERVICE: not inc CARDS: MasterCard, Visa DETAILS: 45 seats. Private parties: 30 main room, 10 private room. Car park. No smoking in dining room. No smoking in 1 dining room. No music ACCOMMODATION: 6 rooms, all with bath/shower. TV. Phone. B&B £49 to £69 (£5)

PAXFORD Gloucestershire map 5

▲ Churchill Arms £

COTSWOLDS GFG 2001 COMMENDED

Paxford GL55 6XH
TEL: (01386) 594000 FAX: (01386) 594005
EMAIL: the_churchill_arms@hotmail.com

COOKING **5**
MODERN EUROPEAN
£20–£42

Opposite the church, with coaching lamps either side of the entrance, and much dry stone walling round about, this sister to Marsh Goose (Sonya Kidney apparently works a couple of days in each; see entry, Moreton-in-Marsh) is an ancient pub with a fine kitchen. Open plan and spacious, its atmosphere often enlivened by a plentiful influx of customers from children upwards, it sports bare wooden furniture, eccentric décor, and a daily-changing menu that responds to the market. Quiet ingenuity is the stock-in-trade, producing a starter of cheese and spring onion fritters spiced with ginger, and a main course of John Dory served on curried aubergine with vinegared shallots: 'it worked!' exclaimed its reporter.

'The sheer freshness, the smells, and the excitement of the food' are what mark out its appeal, perhaps in a dish of warm, nutty, charcoally sauté squid piled on green leaves and wreathed in interestingly marinated mushroom caps. Fine raw materials and pinpoint accurate timing are also typical, giving fillet steak the texture of chocolate mousse for one reporter. French fries are worthy of the name, and vegetables have included a distinguished example of that Cinderella vegetable, buttered curly kale. The fine balance of flavours extends to desserts such as iced blackcurrant terrine with a sharp blackcurrant sauce and crisp caramelised walnut halves. Bread costs £1, and credit card slips are left open, although service consists of little more than food delivery (order and pay at the bar). A short wine list starts with four house wines at £9.50.

CHEFS: Sonya Kidney and Ivan Reid PROPRIETORS: Sonya Kidney and Leo Brooke-Little OPEN: all week 12 to 2, 7 to 9 MEALS: alc (main courses £6.50 to £13.50) SERVICE: not inc CARDS: Delta, MasterCard, Switch, Visa DETAILS: 60 seats. 60 seats outside. Vegetarian meals. Children's helpings. Wheelchair access (not WC). No music. Air-conditioned ACCOMMODATION: 4 rooms, all with bath/shower. TV. Phone. B&B £40 to £60

PENZANCE Cornwall map 1

Harris's

46 New Street, Penzance TR18 2LZ COOKING **2**
TEL: (01736) 364408 FAX: (01736) 333273 ANGLO-FRENCH/SEAFOOD
£37–£54

Very central, with a colour scheme somewhere between lobster and terracotta, this long-standing restaurant majors on fish in its narrow ground-floor dining room (with overflow on to the first-floor bar). The time-honoured style takes in sole goujons, salmon pancakes, poached lobster, and grilled Dover sole with chive butter. Fish and shellfish come from nearby Newlyn, but carnivores are by no means ignored. Game is from local estates, fillet steak is served with béarnaise, and rack of Cornish lamb might be accompanied by celeriac purée and rosemary jus. Straightforward desserts run from treacle tart to crème brûlée, lunches are lighter affairs, and the well-chosen wine list offers good choice under £20. French and Chilean house wines start at £11.50.

CHEF: Roger Harris PROPRIETORS: Roger and Anne Harris OPEN: Mon to Sat 12 to 2, 7 to 9.30 (closed Mon Nov to Easter) CLOSED: 3 weeks winter MEALS: alc (main courses L £6.50 to £10.50, D £15 to £19.50) SERVICE: 10%, card slips closed CARDS: Amex, Delta, MasterCard, Switch, Visa DETAILS: 40 seats. Private parties: 24 main room. No smoking in 1 dining room. Music

PETER TAVY Devon map 1

Peter Tavy Inn

Peter Tavy PL19 9NN COOKING **2**
TEL: (01822) 810348 FAX: (01822) 810835 MODERN EUROPEAN
off A386, 3m NE of Tavistock £17–£34

How long this lively, unpretentious Dartmoor pub has been around depends on your sources, but 400 years seems a reasonable bet. It is certainly the genuine article, sporting flagstone floors, beams and open fireplaces, but the skilful home cooking is not stuck in the past. Order at the bar from blackboards that change twice daily. At lunchtime it's pub grub with a difference, ranging from traditional pies to Thai-spiced vegetable lasagne and a ploughman's featuring no fewer than six local cheeses: Sharpham, Ticklemore goats' and Beenleigh Blue possibly among them. The evening menu extends the repertoire to lamb shank with garlic mash, poached chicken with avocado and prawns, and a platter of ostrich, pheasant, boar, rabbit and venison. Fishy alternatives might include blackened tuna steak with Cajun spices. Inventiveness doesn't stop at dessert stage: try the Turkish delight cheesecake. The list of around three dozen wines keeps prices mostly under £15. House selections are £7.95.

CHEF: Stephen Byrne PROPRIETORS: Graeme and Karen Sim OPEN: all week 12 to 2, 6.30 to 9 CLOSED: 25 Dec MEALS: alc (main courses L £2.50 to £8, D £7 to £13) SERVICE: not inc, card slips closed CARDS: Delta, MasterCard, Switch, Visa DETAILS: 80 seats. 100 seats outside. Private parties: 50 main room. Car park. Vegetarian meals. Children's helpings. No smoking in dining room. Music (£5)

PETWORTH West Sussex **map 3**

Soanes Restaurant

NEW ENTRY

Grove Lane, Petworth GU28 0HY COOKING **4**
TEL/FAX: (01798) 343659 MODERN EUROPEAN
WEB SITE: www.soanes.co.uk £43–£58

Soanes is a seventeenth-century stone farmhouse on the outskirts of a pretty country town. Pre-dinner drinks are taken in the modern conservatory extension, with views over the South Downs, while the dining room is decorated in minimal style with splashes of colourful landscapes. Greg Laskey shows evidence of classical training, though the menu incorporates plenty of modern ideas, and even the more complex ones have a harmonious outcome. A timbale of crab has come with beetroot and avocado, garnished with seared scallops in a lime vinaigrette, while a masterly main course has produced thin slices of rare pigeon breast and foie gras on a dome of truffled mash, served with a rich port sauce.

Inventive fish dishes have included sea bass on rice pilaff with melon and asparagus, and a nostalgic touch is provided by a sorbet between courses. To finish, an assiette of mini-desserts offers good variety, perhaps incorporating sablé of raspberries with clotted cream, orange and lemon crème brûlée, and prune and armagnac ice cream. Mother and daughter team Gill and Alison St Quintin (who also co-chefs) capably and amiably run front-of-house in relaxed style. The serviceable wine list is predominantly French, offering one in each colour from various other countries. House Sauvignon and Merlot from Chile are £14.

CHEFS: Greg Laskey and Alison St Quintin PROPRIETORS: Gillian and Alison St Quintin, and Greg Laskey OPEN: Tue to Sat D 7 to 9.30 (also Sun L once a month, L other days by arrangement) MEALS: alc (main courses £16 to £19) SERVICE: not inc CARDS: Delta, Diners, MasterCard, Switch, Visa DETAILS: 26 seats. 8 seats outside. Private parties: 38 main room. Car park. Vegetarian meals. Children's helpings. No smoking in dining room. Wheelchair access (not WC). No music

The Guide office can quickly spot when a restaurateur is encouraging customers to write recommending inclusion. Such reports do not further a restaurant's cause. Please tell us if a restaurateur invites you to write to the Guide.

PLUMTREE Nottinghamshire **map 5**

Perkins

Old Railway Station, Plumtree NG12 5NA
TEL: (0115) 937 3695 FAX: (0115) 937 6405
EMAIL: perkinsrestaurant@supanet.com
off A606, 2m S of Nottingham

COOKING **2**
MODERN BRITISH/FRENCH
£24–£43

A conservatory extension overlooks the rusty track that still runs behind this brick-built, late-Victorian railway station, and despite its longevity (the Perkinses started up in 1982) the whole place still has a light and fresh appeal. Orders are taken over aperitifs in the bar, where a blackboard lists daily specials, and the repertoire covers a modishly wide range, from Thai-style stuffed squid with sweet chilli dressing, to ham hock and parsley terrine with onion marmalade; from smoked haddock risotto with poached egg, to blade of Scotch beef braised in ale. The Speedy two-course lunch, with two choices per course, is sympathetically priced, as is the midweek fixed-price dinner, and starters from the carte can be taken as bar snacks, so it could hardly be more user-friendly. Orange brioche and butter pudding is served with double cream, or there might be apple and cinnamon crumble with custard. Four house wines start the ball rolling at a very reasonable £9.75, and the rest of the short list is equally encouraging.

CHEFS: Hugh Cocker PROPRIETORS: Tony and Wendy Perkins OPEN: Tue to Sun L 12 to 2 (2.30 Sun), Tue to Sat D 6.30 to 9.45 CLOSED: 1 week Christmas MEALS: alc Tue to Sat (main courses £8 to £13. Set L Tue to Sat £9.75 (2 courses), Set L Sun £11.50 (2 courses) to £14.95, Set D Tue to Thur £14.95 SERVICE: not inc CARDS: Amex, Delta, Diners, MasterCard, Switch, Visa DETAILS: 73 seats. 24 seats outside. Private parties: 30 main room, 30 private room. Car park. Vegetarian meals. No smoking in 1 dining room. Wheelchair access (not WC). Occasional music. Air-conditioned

PLYMOUTH Devon **map 1**

Chez Nous

13 Frankfort Gate, Plymouth PL1 1QA
TEL/FAX: (01752) 266793

COOKING **4**
FRENCH
£44–£53

After 20 years, Jacques Marchal's resolutely French restaurant remains an unpretentious place where high-quality ingredients are seriously and professionally cooked. Just as the décor hits all the Gallic buttons, from Pernod ads to red and white check tablecloths, so too does the food. Bouillabaisse and chateaubriand béarnaise might be augmented by pigeon and foie gras en gelée, grilled cod with pistou, and lambs' sweetbreads with Madeira. Fine materials have included firm, fresh turbot in a sweet pepper sauce, and scallops with mercifully 'no dressing up' beyond some shredded lemon grass, spring onion and a ginger cream sauce.

Ices tend to figure among desserts: perhaps rose-petal with almond gâteau, or cinnamon ice with strawberries soaked in red wine. Although the set menu is marginally down on last year's price, the lack of any concession to more modest pockets, especially at lunchtime, does seem a peculiar omission in a city-centre restaurant. As for service, 'Madame is chatty and easy to get on with'. Fair prices redeem the wine list, which is defiantly written in French and includes a very few 'vins d'autres pays'. Bordeaux and Burgundy sections include some excellent mature vintages, and there is plenty under £20 a bottle from Beaujolais and the Rhône. Six 'vins de la maison' start at £10.50.

CHEF: Jacques Marchal PROPRIETORS: Jacques and Suzanne Marchal OPEN: Tue to Fri L 12.30 to 1.30, Tue to Sat D 7 to 10.30 CLOSED: 3 weeks Feb, 3 weeks Sept, bank hols MEALS: Set L and D £32.50 SERVICE: not inc CARDS: Amex, Diners, MasterCard, Switch, Visa DETAILS: 28 seats. Private parties: 32 main room. No children under 10. Wheelchair access (not WC). Music

PONTELAND Northumberland — map 10

Café 21 £

35 The Broadway, Darras Hall Estate,
Ponteland NE20 9PW
TEL/FAX: (01661) 820357

NEW CHEF
MODERN EUROPEAN
£21–£48

An airy and capacious, double-fronted shop conversion in a well-to-do green-belt district is the home of another of Terence Laybourne's restaurant interests, this one dealing in a mix of traditional and contemporary ideas from seared scallops with black bean vinaigrette, to slow-cooked shoulder of lamb with provençale vegetables, to chocolate vacherin. We were surprised when the restaurant told us in July 2000 that their new chef had started in late 1999 (David Kennedy has worked at 21 Queen Street, Newcastle, and at Odette's in London, see entries), by which time it was too late to send an inspector; and sadly there were no other reports on progress. A short wine list is well-travelled and reasonably priced. House French is £10.50.

CHEF: David Kennedy PROPRIETOR: Terence Laybourne OPEN: Sat L 12 to 2, Mon to Sat D 5.30 to 10.30 CLOSED: bank hols MEALS: alc (main courses £8.50 to £16.50). Set L Sat and D Mon to Fri before 7 £11.50 (2 courses) to £13 SERVICE: not inc CARDS: Amex, Delta, Diners, MasterCard, Switch, Visa DETAILS: 70 seats. Private parties: 70 main room. Vegetarian meals. Children's helpings. No smoking in 1 dining room. Wheelchair access (also WC). Music

POOLE Dorset — map 2

▲ Mansion House

Thames Street, Poole BH15 1JN
TEL: (01202) 685666 FAX: (01202) 665709
EMAIL: enquiries@themansionhouse.co.uk
WEB SITE: www.themansionhouse.co.uk

COOKING **3**
MODERN BRITISH
£26–£43

The success of this comfortable old house near the quay, with its sweeping staircase and Georgian and Victorian furnishings, rests on a foundation of good ingredients 'beautifully cooked and served' as one reporter summed it up. Local suppliers contribute lamb, free-range pork, seafood and West Country cheeses, but the kitchen's lively treatment is what makes them shine: spring roll (of duck confit) with a Thai-flavoured red pepper sauce for one visitor. The repertoire ranges from a modern classic such as scallops with black pudding and pea velouté, via twice-baked cheese soufflé, to good old-fashioned Dover sole meunière.

Vegetarians might be offered a pan-fried risotto and Gorgonzola cake, Saturday dinner brings a roast of the day, and desserts have included fruit gratin and a chocolate and walnut mousse served with caraway-seed ice cream. Value for money is praised. New and Old World wines rub shoulders on a list that was in the process of being updated as the Guide went to press. Up to now it has fielded a fine selection of clarets and Burgundies at reasonable prices, and plenty of half-bottles. Recommended wines of the house include many good-value examples, such as Australian Sémillon, Montagny premier cru and Australian Chenin Blanc. House wines start at £12.50.

CHEF: Gerry Godden PROPRIETORS: Robert Leonard, and Jackie and Gerry Godden OPEN: Sun to Fri L 12 to 2, Mon to Sat D 7 to 9.30 CLOSED: bank hol Mon L MEALS: alc Mon to Fri L (main courses £9 to £14.50). Set L £16.50, Set D £19.50 (2 courses) to £26 SERVICE: not inc CARDS: Amex, Delta, Diners, MasterCard, Switch, Visa DETAILS: 85 seats. Private parties: 100 main room, 14 to 36 private rooms. Car park. Vegetarian meals. Children's helpings. No children under 5 exc Sun L. No smoking in 1 dining room. Occasional music. Air-conditioned ACCOMMODATION: 32 rooms, all with bath/shower. TV. Phone. B&B £65 to £128. Baby facilities (£5)

PORTHLEVEN Cornwall **map 1**

▲ Critchards

The Harbourside, Porthleven TR13 9JA
TEL: (01326) 562407 FAX: (01326) 564444

COOKING **1**
SEAFOOD
£26–£62

A 300-year-old former mill in earthy colours with natural wood and pub-style décor is the setting for this fish restaurant down by the quayside. Porthleven itself is a prime source of fresh fish, and Newlyn is just across the bay, so the range is wide: from John Dory and sea bass to cuttlefish and spider crab, with shark during the summer. A well-laid-out and interesting menu, supplemented by daily specials, turns up anything from zarzuela de mariscos (Catalan shellfish casserole) to Thai fishcakes, while uneven results have varied from underwhelming red mullet and poorly timed sea bass to one reporter's pan-fried gurnard fillets that bore comparison with the best. Non-fishy alternatives range from a starter of goats' cheese and apple tartlet, via pot-roast pheasant to an original Turkish delight ice cream. Long waits remain a problem, but around 40 wines (including a Cornish white) keep prices under control. House French is £11.95.

CHEF: Jo Critchard PROPRIETORS: Steve and Jo Critchard OPEN: Mon to Sat and some Suns in summer D only 6.30 to 9 MEALS: alc (main courses £8 to £26) SERVICE: not inc, card slips closed CARDS: Delta, MasterCard, Switch, Visa DETAILS: 44 seats. Private parties: 30 main room. Vegetarian meals. Children's helpings. No children under 5. No smoking in dining room. Occasional music ACCOMMODATION: 2 rooms, both with bath/shower. TV. B&B £48 to £58 (£5)

'I've eaten fishfood in restaurants all over the world and that was very *good.'*
(On eating in Scotland)

PORTLOE Cornwall map 1

▲ Tregain

Portloe TR2 5QU
TEL: (01872) 501252

COOKING **2**
ENGLISH COUNTRY COOKING
£19–£50

Scarcely a pebble's roll from the 'gobsmackingly lovely' harbour, Tregain occupies a quaint whitewashed cottage. 'Cheerful, inspiring' Clare Holdsworth runs the post office and shop during the day, as well as a café serving cakes and light lunches. Her restaurant opens in the evenings, in a small yellow room with big tables and decorations of local handicrafts. Regional ingredients figure strongly, with clotted cream and butter prominent. The brief menu, on which thick and tasty crab soup is a fixture, is supplemented by specials such as Truro asparagus with hollandaise. Main courses might include brill, simply poached and served with saffron butter; scallops with sorrel-tinged hollandaise; or local fillet steak. Desserts such as a vibrant, tangy summer pudding come inevitably with clotted cream; otherwise there are West Country cheeses. Local cider is an appendage to a short wine list that starts with house wine at £9.50.

CHEF/PROPRIETOR: Clare Holdsworth OPEN: all week L 12 to 3, Mon to Sat D 7 to 8.30 (light meals served all day) MEALS: alc (main courses L £4 to £12, D £9.50 to £18) SERVICE: not inc, card slips closed CARDS: MasterCard, Switch, Visa DETAILS: 22 seats. 16 seats outside. Private parties: 22 main room. Children's helpings. No smoking in dining room. Occasional music ACCOMMODATION: 2 rooms. B&B £22 to £48. Children welcome

PORTREATH Cornwall map 1

Tabb's

Tregea Terrace, Portreath TR16 4LD
TEL/FAX: (01209) 842488

COOKING **2**
MODERN BRITISH-PLUS
£22–£47

By way of celebrating a decade's trading, the Tabbs have added a conservatory-style front, fashioned a more luxurious bar and engineered a better view of the small harbour. One thing that hasn't changed is their commitment to local sourcing: fresh fish from Newlyn, smoked from Penryn, Cornish chickens and their livers, and rabbit and pigeon shot to order. They grow their own herbs and employ assorted techniques to bring welcome variety to the menu: grilling (of sea bass with chive cream and roast peppers), baking (chicken breast with smoked salmon pilaff), pot-roasting (saddle of wild rabbit), and frying (hog's pudding with a mushroom and grain mustard cream). Ice creams include honeycomb and black treacle versions, and the chocolates served with coffee are something of a speciality, available boxed to take away. A brief round-the-world wine list starts with house vin de pays at £9.95.

CHEF: Nigel Tabb PROPRIETORS: Melanie and Nigel Tabb OPEN: Sun L 12.15 to 1.45, Wed to Mon D 7 to 9 CLOSED: 2 weeks Nov, 2 weeks Jan MEALS: alc D (main courses £11 to £18.50). Set L £13.50, Set D £15 SERVICE: not inc, card slips closed CARDS: Delta, MasterCard, Switch, Visa DETAILS: 30 seats. Private parties: 33 main room. Vegetarian meals. Children's helpings. No smoking in dining room. Wheelchair access (not WC). Music (£5)

POULTON-LE-FYLDE Lancashire map 8

▲ River House

Skippool Creek, Thornton-Le-Fylde,
Poulton-le-Fylde FY5 5LF
TEL: (01253) 883497 FAX: (01253) 892083
EMAIL: bill@theriverhouse.org.uk
WEB SITE: www.theriverhouse.org.uk
from roundabout junction of A585 and B5412
follow signs to Skippool Creek

COOKING **3**
FRENCH-PLUS
£34–£57

Just four miles from Blackpool, but a world away from bright lights, funfairs and pleasure beaches, the River House turns its face towards the peace and calm of the muddy Wyre estuary. A doggy welcome is normal (opt for drinks in the conservatory if you prefer to keep your distance), and lengthy conversations with the chef are not unknown: this is a distinctive and original place. It may take a traditional line in most things, but the menu format is new. Choose a starter in the normal way – maybe salmon in white wine and cream, or a sauté of chicken livers – then construct a main course from the list of well-sourced materials: fish from Fleetwood or Scotland, Fylde lamb and local game birds. Next pick out a sauce, from Teriyaki to hollandaise, from rosemary and garlic to coconut and ginger, and Bob's your uncle. The menu notes that sticky toffee (or 'ticky tacky') pudding was first served here in 1958, leaving us to draw our own conclusions about who started the craze, and also offers dark chocolate mousse or rhubarb timbale. The predominantly French wine list may be short on detail but, where it is possible to tell, prices are generally fair. House wines are £12.50.

CHEF/PROPRIETOR: Bill Scott OPEN: Mon to Sat 12 to 2, 7.30 to 9.30 CLOSED: 25 and 26 Dec, 1 Jan MEALS: alc (main courses £16 to £20). Set L and D £25 SERVICE: not inc, card slips closed CARDS: Delta, MasterCard, Switch, Visa DETAILS: 40 seats. Private parties: 40 main room. Car park. Vegetarian meals. No children under 7 at D. Wheelchair access (not WC). Music ACCOMMODATION: 4 rooms, all with bath/shower. TV. Phone. B&B £70 to £90 (£5)

PRESTBURY Cheshire map 8

▲ White House

New Road, Prestbury SK10 4DG
TEL: (01625) 829376 FAX: (01625) 828627
EMAIL: stay@cheshire-white-house.com
WEB SITE: www.thewhitehouse.uk.com
on A538, 2m N of Macclesfield

COOKING **2**
MODERN BRITISH
£25–£67

One of several white-painted buildings near the centre of well-heeled Prestbury, this particular one has a relaxing dining room with close-together tables, and a conservatory extension. The kitchen tries hard to keep on top of developments, and services an ambitious menu of over 20 savoury items on the carte alone. As well as standards such as tiger prawns with garlic and parsley, or calf's liver on olive mash, there is more unusual fare: pear tarte Tatin with Roquefort fritters to start, or hoisin-glazed lamb shank with sweet potato and orange crush. Desserts are something of a highlight, perhaps featuring a stellar chocolate 'galaxy' consisting of a warm Valrhona pudding, a strudel, sorbets, mousses and more besides. Over 50 wines combine interest with variety, and start with decent house French at £13.50.

CHEFS: Ryland Wakeham and Mark Cunniffe PROPRIETORS: Ryland and Judith Wakeham OPEN: Tue to Sun L 12 to 2, Mon to Sat D 7 to 10 CLOSED: 25 Dec MEALS: alc (main courses £11 to £18). Set L Tue to Sat £13.95, Set D Mon to Fri £14.95 (2 courses) to £17.95. Bar menu Tue to Sat L SERVICE: not inc, card slips closed CARDS: Amex, Delta, Diners, MasterCard, Switch, Visa DETAILS: 70 seats. 12 seats outside. Private parties: 40 main room, 28 and 40 private rooms. Car park. Vegetarian meals. Children's helpings. No smoking in restaurant before 2 at L, 10 at D. Wheelchair access (not WC). Music ACCOMMODATION: 11 rooms, all with bath/shower. TV. Phone. Room only £40 to £120. No children under 10

PRESTON Lancashire **map 8**

Simply Heathcotes

23 Winckley Square, Preston PR1 3JJ
TEL: (01772) 252732 FAX: (01772) 203433
EMAIL: brasserie@heathcotes.co.uk
WEB SITE: www.heathcotes.co.uk

COOKING **3**
BRASSERIE
£23–£45

Formerly Heathcote's Brasserie, this successful conversion of a substantial terraced house overlooking a garden square was refurbished in summer 2000: the mural has been papered over, tables now have marble tops, and it has taken the name of its sister operation in Manchester (see entry). Despite such regular items as black pudding (with thyme mash and Lancashire cheese), and Goosnargh duck (with beetroot and orange), there is a sense of vitality about the food: asparagus risotto with lemon and mascarpone, or a refreshing tomato broth with chick peas and spring onions, spiked with a dash of sherry vinegar.

Timing is generally accurate – three precisely cooked noisettes of lamb with fondant potato in a satisfyingly sticky stock reduction at inspection – and side orders of vegetables, charged extra, are not normally needed. Finish perhaps with powerfully flavoured iced aniseed parfait with a well judged compote of blackberries, or sample the cheeses (Brie, Stilton and Lancashire) kept in good condition at room temperature, served with a piquant home-made chutney. Forty wines (including ten by the glass) are listed by price, starting with house French at £11.50.

CHEF: Matthew Nugent PROPRIETOR: Paul Heathcote OPEN: Sun to Fri L 12 to 2.30 (3 Sun), all week D 7 (5 Sat, 6 Sun) to 10 (10.30 Sat, 9.30 Sun) CLOSED: 25 and 26 Dec, bank holidays MEALS: alc exc Sun L (main courses £11 to £14.50). Set L Mon to Fri and Set D Mon to Sat 7 to 8 (5 to 7 Sat) and Sun £10.50 (2 courses) to £12.50, Set L Sun £13.50 SERVICE: 10% (optional, max £20), card slips closed CARDS: Amex, Delta, Diners, MasterCard, Switch, Visa DETAILS: 80 seats. Private parties: 100 main room, 60 and 100 private rooms. Vegetarian meals. Children's helpings. No cigars/pipes in dining-room. Wheelchair access (not WC). Occasional music. Air-conditioned

The text of entries is based on unsolicited reports sent in by readers, backed up by inspections conducted anonymously. The factual details under the text are from questionnaires the Guide sends to all restaurants that feature in the book.

RAMSBOTTOM Greater Manchester map 8

Ramsons Restaurant and Café Bar £

16–18 Market Place, Ramsbottom BL0 9HT
TEL: (01706) 825070 FAX: (01706) 822005
off A56/M66, 4m N of Bury

COOKING 2
ITALIAN
£17–£39

Whatever else, this place – in the Guide last year as the Village Restaurant – is always evolving. Top-drawer materials remain the foundation, and while it is sad that problems with quality and supply have put an end to organic produce, locally sourced meats are still free range. Most ingredients currently hail from Italy, thanks to dapper Chris Johnson's conversion on the road not to Damascus but to San Bonifacio, since when he has applied his customary energy and enthusiasm to sourcing weekly supplies from Milan market. The cellar café-bar is Ramsbottom's answer to an enoteca, serving umpteen types of bruschetta and plates of cured pork.

What cooking there is in the long, narrow, bistro-style ground-floor dining room employs straightforward techniques: chargrilling, for example, to produce a crisp-skinned pink-fleshed Goosnargh duck breast served with good quality, well-timed vegetables. A home-made coarse-textured wild boar terrine has also impressed, although relatively little is now actually produced on the premises: bread and desserts are bought in, as of course are cheeses, perhaps including Robbiola and Gorgonzola. It is easier to choose wines from the cellar directly than tackle the hefty, though informative list. Bottles can then be drunk in the restaurant for a corkage charge, £5 for ordinary wines and £9 for fine wines (those above £15). The range is global, though Italian varieties are favoured.

CHEF: Ros Hunter PROPRIETORS: Ros Hunter and Chris Johnson OPEN: Wed to Sun L 12 to 2.30 (3.30 Sun), Wed to Sat D 6.30 to 9.30 CLOSED: 1 Jan MEALS: alc (main courses £6.50 to £13.50). Set L before 12.45 and D before 7.15 £7.25 (2 courses) to £9.95, Set L Sun £8.50. Café/bar meals available SERVICE: not inc, card slips closed CARDS: Delta, MasterCard, Switch, Visa DETAILS: 40 seats. Private parties: 30 main room, 10 to 25 private rooms. Vegetarian meals. No smoking in dining room. Music (£5)

RAMSGILL North Yorkshire map 8

▲ Yorke Arms 

YORKSHIRE RESTAURANT OF THE YEAR

Ramsgill, nr Pateley Bridge HG3 5RL
TEL: (01423) 755243 FAX: (01423) 755330
EMAIL: enquiries@yorke-arms.co.uk
WEB SITE: www.yorke-arms.co.uk

COOKING 7
MODERN BRITISH
£32–£56

The Yorkshire Dales are well off for converted pubs selling good food, but this one is the tops: an unspoilt, stone-built, creeper-clad Dales house, in a tiny hamlet beside a neatly trimmed triangular green, with polished stone-flagged floors, oak beams, and bare wooden tables. Daily specials augment the carte to produce a generous offering of interesting dishes, from black pudding in brioche with smoked haddock and mustard, to a main course of braised pig's cheek and ox tongue with celeriac, apple, foie gras and greens.

This is satisfying food, although it can be light too. Unfussy descriptions and straightforward ideas belie the subtlety of what arrives on the plate. Cornish crab and spinach lasagne, for example, alternates layers of fresh mace-scented pasta sheets with steamed young spinach leaves and generous dollops of crab meat, ending with a light crusty gratinée topping. First-rate ingredients are simply prepared, using a mix of materials from humble saddle of rabbit to enormous, thick, accurately seared scallops, served with a crisp, dry-fried julienne of vegetables and an unctuous aïoli.

It is finesse that seems to have raised the cooking a notch. Nidderdale mutton pie may sound like a trencherman's dish, but is in fact a delicate compilation of first-class puff pastry enclosing cubes of well-trimmed, flavourful meat in a thick natural gravy, 'even better than anybody's mother used to make'. A locally inspired dish it may be, but its accompanying Chinese leaves, roast garlic cloves, and cannellini beans moistened with a red wine and lamb stock reduction show that culinary intelligence triumphs over cliché.

Desserts tend towards richness, in the shape of pannacotta with raspberries and caramel, or baked cheesecake with a spun-sugar basket containing a compote of lightly poached syrupy strawberries. Bread is charged extra but worth it, service is formal yet friendly. Burgundy, Bordeaux, Italy and Australia are well represented on a 150-strong wine list that starts with 10 house wines, all (except champagne) under £15.

CHEF: Frances Atkins PROPRIETORS: Gerald and Frances Atkins OPEN: all week L 12 to 1.45 (2 Sun), Mon to Sat D 7 to 8.45 (Sun D residents only) MEALS: alc (main courses £10 to £16.50). Light bar L available SERVICE: not inc CARDS: Amex, Delta, Diners, MasterCard, Switch, Visa DETAILS: 70 seats. 30 seats outside. Private parties: 30 main room, 10 to 14 private rooms. Car park. Vegetarian meals. No smoking in dining room. Wheelchair access (not WC). Music ACCOMMODATION: 13 rooms, all with bath/shower. TV. Phone. D,B&B £80 to £130. Rooms for disabled (£5)

REIGATE Surrey — map 3

Dining Room

59A High Street, Reigate RH2 9AE — COOKING **5**
TEL/FAX: (01737) 226650 — MODERN BRITISH
£25–£53

Climb the stairs to a smart, comfortable L-shaped room decorated with flowers, foodie paintings and red and gold curtains, where the menu changes every three weeks: lunch offers no more than a couple of choices per course, while the carte runs to half a dozen. Tony Tobin cooks in a clear-cut modern style with an intelligent approach to flavour combinations: foie gras and chicken liver parfait is served with a Matusalem sherry jelly, and spiced scallops come with coconut crab cakes and a lime and ginger dressing. Variations on themes have included smoked haddock made into a terrine then paired with poached egg and spinach salad, and even when culinary boundaries are crossed, which is often, results are sensible and well defined: grilled veal chop, for example, comes with garam masala potatoes.

Rather than reverting to standby British puds, desserts continue the enterprising approach, taking in piña colada mousse with spiced pineapple, and a chocolate fudge délice accompanied by a star anise and yoghurt ice cream, and by a prune and armagnac compote. The short wine list makes a point of finding good bottles up to around £20, and even the monthly-changing fine wine selection shouldn't break the bank. House vin de pays is £10.95. A new branch, Dining Room 2, has opened at 65 The Broadway, Hayward's Heath, West Sussex (tel. (01444) 417755).

CHEFS: Tony Tobin and Rob Gathercole PROPRIETOR: Elite Restaurants Ltd. OPEN: Sun to Fri L 12 to 2, Mon to Sat D 7 to 10 CLOSED: bank holidays MEALS: alc (main courses £16.50). Set L £10 (2 courses) to 13.50, Set L Sun £25, Set D Mon to Thur £16.95 (2 courses), Set D Fri and Sat £18.95 (2 courses) SERVICE: 12.5% (optional), card slips closed CARDS: Amex, Delta, Diners, MasterCard, Switch, Visa DETAILS: 50 seats. Private parties: 50 main room. No smoking in dining room. Occasional music. Air-conditioned (£5)

RICHMOND Surrey **map 3**

Burnt Chair 🍷

5 Duke Street, Richmond TW9 1HP
TEL: (020) 8940 9488 FAX: (020) 8940 7879 COOKING **3**
EMAIL: connect1@burntchair.com GLOBAL
WEB SITE: www.burntchair.com £30–£53

This unaffected restaurant, a stone's throw from the High Street, continues to be a safe bet for a good meal in a pleasant, welcoming environment. Mr Weenson Oo, its ambitious owner, has chalked up nearly a decade of bonhomie, offering a modern French menu with an international edge. Starters on the carte may include fish soup with rouille, or chunks of duck in a light puff pastry case with slivers of melting foie gras, followed by a tranche of salmon with onion-strewn pea mash, or roast poussin with a ginger mustard Riesling sauce.

The two-course pre-theatre menu is a simpler affair, perhaps including a flan of cod and leeks, or braised steak with apple, onion and potato purée. Cheeses are served with an assortment of leaves and nuts, and the small dessert list may offer chocolate in the form of a rich cake with mint sauce, or as a terrine with a sweet grenache syrup. A devotion to fine and interesting Californian wines is prompted by a belief in their consistent value for money. Burgundy is another favourite, but while quality is undisputed, mark-ups can be steep. House vin de pays, however, is a refreshing £9.75.

CHEF/PROPRIETOR: Weenson Oo OPEN: Tue to Sat D only 6 to 11 CLOSED: 1 week Christmas, 10 days Aug MEALS: alc (main courses £11.50 to £17.50). Set D before 7.30 £15. Cover £1 SERVICE: not inc, 12.5% for parties of 4 or more CARDS: Delta, MasterCard, Switch, Visa DETAILS: 36 seats. Private parties: 36 main room. Vegetarian meals. Children's helpings. No smoking before 11, no cigars/pipes in dining room. Music (£5)

All entries in the Guide are re-researched and rewritten every year, not least because restaurant standards fluctuate. Don't rely on an out-of-date Guide.

Net prices *in the details at the end of an entry indicates that the prices given on a menu and on a bill are inclusive of VAT and service charge, and that this practice is clearly stated on menu and bill.*

Canyon

Riverside, Richmond TW10 6UJ
TEL: (020) 8948 2944 FAX: (020) 8948 2945
EMAIL: canyon@montana.plc.uk
WEB SITE: www.hartfordgroup.co.uk

COOKING **3**
MODERN AMERICAN
£28–£54

Part of the Tex-Mex chain that also embraces Montana, Dakota and Utah (see entries, all London), as well as Idaho (see London Round-up), Canyon has the advantage of a Thames-side location near Richmond Bridge. Expect a few lively flavours, for example in a salad of duck smoked over blackberry tea, incorporating purple plums and spiced walnuts, or in a quail broth with blackened tomato, tortilla shreds and lime. Fish is given similarly robust treatment – chargrilled tuna and roast halibut have both been partnered by sweet-and-sour aubergine – though meats may be given more mainstream preparation: ribeye with béarnaise, or grilled veal chop with sweet potato mash and caramelised onions.

Well-supported weekend brunches bring on Caesar salad and eggs Benedict, and the populist touch is also at work in desserts such as maple-glazed apple pie, strikingly flavoured caramelised banana brûlée, and baked peaches with raspberries and mascarpone. Service can be slow at busy times, but the atmosphere is convivial enough. America dominates the wine list, so prices soon trickle above £20. House French is £11.95.

CHEF: Philippa Martin PROPRIETOR: Hartford Group OPEN: Mon to Fri 12 to 3.30, 6 to 11, Sat and Sun 11 to 4, 6 to 11(10.30 Sun) CLOSED: 25 Dec MEALS: alc (main courses £7 to £15). Set L £14 (2 courses). Brunch menu SERVICE: 12.5%, card slips closed CARDS: Amex, MasterCard, Visa DETAILS: 98 seats. 102 seats outside. Vegetarian meals. Children's helpings. Wheelchair access (also WC). Occasional music. Air-conditioned TUBE: Richmond

Chez Lindsay £

11 Hill Rise, Richmond TW10 6UQ
TEL: (020) 8948 7473 FAX: (020) 8332 0129

COOKING **1**
BRETON
£19–£56

Breton cuisine has fans aplenty in Richmond, judging from the enthusiastic following Lindsay Wotton's restaurant draws in. It's a simply furnished former shop of yellow brick, whose attractions are seafood and pancakes, friendly and unhurried service, and 'belting good value'. Oysters, crabs, clams, winkles and whelks – some hot with garlic butter, others cold with mayonnaise – might start the ball rolling, followed by Normandy-style sole, or notably fresh grilled sea bass with mixed pepper butter. Salads offer alternative starters, and there are meat main courses, but the wide range of galettes and crêpes is hard to resist, filled variously with smoked salmon and sour cream, ham and cheese, or andouille. Sweet ones were the highlights of an inspection meal: a well-flavoured maple syrup version, and one with apples and caramel sauce. Loire wines and Breton ciders star on the drinks list. House wine is £9.95.

Card slips closed *in the details at the end of an entry indicates that the total on the slips of credit cards is closed when handed over for signature.*

CHEFS: Lindsay Wotton and Franck Rivallain PROPRIETOR: Lindsay Wotton OPEN: Mon to Sat 11 to 3, 6 to 11, Sun 12 to 10; crêperie menu also available Mon to Sat 3 to 6 CLOSED: 25 Dec MEALS: alc (main courses £5 to £17.50). Set L Mon to Sat (exc bank hols) £5.99 (2 courses) to £10.99, Set L Sun and bank hols and Set D Sun to Fri £10.99 SERVICE: not inc CARDS: Delta, MasterCard, Switch, Visa DETAILS: 48 seats. Private parties: 50 main room, 36 private room. Vegetarian meals. Children's helpings. No cigars/pipes while others eat. Wheelchair access (not WC). Music (£5)

RIDGEWAY Derbyshire **map 9**

Old Vicarage

Ridgeway Moor, Ridgeway S12 3XW
TEL: (0114) 247 5814 FAX: (0114) 247 7079
EMAIL: eat@theoldvicarage.co.uk COOKING **6**
WEB SITE: www.theoldvicarage.co.uk MODERN BRITISH-PLUS
off A616, on B6054 nearly opposite church £48–£72

One who slogged through bleak countryside in the pouring rain found this handsome stone house standing on a hillside a particularly comforting place to recover. As the Guide went to press, Tessa Bramley was in the process of refurbishing the spacious, ornate rooms, and while she herself now concentrates largely on 'kind and informative' service, the kitchen borrows ideas from a number of food cultures, including Italy, North Africa and India. These are combined into a distinctive style, built on sound classical techniques: for example, pink roast lamb fillet studded with mint and garlic, with two sauces and apricot and almond couscous, accompanied by skewered vegetables and chicken liver.

A mark of the accomplishment is that dishes can be quite intricate without losing their sense of purpose, as in a starter of roast quail marinated in tamarind and pomegranate juice, sitting on strips of carrot and parsnip glazed with cinnamon. Contrasts are well handled – accurately seared sweet scallops paired with a mound of steamed cucumber, garnished with dabs of sevruga caviar – and the plundering of different cuisines has worked to good effect in admirably pot-roast guinea fowl with moist, well-flavoured breast meat and an oriental confit of the thighs, served with noodles and black and white truffles.

The kitchen garden's contribution has included woodruff (in an ice cream reminiscent for one visitor of Dolly Mixtures), while cheeses are served in good condition at room temperature. Pastry work is 'outstanding', bread 'exemplary'. Wines are simply divided by style: rich, full-flavoured whites, for instance, or easy-drinking reds. Although there is little under £20, quality is high, with fine and interesting bottles from around the world. If crisp, light whites are your preference, then perhaps try Hugo Unwooded Chardonnay 1998 from South Australia (£19).

CHEFS: Tessa Bramley, Nathan Smith and Andrew Gilbert PROPRIETOR: Tessa Bramley OPEN: Tue to Fri and Sun L 12.30 to 2.30, Tue to Sat D 7 to 10 CLOSED: 26 Dec, 31 Dec, 1 Jan, bank hol Mons MEALS: Set L Tue to Fri £32 to £43, Set L Sun £32, Set D £32 (exc Sat) to £43 SERVICE: not inc, card slips closed CARDS: Amex, Delta, Diners, MasterCard, Switch, Visa DETAILS: 50 seats. 20 seats outside. Private parties: 50 main room, 6 to 20 private room. Car park. Vegetarian meals. Children's helpings. No smoking in dining room. Wheelchair access (not WC). No music

RIPLEY North Yorkshire **map 9**

▲ Boar's Head 🍷

Ripley HG3 3AY
TEL: (01423) 771888 FAX: (01423) 771509 COOKING **3**
EMAIL: boarshead@boarshead.harrogate.net MODERN EUROPEAN
WEB SITE: www.ripleycastle.co.uk £24–£54

Facing the cobbled square of this nineteenth-century Gothic estate village (the castle is just round the corner), the Boar's Head welcomes with rooms that are comfortably furnished and well laid out, and two options for eating. The bistro menu goes in for venison sausages, lamb casserole, and chorizo risotto with sweet chilli dressing, while the dining room puts on a slightly more ambitious show. A terrine of some sort is usually available – perhaps leek and ham knuckle with a pea dressing, or wild boar with foie gras and prunes – followed by rolled loin of lamb with black pudding, or roast rabbit wrapped in bacon. Accompanying vegetables are along the lines of 'three mange-tout and a piece of sweetcorn', and output has wobbled slightly, in timing and seasoning, for example, but desserts are invariably well reported: perhaps nougatine and amaretto with peach and apricot sauce, or a well-conceived sandwich of banana bread filled with banana ice cream, decorated with chewy strips of dried banana. Service is 'friendly, helpful and French'.

An enthusiastically prepared wine list offers succinct tasting notes, information about growers, and a plethora of personal recommendations including 'Customers' Favourite', 'Fantastic Vineyard' and 'Most Enjoyable'. Mark-ups are fair, ensuring there is plenty to be found below £15, and house wines begin at £12.

CHEF: Steven Chesnutt PROPRIETORS: Sir Thomas and Lady Ingilby OPEN: all week 12 to 2, 7 to 9.30 MEALS: Set L Mon to Sat £10 (2 courses) to £14, Set L Sun £14.95, Set D £25 to £35. Bar/bistro menu available SERVICE: not inc, card slips closed CARDS: Amex, Delta, Diners, MasterCard, Switch, Visa DETAILS: 70 seats. 70 seats outside. Private parties: 40 main room, 18 to 60 private rooms. Car park. Vegetarian meals. Children's helpings. No cigars in dining room. Wheelchair access (also WC). Occasional music ACCOMMODATION: 25 rooms, all with bath/shower. TV. Phone. B&B £95 to £135. Rooms for disabled. Baby facilities. Fishing (£5)

RIPLEY Surrey **map 3**

Michels

13 High Street, Ripley GU23 6AQ COOKING **5**
TEL: (01483) 224777 FAX: (01483) 222940 MODERN FRENCH-PLUS
off A3, 4m SW of Cobham £32–£73

The open-plan layout of this large house, with its sunken-floored bar and ruched curtains, is both clever and attractive, and despite its suburban feel the place is brought to life by a combination of good lighting and the owner's highly proficient oil paintings. A set-price, no-choice, four-course dinner (for the whole table only) offers the option of a glass each of three different wines, while the carte rings up Surrey prices for its brand of French-inspired modern cooking.

Many dishes appear to be labour-intensive, sometimes involving a large number of ingredients, some of them quite luxurious. Consider, for example, a starter of truffle-flavoured pig's trotter made into a galette, served with a truffle- and balsamic-dressed vegetable salad, or a poached duck egg with oyster, topped with lobster and caviar, in a lobster sauce. This is not the sort of stuff to try at home. For the most part, however, dishes go in for variations on more familiar themes: fillets of sea bass, salmon and monkfish served with sauerkraut in a Riesling and juniper cream sauce, or rum baba on pastry cream with tropical fruit. Nine enterprising house wines, starting at £10.95, open a classically oriented French list.

CHEF: Erik Michel PROPRIETORS: Erik and Karen Michel OPEN: Tue to Fri and Sun L 12.30 to 1.30, Tue to Sat D 7.30 to 9 (7 to 9.30 Sat) CLOSED: 2 weeks Jan MEALS: alc (main courses £21 to £23). Set L £21, Set D Tue to Fri £23 to £30 (latter inc wine) SERVICE: not inc CARDS: Amex, Delta, MasterCard, Switch, Visa DETAILS: 45 seats. Private parties: 12 main room, 12 private room. Small car park. Vegetarian meals. No smoking while other eat. Wheelchair access (not WC). No music

ROADE Northamptonshire **map 5**

▲ Roade House

16 High Street, Roade NN7 2NW
TEL: (01604) 863372 FAX: (01604) 862421 COOKING **5**
WEB SITE: www.roadehousehotel.co.uk MODERN BRITISH
off A508, 4m S of Northampton £26–£48

It may look like an ordinary guesthouse from the road, but the business end is round the back, where a hotel extension leads to a light, airy, long bar with sofas, armchairs and a clerestory roof. Beyond is the black-beamed, low-ceilinged, congenial dining room, where Chris Kewley delivers a broadly Anglo-French menu that might take in salt-cod fritters, or a densely packed and well-flavoured parslied ham terrine with broad bean salad. The menu typically starts with something in pastry – half a dozen scraped asparagus stems (fine quality, exactly cooked), with a moat of tangy beurre blanc – and something with a poached egg: perhaps breakfast-like with tomato, fried bread, oyster mushrooms, and chorizo.

Presentation is unfussy – a flawless tart of distinctive Roquefort and shredded leek, for example – and although some dishes are poorly judged, good-quality meats are generally well handled: cooked pink in the case of boneless loin of top-quality spring lamb with onion confit and a well-reduced companionable sauce. Accurate timing also produces moist fish, such as blackened fillet of pepper-coated salmon with a mint and yoghurt dressing. Desserts aim to soothe, with Tia Maria vacherin ('a kind of meringue club sandwich'), and a chocolate and orange cheesecake to rival the best. Bread might be improved, and pressure of numbers at busy times can lead to long waits, but wines are fairly priced, starting with a house quartet at £10.75.

'Smoking is discouraged until 9pm, at which point it began lustily amid an atmosphere of hearty enjoyment.' (On eating in Scotland)

CHEFS: Chris Kewley and Steve Barnes PROPRIETORS: Mr and Mrs C. Kewley OPEN: Tue to Fri and Sun L 12.15 to 1.45, Mon to Sat D 7 to 9.30 MEALS: alc D (main courses £14 to £18). Set L £14.50 (2 courses) to £16 SERVICE: not inc, card slips closed CARDS: Amex, Delta, MasterCard, Switch, Visa DETAILS: 50 seats. Private parties: 58 main room. Car park. Children's helpings. No smoking in dining room. Wheelchair access (also WC). No music. Air-conditioned ACCOMMODATION: 9 rooms, all with bath/shower. TV. Phone. B&B £50 to £75. Rooms for disabled. Baby facilities

ROCHDALE Greater Manchester **map 8**

After Eight Restaurant

Hurst Hill Hotel, 2 Edenfield Road,
Rochdale OL11 5AA
TEL/FAX: (01706) 646432

COOKING **4**
ANGLO-FRENCH
£26–£42

This attractive, stone-built restaurant in a suburban setting is the scene for some classic Anglo-French cooking with an occasional nod towards the East. Vegetarians have their own menu, which might offer chestnut and artichoke pithivier, or tofu and vegetable biryani. Portions are generous, and alcohol and cream frequently feature: a tartlet of rabbit, pheasant, venison, mushrooms and shallots with a red wine gravy, for example, or lemon sole with prawns, served with a white wine, cream and dill sauce.

Fish may be poached or griddled, Barbary duck breast is roasted and served with Chinese noodles, while fillet of beef comes with clapshot. Vegetables, included in the price, are generously supplied. Well-flavoured pear tart with pear ice cream is one way to finish, and pecan and butterscotch pudding has also been recommended. 'Lovely front-of-house staff' are a plus, and a thoughtful wine list goes global, its good value reflected in house wines from £9.90.

CHEF: Geoffrey Philip Taylor PROPRIETORS: Geoffrey Philip Taylor and Anne Taylor OPEN: Mon to Sat D only 7 to 9.30 (L party bookings only) CLOSED: 25 and 26 Dec, 1 Jan, 1 week Jan MEALS: alc (main courses £10 to £15.90) SERVICE: not inc, card slips closed CARDS: Amex, Delta, Diners, MasterCard, Switch, Visa DETAILS: 45 seats. Private parties: 30 main room. Children's helpings. No smoking in dining room. Wheelchair access (not WC). Music (£5)

ROMALDKIRK Co Durham **map 10**

▲ Rose & Crown

Romaldkirk DL12 9EB
TEL: (01833) 650213 FAX: (01833) 650828
EMAIL: hotel@rose-and-crown.co.uk
WEB SITE: www.rose-and-crown.co.uk
on B6277, 6m NW of Barnard Castle

COOKING **2**
TRADITIONAL ENGLISH
£21–£45

This traditional village inn is attractively set in an out-of-the-way location along Teesdale's narrow winding roads, and is popular with walkers. Weekly-changing bar lunches and suppers offer a wide range, from a smoked salmon and prawn bap to chargrilled chump of local lamb, although the standard may not match that of dinner in the oak-panelled dining room, where the format is a set-price four-course menu. Start with a scallop, tomato and grilled pancetta tartlet, or or perhaps baked spinach and Cheddar soufflé, followed by soup, and then pick from around five mains: wood pigeon with root vegetable rösti, say, or baked fillets of plaice with prawns and a herb sauce. Finish with one of three puddings – perhaps lemon cheesecake with lemon-curd ice cream – or English cheeses. Staff are friendly and efficient, and a long list of wines from around the world presents good choice under £20. House Chilean is £9.95.

CHEFS: Christopher Davy and Dawn Stephenson PROPRIETORS: Christopher and Alison Davy OPEN: Sun L 12 to 1.30, Mon to Sat D 7.30 to 9 CLOSED: Christmas MEALS: Set L £13.75, Set D £25. Bar food available SERVICE: not inc, card slips closed CARDS: MasterCard, Switch, Visa DETAILS: 24 seats. 24 seats outside. Private parties: 30 main room. Car park. Vegetarian meals. No children under 6 in dining room. No smoking in dining room. No music ACCOMMODATION: 12 rooms, all with bath/shower. TV. Phone. B&B £62 to £100. Rooms for disabled (£5)

ROMSEY Hampshire **map 2**

Old Manor House

21 Palmerston Street, Romsey SO51 8GF
TEL: (01794) 517353

COOKING **6**
ITALIAN/EUROPEAN
£28–£52

The walls outside the higgledy-piggledy red-brick building in the centre of town are stacked with logs for the fire; inside they are decorated with double rows of the skulls and antlers of deer that have fallen prey to Mauro Bregoli's gun. Were he ever cast away on a desert island, one feels he would never be short of something good to eat. The simplicity of the menu belies the work that goes on behind the scenes. Cotechino with lentils is time-consuming if you make the cotechino yourself, and risotto with wild mushrooms can take half a day if you collect the mushrooms personally, both of which Mauro Bregoli does. Add the deer he shoots, the pork he cures, salamis he makes, the fish he catches, and the result is a DIY object lesson to other chefs.

Raw materials are a treat: for example, a generous fillet of crisp-skinned sea bass, as fresh as it gets, on a smooth celeriac purée, surrounded by a narrow circle of pesto made with the best olive oil. Dishes are freshly and skilfully prepared, with clear-cut, unfussy results. It takes confidence to present food so starkly, as in a large slab of perfectly hung, juicy, flavourful pink venison, accompanied by no more than a single apricot and dried prune, plus a bird's nest of pale pink stewed onion: 'admirable in its simplicity' was an inspector's judgement.

Vegetables are a more predictable side plate collection, but desserts have included a commendably straightforward wedge of chocolate torte with a thin amaretti base and 'no sauce, no garnish'. Professionally baked bread and petits fours are also typical of the care the kitchen takes. France and Italy are the stars of a serious wine list, which includes a few bottles under £20 but mainly targets drinkers with the passion, and pocket, to experiment in the higher echelons. A Mano 1999 Primitivo is an affordable £16.50. Half-bottles are few and far between, but the house selection starts at £11.50.

CHEF: Mauro Bregoli PROPRIETORS: Mauro and Esther Bregoli OPEN: Tue to Sun L 12.15 to 2, Tue to Sat D 7.15 to 9.30 CLOSED: 1 week Christmas to New Year MEALS: alc (main courses £14.50 to £18.50). Set L Tue to Fri £17.50 SERVICE: not inc CARDS: Amex, Delta, MasterCard, Switch, Visa DETAILS: 26 seats. Private parties: 26 main room. Car park. No cigars/ pipes in dining room. No music

ROSS-ON-WYE Herefordshire **map 5**

Faisan Doré (and Pheasants Too)

52 Edde Cross Street, Ross-on-Wye HR9 7BZ COOKING **3**
TEL: (01989) 565751 MODERN EUROPEAN
£26–£43

In an effort to provide a more informal set-up and flexible format, Eileen Brunnarius transformed Pheasants into a gilded Faisan Doré, running it along brasserie lines with bare wooden tables and an à la carte menu. Some customers missed the old style, however, and this year a compromise has been reached, evident in a longer name and choice of menus. The re-instated set-price Pheasants Too version offers the option of a glass of wine with each dish, and takes a relatively traditional line with leeks provençale, followed perhaps by roast rack of lamb and flageolet beans.

The brasserie menu, meanwhile, combines country cooking with a wide-ranging larder, producing spiced Cornish mackerel on a bed of tasty green onion mash, seared tuna with anchovy salsa, and braised lamb's heart stuffed with black pudding, served with buttery chip-shaped parsnips. Vegetables are charged extra, but their high quality and straightforward preparation make them one of the kitchen's strongest suits. Simple desserts have included bread-and-butter pudding, and grilled figs with mascarpone and honey. Long-standing front-of-house man Adrian Wells and his assistant seem 'constantly involved in endless conversations with customers', so prepare for a leisurely evening.

Drinkers are cautioned straight away that 'this is not a traditional wine list', so don't expect fine Bordeaux and Burgundy. Riesling receives star billing in a particularly strong German section, although enthusiasm spreads to most parts of the globe. Wines are arranged by style and grape variety (some intriguingly obscure), with additional headings for 'Cheese Partners' and 'Pudding Partners'. More than 30 wines by the glass are all at generous prices, and house wines start at £10.

CHEF/PROPRIETOR: Eileen Brunnarius OPEN: Tue to Sat D only 7 to 9.30 CLOSED: 24 Dec to mid-Feb, 27 May to 4 June MEALS: alc (main courses £8.50 to £13). Set D Tue to Fri £25 SERVICE: not inc CARDS: Amex, MasterCard, Switch, Visa DETAILS: 22 seats. Private parties: 22 main room, 8 private room. Vegetarian meals. Children's helpings. No smoking in dining room. Wheelchair access (not WC). Music (£5)

ROWDE Wiltshire **map 2**

George & Dragon

High Street, Rowde SN10 2PN COOKING **6**
TEL: (01380) 723053 FAX: (01380) 724738 SEAFOOD
EMAIL: gd-rowde@lineone.net £21–£60

With only half a dozen tables, this is small even by country pub standards. Its motto seems to be that you can eat anything you like as long as it's fish. That is not quite true, since starters might include pork and goose rillettes, cheese soufflé, or a wild mushroom and quail's egg tart with chervil hollandaise. But otherwise the blackboard menu is awash with a range of dishes, from grilled lemon or Dover sole via scallop mousseline to roast hake with aïoli. Behind straightforward descriptions on the menu lies a degree of excellence in freshness, taste and balance. An example might be basic-sounding scrambled egg and smoked salmon cooked to 'creamy perfection'.

Not all reporters are agreed about the benefits of simplicity and elementary presentation, but the consensus is that there is more to the cooking than meets the eye. Cockles, scallops and mussels served with black pasta have been notable for clarity and freshness, and Thai squid salad has come packed with the flavours of chilli, lemon grass and coriander. Desserts, rarely the best course in seafood restaurants, have nevertheless produced highlights such as sliced mango with coconut sorbet and chilli ice cream. The wine list is attractively varied within a small compass and fairly priced. House Vin de Pays d'Oc from Domaine Virginie is £9.50.

CHEFS: Tim Withers, Hannah Seal and Kate Phillips PROPRIETORS: Tim and Helen Withers OPEN: Tue to Sat 12 to 2, 7 to 10 CLOSED: 25 Dec, 1 Jan MEALS: alc (main courses £8 to £25). Set L £10 (2 courses) to £12.50 SERVICE: not inc, card slips closed CARDS: Delta, MasterCard, Switch, Visa DETAILS: 35 seats. 24 seats outside. Private parties: 12 main room. Car park. Vegetarian meals. Children's helpings. No smoking in dining room. No music

RYE East Sussex **map 3**

Landgate Bistro £

5–6 Landgate, Rye TN31 7LH
TEL: (01797) 222829

COOKING **4**
MODERN BRITISH
£22–£36

Step off the street into a small bar, then into a long, thin dining area plainly attired with white-painted brick walls, sewing machine tables, and paper napkins. Toni Ferguson-Lees runs a long menu for a little bistro, but his strength is honest, freshly cooked food, much of it sourced locally. By avoiding frills he makes the most of such simple delights as salmon and salt cod fishcakes – one plain, one with an oriental chilli kick – served with a buttery, eggy, lemony sauce thick with chopped parsley.

While not all reporters have gone away happy, an inspection meal confirmed the appeal of notably fresh and sometimes powerful flavours, not least when it comes to fish: for example a garlic-lover's stew of firm, flavourful cod and whiting with sliced vegetables, accompanied by hot, crisp garlic bread and first-class aïoli. The range extends to lambs' sweetbreads with ginger and coriander, and grilled fillet and kidney of Gloucester Old Spot pork with sage and apple sauce. Desserts, not the strongest suit, have included a summery dish of cherries, served on a thin custard in a biscuit cup. Wines embrace a broad spectrum of modest and reasonably priced bottles. Seven house wines below £12 are also available by the glass.

CHEF: Toni Ferguson-Lees PROPRIETORS: Nick Parkin and Toni Ferguson-Lees OPEN: Tue to Sat D only 7 to 9.30 CLOSED: 2 weeks Christmas, 1 week autumn MEALS: alc (main courses £9 to £13). Set D Tue to Thur £16.50 SERVICE: net prices, card slips closed CARDS: Amex, Delta, Diners, MasterCard, Switch, Visa DETAILS: 30 seats. Children's helpings. No cigars/pipes in dining room. Music (£5)

ST IVES Cornwall **map 1**

Alfresco

Harbourside, Wharf Road, St Ives TR26 1LF
TEL: (01736) 793737 FAX: (01736) 796831 COOKING **4**
EMAIL: alfresco@stivesharbour.com SEAFOOD/MEDITERRANEAN
WEB SITE: www.alfresco@stivesharbour.com £23–£43

Michael Gill's bright seafood restaurant overlooking the harbour has an Italian feel, thanks to its ochre walls hung with local artworks, and a frontage that opens up in good weather. It endeavours to make the best of the fine produce that lands right on its doorstep, with well-prepared and thoughtfully presented dishes drawing ideas mostly from Mediterranean and Thai idioms. The result might be pan-fried red mullet with tomato, capers, tarragon and a balsamic reduction, or steamed mussels with star anise, chilli, lemon grass, ginger and coriander.

Alternatively, a Moroccan-inspired starter of grilled mackerel with couscous and preserved lemon might preface a main course of crisp sea bass with pickled fennel, tomato and tarragon. A few meat and vegetarian options ensure everyone is kept happy, while desserts have included an appealing combination of panettone with fresh fruits. Service is 'pleasant, if a little overworked', value is good, and wines are an attractive bunch starting at a reasonable £9 for house Chilean and South African.

CHEF: Grant Nethercott PROPRIETOR: Michael Gill OPEN: all week 12 to 3 (2 Oct to Dec), 6.30 to 9.30 MEALS: alc (main courses L £6 to £10, D £10 to £16) SERVICE: not inc, card slips closed CARDS: Delta, MasterCard, Switch, Visa DETAILS: 26 seats. 6 seats outside. Private parties: 30 main room. Vegetarian meals. Children's helpings. Wheelchair access (not WC). Occasional music

Porthminster Beach Café

NEW ENTRY

Porthminster Beach, St Ives TR26 2EB COOKING **4**
TEL/FAX: (01736) 795352 GLOBAL
£18–£43

It may sound as if you can stroll up in flip-flops with a beach ball and grab a sandwich from a mobile hut, but there is more to this operation than kiss-me-quick snacks. It does indeed serve tea, coffee and simple lunchtime dishes (and on Sunday evenings there is a barbecue), but the owners have taken advantage of an unsurpassed location and uninterrupted sea views (keep an eye out for dolphins) to move their evening business into more sophisticated territory. The simply and cleanly furnished art deco building incorporates a light and colourful dining room, augmented by a terrace for al fresco eating, and the printed carte is supplemented by a daily specials board.

Other coastlines may come to mind, notably the Mediterranean and Pacific, on a lively menu that offers wok-fried calamari with pistachios, sun-dried tomatoes and chillies in a lime dressing, or grilled scallops with prosciutto and goats' cheese. Meat options have included Moroccan-style braised lamb shank on couscous, and some dishes can be quite busy, judging by chicken marinated in fennel seeds and lemon, served with roast chickpeas, spinach, feta and caramelised balsamic garlic. Baked chocolate pudding with orange praline ice cream has been heartily approved, or go for sticky Riesling-roasted peaches with cinnamon, star anise and mascarpone. Service, which can be stretched at popular times, is willing and amiable. The skimpy-as-a-bikini wine list runs to just eight whites and five reds, none showing any sign of a vintage, but all laudably priced entirely under £17.

CHEFS: Cameron Jennings and Simon Pellow PROPRIETORS: D. Fox, J. Woodcock, R. Symons and T. Symons OPEN: all week L 12 to 4, Mon to Sat D 6.30 to 10 CLOSED: 1 Nov to Mar MEALS: alc (main courses L £5 to £10, D £10 to £15) SERVICE: not inc CARDS: Delta, MasterCard, Switch, Visa DETAILS: 50 seats. 60 seats outside. Private parties: 50 main room. Vegetarian meals. Music

ST KEYNE Cornwall — map 1

▲ Well House

St Keyne PL14 4RN
TEL: (01579) 342001 FAX: (01579) 343891
EMAIL: enquiries@wellhouse.co.uk
WEB SITE: www.wellhouse.co.uk
on B3254, 3m S of Liskeard; at end of village near church follow sign to St Keyne Well

COOKING **4**
MODERN BRITISH
£28–£53

The grey-stone house was built in 1894 by a tea planter returned from Assam, who chose a spot near the restorative waters of St Keyne Well. Proprietor Nick Wainford tells us he is pleased to welcome back Matthew Corner, who was sous-chef here in the mid-1990s and has since done stages in Australia and at Whitechapel Manor in South Molton. There may not be much of a Pacific input to the menu, but the style is perhaps a little simpler than recent incumbents had tended to aim for, given smoked salmon with blinis and crème fraîche for example, but the food is no less satisfying for that, producing a sweet and deeply flavoured lobster and prawn bisque at a May meal.

Dishes are well conceived. Tender pork tenderloin has come with buttered Savoy cabbage with a sauce of white truffle oil and cream, and fillet of beef with dauphinoise potato, tarragon-scented Puy lentils and a leek tartlet. Impressive technique has worked to good effect in a fiercely grilled gratin of strawberries, raspberries, pineapple, kiwi and melon in a passion-fruit-flavoured custard. Service could be improved. France dominates the unfussy wine list, although an effort has been made to provide European and New World alternatives. Prices are reasonable, with house wines from Chile and Australia £9.95 a bottle, £2.25 a glass.

CHEF: Matthew Corner PROPRIETORS: Nick Wainford and Ione Nurdin OPEN: all week 12.30 to 1.30, 7 to 9 MEALS: Set L £14.95 (2 courses) to £18.95, Set D £23.50 (2 courses) to £32.50 SERVICE: not inc, card slips closed CARDS: Amex, Delta, MasterCard, Switch, Visa DETAILS: 32 seats. 18 seats outside. Private parties: 26 main room. Car park. Vegetarian meals. No children under 8 at D. No smoking in dining room. Wheelchair access (also WC). No music ACCOMMODATION: 9 rooms, all with bath/shower. TV. Phone. B&B £70 to £160. Baby facilities. Swimming pool (*The Which? Hotel Guide*)

Although the cuisine style noted at the top of entries has in most cases been suggested to the Guide by the restaurants, some have been edited for brevity or appropriateness.

ST MARGARET'S AT CLIFFE Kent — map 3

▲ Wallett's Court

West Cliffe, St Margaret's at Cliffe CT15 6EW
TEL: (01304) 852424 FAX: (01304) 853430
EMAIL: wc@wallettscourt.com
WEB SITE: www.wallettscourt.com
on B2058, off A258 Dover to Deal road,
3m NE of Dover

COOKING **2**
ANGLO-FRENCH
£30–£65

Very handy for Dover, this magnificently proportioned seventeenth-century manor house combines the roles of hotel, spa and restaurant. Plenty of choice is offered in the busily decorated dining room. An ambitious set-price menu is supplemented by a vegetarian alternative and a five-course 'celebration of Kentish fare', which reflects the prominence given to local materials: wild boar rissoles, jugged hare incorporating armagnac and prunes, and St Margaret's Bay lobster baked with butter, thyme and vanilla. Accurate timing has made the best of materials, including stuffed monkfish tail, served with a grain mustard sauce, and tender if heavily chargrilled organically reared beef fillet, accompanied by dauphinoise potato, wild mushrooms and spinach. Finish perhaps with a thick, creamy ginger crème brûlée with an eggshell-thin topping, accompanied by an enjoyable hot rhubarb compote. The heavily annotated, mostly French wine list spans a wide range of styles and prices, starting at £14.

CHEF: Steven Harvey PROPRIETORS: Chris and Lea Oakley OPEN: all week 12 to 2, 7 to 9 MEALS: Set L £12.50 (2 courses) to £17.50, Set D £27.50 to £40 SERVICE: not inc CARDS: Amex, Delta, Diners, MasterCard, Switch, Visa DETAILS: 60 seats. 10 seats outside. Private parties: 40 main room, 40 private room. Car park. Vegetarian meals. Children's helpings. No children under 8 after 8pm. No smoking in dining room. Occasional music ACCOMMODATION: 17 rooms, all with bath/shower. TV. Phone. B&B £70 to £150. Swimming pool (*The Which? Hotel Guide*) (£5)

ST MARTIN'S Isles of Scilly — map 1

▲ St Martin's on the Isle

Lower Town, St Martin's TR25 0QW
TEL: (01720) 422092 FAX: (01720) 422298
WEB SITE: www.stmartinshotel.co.uk

COOKING **5**
FRENCH/MEDITERRANEAN
£40–£48

Twenty-eight miles from the Cornish coast, the Isles of Scilly are famed for warm weather and sandy beaches. All it takes to reach St Martin's is a short flight, then a boat ride, before being dropped off at the quay some 30 yards from the hotel: 'the sense of isolation is wonderful.' There are splendid views from the first-floor dining room, though hotel guests are given preference for window tables. The menu format is a straightforward choice of around five items per course, and it is difficult to resist the seafood: scallop and Dublin Bay prawn chowder to start, followed by poached sole and salmon in a creamed lobster sauce, or turbot and red mullet with wild fennel beurre blanc.

One or two luxuries are evident – truffled chicken and wild mushroom ravioli – and Patrick Pierre Tweedie seems to relish a few old-fashioned ideas, such as Somerset Brie beignets, and pot-roast guinea fowl with rosemary-infused roast potatoes and onion gravy. In the context, desserts can seem positively exotic, embracing a mango and pineapple mille-feuille with rum sauce, and blueberry tartlet with thyme ice cream. Some 40 assorted wines stay mostly below £20, although there is a reserve list of smarter bottles. House wines in three colours are £13.50.

CHEF: Patrick Pierre Tweedie PROPRIETOR: Peter Sykes OPEN: all week D only 7 to 8.45 CLOSED: Nov to Mar MEALS: Set D £27.50. Bar L available SERVICE: not inc, card slips closed CARDS: Amex, Delta, Diners, MasterCard, Switch, Visa DETAILS: 60 seats. Private parties: 100 main room. Vegetarian meals no evidence of main courses)). Children's helpings. No children under 12. No smoking in dining room. Occasional music ACCOMMODATION: 30 rooms, all with bath/shower. TV. Phone. DB&B £85 to £240. Rooms for disabled. Swimming pool. Fishing (*The Which? Hotel Guide*)

ST MAWES Cornwall **map 1**

▲ Rising Sun

NEW ENTRY

The Square, St Mawes TR2 5DJ
TEL: (01326) 270233 FAX: (01326) 270198

COOKING **3**
MODERN ENGLISH
£22–£39

John Milan decamped from Basset Count House in Carnkie late in 1999 to return to the inn where he was licensee in the '80s, bringing chef Ann Long with him. Stylish décor combines sponge-effect paintwork, blond wood floors and cane and rattan furniture. The cooking style has survived the transition to new premises, right down to the signature oatmeal and raspberry meringue dessert. Before that might come crab and celery soup, rich with flavour yet light, or a colourful main course of rose-pink salmon on ink-black spaghettini with green-flecked minty raita. Meat eaters are equally well catered for, perhaps with a dish combining breast of corn-fed chicken crusted with green pepper paste and boned saddle of rabbit, served with a spot-on red wine sauce. Apart from the meringue, other homely puddings might include warm date and ginger cake with clotted cream. The wine list skims through France, and touches down briefly in southern Europe before heading south of the equator. Red and white house wines start at £10.

CHEF: Ann Long PROPRIETOR: R.J. Milan OPEN: Sun L 12 to 2, all week 7 to 9 MEALS: Set S L £14.50, Set D £24.50. Bar meals available SERVICE: not inc, card slips closed CARDS: Amex, Delta, Diners, MasterCard, Switch, Visa DETAILS: 50 seats. 100 seats outside. Private parties: 50 main room. Car park. Vegetarian meals. Children's helpings. No smoking in dining room. Wheelchair access (also WC). No music ACCOMMODATION: 9 rooms, all with bath/shower. TV. Phone. B&B £40 to £99 (*The Which? Hotel Guide*)

The Guide office can quickly spot when a restaurateur is encouraging customers to write recommending inclusion. Such reports do not further a restaurant's cause. Please tell us if a restaurateur invites you to write to the Guide.

Dining rooms where music, either live or recorded, is never played are signalled by No music *in the details at the end of an entry.*

▲ Tresanton Hotel

Lower Castle Road, St Mawes TR2 5DR
TEL: (01326) 270055 FAX: (01326) 270053
EMAIL: info@tresanton.com
WEB SITE: www.tresanton.com

COOKING **5**
MEDITERRANEAN
£30–£53

Situated at the tip of the Roseland peninsula, this chic hotel commands fine views over the Fal estuary from its wood-panelled dining room, which has something of a nautical feel, and from the adjacent terrace where meals can be taken when weather allows. Peter Robinson arrived to take over the kitchens early in 2000, though the format remains unchanged, with the main dinner menu supplemented by a cheaper menu du jour offering two choices per course; lunch is a lighter affair.

The Mediterranean style has produced starters of moist, creamy crab and corn risotto, and a salad of grilled artichoke, tomatoes and olives with a lemon and honey dressing. Fish is as good as it ought to be in this setting, the catch yielding skilfully cooked turbot roasted on the bone (dressed in lemon, capers and chilli), and halibut with Swiss chard, gnocchi and red pepper dressing. Other options run to Chinese roast duck with garlic greens, and pumpkin and sage ravioli with feta and sauce vierge. Novel dessert ideas have included a liquorice-scented crème brûlée accompanied by a separate pot of blackcurrant compote providing contrasting sharpness and texture. Service is attentive without being overbearing. The wine list is full of imagination and opens with a useful selection by the glass. Prices are on the high side, but start at £10 for Italian red and white.

CHEF: Peter Robinson PROPRIETOR: Olga Polizzi OPEN: all week 12.30 to 2.30, 7 to 9.30 CLOSED: 6 weeks from 6 Jan MEALS: Set L £15 (2 courses) to £20, Set D £24.50 to £33 SERVICE: not inc, card slips closed CARDS: Amex, Delta, MasterCard, Switch, Visa DETAILS: 48 seats. 60 seats outside. Private parties: 50 main room. Car park. Vegetarian meals. Children's helpings. Wheelchair access (not WC). No music ACCOMMODATION: 26 rooms, all with bath/shower. TV. Phone. B&B £127.50 to £250. Baby facilities (*The Which? Hotel Guide*)

SAINT MICHAEL'S ON WYRE Lancashire **map 8**

Mallards

Garstang Road, Saint Michael's on Wyre PR3 0TE
TEL: (01995) 679661

COOKING **1**
MODERN BRITISH
£18–£35

Set in an attractive Fylde village, this pleasant cottage restaurant with rough-cast white walls and ducks everywhere (even dangling from coat-hangers) has been the Steels' pride and joy for 13 years now. John Steel's unashamedly simple cooking aims to please. Honeydew melon with apple and celery salad made a refreshing starter for one reporter on a sultry day, or there may be fishcakes of smoked hake and salmon with garlic and dill mayonnaise, or Bury black pudding on a bed of creamy leeks. Trencherman-sized Barnsley chop comes in the approved fashion with mint sauce and redcurrant jelly. Astringent lemon sorbet or crème brûlée packed with raspberries may well crop up among the verbally announced puddings. Wines include a good half-bottle selection. House French is £9.95.

CHEF: John Steel PROPRIETORS: John and Ann Steel OPEN: Sun L 12 to 2, Mon to Sat D 7 to 9 (9.30 Sat) MEALS: Set L £11.50, Set D £16.50 (2 courses) to £19.95 SERVICE: not inc, card slips closed CARDS: Delta, MasterCard, Switch, Visa DETAILS: 24 seats. Private parties: 34 main room. Car park. Children's helpings. No smoking while others eat. Wheelchair access (also WC). Music (£5)

SALE Greater Manchester map 8

Hanni's

4 Brooklands Road, Sale M33 3SQ
TEL: (0161) 973 6606 FAX: (0161) 972 0469

COOKING **2**
EASTERN MEDITERRANEAN
£26–£46

'We specialise in eastern Mediterranean dishes, especially from Egypt, Lebanon, Greece and North Africa,' writes Jennifer Al-Taraboulsy, a description confirmed by the wide-ranging menu. Starters include a Lebanese-style pizza, and spicy lamb sausage, but most are vegetarian: baba ganoush, spinach and peppers with yoghurt, tabbouleh, and hummus ('the best I can remember,' noted an inspector). Main courses run to stifado, kebabs, a variety of couscous, and tzoog kebab (chargrilled marinated halibut steak). Among desserts, rum baba is found alongside sticky, syrupy baklava and Turkish delight. Service in this family-run establishment is commended as 'extremely pleasant' and fully up to the demands of a full house. Appropriately, Greece, Lebanon and Morocco are represented on the short wine list. House wines from Italy are £10.75.

CHEF: Mr Hoonanian PROPRIETOR: Mohamed Hanni Al-Taraboulsy OPEN: Mon to Sat D only 6 to 10.30 (11 Fri and Sat) CLOSED: 25 and 26 Dec, Good Fri, Easter Mon, last 2 weeks Aug MEALS: alc (main courses £10.50 to £14). Set D Mon to Fri 6 to 7 £10.95 (2 courses) SERVICE: not inc CARDS: Amex, Delta, MasterCard, Switch, Visa DETAILS: 50 seats. Private parties: 50 main room. Vegetarian meals. Children's helpings. Wheelchair access (not WC). Air-conditioned

SANDGATE Kent map 3

▲ Sandgate Hotel

KENT GFG 2001 COMMENDED

Wellington Terrace, The Esplanade,
Sandgate CT20 3DY
TEL: (01303) 220444 FAX: (01303) 220496

COOKING **7**
FRENCH
£35–£70

From the outside this may look like any other nicely done up seafront hotel (you can hear the swish of the waves), but Samuel Gicqueau's smart French cooking has turned it into one of the highlights of the south coast. It has a well-kept but homely feel – 'if you want a place to relax, this is it' – and meals are eaten off immaculately laid tables in the front parlour, where glasses sparkle and service is well paced, responsive and professional.

Local seafood is understandably a strong suit, featuring line-caught sea bass with a mousseline of celeriac, and roast turbot with girolles. The carte begins in classic style with variations on shellfish and foie gras. Impressively fresh langoustines have been served with artichoke hearts and a lobstery shellfish sauce, and scallops come in several forms: with smoked bacon and spinach, or as three large crisply seared ones, stickily soft in the middle, on a circle of sliced potato and leek.

Other supplies run to game from Wadhurst Park, and pink roast rack of Romney Marsh lamb, with an arrangement of provençale vegetables and a thyme-flavoured jus. Truffles frequently appear as a garnish, and there is no shortage of foie gras, from a ballottine with Sauternes jelly, to a seared tranche resting Rossini-style on a tournedos of Aberdeen Angus beef, accompanied by sliced ceps and a truffle-flecked Madeira sauce.

Skilled handling and workmanship extend to desserts of roast William pear with a Szechuan pepper ice cream, and a 'squidgy' oval of Valrhona chocolate, halfway between a mousse and a cake, served with a scoop of coffee ice cream and an almond-flavoured custard. French wines predominate on a hefty list (720 bins), although 'Australie' and 'Chilie' scrape a look-in. Clarets and Burgundies, from a mouthwatering range, are reasonably priced, and detailed tasting notes are in English. All it lacks are a few house/sommelier selections. Prices open at £13.50.

CHEF: Samuel Gicqueau PROPRIETORS: Zara and Samuel Gicqueau OPEN: Wed to Sun L 12.15 to 1.30, Tue to Sat D 7.15 to 9.30 CLOSED: Jan, 1 week Oct MEALS: alc (main courses £17 to £22.50). Set L £22 (2 courses) to £31, Set D £22 to £31 SERVICE: not inc CARDS: Amex, Delta, Diners, MasterCard, Switch, Visa DETAILS: 24 seats. Private parties: 26 main room. Car park. Children's helpings. No smoking in dining room. Wheelchair access (not WC). Music ACCOMMODATION: 14 rooms, all with bath/shower. TV. Phone. B&B £44 to £76. Baby facilities (*The Which? Hotel Guide*)

SAWLEY Lancashire **map 8**

Spread Eagle

Sawley BB7 4NH COOKING 1
TEL: (01200) 441202 FAX: (01200) 441973 MODERN BRITISH
EMAIL: enquiries@spread/eagle.freeserve.co.uk £19–£44

The spacious, airy dining room extension may look a little out of kilter with the stone-built old pub, but the views from its picture windows over the Ribble Valley and Forest of Bowland are a big draw. So, too, is the set lunch, with three or four choices per course: perhaps potted duck and pork rillettes, braised rolled shoulder of lamb, and farmhouse Lancashire cheese. A blackboard of daily dishes supplements the carte, which might offer caramelised red onion tart, followed by seared peppered tuna with coriander-flavoured butter). Although recent reports speak of underpar dishes, the kitchen has also come up with some perfectly decent platefuls, including well-flavoured, crisp-skinned chicken breast in a chopped tomato sauce. Portions are generous, so it takes a large appetite to make it to chocolate fudge brownie, or sticky date and ginger sponge. A short, functional wine list starts with house Argentinian at £10.25.

CHEF: Greig Barnes PROPRIETORS: Steven and Marjorie Doherty OPEN: Tue to Sun L 12 to 2, Tue to Sat D 6 to 9 CLOSED: 25 Dec, 3 weeks Nov MEALS: alc (main courses £8.50 to £13). Set L Tue to Sat £8 (2 courses) to £10.95, Set L Sun £10.95 (2 courses) to £12.95, Set D Tue to Fri 6 to 7 £12.95 SERVICE: not inc, card slips closed CARDS: MasterCard, Switch, Visa DETAILS: 80 seats. Private parties: 30 and 80 private rooms. Car park. Vegetarian meals. Children's helpings. No smoking in dining room. Wheelchair access (also WC). No music

SAXTON North Yorkshire **map 9**

Plough Inn

Headwell Lane, Saxton LS24 9PB
TEL: (01937) 557242 FAX: (01937) 557655
off A162, between Tadcaster and Sherburn in Elmet

COOKING **3**
GLOBAL
£20–£41

The pub, on a corner of the main street, serves baguettes in the bar, and a rather more ambitious blackboard menu of over 20 savoury items in the L-shaped dining room. Pink walls and bare wooden tables retain a sense of informality, and modern gestures from the kitchen run from black pudding on mash via salmon and crab fishcake to Thai-spiced spring rolls. The size of the menu can lead to some rather unconvincing dishes, but among the more reasonable ones have been a professional-looking seafood 'moneybags' parcel, and slow-roast shoulder of lamb (boned and rolled) served with ratatouille. Portions are generous, but those who make it to dessert might encounter straightforward crème brûlée, or plum and apricot compote. Service delivers food to the kitchen's beat, and good value is a feature of the sensibly chosen wine list, which starts with a trio of southern French bottles at £9.95.

CHEFS: Simon Treanor, Richard Hartley and Claire Bridges PROPRIETORS: Simon and Nicky Treanor OPEN: Tue to Sun L 12 to 2, Tue to Sat D 6.30 to 10 CLOSED: 25 and 26 Dec, 1 to 15 Jan MEALS: alc (main courses £10 to £13.50). Set L Sun £13.95 SERVICE: not inc CARDS: Amex, Delta, MasterCard, Switch, Visa DETAILS: 55 seats. 25 seats outside. Private parties: 55 main room. Car park. Vegetarian meals. Children's helpings. No smoking in dining room. Wheelchair access (not WC). Music

SCARBOROUGH North Yorkshire **map 9**

Lanterna

33 Queen Street, Scarborough YO11 1HQ
TEL/FAX: (01723) 363616
WEB SITE: www.lanterna-ristorante.co.uk

COOKING **3**
ANGLO-ITALIAN
£28–£53

'Homely' 'cheerful' and 'unassuming' describe both décor and ambience in this town centre restaurant, while service, led by Rachel Alessio, is efficient and friendly. The menu, as Anglo-Italian as Verdi's *Falstaff*, offers scampi provençale, steak Diane, variously cooked veal escalopes and, for desserts, baked Alaska and zabaglione. Various home-made pastas function as a course on their own or can be bolstered to a main dish with two veg if required.

Starters might include pears baked in red wine with a sauce of gorgonzola and mascarpone, or Savoy salad with croûtons and Dijon sauce. To follow there are daily fish specials, sometimes including Scarborough woof, simply cooked and dressed with lemon juice. Seasonal specialities include fresh white truffles: with veal, chicken, risotto, or on a Piedmontese speciality, tajarin del Monferrato (egg pasta with cream and mushrooms). Wines include their own imports from Piedmont, with Barolo going back to 1990. Sicily and Sardinia are among other Italian regions represented, and house wines are £9.95.

CHEF: Giorgio Alessio PROPRIETORS: Rachel and Giorgio Alessio OPEN: Mon to Sat D only 6.30 to 11 CLOSED: 25 and 26 Dec, 1 Jan, 2 weeks Oct/Nov MEALS: alc (main courses £10.50 to £17.50) SERVICE: not inc, card slips closed CARDS: Delta, MasterCard, Switch, Visa DETAILS: 30 seats. Private parties: 35 main room. Vegetarian meals. Children's helpings. No children under 2. Wheelchair access (not WC). Music. Air-conditioned

SEATON BURN Tyne & Wear **map 10**

▲ Horton Grange

TYNE & WEAR GFG 2001 COMMENDED

Seaton Burn NE13 6BU
TEL: (01661) 860686 FAX: (01661) 860308
EMAIL: andrew@horton-grange.co.uk
WEB SITE: www.horton-grange.co.uk
from A1 take A19 exit; at roundabout take first exit; after 1m turn left, signposted to Brenkley and Dinnington; hotel 2m on right

COOKING **6**
ENGLISH COUNTRY HOUSE
£46–£55

A foursquare, solid-looking stone-built house next to a working farm is where the Shiltons pitched camp over a decade ago, transforming it into one of the premier country-house operations in the north-east. They have succeeded in combining elegance with homeliness, and the summery green conservatory dining room overlooking a Japanese garden, complete with pond, is a pleasing place to sit. Steven Martin has been with Horton Grange since it opened, producing highly refined cooking that is not without a sense of daring. Lightly crumbed fishcakes of fresh salmon are given a chive butter sauce and crowned with deep-fried leeks, and duck and raisin terrine is complemented by a port and redcurrant coulis. A sorbet comes next (perhaps apricot and champagne), and then the stops are pulled out for main courses, such as suprême of halibut with an almond and basil crust on an underlay of creamy saffron mash and a light lemon sauce.

For robust appetites, fillet of Scotch beef is accompanied by black pudding and horseradish cream in a sauce sharpened with red wine vinegar. 'Simply erotic' was the caution-to-the-winds verdict of one who finished with vanilla and raspberry ice cream layered with cashew nut praline in a meringue basket of strawberries. A separate, imaginative vegetarian menu might feature vegetable strudel with deep-fried Brie and 'oriental sauce'. Service is polished and professional, though the perfunctory wine list has room for improvement. Spanish and French house wines are £10.90.

CHEF: Steven Martin PROPRIETORS: Andrew and Sue Shilton OPEN: Mon to Sat D only 7 to 8.30 CLOSED: Christmas and New Year MEALS: Set D £26 (2 courses) to £36 SERVICE: not inc, card slips closed CARDS: Amex, Delta, MasterCard, Switch, Visa DETAILS: 50 seats. Private parties: 70 main room. Car park. Vegetarian meals. Children's helpings. No smoking in dining room. Wheelchair access (also WC). Music ACCOMMODATION: 9 rooms, all with bath/shower. TV. Phone. B&B £59 to £95. Fishing (*The Which? Hotel Guide*) (£5)

'I asked the chef if he shot the rabbit himself and was told, "No, I've got a washer-upper wiv a ferret."' (On eating in Nottinghamshire)

SHEFFIELD South Yorkshire **map 9**

Rafters

220 Oakbrook Road, Nether Green, Sheffield S11 7ED
TEL/FAX: (0114) 230 4819

COOKING **4**
MODERN BRITISH
£34–£41

Despite the sad death of his brother and co-propietor Wayne in a car crash, Jamie Bosworth has resolved to carry on their eight-year-old business, helped out front by other members of the family, and in the kitchen by long-standing assistant Marcus Lane. Pot plants, mock beams and a variety of bottles are part of the simple but effective décor, and a broadly based set-price menu offers three courses with half a dozen choices at each stage. Fresh ingredients and skilful timing are part of the appeal, along with thoughtful combinations and attractive presentation.

Beyond such ubiquitous Mediterranean ideas as baked goats' cheese on tomato and basil salad, or roast loin of lamb with ratatouille, may lie a grilled pork and leek sausage with creamed cabbage, and olive-stuffed chargrilled chicken served with pearl barley. Fish, meanwhile, has included seared salmon with bok choy and a parsley and caper salsa. Desserts employ some popular themes and less familiar variations, such as baked apple bread-and-butter pudding with sticky toffee sauce, or rhubarb crème brûlée with coconut biscuits. Forty-plus wines aim mostly for everyday drinking, including three French house wines under £10.

CHEFS: Jamie Bosworth and Marcus Lane PROPRIETORS: Jamie Bosworth and Joanne Bosworth OPEN: Mon and Wed to Sat D only 7 to 10 CLOSED: 1 week Jan, 2 weeks Aug, bank hols MEALS: Set D £23.95 SERVICE: not inc, card slips closed CARDS: Amex DETAILS: 44 seats. Private parties: 44 main room. Vegetarian meals. Children's helpings. No smoking while others eat. Music

Smith's of Sheffield

34 Sandygate Road, Crosspool, Sheffield S10 5RY
TEL: (0114) 266 6096

COOKING **5**
BISTRO
£25–£55

Major refurbishment was planned as the Guide went to press, and by now just about everything, from bar to kitchen to dining room, should be enlarged and improved. Well-sourced materials are at the heart of the operation, including organic fruit and vegetables, traditional breeds of lamb and pork (Tamworth chops, Old Spot sausages), Orkney beef, and first-rate poultry. For the moment at least the style of cooking remains as it was: a lively mix of ideas ranging from a gâteau of marinated Tuscan vegetables with lemon-scented couscous, to Cajun-spiced chicken with sweet potato crisps and a ketchup made from tomato, mustard and chilli.

Despite the 'let's give them a taste of everything we can think of' impression that this may convey, the approach works a treat, producing a successful starter of smoked duck breast with walnut salad, marinated figs and sage oil, and a dish of Whitby cod served with leek and potato, coriander aïoli and mussel velouté.

Finish perhaps with strawberry and rhubarb crumble, or crème brûlée with peaches. A user-friendly and sympathetically priced wine list starts with house Australian at £9.95 and includes four Domaine Chandon sparklers (from Spain, Australia, Argentina and California).

CHEFS: Richard Smith and Scott Wade PROPRIETORS: Richard and Victoria Smith OPEN: Tue to Sat D only 6.30 to 10 MEALS: alc (main courses £9 to £15). Set D Tue to Fri £17.50 SERVICE: not inc, 10% for parties of 10 or more CARDS: Amex, Delta, MasterCard, Switch, Visa DETAILS: 75 seats. Private parties: 50 main room, 20 private room. Vegetarian meals. Children's helpings. No smoking in dining room. Wheelchair access (not WC). Occasional music. Air-conditioned (£5)

SHELF West Yorkshire **map 8**

Bentley's £

12 Wadehouse Road, Shelf HX3 7PB
TEL: (01274) 690992 FAX: (01274) 690011

COOKING **3**
MODERN BRITISH
£17–£45

Behind a shop front in a stone terrace on the main road to Halifax, the Bentleys offer their brand of contemporary food in a series of small dining rooms (two in the basement) connected by steep stairs. Meals might begin with sharp grilled goat's cheese accompanied by a sweetish grape and shallot salsa, and the partnership of seafood and risotto has been successfully exploited: in a starter of queen scallops on a creamy salmon risotto, and a lunchtime main course of pan-fried mackerel fillets with a sticky smoked mackerel and cheese risotto.

Meat eaters have been offered rump steak with tasty devils on horseback in a Bordeaux sauce, and breast of Gressingham duck with a ham and potato purée, and while desserts may not be the highlight, they have produced an agreeably light treacle pudding. The set lunch and mid-week, early-evening Best Bet deals are good value, service is friendly and informal, and the approachable wine list rarely rises above £20. Four house wines are served in two sizes of glass, with bottle prices starting at £9.50.

CHEFS: Paul Bentley and Anthony Bickers PROPRIETORS: Paul and Pam Bentley OPEN: Tue to Fri L 12 to 2, Tue to Sat D 6 to 9.30 CLOSED: 24 to 31 Dec MEALS: alc (main courses £9 to £16.50). Set L £7.95 (2 courses) to £9.25, Set D Tue to Thur 6 to 7.30 £11.95 (2 courses) to £14.50 (both inc wine) SERVICE: not inc, card slips closed CARDS: Delta, MasterCard, Switch, Visa DETAILS: 68 seats. Private parties: 24 main room, 18 to 24 private rooms. Vegetarian meals. Children's helpings. No smoking in dining room. Music. Air-conditioned

SHEPTON MALLET Somerset **map 2**

▲ Bowlish House

Wells Road, Shepton Mallet BA4 5JD
TEL/FAX: (01749) 342022
on A371 to Wells, ¼m from town centre

COOKING **4**
MODERN FRENCH/BRITISH
£36–£46

Having bought this elegant Palladian mansion towards the end of 1999, Deirdré and John Forde immediately put their personal stamp on the place, installing their own substantial collection of antiques and paintings. The cooking, predicated on simple presentation and good ingredients, has made its mark too, offering simple, well made starters based on familiar ideas such as a parsleyed terrine of ham hock and artichoke, and a soufflé of Shropshire Blue cheese and walnuts. Good materials are evident, for example in a dish of roast monkfish and garlic cloves on black noodles in a rich red wine sauce at inspection. While not all taste combinations work equally well, reporters have praised beef fillet with saffron glazed potatoes, red mullet with caviar and pepper coulis, and pan-fried breast of mallard on Puy lentils and lardons with marsala.

Finish perhaps with crème brûlée flavoured with lavender, chocolate melting pudding, or a selection of unpasteurised English cheeses. Service may lack a professional foundation, but John Forde is a natural and enthusiastic host. Fair prices and fine producers characterise the serious wine list, which includes a judicious blend of old and new. Spanish reds are worth some careful pondering, and ten cheerful house wines at £10.95 a bottle (£2.25 a glass) provide a good range of flavours and fair value.

CHEF: Deirdré Forde PROPRIETOR: John and Deirdré Forde OPEN: Tue to Sat D only 7 to 9.30 (D Sun and Mon and L by arrangement) MEALS: alc D Tue to Thur (main courses £14 to £18). Set D £24.95 SERVICE: not inc, card slips closed CARDS: Delta, MasterCard, Switch, Visa DETAILS: Private parties: 50 main room, 30 private room. Car park. Vegetarian meals. Children's helpings. No smoking in dining room. Occasional music ACCOMMODATION: 3 rooms, all with bath/shower. TV. Room only £58 to £68. Baby facilities

▲ Charlton House, Mulberry Restaurant

Charlton Road, Shepton Mallet BA4 4PR
TEL: (01749) 342008 FAX: (01749) 346362
EMAIL: reservation-charltonhouse@btinternet.com — COOKING **5**
WEB SITE: www.mulberry-england.co.uk — MODERN BRITISH
1 mile from Shepton Mallet on A361 towards Frome — £30–£75

It is 'Mulberry all the way' at this showcase for the brand's furnishings and fabrics, the effect in the dining room being comfortable rather than opulent. Adam Fellows demonstrates a sure hand with his refined, classical style of cooking, producing a range of sunny dishes from chargrilled Mediterranean vegetable terrine to fillet of seabass with crushed potato and sauce vierge. Ingredients are well sourced, including powerfully flavoured duck from the Quantocks (typically roasted, perhaps with a five-spice sauce), locally reared beef and lamb, and Cornish seafood. One or two luxuries creep in – a lattice combining 'robust' rabbit with 'sweet' foie gras – but the style is governed more by the southern palette of flavourings: pesto dressing for a tian of crab and red mullet, or a salad of rocket and basil oil to accompany trout fillet.

Meals might end with unpasteurised farmhouse cheeses, walnut and mascarpone cake with a bitter chocolate ice cream, or an 'epic' wild strawberry soup with fromage frais sorbet. 'Exemplary' service from 'exceptional' staff makes visitors feel at home. Those on the hunt for less expensive fare might try lunch, while those with plenty of money can enjoy a good bottle from the high-quality, stylistically arranged wine list. Prices start around £15.

Dining rooms where music, either live or recorded, is never played are signalled by No music *in the details at the end of an entry.*

CHEF: Adam Fellows PROPRIETORS: Mr and Mrs Roger Saul OPEN: all week 12.30 to 2, 7 to 9.30 MEALS: alc (main courses L £7.50 to £11, D £19 to £25). Set L Mon to Sat £12.50 (2 courses) to £16.50, Set D £35 to £43. Light L available SERVICE: not inc CARDS: Amex, Delta, Diners, MasterCard, Switch, Visa DETAILS: 84 seats. 18 seats outside. Private parties: 84 main room, 24 to 34 private rooms. Car park. Children's helpings. No smoking in dining room. Wheelchair access (also WC). Music ACCOMMODATION: 16 rooms, all with bath/shower. TV. Phone. B&B £100 to £300. Baby facilities. Garden. Swimming pool. Fishing (*The Which? Hotel Guide*)

SHERE Surrey **map 3**

Kinghams

Gomshall Lane, Shere GU5 9HE
TEL: (01483) 202168
just off A25 Dorking to Guildford road
WEB SITE: www.kinghams-restaurant.co.uk

COOKING **4**
MODERN ENGLISH
£31–£51

Tables are shoehorned into this cottagey village restaurant, where small windowpanes and dark beams contribute to the atmosphere. The weekday set-price option is considered good value, but the carte is the showcase for Paul Baker's sometimes busy dishes: perhaps a starter of sauté scallops in a watercress and basil pesto with pasta ribbons, or duck breast with an apple and pear pancake surrounded by sherry vinegar and pink peppercorn sauce. Tatins, confits and marmalades are favoured devices – duck breast might come with a confit of the leg and a ginger and kumquat marmalade – and variety of flavour is achieved without departing too much from conventional wisdom. Fish varies by the day (one reporter enjoyed Dover sole with 'good and well-cooked' vegetables), and desserts have included almond and blackberry soufflé with vanilla ice cream, and a rice pudding cake flavoured with nutmeg, and served with a mango compote and caramel. Service is courteous and friendly, and wines sensibly explore pockets of good value around the world. House French is £10.95.

CHEF/PROPRIETOR: Paul Baker OPEN: Tue to Sun L 12 to 2, Tue to Sat D 7 to 9.30 CLOSED: 25 Dec to 4 Jan MEALS: alc (main courses £10 to £17). Set L £13.95 (2 courses), Set D Tue to Thur £15.95 (2 courses) SERVICE: not inc CARDS: Amex, Delta, Diners, MasterCard, Switch, Visa DETAILS: 50 seats. 20 seats outside. Private parties: 30 main room, 20 and 30 private rooms. Car park. Vegetarian meals. Children's helpings. No smoking in dining room. Wheelchair access (not WC). Occasional music (£5)

'Starters [included] twice-baked cheese soufflé ("a rich creamy soufflé baked twice" is helpfully added to the menu description in case you can't work out what that means).' (On eating in Hampshire)

Several sharp operators have tried to extort money from restaurateurs on the promise of an entry in a guidebook that has never appeared. The Good Food Guide *makes no charge for inclusion.*

SHIPHAM Somerset — map 2

▲ Daneswood House

Cuck Hill, Shipham BS25 1RD
TEL: (01934) 843145 FAX: (01934) 843824
EMAIL: info@danewoodhotel.co.uk
WEB SITE: www.daneswoodhotel.co.uk
S of Bristol off A38 towards Cheddar; hotel on left as you leave the village

COOKING **2**
MODERN BRITISH
£25–£49

Views are 'splendid' from this tall Edwardian-elegant former health hydro, and the atmosphere in its three dining rooms is quite relaxed. Set-price menus bring a range of dishes in broadly country-house mode, from wild rabbit and foie gras terrine to roast Quantock duck breast with braised red cabbage and blackcurrant sauce. Ideas are attractively varied without straying far from the mainstream, taking in mildly curried scallops, or red mullet on a sweet pea guacamole with a lemon grass and chilli nage. Choice is generous, at around half a dozen options per course, and meals might end with lavender-scented crème brûlée, or warm brioche butter pudding with mascarpone ice cream. Staff are friendly, although service can be slow, and a conventional wine list starts with a dozen or more house recommendations between £10 and £16.

CHEF: Heather Matthews PROPRIETORS: David and Elise Hodges OPEN: all week 12.15 to 1.45, 7 to 9.30 (8 Sun) CLOSED: 26 Dec to 3 Jan MEALS: Set L Mon to Sat £15.95 to £29.95, Set L Sun £13.95 (2 courses) to £17.95, Set D £23.95 (2 courses) to £29.95 SERVICE: not inc, card slips closed CARDS: Amex, Delta, Diners, MasterCard, Switch, Visa DETAILS: 50 seats. Private parties: 30 main room, 10 and 14 private rooms. Car park. Vegetarian meals. Children's helpings. No smoking in dining room. Wheelchair access (also WC). Occasional music ACCOMMODATION: 17 rooms, all with bath/shower. TV. Phone. B&B £79.50 to £135. Baby facilities (*The Which? Hotel Guide*) (£5)

SHREWSBURY Shropshire — map 5

Sol

82 Wyle Cop, Shrewsbury SY1 1UT
TEL: (01743) 340560 FAX: (01743) 340552

COOKING **5**
INTERNATIONAL
£29–£45

The warm Latin American glow, produced by paintings of chillies hung on large expanses of yellow ochre and terracotta, is slightly at odds with the '50s-style coffee bar seating, but this split-level former tapas bar wasn't designed with its present purpose in mind. Nevertheless, it is colourful, welcoming, and a place where people feel relaxed. John Williams applies sound skills to well-sourced supplies of Shropshire lamb, Dexter beef and Cornish fish, and produces enjoyable meals. Trios are a feature: for example, a ballottine of foie gras served with rhubarb compote and watercress salad; or a small pile of freshly cooked shelled langoustines mixed with green leaves, set between a clear tomato jelly at one end, and a scoop of gentle horseradish cream at the other.

The confident cooking extends from palpably fresh fish – a small fillet each of John Dory, red mullet and monk – to pink, livery, flavourful breast of squab pigeon on a bed of just-cooked lentils, accompanied by a small leek tart. The theme of an inspection meal seemed to be the chef's desire to play with some slightly unusual combinations, several of which worked well, including a puffy square of well-browned pastry filled with apple and goats' cheese, served with a scoop of caramel ice cream. Service is attentive enough, and the varied wine list is attractively priced, starting with five house wines at £9.95.

CHEF: John Williams PROPRIETORS: John and Debbie Williams OPEN: Tue to Sat 12 to 1.45, 7 to 9.30 CLOSED: 1 week Christmas, 1 week summer MEALS: Set L £19.50, Set D £27.50 SERVICE: not inc, card slips closed CARDS: Amex, Delta, MasterCard, Switch, Visa DETAILS: 45 seats. Private parties: 20 main room, 20 private room. Vegetarian meals. No children under 8. No smoking in dining room. Wheelchair access (not WC). Music

SKIPTON North Yorkshire map 8

Le Caveau

86 High Street, Skipton BD23 1JJ
TEL/FAX: (01756) 794274

COOKING **2**
ANGLO-FRENCH
£22–£39

Descend from street level beneath the Edinburgh Woollen Mill shop to find a small cellar restaurant, with a vaulted stone ceiling, which once served as a prison. Richard Barker cooks a simple, fairly priced menu supplemented by blackboard specials. Since the last Guide some new dishes have entered the repertoire: for example sauté scallops on a bed of Savoy cabbage, and monkfish wrapped in bacon served with a red pepper and coriander butter sauce. Given the Anglo-French orientation of the kitchen, main courses may offer a choice between chicken breast stuffed with tapénade sliced on ratatouille, and roast Deben duck sauced with orange and sage. Crème brûlée is tricked out with diced apricots and apricot liqueur, while the equally alcoholic chocolate rum truffle cake is considered outstanding by a regular. Knowledgeable and friendly service aims to please. Wines, simply listed by colour, come from around the world, with Australia responsible for the lion's share. There is plenty of choice under £15 a bottle, with house Duboeuf £9.25.

CHEF: Richard Barker PROPRIETORS: Brian Womersley and Richard Barker OPEN: Tue to Sat 12 to 2, 7 to 9.30 CLOSED: 1 week spring bank holiday, 2 weeks Aug–Sept MEALS: alc (main courses £9.50 to £14). Set L £6.95 (2 courses), Set D Tue to Thur £13.95 SERVICE: not inc CARDS: Delta, MasterCard, Switch, Visa DETAILS: 28 seats. Private parties: 30 main room, 18 private room. Vegetarian meals. No smoking in dining room. Music (£5)

SOUTHALL Greater London map 3

Brilliant

72–76 Western Road, Southall UB2 5DZ
TEL: (020) 8574 1928 FAX: (020) 8574 0276

COOKING **3**
INDIAN
£27–£56

Customers of Brilliant can now experience not just music but the full visual experience of Indian films, plus the chef's interviews and demonstrations on screen. The 1950s Kenyan origins of the menu account for its mogo-cassava chips, and tandoori tilapia marinated Kenyan-style. Chilli chicken, palak lamb (with spinach), and keema (minced lamb) with peas are some of the many dishes for two to five people. In smaller portions there is ample choice of starters, with conventional seekh kebabs or samosas contrasting with makkai pili pili (spiced corn on the cob), or a boiled egg filled with spices then fried to become masala egg. In the wide assortment of vegetable curries, karahi Mexican mix stands out, alongside potato and aubergine masala with dhal, chickpeas, mater paneer, and okra. Chicken, prawn and lamb curries as well as pilaus and birianis are supported by paratha, naan and roti breads to ensure that no one leaves with hunger unappeased. Note that 10 per cent service is included on the bill, but that fact may not be displayed on menus. House wine is £9.

CHEF: D.K. Anand PROPRIETORS: K.K. and D.K. Anand OPEN: Tue to Fri L 12 to 2.30, Tue to Sun D 6 to 11 CLOSED: Aug MEALS: alc (main courses £6 to £14) SERVICE: 10%, card slips closed CARDS: Amex, Delta, Diners, MasterCard, Switch, Visa DETAILS: 250 seats. Private parties: 120 main room, 120 private room. Car park. Vegetarian meals. Children's helpings. No smoking in 1 dining room. Music. Air-conditioned (£5)

SOUTHWATER West Sussex **map 3**

Cole's

Worthing Road, Southwater RH13 7BS
TEL: (01403) 730456

COOKING **4**
MODERN BRITISH
£25–£53

'Ye Olde Barn', as it says over the front door, is an ancient building well endowed with beams, its small dining room dominated by a brick-built, copper-hooded, floor-to-ceiling fireplace. Two fresh pairs of hands in the kitchen have enabled Elizabeth Cole to extend the repertoire and change the menu more frequently. The carte is certainly generous, offering some two dozen savoury items from twice-baked cheese and mustard soufflé, to buttered asparagus, to duck livers on bubble and squeak.

Grilling and pan-frying, which seem to take precedence over long slow cooking, are applied variously to calf's liver, Scottish fillet steak, and suprême of salmon with asparagus guacamole. Elsewhere, a few bright flavours catch the eye: a mango and basil sauce for filo-wrapped tiger prawns, a sweet chilli dressing for sauté scallops, and a cucumber and tomato salsa for herb-crusted halibut fillet. Desserts span the range from coffee liqueur cheesecake to coconut and lemon-grass crème brûlée, and a serviceable wine list unites the New and Old Worlds in a reasonably priced 50-strong collection. House red and white are £11.25.

CHEFS: Elizabeth Cole, Ian Bradley and Ben Allen PROPRIETORS: the Cole family OPEN: Tue to Fri and Sun L 12 to 2, Tue to Sat D 7 to 9 CLOSED: 1 week Christmas, 2 weeks summer MEALS: alc (main courses £12.50 to £20). Set L £12.95 (2 courses) to £15 SERVICE: not inc CARDS: Amex, Delta, Diners, MasterCard, Switch, Visa DETAILS: 36 seats. Private parties: 26 main room, 10 private room. Car park. Vegetarian meals. Children's helpings. No smoking in dining room. Wheelchair access (also WC). Music (£5)

'In [my wife's] opinion [the fish] was saved by a decent tapénade in a separate serving boat. [My wife] will eat carpaccio of rat if it comes with tapénade.'
(On eating in Suffolk)

SOUTHWOLD Suffolk map 6

▲ Crown Hotel

High Street, Southwold IP18 6DP
TEL: (01502) 722275 FAX: (01502) 727263

NEW CHEF
MODERN BRITISH-PLUS
£26–£40

This bustling white-painted Georgian hotel attempts to be all things to all people, with a maritime-themed bar where locally brewed Adnams beers are served, another which functions as a brasserie and wine bar, and a restaurant where the set-price menu changes twice daily and fresh fish is a speciality. Chris Couborough (who used to work at nearby sister restaurant The Swan) arrived too late for us to receive any feedback about performance. His menus, however, look set to continue the broad-ranging style, taking in Thai-style fishcakes with sweet chilli sauce, turbot with spicy couscous and salsa, and summer pudding with clotted cream. This being the home of Adnams, wines are second to none: a mix of classic, rare and inspirational bottles from around the world. Mark-ups are reasonable with prices for all pockets: there is plenty under £20, while those who can afford great claret will appreciate that Ch. Pétrus 1975 is a bargain £425. Note the monthly-changing list of 20 wines available by the glass.

CHEF: Chris Couborough PROPRIETOR: Adnams Hotels OPEN: all week 12.15 to 2, 7 to 9.30 MEALS: restaurant Set L £15.50 (2 courses) to £18.50, Set D £20.50 (2 courses) to £25.50; bar alc (main courses £9 to £10.50) SERVICE: not inc, card slips closed CARDS: Amex, Delta, Diners, MasterCard, Switch, Visa DETAILS: 70 seats. 10 seats outside. Private parties: 12 main room, 8 to 45 private rooms. Car park. Vegetarian meals. Children's helpings. No children under 5 in restaurant. No smoking in restaurant, no-smoking area in bar. Wheelchair access (also WC). Occasional music ACCOMMODATION: 14 rooms, all with bath/shower. TV. Phone. B&B £50 to £75. Baby facilities (*The Which? Hotel Guide*)

STADDLEBRIDGE North Yorkshire map 9

▲ McCoy's Bistro

Cleveland Tontine, Staddlebridge DL6 3JB
TEL: (01609) 882671 FAX: (01609) 882660
6m NE of Northallerton, at junction of A19 and A172

COOKING **5**
BISTRO
£21–£52

When the turnpike on the road between Yarm and Thirsk was built nearly 200 years ago, the travelling population of the time soon found themselves in need of somewhere to water the horses, and so the Tontine Inn came into being. A large stone house with the feel of a run-down French château, it now houses the McCoy brothers' two-pronged operation that divides into ground-floor dining room (open Saturday night only), and basement bistro (open all week). The casual air is enjoyed for its eccentricity, but there is nothing at all slipshod about Marcus Bennett's cooking.

Menus are long but deliver reliably. Smoked haddock tart comes with a sweet-sharp beurre blanc, the light puff pastry topped with rich onion confit and fine fish. A pair of scallops is topped with hummus and a vegetable spring roll, just to show what assurance the kitchen is capable of. Indeed presentation might at times be fussy, but flavours are not lacking, as evidenced by pork fillet with black pudding, caramelised onions, apple, tortellini of bacon and a cider sauce. Rice pudding with a green apple sorbet has impressed, as has sticky toffee. The wine list, heavier in reds than whites, abounds with good growers, but prices are on the steep side. House French – Chardonnay and Merlot – are £12.75.

CHEF: Marcus Bennett PROPRIETORS: Thomas and Eugene McCoy OPEN: bistro all week 12 to 2, 7 to 10; restaurant Sat D only 7 to 10 CLOSED: 25 and 26 Dec, 1 Jan MEALS: alc (main courses L £7 to £12, D £16 to £18). Set L £9.95 (2 courses) to £11.95, Set D Mon to Thur £16 (2 courses) to £18.50 SERVICE: not inc CARDS: Amex, Diners, MasterCard, Switch, Visa DETAILS: 140 seats. Private parties: 60 main room, 14 and 25 private rooms. Car park. Vegetarian meals. Music. Air-conditioned ACCOMMODATION: 6 rooms, all with bath/shower. TV. B&B £75 to £90

STAITHES North Yorkshire **map 9**

▲ Endeavour

1 High Street, Staithes TS13 5BH
TEL: (01947) 840825

COOKING **2**
SEAFOOD
£27–£48

To succeed so far off the beaten track is, according to one supporter, 'an outstanding achievement'. Part of the secret may lie in that very location – a tiny converted cottage down by the quay – which makes it a natural for local seafood straight from the boats: seasonal lobster (cold in salad or hot with garlic butter), crab (in a mousse with avocado) and plenty of white fish, from cod, with a salad of potato and smoked bacon, to sea bass with an olive and herb crust. A blackboard announces the options, butter and herb sauces help to keep it all simple, and for those who prefer a change there may be nettle soup, braised lamb shanks, or a vegetarian main course such as Turkish zucchini pancakes. After 11 years, writes Lisa Chapman, crème brûlée is still the most popular dessert. Service is 'cheerful, competent and quick', and a modest but sound wine list starts with vin de pays at £8.95.

CHEF/PROPRIETOR: Lisa Chapman OPEN: Tue to Sat and bank hol Sun 12 to 2 (bookings only), 6.45 to 9 CLOSED: Nov, 25 and 26 Dec, mid-Jan to mid-Mar MEALS: alc (main courses £10 to £18) SERVICE: not inc CARDS: none DETAILS: 45 seats. Private parties: 30 main room, 12 and 16 private rooms. Car park. Vegetarian meals. No smoking in dining room. Occasional music ACCOMMODATION: 3 rooms, 2 with bath/shower. B&B £42 to £55 (double room only) (*The Which? Hotel Guide*)

STANTON Suffolk **map 6**

Leaping Hare Vineyard Restaurant

Wyken Vineyards, Stanton IP31 2DW
TEL: (01359) 250287 FAX: (01359) 252256
signposted off A143, 8m NE of Bury St Edmunds

COOKING **1**
MODERN BRITISH
£26–£44

This bright, charming timbered barn restaurant on the Wyken Hall Estate is the sales point for the vineyard's wines and divides into two parts, one as a coffee/tea shop, the other for more serious eating. Game and lamb from the estate, and locally sourced rare-breeds meats, contribute to a modern British menu of sensible length that takes in bacon-wrapped pigeon terrine, and roast rump of beef with béarnaise. Imaginative ideas run from goats'-cheese calzone to a delicately flavoured orange and ginger burnt cream with rhubarb. As befits the restaurant's enterprising nature, all food is made on the premises, including impressive focaccia and ice creams. Service is efficiently managed, and six Wyken wines, from £8.50 a bottle, naturally form part of the small list (which includes eight by the glass). Wyken Bacchus '96, at £3.50 a glass, has been admired as 'aromatic, crisp, with excellent balance'.

CHEF: Peter Harrison PROPRIETORS: Kenneth and Carla Carlisle OPEN: Wed to Sun L 12 to 3.30, Fri and Sat D 7 to 9.30 (also open bank hols) CLOSED: 2 weeks Christmas MEALS: alc (main courses £9 to £14.50). Set L Wed to Fri £12.50 (2 courses) to £16.50 SERVICE: not inc, card slips closed CARDS: MasterCard, Switch, Visa DETAILS: 55 seats. 16 seats outside. Private parties: 12 main room. Car park. Vegetarian meals. Children's helpings. No smoking in dining room. Wheelchair access (also WC). No music (£5)

STOCKCROSS Berkshire **map 2**

▲ Vineyard at Stockcross

Stockcross RG20 8JU
TEL: (01635) 528770 FAX: (01635) 528398
EMAIL: general@the-vineyard.co.uk
WEB SITE: www.the-vineyard.co.uk
just off A4, 2m W of Newbury on B4000

COOKING **5**
ANGLO-FRENCH
£35–£77

'A chap meets the car, escorts you in, and drives the car away', then you are 'greeted and greeted and greeted'. So begins a meal at this slick, modern temple to fine wines and classy food. After witnessing the dramatic fire and water display outside, enjoyment is 'pressed upon you' in the spacious, light and airy split-level rooms. Rich fabrics and comfortable padded seats herald a cosseting style of cooking that runs from lobster terrine to black pudding beignets, from scallops, brill and Dover sole to a lunchtime chump of flavourful lamb with a chimney-high pile of mashed potato and a host of baby vegetables. Contrasts of flavour and texture are carefully managed, taking in velvety celeriac soup, and fresh, full-flavoured and firm red mullet, served with wild mushrooms and a potato purée rich in olive oil.

Dishes are attractively presented – as in a paper-thin pastry tart and crisp, sweet slices of apple, accompanied by caramel sauce and vanilla ice cream – and service from masses of staff is helpful and well paced. Lovers of Californian wines will be in their element as one of the two lists is devoted to the region's vinous delights, starting with two pages of Sir Peter Michael's own wines. International stars are thoroughly represented with superb range and quality on the equally impressive second list. Prices on the whole are high, though there are many good wines under £20, and plenty of half-bottles.

CHEF: Billy Reid PROPRIETOR: Sir Peter Michael OPEN: all week 12 to 2, 7 to 10 (10.30 Sat) MEALS: alc (main courses £20 to £24). Set L £16 (2 courses) to £22, Set D £42 to £75 SERVICE: not inc CARDS: Amex, Delta, Diners, MasterCard, Switch, Visa DETAILS: 74 seats. Private parties: 55 main room, 55 private room. Car park. Vegetarian meals. Children's helpings. No-smoking area. Wheelchair access (also WC). Music. Air-conditioned ACCOMMODATION: 33 rooms, all with bath/shower. TV. Phone. B&B £139 to £435. Rooms for disabled. Baby facilities. Swimming pool (*The Which? Hotel Guide*) (£5)

STOKE BRUERNE Northamptonshire map 5

Bruerne's Lock

NEW ENTRY

5 The Canalside, Stoke Bruerne NN12 7SB
TEL: (01604) 863654 FAX: (01604) 863330
EMAIL: bruernlock@aol.com
WEB SITE: www.bruerneslock.co.uk
off A508, 3½m from M1 junction 15

COOKING **1**
MODERN BRITISH/MEDITERRANEAN
£27–£58

Since its last appearance in the Guide as a main entry in 1996 (in between it has been in the Round-up section), the cellar of this red-brick Georgian building has been converted into a bar, and the terrace overlooking the Grand Union Canal extended. What vintage black and white photographs of the lock-side scene contribute to the atmosphere, the 'galloping Muzak' tends to take away, but this is a place that tries hard. The carte changes every couple of months, the lunch menu weekly (dishes come with verbal descriptions as well), and span the range from mackerel terrine via braised lamb shank to ostrich (flavoured with garlic and rosemary, on a vegetable risotto). Raw materials and technical skills are sound – good-quality beef fillet served with on-plate vegetables at inspection – although the word 'restraint' doesn't seem to form part of the chef's vocabulary, and combinations vary in their effectiveness. Finish perhaps with warm fruit muffin, or glazed lemon meringue tart. Springy, crisp-crusted bread is 'gold medal' stuff, prices are rather high, and 40 or so wines are grouped by style, starting with monthly-changing house wines at £11.95.

CHEF: Nick Collingwood PROPRIETORS: Nigel Hollick and Harry Thuillier OPEN: Tue to Fri and Sun L 12.15 to 2.15, Tue to Sat D 7.15 to 9.30 CLOSED: 1 week from 26 Dec, 1 week Oct MEALS: alc D (main courses £14.50 to £20). Set L £14.50 (2 courses) to £17, Set D Tue to Fri £18. Light L available SERVICE: not inc CARDS: Amex, Delta, MasterCard, Switch, Visa DETAILS: 50 seats. 24 seats outside. Private parties: 36 main room, 14 private room. Car park. Children's helpings. No smoking in dining room. Wheelchair access (not WC). Occasional music

STOKESLEY North Yorkshire map 10

▲ Chapters

27 High Street, Stokesley TS9 5AD
TEL: (01642) 711888 FAX: (01642) 713387

COOKING **3**
MODERN EUROPEAN
£22–£47

Chapters is a modest three-storey hotel in a traditional old Yorkshire market town square, with a terrace – stretching down to the River Leven – where jazz and barbecue weekends are planned for summer. Brown tiled floors and plasterwork, paper tablecloths, and subdued lighting may not make for a scintillating atmosphere, but the food brings its own sparkle. Asian and Mediterranean flavours are usually to the fore, perhaps in spiced fishcake, served with a red Thai rémoulade and coriander and lemon grass dressing, or in a Valencia-style paella incorporating seafood, chicken and chorizo. Fish specials have included griddled tuna with an unusual dressing of pear and olive salsa with orange oil, while desserts might run to prune and armagnac rice pudding, or almond and cherry tart with Horlicks ice cream. A simple, 30-strong wine list starts with house Duboeuf at £9.25.

CHEF: Dave Connelly PROPRIETORS: Alan and Catherine Thompson OPEN: Mon to Sat 12 to 2.30, 6.30 to 9.30 (10 Sat) MEALS: alc (main courses L £6.50 to £12.50, D £11.50 to £17) SERVICE: not inc CARDS: Amex, Delta, Diners, MasterCard, Switch, Visa DETAILS: 60 seats. 40 seats outside. Private parties: 60 main room, 60 private room. Vegetarian meals. Children's helpings. No-smoking area. Wheelchair access (not WC). Occasional music ACCOMMODATION: 13 rooms, all with bath/shower. TV. Phone. B&B £45 to £75. Baby facilities (*The Which? Hotel Guide*) (£5)

STORRINGTON West Sussex **map 3**

Fleur de Sel

Manleys Hill, Storrington RH20 4BT
TEL: (01903) 742331 FAX: (01903) 740649

COOKING **6**
FRENCH
£28–£54

The building on the edge of the village is a typical southern English medley – two or three cottages of various ages knocked together – with a garden at the back and a 'light, airy and stylish' feel inside. Michel Perraud combines skills of a high order with an intelligent approach to flavouring to produce an array of well-balanced dishes. His canvas includes prime fish such as sea bass (on fennel with red pepper sauce), and brill (filled with salmon soufflé on a cider cream sauce), and the lengthy carte allows him to bring on wood pigeon and calf's liver alongside more mainstream rack of lamb and beef fillet.

Ideas such as scrambled egg with smoked salmon and asparagus may not be designed to set the pulse racing, but the strength is a high degree of integrity allied to fine-quality raw materials, producing a well-flavoured sole terrine with prawn sauce, Cornish crab cake with hazelnuts and Dublin Bay prawns, and pink lamb with an olive crust and port sauce. The kitchen's assurance applies equally to desserts, which have taken in chocolate soufflé with pistachio ice cream, and almond macaroon with a prune and armagnac ice cream. Good appetisers and freshly made bread add to the appeal, service is attentive and charming, and the predominantly French list favours the grander wines but offers a few bottles under £20, including house red and white at £12.50.

CHEF: Michel Perraud PROPRIETORS: Bernadette and Michel Perraud OPEN: Tue to Fri and Sun L 12 to 2, Tue to Sat D 7 to 9.30 MEALS: Set L Tue to Fri £12.50 (2 courses) to £31, Set L Sun £16.50 (2 courses) to £20, Set D Tue to Thur £16.50 to £31, Set D Fri and Sat £26 to £31 SERVICE: 12.5% (optional), card slips closed CARDS: Amex, Delta, MasterCard, Switch, Visa DETAILS: 50 seats. Private parties: 54 main room. Car park. No children under 12. No cigars/pipes in dining room. Wheelchair access (not WC). Music

The 2002 Guide will be published before Christmas 2001. Reports on meals are most welcome at any time of the year, but are particularly valuable in the spring (no later than June). Send them to The Good Food Guide, *FREEPOST, 2 Marylebone Road, London NW1 4DF. Or email your report to goodfoodguide@which.net*

Old Forge 🍷

Church Street, Storrington RH20 4LA
TEL: (01903) 743402 FAX: (01903) 742540 — COOKING **4**
EMAIL: contact@oldforge.co.uk — MODERN BRITISH
WEB SITE: www.oldforge.co.uk — £23–£48

Tiny but comfortable rooms live up to the promise of the bow-windowed, cottagey exterior, with low dark beams, old stone ginger-beer bottles and a friendly approach led by Cathy Roberts all hitting the right notes. The cooking is accomplished too, and Clive Roberts brings a sense of balance and judgement to his creative menus. The cream-tea ambience of Storrington might not quite prepare you for grilled spiced ox-tongue with tomato and chilli jam, or braised pork chump with yam mash and lentil jus, but both featured on a spring menu.

Fixed-price deals with nary a supplement in sight keep the format nice and simple, and traditional tastes are catered for alongside the more adventurous: poached skate with spinach, capers and Dijon mustard, and a Sunday-lunch roast beef and Yorkshire pudding. Pot au chocolat is a rich way to finish, or try a refreshing-sounding sorbet of melon, mint and tea. Fine new-wave English cheeses are also on offer. A wine list to suit all palates and price brackets opens with an imaginative choice of house wines at £12 a bottle and that rarest of sights, a tempting list of sparkling wines and champagnes at celebratory prices. Dessert wines by the glass are inviting too.

CHEF: Clive Roberts PROPRIETORS: Cathy and Clive Roberts OPEN: Wed to Fri and Sun L 12.30 to 1.15, Wed to Sat D 7.15 to 9 CLOSED: Christmas to New Year, 2 weeks spring, 2 weeks autumn MEALS: Set L Wed to Fri £11.50 (2 courses) to £30, Set L Sun £15 (2 courses) to £18, Set D £19.25 (2 courses) to £30 SERVICE: not inc, card slips closed CARDS: Amex, Delta, Diners, MasterCard, Switch, Visa DETAILS: 34 seats. Private parties: 14 main room. Children's helpings. No smoking while others eat. Music (£5)

STRATFORD-UPON-AVON Warwickshire — map 5

Boathouse

NEW ENTRY

Swan's Nest Lane, Stratford-upon-Avon CV37 7LS — COOKING **2**
TEL: (01789) 297733 — MODERN EUROPEAN
£27–£54

It is a mystery to many why one of the country's most visited tourist towns can't field a few good restaurants, but things may be changing. This open-plan first-floor dining room, looking like 'an arty interior design shop', runs the length of the building above a working boat yard directly on the river. Views of the RSC theatre, and twinkling lights reflecting off the water at night, add to the appeal. Its short menu may seem routinely trendy but includes a helping of good ideas: from light and tasty polenta fritters with lime and coconut cream, to a dish of lamb (kidneys, sweetbreads and cutlets) served simply with mash and spinach. Main-course materials can be overshadowed by their accompaniments, but the cooking generally combines fine raw materials with sound technical skills. Desserts have produced a light upside-down apple cake, and a worthy Valrhona chocolate cake with a scoop of espresso ice cream. Service is friendly, attentive and well informed, and the short, reasonably priced wine list features a handful from Languedoc-Roussillon. House wines from France and Chile are £11.95.

CHEF: Laurent Courtois PROPRIETOR: William Meredith-Owen OPEN: Wed to Sun L 12 to 2, Mon to Sat D 6 to 10 MEALS: alc (main courses £9.50 to £16). Set L £9.95 (2 courses) SERVICE: not inc CARDS: Amex, MasterCard, Switch, Visa DETAILS: 90 seats. 20 seats outside. Private parties: 100 main room. Car park. Vegetarian meals. Children's helpings. No-smoking area. Music (£5)

Desport's

NEW ENTRY

13–14 Meer Street,
Stratford-upon-Avon CV37 6QB
TEL/FAX: (01789) 269304
EMAIL: bookings@desports.com
WEB SITE: www.desports.co.uk

COOKING 2
MODERN EEUROPEAN
£21–£53

Paul and Julie Desport forsook the world of London's grand hotels (Dorchester and Savoy among them) when they took over this centuries-old, half-timbered, terraced house in the centre of Stratford. A central staircase leads from the ground floor deli/café to a first-floor dining room complete with beams, buttercup yellow walls, and a friendly welcome. Rather than list starters and main courses, the menu simply offers several dishes in two sizes, dividing them according to origin: earth (beetroot risotto), land (honey-baked ham with sage mash), and sea (three medallions of chargrilled monkfish accompanied by a two-tone tower of potato and pea purées). An inventive streak has produced curried fennel souffle with spiced mango chutney, tea-smoked cod with celery and ginger sauce, and hot chocolate and cardamom pudding with peppered pineapple and coconut ice cream. The short wine list provides some decent drinking, with house French £10.50.

CHEF: Paul Desport PROPRIETORS: Paul and Julie Desport OPEN: Tue to Sat 12 to 2, 6 to 10.30 CLOSED: 25 and 26 Dec, 1 Jan, bank hol Mons MEALS: alc (main courses £12 to £17). Set L £10.50 to £14, Set D Tue to Fri £22.95 (2 courses) to £27.95 SERVICE: not inc CARDS: Amex, Delta, Diners, MasterCard, Switch, Visa DETAILS: 54 seats. Private parties: 54 main room. Vegetarian meals. Children's helpings. No cigars/pipes in dining room. Music (£5)

STRETE Devon **map 1**

Laughing Monk

Totnes Road, Strete TQ6 0RN
TEL: (01803) 770639
5m S of Dartmouth, just off A379

COOKING 2
MODERN EUROPEAN-PLUS
£19–£43

'A friendly place to know' was how one visitor summed up Trudy and David Rothwell's converted school off Strete's high street occupying a large L-shaped room painted in warm terracotta. The menu changes regularly to reflect the seasons, with fish coming direct from Brixham or Plymouth markets, but has a modern, Mediterranean slant. A meal might kick off with smoked duck with roasted peppers and orange oil, and progress to roast monkfish with salsa verde. Cream-laden desserts from the sweets trolley could include a cheesecake, or chocolate roulade. The well-priced wine list is categorised by style. House wine is £9.25.

CHEF: David Rothwell PROPRIETORS: David and Trudy Rothwell OPEN: Sun L on last Sun of month 12 to 1.45, Tue to Sat D 7 to 9.30 MEALS: alc D (main courses £11 to £16.50). Set L £12.95, Set D £16.50 SERVICE: not inc, card slips closed CARDS: Delta, MasterCard, Switch, Visa DETAILS: 50 seats. Private parties: 60 main room. Car park. Vegetarian meals with notice. Children's helpings. Wheelchair access (also women's WC). Music

STUCKTON Hampshire **map 2**

▲ Three Lions 

Stuckton Road, Stuckton SP6 2HF
TEL: (01425) 652489 FAX: (01425) 656144
½m SE of Fordingbridge, off A338 but not signposted from it: take the turn just S of Fordingbridge and follow a sign down a narrow country lane

COOKING **7**
ANGLO-FRENCH
£34–£57

Part of the charm of this husband-and-wife operation is that there is no attempt to dissemble. Food so good that it is among the best in the south of England is served in modest, unassuming surroundings. Scrubbed pine furniture lends a cottagey feel, and the menu, chalked on a blackboard in the bar, is as generous in scope as it is spare in tone: galette of smoked haddock, hot pie of minced game and sultanas, or chicken with roast garlic and mustard. Michael Womersley gets day-boat fish from Dorset, mushrooms from the forest, and fruit and vegetables from local growers, and aims for light and precise cooking. Meat is often paired with fruit, producing tender and flavourful venison with plums, sesame-coated Quantock duck with mango, and an unusual starter of lambs' kidneys with braised apricots.

Treatments are varied but never outlandish, yielding seared scallops with an oriental dressing, for example, and there are typically light accompaniments to other seafood: maybe a warm vinaigrette of tomato, garlic and basil for grilled sea bass. Vegetables are 'just as they should be'. Light and lemony treacle tart has drawn praise, as have triangles of lime parfait with passion-fruit sauce, or there may be poached pears with verbena ice cream. A lively and unpretentious wine list offers many bottles around the £15 mark. Up-and-coming producers from south-west France feature strongly, with a 1998 Foxwood Marsanne providing a stimulating alternative to Chardonnay.

CHEF: Michael Womersley PROPRIETORS: Mr and Mrs Womersley OPEN: Tue to Sun L 12 to 2, Tue to Sat D 7 to 9.30 (10 Sat) CLOSED: 2 weeks Jan, 1 week Feb MEALS: alc (main courses £13 to £17). Set L Tue to Fri £13.50 (2 courses) SERVICE: not inc CARDS: Amex, Delta, MasterCard, Switch, Visa DETAILS: 60 seats. 12 seats outside. Private parties: 60 main room. Car park. Vegetarian meals. Children's helpings. No smoking in dining room. Wheelchair access (not WC). Occasional music ACCOMMODATION: 3 rooms, all with bath/shower. TV. B&B £59 to £85. Rooms for disabled. Baby facilities (£5)

The Guide relies on feedback from its readers. Especially welcome are reports on new restaurants appearing in the book for the first time. All letters to the Guide are acknowledged.

STURMINSTER NEWTON Dorset map 2

▲ Plumber Manor

Sturminster Newton DT10 2AF
TEL: (01258) 472507 FAX: (01258) 473370
EMAIL: book@plumber.com COOKING **3**
A357 to Sturminster Newton, take first left to Hazelbury Bryan, on left-hand side after 2m ANGLO-FRENCH £26–£51

Considered 'a gem of a place,' with a calm and peaceful atmosphere, this has been the Prideaux-Brune family home for generations, and a hotel and restaurant for over 25 years. Big paintings in old frames, labradors gently padding about the house, and a log-fired lounge capture the feel of private quarters 'manfully put to use for paying guests'. The food may not be cutting edge, dealing as it does in prawns and avocado with Marie-Rose sauce, roast loin of pork with apple sauce and sage, and an eat-as-much-as-you-like sweets trolley (available when the restaurant is at least a third full) featuring 'lashings of cream'. But the predominantly Anglo-French home cooking style also takes in monkfish with crab mousse, and guinea fowl with Thai curry sauce. Vegetables are served in profusion, and desserts have included Austrian cheesecake, hazelnut and apricot roulade, and lemon ginger crunch. Staff are attentive and polite, and a fairly priced wine list starts with house Vin de Pays d'Oc at £10 and includes a generous supply of half-bottles.

CHEF: Brian Prideaux-Brune PROPRIETOR: Richard Prideaux-Brune OPEN: Sun L 12.30 to 2, all week D 7.30 to 9 CLOSED: Feb MEALS: Set L £17.50, Set D £19.50 (2 courses) to £30 SERVICE: not inc, card slips closed CARDS: Amex, Diners, MasterCard, Switch, Visa DETAILS: 60 seats. Private parties: 45 main room, 14 and 25 private rooms. Car park. Vegetarian meals. Children's helpings. No smoking in 1 dining room. Wheelchair access (also WC). No music ACCOMMODATION: 16 rooms, all with bath/shower. TV. Phone. B&B £80 to £145. Rooms for disabled. Baby facilities (*The Which? Hotel Guide*)

SUDBURY Suffolk map 6

Brasserie Four Seven £

47 Gainsborough Street, Sudbury C10 2ET
TEL/FAX: (01787) 374298 COOKING **1**
EMAIL: fiona@brasserie47.co.uk MODERN BRITISH
WEB SITE: www.brasserie47.co.uk £24–£28

Close to the centre of Sudbury, and next door to Gainsborough's house (now a museum exhibiting some of the master's lesser-known paintings), this informal brasserie with its open-plan kitchen offers contemporary cooking to a knowledgeable Suffolk crowd. Menus move from 'rich, generous, top-notch' fish soup with crunchy croûtons, through chargrilled beef fillet with port and shallot sauce and hand-cut chips, to robust date and walnut pudding with vanilla custard. Vegetarians are catered for imaginatively, perhaps with baked Spanish onion stuffed with couscous, courgette, aubergine and tomato with sliced yam wedges and a watercress sauce. Other inventive preparations have included tomato jelly with pesto, black olives and celery, and coconut-crusted pineapple compote with coconut ice cream. Coffee comes with home-made fudge, and the enthusiastic front-of-house is led by Fiona Green. Wines are priced with restraint, opening with house Bordeaux at £7.95.

CHEF: Fraser Green PROPRIETORS: Fraser and Fiona Green OPEN: Tue to Sat 12 to 1.45, 7 to 9.30 (open for morning coffee and late breakfast) CLOSED: Christmas and New Year MEALS: Set L £4.95 (1 course), Set D £12.50 (2 courses) to £15.50. Light L menu SERVICE: not inc, card slips closed CARDS: Amex, Delta, Diners, MasterCard, Switch, Visa DETAILS: 56 seats. Private parties: 25 main room, 25 private room. Vegetarian meals. Children's helpings. No smoking in 1 dining room. Wheelchair access (not WC). No music. Air-conditioned (£5)

Red Onion Bistro £

57 Ballingdon Street, Sudbury CO10 6DA
TEL: (01787) 376777 FAX: (01787) 883156

COOKING **1**
MODERN EUROPEAN
£15–£33

This veteran of the rural bistro scene, under new ownership since last year, and with a new chef, stakes its Francocentric claim with red-checked curtains, green-checked tablecloths, posters and a blackboard menu. Its attractions are informality, low prices, and sometimes imaginative yet simply cooked dishes. Leek and potato soup, delicately flavoured salmon ceviche, or Greek salad might get things going, followed by guinea fowl with shallots and Puy lentils. Meatless options have included a tarte Tatin of Mediterranean vegetables topped with goats' cheese, while successful desserts have ranged from pannacotta with strawberries, to a comfortingly rich and dense version of chocolate brownies with gooey chocolate sauce. Wines are mostly under the £20 mark, with house wines starting at £7.75.

CHEF: Stuart Mott PROPRIETOR: Red Onion Bistro Ltd OPEN: Mon to Sat 12 to 2, 6.30 to 9.30 CLOSED: Christmas to New Year, bank hols MEALS: alc (main courses £6.50 to £11). Set L £6.75 (2 courses) to £8.75, Set D Mon to Thur £8.75 (2 courses) to £10.75 SERVICE: not inc, card slips closed CARDS: Amex, Delta, MasterCard, Switch, Visa DETAILS: 65 seats. 25 seats outside. Private parties: 60 main room. Car park. Vegetarian meals. Children's helpings. No cigars/pipes in dining room. Wheelchair access (not WC). No music

SUNDERLAND Tyne & Wear **map 10**

Café 21

Wylam Wharf, Low Street, Sunderland SR1 2AD
TEL: (0191) 567 6594 FAX: (0191) 510 3994

COOKING **3**
MODERN FRENCH/BRASSERIE
£26–£52

In the Guide last year as Brasserie 21, the restaurant had a name change as we were about to go to press. If the weather is up to it (and it has been on at least one occasion) the verandah makes a good spot for observing boats bobbing on the river against a backdrop of the National Glass Centre. Apart from a handful of daily and vegetarian dishes – such as lobster and asparagus salad, grilled Dover sole, and field mushroom fritters – the menu is unchanging. Simple seafood is the main preoccupation, typically Morecambe Bay potted shrimps, crab mayonnaise, and fish and chips with mushy peas and tartare sauce. But the menu covers enough territory to satisfy a wide variety of tastes, with salt chilli squid, and non-fishy items such as egg Benedict, thin tomato tart with pesto, and slow-cooked knuckle of ham with braised beans and parsley mash. The plain, reassuring nature of the food extends to desserts of baked Alaska with hot cherries, and French apple tart. Geordie service is relaxed and friendly, and 40-plus wines combine interest and fair value. House Duboeuf is £10.

CHEF: Andrew Brown PROPRIETORS: Terence and Susan Laybourne OPEN: Tue to Sat 12 to 2, 5.30 to 10.30 CLOSED: bank hols MEALS: alc (main courses £9.50 to £16). Set L £12.50 (2 courses) SERVICE: not inc CARDS: Amex, Delta, Diners, MasterCard, Switch, Visa DETAILS: 64 seats. 20 seats outside. Car park. Vegetarian meals. Children's helpings. Wheelchair access (also men's WC). Music

SURBITON Surrey map 3

Luca

NEW ENTRY

85 Maple Road, Surbiton KT6 4AW
TEL: (020) 8399 2365 FAX: (020) 8390 5353

COOKING **4**
GLOBAL
£34–£52

Fusion cooking has come to Surbiton in the shape of this plainly appointed but unmistakably trend-conscious restaurant in a suburban parade of shops. Annie O'Carroll, its chef and co-proprietor, cooked with Peter Gordon in the early days of the Sugar Club (see entry, London), and brings some of the heady mix of his global shopping basket and colourful treatment to her fortnightly-changing menus. Middle Eastern is a favoured mode and seems well understood, judging by an inspector's starter of pink, skewered cubes of lamb successfully partnered with artichoke, fennel, sweet potato, beetroot, cherry tomato and yoghurt.

The juxtaposition of ingredients helps to spark some fizz and crackle, as beetroot and smoked salmon are combined in a risotto, goat's cheese is stirred into mash, and grilled halloumi and marinated chickpeas are served with cumin flatbread and pickled chilli. Results tends to be interesting at the very least, as in a main course of braised belly pork with caramelised crackling and succotash. Desserts make less impact, but tiramisù-like chocolate espresso trifle has pleased, and service might be more clued up, although it gets the tone right. France and Australia form the backbone of the wine list, which showcases some good growers at prices that don't often exceed £20. The house selection starts at £11.

CHEF: Annie O'Carroll PROPRIETORS: Mr and Mrs D.K. O'Carroll OPEN: Sun L 12 to 2.30, Tue to Sat D 6.30 to 10.30 CLOSED: 25 Dec MEALS: alc (main courses £10 to £14.50) SERVICE: 12.5%, card slips closed CARDS: Delta, MasterCard, Switch, Visa DETAILS: 58 seats. Private parties: 55 main room. Vegetarian meals. Children's helpings. No-smoking area. Wheelchair access (not WC). Music. Air-conditioned

The Guide is totally independent, accepts no free hospitality, and survives on the number of copies sold each year.

Restaurateurs justifiably resent no-shows. If you quote a credit card number when booking, you may be liable for the restaurant's lost profit margin if you don't turn up. Always phone to cancel.

SUTTON GAULT Cambridgeshire **map 6**

▲ Anchor Inn

Sutton Gault CB6 2BD
TEL: (01353) 778537 FAX: (01353) 776180
EMAIL: anchor@sutton-gault.freeserve.co.uk
off B1381 Sutton to Earith road, just S of Sutton, 6m W of Ely

COOKING **2**
MODERN BRITISH
£21–£44

While the surrounding watery marshy landscape exerts its own charm, wooden tables and chairs help to maintain the feel of a pub, which this still is; together, they produce an ambience that 'couldn't be bettered'. The kitchen, meanwhile, makes the most of its strong roots, typically featuring a rare breed such as Norfolk Horn lamb alongside a game dish or two: maybe wild pigeon breast, or a Denham Estate venison steak served with braised chicory. Notable successes have included mushroom soup that was 'hot, peppery, full of mushroom and tarragon flavour', and rich and plentiful roast loin of hare with poached leeks. Desserts might include Italian zucotta, cheeses are given strong billing, and service is 'always friendly and timely'. A helpful, varied, good-value wine list includes plenty of bottles under £15, with monthly specials (from £10.95) in place of house wines.

CHEFS: Richard Bradley, Maria Norman, and Will Munford PROPRIETORS: Robin and Heather Moore OPEN: all week 12 to 2, 7 to 9 (6.30 to 9.30 Sat) CLOSED: 26 Dec MEALS: alc (main courses £11 to £15). Set L Mon to Fri £7.50 (2 courses), Set L Sun £16.50 SERVICE: not inc CARDS: Amex, Delta, MasterCard, Switch, Visa DETAILS: 70 seats. 30 seats outside. Private parties: 25 main room. Car park. Children's helpings. No very young children after 8.30. No smoking in dining room. Wheelchair access (also WC). No music ACCOMMODATION: 2 rooms, both with bath/shower. TV. Phone. B&B £50 to £95. Baby facilities (£5)

SWAFFHAM Norfolk **map 6**

▲ Strattons

4 Ash Close, Swaffham PE37 7NH
TEL: (01760) 723845 FAX: (01760) 720458
WEB SITE: www.strattons-hotel.co.uk

COOKING **4**
MODERN EUROPEAN
£38–£45

Evenings begin upstairs in two 'splendidly cluttered' rooms of this Palladian house off the square, amid family memorabilia and visual jokes, and continue in the ground-floor dining room whose plain décor is 'quite a shock after the riot upstairs'. It is a small-scale family operation that makes environmental waves by recycling most of its waste, collecting eggs from its now legendary chickens, and investing heavily in local and organic produce. The simple but imaginative cooking style is set out on a short menu that might begin with salmon and smoked oyster fishcakes served with sweet cucumber pickle, followed by a choice of just one meat, fish or vegetable main course.

Within the broadly European flavour spectrum, a cook's sense of economy produces some interesting variations: pea and mint combined in a sauce to accompany wild sea trout, for example, or made into a jelly and served with fine slices of locally smoked ham alongside a spring cabbage chutney. Roasting is a favoured technique, applied perhaps to local duck suprêmes with a garlic, honey and soy sauce, while vegetarian options have included roast tomato and Chianti risotto 'oozing with rich, charred, tomatoey sweetness'.

British and Irish cheeses in good condition are knowledgeably served with details of type, source, animal, potted history and more, while desserts might run to strawberry granita with lemon curd ice cream, or wild apricot fool. Service is relaxed, the cost is 'serious money for mid-Norfolk but worth it', and wines on the handwritten and well-annotated list – complete with illustrations and witty quotations – are arranged by style and include a wide range from around the world. House wines range from £9 to £13, and eight wines are sold by the glass.

CHEFS: Vanessa Scott and Margaret Cooper PROPRIETORS: Les and Vanessa Scott OPEN: all week D only 6.45 to 9 CLOSED: Christmas MEALS: Set D £30 SERVICE: not inc, card slips closed CARDS: Amex, Delta, MasterCard, Switch, Visa DETAILS: 20 seats. 4 seats outside. Private parties: 8 main room. Car park. Vegetarian meals. Children's helpings. No smoking in dining room. Occasional music ACCOMMODATION: 6 rooms, all with bath/shower. TV. Phone. B&B £70 to £150. Rooms for disabled. Baby facilities. Garden (*The Which? Hotel Guide*)

SWANAGE Dorset **map 2**

Galley

9 High Street, Swanage BH19 2LN
TEL: (01929) 427299

COOKING **3**
MODERN BRITISH/SEAFOOD
£30–£36

The name of this high-street restaurant is reflected in its décor, which features a host of ocean-going memorabilia: hanging nets, ships' lamps and so forth. The cooking, too, has a maritime theme, employing fish enthusiastically and sympathetically. 'We continue to strive for simplicity and perfection,' writes Nick Storer, highlighting the case that the latter is often dependent on the former; to enforce the point, menu descriptions tend to avoid elaboration, which may mean a pleasant surprise when the dish arrives. Poached salmon with sorrel sauce, herb-stuffed baked sea bass, and roast cod served with mushrooms, onions and smoked bacon will strike happy chords with many. Non-fish eaters might be appeased by a combination of venison, rabbit and pigeon in a rich stout sauce with sage dumplings. Desserts might include raspberry pavlova, chocolate prâline mousse or crème brûleé. Wines are stylistically arranged, and there are some good bargains to be had; house Chilean is £8.50.

CHEF: Nick Storer PROPRIETORS: N.D. and M.G. Storer OPEN: all week D only 6.30 to 9.30 CLOSED: 3 weeks Nov, 1 Jan to Easter MEALS: Set D £21.50 SERVICE: not inc, card slips closed CARDS: Amex, Delta, Diners, MasterCard, Switch, Visa DETAILS: 34 seats. Private parties: 30 main room. Vegetarian meals. Children's helpings. No smoking while others eat. Wheelchair access (not WC). Music. Air-conditioned

Prices quoted in the Guide are based on information supplied by restaurateurs. The prices quoted at the top of each entry represent a range, from the lowest meal price to the highest; the latter is inflated by 20 per cent to take account of likely price rises during the year of the Guide.

TADCASTER North Yorkshire **map 9**

▲ Hazlewood Castle, Restaurant 1086

Paradise Lane, Hazlewood, Tadcaster LS24 9NJ
TEL: (01937) 535354 FAX: (01937) 530630
EMAIL: info@hazelwood-castle.co.uk
WEB SITE: www.hazlewood-castle.co.uk
off A64, 3½m SW of Tadcaster

COOKING **2**
MODERN BRITISH
£27–£56

Occupying a barn-like first-floor room, the dining room commemorates the year of the Domesday Book (in which the castle is mentioned). Its rag-rolled walls and bonsai trees do their best to make it feel most unlike an ancient pile. The repertoire is not old-fashioned either, dealing in smoky garlic risotto, lambs' liver with olive mash and red cabbage, and fish from either Fleetwood or Cornwall: red snapper with a sweet-tasting shellfish sauce for one diner. The food does not always live up to ambition, which can be a problem at these prices, but enough reporters are convinced. Cheeses are well presented – half a dozen arranged in order of strength around a plate – and desserts have included a successful orange mousse with mango-flavoured coulis. House Chilean red and white are £14.95.

CHEFS: John Benson-Smith and Matthew Benson-Smith PROPRIETOR: Hazlewood Castle Ltd OPEN: Sun L 12 to 2, Mon to Sat D 6 to 9.30 MEALS: Set L Sun £17.50, Set D 6 to 7 £15.95 (2 courses) to £17.50, Set D Mon to Sat £25 to £35 SERVICE: not inc, card slips closed CARDS: Amex, Delta, Diners, MasterCard, Switch, Visa DETAILS: 80 seats. Private parties: 80 main room. Car park. Vegetarian meals. Children's helpings. No smoking in dining room. Wheelchair access (also WC). Music ACCOMMODATION: 21 rooms, all with bath/shower. TV. Phone. B&B £95 to £300 (*The Which? Hotel Guide*) (£5)

Singers

16 Westgate, Tadcaster LS24 9AB
TEL: (01937) 835121

COOKING **3**
MODERN EUROPEAN
£18–£32

Just about everything that can be is musically themed, from wallpaper to the fairly priced wine list, but the strongest leitmotif running through reports is the warmth and friendliness of staff – 'we instantly felt at home' – who provide generally attentive service. Singers delivers good value (note the early-bird offer) from a balanced, modern menu that might start with melting goats' cheese in filo pastry with an orange-flavoured red pepper dressing, or chargrilled tuna with a grapefruit, chilli and coriander salsa. Successful meat dishes have included crispy duck leg on bubble and squeak, and calf's liver with smoked bacon and black pudding, while among notable desserts has been a lightly set banana crème brûlée with a crispy caramelised topping. As an alternative, a rather 'safe selection' of cheese (with a £1.50 supplement) comes ready plated. House vin de table is £9.25.

London restaurants by cuisine are listed near the front of the book.

CHEFS: David Lockwood and Richard Thompson PROPRIETORS: Philip Taylor and Guy Vicari OPEN: Tue to Sat D only 6 to 9.30 CLOSED: 25 and 26 Dec, 1 week Feb, 1 week Aug MEALS: Set D Tue to Fri 6 to 7 £11.95, Set D Tue to Thur £9.95 (1 course) to £16.95, Set D Fri and Sat £16.95 SERVICE: not inc, card slips closed CARDS: Delta, MasterCard, Switch, Visa DETAILS: 38 seats. Private parties: 38 main room. Vegetarian meals. No children under 5. No smoking in dining room. Wheelchair access (not WC). Music (£5)

TADWORTH Surrey **map 3**

Gemini

28 Station Approach, Tadworth KT20 5AH
TEL/FAX: (01737) 812179

COOKING **3**
FRENCH/MODERN EUROPEAN
£24–£47

Attractive decor, service that is friendly, informative and well-paced, and some imaginative and competent dishes appear to be three good reasons for visiting Robert Foster's dependable local restaurant, which now sports a modern lemon and terracotta bar, and an apricot and dark red dining room in keeping with the cottagey exterior. The kitchen delivers some well-judged tastes and textures. A generous mussel, crab and salmon laksa has been densely flavoured, 'zingy and creamy', while twice-baked Roquefort and spinach soufflé (from the specials board) is light and fluffy, 'like eating cheese feathers'.

By contrast main courses (following a sorbet) can be robust. Crisp and well-trimmed calf's liver has come with pesto, a jus of pan juices and a pyramid of ratatouille, while lamb shank has been served with a full-flavoured gravy of ceps and button onions, and velvety garlic and olive oil mash. Praiseworthy desserts run to a fruit-packed Sauternes jelly of the correct 'wobble factor', and cherry and almond tart with coconut ice cream. Most of the 50 or so widely sourced wines, including eight house wines from £10.50, are under £20.

CHEF/PROPRIETOR: Robert Foster OPEN: Tue to Fri and Sun L 12 to 2.30, Tue to Sat D 7 to 9.30 CLOSED: 2 weeks Christmas MEALS: alc Tue to Fri D (main courses £13.50 to £16.50). Set L £13.50 (2 courses) to £15.50, Set L Sun 17.95, Set D Sat £28.50 SERVICE: not inc CARDS: Amex, Delta, Diners, MasterCard, Switch, Visa DETAILS: 56 seats. 12 seats outside. Private parties: 60 main room. Children's helpings. No children under 12 exc Sun L. No smoking in dining room. Wheelchair access (not WC). Music

TAPLOW Berkshire **map 3**

▲ Cliveden, Waldo's

Taplow SL6 0JF
TEL: (01628) 668561 FAX: (01628) 661837
WEB SITE: www.clivedenhouse.co.uk
off A4, 2m N of Taplow on Cliveden road

COOKING **3**
MODERN EUROPEAN
£68–£112

The huge, grey, angular mansion (owned by the National Trust) was designed by Sir Charles Barry, architect of the Houses of Parliament. Decorated with balustrades and urns, it faces a long parterre, formal box hedges, and the River Thames in the distance. Inside is no less grand, with dark carved wood, exuberantly sculpted fireplaces and enormous tapestries. Waldo's is a small, comfortable basement dining room where John Wood, who arrived just as the last edition of the Guide went to press, continues the luxurious style of his predecessors. He favours such ideas as Jerusalem artichoke and truffle soup, monkfish with lobster risotto, and turns out fine mainstream dishes such as pink, supple, well-flavoured best end of lamb, served with a tian of Mediterranean vegetables and a heavily reduced stock-based sauce.

Desserts are typically paired with an ice cream: basil flavoured to accompany caramelised pineapple tart, or made with cherry and almond milk to partner mildly flavoured cherry soufflé. The year 2000 heralds an overhaul for the Cliveden cellar (bringing more of an international flavour) which should be completed by 2001. The classics remain impressive, with some great years and fine producers, but prices are an obstacle: only one red and one white are under £20 a bottle.

CHEF: John Wood PROPRIETOR: Cliveden Ltd OPEN: Tue to Sat D only 7 to 9.30 MEALS: Set D £58 to £84 SERVICE: net prices, card slips closed CARDS: Amex, Delta, Diners, MasterCard, Switch, Visa DETAILS: 25 seats. Private parties: 35 main room. Car park. Children's helpings. Jacket and tie. No smoking in dining room. Wheelchair access (not WC). Music. Air-conditioned ACCOMMODATION: 38 rooms, all with bath/shower. TV. Phone. Room only £290 to £830. Baby facilities. Swimming pool

TAUNTON Somerset **map 2**

Brazz  £

Castle Bow, Taunton TA1 1LR
TEL/FAX: (01823) 252000

COOKING **2**
MODERN BRITISH
£21–£51

'Every town should have one,' concluded a reporter, and Kit Chapman is doing his best to oblige. Having hit the nail on the head in terms of décor, prices, local meeting point and food, the stylish Brazz now has a kid brother (see entry, Exeter). Bright, shiny, big and bold, it sports a fibre-optic-lit dome, an attention-grabbing aquarium, and delivers a carefully constructed catalogue of brasserie staples and reworked British favourites (among them prawn cocktail and fishcakes), several available in two sizes.

The inventory (overseen, as the Guide went to press, by the Castle's chef Richard Guest) includes a range of salads from Caesar to pink chicken liver to chunky duck on interesting leaves. It also takes in risottos, burgers, grilled steaks, braises and perhaps a tower of crusty liver and bacon with mashed potato. Puddings are more limited in scope, but may include chocolate marquise or rhubarb Bakewell tart, as well as a few ice creams and sorbets. The biggest shortcoming, by a long chalk, is service. Some three dozen wines suit the circumstances, starting with vin de pays at £9.50 and including ten by the glass.

CHEF: Richard Guest PROPRIETORS: the Chapman family OPEN: all week 11.30 to 3, 6.30 to 10.30 MEALS: alc (main courses £5.50 to £15). Set L and D £10 (2 courses) SERVICE: not inc CARDS: Amex, Delta, Diners, MasterCard, Switch, Visa DETAILS: 100 seats. Private parties: 50 main room. Car park. Vegetarian meals. Children's helpings. Wheelchair access (also WC). Occasional music. Air-conditioned

---

Dining rooms where music, either live or recorded, is never played are signalled by No music *in the details at the end of an entry.*

▲ Castle Hotel

Castle Green, Taunton TA1 1NF
TEL: (01823) 272671 FAX: (01823) 336066
EMAIL: reception@the-castle-hotel.com
WEB SITE: www.the-castle-hotel.com

COOKING **5**
MODERN BRITISH
£33–£70

The Chapman family's 50-year tenure at the Castle has been a distinguished one, putting Taunton on the map as far as the Guide and its readers are concerned. Most recently the dining room has been refurbished in muted pinks and greens and, following the departure of Phil Vickery after nine years (just as the last edition of the Guide went to press) new incumbent Richard Guest took on Kit Chapman's long-standing 'English Project'. Guest worked with very French Jean-Christophe Novelli, but his mission here is to develop a distinctive style of English food and cooking, and many of the meat dishes are particularly appealing in this respect: braised oxtail with cauliflower purée, steamed venison pudding, or slow-cooked mutton with buttered greens and gravy.

Raw materials continue to be first class (suppliers are confidently listed on the menu, as they are on the wine list), and technical skills are impressive: for example in three fat, accurately seared scallops on a smooth pea purée spiked with whole peas, and a clever dish of roast quail, stuffed with a poached egg wrapped in spinach, served on freshly made corned beef hash, with underdone lentils and a highly reduced caramelised sauce. Desserts include the Castle's own take on Black Forest gâteau, and cheeses are British, some of them local. Incidentals include first-rate bread, and an impressive line in appetisers: gazpacho for one visitor, layered with red pepper reduction and cucumber froth in a sherry glass. Prices make the food very good value, and restaurant management comes in for praise: its 'effortless communication is to a large extent what good service is all about'. Wines are predominantly French, but with sound European and global selections, and while the list may not be a trail-blazer, mark-ups are reasonable, with several bottles under £15 and plenty of halves. House wines start at £11.50.

CHEF: Richard Guest PROPRIETORS: the Chapman family OPEN: all week 12.30 to 2, 7 to 9.30 MEALS: alc (main courses £15 to £22). Set L and D £18 (2 courses) to £24 SERVICE: not inc CARDS: Amex, Diners, MasterCard, Switch, Visa DETAILS: 65 seats. Private parties: 90 main room, 8 to 90 private rooms. Car park. Vegetarian meals. Children's helpings. No smoking in dining room. Wheelchair access (not WC). No music ACCOMMODATION: 44 rooms, all with bath/shower. TV. Phone. B&B £95 to £145. Rooms for disabled. Baby facilities

The Guide relies on feedback from its readers. Especially welcome are reports on new restaurants appearing in the book for the first time. All letters to the Guide are acknowledged.

'There is a tedious tendency to decorate every plate with a Vietnamese jungle of some wimpy designer lettuce. Thought longingly about Agent Orange.' (On eating in Somerset)

TAVISTOCK Devon **map 1**

▲ Horn of Plenty

Gulworthy, Tavistock PL19 8JD
TEL/FAX: (01822) 832528
EMAIL: enquiries@thehornofplenty.co.uk
WEB SITE: www.thehornofplenty.co.uk
3m W of Tavistock on A390, turn right at Gulworthy Cross

COOKING **6**
GLOBAL
£35–£62

Set in five acres of gardens and orchards with majestic views over the Tamar valley, this 200-year-old stone house was originally built for the Duke of Bedford. This year, the Rostons welcomed long-standing chef Peter Gorton as a co-owner, and the partnership also acquired the Carved Angel (see entry, Dartmouth). Fixed-price menus of half-a-dozen choices per course are the order of the day, and there is some ambitious, though not outlandish, cooking going on. Starters of sauté sesame scallops with roast red pepper and ginger dressing, or baked goats' cheese wrapped in courgette with a lentil balsamic vinaigrette, may be followed by grilled sea bass with asparagus on a prawn sauce, or roast quails with a port and juniper sauce.

Careful timing has been commended, for example of lamb cooked *à point* and served on a bed of aubergines, spinach and ratatouille, and the daily fish specials seem to be a safe bet, judging by Tamar salmon, John Dory and turbot enjoyed on consecutive nights by one reporter. Desserts are tried-and-true classics such as glazed lemon tart with spiced oranges, apple and blackcurrant crumble with vanilla ice cream, or pistachio and banana parfait with caramelised banana. Service is usually 'efficient and attentive', though some reporters have commented on long delays between arriving, ordering and eating. A fine selection of French wines is complemented by a decent New World section, though mark-ups are a little greedy all round. House French is £17 and five wines are available by the glass.

CHEF: Peter Gorton PROPRIETORS: Paul and Andie Roston, and Peter Gorton OPEN: Tue to Sun L 12 to 2, all week D 7 to 9 MEALS: Set L £23.50, Set D £37 SERVICE: not inc CARDS: Amex, Delta, MasterCard, Switch, Visa DETAILS: 50 seats. Private parties: 60 main room, 20 private room. Car park. Vegetarian meals. Children's helpings. No children under 13 at D. No smoking in dining room. Wheelchair access (also WC). Occasional music ACCOMMODATION: 10 rooms, all with bath/shower. TV. Phone. B&B £115 to £200. Rooms for disabled. Baby facilities (*The Which? Hotel Guide*)

All details are as accurate as possible at the time of going to press, but chefs and owners often change, and it is wise to check by telephone before making a special journey. Many readers have been disappointed when set-price bargain meals are no longer available. Ask when booking.

'At the end, the manager urged us to sign a book singing the restaurant's praises, and looked miffed when I declined firmly.' (On eating in Scotland)

TEFFONT EVIAS Wiltshire map 2

▲ Howard's House

WILTSHIRE GFG 2001 COMMENDED

Teffont Evias SP3 5RJ
TEL: (01722) 716392 FAX: (01722) 716820
EMAIL: paul.firmin@virgin.net
WEB SITE: www.howardshousehotel.co.uk
off B3089, W of Dinton and 9½m W of Salisbury, signposted Chicksgrove

COOKING **5**
MODERN BRITISH-PLUS
£26–£55

The Teffont Evias estate consists of a church, a manor house and this seventeenth-century grey-stone dower house whose extensive gardens – a mix of formal and wild (think 'National Trust with weeds') – may be viewed through French windows from the end of the long, narrow, chintzily appointed dining room. A partial change of ownership accounts for it being 'more stylish and sophisticated than before', and the arrival of Boyd McIntosh to beef up the kitchen operation has injected a new spirit of adventure into the cooking, yielding at inspection for example a strikingly flavourful dish of grilled red mullet fillets and a single large scallop, with parsnip crisps, provençale vegetables and lime and lavender oil.

Although some dishes may seem very busy, raw materials are first-class, timing is spot-on, and sauces are a strong point: a top-of-the-range Madeira jus served with smoked Scottish beef on a rosemary and garlic galette, and an exceptionally fine rosemary and thyme gravy accompanying impeccably sourced roast rack of lamb. Attention to detail continues through to desserts of lemon tart with cinnamon custard and an orange and white chocolate sorbet, and strawberry parfait with mango coulis and a strawberry and kiwi salad. Service is well-informed and friendly. The wine list leads with French classics, being especially strong in Burgundy, but prices reflect the pedigree. House wines start at £9.95.

CHEFS: Boyd McIntosh and Paul Firmin PROPRIETOR: Paul Firmin OPEN: Sun L 12.30 to 2, all week D 7.30 to 9.30 CLOSED: Christmas MEALS: alc (main courses £14 to £18). Set L £18.50, Set D £19.95 SERVICE: not inc, card slips closed CARDS: Amex, Delta, Diners, MasterCard, Switch, Visa DETAILS: 30 seats. 10 seats outside. Private parties: 38 main room. Car park. Vegetarian meals. No smoking in dining room. Wheelchair access (not WC). Occasional music ACCOMMODATION: 9 rooms, all with bath/shower. TV. Phone. B&B £70 to £145. Baby facilities (*The Which? Hotel Guide*)

THAME Oxfordshire map 2

▲ Old Trout

29–30 Lower High Street, Thame OX9 2AA
TEL: (01844) 212146 FAX: (01844) 212614
EMAIL: mj4trout@aol.com
WEB SITE: www.theoldtrouthotel.co.uk

COOKING **2**
MODERN EUROPEAN
£22–£50

The two thatched cottages at one end of the wide street that runs through this attractive market town look 'obviously old', give or take a few years, and the beams and flagstone floors provide an attractive setting for some brightly flavoured dishes. Seafood is a strong suit – sweet chilli-seared salmon comes with oysters and a lemon-grass dressing – and the monthly-changing menu is supplemented by daily extras. One of the highlights appears to have been a seafood platter, on a silver stand, containing everything from oysters and lobster claws, via crab and squid, to tuna and sea bass, 'all fresh as can be'. Among alternatives might be shredded duck on wilted greens with a huge pile of crispy noodles. Finish with baked lemon tart, or apple and berry crumble. Casual service may not always impress, although the up-to-date, varietally arranged wine list does, not least for its catholic taste and fair pricing. House wines, chalked on a blackboard, are around £13.50.

CHEF: Mark Jones PROPRIETORS: Mr and Mrs Mark Jones OPEN: Mon to Sat 12 to 2.30, 6.30 to 10 CLOSED: 2 weeks from 24 Dec MEALS: alc (main courses £11.50 to £15). Set L £10.50 (2 courses) to £13 SERVICE: not inc, card slips closed CARDS: Delta, Diners, MasterCard, Switch, Visa DETAILS: 65 seats. 30 seats outside. Private parties: 65 main room, 16 and 26 private rooms. Car park. Vegetarian meals. No smoking in dining room. Music ACCOMMODATION: 7 rooms, all with bath/shower. TV. Phone. B&B £55 to £85 (*The Which? Hotel Guide*)

TITLEY Herefordshire **map 5**

▲ Stagg Inn £

Titley HR5 3RL
TEL: (01544) 230221
EMAIL: stagginn@titley.kc3.co.uk
WEB SITE: www.kc3.co.uk/stagg
on B4355, NE of Kington

COOKING **4**
MODERN BRITISH
£23–£41

A welcoming bar with mugs dangling from the ceiling, real fires and antique furniture help to maintain the feel of a country inn. One of the strengths of Steve Reynolds's cooking is its foundation on carefully sourced materials. Local suppliers come up with traceable Marches beef (served in a choice of three or four ways), organic pork and free-range poultry, while fish arrives from Cornwall. The cooking is admirably restrained – dishes can be 'dead simple' – and while the techniques employed are generally straightforward, timing is good and saucing fundamentally sound.

Favourable results have included pigeon breast with herb risotto, scallops with creamed leeks and black pepper oil, and confit of rabbit leg with lentils and mustard sauce. Vegetarians get a good deal, unpasteurised cheeses include some rarities (Finn, Ragstone, Monkland, Carneddau goats' and Skirrid ewes' milk among them), and puddings run to spiced rhubarb compote, passion-fruit jelly, and caramelised lemon tart. Around 60 wines feature on the fairly priced list, which is weighted towards France but includes a good showing from the rest of the world too. Eight house wines are all £9.50 or £1.70 per glass.

CHEF: Steve Reynolds PROPRIETORS: Steve Reynolds and Nicola Holland OPEN: Tue to Sun 12 to 2, 6.30 to 10 CLOSED: first 2 weeks Nov, 25 Dec MEALS: alc (main courses £9.50 to £14) SERVICE: not inc, card slips closed CARDS: Delta, MasterCard, Switch, Visa DETAILS: 50 seats. 20 seats outside. Private parties: 30 main room. Car park. Vegetarian meals. Children's helpings. No smoking in dining room. No music ACCOMMODATION: 2 rooms, both with bath/shower. TV. B&B £30 to £50 (£5)

denotes an outstanding wine cellar; denotes a good wine list, worth travelling for.

TODMORDEN West Yorkshire map 8

Old Hall **NEW ENTRY**

Hall Street, Todmorden OL14 7AD
TEL: (01706) 815998 FAX: (01706) 810669

COOKING **2**
MODERN EUROPEAN
£21–£48

'Full marks for appearance,' conceded one visitor to this lofty Grade II listed Elizabethan manor house. Large enough to accommodate three dining rooms, its atmospheric setting derives from dark carved wood, a big stone fireplace and sumptuous crimson and gold fabrics. The seasonally changing carte combines regional and global ingredients, producing a hearty starter of black pudding in filo on sweet red cabbage, and simple but tasty roast vegetables with pesto and Parmesan shavings. Dishes are commendably straightforward, along the lines of leek and Gruyère tart, crisp-skinned roast cod fillet with Savoy cabbage and salty bacon, and lamb shank with an enthusiastic quota of sun-dried tomatoes in the sauce. Portions are generous, vegetables plentiful (although 'proper' chips would be a bonus), and desserts might include crème brûlée or tangy lemon tart with raspberry coulis. Service is welcoming, down to earth and helpful, set price meals sound tempting, and a short, serviceable wine list stays mostly under £20.

CHEF: Chris Roberts PROPRIETORS: Nick Hoyle and Madeleine Hoyle OPEN: Tue to Sun L 12 to 2 (2.30 Sun), Tue to Sat D 7 to 9.45 CLOSED: 25 Dec and first week Jan MEALS: alc (main courses £9 to £16). Set L Sun £9.95 (2 courses) to £12.95, Set L Tue to Sat £6.95 (2 courses) SERVICE: not inc CARDS: Delta, Diners, MasterCard, Switch, Visa DETAILS: 70 seats. 20 seats outside. Private parties: 60 main room, 18 to 30 private rooms. Vegetarian meals. Children's helpings. No smoking in 2 dining rooms. Music

TUNBRIDGE WELLS Kent map 3

▲ Hotel du Vin & Bistro

Crescent Road, Tunbridge Wells TN1 2LY
TEL: 01892 526 455 FAX: 01892 512 044
EMAIL: reservations@tunbridgewells.hotelduvin.co.uk
WEB SITE: www.hotelduvin.com

COOKING **4**
MODERN EUROPEAN
£31–£51

Having hit on a successful combination of town-house hotel, relaxed restaurant and first-class wine list, this small group is expanding further, with a new branch in Bristol (see entry). Three interlinked dining rooms, their tall windows overlooking the garden and rooftops, set an informal tone with bare floorboards and wooden tables and chairs, while a modish menu takes a mostly European line.

To cover all bases it alternates between traditional items such as frogs' legs with garlic and parsley, pork with prunes, and Aberdeen Angus ribeye steak with chips, and more contemporary baked cod with artichokes, clams and chorizo. However, quite a few disappointments have been registered over the past year. Desserts come with a recommended glass of wine – fig tart and honey ice cream with sweet Muscat, for instance – and, as might be expected, the 'Screwpull Cellar' wine list is widely travelled and well priced. Quality is high and experimentation is encouraged, with bottles from Morocco and Thailand finding a place. But traditionalists need have no fear since all the great and the good are here. Fifteen wines by the glass kick off at £3.

CHEF: Sam Mahoney PROPRIETORS: Robin Hutson and Gerard Basset OPEN: all week 12 (12.30 Sun) to 1.30 (2 Sun), 7 to 9.30 MEALS: alc exc Sun L (main courses £11.25 to £15.50). Set L Sun £22.50 SERVICE: not inc CARDS: Amex, Delta, Diners, MasterCard, Switch, Visa DETAILS: 70 seats. Private parties: 14 and 70 private rooms. Car park. Vegetarian meals. Children's helpings. Wheelchair access (also WC). No music ACCOMMODATION: 32 rooms, all with bath/shower. TV. Phone. Room only £75 to £139 (*The Which? Hotel Guide*)

TWICKENHAM Greater London **map 3**

McClements

2 Whitton Road, Twickenham TW1 1BJ
TEL: (020) 8744 9610 FAX: (01784) 252967

COOKING **6**
FRENCH
£29–£43

John McClements has made Twickenham a destination for foodie pilgrimages with his impressive original restaurant – now extended into a new room at the back – and its simpler sister establishment (see entry below). Sand-coloured walls are hung with modern prints, table settings are classy, and seats solidly comfortable. Fixed-price menus offer plenty of choice and reflect the fact that there is a lot going on in the kitchen. 'I am suspicious of a dish that needs three lines of description, especially when it is only a starter,' commented a reporter, though the item in question – a Savoy cabbage parcel of crabmeat in a light ginger dressing, served with sesame-coated tuna and tempura-battered king prawns – could not be faulted for ingredients, technique or presentation.

Among recommended main courses have been an agreeably gamey mallard breast with roast potatoes and apples, turnip dauphinois, and a calvados sauce, and peppered venison fillet embellished with a little burger of venison, braised pork belly, chestnuts and fennel. If you can manage them after all that, it is possible to have a plate of five desserts, or perhaps a hot pistachio soufflé with cappuccino parfait. Service has been a little slow at times. The wine list has a nice sense of geographical balance, and includes many classic white and red Burgundies. House wines are £12.50.

CHEF/PROPRIETOR: John McClements OPEN: all week L 12 to 2.30, Mon to Sat D 7 to 11 MEALS: Set L £18, Set D £24 SERVICE: 10%, card slips closed CARDS: Amex, MasterCard, Switch, Visa DETAILS: 45 seats. Private parties: 200 main room. Car park. Vegetarian meals. No-smoking area. Wheelchair access (also WC). No music. Air-conditioned (£5)

TW1

108 Heath Road, Twickenham TW1 4BN
TEL: (020) 8891 0008 FAX: (01784) 240593

COOKING **3**
FRENCH
£26–£44

John McClements's second Twickenham restaurant is a smartly turned-out, intimate place done in blue and cream, with a wooden screen running down the centre. Cooking of impeccable modern pedigree is provided by Stephen Blakemore, whose sense of invention mirrors the proprietor's own. Tiger prawns with roast peppers and fattoush tomatoes, and tenderloin of pork with apricot mustard mash and oyster mushrooms are two of the ways he stimulates imagination and tastebuds alike. The carte is supplemented by a good-value four-course 'gourmet menu', which includes a glass of wine for each course. A sense of the exotic pairs a mango and chilli salsa with grilled scallops, and delivers for dessert a fruit gratin with a rosemary-flavoured cake. Otherwise, it might be hot chocolate mousse with coffee ice-cream. The short wine list is good but pricy, though it opens at £11.

CHEF: Stephen Blakemore PROPRIETOR: John McClements OPEN: all week L 12 to 3 (5 Sun), Mon to Sat D 6.30 to 11.30 MEALS: alc (main courses £11.50 to £14). Set L £12.50 (2 courses), Set D Mon to Fri £21 (inc wine) SERVICE: 10% (optional), card slips closed CARDS: Delta, MasterCard, Switch, Visa DETAILS: 70 seats. 15 seats outside. Private parties: 100 main room. Vegetarian meals. Children's helpings. Wheelchair access (also WC). No music. Air-conditioned (£5)

ULLSWATER Cumbria — map 10

▲ Sharrow Bay

Ullswater CA10 2LZ
TEL: (017684) 86301 FAX: (017684) 86349
WEB SITE: www.sharrow-bay.com — COOKING 7
2m from Pooley Bridge on E side of lake, — ENGLISH
signposted Howtown and Martindale — £44–£66

The nation's senior country-house hotel (it opened in 1948) is like a long-running soap opera, of which visitors need their annual fix. Part of the appeal is that it has not been corporatised but retains its personal and individual character. Service is friendly and unpretentious – there is no snobbery at Sharrow – and Brian Sack still does the rounds, making guests feel 'special'. Even when space is at a premium, it only appears to make visitors more friendly towards each other. The operation works to a time-honoured formula. Dinner is at eight (first courses are served on the dot) and the house rule about cheese is inviolable: it comes after dessert, never before. But good organisation is indispensable, given the pace of things: one couple emerged for coffee after lunch to find others gathering for afternoon tea.

Apart from the fish course, choice is extensive, portions are on the generous side, and dishes are attractively presented and garnished. The range extends from stuffed pig's trotter on pease pudding to al dente ravioli filled with a rich mix of lobster, scallops and truffle in a crayfish sauce, by way of English lamb fillet in a parsley crust with couscous and vegetables. There are changes to the menu, but you may need a microscope to spot them: one couple who enjoyed fillet of halibut with a red pepper coulis in May returned in August to find it served with a yellow pepper coulis. And the veal had been replaced by duckling, and a couple of desserts had changed. Otherwise, Sharrow Bay cruises through people's lives with the poise and serenity of an ocean liner. Desserts are comforting, none more so than icky sticky toffee sponge, although tiramisù and bread-and-butter pudding give it a run for its money.

Talking of which, value is considered good compared with other country-house hotels, and breakfasts are reckoned among the best available. Celebrated regions, good vintages and reasonable prices characterise the newly formatted wine list. With 24 wines by the glass (ranging from £3.95 to £8.75), it is sommelier James Payne's intention that classic Sharrow dishes can be matched, course by course, with an ideal wine.

CHEFS: Johnnie Martin and Colin Akrigg PROPRIETOR: Brian Sack OPEN: all week 1 to 1.30, 8 to 8.30 CLOSED: early Dec to early Mar MEALS: Set L £36.25, Set D £47.25 SERVICE: net prices, card slips closed CARDS: Delta, MasterCard, Switch, Visa DETAILS: 60 seats. Private parties: 35 main room. Car park. No children under 13. Jacket and tie. No smoking in dining room. Wheelchair access (also WC). No music. Air-conditioned ACCOMMODATION: 26 rooms, all with bath/shower. TV. Phone. D,B&B £100 to £400. No children under 13 (*The Which? Hotel Guide*)

ULVERSTON Cumbria **map 8**

▲ Bay Horse Hotel

Canal Foot, Ulverston LA12 9EL
TEL: (01229) 583972 FAX: (01229) 580502
EMAIL: reservations@bayhorse.furness.co.uk
off A590; just before centre of Ulverston, follow signs to Canal Foot
WEB SITE: www.furness.co.uk/bayhorse

COOKING **4**
ENGLISH COUNTRY HOUSE
£28–£50

Perseverance may be needed to locate this former staging-post on the Leven Estuary, hidden beyond the industrial environs of Ulverston on the edge of Morecambe Bay. This is part-owner John Tovey country, his inimitable style apparent not least when the pubby bar is abandoned in favour of the dining room and its pretty conservatory as the curtain goes up on synchronised eating at 7.30pm precisely. The menu is catholic in conception: no unusual combinations, just tried-and-tested marriages of ingredients that may include toasted goat's cheese with air-dried Cumbrian ham, and Norfolk guinea fowl with lemon and thyme.

Good materials generally lay a firm foundation – pan-fried medallions of venison in a rich game and chestnut sauce, for example – although there have been disappointments with fish, and the copious quantity of vegetables can provide a challenge to the main item rather than helping it along. Successful desserts have included thick brûléed chocolate mousse, and orange cheesecake on a first-rate macadamia nut base. Culinary archaeologists may like to note that butter is still fashioned into swans. Service is efficient, and breakfast gets the thumbs up. A plethora of New World Chardonnays and Sauvignon Blancs dominate the white wine selection, while there are slightly more adventurous choices among the reds. Prices are up on last year, although there is still plenty of choice between £15 and £20.

CHEFS: Robert Lyons and Esther Jarvis PROPRIETORS: Robert Lyons and John Tovey OPEN: Tue to Sat L 12 to 1.30, all week D 7.30 for 8 (1 sitting) MEALS: alc (main courses £17 to £18). Set L £17.75 SERVICE: 10%, card slips closed CARDS: Delta, MasterCard, Switch, Visa DETAILS: 50 seats. Private parties: 50 main room. Car park. Vegetarian meals. No children under 12. No smoking in dining room. Wheelchair access (also WC). Music ACCOMMODATION: 9 rooms, all with bath/shower. TV. Phone. D,B&B £90 to £170. No children under 12 (*The Which? Hotel Guide*)

The Guide always appreciates hearing about changes of chef or owner.

UPPER SLAUGHTER Gloucestershire map 5

▲ Lords of the Manor

Upper Slaughter GL54 2JD
TEL: (01451) 820243 FAX: (01451) 820696
EMAIL: lordsofthemanor@btinternet.com
WEB SITE: www.lordsofthemanor.com
turn W off A429, 3m S of Stow-on-the-Wold

COOKING **7**
MODERN FRENCH
£45–£107

Large, comfortable country houses may be ten a penny in the Cotswolds (this used to be a vicarage), but despite the peaceful surroundings this is no sleepy backwater. John Campbell's cooking has moved up a notch since last year, exhibiting greater clarity and sense of purpose. Meals might start with a drink on the lawn in summer, or perhaps in the clubby Chesterfield-strewn bar lounge, where the menu's unusual format makes itself known. Instead of being offered an appetiser with the chef's compliments, there is a mini menu – three to choose from – perhaps including a slice of boudin blanc with a smear of cumin-infused sauce, or a mouthful of chicken and foie gras terrine. A three-way choice also precedes dessert.

The dining room hints at some of the luxuries to come on the carte, not so much on account of its old-fashioned paintings and big flower display, but because, at least for one couple, it smelled powerfully of the truffles that crop up, for example, in a sensuous, creamy-grey, deep-flavoured velouté of wild mushrooms with truffle tortellini. Despite their apparent simplicity, dishes can involve a lot of work, many stages of preparation, and several components, but these are all done without losing sight of the point of the dish: as in an expertly made risotto of shellfish topped with a few spinach leaves and a Parmesan crisp, doused in a bouillabaisse froth.

Timings are spot on throughout, and materials top quality: for example roast rump of organic Highgrove lamb, pink as can be, with thin crisp fat, in a resolutely strong and sweet reduction. The kitchen's clear focus has produced some interesting and intelligent combinations too. Stiffly fresh fillet of turbot has come on chlorophyll mash with a few flakes of oxtail to emphasis its sticky meaty character, and a delicate peach mousse is cleverly partnered by a basil ice cream. The menu has one more surprise in store. Instead of a cheeseboard, three cheese options are served from the kitchen: one of them a baked wedge of Sharpham with a quail's egg yolk, fried brioche and a small salad. Wines are mostly French, and prices mostly high, although a few Italians and South Americans bring variety and some relief for the pocket.

CHEF: John Campbell PROPRIETOR: Empire Ventures Ltd OPEN: all week 12 to 2 (2.30 Sun), 7 to 9.30 MEALS: alc (main courses £19.50 to £26). Set L £14.95 (2 courses) to £17.95, Set D £79 (inc wine) SERVICE: 12.5%, card slips closed CARDS: Amex, Delta, Diners, MasterCard, Switch, Visa DETAILS: 50 seats. 25 seats outside. Private parties: 50 main room, 20 to 25 private rooms. Car park. Vegetarian meals. No children under 10. No smoking in dining room. Wheelchair access (also men's WC). No music ACCOMMODATION: 27 rooms, all with bath/shower. TV. Phone. B&B £99 to £295. Rooms for disabled people (*The Which? Hotel Guide*)

All entries, including Round-ups, are fully indexed at the back of the Guide.

VIRGINSTOW Devon **map 1**

▲ Percy's at Coombeshead

Virginstow EX21 5EA
TEL: (01409) 211236 FAX: (01409) 211275
EMAIL: info@percys.co.uk
WEB SITE: www.percys.co.uk
follow signs to Percy's at Coombeshead from Gridley corner on A388, or from B3218 at Metherell Cross junction

COOKING **5**
MODERN BRITISH
£32–£57

The Bricknell-Webbs have laudable aims for the well-restored 400-year-old Devon longhouse they run as a restaurant-with-rooms. The two dining rooms – one with polished wooden floors, the other carpeted, both with assorted food-based pictures – are overseen by the well-informed Tony, while Christina is committed to fresh seasonal organic produce, supplying her kitchen with home-grown vegetables, salads and herbs, and lamb and eggs from the Coombeshead estate. Careful sourcing also includes local game, organic beef and Cornish fish.

While the passion is in the ingredients, a short, modern menu also reveals a knack for blending flavours to maximise their quality, taking in tender squid on an imaginative leafy salad, a warm salad of tiger prawns and scallops with dill mustard and honey, and moist, pink Aylesbury duck with a well-judged lavender glaze. Copious vegetables have included flavourful al dente carrots, courgette flowers, spinach and potato. To finish, lemon tart has been less successful than a triumphant Grand Marnier and chocolate pudding with star anise ice cream. Meals begin with 'dense, aromatic' home-made breads (potato, swede and cumin among them), and a short, readable wine list of sense and style offers eight wines by the glass from £2.50 and house wines from £9.95.

CHEF: Christina Bricknell-Webb PROPRIETORS: Christina and Tony Bricknell-Webb OPEN: all week 12.30 to 2, 6.30 to 9 MEALS: alc (main courses £16 to £20). Set L £16.50 (2 courses), Set D £28.50. Bar L available SERVICE: not inc, card slips closed CARDS: Amex, Delta, MasterCard, Switch, Visa DETAILS: 36 seats. 50 seats outside. Private parties: 40 main room, 14 to 26 private rooms. Car park. Vegetarian meals. Children's helpings. No children under 12 exc residents. No smoking in dining room. Wheelchair access (not WC). Music ACCOMMODATION: 8 rooms, all with bath/shower. TV. Phone. B&B £59.50 to £99.50. Rooms for disabled. Baby facilities (*The Which? Hotel Guide*)

The text of entries is based on unsolicited reports sent in by readers, backed up by inspections conducted anonymously. The factual details under the text are from questionnaires the Guide sends to all restaurants that feature in the book.

'Owners [were] nowhere in evidence, except in pictures extolling their welcome.'
(On eating in Scotland)

The Guide office can quickly spot when a restaurateur is encouraging customers to write recommending inclusion. Such reports do not further a restaurant's cause. Please tell us if a restaurateur invites you to write to the Guide.

WALDLEY Derbyshire map 5

▲ Beeches **NEW ENTRY**

Waldley, Doveridge DE6 5LR
TEL: (01889) 590288 FAX: (01889) 590559
EMAIL: beechesfa@aol.com
WEB SITE: beechesrestaurant.com
going E on A50 take Doveridge slip road to top, turn L and at Waldley turn R

COOKING **4**
MODERN BRITISH
£24–£56

One of the plus points at this sprawling farmhouse set in peaceful countryside is that it has not had too much money thrown at it, so preserving its 'unprecious' feel. Indeed it is all rather pub-like, with lots of wood and a cheerful, straight up, country style dining room that may suggest steak and kidney pie rather than its more urbane offerings of smoked salmon and foie gras on potato galette, or sea bass with sauce vierge. There are two eating areas, but the brasserie menu – seared tuna loin with salsa and coriander dressing, or Old Spot sausages with chive mash – is also available in the dining room.

Plates are artistically arranged – a pretty mosaic of ham and leek terrine for example, with lentil purée and a mustardy mayonnaise – and there are lots of flourishes. Despite that, nothing appears over-elaborate or contrived, not even in an inspector's dish of Goosnargh duck (pink roast breast and properly made confit leg) accompanied by beetroot batons, artichoke bits, shredded onion, various kinds of cabbage and more. Desserts are decently rendered, and wines offer good choice under £20 without bothering to list vintages. House Costières de Nîmes is £9.95.

CHEF: Barbara Tunnicliffe and Stephen Oppenhagen PROPRIETORS: Paul and Barbara Tunnicliffe OPEN: all week L 12 to 2, D 7 (6 Sun) to 9 (8 Sun) CLOSED: Christmas MEALS: alc (main courses restaurant £15.95 to £19.95, brasserie £6.50 to £9.50) SERVICE: not inc CARDS: Amex, Delta, MasterCard, Switch, Visa DETAILS: 60 seats. 15 seats outside. Private parties: 24 main room, 12 to 24 private rooms. Car park. Vegetarian meals. No smoking in dining room. Wheelchair access (also WC). No music ACCOMMODATION: 10 rooms, all with bath/shower. TV. Phone. B&B £45 to £72. Baby facilities (*The Which? Hotel Guide*) (£5)

WALKINGTON East Riding of Yorkshire map 9

▲ Manor House

Northlands, Newbold Road, Walkington HU17 8RT
TEL: (01482) 881645 FAX: (01482) 866501
EMAIL: derek@the-manor-house.fsbusiness.co.uk
WEB SITE: www.the-manor-house.co.uk
off B1230 towards Beverley from Walkington

COOKING **2**
MODERN BRITISH
£29–£69

Surrounded by parkland and set in its own ample grounds, this family-run Victorian manor with a conservatory dining room offers enterprising four-course dinners, plus a cheaper three-course menu with less choice on weekday evenings. Main menus typically offer half a dozen options for first and second courses, 'All For The Sum Of Thirty Pounds & No Pence', although items such as foie gras and lobster attract a supplement. Derek Baugh uses game from his own shoot in, perhaps, shredded pheasant and leek confit with grape chutney and a

Thai sauce, which after soup or sorbet might be followed by pan-fried 'fishes of the day' with Mediterranean vegetables, or rondelle of pork confit with a creamy prune and calvados reduction. Finish with cherry and almond sponge with a black cherry coulis, or mille-feuille of strawberries and cream. Over 150 wines encompass both rare and vintage clarets as well as provide a fair showing under £20. Five house wines are £11.95 or £13.95.

CHEF: Derek Baugh PROPRIETORS: Derek and Lee Baugh OPEN: Mon to Sat D only 7 to 9.15 CLOSED: 25 and 26 Dec, 1 Jan, bank hol Mons MEALS: Set D Mon to Fri £18.50 and Mon to Sat £30 SERVICE: not inc, card slips closed CARDS: MasterCard, Switch, Visa DETAILS: 50 seats. Private parties: 40 main room, 24 and 40 private rooms. Car park. No children under 12. No cigars/pipes in dining room. Music ACCOMMODATION: 7 rooms, all with bath/shower. TV. Phone. Room only £65 to £100 (£5)

WAREHAM Dorset **map 2**

▲ Priory Hotel

Church Green, Wareham BH20 4ND
TEL: (01929) 551666 FAX: (01929) 554519 — COOKING **4**
EMAIL: reception@theprioryhotel.co.uk — MODERN ENGLISH
WEB SITE: www.theprioryhotel.co.uk — £31–£74

A manicured lawn sweeps down to the tidal river from this sixteenth-century Priory, and although it was converted to a hotel in 1976 the fabric still feels ancient. The kitchen, visible at one end of the beamed and flag-floored cellar dining room, takes a rather traditional view, dealing in a starter plate of smoked salmon and crab with avocado and pink grapefruit, and fillet of beef with green peppercorns and brandy cream. But there are more up-to-date ideas too, including a fine seafood and asparagus terrine with a fennel and saffron dressing, and praiseworthy goats'-cheese crostini with a red pepper and basil dressing.

Expect simple but classic desserts of caramelised lemon tart or chocolate and pistachio fondant. Diners seem to come off better than lunchers, who fail to benefit from the Priory's full attention; indeed, it could almost be a different team in the kitchen. A skilfully annotated wine list offers fine wines from France and Germany alongside an enlightened choice from the New World. There is a small selection of English wines too. Mark-ups are reasonable but one reporter was disappointed to find that his first two choices were unavailable. House Chardonnay and Pinot Noir from Domaine Laroche are £12.50.

CHEF: Stephen Astley PROPRIETORS: Stuart and John Turner OPEN: all week 12.30 to 2, 7.30 to 10 MEALS: alc (main courses £19 to £24.50). Set L Sun £21.50, Set D £27.50 to £32.50. Light L available SERVICE: not inc, card slips closed CARDS: Amex, Delta, Diners, MasterCard, Switch, Visa DETAILS: 45 seats. 40 seats outside. Private parties: 45 main room, 25 to 45 private rooms. Car park. Vegetarian meals. Children by arrangement. No smoking in dining room. Music ACCOMMODATION: 19 rooms, all with bath/shower. TV. Phone. B&B £80 to £240. Children by arrangement (*The Which? Hotel Guide*)

The Guide is totally independent, accepts no free hospitality, and survives on the number of copies sold each year.

WARMINSTER Wiltshire — map 2

▲ Bishopstrow House

Warminster BA12 9HH
TEL: (01985) 212312 FAX: (01985) 216769
EMAIL: enquiries@bishopstrow.co.uk
WEB SITE: www.slh.com
on B3414, 1½m E of Warminster

COOKING **4**
ENGLISH COUNTRY HOUSE
£28–£73

Swagged about with ivy and rambling roses, this late-Georgian edifice – with its pools, tennis courts, and wrought-iron tables and chairs arranged on immaculate lawns for summer-evening aperitifs – offers the country-house idiom at full strength. The carte is joined in the evenings by a fixed-price deal with a few supplements (and extra charges for vegetables). Dishes are thoughtfully composed, often showing a fine sense of balance, as in well-timed chargrilled scallops on goats'-cheese crostini with asparagus spears and a thin smear of hot chilli jam. An emphasis on light, low-cholesterol dishes brings fish centre stage: pavé of salmon with fennel and crayfish risotto, and roast sea bass with truffled mash, wild mushrooms and a sauce of ceps have both garnered praise. Those who aren't counting the calories might opt for confit of Quantock duck with braised Puy lentils, leeks and pancetta.

If the diet really has been thrown to the winds, finish with sticky toffee pudding with butterscotch sauce and vanilla ice cream or, if not, a chilled soup of summer berries scented with rose-water and served with a dab of lemon and mint sorbet. Service, in a mixture of European accents, is charming and solicitous. The extensive wine list will delight aficionados, but only if money is not the prime concern. House wines, imaginatively, are Argentinian blends at £13.50.

CHEF: Chris Suter PROPRIETORS: Howard Malin, Andrew Leeman and Simon Lowe OPEN: all week 12.15 to 2.15, 7.30 to 9 (9.30 Fri and Sat) MEALS: alc (main courses £5 to £12.50). Set D £35 SERVICE: 15% (optional), card slips closed CARDS: Amex, Delta, Diners, MasterCard, Switch, Visa DETAILS: 70 seats. 50 seats outside. Private parties: 65 main room, 22 private room. Car park. Vegetarian meals. Children's helpings. No smoking in dining room. Music ACCOMMODATION: 32 rooms, all with bath/shower. TV. Phone. B&B £99 to £320. Baby facilities. Swimming pool. Fishing (*The Which? Hotel Guide*)

WARWICK Warwickshire — map 5

Cellar

NEW ENTRY

5–6 The Knibbs, Smith Street, Warwick CV34 4UW
TEL/FAX: (01926) 400809

COOKING **3**
MODERN BRITISH/PROVENÇALE
£20–£42

The name can't have been difficult to decide on. Once part of the sandstone tunnelling that led to the castle, the candlelit, vaulted cellar has taken on a more romantic air of late. Terracotta pots of dried lavender tied with raffia give a clue that Provence and the Mediterranean are the inspiration for the whole enterprise. Although the owners spent several years there, the menu is by no means traditional French, taking in starters of salmon marinated in lemon and dill, Tuscan tomato soup, and roast pigeon on a corn cake with sweet beetroot glaze. Neither do you find much red curry on the Côte d'Azur, but the well-balanced one sampled by our inspector used very fine 'sweet and chewy' king prawns. Vegetables are first class too, while desserts have included standard crème brûlée, and tarte Tatin with a pleasing combination of taste and texture. Bread is charged extra, service is friendly, and a diminutive wine list stays mostly under £20. House South African is £9.50.

CHEF: Richard Smallridge PROPRIETORS: Richard Smallridge and Faye Imrie OPEN: Tue to Sat 12 to 2, 7 to 9.30 (10 Sat); Sun L by arrangement only CLOSED: 26 Dec to 5 Jan MEALS: alc (main courses £5.50 to £15). Set L and D £15. Light L Tue to Sat SERVICE: not inc, 10% for parties of 8 or more CARDS: Delta, MasterCard, Switch, Visa DETAILS: 44 seats. 20 seats outside. Private parties: 44 main room. Vegetarian meals. Children's helpings. No cigars/pipes in dining room. Music (£5)

Findons

7 Old Square, Warwick CV34 4RA
TEL: (01926) 411755 FAX: (01926) 400453

COOKING **3**
MODERN BRITISH
£24–£62

Occupying the ground floor of an elegant eighteenth-century town house, and convincingly decorated in period style, Findons feels very much a special-occasion venue. Yet it is not stuffy, one parent commenting that her three- and seven-year-olds were made to feel welcome by the attentive, smiling waitresses. In contrast with the surroundings, the menu shows modern sensibilities and an inventive streak, perhaps opening with smoked Loch Fyne salmon with a salpicon of salmon caviar, cucumber and beetroot, or chicken livers with thyme and lemon salsa.

Main courses take up the contemporary baton too, in the shape of cannon of lamb served with cumin-scented couscous and a mint and coriander jus, or chilli risotto made with wild rice, incorporating field mushrooms and vanilla oil. Fillet of Scotch beef with garlic mash and red wine jus is about as conservative as it gets, though bread-and-butter pudding also makes an appearance, next to chocolate and pistachio timbale with mint and crème de menthe coulis. Most of the 50-odd wines are under £20, with house wines £10.95.

CHEFS: Sean Rouse and Michael Findon PROPRIETOR: Findon & Williams Ltd OPEN: Mon to Fri L 12 to 2, Mon to Sat D 7 to 9.30 CLOSED: bank hols MEALS: alc (main courses £11 to £19). Set L £4.95 (1 course) to £13.95, Set D £15.95 (2 courses) SERVICE: not inc, 10% for parties of 8 or more CARDS: Amex, Delta, Diners, MasterCard, Switch, Visa DETAILS: 50 seats. 20 seats outside. Private parties: 36 main room, 14 and 36 private rooms. Vegetarian meals. No children under 8 at D. Wheelchair access (not WC). Music

'We considered the chef's '"Special Winter Menu" but it was identical to his "Special Autumn Menu" and we had that last time.' (On eating in Sussex)

All entries in the Guide are re-researched and rewritten every year, not least because restaurant standards fluctuate. Don't rely on an out-of-date Guide.

WATERHOUSES Staffordshire map 5

▲ Old Beams

Leek Road, Waterhouses ST10 3HW
TEL: (01538) 308254 FAX: (01538) 308157
on A523, 7m SE of Leek

COOKING **6**
MODERN BRITISH
£34–£71

The welcome, atmosphere and service all please reporters at this roadside restaurant. A quiet conservatory at the back is set in a small garden, with tables outside for drinks in fine weather, and one word seems to sum up the majority view: excellence. The cooking may be conservative, but it still delivers: roast cod on a bed of creamed leeks to start, or white bean soup with truffle, followed by lambs' sweetbreads and kidneys in a tarragon sauce. There are luxuries – scallop mousse with langoustine ravioli, for example – but humbler materials have excited just as much interest: loin of rabbit, for instance, served with ravioli stuffed with minced rabbit. There is always a fish of the day, and a vegetarian option in the evenings.

Desserts tend to soothe, with raspberry trifle on a strawberry coulis, a hot soufflé, or chocolate pavé on a coffee bean sauce. Skills and accomplishment extend to incidentals (bread is good), and portions are generous, although reporters are divided on the question of value: if in doubt, go for lunch. An exciting range of global wines characterises the enthusiastic, well-priced list, where quality rather than quantity is the dominant philosophy. New World Pinot Noirs jostle their Burgundian rivals with an informality that belies some very fine producers. There is lots of good drinking under £20, and plenty of half-bottles, though only two wines are offered by the glass.

CHEF: Nigel Wallis PROPRIETORS: Nigel and Ann Wallis OPEN: Fri and Sun L 12 to 1.30, Tue to Sat D 7 to 9 CLOSED: Jan MEALS: alc D (main courses £12.50 to £20). Set L £16.95 (2 courses) to £23 SERVICE: none, card slips closed CARDS: Amex, Delta, Diners, MasterCard, Switch, Visa DETAILS: 36 seats. 6 seats outside. Private parties: 45 main room, 10 to 26 private rooms. Car park. Vegetarian meals. Children's helpings. No smoking in dining room. Wheelchair access (also women's WC). Occasional music ACCOMMODATION: 5 rooms, all with bath/shower. TV. Phone. B&B £65 to £120. Rooms for disabled. Baby facilities (*The Which? Hotel Guide*) (£5)

WATERMILLOCK Cumbria map 10

▲ Rampsbeck Hotel

Watermillock CA11 0LP
TEL: (017684) 86442 FAX: (017684) 86688
EMAIL: enquiries@rampsbeck.fsnet.co.uk
WEB SITE: www.rampsbeck.fsnet.co.uk
on A592 Penrith to Windermere road

COOKING **3**
ANGLO-FRENCH
£35–£60

Impressions get off to a good start at this attractive-looking eighteenth-century country-house hotel with splendid views of Ullswater and the fells. An Anglo-French approach takes in hearty braised pig's trotter with smoked Cumberland sausage, and a cassoulet of mussels and scallops (with noodles in a saffron sauce), as well as dealing in luxuries such as foie gras and truffles from time to time. Not all combinations are deemed succesful, flavours may sometimes be muted, and the 'twiddly bits' (sorbets and chocolates, for example) may not be quite up to snuff, but the kitchen has turned out first-class slightly pink venison as well as 'correctly cooked and tastily sauced' red mullet with ratatouille dressing. Good pastry work has made a success of nectarine tartlets to finish. Service is 'gracious, professional and attentive'. Wines from around the world are arranged according to style, with an index by country. Pithy tasting notes add to the user-friendliness, prices are fair throughout, and house wines start at £11.25

CHEF: Andrew McGeorge PROPRIETORS: T.I. and M.M. Gibb, and Mrs M.J. MacDowall OPEN: all week 12 to 1 (bookings only Mon to Sat), 7 to 8 CLOSED: mid-Jan to mid-Feb MEALS: Set L £26, Set D £29 to £39.50. Bar L available SERVICE: not inc, card slips closed CARDS: Delta, MasterCard, Switch, Visa DETAILS: 40 seats. Private parties: 70 main room, 15 private room. Car park. Vegetarian meals. Children's helpings. No children under 6. No smoking in dining room. No music ACCOMMODATION: 20 rooms, all with bath/shower. TV. Phone. B&B £60 to £190 (*The Which? Hotel Guide*)

WATH-IN-NIDDERDALE North Yorkshire **map 8**

▲ Sportsman's Arms

Wath-in-Nidderdale, Pateley Bridge HG3 5PP
TEL: (01423) 711306 FAX: (01423) 712524
off B6265, 2m NW of Pateley Bridge

COOKING **4**
ENGLISH/FRENCH
£24–£46

The village and surrounding moors and farmland provide most of the produce used in the kitchen at this remote sporting hotel (in a prime spot for grouse shooting) and daily fish supplies come from Whitby. The slate-floored bar is formal by pub standards (with tablecloths and napkins), but less so than the light, airy dining room, where white walls are hung with duck-hunting prints, and tables are set with highly polished silver. The cooking by contrast is an unpretentious blend of traditional and modern ideas, ranging from beef fillet with green peppercorns and mustard to best end of lamb with olive mash, roast garlic and cherry tomatoes.

Locally smoked trout on rösti topped with crème fraîche was a successful starter at inspection, while main courses have produced notably fresh turbot given added lift by roast peppers and a lime-scented basil paste. Among game dishes, rare saddle of wild venison has come in a red wine, chestnut and cranberry sauce. Finish with homely apple pie or a selection of local and French cheeses. Service is 'intelligent and charming'. An extensive and fairly priced wine list majors in Bordeaux and Burgundies with smaller selections from elsewhere. A dozen house recommendations start around £12.

CHEFS: Ray Carter PROPRIETORS: Ray and Jane Carter OPEN: Sun L 12 to 2, Mon to Sat D 7 to 9 CLOSED: 25 Dec MEALS: alc D (main courses £8 to £16.50). Set L Sun £15.80. Bar meals available all week L and D SERVICE: not inc, card slips closed CARDS: MasterCard, Switch, Visa DETAILS: 70 seats. 30 seats outside. Private parties: 50 main room, 12 private room. Car park. Vegetarian meals. Children's helpings. No smoking in dining room. Wheelchair access (not WC). No music ACCOMMODATION: 13 rooms, all with bath/shower. TV. Phone. B&B £45 to £90. Rooms for disabled. Fishing (*The Which? Hotel Guide*) (£5)

Card slips closed *in the details at the end of an entry indicates that the total on the slips of credit cards is closed when handed over for signature.*

WELLS Somerset — map 2

Ritcher's

5 Sadler Street, Wells BA5 2RR
TEL: (01749) 679085 FAX: (01749) 673866

COOKING **4**
FRENCH
£16–£40

Not far from the cathedral and market place in this pint-sized city, down a passageway between shops, Ritcher's is a small but bustling restaurant catering to a tenacious local clientele. The approach front and back is conscientious and informed, keeping abreast of modern ideas as well as the passing seasons. A pair of lunchers in January were impressed by the counterpointing flavours in an avocàdo flan served with lime sauce, and also in tarragon-seasoned guinea fowl with parsnip crisps. Menus are fixed-price, with daily-changing fish and vegetarian specials supplementing the likes of calf's liver with wild mushroom ragoût and truffled mash, or leg of lamb stuffed with prunes, armagnac and smoked bacon and served with a sweet rosemary jus. Equal thought goes into desserts, for example a tart-and-sweet bread-and-butter pudding made with lemon curd and brioche. An imaginative wine list is stylistically grouped, and prices are mostly quite cheering. International house selections start at £9.95.

CHEF: Nick Hart PROPRIETORS: Kate Ritcher and Nick Hart OPEN: all week 12 to 2, 7 to 9.30 (10 Sat) CLOSED: 1 Jan MEALS: Set L £7.50 (2 courses) to £8.50, Set D £15.50 (2 courses) to £18.50 SERVICE: not inc, card slips closed CARDS: Delta, MasterCard, Switch, Visa DETAILS: 40 seats. 12 seats outside. Private parties: 24 main room. Vegetarian meals. Children's helpings. No children under 10 at D. No cigars/pipes while others eat. Wheelchair access (not WC). Music. Air-conditioned

WELWYN GARDEN CITY Hertfordshire — map 3

▲ Auberge du Lac 🍷

NEW ENTRY

Brocket Hall, Welwyn Garden City AL8 7XG
TEL: (01707) 368888 FAX: (01707) 368898
EMAIL: aubergedulac@brocket-hall.co.uk

COOKING **5**
MODERN FRENCH-PLUS
£36–£80

A long drive leads to this brick-built, green-shuttered former hunting lodge in the grounds of a stately home, where ladies are handed menus without prices. Some men probably wish theirs were blank too, the better to enjoy the evening before the bill arrives; but if money is not a pressing concern, then here is a kitchen that delivers some good dishes. Pascal Breant grafts a few oriental ideas on to a fundamentally French framework, producing for example an imaginative sweet and crunchy galette of prawn and water chestnut with a buttery coriander sauce. Otherwise the food is in the more European mould of cured salmon and Jersey potato terrine, or calves' sweetbreads with wild mushrooms.

Results may not always be as sure-footed as ambition requires, but an inspection meal nevertheless produced immaculately fresh John Dory and red mullet, served with vivid provençale accompaniments of tomatoes and tapénade, and a seven-hour-baked leg of lamb: an 'unctuous gamey-tasting' dish with a rich sticky jus. If English and French farmhouse cheeses, or a savoury Reblochon tart don't tempt, then try a thin pear tart with matching sorbet, or warm apple soufflé with calvados sauce and thyme sorbet. Service is attentive without being fussy.

There is very little under £20 on the wine list, whose traditional preoccupation takes in many fine clarets and Burgundies, a lot of them in three figures. The publicity brochure invites you to try Mouton-Rothschild 1982 with the cheese course: fine if you have £745 to spare. A few New World wines surface towards the back, and 25 wines by the glass start at £5. House wines are £15.

CHEF: Pascal Breant PROPRIETOR: CCA International OPEN: Tue to Sun L 12 to 2.30, Tue to Sat D 7 to 10.30 MEALS: Set L Tue to Sat £25 inc wine, Set L Sun £27, Set D £38 SERVICE: 10%, card slips closed CARDS: Amex, Diners, MasterCard, Switch, Visa DETAILS: 70 seats. 50 seats outside. Private parties: 10 main room, 16 private room. Car park. Vegetarian meals. Children's helpings. No cigars/pipes in dining room. Wheelchair access (not WC). Music. Air-conditioned ACCOMMODATION: 16 rooms, all with bath/shower. TV. Phone. B&B £138 to £300. Baby facilities

WEST BAY Dorset **map 2**

Riverside Restaurant

West Bay DT6 4EZ COOKING **2**
TEL: (01308) 422011 SEAFOOD
off A35, 1m S of Bridport £23–£59

It is such a sensible idea to have an informal, no-nonsense seafood restaurant perched on the harbour like this 'that you wonder why it's such a rarity in the UK'. Enough customers appreciate its value to have kept the Watsons going for 35 years. As one summed up, 'What you want from a fish restaurant is fresh fish cooked to exactly the right degree, and this is pretty much what we got.' Among successes have been 'the freshest of fresh' crab with mayonnaise, and a textbook brandade that was creamy, unctuous, heavy on the garlic and 'uncompromisingly salty'. Given a slight tendency towards over-elaboration, it is advisable to stick to simpler dishes of grilled whole fish, served with salad or thin, crisp, well-browned and plentiful chips. Desserts tend to be homely, along the lines of rice pudding with winter fruits, or treacle tart and cream, and service for the most part is obliging and well informed. Half a dozen wines by the glass head up a well-chosen and fairly priced list, most of which is comfortably under £20 a bottle.

CHEFS: Nic Larcombe, Paul Morey and Jake Platt PROPRIETORS: Arthur and Janet Watson OPEN: Tue to Sun L 12 to 2.15, Tue to Sat D 6.30 to 9 (open Sun D and Mon on bank hols) CLOSED: 1 Dec to mid-Feb MEALS: alc (main courses £10.50 to £25). Set L weekdays only Oct to Apr £10.50 (2 courses) to £13.50 SERVICE: not inc, card slips closed CARDS: Delta, MasterCard, Switch, Visa DETAILS: 80 seats. 25 seats outside. Private parties: 70 main room, 20 private room. Vegetarian meals. Children's helpings. Wheelchair access (not WC). Occasional music

indicates that smoking is either banned altogether or that a dining-room is maintained for non-smokers. The symbol does not apply to restaurants that simply have no-smoking areas.

If a restaurant is new to the Guide this year (did not appear as a main entry in the last edition), NEW ENTRY *appears opposite its name.*

WEST ILSLEY Berkshire map 2

Harrow Inn

West Ilsley RG20 7AR | COOKING **3**
TEL: (01635) 281260 FAX: (01635) 281139 | MODERN BRITISH
1½m off A34, 10m N of Newbury | £27–£41

Standing opposite a cricket field and duck pond in a sleepy rural village, and exuding a laid-back and unpretentious atmosphere, the seventeenth-century Harrow is every bit the archetypal English country inn. Recognisably pubby décor reinforces the image, but a quick perusal of the extensive blackboard menus hints that this is a cut above the ordinary. The cooking, in a homely-yet-modern vein, shows confidence and sureness of touch, typically producing grilled goats' cheese on a walnut salad with shallot and cassis dressing, and braised chump of pork with home-made sausage and caramelised red cabbage. At the more inventive end of the scale might be pan-seared scallops with orange, cardamom and vanilla dressing, while those in search of comfort should be content with tender, pink chargrilled lambs' liver and bacon with creamy mash. A separate puddings board might offer hot caramel soufflé, and grapefruit cream with honey ice cream. Eight house wines at £10.95 (£2 a glass) head up a decent selection at not unreasonable prices.

CHEF: Scott Hunter PROPRIETORS: Scott Hunter and Emily Hawes OPEN: all week 12 to 2, 7 to 9 (later Fri and Sat) CLOSED: no food Mon D and Sun D end Nov to Feb exc special occasions MEALS: alc (main courses £10 to £12); snacks available SERVICE: not inc, 10% for parties of 8 or more, card slips closed CARDS: Delta, MasterCard, Switch, Visa DETAILS: 55 seats. 30 seats outside. Private parties: 40 main room. Children's helpings L. No children under 12 at D. No smoking in dining room. Occasional music

WEST TANFIELD North Yorkshire map 9

▲ Bruce Arms

Main Street, West Tanfield HG4 5JJ | COOKING **4**
TEL: (01677) 470325 FAX: (01677) 470796 | MODERN ENGLISH
£20–£39

Describing itself as a bistro with bedrooms, the Bruce Arms holds its own in a county that is well off for rural food pubs. Old beams, log fires, tankards, coaching lamps and a stone and wood bar are all standard issue, but the ever-changing blackboard menu offers lots of choice and takes the trouble to incorporate a few seasonal and local ingredients. Wensleydale cheese appears in a twice-baked soufflé, black pudding is served with a poached egg and hollandaise, and wild mushrooms have lent character to a moist risotto doused in truffle oil.

Dishes are all the better for being simply conceived and presented, and accurate timing helps to get the best out of first-class materials: sweet, pink rack of lamb on a potato cake spiked with mint leaves for example, or a whole roast sea bass, with lemon grass inside and out, served with a tangy lemon sauce. Desserts revert to more traditional mode with crème brûlée, strawberry pavlova and iced chocolate terrine. Service is enthusiastic, and around 40 fairly priced wines (whites rated for sweetness, reds for body) start with house Californian at

£9.25; in addition to large and small glass sizes, a few are also available as 'small bottles' (185ml) for £2.80.

CHEF: Geoff Smith PROPRIETORS: Geoff Smith and Amanda Donkin OPEN: Thur to Sun (Tue to Sun Apr to Sept) L 12 to 2, Mon to Sat D 6.30 to 9.30 CLOSED: 31 Dec MEALS: alc (main courses £9 to £14.50). Set L Sun £8.75 (1 course) to £12.25. Light L available Tue to Sat SERVICE: not inc, card slips closed CARDS: Delta, MasterCard, Switch, Visa DETAILS: 40 seats. 16 seats outside. Private parties: 24 private room. Car park. Vegetarian meals. Children's helpings. Music ACCOMMODATION: 3 rooms, all with bath/shower. TV. B&B £35 to £50. No children under 14

WETHERSFIELD Essex **map 6**

Dicken's

The Green, Wethersfield CM7 4BS
TEL/FAX: (01371) 850723

COOKING **3**
MODERN BRITISH
£23–£46

This small pink-painted building overlooking the village green is a mixture of cottagey and medieval, combining wrought-iron chandeliers, an old stone fireplace and minstrels' gallery. Owner John Dicken divides his time between here and the recently acquired White Hart (see entry, Great Yeldham), but the cooking remains in the same up-to-date style, offering intensely flavoured smooth fish soup with mussels, and grilled English goats' cheese with a pear and rocket salad. Among main courses, cod is given a Welsh rarebit glaze with plum tomatoes and red onions, and there may also be guinea fowl with black pudding and cabbage, or sea bass with a watercress and parsley risotto. Desserts let the side down at inspection, though another reporter couldn't fault his cinnamon parfait and caramelised apples. Service is pleasant and correct, despite occasionally being reduced to autopilot when things get busy. Wines are grouped by style, the mark-ups a touch heavy, though a dozen 'Personal Selections' open with Côtes de Duras at £10.50.

CHEF/PROPRIETOR: John Dicken OPEN: Wed to Sun L 12.30 to 2, Wed to Sat D 7.30 to 9.30 CLOSED: bank hols, 24-26 Dec., 1 Jan MEALS: alc (main courses £11 to £15.50). Set L Wed to Sat £10 (2 courses), Set L Sun £19 SERVICE: not inc CARDS: Delta, MasterCard, Switch, Visa DETAILS: 60 seats. 12 seats outside. Private parties: 36 main room, 10 to 18 private rooms. Car park. Vegetarian meals. Children's helpings. Wheelchair access (also WC). Occasional music (£5)

WHITBY North Yorkshire **map 9**

Magpie Café £

14 Pier Road, Whitby YO21 3PU
TEL: (01947) 602058 FAX: (01947) 601801
EMAIL: ian@magpiecafe.co.uk
WEB SITE: www.magpiecafe.co.uk

COOKING **2**
SEAFOOD
£16–£47

This three-storey white-fronted house overlooking Whitby's harbour dates from the mid-eighteenth century and has been a café since before the war. It may look a little grand from outside, but inside you will find a cheerfully busy fish restaurant, so busy indeed that regulars seem to take the almost inevitable queuing in their stride. Locally caught fish is professionally presented, and extends to plump pieces of monkfish tail, skate wing, and a gratinated cheesy pasta dish with haddock. Lobster thermidor is usually available for those on a spree. Meat eaters might go for fillet steak in pepper sauce, but that would hardly be entering into the spirit of the place. Finish with the likes of hazelnut meringue served with boozy bananas and cream. Service is hugely welcoming, though you are asked to be patient while the fish is prepared. The short wine list is predominantly French, but prices are perfectly fair, starting at £7.95.

CHEFS: Ian Robson and Paul Gildroy PROPRIETORS: Ian Robson and Alison McKenzie-Robson OPEN: all week 11.30 to 9 CLOSED: 22 to 25 Dec, mid-Jan to mid-Feb MEALS: alc (main courses £4.50 to £17) SERVICE: not inc, card slips closed CARDS: Delta, MasterCard, Switch, Visa DETAILS: 98 seats. Private parties: 50 main room. Vegetarian meals. Children's helpings. No smoking in dining room. Occasional music. Air-conditioned (£5)

WHITCHURCH Hampshire **map 2**

Red House £

21 London Street, Whitchurch RG28 7LH
TEL: (01256) 895558

COOKING **2**
GLOBAL
£18–£36

A sixteenth-century coaching inn close to the River Test, the Red House is part busy pub, part informal restaurant. In the dining area, large mirrors lend a feeling of expansiveness, but the simple wooden tables and shelves crowded with home-made produce maintain an air of the domestic. Shannon Wells's cooking keeps things relatively straightforward – mushroom and mustard cream soup with garlic croûtons, or roast pheasant with pearl barley and a Madeira sauce, for example – but diversity might come in the shape of a meaty and succulent roast duck leg with a clean-tasting pineapple and chilli salsa. Occasional theme nights have included a showcasing of Italian cooking, while blackboards should be consulted for details of specials, including steaks and puddings. The latter seem to round up many of today's favourites, from tiramisù to bread-and-butter pudding with butterscotch sauce. Service is youthful and enthusiastic, and all wines bar the single champagne and premier cru Chablis are under £20. House choices start at £8.80.

CHEF: Shannon Wells PROPRIETORS: Shannon and Caroline Wells OPEN: all week L 12 to 2, D 6.30 (7 Sun) to 9.30 CLOSED: 25 Dec MEALS: alc (main courses L £5 to £13.50, D £7 to £13.50) SERVICE: not inc, card slips closed CARDS: MasterCard, Switch, Visa DETAILS: 36 seats. 40 seats outside. Private parties: 28 main room. Car park. Vegetarian meals. No smoking in dining room. Occasional music

---

Occasional music *in the details at the end of an entry means live or recorded music is played in the dining room only rarely or for special events.* No music *means it is never played.*

'It's a bit hard to tell whether every main course comes with the same vegetables when you're the only person in the dining room.' (On eating in the Midlands)

WHITSTABLE Kent map 3

Whitstable Oyster Fishery Co 

Royal Native Oyster Stores, The Horsebridge,
Whitstable CT5 1BU
TEL: (01227) 276856 FAX: (01227) 770666
WEB SITE: www.oysterfishery.co.uk

COOKING **1**
SEAFOOD
£26–£56

Whitstable cultivates an old-fashioned image – 'you can't miss the point that this is Dickens country' – and the bare-floored, brick-walled seafood restaurant is the sort of place that has 'probably ebbed and flowed with the tide of culinary fashion'. Its seaside ambience is just right for the slate of dishes that runs from oysters (natives in winter, otherwise Scottish), through scallops in bacon, and chargrilled sardines, to whole grilled Dover soles and sea bass fillets. Weekends bring plates of crab, whelks, shrimps and langoustines, and desserts are as simple as can be. Service may blow hot and cold but this remains at heart a relaxed place. A short wine list opens with Muscadet and Chilean Chardonnay at £9.95.

CHEFS: Richard and James Green, Dave Foster and John Gyena PROPRIETOR: Whitstable Oyster Fishery Co OPEN: Tue to Sun L 12 to 2 (2.30 Sat, 3.30 Sun), Tue to Sat D 7 (6.30 Sat) to 9 (10 Sat) MEALS: alc (main courses £8.50 to £23) SERVICE: 10% (optional), card slips closed CARDS: Amex, Delta, Diners, MasterCard, Switch, Visa DETAILS: 140 seats. 50 seats outside. Private parties: 16 main room. Children's helpings. Music

WICKHAM Hampshire map 2

▲ Old House

The Square, Wickham PO17 5JG
TEL: (01329) 833049 FAX: (01329) 833672
EMAIL: enq@theoldhousehotel.co.uk

COOKING **4**
MODERN BRITISH
£25–£51

The Old House sits on Wickham's market square, a tranquil enough setting, though less than five minutes' drive from the M27. Despite a change of ownership since the last edition of the Guide, Nicholas Ruthven-Stuart has not deserted his post in the kitchen, so consistency is maintained. Eating takes place in a barn extension, a high-ceilinged space with A-shaped beams and windows on three sides overlooking the gardens. Voguish contemporary ingredients are brought to bear on what is essentially the British country-house mode: miniaturised ratatouille vegetables may form the topping for a grilled goats' cheese tartlet, and wild mushroom risotto is enriched with truffle oil.

Trios of meat or fish are one way of making people feel looked after at main-course stage, whether it be beef, lamb and venison with caramelised shallots in red wine sauce, or monkfish, salmon and cod as a fricassee with curried coriander sauce. Bread-and-butter pudding, cherry and almond tart, or a version of St-Emilion au chocolat with orange crème anglaise may crop up among crowd-pleasing desserts. Wines are grouped by type. While prices may not be giveaway, a good selection of half a dozen house wines starts with South Africans at £10.95.

CHEF: Nicholas Ruthven-Stuart PROPRIETOR: John and Gloria Goodacre OPEN: Tue to Sun L 12 to 2, Mon to Sat D 7 to 9.30 CLOSED: 26 Dec to 5 Jan MEALS: alc (main courses £14 to £16.50). Set L £10 (2 courses) to £15, Set D £19.95 to £23.50 (both 2 courses) SERVICE: not inc,12.5% for parties of 6 or more CARDS: Amex, Delta, MasterCard, Switch, Visa DETAILS: 36 seats. Private parties: 40 main room, 14 private room. Car park. Children's helpings. No smoking in dining room. Wheelchair access (not WC). No music ACCOMMODATION: 9 rooms, all with bath/shower. TV. Phone. B&B £60 to £80 (£5)

WILLITON Somerset — map 2

▲ White House

11 Long Street, Williton TA4 4QW — COOKING **6**
TEL: (01984) 632777 — ENGLISH/MEDITERRANEAN
£46–£55

The house – it is indeed very white – is on the main road that runs through this slip of a Somerset village. A neoclassical Georgian façade with green-shuttered windows and two tall palm trees set before it create a faintly surreal impression. Dick and Kay Smith are experienced hoteliers, concentrating their efforts on summer and early autumn only, when the restaurant is open for dinner every night. The dining room is done out in autumnal tones, with hessian walls and some exposed stone, a muted backdrop for some vividly fresh, intelligent cooking.

Despite the small compass of the short menus, there is plenty of contrast between dishes. The simple, colourful Mediterranean end of the spectrum is evident in a starter of seven thin scallop slices, seared nut-brown and dressed with olive oil, diced tomato, lemon juice and herbs (including basil, tarragon and chervil), while a heartier vein has shown up in noisettes of local wild roe deer, crosshatched with stripes from the chargrill, flawlessly supported by velvety parsnip purée, redcurrant sauce and red wine gravy.

As this is a summer venue, vegetables and fruits all have a distinctly seasonal bloom about them, be it loganberries that go into a crème brûlée, or gooseberries and cherries that come with a wedge of polenta and almond cake and pannacotta. Incidentals are exemplary, breads exceptional. A varied selection of house wines sets the tone for a shrewd and affectionately produced wine list. An impressive range of mature clarets and Rhônes is balanced by an inspiring line-up from Bandol. Wines from Spain, Germany, Italy and the New World are equally tempting, and it is worth considering one of the nine dessert wines offered by the glass. There are plenty of half-bottles, and pricing is fair all round, starting at £12.

CHEFS/PROPRIETORS: Dick and Kay Smith OPEN: all week D only 7 to 8.30 CLOSED: Nov to mid-May MEALS: Set D £33.50 SERVICE: not inc CARDS: none DETAILS: 22 seats. Private parties: 6 main room. Car park. Children's helpings. No smoking in dining room. Wheelchair access (not WC). No music ACCOMMODATION: 10 rooms, all with bath/shower. TV. Phone. Room only £52 to £110. Rooms for disabled. Baby facilities

'I think the worst of my evening was to sit and watch the barman eat ice cubes.'
(On eating in Oxfordshire)

WILMINGTON East Sussex — map 3

▲ Crossways

Lewes Road, Wilmington BN26 5SG
TEL: (01323) 482455 FAX: (01323) 487811
EMAIL: crossways@fastnet.co.uk
on A27, 2m W of Polegate

COOKING **4**
MODERN BRITISH
£38–£49

Shielded from the main road by a pretty garden, the square Georgian house is warmly and attractively done out with pink carpets and drapes, comfortable chairs, fine napery and fresh flowers. A monthly-changing menu of four courses (one of them an intermediate soup such as creamy parnsip) is both printed and affably recited at table by Mr Stott or Mr James. Simplicity is a keynote, with an emphasis on first-class ingredients put together in combinations that generally work well, among them a creamy smoked salmon and mushroom bake, and a devilled breast and leg of Gressingham duck scented with lemon grass and ginger.

Inspiration comes from several sources. If some dishes have a traditional French ancestry – poulet en croûte, pork Normandy, or sauté calf's liver with a sauce of Dubonnet, orange and tomato – there might also be sesame prawn noodles, or Cajun-style slices of wild boar tenderloin. Portions tend to be large, and the food sometimes rich, making a light dessert such as lime mousse with citron sauce all the more appealing. Service combines easy bonhomie and professionalism. Four out of five house wines on the carefully chosen list are English, the fifth a red from Chile at £10.95.

CHEFS: David Stott and Juliet Anderson PROPRIETORS: David Stott and Clive James OPEN: Tue to Sat D only 7.30 to 8.30 CLOSED: 24 Dec to 24 Jan MEALS: Set D £28.95 SERVICE: not inc, card slips closed CARDS: Delta, MasterCard, Switch, Visa DETAILS: 24 seats. Private parties: 6 main room. Car park. Vegetarian meals require pre-booking. No children under 12 in dining room. No smoking in dining room. Wheelchair access (not WC). Occasional music ACCOMMODATION: 7 rooms, all with bath/shower. TV. Phone. B&B £49 to £80.

WILMSLOW Cheshire — map 7

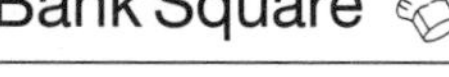

Bank Square

4 Bank Square, Wilmslow SK9 1AN
TEL: (01625) 539754 FAX: (01625) 539813

COOKING **3**
MODERN EUROPEAN
£22–£52

The setting, as the name indicates, is a converted former bank on a corner site in the centre of town. On the ground floor is a minimalist modern bar; upstairs is a smart, cleanly designed dining room with tables separated by wrought-iron dividers. Modern brasserie cooking defines the style, the kitchen delivering sauté foie gras on wilted spinach with glazed goats' cheese and a chilli dressing (an improbable combination that nevertheless impressed an inspector), honeyed Chinese duck with spring onions and ginger, and a main course of top-drawer calf's liver and bacon on chive mash with roasted fennel and a redcurrant sauce. Fish dishes have included lemon-battered hake with basil pesto, and the kitchen even stretches to lobster Thermidor. Warm clafoutis with calvados ice cream, and a trio of chocolate have been successful desserts. Service is pleasant enough, but you may need patience between courses. The wine list is short and to the point, with pithy tasting notes and something for everyone in the under £20 price bracket. South African Chenin and Pinotage are £12.70.

CHEFS: Glenn Barry and Steven Adams PROPRIETORS: Janet and David Rivett OPEN: Mon to Sat 12 to 2.30, 6.30 to 10 CLOSED: 26 Dec, 1 Jan MEALS: alc (main courses £12 to £18). Set L £10.95 (2 courses) to £13.50, Set D Mon to Fri before 7.30 £10.95 (2 courses) to £13.50, Set D Mon to Fri after 7.30 and Sat before 7.30 £13.50 (2 courses) to £15.95. Bar meals available SERVICE: not inc CARDS: Amex, Delta, MasterCard, Switch, Visa DETAILS: 52 seats. Private parties: 65 main room. Vegetarian meals. Children's helpings. No cigars/pipes in dining room. Occasional music. Air-conditioned (£5)

WINCHCOMBE Gloucestershire map 5

▲ Wesley House

High Street, Winchcombe GL54 5LJ
TEL: (01242) 602366 FAX: (01242) 609046 COOKING **3**
EMAIL: reservations@wesleyhouse.co.uk ANGLO-FRENCH
WEB SITE: www.wesleyhouse.co.uk £22–£60

Walk straight off the main street into a reception area, and up a few steps to an open-plan dining room that stretches to the back of this fifteenth-century building. Start perhaps with a terrine (of fish or smoked chicken), or salad (smoked salmon and poached egg), and go on to wood pigeon on apple and sage rösti. There is a tendency towards decorative effects, but dishes generally turn out well, for example a supple and juicy loin of English lamb accompanied by scallop mousse, smitane sauce, tiny pickling onions and a chickpea chutney.

The kitchen navigates a course between voguish towers on the one hand, and an old-fashioned side plate of vegetables tied in bundles on the other, and while the relative safety of advance preparation may be preferred to the excitement of last-minute cooking, a freshly made prune and armagnac tart has impressed, not least for its fine pastry. Service from owner Matthew Brown is amiable and chatty, and the wine list offers a good opportunity to sample South African wines. The top names are all here: Mulderbosch, Meerlust, Thelema and Hamilton Russell, along with a sound French selection and a smattering of other New World choices. Wines of the month start at £11.50.

CHEF: James Lovatt PROPRIETOR: Matthew Brown OPEN: all week L 12 to 2, Mon to Sat D 6.45 to 9 CLOSED: 10 to 24 Jan MEALS: alc (main courses £9 to £16.50). Set L £8.95 (2 courses) to £12.50, Set D Mon to Fri before 7.45 £15.50 (2 courses) to £18.50, Set D £23.50 (2 courses) to £28.50 SERVICE: not inc CARDS: Amex, Delta, MasterCard, Switch, Visa DETAILS: 50 seats. 16 seats outside. Private parties: 60 main room. Children's helpings. No smoking in dining room. Wheelchair access (not WC). Music ACCOMMODATION: 6 rooms, all with bath/shower. TV. Phone. B&B £48 to £80. No young children (exc babies). Baby facilities (*The Which? Hotel Guide*) (£5)

The cuisine styles noted at the tops of entries are only an approximation, often suggested to us by the restaurants themselves. Please read the entry itself to find out more about the cooking style.

WINCHESTER Hampshire **map 2**

▲ Hotel du Vin & Bistro

Southgate Street, Winchester SO23 9EF
TEL: (01962) 841414 FAX: (01962) 842458
EMAIL: admin@winchester.hotelduvin.co.uk
WEB SITE: www.hotelduvin.com

NEW CHEF
MODERN EUROPEAN
£35–£51

This small chain is expanding. With branches already in Tunbridge Wells and Bristol, it expects to open one in Birmingham in spring 2001. Under these circumstances chefs move around, and it is all change at the stoves here, with former sous-chef Gareth Longhurst due to head up the kitchen as the Guide went to press. Reports are particularly welcome, but the distinctive style is likely to remain: a blend of informal surroundings – polished wood and lots of bottles – and a cheerfully broad repertoire that runs the gamut from salad niçoise via barbecued belly pork to smoked chicken spring roll with sweet chilli sauce. The wine list is full of glorious bottles from around the world, including reasonably priced staples from classic French regions, and up-to-date wines from Uruguay, Greece, Switzerland, Thailand and Mexico. Four own-label French wines are priced from £11.50, and up to six wines are available by the glass on a daily-changing list.

CHEF: Gareth Longhurst PROPRIETOR: Alternative Hotel Company OPEN: all week 12 to 1.45, 7 to 10 MEALS: alc Mon to Sat L, all week D (main courses £11 to £15). Set L Sun £23.50 SERVICE: not inc, card slips closed CARDS: Amex, Delta, Diners, MasterCard, Switch, Visa DETAILS: 65 seats. 30 seats outside. Private parties: 48 main room, 12 to 48 private rooms. Car park. Vegetarian meals. Children's helpings. No cigars/pipes in dining room. Wheelchair access (also WC). No music ACCOMMODATION: 23 rooms, all with bath/shower. TV. Phone. Room only £89 to £185. Rooms for disabled (*The Which? Hotel Guide*)

Hunters

5 Jewry Street, Winchester SO23 8RZ
TEL/FAX: (01962) 860006

NEW CHEF
MODERN BRITISH
£23–£44

With a fresh, clean look, and close-together tables, Hunters plays host to business folk at lunch, and brings out the candles for dinner. Local lad Simon Lakey arrived to head up the kitchen just as the Guide went to press, overseeing a menu (generous for the circumstances) that takes in moules marinière, and chicken Caesar salad, as well as lime seared scallops, and roast lamb with swede purée, followed by warm chocolate brownie with hot fudge sauce. Reports on progress are particularly welcome. A mixed list of around 60 wines, with fair choice under £20, starts with house French at £9.95.

CHEF: Simon Lakey PROPRIETOR: David Birmingham OPEN: Mon to Sat 12 to 2, 6.30 to 10 CLOSED: 24 Dec to 3 Jan MEALS: alc (main courses £7 to £13). Set L £9.95 (2 courses) to £12.95, Set D Mon to Fri £9.95 (2 courses) to £12.95 SERVICE: not inc, 10% for parties of 6 or more CARDS: Amex, Delta, Diners, MasterCard, Switch, Visa DETAILS: 45 seats. Private parties: 15 main room, 25 private room. Vegetarian meals. No children under 5. No-smoking area. Wheelchair access (not WC). Occasional music (£5)

Old Chesil Rectory

1 Chesil Street, Winchester SO23 0HU
TEL: (01962) 851555 FAX: (01962) 869704

COOKING **6**
MODERN BRITISH
£33–£58

Dating from the fifteenth century, the Rectory has been decorated with style and sensitivity to allow appreciation of its characterful half-timbered architecture, much of it original. Philip Storey prides himself on using local supply lines wherever possible, making them the basis for boldly flavoured seasonal cooking that manages to avoid over-elaboration and voguish flourishes. Instead, he concentrates on important details: one reporter's wild mushroom risotto in autumn, for example, was considered outstanding for both flavour and spot-on texture.

Partnerships are typically interesting and well considered, be it a soup combining smoked haddock and Jerusalem artichoke, a pairing of veal loin and liver, or pork with black pudding, served with mustard mash and a spinach and apple vinaigrette. Desserts might explore variations on a theme, such as a trio of pear (including pie, parfait and poached fruit), or take a traditional line in chocolate tart with coffee anglaise. Restaurant manager Gary Nicholls is mentioned in dispatches for his agreeably attentive yet unobtrusive service. Wines open with an enterprising slate of house offerings, from £13.95, and continue with a stylistically arranged selection of generally well-sourced bottles.

CHEF: Philip Storey PROPRIETORS: Philip and Catherine Storey OPEN: Tue to Sat 12 to 2, 7 to 9.30 CLOSED: Christmas to first week Jan, first week Aug MEALS: Set L £16 (2 courses) to £20, Set D £28 (2 courses) to £34 SERVICE: not inc CARDS: Delta, Diners, MasterCard, Switch, Visa DETAILS: 45 seats. Private parties: 40 main room, 10 to 20 private rooms. Children's helpings. No smoking in 1 dining room. Occasional music (£5)

▲ Wykeham Arms

75 Kingsgate Street, Winchester SO23 9PE
TEL: (01962) 853834 FAX: (01962) 854411

COOKING **2**
MODERN BRITISH/MEDITERRANEAN
£20–£40

Hard by the cathedral and college, Wykeham Arms is a friendly, down-to-earth and popular pub-restaurant, decked out with assorted school and sporting paraphernalia. Meals are eaten off well-worn scrubbed pine tables: simple lunches of sandwiches or smoked haddock kedgeree, and dinners that range from baked stuffed aubergine with halloumi to monkfish on Puy lentils with a curried vegetable cream sauce. Materials are sound, and simple but effective treatment has produced a well-flavoured fennel, leek and potato soup, and lightly fat-encrusted cutlets of tasty Hampshire Down lamb served with buttery herby polenta and Madeira sauce. Desserts run to pineapple Tatin with mascarpone ice cream, and carrot and ginger pudding with fudge sauce. Service is cheerful and informed. The wine list comes helpfully in two parts: a straight list, then a heavily annotated version. Bottles are fairly priced and globally sourced, although Burgundy remains a highlight. House wines from France and Chile start at £10.95.

CHEFS: Wendy Moore, Nicola Saunders and Gary Stickland PROPRIETOR: George Gale & Co. Ltd OPEN: Mon to Sat 12 to 2.30, 6.30 to 9 CLOSED: 25 Dec MEALS: alc (main courses L £5 to £7, D £10 to £13.50) SERVICE: not inc, card slips closed CARDS: Amex, Delta, Diners, MasterCard, Switch, Visa DETAILS: 75 seats. 30 seats outside. Private parties: 8 main room. Small car park. Vegetarian meals. No children under 14. No smoking in 2 dining rooms. No music ACCOMMODATION: 13 rooms, all with bath/shower. TV. Phone. B&B £45 to £117.50. No children under 14 (*The Which? Hotel Guide*)

WINDERMERE Cumbria **map 8**

▲ Gilpin Lodge 

Crook Road, Windermere LA23 3NE
TEL: (015394) 88818 FAX: (015394) 88058
EMAIL: hotel@gilpin-lodge.co.uk
WEB SITE: www.gilpin-lodge.co.uk
on B5284, 2m SE of Windermere

COOKING **4**
MODERN BRITISH
£28–£65

In a peaceful setting well away from crowds and congestion, this long, low, blindingly white stone building is kept to meticulous housekeeping standards, yet offers a commendably flexible approach to eating arrangements. There are three dining rooms, one with a conservatory extension, and good-value lunch can be one course only if preferred: anything from a chicken sandwich to calf's liver with sage fritters and Cumbrian bacon. Supplies are well sourced, taking in Holker Hall pheasant, Mansergh Farm lamb, Wabberthwaite sausages and hams, Flookburgh shrimps (perhaps in a moulded risotto, with a sparse lemon and dill butter dressing), and Lyth Valley damsons.

Technically proficient cooking has turned out a puff pastry mille-feuille layered with Mediterranean vegetables and mozzarella, and a crisp-skinned, well-flavoured breast of corn-fed chicken (this from Perigord apparently) on coriander mash. Components may not always be compatible, and desserts may not be the strongest suit, but quantities are generous and bread is first rate. Well-priced and well-chosen wines from France, the rest of Europe and the New World are accompanied by succinct tasting notes and include seven wines by the glass from six countries. Grant Burge 80-year-old Vine Shiraz from South Australia comes highly recommended at £24.95. House wines start at £12.50.

CHEF: Grant Tomkins PROPRIETORS: John and Christine Cunliffe OPEN: all week 12 to 2.30, 7 to 9 MEALS: alc L Mon to Sat (main courses £8.50 to £12). Set L Sun £17.50, Set D £35 SERVICE: not inc, card slips closed CARDS: Amex, Delta, Diners, MasterCard, Switch, Visa DETAILS: 60 seats. 24 seats outside. Private parties: 26 main room, 12 and 26 private rooms. Car park. Vegetarian meals. No children under 7. No smoking in dining room. Wheelchair access (not WC). Music ACCOMMODATION: 14 rooms, all with bath/shower. TV. Phone. D,B&B £100 to £250. Rooms for disabled. No children under 7 (*The Which? Hotel Guide*) (£5)

All entries, including Round-ups, are fully indexed at the back of the Guide.

'Crisp fillet of cod with butter beans, asparagus and herb bouillon. The piece of cod that passeth all understanding. We'll say amen to that.' (On eating in Lancashire)

▲ Holbeck Ghyll

Holbeck Lane, Windermere LA23 1LU
TEL: (01539) 432375 FAX: (01539) 434743
EMAIL: accommodation@holbeck-ghyil.co.uk
WEB SITE: www.holbeck-ghyll.co.uk
off A591, take Holbeck Lane 3m N of Windermere
signposted Troutbeck; hotel is ½m on left

NEW CHEF
MODERN EUROPEAN
£30–£81

This well-kept, characterful hotel has a breathtaking panoramic view over Lake Windermere. To take full advantage, it is probably best to eat on the terrace on a sunny summer evening, although the oak-panelled dining room has its own charm too, with a few references to art nouveau. The cooking so far has focused on refined Modern European ideas, from a boudin of oyster with watercress purée, via Périgord pigeon with stuffed cabbage, to a chocolate and pistachio pyramid. But David McLaughlin arrived just as the Guide went to press, too late for us to receive any reports on his progress. The wine list is wide-ranging, although a decent bottle can easily bump up the bill. Four house wines are priced from £16 to £17.50.

CHEF: David McLaughlin PROPRIETORS: David and Patricia Nicholson OPEN: all week 12.30 to 2, 6.45 to 9.30 MEALS: Set L £19.50, Set D £42.50. Light L and afternoon tea available SERVICE: not inc, card slips closed CARDS: Amex, Delta, Diners, MasterCard, Switch, Visa DETAILS: 50 seats. 20 seats outside. Private parties: 65 main room. Car park. Vegetarian meals. No children under 8 at D. No smoking in dining room. Wheelchair access (not WC). No music ACCOMMODATION: 20 rooms, all with bath/shower. TV. Phone. D,B&B £95 to £300. Baby facilities (*The Which? Hotel Guide*) (£5)

Jerichos

Birch Street, Windermere LA23 1EG
TEL/FAX: (015394) 42522
EMAIL: enquiries@jerichos.co.uk
WEB SITE: www.jerichos.co.uk

COOKING **5**
ENGLISH
£30–£48

At the end of a quiet terrace, up a flight of slate steps, Jerichos can radiate a private party atmosphere with its bright colours, developing collection of pictures, and a glimpse into the kitchen. The menu changes weekly but follows a regular format. Despite a soup (such as pea and pear with watercress and mustard), starters can be quite busy and hearty, some sounding like main courses in miniature: stuffed pork fillet on creamed swede with caramelised apple wedges and Madeira sauce, for example.

Chargrilled Scotch beef fillet is a regular main course, usually served with tomatoes, mushrooms, red wine sauce and fries. There is generally a chicken dish (breast stuffed with smoked Lancashire cheese, garlic and rosemary), and one involving best end of Lakeland lamb (maybe curry-crusted on mash with peppered Savoy cabbage), while other options range from risotto via skate wing with tomato and onion salsa, to richly gravied calf's liver on mash with lentils. Finish with a comforting dessert such as pistachio, apricot and honey sponge, or chocolate and mascarpone cheesecake. Meals are helped by personable and well-paced service from Jo Blaydes, and by a briefly annotated, well-priced wine list that takes the New World as seriously as it does Europe. House wines are £11.75 (£3.25 a glass).

CHEFS: Chris Blaydes and Sarah Connolly PROPRIETORS: Chris and Joanne Blaydes OPEN: Tue to Sun D only 6.45 to 9.30 CLOSED: 2 weeks Nov/Dec, 25 and 26 Dec, 1 Jan, 1 week Feb MEALS: alc (main courses £12.50 to £17) SERVICE: not inc CARDS: Delta, MasterCard, Switch, Visa DETAILS: 36 seats. Private parties: 24 main room, 16 and 24 private rooms. Vegetarian meals. No children under 12. No smoking in dining room. Music

▲ Miller Howe

Rayrigg Road, Windermere LA23 1EY
TEL: (015394) 42536 FAX: (015394) 45664
EMAIL: lakeview@millerhowe.com
WEB SITE: www.millerhowe.com
on A592, between Windermere and Bowness

COOKING **6**
ENGLISH COUNTRY HOUSE
£26–£58

Once recovered from the brio of golden cherubs suspended from plum-coloured ceilings, and a dining room bright with silver, sparkling glassware and crisp white linen – reporters find a hotel in good shape. The custom of all sitting down together for dinner is an established part of the theatre: in fact there is a curtain across the dining room, and 'it did indeed go up.' The menu is idiosyncratically laid out, offering a set meal on one sheet, with options on another; by sticking to the recommended items, one diner found himself eating chicken liver pâté followed by fried turkey liver, but such occurrences are rare. More typically, a meal might begin with foie gras and rocket risotto, followed by poached turbot (there is no choice of second course), then roast loin of suckling pig.

The style picks up on contemporary ideas, and fish tends to get upbeat treatment – seared scallops, with lime, chilli and tequila in the dressing and a friture of root ginger to accompany – while meats may be dealt with rather more conventionally: chargrilled steak for example comes with a steak and kidney pudding (thank you, Gary Rhodes). Finish, perhaps, with armagnac parfait covered in a spun-sugar basket. Staff are attentive, friendly and professional, and after the show the cast – usually in the form of Susan Elliott – comes round and chats to the audience; the part of 'the perfect host' is played by Charles Garside. New World wines, particularly from South Africa, predominate on an extensive and resourceful list. Few bottles come in under £20, although there are plenty of halves, and two wines by the glass change nightly to suit the set menu.

CHEF: Susan Elliott PROPRIETOR: Charles Garside OPEN: all week 12.30 to 1.30, 8 (1 sitting) CLOSED: Jan MEALS: Set L Mon to Sat £15, Set L Sun £18.50, Set D £35 SERVICE: not inc, card slips closed CARDS: Amex, Diners, MasterCard, Switch, Visa DETAILS: 68 seats. Private parties: 68 main room, 30 and 40 private rooms. Car park. Vegetarian meals. No children under 8 at D. No smoking in dining room. Wheelchair access (also WC). Music. Air-conditioned ACCOMMODATION: 12 rooms, all with bath/shower. TV. Phone. D,B&B £90 to £250. No children under 8 (*The Which? Hotel Guide*)

The Guide office can quickly spot when a restaurateur is encouraging customers to write recommending inclusion. Such reports do not further a restaurant's cause. Please tell us if a restaurateur invites you to write to the Guide.

WINKLEIGH Devon map 1

Pophams

Castle Street, Winkleigh EX19 8HU
TEL: (01837) 83767

COOKING **5**
MODERN BRITISH
£27–£42

Melvyn Popham and Dennis Hawkes pitched their tent in this little Devon village back in the mid-1980s and have stuck to the same winning formula ever since. They cater for just ten covers at capacity on three lunchtime sessions each week, chalking the short menu on the blackboard each day and inviting you to bring your own bottle, which will be opened without charge. (If you forget, the post office next door is licensed.) One trio have booked in for a birthday celebration for each of the last three years, appreciating the idiosyncrasy as well as the cooking. Last time, they enjoyed a fine, simple starter of Parma ham with figs, rocket and Parmesan, although they might also have been offered roast cod with tomato, ginger and garlic, or a bowl of leek and watercress soup. Main-course meats from a quality butcher are carefully handled: best end of lamb is boned out and stuffed with spinach and thyme, then encased in puff pastry and sauced with Madeira. Lemon tart with vanilla ice cream is one way to finish, or there might be a single cheese, such as Shropshire Blue, served at its peak. Dennis Hawkes's front-of-house approach elicits greater appreciation than many more formal places, and he is very good with the corkscrew.

CHEF: Melvyn Popham PROPRIETORS: Melvyn Popham and Dennis Hawkes OPEN: Wed to Fri L only 11.45 to 1.30 CLOSED: Feb MEALS: alc (main courses £14 to £16). Unlicensed but BYO (no corkage) SERVICE: not inc, card slips closed CARDS: MasterCard, Visa DETAILS: 10 seats. Private parties: 10 main room. No children under 14. No smoking in dining room. Occasional music. Air-conditioned

WINTERINGHAM North Lincolnshire map 9

▲ Winteringham Fields

Winteringham DN15 9PF
TEL: (01724) 733096 FAX: (01724) 733898
EMAIL: wintfields@aol.com
WEB SITE: www.winteringhamfields.com

COOKING **9**
PROVINCIAL FRENCH/SWISS
£42–£102

A converted farmhouse in an unremarkable village a few miles west of the Humber Bridge may not seem the likeliest spot for a top-class restaurant, but life is often like that. Forget minimalism. Dark wood, a crowded conservatory, and rooms stuffed with Victorian antiques and curios may convey a somewhat heavy and serious air, but the small marble-floored dining room is most agreeable, with eye-catching painted ostrich eggs parked on each table. If this is 'cuisine at its haute-est', it is also exciting, the few disappointments over the year being far outweighed by compliments and superlatives. The carte offers plenty of choice (including a few fish dishes that can be taken as either first or main courses) without being overwhelming, and the three-course set meal is reasonably priced.

Individuality and flair are part of the style, for example in a complex but 'inspired' pot-au-feu of scallops and confit calf's liver in a copious broth of duck, Madeira and galangal; or in foie gras paired with rhubarb and ginger. Cooking combines a classical approach and flawless technique with innovation in such a way that the food is both reliable and stimulating: in rolled rack of Lincolnshire lamb, for example, accompanied by a suet pudding filled with offal, and a brochette of sweet, candied aubergine. Flavours picked up from the Orient and Maghreb are integrated successfully into the repertoire, producing a range of dishes from marlin steak with lime noodles to chermoula of cod with aromatic couscous.

Even simple dishes are a treat – fillet of brilliantly fresh brill on a thin bordelaise sauce, accompanied by airy 'elongated balloons' of soufflé potato – all helped by well-sourced ingredients, from Grimsby fish to organic pork reared in the village, and vegetables and herbs from the kitchen garden. Gimmicks are conspicuous by their absence, although presentation is striking, and a kitsch jokiness sometimes lightens the seriousness: as in a trompe l'oeil dessert consisting of a cup of coffee and chocolate cream topped with whipped cream and powdered chocolate, with nougat sugar lumps and the word 'cappuccino' stencilled on the plate.

The cheese trolley is one of the best, its varied contents (including a strong British showing) kept in impeccable condition and knowledgeably described. Attention to detail is a characteristic of the whole operation, evident, for example, in the waves of skilfully produced appetisers (including 'dazzling' breadcrumbed cubes of truffle-flavoured foie gras). Service from Annie Schwab and 'hordes of cheerful, attentive young men', several of whom have been here for some years, is generally considered second to none. A lengthy, global wine list includes European classics and is unusual for its Swiss selection. While quality is undisputed, prices are high, with house wines from Italy, France and Chile starting at £17.50. Advice from the knowledgeable young sommelier can be safely sought, however, without the fear that you will be steered towards the stratosphere.

CHEF: Germain Schwab PROPRIETORS: Germain and Annie Schwab OPEN: Tue to Sat 12 to 1.30, 7 to 9.30 CLOSED: 2 weeks from 24 Dec, last week Mar, first week Aug, bank hols MEALS: alc (main courses £26 to £30). Set L £26, Set D £29 to £58 SERVICE: not inc, card slips closed CARDS: Amex, Delta, MasterCard, Switch, Visa DETAILS: 42 seats. Private parties: 10 main room, 10 private room. Car park. No smoking in dining room. Wheelchair access (not WC). No music ACCOMMODATION: 10 rooms, all with bath/shower. TV. Phone. Room only £75 to £150. Rooms for disabled (*The Which? Hotel Guide*)

Several sharp operators have tried to extort money from restaurateurs on the promise of an entry in a guidebook that has never appeared. The Good Food Guide *makes no charge for inclusion.*

indicates that smoking is either banned altogether or that a dining-room is maintained for non-smokers. The symbol does not apply to restaurants that simply have no-smoking areas.

WITHERSLACK Cumbria map 8

▲ Old Vicarage

Church Road, Witherslack LA11 6RS
TEL: (015395) 52381 FAX: (015395) 52373
EMAIL: hotel@oldvicarage.com
WEB SITE: www.oldvicarage.com
off A590, take first left in village to church

COOKING **3**
MODERN BRITISH/FRENCH
£23–£59

Handy for walking the low-lying southern fells, with views over Morecambe Bay, the house feels warm and lived in. With a recent kitchen refit behind him, James Brown is turning increasingly to local and organic materials, from Hawkshead organic trout, via Holker Estate venison and Howbarrow Farm fruit and vegetables, to Dexter beef from the nearby Stanley Estate. The sometimes lengthy menu descriptions embrace largely mainstream or traditional ideas, such as grilled breast and confit leg of Gressingham duck on Puy lentils, or kedgeree enclosed in paupiettes of fresh and accurately cooked lemon sole, topped with a poached egg and hollandaise, a sort of 'fish Benedict'.

Cheeses are kept in good condition, and desserts might include a wedge of fig and banana tart, or rhubarb and orange Eve's pudding with custard. Note the early-bird option of the same dinner menu at a reduced price. Wines are a blend of New and Old Worlds and feature interesting bottles from Australia and Italy in particular. While there are few under £20 in the special house selections, house white starts at £11.50 and red at £13.

CHEF: James Brown PROPRIETORS: the Brown and Reeve families OPEN: Sun L 12.30 to 1.30, all week D 6 to 9 MEALS: alc D 7 to 9 (main courses £12.50 to £20). Set L £12.50 (2 courses) to £15.50, Set D 6 to 7 £12.50 (2 courses) to £15.50 SERVICE: not inc, card slips closed CARDS: Amex, Delta, MasterCard, Switch, Visa DETAILS: 40 seats. Private parties: 20 main room, 12 private room. Car park. Vegetarian meals. Children's helpings. No smoking in dining room. Wheelchair access (not WC). Music ACCOMMODATION: 13 rooms, all with bath/shower. TV. Phone. B&B £65 to £158. Rooms for disabled. Baby facilities (*The Which? Hotel Guide*) (£5)

WOKINGHAM Berkshire map 3

Rose Street

6 Rose Street, Wokingham RG40 1XH
TEL: (0118) 978 8025 FAX: (0118) 989 1314

COOKING **4**
MODERN ANGLO-FRENCH
£26–£60

Occupying a sixteenth-century building in the town centre, with ancient floorboards, beamed ceilings, assorted carpets and simple wooden tables, Rose Street makes modern Anglo-French food its stock in trade. Caesar salad may start the ball rolling, or pan-fried foie gras with a confit of apples and kumquats, followed by English lamb cutlets, or a dish of beef fillet with braised oxtail. But the style is flexible enough to take in seared scallops and Szechuan spiced tuna with mizuna leaves and a mirin and wasabi dressing. Enterprising combinations run to sautéed chicken livers with an escabèche of artichokes and peppers in a chocolate and raspberry vinegar cream; and cod fillet sharing the plate with a cod and crab fishcake, a mussel and chorizo risotto, and crab bisque. Among desserts, passion fruit comes four ways – brûlée, mousse, parfait and sorbet – and crêpes suzette, for some reason, are 'subject to availability'. Wines concentrate on France, but the choice elsewhere is a bit livelier. House vin de table is £10.95.

CHEF: Paul Scott PROPRIETOR: John Read OPEN: Mon to Sat 12 to 2.30, 7 to 10 CLOSED: 25 to 26 Dec, 1 Jan, L bank hols MEALS: alc (main courses £12 to £20). Set L £14 (2 courses) to £18, Set D £42.50 SERVICE: not inc CARDS: Amex, Delta, MasterCard, Switch, Visa DETAILS: 46 seats. Private parties: 18 main room, 10 to 18 private rooms. Vegetarian meals. Children's helpings. No smoking in 1 dining room. Wheelchair access (also women's WC). Music (£5)

WOODBRIDGE Suffolk map 6

Captain's Table £

3 Quay Street, Woodbridge IP12 1BX
TEL: (01394) 383145 FAX: (01394) 388508

COOKING **4**
MODERN BRITISH
£19–£34

Pascal Pommier's hands-on style adds much to the appeal: when not behind the stoves, he is out serving and clearing up with the rest of the staff in the airy, light, timbered rooms that make up this smart yet informal restaurant near the water. Keenly priced menus focus on simplicity and bring to the fore invention delivered with a light touch: for example in crab samosas with a chilli-flavoured dipping sauce, plain, fresh rock oysters, and 'good, honest' ham hock terrine with a heap of sweet red onion marmalade. Reporters have praised tender braised lamb shank on creamy mash with a tasty red wine sauce, moist fillets of sea bass with a fennel and Pernod cream sauce, and slow-roasted marinated duck leg with red cabbage. Desserts too have pleased: iced armagnac soufflé with poached prunes, and light and bouncy chocolate sponge with rich, boozy white chocolate and tequila sorbet. Service is 'swift, professional and charming', and the well-rounded, ungreedy wine list, where only a handful of bottles are over £20, offers seven wines by the glass from £1.80. Bottle prices start at £8.95.

CHEF: Pascal Pommier PROPRIETORS: Jo and Pascal Pommier OPEN: Tue to Sun and bank hol Mon L 12 to 2 (3 Sun), Tue to Sat and bank hol Sun and Mon D 6.30 to 9 (10 Fri and Sat) CLOSED: 2 weeks Jan MEALS: alc (main courses £5.50 to £10.50) SERVICE: not inc, card slips closed CARDS: Delta, MasterCard, Switch, Visa DETAILS: 50 seats. 30 seats outside. Private parties: 34 main room, 19 to 34 private rooms. Car park. Vegetarian meals. No smoking in 1 dining room. Wheelchair access (not WC). No music

WOODSTOCK Oxfordshire map 2

▲ Feathers Hotel

Market Street, Woodstock OX20 1SX
TEL: (01993) 812291 FAX: (01993) 813158
EMAIL: enquiries@feathers.co.uk
WEB SITE: www.feathers.co.uk

COOKING **5**
MODERN EUROPEAN
£32–£73

Enter the old inn through a hotel lobby, where a singing canary entertains, and progress to an English country-style dining room with yellow walls, blue and yellow curtains and upholstery. A modern European carte is the focus of attention, offering an appealing array of dishes from langoustine beignets with herb mash and tartare sauce to canon of lamb wrapped in puff pastry with provençale herbs. Ambition is high, and quite a few items consist of several parts, for example a collar of bacon combined with black pudding, a turnip and morel mousseline, white truffle oil and foie gras with parsnip crisps. And that is just a starter.

Options extend to a couple of six-course tasting menus, one devoted exclusively to fish; indeed, seafood is well handled, taking in hand-dived roast scallops with split-pea casserole, and baked sea bass with ratatouille, black olives, rouille and pesto juices. The cooking, however, highlights one of the problems of restaurants that open all week: if the head chef cannot be there all the time (and he appears not to have been at inspection), and if the kitchen does not perform well in his absence, then disappointments are inevitable.

Desserts might take in warm plum tart, or a recommended creamy textured, zesty lemon posset. The 12.5 per cent service charge 'does not feel optional', nor does it seem appropriate considering how much service needs sharpening up. Wines are well-chosen across the board in terms of quality and variety, and half-bottles are plentiful, but prices rise steeply. Seven house wines start with Duboeuf red and white at £11.75.

CHEF: Mark Treasure PROPRIETOR: Empire Ventures Ltd OPEN: all week 12.30 to 2.15, 7.30 to 9.15 MEALS: alc D (main courses £18.50 to £22.50). Set L Mon to Sat £17.50 (2 courses) to £21, Set L Sun £20.50, Set D £48. Bar meals available SERVICE: 12.5% (optional), card slips closed CARDS: Amex, Delta, Diners, MasterCard, Switch, Visa DETAILS: 60 seats. 60 seats outside. Private parties: 60 main room. Vegetarian meals. No smoking in dining room. Music. Air-conditioned ACCOMMODATION: 22 rooms, all with bath/shower. TV. Phone. B&B £115 to £290 (*The Which? Hotel Guide*) (£5)

WORCESTER Worcestershire **map 5**

Brown's

24 Quay Street, Worcester WR1 2JJ
TEL: (01905) 26263 FAX: (01905) 25768

COOKING **3**
ANGLO-FRENCH
£25–£50

The Tansley partnership has run this converted Worcester corn mill as a restaurant for 20 years now. Readers appreciate the elegant décor, the bucolic tranquillity of the view, where swans glide by on the River Severn, and the reliable country-house style of cooking. Fixed-price menus try not to startle with way-out combinations, preferring instead mussel gratin on spinach with white wine and Gruyère sauce, or smoked haddock with tomato concassé, followed perhaps by spatchcock quails with herbed couscous and red wine sauce. Vegetarian dishes are thoughtfully handled, producing mushroom and cashew-nut terrine with green peppercorn sauce. Warm apple and mincemeat pudding, or tiramisù with ginger, offers comfort at dessert stage. Highly professional service is generally commended. Wines are predominantly French, the list opening in classical mode with a run of serious clarets and then white Burgundies, but Australia gets a fair crack of the whip too. French and Australian house wines start at £11.95.

CHEFS: W.R. Tansley and L. Jones PROPRIETORS: W.R. and P.M. Tansley OPEN: Tue to Fri and Sun L 12.30 to 1.45, Tue to Sat D 7.30 to 9.45 CLOSED: 24 to 31 Dec MEALS: Set L Tue to Fri £19.50, Set L Sun £25, Set D £35.50 SERVICE: net prices, card slips closed CARDS: Amex, Delta, MasterCard, Switch, Visa DETAILS: 100 seats. Private parties: 90 main room. Vegetarian meals. No children under 8. No-smoking area. Wheelchair access (also WC). No music

WORFIELD Shropshire map 5

▲ Old Vicarage Hotel

Worfield WV15 5JZ
TEL: (0800) 096 8010 and (01746) 716497
FAX: (01746) 716552
EMAIL: admin@the-old-vicarage.demon.co.uk
2m N of A545, 3m E of Bridgnorth
WEB SITE: www.oldvicarageworfield.com

COOKING **3**
MODERN EUROPEAN
£31–£70

The tall-chimneyed, red-brick Edwardian building comes with a croquet lawn, a conservatory for pre-meal drinks, and a brace of dining rooms with parquet floors, floral curtains and lots of prints on yellow walls. It feels like it could revert to a vicarage at fairly short notice. Dinner is priced according to main course, yielding a difference of around £13, for example, between beef fillet with Madeira jus and a vegetarian galette of griddled aubergine and tomato with goats' cheese, asparagus and pesto. The food seems rather ambitious for the circumstances, but the kitchen has turned out a satisfactory terrine of pork and Toulouse sausage with a fruity plum relish, and a well-judged breast of guinea fowl with lentils in a rich stock sauce. Meats are cooked 'medium rare/pink' unless ordered otherwise.

Menus take some advantage of the seasons, producing in summer a starter of chargrilled asparagus, and a couple of strawberry desserts, one of them combining sorbet with a clear, concentrated and notably effective soup. Affordable wines from Bordeaux and Burgundy are high points on an enthusiastic wine list, a broadly based selection that brings together many fine bottles from around the world. Around 100 half-bottles ensure varied and exciting drinking is possible. French house wines are £14.50.

CHEFS: Richard Arnold and Blaine Reed PROPRIETORS: Peter and Christine Iles OPEN: Sun to Fri L 12 to 1.45, all week D 7 to 9 MEALS: Set L £18.50, Set D £22.50 to £36 SERVICE: not inc CARDS: Amex, Delta, MasterCard, Visa DETAILS: 42 seats. Private parties: 20 main room, 10 to 12 private rooms. Car park. Vegetarian meals. Children's helpings. No smoking in dining room. Wheelchair access (also WC). Occasional music ACCOMMODATION: 14 rooms, all with bath/shower. TV. Phone. B&B £75 to £175. Rooms for disabled. Baby facilities (*The Which? Hotel Guide*) (£5)

WORLESTON Cheshire map 5

▲ Rookery Hall

Main Road, Worleston CW5 6DQ
TEL: (01270) 610016 FAX: (01270) 626027
EMAIL: rookery@aol.com
WEB SITE: www.mywebpage.net/rookeryhall
on B5074, 2½m N of Nantwich

COOKING **3**
MODERN EUROPEAN
£29–£74

Built in 1816, the sumptuous and elegant hall reputedly has one of the most beautiful dining rooms in the country, with antique tables and views of the lush Cheshire countryside. The cooking is full-dress country-house style, offering complex treatment of generally high-quality materials. An ambitious menu makes enticing reading – raviolo of smoked cod on a thick, well-flavoured gazpacho coulis, topped with deep-fried rocket leaves – although there is a sense of dishes striving so hard to impress that they can lose a proper sense of direction.

Nevertheless the kitchen has produced roast breast and thigh of pheasant (unseasonally served in April) with a fine game stock, and pink, well-flavoured roast loin of Scottish lamb, partnered by smoked garlic dumplings. 'Impeccable' British and Irish cheeses are followed by interesting desserts that have included beignets of puréed fruit redolent of cinnamon, alongside a scoop of cocoa sorbet in a toffee container. Bread and appetisers are first class, staff make a big effort to be welcoming and helpful, and there is a fine-wine list in addition to a short global one whose price fulcrum is around £25. Prices start at £16.

CHEF: Craig Grant PROPRIETORS: Hand Picked Hotels and Arcadian OPEN: Sun to Fri L 12 to 2, all week D 7 to 9.30 MEALS: alc L (main courses £12 to £12.50). Set L £10.99 (2 courses), Set D £39.50, Set D Fri and Sat £45 SERVICE: not inc CARDS: Amex, Delta, Diners, MasterCard, Switch, Visa DETAILS: 34 seats. Private parties: 30 main room, 14 to 66 private rooms. Car park. Vegetarian meals. Children's helpings. Wheelchair access (also WC). No music ACCOMMODATION: 45 rooms, all with bath/shower. TV. Phone. B&B £95 to £155. Rooms for disabled. Fishing

WYE Kent **map 3**

▲ Wife of Bath

4 Upper Bridge Street, Wye TN25 5AF
TEL: (01233) 812540 FAX: (01233) 813630
EMAIL: reservation@wifeofbath.com
WEB SITE: www.wifeofbath.com
just off A28, Ashford to Canterbury road

COOKING **3**
MODERN EUROPEAN/FAR EASTERN
£25–£46

In medieval times, Wye may well have been one of the last stops a pilgrim would make on the Canterbury trail, but this timber-framed house wasn't built until the mid-eighteenth century. The Chaucerian theme is still played for all it's worth at John Morgan's establishment, however, right up to 'The Squire' and 'The Prioress' in place of 'Gents' and 'Ladies'. Despite that, the cooking is as up to date as can be, Robert Hymers having refined his enterprising style here over the past decade.

A Far Eastern mode is clearly popular – even roast cod may arrive with a Thai red curry sauce – but not at the expense of, for example, peppered beef fillet classically sauced with cognac and cream. Home-made ice creams and sorbets are always on offer, and the chef's medley comes with all the usual sponges, mousses and coulis. John Morgan personally leads the meeting and greeting, and the tone is readily friendly. Bordeaux and Burgundy head the list of wines, but there is sufficient southern-hemisphere interest to keep prices within reason. Chilean Sauvignon Blanc and Merlot open the house wines at £13.50.

CHEF: Robert Hymers PROPRIETOR: John Morgan OPEN: Tue to Sat 12 to 1.45, 7 to 9.45 CLOSED: 1 week from 25 Dec MEALS: alc (main courses £11 to £16). Set L £10 (2 courses) to £13.95, Set D £23.75 SERVICE: not inc CARDS: Amex, Delta, Diners, MasterCard, Switch, Visa DETAILS: 50 seats. Private parties: 50 main room. Car park. Vegetarian meals. Children's helpings. No pipes in dining-room. Wheelchair access (not WC). No music ACCOMMODATION: 6 rooms, all with bath/shower. TV. Phone. B&B £45 to £90. Garden (*The Which? Hotel Guide*)

YARM Stockton-on-Tees map 10

Chadwick's

104B High Street, Yarm TS15 9AU
TEL: (01642) 788558 FAX: (01642) 788344

COOKING **4**
MODERN EUROPEAN
£22–£52

Fizzing with life, this self-styled Continental café comes with marble-topped tables, a zinc-covered bar, faux marble pillars, and colourful modern paintings on a culinary theme. The cooking is based on sound raw ingredients (fish is a strength), which are subject to some modern treatments, producing an attractively varied menu supplemented by blackboard specials. A strong Italian input is responsible for antipasti, and lunchtime dishes of pasta or perhaps hot chicken with red pesto and provolone on ciabatta.

Fish might take take the form of seared scallops with yoghurt, coriander and spicy aubergine, and even humble fish pie is fresh-tasting, with a well-browned cheesy topping and a creamy sauce. Meat options range from a Thai chicken and vegetable curry to calf's liver and bacon with pan haggerty. Desserts may not be quite as professional as the rest, but have included lemon cheesecake and strawberry pavlova. Service is friendly and cheerful, and wines on the 40-strong list (with plenty under £20) are French, Italian or from the New World, with a maverick from Greece. House Duboeuf is £10.95.

CHEFS: Philip Vaux and David Brownless PROPRIETOR: David Brownless OPEN: Tue to Sat 12 to 2.30, 5.30 to 9.30, plus Sun L once a month Apr to Sept CLOSED: 1 week Oct MEALS: alc (main courses L £6 to £9.50, D £13 to £16) SERVICE: not inc CARDS: Amex, Delta, MasterCard, Switch, Visa DETAILS: 70 seats. Private parties: 70 main room. Children's helpings. No smoking in 1 dining room. Music

YARMOUTH Isle of Wight map 2

▲ George Hotel

Quay Street, Yarmouth PO41 0PE
TEL: (01983) 760331 FAX: (01983) 760425
EMAIL: res@thegeorge.co.uk

COOKING **5**
MODERN BRITISH
£44–£57

The George occupies an enviable spot overlooking the Solent, near the streets of shops where tourists congregate and the ferry comes and goes. It is an ancient building, where dinners are taken in a fine old candlelit dining room with painted panels and an atmosphere that befits its maturity. For the best view, find the bright sunny yellow Brasserie, which serves deep-fried cod cakes, mussel and smoked haddock risotto, and braised lamb shank. For the best food, stay with the dining room and its fixed-price, three-course dinners of often complex dishes: perhaps a trio of duck incorporating rillettes, foie gras and a ravioli of honey-flavoured duck.

Materials range from roast loin of rabbit (with leek and rabbit tortellini on a ginger sauce) to smoked ribeye of Glenbervie beef, and while dishes may not always ignite passion, ability levels are high and timing is accurate. Combinations are sensible, even if they are not always expected, as in a starter of squab pigeon with veal sweetbread and white onion purée, or a mille-feuille of red mullet and pork skin with lime and artichoke. Trios might recur at dessert stage (chocolate as ice cream, soup, and deep-fried), where there might also be a rhubarb mousse with blueberries poached in liquorice. Arranged in price bands, a global wine selection starts at £11.50 and rises to three-figure sums for fine clarets dating back to 1937. Half-bottles are plentiful, and around a dozen wines are available by the glass.

CHEF: Kevin Mangeolles PROPRIETORS: Jeremy and Amy Willcock, and John Illsley OPEN: Tue to Sat D only 7 to 10 MEALS: Set D £39.50 SERVICE: none, card slips closed CARDS: Amex, Delta, MasterCard, Switch, Visa DETAILS: 30 seats. Private parties: 20 main room. No children under 10. No music. Air-conditioned ACCOMMODATION: 17 rooms, all with bath/shower. TV. Phone. B&B £85 to £192.50 (*The Which? Hotel Guide*)

YORK North Yorkshire **map 9**

Melton's

7 Scarcroft Road, York YO23 1ND COOKING **5**
TEL: (01904) 634341 FAX: (01904) 635115 MODERN BRITISH
£22–£40

'We have no intention of going posh,' writes Lucy Hjort in reporting the face-lift of Melton's, now with banquette seating under both murals, as well as mirrors and wood panelling. Priorities remain as before, starting with well-sourced ingredients that feed an attractively varied menu. The fixed priced dinner has gone (except for early birders), replaced by a carte that might offer beignets of corn and Wensleydale cheese, followed by rabbit leg escalopes with bacon and a herb crust. Fish and vegetarian dishes are given due prominence, and materials are enticingly combined, for example in pan fried red mullet on a warm spiced aubergine salad with pepper and chilli salsa.

Even those for whom Melton's is an old favourite are capable of being pleasantly surprised: in one case by hot prune and brandy soufflé. Pudding lovers might otherwise be hard pushed to choose between Yorkshire curd tart soufflé, and spiced fruit and nut cookie ice cream with orange sauce. Service is pleasant, easy-going, and free of charge (like mineral water and coffee). The enthusiastic wine list offers an intelligent selection from Old and New Worlds, combined with a maximum mark-up policy of £10, which naturally favours those who wish to drink more expensive wines. However, there is plenty under £20, and instructive tasting notes and cross-referencing suggestions are friendly and educational. The Hjorts plan to open a café brasserie in the city in 2001.

CHEFS: Adam Holliday and Michael Hjort PROPRIETOR: Michael and Lucy Hjort OPEN: Tue to Sun L 12 to 2, Mon to Sat D 5.30 to 10 CLOSED: 3 weeks Christmas, 1 week Aug MEALS: alc (main courses £11 to £15). Set L and D 5.30 to 6.15 £16 SERVICE: net prices, card slips closed CARDS: Delta, MasterCard, Switch, Visa DETAILS: 40 seats. Private parties: 34 main room, 16 private room. Vegetarian meals. Children's helpings. No smoking in 1 dining room. Wheelchair access (not WC). Music. Air-conditioned (£5)

Net prices *in the details at the end of an entry indicates that the prices given on a menu and on a bill are inclusive of VAT and service charge, and that this practice is clearly stated on menu and bill.*

▲ Middlethorpe Hall

Bishopthorpe Road, York YO23 2GB
TEL: (01904) 641241 FAX: (01904) 620176
EMAIL: info@middlethorpe.com
WEB SITE: www.middlethorpe.com

COOKING **3**
MODERN BRITISH
£29–£53

Built in 1699, Middlethorpe Hall is a country house close to the city, not unlike Buckingham Palace in that respect. Restoration by Historic House Hotels has been sympathetic, and everything is on a big scale: substantial gardens, loads of antiques and three dining rooms, for example. As for restauration, a couple who dined several days running were impressed by the food's consistency, use of good materials and clear and distinctive flavours. A few classy ingredients are called for, if only to match the surroundings. Watercress soup comes with poached oysters, sea bass with asparagus, celery and a herb sauce, but the kitchen is equally at home with quail ravioli, roast lamb with a tian of aubergines, and pig's trotter stuffed with sweetbreads. Soft, indulgent textures are a feature of desserts, such as hot chocolate fondant, mandarin parfait, or caramel soufflé. Service is 'friendly and effective'. A big spread of vintage champagnes kicks off a lengthy, varied list in which prices reflect the luxury of the location, though careful searching reveals a few bottles under £20. Fifteen wines are offered by the glass, and house wines – the same in all Historic House Hotels – start at £13.90.

CHEF: Martin Barker PROPRIETOR: Historic House Hotels Ltd OPEN: all week 12 to 1.45, 7 to 9.45 CLOSED: 25 Dec and 31 Dec (open for residents) MEALS: Set L Mon to Fri £15.50 (2 courses) to £18.50, Set L Sun £20, Set D £34 SERVICE: net prices, card slips closed CARDS: Delta, MasterCard, Switch, Visa DETAILS: 60 seats. Private parties: 50 private room. Car park. Vegetarian meals. No children under 8. Jacket and tie. No smoking in dining room. No music ACCOMMODATION: 30 rooms, all with bath/shower. TV. Phone. Room only £105 to £260. Swimming pool (*The Which? Hotel Guide*)

Scotland

ABERDEEN Aberdeen **map 11**

Faraday's

2 Kirk Brae, Cults, Aberdeen AB15 9SQ
TEL/FAX: (01224) 869666
EMAIL: kapcot@aol.com
on A93, 3m from city centre

COOKING **2**
TRADITIONAL
£21–£46

Apart from the heavy lifting gear visible in the ceiling, you would never know this used to be an electricity substation, unless of course the name gave it away. The unfussy but well-kept surroundings are appreciated for their lack of affectation, as is the no-nonsense food: sweet pickle dill herrings with a potato and beetroot salad, seafood pie with either a pastry or potato topping, and venison with a blackcurrant and Madeira sauce. Lunch is, if anything, even more casual in style, with shepherd's pie, fish rissoles, and meat roll with chappit tatties; a regular puts in a good word for the accompanying vegetables, of which roast potatoes, beetroot, and cauliflower in cheese sauce are typical. Finish maybe with poached pear, served with home-made ice cream and toffee sauce, and drink from a short, standard wine list that starts with five house wines at £13.50.

CHEF/PROPRIETOR: John Inches OPEN: Tue to Sat 12 to 1.30, 7 to 9.30 CLOSED: 1 week from 26 Dec MEALS: alc L (main courses £5.50 to £14). Set D Tue to Thur £18.50, Set D Fri and Sat £21.50 SERVICE: 10%, card slips closed CARDS: Amex, Delta, MasterCard, Switch, Visa DETAILS: 40 seats. Private parties: 40 main room. Car park. Vegetarian meals. Children's helpings. No smoking before 2 at L, 10 at D. Wheelchair access (also WC). Music. Air-conditioned (£5)

Silver Darling

Pocra Quay, North Pier, Aberdeen AB11 5DQ
TEL/FAX: (01224) 576229

COOKING **4**
SEAFOOD
£31–£53

A bright, cheerful first-floor dining room sets the mood admirably, with panoramic views of the harbour entrance, the North Sea and Aberdeen foreshore. Didier Dejean has made barbecued seafood a speciality during the fifteen years he has been cooking here; a selection of fish from the daily market might typically be served with a sweet red pepper coulis and basil olive oil. Such commendable restraint is balanced elsewhere by classic treatments of bourride provençale, and wider-ranging ideas such as a cassoulet of salmon with chorizo, or red snapper marinated in soy, ginger and garlic, served with a Thai vinaigrette and stir-fried vegetables. Meals might begin with soup, a warm fish salad, or perhaps just half a dozen oysters, and end with chocolate marquise, or warm apple and pear tart with a red wine caramel sauce. A short, annotated list of predominantly French white wines starts with house Haut Poitou at £9.90.

CHEF: Didier Dejean PROPRIETORS: Didier Dejean and Catherine Wood OPEN: Sun to Fri L 12 to 2, all week D 7 to 9.30 CLOSED: Sun Oct to April, 2 weeks Christmas/New Year (exc 31 Dec) MEALS: alc D (main courses £13.50 to £18.50). Set L £19.50 (2 courses) to £23 SERVICE: not inc, card slips closed CARDS: Amex, Delta, Diners, MasterCard, Switch, Visa DETAILS: 55 seats. Children's helpings. Wheelchair access (also WC). Music

ABERFELDY Perthshire & Kinross map 11

▲ Farleyer House

Aberfeldy PH15 2JE
TEL: (01887) 820332 FAX: (01887) 829430
EMAIL: reservations@farleyer.com
WEB SITE: www.farleyer.com
on B846, Aberfeldy to Kinloch Rannoch road, 1½m W of Weem

COOKING 3
MODERN EUROPEAN
£29–£45

Whether in the relaxed bistro, or in the more formal dining room with its old pine doors, modern carver chairs in dark stained wood, and vibrantly coloured modern paintings, the kitchen makes a point of sourcing native produce. Beef and lamb are local, and Tay salmon, Highland venison, and even ptarmigan have all appeared on the menu. Materials (including smoked ham, lamb and venison) are put through a modern mill, producing turbot, for example, with polenta and sweet pepper salsa. While results may be uneven, reporters have been more than happy with a baked filo parcel of Aberfeldy cheese with onion marmalade and walnut dressing, and griddled mountain hare fillet served with rhubarb and ginger compote, redcurrant salsa and whisky jus. Among desserts, iced tiramisù parfait has gone down a treat, and so has the young, friendly and professional service. Wines cover a wide range and have an eye for quality, but there is choice under £20, including a dozen house recommendations starting at £11.

CHEF: Kieran Grant PROPRIETOR: Janice Reid OPEN: all week 12 to 2.30, 6 to 9.30 MEALS: alc (main courses £10 to £16) SERVICE: not inc CARDS: Amex, Delta, Diners, MasterCard, Switch, Visa DETAILS: 110 seats. 20 seats outside. Private parties: 60 main room, 30 to 40 private rooms. Car park. Vegetarian meals. Children's helpings. No smoking in 1 dining room. Wheelchair access (also WC). Music ACCOMMODATION: 19 rooms, all with bath/shower. TV. Phone. B&B £60 to £120. Rooms for disabled. Baby facilities. Fishing (£5)

'The tables were sticky and so was the floor. The whole place looked as if a good scrubbing would do no harm. . . . Mercifully, neither of us was ill afterwards, but our digestive systems are pretty robust.' (On eating in Yorkshire)

The Guide is totally independent, accepts no free hospitality, and survives on the number of copies sold each year.

ABOYNE Aberdeenshire — map 11

▲ White Cottage

Dess, Aboyne AB34 5BP
TEL/FAX: (013398) 86265
On A93 2½m E of Aboyne

COOKING **4**
MODERN EUROPEAN
£25–£47

The Cottage (only the porch is white) is a restaurant-with-a-room (just the one). Dining takes place in either a low-ceilinged room or a small conservatory extension, the latter containing a glass-fronted stove and enjoying a nocturnal view of a tiny patch of lawn with an illuminated little fountain. Country-house grandeur this is not. The Mills run a tight ship, and impress reporters with the range of their output. Chicken parfait with leeks, or a creamed soup of organic spinach and Swiss chard, might precede Aberdeen Angus fillet cooked in claret, a flavourful version of beef stroganoff made with crème fraîche, or a bourride of mussels, turbot and cod. Meals may well end with plum, prune and armagnac tart, passion-fruit soufflé or zesty lemon tart. Guigal Côtes du Rhône, Durup Chablis and Bonny Doon Californian Riesling are among the temptations on a wine list that offers a succinct global selection. House wines from France and South Africa are £12.80.

CHEF: Laurie Mill PROPRIETORS: Laurie and Josephine Mill OPEN: Tue to Sat 11.30 to 2.30, 7 to 9 CLOSED: 4 days Christmas, 1 week after Easter, 1 week July MEALS: alc L (main courses £8.50 to £15). Set D £29.50 SERVICE: not inc CARDS: Diners, MasterCard, Switch, Visa DETAILS: 45 seats. 12 seats outside. Private parties: 60 main room, 30 private room. Car park. Children's helpings. No smoking in dining room. Wheelchair access (also WC). Occasional music ACCOMMODATION: 1 room. B&B £26 to £52

ACHILTIBUIE Highland — map 11

▲ Summer Isles Hotel

Achiltibuie IV26 2YG
TEL: (01854) 622282 FAX: (01854) 622251
EMAIL: smilehotel@aol.com
WEB SITE: www.summerisleshotel.co.uk
take A835 to Drumrunie, 10m N of Ullapool, then single-track road for 15m; hotel 1m past Achilitbuie on left

COOKING **5**
MODERN EUROPEAN
£44–£53

A visit to Summer Isles begins with a 15-mile drive along a twisting single-track road past lochs and hills, before reaching the 'breathtaking' scene; windows in the blue and gold dining room face west, making the most of magical sunsets over the islands. Dinner is five courses with no choice before dessert; portions are adjusted for quantity, and it helps to like seafood, which might appear in the form of langoustines and spiny lobsters with basil aïoli, or seared scallops with a beremeal loaf. The best dishes show restraint and sound judgement, for example 'exquisitely fresh and just-cooked' chargrilled halibut served with leaves and herbs, or 'brilliant' local lamb fillet on a rustic bed of haricot beans, with a shredded potato and courgette cake and a first-class rosemary-flavoured gravy.

Scottish and English cheeses in first-class condition come with biscuits and a bowl of fruit, and a lavish display of desserts is wheeled round on a trolley: raspberry and strawberry pavlova with 'crisp, tacky meringue'; lemon curd roulade that was 'a marvel of lightness'; chocolate velvet tart; and sticky toffee pudding. Extras, according to one visitor, are less grand and sumptuous than previously, although bread – a home-baked buckwheat loaf straight from the oven – is as good as ever. Gerry Irvine and helpers are 'friendly, attentive and effective'. A hefty wine list incorporates fine bottles from around the world, and a choice selection of clarets is dominated by the legendary Ch. Pétrus 1982 for £1,500. Less extravagant drinkers might prefer Alta Vista Malbec from Argentina at £11.50. Seven wines are available by the glass, one changing daily to complement the first course.

CHEF: Chris Firth-Bernard PROPRIETORS: Mark and Geraldine Irvine OPEN: all week 12.30 to 2, 8pm (1 sitting D) CLOSED: mid-Oct to Easter MEALS: Set D £38. Light L menu SERVICE: net prices, card slips closed CARDS: MasterCard, Switch, Visa DETAILS: 28 seats. Private parties: 8 main room. Car park. Vegetarian meals. Children's helpings. No children under 6. No smoking in dining room. No music ACCOMMODATION: 13 rooms, all with bath/shower. Phone. B&B £55 to £200. No children under 6. Fishing (*The Which? Hotel Guide*)

ACHNASHEEN Highland **map 11**

▲ Loch Torridon Hotel

NEW ENTRY

Loch Torridon, Achnasheen IV22 2EY
TEL: (01445) 791242 FAX: (01445) 791296
WEB SITE: www.lochtorridonhotel.com

COOKING **3**
MODERN BRITISH
£50–£60

This Victorian shooting lodge in full baronial rig is set in wild, romantic country at the head of a sea loch in Wester Ross. It is not so much grand, felt one visitor, as reminiscent of 'my granny's living room', with heavy sofas, log fires and antlered stag heads hanging on the walls. Some granny. The owners appear to have 'a good grasp of what a Highland restaurant ought to offer', which, given the location, understandably includes locally caught crab, langoustines and dived scallops, as well as Gairloch salmon with asparagus and hollandaise, and perhaps roast monkfish with baby fennel and sauce vierge.

But this is not a seafood restaurant, since it also delivers plum tomato tart with fresh sharp flavours, powerfully flavoured marinated venison, and roast quail served with spinach, rösti and carrot spaghetti in a well-judged red wine sauce. On-plate vegetables at inspection could have been more accurately timed, but a thin-crusted lemon tart with raspberry sorbet was a hit. Service is friendly, and although prices are generally high, the wine list manages to find some serviceable bottles under £20, including eight house suggestions.

CHEF: Neil Dowson PROPRIETORS: David and Geraldine Gregory OPEN: all week D only 7.15 to 8.45 MEALS: Set D £38. Light L available 12.30 to 2 SERVICE: not inc, card slips closed CARDS: Amex, Delta, Diners, MasterCard, Switch, Visa DETAILS: 40 seats. Private parties: 40 main room, 15 private room. Car park. Vegetarian meals. Children's helpings. No children under 10. No smoking in dining room. Wheelchair access (not WC). No music ACCOMMODATION: 20 rooms, all with bath/shower. TV. Phone. B&B £50 to £260. Rooms for disabled. Baby facilities. Fishing

ALEXANDRIA Dumbarton & Clydebank map 11

▲ Cameron House, Georgian Room

Loch Lomond, Alexandria G83 8QZ
TEL: (01389) 755565 FAX: (01389) 759522
EMAIL: devere.cameron@airtime.co.uk
WEB SITE: www.cameronhouse.co.uk
off A82, ½m N of Balloch roundabout, 1m S of Arden

COOKING **6**
MODERN EUROPEAN
£32–£99

Victorian portraits and landscapes decorate the baronial-style house, whose serene setting provides 'outstandingly beautiful' views over Loch Lomond. Well-spaced tables and heavy napery in the first-floor dining room indicate a seriousness of intent that the menu soon confirms, not least by its price (although dinner is accompanied by live piano or guitar music). Peter Fleming's contemporary European approach combines native materials and a few luxuries in a seamless display of confident dishes. West Coast fish might come together with asparagus and truffled potato purée in a curry emulsion, oyster fritters are served with spinach and a tapénade dressing, and roast loin of venison is given a bitter chocolate and thyme dressing.

The kitchen employs humbler materials, such as black pudding (in a 'pan-fried terrine' with white haricot beans and tomato) and saddle of rabbit with prunes and grenadine syrup, but is not afraid to let rip when occasion demands: for example in a casserole of lobster and seared Oban langoustines accompanied by langoustine ravioli on a keta caviar cream. A hot soufflé typically features among desserts (banana, passion fruit, or apple and pear) but there is plenty more to tempt, including coconut parfait with pineapple crisps, and cappuccino mouse with a whisky sabayon and chocolate croquant. Globally sourced wines are geared towards those who are looking for quality, and priced accordingly. Look to Italy and Spain for a few bins under £20. Eleven wines by the glass start at £4.50.

CHEF: Peter Fleming PROPRIETOR: De Vere Hotels OPEN: Tue to Fri L 12 to 1.45, Tue to Sun D 7 to 9.45 CLOSED: 26 Dec, bank hols MEALS: alc (main courses £24 to £35). Set L £17.50 (2 courses) to £21, Set D £41.50 to £47 SERVICE: not inc, card slips closed CARDS: Amex, Delta, Diners, MasterCard, Switch, Visa DETAILS: 45 seats. Car park. Vegetarian meals. No children under 14. Jacket and tie. No smoking in dining room. Music. Air-conditioned ACCOMMODATION: 96 rooms, all with bath/shower. TV. Phone. B&B £110 to £300. Rooms for disabled. Baby facilities. Swimming pool. Fishing

---

'It was a Saturday night and the place was packed . . . . There was an undiscovered youthful version of Paula Yates, partnered by a cross between Tom Jones and Bob Geldof. . . . There was a cross between Laurence Llewelyn-Bowen and Neanderthal man. There was a man in a short-sleeved shirt who had heavily tattooed arms and who emptied his vegetable side plate by holding it upside down above his main-course plate. And there was a man who moved his gratin dauphinois from the serving dish on to his main-course plate by means of a spoon and all the fingers of his left hand. I just thought I'd mention the highlights of the evening.' (On eating in Hampshire)

ALYTH Perthshire & Kinross map 11

▲ Drumnacree House £

St Ninians Road, Alyth PH11 8AP
TEL/FAX: (01828) 632194/633355
EMAIL: allan.cull@virgin.net
turn off A926 Blairgowrie to Kirriemuir road to Alyth; take first left after Clydesdale Bank; hotel entrance is 300 metres on right

COOKING **3**
MODERN BRITISH-PLUS
£21–£38

There are two parts to this operation: a formal hotel dining room with a set-price dinner for residents, and a cheerful, informal, child-friendly bistro – 'a good place to take hungry adolescents' – which seems to attract most attention. Here, pink and orange predominate, and Alan Cull works at his wood-burning stove and chargrill for all to see, turning out Aberdeen Angus ribeye steak with a mustard and stout sauce, and whole suckling pig for parties of eight or more.

Winter might bring potted venison with redcurrant jelly, and hearty cassoulet, while old Drumnacree standbys such as Louisiana gumbo and blackened chicken help to ring the changes. Temperature control of a wood-fired oven can be tricky, resulting in more charring and textural compromise than is ideal, but the generally sound, tasty and unpretentious food still appeals for value, particularly at lunch. The dining-room style ranges from Arbroath smokie mousse, via tarragon penne with salad, to French apple tart. A short wine list (even shorter in the Bistro) starts with house red and white Grenache at £9.

CHEF: Allan Cull PROPRIETORS: Allan and Eleanor Cull OPEN: Tue to Sun 12 to 1.45, 6.30 to 9 MEALS: bistro alc (main courses L £4 to £5.50, D £7.50 to £13); hotel Set D £20 (residents only) SERVICE: not inc, card slips closed CARDS: Amex, Delta, MasterCard, Switch, Visa DETAILS: 40 seats. Private parties: 40 main room, 32 private room. Car park. Vegetarian meals. Children's helpings. No cigars/pipes in dining room. Wheelchair access (also women's WC). Music ACCOMMODATION: 6 rooms, all with bath/shower. TV. B&B £48.50 to £90 (£5)

ANSTRUTHER Fife map 11

Cellar

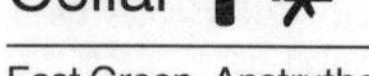

East Green, Anstruther KY10 3AA
TEL: (01333) 310378 FAX: (01333) 312544

COOKING **6**
MODERN SEAFOOD
£25–£48

After 18 years, Peter Jukes still cooks daily at this east coast institution, where décor remains unchanged from one year to the next: old awards hang on the rough stone walls, floors are tiled, tables are converted sewing machines, and a generally old-fashioned air pervades. Fish is the draw, and the majority of dishes don't change much. Smoked haddock omelette, crab salad with mayonnaise, or lobster and smoked salmon quiche might all have appeared on the menu a decade ago. This is because the cooking is no more, and no less, ambitious than to make the most of its simple, fresh and regularly available materials.

What it does do, however, is reflect the seasons: as mussels fade or haddock thins out, first-class lobster comes on stream, along with crab and dived scallops: three juicy slices, full of flavour, with a sun-dried tomato dressing. Inspection revealed a few lapses, not least in seasoning, but the kitchen has also turned out well-timed cod with basil mash and pesto, and intensely flavoured crayfish bisque, well served by 'good bits of fish and a cheesy flavour'. Desserts run to hazelnut praline terrine with a red berry coulis, and vanilla ice cream with hot butterscotch. The handwritten wine list brings together top producers from around the world. A strong white Burgundy section provides excellent accompaniments to fish, and numerous half-bottles facilitate the perfect food/wine combination, though prices can be a bit steep. House wines start at £15.

CHEF/PROPRIETOR: Peter Jukes OPEN: Wed to Sat L 12.30 to 1.30, Mon to Sat D 7 to 9.30 CLOSED: Mon D Nov to March MEALS: alc L (main courses £6.50 to £16). Set D £28.50 SERVICE: not inc, card slips closed CARDS: Amex, Delta, Diners, MasterCard, Switch, Visa DETAILS: 32 seats. Private parties: 32 main room. No children under 8. No smoking in dining room. Occasional music

ARCHIESTOWN Moray **map 11**

▲ Archiestown Hotel

Archiestown AB38 7QL
TEL: (01340) 810218 FAX: (01340) 810239

COOKING **2**
INTERNATIONAL
£26–£53

'After the grand baronial hotels of Scotland, it is a relief to find such a down-to-earth hotel,' commented one visitor. The 'junk-shop' surroundings – eccentric even by the hotel's own admission – provide an informal background, while a daily-changing blackboard menu majors on seafood. Judith Bulger does her best to intercept first-class produce from Scottish waters on its way to the markets of London, Madrid or wherever, and what seafood she gets – turbot, halibut, sole, plaice or scallops – she serves 'very simply and in serious quantities'. As well as langoustines mayonnaise, fish pie, and cod with parsley sauce, there may also be oxtail braised in port, or devilled kidneys, although it is probably best to avoid the chicken tikka. A standard range of desserts includes crème caramel and treacle pudding, while a short but well-chosen and mostly French wine list starts with house Vin de Pays d'Oc from Domaine Virginie at £12.

CHEF: Judith Bulger PROPRIETORS: Judith and Michael Bulger OPEN: all week 12.30 to 1.45, 7 to 8.45 CLOSED: 1 Oct to 9 Feb MEALS: alc (main courses £6.50 to £18.50). Min £10 D and Sun L SERVICE: not inc, card slips closed CARDS: MasterCard, Visa DETAILS: 40 seats. 12 seats outside. Private parties: 25 main room, 20 private room. Car park. Children's helpings. No music ACCOMMODATION: 9 rooms, 7 with bath/shower. TV. Phone. B&B £25 to £90. Baby facilities (*The Which? Hotel Guide*) (£5)

▲ *means accommodation is available.*

All entries in the Guide are re-researched and rewritten every year, not least because restaurant standards fluctuate. Don't rely on an out-of-date Guide.

ARISAIG Highland map 11

▲ Arisaig House

Beasdale, by Arisaig PH39 4NR
TEL: (01687) 450622 FAX: (01687) 450626
EMAIL: arisaighse@aol.com
WEB SITE: www.arisaighouse.co.uk
on A830, 3m E of Arisaig, 1m from Beasdale station

COOKING **6**
FRANCO-SCOTTISH
£38–£65

A clock on the roof of this fine granite hotel, set in a charming location by a loch, runs slow, as if to indicate that 'life here is, quite sensibly, a few minutes behind the rest of the world'. There is nothing to show the cooking dragging its feet, however: the four-course dinner menu offers a handsome, up-to-date selection of locally sourced Scottish fish and game peppered with the likes of rocket, pesto and aged Balsamic vinegar. Among starters might be prime Scotch beef given the carpaccio treatment with chilled oyster cream and Parmesan tuiles, a navarin of local seafood infused with saffron, and a more traditional 'deeply flavoursome' game terrine.

The second course is sorbet, salad or soup, the latter perhaps of Jerusalem artichoke with truffle oil. Splendid beef fillet with a 'basso profundo' red wine sauce might come next, or maybe halibut with sun-dried tomatoes, toasted pine kernels and garden greens. Dark chocolate fondant with pistachio ice cream, and apple tart with calvados ice cream have been successful desserts. An extensive, globe-trotting wine list has plenty of fine clarets for those who can afford to splash out, while house wines start at £14.50 and there are eight wines by the glass.

CHEF: Duncan Gibson PROPRIETORS: John, Ruth and Andrew Smither, and Alison WIlkinson OPEN: all week 12.30 to 2, 7.30 to 8.30 CLOSED: Dec to Feb MEALS: Set L £25, Set D £39.50. Bar meals available SERVICE: not inc, card slips closed CARDS: MasterCard, Switch, Visa DETAILS: 32 seats. 12 seats outside. Car park. Vegetarian meals. No children under 10. No smoking in dining room. No music ACCOMMODATION: 12 rooms, all with bath/shower. TV. Phone. B&B £125 to £290 (*The Which? Hotel Guide*)

AUCHMITHIE Angus map 11

But 'n' Ben £

Auchmithie DD11 5SQ
TEL: (01241) 877223 FAX: (01241) 430901
on coast, 3m NE of Arbroath, off A92

COOKING **2**
SEAFOOD/TRADITIONAL SCOTTISH
£17–£38

Waves crash on the craggy shore below Auchmithie and can be enjoyed from the dining room of the Horns' homely restaurant. A quarter of a century in the business has not dulled their enthusiasm for traditional Scottish cooking with an emphasis on seasonality. Arbroath is but a hop down the coast, and its fabled smokies turn up in many guises on the menus: in pancakes, flans and mousses. There are Loch Fyne oysters and mussels too (the latter done in white wine and garlic), rainbow trout pan-fried in butter and almonds, and Aberdeen Angus steaks with a choice of peppercorns: crushed black, or whole green with cream. Afters are served from a trolley, and coffee comes with rum and coconut truffles.

The short wine list keeps prices sensible, even for the fine wine section. House French is £9.50.

CHEFS: Angus and Margaret Horn PROPRIETORS: Margaret, Iain and Angus Horn OPEN: Wed to Mon L 12 to 2.30, Wed to Sat and Mon D 7 to 10 CLOSED: 1 Jan MEALS: alc (main courses £5.50 to £13.50) SERVICE: not inc, card slips closed CARDS: Amex, Delta, Diners, MasterCard, Switch, Visa DETAILS: 40 seats. Private parties: 40 main room. Car park. Vegetarian meals. Children's helpings. No smoking in dining room. Wheelchair access (also WC). No music (£5)

AUCHTERARDER Perthshire & Kinross — map 11

▲ Auchterarder House

Auchterarder PH3 1DZ
TEL: (01764) 663646 FAX: (01764) 662939
EMAIL: auchterarder@wrensgroup.com
WEB SITE: www.wrensgroup.com

COOKING **2**
MODERN SCOTTISH
£27–£63

Owned by the same group as Cringletie House (see entry, Peebles), and as baronial as one would expect of a mansion set in seventeen acres just two miles from Gleneagles, Auchterarder takes a similarly refined and labour-intensive approach to cooking. Pink breast of milk-fed pigeon, for example, has been served on a little roulade of duck and Parma ham, with baby vegetables and a sherry vinegar sauce. And that's just a starter. Loins of lamb or venison typically share the main-course stage (there are usually two choices) with fish: perhaps cod with rocket pesto in puff pastry on a champagne and caviar sauce.

Any questions about value are answered by a lunch menu that might start with a warm mosaic of quail and pied de mouton mushrooms with truffle and foie gras, progress to grilled John Dory fillets with langoustine tortellini, and finish with sticky toffee pudding served with prune and calvados ice cream. An elegant and concise list concentrates on fine wines from France but pitches enough bins from the New World to satisfy less traditional palates. House wines start at £16.50.

CHEF: Willie Deans PROPRIETOR: Wren's Hotel Group OPEN: all week 12 to 2, 7 to 9.30 MEALS: Set L Mon to Sat £16.50, Set L Sun £18.50, Set D £39.50 SERVICE: not inc CARDS: Amex, Delta, Diners, MasterCard, Switch, Visa DETAILS: 70 seats. Private parties: 70 main room, 20 and 30 private rooms. Car park. No children under 12. Jacket and tie. No smoking in dining room. Occasional music ACCOMMODATION: 15 rooms, all with bath/shower. TV. Phone. B&B £125 to £350. No children under 12 (*The Which? Hotel Guide*)

'The "napkin" looked like and had the texture of a duster, so on the principle that if something looks like a duck and quacks like a duck, it probably is a duck, then I believe that we had dusters rather than napkins.' (On eating in London)

The text of entries is based on unsolicited reports sent in by readers, backed up by inspections conducted anonymously. The factual details under the text are from questionnaires the Guide sends to all restaurants that feature in the book.

AULDEARN Highland map 11

▲ Boath House

Auldearn IV12 5LE
TEL: (01667) 454896 FAX: (01667) 455469
EMAIL: wendy@boath-house.demon.co.uk
WEB SITE: www.boath-house.com
on A96, 2m E of Nairn

COOKING 5
FRANCO-SCOTTISH
£28–£45

Set back from the main road, this Georgian mansion, built in the 1820s and set in 20 acres, could easily be mistaken for a stately home, at least from outside. The dining room, which looks out on lawns and an ornamental lake, has had perhaps the most sympathetic refurbishment, sporting a marble fireplace, crystal candlesticks and white damask cloths. The kitchen is a busy one, making good use of local resources (including its own garden in summer), and menus are intelligent and well balanced.

Presentation is a strong suit and, at their best, dishes are full of both interest and flavour, among them a 'star' soup of butternut squash and carrot sprinkled with roasted seeds, and carpaccio of tuna with a crust of oriental herbs and spices and a sweet chilli dressing. Standards can see-saw a little, but among successes have been first-rate tender pink Aberdeen Angus beef fillet with a Madeira and thyme sauce, and a couple of desserts: a 'wondrous' passion-fruit sorbet accompanying a simple, classic crème brûlée, and a 'sumptuous' chocolate truffle and blackberry torte with an intriguingly flavoured pumpkin sorbet. Bread is a highlight too, and service from the owners and helpers is friendly, efficient and unobtrusive. Wines under £20 account for nearly half of the 100-strong list, including six house selections from £10.75, and quality and value are good across the board.

CHEF: Charles Lockley PROPRIETORS: Don and Wendy Matheson OPEN: Thur to Sun L 12.30 to 2, Wed to Sun D 7 to 9 MEALS: Set L £18.95, Set D £27.50 SERVICE: not inc CARDS: Amex, Delta, MasterCard, Switch, Visa DETAILS: 36 seats. Private parties: 28 main room, 8 private room. Car park. Vegetarian meals. Children's helpings. No smoking in dining room. Wheelchair access (also WC). Occasional music ACCOMMODATION: 6 rooms, all with bath/shower. TV. Phone. Rooms for disabled. Baby facilities. Fishing (*The Which? Hotel Guide*) (£5)

AYR South Ayrshire map 11

Fouters Bistro

2A Academy Street, Ayr KA7 1HS
TEL: (01292) 261391 FAX: (01292) 619323
EMAIL: qualityfood@fouters.co.uk
WEB SITE: www.fouters.co.uk

COOKING 3
MODERN SCOTTISH
£20–£47

Now decorated in bright terracotta, blue and white, this cellar bistro-restaurant is turning increasingly to the Mediterranean for inspiration. Native ingredients remain the foundation, from lamb and beef to fish and game, producing steamed Shetland mussels, Carrick venison in juniper sauce, and chargrilled fillet and sirloin steaks. While conventional chicken liver pâté, or Gressingham duck with a port sauce, are still central to the repertoire, there is usually a more exotic option available, such as Hebridean salmon with couscous and a provençale sauce. Desserts plough a more traditional furrow in the form of lemon tart or bread-and-butter pudding, as do most of the 40-plus wines, which start with house French at £12.95.

CHEFS: Laurie Black and Laurent Labede PROPRIETORS: Laurie and Fran Black OPEN: Mon to Sat 12 to 2, 5.30 to 10 CLOSED: 25 and 26 Dec, 1 to 3 Jan MEALS: alc (main courses L £5 to £10, D £8 to £14.50) SERVICE: not inc CARDS: Amex, Diners, MasterCard, Switch, Visa DETAILS: 38 seats. Private parties: 20 main room, 20 private room. Children's helpings. No smoking in 1 dining room. Music. Air-conditioned (£5)

BALLATER Aberdeenshire map 11

▲ Balgonie Country House

Braemar Place, Ballater AB35 5NQ — COOKING **3**
TEL/FAX: (013397) 55482 — MODERN SCOTTISH
off A93, on W outskirts of Ballater — £30–£51

Built in the early 1900s in four acres on the edge of the village, Balgonie is furnished in period character, its tasteful dining room decorated in soft pastel colours. A straightforward four-course dinner menu, soundly based on good materials, might offer local partridge on shallot Tatin, or fillet of Aberdeen Angus with lyonnaise potatoes in a red Burgundy sauce. After vegetable soup, chicken liver parfait, or occasionally a more unusual item such as Clonakilty black pudding topped with a poached quail's egg, comes a second course of maybe chicken-filled spring roll, or deep-fried salmon fishcake.

Herbs are used to aromatise sauces – tarragon cream for chicken breast on crisp polenta cake, rosemary jus for braised veal – and desserts tend towards richness in the shape of chocolate sponge pudding served with whisky parfait, or banana and coconut chiboust cream in a nougatine box. Around 50 wines span a good range of styles and prices, starting at £16.75, with six offered by the glass.

CHEF/PROPRIETOR: John G. Finnie OPEN: all week 12.30 to 2 (reservations only), 7 to 9 CLOSED: 5 Jan to 10 Feb MEALS: Set L £18.50, Set D £30 SERVICE: not inc, card slips closed CARDS: Amex, Delta, Diners, MasterCard, Switch, Visa DETAILS: 30 seats. Private parties: 30 main room. Car park. Children's helpings. No smoking in dining room. No music ACCOMMODATION: 9 rooms, all with bath/shower. TV. Phone. B&B £50 to £115. Baby facilities (*The Which? Hotel Guide*) (£5)

Net prices *in the details at the end of an entry indicates that the prices given on a menu and on a bill are inclusive of VAT and service charge, and that this practice is clearly stated on menu and bill.*

'The GFG certainly seems to have got their number as far as the cooking is concerned (the décor and atmosphere is another matter - or can't you bring yourself to be as rude as honesty would entail?)' (On eating in the Midlands)

▲ Darroch Learg

SCOTLAND GFG 2001 COMMENDED

Braemar Road, Ballater AB35 5UX
TEL: (013397) 55443 FAX: (013397) 55252
EMAIL: nigel@darroch-learg.demon.co.uk
WEB SITE: www.darroch-learg.demon.co.uk
off A93 Ballater to Braemar Road at western edge of village

COOKING **6**
MODERN SCOTTISH
£30–£54

Views from the stylish conservatory-style dining room of this nineteenth-century country house extend over Ballater and Deeside, which would be a draw even without the talented David Mutter at the stoves. Dinner is where the energy is concentrated, in three courses with half a dozen choices for each. The first majors on liver and shellfish in classic French fashion, and materials are sourced from the top end of the market. Foie gras, for example, might turn up in a parfait with chicken livers, accompanied by fig jam, or as a hefty chunk encased in pasta, served with onion jam and pesto-dotted Parmesan cream, to produce an inspector's 'best dish of the year'. Well-flavoured tortellini of crab and langoustine with shellfish sauce is another outstanding starter, and smoked haddock has also triumphed, served in a velouté with Jersey Royal potatoes

Remarkably few disappointments are registered in the dishes reported on, suggesting that they are carefully honed before taking their place in the repertoire, among them celeriac and truffle oil soup; breast of duck with asparagus, white haricot beans, a boudin and a rich truffle cream sauce; and fillet of veal with potato and butternut squash gratin, lentils and a gently sage-infused sauce. Fish also impresses for both freshness and accuracy of cooking. To finish, the dish to go for is apparently a huge plateful of house desserts including mini lemon tart, hazelnut terrine, intense chocolate tear, crème caramel and plum ravioli, all described in superlatives. Service from Nigel Franks and staff is charming, attentive, and not only friendly but child-friendly. Lovers of New World wines will enjoy the Australian, New Zealand and Californian sections on a list that covers most major wine-producing countries, while traditionalists will be reassured with top bins from Bordeaux, Burgundy and the Rhône. The mark-up policy is such that it pays to drink more expensively, which is just as well since there is very little under £15.

CHEF: David Mutter PROPRIETORS: the Franks family OPEN: all week 12.30 to 2, 7 to 9 CLOSED: Christmas, Jan (open New Year) MEALS: Set L £19.50, Set D £33. Light L available Mon to Sat SERVICE: net prices, card slips closed CARDS: Amex, Delta, Diners, MasterCard, Switch, Visa DETAILS: 48 seats. 10 seats outside. Private parties: 62 main room. Car park. Vegetarian meals. Children's helpings. No smoking in dining room. Wheelchair access (not WC). No music ACCOMMODATION: 18 rooms, all with bath/shower. TV. Phone. D,B&B £73 to £204. Rooms for disabled. Baby facilities (*The Which? Hotel Guide*)

The cuisine styles noted at the tops of entries are only an approximation, often suggested to us by the restaurants themselves. Please read the entry itself to find out more about the cooking style.

▲ Green Inn 🍷

9 Victoria Road, Ballater AB35 5QQ
TEL/FAX: (013397) 55701

COOKING **5**
MODERN SCOTTISH
£41–£49

The big, square, cottagey dining room is awash with pastel colours and crammed with tables, and if it is not bang up to date – one visitor felt 'transported back 15 or 20 years' – the food makes amends by combining a traditional Scottish approach with a few more contemporary ideas. Haggis, for example, is made into a mousse and stuffed inside guinea-fowl breast, and prune and frangipane flan comes with a whisky ice cream. Materials indicate good sourcing, from local wild venison via dived scallops to foie gras, served with a stickily sweet shallot and raisin sauce. First-class fish has impressed particularly, for both quality and timing, including turbot (with potato galette in a fine stock and white wine sauce) and halibut (with scallops in a tomato and basil sauce).

There is a sense that some dishes may not integrate components as well as they might, as an inspector found with a starter of flavourful duck accompanied by black pudding, apple purée and soy sauce. Although a few other items let down an inspection meal, reporters have been quick to praise twice-baked cheese soufflé, and roast partridge on a bed of cabbage leaves with root vegetables, mushrooms and a Riesling sauce. Finish with steamed syrup sponge or cappuccino crème brûlée. A well-balanced and classy selection of wines combines fine clarets (Chateau Talbot 1985 is fairly priced at £56.10), with inspiring bottles from Austria, Spain and the New World. Four house wines start at £11.60.

CHEF: Jeffrey Purves PROPRIETORS: Jeffrey and Carol Purves OPEN: all week D only 7 to 9 CLOSED: 2 weeks Oct, Sun and Mon Oct to March MEALS: Set D £26.50 (2 courses) to £31 SERVICE: not inc, card slips closed CARDS: Amex, Diners, MasterCard, Switch, Visa DETAILS: 32 seats. Private parties: 8 main room. Children's helpings. No smoking while others eat. Wheelchair access (not WC). Music. Air-conditioned ACCOMMODATION: 3 rooms, all with bath/shower. TV. D,B&B £60 to £119. Baby facilities (£5)

BALQUHIDDER Stirling **map 11**

▲ Monachyle Mhor

Balquhidder FK19 8PQ
TEL: (01877) 384622 FAX: (01877) 384305
EMAIL: monachylemhorhotel@balquhidder.freeserve.co.uk
WEB SITE: www.monachylemhor.com

COOKING **4**
MODERN SCOTTISH
£24–£46

Stunning scenery surrounds this country-estate hotel, a world away from metropolitan bustle. A walled garden, where guests are free to wander, is where many of Tom Lewis's vegetables and herbs come from, and game is locally shot. The cooking has grown grander by degrees in recent years, and is all the more appreciated by many for that. One reporter began a gamey autumn dinner with tender grouse breasts accompanied by a generous lump of foie gras before proceeding to an impeccable main course of guinea fowl.

Fish dishes, too, have pleased, such as seared scallops with braised chard and lemon grass, and lemon sole on a bed of spinach with fennel and Noilly Prat sauce. Bitter chocolate tart to finish has been 'disgracefully decadent', served with two fine home-made ice creams, one chocolate and walnut, the other brown bread and cinnamon. Service is thoroughly obliging. The classically inclined wine list does the bulk of its business in France. Look to Australia and Chile for price relief, or to a house wine selection that starts at £9.30.

CHEF: Tom Lewis PROPRIETORS: Rob, Jean and Tom Lewis OPEN: all week 12 to 2, 7 to 8.45 MEALS: alc (main courses £8 to £15). Set L £17.50, Set D £29. Snacks available 2 to 4 SERVICE: not inc, card slips closed CARDS: Delta, MasterCard, Switch, Visa DETAILS: 40 seats. 20 seats outside. Private parties: 40 main room, 14 and 20 private rooms. Car park. Vegetarian meals. Children's helpings. No children under 8. No smoking in dining room. Wheelchair access (also WC). No music ACCOMMODATION: 10 rooms, all with bath/shower. TV. Phone. B&B £45 to £90. Baby facilities. Fishing (*The Which? Hotel Guide*)

BLAIR ATHOLL Perthshire & Kinross **map 11**

Loft

Blair Atholl, by Pitlochry PH18 5TE — COOKING **2**
TEL: (01796) 481377 — MODERN SCOTTISH/MEDITERRANEAN
FAX: (01796) 481511 — £28–£41

Occupying a nineteenth-century loft at the corner of a short terrace of stone houses, this hotel and spa complex misses no opportunity to offer a bite to eat, from snacks and light lunches in the conservatory and on the roof terrace overlooking the swimming pool, to a fully fledged dining room. If décor hints at the Côte d'Azur, so too does the food, offering gazpacho with roast Mediterranean vegetables, and seared tuna with pesto creamed potatoes and provençale vegetables. Since the last edition of the Guide Graham Horne has moved up from sous chef to oversee the whole show, adding sweetcorn and mascarpone ravioli with truffle oil and wild mushrooms to more mainstream ideas such as roast loin of lamb with aubergine and fennel confit. Finish perhaps with chocolate tart served with raspberry coulis and cinnamon ice cream. The wine list claims to be 'growing by the week' and now extends to around 30 global bins, with about a dozen fine clarets and Burgundies. House Australian is £9.50.

CHEF: Graham Horne PROPRIETORS: Mrs P.M. Richardson and family OPEN: all week 12 to 2, 6 to 9 CLOSED: Mon to Thur Jan to Mar MEALS: alc (main courses £12 to £15). Set L Sun £6.95 (2 courses). Light L available SERVICE: not inc CARDS: Amex, Delta, MasterCard, Switch, Visa DETAILS: 56 seats. 30 seats outside. Private parties: 56 main room, 22 to 34 private rooms. Car park. Vegetarian meals. Children's helpings. No smoking in 1 dining room. Music. Air-conditioned

---

'If you could give just the slightest hint in the entry that this is the place to go if you're a pretentious gourmet nincompoop, that would be nice'. (On eating in Wales)

indicates that smoking is either banned altogether or that a dining-room is maintained for non-smokers. The symbol does not apply to restaurants that simply have no-smoking areas.

BLAIRGOWRIE Perthshire & Kinross map 11

▲ Kinloch House

Blairgowrie PH10 6SG
TEL: (01250) 884237 FAX: (01250) 884333
EMAIL: reception@kinlochhouse.com
WEB SITE: www.kinlochhouse.com
on A923, 3m W of Blairgowrie towards Dunkeld

COOKING **4**
SCOTTISH
£22–£55

Immaculate housekeeping and top-quality service are part of the draw at this ivy-covered stone-built Victorian house dating back to 1840, whose 25 acres and oak-panelled hall set the scene for a comfortable and relaxing time. Supplies are taken seriously, including locally butchered Aberdeen Angus beef, free-range poultry and eggs, and vegetables from the walled garden. Dishes on the four-course set-price menu can be exchanged for items on the Scottish menu (such as whisky-marinated salmon or Arbroath smokies), or supplemented by regularly appearing Kyle of Lochalsh scallops and prawns, or steak three ways, all for an extra charge.

Butter and alcohol often play a starring role in sauces, and game features prominently in winter: perhaps fillet of hare with red cabbage, partridge stuffed with wild mushrooms, or pigeon breasts topped with a 'bagel-like' Yorkshire pudding crust and served with pea purée. Vegetables might be improved, but the kitchen has also turned out 'perfectly cooked and executed' smoked haddock risotto with asparagus, and tarte Tatin with a buttery caramel ice cream. Classed-growth clarets feature strongly on the friendly wine list, which combines serious bottles with simple write-ups. France is given full attention though choice bins from the New World provide sound alternatives. Half-bottles are well-priced and plentiful. House wines start at £14.95.

CHEF: Bill McNicoll PROPRIETORS: the Shentall family OPEN: Sun L 12.30 to 2, all week D 7 to 9.15 MEALS: alc L (main courses £5.50 to £11.50). Set L £17.50, Set D £34.50. Bar L available all week SERVICE: none, card slips closed CARDS: Amex, Delta, Diners, MasterCard, Switch, Visa DETAILS: 55 seats. Private parties: 50 main room, 16 private room. Car park. Vegetarian meals. Children's helpings. No children under 7 in dining room. Jacket and tie. No smoking in dining room. Wheelchair access (also WC). No music ACCOMMODATION: 20 rooms, all with bath/shower. TV. Phone. D,B&B £101 to £260. Rooms for disabled. Baby facilities. Swimming pool. Fishing (*The Which? Hotel Guide*)

BOWMORE Argyll & Bute map 11

▲ Harbour Inn

The Square, Bowmore PA43 7JR
TEL: (01496) 810330 FAX: (01496) 810990
EMAIL: harbour@harbour-inn.com
WEB SITE: www.harbour-inn.com

COOKING **2**
MODERN EUROPEAN
£26–£56

Last year we reported that Scott Chance had won the much-coveted World Porridge-Making title, and this year he has won it again. Of course, you will have to stay over and take breakfast at this small, well-run inn on Islay in order to avail yourself. Those visiting for lunch or dinner may instead enjoy robust starters of flash-fried woodcock with smoked bacon and orange, or roast fillet of hare in a potato and celeriac 'mille-feuille', followed perhaps by stir-fried monkfish with a ginger glaze, or lamb's liver and Stornoway black pudding on onion soubise. The local 17-year-old single malt goes into a chocolate gâteau, or it can be taken straight from the extensive listing of whiskies. An imaginative, fairly priced wine list kicks off with house French at £9.95.

CHEF: Scott Chance PROPRIETORS: Scott and Wendy Chance OPEN: all week 12 to 2.30, 6 to 9 CLOSED: Sun Oct to Easter MEALS: alc (main courses £10.50 to £24) SERVICE: not inc CARDS: Amex, Delta, MasterCard, Switch, Visa DETAILS: 44 seats. Private parties: 40 main room. Vegetarian meals. Children's helpings. No smoking in dining room. Wheelchair access (also men's WC). No music ACCOMMODATION: 8 rooms, all with bath/shower. TV. Phone. B&B £37.50 to £60. Rooms for disabled. Baby facilities (*The Which? Hotel Guide*) (£5)

CAIRNDOW Argyll & Bute — **map 11**

Loch Fyne Oyster Bar £

Clachan, Cairndow PA26 8BH — COOKING **2**
TEL: (01499) 600236 FAX: (01499) 600234 — TRADITIONAL SEAFOOD
on A83, at head of Loch Fyne — £21–£42

The converted cow byre at the head of the loch represents many people's idea of just what a seafood restaurant should be. A shop sells a wide range of take-away items, and the dining room and conservatory aim to serve up simple plates of smoked salmon, oysters and mixed shellfish, keeping the cooking to a minimum. It is rarely more complicated than mussels marinière, queen scallops with garlic butter, or a daily dish from the board such as 'fresh and crisply pan-fried' trout. Reports and an inspection, however, suggest that the kitchen has been pushed to meet even such simple aims with customary success: materials and handling have been below par, and service has not been up to the standard of previous years either. The advice is to make for the simplest items of all – strongly smoked roast bradan orach is 'uniquely moreish' – and don't expect large portions. Finish perhaps with apple crumble or a well-chosen Scottish cheese, and consider the wine list's advice to drink sharp Gros Plant (£10.95) with oysters.

CHEFS: Morag Keith and Tracy Wyatt PROPRIETORS: John Noble and Andrew Lane OPEN: all week 9 to 9 (9 to 6 Mon to Fri Nov to March) CLOSED: 25 and 26 Dec, 1 and 2 Jan MEALS: alc (main courses £6 to £13) SERVICE: not inc CARDS: Amex, Delta, Diners, MasterCard, Switch, Visa DETAILS: 120 seats. Private parties: 40 main room, 40 private room. Car park. Vegetarian meals. Children's helpings. No smoking in dining room. Wheelchair access (also WC). Occasional music

The 2002 Guide will be published before Christmas 2001. Reports on meals are most welcome at any time of the year, but are particularly valuable in the spring (no later than June). Send them to The Good Food Guide, *FREEPOST, 2 Marylebone Road, London NW1 4DF. Or email your report to goodfoodguide@which.net*

indicates that there has been a change of chef since last year's Guide, and the Editor has judged that the change is of sufficient interest to merit the reader's attention.

CLACHAN-SEIL Argyll & Bute — map 11

▲ Willowburn Hotel

NEW ENTRY

Clachan-Seil, Isle of Seil PA34 4TJ
TEL: 01852 300276 FAX: 01852 300597
EMAIL: willowburn.hotel@virgin.net
WEB SITE: www.willowburn.co.uk
from Oban take A816 S for 8m; then take B844, following signs for Seil Island and Luing, for 7m; after hump-backed bridge Willowburn is 400m on left

COOKING **2**
MODERN SCOTTISH
£33–£40

The long, low-lying bungalow is a small, friendly hotel with above-average, keenly-priced food for these parts. It boasts a chintzy lounge for drinks, a few watercolours, and rare conversational pieces including a couple of dinosaur bones. Four-course meals plus coffee might start with a terrine of Dunsyre Blue cheese, followed by a punchy elderberry and beer sorbet or a cream-enriched pea and pear soup. Seafood offerings extend to prawns, lobster and crab (perhaps baked in a herb and cheese crust) from the waters between Corryvreckan and Mull, as well as native Angus beef (stuffed with cheese on a whisky cream sauce) and roast rack of richly flavoured hill farmed lamb, which has been served unusually as a first course. Vegetables come from local market gardeners and the hotel's own plot, although an inspector felt the kitchen didn't get the best out of them. Desserts on the other hand are a high point, running to a fine honey and Lagavulin ice cream, and a swan shaped meringue with chocolate and a well-judged strawberry coulis. A fair choice of wines under £20 starts with five house wines at £9.95.

CHEF: Chris Mitchell PROPRIETORS: Chris Mitchell and Jan Wolfe OPEN: all week D only 7 to 8 CLOSED: Jan and Feb MEALS: Set D £25 SERVICE: not inc, card slips closed CARDS: Delta, MasterCard, Switch, Visa DETAILS: 24 seats. Private parties: 10 main room. Car park. Vegetarian meals. Children's helpings. No smoking in dining room. Music ACCOMMODATION: 7 rooms, all with bath/shower. TV. D,B&B £58 to £116. Baby facilities (*The Which? Hotel Guide*) (£5)

COLBOST Highland — map 11

▲ Three Chimneys

SCOTLAND GFG 2001 COMMENDED

Colbost, by Dunvegan, Isle of Skye IV55 8ZT
TEL: (01470) 511258 FAX: (01470) 511358
EMAIL: eatandstay@threechimneys.co.uk
WEB SITE: www.threechimneys.co.uk
on B884, 4m W of Dunvegan

COOKING **5**
MODERN SCOTTISH
£31–£73

The Spears and their staff create a friendly atmosphere at this brace of white-painted crofters' cottages next to the Colbost Folk Museum. The rustic tone set by sympathetic restoration, stone walls, rough plaster and simply laid bare wooden tables is appreciated as much as the accommodation, where 'beds are on raised platforms so you can see the sea'. Among local produce to feature is an enviable range of seafood that might appear as twice-baked Bracadale crab soufflé, grilled Skye cod with tapénade and basil mash, or sweet, firm langoustines caught that morning, in a salad made with dressed organic leaves from Glendale (three miles away).

As avid campaigners for Skye's produce, the Spears set an example with their fillet of well-hung Highland beef in a mushroom and Madeira sauce, and loin of lamb accompanied by curly kale mash and honey roast roots. Prices may be considered high (and there is usually a supplement or two), but the three-course deal includes desserts such as dark chocolate tart with white chocolate sauce, and warm plum torte with spiced plum sauce and cinnamon ice cream. Plenty of wines under £20 are included on the elegantly compiled list, which features France, Germany, Italy and the New World, plus a fine Old Wine selection at the back highlighting one or two lesser vintages for those who like to gamble. House white from Tuscany is £14.25.

CHEF: Shirley Spear PROPRIETORS: Eddie and Shirley Spear OPEN: Mon to Sat L 12.30 to 2.30 (phone to check L times in winter), all week D 6.30 to 9.30 CLOSED: 3 weeks Jan MEALS: Set L £12.50 (2 courses) to £19.95, Set D £24 (2 courses) to £34.95 SERVICE: not inc CARDS: Amex, Delta, MasterCard, Switch, Visa DETAILS: 32 seats. 6 seats outside. Private parties: 21 main room, 21 to 60 private rooms. Car park. Vegetarian meals. Children's helpings. No smoking in dining room. Wheelchair access (not WC). No music ACCOMMODATION: 6 rooms, all with bath/shower. TV. Phone. B&B £95 to £140. Rooms for disabled. Baby facilities (*The Which? Hotel Guide*) (£5)

CUPAR Fife **map 11**

Ostlers Close 🍷

25 Bonnygate, Cupar KY15 4BU — COOKING **5**
TEL: (01334) 655574 — MODERN SCOTTISH
WEB SITE: www.ostlersclose.co.uk — £25–£57

If a degree of inertia seems to be creeping over the operation, it may be because the Grahams have spent 20 years in this small stone-built cottage. The atmosphere usually has a buzz about it (although nobody would object if the décor had an overhaul), and if some dishes go back a decade or more, it is the job of daily specials to ring the changes: perhaps pig's trotter stuffed with oxtail on a richly flavoured red wine sauce. The foundation of properly sourced materials remains as important as ever, and the kitchen is well stocked with organic vegetables, free-range ducks, dived scallops (seared and served with sweet potato risotto for one reporter), potato varieties grown specially for them, local game in season, fresh fish ('a cracking piece of monkfish'), home-grown herbs, well-hung beef, and rare-breed lamb.

A number of different vegetables (identical whatever the main course) are served on a side plate, perhaps including a spinach cream tart, or courgettes with tomato. Presentation is not a strong point, and desserts are not a highlight. 'We enjoyed a good meal, but not a memorable meal,' sums up the tone of reports. Service is friendly, and wines are an unpretentious selection of just over 100 bottles from around the world. The handwritten list includes helpful tasting notes and recommendations. There are numerous half-bottles, and Chilean house wines start at £11.50 for Concha y Toro Chardonnay.

CHEF: James Graham PROPRIETORS: James and Amanda Graham OPEN: Tue, Fri and Sat L 12.15 to 2, Tue to Sat D 7 to 9.30 CLOSED: 25 to 26 Dec, 1 and 2 Jan MEALS: alc (main courses L £9 to £12.50, D £15.50 to £18.50) SERVICE: not inc, card slips closed CARDS: Amex, Delta, MasterCard, Switch, Visa DETAILS: 28 seats. Private parties: 22 main room. Children's helpings. No children under 6 at D. No smoking while others eat. No music (£5)

DALRY North Ayrshire **map 11**

Braidwoods

Drumastle Mill Cottage, Dalry KA24 4LN
TEL: (01294) 833544 FAX: (01294) 833553 — COOKING **6**
1m off A737 on Dalry to Saltcoats road — MODERN SCOTTISH
WEB SITE: www.braidwoods.co.uk — £26–£48

Against a peaceful rural background, Keith and Nicola Braidwood ply a dedicated trade in a pair of converted, whitewashed millers' cottages. Locally sourced produce plays a key role in a repertoire that stays with dishes it knows well, and the contemporary style is simple and uncluttered. Dinner, for example, may centre round roast Aberdeen Angus fillet with spinach and wild mushroom jus, or honey-glazed breast and confit leg of Gressingham duck with Arran mustard jus. Choice may be limited, but the options offer variety: starters of Caesar salad, perhaps, or plum tomato and basil risotto with scallops, or foie gras and chicken liver parfait with gooseberry chutney.

The second course is not just a token sorbet either, but a real dish: maybe warm Parmesan tart with leaves and a red pepper coulis, or smoked Finnan haddock and saffron soup. Desserts, meanwhile, have featured crème brûlée (of rhubarb, and banana) as well as a dark chocolate and maple tart, but there is also competition from Iain Mellis cheeses. Around 50 wines cover familiar territory, and eight or so house wines start at £12.95.

CHEFS/PROPRIETORS: Keith and Nicola Braidwood OPEN: Wed to Sun L 12 to 1.45, Tue to Sat D 7 to 9 CLOSED: first 3 weeks Jan, 2 weeks Sept/Oct MEALS: Set L Wed to Sat £14.50 (2 courses) to £17, Set L Sun £18, Set D £27.50 to £30 SERVICE: not inc, card slips closed CARDS: Amex, Delta, Diners, MasterCard, Switch, Visa DETAILS: 24 seats. Private parties: 14 main room. Car park. Children's helpings. No smoking in dining room. No music

DERVAIG Argyll & Bute **map 11**

▲ Druimard Country House

Dervaig, Isle of Mull PA75 6QW
TEL/FAX: (01688) 400345 — COOKING **4**
WEB SITE: www.smoothound.co.uk/hotels/druimard.html — EURO-SCOTTISH
£37–£44

Dervaig, in north-west Mull, can hardly be considered on the way to anywhere, so a visit has to be a special trip. Part of the draw is the view over Glen Bellart, part the Victorian manse itself, part the theatre (around whose opening times meals are arranged when it is in operation), and yet another part the five-course dinners that Wendy Hubbard cooks in homely Euro-Scottish style. Some of Mull's own produce finds its way on to the menu, supplemented by the kitchen's own herbs and salad items in season.

After a starter of salmon tartare, or a puff pastry case of chicken livers, comes a soup or sorbet, then the centrepiece: maybe monkfish with a saffron and mussel sauce, or herb-crusted loin of Scottish lamb with couscous. Dessert is the only course to offer a choice – on one occasion between chocolate creme fraîche torte, vanilla meringues filed with lemon cream, and steamed syrup pudding – and cheese brings down the curtain. Around half the 40 wines are French, and prices are fair, starting with house Côtes de Duras at £9.50.

CHEF: Wendy Hubbard PROPRIETORS: Haydn and Wendy Hubbard OPEN: all week D only 7 (6.30 when theatre playing) to 8.30 CLOSED: Nov to end March MEALS: Set D £28.50 SERVICE: not inc CARDS: MasterCard, Visa DETAILS: 28 seats. Private parties: 20 main room. Car park. Vegetarian meals. Children's helpings. No smoking in dining room. Wheelchair access (not WC). Music ACCOMMODATION: 7 rooms, all with bath/shower. TV. Phone. D,B&B £72 to £152. Rooms for disabled. Baby facilities (*The Which? Hotel Guide*)

DORNOCH Highland map 11

▲ 2 Quail

Castle Street, Dornoch IV25 3SN
TEL: (01862) 811811 COOKING **4**
EMAIL: enquiries@2quail.co.uk MODERN EUROPEAN-PLUS
WEB SITE: www.2quail.co.uk £39–£46

Barely 200 yards from the thirteenth-century cathedral, and not a million miles from the golfing at St Andrews, the Carrs' intimately proportioned restaurant-with-rooms occupies a terrace conversion. Warm hues of ochre and russet predominate within, and there is a heartening resistance to extraneous flounce in both the front-of-house approach and the cooking style. Leek flamiche with bitter salad leaves might set the ball rolling at dinner, or there may be langoustine risotto with crisp-fried ginger and spring onions. A stunning creamy basil risotto with 'contrastingly sharp' tomato sauce has lifted a spring main course of baked salmon; and loin of lamb with roast vegetables, including asparagus, has also been highly rated. Two sweet things are offered alongside cheese with oatcakes, and have included 'truly memorable' pear and ginger sticky upside-down pudding. An adventurous wine list is arranged in price order, beginning with Vins de Pays d'Oc at £13.

CHEF: Michael Carr PROPRIETORS: Michael and Kerensa Carr OPEN: Tue to Sat D only 7.30 to 9.30 CLOSED: 2 weeks Feb to Mar MEALS: Set D £28.50 SERVICE: not inc CARDS: Amex, Delta, MasterCard, Switch, Visa DETAILS: 18 seats. Private parties: 10 main room, 8 and 10 private rooms. Car park. Vegetarian meals. No smoking in 1 dining room. Occasional music ACCOMMODATION: 3 rooms. TV. B&B £25 to £80. No children under 10

Several sharp operators have tried to extort money from restaurateurs on the promise of an entry in a guidebook that has never appeared. The Good Food Guide *makes no charge for inclusion.*

Card slips closed *in the details at the end of an entry indicates that the total on the slips of credit cards is closed when handed over for signature.*

DUNKELD Perthshire & Kinross — map 11

▲ Kinnaird

Kinnaird Estate, Dunkeld PH8 0LB
TEL: (01796) 482440 FAX: (01796) 482289
EMAIL: enquiry@kinnairdestate.com
WEB SITE: www.kinnairdestate.com
from A9 2m N of Dunkeld, take B898, signposted Kinnaird, for 4½m

COOKING **6**
MODERN EUROPEAN
£43–£71

A 'stunning' vista extends from the dining room of this lavishly proportioned, predominantly Edwardian mansion, over beautifully maintained grounds down to the River Tay. Attractive frescoes make the room itself feel light and, given the scale of things (the estate covers 9,000 acres), quite intimate. It still has the air of a grand family home, and is a place to 'relax and savour the good things in life', among them the fruits of Trevor Brooks's kitchen. He relies on small local producers for Black Face lamb and Highland beef (maybe served on a potato and truffle torte), along with spring and summer vegetables, plus game, salmon, trout and eels from the estate. Diver-picked scallops are sourced from Loch Linnhe, perhaps skewered and served with asparagus, and some of the fish comes from Cornwall, for example sea bass, served as a starter with goats' cheese, new potatoes and rocket.

The broadly European thrust of the menu has taken in a thin pastry tart combining plum tomato with basil and olive, main course breast of duck with choucroute, and saddle of hare with maple-roast squash. Desserts maintain the classical impetus with pannacotta, tarte Tatin, and bitter chocolate mousse with caramelised walnuts and coffee ice cream. Service is warm, friendly and courteous. Traditional French wines reign supreme on the classy, though pricey, list. California and Australia offer strong support, but for the odd bottle under £20 (prices start at £18) 'French Country Wines' offer the best option.

CHEF: Trevor Brooks PROPRIETOR: Constance Ward OPEN: all week 12.30 to 1.45, 7.15 to 9.30 CLOSED: Mon to Wed in Jan and Feb MEALS: Set L £30, Set D £45 SERVICE: not inc, card slips closed CARDS: Amex, MasterCard, Switch, Visa DETAILS: 36 seats. Private parties: 30 main room, 16 private room. Car park. Vegetarian meals. No children under 12 in dining room. Jacket and tie. No smoking in dining room. Wheelchair access (also WC). No music ACCOMMODATION: 9 rooms, all with bath/shower. TV. Phone. D,B&B £300 to £440. Rooms for disabled. No children under 12 in accommodation. Fishing (*The Which? Hotel Guide*)

EDINBURGH Edinburgh — map 11

Atrium

10 Cambridge Street, Edinburgh EH1 2ED
TEL: (0131) 228 8882 FAX: (0131) 228 8808

COOKING **2**
MODERN EUROPEAN
£29–£56

Part of a modern office complex close to the Usher Hall and Lyceum and Traverse Theatres, Atrium is considered 'smart to the point of parody, perhaps, but cleverly done'. Railway-sleeper tables have been replaced by better-finished wood, although the desperately inefficient lighting still doesn't make it easy to read the contents of the heavy metal menu holders. Set-price options offer just a couple of choices per course, while the carte is a bit more generous. The style owes much to Italy and the Mediterranean, taking in vitello tonnato, a satisfyingly chunky, chervil-flavoured fish soup, and usually a risotto or two: at inspection a creamy-textured, well-timed chicken-liver version, richly flavoured with stock, cheese and saffron. Some dishes are rather more ambitious than the kitchen can comfortably handle, but it has turned out a creditable raspberry crème brûlée with a faint wobble, crisp glaze, and matching sorbet. Service has varied from 'zany' to 'pretentious'. Wines are well chosen and include fine French classics alongside rising New World stars and some interesting aperitifs. However, mark-ups are high, with little under £20 even on the 'Quick Selection' page. The 'Sommelier's Selection' cannot find anything to recommend below £37. French House wines are 12.50.

CHEF: Neil Forbes PROPRIETORS: Andrew and Lisa Radford OPEN: Mon to Fri L 12 to 2, Mon to Sat D 6.30 to 10 (Mon to Sat 12 to 2.30, 6.30 to 10.30 during Festival) CLOSED: D 24 Dec to 3 Jan MEALS: alc (main courses L £11.50 to £13, D £13.50 to £18.50). Set L £14 (2 courses) to £18, Set D £25. Tasting menu available SERVICE: not inc CARDS: Amex, Delta, Diners, MasterCard, Switch, Visa DETAILS: 65 seats. 100 seats outside. Private parties: 100 main room, 100 private room. Vegetarian meals. Children's helpings. Wheelchair access (also WC). No music. Air-conditioned (£5)

▲ Balmoral, Number One

1 Princes Street, Edinburgh EH2 2EQ — COOKING **5**
TEL: (0131) 557 6727 FAX: (0131) 557 8740 — MODERN EUROPEAN
WEB SITE: www.rfhotels.com — £35–£78

The spacious, red-lacquered, mirrored dining room, housed in the nether regions of the grand hotel by Waverley station, tends to attract a business clientele and is priced accordingly. Nevertheless, it may be viewed as good value, given that Jeff Bland is a talented and confident chef. Among dishes that pleased at inspection were a 'jazzy green' pea and smoked bacon cappuccino soup with a swirl of frothy cream, and an appealingly boozy and lightly spiced terrine of foie gras and Monbazillac jelly. If starters such as salmon and turbot carpaccio with fennel and tomato confit have a contemporary feel, main courses are in largely traditional vein: grilled fillet of beef with bourguignon sauce, or roulade of Dover sole garnished with langoustines and scallops.

The three-course Market Menu provides an attractively priced alternative to the carte and features a roast from the trolley: best end of lamb on Monday, rib of beef on Wednesday. Impressive desserts have included a light, moussey, deeply flavoured chocolate terrine with a tang of fresh orange, and homely creamed rice pudding with apricots. Service is formal but can be 'rather amateurish', and the expensive wine list is not for the faint-hearted, with few bottles below the £20 mark. Wines by the glass are from £4.75.

CHEF: Jeff Bland PROPRIETOR: RF Hotels OPEN: Mon to Fri L 12 to 2, all week D 7 to 10 (10.30 Fri and Sat) MEALS: alc (main courses £20 to £22.50). Set L £16.95 (2 courses) to £19.95, Set D £35 to £50 SERVICE: not inc, 12.5% for parties of 6 or more CARDS: Amex, Diners, MasterCard, Switch, Visa DETAILS: 60 seats. 30 seats outside. Private parties: 80 main room, 6 to 450 private rooms. Vegetarian meals. Children's helpings. No-smoking area. No cigars in restaurant. Music. Air-conditioned ACCOMMODATION: 186 rooms, all with bath/shower. TV. Phone. B&B £153 to £825. Rooms for disabled. Baby facilities. Swimming pool

Blue Bar Café 🍷

Cambridge Street, Edinburgh EH1 2ED
TEL: (0131) 221 1222 FAX: (0131) 228 8808

COOKING **3**
MODERN BRITISH
£21–£46

Sitting above the Atrium (see entry) in the same complex that includes the Traverse Theatre, and next to the Usher Hall, the Blue Bar is certainly in the thick of what's happening. Although the price structure is intended to be gentler than downstairs, there is no stinting on impeccable Scottish produce. 'Blue sausages' are not the latest way-out ingredient, but a selection of house specialities that may well take in Moroccan lamb or beef with ginger and black bean versions. Otherwise, simple and eclectic are the watchwords for David Haetzman; among the lighter starters, seared scallops with cauliflower purée and shiitake mushrooms sit alongside duck spring rolls with sweet chilli syrup.

A certain robustness permeates main courses, whether in salmon with mussels, spaghetti and tomato confit, or more familiar horseradish-crusted ribeye steak with mustard mash. A trio of well-chosen cheeses with walnut bread is offered for those who do not fancy contemporary nursery puddings such as chocolate brownie cake or Malteser ice-cream. Although only one page long, the wine list is cannily selected to offer a wide range of interesting wines at very good prices. There is little over £20 (now that makes a change), and even champagne is competitively priced. Eleven wines are available by the glass, and house wines from Argentina are £11.55.

CHEF: David Haetzman PROPRIETORS: Andrew and Lisa Radford OPEN: Mon to Sat 12 to 3, 6 to 11 (open Sun during Festival) MEALS: alc (main courses £8.50 to £12.50). Set L £9 (2 courses) to £12, Set D Sun to Thur before 7.30 £11 (2 courses) to £14 SERVICE: not inc, 10% for parties of 8 or more CARDS: Amex, Delta, Diners, MasterCard, Switch, Visa DETAILS: 110 seats. Private parties: 110 main room. Vegetarian meals. Children's helpings. No-smoking area. Wheelchair access (also WC). Music. Air-conditioned (£5)

▲ The Bonham

35 Drumsheugh Gardens, Edinburgh EH3 7RN
TEL: (0131) 623 9319 FAX: (0131) 226 6080
EMAIL: restaurant@thebonham.com
WEB SITE: www.thebonham.com

COOKING **4**
MODERN SCOTTISH
£26–£52

A typical Edinburgh townhouse conversion, the Bonham Hotel sports a seriously trendy restaurant that is admired for its taste and minimalism, polished wooden floors, and gigantic mirrors that give it the feel of a larger room. The diverse ingredients and bright combinations of flavours, textures and colours that appear on the menus give clues as to Pelham Hill's globetrotting background. Chickpea, coriander and chilli soup appears alongside smoked haddock kedgeree with toasted brioche for starters, while main courses range from guinea fowl with sweetcorn fritters to rack of lamb on spicy couscous with apricot and mint sauce.

The kitchen does not shirk the burger, offering a chilli version with fries and a garlic and shallot butter on the 'bargain' set-price lunch menu, alongside black olive and basil risotto, niçoise salad with seared rare tuna, and orange and

Cointreau rice pudding. Top-notch coffee is served with brownies, and well-trained waitresses deliver efficient service. The carefully chosen wine list, with its succinct descriptions, includes Canada and Switzerland among more usual global choices. House wine is £13.50 and six wines by the glass are from £3.50.

CHEF: Pelham Hill PROPRIETOR: Peter Taylor OPEN: all week 12 to 2.30, 6.30 to 10 (9.30 Sun) CLOSED: 3 to 7 Jan MEALS: alc (main courses L £6.50 to £8.50, D £13 to £16.50). Set L £13.50 (2 courses) to £16.50 SERVICE: not inc CARDS: Amex, Delta, Diners, MasterCard, Switch, Visa DETAILS: 60 seats. Private parties: 60 main room, 24 private room. Vegetarian meals. No smoking area. Wheelchair access (also WC). Music ACCOMMODATION: 48 rooms, all with bath/shower. TV. Phone. B&B £135 to £295. Rooms for disabled. Baby facilities (*The Which? Hotel Guide*)

Café St-Honoré

34 NW Thistle St Lane, Edinburgh EH2 1EA
TEL: (0131) 226 2211 FAX: (0131) 624 7905

COOKING **1**
MODERN BISTRO
£23–£47

'One could have imagined one was dining in Montmartre,' declared a satisfied visitor to this old stalwart hidden away down a 'funny little lane'. The warmly dark room is done up with distressed mirrors and ornate lamps reminiscent of fin-de-siècle Paris. A long menu strays from typical bistro fare – steak au poivre with frites, or duck confit, for example – into contemporary dishes, or combinations of both, which may include scallop salad with boudin noir and chilli, or cod with couscous. French cheeses mingle with chocolate brownies for afters, and a crème brûlée was up to one diner's exacting standards. Service is 'relaxed'. The lengthy, ungrasping wine list includes a house Pays d'Oc Chardonnay at £9.75.

CHEFS: Chris Colverson and John Winnik PROPRIETORS: Chris and Gill Colverson OPEN: Mon to Fri L 12 to 2.15, Mon to Sat D 5 to 10 (all week L and D during Festival) CLOSED: 1 week Oct, 3 days Christmas, 3 days New Year MEALS: alc L and after 7 D (main courses L £8 to £14.50, D £14 to £17.50). Set D 5 to 7 £9 (2 courses) to £18 SERVICE: not inc, 10% for parties of 8 or more CARDS: Amex, Delta, Diners, MasterCard, Switch, Visa DETAILS: 56 seats. Private parties: 40 main room, 14 to 26 private rooms. Vegetarian meals. Children's helpings. No smoking in 1 dining room. Wheelchair access (not WC). Music

Fishers £

1 The Shore, Leith, Edinburgh EH6 6QW
TEL/FAX: (0131) 554 5666

COOKING **2**
INTERNATIONAL SEAFOOD
£23–£42

A former pub at one end of the waterfront in Leith, Fishers consists of a dark, bustling bar and a lighter, calmer restaurant that overlooks the shore. Appropriately for the location, there is plenty of seafood on the menu, and much of it impresses. Artful timing and impeccable fish lifted a starter tart of smoked haddock and oyster mushrooms out of the ordinary. Some dishes would be better appreciated by reporters if they were simpler: 'beautifully fresh' grilled turbot with ginger and orange hollandaise is about as straightforward as it gets.

Otherwise, there may be a fashionable pairing of scallops and black pudding, which won over a doubter, though its accompaniments of banana and a dressing of spiced rum, passion fruit and habañero chillies tended to upset the balance a bit. Non-fishy options have included a rich terrine of chicken, pigeon and pistachios with caramelised orange and rosemary jus. Finish more simply with something like peach ice cream in a brandy-snap basket. Hard-pressed service manages to cope well. Wines are an exciting global range, selectively annotated and carefully chosen to suit all palates and prices. Nine are available by the glass, and two pages of fine wines include Australia's Penfolds Grange. House French starts at £9.75.

CHEFS: Mary Walker and Brendan Sugars PROPRIETORS: Graeme Lumsden and James Millar OPEN: all week 12 to 10.30 CLOSED: 25 and 26 Dec, 1 and 2 Jan MEALS: alc (main courses £9 to £15) SERVICE: not inc CARDS: Amex, Diners, MasterCard, Switch, Visa DETAILS: 46 seats. 20 seats outside. Private parties: 30 main room. Vegetarian meals. Wheelchair access (not WC). Music

Haldanes

39A Albany Street, Edinburgh EH1 3QY
TEL: (0131) 556 8407 FAX: (0131) 556 2662
EMAIL: gkelso1547@aol.com
WEB SITE: www.haldanesrestaurant.com

COOKING **3**
MODERN SCOTTISH
£25–£57

Haldanes, in the basement of a Georgian-built hotel, is an elegant place to dine, its décor more in keeping with an opulent country house (complete with small walled garden) than its city-centre location would suggest. Prime Scottish produce is the backbone of the set-price menus, which might offer Shetland crab cake with a vegetable salsa and chilli dressing, or roast Pentland pheasant served with a red wine, bacon and shallot sauce. A Highland element is evident in the cooking too – a starter of haggis baked in filo is accompanied by roast turnips and a whisky sauce, for example – while beef fillet with a choice of sauces is a permanent fixture.

Although timing and saucing were a disappointment at inspection, puddings that have impressed include honey parfait with roast strawberries, and dark chocolate terrine with mango coulis. Note that a number of dishes attract fairly hefty supplements. Service can be rushed at busy times. Around 75 bottles feature on the list, divided between France and the rest of the world, with about a third dipping below £20. House wines, from South Africa and France, are £12.75.

CHEF: George Kelso PROPRIETORS: George and Michelle Kelso OPEN: Tue to Fri L 12 to 1.30, all week D 6 to 9.30 CLOSED: 25 and 26 Dec MEALS: Set L £12 (2 courses) to £15, Set D £25.50 SERVICE: not inc CARDS: Amex, Delta, Diners, MasterCard, Switch, Visa DETAILS: 50 seats. 6 seats outside. Private parties: 40 main room, 14 and 20 private rooms. Vegetarian meals. Children's helpings. No smoking in dining room. Occasional music (£5)

The Guide relies on feedback from its readers. Especially welcome are reports on new restaurants appearing in the book for the first time. All letters to the Guide are acknowledged.

Kalpna £

2–3 St Patrick Square, Edinburgh EH14 1AJ
TEL: (0131) 667 9890 FAX: (0131) 443 9523

COOKING 2
INDIAN
£14–£38

Ajay Bhartdwaj's hospitable, brightly decorated restaurant offers a wide range of Indian vegetarian cooking, with South Indian dosas alongside the Gujarati and Punjabi dishes at the heart of the menu. Additional specialities include Kashmiri stuffed, baked potatoes with a combination of sauces described as piquant, almond, saffron and tomato butter honey. An easy way into this cuisine is a thali (one-plate meal), which is available in several versions, including one for vegans and one that features kachori (stuffed lentil pasty); mushroom curry; crushed roasted aubergines; navratan kurma of mixed vegetables; fresh fruits and nuts in a cream and saffron sauce; and, of course, dal, rice, bread, pickles, yoghurt and a sweet. Among starters are bhel poori, and the unusual aloo firdoshi: potato barrels stuffed with pistachio, raisins and coriander. Lunch is a particularly good-value buffet. House wine is £8.50.

CHEF/PROPRIETOR: Ajay Bhartdwaj OPEN: Mon to Sat L 12 to 2, all week D 5.30 to 10.30 (11 Fri and Sat May to Sept) CLOSED: 25 and 26 Dec, 1 Jan, L Sat and D Sun from Oct to April MEALS: alc D (main courses £4 to £7.50). Set buffet L £5, Set D £10 to £15 SERVICE: 10%, card slips closed CARDS: Visa (no credit cards accepted at L) DETAILS: 65 seats. Private parties: 60 main room, 30 private room. No smoking in dining room. Wheelchair access (not WC). Occasional music

Martins

70 Rose Street North Lane, Edinburgh EH2 3DX
TEL: (0131) 225 3106 FAX: (0131) 220 3040

COOKING 4
MEDITERRANEAN
£28–£58

Narrowly off the beaten track, down a cobbled back lane, Martin's provides welcome relief from the hustle and bustle of the city centre. Bright, colourful interiors make an impact none the less, and the Ironses' friendly approach radiates confidence. Organic vegetables and unpasteurised cheeses from 'suppliers with integrity' are the order of the day on David Romanis's attractive Mediterranean-inspired menu. Earthy treatments have included cod crusted with garlic and herbs in a broth of mixed beans and chorizo with coriander pesto, and braised lamb shank with tarragon mash in a red wine and rosemary sauce. Twice-baked cheese and chive soufflé with provençale balsamic dressing offers a lighter alternative.

Lemon curd tartlets with mango mascarpone cream, and ginger and golden syrup pudding with toffee sauce and grilled pineapple are typically sticky desserts, though the impeccable Scottish and Irish cheeses will prove hard to pass up for many. A cleverly chosen wine list features sound, interesting bottles from around the world, although France receives due reverence. Pithy tasting notes and good mark-ups add to the overall appeal. Seven wines by the glass start at £2.15.

CHEF: David Romanis PROPRIETORS: Martin and Gay Irons OPEN: Tue to Fri L 12 to 2, Tue to Sat D 7 to 10 (6.30 to 11 during Festival) CLOSED: 1 week Oct, 4 weeks from 24 Dec, 1 week June/July MEALS: alc (main courses L £9 to £11.50, D £15 to £20.50). Set L £12.50 (2 courses), Set D £25 SERVICE: not inc, 10% for parties of 6 or more CARDS: Amex, Delta, Diners, MasterCard, Switch, Visa DETAILS: 56 seats. Private parties: 30 main room, 8, 18 private rooms. Vegetarian meals. No children under 8. No smoking in dining room. Wheelchair access (not WC). No music

Restaurant Martin Wishart

54 The Shore, Leith, Edinburgh EH6 6RA
TEL: (0131) 553 3557 FAX: (0131) 467 7091

COOKING **6**
MODERN FRENCH
£24–£55

A modest shop front leads into an unassuming, and simply but effectively decorated open space with discreet lighting and big tables. So far so ordinary, but compliments pour in for Martin Wishart's accomplished cooking, several meals being hailed as a triumph. 'Serious, confident cooking of a high order' is how one visitor summed it up on the strength of a meal that began with an assiette of oysters: two lightly poached with tagliatelle in a champagne sauce, topped with caviar; two raw, accompanied by smoked salmon and herbs in aspic; and two deep-fried with ginger and other 'Chinesey bits'.

Despite a few luxuries – lobster ravioli on an oyster velouté, or partridge breast with foie gras and black truffle – materials are enterprisingly chosen to include a few relatively humble ones: saddle of rabbit, pot-roast pig's cheek, or a tartlet of salt cod on a delicately seasoned tomato base. Sauces make up in flavour what they may lack in quantity: an unctuous 'sublimation' of mushrooms, cream and wine to accompany fresh, firm lemon sole fillets with buttered spinach for example. Others derive their depth from good stock properly reduced.

Skills extend from accurate timing to sensitive marrying of ingredients, evident for example in a refreshing glazed lemon tart with praline ice cream and raspberry coulis. Not every dish is faultless, but the satisfaction level is high. Prices are considered reasonable (at lunch, 'a virtual give-away'), and the charming, bubbly French maîtresse d' keeps an eye on everything. Wines, listed by price (from £11 upward), are a short, sharp, well-chosen selection from leading regions, with no passengers.

CHEF/PROPRIETOR: Martin Wishart OPEN: Tue to Fri L 12 to 2, Tue to Sat D 6.30 to 10 (10.30 Fri and Sat) CLOSED: 25 Dec, 1 Jan MEALS: alc D (main courses £14.50 to £18.50). Set L £12.50 (2 courses) to £14.50 SERVICE: not inc CARDS: Delta, MasterCard, Switch, Visa DETAILS: 32 seats. Private parties: 36 main room. Children's helpings. Smoking permitted after 2.30 L, 10 D. Wheelchair access (also WC). Music

NEW CHEF *is shown instead of a cooking mark where a change of chef occurred too late for a new assessment of the cooking.*

Not inc *in the details at the end of an entry indicates that no service charge is made and any tipping is at the discretion of the customer.*

Rhodes & Co

NEW ENTRY

3–15 Rose Street, Edinburgh EH2 2YJ
TEL: (0131) 220 9190 FAX: (0131) 220 9199

COOKING **4**
MODERN BRITISH
£23–£46

Gary Rhodes has lent his name to another branch of this mini chain (see entry, Manchester), with plans for others in the works. This one has a ground-floor bar done in glass, marble, leather and steel, with an informal and rather minimalist dining room in wood and chrome above it. Comforting British cooking is the bedrock – black pudding with toasted goats' cheese and roast tomatoes, or well-executed eggs Benedict – and the generally straightforward dishes use sound ingredients, prepared with few gimmicks: a sharp Caesar salad, for example, or a small porcelain cauldron of creamy-rich chicken liver parfait sealed with butter, accompanied by a sharp-sweet Bramley apple jelly chopped into cubes.

Main courses arrive as described (there is a charge for extra vegetables), taking in three golden salmon fishcake balls set in a foaming lemon butter sauce, and pink duck breast served with spicy plums and a slick of sauce redolent of cinnamon and cloves. This being a restaurant with pretensions to modernity, froths are much in evidence: applied to carrot and tarragon soup to start, and a raspberry crème brûlée. Alternatively, finish with fettuccini crêpes suzette: a pancake cut into ribbons and tossed with pieces of orange in a rich sharp sauce 'interestingly lacking in alcohol'. Service might be more astute and friendly, and around three dozen wines stay mostly under £25. House vin de pays is £9.95.

CHEF: Paul Malinen PROPRIETORS: Jenners and Sodexho OPEN: all week L 12 to 2.30 (3 Sun), Mon to Sat D 6 to 10.30 MEALS: alc (main courses £7.50 to £14). Set L and D before 7 £12 (2 courses). Bar meals available SERVICE: 10% (optional), card slips closed CARDS: Amex, Delta, Diners, MasterCard, Switch, Visa DETAILS: 90 seats. 24 seats outside. Private parties: 60 main room. Vegetarian meals. Children's helpings. Wheelchair access (also WC) to downstairs bar only. Music. Air-conditioned

Shore £

3–4 The Shore, Leith, Edinburgh EH6 6QW
TEL.FAX: (0131) 553 5080

COOKING **2**
SEAFOOD
£22–£44

This eighteenth-century building of handsome grey Edinburgh stone boasts large west-facing windows overlooking the Water of Leith. Friendly, informal service and 'consistently imaginative' cooking are what draw regulars back, plus the emphasis on fish and shellfish. Smoked haddock accompanies leeks in a full-flavoured soup, while squid are given a garlic stuffing and come with courgettes, pine nuts and tomato. Meatier fish are well served by their preparations too, balsamic-flavoured aubergines appearing with grilled cod, thought-provoking ratatouille and herbed yoghurt the medium for sea bass. Simple puddings, such as sticky toffee, fruit crumble, or orange and ginger cheesecake, bring things to a satisfying conclusion. Wines tilt towards the white axis, there is plenty of choice, and prices stay reasonable. House Côtes du Roussillon in red and white is £9.90.

CHEFS: Innes Gibson and Alison Bryant PROPRIETOR: Stuart Linsley OPEN: all week 12 to 2.30 (12.30 to 3 Sun), 6.30 to 10 CLOSED: 25 and 26 Dec, 1 and 2 Jan MEALS: alc (main courses L £7.50 to £10, D £9 to £16) SERVICE: not inc, 10% for parties of 8 or more CARDS: Amex, Delta, Diners, MasterCard, Switch, Visa DETAILS: 36 seats. 12 seats outside. Private parties: 36 main room. Vegetarian meals. Children's helpings. No smoking in dining room. Wheelchair access (not WC). Occasional music (£5)

Skippers

1A Dock Place, Leith, Edinburgh EH6 6LU	COOKING **2**
TEL: (0131) 554 1018 FAX: (0131) 553 5988	SEAFOOD
WEB SITE: www.skippers.co.uk	£22–£48

'Quite a lesson for others,' noted a reporter: 'ensure that the fish is the best possible and treat it simply and sympathetically.' And indeed this seems to sum up the kitchen's philosophy at this converted pub, now a memorabilia-bedecked informal bistro specialising in fish. Short descriptions of dishes on the daily-changing menus are of the no-nonsense school of menu-speak. Potted shrimps, gravad lax with dill and mustard dressing, and roasted monkfish with red pepper sauce put you in the picture. Equally, the kitchen turns out grilled asparagus with melted goats' cheese, and loin of lamb with garlic mash, followed by banoffi cheesecake or lemon and lime tart. The helpfully annotated, ungrasping wine list opens with a house selection ranging from £9.75 to £11.50.

CHEFS: Kerr Marrian and Stewart Thrumble PROPRIETORS: Karen Miller and Gavin Ferguson OPEN: all week L 12.30 to 2 (2.30 Sun), Mon to Sat D 7 (6.30 during Festival) to 10 CLOSED: 24 to 26 Dec, 31 Dec to 2 Jan, 1 week Feb/Mar, 1 week Sept MEALS: alc (main courses L £8 to £15.50, D £12 to £17.50). Set L £10.50 (2 courses) to £13.50 SERVICE: not inc, 10% for large tables CARDS: Amex, Delta, MasterCard, Switch, Visa DETAILS: 56 seats. 16 seats outside. Private parties: 25 main room, 25 private room. Wheelchair access (also WC). Music

Tower Restaurant

Museum of Scotland, Chambers Street,	COOKING **2**
Edinburgh EH1 1JF	SEAFOOD/MODERN BRITISH
TEL: (0131) 225 3003 FAX: (0131) 247 4220	£31–£64

Sited above the crouching 'sandstone Sphinx' that is the nation's museum, the long, thin dining room takes full advantage of its setting, offering dramatic views of the city. Seafood is a strong suit on a menu that opens with oysters, lobster and a plateau de fruits de mer, and among dishes that have caught readers' attention are beetroot cured salmon, crab with lime mayonnaise, and smoked haddock risotto with a poached egg and Parmesan shavings. But choice is plentiful, extending to sushi, onion soup, aubergine lasagne, and grills of ribeye steak, calf's liver and sea bass. Desserts, like the rest, cater for a wide range of tastes, taking in elderflower and pickled ginger crème brûlée, and chocolate truffle torte. Wines are sorted by price band, with modest choice under £20 and many tempting bottles above. House wines start at £12 (£2 a glass).

See inside the front cover for an explanation of the symbols used at the tops of entries.

CHEF: Steven Adair PROPRIETOR: James Thomson OPEN: all week L menu 12 to 6, D menu 6 to 11 CLOSED: 25 and 26 Dec MEALS: alc (main courses L £9 to £13, D £12 to £24). Set pre- and post-theatre D available SERVICE: not inc; 10% (optional) for parties of 8 or more CARDS: Amex, Delta, Diners, MasterCard, Switch, Visa DETAILS: 70 seats. 40 seats outside. Private parties: 70 main room. Vegetarian meals. No smoking in dining room. Wheelchair access (also WC). Music. Air-conditioned

Tuscan Square

30B Grindlay Street, Edinburgh EH3 9AX — COOKING **3**
TEL: (0131) 229 9859 — MODERN SCOTTISH/MEDITERANNEAN
FAX: (0131) 221 9515 — £18–£41

Conveniently close to the Lyceum Theatre, Tuscan Square comes in two parts. A ground-level café-bar is open for sandwiches, pasta and light meals from noon to 11pm, while the first-floor dining room, with basic but comfortable seating, offers a monthly-changing menu that owes a debt to other countries apart from just Italy. Alongside cod with smoked salmon risotto, or a filo parcel of buffalo mozzarella with tomato and basil might be Thai vegetable broth with chicken dumplings, and rump of lamb with mustard sauce. The fixed-price dinner menu has gone, but the carte remains reasonably priced, offering fairly simple but deftly handled food with 'good strong flavours'. Cheeses are a mix of Italian and Scottish, while desserts favour tiramisù, fresh fruit minestrone, and chocolate pecan pie. Twenty varied wines, mostly under £20, start with house Chilean at £10.95.

CHEF: Iain McMaster PROPRIETORS: Iain McMaster and Ferrier Richardson OPEN: Tue to Sat 12 to 2.30, 5.30 to 11 CLOSED: 25 and 26 Dec, 1 and 2 Jan MEALS: alc (main courses £11). Set L £9.95 CARDS: Amex, Delta, MasterCard, Switch, Visa DETAILS: 80 seats. 30 seats outside. Private parties: 50 main room, 30 and 50 private rooms. Vegetarian meals. Children's helpings. No-smoking area. Wheelchair access (also WC). Music. Air-conditioned

Valvona & Crolla Caffè Bar

19 Elm Row, Edinburgh EH7 4AA
TEL: (0131) 556 6066 FAX: (0131) 556 1668 — COOKING **2**
EMAIL: caffe@valvonacrolla.co.uk — ITALIAN
WEB SITE: www.valvonacrolla.co.uk — £23–£54

The caffè bar is a logical extension of the Contini family's 65-year-old delicatessen business. Since they import cheeses, hams, oils, vinegars, and fruit and vegetables from Milan market twice a week, it seems only sensible to combine them with their own baked bread, plus a few locally available items. The result is a lunchtime slate of dishes, mostly under £10, that range from pizza, via Sardinian tomatoes dressed with sheep's milk cheese and olive oil, to monkfish with bruschetta and herb salad. One who enjoyed a steak sandwich of Italian bread and Scottish beef thanked his God it wasn't the other way round.

Italian classics among desserts include pannacotta, and crumbly lemon polenta cake. Most reporters are happy, although one noted that it can get ragged around the edges during Festival time. A thousand bottles from the length and breadth of Italy dominate the stunning wine list. Internationally recognised producers Gaja, Antinori and Conterno are well represented and at reasonable prices. For those seeking plainer drinking, 10 to 12 house wines change weekly, and start at £7.99 a bottle, £2.75 a glass.

CHEFS/PROPRIETORS: the Contini family OPEN: Mon to Sat L 12 to 3, D 6 to 9 2 evenings per month and Mon to Sat last 3 weeks Aug, first week Sept CLOSED: 25 and 26 Dec, 1 and 2 Jan MEALS: alc L (main courses £8 to £13). Set D £35 SERVICE: not inc CARDS: Amex, Delta, MasterCard, Switch, Visa DETAILS: 80 seats. Private parties: 80 main room, 40 private room. Vegetarian meals. Children's helpings. No smoking in dining room. Wheelchair access (also WC). Music. Air-conditioned

Vintners Rooms 🍷 $*

The Vaults, 87 Giles Street, Leith, Edinburgh EH6 6BZ
TEL: (0131) 554 6767 FAX: (0131) 467 7130

COOKING **4**
FRENCH-PLUS
£25–£54

Chandeliers and cherubs are part of the atmospheric fittings at this eighteenth-century monument to the wine trade. It sports a large bar and a small dining room, where Tim Cumming's largely French-inspired style of cooking gently keeps pace with the times. Perhaps unsurprisingly, alcohol creeps into the menu here and there – boudin blanc with an apple muscat purée, or partridge 'boulette' with a cup of bouillon and a glass of marsala – and seafood understandably features, from scallops with risotto nero to grilled sea bass fillet with red pepper dressing.

Saucing may not always be as distinctive as it promises, but the kitchen has turned out sweet and tasty scallops in a smooth mussel sauce, as well as freshly baked bread, well-kept Scottish cheeses, and a range of desserts from chocolate parfait to a terrine of prune and armagnac ice cream with plum sauce. Service is 'friendly if a little brisk'. Wines pay homage to classical French regions, but there is flair and value to be found in the New World too. Seven wines are available by the glass, with bottle prices starting at £12.

CHEF: Tim Cumming PROPRIETORS: A.T. and S.C. Cumming OPEN: Mon to Sat 12 to 2, 7 to 10 CLOSED: 2 weeks Christmas to New Year MEALS: alc D (main courses £14.50 to £19). Set L £11.50 (2 courses) to £15 SERVICE: not inc CARDS: Amex, Delta, MasterCard, Switch, Visa DETAILS: 60 seats. Private parties: 34 main room. Vegetarian meals. Children's helpings. No smoking in 1 dining room. Wheelchair access (not WC). No music

Winter Glen

3A1 Dundas Street, Edinburgh EH3 6QG
TEL: (0131) 477 7060 FAX: (0131) 624 7087

COOKING **3**
MODERN BRITISH
£33–£54

Stone-built Winter Glen, conveniently near the New Town, has the considerable merit of great comfort, helped by old-fashioned, capacious chairs and well-spaced tables. Menus revolve around standard materials, from chicken breast to Scottish salmon, many of which are treated to a range of fashionable add-ons: smoked salmon sausage on olive mash with black pudding, for example, or spiced crab cake with cumin, coriander and a citrus lime caramel. Large portions are served on huge white plates, among them a two-inch-thick, accurately cooked Aberdeen Angus fillet, 'a whopping amount of venison', and a starter of high-quality, exactly timed pink chicken livers tossed in butter and placed in a crisp filo basket. Cold rice pudding with cinnamon and a prune compote might be the pick of desserts. Uninformed service was one of the letdowns at inspection – 'I enquired about the Scottish cheeses on offer, and was told Brie and Stilton' – and incidentals from bread to coffee could be improved. Around 30 wines feature on the French-dominated list, which also touches down elsewhere in Europe and in the New World. Four house wines from France start at £12.50 or £2.95 per glass.

CHEF: Graham Winter PROPRIETORS: Blair Glen and Graham Winter OPEN: Mon to Fri L 12 to 2, Mon to Sat D 6.30 to 'late' CLOSED: 25 and 26 Dec, 1 Jan MEALS: alc L (main courses £13 to £19). Set D £23 (2 courses) to £26 SERVICE: not inc CARDS: Amex, Delta, MasterCard, Switch, Visa DETAILS: 60 seats. Private parties: 40 main room, 25 and 35 private rooms. No children under 14 at D. No smoking before 2 at L, 9 at D. Music. Air-conditioned

EDNAM Borders **map 11**

▲ Edenwater House

Ednam TD5 7QL COOKING **5**
TEL/FAX: (01573) 224070 MODERN BRITISH
on B6461, 2m N of Kelso £39–£47

The Kellys have bought themselves a fine home with attractive views of the river, furnished it for their own pleasure, and seem to delight in sharing it with admiring visitors for a few days. It is an old stone-built manse next to the church, with a small, relaxed dining room open to non-residents just three nights a week. The pattern is four courses, the main coming either second or third in the running order. This is the only one with a choice: perhaps guinea fowl on a bed of spinach with a wild mushroom crêpe, or pink roast saddle of venison sliced on to celeriac and potato mash, accompanied by a sweet pear and a redcurrant and port sauce.

Fish typically turns up at the start, in the form of a mille-feuille of scallops and asparagus, or seared salmon on spinach and ceps with a coriander and lemon balm sauce. Unusual combinations occasionally surface – perhaps asparagus and coconut soup – but this is not experimental cooking, and dishes taste as if they have been tried and tested to get the balance of flavours right. That seems to have happened in the case of a thin bitter chocolate box containing a raspberry mousse, surrounded by four kinds of berry in a raspberry coulis. 'Courteous, talkative and enthusiastic' Jeff Kelly oversees a quality-conscious wine list that doesn't ignore modest requirements. House vin de pays is £11.

CHEF: Jacqui Kelly PROPRIETORS: Jacqui and Jeff Kelly OPEN: Thur to Sat D only 8 to 8.30 (open all week for residents) CLOSED: first 2 weeks Jan MEALS: Set D £30 SERVICE: net prices CARDS: Access, Visa DETAILS: 16 seats. Private parties: 18 main room. Car park. Vegetarian meals. No smoking in dining room. Wheelchair access (not WC). No music ACCOMMODATION: 3 rooms, all with bath/shower. TV. B&B £55 to £75. No children under 10. Fishing (*The Which? Hotel Guide*)

Report forms are at the back of the book; write a letter if you prefer; or email us at goodfoodguide@which.net

ERISKA Argyll & Bute **map 11**

▲ Isle of Eriska

Ledaig, Eriska PA37 1SD
TEL: (01631) 720371 FAX: (01631) 720531
EMAIL: office@eriska-hotel.co.uk
WEB SITE: www.eriska-hotel.co.uk
off A828, 12m N of Oban

COOKING **6**
SCOTTISH
£46–£55

Driving along winding roads, across the quaint bridge, is a prelude to a 'peculiarly enchanting experience'. There is little else on Eriska apart from wildlife and this baronial-style granite and sandstone house, where an 'amiably patrician' Beppo Buchanan-Smith welcomes visitors. Space is not at a premium, so there is room to relax in capacious chairs in one of several log-fired sitting rooms, where friendly staff bring drinks and appetisers, until a gong is struck and dinner begins. The format is six courses, though not everybody makes it to the end without passing up something.

Seafood features prominently, from exemplary local oysters, to poached home-smoked cod with a mustard crust on a wild herb and broom bud salad. The kitchen uses mainly native ingredients with a few cosmopolitan contributions: couscous to accompany fish terrine with dill vinaigrette, and okra in a chicken soup. One main course usually arrives on a huge covered trolley, the waiter offering to carve whatever cut you fancy from an enormous side of flavourful roast beef. Creamy, boldly flavoured horseradish sauce is a bonus, as is the thin, tasty gravy poured over a decent Yorkshire pudding.

Desserts can be a high point – 'profoundly flavoursome' chocolate fondant with a scoop of rich chocolate ice cream in a crunchy biscuit cup – although pastrywork is not up to the standard of the rest of the output. Cheeses are varied and interesting, but could be better described. Wines are favourably priced, with many bottles below £15 that would be considerably higher elsewhere. Half the list is French, including first-growth clarets and Alsatian wines exclusively from Trimbach. Lovers of vintage port will find plenty to choose from. Prices kick off at £8.80 for a Vin de Pays d'Oc Merlot.

CHEF: Robert MacPherson PROPRIETORS: the Buchanan-Smith family OPEN: all week D only 8 to 9 MEALS: Set D £37.50 SERVICE: not inc, card slips closed CARDS: Amex, Delta, MasterCard, Switch, Visa DETAILS: 40 seats. Private parties: 20 main room. Car park. Vegetarian meals. Jacket and tie. No smoking in dining room. Wheelchair access (not WC). No music ACCOMMODATION: 17 rooms, all with bath/shower. TV. Phone. B&B £120 to £260. Rooms for disabled. Baby facilities. Swimming pool. Fishing (*The Which? Hotel Guide*)

'Unusually, in London, the restaurant is a no-smoking area – a godsend in this area of ladies who lunch on a few shreds of lettuce and a packet of fags.'
(On eating in London)

The cuisine styles noted at the tops of entries are only an approximation, often suggested to us by the restaurants themselves. Please read the entry itself to find out more about the cooking style.

FAIRLIE North Ayrshire — map 11

▲ Fins £ — NEW ENTRY

Fencefoot Farm, Fairlie KA29 0EG
TEL: (01475) 568918 FAX: (01475) 568921
EMAIL: fencebay@aol.com
WEB SITE: www.fencebay.co.uk
on A78, 1m S of Fairlie

COOKING **2**
SEAFOOD
£19–£54

Formerly a *Good Food Guide* Round-up entry, this converted byre attached to a fish farm shop on the Ayrshire coast is a seafood specialist. Fish motifs abound, and materials are as well sourced as anywhere: much of it local, some of it landed from their own fishing boat, some smoked in-house. Lobsters are kept live in sea-water tanks on site, and rainbow trout are farmed here too. Shellfish stood out particularly at inspection: a generous heap of juicy squat lobster tails tossed in butter, and five fat, springy, accurately seared scallops with their corals in an improvable smoked salmon and crème fraîche sauce. Oysters are probably best eaten 'au naturel', although they also come cooked. To finish, vanilla and ginger parfait have been recommended, while traditionalists are offered a treacly-tasting toffee pudding. Service is warm and well-informed, and children are made welcome. A reasonably priced wine list favours France and stays mostly below £20, with house wines starting at £9.50.

CHEFS: Gillian Dick, Jill Thain and Jane Burns PROPRIETORS: Jill and Bernard Thain OPEN: Tue to Sun L 12 to 2.30, Tue to Sat D 6.45 to 9.30 CLOSED: 25 and 26 Dec, 1 and 2 Jan MEALS: alc (main courses £6.50 to £23). Set L Tue to Thur £7.50 (2 courses), Set D Tue to Thur £10 (2 courses) SERVICE: not inc, card slips closed CARDS: Amex, Delta, MasterCard, Switch, Visa DETAILS: 32 seats. Private parties: 32 main room. Car park. Vegetarian meals. No smoking in dining room. Wheelchair access (also WC). Music ACCOMMODATION: 2 rooms. B&B £15 to £40. Baby facilities (£5)

FORT WILLIAM Highland — map 11

Crannog 

Town Pier, Fort William PH33 7NG
TEL: (01397) 705589 FAX: (01397) 705026
WEB SITE: www.crannog.net

COOKING **2**
SEAFOOD
£18–£49

Neat and attractive, 'spick and span', with delightful views at the head of Loch Linnhe (Crannog has its own fishing boat and smokehouse), this is not a place for meat eaters or vegetarians, but for lovers of simply cooked seafood. West Coast langoustines come with garlic and herb butter, creamy Cullen skink is well judged, and a savoury seafood tart is 'chock full of seafood flavours'. The straightforward menu is supplemented by blackboard specials, such as first-rate sautéd Islay scallops served with a velvety crayfish essence on a little mound of saffron rice, or baked fillet of Mallaig shark with asparagus and shallot butter. Main courses come with buttered potatoes and green salad, and uncomplicated desserts run to crisp lemon and lime tart with kumquat sauce, and above-average vanilla ice cream with raspberry sauce. Around 20 (mainly white) wines start with house Chasan Chardonnay at £12.95 and stay mostly below £20.

CHEF: Garry Dobbie PROPRIETOR: Crannog Ltd OPEN: all week 12 to 2.30, 6 to 9.30 (10.30 in summer) CLOSED: 25 and 26 Dec, 1 and 2 Jan MEALS: alc (main courses £10 to £18). Light L available SERVICE: not inc CARDS: MasterCard, Switch, Visa DETAILS: 65 seats. 20 seats outside. Private parties: 35 main room. Car park. Children's helpings. No smoking in 1 dining room. Wheelchair access (also WC). Occasional music (£5)

▲ Inverlochy Castle

Torlundy, Fort William PH33 6SN
TEL: (01397) 702177 FAX: (01397) 702953
EMAIL: info@inverlochy.co.uk
WEB SITE: www.inverlochy.co.uk
3m N of Fort William on A82

COOKING **6**
MODERN EUROPEAN
£38–£74

Spectacularly situated in landscaped grounds in the shadow of Ben Nevis, Inverlochy Castle 'couldn't be classier if it was a royal palace'; indeed Queen Victoria lived here for a while in 1873, ten years after it was built. With an entrance hall two storeys high, crystal chandeliers, antique paintings and the smell of wood smoke, it is the antithesis of a chain hotel. Simon Haigh's four-course dinners (the second a no-choice soup such as roast tomato or curried parsnip) employ native materials from roast saddle of hare to Loch Linnhe prawns. Among the more unusual items are poached salmon cheeks, served in puff pastry with a salmon mousse, and roast teal accompanied by creamed endive and quince purée.

Many dishes inhabit ostensibly familiar territory – warm asparagus mousse with home-smoked salmon, for instance, or grilled fillet of Charolais beef with horseradish hollandaise – but the cooking avoids clichés: tuna fishcakes are served in a mushroom and toasted sesame bouillon, and Isle of Skye crab is sandwiched between potato tuiles with crushed avocado. Desserts run from a simple plate of warm berries served with clotted cream and a sablé biscuit, via old-fashioned crêpes suzette, to indulgent hot chocolate tart with orange sauce. An impeccable though conservative wine list features mature clarets and grand cru Burgundies, some at quite high prices. More could be done for modest budgets, although a few bottles under £20 can be found in the New World sections, and Justerini & Brooks claret and white Burgundy are a respectable £17.

CHEF: Simon Haigh PROPRIETOR: Inverlochy Castle Ltd OPEN: all week 12.30 to 1.45, 7 to 9.15 CLOSED: 7 Jan to 12 Feb MEALS: Set L £23 (2 courses) to £28.50, Set D £50. Light L available SERVICE: not inc, card slips closed CARDS: Amex, Delta, MasterCard, Switch, Visa DETAILS: 34 seats. Private parties: 34 main room, 15 private room. Car park. Children's helpings. Jacket and tie. No smoking in dining room. Wheelchair access (not WC). No music ACCOMMODATION: 17 rooms, all with bath/shower. TV. Phone. B&B £180 to £480. Baby facilities. Fishing (*The Which? Hotel Guide*)

(£5) *indicates that the restaurant has elected to participate in the* Good Food Guide *voucher scheme. For full details, see page 6.*

denotes an outstanding wine cellar; *denotes a good wine list, worth travelling for.*

GLASGOW Glasgow **map 11**

▲ Arthouse Hotel, Arthouse Grill

NEW ENTRY

129 Bath Street, Glasgow G2 2SY
TEL: (0141) 221 6789 FAX: (0141) 221 6777
WEB SITE: www.arthousehotel.com

COOKING **3**
MODERN EUROPEAN
£21–£57

This former educational establishment now houses a new hotel and restaurant, adding further lustre to Glasgow's already thriving gastronomic scene. There is a ground-floor dining room replete with early-twentieth-century stained-glass panels, but this caters only for party bookings. Downstairs, the Arthouse Grill incorporates a Guinness and oyster bar, as well as a Japanese teppanyaki grill, and on weekend evenings particularly the joint fairly jumps. Glossy, buttery field mushrooms are served on bruschetta with sun-dried tomatoes and Parmesan, while chargrilled halibut with hollandaise and tapénade delivered a fine piece of sensitively cooked fish at inspection. Other offerings include jumbo pork chop with caramelised apples, sage and cranberry relish, or harissa-braised lamb shank with gremolata and minted couscous. Desserts take in well-made lemon tart with a sharp lime syrup, and pineapple upside-down cake with crème anglaise. The wine list is a short, sensible collection with a pair of fancy Burgundies at the top end, and southern French house wines for £9.95 at the other.

CHEF: John Quigley PROPRIETOR: K. Skey OPEN: all week 12 to 11 MEALS: alc (main courses £7.50 to £20). Set L Mon to Fri 12 to 5 £9.95 (2 courses) to £12.50. Teppanyaki Mon to Sat 12 to 3, 6 to 10 SERVICE: not inc, card slips closed CARDS: Amex, Delta, Diners, MasterCard, Switch, Visa DETAILS: 90 seats. Private parties: 20 main room, 60 private room. Vegetarian meals. Children's helpings. Wheelchair access (also WC). Music ACCOMMODATION: 65 rooms, all with bath/shower. TV. Phone. Room only £70 to £140. Rooms for disabled

Buttery

652 Argyle Street, Glasgow G3 8UF
TEL: (0141) 221 8188 FAX: (0141) 204 4639

COOKING **2**
MODERN SCOTTISH
£29–£68

Under new ownership since last year, and with a new chef, this old-stager beguiles visitors with its large mirrored bar, heavy furniture, impressive paintings, dark oak panelling, and the general air of 'an exclusive Victorian club'. Roaming freely around Europe, the menu picks up on lots of contemporary ideas from a pressed potato and sardine terrine, via a wholemeal tartlet of field mushrooms with lamb loin and liquorice sauce, to a ballottine of chicken on creamed lentils with a white truffle and porcini sauce. The style is ambitious and occasionally inventive – apple and rosemary tart with Lancashire cheese (or, in our inspector's case, without it) – but fresh materials and accurate timing have made a success of, for example, seared fillet of brill in a light buttery sauce with mussels and braised fennel. Service is friendly and attentive. Wines favour those with more than £20 to spend, although house French is £12.95.

CHEF: Ian Mackie PROPRIETOR: Punch Retail Ltd. OPEN: Mon to Fri L 12 to 2.30, Mon to Sat D 7 to 10.30 CLOSED: 25 Dec, 1 Jan MEALS: alc (main courses £14 to £20). Set L £17.50 (2 courses) to £19.50 SERVICE: 10% (optional), card slips closed CARDS: Amex, Delta, Diners, MasterCard, Switch, Visa DETAILS: 50 seats. Private parties: 50 main room, 10 private room. Car park. Vegetarian meals. Children's helpings. No cigars/pipes in dining room. Wheelchair access (not WC). Music. Air-conditioned

Café Gandolfi £

64 Albion Street, Glasgow G1 1NY
TEL: (0141) 552 6813 FAX: (0141) 552 8911

COOKING **2**
INTERNATIONAL
£17–£34

The Café is seemingly always open, as cafés traditionally are, although the variety and quality of what's on offer elevate this one into another class. You might start the day here with eggs en cocotte and toast, or pitch up at lunchtime, as one reader did, to enjoy crispy bacon and avocado salad with warm vinaigrette, served with fine home-made wholemeal bread. A quarterly-changing menu tries out dishes such as Stornoway white pudding with roasted apple and onions, or grilled sea bass with tomato and beetroot risotto. Clootie dumpling with butterscotch is an evocative sort of pudding in Glasgow, and walnut tart has been commended. An imaginative choice of wines includes many by the glass. House French is £2.85 for a large glass, £9.95 the bottle.

CHEFS: Margaret Clarence, Alasdair Braidwood and Michael Clarence PROPRIETOR: Seumas MacInnes OPEN: Mon to Sat 9am to 11.30pm, Sun noon to 11.30pm MEALS: alc (main courses £5.50 to £10.50) SERVICE: not inc, 10% for parties of 6 or more CARDS: Delta, MasterCard, Switch, Visa DETAILS: 65 seats. Private parties: 65 main room. Vegetarian meals. No children after 8.30pm. No-smoking area. Wheelchair access (not WC). Music

Eurasia

NEW ENTRY

150 St Vincent Street, Glasgow G2 5NE
TEL: (0141) 204 1150 FAX: (0141) 204 1140

COOKING **4**
SCOTTISH/ORIENTAL FUSION
£29–£74

Ferrier Richardson's latest venture, a bold, confident successor to Yes (which is still operating, under new ownership), is a large, stylish, open-plan wood and glass affair with tables looking on to the street, and an open-to-view kitchen at the far end. Oriental influences have now developed into a full-blown fusion menu, taking in vegetable and chilli chicken spring rolls, a tomato, ginger and jasmine soup, and Thai-cured items such as duck (with orange and cardamom) or salmon (with hot-and-sour vegetables and a lime dressing).

Scottish produce underlies the operation, including first-rate tender beef fillet topped with an impressive selection of wild mushrooms, accompanied by a rich and sticky stock and oyster sauce. Other touchstones include teriyaki beef, tempura fish, green curry, and desserts such as lemon grass rice pudding, or grapefruit and figs with a nutty gratin of almond cream, the star of an inspection meal. Breads are 'pretty good', service is 'OK', and the list of well over 100 wines, mostly French, includes a decent selection of half-bottles and opens with four house wines at £14.95.

CHEFS: Ferrier Richardson and Steven Caputta PROPRIETOR: Ferrier Richardson OPEN: Mon to Fri L 12 to 2.30, Mon to Sat D 7 to 11 CLOSED: bank hols MEALS: Set L £13.95 (2 courses) to £16.95, Set D £25.95 (2 courses) to £32.50 SERVICE: not inc CARDS: Amex, Delta, Diners, MasterCard, Switch, Visa DETAILS: 180 seats. Private parties: 150 main room, 12 to 24 private rooms. Wheelchair access (also WC). Music. Air-conditioned

▲ Nairns

13 Woodside Crescent, Glasgow G3 7UP
TEL: (0141) 353 0707 FAX: (0141) 331 1684
EMAIL: info@nairns.co.uk
WEB SITE: www.nairns.co.uk

COOKING **3**
MODERN SCOTTISH
£29–£51

Combining minimalist grey with powerful black and white abstract photographs and white napery, this basement restaurant makes a bold bid for modernity. Nick Nairn's crusading zeal is evident in some first-class materials, and anyone looking for an agreeable gathering of fine Scottish protein, well sourced and precisely cooked, will most likely enjoy themselves. A feeling for tradition runs through the repertoire, producing fishcakes with mushy peas, and seared cod with asparagus hollandaise and poached egg.

Despite a few minuses (tomato soup 'best avoided', accompaniments not up to main-course standard), the kitchen has produced chunky pink seared chicken livers in a sharp red wine jus, well-flavoured crispy salmon, and rare chargrilled sirloin steak that 'yielded juicily to the touch', its accompanying Puy lentils adding scrunch to the gravy. To finish, warm chocolate cake comes with softly whipped cream, and lemon tart is a creamy rather than tangy version. Service could be sharper. Wines include many good bottles, although most are over £20. House South African is £14.50.

CHEF: Derek Blair PROPRIETORS: Nick and Topher Nairn OPEN: Mon to Sat 12 to 2, 6 to 9.30 CLOSED: 25 and 26 Dec, 1 and 2 Jan MEALS: Set L £13.50 (2 courses) to £17, Set D £27.50 SERVICE: not inc CARDS: Amex, Delta, Diners, MasterCard, Switch, Visa DETAILS: 75 seats. Private parties: 40 main room, 40 private room. Vegetarian meals. Children's helpings. No smoking before coffee. Music. Air-conditioned ACCOMMODATION: 4 rooms, all with bath/shower. TV. Room only £110 to £140 (*The Which? Hotel Guide*) (£5)

Number Sixteen £

NEW ENTRY

16 Byres Road, Glasgow G11 5JY
TEL: (0141) 339 2544 FAX: (0141) 576 1505

COOKING **3**
MODERN BRITISH
£14–£33

Aisla and Rupert Staniforth (who has cooked at a number of restaurants in the Guide, including the Old Vicarage at Ridgeway and Marsh Goose at Moreton-in-Marsh) took over this small, split-level restaurant (once a branch of Pierre Victoire) at the end of 1999. It has a lot of competition hereabouts, but also plenty going for it, not least a sensible menu that incorporates variety without trying to be too ambitious. Fish and vegetable dishes outnumber meat main courses, and the repertoire extends from chicken with a sharp red pepper pesto, to mushroom and creme fraîche risotto with a poached egg.

Good timing has made a success of moist caramelised scallops (on artichoke purée with Parma ham and lemon cream), and 'well-hung, tender, flavoursome' ribeye steak served with both red wine butter and a horseradish and parsley sauce. Desserts might take in raspberry and pistachio iced terrine, as well as warm prune and armagnac tart with caramel ice cream, and a list of around 20 modestly priced wines starts with house French Sauvignon Blanc and Spanish Tempranillo at £10.50.

CHEF: Rupert Staniforth PROPRIETORS: Rupert and Aisla Staniforth OPEN: Mon to Sat 12 to 2.30, 5.30 to 10 CLOSED: Christmas, first 2 weeks Jan MEALS: alc (main courses L £6 to £8, D £8 to £12). Set D before 6.30 £9.50 (2 courses) to £11.50 SERVICE: not inc, 10% for parties of 8 or more CARDS: Delta, MasterCard, Switch, Visa DETAILS: 42 seats. Private parties: 42 main room. Vegetarian meals. Children's helpings. No music

▲ One Devonshire Gardens

1 Devonshire Gardens, Glasgow G12 0UX
TEL: (0141) 339 2001 FAX: (0141) 337 1663 — COOKING **6**
EMAIL: onedevonshire@btconnect.com — FRANCO-SCOTTISH
WEB SITE: www.one-devonshire-gardens.co.uk — £45–£73

Set in an attractive area of trees, parks and grand houses in the West End, the three properties that make up this address came under new ownership in March 2000. The dining room is still decorated in comfortable bourgeois style, with high ceilings, big windows and enormous potted palms (though there are plans for refurbishment), and Andrew Fairlie remains as head chef. He presides over a menu with strong classical European foundations: risotto milanese, Toulouse cassoulet, and roast breast of squab pigeon with braised cabbage and truffled gnocchi.

The kitchen is commended for keeping its priorities firmly in place (and not wasting time on lavish incidentals), producing a smooth, balanced cream of Jerusalem artichoke soup, and a simple, elegant, understated dish of crispy roast skate wing with spinach and fondant potato. Presentation is attractive – splayed spring onions, courgette, avocado and artichokes decorating a plate of duck carpaccio – and, though portions can be large, the food is characterised by 'richness without heaviness': for example braised oxtail with a 'dense but light' stuffing of wild mushrooms in a 'gooey' sauce.

The star of an inspection meal was a spiced mulled wine soufflé with perfect consistency and well-balanced flavours. Service is 'not stuffy in the least, in fact quite chummy', though prices on the French-dominated list of almost 300 wines aren't quite as friendly. House selections start at £19 and even the cheapest half-bottle is over £15.

CHEF: Andrew Fairlie PROPRIETOR: Residence International OPEN: Sun to Fri L 12.15 to 2, all week D 7.15 to 10 MEALS: alc D (main courses £16.50 to £19.50). Set L Mon to Fri £21 (2 courses) to £27.50, Set L Sun £27.50 SERVICE: not inc, card slips closed CARDS: Amex, Delta, Diners, MasterCard, Visa DETAILS: 40 seats. Private parties: 50 main room, 12 to 32 private rooms. Vegetarian meals. Children's helpings. Jacket and tie. No smoking in dining room. Music ACCOMMODATION: 27 rooms, all with bath/shower. TV. Phone. Room only £145 to £230. Baby facilities (*The Which? Hotel Guide*)

La Parmigiana

447 Great Western Road, Glasgow G12 8HH
TEL: (0141) 334 0686 FAX: (0141) 332 3533

COOKING **2**
ITALIAN
£17–£53

An Italian restaurant much favoured by the Italian community, La Parmigiana draws support from others too. It may feel a little cramped when full, but what draws people are 'a happy atmosphere' and Sandro Giovanazzi's assured modern cooking. Set-lunch and pre-theatre menus offer excellent value, particularly for generously served fish and shellfish stews. Pasta dishes – lobster ravioli in basil cream sauce, for example – have been praised, as has 'pink and juicy' calf's liver with agrodolce shallots and pancetta. Recommended puddings have included marbled mousse of dark and white chocolate served with pear, or you might try crêpe gâteau with lemon and lime syrup. Apart from a couple of champagnes, the wine list is wholly Italian, the country anatomised into its regions and the choices sound. House wines are a southern Trebbiano at £12.10 and a northern Merlot at £12.50.

CHEF: Sandro Giovanazzi PROPRIETORS: Angelo and Sandro Giovanazzi OPEN: Mon to Sat 12 to 2.30, 6 to 11 CLOSED: 25 and 26 Dec, 1 and 2 Jan, Easter Mon MEALS: alc (main courses £11.50 to £16). Set L £9.10, Set D 6 to 7.30 £9.50 (2 courses) to £11.50 SERVICE: not inc CARDS: Amex, Delta, Diners, MasterCard, Switch, Visa DETAILS: 60 seats. Private parties: 60 main room. Vegetarian meals. Children's helpings. No cigars/pipes in dining room. Music. Air-conditioned (£5)

Puppet Theatre

11 Ruthven Lane, G12 9BG
TEL: (0141) 339 8444 FAX: (0141) 339 7666
EMAIL: puppet@bigbeat.co.uk

COOKING **5**
MODERN EUROPEAN
£26–£64

Down a cobbled lane off Byres Road, the throbbing main artery of Glasgow's trend-setting West End, is the Puppet Theatre. Snug and dimly lit Edwardian interiors, together with an oddly shaped conservatory extension, lend the place plenty of offbeat yet romantic character. The name is a flight of fancy only; no marionettes perform here. Hervé Martin does, however, and the idiom of the cooking is as contemporary as the décor is quaintly retro. He avoids clichés, but does not set out to be different for the sake of it; rather he knows how to invent without compromising the basic rules pertaining to flavour and texture, turning up a starter of impressively light asparagus mousse for example, topped with thin, crunchy carrot crisps, surrounded by trompette mushrooms, all in a chervil broth.

Oriental ideas are used to full effect in main courses such as seared cod on aromatically peppery bok choy, and a well-conceived dish of tender but resilient monkfish wrapped sushi-like in arami seaweed with a midnight-black squid ink sauce. Full marks for invention have gone to a dessert of apple cobbler of perfect texture, served with a cider reduction, and a stunning ice cream of beetroot and vanilla with a dried apple crisp. Other options might include a hot soufflé of roast mango and gin served with chocolate sorbet. Service has been commended as 'absolutely ace'. Wines are divided into 'classic' and 'modern' by colour, and the list includes a good selection of aperitifs. Eight wines are available by the glass, with house wines starting at £13.

CHEF: Hervé Martin PROPRIETORS: Ron McCulloch and George Swanson OPEN: Tue to Fri and Sun L 12 to 2.30, Tue to Sun D 7 to 10.30 CLOSED: 26 Dec, 1 and 2 Jan MEALS: alc (main courses L £8.50 to £11, D £8 to £21.50) SERVICE: not inc CARDS: Amex, Delta, MasterCard, Switch, Visa DETAILS: 65 seats. Private parties: 26 main room, 12 to 16 private rooms. Small car park. Vegetarian meals. No children under 12. No smoking in 1 dining room. Music

Rogano

11 Exchange Place, Glasgow G1 3AN — COOKING **2**
TEL: (0141) 248 4055 FAX: (0141) 248 2608 — SEAFOOD
WEB SITE: www.rogano.co.uk — £25–£61

Proclaiming itself 'the oldest surviving restaurant in Glasgow', Rogano is a fine example of art deco styling. It was fitted out in 1935, as the Queen Mary was being built on the Clyde, and remains a winner on this count. Seafood is a draw: from plain oysters, to salmon and scallop sashimi, by way of the ever-present fish soup with rouille and croûtons, and simply treated main courses such as halibut au gratin, grilled lemon sole and lobster thermidor. Meat dishes are in the minority, but might run to rack of lamb with a rosemary crust, or an individual beef Wellington with truffle sauce. Finish with steamed apple and cinnamon pudding, or rhubarb soup with frozen tangerine mousse. Wine mark-ups tend to be high, with the result that bottles under £20 are few and far between, although house Bordeaux is £10.95.

CHEF: William Simpson PROPRIETOR: Punch Taverns OPEN: all week 12 to 2.30, 6.30 to 10.30 CLOSED: 25 Dec, 1 Jan MEALS: alc (main courses £18 to £32.50). Set L £17 SERVICE: 12.5% (optional), card slips closed CARDS: Amex, Delta, Diners, MasterCard, Switch, Visa DETAILS: 60 seats. Private parties: 60 main room, 20 private room. Vegetarian meals. No smoking before 2 L and 10 D. Wheelchair access (not WC). Music. Air-conditioned (£5)

78 St Vincent 

78 St Vincent Street, Glasgow G2 5UB
TEL: (0141) 248 7878 FAX: (0141) 248 4663 — COOKING **1**
EMAIL: frontdesk@78stvincent.com — BRASSERIE
WEB SITE: www.78stvincent.com — £25–£50

The feel of a turn-of-the-century (twentieth, not twenty-first) French brasserie is the atmosphere aimed for at this central Glasgow address, which explains the high ceilings, marble staircase and swagged red curtains, although the cooking will strike more contemporary notes. Seared springy-textured scallops have come with a frothy nage of their corals, smoked bacon and watercress salad, and beef fillet has also impressed, served in a plentiful reduction of red wine and shallots and accompanied by parsley purée. Although vegetables have disappointed and not all desserts have pleased, a zingy layer of mango has helped to make a success of crisply caramelised crème brûlée. Service is friendly enough, but could be a bit more informed. Wines are well chosen, kicking off with a house selection that starts at £12.95 for a bottle, or £4.35 for a large measure that turns out to be a third of a bottle.

CHEF: Stuart Wilson PROPRIETOR: Mike Conyers OPEN: all week 12 to 3, 5 to 10.30 (10.45 Fri and Sat, 10 Sun) CLOSED: 25 Dec MEALS: Set L £10.95 (2 courses) to £13.95, Set D £20 (2 courses) to £24.50 SERVICE: not inc, card slips closed, 10% for parties of 7 or more CARDS: Amex, Delta, Diners, MasterCard, Switch, Visa DETAILS: 116 seats. Private parties: 68 main room, 16 private room. Vegetarian meals. Children's helpings. No smoking in dining room. Wheelchair access (also WC). No music (£5)

Stravaigin

26 Gibson Street, Hillhead, Glasgow G12 8NX
TEL: (0141) 334 2665 FAX: (0141) 334 4099
EMAIL: bookings@stravaigin.com
WEB SITE: www.stravaigin.com

COOKING **4**
GLOBAL
£34–£47

The menu at Colin Clydesdale's bright, modern basement restaurant takes in ideas from as far afield as Cuba and China, applying them to fine native ingredients, including Aberdeen Angus beef and West Coast fish. The style typically produces a range of starters from light Burmese seafood broth with spiced potatoes, to seared lambs' kidneys (rare enough to be deemed 'not for the faint-hearted') in a rich marsala sauce with pumpkin ravioli and lemon pesto. To follow might be a rustic dish of flavoursome rabbit with Puy lentils; poussin with burnt onion polenta and roasted garlic sauce; or perhaps mullet on a bed of noodles with a Thai-flavoured broth containing mussels and mushrooms. East meets West in a dessert of hazelnut and goat's-cheese tart with chillies and plums; otherwise, there may be a rich Belgian chocolate cushion crowned with ice cream in a Kahlua sauce, or Scottish cheeses with quince jelly and bannocks. The helpfully annotated wine list features some unusual bottles – including a white Châteauneuf du Pape – and is reasonably priced, starting with house wines at £11.25.

CHEF/PROPRIETOR: Colin Clydesdale OPEN: Fri and Sat L 12 to 2.30, Tue to Sun D 5 to 11.30 CLOSED: 25 and 26 Dec, 1 and 2 Jan MEALS: Set D £20 (2 courses) to £25. Café/bar menu available SERVICE: not inc CARDS: Amex, Delta, Diners, MasterCard, Switch, Visa DETAILS: 75 seats. Private parties: 75 main room. Vegetarian meals. Children's helpings. No smoking before 10. Music. Air-conditioned (£5)

Ubiquitous Chip

12 Ashton Lane, Glasgow G12 8SJ
TEL: (0141) 334 5007 FAX: (0141) 337 1302
EMAIL: mail@ubiquitouschip.co.uk
WEB SITE: www.ubiquitouschip.co.uk

COOKING **4**
SCOTTISH
£33–£67

Now in its twenty-ninth year, the Chip continues to attract praise for its appealing setting down a cobbled mews, its ambience, and the flair of chef and owner Ronnie Clydesdale. The menu gives a measure of his passions: to make use of carefully sourced Scottish produce and 'treat it in a simple, wholesome and imaginative way but never losing sight of the tradition'. Wild Dumfries-shire rabbit thus fetches up with cinnamon and olive mash, while Troon-landed cod arrives with star anise sauce. Heather honey, Orkney organic salmon, Perthshire pork, Aberdeen Angus beef, West Coast squid, and Ayrshire

Bonnet cheese find their way on to the Chip's two menus, one in the brasserie-style Upstairs and the other in the more traditional dining room next to the pretty courtyard with its greenery.

Wood pigeon has been singled out for commendation, while Laphroaig salmon, free-range pork and bacon, and pears with maple syrup 'made my daughter's twenty-first'. Staff are informative and attentive. Fine wines from Bordeaux, Burgundy and the Rhône are complemented by an extensive German section and plenty of star bottles from the New World. Mark-ups are reasonable, and a smattering of halves cater for those who want to mix and match. House red, white and rosé are all £12.95, or £3.25 for a small glass, £5.20 for a large.

CHEF/PROPRIETOR: Ronald Clydesdale OPEN: all week 12 to 2.30, 5.30 to 11 CLOSED: 25 Dec, 1 Jan MEALS: Set L £18.95 (2 courses) to £23.95, Set D £27.95 (2 courses) to £32.95 SERVICE: not inc CARDS: Amex, Delta, Diners, MasterCard, Switch, Visa DETAILS: 80 seats. 60 seats outside. Private parties: 80 main room, 20 private room. Vegetarian meals. Children's helpings. Wheelchair access (also WC). No music (£5)

GULLANE East Lothian **map 11**

▲ Greywalls

Muirfield, Gullane EH31 2EG
TEL: (01620) 842144 FAX: (01620) 842241
EMAIL: hotel@greywalls.co.uk
WEB SITE: www.greywalls.co.uk
on A198, at E end of Gullane

COOKING **5**
MODERN BRITISH
£429–£58

The impending (though possibly temporary) closure of La Potinière after 25 years will disappoint many readers, but Greywalls still flies the local flag, catering for visitors who come out from Edinburgh, or who take their golf seriously enough to play at Muirfield. The elegant Lutyens house has 'wonderful' gardens, comfortable lounges, and a history to rival almost anywhere in the Guide, including Ullswater's Sharrow Bay (see entry): both opened in 1948. Three-course lunches and four-course dinners make use of regional materials, a few of them organic, many from the sea: wafers of peat-smoked Shetland salmon, served with caper berries and lemon oil, or carpaccio of Isle of May scallops with coconut and coriander dressing.

Red meat is an equally strong suit, however, judging by loin of venison with honey-roast parsnips and creamed cabbage, and a very fine tournedos of Angus beef fillet with a ragoût of bacon, wild mushrooms and shallots. Welsh rarebit might feature as an alternative to desserts of chocolate and pistachio parfait, or summer berries served with blackcurrant sorbet. Service is 'friendly and attentive', and an impressive wine list is weighted towards classics from Bordeaux and Burgundy, providing an opportunity for those who can afford it to taste some rare older vintages (Ch. Calon-Ségur 1928 at £650, for example). But there is plenty of unusual and experimental drinking in all price brackets, a smattering of useful halves and ten wines by the glass starting at £2.60.

'They don't need butter and cream to stop your heart, the prices do this by themselves.'
(On eating in Berkshire)

CHEFS: Simon and Matthew Burns PROPRIETORS: Giles and Ros Weaver OPEN: all week 12.30 to 1.45, 7.30 to 9.15 CLOSED: Nov to Mar MEALS: Set L Mon to Sat £15 (2 courses) to £17.50, Set L Sun £20, Set D £37.50 SERVICE: not inc, card slips closed CARDS: Amex, Delta, Diners, MasterCard, Switch, Visa DETAILS: 50 seats. 12 seats outside. Private parties: 35 main room, 20 private room. Car park. Children's helpings. Jacket and tie at D. No smoking in dining room. Wheelchair access (not WC). No music ACCOMMODATION: 23 rooms, all with bath/shower. TV. Phone. B&B £105 to £210. Rooms for disabled. Baby facilities (*The Which? Hotel Guide*) (£5)

INVERKEILOR Angus map 11

▲ Gordon's

NEW ENTRY

32 Main Street, Inverkeilor DD11 5RN
TEL/FAX: (01241) 830364
off A92 from Arbroath to Montrose

COOKING **4**
MODERN SCOTTISH
£20–£44

Find this small restaurant with its stone-slabbed floor and beamed ceiling in a terrace on an inauspicious street in a little town near the stunning beaches of Lunan Bay. Gordon's is very much a family concern, son Garry joining father Gordon at the stoves. They have chosen their suppliers cannily, and the marriage of good sourcing and considerable assurance in technique has produced some fine results: an intensely flavoured soup of roast red peppers and plum tomatoes with pesto crème fraîche, for example.

Combinations that might sound a little daunting in description turn out to work well: salmon stuffed with a rarebit mixture of Finnan haddock, cheese and mustard, or guinea fowl with haggis champit and crispy noodles, served with a Drambuie jus that was 'pleasantly sweet' without overpowering the good stock base. Large portions may leave little room for pudding, but those who have paced themselves will be ready to tackle shortbread and Atholl brose torte with forest fruit coulis, or a pyramid of chocolate and Malibu marquise with orange and apricot syrup. Wines don't quite show the same imaginative flair as the cooking, but prices are kept on a tight rein, with house French £9.80.

CHEFS: Gordon and Garry Watson PROPRIETORS: Gordon and Maria Watson OPEN: Tue to Fri and Sun L 12 to 1.45, Tue to Sat D 7 to 9 CLOSED: last 3 weeks Jan, 2 weeks Oct to Nov MEALS: alc (main courses £11 to £15.50) SERVICE: not inc, card slips closed CARDS: Delta, MasterCard, Switch, Visa DETAILS: 24 seats. Private parties: 20 main room. Car park. Vegetarian meals. Children's helpings. No children under 12 at D. No smoking in dining room. Wheelchair access (not WC). No music ACCOMMODATION: 2 rooms, both with bath/shower. TV. B&B £35 to £45 (double room. No children under 6

▲ means accommodation is available.

All entries, including Round-ups, are fully indexed at the back of the Guide.

Restaurateurs justifiably resent no-shows. If you quote a credit card number when booking, you may be liable for the restaurant's lost profit margin if you don't turn up. Always phone to cancel.

INVERNESS Highland map 11

▲ Culloden House

Culloden, Inverness IV2 7BZ
TEL: (01463) 790461 FAX: (01463) 792181
EMAIL: info@cullodenhouse.co.uk
WEB SITE: www.cullodenhouse.co.uk
from Inverness take A96 to Nairn, turn right after 1m, then left at Culloden House Avenue

COOKING **2**
INTERNATIONAL
£35–£60

This grand Georgian mansion with its Adam plaster reliefs, spacious high-ceilinged rooms and marble fireplaces has not been modernised more than is absolutely necessary. 'There are not too many frills here,' observed one visitor, 'and not many letdowns.' Its rather old-fashioned style includes a mid-meal sorbet, and such offerings as avocado with orange and grapefruit segments, and melon with Parma ham. Alongside tourist favourites of smoked salmon, or venison collops with potato and cabbage rösti, come West coast scallops with garlic butter, duck with Puy lentils, and puddings of chocolate truffle cake, and glazed pear with vanilla parfait and bitter chocolate sorbet. Eleven wines by the glass head up an extensive and wide-ranging list, and although prices can be on the high side there are a few bottles under £20.

CHEF: Michael Simpson PROPRIETOR: North American Country Inns OPEN: all week 12.30 to 2, 7 to 8.45 MEALS: alc L (main courses £12 to £18). Set D £35 SERVICE: not inc, card slips closed CARDS: Amex, Delta, Diners, MasterCard, Switch, Visa DETAILS: 60 seats. Private parties: 60 main room, 40 to 60 private rooms. Car park. Vegetarian meals. No children under 14. Jacket and tie. No smoking in dining room. No music ACCOMMODATION: 28 rooms, all with bath/shower. TV. Phone. B&B £145 to £270. No children under 10 exc babies. Baby facilities

▲ Dunain Park

Inverness IV3 8JN
TEL: (01463) 230512 FAX: (01463) 224532
EMAIL: dunainparkhotel@btinternet.com
WEB SITE: www.dunainparkhotel.co.uk
on A82 to Fort William, 1m from town boundary

COOKING **2**
SCOTTISH
£37–£55

The unpretentious Georgian house, plainly but comfortably furnished, sits in extensive grounds just outside Inverness, where Ann Nicoll serves a style of food that keeps up to date without losing its traditional identity. Aberdeen Angus sirloin steak forms a centrepiece, served any of six ways, but there may also be Shetland salmon fillet baked in sea salt, with new potatoes and sorrel sauce, or breast of pheasant on potato and lentil mash. Cajun-spiced seafood in a tomato and bean broth is a fairly contemporary way to start, carrot and lovage soup more old-fashioned. Sweets are 'help yourself from the buffet', service is efficient and accommodating, and wines cover a good spread of styles and regions, with one or two bargains to unearth. House wines are £14.

'The staff are not robots, they're absolute zombies.' (On eating in Wales)

CHEF: Ann Nicoll PROPRIETORS: Ann and Edward Nicoll OPEN: all week D only 7 to 8.30 MEALS: alc (main courses £16 to £18). Set D £25 SERVICE: not inc, card slips closed CARDS: Amex, Delta, MasterCard, Switch, Visa DETAILS: 36 seats. Private parties: 8 main room. Car park. Vegetarian meals. Children's helpings. No smoking in dining room. Wheelchair access (not WC). No music ACCOMMODATION: 13 rooms, all with bath/shower. TV. Phone. B&B £138 to £198 (double room). Rooms for disabled. Baby facilities. Swimming pool (*The Which? Hotel Guide*) (£5)

KILCHRENAN Argyll & Bute map 11

▲ Taychreggan

NEW ENTRY

Kilchrenan PA35 1HQ
TEL: (01866) 833211 or 833366
FAX: (01866) 833244
EMAIL: info@taychregganhotel.co.uk
WEB SITE: www.taychregganhotel.co.uk
on B845, 7m S of Taynuilt

COOKING **4**
MODERN SCOTTISH
£46–£55

The peaceful location beside Loch Awe is romantic, although whoever built the old stone house with its cobbled courtyard – formerly a drovers' inn – did not take as much advantage of the views as they might. Dinner is four courses, with two or three options at each stage, and skills are evident in a classically executed beurre blanc to accompany roast salmon fillet rubbed with sea salt, and in a rich truffle jus that partnered a pigeon breast starter: impeccably timed rare slices assembled into a pyramid, with deftly roast shallots. Roast saddle of full-flavoured venison was equally well-handled at inspection, served with long shafts of rosemary scented salsify.

Vegetables are mostly successful, and vegetarians are treated well, judging by a starter of roasted hazelnuts, almonds and cashews arranged around a dainty Parmesan basket with perkily dressed fresh frilly greens. The second course offers a choice between sorbet and soup (broccoli and Brie perhaps, or carrot and sweetcorn), and desserts run to profiteroles with apricot ice cream, or an intense chocolate marquise. Canny purchasing extends to Scottish cheeses (served after dessert), and to cognacs, malt whiskies and a largely French collection of wines that starts with house Vin de Pays d'Oc at £13.95.

CHEF: Jerome Prodanu PROPRIETOR: Annie Paul OPEN: all week D only 7.30 to 8.45 MEALS: Set D £35. Bar L available SERVICE: not inc, card slips closed CARDS: Amex, MasterCard, Switch, Visa DETAILS: 40 seats. Private parties: 50 main room. Car park. Vegetarian meals. No children under 14. No smoking in dining room. Music ACCOMMODATION: 19 rooms, all with bath/shower. Phone. B&B £71 to £164. No children under 14. Fishing (*The Which? Hotel Guide*)

---

indicates that smoking is either banned altogether or that a dining-room is maintained for non-smokers. The symbol does not apply to restaurants that simply have no-smoking areas.

£ *means that it is possible to have a three-course meal, including coffee, half a bottle of house wine and service for £25 or less per person, at any time the restaurant is open, i.e. at dinner as well as lunch. It may be possible to spend considerably more than this, but by choosing carefully you should find £25 or less achievable.*

KILLIECRANKIE Perthshire & Kinross map 11

▲ Killiecrankie Hotel

Killiecrankie PH16 5LG
TEL: (01796) 473220 FAX: (01796) 472451
EMAIL: enquiries@killiecrankiehotel.co.uk
WEB SITE: www.killiecrankiehotel.co.uk
off A9, 3m N of Pitlochry

COOKING **3**
GLOBAL
£42–£51

A scene of slaughter during the Jacobite rebellion in 1689, Killiecrankie is now a tranquil place, on a recommended walking route through a National Trust for Scotland Reserve. Shielded from the A9, beside the River Garry, the hotel offers a welcome pit-stop for travellers, where Mark Easton's cooking is founded on a bedrock of Aberdeen Angus beef, and native game, fish and shellfish. To these are added the contents of a global store cupboard, producing, for example, steamed Shetland mussels in a chilli, coconut and coriander broth, and goujons of Gressingham duck stir-fried with broccoli, mange-tout and noodles in a honey and ginger sauce. A European strand is also evident, as the food appeals across a broad spectrum: from smoked chicken and saffron risotto via herb-crusted cod with beurre blanc to glazed lemon tart or baked Alaska. Four-course meals end with cheese, coffee is included, and the 50-strong wine list includes some enterprising and good-value choices, as well as a handful of house wines and half-bottles. Prices start at £12.

CHEF: Mark Easton PROPRIETORS: Colin and Carole Anderson OPEN: all week D 7 to 8.30 CLOSED: Jan, Mon and Tue Dec to March MEALS: Set D £32.50. Bar meals available L SERVICE: not inc, card slips closed CARDS: Delta, MasterCard, Switch, Visa DETAILS: 30 seats. Private parties: 12 main room. Car park. Vegetarian meals. Children's helpings. No children under 5 at D. No smoking in dining room. No music ACCOMMODATION: 10 rooms, all with bath/shower. TV. Phone. D,B&B £66 to £178 (*The Which? Hotel Guide*)

KINCLAVEN Perthshire & Kinross map 11

▲ Ballathie House

Kinclaven, By Stanley PH1 4QN
TEL: (01250) 883268 FAX: (01250) 883396
EMAIL: email@ballathiehousehotel.com
WEB SITE: www.ballathiehousehotel.com
off B9099, take right fork 1m N of Stanley

COOKING **2**
MODERN SCOTTISH
£27–£58

A mile-long drive leads through trees and rhododendrons to an attractively furnished and decorated baronial building 'idyllically situated' beside the River Tay. Elegant rooms and soft colours add to the appeal, while the kitchen seeks to tread a line between traditional and modern. Dill-cured salmon with a grain mustard dressing, and beef fillet with a brandy and peppercorn sauce share the menu with loin of lamb and couscous, and monkfish with leek mash and cumin-roasted courgettes. Presentation is attractive: 'cooking for the eyes', one called it. Scottish cheeses provide an alternative to iced mint terrine or strawberry crème brûlée. A selection of 12 house wines, starting at £11.75, are also offered by the glass and half-carafe, making good-value drinking a flexible affair. Prices are reasonable throughout the extensive and catholic list, which includes a fine selection of clarets.

CHEF: Kevin MacGillivray PROPRIETOR: Ballathie House Hotel Co Ltd OPEN: all week L 12.30 to 2, D 7 to 9 MEALS: Set L £15 (2 courses) to £18.50, Set D £35 SERVICE: not inc CARDS: Amex, Delta, Diners, MasterCard, Switch, Visa DETAILS: 70 seats. Private parties: 90 main room, 16 and 32 private rooms. Car park. Vegetarian meals. Children's helpings. Jacket and tie. No smoking. Wheelchair access (also WC). No Music ACCOMMODATION: 27 rooms, all with bath/shower. TV. Phone. D,B&B £95 to £125. Rooms for disabled. Baby facilities. Fishing

KINGUSSIE Highland **map 11**

▲ The Cross

Tweed Mill Brae, Ardbroilach Road,
Kingussie PH21 1TC COOKING **6**
TEL: (01540) 661166 FAX: (01540) 661080 MODERN SCOTTISH
WEB SITE: www.thecross.co.uk £48–£58

Just a few hundred yards from the crossroads at centre of the village, this former water-powered tweed mill occupies four acres of semi-wilderness beside the Gynack burn, where modern art looks very much at home among the rough stone walls and heavy beams. 'Exemplary meal and great atmosphere,' summed up one who also appreciated Tony Hadley's dry, laconic wit, which soon breaks the ice and gets diners talking to each other. Five-course dinners typically start with seafood – West Coast prawns with an avocado salad maybe, or Shetland scallops with Thai-dressed noodles – followed by a soup such as creamy butter-bean. A salmon or smoked haddock fishcake might come next, and so far there is no choice.

If this sounds all rather ordinary, do not be taken in. The lack of flannel in menu descriptions belies the labour that goes into each dish. One visitor's roast cod fillet proved to be 'a deceptively simple description for the juiciest, most perfectly judged slab of top-notch fresh cod I can ever remember eating'. It came with a fresh herb crust 'a million miles from the usual stale sawdust that passes for a herb crust'. This is not overworked or complex cooking, just skilful and appealing. Main course offers a two-way choice, typically between meats such as fillet of beef, or breast of Ayrshire guinea fowl, as does dessert: one who could not decide between pear and almond tart and dark chocolate cheesecake simply ate both. The cheeseboard is 'unusual and unmissable', with some real stunners sourced from around the UK.

France is deliberately absent from the enthusiastic wine list, which covers the rest of the world in exemplary fashion. Marvellous bottles from California, Australia and South America are temptingly priced, and the lack of French staples provides a catalyst for experimentation. Can't cope without claret? Try Santa Ema Merlot Reserve 1996 from Chile (£16.85), or South Africa's Thelema Cabernet Sauvignon 1994 (£26) for a stimulating alternative. Prices start around £10, with a wide choice under £20.

New main entries and restaurant closures are listed near the front of the book.

CHEFS: Ruth Hadley and Becca Henderson PROPRIETORS: Tony and Ruth Hadley OPEN: Wed to Mon D only 7 to 8.30 CLOSED: 1 Dec to 28 Feb MEALS: Set D £37.50 SERVICE: not inc, card slips closed CARDS: Delta, MasterCard, Switch, Visa DETAILS: 24 seats. Private parties: 30 main room. Car park. No children under 8. No smoking in dining room. Wheelchair access (also WC). No music ACCOMMODATION: 9 rooms, all with bath/shower. Phone. D,B&B £115 to £230. No children under 8 (*The Which? Hotel Guide*)

LINLITHGOW West Lothian **map 11**

▲ Champany Inn

Champany Corner, Linlithgow EH49 7LU
TEL: (01506) 834532 FAX: (01506) 834302
EMAIL: info@champany.com COOKING **6**
WEB SITE: www.champany.com SCOTTISH
2m NE of Linlithgow at junction of A904 and A803 £36–£78

Few restaurateurs can have been more cheered by the resumption of normal service after the beef-on-the-bone ban than Clive and Anne Davidson, whose lives are dedicated to serving up prime cuts of Aberdeen Angus. Theirs is the sort of place that gives 'traditional' a good name, with an old stone-built, wooden-raftered round house set with polished tables, and an eminently straightforward approach to food: find the best beef and cook it simply. Hanging time is generally three weeks, after which the meat is butchered in-house and served in a variety of cuts from pope's eye to porterhouse, from ribeye to strip loin. It may only be chargrilled steak, but 'it simply doesn't get any better than this'.

By way of variety, there are Loch Gruinart oysters, lobsters from a tank, and salmon plain or smoked. The food is lightly cooked to retain proper texture – be it asparagus in a salad, West Coast scallops, or 'pink and tender' lamb – and only an occasional hiccup mars the smooth progression of first-class dishes. The same quality beef is also made into burgers, which form the mainstay of the Chop and Ale House. For dessert there could be lemon meringue pie, or spotted dick. Service is 'well nigh perfect'. Finding the perfect red wine to accompany the beef may prove an unexpected dilemma. The 32,000-bottle cellar contains an overwhelming range of red Burgundy, Bordeaux, South African Pinotage, Australian Shiraz, Californian Merlot and so on, though white wine drinkers are well catered for too. The costs of keeping such an extensive collection are reflected in the prices and there is little under £20, though own-label house wines begin at £14.50.

CHEFS: David Gibson, Clive Davidson and Kevin Hope PROPRIETORS: Clive and Anne Davidson OPEN: Mon to Fri L 12.30 to 2, Mon to Sat D 7 to 10 CLOSED: 25 and 26 Dec, 1 and 2 Jan MEALS: alc (main courses £15.50 to £27.50). Set L £16.75 (2 courses) SERVICE: 10%, card slips closed CARDS: Amex, Delta, Diners, MasterCard, Switch, Visa DETAILS: 50 seats. 20 seats outside. Private parties: 50 main room, 30 private room. Car park. Vegetarian meals. No children under 8. Wheelchair access (also WC). No music ACCOMMODATION: 16 rooms, all with bath/shower. TV. Phone. B&B £95. Rooms for disabled

Occasional music *in the details at the end of an entry means live or recorded music is played in the dining room only rarely or for special events.* No music *means it is never played.*

LOCHINVER Highland map 11

▲ The Albannach

Baddidarroch, Lochinver IV27 4LP
TEL: (01571) 844407 FAX: (01571) 844285

COOKING 5
MODERN SCOTTISH
£40–£48

Local walks and boat-trips, and magnificent views across the harbour to Suilven and the Assynt Mountains, make this 'an absolute must' for anyone travelling in the remote north-west. Much of The Albannach's produce is wild or free-range, and from as close to Lochinver as possible: vegetables are grown by local crofters, fish and shellfish come directly from small boats landing at the pier. The five-course format typically starts with 'beautifully fresh and superbly prepared' seafood, such as dressed crab with celeriac rémoulade, grilled langoustines with lemon butter, or roast cod on creamed leeks. A salad or soup follows: perhaps leek and tarragon, or wild mushroom with mustard. Although there is no choice, meals are balanced and results doubtless helped by having not one but two hands-on chefs/proprietors.

The well-sourced materials are managed with care and intelligence. Meats might take in fillet of Highland lamb on Puy lentils with a root vegetable tartlet, and dishes come complete: juniper cabbage, asparagus tips and paprika potatoes, for example, accompanying pan-fried breast of guinea fowl with cider sauce. Occasionally the meat and fish order is reversed, with a starter of wood pigeon breast and a main course of roast turbot with hollandaise. Cheeses come in pairs, at least one of them Scottish (Munster and Mull Cheddar, perhaps), while desserts run to lemon soufflé torte with berry fruits, and hot chocolate fondant with caraway ice cream. Service is friendly and helpful, and wines are mostly French, although due homage is paid to the New World. Prices are very fair, with house wines starting at £8.

CHEFS/PROPRIETORS: Colin Craig and Lesley Crosfield OPEN: all week D only 8 (1 sitting) CLOSED: 1 Dec to 15 Mar MEALS: Set D £32 SERVICE: not inc, card slips closed CARDS: Delta, MasterCard, Switch, Visa DETAILS: 18 seats. Private parties: 24 main room. Car park. No children under 12 in restaurant. No smoking in dining room. No music ACCOMMODATION: 5 rooms, all with bath/shower. Phone. D,B&B £84 to £168. No children under 12 in hotel (*The Which? Hotel Guide*)

MOFFAT Dumfries & Galloway map 11

▲ Well View

Ballplay Road, Moffat DG10 9JU
TEL: (01683) 220184 FAX: (01683) 220088
EMAIL: info@wellview.co.uk
WEB SITE: www.wellview.co.uk

COOKING 4
SCOTTISH-FRENCH
£22–£45

Quiet colours set the tone in this late-Victorian house and, although it is not a grand place, the five-course menu (augmented by generous canapés, mid-meal sorbet, coffee and sweetmeats) is characterised by 'meticulous attention to detail'. Combinations are well chosen, for example in a rich, meaty and professionally made terrine of chicken livers and Puy lentils complemented by a zigzag of sweet raspberry sauce. Timings are spot-on, and the food is 'a pleasure to eat', the highlight at one meal being salmon fillet with a translucent interior and crisp Parmesan crumb topping, served with a creamy dill-flecked Chardonnay sauce.

Dishes are simply conceived and textures taken into account, as in a rare fillet of organic beef, topped with an aubergine crisp, on roasted vegetables, surrounded by a dark, rich sauce of reduced meat stock. Large chunks of freshly cut cheese are delivered on a board, and pudding offers the only choice: perhaps between a chocolate pot with whipped cream, and a triangle of crisp filo wrapped around almond cream, served with butterscotch sauce, vanilla custard, and a milky rum and raisin ice cream. The brisk and unfussy wine list includes bins from around the world although France and Germany receive most attention. House selections start at a reasonable £12, and four or so wines of the day are featured on the menu.

CHEF: Janet Schuckardt PROPRIETORS: Janet and John Schuckardt OPEN: Mon to Fri L 12.30 to 1.25, all week D 6.30 to 8.30 (booking essential Sun L and D) MEALS: Set L £14, Set D £28 SERVICE: none, card slips closed CARDS: Amex, Delta, MasterCard, Switch, Visa DETAILS: 26 seats. Private parties: 20 main room, 6 private room. Car park. No children under 5 at D. No smoking in dining room. Wheelchair access (not WC). No music ACCOMMODATION: 6 rooms, all with bath/shower. TV. B&B £53 to £100. Baby facilities (*The Which? Hotel Guide*) (£5)

MUIR OF ORD Highland **map 11**

▲ The Dower House

Highfield, Muir of Ord IV6 7XN
TEL/FAX: (01463) 870090
EMAIL: tgfg@thedowerhouse.co.uk
on A862, 1m N of Muir of Ord
WEB SITE: www.thedowerhouse.co.uk

COOKING **3**
MODERN BRITISH
£41–£50

Set in three acres, with antlers over the door and antique furniture inside, this Victorian bungalow maintains the atmosphere of a particularly quiet and intimate private home. The sentiment is echoed in the 'dinner party' food that Robyn Aitchison has been serving up for over a dozen years. Dinner is indeed the main meal, consisting of three courses, typically with no choice before dessert, the only other option then being farmhouse cheese.

Its appeal is a straightforward style that might take in a risotto (of asparagus, or red wine) to start, followed by turbot with a herb relish, or maybe fillet of lamb with roast vegetables to follow. Materials extend from chanterelles (served with a starter of creamed eggs), to a collection of interesting leaves and fresh herbs that turned up in one reporter's lobster salad, via fillet of local beef, and raspberries that might be turned into a soufflé. Wines are an interesting blend of French classics and New World finds. Australia, New Zealand and South Africa are all well-represented, and plenty of halves make up for there only being two wines available by the glass. House French is £15.

The Guide's longest-serving restaurants are listed near the front of the book.

CHEF: Robyn Aitchison PROPRIETORS: Robyn and Mena Aitchison OPEN: all week D only 8 to 9.30 (L by arrangement) CLOSED: 25 Dec MEALS: Set D £30 SERVICE: not inc, card slips closed CARDS: Delta, MasterCard, Switch, Visa DETAILS: 26 seats. 6 seats outside. Private parties: 28 main room. Car park. Children's helpings. No smoking in dining room. Wheelchair access (also WC). No music ACCOMMODATION: 6 rooms, all with bath/shower. TV. Phone. B&B £45 to £150. Baby facilities (*The Which? Hotel Guide*)

NAIRN Highland **map 11**

▲ Clifton House

Viewfield Street, Nairn IV12 4HW
TEL: (01667) 453119 FAX: (01667) 452836
EMAIL: macintyre@clifton-hotel.co.uk
WEB SITE: www.clifton-hotel.co.uk
W of town roundabout on A96

COOKING **4**
MODERN SCOTTISH
£28–£47

The theatrical feel of this Victorian town house – the Macintyre home – extends from the bold red, gold and black wallpapered drawing room to the treasure trove of paintings, objets d'art, flowers and soft furnishings that litter the rest of the public rooms. Gordon Macintyre's other passions include good sourcing of raw materials for his guests and a 'fantastic' wine list. Free-range chicken and eggs are local, and simply cooked lobster at dinner might be taken from the sea 'at 6.30pm that day. How fresher can you get?' To-the-point handwritten menus list dishes without flummery and in French.

Throwbacks to a simpler, less vogue-ish style of cooking – egg mayonnaise, smoked salmon mousse, braised leg of lamb – are balanced by an occasional nod to fashion such as a ginger, tapénade and mozzarella stuffing for chicken breast. Caramel custard and chocolate vacherin have appeared among desserts, home-made bread is 'tasty and wholesome', and service is 'wonderful'. The beautifully presented wine list urges diners to drink and be merry, and it is difficult not to succumb, with mature wines from Bordeaux and Burgundy leading the way, and an impeccable selection of pudding wines bringing up the rear. Though great names abound, prices are very fair, with good bottles to be found under £15. Around 14 wines are offered by the glass, starting at £2.50.

CHEFS: J. Gordon and Charles Macintyre PROPRIETOR: J. Gordon Macintyre OPEN: all week 12.30 to 1, 7.30 to 9.30 CLOSED: mid-Dec to mid-Jan MEALS: alc (main courses £12 to £18) SERVICE: none, card slips closed CARDS: Amex, Diners, MasterCard, Visa DETAILS: 45 seats. Private parties: 40 main room, 12 private room. Car park. Vegetarian meals. Children's helpings. No smoking in 1 dining room. Music ACCOMMODATION: 12 rooms, all with bath/shower. B&B £60 to £107 (*The Which? Hotel Guide*) (£5)

'Garnishes they were very keen on; in fact, it got very silly, with lump fish and strawberries on everything. I even got a strawberry on my breakfast kipper!'
(On eating in Yorkshire)

Although the cuisine style noted at the top of entries has in most cases been suggested to the Guide by the restaurants, some have been edited for brevity or appropriateness.

NEWTON STEWART Dumfries & Galloway — map 11

▲ Kirroughtree Hotel

Newton Stewart DG8 6AN
TEL: (01671) 402141 FAX: (01671) 402425
EMAIL: kirroughtree@n-stewart.demon.co.uk
WEB SITE: www.macmillanhotels.com
off A712, just outside Newton Stewart

COOKING **2**
MODERN EUROPEAN
£22–£49

Four-course dinners are the main business at this eighteenth-century house, set in landscaped gardens just off the road between Dumfries and Stranraer. Ian Bennett's broadly European approach takes a country house route, in which a mille-feuille of wood pigeon might be combined with lentil salad and port sauce, and seared Solway scallops given a dressing of orange, cardamom and vanilla oil. Main courses are complete in themselves, featuring perhaps guinea fowl on mashed potato with Savoy cabbage, wild mushrooms, garlic confit and Albufera sauce. Meals begin with a soup, or maybe cod brandade, and end with a choice of Scottish cheeses or dessert: cinnamon soufflé with Glayva cream, or a tartlet of chocolate and raspberries with vanilla sauce and lemon sorbet. Wines (more than half of them French) span a wide range, starting with house Vin de Pays d'Oc at £13.75, and extending to a handful of clarets in three figures.

CHEF: Ian Bennett PROPRIETOR: McMillan Hotels Ltd OPEN: all week 12 to 1.30, 7 to 9 CLOSED: 3 Jan to mid-Feb MEALS: alc L Mon to Sat (main courses £10.50 to £13.50). Set L Sun £13.50, Set D £30 SERVICE: not inc, card slips closed CARDS: Amex, Delta, MasterCard, Switch, Visa DETAILS: 50 seats. Private parties: 24 main room. Car park. Vegetarian meals. No children under 10. Jacket and tie. No smoking in dining room. Occasional music ACCOMMODATION: 17 rooms, all with bath/shower. TV. Phone. D,B&B £78 to £220. No children under 10 (*The Which? Hotel Guide*)

PEAT INN Fife — map 11

▲ Peat Inn

Peat Inn KY15 5LH
TEL: (01334) 840206 FAX: (01334) 840530
EMAIL: reservations@thepeatinn.co.uk
at junction of B940 and B941, 6m SW of St Andrews

COOKING **6**
SCOTTISH
£30–£61

An open log fire usually awaits in the lounge of this white-painted former coaching house at the crossroads. Considered a classy place to eat – people usually dress up – its nooks and crannies are filled with 'splendidly middle-aged fittings and fixtures'. Indeed, it is indisputably old-fashioned, and 'you will be met with courtesy and efficiency', while the kitchen tends to turn its back on culinary trends. David Wilson makes his own position clear: any chef can now acquire exotic ingredients, which may open up lots of new possibilities, 'but is it really what we should be doing?' His aim is to reflect the region and the seasons, at least as far as the main ingredients are concerned.

Cooking tends to be light, so meat and seafood can come very rare, but materials are first-rate, from 'gargantuan' scallops on buttery leeks to 'knockout' beef fillet on a crunchy potato cake surrounded by a rich Madeira sauce.

Presentation has been equally impressive, from a colourful herb salad with prawns, scallops, roast red pepper and black olives, to roast duck with a fragrant spice-rubbed skin, in a pool of lime-flavoured oil. Despite some inconsistencies, most dishes succeed, for example a trio of caramel desserts, incorporating a miniature apple tart, an intensely flavoured crème caramel, and a creamy ice cream in a small pool of toffee sauce. Prices may appear high to some, 'fine' to others.

The helpful and unpretentious wine list features top-quality wines from France, Germany and the New World. The white Burgundy section is notable, followed by a page of Chardonnays from other countries. Fair mark-ups encourage experimentation and make it worthwhile spending a bit more than usual. House wines are £16.

CHEF: David Wilson PROPRIETORS: David and Patricia Wilson OPEN: Tue to Sat 12.30 to 1, 7 to 9.30 CLOSED: 25 Dec, 1 Jan MEALS: alc D (main courses £16 to £19). Set L £19.50, Set D £28 SERVICE: not inc, card slips closed CARDS: Amex, Delta, Diners, MasterCard, Switch, Visa DETAILS: 48 seats. Private parties: 24 main room, 12 to 24 private rooms. Car park. Vegetarian meals. Children's helpings. No smoking in dining room. Wheelchair access (also WC). No music ACCOMMODATION: 8 rooms, all with bath/shower. TV. Phone. B&B £75 to £145. Rooms for disabled (*The Which? Hotel Guide*)

PEEBLES Borders **map 11**

▲ Cringletie House

Eddleston, Peebles EH45 8PL
TEL: (01721) 730233 FAX: (01721) 730244
EMAIL: enquiries@cringletie.com
WEB SITE: www.cringletie.com
on A703, 2m N of Peebles

COOKING **5**
MODERN SCOTTISH
£24–£56

'Unpretentious luxury' is the style at this grand baronial mansion, lavishly decorated with antiques and paintings. Set in 30 acres, including a walled kitchen garden that supplies vegetables and soft fruits in summer, it takes a glossy, modern approach to haute cuisine. Dinner is the marginally more extravagant meal, alternately whipping up light froths and cappuccinos (of oyster, for example, to accompany a starter of scallops, langoustine tails and white asparagus) and adding depth to other sauces with port or Madeira (perhaps to accompany a brace of boneless quail stuffed with trompettes).

Materials are treated sympathetically: loin of red deer (meat comes from a local estate) with lentils and pearl barley, or breast of wood pigeon with wild mushrooms and a mustard dressing. Desserts are no less intriguing: crème caramel comes with fudge nuggets, and Traquair ale adds an unusual note to a dark chocolate gâteau served with bitter orange compote. Ten house recommendations at £14.50 head up an enterprising list that neatly balances Old and New Worlds.

The Guide office can quickly spot when a restaurateur is encouraging customers to write recommending inclusion. Such reports do not further a restaurant's cause. Please tell us if a restaurateur invites you to write to the Guide.

CHEF: Gregg Russell PROPRIETOR: Wrens Hotel Group OPEN: all week 12.30 to 2, 7 to 9 (afternoon tea 3.30 to 5, breakfast 7.30 to 10) MEALS: Set L Mon to Sat £10.95 (2 courses) to £14.95, Set L Sun £17, Set D £32.50 to £35. Light L menu available May to Oct SERVICE: not inc, card slips closed CARDS: Amex, Delta, MasterCard, Switch, Visa DETAILS: 50 seats. Private parties: 60 main room, 10 and 20 private rooms. Car park. Vegetarian meals. Children's helpings. No smoking in dining room. Occasional music ACCOMMODATION: 14 rooms, all with bath/shower. TV. Phone. B&B £75 to £180 (£5)

PERTH Perthshire & Kinross **map 11**

Let's Eat/Let's Eat Again

77 Kinnoull Street, Perth PH1 5EZ
TEL: (01738) 643377 FAX: (01738) 621464
33 George Street, Perth PH1 5LA
TEL: (01738) 633771

COOKING **3**
MODERN EUROPEAN
£22–£43

This smart but casual pair of restaurants, with their warm atmosphere and friendly, efficient service, offer 'unrivalled value for money locally'. The restaurants' aim to be all things to all men may be motivated by sheer instinct for survival, but it packs in plenty of variety: a simply presented three-cheese and red onion tart with tomato fondue, fillet of sea bass in a squat lobster sauce with spinach, and pigeon breast, 'rosy, tender, full of flavour', with a rich-tasting wild mushroom risotto. Menus change often enough to keep up interest for regulars, helping to make the two venues 'high on our list of favourite places' for one couple. For another it is 'the sort of place you could dine at twice a week and not tire of'.

A sensible approach to materials combines a commitment to quality – dived scallops with prawn-flavoured oil – with a few less expensive cuts such as shin of beef or oxtail. Local, and by definition seasonal, ingredients such as asparagus and sea kale play their part too (look to the blackboard for the most up-to-date offerings) while desserts have included steamed chocolate pudding with caramelised banana, and a very custardy bread-and-butter pudding. Lunchtime snackers are encouraged to drop in for one or two starters, a glass of wine and a coffee, and a short, fairly priced wine list kicks off with house South African at £10.50 and French at £9.75.

CHEFS: Tony Heath, Graeme Pallister, Michael Pallister and David Auld (Let's Eat); Neil Simpson and Richard Paton (Let's Eat Again) PROPRIETORS: Tony Heath and Shona Drysdale OPEN: Tue to Sat 12 to 2, 6 to 9.30 (9.45 Let's Eat) CLOSED: 2 weeks Jan, 2 weeks July (Let's Eat); 2 weeks Feb, 2 weeks July (Let's Eat Again) MEALS: alc (main courses £7.50 to £15) SERVICE: not inc, card slips closed CARDS: Amex, Delta, MasterCard, Switch, Visa DETAILS: 70 seats. Private parties: 70 main room (Let's Eat). 36 seats. Private parties: 30 main room (Let's Eat Again). Vegetarian meals. Children's helpings. No smoking in dining room. Wheelchair access (also WC)(Let's Eat). Occasional music (£5)

Prices quoted in the Guide are based on information supplied by restaurateurs. The prices quoted at the top of each entry represent a range, from the lowest meal price to the highest; the latter is inflated by 20 per cent to take account of likely price rises during the year of the Guide.

PORT APPIN Argyll & Bute **map 11**

▲ Airds Hotel

Port Appin PA38 4DF
TEL: (01631) 730236 FAX: (01631) 730535
EMAIL: airds@airds-hotel.com
WEB SITE: www.airds-hotel.com
2m off A828, on E shore of Loch Linnhe

COOKING **7**
MODERN BRITISH
£57–£69

The setting on the edge of a tiny village not far from the shore is considered 'idyllic' even in winter. The house is neat and well kept, modest rather than luxurious (although the armchairs are easy to sink into), and the homely approach of the Allens (who have spent 25 unbroken years in the Guide) is a 'godsend in these days of faceless, formula hotels'. Food and wine orders are required a little before dinner, which lays on four good-value courses using flawlessly fine ingredients at every turn: from a humble starter of baked goats' cheese on a crisp croûton with an olive oil and coriander dressing, to roast loin of venison rivalling the best, sitting on a potato cake with a surfeit of red cabbage.

Impeccable sourcing runs to steak, scallops, sea bass, wild mushrooms, all prepared with a combination of skill, simplicity and flair. Seafood highlights have included poached lobster on an unfashionable but successful avocado salad with gazpacho sauce, garnished with fennel and coriander, and a fillet of salty-skinned sea bass with squat lobsters on a chive velouté. Meals offer a balanced selection. After a second-course no-choice soup, such as silky, truffle-flecked Jerusalem artichoke, might come fillet of cod on creamed white beans, or breast of corn-fed chicken with wild mushrooms and tarragon sauce.

Confident desserts take in baked peaches with a light elderflower and lemon mousse, and a buoyant, spongy date pudding with walnut sauce. Appetisers and fine, chewy-textured bread are of 'outstanding quality', and although tea and coffee are ordinary, petits fours are first rate, and breakfast is worth staying for. Service is friendly, knowledgeable and unstuffy. Quality is consistent on the 250-bottle wine list, and lovers of Burgundy will be entranced by the selections. Although France remains dominant, California and Italy are not neglected, and numerous half-bottles make choosing between great wines a little simpler. There is not much under £20, though house Burgundy starts at £16.50.

CHEFS: Graeme Allen and Steve McCallum PROPRIETORS: the Allen family OPEN: all week D only 7.30 to 8.30 CLOSED: 20 to 27 Dec, 6 to 26 Jan MEALS: Set D £45. Light L available 12.30 to 1.30 SERVICE: not inc, card slips closed CARDS: MasterCard, Switch, Visa DETAILS: 36 seats. Private parties: 40 main room. Car park. Children's helpings. No children under 8 in dining room. No smoking in dining room. No music ACCOMMODATION: 12 rooms, all with bath/shower. TV. Phone. D,B&B £196 to £298. Baby facilities. Fishing (*The Which? Hotel Guide*)

Card slips closed *in the details at the end of an entry indicates that the total on the slips of credit cards is closed when handed over for signature.*

▲ Pierhouse £

Port Appin PA38 4DE
TEL: (01631) 730302 FAX: (01631) 730400
EMAIL: pierhouse@btinternet.com
off A828, on E shore of Loch Linnhe, opposite Lismore ferry

COOKING **3**
SEAFOOD
£20–£50

The location beside Loch Linnhe could hardly be bettered, with views across to Lismore and (in fine weather) beyond to Mull and the Morvern Hills. 'Talk about fresh!' exclaimed one visitor who strolled the few yards to the pier itself where fish and shellfish are landed. As to cooking, the enterprise is a modest one, not averse to buying in a few items that many restaurants would make in their own kitchen, and happy to lay on old-fashioned avocado and prawns in marie-rose sauce, or deep-fried Camembert, but the freshness of plainly presented seafood (particularly shellfish) is the real draw: oysters, chargrilled scallops, lobster thermidor, langoustines with cucumber mayonnaise, or a big platter for those who want a feast on a plate. There is meat too – fillet or sirloin steak with French fries – and vegetarians get a good deal, from pasta to salads: 'even the obligatory nut cutlets were fresh and home made'. Fifty-plus wines are fairly priced, starting with a short house selection under £15.

CHEF: Rita Thomson PROPRIETORS: David and Liz Hamblin OPEN: all week 12.30 to 2.30, 6.30 to 9.30 CLOSED: 25 and 26 Dec MEALS: alc (main courses £7 to £20) SERVICE: not inc, card slips closed CARDS: Delta, MasterCard, Switch, Visa DETAILS: 70 seats. 24 seats outside. Car park. Vegetarian meals. Children's helpings. No smoking in dining room. Wheelchair access (also WC). Music ACCOMMODATION: 12 rooms, all with bath/shower. TV. Phone. B&B £45 to £90. Baby facilities (£5)

ST ANDREWS Fife map 11

West Port

NEW ENTRY

170–172 South Street, St Andrews KY16 9EG
TEL: (01334) 473186 FAX: (01334) 479732

COOKING **4**
GLOBAL FUSION
£20–£47

Hard by the old archway entrance to town, West Port is a thoroughly up-to-date multi-faceted operation, taking in a café-bar, walled beer garden and a large restaurant, where bare white walls and a stripped wood floor are offset on chilly days by a roaring open fire. Alan Matheison cooked at the Atrium (see entry, Edinburgh) before moving here in 1999, bringing his globetrotting cooking style with him. Crab and lobster sushi roll with udon noodles, wasabi and soya might start a meal in one part of the world, before moving to a different continent for a main-course breast and confit leg of squab pigeon with cabbage and bacon and a red wine sauce. A dessert of pineapple Tatin with coconut sorbet and fennel and chilli syrup will send the compass spinning. Performance at inspection was uneven, but high points included a fine Caesar salad, and well-rendered deep-fried cod that came with a potato and spring onion salad with crème fraîche and pesto. Presentation throughout is impressive, and staff are efficient and friendly. An enterprising choice of stylistically grouped wines and a good selection of malts make for assured drinking pleasure. Prices are fair, opening at £10.50, and over a dozen wines are available by the glass.

CHEF: Alan Matheison PROPRIETORS: Mr and Mrs T.R. Waterbury OPEN: Tue to Sun 12 to 2 (2.30 Sat and Sun), 6.30 to 9.45 MEALS: alc (main courses L £4.50 to £6.50, D £9.50 to £15.50). Bar meals available SERVICE: not inc, 10% (optional) for parties of 8 or more CARDS: Amex, Delta, MasterCard, Switch, Visa DETAILS: 72 seats. Private parties: 40 main room. Vegetarian meals. No smoking in dining room. Wheelchair access (also WC). Music

ST MARGARET'S HOPE Orkney **map 11**

▲ The Creel

Front Road, St Margaret's Hope KW17 2SL
TEL: (01856) 831311
EMAIL: alan@the creel.freeserve.co.uk
WEB SITE: www.thecreel.co.uk
off A961, 13m S of Kirkwall, on South Ronaldsay

COOKING **7**
MODERN SCOTTISH
£35–£52

'The magic of Orkney keeps pulling us back', wrote one couple. 'We return again and again for the place, the food and the people', confessed another. The house may be unprepossessing, but visitors who stay several days find the quality unwavering, and the range of fish impressive: over three nights, one couple counted fourteen different white fish, not to mention crab, lobster, scallops and two kinds of mussel. A short menu of four starters and three mains suits the circumstances well, thanks to the outstanding quality of ingredients, and to Alan Craigie's skill and attention to detail.

Soups range from mussel and coriander to a superior chunky broth of smoked haddock. Warm salads provide an alternative beginning: masses of sweet, tender cockles piled over a mound of green leaves, with a generous pool of garlic butter, or Parton salad, nothing to do with Dolly, but referring to 'pristinely fresh' crabmeat, served in the shell, on an interesting mix of leaves dressed with herb-infused olive oil and lemon mayonnaise. Mains typically contrast two fishy elements: firm-fleshed ling with softer, creamier hake, or a confident and sophisticated plate of halibut surrounded by small, crispy sea bream fillets with a moist, oily interior. Already generous in quantity (a characteristic of the food), these come with finely shredded leek and two kinds of potato: fluffy, buttery, herb-flecked mash, and waxy new potatoes. Dishes are attractively presented without being prissy.

Given the large portions, it is understandable if desserts rarely feature in correspondence, although summer fruit parfait appears to be a winner: studded with local raspberries, redcurrants and blackcurrants, it is accompanied by a thin, crisp brandy-snap basket (as are most desserts) cupping a scoop of the local ice cream, overlaid with a lattice of white and dark chocolate strands. Beremeal bannocks and golden-coloured soda bread are an added attraction. There is still scope for bringing the 20-strong wine list up to the standard of the food, but no doubting the quality of what is available. House Australian is under £10.

CHEF: Alan Craigie PROPRIETORS: Alan and Joyce Craigie OPEN: all week D only 7 to 9.30 CLOSED: 2 weeks Oct, Jan and Feb MEALS: alc (main courses £15.50 to £21.50) SERVICE: not inc, card slips closed CARDS: MasterCard, Visa DETAILS: 34 seats. Private parties: 40 main room. Car park. Children's helpings. No smoking in dining room. Wheelchair access (also WC). No music ACCOMMODATION: 3 rooms. TV. Room only £45 to £65

SPEAN BRIDGE Highland **map 11**

▲ Old Pines

Spean Bridge PH34 4EG
TEL: (01397) 712324 FAX: (01397) 712433
EMAIL: goodfood@oldpines.co.uk
WEB SITE: www.oldpines.co.uk

COOKING **4**
MODERN SCOTTISH
£33–£47

The Barbers fill a special niche in this part of the world, not only welcoming families to their chalet-type buildings in a stand of pine trees off the Fort William to Inverness road, but treating them in a sensible and grown-up way. Younger children are given high tea in the family kitchen, and looked after while parents eat in a calm dining room. A policy of sourcing local, organic and seasonal produce is vigorously pursued, helped along by a poly tunnel that yields fruit, vegetables, herbs and saladings. Flavours tend to avoid the global-fusion end of the spectrum in favour of Mallaig fish soup with garlic mayonnaise, or turbot with red onion butter sauce (sauces are not mere slicks either, but the kind 'needing a sauce spoon for full enjoyment').

Local, dark, gamey-flavoured Lochaber lamb is a speciality in summer, as one couple discovered: cold lamb sandwiches were so good at lunch, they returned for dinner of Loch Linnhe prawns, Skye diver-caught scallops and 'beautifully prepared' roast lamb. Desserts, from lemon posset with brambles to marmalade cloutie dumpling, are followed by Scottish cheeses. Wines are becomingly increasingly attractive, helped by a friendly mark-up policy, and in place of house wines the Barbers establish guests' preferences and open bottles accordingly. Prices start at £10.50. Bottled Scottish beers are another delight.

CHEF: Sukie Barber PROPRIETORS: Bill and Sukie Barber OPEN: all week D only 8pm (1 sitting, occasionally 7.30 in winter, April to Sept Sun D residents only) MEALS: Set D £24.50 to £30. Light meals available all day SERVICE: not inc, card slips closed CARDS: MasterCard, Switch, Visa DETAILS: 30 seats. 10 seats outside. Private parties: 30 main room. Car park. Vegetarian meals. Children's helpings No babies/young children in dining room at D. No smoking in dining room. Wheelchair access (also WC). No music ACCOMMODATION: 8 rooms, all with bath/shower. D,B&B £60 to £150. Rooms for disabled. Baby facilities (*The Which? Hotel Guide*) (£5)

STEIN Highland **map 11**

▲ Lochbay £

1–2 Macleod Terrace, Stein, Isle of Skye IV55 8GA
TEL/FAX: (01470) 592235

COOKING **1**
FISH
£18–£42

This tiny restaurant retains the character of the two white-painted fishermen's cottages from which it grew, and the Greenhalghs, who have been here since 1983, do the sensible thing by specialising. They are warm and welcoming hosts, making guests feel 'valued and special', and seem to know everything about fish. Freshness is a guiding principle – prawns (perhaps in garlic butter) are highly rated, as are 'moist' crab and 'juicy' lobsters (boiled or grilled) – and the cooking is commendably plain, so that flavours are 'not swamped by unnecessary garnishes, which was much appreciated'. The gamut runs from rich fish soup to a shellfish platter for two, and hearty sweets might include chocolate bread-and-butter pudding, and cloutie dumpling. A short drinks list features Scottish wines and liqueurs, and house red and white at £9.50 a litre.

CHEFS/PROPRIETORS: Margaret and Peter Greenhalgh OPEN: Mon to Fri 12 to 2.30, 6 to 9 CLOSED: Oct to Easter MEALS: alc (main courses £6 to £19). Snacks available L SERVICE: not inc CARDS: MasterCard, Visa DETAILS: 24 seats. 8 seats outside. Private parties: 6 main room. Car park. Children's helpings. No smoking in dining room. Music ACCOMMODATION: 2 rooms, both with bath/shower. TV. B&B £28 to £46

STONEHAVEN Aberdeenshire **map 11**

Tolbooth £

Old Pier, Stonehaven AB39 2JU COOKING **3**
TEL/FAX: (01569) 762287 SEAFOOD
15m S of Aberdeen on A90 £23–£47

The attractive setting – a first-floor room overlooking the harbour – has been enhanced with more furniture and a few extras, but the essential simplicity remains. Former co-owner and chef Jean-François Meder has left, and Chris McCarrey has returned to the kitchen, overseeing a slightly different format: a free-ranging 'eat what you like in the order you like it' menu. Dual pricing helps to increase the options.

The strength is fresh native seafood, supplemented occasionally by exotic items such as shark. Supplies from Aberdeen market dictate what is available, and the quality of produce makes a significant contribution to the outcome. At one end of the spectrum might be homely Cullen Skink, or steamed cockles and mussels in heather ale, at the other chargrilled squid with a honey, mint and chilli dressing, or a papillote of monkfish and king prawns in red Thai coconut curry sauce. Meat eaters might prefer pork tenderloin with wild mushrooms, or pigeon breasts with bok choy and hoisin sauce, and toasted coconut ice cream should make a refreshing finish. A resourceful wine list plays fair by most pockets and tastes up to a ceiling of £40. House wines are £9.

CHEF/PROPRIETOR: Chris McCarrey OPEN: Tue to Sat D only 6 to 9.30 CLOSED: 3 weeks after Christmas, 1 week Oct MEALS: alc (main courses £9 to £18) SERVICE: not inc CARDS: Delta, MasterCard, Switch, Visa DETAILS: 44 seats. Private parties: 40 main room. Vegetarian meals. No children under 8. No cigars/pipes in dining-room. Music (£5)

'Bread [was] undoubtedly produced on the premises, because no self-respecting baker's shop or supermarket would sell such drab, stale, misjudged stuff.'
(On eating in Dorset)

Net prices *in the details at the end of an entry indicates that the prices given on a menu and on a bill are inclusive of VAT and service charge, and that this practice is clearly stated on menu and bill.*

STRONTIAN Highland map 11

▲ Kilcamb Lodge

Strontian PH36 4HY
TEL: (01967) 402257 FAX: (01967) 402041
EMAIL: kilcamblodge@aol.com
WEB SITE: www.lochaber.com
on A861, by N shore of Loch Sunart

COOKING **4**
MODERN SCOTTISH
£22–£47

Outstanding views across Loch Sunart are part of the appeal at what history books describe as 'an old church and barracks used in the 1745 uprising'. Peter and Anne Blakeway continue to provide hospitality in the family tradition, and Neil Mellis's cooking seems to have gained maturity and confidence, helped by a stack of native materials: Angus beef, Perthshire lamb, Mingarry venison, Shetland salmon, plus lobsters and langoustines from the loch. Indeed, visitors who wish may pile in the hotel's boat and help to catch their own dinner.

Such freshness impressed an inspector, whose casserole of squat lobster (caught only hours earlier) was topped with a crisp paper-thin slice of courgette and long shreds of cucumber, in a pool of beurre blanc. Simple techniques such as roasting and grilling also make the best of meat, while successful desserts have included a light, crisp pastry case with a rich, dark treacle and walnut filling. Lunch is a lighter affair, taking in perhaps warm ciabatta with Argyll smoked ham, mushroom ragoût and a poached egg. Styles are fastidiously logged on the global wine list (by number for whites, by letter for reds), which caters for all pockets and includes eight by the glass. A house selection starts at £9.75.

CHEF: Neil Mellis PROPRIETORS: Peter and Anne Blakeway OPEN: all week 12 to 2, 7.30 (1 sitting D) CLOSED: Dec to Feb exc New Year MEALS: alc L (main courses £5.50 to £7.50). Set D £29.50 SERVICE: not inc, card slips closed CARDS: Delta, MasterCard, Switch, Visa DETAILS: 28 seats. Private parties: 28 main room. Car park. Vegetarian meals. Children's helpings. No children under 8. No smoking in dining room. Wheelchair access (not WC). No music ACCOMMODATION: 11 rooms, all with bath/shower. TV. Room only £48 to £130. Baby facilities. Fishing (*The Which? Hotel Guide*)

SWINTON Borders map 11

▲ Wheatsheaf

Main Street, Swinton TD11 3JJ
TEL: (01890) 860257 FAX: (01890) 860688
on A6112, Coldstream to Duns road

COOKING **3**
MODERN SCOTTISH
£21–£46

The Reids are 'welcoming and enthusiastic', declared one reporter after a satisfying visit to this good-value, stone-built restaurant-with-rooms facing the village green. The rather dark old dining room has been augmented by a bright new room with a vaulted pine ceiling, which provids an alternative setting for local and organically sourced produce offered on lunch, dinner and bar menus. Buccleuch beef, Highland venison – perhaps with spicy red cabbage and a juniper and Cassis sauce – Borders lamb, wild mushrooms and a neighbour's organic herbs are brought into play.

Simplicity is a keynote (a starter of asparagus with hollandaise for instance), and accurately timed fish is a strength of main courses: pan-fried sea bass on crushed new potatoes with olive oil, basil and parsley. Less than expert saucing can throw things off balance, and some dishes are only partially successful, but a hearty new season's rhubarb and almond tart with Tweedside honey ice cream fitted the bill for one reporter. Scottish farmhouse cheeses are served in prime condition, partnered by equally impressive home-made oatcakes. Service is pleasant and willing, and the 100-strong wine list, mostly under £20, is globally sourced, with six house wines £10.65 (£2.20 per glass).

CHEF: Alan Reid PROPRIETORS: Alan and Julie Reid OPEN: Tue to Sun 12 to 2.15, 6.30 to 9.30 (residents dinner only Mon D, and Sun D Oct to Apr) MEALS: alc (main courses L £7 to £12.50, D £9 to £16) SERVICE: not inc, card slips closed CARDS: Delta, MasterCard, Switch, Visa DETAILS: 44 seats. 20 seats outside. Private parties: 28 main room, 18 private room. Car park. Vegetarian meals. Children's helpings. No smoking in dining room. Wheelchair access (not WC). No music ACCOMMODATION: 7 rooms, all with bath/shower. TV. B&B £49 to £98. Baby facilities (*The Which? Hotel Guide*)

TROON South Ayrshire **map 11**

▲ Lochgreen House

Monktonhill Road, Southwood, Troon KA10 7EN
TEL: (01292) 313343 FAX: (01292) 318661 — COOKING **5**
EMAIL: lochgreen@costley-hotels.co.uk — FRANCO-SCOTTISH
WEB SITE: www.costley-hotels.co.uk — £30–£64

The house looks out to mature trees, well-shaved lawns, and neat flower beds 'raked to within an inch of their lives', while family portraits and landscapes combine with an impressive malt bar to make the inside feel characterful, relaxed, happy and comfortable. The thrust of the Franco-Scottish menu is towards traditional ideas such as whole Dover sole with parsley potatoes, or beef tournedos Rossini, backed up by terrine of ham hock with lentils and sauce gribiche, or foie gras served two ways – warm and chilled – with oranges and green beans.

In an effort to cover the whole spectrum, first courses range from a refreshing-sounding plate of seasonal fruit with basil sorbet to a considerably more substantial confit duck leg, served with both a risotto of Toulouse sausage and a bean cassoulet. As ever in Scotland, seafood makes an important contribution, perhaps a warm salad of Dublin Bay prawns with asparagus, or a salmon and langoustine gratin, while desserts aim to soothe with sherry trifle, chocolate torte, and rice pudding with rhubarb and ginger. A global wine list is fairly priced and includes helpful annotations, six recommendations from a local wine merchant, and six house wines starting at £14.50 (£3.75 per glass). Whisky lovers will be happy to note they have 140 to choose from.

'I was greeted with "Are there two of you?" I said, "No, I'm unique"'
(On eating in Northamptonshire)

CHEF: Andrew Costley PROPRIETORS: William and Catherine Costley OPEN: all week 12 to 2, 7 to 9 MEALS: alc L (main courses £14.50 to £22.50). Set L £19.95, Set D £29.95 SERVICE: not inc, card slips closed CARDS: Amex, Delta, MasterCard, Switch, Visa DETAILS: 100 seats. Private parties: 45 main room, 14 and 45 private rooms. Car park. Vegetarian meals. Children's helpings. No smoking in dining room. Wheelchair access (also WC). Music. Air-conditioned ACCOMMODATION: 15 rooms, all with bath/shower. TV. Phone. D,B&B £125 to £195. Rooms for disabled. Baby facilities (*The Which? Hotel Guide*)

MacCallums' Oyster Bar

The Harbour, Troon KA10 6DH
TEL/FAX: (01292) 319339

COOKING **3**
SEAFOOD
£23–£50

The setting, right on the harbour with a view of fishing boats and frolicking seals, could hardly be more appropriate. On warm days, French windows open to let in a cooling sea breeze and the call of gulls. As well as oysters, waitresses in navy-blue aprons deliver the freshest seafood from a varied and imaginative menu that takes in starters such as a thin escalope of seared salmon with spinach and lemon cream, and sweet grilled langoustines with garlic butter. Among main courses might be a generous assemblage of moist, crisp-skinned John Dory and red mullet, supplemented by trout, monkfish and lemon sole, all in a chive cream sauce. Otherwise, a superior version of a national dish features cod fried in a light batter accompanied by crunchy chips, home-made tartare sauce with a strong taste of capers, and mushy peas with little pieces of bacon. Finish with rhubarb crème brûlée, or rice pudding and Bramley apple pots. Chilean Chardonnay and Sauvignon at £9.50 kick off the serviceable wine list, which is weighted to whites.

CHEF: Nick Wright PROPRIETORS: John and James MacCallum OPEN: Tue to Sun L 12 to 2.45 (3.30 Sun), Tue to Sat D 7 to 9.45 CLOSED: 2 weeks from 25 Dec MEALS: alc (main courses L £7.50 to £9.50, D £12 to £18.50) SERVICE: not inc CARDS: Delta, MasterCard, Switch, Visa DETAILS: 43 seats. Private parties: 30 main room. Car park. Vegetarian meals. Children's helpings. Wheelchair access (also WC). Music

UIG Western Isles **map 11**

▲ Baile-na-Cille

Timsgarry, Uig, Isle of Lewis HS2 9JD
TEL: (01851) 672242 FAX: (01851) 672241
EMAIL: randjgollin@compuserve.com
WEB SITE: ourworld.compuserve.com/homepages/randjgollin
take B8011 to Uig, then right down track on to shore

COOKING **1**
MODERN EUROPEAN
£30–£36

One reporter who spent seven weeks sailing up the coast of Scotland from Peterhead to the Orkneys, then down the north-west coast to Skye, stopped off at Uig for a memorable meal and a dose of the eccentric, entertaining, hospitable and child-friendly Richard Gollin. He offers no menu and no wine list. A set meal is prepared based on what he enjoys cooking, plus 'requests and comments of those who have booked', and special diets (such as vegetarian) are increasingly catered for. The island produces lamb, salmon and venison, and the village smokehouse is another good source of supply. Meals tend to be simple affairs: guacamole, rainbow trout, and ice cream with strawberries on one occasion, smoked venison, chicken with tarragon, and chocolate bread-and-butter pudding on another, ending in each case with cheese ordered from France via the Internet. The wine cellar consists of two shelves and a fridge, with just two prices, £8.50 and £12.50, but the main supplier is Yapp Bros so quality is assured.

CHEFS/PROPRIETORS: Richard and Joanna Gollin OPEN: all week D only 7pm (1 sitting) CLOSED: Oct to March MEALS: Set D £24 SERVICE: net prices, card slips closed CARDS: MasterCard, Visa DETAILS: 30 seats. Private parties: 30 main room. Car park. Vegetarian meals. Children's helpings. No smoking in dining room. No music ACCOMMODATION: 12 rooms, all with bath/shower. B&B £24 to £78. Baby facilities

ULLAPOOL Highland map 11

▲ Altnaharrie Inn

Ullapool IV26 2SS
TEL: (01854) 633230

COOKING **9**
SEAFOOD/MODERN EUROPEAN
£76–£92

Altnaharrie is 'stunning, beautiful and remote'. The old drovers' inn, white-washed and hung with creepers, thrives on a blend of romantic loch-side location, intimacy and lack of pretension, helped along by tranquillity and unobtrusive comfort. Small rooms with narrow doorways are furnished traditionally, with books, log fires, and captivating flower arrangements. The dining room struck one visitor as a 'luxurious interpretation of Shaker style' in its combination of simplicity and pretty detail, with Turkish rugs, brass candlesticks, and lace mats on bare wooden tables. Scandinavian good taste is evident everywhere, not least in Gunn Eriksen's own tapestries that hang on the walls. She is clearly a one-off, who works unaided in the kitchen: how different from most other leading restaurants which typically require a large brigade distributed over several departments.

Seafood's prominent role is well-attested, in a warm salad of lobster, in a dish of langoustines and scallops in champagne jelly, and in a 'knockout' starter of 'mountains of scallop flesh' accompanied by three sauces: roast pumpkin, meat jus, and an unbeatable frothy and creamy-textured scallop and Sauternes reduction. Soups, the second of four no-choice courses, are equally accomplished, from artichoke with quail and foie gras, to a clear sherry-infused crab version with a tiny crab-filled puff pastry mound in the centre and claws arranged round it.

Dishes owe their success partly to prime materials, and are full of interest and flavour without relying on exotic inputs. Many are based on standard, basic partnerships, although often with an intriguing or unexpected spin. A main course of squab pigeon illustates the point, served conventionally enough with a slice of foie gras (all timings accurate), but also with a mellow 'cake' made from chicken livers, mushrooms and grapes. Saucing in this case included one made from pigeon jus and Burgundy, the other with rowan jelly.

British, Irish and French cheeses from a long list, 'all in perfect condition', are followed by up to four desserts. These are not only 'as pretty as a picture' but also avoid excessive sweetness: chocolate mousse with two chocolate ice creams; slices of warm pineapple with a cloudberry ice cream; and an apple-shaped layering of apple and pastry, served with calvados ice cream and caramel sauce. Fred Brown's discreet and 'intuitive' service is second to none. Wine orders are taken a couple of hours before dinner begins. Traditionalists will be pleased with the predominantly French list, which provides a sound and extensive selection of Bordeaux and Burgundy, though the New World does get a look in. Prices are fair throughout, and a plentiful and varied list of half-bottles facilitates food matching. House wines start at £11.50.

CHEF: Gunn Eriksen PROPRIETORS: Fred Brown and Gunn Eriksen OPEN: all week D only 8pm (1 sitting) CLOSED: Nov to April (exc some weekends) MEALS: Set D £70 SERVICE: none, card slips closed CARDS: Amex, Delta, MasterCard, Switch, Visa DETAILS: 18 seats. Private parties: 16 main room. Car park. Children's helpings. No children under 8. No smoking in dining room. No music ACCOMMODATION: 8 rooms, all with bath/shower. D,B&B £165 to £410. No children under 8 (*The Which? Hotel Guide*)

WALLS Shetland **map 11**

▲ Burrastow House

Burrastow, Walls ZE2 9PD
TEL: (01595) 809307 FAX: (01595) 809213
EMAIL: burr.hs.hotel@zetnet.co.uk
WEB SITE: www.users@zetnet.co.uk/burrastow-house-hotel
at Walls drive to top of hill, turn left, then follow road for 2m to Burrastow

COOKING **3**
MODERN EUROPEAN
£19–£46

One family was advised before going to 'take the boat ride and the lobster'. The water was rough 'but the same could not be said about Burrastow House', which is eccentric maybe, but friendly, with a peat fire in the small oak-panelled dining room (in August) and a bright conservatory for warmer days. The lobsters, incidentally, awaiting their turn for dinner in crates in the loch, are 'enormous monsters', and just one of many items sourced from nearby: locally caught halibut has come with an orange butter sauce, and steamed Shetland sea trout with pickled ginger. Meat is by no means neglected, taking in fillet of Linga lamb with pearl barley risotto for example, and there is always a vegetarian main course option on the short daily-changing carte: perhaps roasted vegetables with polenta, or goats'-cheese soufflé. Greengage ice cream comes recommended, or there may be trifle, or chocolate pancakes. Bo Simmons goes out of her way to cater for special dietary needs, serving up wheat-free bread for one visitor. A few organic wines pepper the fairly priced, 50-strong list, including two house wines at £9.95.

The text of entries is based on unsolicited reports sent in by readers, backed up by inspections conducted anonymously. The factual details under the text are from questionnaires the Guide sends to all restaurants that feature in the book.

CHEF: Bo Simmons PROPRIETORS: Bo Simmons and Henry Anderton OPEN: Tue to Sun L 12 to 2.30, Tue to Sat D 7.30 to 9 CLOSED: 24 Dec to early March MEALS: alc D (main courses £13 to £18). Set L £12.50 SERVICE: not inc CARDS: Amex, Delta, MasterCard, Switch, Visa DETAILS: 25 seats. Private parties: 12 main room, 25 private room. Car park. Vegetarian meals. Children's helpings. No smoking in dining room. Wheelchair access (also WC). Occasional music ACCOMMODATION: 5 rooms, all with bath/shower. D,B&B £75 to £170. Rooms for disabled. Baby facilities. Fishing (*The Which? Hotel Guide*) (£5)

Wales

ABERDOVEY Gwynedd map 7

▲ Penhelig Arms Hotel

Terrace Road, Aberdovey LL35 0LT
TEL: (01654) 767215 FAX: (01654) 767690
EMAIL: penheligarms@saqnet.co.uk
on A493 Tywyn to Machynlleth road, opposite Penhelig station

COOKING **2**
MODERN BRITISH
£19–£45

The extensive menu at this comfortable pub/hotel extends to a choice of nine or ten starters, around twelve main courses and maybe eight 'weighty' puds. Although it goes in for a fair amount of cheese and other dairy content, fish gets a respectable showing in the shape of haddock, monkfish, cod, prawns or mullet; and the grilled sardines are 'always fresh'. Meat eaters are well served by lamb, pork, kidneys, beef and duck, usually subject to Italian or French influences but with some nods to the Far East. The kitchen has its hands full with the addition of a good-value specials board, and will even down tools to make you a sandwich. Finish perhaps with a frangipane or treacle tart. 'Charming' staff add to the enjoyment, while the wine list brims with exciting bottles and enthusiastic suggestions delightfully presented. It is priced sympathetically too, and features 14 regularly changing wines by the glass, allowing guests to cater for each course separately. Respect for Italy is instantly apparent with the Salice Salentino Riserva from Puglia promising Mediterranean sunshine at £12.50. Ten house wines start at £10.

CHEF: Jane Howkins PROPRIETORS: Robert and Sally Hughes OPEN: all week 12 to 2.15, 7 to 9.30 CLOSED: 25 and 26 Dec MEALS: alc L Mon to Sat (main courses £6 to £10.50). Set L Sun £13.50, Set D £21. Bar meals available SERVICE: not inc, card slips closed CARDS: Delta, MasterCard, Switch, Visa DETAILS: 36 seats. Private parties: 20 main room. Car park. Children's helpings. No smoking in dining room. No music. Air-conditioned ACCOMMODATION: 10 rooms, all with bath/shower. TV. Phone. B&B £39.50 to £79 (*The Which? Hotel Guide*) (£5)

'Trying to get the waiter's attention to order our wine was, well, difficult, despite the fact that we are sitting in a tiny dining room. After speaking and then eventually shouting to him and being completely ignored, I found a use for the bell placed on the table and, feeling like Michael Winner, proceeded to make enough of a racket that eventually one of the waitresses wandered over and duly took the wine order.' (On eating in London)

ABERSOCH Gwynedd map 7

▲ Porth Tocyn Hotel

Bwlch Tocyn, Abersoch LL53 7BU
TEL: (01758) 713303 FAX: (01758) 713538
EMAIL: porthtocyn.hotel@virgin.net
WEB SITE: www.porth-tocyn-hotel.co.uk
on minor road 2m S of Abersoch through hamlets of Sarn Bach and Bwlchtocyn

COOKING **4**
MODERN EUROPEAN
£27–£48

Sitting on a gentle rise above Cardigan Bay, with magnificent views across to Snowdonia's peaks, Porth Tocyn has been a family concern for over half a century. It is a happy seaside establishment teeming with well-trained staff, the interiors a warren of corridors and elegant rooms (refurbished over the winter), the style old-fashioned: dinner is announced by a gong. Since last year the five-course dinner has been trimmed to four, with marginally more choice at each stage, and extra help has arrived in the kitchen. A starter of calf's liver with lamb's sweetbreads on a warm shallot and garlic tart with cider jus proves the kitchen can handle lightness, timing, and sweetness simultaneously. Main-course fish dishes have included salmon on a first-class risotto with parsley pesto, while saddle of venison comes with a Madeira sauce and sultanas. For those taking more than two courses, a pudding comes next – perhaps chocolate brandy cake or kumquat and orange mousse – followed by cheese and fruit. A reshuffling of the wine list has seen greater emphasis placed on the New World, although France remains well represented. Six varied house wines start at £12.50 and include bins from Argentina and Chile.

CHEFS: Louise Fletcher-Brewer, Guy Lamble and Gary Moreton-Jones PROPRIETORS: the Fletcher-Brewer family OPEN: Sun L 12.15 to 2, all week D 7.30 to 9 CLOSED: mid-Nov to Easter MEALS: Set L £18, Set D £23.50 (2 courses) to £30 SERVICE: not inc, card slips closed CARDS: MasterCard, Switch, Visa DETAILS: 50 seats. 30 seats outside. Private parties: 50 main room. Car park. Vegetarian meals. Children's helpings No children under 7 at D. No smoking in dining room. No music ACCOMMODATION: 17 rooms, all with bath/shower. TV. Phone. B&B £49 to £119. Rooms for disabled. Baby facilities. Swimming pool (*The Which? Hotel Guide*)

BASSALEG Newport map 4

Junction 28

Station Approach, Bassaleg NP10 8LD
TEL: (01633) 891891 FAX: (01633) 895978
from M4 junction28 take A468 towards Caerphilly, turn right at Tredegar Arms and take first left

COOKING **2**
MODERN BRITISH
£18–£45

This large restaurant, once Bassaleg's railway station, is off the M4's junction 28: hence the name. It emulates a busy station by packing in the crowds, but the parallel stops there as the décor is smooth and smart, with a large bar, deep-pile carpet and interconnecting rooms with bamboo screen dividers. Staff are efficient and the thoughtful owner is much in evidence. What might seem to be a 'conveyor-belt operation', albeit a slick one, is to be marvelled at as there are no fewer than 22 starters and 25 main courses on an easy-to-access modern British menu with vegetarian, meat and fish headings. A bargain basement 'Evening

Flyer' menu attracts too, with an equally rounded choice, which may include duck rillettes with onion and ginger marmalade, Cajun loin of pork with parsnip purée, and treacle sponge pudding. Sunday lunch has been considered 'exceptional value', and reasonable prices – plus variety and quality – are keynotes of the global wine list, which includes a canny selection of half-bottles, and three house wines at £9.95.

CHEF: Jon West PROPRIETORS: Jon West and Richard Wallace OPEN: all week L 12 to 2 (4 Sun), Mon to Sat D 5.30 to 9.30 CLOSED: last week July and first week Aug MEALS: alc (main courses £7.50 to £16). Set L Mon to Sat £8.95 (2 courses) to £10.45, Set L Sun £9.95 (2 courses) to £11.95, Set D 5.30 to 7 £11.95 SERVICE: not inc, card slips closed CARDS: Delta, MasterCard, Switch, Visa DETAILS: 165 seats. Private parties: 60 main room, 12 and 60 private rooms. Car park. Vegetarian meals. Wheelchair access (also WC). Music. Air-conditioned

BEAUMARIS Isle of Anglesey **map 7**

▲ Ye Olde Bulls Head

WALES GFG 2001 COMMENDED

Castle Street, Beaumaris LL58 8AP
TEL: (01248) 810329 FAX: (01248) 811294

COOKING **4**
MODERN EUROPEAN
£20–£48

After a period of refurbishment the Bulls Head, which first did business in the fifteenth century, now has two separate places to eat: a main first-floor dining room, and a modern conservatory-style brasserie on the ground floor. The former is newly decorated, its pale oak beams set off by dramatic shades of purple, blue and burgundy, with huge porthole-shaped mirrors fore and aft. The kitchen thrives on local materials, often given exotic treatment: leek terrine with truffle potatoes, loin of lamb with an olive crust and ratatouille, or sweet scallops on stir-fried vegetables, with a light soy and scallop liquor sauce. Results have ranged from a rather 'heavy combination' of notably fresh halibut steak with Welsh rarebit and herb salsa, via lamb kidneys with mushrooms, chillies and mustard, to first-rate lemon tart with raspberry sorbet. Service at inspection was 'charming, friendly and slow'. A broad selection of reasonably priced wines includes French classics and intelligently selected bins from the New World. Te Motu Cabernet Merlot from Waiheke Island, New Zealand (£25.95) is specially recommended. House wines from France, South Africa and Argentina are served by the bottle (£13.75), half-carafe (£7) and glass (£3.50).

With its Welsh slate floor and lime green walls, the non-bookable brasserie feels light and airy. Combining first-class ingredients and uncomplicated cooking (the chargrill is much in evidence), it offers a selection of starters (Arbroath smokies baked with cream and Parmesan), sandwiches (pastrami), seafood (tuna with ginger, garlic and coriander), pasta (pumpkin tortellini) and meat dishes (ribeye steak with mash and butter beans). This is a professional operation with reasonable prices, prompt service and some two dozen wines (ten by the glass) under £20.

The text of entries is based on unsolicited reports sent in by readers, backed up by inspections conducted anonymously. The factual details under the text are from questionnaires the Guide sends to all restaurants that feature in the book.

CHEF: Ernst Van Halderen PROPRIETOR: Rothwell and Robertson Ltd OPEN: restaurant Mon to Sat D only 7 to 9.30; brasserie all week 12 to 2, 6 to 9 CLOSED: 25 and 26 Dec, 1 Jan MEALS: restaurant Set D £27.50; brasserie alc (main courses £4.50 to £12) SERVICE: not inc CARDS: Amex, Delta, MasterCard, Switch, Visa DETAILS: 45 seats. Private parties: 25 main room, 15 private room. Car park. Children's helpings. No children under 7 in restaurant. No smoking in dining room. No music ACCOMMODATION: 15 rooms, all with bath/shower. TV. Phone. B&B £53 to £85. Baby facilities (*The Which? Hotel Guide*)

BROAD HAVEN Pembrokeshire **map 4**

▲ Druidstone £

Druidston Haven, Broad Haven SA62 3NE
TEL: (01437) 781221 FAX: (01437) 781133
from B4341 at Broad Haven turn right at sea; after 1½m turn left to Druidston Haven; hotel ¾m on left

COOKING **2**
GLOBAL FUSION
£18–£37

Druidstone is a late-Victorian stone farmhouse perched dramatically on a clifftop overlooking St Brides Bay, braving the Atlantic westerlies. Rod and Jane Bell have run the hotel since 1972, happily catering to a broad mix of custom, from school-age outward-bounders to regulars of some seniority. Choose between bar or dining-room for eating: both are refreshingly informal. From the blackboard bar menu, open-cap mushrooms stuffed with nuts and herbs have been good, the filling 'crunchy, with a savoury yet slightly sweet tang', while 'fresh, flaky, sea-clean' haddock fillets with tomato and basil have also impressed. Grander dishes might include turkey escalope sauced with green peppercorns and brandy, and lamb chops with rhubarb and pickled ginger glaze. Good pastry and lively fruit flavours have distinguished hot apple and raspberry tart. Not everything at inspection quite came up to snuff, but this is an idiosyncratic and charming place none the less. Virtually every bottle on the wine list ducks below the £20 barrier, with house French £7.

CHEFS: Rod and Jane Bell, Angus Bell, John Lewis and Donna Banner PROPRIETORS: Rod and Jane Bell OPEN: Sun L 1 to 2, Mon to Sat D 7.30 to 9.30 CLOSED: Mon to Thur third week Nov to third week Dec, Mon to Thur third week Jan to third week Feb MEALS: alc (main courses L £7 to £9, D £7 to £15) SERVICE: not inc, card slips closed CARDS: Amex, Delta, MasterCard, Switch, Visa DETAILS: 36 seats. 40 seats outside. Private parties: 36 main room, 12 private room. Car park. Vegetarian meals. Children's helpings. No smoking while others eat. Wheelchair access (also WC). No music ACCOMMODATION: 9 rooms. B&B £40 to £80. Baby facilities (*The Which? Hotel Guide*)

The Guide office can quickly spot when a restaurateur is encouraging customers to write recommending inclusion. Such reports do not further a restaurant's cause. Please tell us if a restaurateur invites you to write to the Guide.

The 2002 Guide will be published before Christmas 2001. Reports on meals are most welcome at any time of the year, but are particularly valuable in the spring (no later than June). Send them to The Good Food Guide, *FREEPOST, 2 Marylebone Road, London NW1 4DF. Or email your report to goodfoodguide@which.net*

CAPEL GARMON Conwy map 7

▲ Tan-y-Foel

Capel Garmon, nr Betws-y-Coed LL26 0RE
TEL: (01690) 710507 FAX: (01690) 710681
EMAIL: tanyfoel@wiss.co.uk
WEB SITE: www.tyfhotel.co.uk
take turning marked Capel Garmon and Nebo from A470 about halfway between Betws-y-Coed and Llanrwst

COOKING **4**
MODERN BRITISH-PLUS
£34–£53

Whether the interior of this rural, family-run hotel strikes visitors as 'sophisticated' or rather 'out of character' with the rest of the building, they all agree that the contrast between the old farmhouse and its colourful, comfortable, 'impeccably kept' remodelling is marked. There is agreement too on the excellence of Janet Pitman's cooking. With a decade under her belt, she has good supply lines to Welsh Black beef, Conwy Valley lamb and fish caught off Anglesey, which provide the basis for a simple-format three-course dinner (two choices at each stage). Steamed sea bass, for example, has arrived on wasabi mash with a turmeric and ginger sauce, and Welsh venison has been partnered by buttered curly kale and roast baby beetroot. While Asian spicings give a lift to starters such as seared tuna (marinated in coriander and lime with a chilli salsa), more traditional desserts take in frangipane and pear tart, or baked vanilla custard and strawberries. As for hospitality, 'from the minute we arrived to the time we departed we couldn't have been looked after in a more professional manner'. A varied wine list includes a sound representative selection from France as well as bottles from the New World. House wines start at £15.

CHEF: Janet Pitman PROPRIETORS: Peter and Janet Pitman OPEN: all week D only 7.30 to 8.30 (light lunches Mon to Thur 12.30 to 2) MEALS: Set D £25 to £30 (pre-booking essential) CLOSED: Christmas SERVICE: not inc CARDS: Amex, Delta, Diners, MasterCard, Switch, Visa DETAILS: 16 seats. Car park. No children under 7. No smoking in dining room. No music ACCOMMODATION: 7 rooms, all with bath/shower. TV. Phone. B&B £70 to £150. No children under 7 (*The Which? Hotel Guide*)

CARDIFF Cardiff map 4

Armless Dragon 

97 Wyeverne Road, Cathays, Cardiff CF2 4BG
TEL: (029) 2038 2357 FAX: (029) 2038 2055

COOKING **1**
MODERN WELSH
£17–£37

Since arriving towards the end of 1999, new brooms Paul and Martine Lane have winkled out a supply of quality local produce for their contemporary Welsh restaurant in the student quarter. Some flavour combinations turn out well, such as crunchy deep-fried mushroom and almond toast triangles with a spicy peanut dip, and warm smoked chicken sausage with an 'excellent and necessary foil' of red onion marmalade; others are perhaps a bit too brave. Deep-fried laver balls with sunflower and sesame seeds, and roast Monmouthshire pork with cockle and coriander sauce sum up their eclectic outlook 'but with our feet firmly in

Wales'. 'Quantities could be more modest' for those with an eye on white chocolate and coconut crème brûlée, or spiced ginger cake with rhubarb compote, and 'presentation could be tightened up'. Wines are a modestly priced half-French, half-elsewhere collection, opening with half a dozen house wines from £8.90.

CHEF: Paul Lane PROPRIETORS: Paul and Martine Lane OPEN: Tue to Fri L 12 to 2, Tue to Sat D 7 to 10 (also pre- and post-theatre D Fri and Sat by arrangement) CLOSED: 25 and 26 Dec MEALS: alc (main courses £9 to £14). Set L £7.90 (2 courses) to £9.90 SERVICE: not inc CARDS: MasterCard, Switch, Visa DETAILS: 48 seats. Private parties: 55 main room. Vegetarian meals. Children's helpings. No smoking in dining room. Wheelchair access (not WC). Music (£5)

Le Cassoulet

5 Romilly Crescent, Canton, Cardiff CF1 9NP — COOKING **3**
TEL/FAX: (029) 2022 1905 — FRENCH
EMAIL: lecassoulet@ukonline.co.uk — £26–£52

Framed French cartoons and pictures of the Stade Toulousain rugby team confirm that Le Cassoulet is as French as they come, although the immersion course is tempered by English translations on the menu. Despite a new pair of hands in the kitchen, classical French provincial touchstone dishes prevail, from cassoulet Toulousain itself via foie gras confit to crème brûlée. The careful, precise cooking uses well-sourced ingredients, though sometimes the various strands of a dish may not come together as they should, seeming to justify their inclusion 'on looks alone'. On the other hand, 'pink, tender' Welsh lamb with a mustard seed crust, served with a sweet potato galette and roasted artichoke hearts, has offered a good variety of complementary tastes, and apple and pear crêpe with two tiny additions – a crème brûlée and a floating island – has been deemed a 'real treat'. 'Formidable' cheeses (at least 20, all labelled and in good condition) are left at the table. Service is 'impeccable, welcoming and spontaneous'. The 70-plus wine list, firmly rooted in France of course, offers around a third under the £20 mark. House vin de pays is £11.50.

CHEF: Yvonnick Le Roy PROPRIETORS: Gilbert and Claire Viader OPEN: Tue to Sat 12 to 2, 7 to 10 (post-theatre D by arrangement) CLOSED: 2 weeks Christmas, 2 weeks Aug MEALS: alc (main courses L £8.50, D £14 to £17.50) SERVICE: not inc CARDS: Amex, Delta, Diners, MasterCard, Switch, Visa DETAILS: 40 seats. Private parties: 40 main room. Vegetarian meals. Children's helpings. No cigars/pipes in dining room. Occasional music (£5)

Le Gallois

WALES NEWCOMER OF THE YEAR — **NEW ENTRY**

6–8 Romilly Street, Canton, Cardiff CF11 9NR — COOKING **4**
TEL: (029) 2034 1264 FAX: (029) 2023 7911 — MODERN EUROPEAN
EMAIL: le.gallois@virgin.net — £21–£60

Le Gallois is located in a row of shops in the 'media' district, and a split-level yellow and blue art nouveau interior, decked out with metal balustrades and mirrors, makes for an atmosphere that is stylish, modern and relaxed. Ex-London Hilton and Canteen chef Padrig Jones serves up an indulgent version of Modern European cooking that takes in soft-boiled eggs with caviar and toast soldiers, creamily rich Mediterranean fish soup, and a 'mountain' of thick juicy scallop slices on watercress leaves and potato croûtons, admirably set off with a sweet-and-sour relish. Other successes have included pot roast pig with Alsace bacon, truffle and chive mash, and a plate of duck three ways: pink breast, lightly fried liver, and a roundel of satisfying duck black pudding, all served with cabbage, Puy lentils and mash. Desserts of warm egg custard tart, and hot chocolate fondant with stem ginger ice-cream have also pleased. Lunch is considered good value with plenty of choice, and bread is first class. Service is knowledgeable but can be stretched at busy times. The French-dominated wine list features some quality clarets and also takes a brisk trot around the world by way of Greece and Wales. Ten wines are sold by the glass, with house vin de pays £2.30 (£10.95 the bottle).

CHEFS: Padrig Jones and Mark Freeman PROPRIETORS: Graham and Anne Jones and family OPEN: Tue to Sat 12 to 2.30, 6.30 to 10.30 CLOSED: 1 week Christmas, 3 weeks Aug MEALS: Set L £9.95 (2 courses) to £27, Set D £22 (2 courses) to £32 SERVICE: not inc, card slips closed, 10% for parties of 6 or more CARDS: Amex, Delta, MasterCard, Switch, Visa DETAILS: 60 seats. Private parties: 60 main room. Car park. Vegetarian meals. Children's helpings. No-smoking areas, No cigars/pipes in dining room. Wheelchair access (also WC). Occasional music. Air-conditioned

Gilby's

Old Port Road, Culverhouse Cross,
Cardiff CF5 6DN
TEL: (029) 2067 0800 FAX: (029) 2059 4437
WEB SITE: www.gilbysrestaurant.co.uk

COOKING **3**
MODERN EUROPEAN
£22–£58

Anyone tempted to describe this 100-seater as barn-like will be closer to the truth than they might expect. The eighteenth-century cattle shed and tithe barn have been cleverly adapted, with outside seating and an open-to-view kitchen, fronted by a fine display of fresh fish and shellfish. The seafood strand aims for the luxury end of the market with oysters, caviar and lobster three ways, not to mention plain grilled Dover sole and sea bass, but also takes in monkfish tempura, Pembrokeshire crab risotto, and prawn cocktail. A parallel theme is explained by the fact that Anthony Armelin's father is Venetian, and his mother is from Emilia-Romagna. Alongside bangers and mash or 'first-class' fish and chips, therefore, expect to find beef carpaccio, and perhaps deep-fried balls of saffron risotto filled with dolcelatte on a porcini-infused sauce. Desserts might feature tiramisù, chocolate marquise, and brioche bread-and-butter pudding. Service is both friendly and efficient and, except for champagne, the concise wine list stays below £20 and offers ten wines by the glass, including two Italian organics. The house selection starts at £10.95.

CHEFS: Anthony Armelin and Martyn Cornock PROPRIETOR: Anthony Armelin OPEN: Tue to Sun L 12 to 2.30 (3.30 Sun), Tue to Sat D 6 to 10.30 MEALS: alc (main courses £10 to £22). Set L Tue to Sat £8.95 (2 courses), Set L Sun £7.95 (1 course) to £14.95, Set D Tue to Fri £12.95 SERVICE: not inc CARDS: Amex, Delta, MasterCard, Switch, Visa DETAILS: 100 seats. 29 seats outside. Private parties: 24 main room. Car park. Vegetarian meals. No children under 7. No smoking in dining room. Wheelchair access (also WC). Music (£5)

▲ St David's Hotel & Spa

Havana Street, Cardiff Bay, Cardiff CF10 5SD
TEL: (029) 2031 3018 FAX: (029) 2048 7056
EMAIL: reservations@thestdavidshotel.com
WEB SITE: www.rfhotels.com

COOKING **4**
MODERN EUROPEAN
£33–£59

Standing out starkly on the waterfront, in a prime position facing Cardiff Bay, the hotel looks for all the world like an ocean liner. Beyond the foyer and atrium a large bar leads to a similarly themed dining room with waves everywhere, and waiters done up in ship's steward uniforms. But it is all carried out with 'restrained stylishness'. In these circumstances seafood would be conspicuous were it absent; in fact it accounts for nearly half the main courses on the carte, from a simple grilled tranche of halibut, via brill with a crab crust in roast langoustine sauce, to seared sea bass in a champagne and caviar sauce. Other native materials are used to produce potato-crusted loin of Pembrokeshire lamb with roast garlic, and fillet of Welsh Black beef Rossini. The broadly based cooking also takes in seared scallops with sweet chilli dressing, and Pant-ys-gawn goats'-cheese soufflé with grilled asparagus, ending with old-fashioned desserts of profiteroles or Grand Marnier pancakes. Set-price market menus change weekly, and children get their own bill of fare. Helpful and friendly staff serve with 'dignified informality'. The long wine list has gone, replaced by a short global one that starts around £16.

CHEF: Martin Green PROPRIETOR: RF Hotels OPEN: all week 12.30 to 2.30 (3 Sat and Sun), 6.30 to 10.30 MEALS: alc (main courses £12.50 to £18). Set L £14.95 to £19.95 (all 2 courses), Set D £20 (2 courses) to £25 SERVICE: not inc CARDS: Amex, Delta, Diners, MasterCard, Switch, Visa DETAILS: 110 seats. 40 seats outside. Private parties: 110 main room. Car park. Vegetarian meals. Children's helpings. No smoking in dining room. Wheelchair access (not WC). Music. Air-conditioned ACCOMMODATION: 136 rooms, all with bath/shower. TV. Phone. Room only £115 to £160. Rooms for disabled. Baby facilities. Swimming pool

Woods Brasserie

Pilotage Building, Stuart Street, Cardiff Bay,
Cardiff CF10 5BW
TEL: (029) 2049 2400 FAX: (029) 2048 1998

COOKING **4**
MODERN EUROPEAN
£25–£58

Reporters are struck by the cool modern style – polished wood, glass and stainless steel – that has transformed the old Pilotage Building down by the dock. The brasserie's contribution to this fast-improving area of the city is a generous slate of well-presented and -served contemporary dishes, taking inspiration from both the Mediterranean and Pacific Rim. Among the offerings might be bang-bang chicken with peanut sauce, or Aberdeen Angus fillet with Gorgonzola polenta. Rump of Welsh salt-marsh lamb has also turned up, served with red onion tarte Tatin. The style is lively enough to surprise and delight with its imaginative ideas while staying the right side of flamboyance, producing, for example, wild mushroom and chestnut soup, and crab and sweetcorn spring rolls with harissa vinaigrette. At the same time it appeals to traditionalists with fish and chips, omelette Arnold Bennett, and desserts from Eton mess to chocolate nemesis. Service is 'friendly, efficient and prompt', and the 40-plus wines cover a lot of territory, much of it for less than £20. House Australian is £11.95 (white) and £12.95 (red).

CHEF: Martyn Peters PROPRIETORS: Martyn and Deborah Peters OPEN: Tue to Sat L 12 to 2, Sun L 11.30 to 3, Tue to Sat D 7 to 10 CLOSED: 1 week autumn, Christmas and New Year, 1 week spring, bank hols MEALS: alc (main courses £7 to £18) SERVICE: not inc CARDS: Amex, Delta, Diners, MasterCard, Switch, Visa DETAILS: 90 seats. 30 seats outside. Private parties: 60 main room, 30 and 60 private rooms. Vegetarian meals. Children's helpings. Wheelchair access (also WC). Music. Air-conditioned

CLYTHA Monmouthshire — map 2

▲ Clytha Arms

Clytha NP7 9BW
TEL/FAX: (01873) 840206
off old Abergavenny to Raglan road, S of A40, 6m E of Abergavenny

COOKING **4**
MODERN WELSH
£22–£45

For one supporter, this slate-roofed pub, part of an estate bordering the River Usk, remains 'as popular and reliable an eating place as ever'. Beverley Canning keeps busy out front in the low-ceilinged dining room with its linen-covered tables and spindly tea room chairs, while father and daughter cook with assurance. Although the menu is relatively long, dishes are pleasingly simple, taking in jugged hare with herb dumplings, and leg of lamb steak with glazed shallots. Seafood is a strong suit, yielding starters of mussels and clams with roast garlic, leek and laverbread rissoles with pickled beetroot, and highly recommended seafood soup. Carefully sourced materials combine with a generous hand in the kitchen to produce, for example, a Sunday lunch of 'outstandingly good' roast Welsh Black beef with copious vegetables. Among desserts to draw praise are a light Sauternes cream with spiced prunes, and treacle pudding with custard. Eight house wines at £8.95 head up an enthusiastic 75-strong list that includes a trio of Welsh wines.

CHEFS: Andrew Canning and Sarah Canning PROPRIETORS: Andrew and Beverley Canning OPEN: all week L 12.30 to 2.30, Tue to Sat D 7.30 to 9.30 CLOSED: Mon L Sept to April MEALS: alc Tue to Sat L and D (main courses £12 to £15.50). Set L Sun £13.95. Bar menu available SERVICE: not inc, card slips closed CARDS: Amex, Delta, Diners, MasterCard, Switch, Visa DETAILS: 50 seats. 40 seats outside. Private parties: 55 main room, 15 to 55 private rooms. Car park. Vegetarian meals. Children's helpings. No smoking in dining room. Wheelchair access (not WC). No music ACCOMMODATION: 4 rooms, all with bath/shower. TV. Room only £45 to £70 (*The Which? Hotel Guide*) (£5)

COLWYN BAY Conwy — map 7

Café Niçoise £

124 Abergele Road, Colwyn Bay LL29 7PS
TEL: (01492) 531555

COOKING **4**
MODERN EUROPEAN
£19–£43

The inviting appearance of this former shop, its windows hung with bright fabric, livens up Colwyn's otherwise unremarkable main street, and the welcome inside from 'friendly, caring and courteous' Lynne Swift is just as warm. Carl Swift's assured modern cooking, meanwhile, takes in salade lyonnaise, a crisp filo pastry parcel oozing 'silky' Camembert, and chicken with provençale vegetables. Wider influences are apparent, too, in roast salmon with lemon grass and ginger, and a generous portion of baked cod 'still tasting of the sea and cooked just right', served in a curry sauce with Bombay potato. A delicate glazed lemon tart with a serving of lemon ice cream made a 'glorious' end to one reporter's meal. The set-price *menu touristique* remains a bargain, and the list of 50-plus wines (mostly French) includes ten half-bottles and seven house recommendations from £7.95.

CHEFS: Carl Swift and Chris Jackson PROPRIETORS: Carl and Lynne Swift OPEN: Wed to Sat L 12 to 2, Mon to Sat D 7 to 10 CLOSED: 25 and 26 Dec, 1 Jan, 1 week Jan, 1 week June MEALS: alc (main courses £5 to £14). Set L £12.75 (2 courses) to £14.95, Set D £12.75 (2 courses) to £14.95 SERVICE: not inc, card slips closed CARDS: Amex, Delta, MasterCard, Switch, Visa DETAILS: 32 seats. Private parties: 30 main room. Vegetarian meals. Children's helpings. No-smoking area. Music (£5)

CRICCIETH Gwynedd **map 7**

Tir-a-Môr 🍷

1–3 Mona Terrace, Criccieth LL52 0HG COOKING **3**
TEL: (01766) 523084 FAX: (01766) 523049 MODERN WELSH/SEAFOOD
£28–£45

Meaning 'land and sea', the name of this welcoming, unpretentious bistro is reflected in its regularly updated carte and daily-changing blackboard menu featuring locally landed fish and seafood: perhaps seared Anglesey scallops with capers and sage, or baked sea bass with fresh herb butter. Clare Vowell's enthusiasm for local produce, and for techniques such as pickling and curing, is apparent in a 'truly tasty' starter of home-cured Lleyn rose beef with sharply pickled vegetables, and a 'rich, creamy' cod and thyme pie topped with Hen Sir (a locally made cheese). An Italian influence is also evident in bagna cauda, baked potato gnocchi with tomato and basil, and desserts of pannacotta, or spumone amaretto. Some reporters feel that the vast choice puts a strain on the small kitchen but it 'copes admirably most of the time' and most agree that the cooking's flair makes it worth the occasional long wait. Martin is a cheerful front-of-house presence, aided by Welsh-speaking waitresses. Arranged according to style rather than geographical region, the 80-strong wine list includes an intelligent global selection, all enticingly priced. House wines start at £10.95.

CHEF: Clare Vowell PROPRIETORS: Clare and Martin Vowell OPEN: Mon to Sat D only 7 to 9.30 (booking essential Fri and Sat) CLOSED: Christmas to end Jan MEALS: alc (main courses £10 to £17) SERVICE: not inc CARDS: Delta, MasterCard, Switch, Visa DETAILS: 35 seats. Private parties: 25 main room. Vegetarian meals. No children under 7. Wheelchair access (not WC). Music

All details are as accurate as possible at the time of going to press, but chefs and owners often change, and it is wise to check by telephone before making a special journey. Many readers have been disappointed when set-price bargain meals are no longer available. Ask when booking.

CRICKHOWELL Powys map 4

▲ Bear Hotel

High Street, Crickhowell NP8 1BW
TEL: (01873) 810408 FAX: (01873) 811696 NEW CHEF
EMAIL: bearhotel@aol.com MODERN WELSH
WEB SITE: www.bearhotel.co.uk £26–£45

Converted coaching inns may come ten to the groat these days, but here is one with charm and elegance, set among the hills of the Brecon Beacons National Park. There are two eating areas: a large, informal, oak-beamed space with rugs laid over the old slate-slabbed floor, and a smaller, more intimate room that accommodates a mere two dozen covers. Local meats such as lamb and venison have been mainstays of the menu, and fish has been adventurously treated, but Anthony Jones arrived at the stoves just as the Guide was going to press, and we welcome reports of the new kitchen regime. Wines are grouped by style, the selections not startlingly original but serving their purpose reasonably well. House French is £8.95.

CHEF: Anthony Jones PROPRIETORS: Judy and Stephen Hindmarsh OPEN: Sun L 12 to 2, Mon to Sat D 7 to 9.30 CLOSED: 25 Dec MEALS: alc (main courses £9.50 to £17) SERVICE: not inc CARDS: Amex, Delta, MasterCard, Switch, Visa DETAILS: 90 seats. 30 seats outside. Private parties: 60 main room, 25 and 30 private rooms. Car park. Vegetarian meals. No-smoking area. Wheelchair access (also WC). No music ACCOMMODATION: 35 rooms, all with bath/shower. TV. Phone. B&B £49.50 to £120. Rooms for disabled. No children under 6 (*The Which? Hotel Guide*)

Nantyffin Cider Mill Inn

Brecon Road, Crickhowell NP8 1SG
TEL/FAX: (01873) 810775 COOKING **2**
WEB SITE: www.cidermill.co.uk MODERN WELSH-PLUS
1½m W of Crickhowell at junction of A40 and A479 £26–£47

The converted grey-stone cider mill's three eating areas – bar, bistro, restaurant – are presided over by chef-proprietor Sean Gerrard. He blends regional and organic produce with myriad global ingredients to create unusual combinations, particularly in starters such as American-style crabcakes with a Seville orange and saffron coleslaw. Occasionally, dishes might do with paring down, as in an inspector's creamy but heavily garnished saffron and mussel risotto, though a griddled ribeye of Welsh Black beef on mustardy mash has shown off top-quality raw materials at their best. Desserts have included a 'sticky, spicy' pear poached in red wine, ginger and cardamom. Staff are hard-working, not least the enthusiast behind the bar, sporting a 'so many wines . . . so little time' T-shirt. The wine list features a fashionable range of New World bottles that are well priced and intelligently written up. Wines of the month allow for even more variety. Five house wines include South African Danie de Wet's unoaked Chardonnay and cost £12.95.

▲ *means accommodation is available.*

CHEF: Sean Gerrard PROPRIETORS: Sean Gerrard and Glyn Bridgeman OPEN: Tue to Sun 12 to 2.15, 6.30 (7 Sun) to 9.30 CLOSED: 1 week Jan, 1 week Nov MEALS: alc (main courses £8 to £15). Bar L available SERVICE: not inc, card slips closed CARDS: Amex, Delta, MasterCard, Switch, Visa DETAILS: 90 seats. 50 seats outside. Private parties: 60 main room. Car park. Vegetarian meals. Children's helpings. No smoking in dining room. Wheelchair access (also WC). Occasional music (£5)

DOLGELLAU Gwynedd **map 7**

Dylanwad Da

2 Ffôs-y-Felin, Dolgellau LL40 1BS
TEL: (01341) 422870

COOKING **2**
BISTRO
£22–£39

Dylan Rowlands went straight to the pun on his name in calling his small, fresh-looking bistro the Welsh for 'good welcome'. His smiling staff dispense well-timed service to all comers. The formula is five starters, usually including a salad, a soup or broth, and a pasty or turnover, then six main courses always with a proper vegetarian dish among them, such as Glamorgan sausages, and black-eyed bean casserole. But the main thrust is the meat: Welsh beef turned Spanish with tomatoes, basil and chorizo, or lamb done like boeuf bourguignon. Curried monkfish or salsa-fied hake might be the fish option, and vegetables are also vehicles for some judicious spicing. For 'pwdin' Mr Rowlands offers four, among them tarte aux pruneaux, or lemon ice cream with a lemon sauce, plus local cheeses. 'Wine is an area of growing interest,' he asserts, offering an unpretentious and pithy wine list that combines safe drinking – Berry Brothers Good Ordinary Claret (£11.10) – with more adventurous bottles such as Mission Hill Pinot Blanc from Canada (£12.80). Prices are competitive, with most bottles under £20, and house wines £9.40.

CHEF/PROPRIETOR: Dylan Rowlands OPEN: Tue to Sat (Tue to Sun summer, all week Easter and Whitsun) D only 7 to 9 CLOSED: 6 weeks Feb/Mar MEALS: alc (main courses £9 to £14.50). Set D £15 SERVICE: not inc CARDS: none DETAILS: 30 seats. Private parties: 30 main room. Vegetarian meals. Children's helpings. No smoking in dining room. Wheelchair access (not WC). Music (£5)

EGLWYSFACH Powys **map 7**

▲ Ynyshir Hall

Eglwysfach SY20 8TA
TEL: (01654) 781209 FAX: (01654) 781366
EMAIL: info@ynyshir-hall.co.uk
WEB SITE: www.ynyshir-hall.co.uk
off A487, 6m SW of Machynlleth

COOKING **5**
MODERN BRITISH
£32–£59

The décor makes a dramatic impression at this peaceful retreat. Based throughout on strong colours, it features Rob Reen's bold, accomplished oil paintings, with spacious tables, comfortable chairs and cheerful lighting adding to the dining room's appeal. Materials for the three-course set-price meals are well sourced, taking in Brecon venison, Cardiganshire cheese, and local shellfish: perhaps a generous plate of 'sweet and fresh' warm brown shrimps, calamari and mussels, with a pool of garlicky aïoli for dipping. Equally fresh steamed sea bass has arrived on a bed of potatoes with a glossy and lightly tarragoned beurre blanc, while a robust daube of Welsh black beef, cooked for hours until the meat was 'the colour of old wood', proved the highlight of a winter meal.

Dishes tend to be elaborate – fillet of red mullet comes with a lobster soufflé and warm lobster salad, for example – but when they work the combinations can certainly wow visitors. 'A dish for hedonists' is how one of them described a box made from thin crisps of apple, with apple confit set on top of creamy rice pudding containing fat, juicy sultanas, all topped with Horlicks ice cream. As for service, 'the Reens could give lessons in how to be the perfect hosts'. Fine old wines from Bordeaux and Burgundy are the star attraction on a hefty wine list, which includes a page devoted to the wines of Austrian Willi Opitz. Those seeking less costly drinking would do well to concentrate on Chile or southern France. Half-bottles are plentiful, house wines start at £15 and there are 12 wines offered by the glass.

CHEF: Chris Colmer PROPRIETORS: Rob and Joan Reen OPEN: all week 12.30 to 1.30, 7.30 to 8.45 CLOSED: 4 to 25 Jan MEALS: Set L £21.50, Set D £35 SERVICE: not inc, card slips closed CARDS: Amex, Delta, Diners, MasterCard, Switch, Visa DETAILS: 35 seats. Private parties: 28 main room, 16 private room. Car park. No children under 9. No smoking in dining room. Occasional music ACCOMMODATION: 10 rooms, all with bath/shower. TV. Phone. B&B £95 to £200. No children under 9 (*The Which? Hotel Guide*)

FISHGUARD Pembrokeshire **map 4**

▲ Three Main Street

3 Main Street, Fishguard SA65 9HG
TEL: (01348) 874275 FAX: (01348) 874017

COOKING **5**
MODERN EUROPEAN
£23–£46

Considered Pembrokeshire's best restaurant by reporters, this unassuming Georgian town house is a 'delightful, well-run operation' with old oak furniture, a well-proportioned dining room, and a rich, comforting feel. Over the 11 years they have been here, Marion Evans and Inez Ford have been keen to run 'the kind of restaurant that we would like to eat at', imagining themselves in the role of paying customers, the better to understand what their own customers want. Judging by the endorsements, they seem to have got the hang of it.

High-quality ingredients are at the heart of things, many coming from close to home. Seafood includes line-caught sea bass baked with fennel, and 'scallops to drive miles for', seared and served with sweet chilli sauce and crème fraîche on watercress salad. Traditional ideas and partnerships predominate – loin of lamb from the Preseli hills with mint jelly and port sauce – although the kitchen also keeps in touch with developments by serving up crostini of smoked duck breast on spiced red onion marmalade. 'Precise cooking' is the unifying theme. Farmhouse cheeses provide a viable alternative to desserts of lemon meringue tartlet, or iced chocolate praline and raisin parfait, and three dozen wines deliver much of interest at fair prices, which start with vin de pays at £10.50.

All entries, including Round-ups, are fully indexed at the back of the Guide.

CHEF: Marion Evans PROPRIETORS: Marion Evans and Inez Ford OPEN: Tue to Sat 12 to 2, 7 to 9 CLOSED: Feb; phone to check during winter MEALS: alc L (main courses £5.50 to £7.50). Set D £23 (2 courses) to £28 SERVICE: not inc CARDS: none DETAILS: 35 seats. Private parties: 18 main room, 14 private room. Vegetarian meals. Children's helpings. No smoking in dining room. Wheelchair access (not WC). No music ACCOMMODATION: 3 rooms, all with bath/shower. TV. B&B £60 to £70 (double room) (*The Which? Hotel Guide*)

GANLLWYD Gwynedd map 7

▲ Plas Dolmelynllyn

Ganllwyd LL40 2HP
TEL: (01341) 440273 FAX: (01341) 440640
EMAIL: info@dolly-hotel.co.uk
WEB SITE: www.dolly-hotel.co.uk
on A470, 5m N of Dolgellau

COOKING **1**
MODERN WELSH
£33–£39

The setting is an impressive stone-built hall dating back some 450 years, in the lea of the Rhinog range, with the Coed y Brenin National Park on the doorstep. Joanna Reddicliffe's four-course dinners allow minimal choice, but offer a degree of invention in starters of cockle and sweetcorn fritters, or a Stilton and white port pâté served with a pecan galette. After soup or sorbet comes a trio of main courses such as venison with leek crumble and rosemary gravy, chicken ballottine with apricot and almonds, or vegetable tajine with honeyed couscous and salted chickpeas. To finish, options have included croissant and butter pudding with saffron and cardamom, and an intriguing savoury of smoked Cheddar and pear rarebit with sweet marrow chutney. The enthusiastically annotated wine list includes many bottles under £15 and brings together an interesting range of styles from around the world. Producers are cleverly sourced, established names rubbing shoulders with more obscure ones. Try red Quinta do Crasto (£13.25) from Portugal, made by Australian wine-maker David Baverstock. Prices start at £9.75, and six wines are available by the glass.

CHEF: Joanna Reddicliffe PROPRIETORS: Jonathan Barkwith and Joanna Reddicliffe OPEN: all week D only 7 to 8.30 CLOSED: 1 Nov to 28 Feb MEALS: Set D £24.50 SERVICE: not inc, card slips closed CARDS: Amex, Delta, Diners, MasterCard, Switch, Visa DETAILS: 20 seats. Private parties: 36 main room. Car park. Vegetarian meals. Children's helpings. No children under 8. No smoking in dining room. Wheelchair access (not WC). No music ACCOMMODATION: 10 rooms, all with bath/shower. TV. Phone. B&B £45 to £120. Baby facilities. Fishing (*The Which? Hotel Guide*) (£5)

HARLECH Gwynedd map 7

▲ Castle Cottage

Pen Llech, Harlech LL46 2YL
TEL/FAX: (01766) 780479
EMAIL: gh.roberts:talk21.com
WEB SITE: www.lokalink.co.uk/harlech/castlecottage

COOKING **2**
MODERN WELSH
£31–£41

As names go, this one accurately sums up the old cottage just a couple of hundred yards from the castle, easily recognisable by its slate roof and white-painted frontage. Glyn Roberts builds his dinner menus around native produce: grilled ribeye steak of Welsh Black beef on olive oil mash with wild mushroom sauce, for example, or herb-roasted rack of local lamb on parsnip purée with a wine and rosemary sauce. The style is kept simple enough – cream of broccoli and Stilton soup, or grilled asparagus on tomato with basil and capers – and alcohol is a typical saucing standby, from white wine to Cognac to Madeira. Finish with cheese, a cheesy savoury, or perhaps a dessert such as brown bread-and-butter pudding with banana ice cream. An up-to-date and good-value wine list starts with a sensible dozen under £15.

CHEF: Glyn Roberts PROPRIETORS: Glyn and Jacqueline Roberts OPEN: all week D only 7 to 9.30 (8.30 off-season) CLOSED: 3 weeks Feb MEALS: Set D £23 SERVICE: not inc, card slips closed CARDS: Delta, MasterCard, Switch, Visa DETAILS: 45 seats. Private parties: 45 main room. Vegetarian meals. Children's helpings. No smoking in dining room. Wheelchair access (not WC). Occasional music ACCOMMODATION: 6 rooms, 4 with bath/shower. B&B £28 to £59. Baby facilities (*The Which? Hotel Guide*) (£5)

HAWARDEN Flintshire map 7

The Brasserie

NEW ENTRY

68 The Highway, Hawarden CH5 3DH
TEL: (01244) 536353 FAX: (01244) 520888

COOKING **4**
MODERN EUROPEAN
£21–£39

Some readers may remember a Swiss restaurant on this site a few years ago. In its new incarnation, with new owners, it delivers a cheerful, informal brasserie style of food in a warm and friendly atmosphere. The tone is enthusiastic, the style light, and flavours well defined: a tower of poached salmon flakes, for example, mixed with thinly sliced new potatoes coated in crème fraîche, with coriander leaves to perk it all up; or a warm charlotte of goats' cheese and roast tomato with rocket and basil oil. Ingredients are sound and favour the mainstream, while combinations are generally interesting. Crispy duck with chorizo and a Mediterranean vegetable confit is a regular item, or there may be a torte of black and white puddings with caramelised apples and onions. Textures are well managed too: raspberry ripple cheesecake manages to be both 'light and fluffy' and 'creamy and sumptuous', a feat equalled by sticky toffee pudding. In the weekly cycle, Saturday evening brings two sittings, and on Sunday and Monday evenings the carte gives way to a set-price meal for two. Twenty sensibly priced wines start with house Italian at £9.95.

CHEF: Mark Jones PROPRIETORS: Neal Bates and Mark Jones OPEN: Sun to Fri L 12 to 2, all week D 6.45 to 9.15 MEALS: alc D Tue to Sat (main courses £9 to £14). Set L £9.95 (2 courses) to £12.50, Set D Sun and Mon £25 (2 courses) to £29 (Set D prices are for 2 people) SERVICE: not inc CARDS: Delta, MasterCard, Switch, Visa DETAILS: 35 seats. Private parties: 30 main room, 25 private room. Vegetarian meals. Children's helpings. Wheelchair access (not WC). Music. Air-conditioned

---

£ *means that it is possible to have a three-course meal, including coffee, half a bottle of house wine and service for £25 or less per person, at any time the restaurant is open, i.e. at dinner as well as lunch. It may be possible to spend considerably more than this, but by choosing carefully you should find £25 or less achievable.*

LLANARMON DYFFRYN CEIRIOG Wrexham map 7

▲ West Arms £

Llanarmon Dyffryn Ceiriog LL20 7LD
TEL: (01691) 600665 FAX: (01691) 600622
EMAIL: gowestarms@aol.com
off A5 Llangollen to Oswestry road at Chirk, then follow B4500 for 11m

COOKING **1**
WELSH
£21–£40

The old-fashioned, unstuffy rural inn, where rough-plastered stone meets low black beams and inglenook fireplaces, is now presided over by Geoff Leigh-Ford, a relaxed, unpretentious, warm-hearted natural host. Grant Williams has stayed on under the change of ownership, serving up bar food as well as a short menu that might take in moules marinière, and gammon steak with either egg or pineapple. Some dishes tend to be more ambitious than is wise (meat baked in pastry or brioche is a case in point), but good-quality grilled fillet of brill in a properly made butter sauce has made a 'fresh impression'. Steamed chocolate pudding comes with toffee sauce, and tangy lemon tart with chopped nuts. Bread is first class, and the inn can also count reasonable prices in its favour. Wines stay mostly under £20, including a house trio at £10.90.

CHEF: Grant Williams PROPRIETORS: Geoff and Gill Leigh-Ford OPEN: all week 12 to 2, 7 to 9 MEALS: alc (main courses £7 to £13). Set D £21.90 to £24.90 SERVICE: not inc, card slips closed CARDS: MasterCard, Switch, Visa DETAILS: 60 seats. 25 seats outside. Private parties: 70 main room, 80 and 100 private rooms. Car park. Vegetarian meals. Children's helpings. No smoking in dining room. Wheelchair access (also WC). Music ACCOMMODATION: 15 rooms, all with bath/shower. TV. Phone. B&B £44.50 to £79. Rooms for disabled. Fishing (*The Which? Hotel Guide*)

LLANBERIS Gwynedd map 7

Y Bistro

43–45 High Street, Llanberis LL55 4EU
TEL/FAX: (01286) 871278
EMAIL: ybistro@fsbdial.co.uk
WEB SITE: www.ybistro.co.uk
off A4086, at foot of Mount Snowdon

COOKING **2**
MODERN WELSH
£32–£38

Sheltering in the imposing shadow of Mount Snowdon, Llanberis is unusually well-provided with eating places, but the Robertses' homely, well-run bistro, now into its third decade, still seems to be the jewel in the crown. The fixed-price dinner menus are bilingual and offer classically rich food that's a cut or two above the domestic. A starter featuring local black pudding comes with creamy calvados sauce and apple purée, for example. Main courses major on meats, with generally one fish and one vegetarian option, although even the lemon sole with salmon mousseline may be accompanied by smoked bacon. Finish with pannacotta and raspberries or Snowdon pudding, a steamed fruit suet sponge with lemon sherry sauce. France heads up the fairly priced wine list, which includes a Welsh sparkling rosé as well as house wines at £9.50.

CHEF: Nerys Roberts PROPRIETORS: Danny and Nerys Roberts OPEN: all week D only 7.30 to 10 CLOSED: Sun and Mon in winter MEALS: Set D £24 SERVICE: not inc, card slips closed CARDS: Delta, MasterCard, Switch, Visa DETAILS: 50 seats. Private parties: 42 main room, 10 private room. Vegetarian meals. Children's helpings. No smoking in dining room. Wheelchair access (not WC). No music (£5)

LLANDDEINIOLEN Gwynedd map 7

▲ Ty'n Rhos

Seion, Llanddeiniolen LL55 3AE
TEL: (01248) 670489 FAX: (01248) 670079
EMAIL: enquiries@tynrhos.co.uk
WEB SITE: www.tynrhos.co.uk
off B4366, 5m NE of Caernarfon on road signposted Seion

COOKING **4**
BRITISH/WELSH
£23–£48

This immaculately decorated and appointed former farmstead is set in prime countryside, with jaw-dropping views from the conservatory and dining room across the Menai Strait to Anglesey, and from the lounge inland to Snowdonia. Local and regional ingredients are a mainstay, from Welsh lamb (braised shoulder with a tartlet of kidneys) via Black beef (with an oxtail 'crust') to a crop of herbs and vegetables from the kitchen garden. While the set menu offers no choice, the carte is more than generous and brings a degree of enterprise to familiar ideas in the form of black pudding risotto with a poached egg, for example, or home-cured gravad lax of haddock with cucumber relish. A similar approach applies to desserts, which may combine warm treacle tart with rhubarb sorbet, or jellied strawberries with Welsh honey ice cream. Cheeses are mostly Welsh, service is 'informed and attentive', and wines on the 60-plus list are arranged by style and include helpful notes, with the majority under £20. Ten house wines are £11.50, or £4 per 250ml glass.

CHEFS: Carys Davies and Ian Cashen PROPRIETORS: Lynda and Nigel Kettle OPEN: all week L 12 to 2, Mon to Sat D 7 to 9.30 CLOSED: Christmas MEALS: alc D (main dishes £13 to £19). Set L £12.95, Set D £22.50 (£19.50 for residents) SERVICE: not inc, card slips closed CARDS: Amex, Delta, MasterCard, Switch, Visa DETAILS: 35 seats. Private parties: 25 main room, 20 private room. Car park. Vegetarian meals. Children's helpings. No children under 6. No smoking in dining room. Wheelchair access (2 steps; not WC). Occasional music. Air-conditioned ACCOMMODATION: 14 rooms, all with bath/shower. TV. Phone. B&B £55 to £110. Rooms for disabled. No children under 6 (*The Which? Hotel Guide*)

LLANDEILO Carmarthenshire map 4

▲ Cawdor Arms

Rhosmaen Street, Llandeilo SA19 6EN
TEL: (01558) 823500 FAX: (01558) 822399
EMAIL: cawdor.arms@btinternet.com
WEB SITE: www.cawdor-arms.co.uk

COOKING **3**
MODERN BRITISH
£25–£42

Welsh produce is celebrated at this 200-year-old coaching inn, and the sourcing of Carmarthenshire lamb, St David's duck, and fish and crab from the Gower take pride of place on its good-value set menus. A formal country-house atmosphere pervades the dark wood-floored dining room, with its well-spaced tables, and subdued lighting enhanced by candle-style table lamps. 'Judicious' cooking with 'flair' veers between traditional Sunday lunch roasts and contemporary Franco-Italian touches with an occasional nod towards the East. Start perhaps with rillettes of St David's duckling and rhubarb with piccalilli, followed by well-timed monkfish with spring onions and ginger, or grilled fillet of Welsh beef wrapped in smoked bacon with a rarebit glaze, all of them 'flamboyantly garnished'. Warm Bakewell tart with properly cooked frangipane finished off an inspector's meal, or there might be lemon curd mousse. Service is 'friendly and helpful', and, except in the fine wine section, the fairly priced wine list rarely gets above £20. Three house wines are £9.90 a bottle, £3.60 a large glass.

CHEF: Rod Peterson PROPRIETORS: John, Sylvia and Jane Silver OPEN: all week L 12 to 2, Mon to Sat D 7.30 to 9 MEALS: Set L £11.95 (2 courses) to £14.95, Set D £21. Light L available Mon to Sat SERVICE: not inc, card slips closed CARDS: Amex, Delta, MasterCard, Switch, Visa DETAILS: 100 seats. 30 seats outside. Private parties: 110 main room, 24 private room. Car park. Vegetarian meals. Children's helpings. No smoking in dining room. Wheelchair access (not WC). Music ACCOMMODATION: 17 rooms, all with bath/shower. TV. Phone. B&B £45 to £75. Baby facilities (*The Which? Hotel Guide*) (£5)

LLANDEWI SKIRRID Monmouthshire — **map 4**

Walnut Tree Inn

Llandewi Skirrid NP7 8AW — COOKING **7**
TEL: (01873) 852797 — ITALIAN
on B4521, 3m NE of Abergavenny — £38–£67

After all this time – the Taruschios started here in 1963 – the Walnut Tree still has the capacity to arouse passion. Some fall ardently in love with it, others find it so unlike their preconceived idea of a fine restaurant that they despair. It was what some might call a 'gastro pub' long before the term was invented, and is the antithesis of flash, formal country-house eating. For many this is an integral part of its charm. If the Taruschios bothered to produce a glossy brochure (which, thankfully, they don't), it might tell visitors not to expect an effusive welcome, or a professional maitre d' to sweep them into a smartly furnished dining room with vast tables and acres of space. Be prepared instead for informal seating, especially in the crammed-to-capacity bar, for paper napkins, for no credit cards, and for a long menu worthy of a metropolitan brasserie: over three dozen savoury items and nearly half as many puddings.

The style of food, too, is a welcome antidote to much that is served up elsewhere these days, since it makes a virtue of simple materials: a pie of mussels, cockles, bacon and leek; ox tongue with cannellini beans; and marinated sardines and mackerel. Not all dishes, it has to be said, work equally well, but among successes are a couple of Walnut Tree classics: Lady Llanover's salt duck, and the 'magnificent' vincisgrassi maceratese (pasta with porcini mushrooms, truffles and Parma ham), although even this fails to please all reporters. Pasta and rice show up well – first-rate spaghetti with cockle sauce, and risotto primavera – and sweets have produced old fashioned rum baba and a 'divine' trio of chocolate desserts. Italy and France vie for top billing on the cleverly selected wine list, supported by a fine selection from other countries.

The top names are all there, and though few bargains are to be had, there is lots to enjoy under £20.

CHEF: Franco Taruschio PROPRIETORS: Franco and Ann Taruschio OPEN: dining room Tue to Sat D only 7 to 10.15, bar/bistro all week 12 to 3, 7 to 10.15 CLOSED: 1 week Christmas, 2 weeks Feb MEALS: alc (main courses £10.50 to £20). Cover £1 SERVICE: not inc CARDS: none DETAILS: 100 seats. 30 seats outside. Private parties: 40 main room. Car park. Vegetarian meals. Children's helpings. Wheelchair access (also WC). No music. Air-conditioned

LLANDRILLO Denbighshire map 7

▲ Tyddyn Llan

WALES GFG 2001 COMMENDED

Llandrillo LL21 0ST
TEL: (01490) 440264 FAX: (01490) 440414
EMAIL: tyddynllanhotel@compuserve.com
WEB SITE: www.tyddynllan.co.uk
on B4401, 4½ miles S of Corwen

COOKING **6**
MODERN BRITISH
£27–£48

Looking 'beetle-browed' against a backdrop of the Berwyn Mountains, this rough-stone, slate-roofed, peaceful old farmhouse goes in for striking greyish blues and flowery yellows inside, perhaps a consequence of the Kindreds' artistic leanings (Peter runs courses). Matthew Haines, head chef since May 2000, carries on where his predecessors left off, cooking in modern British style helped by a fair quota of Mediterranean ideas and by some fine raw materials, including fish and shellfish. Clear flavours characterise the dishes, with not an unnecessary ingredient, let alone garnish, in sight. One meal, for example, began with three big, fat, superbly fresh and nuttily roasted scallops arranged around a sensuous cauliflower purée, encircled in turn by a thin dribble of classically made pesto.

Other impeccable ingredients have included juicy loin fillet of local lamb with a thin coriander-flavoured crust, set beside a mound of copybook couscous, warmly and subtly spiced. Saucing is technically sound, and cheese is a sensibly limited selection (Stilton, Brie and Yarg for one diner) accompanied by freshly baked biscuits. The work that goes into desserts is impressive too: for example, a tall, thin pyramid made from caramel, chocolate and chopped pistachios surmounted by a biscuit question mark ('a bit corny but rather nice'), enclosing a silky, intense chocolate and pistachio mousse.

Appetisers make a good impression at the outset, and bread, according to an expert, is 'terrific'. Value for money is praised, vegetarians get their own menu, and relatively simple lunches run to salmon steak in a cream and white wine sauce. Service is bright, knowledgeable and quite relaxed. Wines are shrewdly chosen to provide a good cross section of styles, and prices are fair. Around ten house recommendations between £13.50 and £17.50 start the ball rolling.

CHEF: Matthew Haines PROPRIETORS: Peter and Bridget Kindred OPEN: Tue to Sun L 12.30 to 2, all week D 7 to 9 MEALS: alc L (main courses £9 to £10.50). Set L Sun £15.50, Set D £25 to £27 SERVICE: not inc, card slips closed CARDS: Amex, Diners, MasterCard, Switch, Visa DETAILS: 60 seats. 10 seats outside. Private parties: 50 main room, 35 private room. Car park. Vegetarian meals. Children's helpings. No smoking in dining room. Wheelchair access (also men's WC). Music ACCOMMODATION: 10 rooms, all with bath/shower. TV. Phone. B&B £67.50 to £140. Baby facilities. Fishing (*The Which? Hotel Guide*) £5

LLANDUDNO Conwy map 7

▲ Bodysgallen Hall

Llandudno LL30 1RS
TEL: (01492) 584466 FAX: (01492) 582519
EMAIL: info@bodysgallen.com
WEB SITE: www.bodysgallen.com
off A470, 2m SE of Llandudno

COOKING **3**
COUNTRY HOUSE
£26–£62

Magnificently maintained by Historic House Hotels, Bodysgallen is set in acres of mature parkland with formal gardens on many levels, huge box trees, long hedges, and water tumbling into a fish pond. Large oil paintings, crisp napery and traditional silver lend the dining room a formal feel, an impression bolstered by correct and attentive service. Dishes can be busy, in typical country-house style, but include some alluring combinations, particularly among starters: lobster niçoise salad with chilli couscous, for example, or a tartlet combining roast squab and chorizo with parsnip purée and lentils.

Sound materials are evident, in grilled Dover sole (well timed) with a sharp lemon and herb butter, and well-flavoured breast of maize-fed chicken with roasted vegetables. The cooking, however, varies from improvable risotto (an accompaniment to several dishes) to a successfully chunky, bouncy, warm sausage of crab, lobster and scallop in a light shellfish cream sauce. Desserts are equally industrious, producing caramelised banana and rice pudding tart with honey ice cream, and hot chocolate fondant with white chocolate sauce and coffee ice cream. Wines offer a broad if fairly standard selection from the Old and New Worlds, enlivened by intelligent tasting notes. Prices reflect the magnificence of the setting, although there is plenty under £20. House white from Rueda (Spain) is £12.75.

CHEF: David Thompson PROPRIETOR: Historic House Hotels OPEN: all week 12.30 to 1.45, 7 to 9.30 MEALS: Set L £14.50 (2 courses) to £17.50, Set D £33.90 SERVICE: net prices, card slips closed CARDS: Delta, MasterCard, Switch, Visa DETAILS: 60 seats. Private parties: 40 main room, 40 private room. Car park. Vegetarian meals. No children under 8. Jacket and tie. No smoking in dining room. Wheelchair access (also WC). Music. Air-conditioned ACCOMMODATION: 35 rooms, all with bath/shower. TV. Phone. Room only £104 to £235. Rooms for disabled. No children under 8. Swimming pool (*The Which? Hotel Guide*)

▲ Martins

11 Mostyn Avenue, Craig-y-Don,
Llandudno LL30 1YS
TEL: (01492) 870070 FAX: (01492) 876661
EMAIL: martins@walesuk4.freeserve.co.uk
WEB SITE: www.smoothhound.co.uk/hotels/martins2.html

COOKING **3**
ANGLO-FRENCH
£25–£54

The dining room and front parlour of an Edwardian house have been knocked into one and filled with small tables: once they are laid with all the accoutrements 'it doesn't do to sneeze'. 'Old-fashioned' doesn't begin to describe the décor, according to one visitor, but most are agreed on the worth of the 'thoroughly professional' food. Choice extends from pigeon breast salad, via

Welsh lamb with creamed leeks, to fish and game in season, and the Anglo-French style takes in Stilton and chestnut pâté with Cumberland sauce, as well as grilled sea bass fillet with a sea urchin sauce. Most other sauces plough a traditional furrow, from herb butters to a generous drinks cabinet full: basil and champagne with steamed Dublin Bay prawns, apples and calvados with slow-roast duck, not to mention a slug each of Cointreau and Tia Maria in the chocolate mousse. Muzak can be irritating, but supporters praise value for money, and service is 'friendly and welcoming'. A short wine list starts with house vin de pays at £11.50.

CHEF: Martin James PROPRIETORS: Martin James and Jan Williams OPEN: Wed to Sat 12 to 2, 6 to 9 (pre-theatre bookings from 5.30 to 7) CLOSED: 2 weeks in Jan MEALS: alc (main courses £15 to £23). Set L £9.95 (2 courses), Set D to 7.30 £17.95 SERVICE: not inc, card slips closed CARDS: Amex, Delta, Diners, MasterCard, Switch, Visa DETAILS: 36 seats. 10 seats outside. Private parties: 36 main room. Vegetarian meals. Children's helpings. No very young children. Jacket and tie. No smoking in dining room. Wheelchair access (not WC). Music ACCOMMODATION: 4 rooms, all with bath/shower. TV. B&B £27.50 to £59. No children (£5)

Richard's

7 Church Walks, Llandudno LL30 2HD
TEL: (01492) 875315

COOKING **2**
MODERN BRITISH-PLUS
£27–£45

A basement bistro with a restaurant above comprise Richard Hendey's efficient and conscientious operation, in which the focus is on fine raw ingredients. A single, menu throughout offers a wide and often imaginative choice, along the lines of warm salad of black pudding with Bramley apples, smoked bacon, mushrooms, grapes and barbecue sauce; or Conwy mussels with champagne cream served with black tagliatelle and spinach. Meats, on the other hand, are often given classic treatment, as in loin of Welsh lamb with redcurrants, garlic and rosemary. 'Fresh, attractively presented' fish – halibut and sea bass were lauded by one reporter – add to the repertoire, and 'after-dinner indulgences', as the menu has it, might include a chocoholic's chocolate platter, or old-English trifle. Service is keen to please, while the wine list scours the world for stimulating flavours, opening with 11 house wines from £9.95.

CHEF/PROPRIETOR: Richard Hendey OPEN: all week D only 5.30 to 11 CLOSED: 3 days at Christmas MEALS: alc (main courses £11 to £15) SERVICE: not inc, card slips closed CARDS: Amex, Delta, Diners, MasterCard, Switch, Visa DETAILS: 50 seats. Private parties: 30 main room. Vegetarian meals. Children's helpings. Music

'[Customer to waiter:] "I'd like a tomato juice with everything in it, but no ice because I'm driving."' (On eating in Scotland)

Several sharp operators have tried to extort money from restaurateurs on the promise of an entry in a guidebook that has never appeared. The Good Food Guide *makes no charge for inclusion.*

▲ St Tudno Hotel

Promenade, Llandudno LL30 2LP
TEL: (01492) 874411 FAX: (01492) 860407
EMAIL: sttudnohotel@btinternet.com
WEB SITE: www.st-tudno.co.uk

COOKING **3**
MODERN EUROPEAN
£27–£56

'Worth visiting Llandudno for,' concluded one visitor to this hotel near the pier. Reporters may be divided in their opinions of the décor ('something more imaginative could be done,' reckoned one) but all agree that food is the draw: 'pleasing to the eye and beautifully cooked' is a typical endorsement. A seasonal carte is supplemented by a daily one, with freedom to move between the two, while lunch offers a set-price option of two or three courses. Seafood makes its presence felt in the shape of crab tart, fish soup, and monkfish with prawn risotto and caper sauce, while fillet of Welsh Black beef is a regular item. Vegetarians are well looked after, perhaps with a puff pastry tartlet of spinach, asparagus and poached egg, and desserts run to pecan tart with clove ice cream, and lemon mousse with toffee sauce. Service is polite, attentive but not intrusive. The hefty wine list kicks off with six pages devoted to wine-growers which the Blands have visited. Homage is paid to Willi Opitz (Austria), d'Arenberg (South Australia) and Château Musar from the Lebanon. High quality and favourable prices epitomise the entire selection. House specials start at £10.30.

CHEF: David Harding PROPRIETORS: Martin and Janette Bland OPEN: all week 12.30 to 1.45, 7 to 9.30 (9 Sun) MEALS: alc D (main courses £14.50 to £18.50). Set L Mon to Sat £15.50 (2 courses), Set L Sun £16.95, Set D £35 SERVICE: not inc, card slips closed CARDS: Amex, Delta, Diners, MasterCard, Switch, Visa DETAILS: 60 seats. Private parties: 70 main room. Car park. Vegetarian meals. Children's helpings. No children under 6 in dining room. No smoking in dining room. Wheelchair access (notWC). Music. Air-conditioned ACCOMMODATION: 20 rooms, all with bath/shower. TV. Phone. B&B £60 to £260. Rooms for disabled. Baby facilities. Swimming pool (*The Which? Hotel Guide*) (£5)

LLANFIHANGEL NANT MELAN Powys **map 4**

▲ Red Lion Inn £

Llanfihangel Nant Melan LD8 2TN
TEL/FAX: (01544) 350220
on A44 Rhayader to Kington road, 3m W of New Radnor

NEW CHEF
MODERN EUROPEAN
£17–£38

After the best part of a decade at this isolated group of buildings beside the busy A44, Keith and Elizabeth Johns have retired and son Gareth has moved on. They will be missed as much for their unassuming friendliness and warm hospitality as for their championing of native produce. New owners David and Annie Browne are undertaking thorough refurbishment, including expansion of guest accommodation, and have recruited André Cluzeau from the Riverside Inn (see Round-up entry, Aymestrey) to take over the kitchen. He arrived too late for the Guide to make an assessment, but an early menu showed promise in the form of foie gras terrine with spicy apple sauce, Penrhyn mussels with cream and herbs, beef fillet with Anna potatoes and red wine, seared scallops in a spring vegetable stew, and lemon cream tart. Reports please.

CHEF: André Cluzeau PROPRIETORS: David and Annie Browne OPEN: all week 12 to 2, 6.30 to 9.45 MEALS: alc (main courses L £5 to £7, D £7.50 to £14.50) SERVICE: not inc, card slips closed CARDS: Amex, Delta, Diners, MasterCard, Switch, Visa DETAILS: 36 seats. Private parties: 20 main room. Car park. Vegetarian meals. Children's helpings. No smoking in 1 dining room. Occasional music ACCOMMODATION: 5 rooms, all with bath/shower. TV. B&B £25 to £45. Rooms for disabled

LLANGAMMARCH WELLS Powys map 4

▲ Lake Country House 

Llangammarch Wells LD4 4BS COOKING **3**
TEL: (01591) 620202 FAX: (01591) 620457 MODERN BRITISH
off B483 at Garth, 6m W of Builth Wells £28–£51

The 50 acres of grounds surrounding this half-timbered mock Victorian-Edwardian house are rich in wildlife and 'a paradise for fishermen'. Inside, a spacious hall with an oak staircase leads to an intimate, modern bar, and a pale yellow, if rather dark, dining room. Sean Cullingford, who took over the kitchen as the last edition of the Guide appeared, cooks with a degree of sophistication, helped by the occasional luxury: a creamy celeriac and apple soup with summer truffle cream, well-rendered gazpacho with red mullet, or a pile of nuttily dressed leaves surrounded by chunks of Cornish lobster and lightly seared scallops.

Good timing leads to 'moist and tender' John Dory with leeks and Veronique sauce, and a thick, pink fillet of beef topped with a thin slice of foie gras, in a well-reduced port sauce. Balance is evident, not least among desserts such as an expertly made hot chocolate fondant oozing molten chocolate, with an orange flavoured crème anglaise. Jean-Pierre Mifsud is a kind and welcoming host, although an inspection meal found the kitchen to be operating in slow motion. Those daunted by the bulk of the 25-page wine list can happily peruse two pages of intelligent house selections instead. Although it is global in content, lovers of fine claret and malt whisky are particularly well catered for. French medium red and dry white are both £11.50

CHEF: Sean Cullingford PROPRIETORS: Mr and Mrs J.P. Mifsud OPEN: all week 12.30 to 2, 7.30 to 9.15 MEALS: Set L £17.50, Set D £30 SERVICE: not inc, card slips closed CARDS: Amex, Delta, Diners, MasterCard, Switch, Visa DETAILS: 40 seats. Private parties: 85 main room, 40 private room. Car park. Vegetarian meals. Children's helpings. Jacket and tie. No smoking in dining room. Wheelchair access (not WC). No music ACCOMMODATION: 19 rooms, all with bath/shower. TV. Phone. B&B £90 to £205. Rooms for disabled. Baby facilities. Fishing (*The Which? Hotel Guide*) (£5)

'The menu is written in Estuary English with a smattering of "Del Boy" French.'
(On eating in Essex)

The Guide relies on feedback from its readers. Especially welcome are reports on new restaurants appearing in the book for the first time. All letters to the Guide are acknowledged.

LLANRHIDIAN Swansea map 4

Welcome to Town

Llanrhidian SA3 1EH
TEL: (01792) 390015
WEB SITE: www.welcometotowngower.org.uk
on B4295, 10m W of Swansea

COOKING **1**
MODERN WELSH
£23–£36

Overlooking 5,000 acres of the Llanrhidian marsh and Loughor Estuary, this long, whitewashed country inn opposite the church is indeed a friendly and hospitable place. Sheila Allen starts with Welsh produce, including lamb and Black beef, and puts them through a modern mill. Starter salads on the monthly-changing menu might include an unusual savoury mix of laverbread, leek, cockles and bacon, followed perhaps by Gower fish stew (incorporating trout, monkfish, salmon and crevette), or rack of Welsh lamb with garlic and coriander mash. Pastry work is a strength, featuring in tarts of caramelised onion to begin, and apple and raspberry crumble, or Tia Maria, to finish. Alternatively, there might be coconut cream rice pudding with Thai spices, or chocolate and brandy brioche pudding. Two dozen modest (and modestly priced) wines start with house Chilean at £10.

CHEF: Sheila Allen PROPRIETORS: the Allen family OPEN: Tue to Sat 12.30 to 1.45, 7 to 8.30 CLOSED: bank hols MEALS: alc (main courses L £7.50 to £12, D £9.50 to £12). Light L available SERVICE: not inc, card slips closed CARDS: Amex, Delta, MasterCard, Switch, Visa DETAILS: 36 seats. Car park. Vegetarian meals. No children under 14 at D. No smoking in dining room. Wheelchair access (also WC). Music (£5)

LLANSANFFRAID GLAN CONWY Conwy map 7

▲ Old Rectory Country House

Llanrwst Road, Llansanffraid Glan Conwy,
nr Conwy LL28 5LF
TEL: (01492) 580611 FAX: (01492) 584555
EMAIL: info@oldrectorycountryhouse.co.uk
WEB SITE: www.oldrectorycountryhouse.co.uk
on A470, 1m S of junction with A55

COOKING **6**
MODERN BRITISH/FRENCH
£42–£50

With serene views across the garden to the estuary and castle, the Old Rectory offers a 'top-class dining experience'. Carved wooden panelling abounds, floral rugs on parquet floors lend an 'old-fashioned domestic' feel to the dining room, and the Vaughans' art collection and accumulated treasures range from antiques to 'tongue-in-cheek kitsch'. The fact that everybody sits down at the same time gives it a house party atmosphere, a feeling reinforced by the absence of any choice before dessert.

Wendy Vaughan comes across as a perfectionist who takes immense care over details, although she is less inclined to take risks. What the cooking may lack in excitement, however, it makes up for in its strikingly fresh materials and skilful handling: a rough mousse of smoked haddock, for example, wrapped in smoked salmon leaves, topped by an unbeatable roast scallop, surrounded and well balanced by thin ribbons of pesto and red wine sauces. The wrapping idea has cropped up elsewhere too, for instance in a chargrill-striped fillet of locally reared Welsh Mountain lamb accompanied by minced lamb and lentils rolled up in spinach leaves.

Come dessert, a tray is borne from table to table with both puddings on display, 'rather like a small-scale version of ye olde sweet trolley'. Among its offerings might be a wedge of warm pear and almond tart made with rich, crumbly shortcrust pastry (a definite strength), with a sophisticated pear-flavoured toffee sauce. Alternatives might include locally made ice creams or grilled goats' cheese. Affable and courteous service from Michael Vaughan is 'second to none'. A good-value wine list pays homage to the regions of classical France and Germany yet maintains a healthy enthusiasm for New World pioneers. Great care has been taken to provide a long list of half-bottles; French house wines are £15.90.

CHEF: Wendy Vaughan PROPRIETORS: Michael and Wendy Vaughan OPEN: all week D only 7.30 for 8 (1 sitting) CLOSED: 20 Dec to 1 Feb MEALS: Set D £29.90 SERVICE: not inc, card slips closed CARDS: Delta, MasterCard, Switch, Visa DETAILS: 16 seats. Private parties: 12 main room. Car park. No smoking in dining room. No music ACCOMMODATION: 6 rooms, all with bath/shower. TV. Phone. B&B £79 to £149. No children under 5, exc babies under 6 months (*The Which? Hotel Guide*)

LLANWRTYD WELLS Powys **map 4**

▲ Carlton House

WALES OF THE YEAR RESTAURANT

Dolycoed Road, Llanwrtyd Wells LD5 4RA
TEL: (01591) 610248 FAX: (01591) 610242
EMAIL: info@carltonrestaurant.co.uk
WEB SITE: www.carltonrestaurant.co.uk

COOKING **6**
MODERN BRITISH
£32–£46

The setting – a red-painted three-storeyed house near the crossroads – may not be the most attractive in Wales, but several delighted readers are quick to assert that appearances aren't everything. Since last year 'we have had to give lunches the boot', writes Mary Ann Gilchrist, 'because they just didn't take off'. At dinner the carte has gone too, and a brace of no-choice menus now offer two to four courses: one may be centred on baked fillet of cod, the more expensive on roast best end of Welsh lamb. Dishes are no more complex than they need to be, and often rely on established partnerships, such as honey-roast Gressingham duck on shredded Savoy cabbage with a rhubarb compote.

In terms of ideas, raw materials and cooking skills, however, the food has produced 'astounding' results. A first course of crab, stirred into freshly made tagliolini (along with olive oil, chillies and coriander), and topped with half a dozen well-timed scallops, showed off the straightforward and unpretentious nature of the cooking. Materials are sensibly sourced – seared Towy sewin with squid ink pasta and Hereford asparagus for a summer visitor – and the cooking's simple perfection extends to desserts such as intensely flavoured warm chocolate fondant with home-made caramel ice cream.

Incidentals are of a high standard, value for money is unusually good – 'if there is better value I would like to hear about it' – and staff are professional and helpful. Quiet, self-effacing and affable Alan Gilchrist's wise and appropriate wine recommendations are much appreciated. The intelligent global list provides plenty of original and exciting drinking under £20, although a claret devotee can spend far more on a few well-selected, pricier bottles. House champagne is a very reasonable £23.50; house Chilean is £9.95 (£2.75 a glass).

CHEF: Mary Ann Gilchrist PROPRIETORS: Alan and Mary Ann Gilchrist OPEN: Mon to Sat D only 7 to 8.30 CLOSED: 10 to 27 Dec MEALS: Set D £18 (2 courses) to £29.50 SERVICE: not inc, card slips closed CARDS: Delta, MasterCard, Switch, Visa DETAILS: 14 seats. Private parties: 12 main room. Vegetarian meals. No children under 6. No smoking in dining room. No music ACCOMMODATION: 7 rooms, all with bath/shower. TV. B&B £30 to £75 (*The Which? Hotel Guide*)

LLYSWEN Powys map 4

▲ Griffin Inn

Llyswen LD3 0UR
TEL: (01874) 754241 FAX: (01874) 754592
EMAIL: info@griffin-inn.freeserve.co.uk
WEB SITE: www.griffin-inn.co.uk
on A470 Builth Wells to Brecon road

COOKING **1**
TRADITIONAL COUNTRY COOKING
£23–£42

Four generations of the Stockton family run the ivy-covered fifteenth-century sporting inn, the sporting referring mainly to fishing on the nearby River Wye. Stuffed trophies in glass cases form part of the décor in the bar, and locally caught salmon and sewin have both appeared on the menu, the latter served in small fillets with two sauces: tomato and vermouth, and a beurre blanc. Careful sourcing also includes Brecon venison, moorland lamb and Radnor wild berries, while a daube of Welsh Black beef with herbs, red wine and a 'lusciousness from long, slow cooking', won plaudits from an inspector. Welsh cheeses are on offer and locally made ice creams partner desserts such as lemon crunch and sticky toffee pudding. Service ranges from 'slow' to 'fairly quick'. The short wine list includes some well-known names and eight wines by the glass from £2.25.

CHEFS: Andrew Addis-Fuller, Richard Stockton and Richard Gardener PROPRIETORS: Richard and Dianne Stockton OPEN: Sun L 12 to 2, Mon to Sat D 7 to 9 CLOSED: 25 and 26 Dec MEALS: alc D (main courses £10 to £14). Set L Sun £15.85. Light L available Mon to Sat SERVICE: not inc, card slips closed CARDS: Amex, Delta, Diners, MasterCard, Switch, Visa DETAILS: 70 seats. 16 seats outside. Private parties: 40 main room, 14 to 30 private rooms. Car park. Vegetarian meals. Children's helpings. No smoking in dining room. No music ACCOMMODATION: 7 rooms, all with bath/shower. TV. Phone. B&B £45 to £80. Baby facilities (*The Which? Hotel Guide*) (£5)

NANTGAREDIG Carmarthenshire map 4

▲ Four Seasons

Cwmtwrch Farm Hotel, Nantgaredig SA31 7NY
TEL: (01267) 290238 FAX: (01267) 290808
EMAIL: jen4seas@aol.com
WEB SITE: www.visit-carmarthenshire.co.uk/fourseasons
on B4310, ½m N of Nantgaredig

COOKING **3**
MODERN BRITISH
£33–£44

This sympathetic conversion of a stone-built farmhouse into a restaurant-with-rooms is considered a successful fusion of traditional and modern. A conservatory extension and terrace have been added at the front, for outside eating and pre-dinner drinks, and the dining room, with its pine furniture, roughly plastered walls and collection of farm implements, offers a glimpse of action at the stoves. Produce is fresh and often local – Carmarthen ham, Brechfa smoked salmon, Welsh salt-marsh lamb and Black beef – and the honest, wholesome food is delivered in generous portions: crab and asparagus tart, for example, or rack of Welsh lamb with a rosemary flavoured aubergine caponata. Desserts have included well-made raspberry crème brûlée with a brittle topping, and 'mercifully un-sweet' peach and almond tart, while cheeses run to Llanboidy and Penybont. Service is 'efficient without any frills', and around 50 wines, mostly under £20, provide decent drinking. Three house wines are £10.

CHEFS/PROPRIETORS: Charlotte Pasetti and Maryann Wright OPEN: Tue to Sat D only 7.30 to 9.30 CLOSED: Christmas MEALS: Set D £25 SERVICE: not inc, card slips closed CARDS: Delta, MasterCard, Switch, Visa DETAILS: 45 seats. 12 seats outside. Private parties: 45 main room. Car park. Vegetarian meals. Children's helpings. No children under 5 (exc residents). No smoking in dining room. Wheelchair access (not WC). Music ACCOMMODATION: 6 rooms, all with bath/shower. TV. B&B £40 to £80. Rooms for disabled. Baby facilities. Swimming pool (*The Which? Hotel Guide*) (£5)

NEWPORT Pembrokeshire **map 4**

▲ Cnapan

East Street, Newport SA42 0SY COOKING **2**
TEL: (01239) 820575 FAX: (01239) 820878 TRADITIONAL
WEB SITE: www.online-holidays.net/cnapan £18–£44

Fashioned from two rooms of a town house, and setting out its stall with lace tablecloths and fresh flowers, Cnapan has a 'comfortable Laura Ashley feel to it'. Modest, family-run and welcoming, it offers a homely style of cooking along the lines of stuffed red pepper, duck breast with soured black cherry sauce, and a herby crêpe filled with mushrooms, Stilton and coriander. In addition to Welsh lamb and beef (perhaps fillet steak with garlic butter), Judith Cooper manages to lay her hands on lobster, crab and some local organic vegetables: spinach and broccoli roulade and roast vegetable tart have been among the meatless options. Desserts run from a variation on trifle, via chocolate and rum mousse, to a sticky apple and apricot shortcake with butterscotch sauce. Lunches are lighter. An unassuming wine list includes native Monnow Valley, and prices start at £9.50.

CHEF: Judith Cooper PROPRIETORS: Eluned and John Lloyd, and Michael and Judith Cooper OPEN: Wed to Mon L 12 to 2, Mon and Wed to Fri D 6.30 to 8.45 CLOSED: 25 and 26 Dec, Jan and Feb. MEALS: alc (main courses L £6 to £9, D £12 to £18) SERVICE: not inc, card slips closed CARDS: Delta, MasterCard, Switch, Visa DETAILS: 36 seats. 24 seats outside. Private parties: 36 main room. Car park. Vegetarian meals. Children's helpings. No smoking in dining room. Wheelchair access (also WC). Occasional music ACCOMMODATION: 5 rooms, all with bath/shower. TV. B&B £35 to £56. Baby facilities (*The Which? Hotel Guide*)

'Service . . . plumbed new depths for me: young girls who don't know what the daily soup is, who can't tell you what the house wines are even when they're confronted with the wine list, who don't remove unused place settings, and don't pick up a customer's blazer that has fallen on the floor.' (On eating in Hampshire)

PEMBROKE Pembrokeshire map 4

Left Bank

63 Main Street, Pembroke SA71 4DA
TEL: (01646) 622333
WEB SITE: www.leftbankrestaurant.co.uk

COOKING **2**
FRENCH
£34–£40

This converted old bank is a pleasantly informal, comfortable and convivial place to dine. A sensibly limited menu (four choices per course at dinner) sets its sights high, and the cooking is done with enthusiasm and a degree of skill. Local supplies play a part, although (an inspector felt) without taking as much advantage of the seasonal abundance as might be expected. Presentation is a strength – a mixed chowder containing a huge, well-timed scallop surrounded by chunks of cod and monkfish, in a light fishy broth – although results can be patchy: from a disappointing dish of lamb with couscous at inspection to a 'magnificent' fillet of Welsh Black beef with parsley purée, parsnip crisps and a deeply flavourful sauce. Also hitting the spot has been a silky-textured dark chocolate mousse with raspberry sorbet and chocolate wafers. Lunches are lighter and reasonably priced. Service is willing and friendly, and 40-plus wines offer good value, starting with a handful of house wines under £10.

CHEFS: Andrew Griffith and Becky Bradshaw PROPRIETORS: Andrew and Emma Griffith, and Sue Wharrad OPEN: Tue to Sat 12 to 2.30, 7 to 9.30 CLOSED: 24 to 26 Dec, 2 weeks Jan MEALS: alc L (main courses around £5), Set D £19.50 (2 courses) to £24.50 SERVICE: not inc, card slips closed CARDS: Delta, MasterCard, Switch, Visa DETAILS: 30 seats. Private parties: 40 main room, 40 private room. Vegetarian meals. Children's helpings. No smoking in 1 dining room. Music (£5)

PONTFAEN Pembrokeshire map 4

Tregynon Farmhouse

Gwaun Valley, Pontfaen SA65 9TU
TEL: (01239) 820531 FAX: (01239) 820808
EMAIL: tregynon@online-holidays.net
WEB SITE: www.online-holidays.net/tregynon
at junction of B4313 and B4329, take B4313 towards Fishguard, then take first right, and first right again

COOKING **1**
MODERN BRITISH
£30–£44

Perched on the side of the Preseli Montains, this sixteenth-century stone-built farmhouse has been home to Peter and Jane Heard for over 20 years. At the heart of the operation is a rotating menu which prides itself on not repeating dishes (or canapés or vegetables) for the sake of those who stay. The business of ordering food well in advance doesn't go down well with reporters, who wonder why it is necessary, but the kitchen seems equally at home with last-minute preparation – a pastry case of kidneys in mustard sauce – as it is with slow-cooked, herb-crusted loin of Preseli lamb with a fresh-tasting rosemary and elderberry sauce. Finish perhaps with 'vibrantly fruity' summer fruit bombe, or a gooey, crunchy-topped, whisky-infused bread-and-butter pudding, and drink from a global list of wines that are graded according to sweetness and body. A Special

Selection (from £11.50 for red and white Touraine) offers particular value for money, and the range of half-bottles has been enhanced.

CHEFS/PROPRIETORS: Peter and Jane Heard OPEN: Mon to Wed, Fri and Sat D only 7.30 to 8.30 CLOSED: Christmas MEALS: Set D £21.95 SERVICE: not inc CARDS: Delta, MasterCard, Switch, Visa DETAILS: 24 seats. Private parties: 14 main room, 10 private room. Car park. Vegetarian meals. No children under 6. No smoking in dining room. Music

PORTHGAIN Pembrokeshire map 4

Harbour Lights

Porthgain, nr St David's SA62 5BL
TEL: (01348) 831549 FAX: (01348) 831193
EMAIL: info@wales-pembs-art.com
off A487 at Croesgoch, 4m W of Mathry

COOKING **4**
MODERN WELSH
£35–£43

Three stone cottages have been knocked together to form a long, low, 'delightfully characterful' restaurant in this picturesque fishing bay. Candlelit, with wooden floors, tables and beams, its dark terracotta walls hung with local paintings, it exudes a 'professional yet informal feel'. Anne Marie Davies uses local materials in a simple and sensible way, harvesting laver from the rocks for example, to serve as a starter with cockles, organic smoked bacon and Llangloffan cheese.

Much of the seafood is landed at the harbour jetty, including famed Porthgain lobsters and crabs, the latter mildly spiced and baked with cream. Sewin also finds its way on to the table in season, served plainly with chive butter sauce, although meat is not forsaken – a chargrilled organic steak comes admirably unadorned except for garlic and parsley butter – and one of the four main course choices is vegetarian. Finish with banoffi pie, lemon and ginger sorbet, or a little pot of chocolate, and drink from what must be one of the shortest wine lists in Wales: four reds and four whites, all French, starting at £10.50.

CHEFS: Anne Marie Davies and Bernadette Lomax PROPRIETOR: Anne Marie Davies OPEN: all week D only 6.30 to 9 MEALS: Set D £25 SERVICE: not inc CARDS: Delta, MasterCard, Switch, Visa DETAILS: 27 seats. 16 seats outside. Car park. No smoking in dining room. Wheelchair access (not WC). Music

PORTMEIRION Gwynedd map 7

▲ Hotel Portmeirion

Portmeirion LL48 6ET
TEL: (01766) 770000 FAX: (01766) 771331
EMAIL: hotel@portmeirion-village.com
WEB SITE: www.portmeirion.com
off A487, signposted from Minffordd

COOKING **2**
MODERN WELSH-PLUS
£18–£51

Everybody falls for the charms of the Italianate village, built by Sir Clough Williams-Ellis over the course of nearly 50 years, beginning in the 1920s. It may be best known as the location of the 1960s TV series *The Prisoner*, but it has also attracted George Bernard Shaw, H.G. Wells and Noël Coward. Pleasant staff contribute to a warm ambience in the curvilinear, ruche-curtained dining room (though note you will not be allowed in if you are wearing jeans). To start, salads might combine duck breast with kiwi and mango, vegetables are piled into filo baskets and topped with grated Welsh Cheddar, and for main course, loin of pork has arrived with traditional apple compote. Desserts may not be a highlight, although expect bara brith-and-butter pudding among the offerings. The bilingual wine list manages to be both sophisticated and user-friendly. It opens with a cluster of well-chosen bottles under £15 and continues with a global selection of top-quality wines, including one from Wales. Mark-ups are reasonable and become virtually negligible the finer the wine. Ch. Lafite 1983 is therefore a bargain at £110.

CHEFS: Billy Taylor, Colin Pritchard, Steven Rowlands, Kevin Williams and Olivier Piffaudat PROPRIETOR: Portmeirion Ltd OPEN: Tue to Sun L 12.30 to 2, all week D 7 to 9.45 CLOSED: 7 Jan to 2 Feb MEALS: Set L Tue to Sat £11 to £13.50, Set L Sun £15, Set D £33 SERVICE: not inc, card slips closed CARDS: Amex, Delta, Diners, MasterCard, Switch, Visa DETAILS: 100 seats. Private parties: 100 main room, 14 and 35 private rooms. Car park. Vegetarian meals. Children's helpings. No smoking in dining room. No music ACCOMMODATION: 40 rooms, all with bath/shower. TV. Phone. Room only £90 to £170. Baby facilities. Swimming pool (*The Which? Hotel Guide*)

PWLLHELI Gwynedd map 7

▲ Plas Bodegroes

Nefyn Road, Pwllheli LL53 5TH
TEL: (01758) 612363 FAX: (01758) 701247
EMAIL: gunna@bodegroes.co.uk
WEB SITE: www.bodegroes.co.uk
on A497, 1m W of Pwllheli

COOKING **7**
MODERN BRITISH
£22–£55

The elegant Georgian manor house, reached by an avenue of 200-year-old beech trees, is a 'haven of peace and tranquillity' with secluded, well-kept gardens and a wisteria-covered veranda. Its calm tone is partly attributable to smart blond wood, sea-green walls and contemporary Welsh paintings, and partly to Gunna Chown, whose elegance, cool charm and welcoming manner put everyone at ease. The food's corresponding directness and simplicity is a mark of its strength. It may be rooted in traditional ideas, but these can sometimes be from other traditions – a pigeon, foie gras and almond pastilla, for example – and in any case are subject to a contemporary approach. A fishcake starter might combine scallop and smoked haddock, and come with puddles of sharp tartare sauce, or it may be spiced up with a chilli and goats'-cheese relish.

Native materials are prominent, from seafood to free range poultry, and among impressive examples of their use have been a 'simple, satisfying' warm salad of chargrilled monkfish with Carmarthen ham and mushrooms. While offal may not play a central role in the cooking, it does make occasional cameo appearances: pork tenderloin with kidney and black pudding, or a saddle of lamb in light puff pastry, with a stuffing of kidney and mushroom, served in a powerful jus infused with rosemary. Occasional small slips do little to mar the overall impression of Chris Chown being very much on form, not least when it comes to desserts. One that stands out consists of two thin, crunchy, heart-shaped cinnamon biscuits filled with apple and rhubarb, alongside a dollop of apple and rhubarb sorbet in a puddle of elderflower custard, the whole dish attractively presented and subtly flavoured. France takes centre stage on the extensive wine list, with the food-matching abilities of Alsace strongly recommended. Italy and the New World are also given star billing, and 60 half-bottles across the spectrum encourage experimentation. House wines start at £12.

CHEF: Chris Chown PROPRIETORS: Chris and Gunna Chown OPEN: Sun L 12 to 2, Tue to Sat D 7 to 9 (9.30 summer) CLOSED: Dec to Feb MEALS: alc D (main courses £15 to £21). Set L Sun £12.50, Set D £24.50 SERVICE: not inc, card slips closed CARDS: Delta, MasterCard, Switch, Visa DETAILS: 40 seats. Private parties: 40 main room, 16 private room. Car park. No smoking in dining room. Wheelchair access (also WC). Occasional music ACCOMMODATION: 11 rooms, all with bath/shower. TV. Phone. B&B £35 to £60. Baby facilities (*The Which? Hotel Guide*)

REYNOLDSTON Swansea map 4

▲ Fairyhill

Reynoldston SA3 1BS
TEL: (01792) 390139 FAX: (01792) 391358
EMAIL: postbox@fairyhill.net
WEB SITE: www.fairyhill.net

COOKING **4**
MODERN WELSH
£34–£51

Fairyhill – or is this fairyland? – is a fine creeper-clad eighteenth-century house set in acres of grassland, woodland and orchards in the Gower Peninsula with ducks in its pond, trout in its stream, and the owners much in evidence. Start with canapés and drinks in the drawing room or on the large patio, before moving to an agreeable dining room or conservatory for set menus that make much use of local produce: such as laverbread, Penclawdd cockles, sewin and Welsh Black beef. Asian and Mediterranean influences are brought to bear, producing a 'sticky, soft and melting' lemon risotto cake topped with crisp aubergine rings, and a lemon and thyme infused roast chicken ('just like chicken used to taste') with vegetable spaghetti. Imaginative desserts have included rosé wine and honey fruit jelly with blue curaçao sorbet, and rich poached plum syllabub with toasted oatmeal. Whole pages are devoted to the wines of Jean Coche Dury from Burgundy and Stephen Henschke from Australia on a thrilling list that sources an impressive range from both hemispheres. Prices are reasonable, with plenty of wines below £20 (some of them highlighted at the front of the list, though there are more inside). House wines start at £12.50

CHEFS: Adrian Coulthard and Bryony Jones PROPRIETORS: Peter and Jane Camm, Andrew Hetherington and Paul Davies OPEN: all week 12.30 to 1.30, 7.30 to 8.45 CLOSED: 26 Dec to 6 Jan MEALS: Set L £14.50 (2 courses) to £17.50, Set D £25 (2 courses) to £32 SERVICE: not inc, card slips closed CARDS: Amex, Delta, MasterCard, Switch, Visa DETAILS: 60 seats. 20 seats outside. Private parties: 52 main room, 40 to 52 private rooms. Car park. Vegetarian meals. No children under 8 at D. No smoking in dining room. Music ACCOMMODATION: 8 rooms, all with bath/shower. TV. Phone. B&B £95 to £190. No children under 8 (*The Which? Hotel Guide*)

Prices quoted in the Guide are based on information supplied by restaurateurs. The prices quoted at the top of each entry represent a range, from the lowest meal price to the highest; the latter is inflated by 20 per cent to take account of likely price rises during the year of the Guide.

ST DAVID'S Pembrokeshire map 4

Morgan's Brasserie

20 Nun Street, St David's SA62 6NT
TEL/FAX: (01437) 720508
EMAIL: morgans@stdavids.co.uk
WEB SITE: www.stdavids.co.uk/morgans

COOKING **3**
FISH/MODERN BRITISH
£26–£45

With its simple approach to good dining and smart townhouse setting, Morgan's adds to the already numerous attractions of the charming city of St David's. A short printed carte offers such temptations as confit duck on a pear and potato rösti with port and redcurrant, but the main draw is undoubtedly the daily-changing blackboard featuring fish and seafood landed daily at nearby Milford Haven. Straightforward treatments are the order of the day – sewin comes with a tomato and basil vinaigrette, bass with laverbread and cockles, and seared scallops on a bouillabaisse sauce – and accurate cooking and restraint with accompanying flavours allow the fish to remain the star of the show. Start with tiger prawns deep-fried in filo pastry with sweet-and-sour chilli dressing, and finish with pear and almond tart with rum and raisin ice cream, or perhaps Baileys crème brûlée. The respectable wine list keeps prices within the reach of most drinkers; house French is £10 (£2.25 a glass).

CHEF: Ceri Morgan PROPRIETORS: Ceri and Elaine Morgan OPEN: Mon to Sat D only 7 to 9 (10 during St David's Cathedral festival week) CLOSED: Jan, Feb and occasional days in low season (phone to check) MEALS: alc (main courses £9.50 to £16.50) SERVICE: not inc, card slips closed CARDS: Amex, MasterCard, Switch, Visa DETAILS: 34 seats. Private parties: 20 main room. Vegetarian meals. Children's helpings. No smoking in dining room. Music

SWANSEA Swansea map 4

La Braseria £

28 Wind Street, Swansea SA1 1DZ
TEL: (01792) 469683 FAX: (01792) 470816
WEB SITE: www.scoot.co.uk/la_braseria

COOKING **1**
SPANISH
£18–£43

This is Spain via south Wales in all its hearty conviviality, where a sprinkling of sawdust on the floor should dissuade anybody from standing on undue ceremony. Choose from the meat and fish offerings displayed in chiller cabinets, and expect a fair amount of chargrilling. Exemplary fresh calamares and sardines got the nod from one pair of reporters, who went on to enjoy a Segovian speciality of roast suckling pig, and one of the signature dishes, sea bass baked in coarse salt. Other selections include devilled chicken livers, and stuffed aubergine for the veggies. Everything comes with a baked potato or chips, with side salads extra. House Spanish is £9.85 a bottle, and three types of Rioja are offered by the glass from £1.75.

CHEF: Ian Wing PROPRIETOR: Manuel Tercero OPEN: Mon to Sat 12 to 2.30, 7 to 11.30 CLOSED: 25 and 31 Dec MEALS: alc (main courses £8 to £15.50). Set L £6.95 (2 courses) SERVICE: not inc, card slips closed CARDS: Amex, Delta, Diners, MasterCard, Switch, Visa DETAILS: 170 seats. Private parties: 100 main room. Vegetarian meals. No prams or pushchairs. Wheelchair access (also WC). Music. Air-conditioned

Hanson's

Pilot House Wharf, Trawler Road, Swansea Marina, Swansea SA1 1UN
TEL: (01792) 466200 FAX: (01792) 201774

COOKING **3**
MODERN BRITISH/SEAFOOD
£21–£43

Head for the working part of the waterfront and the Maritime and Industrial Museum, and find the restaurant above a fishing tackle shop, where the simple bistro atmosphere is helped by gold, mustard and cream colours, and by views of the River Tawe. The menu mixes plain, old-fashioned items – prawn and avocado salad with a dill and lemon dressing, well-rendered chicken liver pâté with toast, and steak Diane 'cooked rare' – with crispy aromatic duck on Chinese pancakes, or perhaps a salad incorporating baked aubergine, red pepper, mozzarella and sun-dried tomato. Fish is a strength, the day's offerings listed on a blackboard: maybe poached salmon with hollandaise sauce, or seafood thermidor. Food is cooked in a no-nonsense style without fancy decoration, and meals might end with chocolate torte or crème brûlée. Staff are generally helpful and friendly, and around 30 wines stay mostly under £20, starting with house French at £9.65.

CHEFS: Andrew Hanson and Jonathan Crandon PROPRIETORS: Andrew Hanson and Helen Tennant OPEN: all week L 12 to 2, Mon to Sat D 6.30 to 9.30 CLOSED: 25 and 26 Dec MEALS: alc (main courses £8 to £15). Set L £9.95 (2 courses) to £12.95 SERVICE: not inc, card slips closed CARDS: Delta, MasterCard, Switch, Visa DETAILS: 50 seats. Private parties: 50 main room. Vegetarian meals. Children's helpings. Music (£5)

TALSARNAU Gwynedd **map 7**

▲ Maes-y-Neuadd

Talsarnau LL47 6YA
TEL: (01766) 780200 FAX: (01766) 780211
EMAIL: maes@neuadd.com
WEB SITE: www.neuadd.com
off B4573, 1m S of Talsarnau

COOKING **4**
MODERN WELSH
£22–£51

A beautiful setting and luxurious appointments are part of the draw at this low-ceilinged house, whose history dates back to the fourteenth century. Lunches revolve around a daily special – cottage pie on Monday, smoked haddock omelette on Wednesday – while dinners extend from three courses upwards. Anyone going the whole hog might start with a deep-fried parcel of duck confit followed by soup: in one case strips of tomato flesh in a clear vegetable stock with a basil soufflé 'crust'. Fish, perhaps lemon sole with capers, precedes the main course, which might offer loin of venison with bubble and squeak, or roast monkfish with creamed leeks. Welsh lamb is a fixture, as is a vegetarian option, and desserts constitute a 'grand finale' in country-house style, with lemon and lime tart perhaps, or roast pineapple with caramel sauce. Enticing quotes from Hugh Johnson accompany several of the wines on this 150-strong list, which is lovingly compiled and attended to regularly. Alsace and the Rhône have received a recent boost, and although European wines predominate there is a fine New World presence. A suggested trio of wines by the glass solves the dilemma of finding one bottle to suit an entire meal. House French starts at £11.95.

CHEF: Peter Jackson PROPRIETORS: Mr and Mrs Slatter, and Mr and Mrs Jackson OPEN: all week 12 to 1.45, 7 to 9 MEALS: Set L Mon to Sat £9.50 (1 course) to £13.75, Set L Sun £14.95, Set D £27 to £34. Bar L available SERVICE: not inc, card slips closed CARDS: Amex, Delta, Diners, MasterCard, Switch, Visa DETAILS: 60 seats. 12 seats outside. Private parties: 60 main room, 12 private room. Car park. Vegetarian meals. Children's helpings. No children under 7 at D. No smoking in dining room. Wheelchair access (also WC). Occasional music ACCOMMODATION: 16 rooms, all with bath/shower. TV. Phone. D,B&B £90 to £230. Rooms for disabled. Baby facilities (*The Which? Hotel Guide*) (£5)

WHITEBROOK Monmouthshire **map 2**

▲ Crown at Whitebrook

Whitebrook NP25 4TX
TEL: (01600) 860254 FAX: (01600) 860607
EMAIL: crown@whitebrook.demon.co.uk
leave A466 at Bigsweir bridge, 6m S of Monmouth; follow signs to Whitebrook; hotel is 2m on left

COOKING **4**
MODERN EUROPEAN
£25–£49

Set against a steep hillside in an isolated straggly village a mile from the River Wye, and styling itself a restaurant-with-rooms, the Crown is under new ownership. Its floral fabrics, glossy black beams, lighting and table settings may not be to everyone's taste, but Mark Turton stays on in the kitchen, and the set-price-menu format remains unchanged. A broadly European approach takes in seafood ravioli on laverbread, flavour-packed mushroom soup, and rack of supple, tasty Welsh lamb with a tapénade crust, served with a roasted pepper tart and a heavily reduced stock-based sauce. Vegetables (eight of them) come crammed on a side plate, and while flavours may not always reach their full potential, technical skills are sound, showing to good effect in bread and pastry, for example.

When they are not being 'seriously garnished', dishes might be fashioned into a trio of something: perhaps salmon (gravad lax, smoked on a blini, and a warm wobbly mousse) or bananas (incorporating pannacotta, a tart and ice cream). Desserts have proved a hit, not least when they combine flavours, textures and temperatures well, as in apple Tatin with clove ice cream and caramel sauce. Meals are well paced. Informal, enthusiastic tasting notes are peppered throughout the chunky wine list, which concentrates on France but includes sound New World offerings and a page of Riojas. House wines vary constantly, aim to be 'inexpensive yet interesting', and begin at £9.95.

CHEF: Mark Turton PROPRIETORS: Angela and Elizabeth Barbara OPEN: Tue to Sun L 12 to 1.45, all week D 7 to 9 CLOSED: 2 weeks Jan, 2 weeks Aug MEALS: Set L £15.95, Set D £27.95. Light L available SERVICE: not inc CARDS: Amex, Delta, Diners, MasterCard, Switch, Visa DETAILS: 32 seats. Private parties: 20 main room, 14 private room. Car park. Vegetarian meals. Children's helpings. No children under 12. No smoking in dining room. Wheelchair access (not WC). No music ACCOMMODATION: 12 rooms, all with bath/shower. TV. Phone. B&B £50 to £130. No children under 12 (*The Which? Hotel Guide*) (£5)

See inside the front cover for an explanation of the symbols used at the tops of entries.

WOLF'S CASTLE Pembrokeshire map 4

▲ The Wolfe

Wolf's Castle SA62 5LS
TEL: (01437) 741662 FAX: (01437) 741676

COOKING **1**
MODERN BRITISH
£28–£44

Beside a main road, but set in beautiful countryside between Fishguard and Haverfordwest, this pub's Italianate feel reflects the owner's nationality (look for the aperitifs and grappas). There are three dining rooms to choose from, and just as materials hail from many sources – foie gras from France, salmon from Scotland, butter from the village, and 'local' sewin served with ginger and white wine – so dishes cover a lot of territory, from Welsh country pork pâté to Alabama prawn salad. Black beef is a regular fixture (perhaps flamed in brandy with cream), while desserts have included chocolate brioche pudding, and a simple dish of mascarpone with fresh raspberries. The Italian section of the wine list is the most interesting and offers fair value. Prices start below £10 and don't rise much above £20.

CHEF: Mike Lewis PROPRIETORS: Gianni and Jacqueline Di Lorenzo OPEN: all week 12 to 2, Mon to Sat D 7 to 9 CLOSED: Mon Nov to Easter MEALS: alc (main courses £10 to £17.50). Bar meals available all week L and D SERVICE: not inc, card slips closed CARDS: Delta, MasterCard, Switch, Visa DETAILS: 75 seats. 20 seats outside. Private parties: 25 main room, 25 private room. Car park. Vegetarian meals. Children's helpings. No smoking in dining room. Wheelchair access (also women's WC). Occasional music ACCOMMODATION: 3 rooms, 1 with bath/shower. TV. B&B £40 to £50 (*The Which? Hotel Guide*) (£5)

Channel Islands

GOREY Jersey — map 1

Jersey Pottery Restaurant

Gorey JE3 9EP
TEL: (01534) 851119
FAX: (01534) 856403
EMAIL: jsypot@itl.net

COOKING **1**
MODERN BRITISH/FISH
£23–£60

The glass-roofed restaurant, part of a pottery set in a garden, focuses on fresh local ingredients, with fish centre-stage. Meaty butterflied prawns may precede baked cod in a herb crust, or a whole chancre crab 'to pick yourself or dressed with salad'. For meat eaters there's piri-piri spatchcock baby chicken, or wok-fried pepper duck with bean sprouts, while vegetarians might want to try Mediterranean vegetable hotpot. Desserts from the buffet include mille-feuilles, tarts, mousses and berries. Despite the bustle, staff remain courteous, friendly and professional. The reasonably priced 90-strong wine list has house choices from £8.95

CHEF: Tony Dorris PROPRIETORS: the Jones family OPEN: Tue to Sun L only 12 to 2.30 CLOSED: 10 days Christmas, Tues after bank hols MEALS: alc (main courses £6.50 to £27) SERVICE: net prices, card slips closed CARDS: Amex, Delta, Diners, MasterCard, Switch, Visa DETAILS: 300 seats. 60 seats outside. Private parties: 300 main room. Car park. Vegetarian meals. Children's helpings. No-smoking area. No pipes in dining room. Wheelchair access (also WC). Occasional music

Suma's

Gorey JE3 6ET
TEL: (01534) 853291
FAX: (01534) 851913

COOKING **4**
MODERN EUROPEAN
£21–£46

Suma's is smack by the harbour, with a good view of Mont Orqueil Castle. Opened in 1997 as a sibling to Longueville Manor (see entry, St Saviour), it is carved out of a hillside and designed in colourful modern style, with some vivid contemporary paintings on show. Shaun Rankin, formerly a sous-chef at Longueville, arrived at the beginning of 2000 to head up the kitchen, and has maintained the dashingly inventive culinary style. A variation on Caesar salad with calamari and grilled mackerel pleased one reporter, while a maritime translation of cassoulet made with sea bass incorporated a memorable sausage of lobster, as well as the customary foil of beans and lardons. Pairing grilled scallops with braised oxtail and chestnuts is an arresting way to start, and main courses include an unusual partnership of grilled calf's liver with braised ham hock and pease pudding. Desserts of carrot and coconut cake with hazelnut and pear praline, and a novel rendition of banana split, were the highlights of one meal. Efficient and unobtrusive service makes everything run smoothly. A thoughtfully compiled modern wine list opens with southern French house wines at £8.75 (white) and £9 (red).

CHEF: Shaun Rankin PROPRIETORS: Malcom Lewis and Susan Dufty OPEN: all week L 12 to 2.30, Mon to Sat D 6.30 to 10 CLOSED: 22 Dec to 20 Jan MEALS: alc (main courses £9 to £16.50). Set L Mon to Sat £11.50 (2 courses) to £14.50, Set L Sun £15.75 SERVICE: net prices, card slips closed CARDS: Amex, Delta, Diners, MasterCard, Switch, Visa DETAILS: 45 seats. 16 seats outside. Vegetarian meals. Children's helpings. Music. Air-conditioned

ST BRELADE Jersey **map 1**

▲ Sea Crest

La Route du Petit Port, St Brelade JE3 8HH
TEL: (01534) 746353
FAX: (01534) 747316
EMAIL: seacrest@super.net.uk
WEB SITE: www.jerseyisland.com/stbrelade/seacrest

NEW CHEF
MODERN EUROPEAN/SEAFOOD
£23–£75

The interiors of this roadside restaurant are bedecked with an enviable collection of fine twentieth-century paintings, including the odd Picasso. Andrew Waugh took over the stoves just as the Guide went to press, but no major changes were planned for the vein of fresh, seafood-based cooking for which the hotel has been celebrated. Fishermen deliver their catch direct to the kitchen door, which may translate into a scallop and Parma ham brochette, or grilled fillets of sea bass served with coriander mash and steamed bok choy. Meat eaters might prefer half a crispy duck with roast parsnips and an orange-flavoured sauce, while desserts have offered spiced Amaretto and chocolate truffle torte with a black cherry 'ragoût'. Professional, caring service has been praised. The wine list is a very old-school document, heavy on French luxuries, with some New World wines providing price relief. House wines are Australian blends from Rosemount at £12.50.

CHEF: Andrew Waugh PROPRIETORS: Julian and Martha Bernstein OPEN: Tue to Sun 12.30 to 2, 7.30 to 10 CLOSED: Feb, Sun D Nov to Apr MEALS: alc (main courses £12.50 to £25). Set L Tue to Sat £14.50, Set D Tue to Fri £19.75 SERVICE: not inc CARDS: Amex, Delta, MasterCard, Switch, Visa DETAILS: 70 seats. 20 seats outside. Private parties: 70 main room. Car park. Children's helpings. No cigars/pipes in dining room. Music. Air-conditioned ACCOMMODATION: 7 rooms, all with bath/shower. TV. Phone. B&B £65 to £130. Baby facilities. Swimming pool
(£5)

Prices quoted in the Guide are based on information supplied by restaurateurs. The prices quoted at the top of each entry represent a range, from the lowest meal price to the highest; the latter is inflated by 20 per cent to take account of likely price rises during the year of the Guide.

ST SAVIOUR Jersey **map 1**

▲ Longueville Manor

St Saviour JE2 7WF
TEL: (01534) 725501
FAX: (01534) 731613
EMAIL: longman@itl.net
WEB SITE: www.longuevillemanor.com

COOKING **6**
MODERN EUROPEAN
£28–£84

An oak-panelled room in a thirteenth-century manor house is the setting for one of the Channel Islands' more sumptuous dining experiences. Andrew Baird is not short of inventive ideas, and his combinations invariably make sense, producing roast quail partnered with glazed apple, Lancashire black pudding and bacon, as well as beef casserole served with wild mushrooms, Yorkshire pudding and horseradish 'hollandaise'. His style is refined, and materials are sound and competently handled: grilled local scallops for example, come with a simple salad of artichoke, French beans and bacon.

Certain dishes are flagged for their low salt, fat and carbohydrate content, including a seafood ragoût that comes with wilted greens and vegetables from the hotel's own garden. Imaginative desserts have included roast bananas with hot chocolate samosas, and passion-fruit charlotte with a salsa of exotic fruits. Service is clockwork-smooth and highly professional, and the wine list is encyclopedic, giving the New World a fair shout but saving its most exhaustive efforts for France. You can spend £895 on Lafite-Rothschild '59 if you've a mind, or £2.95 on a large glass of Languedoc Cabernet Sauvignon. House wines start at £9.75.

CHEF: Andrew Baird PROPRIETORS: Malcolm Lewis and Susan Dufty OPEN: all week 12.30 to 2, 7 to 9.30 MEALS: alc (main courses L £9.50 to £17, D £18 to £25.50). Set L £16 (2 courses) to £20, Set D £42 to £70 (inc wine) SERVICE: net prices, card slips closed CARDS: Amex, Delta, Diners, MasterCard, Switch, Visa DETAILS: 65 seats. 20 seats outside. Private parties: 65 main room, 14 and 18 private rooms. Car park. Vegetarian meals. Children's helpings. No smoking in 1 dining room. Wheelchair access (not WC). No music ACCOMMODATION: 32 rooms, all with bath/shower. TV. Phone. B&B £155 to £280. Baby facilities. Swimming pool

Northern Ireland

BALLYCLARE Co Antrim **map 16**

Ginger Tree

29 Ballyrobert Road, Ballyclare BT36 4TL
TEL: (01232) 848176 FAX: (01232) 844077

COOKING **4**
JAPANESE
£23–£63

A Victorian farmhouse set off the road in rural County Antrim provides a singular, and popular, location for Japanese cooking. To acclimatise diners, the owners (who both take a turn in the kitchen) have decorated their long, thin restaurant with various Far Eastern artefacts, including a painting of a samurai. Food has been tempered to local tastes – 'if there is a Japanese equivalent of country cooking, this is it' – but dishes (well-explained on the menu) adequately cover the fundamentals of the cuisine. Well-balanced seven-course set meals might be centred on beef yakinikufu (thin slices cooked in a saké, garlic, ginger and soy sauce), or tempura prawns and vegetables. Alternatively, from the two-course 'Osaka Menu', start with zaru soba (cold buckwheat noodle served with wasabi mustard and a dipping sauce) or yakitori (skewer of grilled chicken and onion), and follow with grilled eel on rice, or chicken in sweet-and-sour sauce. Sashimi (the raw salmon variety only) is served on Friday and Saturday. Banana stuffed with sweet soybean paste is one way to conclude. Saké comes in two pot sizes, and the wine list includes a varied choice of halves. House wine is £11.50.

CHEFS/PROPRIETORS: Elizabeth English Wylie and Shotaro Obana OPEN: Mon to Fri L 12 to 2, Mon to Sat D 6.30 to 8.30 CLOSED: 24 to 26 Dec, 12 to 13 July MEALS: alc (main courses £10 to £17.50). Set L £13.95, Set D £15.95 to £32 SERVICE: not inc CARDS: Amex, Delta, Diners, MasterCard, Visa DETAILS: 60 seats. Private parties: 70 main room. Car park. Vegetarian meals. Children's helpings. No-smoking area. Wheelchair access (also WC). Music. Air-conditioned (£5)

The Guide relies on feedback from its readers. Especially welcome are reports on new restaurants appearing in the book for the first time. All letters to the Guide are acknowledged.

The cuisine styles noted at the tops of entries are only an approximation, often suggested to us by the restaurants themselves. Please read the entry itself to find out more about the cooking style.

BANGOR Co Down map 16

Shanks

The Blackwood, 150 Crawfordsburn Road, Bangor BT19 1GB
TEL: (028) 9185 3313 FAX: (028) 9185 2493

COOKING **6**
MODERN EUROPEAN
£29–£68

There are two levels at the Millars' fashionable Bangor restaurant in the middle of a golf course on the Clandeboye estate of the Marchioness of Dufferin and Ava. Upstairs is a bright, spacious room with chunky modern sofas, unusually shaped chairs and a piano, while downstairs (equally light and airy) boasts half a dozen large Hockneys and a view of the kitchen's activity. And action there is aplenty, not least on the plate. Dishes are variously spiked with lively accompaniments of coriander salsa, truffle oil, mustard vinaigrette and lemon aïoli, and built into towers. Soup, naturally, is frothed into a cappuccino – a triumphant pea, ham and mushroom for one visitor – while chargrilled squid has been stacked with crisp-fried, spinach-wrapped aubergine slices on a plate colourfully glazed with tomato chilli oil.

Presentation enhances what is being served, evident in a dish of grilled and sliced chicken breast on coarsely chopped avocado salsa, accompanied by a mini tortilla of melted blue cheese. Desserts at inspection did not match up to the rest, although they might offer chocolate tart with banana sorbet, and spiced apple soup with cinnamon ice cream. Breads are first class, and service is courteous and attentive. A well-chosen, competitively priced, global wine list runs to top names from Bordeaux, Italy, Australia and California. Six are available by the glass, and house French is £12.50.

CHEF: Robbie Millar PROPRIETORS: Robbie and Shirley Millar OPEN: Tue to Fri L 12.30 to 2.30, Tue to Sat D 7 to 10 MEALS: Set L £14.95 (2 courses) to £18.95, Set D £32.50 SERVICE: not inc, 10% for parties of 6 or more CARDS: Amex, MasterCard, Switch, Visa DETAILS: 60 seats. Private parties: 16 main room, 30 private room. Car park. Vegetarian meals. Children's helpings. No smoking in 1 dining room. Wheelchair access (also WC). Occasional music

BELFAST Co Antrim map 16

La Belle Epoque £

61 Dublin Road, Belfast BT2 7HE
TEL: (028) 9032 3244 FAX: (028) 9020 3111

COOKING **2**
MODERN FRENCH
£19–£38

A popular brasserie on the edge of the student quarter, La Belle Epoque pulls in the crowds with a combination of vivacious atmosphere and bold, contemporary cooking. Intrepid flavours are evident in a mille-feuille of pastrami with a vinaigrette of gherkins, capers and spring onions, while salmon comes with rhubarb purée. Menus are in French (with English translation) but ingredients and treatments often come from further afield: roast ostrich fillet sauced with white wine, cream and mushrooms, and boneless loin of lamb served with a chilli, soy and oyster sauce. Vegetarians might be drawn to a Mexican galette containing spiced ratatouille. A peach poached in Sauternes syrup served with Campari sorbet is one alternative to the impeccably Gallic house special, crêpes suzette. Some tempting bottles from France and Australia adorn a better-than-average wine list, although vintages are not stated. House wines start at around £9.

CHEF: Alan Rousse PROPRIETORS: Alain Rousse, J. Delbart and G. Sanchez OPEN: Mon to Fri L 12 to 5, Mon to Sat D 5.30 to 11 CLOSED: 25 and 26 Dec, 12 and 13 July MEALS: alc (main courses L £5 to £9, D £7 to £12.50). Set L £6.25 (2 courses), Set D Mon to Fri £16 SERVICE: not inc CARDS: Amex, Delta, Diners, MasterCard, Switch, Visa DETAILS: 84 seats. Private parties: 40 main room, 24 private room. Music

Cayenne

NEW ENTRY

7 Lesley House, Shaftesbury Square,
Belfast BT2 7DB
TEL: (028) 9033 1532 FAX: (028) 9026 1575

COOKING **2**
GLOBAL
£25–£46

In premises that were formerly Roscoff, and which are still owned by Paul and Jeanne Rankin, there has been a change of tack. As we went to press, they were looking for a new site to which to transfer the Roscoff formula, and the old Shaftesbury Square place has now become – with the help of fragments of the Belfast telephone directory decorating the walls – a modern bistro as spicy as it sounds. Indian, Thai, Chinese and Italian influences are all discernible, and highlights have included impressively accurate risotto primavera (verdant with broad beans, peas and spinach) and generous calf's liver with Puy lentils, buttery mash, and a creamy variation on salsa verde. Lemon-grass crème brûlée at inspection was outshone by steamed ginger pudding served with baked bananas, butterscotch sauce and crème fraîche. The varietally arranged wine list is sensibly priced in keeping with the tone, and there is an enterprising slate of cocktails. Wine prices start at £12.50.

CHEFS/PROPRIETORS: Paul and Jeanne Rankin OPEN: Mon to Fri L 12.30 to 2.30, Mon to Sat D 6 to 11.15 CLOSED: 25 and 26 Dec, 1 Jan, Easter Mon and Tue, 12 and 13 July MEALS: alc (main courses £8.50 to £12.50). Set L £14.50 SERVICE: not inc, 10% for parties of 6 or more CARDS: Amex, Diners, MasterCard, Switch, Visa DETAILS: 80 seats. Private parties: 80 main room. Vegetarian meals. Children's helpings. No-smoking area. Wheelchair access (also WC). Music. Air-conditioned

▲ Metro

13 Lower Crescent, Belfast BT7 1NR
TEL: (028) 9032 3349 FAX: (028) 9032 0646
{30EMAIL: info@crescenttownhouse.com

COOKING **2**
MODERN EUROPEAN
£20–£59

Listed last year in the Guide as 'Crescent Townhouse, Metro', the restaurant tells us a simple 'Metro' will do this year. Set in the heart of the Botanic Avenue district of Belfast, a little way south of the city centre, it is a contemporary urban brasserie with a lively, bustling ambience. As well as a bar menu offering staples of filled baked potatoes, tortilla wraps, and pork and leek sausages with mash and gravy, the brasserie menu encompasses Thai fishcakes with red curry sauce and rice, and roast cod with ratatouille sauce. Robust appetites will appreciate main courses along the lines of sage-roasted chicken breast served with Toulouse sausage and penne pasta in a grain mustard cream sauce. Apposite dessert pairings might include mango sorbet with lemon tart, or balsamic strawberries with pannacotta. The wine list contains plenty of vivacious flavours, with a strong showing of New World bottles, and opens at £10 for Australian blends from Hardy's.

CHEFS: Aaron Loughron and Karl Taylor PROPRIETOR: Wine Inns Ltd OPEN: Mon to Sat D only 6 to 9.30 (10 Fri and Sat) CLOSED: 25 and 26 Dec, 1 Jan MEALS: alc (main courses £9 to £15). Set D before 8 Mon to Fri £9.95 (2 courses) to £12.50. Bar meals available L 12 to 3 SERVICE: not inc, card slips closed CARDS: Amex, Delta, MasterCard, Switch, Visa DETAILS: 65 seats. Private parties: 60 main room. Vegetarian meals. Children's helpings. No cigars/pipes in dining room. Wheelchair access (also WC). Music. Air-conditioned ACCOMMODATION: 11 rooms, all with bath/shower. TV. Phone. B&B £55 to £100. Baby facilities (£5)

Nick's Warehouse 🍷

35 Hill Street, Belfast BT1 2LB
TEL/FAX: (02890) 439690
EMAIL: nicks@warehouse.dnet.co.uk
WEB SITE: www.nickswarehouse.co.uk

COOKING **5**
GLOBAL
£29–£43

Find Nick Price's warehouse-conversion restaurant among the narrow cobbled streets and redbrick buildings of Belfast's cathedral quarter. Once a Bushmills whiskey depot, it formerly dispensed flagons of the good stuff to a discerning Ulster clientele. Despite having been a restaurant for over a decade now, it retains a feeling of up-to-the-minute voguishness, in the exposed-brick décor, the open kitchen (complete with 'manic chefs creating flames', as the literature has it) and Nick Price's daily-changing menus.

World-larder stuff is the business here, and the lunchtime menu alone might take in Mexican beef enchilada with guacamole, naan bread pizza, grilled haddock on mash with Asian pesto, and Cajun roast chicken with pineapple. Although timing may miss a beat occasionally, the Babel of culinary tongues generally works well, progressing seamlessly from seafood chowder, via rare-breed pork with mushroom tagliatelle, to a hunk of Cashel Blue cheese. Desserts are low key but still inventive: tiramisù is turned into a terrine and served with a coffee and rum sauce, while poached pear comes with mandarin sorbet and raspberry compote. Service has engendered variable impressions, from laid-back to rushed. Unpretentious and intelligently selected, the global wine list maintains quality while keeping prices refreshingly low. A separate fine wine list and the 'Nobody Expects – The Spanish Wine List' will keep wine buffs thoroughly content. Eight house wines are all £9.90.

CHEF: Nick Price PROPRIETORS: Nick and Kathy Price OPEN: Mon to Fri L 12 to 3, Tue to Sat D 6 to 9.30 (10 Fri and Sat) CLOSED: 25 and 26 Dec, Easter Mon and Tue, 12 July MEALS: alc (main courses £10.50 to £14.50). Bistro menu available at L SERVICE: not inc, 10% (optional) for parties of 5 or more CARDS: Amex, Delta, Diners, MasterCard, Switch, Visa DETAILS: 180 seats. Private parties: 90 main room, 50 private room. Vegetarian meals. Children's helpings. Wheelchair access (also WC). Music. Air-conditioned

Although the cuisine style noted at the top of entries has in most cases been suggested to the Guide by the restaurants, some have been edited for brevity or appropriateness.

Restaurant Michael Deane

38–40 Howard Street, Belfast BT1 6PD | COOKING **6**
TEL: (028) 9033 1134 FAX: (028) 9056 0001 | MODERN EUROPEAN-PLUS
WEB SITE: www.deanesbelfast.com | £47–£81

As the Guide went to press some refurbishment was planned and a name change – no longer is it simply Deane's – was taking place. A Hollywood-style sweeping staircase leads up to the main dining room, where welcoming staff will usher you to one of the well-upholstered sofas (expect more of those after the refurbishment) for a look at the menu. Michael Deane's assured way with classical techniques and his fertile culinary imagination ensure that surroundings don't overshadow the cooking. Menus read well, and inspiration is drawn from around the world.

This produces an intriguingly varied mix that runs from a hotpot of monkfish with shiitakes and lemon grass, to a more loin-girding starter of Clonakilty black pudding with roast squab, foie gras, asparagus and potato. Equally energetic main courses take in crisped salmon with spiced risotto, bok choy and chilli, as well as cannon of lamb paired with 'whipped and fried' parsnips. Desserts may be a little quieter, offering pear caramel, and warm chocolate tart with white chocolate ice cream. Downstairs is Deane's Brasserie, where simpler dishes are available. An extensive wine list offers plenty of expensive French classics, but there is some price relief in the rest of Europe and the New World. Pedigree selections allow for confidence in choosing. Sixteen house wines start at £12.50.

CHEF: Michael Deane PROPRIETORS: Michael Deane, and Lynda and Brian Smyth OPEN: Tue to Sat D only 7 to 9.30 CLOSED: Christmas, New Year, Easter, 1 week July MEALS: Set D £25.50 to £55. Brasserie menu available downstairs SERVICE: not inc, 10% for parties of 6 or more CARDS: Amex, Delta, MasterCard, Switch, Visa DETAILS: 40 seats. Private parties: 40 main room. Vegetarian meals. No cigar/pipes in dining room. Music. Air-conditioned

HOLYWOOD Co Down **map 16**

Fontana 🍷 £

61A High Street, Holywood BT18 9AE | COOKING **2**
TEL: (028) 9080 9908 FAX: (028) 9080 9912 | GLOBAL
£19–£36

Feeling larger than it appears from outside, Fontana's new-wave look is reinforced by modern wall-hangings, big leafy pot plants and funky music. Keeping abreast of global trends is the name of the game, and menus are likely to veer from Caesar salad to laksa, and from tomato tortilla roll with chicken, salsa and guacamole to steak sandwich. And that's just for lunch. Dinner expands to take in skate wing capers and lemon butter, bacon and blue cheese risotto, and slow roast spring lamb served with polenta and salsa rossa. To finish there might be chargrilled plums with amaretto ice cream, or chocolate brownies with vanilla ice cream. Although the wine list is notably short, and doesn't do vintages, it nevertheless contains interesting and well-priced bottles from around the world, and makes an effort to present a wide range of grapes and styles. Abadia Retuerta Rivola from Spain comes recommended at £18.50, and there is a decent choice around the £12 mark.

CHEF: Colleen Bennett PROPRIETORS: Colleen Bennett and Stephen McAuley OPEN: Tue to Fri L 12 to 2.30, Sun L 11 to 3, Tue to Fri D 5 to 9.30, Sat D 6.30 to 10 CLOSED: 25 Dec, 1 Jan, 10 to 17 July MEALS: alc L (main courses L £5 to £8.50), Set L and D £8.50 (2 courses) to £10.50 SERVICE: not inc, 10% for parties of 6 or more CARDS: Delta, MasterCard, Switch, Visa DETAILS: 56 seats. 12 seats outside. Private parties: 40 main room. Vegetarian meals. Children's helpings. No cigars/pipes in dining room. Music

LIMAVADY Co Londonderry **map 16**

The Lime Tree £

60 Catherine Street, Limavady BT49 9DB
TEL: (028) 7776 4300

COOKING **2**
MODERN EUROPEAN
£14–£40

Warm, unforced hospitality is a strong point at the Matthewses' market-town restaurant, which occupies one ground-floor room of a large old house. Further assets are the excellent-value business lunch and early-bird dinner. For the latter, choose from the likes of duck confit in red wine with tomatoes, mushrooms and tarragon, or fresh fish from Donegal, served with pasta and a cream sauce. Salmon and courgette tart at a summer lunch featured a delicate pastry base heaped with fish. The carte, meanwhile, offers sauce-based cookery of some panache (sautéed lambs' kidneys in a pastry case with red wine and shallots, for example), and the occasional modern turn such as monkfish dressed with chilli oil. Meals might end with white chocolate cheesecake or 'tangerine dream'. Wines cover a global range from Argentina to Lebanon, with house French and Australian at £9.25.

CHEF: Stanley Matthews PROPRIETORS: Stanley and Maria Matthews OPEN: Wed to Fri and Sun L 12 to 2, Wed to Sun D 6 to 9 (9.30 Sat, 8.30 Sun) CLOSED: 1 week Nov, 1 week Feb/March, 1 week July MEALS: alc Wed to Fri L, Wed to Sun D (main courses L £5.50 to £7.50, D £9 to £15). Set L Wed to Fri £6.95, Set D before 7 Wed to Fri and Sun £12.95 SERVICE: not inc CARDS: Amex, Delta, MasterCard, Switch, Visa DETAILS: 30 seats. Private parties: 34 main room. Vegetarian meals. Children's helpings. No cigars/pipes in dining room. Wheelchair access (also WC). Music

PORTRUSH Co Antrim **map 16**

Ramore 🍷

The Harbour, Portrush BT56 8BN
TEL: (028) 7082 4313 FAX: (028) 7082 3194

NEW CHEF
MODERN EUROPEAN
£30–£50

Ramore's field of operations comprises a pub, wine bar and restaurant, each with its own separate entrance. The restaurant is sharp and minimal in style, and features that modern sine qua non, an open-plan kitchen. Cool jazz plays, staff swish about in monochrome attire and, if you ignore the car park, there is a view over to the harbour. As the Guide was going to press, George McAlpin brought in a new pair of hands to take over the kitchen. On the basis of new menus, it seems modern brasserie-style cooking will still be the name of the game, offering perhaps Dubin Bay prawn and artichoke salad with a lemon cream, fillet of lamb with 'Asian ratatouille', aïoli and pesto, and desserts of Eton Mess or chocolate nemesis. Wines are a varied global selection, six by the glass making up for a lack of half-bottles. Prices are generous with 50 per cent of bottles under £10. Reports please.

CHEF: Saleem Ahmed PROPRIETORS: George and Jane McAlpin OPEN: Tue to Sat D only 6.15 to 10.15 CLOSED: 24 to26 Dec, 1 Jan MEALS: alc (main courses £10 to £14) SERVICE: not inc CARDS: Delta, MasterCard, Switch, Visa DETAILS: 60 seats. Private parties: 60 main room. Vegetarian meals. Wheelchair access (not WC). Music

Republic of Ireland

We have not given marks for cooking for the Republic of Ireland entries because of a shortage of reports; please do give us feedback should you visit. To telephone the Republic from mainland Britain, dial 00 353 followed by the number listed, but dropping the initial 0. Prices are quoted in Irish punts.

ADARE Co Limerick **map 16**

▲ Adare Manor 

Adare
TEL: (061) 396566 FAX: (061) 396124
EMAIL: reservations@adare.com
WEB SITE: www.adaremanor.ie

GLOBAL
£51–£78

Adare Manor is grand even by country-house standards (it has been compared to Versailles), and enjoys a wonderful setting in 900 acres of gardens, which includes a golf course. The new chef's menus are a verbal feast, seldom listing fewer than five ingredients in a dish and often more. Mediterranean and Irish flavours typically meet in a panaché of Atlantic seafood with fennel and garlic, or a salad of local leaves with smoked chicken, quails' eggs, avocado and white truffle oil. Dinner might typically begin with a terrine (chicken and wild mushroom with leek), followed by cream of celeriac and smoked bacon soup. For mains, rump of lamb has been marinated, smeared with tapénade and served with a moussaka of vegetables, as well as a wild mushroom and spinach fondue. Finish perhaps with rhubarb parfait served with a warm compote of apple and cinnamon. The splendour of the manor itself is reflected in a wine list containing many great wines at matching prices, including Sauzet's Bâtard Montrachet 1990 at £520, and Ch. Lynch-Bages 1945 at £1,700. For more modest tastes, house wines are £18.

CHEF: Thomas Andrews PROPRIETOR: Tom Kane OPEN: all week D only 6.30 to 9.30 MEALS: alc (main courses £18.50 to £23). Set D £36.50 to £39.50. Bar meals available 11 to 5.30 SERVICE: not inc CARDS: Amex, Diners, MasterCard, Visa DETAILS: 70 seats. Private parties: 100 main room, 30 to 180 private rooms. Car park. Vegetarian meals. Children's helpings. Jacket and tie. No smoking in 1 dining room. Wheelchair access (not WC). Music ACCOMMODATION: 63 rooms, all with bath/shower. TV. Phone. Room only £180 to £450. Rooms for disabled. Swimming pool. Fishing

---

Report forms are at the back of the book; write a letter if you prefer; or email us at goodfoodguide@which.net

---

AHAKISTA Co Cork **map 16**

Shiro

Ahakista, County Cork
TEL: (027) 67030 FAX: (027) 67206
EMAIL: pilzw@gofree.indigo.ie JAPANESE
on coast road from Durrus towards Sheep's Head £59–£76

Kei and Werner Pilz aptly call it their Japanese Dinner House. The setting, a country cottage surrounded by trees and sculpture in the grounds, is a happy meeting of Eastern and Western hemispheres. True to Irish tradition, the format is a five-course set-price menu, but in Japanese style some items are listed by cooking method, not ingredients. The daily menu starts with zensai, seasonal appetisers, and perhaps 'azuke-bachi', comprising egg and sushi snacks. After soup followed by green tea sorbet, diners choose from seven main courses which might include tempura, sashimi, or sushi of unspecified components; teriyaki beef; wild salmon in a light, creamy ginger and lemon sauce; or a bamboo skewer of chicken and sheep's liver with a spicy-sweet sauce. Home-made ice cream is the customary dessert, and as a change from oaked Chardonnay, why not finish with Japanese oak-smoked tea? Drink hot saké, £18, or consider a short, mostly French, wine list, with bottles from £12.

CHEF: Kei Pilz PROPRIETORS: Kei and Werner Pilz OPEN: all week D only 7 to 9 CLOSED: Christmas and New Year MEALS: Set D £45 (5 courses) SERVICE: 10%, card slips closed CARDS: Amex, Diners, MasterCard, Visa DETAILS: 17 seats. Private parties: 12 main room, 5 private room. Car park. Vegetarian meals. No children under 14. No smoking in 1 dining room. Music

BALLYDEHOB Co Cork **map 16**

Annie's

Main Street, Ballydehob EUROPEAN
TEL: (028) 37292 £29–£41

'Suffice to say we are still here after 17 years,' writes Anne Barry, and indeed western Cork might be the scene of an uprising if she decided to change anything about her small, busy restaurant on the main road through the village. An English family seemed to enjoy every minute of it, not least their five-year-old, who was furnished with a complimentary bowl of chips and ketchup. For those over five, crab and avocado cocktail, prime sirloin steak in garlic butter, and apricot and almond tart should do very nicely. The place is run with an exemplary sense of hospitality. Wines are a carefully chosen, French-led selection, with six house wines at £12.

CHEFS/PROPRIETORS: Dano and Anne Barry OPEN: Tue to Sat D only 6.30 to 9.30 CLOSED: Oct and Nov, 24 to 26 Dec, bank hols exc 17 Mar MEALS: alc (main courses £14 to £16). Set D £22.50 to £24.50 SERVICE: not inc CARDS: MasterCard, Visa DETAILS: 24 seats. Private parties: 24 main room. Children's helpings. No cigars/pipes in dining room. Wheelchair access (not WC). Music

BALLYLICKEY Co Cork **map 16**

▲ Ballylickey Manor, Le Rendez-Vous

Ballylickey, Bantry Bay
TEL: (027) 50071 FAX: (027) 50124

FRENCH
£32–£68

A 300-year-old former shooting lodge within earshot of Bantry Bay, Ballylickey Manor has been under the same ownership since just after the war. The gleaming white façade rises from lush gardens, and the accent in the dining room has always been modern French. A fixed-price menu supplements the expansive carte, and the cooking is full of assured classical technique. Local scallops are served with smoked ham, cabbage and pistou, while black sole fillets are presented à la grenobloise with lemon and capers. Braised stuffed oxtail indicates a robust approach to meat cookery, and puddings explore such byways as rhubarb gratin, or crème renversée au thé, which brings whole new meaning to the phrase 'cream tea'. An exclusively French wine list kicks off at £17 for house claret.

CHEFS: Thierry Laurier and Pascal Kirsch PROPRIETORS: Mr and Mrs Graves OPEN: Thur to Tue L 1 to 2, all week D 7 to 9.30 CLOSED: Nov to Apr MEALS: alc (main courses £14 to £18). Set L £18, Set D £30 SERVICE: 10%, card slips closed CARDS: Amex, Diners, MasterCard, Visa DETAILS: 30 seats. 15 seats outside. Private parties: 10 main room. Car park. No children under 4 at D. Jacket and tie. No smoking in dining room. Wheelchair access (not WC). Occasional music ACCOMMODATION: 11 rooms, all with bath/shower. TV. Phone. B&B £100 to £220. Baby facilities. Swimming pool. Fishing

BALLYVAUGHAN Co Clare **map 16**

▲ Gregans Castle 

Ballyvaughan
TEL: (065) 7077005 FAX: (065) 7077111
EMAIL: res@gregans.ie
WEB SITE: www.gregans.ie
on N67, 3½m S of Ballyvaughan

FRENCH
£42–£67

Try to grab a window table if you can, advises a reporter, the better to appreciate the extraordinary natural light show formed by the sunset reflecting off Galway Bay on to the limestone hills in the distance. Most nights, a harpist or pianist plays in the dining-room. It all forms an atmospheric setting for new chef Regis Herviaux to ply his skills. Aumonière of garlicky poultry livers with pancetta, mushrooms and goose fat might start a meal in thoroughly Gallic fashion, but simpler tastes are not neglected: witness grilled Dover sole with saffron butter. Vegetarians may be offered asparagus risotto served with pesto made from roast red peppers, while carnivores could be drawn to roast leg of local lamb with a dressing of fresh garden mint. Sixteen organic wines (including house wines at £15) appear on the lengthy list, which offers an astute selection from around the world.

The Guide always appreciates hearing about changes of chef or owner.

CHEF: Regis Herviaux PROPRIETORS: the Haden family OPEN: all week D only 7 to 8.30 CLOSED: Nov to Mar MEALS: alc (main courses £19 to £29). Set D £36 SERVICE: not inc, card slips closed CARDS: Amex, MasterCard, Visa DETAILS: 60 seats. Private parties: 60 main room. Car park. Vegetarian meals. Children's helpings. No-smoking area. Wheelchair access (not WC). Music ACCOMMODATION: 22 rooms, all with bath/shower. Phone. B&B £89 to £280. Baby facilities

BANTRY Co Cork map 16

▲ Larchwood House

Pearsons Bridge, Bantry MODERN IRISH
TEL: (027) 66181 £34–£43

This pretty little house hardly looks big enough to be a guesthouse, let alone a restaurant seating 30 at well-spaced tables. Varied but unselfconscious décor in the dining room takes in rococo cabinets, wooden sculptures, dried flowers and an Indian brass lamp. Six-course dinners might typically kick off with potato cake with chicken and bacon, or a seafood casserole, with a soup next: carrot and coriander, say, or chicken and chive. There are normally half a dozen main-course choices, perhaps including fillet steak with pepper sauce, duckling with plum sauce, or perfectly cooked fillet of John Dory with sesame seeds. Desserts offer the widest selection, ranging from bread-and-butter pudding to an unusual speciality combining a light, jelly-like blob made from carrageen moss with a generous quantity of rhubarb coulis. Service has at times seemed amateurish, but always aims to please. House wines are £13, and the well-annotated list includes decent wines from Spain, Italy, Germany and the New World as well as France.

CHEF/PROPRIETOR: Sheila Vaughan OPEN: Mon to Sat D only 7 to 9.30 CLOSED: limited opening in winter MEALS: Set D £24 to £26 SERVICE: not inc, card slips closed CARDS: Amex, Diners, MasterCard, Visa DETAILS: 30 seats. Private parties: 13 main room. Car park. Children's helpings. No smoking in 1 dining room. Wheelchair access (not WC). Music ACCOMMODATION: 4 rooms, all with bath/shower. B&B £25 to £50. Fishing (£5)

BLACKLION Co Cavan map 16

▲ MacNean Bistro

Blacklion MODERN IRISH
TEL: (072) 53022 FAX: (072) 53404 £23–£60

A family-run restaurant and guesthouse in the north of the Republic, the MacNean prides itself on using local and naturally grown produce in a style of cooking that combines Irish ways with world influences. That translates into roast scallop with cabbage, five-spice and white beans; prawn bisque with coconut milk; and loin of lamb with a leek and mushroom vol-au-vent and curry oil. The carte and fixed-price menus are bolstered by the options of a menu surprise or a tasting menu of fish dishes, so the kitchen clearly has its work cut out. Clichés are avoided at pudding stage, with offerings such as roast figs with lime ice cream and waffles, or warm chocolate fondant with chestnut and whiskey ice cream. The wine list has expanded but is still strongest in France, although the international slate of house wines shows imagination. Prices open at £12.50.

CHEF: Neven Maguire PROPRIETORS: Vera and Neven Maguire OPEN: Sun L 12.30 to 3.30, Tue to Sun D 6 to 9.30 CLOSED: 1 week Oct, 4 days at Christmas MEALS: alc (main courses £13 to £16). Set L £15, Set D £32 to £39 SERVICE: not inc CARDS: Amex, MasterCard, Visa DETAILS: 50 seats. Private parties: 50 main room, 15 private room. Car park. Vegetarian meals. Children's helpings. No smoking in dining room. Wheelchair access (not WC). Music ACCOMMODATION: 5 rooms, all with bath/shower. TV. Phone. B&B £25 to £55. Baby facilities

CASHEL Co Tipperary **map 16**

Chez Hans 🍷

Moor Lane, Cashel — MODERN EUROPEAN
TEL: (062) 61177 — £34–£57

A short trot off the main Dublin to Cork road, and well signposted, is the Matthiae family's restaurant in a converted church. Jason is currently in charge of the kitchen, and appears to relish a contemporary and largely southern European approach. Tagliatelle of spinach with smoked salmon and chives, or duck risotto with chorizo and mushrooms, may be alternative places to start. Then one might opt for the simplicity of Dover sole cooked on the bone and served à la meunière, or the greater intricacy of a veal cutlet wrapped in Parma ham, stuffed with the local (internationally renowned) Cashel Blue cheese and accompanied by spring onion mash and wild mushrooms. Vegetarian risotto and pasta variations are always available. A resourceful wine list takes in some good selections from the Americas, as well as famous French names, and the house range opens at £13.

CHEF: Jason Matthiae PROPRIETORS: Hans-Peter and Jason Matthiae OPEN: Tue to Sat D only 6 to 10 CLOSED: 3 days Christmas, last 2 weeks Jan, first week Sept MEALS: alc (main courses £14 to £18). Set D £27.50 SERVICE: not inc CARDS: MasterCard, Switch, Visa DETAILS: 80 seats. Private parties: 80 main room. Car park. Vegetarian meals. Children's helpings. No cigars/pipes in dining room. Wheelchair access (not WC). Occasional music

CASTLEBALDWIN Co Sligo **map 16**

▲ Cromleach Lodge

Castlebaldwin, via Boyle
TEL: (071) 65155 FAX: (071) 65455
EMAIL: info@cromleach.com — MODERN IRISH
WEB SITE: www.cromleach.com — £44–£68

The waters of Lough Arrow and the mountains beyond are on view from this summerhouse in the country, whose short carte offers a balanced choice using local organic produce in modern Irish style. That could mean starting with cod fillet with a sun-dried tomato crust, quail breasts with glazed barley, or Roquefort and walnut tartlet on redcurrant coulis. Soup or salad can be taken as a separate course after starters, and then comes a sorbet. Typical main courses are loin of lamb with lentils, seared wild Atlantic salmon with creamy spring onions, and fillet of Sligo beef with bacon julienne. Desserts can be as tempting as iced pineapple soufflé on rich chocolate torte, or layered coffee and ginger gâteau with chicory anglaise. Before classic clarets and mainly New World bottles, the wine list has 13 each of red and white house recommendations, starting at £14.95.

CHEF: Moira Tighe PROPRIETORS: Christy and Moira Tighe OPEN: all week D only 6.30 to 8.30 CLOSED: Nov to Feb MEALS: alc (main courses £19). Set D £40 SERVICE: not inc CARDS: Amex, Diners, MasterCard, Visa DETAILS: 50 seats. Private parties: 24 main room, 6 to 26 private rooms. Car park. Vegetarian meals. Children's helpings. No children under 7. No smoking in dining room. Wheelchair access (not WC). No music ACCOMMODATION: 10 rooms, all with bath/shower. TV. Phone. B&B £79 to £198. Rooms for disabled. Fishing

CORK Co Cork **map 16**

Crawford Gallery Café £

Emmet Place, Cork
TEL: (021) 274415 FAX: (021) 652021 IRISH/BRITISH
WEB SITE: www.ballymaloe.ie £20–£29

The Allen family of Ballymaloe fame (see entry, Shanagarry) have the franchise for the café in Cork's main art gallery, where the emphasis at lunchtime is on fresh fish landed at nearby Ballycotton. Fish pie with green salad, or fishcakes with chilli salsa and tartare sauce might well be on offer, while meat eaters might choose casseroled pork with Normandy mustard and glazed apples, or braised lamb with haricots, tomatoes and rosemary, both served with champ and pea purée. Finish with Irish coffee meringue with whiskey cream, or rhubarb cake. Breakfasts and afternoon teas are available too. House wine is £11 (£2.30 a glass).

CHEF: Michele Sheilds PROPRIETORS: Fern and Hazel Allen OPEN: Mon to Sat 10 to 5 CLOSED: 24 Dec to 3 Jan MEALS: alc (main courses £6 to £8.50). Set L £13 SERVICE: not inc CARDS: MasterCard, Visa DETAILS: 70 seats. Private parties: 70 main room, 150 private room. Vegetarian meals. Children's helpings. No-smoking area. Wheelchair access (also WC). Occasional music

DINGLE Co Kerry **map 16**

▲ Half Door

3 John Street, Dingle
TEL: (066) 9151600 FAX: (066) 9151883 MODERN IRISH
EMAIL halfdoor@iol.ie l £27–£76

Perched on the Kerry peninsula, jutting out into the Atlantic, Dingle is well served by good restaurants. This one majors in sea-fresh fish and shellfish, perhaps a gratinated crab first course, or salmon escalope in a garlic beurre blanc, followed by boiled lobster chosen from the tank, or roast cod on a bed of potatoes and chives. Meat eaters might opt for chargrilled sirloin steak in peppercorn sauce, while homely desserts include pear and apple crumble, or Bailey's cheesecake. The broad-minded wine list offers classic clarets and Burgundies to aficionados, as well as an upmarket range of bottles from around the world. There is always a featured wine of the month, and the international house selections start at £13.

CHEF/PROPRIETOR: Denis O'Connor OPEN: Tue to Sat L 12.30 to 2, Mon to Sat D 6 to 10 CLOSED: Jan and Feb MEALS: alc (main courses £8 to £35) SERVICE: not inc CARDS: MasterCard, Visa DETAILS: 50 seats. Private parties: 20 main room. Vegetarian meals. Children's helpings. No smoking in 1 dining room. Wheelchair access (not WC). Music. Air-conditioned ACCOMMODATION: 7 rooms, all with bath/shower. TV. Phone. B&B £25 to £100. Rooms for disabled

DONEGAL Co Donegal **map 16**

▲ Harvey's Point

Lough Eske, Donegal
TEL: (073) 22208 FAX: (073) 22352
EMAIL: harveyspoint@eircom.ie MODERN EUROPEAN
WEB SITE: www.commerce.ie/harveys-pt £20–£46

A mere four miles out of Donegal, Marc Gysling's country hotel has seen some structural changes that were completed in April 2000. It still looks like an expansive chalet transplanted from the proprietor's native Switzerland, but now the lounge has been refurbished and the restaurant extended down to the shores of Lough Eske, giving a close-in picture of the unruffled view. The gentle style of European cooking continues serenely too, encompassing a salad of goats' cheese wrapped in Parma ham, feuilleté of confit quail with red wine sauce, and main courses that take in monkfish with steamed potatoes and grain mustard sauce, as well as textbook tournedos Rossini. And then, to complete the sense of cosseting, along comes a two-tone mousse of chocolate and orange served with raspberry coulis. There is even caramelised banana in the crème brûlée. House wines are £12.50.

CHEF/PROPRIETOR: Marc Gysling OPEN: all week 12.30 to 2.30, 6.30 to 9.30 CLOSED: Sun D, Mon and Tue Nov to Mar MEALS: alc (main courses L ££8.50 to £10, D £15 to £18.50). Set L £12.95, Set D £30 SERVICE: net prices, card slips closed CARDS: Amex, Diners, MasterCard, Visa DETAILS: 120 seats. Private parties: 100 main room, 100 to 300 private rooms. Car park. Vegetarian meals. Jacket and tie. No smoking in dining room. Wheelchair access (also WC). Music. Air-conditioned ACCOMMODATION: 20 rooms, all with bath/shower. TV. Phone. B&B £64 to £110

DOUGLAS Co Cork **map 16**

Lovetts

Churchyard Lane, off Well Road, Douglas
TEL: (021) 294909 FAX: (021) 294024 MODERN EUROPEAN
EMAIL: lovetts@indigo.ie £26–£55

The crediting of local supply lines on the menu at the Lovetts' restaurant, not far south of Cork city, is a testament to the conscientious approach here. Seasonal oysters, free-range chickens, local venison and farmhouse cheeses are among the fine things on offer, in both the brasserie and main dining room. Filo cigars of crab and coriander with a salsa of watercress and tomato might start things off, and be followed by that venison, served with spiced oranges in an apricot brandy sauce. Vegetarians have their own menu, which may include chickpea burger with feta and tapénade, before everyone reunites for pudding. Both Old and New Worlds are well represented on a lengthy wine list which includes star producers and many much sought-after bottles. Mark-ups, consequently, are not cheap. House Vins de Pays de L'Herault are £14.

CHEF: Marie Harding PROPRIETORS: the Lovett family OPEN: Tue to Sat D only 6 to 10 CLOSED: 1 week Christmas, 2 weeks Aug, bank hols MEALS: alc (main courses £9 to £18). Set vegetarian D £15.50 (2 courses). Brasserie menu available SERVICE: not inc, card slips closed CARDS: Amex, MasterCard, Visa DETAILS: 70 seats. Private parties: 50 main room, 24 and 50 private rooms. Car park. Vegetarian meals. Children's helpings. No smoking in 1 dining room. Wheelchair access (not WC). Music

DUBLIN Co Dublin **map 16**

▲ Clarence, Tea Room

6–8 Wellington Quay, Dublin 2
TEL: (01) 6709000 FAX: (01) 6707800 MODERN IRISH/EUROPEAN
WEB SITE: www.theclarence.ie £28–£62

Early 2000 brought a change of ownership at this stylish hotel, but a new chef has retained most of his predecessor's menu, and it looks as though standards are being maintained. A starter combining mustard-cured and tartare salmon with marinated cucumber is new, as is a dessert of warm crispy pear amandine with Williams schnapps ice cream. Otherwise, expect simply roasted scallops with new potatoes, rump of lamb with crushed minted potatoes, and bitter chocolate fondant. House wines are £15, though the whole list was about to be revised when the Guide went to press.

CHEF: Antony Ely PROPRIETOR: Clarence Hotel OPEN: Mon to Fri L 12 to 3, all week D 6.30 to 11 CLOSED: bank hols MEALS: alc (main courses £15 to £19). Set L17 SERVICE: not inc, 12.5% for parties of 8 or more CARDS: Amex, Diners, MasterCard, Visa DETAILS: 90 seats. Private parties: 80 private room. No-smoking area. Wheelchair access (also WC). Music. Air-conditioned ACCOMMODATION: 50 rooms, all with bath/shower. TV. Phone. Room only £195 to £1,500. Rooms for disabled

Commons 

Newman House, 85–86 St Stephen's Green,
Dublin 2 MODERN IRISH/FRENCH
TEL: (01) 4780530 FAX: (01) 4780551 £34–£90

Under a vaulted ceiling in a splendid Georgian-style building, this basement dining room is wide and spacious, its modern artworks celebrating literary associations with James Joyce and Gerard Manley Hopkins. Just as the Guide went to press, Aidan Byrne (with experience at Peacock Alley, Dublin; see entry) arrived to take over the stoves. We cannot know what will follow, but it will be surprising if the Irish-French accent is not maintained. Luxury materials have typically featured (oscietra caviar with sea bass for example), although more humble ones might turn up in an oxtail version of shepherd's pie. Various ways with chocolate – perhaps a fondant with milk ice cream – have been favoured puddings. Service, also Franco-Irish, is charming. The wine list starts with a dozen house selections from £17 and goes on to a diverse range that includes many French classics as well as big names from elsewhere.

CHEF: Aidan Byrne PROPRIETORS: Mike and Maggi Fitzgerald OPEN: Mon to Sat 12.30 to 2.15, 7 to 10.15 CLOSED: 1 week Christmas, bank hols MEALS: alc (main courses £20 to £30). Set L £22 SERVICE: not inc CARDS: Amex, Diners, MasterCard, Visa DETAILS: 60 seats. 20 seats outside. Private parties: 70 main room, 26 to 60 private rooms. Children's helpings. No-smoking area. Music

Le Coq Hardi

35 Pembroke Road, Dublin 4 FRENCH-PLUS
TEL: (01) 6689070 FAX: (01) 6689887 £38–£94

In a Georgian house in the chic district of Ballsbridge, James O'Sullivan has been cooking on a grand scale for 20 years now. The predominantly French style accommodates other culinary idioms, producing roast monkfish tail on bok choy with a star anise and Pernod cream, and a terrine is formed from prize-winning Clonakilty black and white puddings. The heart of the menu centres on dishes such as langoustine and crab bisque with cognac, and herb-crusted rack of Wicklow lamb with a thyme jus, while the eponymous signature dish is a bacon-wrapped chicken breast stuffed with potato, apple and ham, and pot-roasted with Irish whiskey. Lemon tart with raspberry coulis is an appropriate way to finish. Lovers of fine vintage wines will imagine they have died and gone to heaven. Classed-growth clarets, thoroughbred Burgundies, and even Rhônes back to 1961 will all delight, and the good news is they still haven't sold out of the 1870 Mouton-Rothschild. Deep pockets will be needed to explore it all. Guigal's Côtes du Rhône is £18.

CHEF: James O'Sullivan PROPRIETOR: John Howard OPEN: Mon to Fri L 12.30 to 2.30, Mon to Sat D 7 to 10.45 CLOSED: 2 weeks Christmas, 2 weeks Aug MEALS: alc (main courses £21 to £28). Set L £24.50 SERVICE: 12.5%, card slips closed CARDS: Amex, Diners, MasterCard, Visa DETAILS: 50 seats. Private parties: 50 main room, 4 to 35 private rooms. Car park. Jacket and tie. No smoking in 1 dining room. No music. Air-conditioned

L'Ecrivain

109A Lower Baggot Street, Dublin 2
TEL: (01) 6611919 FAX: (01) 6610617
EMAIL: enquiries@lecrivain.com MODERN IRISH/FRENCH
WEB SITE: www.lecrivain.com £26–£68

A portrait gallery of Irish literary notables explains the name and provides visual interest at the Clarkes' restaurant. For a pair from England who went on a gastro-tour of the Republic, L'Ecrivain turned out to be the highlight. They appreciated Derry Clarke's enterprising modern cooking, which takes in dishes such as honey-roast root vegetable soup with buttermilk, and fillet of John Dory with caramelised fennel. A separate vegetarian menu furnishes plenty of choice, including an unusual main course of French onion tart served with saffron ice cream and crisp celery. Coffee is served with chocolate truffles. An overhauled (since the last Guide) wine list offers 14 by the glass from around the world.

Classical French regions are nevertheless given precedence, although mark-ups for clarets are severe. House Chilean is £15 a bottle.

CHEF: Derry Clarke PROPRIETORS: Derry and Sallyanne Clarke OPEN: Mon to Fri L 12.30 to 2, Mon to Sat D 7 to 11 CLOSED: bank hols MEALS: alc D (main courses £18.50 to £23.50). Set L £13.50 (2 courses) to £16.50, Set D £33 SERVICE: 10% on food only CARDS: Amex, Diners, MasterCard, Visa DETAILS: 120 seats. 30 seats outside. Private parties: 90 main room, 24 private room. Vegetarian meals. Children's helpings. No smoking in 1 dining room. Wheelchair access (also WC). Music. Air-conditioned

Les Frères Jacques

74 Dame Street, Dublin 2 — FRENCH
TEL: (01) 6794555 FAX: (01) 6794725 — £23–£69

Traditional French cuisine with an eye on lightness and seasonality is what Jean-Jacques Caillabet has always prided himself on offering Dublin from his intimate restaurant next to the Olympia Theatre. Chefs may come and go, but the standard remains high, as demonstrated by a beautifully textured 'boudin blanc' of monkfish on chopped tomato, competently cooked salmon with braised fennel, and melting lamb fillet with a plum and ginger sauce. Meals might end with poached pear with red wine coulis, or classic lemon tart with yoghurt sorbet. The wine list finds a little space for foreigners, but the broad thrust is French and classical. House wine in all three colours is £11.

CHEF: Daragh Kavanagh PROPRIETOR: Jean-Jacques Caillabet OPEN: Mon to Fri L 12.30 to 2.30, Mon to Sat D 7.15 to 10.30 (11 Fri and Sat) CLOSED: D 24 Dec to 4 Jan, bank hols MEALS: alc (main courses L £6.50 to £9.50, D £17 to £25). Set L £13.50, Set D £21 SERVICE: 12.5% (optional) CARDS: Amex, Diners, MasterCard, Visa DETAILS: 65 seats. Private parties: 40 main room, 20 and 40 private rooms. No smoking in 1 dining room. Music. Air-conditioned

Jacob's Ladder

NEW ENTRY

4 Nassau Street, Dublin 2 — MODERN IRISH
TEL: (01) 6703865 FAX: (01) 6703868 — £25–£57

The upstairs dining room overlooks the lawns of Trinity College, where you may see a sedate game of cricket being played on a summer evening. In this peaceful setting, Adrian Roche offers highly polished modern Irish cooking. His menus might deliver sauté scallops with roast beetroot and spiced lentils, or marinated salmon served with a leek and bacon quiche and fried oysters in a grain mustard dressing. It is not uncommon to find lots of ingredients in one dish. Shellfish coddle is a signature starter; a variation on Dublin coddle (made with pork sausages), it is a light but generous stew of mussels, clams, prawns, a salmon sausage and vegetables. Main courses might extend to roast duck breast with bok choy and a cassis sauce, or roast rump of lamb with leek and goats'-cheese parcels. Finish with rum and raisin brûlée with rum ice cream, or a parfait of Bailey's accompanied by a pear poached in coffee. The short wine list is tilted towards sunny New World flavours, with a spread of Languedoc varietal house wines at £12.

CHEF: Adrian Roche PROPRIETORS: Adrian and Bernie Roche OPEN: Tue to Sat 12.30 to 2.30 (2 Sat), 6 (7 Sat) to 10 CLOSED: 3 weeks from 24 Dec, 1 week Aug MEALS: alc (main courses L £8 to £9.50, D £13.50 to £19). Set D £25 SERVICE: not inc CARDS: Amex, Diners, MasterCard, Visa DETAILS: 80 seats. Private parties: 50 main room, 50 private room. Vegetarian meals. No smoking while others eat. Music (£5)

Mermaid Café

69–70 Dame Street, Dublin 2 MODERN EUROPEAN
TEL: (01) 6708236 FAX: (01) 6708205 £23–£53

Bare varnished floorboards, chunky pine tables and an open-plan kitchen set the contemporary design tone at the Mermaid, a bustling, trend-conscious restaurant a couple of doors up from the Olympia Theatre. Weekly-changing menus acknowledge an east-coast American influence, visible in New England crab cakes with piquant mayonnaise, and mussel and smoked fish chowder with celery biscuits. The pick of the day's catch goes into giant seafood casseroles with Thai aromatic seasonings, while meat eaters might be regaled with calvados-marinated pork fillet with apple mash and gingered leeks. Pecan pie with maple ice cream sounds the east-coast note again, or stay local for a pair of Irish cheeses served with spiced apples. A short but well-focused wine list concentrates predominantly on exciting bottles from the New World, many of which are imported direct. House French is £12.95 a bottle.

CHEFS: Ben Gorman and Temple Garner PROPRIETORS: Mark Harrell and Ben Gorman OPEN: all week 12.30 to 2.30 (12 to 3.30 Sun), 6 to 11 CLOSED: 24–25 and 31 Dec, 1 Jan, Good Fri MEALS: alc (main courses L £6 to £9, D £11 to £19). Set L £18.50, Set D £23.50 SERVICE: not inc, 12.5% for parties of 5 or more CARDS: MasterCard, Visa DETAILS: 60 seats. Private parties: 60 main room, 28 private room. Vegetarian meals. Children's helpings. No-smoking area. Wheelchair access (also WC). Music. Air-conditioned

Patrick Guilbaud

21 Upper Merrion Street, Dublin 2 MODERN IRISH/FRENCH
TEL: (01) 6764192 FAX: (01) 6610052 £64–£104

'Still reigns supreme' and 'easily the best meal I've had this year' are two of the plaudits the Guide received this year about this smart restaurant in the Merrion Hotel opposite government buildings. Modern Irish cuisine (with a French accent) using seasonal domestic produce is the guiding principle of Guillaume Lebrun's menus, which take the form of a fixed-price lunch as well as a carte. The style is robust, with roast scallops appearing on rabbit confit, and roast squab pigeon accompanied by a parcel of stuffed cabbage and a spiced Madeira jus. Deserts range from a straightforward banana Tatin with rum ice cream, to a plate combining iced milk chocolate mousse and bitter chocolate coulis with caramel ice cream and croquant. The full wine list is never sent to us, but as an indication house wines start at £22.

Although the cuisine style noted at the top of entries has in most cases been suggested to the Guide by the restaurants, some have been edited for brevity or appropriateness.

CHEF: Guillaume Lebrun PROPRIETOR: Patrick Guilbaud OPEN: Tue to Sat 12.30 to 2.15, 7.30 to 10.15 CLOSED: first week Jan MEALS: alc (main courses £24 to £29). Set L £22 (2 courses) SERVICE: not inc CARDS: Amex, Diners, MasterCard, Visa DETAILS: 90 seats. 20 seats outside. Private parties: 90 main room, 25 private room. Car park. Vegetarian meals. No-smoking area. No music. Air-conditioned

Peacock Alley

109 St Stephen's Green, Dublin 2
TEL: (01) 4787015 and 4787028
FAX: (01) 4787043

MODERN IRISH
£45–£107

The cooking at this Conran-designed venue near St Stephen's Green shopping centre is nothing if not fashionable. Start perhaps with roasted foie gras paired with rhubarb, kumquat and a caramel sauce, or maybe truffled goats' cheese and potato roulade with Parmesan cream and frisée. Seafood tends to be given upbeat treatment – crab roulade with coriander, lemon and horseradish, or John Dory with galette potato and a pea casserole – while weighty meat dishes tend to be roasted and come with root vegetables: perhaps saddle of venison with roast parsnips, or or beef fillet with braised beetroot. Desserts tempt with mango rice pudding, lemon tart with raspberries, and chocolate hazelnut cake with florentines. Wines are an opulent selection, both in terms of variety and price, as befits the cooking. The sommelier's selection starts at £22.

CHEF/PROPRIETOR: Conrad Gallagher OPEN: Mon to Sat 12.30 to 2.15, 6.30 to 10.45 CLOSED: 24 to 26 Dec, bank hols MEALS: alc (main courses £20 to £29). Set L £20 (2 courses) to £30, Set D £50 to £70 SERVICE: not inc CARDS: Amex, Diners, MasterCard, Visa DETAILS: 120 seats. Private parties: 120 main room, 20 private room. Vegetarian meals. No children under 12. No smoking in 1 dining room. Wheelchair access (also WC). Music. Air-conditioned

Roly's Bistro

7 Ballsbridge Terrace, Dublin 4
TEL: (01) 6682611 FAX: (01) 6608535

IRISH-FRENCH
£20–£51

There may not be much of the bistro in the scale of the outfit – two floors in the Ballsbridge district of Dublin, and another branch in Palm Beach, Florida – but regulars seem to appreciate the comforting style of home cooking that Roly's specialises in. That doesn't mean that Paul Cartwright is afraid of occasional innovation – which he introduces in the form of, for example, crab claws with linguine dressed in garlic, ginger and coriander – but the backbone of the menus is to be found in smoked mackerel with soured cream and lime, braised oxtail with Toulouse sausage and beans, and chicken breast stuffed with Clonakilty black pudding, served with mashed potato and port sauce. Crème brûlée to finish comes with praline ice cream and peanut butter cookies. House wine, on a list of 88 bottles, is £11.50.

Not inc *in the details at the end of an entry indicates that no service charge is made and any tipping is at the discretion of the customer.*

CHEF: Paul Cartwright PROPRIETORS: John and Angela O'Sullivan, and Colin O'Daly OPEN: all week 12 to 3, 6 to 10 MEALS: alc (main courses £11 to £16.50). Set L £12.50, Set D before 6.45 £12.95 (2 courses) to £14.95 SERVICE: 10% CARDS: Amex, Diners, MasterCard, Visa DETAILS: 150 seats. Private parties: 12 main room, 40 private room. Vegetarian meals. No-smoking area. Wheelchair access (also WC). Music. Air-conditioned

Thornton's

1 Portobello Road, Dublin 8 MODERN IRISH
TEL: (01) 4549067 FAX: (01) 4532947 £37–£90

Location may not have been uppermost in Kevin Thornton's mind when he set up shop in 1995 away from the elegant Georgian centre, but his cooking would be welcome anywhere. It may be classic, timeless and luxurious, but it is also joyful and exuberant, relishing the juxtaposition of John Dory with a tomato and garlic tartlet, or spring lamb with a courgette clafoutis. It is generous with expensive ingredients, producing starters of white asparagus mousse with truffle vinaigrette, and lobster ravioli with vegetable linguine and lobster coral sauce. Passion is equally evident, however, in more prosaic-sounding bacon and cabbage terrine with leek sauce, or the house speciality of roast suckling pig and trotter with a potín (Irish alcohol made from potatoes)sauce. A menu surprise runs to eight courses, and suave service maintains high standards. As well as going for the big French guns, wines cherry pick their way around Spain, Italy, Australia, and North and South America, producing a confidence-inspiring list. Such quality doesn't come cheap, but house wines start at £15.

CHEF: Kevin Thornton PROPRIETORS: Kevin and Muriel Thornton OPEN: Fri L 12.15 to 2.30, Tue to Sat D 6.30 to 10.30 CLOSED: 2 weeks Christmas, bank hols MEALS: alc (main courses £27 to £29). Set L £25, Set D £59 SERVICE: 12.5% CARDS: Amex, Diners, MasterCard, Visa DETAILS: 40 seats. Private parties: 50 main room, 16 to 35 private rooms. Vegetarian meals. Children's helpings. No smoking in 1 dining room. Music. Air-conditioned

DURRUS Co Cork **map 16**

▲ Blairs Cove House

Durrus
TEL: (027) 61127 FAX: (027) 61487
EMAIL: blairscove@eircom.net MODERN IRISH
1½m out of Durrus on Barleycove to Goleen road £44–£53

This 270-year-old country house sits atop a promontory over Dunmanus Bay, where the Gulf Stream brings a touch of the subtropical. Sabine De Mey's menus offer an extensive choice of main courses, with fish the leading edge: broiled hake with spiced couscous, horseradish-crusted salmon, and steamed John Dory with balsamic vinaigrette among the options. Starters and desserts are served buffet-style. The wine list makes a good fist of covering the globe, and prices are not unreasonable. The house selection is uniformly pegged at £12.50.

denotes an outstanding wine cellar; denotes a good wine list, worth travelling for.

CHEF: Sabine De Mey PROPRIETOR: Philippe De Mey OPEN: Tue to Sat D only 7 to 9.30 CLOSED: Nov to Mar MEALS: Set D £32 SERVICE: not inc, card slips closed CARDS: Diners, MasterCard, Visa DETAILS: 75 seats. Private parties: 40 main room. Car park. Vegetarian meals. Children's helpings. No cigars/pipes in dining room. Music ACCOMMODATION: 3 rooms. TV. Phone. B&B £60 to £140. Baby facilities

GOREY Co Wexford — map 16

▲ Marlfield House

Courtown Road, Gorey
TEL: (055) 21124 FAX: (055) 21572
EMAIL: info@marlfieldhouse.ie
WEB SITE: www.marlfieldhouse.com

MODERN FRENCH
£36–£81

A family-run country house on a majestic scale, Marlfield is now in its twenty-second year of operation as a hotel. Woodland walks and a rose garden are among the outdoor attractions, while the public rooms are awash with fine paintings and antiques, and the conservatory dining room with fresh flowers. Henry Stone uses plenty of herbs from the kitchen garden in his classically oriented fixed-price menus, which cover a range from terrine of ham knuckle and foie gras with apple and truffle dressing, to pan-fried turbot with an asparagus and pea purée and lobster sauce. An intermediate course offers soup, salad or sorbet. Desserts maintain the inventiveness with rhubarb frangipane tart, or mixed nut parfait with butterscotch sauce, or there are well-kept Irish cheeses. The wine list knows its Onions when it comes to the pre-eminent regions of France, but the selections from elsewhere are not bad either. Prices generally reflect the opulence of the place, starting at £16.

CHEF: Henry Stone PROPRIETORS: Mary and Ray Bowe OPEN: all week 12.30 to 1.45, 7 to 9 (9.30 Sat) CLOSED: mid-Dec to end Jan MEALS: Set L £24 to £25, Set D £37 to £42. Light L available Mon to Sat SERVICE: not inc, card slips closed CARDS: Amex, Diners, MasterCard, Switch, Visa DETAILS: 65 seats. Private parties: 20 main room, 20 private room. Car park. Vegetarian meals. Children's helpings at L. No children under 10 at D. Jacket and tie. No smoking in dining room. Wheelchair access (also WC). No music. Air-conditioned ACCOMMODATION: 20 rooms, all with bath/shower. TV. Phone. B&B £85 to £520. Rooms for disabled. Baby facilities (£5)

HOWTH Co Dublin — map 16

▲ King Sitric

East Pier, Howth
TEL: (01) 8325235 FAX: (01) 8392442
EMAIL: info@kingsitric.ie
WEB SITE: www.kingsitric.com

SEAFOOD
£28–£84

After some serious rebuilding and refurbishing – the restaurant was closed for nine months in 1999 – the dining room has moved to the first floor and enjoys commanding sea views. The cooking, however, hasn't missed a beat, once again turning out refined seafood dishes such as crab baked in buttermilk, or grilled plaice served on shredded cabbage and bacon with a mint dressing. Main courses on the carte provide a wealth of choice, from poached turbot with hollandaise, via roast monkfish with mushrooms in a wholegrain mustard sauce, to classic lobster thermidor. If you really don't want fish, there is sirloin steak in red wine sauce. Irish cheeses or perhaps pineapple and coconut parfait might be a good way to finish. The extensive and serious wine list is strongest in Bordeaux and Burgundy (Chablis is a major passion), but it is also authoritative in its rest-of-the-world selections, and prices are demonstrably fair. House French starts at £13.50.

CHEF: Aidan MacManus PROPRIETORS: Aidan and Joan MacManus OPEN: Mon to Fri L 12.30 to 2.15, Mon to Sat D 6.30 to 10.30 CLOSED: Christmas, bank hols MEALS: alc (main courses £16.50 to £40). Set L £15 (2 courses) to £18.50, Set D £32 SERVICE: not inc CARDS: Amex, Diners, MasterCard, Visa DETAILS: 70 seats. Private parties: 80 main room. Children's helpings. No music. Air-conditioned ACCOMMODATION: 8 rooms, all with bath/shower. TV. Phone. B&B £65 to £150. Rooms for disabled. Baby facilities (£5)

KANTURK Co Cork **map 16**

▲ Assolas Country House

Kanturk
TEL: (029) 50015 FAX: (029) 50795
EMAIL: assolas@eircom.net
WEB SITE: www.assolas.com
signposted from N72, NE of Kanturk, 8m W of Mallow

MODERN IRISH
£41–£50

The seventeenth-century manor house in its tranquil setting in the west of Cork has been home to the Bourke family since the time of the Great War. Hazel Bourke's sourcing of raw materials is impeccable, with oysters from Rosscarberry, mussels from Kenmare, locally raised meats, and fruits and vegetables from her own kitchen garden. She keeps the cooking simple, the better to let the ingredients shine, steaming those mussels with olive oil and herbs, perhaps, and serving roast loin of lamb with garden mint jelly. Hot duck confit with green salad, followed by herb-crusted baked monkfish tail might be another way to go about it. Desserts are served from a trolley, or there are fine regional cheeses. France leads the wine list, with a small showing each of Spanish and Italian bottles. Prices start at £15.

CHEF: Hazel Bourke PROPRIETORS: the Bourke family OPEN: all week D only 7 to 8 CLOSED: Nov to Mar MEALS: Set D £30 SERVICE: none, card slips closed CARDS: MasterCard, Visa DETAILS: 20 seats. Private parties: 20 main room. Car park. Children's helpings. No children under 8 at D. No cigars/pipes in dining room. Wheelchair access (not WC). No music ACCOMMODATION: 9 rooms, all with bath/shower. Phone. B&B £65 to £170. Baby facilities. Fishing

All details are as accurate as possible at the time of going to press, but chefs and owners often change, and it is wise to check by telephone before making a special journey. Many readers have been disappointed when set-price bargain meals are no longer available. Ask when booking.

KENMARE Co Kerry **map 16**

▲ Park Hotel Kenmare

Kenmare
TEL: (064) 41200 FAX: (064) 41402
EMAIL: phkenmare@iol.ie
WEB SITE: www.parkkenmare.com

MODERN IRISH
£53–£84

The Park is the sort of swashbuckling grand hotel where you mustn't be surprised to encounter a suit of armour halfway up the stairs, and where a view of watery tranquillity – in this case, Kenmare Bay – may be enjoyed from the dining room. Joe Ryan's menus may read elaborately, yet what turns up on the plate usually makes sense: for instance a local black pudding served with an olive and tomato pesto on home-baked soda bread. The carte is helpfully flagged with healthy-eating options for the conscientious, and anyone looking to bump up their garlic levels might try a main-course Mediterranean vegetable pavé with aïoli, hummus and a garlic cracker. Fish gets a good showing, and meats take in ideas such as a duck breast with noodle salad, accompanied by a spring roll of leg confit and a bitter orange sauce. Finish perhaps with a papillote of warm tropical fruits on a bed of mixed fruits and roasted coconut. Grand wines from predictable regions suit the setting, and an unerring eye picks out quality wherever it settles. Look to Spain and Italy for variety, Australia and New Zealand for dependability, and California for both. Four house wines under £22 are also available by the glass.

CHEF: Joe Ryan PROPRIETOR: Francis Brennan OPEN: all week D only 7 to 9 CLOSED: Nov to 23 Dec, 2 Jan to Easter MEALS: alc (main courses £19.50 to £24). Set D £40 SERVICE: not inc, card slips closed CARDS: Amex, Diners, MasterCard, Visa DETAILS: 80 seats. 30 seats outside. Private parties: 120 main room, 35 private room. Car park. Vegetarian meals. Children's helpings. No children under 10 at D. No-smoking area. Wheelchair access (not WC) ACCOMMODATION: 49 rooms, all with bath/shower. TV. Phone. B&B £132 to £484. Rooms for disabled. Baby facilities

▲ Sheen Falls Lodge, La Cascade  

Kenmare
TEL: (064) 41600 FAX: (064) 41386
EMAIL: info@sheenfallslodge.ie
WEB SITE: www.sheenfallslodge.ie
follow signs for Glengariff from Kenmare; hotel signposted after about ½m

MODERN IRISH
£57–£68

In April 2000 Chris Farrell, a sous-chef here for three years, stepped into the shoes of Fergus Moore as head chef, a pretty tough act to follow. The dining room looks out over rushing water – hence the name – and the cooking is elegant enough to suit the lush surroundings. Much use is made of local organic produce, which might turn up as salmon smoked in-house, served with herb-dressed new potatoes and tapénade toast, or as a main course of scallops with pancetta, braised salsify and rocket pesto. Meat options have included corn-fed chicken breast topped with foie gras, served with spinach, wild mushrooms and morel cream, while desserts have yielded fig and almond tart with caramel sauce; Irish farmhouse cheeses with Parmesan biscuits are the alternative. No fewer than 18 countries are represented (some by only a single bottle) on an epic wine list that majors on the bewildering choice that France affords, from acres of Bordeaux and Burgundy to such less usual appellations as Irouléguy. A sommelier's selection offers a short cut, and prices open at £19 for Mastroberardino's Lacryma Christi del Vesuvio.

CHEF: Chris Farrell PROPRIETOR: Bent Hoyer OPEN: all week D only 7.15 to 9.30 CLOSED: 3 to 23 Dec, 2 Jan to 2 Feb MEALS: Set D £40 SERVICE: not inc, card slips closed CARDS: Amex, Diners, MasterCard, Visa DETAILS: 80 seats. Private parties: 120 main room, 20 to 60 private rooms. Car park. Vegetarian meals. Children's helpings. No smoking in 1 dining room. Wheelchair access (also WC). Music ACCOMMODATION: 61 rooms, all with bath/shower. TV. Phone. Room only £168 to £258. Rooms for disabled. Baby facilities. Swimming pool. Fishing

KILKENNY Co Kilkenny **map 16**

▲ Lacken House

Dublin Road, Kilkenny, Co Kilkenny
TEL: (056) 61085 FAX: (056) 62435
EMAIL: info@lackenhouse.ie

MODERN IRISH
£37–£58

New owners took over this white-fronted nineteenth-century house in Ireland's medieval capital just as the Guide went to press, though Nicola O'Brien, a mainstay in the kitchen under the previous regime, continues at the stoves. There are plans for refurbishment in the winter, and perhaps an updating and expanding of menus, but if they follow current form they might include tian of crab served on minted potatoes and topped with crème fraîche, followed by fillet of beef with Cashel Blue sauce, or roast duckling with orange star anise sauce served with rösti. The wine list makes a commendable effort to look beyond France. House Chilean and French (two of each) are £13.

CHEF: Nicola O'Brien PROPRIETORS: Trevor and Jackie Toner OPEN: Tue to Sat D only 6.30 to 10 CLOSED: 1 week Christmas MEALS: alc (main courses £14.50 to £20). Set D £25 SERVICE: not inc, card slips closed CARDS: MasterCard, Visa DETAILS: 30 seats. 20 seats outside. Private parties: 45 main room, 20 private room. Car park. Vegetarian meals. Children's helpings. No-smoking area. No music. Air-conditioned ACCOMMODATION: 8 rooms, all with bath/shower. TV. Phone. B&B £30 to £60

LETTERFRACK Co Galway **map 16**

▲ Rosleague Manor

Letterfrack
TEL: (095) 41101 FAX: (095) 41168
EMAIL: themanor@anu.ie
on N59 to Westport, 7m NW of Clifden

IRISH COUNTRY HOUSE
£27–£59

Overlooking sheltered Ballinakill Bay, right by the unspoiled Connemara National Park, this early-nineteenth-century manor house is magnificently sited. Rosie Curran, who has worked here on and off since 1997, is back at the stoves again. Seafood and local lamb are specialities of the kitchen, the former perhaps appearing at dinner as seared scallops with creamed leeks and a saffron sauce, the latter as a main-course serving of the loin with roasted peppers and a rosemary jus. The ever-popular fruity duck treatment might involve pairing a Barbary breast with caramelised pears and orange segments, while those who prefer to wait until dessert for their fruit might be rewarded by iced nougatine with mango and raspberry coulis. Lunch can be something of a hit or miss affair. The wine list is very fairly priced for Ireland, opening with house wines at £13.

CHEF: Rosie Curran PROPRIETORS: the Foyle family OPEN: all week 12.45 to 2.30, 8 to 9.30 CLOSED: early Nov to mid-Mar MEALS: alc (main courses L £6.50 to £10.50, D £14 to £21). Set D £30 SERVICE: not inc, card slips closed CARDS: Amex, MasterCard, Visa DETAILS: 65 seats. Private parties: 65 main room. Car park. Children's helpings. No smoking in dining room. No music ACCOMMODATION: 20 rooms, all with bath/shower. TV. Phone. B&B £50 to £150. Rooms for disabled. Baby facilities (£5)

LISDOONVARNA Co Clare **map 16**

▲ Ballinalacken Castle

NEW ENTRY

Lisdoonvarna, Doolin
TEL/FAX: (065) 7074025
EMAIL: ballinalackencastle@eircom.net
WEB SITE: www.ballinalackencastle.com
on R477, 2m N of Doolin

MODERN IRISH
£27–£48

Alhough the road leading to the castle may be long and difficult, the stunning scenery makes it all worthwhile. The castle is actually a house built in 1840 next to a Norman-looking keep, with commanding views of the cliffs of Moher and the Atlantic. In the rather Victorian ambience of the dining room, some impeccably modern food is served, mixing and matching Mediterranean and Eastern modes in ways that work well. Thai-spiced salmon spring roll with lemon grass, pesto couscous and a basil and pepper dressing is a United Nations of a starter that has been highly commended. Grilled turbot might be partnered with seared scallops and red pepper cream, while sound technique is evident in sauté beef fillet presented on garlic and herb mash and sauced with brandy and grain mustard. Vegetables are served in copious quantities, and for dessert crème brûlée arrives flavoured with ginger, and served with a honey wafer and prune and armagnac ice cream. Professional service and a concise and fairly priced wine list, opening with house Anjou at £12, complete the deal.

CHEF: Frank Sheedy PROPRIETOR: Denis O'Callaghan OPEN: Wed to Mon D only 7 to 8.45 CLOSED: early Oct to mid-Apr MEALS: alc (main courses £11 to £18) CARDS: Amex, MasterCard, Visa DETAILS: 40 seats. Car park. Vegetarian meals. No smoking in dining room. Music ACCOMMODATION: 13 rooms, all with bath/shower. TV. Phone. B&B £35 to £45

▲ Sheedys

Lisdoonvarna
TEL: (065) 7074026 FAX: (065) 7074555
EMAIL: sheedys@gofree.indigo.ie

MODERN IRISH
£25–£49

Renovations to this former farmhouse, built in the eighteenth century, have artfully exposed sections of the original stonework, which combine with areas painted terracotta and dark blue to create a style the owners characterise as 'the old with the new'. John Sheedy has a go at fulfilling that rubric with his cooking too, using traditional ingredients (Bonina black pudding for one), and offering dishes such as seafood chowder or Dover sole on the bone with garlic butter, alongside some modern flourishes. A starter of prawn spring rolls, with tomato and chilli jam and rocket salad, might be followed by loin of lamb with parsnip purée and a gravy of balsamic and mint. Desserts have included parfait of passion-fruit and toasted coconut served with raisins soaked in Malibu syrup, but also sticky toffee pudding for more cautious palates. Service is swift and efficient. Wines from southern Europe and the southern hemisphere kick off with Languedoc Sauvignon Blanc and Merlot at £13.

CHEF: John Sheedy PROPRIETORS: Martina and John Sheedy OPEN: all week D only 6 to 9 CLOSED: 31 Oct to 17 Mar MEALS: alc (main courses £13 to £18.50). Set D before 7 £15.95. Bar seafood menu available L and D SERVICE: not inc, card slips closed CARDS: Amex, MasterCard, Visa DETAILS: 35 seats. Private parties: 35 main room. Car park. Vegetarian meals. Children's helpings. No smoking in dining room. Wheelchair access (also men's WC). Music. Air-conditioned ACCOMMODATION: 11 rooms, all with bath/shower. TV. Phone. B&B £45 to £65. Baby facilities (£5)

MALLOW Co Cork **map 16**

▲ Longueville House

Mallow, Co Cork
TEL: (022) 47156 FAX: (022) 47459
EMAIL: info@longuevillehouse.ie
WEB SITE: www.longuevillehouse.ie
3m W of Mallow on N72 Killarney road

MODERN IRISH/FRENCH
£48–£57

The supply network is enviable: lamb and pork come from the O'Callaghans' own farm, fruit and vegetables are provided by the walled kitchen garden, and salmon and trout are caught in the nearby Blackwater River. With such ingredients to hand, son William O'Callaghan turns out dishes such as roast loin of lamb with a confit of the leg, and garden vegetable lasagne and golden oregano sauce. Guinea-fowl breast comes with a gâteau of red cabbage (with sultanas and apple) and a sauce of nutmeg (with cinnamon and vanilla). Strawberry vacherin with white chocolate sorbet is among the luxurious-sounding desserts. Opulent clarets and Burgundies are the bedrock of the list, but there are nods to other areas too. House wines start at £15.

CHEF: William O'Callaghan PROPRIETORS: the O'Callaghan family OPEN: all week D only 6.30 to 9 CLOSED: mid-Dec to early Mar MEALS: Set D £36. Bar menu 12.30 to 5 SERVICE: not inc, 10% for parties of 8 or more CARDS: Amex, Diners, MasterCard, Switch, Visa DETAILS: 74 seats. Private parties: 40 main room, 16 and 18 private rooms. Car park. Vegetarian meals. Children's helpings. No smoking in 1 dining room. Wheelchair access (not WC). No music. ACCOMMODATION: 22 rooms, all with bath/shower. TV. Phone. D,B&B £65 to £250. Baby facilities. Fishing (£5)

Occasional music *in the details at the end of an entry means live or recorded music is played in the dining room only rarely or for special events.* No music *means it is never played.*

MIDLETON Co Cork map 16

Farmgate

Coolbawn, Midleton
TEL/FAX: (021) 4632771

TRADITIONAL IRISH
£11–£37

Local fish and shellfish, free-range poultry and organic lamb are on the menu at this busy, spacious restaurant in the centre of town. Getting the thumbs-up from reporters have been warm salad of ginger- and soy-marinated chicken with roasted red peppers and garlic potatoes, and fruit pavlova. Lamb might be served as a rack on a bed of leeks and potatoes with rosemary and garlic jus, while salmon has come with tomato provençale and scallion butter. A serviceable wine list opens with house Spanish at £12.

CHEFS: Máróg O'Brien and David Doran PROPRIETOR: Máróg O'Brien OPEN: Mon to Sat L 12 to 4, Wed to Sat D 6.30 to 9.45 CLOSED: 25 Dec to 2 Jan MEALS: alc (main courses L £5 to £9, D £8 to £16) SERVICE: not inc CARDS: MasterCard, Visa DETAILS: 60 seats. 25 seats outside. Private parties: 20 main room, 20 private room. Vegetarian meals. Children's helpings. No smoking in 1 dining room. Wheelchair access (also WC). Music. Air-conditioned

MOYCULLEN Co Galway map 16

Drimcong House

Moycullen, Galway
TEL: (091) 555115 and 555585 FAX: (091) 555836
EMAIL: drimcong@indigo.ie
on Galway to Clifden road, 1m W of Moycullen

MODERN IRISH
£39–£47

Herbs and vegetables from the grounds of this 300-year-old house feature in Gerry Galvin's varied and imaginative cooking. Many dishes on the set-price menu of three to five courses suggest metropolitan simplicity allied to rural sophistication, as in tomato and olive salsa to accompany a grilled fish fillet, or oysters grilled with goats' cheese, bacon and lovage. Equally appealing are main dishes such as confit duck leg with pan-fried breast and a foie gras sauce, a warm seafood gâteau, and meltingly rare pan-fried pigeon breast. A reporter's flawless passion-fruit soufflé, at a supplement of £3, came decorated with nasturtium and borage, while coffee or tea is accompanied by little chocolate fruit cakes. Vegetarians have options on both the main menu and on a separate vegetarian page. Pre-dinner drinks are taken in a relaxing room with an open fire, and service is 'friendly but not overbearing'. A global range of wines, with classical French leanings and enthusiastic tasting notes, is helpfully arranged by style. House wines are £13.50.

CHEF: Gerry Galvin PROPRIETORS: Gerry and Marie Galvin OPEN: Tue to Sat D only 7 to 9.30 CLOSED: Christmas to March MEALS: Set D £26 to £30 SERVICE: not inc CARDS: Amex, Diners, MasterCard, Visa DETAILS: 50 seats. Private parties: 50 main room, 10 to 25 private rooms. Car park. Vegetarian meals. Children's helpings. No smoking in dining room. Wheelchair access (also WC). Music

All entries, including Round-ups, are fully indexed at the back of the Guide.

NEWPORT Co Mayo map 16

▲ Newport House

Newport, Co Mayo
TEL: (098) 41222 FAX: (098) 41613
EMAIL: kjt1@anu.ie

IRISH/FRENCH
£46–£66

Salmon and sea trout fishing from river or loughs is a major attraction at this elegant, creeper-covered Georgian mansion. Lunch is light and casual, the big event a six-course dinner. One of four starters is usually home-smoked wild salmon, while others might take in baked goats' cheese, fried fillets of brill, or, for devoted carnivores, terrine of black pudding with rhubarb purée and Madeira sauce. Local Clew Bay oysters are an optional extra, and main courses favour fish – perhaps pan-fried turbot with creamed leeks in a white wine and saffron sauce – though meat and poultry also feature: maybe roast poussin with glazed vegetables and a mustard, tarragon and brandy sauce.

After salad, and cheese, desserts might take in home-made sorbets and ice creams, and fruit-based temptations such as poached pear with honey and walnut ice cream. For those craving greater variety the chef 'will vary a dish on request'. Impressive listings from Bordeaux, Burgundy and the Rhône provide plenty to plough through, while a concise selection of house recommendations offers a nifty short cut. Australia and Italy provide many fine bottles, though there are few bargains to be had. House Côtes du Rhône (Guigal) is £17 (£3.50 per glass).

CHEF: John Gavin PROPRIETORS: Kieran and Thelma Thompson OPEN: all week D only 7 to 9.30 (light L 12 to 2.30) CLOSED: Oct to 18 Mar MEALS: Set D £34. Light L menu SERVICE: not inc, card slips closed CARDS: Amex, Diners, MasterCard, Visa DETAILS: 38 seats. Private parties: 12 main room. Car park. Children's helpings. No smoking in dining room. Wheelchair access (not WC). No music ACCOMMODATION: 18 rooms, all with bath/shower. Phone. B&B £79 to £164. Rooms for disabled. Baby facilities. Fishing

OUGHTERARD Co Galway map 16

▲ Currarevagh House

Oughterard, Connemara
TEL: (091) 552312 and 552313 FAX: (091) 552731
EMAIL: currarevagh@ireland.com
4m NW of Oughterard on Hill of Doon lakeshore road

IRISH COUNTRY HOUSE
£31–£37

Meals at this Victorian family home, set in beautiful Connemara countryside near the shore of Loch Corrib, follow an unchanging formula of five courses served at 8pm. Modern ideas contrast with traditional ones: grilled goats' cheese and tomatoes on ciabatta, or fillets of brill with a pesto crust on the one hand, roast leg of lamb with mint sauce, or roast beef with Yorkshire pudding and horseradish sauce on the other. Thought goes into the balance of the menus. For example, criterion soup (the Hodgsons' name for a rich meat broth from their stockpot) is followed by baked Corrib trout, then chicken wrapped in Parma ham with polenta cakes and mustard sauce, with hot lemon sponge and, as always, Irish cheeses to finish. Occasionally, soup may be dropped, and a savoury, such as mushrooms en croûte, may be served after dessert. Seconds are offered, though choice is not (but special requirements can be catered for with notice). House wines are £10.80 and £11.90, and the mainly French list, with a useful page of half-bottles, is reasonably priced.

CHEF: June Hodgson PROPRIETORS: Harry and June Hodgson OPEN: all week D only 8 (1 sitting) CLOSED: 15 Oct to 1 Apr MEALS: Set D £22.50 SERVICE: 10%, card slips closed CARDS: MasterCard, Visa DETAILS: 30 seats. Private parties: 10 main room. Car park. Children's helpings. No smoking in dining room. No music ACCOMMODATION: 15 rooms, all with bath/shower. B&B £55 to £125. Fishing

SHANAGARRY Co Cork map 16

▲ Ballymaloe House

Shanagarry, nr Midleton
TEL: (021) 4652531 FAX: (021) 4652021
EMAIL: res@ballymaloe.com
WEB SITE: www.ballymaloe.com
2m outside Cloyne on Ballycotton road

IRISH/INTERNATIONAL
£30–£55

Ballymaloe is a large, well-established operation with many sectors – hotel, farm, cookery school and restaurant – and at the heart of it all are warm hospitality and conscientious, seasonally motivated cooking of considerable flair. Daily-changing menus might offer hot cucumber soup with dill cream, proceeding to roast home-grown pork with apple sauce and red cabbage, or spiced goujons of turbot with aïoli and chilli salsa. 'Rory's refined fish and chips' is one way of selling comfort food, or opt for steak and kidney tart with spiced aubergines. Finish with Irish farmhouse cheeses, yoghurt and cardamom mousse with a citrus fruit salad, or Worcesterberry tart. The extensive wine list is especially strong in French classics, as well as half-bottles. House Duboeuf is £15.

CHEF: Rory O'Connell PROPRIETORS: the Allen family OPEN: Mon to Sat L 1 to 1.30 (1 sitting), all week D 7 to 9.30 (Sun buffet only) CLOSED: 23 to 27 Dec, 7 to 14 Jan MEALS: Set L £19.50, Set D £34.50 SERVICE: not inc, card slips closed CARDS: Amex, Delta, Diners, MasterCard, Visa DETAILS: 100 seats. Private parties: 10 main room, 8 to 32 private rooms. Car park. Vegetarian meals. Children's helpings. No children under 10. No smoking in 1 dining room. No music ACCOMMODATION: 33 rooms, all with bath/shower. Phone. B&B £80 to £160. Rooms for disabled. Baby facilities. Swimming pool

WATERFORD Co Waterford map 16

Dwyers

8 Mary Street, Waterford
TEL: (051) 877478 FAX: (051) 877480
EMAIL: dwyerest@tinet.ie

FRENCH/IRISH
£23–£46

The Dwyers have given their dining room an extensive refurbishment since last year's Guide, the more modern feel thrown into relief by a display of antique and unusual glass. In the kitchen, things remain much as before, which is to say inventive and inspiring. Kidneys of spring lamb with caramelised shallots and oloroso sherry is an elegant way to start a dinner, and may be followed by an intermediate soup, such as lettuce or gazpacho, before a main dish that may take in anything from Thai green vegetable curry to honey-roast loin of bacon with cabbage and apple. Fish gets a look-in too, perhaps in the form of chargrilled salmon with a herb sauce. Tiramisù or strawberry mille-feuille are among the sweet things. Wines are an intelligent international selection, their prices opening at £10.

CHEFS: Martin Dwyer and Declan Coughlan PROPRIETORS: Martin and Sile Dwyer OPEN: Mon to Sat D only 6 to 10 CLOSED: 1 week Christmas, bank hols MEALS: alc (main courses £12 to £16.50). Set D 6 to 7 £15 SERVICE: not inc CARDS: Amex, Diners, MasterCard, Visa DETAILS: 36 seats. Private parties: 20 main room, 8 private room. Vegetarian meals. Children's helpings. No smoking in 1 dining room. Wheelchair access (also WC). Music (£5)

Round-ups

Looking for a suitable place to eat can be a lottery, especially if you are travelling around the country with no set plans in mind. The Round-up section is intended to provide some interesting gastronomic possibilities, whether you find yourself in a strange city centre or the northern outposts of Scotland. Pubs are becoming increasingly valuable as sources of high-quality food, but the listings also include modest family-run enterprises in country towns, racy café/bars and ethnic restaurants in big cities, and a sprinkling of hotel dining rooms in all parts of the land. Dip into this section and you are almost bound to find somewhere that suits your needs and pocket. Entries are based on readers' recommendations supported by inspectors' reports. Sometimes restaurants appear in the Round-ups instead of the main entry section because seasonal closures or weekly openings limit their usefulness, or because there are changes in the air, or because positive feedback has been thin on the ground. Reports on these places are especially welcome, as they help to broaden our coverage of good eating places in Britain. Round-up entries (outside London) are arranged alphabetically by locality within England, Scotland, Wales, Channel Islands and Northern Ireland.

England

• **ALDEBURGH** (Suffolk)
Café 152 152 High Street, (01728) 454152. A small, comfortably spaced room serving 'the freshest of fish', such as halibut in a simple butter and herb sauce, or perfectly cooked cod and good chips. Others have praise for rich onion soup, 'first-rate' tiny three-cheese soufflé, green bean salad with artichoke hearts, steamed ginger pudding with roasted pears, and good coffee. Cheerful service. Wines are from Adnams. Open Tue to Sun (and Mon in summer).

• **AMERSHAM** (Buckinghamshire)
Gilbey's 1 Market Square, (01494) 727242. Wines are sold at shop prices here, and in Gilbey's in Ealing (see London Round-ups), and the food is suitably simple to help show them at their best. There are no starters on the set menu, but main dishes might be garlic and herb chicken breast with red wine risotto, or vegetarian lasagne. A la carte dishes, some dual-priced as starters and mains, include salad of slow-roasted fennel and tomatoes, Gruyère and shallot tart, and potted ham with home-made piccalilli. Follow perhaps with salmon wrapped in Savoy cabbage, and finish with banana and toffee sponge. Open all week.

• **ARDINGTON** (Oxfordshire)
Boar's Head Church Street, (01235) 833254. The wisteria was flourishing in this quintessential English village for one summer visitor, and the owner's cheerful welcome added to the feeling of comfort. The pub may be quaint, but the cooking is unashamedly modern: fritto misto, fennel risotto with parsley pesto, roast monkfish with lime and nero sauce, and shredded duck are joined by more traditional dishes such as beef and onion pie. 'Sublime' pavlova finished one meal. Look out for the bin-ends on the wine list. Closed Sun D.

• **AYMESTREY** (Herefordshire)
Riverside Inn Aymestrey, (01568) 708440. Changes are afoot at this lovely sixteenth-century half-timbered inn by the River Lugg, with a new chef due to arrive as the Guide went to press, but Val and Steve Bowen's philosophy is unlikely to change, and menus will most probably continue to feature local produce and home-grown salads and vegetables, with home-brewed beers in the bar. A terrace by the riverside makes for pleasant al fresco dining in summer. Four house

wines at £9.95 are also available by the carafe or half-carafe. Open all week.

• **Barham** (Kent)

Old Coach House Dover Road, (01227) 831218. The simple menu of this restaurant-with-rooms – run by Jean-Claude Rozard for the past 13 years – reflects the owner's Gallic origins with fish soup, moules marinière, langoustines with mayonnaise, and steak au poivre. Look out for daily blackboard specials, which focus on local and home-grown produce: white asparagus hollandaise, lobster soufflé, bouillabaisse, and turbot béarnaise might appear depending on what local suppliers bring, or the seasons provide. Open all week D.

• **Barnard Castle** (Co Durham)

Blagraves House The Bank, (01833) 637668. Named after the family that owned it in the seventeenth century, the house actually dates back to Elizabethan times when it was the Boar's Head inn. Hospitality is nowadays administered by Elizabeth and Kenneth Marley. They open for dinner only, five nights a week (Tue to Sat), offering a generous carte and set-price menu in the first-floor dining room. Meals typically begin with risotto of Mediterranean vegetables, or coarse chicken and leek terrine, followed by beef Wellington, sauté calves' liver and bacon, or roast seafood with a Chablis sauce. Home-made ice creams come in flavours such as lemon curd, cinder toffee, or Turkish delight. Open Tuesday to Saturday.

• **Barnstaple** (Devon)

Lynwood House Bishop's Tawton Road, (01271) 343695. Close to Exmoor and Dartmoor, and only a mile from the town centre, this Victorian gentleman's residence has been run by the Roberts family for over 30 years. Plenty of local produce is used in the kitchen, particularly fish from Clovelly and St Mawes. The house speciality is the 'seafood pot' of assorted fish on a bed of rice with white wine and cream sauce. Other options might include duck liver pâté, or chunky fish soup, followed by crab pancakes, grilled Dover sole with parsley butter, or pan-fried local lamb with red wine sauce. Crème caramel is a typical dessert. Closed Sat L and Sun.

• **Barton on Sea** (Hampshire)

Oysters Marine Drive, (01425) 627777. First impressions of this elegant, modern clifftop restaurant bode well. The view is great, whether outwards over the Solent or inwards to the open-plan kitchen. A weekly-changing menu offers inventive, modern fish cooking, with occasional meat interlopers: roast rack of Dorset lamb with crunchy herb and mustard topping, for example. Starters of salmon rillettes, or sardines with tomato and fennel, might be followed by cod ceviche with spicy avocado purée, or tuna piccata on pipérade, with brioche pain perdu to finish. 'Quick, non-intrusive' service, and a good selection of wines are other pluses. Accommodation available. More reports, please.

• **Barton-upon-Humber** (North Lincolnshire)

Elio's 11 Market Place, (01652) 635147. Eat al fresco in the courtyard in summer, or in the tile-floored dining room decorated with Venetian masks, at this long-standing trattoria. Fish predominates, the daily specials blackboard typically offering scallops in garlic butter with asparagus, chargrilled tuna with salsa verde, or sea bass with fennel sauce. The rest of the menu is a traditional range of pizzas, pasta and meat dishes such as saltimbocca alla romana, or chicken cacciatora. Exclusively Italian wines start at £9.25 a litre. Accommodation in two rooms is now available. Open Tue to Fri L and Mon to Sat D.

• **Baslow** (Derbyshire)

Cavendish Hotel Baslow, (01246) 582311. 'First-class service' and superb views over the Chatsworth estate are reason enough to visit this well-bred hotel, but the food also deserves a mention. Reporters have enjoyed informal meals in the conservatory, where you can eat a little or a lot (afternoon tea is also served here). Mushroom and oxtail soups are praised, along with asparagus in a walnut oil dressing (a blackboard extra); Chatsworth sausages and mash, and lemon sole with 'crisp, floury, Stonehenge' chips arrive attractively on colourful plates, rounding off with vanilla rice pudding with lemon curd ice cream. Open all week.

• **Bath** (Bath & N.E. Somerset)

Firehouse Rôtisserie 2 John Street, (01225) 482070. Expect something 'slightly different' in this light, airy Georgian building, whose Californian/ South-western cuisine also embraces the food of Louisiana and the Mediterranean. Giant green-lipped mussels come with Caribbean habañero dip, goats' cheese crostini with pesto Genovese. LA-style gourmet pizzas are topped with Louisiana chicken sausage, or artichoke hearts, pesto, sun-dried tomatoes and Pecorino. The rôtisserie and grill contribute Santa Fe grilled chicken quesadilla, and Bourbon barbecued free-range loin of pork stuffed with apricots, melted onions and red eye gravy. Short list of interesting, fairly priced wines from £10.95. Closed Sun.

Hole in the Wall 16 George Street, (01225) 425242. Although reborn as a brasserie, open all day, and smartly refurbished by owner Chris Chown, the calm, serene ambience, is unchanged. Of some fifteen choices on the carte many are priced as starters or main dishes. Mediterranean and eastern influences appear in confit duck leg with spicy tamarind sauce, and seared swordfish with fennel, mango and kumquat chutney. More impressive may be the simplicity of juicy, pink rack of lamb with pea and mint purée. 'Dense, creamy, well-flavoured' home-made ice creams come in such flavours as plum, apple and calvados. Wines are reasonably priced. Open Mon to Sat.

Rendez Vous Provençal 2 Margarets Buildings, (01225) 310064. French owned and run, this small restaurant close to the Royal Crescent is aptly named and popular with locals: 'most of the clientele were on first-name terms with staff'. Reporters recommend goats' cheese and spinach tartlet, and Toulouse sausage with couscous, taken respectively from the evening carte and set lunch menus. Fishcakes with seafood sauce, and chicken with green peppercorn sauce, are other options at dinner; finish with strawberry tartlet. Closed Sun.

Woods 9–13 Alfred Street, (01225) 314812. Expect good-value set-price menus, plus a short carte and daily specials at this brasserie in a Georgian terraced house, located in a cul-de-sac opposite the Assembly Rooms. Pork and pheasant terrine and braised shank of lamb with Madeira sauce are typical, while the dessert menu is titled 'Cholesterol Corner': choose blackberry parfait or Grand Marnier crème brûlée. A dozen wines are available by the glass from a list with helpful descriptions. Open all week.

• **Beetham** (Cumbria)

Wheatsheaf Beetham, (015395) 62123. A sixteenth-century village inn by a river, just off the A6, has been converted to a restaurant (a small bar remains) on two levels with the main dining room upstairs. The light lunch menu has open sandwiches, while the set menu (available at lunchtime and early evening) has three choices at each course. Recommendations have been registered for black pudding and pork terrine followed by fillet of Scotch beef with a selection of vegetables; half-portions are available for children. Short, mainly New World wine list. Open all week.

• **Bilbrough** (North Yorkshire)

Three Hares Main Street, (01937) 832128. Dine under beamed ceilings, with log fires and scented candles adding their bit to the atmosphere, at this smart country inn in an affluent village a few miles from York. The tenor of both bar and restaurant menus is British-Continental, taking in corn-fed chicken with Puy lentils and dauphinoise potatoes, and monkfish on a mound of tomato and pepper dice, served with two sauces. Ice creams are a forte, a black cherry and kirsch one complementing an almond and pear tart, or a nutmeg version accompanying three little custard tarts. Drink real ales or something from the mostly New World wine list. Open Tue to Sun L, Tue to Sat D.

• **Birmingham** (West Midlands)
Berlioz Burlington Hotel, 120 New Street, (0121) 643 9191. 'Quiet, attentive and unobtrusive' service has been praised in this sumptuous hotel restaurant. The carte delivers plenty of fish: perhaps fishcake with green pea risotto, or char-grilled smoked salmon with latkes as starters, and sea bream with a sweet pepper coulis or John Dory with spring onion and tomato salsa as main courses. The meat interest extends to peppered duck breast with a red onion marmalade, or traditional Scotch beef. A table d'hôte menu offers three choices at each course. Open all week.
Café Ikon Ikon Gallery, Oozells Square, Brindley Place, (0121) 248 3226. This converted Victorian school, housing a contemporary art gallery with a bustling café, is a popular venue with crowds of young people and a good place for a light lunch of hearty and reasonably priced tapas and raciones after viewing the exhibits. Anchovies and garlic bread, grilled sardines, and chorizo al Jerez are typical, and paella (for two people) has been enthusiastically endorsed. Open all day until 11 Tue to Sat, and Sun until 6.
Maharaja 23–25 Hurst Street, (0121) 622 2641. Major refurbishment of this modest restaurant was due as the Guide went to press, but the long-running menu is unlikely to change. It offers mostly conventional northern Indian dishes – prawn bhuna with pilau rice has been approved, and tandoori specialities include seekh kebab – though diners are encouraged to ask about the chef's daily specials: more unusual items include K. K. mattar (lotus root with peas) and 'Maharaja tikkian' (fried patty of 'smashed' potato, peas and spices). House wine is £7.70. Closed Sun.
San Carlo 4 Temple Street, (0121) 633 0251. The 'vibrant' San Carlo, with its swish interior, is one of a small chain offering modern Italian food with a remarkable 150 dishes to choose from; an additional blackboard selection of fish makes decision-making even more difficult. The usual trattoria-style food is evident in Parma ham and melon, cured beef, or prawn cocktail, with a large range of pizzas, chargrilled meats and pasta dishes to follow. Open all week.

• **Bishop's Stortford** (Hertfordshire)
The Lemon Tree Water Lane, (01279) 757788. Two bright and stylish rooms, painted in Mediterranean colours of terracotta and yellow, with a relaxed atmosphere, form this restaurant in a Georgian terraced property, located down an obscure back lane (it is advisable to phone for directions). The food, like the décor, is modern European, the set-lunch menu producing on one occasion a rich, smooth fish soup with rouille, and terrine of ham, foie gras and apricot, followed by slow-roast belly of pork, and seared salmon with stir-fried cabbage. Finish with vanilla parfait with caramelised banana. Open Tue to Sat and Sun L. More reports please.

• **Blackpool** (Lancashire)
Kwizeen 47–49 King Street, (01253) 290045. Even restaurant consultant Patrick McDonald, as seen on TV, couldn't persuade owners Tony Beswick and Marco Calle-Calatayud to change the name of their restaurant, so Kwizeen it remains. The innovative menu might start with roast pigeon in liquorice sauce, or marinated salmon en croûte with sweet piccalilli, with maybe fillet steak and king prawns with marsala sauce to follow from a reasonably priced carte. A bargain lunch is £5.50 for two courses. Lemon tart, 'a model of its kind', has been served with sweet basil ice cream. Closed Sun.

• **Blewbury** (Oxfordshire)
Blewbury Inn London Road, (01235) 850496. The innovative menu at this country pub restaurant betrays the Gallic origins of chef-proprietor Franck Peigne, but he takes inspiration from all over the world. Starters of cured venison with Moroccan tabbouleh, Brittany pancakes with smoked salmon, and a terrine of

lobster demonstrate the serious intentions of the kitchen. Sea bass with tempura king prawns, and shiitake and artichoke risotto with Swiss chard, have been main courses during the summer. Vegetables and salads are extra. Complex desserts might include prune and Armagnac parfait with ginger tea bread, and lemon tartlet with mango sorbet. Closed Mon L and Sun.

• **Bradford** (West Yorkshire)
Symposium 7 Albion Road, Idle, (01274) 616587. This lively wine bar and restaurant justifies both descriptions with an extensive list of wines from £7.50 and an adventurous menu. Typical offerings are crab and langoustine bisque or tartlet of smoked chicken and haggis, followed by lamb shank with parsnip couscous and a bitter-sweet orange and ginger sauce. The two-course business lunch at £6.95 could include terrine of game pâté with pear chutney, and lamb's liver with creamy cabbage or spaghetti with spinach. Open Tue to Fri and Sat D.

• **Brighouse** (West Yorkshire)
Brook's 6–8 Bradford Road, (01484) 715284. Slightly exotic, this dinner-only bistro (it opens at 6pm) offers starters of cold-sliced, five-spiced belly pork on Japanese yakisoba noodle salad with chilli sugar, and grilled squid satay with satay cream sauce. Main dishes might include braised lamb shoulder, smoked bacon and Puy lentils, or pigeon breasts on bubble and squeak with blueberry juice. Desserts come home with summer pudding, apple and blackberry pie, or chocolate cheesecake with black cherries. The inclusion, among 'favourite specials', of warm Spam fritters on salad probably makes it unique in the Guide. Open all week D (L Dec only).

• **Brighton** (East Sussex)
Bushby's Brasserie 24 Ship Street, (01273) 321233. This centrally located converted shop in the famous Lanes area of the town takes an international route on its menu. Thai dressing with salmon fishcakes, buffalo mozzarella wrapped in vine leaves, and roulade of smoked salmon and trout are typical starters. Main courses of roast duck breast with plum sauce and game chips, or sea bass on a bed of poppadoms, continue the globetrotting. Daily specials have included chargrilled ostrich steak (with game chips again) and Sussex pork and leek sausages. Open all week.

• **Brinkworth** (Wiltshire)
Three Crowns Brinkworth, (01666) 510366. Very much a dining pub, the blackboard menu lists no starters, but no matter as main dishes are substantial. Lunchtime snacks are mainly traditional (salads, sausages and rolls), while the blackboard menu (available lunch and dinner) might include wild boar with Stilton and apricots in a creamy rich sauce, or smoked chicken in mustard sauce. The repertoire includes pies of steak and kidney, lamb and mint, veal and mushroom or seafood, while fish may be as exotic as a duo of barramundi and blue marlin. Firmly traditional desserts include a wicked sticky toffee pudding. Open all week.

• **Bristol** (Bristol)
Blue Goose 344 Gloucester Road, (0117) 942 0940. The eponymous bird is easily spotted above the doorway of this converted corner shop on the A38. Inside, the blue theme is continued to good effect. Lively, modern menus might offer butternut squash lasagne with goats' cheese cream and calypso spiced sauce to start, perhaps followed by pot au feu of cod with sugar-snap peas and shiitake mushrooms, or lamb niçoise with rösti and candied aubergine. Sweets are even wackier creations such as deep-fried coconut ice cream, or plum tomato and vanilla Tatin. Two dozen wines stay under £20. Open Mon to Sat D only.
Tico Tico 24 Alma Vale Road, (0117) 923 8700. A light and airy shop conversion off Whiteladies Road, whose yellow walls and closely set tables with plastic cloths produce a lively and informal atmosphere. Described as a 'brasserie with modern cooking', it has produced Caesar salad with goats' cheese bruschetta, chargrilled tuna, and Poire William sticky sponge pudding with

vanilla sauce. Friendly service and a small international wine list; bread is charged extra. Open Tue to Sat D only.

• **Brockenhurst** (Hampshire)
Thatched Cottage 16 Brookley Road, (01590) 623090. The small, comfortable and elegant oak-beamed dining room of this quaint and pretty cottage has a view of the open-plan kitchen where chefs go quietly about their modern cooking, using ingredients from the New Forest and locally landed seafood. Wild mushroom pancake, or tempura and sushi of salmon are typical starters, perhaps followed by a just-cooked, de-shelled half lobster, or fillet of beef marinated in Guinness with basil mash. Imaginative if pricey wine list. Accommodation available. Open Tue to Sun L, Tue to Sat D.

• **Bromfield** (Shropshire)
Cookhouse Bromfield, (01584) 856565. This roadside eaterie is a light and airy all-day café from 11 to 6.30, then turns into a bistro in the evening. Start the day with an American breakfast: pancakes and maple syrup (served between 9–11am), or hold on until the 'In and Out' lunch menu, offering watercress soup, breast of chicken and lemon tart. Reporters have commended chargrilled salmon on creamy tagliatelle and bread-and-butter pudding in the evening bistro. Good real ales, and young helpful staff. Open all week.

• **Broxton** (Cheshire)
Frogg Manor Nantwich Road, (01829) 782629. John Sykes, the 'only mildly eccentric' host of this eighteenth-century manor, which enjoys views of the Welsh mountains, offers a menu priced at 30 guineas: just one of many unusual features. The vast choice extends to no fewer than six pages, and the cooking ranges from traditional English fare such as steak pie, to dishes as far-flung as Mongolian chicken, or chicken 'Montezuma' (South American style). In between might be poached pear and Roquefort salad, or pan-fried halibut rolled in oats, with apples Suzette or bread-and-butter pudding to finish. Open all week.

• **Burgh Le Marsh** (Lincolnshire)
Windmill 46 High Street, (01754) 810281. In the shadow of a working windmill, which produces flour for the home-baked bread, this Lincolnshire restaurant offers a friendly atmosphere and a 'cheery smile' from the helpful staff and owners. Pan-fried salmon fishcake on a spicy tomato sauce has been a successful starter, while mains might take in poached fillet of sea bass in a basil hollandaise, or half a wild mallard duckling in a rich chasseur sauce. Pecan tart with cream has been a well-received dessert. Open Sun L, Tue to Sat D.

• **Bury St Edmunds** (Suffolk)
Ravenwood Hall Rougham, (01359) 270345. This family-run sixteenth-century country hotel and restaurant offers good choice in its two- or three-course set-price menu. There are a few oriental surprises, such as a starter of crispy fried teriyaki beef strips on a bean salsa, but more typical of the style are mushrooms baked with Marsala in filo pastry, or scallops with duchesse potato, smoked bacon and spinach in cheese sauce. A reporter's excellent salmon fillet would have been even better without the elaborate accompanying vegetables. Vegetarian choices might include courgette charlotte or sun-dried tomato risotto. Open all week.

• **Buxton** (Derbyshire)
Columbine 7 Hall Bank, (01298) 78752. This simple restaurant has many small rooms, including a cellar for smokers, and offers a light lunch menu of pasta, hot salads or baguettes, plus a mostly European carte running from Cornish crab pâté to rack of lamb with sauté kidneys; vegetarians are catered for with a separate menu. Daily specials might include sea bass baked with lemon and tarragon. Desserts are also featured on blackboards: perhaps hot chocolate kumquat cake. Open L Thur to Sat (summer only); D Mon to Sat (closed Tue in winter).

• **Cambridge** (Cambridgeshire)
Charlie Chan 14 Regent Street, (01223) 359336. Dramatic tinted glass at the entrance leads to both conventional ground-floor and nightclub-like first-floor rooms, the latter sporting a chrome bar, mirrored wall, and well-spaced round tables on a dark blue carpet. Helpful advice from a friendly waiter led a reporter to a pleasing meal of lightly battered king prawns, deep-fried aubergine, chicken and sweetcorn soup, aromatic duck with a truly crisp skin, lemon chicken, and soft discs of sliced scallop in a hot red sauce with ginger, chilli, carrot, onion and water chestnuts. Toffee bananas, plain lychees and Chinese tea made a refreshing finish. Open all week.
Loch Fyne 37 Trumpington Street, (01223) 362433. What used to be the Little Rose pub is now a branch of this growing chain, with a buzzy atmosphere, and friendly and efficient service. As at the original in Cairndow (see main entry, Scotland), Loch Fyne oysters are the centrepiece, whether on ice accompanied by a hot sausage, or baked with spinach and cheese. Otherwise, the excellent fish and seafood ranges from bradan orach (strongly smoked salmon) to a full-blown shellfish platter. Main dishes might be chargrilled halibut with pesto, or herb-crusted roast cod. Also a short, good-value wine list; and a shop selling their own products. Open all week.
Sala Thong 35 Newnham Road, (01223) 323178. Service is charming and unobtrusive in this cheerful, unpretentious, basically decorated eating house, with sweetly melodic Thai background music. Start perhaps with hot and sour chicken coconut soup with galangal. To follow might be mild green chicken curry, stir-fried pork with ginger, and fried prawns in light crisp batter coated with a 'wonderfully gloopy' peanut sauce. Light and delicate tapioca pudding with palm seed and lotus nuts is far removed from old school dinners, while grass jelly drink is 'nicer than you would expect'. Open all week.

• **Caunton** (Nottinghamshire)
Caunton Beck Main Street, (01636) 636793. Food is served every day of the year from 8am to 11pm in the light, airy rooms of this 100-year-old beamed pub. Seasonal, daily and sandwich menus are available all day, with 'express' meals from 12 noon (except Saturday evenings), while breakfast can be taken in the morning or by late risers from 3 to 6pm. Cooking styles range from traditional English breakfast to modish cod fillet with olive oil mash, or breast of chicken with tarragon and prawn mousse. There are multiple wine lists too, with four house wines at £10.45, and another 40, listed by style, on the main list.

• **Cheltenham** (Gloucestershire)
Beaujolais 15 Rotunda Terrace, (01242) 525230. Despite the name, the description as 'restaurant français' and the snails in puff pastry with garlic butter, the menu is more modern British than French. A good-value table d'hôte (Tue to Sat L £7.95, Tue to Thur D £10.95) might offer marinated seafood salad, followed by lamb leg steak with redcurrants, or goats' cheese and tomato tartlet, with chocolate parfait or English cheeses to finish. A la carte possibilities are mild curried smoked haddock korma with onion and coriander naan bread, or chicken breast on artichoke heart and pine kernel salad. A characteristically imaginative dessert is apple and cinnamon bread-and-butter pudding with butterscotch sauce and cider sorbet. Open Tue to Sat.
Daffodil 18–20 Suffolk Parade, (01242) 700055. One might wonder why this 'young, stylish' place among the spa's antique shops isn't called Fred and Ginger or Oscar, since you eat where the seats of this old cinema used to be and watch the action in the kitchen where the screen once was. Main courses that have notched up notices include juicy steak Diane on rösti, with good, simple vegetables; sea bass with Chinese stir-fried greens and crispy noodles; and haddock with polenta. Birthday

celebrants were pleased with their Genoese iced sponge cake. Coffee is good and service is efficient, if sometimes jokey. Closed Sun.

• **Chettle** (Dorset)
Castleman Hotel Chettle, (01258) 830096. In this solidly traditional small country-house hotel the daily menu uses local produce in mostly classical style, but often incorporating novel ideas. Examples include potted trout with cream cheese and dill, and warm chicken and bacon salad with shallot and cassis dressing. Mediterranean-style fish soup might use bass, scallops, monkfish and brill, and a typical vegetarian option is aubergine, kidney bean, red pepper and mozzarella Wellington. Desserts are mostly light and fruit-based, although toffee and banana sponge with custard, or white chocolate cheesecake with poached apricots, are today's variations on familiar dishes. Open Sun L, all week D.

• **Chichester** (West Sussex)
Comme Ça 67 Broyle Road, (01243) 788724. The restaurant and garden room are decked about with hanging baskets, hops and dried flowers, and lead to an enclosed patio for al fresco eating. In this attractive setting all-French meals are beautifully presented and attentively served. Successes reported this year include crab and Gruyère tartlet, chicken with blackcurrant and pink peppercorn sauce, and pear and chocolate soufflé. Fish and seafood might feature as mussels in cider, or cod with orange and pistachio sauce. 'Les glaces' may include gin and lavender. Sunday lunch is quite an event. Closed Sun D and Mon.

• **Chillesford** (Suffolk)
Froize Inn Chillesford, (01394) 450282. Local dialect is responsible for Froize, referring to Orford Friary close to this fifteenth-century pub. Local fish is well represented on both bar and restaurant menus: Butley Creek oysters, bacon-wrapped scallops or seafood froize (a stuffed pancake) might be among the options, but that depends on availability and the season. Chef/proprietor Alistair Shaw makes the most of his local smokers and butchers, offering smoked duck with a balsamic dressing, and beef and beer pie. Snacks including salads and cobbers (Suffolk brown rolls) are available from the bar. Closed Mon.

• **Chipping Campden** (Gloucestershire)
Cotswold House The Square, (01386) 840330. Christa and Ian Taylor have acquired this honey-coloured Georgian Cotswold stone hotel and installed Roux-trained chef Alan Dann, who majors on luxury ingredients and extravagant presentation. Duck foie gras, lobster, crab, and queen scallops are typical ingredients, sometimes combined into towers, swirls and other feats of artistry. Main courses could include red bream with marinated squid and saffron sauce, or veal and Bayonne ham with cep risotto and sage sauce. Mascarpone ice cream speared with carrot strips accompanies a tiny strawberry and almond filo tartlet. Reports please. Hicks Brasserie is also on the site and altogether different (Caesar salad and braised lamb shank). Open all week D and Sun L.

• **Chittlehamholt** (Devon)
Highbullen Chittlehamholt, (01769) 540561. Standing on high ground in extensive parkland, this relaxed, informal Victorian Gothic-style mansion is a well-appointed hotel offering plenty of sporting activities, including its own golf course, fishing, indoor swimming pool, and tennis courts. Good home cooking at dinner offers the likes of curried mushrooms, grilled sweetbreads on croûtons, and black pudding on parsnip mash, followed by lamb en croûte, duck breast with juniper and red wine, or seafood au gratin. Desserts might include sticky toffee pudding or chocolate pot with Grand Marnier. Light lunches are served in the bar. Open all week.

• **Clifford's Mesne** (Gloucestershire)
Yew Tree Inn May Hill, (01531) 820719. Paul and Anna Hackett are still settling into this old cider press of a pub in the depths of rural Gloucestershire. Downstairs is the bar, popular with walkers, and upstairs the stone-walled

restaurant. 'Ambitious' and 'trendy' menus, carefully sourced, offer five choices at each stage. This might mean asparagus with hollandaise, or a fish soup with saffron and Ricard to start with, followed by chargrilled fillet of smoked beef with beetroot, or a well-balanced dish of lamb with spicy couscous and a white port mint sauce. The wine list is 'just right', with half-a-dozen red and white house choices. Sunday lunch is traditional. Closed Mon.

• **Coggeshall** (Essex)

Baumann's Brasserie 4–6 Stoneham Street, (01376) 561453. Mark Baumann's lively restaurant, with its smartly set tables, wooden floors, and walls covered in pictures and mirrors, is every inch a brasserie. That goes for the menu too, where classic Caesar salad, coconut crab cake with pickled cockles, and griddled prawns yakitori set the tone at first courses. Mains range from British bangers with sticky cheese and bacon mash, to glazed duck with stir-fried greens and oranges, and 'Billingsgate Best' fish. Opt for Belgian waffles with toffee syrup to finish. Closed Sat L, Sun D and all day Monday.

• **Colchester** (Essex)

North Hill Exchange Brasserie 19 North Hill, (01206) 769988. This Georgian-fronted restaurant, formerly an ironmonger's (which explains the listed kettle hanging over the door), offers modern European brasserie cooking on a generous carte, supplemented by a daily set-price option (Mon to Fri L and D, 3 courses £12.50) and light snacks. Californian butternut squash soup, or Isle of Wight crab salad, might be followed by grilled sea bass fillets with ginger, garlic and soy; Scotch beef with Roquefort butter; or honey-roast duck with rösti and apple sauce. Maple syrup crème brûlée with almond Budapest biscuits, or waffles with hot chocolate sauce, may appeal for dessert. Closed Sat L and Sun.

Warehouse Brasserie 12 Chapel Street North, (01206) 765656. Located by the stage door of the Warehouse theatre, the brasserie creates a smart impression with a green awning over its entrance, leading to a high-ceilinged, salmon-pink dining room, with some tables on raised areas and a gallery over the bar. French influences dominate the cooking, with a few modern twists, and smoking, parcelling and stuffing are favoured techniques. Start perhaps with goats' cheese in filo pastry, or smoked chicken and coconut roll with banana chutney, then move on to pork and prune roulade with a mustard and wine sauce, finishing with crème brûlée. Open Tue to Sat.

• **Constantine** (Cornwall)

Trengilly Wartha Inn Nancenoy, (01326) 340332. The inn lies in gardens and meadows in wooded Polpenwith creek, a mile from the village of Constantine. Plenty of vegetarian choice – courgette and ricotta cheese boudin, or leek and asparagus croustade – as well as fish and other local produce go to make up this dining pub-cum-hotel's bar meals and two- or three-course dinners. Blackboards and printed menus appeal with wild rabbit terrine, Cornish venison with cabbage and pearl barley, and garlicky monkfish with baby broad beans. Chocolate and prune tart or the best of West Country cheeses are ways to finish. As many as 20 wines can be had by the glass, and the Maguire and Logan families make the most of the inn's freehouse status, offering a good range of real ales. Open all week.

• **Coppull Moor** (Lancashire)

Coppull Moor 311 Preston Road, (01257) 792222. Barry Rea has been at the helm of his small restaurant for ten years, and the format of five courses at dinner and four for Sunday lunch is a tried-and-tested one. The former might include home-made pasta with seafood, followed by tomato and red onion soup, fillet of Whitby trout, and honey roasted spring lamb, with a rhubarb crème brûlée to finish. Sunday lunch may consist of spinach, crab and smoked salmon roulade, spring vegetable soup, beef fillet and sticky toffee pudding. Open Sun L, Tue to Sun D.

• **Corbridge** (Northumberland)
The Valley Old Station House, Station Road, (01434) 633434. This is an Indian restaurant with a difference, set in an old station house. Special features include the 'Passage to India' train service from Newcastle on which a waiter serves drinks and takes your order, which will be ready by the time you arrive at the restaurant. Added to the full range of curry house favourites on the long menu is a page of sometimes unusual chef's recommendations, such as rajha chingri sagwala (king prawns cooked with fresh spinach), and mangsho pesta ke shadi (topside of beef cooked with mild spices and pistachios). Recent refurbishment has brought, among other things, ostrich hide seating to the bar area. Open Mon to Sat D only.

• **Corby Glen** (Lincolnshire)
Woodhouse Inn Corby Glen, (01476) 550316. In this nineteenth-century stone-built inn, owned and run by Michael and Linda Pichel-Juan, a 'symphony of pinks strikes a warm if idiosyncratic chord'. In its cottage garden is a unique wood-burning Sardinian oven, used only at weekends to roast beef, pork and lamb. Sardinian spiced sausage may be on the menu as well, but bistro-style fare such as steak, grilled salmon, or mushroom stroganoff tend to predominate. Desserts are as thoroughly English as treacle tart, or blackberry and apple crumble. Mr Pichel-Juan's recommendations of his Sardinian wines (offered by the glass, part-bottle or bottle) have been approved. Open all week.

• **Diss** (Norfolk)
Weaver's Wine Bar Market Hill, (01379) 642411. In this medieval building there is plenty of choice, both in wines – a dozen by the glass, two dozen at £11.95 – and in the carte and fixed-price menus. Consider avocado with prawns to start, or quenelles of smoked haddock mousseline with asparagus and soft poached egg in a crêpe. Main dishes range from pan-fried skate wing with black butter and capers to lightly poached breast of pigeon sliced and draped over sweet pickled red cabbage with a white onion and bread sauce. They suggest allowing an hour and a half to fully enjoy the long lunch menu. Open Tue to Fri L, Tue to Sat D.

• **Doddiscombsleigh** (Devon)
Nobody Inn Doddiscombsleigh, (01647) 252394. The name was appropriate at one time in this charming inn's long history. Now there are crowds, especially at lunchtime, efficiently served from a vast, mainly traditional, repertoire of bar meals, including such dishes as local ostrich liver and juniper berry pâté: an old regional speciality? The long restaurant menu occasionally ventures as far as France for inspiration, and is supplemented by other dishes cooked to advance order: half a roast duckling with orange sauce, for example. The list of West Country cheeses has extended to over 50, and the 600-strong wine list is an education. Bar open all week, restaurant open Tue to Sat D only.

• **Elton** (Cambridgeshire)
Loch Fyne Oyster Bar The Old Dairy, (01832) 280298. An excellent stop-off point for the A1. One of the sister restaurants of the original in Cairndow (see main entry, Scotland), serving oysters on ice, bradan orach (strongly smoked salmon), scallops, plus seafood platters, a hot vegetarian pie, sausages and steak for non-fish eaters. A short well-priced wine list offers six half-bottles and four by the glass. Closed Sun D.

• **Evershot** (Dorset)
Acorn Inn Fore Street, (01935) 83228. 'Tess of the d'Urbervilles was here' has not so far been found carved on a beam in this sixteenth-century village pub, but it could be. Dishes on the long and ambitious blackboard menu have included mushroom and hazelnut pâté, and a salad of baked goats' cheese with raspberry vinaigrette to start, followed by grilled tuna steak on caramelised onions and sweet pepper, or oriental-style roast duck breast. There are simpler, more traditional dishes too, and a short, basic bar menu. Open all week.

• **Evesham** (Worcestershire)
Evesham Hotel Coopers Lane, (01386) 765566. Originally a farmhouse, later modernised, the sixteenth-century building's grounds contain six mulberry trees and a magnificent Cedar of Lebanon. A reporter enjoyed crab with Brie followed by smoked chicken pasta, and the somewhat quirky menu runs to devilled chicken livers, Taiwanese chicken, and smoked salmon royale among starters. Veal steak Kenvail and Maltaise quail might be main courses; lengthy descriptions unravel any mysteries in the names of dishes. Equally idiosyncratic puddings have been Walpole treacle tart and spiced Sangria jelly. Open all week.
Riverside The Parks, Offenham Road, (01386) 446200. The declared intention of Vincent and Rosemary Willmott is to make their riverside hotel 'a real home', and their menus (a table d'hôte dinner at £29.85) begin with an assiette de crudités. There are modern touches, such as deep-fried blue cheese polenta with tomato salsa, or spicy marinated strips of chicken on stir-fry vegetables, but more typical dishes are salmon fishcakes with tartare sauce, mulligatawny soup, half a crisp roast duckling, and meringues with fresh strawberries and cream. Closed Sun D and all day Mon.

• **Exeter** (Devon)
Galley 41 Fore Street, Topsham (01392) 876078. Chef-proprietor Paul Da-Costa-Greaves is a man with a mission. His 300-year-old cottage with splendid views of the Exe and hills beyond is the setting for a seriously fishy menu. His style touches on many influences, including Cajun and Thai spicing with a fair mix of French saucing and Mediterranean ingredients. John Dory with Bombay potatoes and a vast slab of turbot may be preceded by a spicy crab salad or Thai fishcakes. Meat and vegetarian dishes must be requested specifically, and desserts might offer tiramisù or lemon and vanilla cheesecake. Open Thur to Sun L, Tue to Sun D.

• **Flitwick** (Bedfordshire)
Flitwick Manor Church Road, (01525) 712242. A splendid Georgian house in beautiful grounds next to the church at the edge of the village; for fun you can stroll through the tunnel folly, or inspect all the sardine dishes in the lounge. Poached ham hock and braised lentil terrine with a mustardy dressing is a typical starter, followed by sea bass with a warm snail and black olive vinaigrette, or mille-feuille of grilled halloumi. Finish perhaps with rhubarb crumble soufflé, or a tart of figs with ruby port ice cream. Open all week.

• **Folkestone** (Kent)
Pauls 2A Bouverie Road West, (01303) 259697. The joint chef-patron of this relaxed bistro says they are trying to 'get away a little from too much cream', although customers still lap it up. A devoted member of the fan club might enjoy creamy mushroom soup with chopped almonds, or mussels and prawns baked in cream with Chablis and Parmesan, then roasted quail with a creamy asparagus and sherry sauce. Desserts from the trolley mine a similar vein. Other clubs which don't require membership are the lunch club buffet at £4.95, and the three-course supper club at £9.95. A carvery menu replaces the carte for Sunday lunch. House wines are £8.65.

• **Forton** (Lancashire)
Bay Horse Inn Bay Horse, Forton, (01524) 791204. Modern pub food is served in this traditional eighteenth-century coaching inn, originally a post office, with log fires and a garden as added attractions. The same menu is offered in the bar and dining room. Reports have commended terrine of chicken and black pudding, and mushroom and tarragon soup among starters, while main courses might run to scallop and monkfish kebab, shank of lamb with potato and swede mash, or seared salmon with spinach and sweet chilli sauce. Finish with yoghurt pannacotta with honeycomb, or a

selection of British cheeses. Open Tue to Sat.

El Nido Whinney Brow Lane, (01524) 791254. There is little Spanish in the three-course early-bird dinner at £10.95, but brasserie and à la carte menus are more Iberian, with conventional 'Continental' dishes too. For the real fiesta, go for the £15.50 table d'hôte, where avocado and smoked chicken salad with chilled cucumber is dressed with garlic, lime and sesame seeds, or eggs are baked with prawns in a cream sauce. To follow consider sliced spiced duck breast with a port and berry sauce or gammon steak with prunes and a sherry sauce. Useful Spanish wines too. Open Sun L and Tue to Sun D.

• **Fotheringhay** (Northamptonshire)

Falcon Inn Fotheringhay, (01832) 226254. Part of the Huntsbridge partnership (within striking distance of Huntingdon and Cambridge), along with the Pheasant at Keyston, the Three Horseshoes at Madingley and the Old Bridge in Huntingdon (see main entries). Here, Ray Smikle is the chef, following the group formula of 'a little or lots, whatever you fancy'. The general menu or indeed the 'bargain lunches' might consist of duck spring rolls with a spicy Asian coleslaw, then Moroccan sweet spiced summer vegetables, or lamb's liver with mash and rosemary gravy. The same approach extends to sweets such as black cherry and almond tartlet with passion fruit and guava sorbet. The Falcon is still proud to be a pub complete with games and Adnams beers, and has an attractive and evenly marked-up wine list. Closed Mon L.

• **Fressingfield** (Suffolk)

Fox and Goose Fressingfield, (01379) 586247. Situated in the heart of the village, this sixteenth-century building with old beams and a tiled floor has had the church as its freeholder from the very beginning. Choose from a bar snack menu offering Caesar salad or a steak sandwich, or more substantial dishes from the fixed-price menu and carte: pork and herb terrine with chutney, green Thai chicken curry, and baked sharp lemon tart. Sunday lunch is a traditional roast; children's and vegetarian menus are also available. Open all week. .

• **Frome** (Somerset)

Croft's 21 Fromefield, (01373) 472149. A 'modest, no fuss' sort of place on one of the main roads into Frome that is nevertheless quite quiet. Every two months the Brothertons put on a Thai week (Sara Brotherton is Thai), introducing authentic tastes of deep-fried meat pancakes, red beef curry with aubergines, and sweet dumplings in coconut milk. Then they return to a more familiar set meal of five choices at each stage, perhaps smoked salmon stuffed with smoked trout mousse, honey-braised lamb shank, and apple charlotte or a fruity meringue. Open D Tue to Sat.

• **Gedney Dyke** (Lincolnshire)

Chequers Main Street, (01406) 362666. This white pub with a red clay pantile roof is 'one of the best places to eat in the Fens', according to a regular. Fish is a speciality, although meat dishes are not neglected: Gloucester Old Spot in assorted cuts, pigeon breast and Lincoln Red steaks all make an appearance. Locally supplied fish choices are offered on the chalkboard, perhaps sea bream in pesto, while Thai crab cakes, and smoked salmon and Puy lentil tartlet, are on the carte. Desserts include banoffi pie or white chocolate mousse. Open all week.

• **Gillan** (Cornwall)

Tregildry Hotel Gillan, (01326) 231378. The dramatic clifftop position of the hotel makes for excellent views from the dining room, which caters mainly for staying guests, offering a daily-changing set-price menu of three choices per course. Starters always include a soup, such as smoked haddock chowder with bacon, as well as something like crab salad with tarragon mayonnaise. Chargrilled ribeye steak with fries is likewise a fixture among main courses, other options perhaps taking in brill fillet with Muscat and pink grapefruit sauce. There is no need to choose between desserts or cheese since both come as part of the price. Open all week D only, Mar to Oct.

• **Gosfield** (Essex)
Green Man The Street, (01787) 472746. The lunchtime cold table at this Greene King pub remains a strength, according to a regular, who singles out the rib of beef and tongue for special praise; other options include whole dressed salmon and home-cooked ham. In the evening, long blackboard menus offer wide-ranging options, from chicken liver pâté to Thai crab cakes for starters, and main courses such as pork and apple casserole, or lamb chops with port and cranberry sauce. From the sweet trolley, home-made fruit pies are recommended. The beer is fresh and wines are good value. No food Sun D.

• **Grampound** (Cornwall)
Eastern Promise 1 Moor View, (01726) 883033. This Chinese restaurant naturally specialises in local seafood cooked in many styles: mussels and scallops steamed in their shells are starters, crab and lobster (ordered in advance) are braised with ginger and spring onion or black bean sauce, sea bass is steamed whole with the same garnish while salmon can be stir fried with mango. Meat is not neglected and as well as chicken, pork and beef, there is lamb prepared four ways. No smoking in the restaurant nor is there any service charge or tipping. Open D all week, exc Wed.

• **Great Whittington** (Northumberland)
Queens Head Great Whittington, (01434) 672267. Near the historic village of Corbridge, this former coaching inn in 'award-winning' Great Whittington offers daily supplies of fresh fish, which may turn up as seared scallops on a bean salad or halibut with deep fried pancetta. Local game is offered on the carte: venison medallions matched with chestnuts and a thyme Burgundy sauce along with 'first-rate' lamb's liver. Desserts may be 'the best bread-and-butter pudding I can remember'. Good service too. Closed Mon.

• **Great Yarmouth** (Norfolk)
Seafood Restaurant 85 North Quay, (01493) 856009. Fish lovers will appreciate the extensive menu which lists no fewer than 16 piscine starters including oysters, kalamari, taramasalata and whitebait, while equally fishy grilled, poached or sauced mains number a whopping 19. Lobster is taken straight from the tank and given a thermidor, Mornay or garlic butter treatment. Steaks or surf and turf can be had too, as well as baked cheesecake and summer pudding for desserts. This 'warm, welcoming' restaurant is run by Greek Cypriots Chris and Miriam Kikis. Closed Sat L and all day Sun.

• **Grimsthorpe** (Lincolnshire)
Black Horse Inn Grimsthorpe, (01778) 591247. This may be a quintessential rural pub – old stone building, hanging baskets, etc. – but the cooking is more ambitious than average pub food. Starters might include roast quail with a redcurrant marmalade and quails' eggs, while 'particularly praiseworthy' mains might take in Barbary duck breast with caramelised apple, or ribeye of Lincoln Red beef with a bacon and cabbage cake. Rhubarb crumble is a typical dessert. Wines on the lengthy list start at around £10. Open all week.

• **Grimston** (Norfolk)
Congham Hall Lynn Road, (01485) 600250. This elegant Georgian manor changed hands late in 1999, with new chef James Parkinson coming on board after stints working for the likes of Gordon Ramsay and John Burton-Race (see eponymous main entries, London). His modern British cooking style shows French influences and takes inspiration from the abundant home-grown produce. Dinner typically opens with dishes like pithiviers of pigeon and foie gras with artichoke mousseline, or potted crab with coriander and a vinaigrette of King's Lynn shrimps, while main courses might include roast beef fillet with foie gras dumplings and Burgundy jus, or curried cod with cauliflower purée and

chive velouté, with hot chocolate fondant to finish. Open all week.

• **Guildford** (Surrey)

The Gate 3 Milkhouse Gate, (01483) 576300. Once a milking shed, the Gate is off an alleyway in the oldest part of Guildford. This 'welcoming small restaurant' with 'efficient' service delivers modern British set and à la carte menus. Thai vegetable risotto or tuna salad with sweet sherry dressing might be on the set menu, with the carte including mille-feuille of Parma ham crackling, and sea bass with chorizo oil. Desserts range from kumquats mulled in port with white chocolate ice cream to apple and calvados crêpes. Open Tue to Sat.

• **Harrogate** (North Yorkshire)

Bettys 1 Parliament Street, (01423) 502746. This is the original of these very English tea rooms, scattered throughout North Yorkshire, which supplement the usual staples – salads, sandwiches, soups, cakes, scones etc. – with light lunches that might include Betty's Yorkshire rarebit, Swiss alpine macaroni, or mushroom sausages. Open all week.

Oliver's 24 24 King's Road, (01423) 531838. This bright restaurant in a Victorian house offers imaginative modern Yorkshire cooking with Italian influences (chef Dean Sowden has won an award for his risottos). At the simpler end of the scale might be Whitby cod with Jersey royals and tartare sauce; at the other might be poached smoked haddock with smoked cheese and chive mash and a mustard velouté, or pan-fried pork tenderloin with sage and onion risotto and balsamic dressing. Desserts range from hazelnut praline pannacotta with poached pears and chocolate sauce to vanilla crème brûlée with crushed Smarties. Bar open Tue to Sat all day and Mon D, restaurant open Mon to Sat D only.

Rick's Just for Starters 7 Bower Road, (01423) 502700. Although it's far from 'fast food' you can eat quickly, as did the reporter who specially praised bread, soup and crêpes enjoyed in flying visits. Many dishes are priced as starters or main courses, and there is plenty for vegetarians – mushroom and pepper pâté, melon with figs, or Rick's pastry box of oyster mushrooms in port cream sauce. Smørgasbørd for two is £9.50, steaks come with traditional garnish or a choice of two sauces, and baked chicken breast is stuffed with apple and apricot. Closed Sun L.

• **Harrow** (Greater London)

Golden Palace 146–150 Station Road, (020) 8863 2333. Behind the striking white facade is an attractive interior with blonde wood, and spectacular flower arrangements. The carte is quite long and among extra specialities are stir-fried chicken with mixed fruits, steamed tofu with dried scallop and diced chicken, and marrow with dried shrimps and vermicelli hotpot. Vegetarians can enjoy fried dried turnips, Chinese mushrooms, straw mushrooms in a black pepper sauce or vegetarian set meals. Dim sum are on the main menu and available in the evening too. Open all week.

• **Harvington** (Worcestershire)

Mill at Harvington Anchor Lane, (01386) 870688. An idyllic setting on the banks of the River Avon, just outside the village, make this Georgian red-brick mill a very pleasant place to be in fine weather. Dinner in the main restaurant might begin with chicken, wild mushroom and venison terrine, or spicy prawn dumplings with an oriental sauce, before pork tenderloin stuffed with Parma ham and mozzarella, or grilled tuna loin with gazpacho dressing. Finish perhaps with sticky toffee pudding. Light lunches in the Chestnut Tree bar might include beef stroganoff, lemon sole with parsley, caper and lemon butter, or Colin's pork pie. Open all week.

• **Helston** (Cornwall)

Nansloe Manor Meneage Road, (01326) 574691. This handsome family-run Georgian manor house is set in woodland at the end of a long drive and offered 'an enchanting evening' for one couple. A fixed-price three-course menu has produced ragoût of Cornish mussels and tiger prawns, followed by roasted duck with a vegetable risotto, and finishing with spiced chocolate bread-and-butter pudding with chocolate ice cream. Service has been pleasant and friendly. Open all week D and Sun L; light lunches Mon to Fri.

• **Hereford** (Herefordshire)
Café at All Saints High Street, (01432) 370415. This wholefood/vegetarian café is probably the only establishment in the Guide run by a working priest; all profits go towards the upkeep of the Grade I listed medieval church in which it is set. Though it is an informal self-service café, the food is worthy of serious attention. Soup of the day might be fennel, green pea, parsley and lemon, and main dishes have included a salad of local asparagus with roast courgette, spinach and shavings of Skirrid cheese. There are also good sandwiches, ploughman's, cakes and organic ice creams. Closed Sundays, of course, otherwise open 8.30 to 5.30, and for dinner (booking essential) on the last Friday of the month.

• **Houghton Conquest** (Bedfordshire)
Knife & Cleaver The Grove, (01234) 740387. This converted pub with Victorian-style conservatory restaurant standing opposite the village church also boasts a terrace with fountain and an orchard garden. A mainly European-influenced menu has plenty of fish, listed as market specials, and reasonably priced three-course dinners might include Mediterranean fish soup, followed by leg of Welsh lamb and finishing with pecan pie. Closed Sat L and Sun D.

• **Hovingham** (North Yorkshire)
Worsley Arms Hovingham, (01653) 628234. Anthony and Sally Finn have taken over at the honey-coloured coaching inn and clearly mean to make wine a big thing, with plans to open up the cellars so that guests can choose their bottles straight from the bins. House wines are £11 to £16, with eight by the glass. The Cricketer's Bistro (open every day for lunch and dinner) is an alternative to the rather formal dining room, where menus offer pork either as cutlet with Parmesan polenta and roast ratatouille, or on a successful black pudding mash with a rich cider jus; braising and searing are two favourite techniques. 'Excellent' baked egg custard with red fruit coulis, or orange posset for pudding. Open all week D and Sun L.

• **Ilkley** (West Yorkshire)
Bettys 34 The Grove, (01943) 608029. Tea and cakes are not the only thing on offer at this quaint English tea room, one of a mini-chain in North Yorkshire. As well as soups, sandwiches, salads and pasta, expect to find more substantial daily specials, as well as a full English breakfast. Given the status of the Bettys brand in these parts, expect queues out of the door in the height of the tourist season. Open all week.

• **Ipswich** (Suffolk)
Scott's Brasserie 4A Orwell Place, (01473) 230254. Comfortable, first-floor brasserie in a row of shops a little away from the town centre. Choosing Scott's hors d'oeuvre platter (for two) would be a good way to try various starters: feta cheese and basil tart, duck and spring onion samosas, and Brie, chive and walnut pâté. Venison sausages arrive on a cheesy mash, or you could go for caramelised pork steaks with lentils and hoisin sauce for main course, with black cherry clafoutis or 'rather good' blackberry and mascarpone crème brûlée afterwards. Wine prices are reasonable, with house wine £10.75. Closed Sat L and all day Sun.

• **Kelsale** (Suffolk)
Hedgehogs Kelsale, (01728) 604444. Spot the chef out in the cottage garden collecting herbs for the good-value two- or three-course menu. Among successful starters this year have been cheese beignets with basil and mozzarella, and duck and game terrine with rhubarb chutney. These might be followed by roast pigeon breast with chorizo and red cabbage, or baked cod with creamed leeks. Well-presented puddings might include cherry cheesecake, or pancakes or meringues in some guise. Attentive, efficient service and an adequate, fairly

priced wine list. Open Wed to Fri and Sun L, Tue to Sat D.

• **KIBWORTH BEAUCHAMP** (Leicestershire)
Firenze 9 Station Street, (0116) 279 6260. Lino Poli cooks and wife Sarah cheerily runs front-of-house in this small, sunnily decorated open-plan restaurant smartly done out with Florentine pictures on the walls. The menu sounds an Anglo-Italian note, and has delivered fresh langoustines wrapped in pancetta, accompanied by leaves 'with a fine nutty, balsamic dressing'; and 'wonderfully tender' lamb with sweetbreads, peas and mint; and poached peach with amaretti, and rich and creamy pannacotta. Portions tend to be generous, and wines are mostly Italian. Open Tue to Fri and Sat D.

• **KING'S LYNN** (Norfolk)
Riverside King's Lynn Arts Centre, 27 King Street, (01553) 773134. In the 500-year-old timbered building which houses the Arts Centre, the restaurant has a delightful setting overlooking the river. Generous bowls of mussels, leek soup, and Arbroath smokies have been approved starters, as well as a main course of lambs' liver and bacon on mash with good vegetables, and plum and almond tart. Light lunch dishes are also available. Service has been good too. Closed Sun.

• **KINTBURY** (Berkshire)
Dundas Arms 53 Station Road, (01488) 658263. Located on a little island between canal and river, this long-established pub-restaurant draws wine-lovers for David Dalzell-Piper's superb list, over 200-strong, and for his traditional English menus with a few Mediterranean incursions. Home-cured gravlax, home-potted shrimps, and grilled scallops have been praised, as have main courses of roast duck breast, steak, and fried pigeon breast with wild mushrooms. Other classic dishes might include calves' liver and bacon, or rabbit with aubergine purée and mustard sauce. For puddings there is frozen coffee and praline mousse, or apricot crème brûlée, and on the bar menu you could find bang bang chicken salad alongside steak and kidney pie. Closed all day Sun and Mon D.

• **KNIGHTWICK** (Worcestershire)
The Talbot Knightwick, (01886) 821235. Sisters Annie and Wiz Clift show admirable devotion to seasonal and local produce at their fourteenth-century family-run pub by the River Teme. What they can't produce themselves, or gather from the wild, they buy from local farmers, the only exception to the rule being fish, which is delivered daily from Cornwall or Wales. The restaurant menu might offer pickled octopus salad, home-made black pudding, a platter of home-cured meats, cider-roasted pork loin stuffed with mushrooms and kidney, or loin of lamb stuffed with crab, garlic and ginger and served on laverbread mash, while the bar menu goes in for simpler fare. Drink home-brewed beers. Open all week.

• **KNUTSFORD** (Cheshire)
Belle Epoque 60 King Street, (01565) 633060. The art nouveau-style interior may seem ostentatious to some, just what's needed for others, as the setting for traditional English cooking with an occasional Italian twist. Recommended have been Caesar salad, seared pork fillet, and duck breast 'cooked pink and tender', or there might be garlic mushroom tart, followed by saddle of rabbit stuffed with vegetables, or calf's liver with mash and Madeira gravy. Finish with apple pie with calvados, or British and Irish cheeses. Prices are not cheap, but portions are generous and technique generally good. The wine list includes a good smattering of half-bottles and half-litres. Closed Sat L and Sun.

• **LAVENHAM** (Suffolk)
The Swan High Street, (01787) 247477. Leaded windows, thick beams, heavy wrought-iron candelabras and a gallery lend a distinctive medieval feel to the comfortable, attractive dining room in this wonderful old building in picturesque Lavenham. Cooking is mostly of a traditional nature: perhaps gâteau of crab and avocado, or parsley and ham terrine among starters, followed by

chicken with leeks and a port sauce, rolled plaice fillets with a prawn cream sauce, or beef fillet with white wine and shallots. Home-made desserts are the likes of treacle tart, or baked Bramley apple with sauce anglaise. Open all week.

• **Leeds** (West Yorkshire)

Bibis Minerva House, (0113) 243 0905. Always busy, the draw is the lively atmosphere and extensive Italian menu of antipasti, blackboard specials, grills, vegetarian dishes, pizza and pasta. Specialities include fillet steak with truffled foie gras and Madeira sauce, and breadcrumbed chicken stuffed with Taleggio and Parmesan, while pizzas – the house version is topped with mozzarella, dolcelatte, Parma ham and tomato – are always popular. 'Good service.' Open all week.

Brio 40 Great George Street, (0113) 246 5225. On a central corner site behind the town hall, this modern, minimalist, cool venture with a bustling atmosphere offers a real taste of Italy. Recommended dishes have been pasta stuffed with spinach, grilled sea bream, and a light panettone bread-and-butter pudding with crème anglaise. Otherwise choose from twelve starters, nine pasta dishes and nine main courses, plus daily specials that might include 'melt-in-the-mouth' salmon. Friendly and efficient service. Closed Sun.

Bryan's 9 Weetwood Lane, (0113) 278 5679. This is where you come for 'the finest fish and chips anywhere', writes a reporter who regularly detours over 50 miles for them. Starters include the 'prawn speciality' of king, butterflied and kebab styles, home-made mackerel pâté and Thai fishcakes. Seafood pizza and pasta are offered too but Bryan's raison d'être is fish fried in beef dripping. It comes in various sizes, with most also available grilled. Halibut and whole lemon sole on the bone have been particularly praised, so have chips, mushy peas, and even the bread and butter. House wine is £9.25 per litre. Open all week.

Olive Tree Oaklands, (0113) 256 9283. This Greek-Cypriot taverna, in a Victorian building on the city ring road, represents both cultures, with interesting Greek wines outnumbering the Cypriot. Locally sourced lamb is used for dishes such as moussaka, kleftiko and arni me frouta (stuffed with apricots, prunes and apples with apricot sauce), while chicken is cooked in styles associated with Zakinthos, Hydra and mainland Greece, some using home-made yoghurt. Meze can be chosen à la carte or as a set selection at £15. Trifle, not typical of Yorkshire, incorporates apricot jam, rosewater, egg custard and almonds. Open all week.

Paris Calverley Bridge, (0113) 258 1885. Under the same ownership as Leodis (see main entry), this roomy restaurant in a Victorian building offers a similar modern British brasserie-style menu. Plenty of fish and seafood appear, mostly seared or grilled, with perhaps tandoori monkfish with coriander risotto among starters, mains taking in grilled lemon sole on a broth of Parma ham and prawns. Other options might be charred pigeon breast with leek, apple and black pudding, followed by roast duck breast with parsnip fritters. Tempting puds are based on chocolate or fruit. There is an impressive list of around 150 wines, and a set-price lunch deal (also Sat D) includes wine. Closed Sat L.

• **Lichfield** (Staffordshire)

Chandlers Corn Exchange, Conduit Street, (01543) 416 688. High vaulted ceilings and stained-glass windows might lend a church-like look, but the atmosphere in the spacious brasserie-style dining room is buzzy. Menus scan the Orient and Med to produce blackened duck breast with sesame and ginger, and then maybe saddle of rabbit, or chicken tournedos. Reasonably priced set-price deals supplement the carte, and a 'fresh fish board' might list marinated tiger prawns with lime leaf and ginger, or half-lobster with sun-dried tomato hollandaise. Desserts have included truffle mousse with champagne and strawberries. Open all week.

• **Little Bedwyn** (Wiltshire)
Harrow Inn Little Bedwyn, (01672) 870871. Ambitious menus in this pub-restaurant offer simple classics and less simple, eclectic cooking. They look Eastward for tandoori seafood fillets with mint yoghurt, or roast free-range quails with oriental spices. More often, though, the focus is on modern versions of traditional dishes: grilled turbot with spinach and fresh summer truffles, or confit of Gascon duck, honey and thyme. A reporter's 'splendidly cooked' grey-leg partridge confirmed Roger and Sue Jones's wise sourcing of materials: game from local shoots, shellfish from Brixham market and foie gras, truffles and poultry from Rungis. Alcoholic desserts have included peach Melba, and sherry poured over vanilla ice cream with marinated raisins. Wide-ranging, fairly priced wine list, from £12.50. Closed Sun D and Mon.

• **Little Eccleston** (Lancashire)
The Smithy Cartford Lane, (01995) 670485. A fine conversion of buildings into a family-run restaurant with traditional country atmosphere, summed up by the horse brasses on display. The Gibson family offer an early evening set menu at just over ten pounds (cheaper for children), perhaps potted salmon and chicken liver pâté followed by poached salmon with prawn sauce or steak Diane. Dishes on the carte are along the same lines: Fleetwood smokie, roast rack of lamb and beef Wellington. Closed Sun D and all day Mon.

• **Liverpool** (Merseyside)
North Garden 28 Nelson Street, (0151) 709 4247. The new, enlarged, redecorated North Garden, with waiters in smart silk waistcoats, impressed an experienced Chinese inspector. After well-flavoured soups, roast duck 'was a real treat with a deep red skin and a melt in the mouth texture and superb taste'. Soy chicken too 'could not be faulted'. Homely is his word for halibut hotpot, its pieces of fillet, lightly coated with batter in rich oyster sauce and the pot lined with Chinese leaves and crispy pork. Another hotpot providing a 'taste of home-cooked comfort food' is yam and belly pork.

• **Longdon Green** (Staffordshire)
The Red Lion Inn Longdon Green, (01543) 490250. This neat and well-appointed family-run pub uses local producers or suppliers for all the meat and vegetables on its long, ambitious menu. Among 'grills' are the expected steaks, chicken and lamb, but also fried cod, steak and mushroom pie, and curry of the day. In the dinner menu Eastern influence shows in Thai, Oriental and tandoori chicken, but for a reporter the cooking that made his Sunday lunch so enjoyable was more homely. It included salmon in a parcel with butter lemon sauce, accompanied by courgettes and carrots with coriander, with warmed marmalade cake and ice cream as a very happy ending. Closed Sun D, and Mon exc bank hols.

• **Lower Oddington** (Gloucestershire)
Fox Inn Lower Oddington, (01451) 870555. New owners of this pretty Cotswold pub are Kirk and Sally Ritchie (formerly managers at Lygon Arms, Broadway, see main entry). Their keen interest in wine shows in the well-chosen, fairly priced list, and a displayed collection of corkscrews and other wine antiques. The modern menu has included baked sardines with lemon and herb butter, lamb tajine with couscous, and steak and mushroom pie, while blackboard specials might be shoulder of lamb with a garlic, sage and cider sauce, and in a happy deviation from the obvious, a sticky almond cake with poached summer fruits. Open all week.

• **Low Laithe** (North Yorkshire)
Carters Knox Manor Summer Bridge, (01423) 780607/780473. Upstairs at this 250-year-old former silk mill is a beamed dining room, full of clocks, where Yorkshire produce gets turned into modern dishes such as best end of Nidderdale lamb with herb crust and roasted garlic, Wensleydale-stuffed chicken breast with port and redcurrant

sauce, or grilled Scarborough woof on red onions with a chorizo and tomato dressing. Downstairs is a more-informal bar/bistro where blackboards of daily specials supplement printed menus. For dessert, think in terms of banana and blueberry bread-and-butter pudding. Accommodation available. Open all week.

• **Lymington** (Hampshire)

Old Bank House 68 High Street, (01590) 671128. This handsome pillared building (apparently named after the geographical feature it was built on, rather than a money-lending institution) is a fine setting for English and Mediterranean cooking, the good-value menus typically offering seared scallops with chilli and bacon, Caesar salad, smoked haddock fishcakes, or chargrilled calves' liver with mustard mash. Additional daily specials might be grilled sardines and lamb, rosemary and redcurrant sausages with mash and onion gravy. Finish with Balsamic marinated strawberries. Closed Sat L and Sun exc bank hol weekends.

• **Maiden Newton** (Dorset)

Le Petit Canard Dorchester Road, (01300) 320536. This village restaurant is a compact place with seascape prints on the walls and fairy lights twinkling from the ceiling beams. Ambitious fixed-price evening menus might start with 'fresh, well-timed' scallops from West Bay, or prawn and monkfish brochette on saffron risotto with garlic butter, before moving on to paprika-spiced pork fillet on celeriac rösti or a roast breast of Gressingham duck with an apple and oriental-spiced chutney. Mango sorbet and black pepper ice cream make a with-it dessert combination, although an alternative might be dark chocolate mousse torte with vanilla anglaise. Wines start at £12.50. Open Tue to Sat D only.

• **Manchester** (Greater Manchester)

Café Exchange Royal Exchange Theatre, St Ann's Square (0161) 932 6666. The café is open for lunch then re-opens as a brasserie for pre-theatre meals. A fixed-price menu of two courses and coffee for £10.95, three for £13.75, offers three choices per course, perhaps starting with carrot and coriander soup, chicken and broccoli terrine, or peppered salmon salad, with braised lamb shank, baked cod, or Thai vegetable curry as main course options. Specials continue the Mediterranean theme with chilled gazpacho finished with seafood, or seared salmon on squid ink linguini. Closed Sun.

Market Restaurant 104 High Street, (0161) 834 3743. Thirties style décor, lots of bric-à-brac and interesting glassware and crockery contribute to the appeal of this long-standing restaurant just off Piccadilly. A culinary mix from couscous to polenta, and salsas to gado-gado, punctuate the menu. Recommended this year are baked ham and asparagus with garlic butter, smoked salmon wrapped in lemon sole with hollandaise, plus Cajun black-baked turkey breast with mango salsa; finish with hazelnut and passion fruit roulade.

Pearl City 33 George Street, (0161) 228 7683. This Chinatown restaurant's long menu is mainly Cantonese, but a few Szechuan specialities share a page with sweet-and-sour dishes. Dim sum include such rarities as steamed tripe, and fried shredded duck meat rolls. Set meals are more imaginative than usual. The £15.50 combination menu for two, offers three soups, followed by five second courses chosen from twelve, including dim sum, spare ribs, and chicken wings. Then pick two out of four main courses with yung chow rice or two sorts of noodles. Open all week.

Sanam 145–151 Wilmslow Road, (0161) 224 1008/8824. Minor refurbishment aside, Sanam continues much as before, providing the same high-quality Indian food that has been its stock in trade for 30 years. The dishes are from the standard repertoire: chicken tikka has been a successful starter, while king prawn karahi was less impressive. It is the home-made sweets, however, that are the greatest strength: gulub jamun, ras malai, kulfi and various burfi among them. Open all week.

Stock 4 Norfolk Street, (0161) 839 6644. This spacious Italian restaurant in the domed hall of the old stock exchange building is the sister restaurant of Mauro's in Bollington; Enzo Mauro cooks at Stock. Fortnightly changing menus offer a good selection of antipasti – aubergine slices or fresh mussels among them – with main courses of breast of duck or baked sea bass; for dessert try chocolate and Amaretto pannacotta or apple and marzipan strudel. Closed Sun.

• **MELMERBY** (Cumbria)

Village Bakery Melmerby, (01768) 881515. Open all week for breakfast, light meals, lunch and afternoon tea, this long-standing establishment prides itself on using only organic ingredients and making everything on the premises. Try oak smoked Inverawe kippers, deep-filled quiche of the day or potato and parsley pie; finish with rhubarb fool. Scones and cakes are a must for tea. Baking equipment is for sale and bread-making courses are also held. Dinner is available every couple of months or so with a theme; check for details. Open all week L.

• **MERLEY** (Dorset)

Les Bouviers Oakley Hill, (01202) 889555. Now in its tenth year, this 'higgledy-piggledy' restaurant with its tiny rooms and conservatory keeps alive the tradition of dome lifting, the task performed by the French staff. The 'Menu Surprise' may offer wild mushroom gâteau, charred cod with spring onion purée and wood pigeon with pickled beetroot. There are often themed evening set menus; one for the chef of the year competition included loin of lamb with a balsamic reduction, and a 'study of British apples' in various dessert guises. Closed Sat L and Sun D.

• **MOUSEHOLE** (Cornwall)

Cornish Range 6 Chapel Street, (01736) 731488. Andrew Ryan's restaurant is situated down a narrow street in the heart of this quintessential Cornish harbourside village, and menus make the most of the local environment for fish, meat, cheese and vegetables. Décor has been updated and the work of local artists adds vibrancy to the room. Chef David Rashleigh's menus follow the catch and the season, with smoked salmon fillet with horseradish cream, and whole red mullet with black chilli olives among fish choices on one summer menu. Or find Cornish spring lamb or seared baby squid, and finish with peasant apple pie or local cheeses. This year two letting bedrooms have been added. Open Thur to Sat D and Sun L Nov to Easter, all week D Dec to Oct.

• **NEWARK** (Nottinghamshire)

Café Bleu 14 Castle Gate, (01636) 610141. Brasserie by day, restaurant at night, featuring live jazz four times a week, with classical music on Fridays, French folk on Saturday afternoons, and flamboyant works from a local artist on the walls. Dishes have strong French leanings, so there may be asparagus and sweet potato soup, fish terrine, succulent and plentiful pan-fried scallops, and crème brûlée. Other menu choices have included Tuscan roast cod with white beans and tarragon, and beef fillet on blue cheese mash. Service is 'friendly, but not overly so', and wines extensive. Closed Sun.

• **NEWCASTLE UPON TYNE** (Tyne & Wear)

Leela's 20 Dean Street, (0191) 230 1261. Leela cooks the food of Kerala in her family-run restaurant, which claims to be the only South Indian in the English north-east. Although not exclusively vegetarian it offers a wide choice of vegetarian starters such as paper dosa (thin rice and lentil pancakes), uthappam (a raised soft pancake), and various vadas (savoury 'doughnuts'), as well as a vegetarian thali at £8.50. Non-vegetarians can choose perhaps chuttathu (marinated spiced pork baked in foil and served with spiced apple salad). There are unusual deserts as well as sorbets and kulfi, (Indian ice-cream). Service is 'charming'. Closed Sun.

• **NEWENT** (Gloucestershire)

Three Choirs Restaurant Newent, (01531) 890223. The restaurant has a restful ambience and pleasant service, and overlooks the vineyards that produce the Three Choirs wines, all 20 of which are available by the glass, supplemented by a few non-English bottles. Among recommended dishes have been starters of English goats' cheese salad, and pork terrine with chutney, followed by pan-fried calf's liver, and grilled fillet of beef with mushrooms. Puddings might be lemon and lime tart or chocolate and orange roulade. One-day cookery courses are also on offer. Closed Sun D and all day Mon.

• **Newmillerdam** (West Yorkshire)
On The Edge Newmillerdam, (01924) 253310. Closely packed tables, ironwork chairs and candlelight lend a café feel to this new restaurant in a stone cottage next to an inn on the edge of the Newmillerdam country park. Main courses seem to be of a higher standard than everything else: reports have praised rack of lamb with a rich rosemary jus and equally well-cooked guinea fowl. Starters might be Thai mussels in a spicy coconut milk sauce, or salmon and Parmesan tart, while desserts typically include bread-and-butter pudding. Limited wine list. Accommodation available. Open Mon to Sat and Sun L.

• **Northallerton** (North Yorkshire)
Bettys 188 High Street, (01609) 775154. Don't be surprised to find yourself queuing outside one of the branches of this popular mini chain dotted around North Yorkshire. A quaint tea room feel is borne out by the food on offer: soups, sandwiches, cheese on toast, cakes and so on. Daily specials are also available for those looking for a heartier lunch, perhaps rösti topped with smoked chicken and asparagus.

• **North Bovey** (Devon)
Blackaller Hotel North Bovey, (01647) 440322. Dating from the seventeenth century, originally a woollen mill, this small hotel in 'an idyllic setting by the riverside' has attracted plaudits from reporters for relaxed, efficient service as well as its food. Daily-changing menus are based on fresh local produce, often given an inventive global touch: butternut squash soup with coconut milk, shank of lamb with Thai spices, and grilled salmon fillet with a pesto and Parmesan crust, for example. Brown sugar meringues with strawberries, or perhaps whisky and marmalade bread-and-butter pudding can round off a meal. Open Tue to Sat D only.

• **North Huish** (Devon)
Brookdale House North Huish, (01548) 821661. This late-Victorian country house stands at the bottom of a deep combe and, appropriately, offers short set menus in the country-house mode. First courses may feature home-cured salmon with a citrus-dressed salad, or duck and chicken liver parfait with toasted brioche, while main courses extend to best end of lamb with garlic and chive potato mash, or grilled turbot with spinach and saffron cream. Desserts are likely to include a selection of ice creams and sorbets plus perhaps hot chocolate fondant sponge, or glazed lemon tart. Accommodation available. Open all week.

• **Northleach** (Gloucestershire)
Old Woolhouse Market Place, (01451) 860366. On the market square stands the Astics' unmarked restaurant, rough stone walls without, rough stone walls within. Jacques Astic sticks to a narrow repertoire, menus recited to diners by his wife, so as for the past 25 years you are likely to come upon brill or turbot in red wine, chicken in vinegar sauce, or calf's liver and kidneys in cassis sauce, then freshen up with a classically dressed salad. Cheese is St Marcellin, since M. Astic is a Lyonnais. Strawberry shortcake, strawberry ice cream, or apple tart to finish. Open Tue to Sat D.

• **Norwich** (Norfolk)
The Aquarium 22 Tombland, (01603) 630090. 'Our favourite venue for lunch in Norwich,' declared one contented couple about this modern restaurant and bar with a globetrotting menu. Crispy duck salad or griddled aubergine with rocket and Parmesan shavings kick things off, with a touch of Spain in roast cod with chickpea and chorizo stew, and the

East in bang bang chicken. Closer to home, crab and asparagus come in a soup, and beef with horseradish mash. Closed Sun.

By Appointment 25–29 St Georges Street, (01603) 630730. Dinner only is served from Tuesday to Saturday at this restaurant-with-rooms in a pink sixteenth-century cottage. Unusual features include the series of tiny antique-furnished dining rooms, a menu displayed on a gilt-edged blackboard, and the flamboyant and friendly owners. The food is a little different too, taking in starters of king prawns flambé in Pernod, or smoked salmon with avocado ice cream. For main course there may be roasted suckling pig with parsnip chips, or beef fillet served with rich red wine sauce on a brioche with pâté. Dessert might be pineapple tarte Tatin with tamarind ice cream.

• **Nottingham** (Nottinghamshire)

Saagar 473 Mansfield Road, (0115) 962 2014/969 2860. Even by Indian standards, the menu of this pleasant restaurant provides a remarkably wide choice with more than 40 ways of preparing chicken. As well as the usual tikka, there are variations such as kastoori hasina, Kashmiri, makhani, newabi and nizami, while curries range from 'sweet and mild' begum bahar to medium hot nargisi with minced lamb and egg, or hot Punjabi with green chilli and yoghurt. Set meals at £32 for two include a tandoori special and an eid (festival) special including lamb tikka topped with cheese and a tandoori mixed grill. House wines are £11.50 per litre. Closed Sun L.

• **Odiham** (Hampshire)

Grapevine 121 High Street, (01256) 701122. Comfortable, attractive high-street dining room offering generous portions of interesting contemporary cooking: pear and watercress soup, tender venison with celeriac and rosemary purée and a fig and port sauce, grilled lemon sole with asparagus and hollandaise, and puddings such as butterscotch tart and spotted dick. Two-course lunches and early-evening menus offer good value. Closed Sat L and all day Sun.

• **Orford** (Suffolk)

Butley-Orford Oysterage Market Hill, (01394) 450277. The Oysterage method of hot-smoking uses whole oak logs, so it may be difficult to match on your garden barbecue. Instead visit this smokehouse-cum-shop-cum-tea house for smoked sardines, fish pâté, salmon, cod roe, trout, even chicken and maybe other specials from the blackboard. Their own Butley oysters are £6.20 per half-dozen, and a selection of smoked fish and oysters is £8.80. Cooked dishes may include prawns in garlic oil, pork and cockle stew, and scalloped prawns in a cheese sauce with potato topping. Open all week summer; closed Mon to Thur D in winter.

• **Oxford** (Oxfordshire)

Fishers 36–38 St Clements Street, (01865) 243003. Barbary duck is the exception proving that fish rules at Fishers. Baked, grilled, poached and smoked are the treatments proclaimed by written and blackboard menus, to which can be added seared (tuna or scallops), roast (cod), pan-fried (king prawns), deep-fried (squid), and even fish and chips with mushy peas and gherkins. Shellfish platters and bouillabaisse offer a multitude of flavours, while mussels, Whitstable oysters or smoked salmon suit simpler tastes. Modern eclectic ideas include chilli, lemon grass and coriander with grilled plaice; or mango and lime pavlova with mascarpone cream. Wide windows allow views into and from this restaurant, which maintains good service even when most crowded. House wines start at £2.75 per glass. Closed Mon L.

Restaurant Elizabeth 82 St Aldates, (01865) 242230. Now in its thirty-fifth year of ownership by Antonio Lopez, this traditional restaurant is housed in one of the oldest occupied buildings in Oxford. Menus draw inspiration from France, Spain and Greece, offering pipérade (eggs with sweet pimento and tomato) or snails to start, then boeuf stroganoff, or breast of chicken with a cognac, white wine and cream sauce. Desserts run to mousse au chocolat, and sorbet au champagne. Three-course set lunches are available for £16. Exclusively Old World 200-strong wine list, with a half-litre of house vin blanc or rouge £8. Closed Mon.

• **Penrith** (Cumbria)

A Bit on the Side Brunswick Square, (01768) 892526. This small, intimate restaurant, with friendly staff and 'interesting' quotations on the walls, offers reasonably priced dishes with a distinct Mediterranean beat. Start with warm goats'-cheese and caramelised onion tart, or roasted red pepper soup with crème fraîche, and then perhaps choose roast duck breast with minted couscous, or pan-fried halibut with basil and Parmesan mash. Pineapple tarte Tatin with coconut ice cream and caramel sauce is one way to finish; if you can't choose, try 'A Grand Bit on the Side' for a selection of puddings. Closed Sat and Sun L and all day Mon.

• **Rockbeare** (Devon)

Jack in the Green London Road, (01404) 822240. A five-mile jaunt from Exeter on the old A30, this welcoming pub serves a contemporary menu. Bangers with mustard mash, minted pea and prawn risotto, Thai-style crab cakes – and those are just the bar snacks. The restaurant menu offers two or three courses, perhaps chicken and hazelnut terrine with curry oil, followed by Scottish salmon with leeks and cider vinegar dressing, and finishing with steamed chocolate sponge with Grand Marnier parfait. The large wine list has plenty of choice under £15. Open all week.

• **Roydhouse** (West Yorkshire)

Three Acres Inn Roydhouse, (01484) 602606. A four-pronged operation applies at this former coaching inn just ten minutes from the M1 south of Huddersfield: it is a restaurant, a seafood bar, a deli and a hotel. The three-course lunch menu at £16.95 offers a fairly wide choice at each stage – maybe a salad of hot-smoked salmon with quails' eggs, followed by oxtail casserole, then rhubarb and macaroon crumble – while the even more extensive dinner carte might turn out Peking duck salad with egg noodles, then roast rack of spring lamb with hotpot potatoes, or omelette Arnold Bennett, and finish with assiette of banana or cheeses from the deli. Vegetarians get a fair look-in, and the bar menu provides imaginative sandwiches. Open all week.

• **Saffron Walden** (Essex)

Old Hoops 15 King Street, (01799) 522813. The smart, traditional first-floor dining room is a pleasant setting for Ray Morrison's food, which starts simply: perhaps with French onion soup on the evening set menu, or potted shrimps for lunch. Main courses of medallions of pork with apples and calvados, or lamb dijonnaise show that France is often the inspiration, with pear and pine nut strudel or strawberries Romanoff as international puddings. Closed Sun and Mon.

• **Seaview** (Isle of Wight)

Priory Bay Hotel Priory Drive, (01983) 613146. This elegantly restored country-house hotel stands in a 70-acre estate, encompassing a stretch of coastline. Its beach café-restaurant specialises in seafood, while in the hotel dining room the set menu, £23 for three courses, might include carpaccio of halibut, or carrot and tarragon soup, followed by tuna provençale. A la carte menus may feature local lobster as a bisque or in a salad among starters, or grilled as a main course, alongside rack of lamb with garlic sauce, and fillet of beef with morels. House wines from £12. Open all week.

Seaview Hotel High Street, (01983) 612711. The Haywards have run this hotel and its two contrasting restaurants for over 20 years. The main dining room features crisp white linen, flowers and several clocks, while the Sunshine Room is nautically themed, with various model ships on display. In both, menus are based on the island's produce, especially fish from local fishermen, cooked in a modern British style. Isle of Wight tomato summer pudding, or crab tartlet with hollandaise might precede roasted duck leg with ginger and plum sauce or local lobster thermidor, with chocolate mousse with pistachios, or Mrs Minghella's ice cream to finish. Closed Sun D.

• **Sheffield** (South Yorkshire)
Greenhead House 84 Burncross Road, (0114) 246 9004. A friendly atmosphere pervades this family-run restaurant. Meals are priced according to the main course choice, but might start with salad of smoked duck breast, or globe artichoke stuffed with mushrooms and topped with Gruyère. Next comes soup, maybe celery and lovage, or sorbet, then perhaps grilled Scottish salmon on crab risotto, or sautéed fillet steak with chicken livers, bacon and marjoram. Desserts are mainly fruit-based concoctions such as blackberries with vanilla custard and pistachio praline. Light lunches might offer toasted ciabatta rolls or lamb casserole. Open Thur and Fri L, Wed to Sat D.

Mediterranean 271 Sharrow Vale Road, (0114) 266 1069. Specialising in fish and tapas, this restaurant lives up to its name. Tapas at lunch and early evening cover a wide range, from seafood salad, marinated anchovies, venison sausage, and shrimp dumplings. North Africa is represented in Moroccan chicken with couscous, and a Spanish influence is found in a stew of cod, salmon, squid, mussels, cockles and tuna. The main menu might take you from quail salad to pecan pie via fillet of snapper with tarragon beurre blanc. Closed Sun.

• **Shepton Mallet** (Somerset)
Blostin's 29 Waterloo Road, (01749) 343648. Blostin's, situated just outside town and decorated in homely style, has been under the ownership of Nick and Lynne Reed for more than 15 years now, and remains largely unchanged from one year to the next. Nick's cooking follows a tried-and-tested route, old favourites on the menu including salmon mousse wrapped in smoked salmon, and rack of spring lamb with herb crust and rosemary sauce. Other dishes might be stir-fried squid with leeks, ginger and garlic, or duck breast with poached pears and cassis. White chocolate and Malteser ice cream might finish a meal. Open Tue to Sat D only.

• **Sinnington** (North Yorkshire)
Fox and Hounds Sinnington, (01751) 431577. The refurbished, non-smoking restaurant of this old coaching inn fuses rural tradition and metropolitan fashion on its long menu. Starters of salmon, crab and sweet potato cakes with red chilli and fennel salsa, or marinated smoked venison and fig salad could be followed by a Sinnington mixed grill of rump steak, lamb and pork chops, gammon, black pudding, sausage and egg. Alternatively, choose something lighter such as grilled whole plaice with citrus butter. Those with an enthusiastic appetite might also enjoy white chocolate parfait with orange sorbet, or sticky toffee pudding with caramel sauce. Open all week.

• **Southall** (Greater London)
Gifto's Lahore Karahi 162–164 The Broadway, (020) 8574 8602. 'The fastest food in the west (or east),' recorded one visitor to this large, buzzing, eating house who paid the very small bill for his three-course meal within an hour of arriving. Lighting is by plastic chandeliers, and a mural painting of Gifto's food emporium decorates a corner of the room. Skewered tikkas and kebabs are barbecued behind a glass screen while larger pieces of chicken, fish, lamb chops and quail come from the tandoor. 'Lahore dishes' are curries such as methi chicken, or tinda gosht (baby gourd with lamb). Unlicensed, so drink lassi or BYO. Open all week noon to 11.30.

• **Stockland** (Devon)
Kings Arms Inn Stockland, (01404) 881361. This old pub in an isolated village has two bars and a dining room, all serving the same blackboard menu; a snack menu is also available at lunchtime Monday to Saturday, offering things like scrambled eggs with smoked salmon, or Stilton mushrooms. Dishes on the main menu might be moules marinière, or grilled scallops with sweet chilli sauce, followed by venison steak with red wine

sauce on a celeriac and potato mash, or rack of local lamb with rosemary and red wine jus, finishing with tangy lime mousse. An extensive wine list includes 14 house wines. Open all week.

• **Stoke Holy Cross** (Norfolk)
Wildebeest Arms Norwich Road, (01508) 492497. The Wildebeest is a pub and restaurant ornamented with spears and wooden masks to evoke Africa. Under a new chef, Szechuan chicken livers with roasted pineapple and couscous is now the exception among such Anglo-European dishes as smoked haddock fishcake with coriander salad, pickled cucumber and tartare sauce, or baked goats' cheese and provençale vegetable tart with pesto. Finish with treacle tart. Service has lacked grace at times. Open all week.

• **Stowmarket** (Suffolk)
Tot Hill House Tot Hill, (01449) 673375. The pretty pink dining room in a handsome building just off the A14 is the setting for the 'enthusiasm and attention to detail' of owners Mary and Christopher Bruce. Lunch and dinner menus are in the modern British mode: crab strudels with Thai dipping sauce, and a goats' cheese tart with red onion marmalade set the tone at first courses, followed by sea bass with roasted fennel, or lamb with minted bread sauce. Finish with an iced tiramisù parfait. Booking advisable. Closed Mon, Tues and Sun D.

• **Stratford-upon-Avon** (Warwickshire)
Russons 8 Church Street, (01789) 268822. This small place with a friendly atmosphere is especially useful for lunch and pre-theatre suppers. The long menu specialises in fish and seafood, such as warm scallop salad, grilled lemon sole, or tiger prawn and tropical fruit kebab, but there are also plenty of non-fish options such as toad-in-the-hole, stir-fried vegetables and noodles, herb-crusted rack of lamb with redcurrant sauce, and roast guinea fowl in a cider sauce. 'Very good chips.' Cappuccino sundae or banana fritters will fill up any corners. Wines are fairly priced. Closed Sun and Mon.

• **Studland** (Dorset)
Shell Bay Ferry Road, (01929) 450363. This small restaurant has views across Poole Bay to Brownsea Island. Expect plain wooden tables, paper napkins and fishy stencils on the walls, plus an almost entirely seafood menu (one vegetarian and one meat dish are available). The daily-changing menu has seen John Dory, mussels and scallops, plus skate with chips, mackerel with bubble and squeak or roast cod with spring greens and lentils. Desserts might be chocolate mousse or warm pear and almond tart. Service is friendly and unobtrusive, and the short wine list is mostly white. Open all week summer; reduced opening in winter.

• **Swanage** (Dorset)
Cauldron Bistro 5 High Street, (01929) 422671. Generous portions and excellent fresh fish are two features of Terry Flenley's down-to-earth cooking at his simply decorated bistro, where chips might appear next to caviar on the menu. Expect grilled whole sea bass, which may be brought out for inspection before cooking, local crab on toasted brioche, or wok-cooked scallops with tomatoes, bacon and pasta among seafood options, while meat dishes might take in loin of Dorset lamb with wild mushrooms and couscous, or chicken cooked on hot coals and served with lime and ginger sauce. Finish perhaps with Irish coffee crème brûlée. Open Thur to Sun L, Tue to Sun D.

• **Tadpole Bridge** (Oxfordshire)
Trout Tadpole Bridge, (01367) 870382. Under the same ownership as the Fox in Corscombe (see main entry) and the Acorn in Evershot (see Round-up entry), this untarnished, original Thameside pub, with décor taking in gorgeous woodwork and a huge fish in a glass case, is the setting for some ambitious modern British cooking. One reporter's meal started with mousseline of Cornish king scallops on a courgette ring with lemon dressing, followed by peppery Scotch fillet steak with tarragon cream, each dish featuring 'well above average' raw

materials. Finish with chocolate and raspberry sponge with orange crème anglaise. Closed Sun D.

• **Tavistock** (Devon)

Neil's 27 King Street, (01822) 615550. This small converted farmhouse is run single-handed by Janet Neil who successfully combines the roles of chef and waitress, seemingly without effort. Her cooking champions organic, free-range and local produce – Dartmoor venison has been singled out for particular praise – and menus blend modern and traditional ideas, to produce wild mushroom and herb risotto, or seafood couscous with crab sauce to start, followed by herb-crusted cod fillet, or roast stuffed guinea fowl with Meaux mustard sauce. Chocolate cheesecake rounds off a meal. Open Tue to Sat D only.

• **Tetbury** (Gloucestershire)

Calcot Manor (01666) 890391 The handsome Cotswold stone house and restored outbuildings are the impeccable setting for the conservatory restaurant (open all week) and Gumstool Inn (open all week; food served all day Sat and Sun). The former offers a modern menu in comfortable and light surroundings, taking in perhaps slow-roasted duck confit, or griddled scallops to start, followed by osso buco or roast turbot. The Gumstool Inn is smartly decorated but the flagstone floors and daily specials board confirm its pub credentials; the long menu features Caesar salad, Thai-spiced crab cakes and good-quality sausages with spring onion mash. The hotel is popular with families.

• **Thirsk** (North Yorkshire)

Charles' Bistro Bakers Alley, (01845) 527444. Service is 'bright and breezy', and the ambience has 'a touch of hippiness', thought one visitor to Vicky Charles's little place, behind a bank in the middle of town. The lemon and lime coloured dining room is enlivened – although some use another word – by light music played loudly. A one-course lunch at £4.95, bread and vegetables included, might be salmon fishcake with lemon butter sauce or Basque pork, 'a wholesome peasant dish' of beans, pork and chorizo sausage in a rich, tasty, tomato and garlic sauce. A crisp shortcrust pastry tart with sliced pears in cinnamon custard might follow. House wines £8.50. Open Tue to Sat L, Wed to Sat D.

• **Torquay** (Devon)

Mulberry House 1 Scarborough Road, (01803) 213639. This Victorian corner terraced house, with accommodation for six guests, has a restaurant patronised by locals and tourists alike. An eclectic set-price menu is available for dinner all week and for lunch at weekends in the elegant dining room with its relaxing ambience. One reporter enjoyed a lunch of Brixham scallop brochette and 'succulent' pork shoulder so much that he returned for a Sunday lunch of superb roast Aberdeen Angus beef. 'Splendid' fresh vegetables and desserts of apple charlotte and lemon soufflé completed the happy experience. Open Fri to Sun L, Mon to Sat D; residents only Mon and Tue D.

No 7 Fish Bistro 7 Beacon Terrace, (01803) 295055. A small seafood bistro with blackboard menus, 'caring' staff and 'superb' local crab and lobster, plus mussels, oysters, whole sole, plaice and combination platters. Start with a pot of creamy curried prawns and go on to a selection of fish cooked in tempura batter. Pasta, chicken and steak are available for non-fish eaters (but not listed on menus). Good choice of reasonably priced wines. Closed Sun and Mon winter, and L Sun and Mon in summer.

• **Tresco** (Isles of Scilly)

Island Hotel Tresco, (01720) 422883. The sea view from the hotel might disclose an unusual aspect of the chef's job description. For among lobsters, steaks and seafood platters on the table d'hôte menu, you will find 'chef's catch of the day'. Four ways with lobster include poached with saffron cream sauce, and cold with Bryher crab and prawn. Start perhaps with fried chicken livers on champ with crispy bacon, go on to chilled wild berry and calvados soup, a sorbet, then salmon, cod, lamb or chicken, followed by island fresh fruit salad with Malibu and flaked coconut. The hotel is closed from Nov to early March; restaurant open all week.

• **Tunbridge Wells** (Kent)
Sankey's 39 Mount Ephraim, (01892) 511422. Hands-on chef-patron Guy Sankey has been at the helm of this seafood restaurant and oyster bar, also incorporating a cellar wine bar, for nearly 15 years. The handsome building is crammed with bric-à-brac and paintings by local artists, and menus are displayed on blackboards. The simple style might produce Whitstable oysters or kiln-roasted salmon for starters, while mains go in for grilling of sea bass or halibut, fish and chips, and seafood platters. Fillet steak or duck will pacify carnivores. There is a terrace and patio for al fresco eating. Closed Sun.

• **Twickenham** (Greater London)
Brula 13 Crown Road, (020) 8892 0602. Small restaurant with yellow walls and paper tablecloths. A good-value set-price menu offers just three choices per course, with four on the evening carte. The name comes from Bruce Dunnett and Lawrence Hartley, who formerly worked at the Ivy and Bibendum respectively (see main entries, London). Approved dishes have included veal terrine, followed by chicken with herbs on a field mushroom, and grilled monkfish. Desserts might be summer compote, or try some excellent cheese. No credit cards. Closed Sun and Mon.

Loch Fyne Restaurant 175 Hampton Road, (020) 8255 6222. One of a chain of Scottish seafood restaurants based on the original in Cairndow (see main entry, Scotland), offering value for money and efficient service from tartan-clad staff. The menu is almost exclusively fish and seafood, with oysters and smoked salmon from Loch Fyne the main stars. Salmon may be kiln-roasted or turned into gravadlax, while skate wings may be done classically with capers in butter. 'Wonderfully fresh' roast halibut came with a large pool of pesto and roast fennel and courgettes. Finish with crème brûlée or chocolate and nut tart. Open all week.

• **Westfield** (East Sussex)
Wild Mushroom Woodgate House, Westfield Lane, (01424) 751137. Set in a quiet part of East Sussex, this restaurant has earned particular praise for its good-value Sunday lunch, with chargrilled pork belly and sea bass singled out. The carte has provided salmon sausage with a winkle and champagne sauce, and asparagus mousse as starters, followed by Gressingham duck with blackcurrant sauce, and Scotch beef with morels and Madeira sauce. Chocolate mousse or home-made ice creams have been successful puddings. Closed Sat L and Sun D, and all day Mon.

• **Weybourne** (Norfolk)
Gasche's The Street, (01263) 588220. Small but well-formed thatched restaurant with two dining rooms, lounge, bar and patio garden for fine weather. Weekly-changing lunch and dinner menus offer a choice of styles: prawn cocktail at one extreme, tiger prawns in cream sauce in puff pastry, or Gasche's smokie with garlic bread at the other. Main dishes are varied too, as in steamed beef and Guinness suet pudding, or crab-crusted cod with spinach on shrimp bisque. Desserts might include blackberry and apple pie with custard or variations on a pavlova theme. Closed Sun D and Mon.

• **Weymouth** (Dorset)
Abbotsbury Seafood Bar Abbotsbury Oyster Farm, (01305) 788867. Right on the edge of the sea near Portland Bill, this small restaurant is an outlet for the produce of the oyster farm, but there is also a huge display of other fish and seafood items, behind which is the open kitchen where food is prepared in full view. One enthusiastic reporter enjoyed plainly cooked whitebait and mussels served with salad and bread followed by a hot crab and shellfish feast including the 'creamiest crab meat I have ever had'. Open Easter to 30 Sept, all week L, Thur to Sat D; phone to check winter opening.

Booking advisable for D.

Perry's 4 Trinity Road, (01305) 785799. Alan, Vivian and Raymond Hodder have run Perry's, a mainly fish restaurant overlooking the harbour, for a decade. Half the extensive menu is on blackboards: Loch Fyne mussels, shellfish soup, bass with olive oil and citrus dressing, and Portland lobster. The main menu includes meat dishes – confit of duck with a honey and lemon glaze – and something for vegetarians, such as grilled goats' cheese with red pepper relish. Desserts might be lemon mousse with raspberry coulis. Closed Mon and Sat L, and Sun D in winter.

• **Whimple** (Devon)

Woodhayes Whimple, (01404) 822237. Woodhayes is a small, elegant Georgian country house offering a high standard of guest accommodation with a homely atmosphere. House-party-style lunches and dinners are also available by arrangement for groups (min 6, max 20), and the cooking is by co-owner Lynda Katz. She prepares a no-choice five-course menu that might open with courgette and mint soup, followed by salmon on lemon pasta with saffron salsa, then apricot-glazed roast duck breast, with ricotta lemon tart for dessert, and Devon cheeses with home-made oat cakes to finish. Open Mon to Sat D only; closed Oct to March.

• **Willington** (Co Durham)

Stile 97 High Street, (01388) 746615. Jenny James, chef at this former miner's cottage since 1984, is magpie-like in her cooking style, borrowing from France, Morocco, Italy and the Far East without losing touch with British dishes, such as rump steak pie. Braised lamb shank with couscous crosses boundaries, while duck confit with lentils, and gougère with ratatouille define French comfort food. Choose mussels or black pudding for starters, marmalade ice cream with shortbread to finish. Wine-tasting sessions are held regularly, and in summer Sunday lunch buffets can be provided by arrangement. Open Wed to Sat D only.

• **Wingfield** (Suffolk)

De La Pole Arms Church Road, Wingfield, (01379) 384545. Historic Wingfield church is a stone's throw away from this 'charming' cream-painted sixteenth-century village pub. House specialities include Irish stew with parsley dumplings, and bowls of mussels or mixed seafood – mussels, crayfish and prawns for one reporter. Try kiln-roasted salmon on pasta, or ribeye steak with chunky chips. Hot Jamaican bananas with rum, and maple cheesecake are possible desserts. Open all week.

• **Woburn** (Bedfordshire)

Paris House Woburn Park, (01525) 290692. A black and white timbered house in the Duke of Bedford's Woburn Park estate is the fine setting for a sophisticated restaurant where chef-proprietor Peter Chandler offers classic French cooking. Dining options include a carte, a 'gastronomique' menu, and a set lunch, the latter typically offering French onion soup followed by rack of lamb with rosemary, and pear charlotte to finish. More ambitious dishes on the main menu might include smoked haddock and leek tart with red pepper coulis, salmon in champagne sauce, and hot raspberry soufflé. Closed Mon and Sun D.

• **Wrightington** (Lancashire)

High Moor High Moor Lane, (01257) 252364. This traditional coaching inn, high up on the Lancashire moors, dates from 1642 and the low, beamed ceiling gives it a definite 'olde worlde' feel. Menus comprise an extensive carte plus a set-price 'early doors' option, and cooking veers from the modern – roast scallops with chicory and foie gras butter, or roast best end of lamb in filo pastry with feta and sun-dried tomatoes – to such traditional items as ham hock terrine, or deep-fried cod with chips and mushy peas. Finish perhaps with crème brûlée with whisky and blueberries. Service is 'friendly and attentive'. Good-value wines start at £9.95. Closed Sat L and Mon.

Mulberry Tree Wrightington Bar, (01257) 451400. Newly opened by Mark Prescott, once of the White Hart in Nayland (see main entry, England), this restaurant has a large open bar and separate dining room. Early reports reveal excellent use of local produce, with nettle and lovage soup, followed by a confit of rabbit leg with wild mushrooms on spicy mash. Other main courses might be breast of Goosnargh duck with pear chutney, or whole roast lemon sole. Dessert may be nougat glacé with raspberry coulis or bread-and-butter pudding with apricot sauce. A bar menu offers ploughman's, club sandwich or cod and chips. Reports please. Closed all day Mon and Tue L.

• **Yattendon** (Berkshire)
Royal Oak The Square, (01635) 201325. This traditional old stone-built hotel has a bar, which functions as a watering hole for locals (and their dogs), plus a brasserie (open all week L and D) with a rural atmosphere, and a more formal restaurant (open Mon to Sat D only) with tablecloths and sparkling cutlery. The cooking has registered some disappointments of late, but one reporter enjoyed 'nicely seared, crisp-skinned' sea bass, and fillet steak with pickled walnut sauce and pearl barley risotto. Service is polished and French.

• **York** (North Yorkshire)
Bettys 6–8 St Helen's Square, (01904) 659142. The York branch of the mini chain of English tea rooms provides much the same options as the others: from tea and cakes to more substantial daily specials of prosciutto, mushroom and cream cheese open sandwich, or sausage and mash. Open all week.

Blue Bicycle 34 Fossgate, (01904) 673990. A pleasant atmosphere and good service are characteristics of this small restaurant in the centre of York. Tian of crab and scallop starters have been described as 'zingingly fresh'; other dishes might be salad of home-smoked venison with lime and coriander salsa, fillets of John Dory with chicory and tarragon sabayon, or turbot with mussel and chive cream, with butterscotch and Bailey's cream cheesecake to finish. Open daily from noon to 10pm. Signs are that this is a restaurant on the up; more reports please.

Scotland

• **Biggar** (South Lanarkshire)
Culter Mill Coulter Village, (01899) 220950. Douglas and Betty Collins, who brought their ancient mill back to life so effectively ten years ago, seem to enjoy a bit of alliteration on the menu front. Hence feta and filo (a pastry parcel of the cheese and spinach on hollandaise) and parfait and pear (chicken liver pâté with pear chutney and oatcakes). Otherwise the generous choice might run to minestrone or five-spiced chicken won tons, followed by wild rabbit casserole, or salmon and crab gâteau. Finish perhaps with chargrilled Amaretto peaches with iced ginger cream. Open Wed to Sun.

• **Broadford** (Highland)
Creelers Seafood Bistro Broadford, (01471) 822281. Closed only at Christmas and New Year, Creeler's makes use of Skye's natural larder, with fish the main focus. There might be Loch Eishort mussels steamed in white wine and garlic, or stuffed squid, while the house speciality is seafood gumbo. Cajun steak or haggis will satisfy meat eaters, and vegetarians are catered for too. Finish with local cheeses or bread-and-butter pudding. Wines are mostly French and start at £9.50. Open all week.

• **Canonbie** (Dumfries & Galloway)
Riverside Inn Canonbie, (013873) 71295/71512. The Riverside is an attractive border pub-cum-hotel with restaurant, and makes a useful stopping-off point to and from Scotland. The split-level bar with a predominance of copper feels the part and shares much the same menu as the dining room. Curried parsnip soup or a bowl of mussels might be among starters on the fixed-price menu, followed by corn-fed Lancashire duck or Buccleuch ribeye steak. Find

air-dried Cumbrian ham, home-made fish pie and thick Barnsley chop on the blackboard. Bar open all week L and D; restaurant open all week L (bookings only), Tue to Sat D.

• **Crieff** (Perthshire & Kinross)

Bank Restaurant 32 High Street, (01764) 656575. Bill McGuigan cooks while wife Lilias runs front-of-house and doubles as pastry chef at this bistro in the centre of town. Their modern Scottish cooking makes good use of local supplies, including Buccleuch estate beef, local heather-fed lamb and organic veg from Arran. A typical meal might start with goats'-cheese and onion tartlet, followed by ribeye steak with a rosemary and garlic sauce. Burnt Glayva cream is a perennial favourite dessert, otherwise there may be Tobermory cheddar with oatcakes. Closed Mon and Sun D.

• **Crinan** (Argyll & Bute)

Crinan Hotel Crinan, (01546) 830261. The location is spectacular, even by Argyll coast standards, and Lock 16 restaurant (Tue to Sat D only) has the very best of views. Situated on the top floor of the hotel, it focuses on freshly caught seafood, for example Jura lobster 'just caught at 17.00 hrs today'. Loch Etive mussels poulette, or locally smoked wild salmon might be followed by glazed lemon tart, or a selection of Scottish cheeses and coffee on the fixed-price dinner menu. The hotel's second restaurant, the Westward, (all week D only), provides an ambitious menu, perhaps ham hock terrine, roast loin of venison and iced fig parfait. There is also a bar serving light L and D all week.

• **Darvel** (East Ayrshire)

Scoretulloch House Darvel, (01560) 323331. Idyllic views come complete with binoculars and bird books for twitchers at this sympathetically restored mill cottage. Four-course set-dinner menus in the restaurant proper might turn out home-smoked salmon, followed by Thai chicken soup, then bacon steaks stuffed with apple and raisins and served with three colours of cabbage, or whole poussin with kumquat sauce, and finally apple strudel. Oscar's Brasserie's offers simpler fare: perhaps fishcakes, venison burgers or fish and chips. Open all week.

• **Edinburgh** (Edinburgh)

Fitz Henry 19 Shore Place, Leith, (0131) 555 6625. Good service and relaxed formality are part of the appeal in this dockside setting. The imaginative menu might start with dressed crab and celeriac rémoulade, or petit aïoli of salt cod with spring vegetables. Braised lamb with mushy peas is a successful main course, and saddle of rabbit with bulgur wheat and a saffron, raisin, and pine nut broth demonstrates the menu's ambition. Among sophisticated desserts is apple crème brûlée with raisin and apple jus. Closed Sun.

Howie's 208 Bruntsfield Place, (0131) 221 1777. 'Not luxuriously furnished but well polished,' writes a regular customer of this restaurant with branches at 63 Dalry Road, 75 St. Leonard's Street and 4–6 Glanville Place. Two-course lunches and three-course dinners are good value. Straightforward starters might include pan-fried pigeon with red cabbage jus, and among one day's main dishes were roast rib of beef in a port sauce, poached red snapper with an orange velouté, and salmon steak with red pepper and dill sauce. To finish there was poached pear with red wine syrup, to make it a red letter day. Fully licensed, but BYO for a small corkage charge. Open all week.

• **Gattonside** (Borders)

Hoebridge Inn Gattonside, (01896) 823082. At their coaching inn on the banks of the Tweed, the Rennies are calling increasingly on local and seasonal produce for their monthly-changing menus, and now have regular supplies of rare-breed beef, pork and lamb, plus game in season. Daily specials might include cream of nettle soup, and chargrilled saddle of Blackface lamb with black pudding and kidneys. The main menu takes in salad of smoked Teviot trout, perhaps followed by soy and ginger glazed Barbary duck with sweet-and-sour onion won tons and drunken raisins. To finish, there might be lemon curd ice cream, rhubarb cheesecake, or British and Irish cheeses. Open Tue to Sun D only.

• **Glasgow** (Glasgow)

Air Organic 36 Kelvingrove Street, (0141) 564 5200. On a corner site with a bar and outside terrace, plus a large, airy first-floor dining room; expect pleasant service and *mostly* organic food with Far Eastern leanings. Menus in the form of airline tickets offer tempura vegetables and miso broth, Thai watermelon stew, and peppered bluefin tuna salad with croûtons. Desserts are suitably global: red berry pavlova with Chantilly cream, white chocolate and lemon cheesecake, or sweet tempura bananas. The organic wine list starts with house French at £10.50. Open all week.

Gamba 225A West George Street, (0141) 572 0899. Under a busy city street, Gamba's menu invites indulgence. Except for Bayonne ham in a Caesar salad, and fillet of beef with black pudding mash, it is all seafood, with such starters as a terrine of sole, lobster and leek with Thai jelly, or sea trout tartare. Whole roast sea bream comes with chilli syrup, roast peppers and soy, and seared turbot on prawn salsa relish with coriander. An ascetic option is simply grilled lemon sole, but there is nothing frugal about desserts, given white and bitter chocolate cream with Tia Maria and pistachio. Closed Sun.

Killermont Polo Club 2022 Maryhill Road, (0141) 946 5412. The authentic polo club décor is not the only unusual feature of this Indian restaurant. As well as traditional dishes, the menu also includes many dum pukht dishes, a name that denotes slow, gentle cooking. This method produces chandi kaliyan (lamb in an aromatic gravy with nuts and saffron) and baghar-e-baingan (aubergines cooked with tamarind, sesame seeds, peanuts and coconut), while the tandoor turns out chicken tikka, and king prawns marinated in yoghurt and spices; the tawa (griddle) is used for a vegetarian starter of potato cakes stuffed with spiced peas and apricots. All main courses come with rice, vegetables and dhal. Closed Sun L.

Lux 1051 Great Western Road, (0141) 576 7576. In this converted railway station, the Stazione brasserie is at ground level, the bar occupies the first floor, and Lux itself is above. Décor is 'spartan-minimalist' and lighting is low. The cooking has sometimes failed to satisfy the expectations aroused by an interesting modern menu, but breast of wood pigeon with skirlie and blackcurrant and rosemary jus has been commended, while banana and chocolate crêpes with toffee took someone devoted to those ingredients a long way towards heaven. Staff are cheerful and efficient. Open Tue to Sat D only.

Mitchells/Mitchells West End 157 North Street, (0141) 204 4312, and 31–35 Ashton Lane, (0141) 339 2220. Two useful neighbourhood restaurants offering pre-theatre menus, set-price lunches and an evening carte. Typical dishes might include Caesar salad, or chicken liver pâté, followed by escalope of pork fillet with noodles, or a crépinette of West Coast sea fish with lobster sauce glaze. Round things off with steamed lemon sponge, or strawberry shortbread tower. For a £2.75 corkage charge, customers may bring their own wine most evenings (Mon to Thur North Street, Mon to Sat Ashton Lane). Open Mon to Fri L, Mon to Sat D (North Street) and Mon to Sat D only (Ashton Lane).

Rococo 202 West George Street, (0141) 221 5004. 'Casual gourmet dining' is the stated aim of this light, airy, basement café-bar, which appeals to a broader age-range than the strong colours and loud music might suggest. Gourmet is an appropriate word for a carte that offers foie gras parfait, or warm Scottish lobster served with 'poached' potatoes, baby leeks, truffled vichyssoise and caviar Chantilly. The set lunch might offer Caesar salad, prepared at table, followed by steak or chicken with well-executed sauces. Portions are large, as is the wine list, which opens at £16. Closed Sun.

Two Fat Ladies 88 Dumbarton Road, (0141) 339 1944. No relation of anyone you may have seen on TV (but see following entry), rather a reference to the street number. Short pre-theatre and lunch menus are available, but the open kitchen also delivers fixed-price dinner menus of two to four courses, which might start with venison sausage, before roast lamb with oatmeal and pistachio stuffing. But fish is the mainstay of the menu: grilled sea bass with salsa verde, or wild sea trout with sesame seeds and teriyaki sauce, typify the local produce prepared with sauces and garnishes from far and wide. Open Fri and Sat L, Tue to Sat D.

• **Haddington** (East Lothian)
Garden Café Lennoxlove House, (01620) 823720. Garden Café exactly describes the setting and simple décor of Clarissa Dickson-Wright's place. Modestly priced dishes can be as straightforward as sausage and mash with beans and gravy, or cream of basil penne pasta with asparagus and sun-dried tomatoes. More exciting starters include warm artichoke and almond salad topped with beans, or stuffed lamb fillet and couscous salad. There are eastern touches in Thai-style green curry, or stir-fried chicken and melon with rice noodles and pecans. Among appealing deserts are Rosie's home-made chocolate tart with crème anglaise, and Crunchie meringue with orange and ginger glaze. Open Tue to Sun L and Thur to Sat D.

• **Kinfauns** (Perthshire & Kinross)
Kinfauns Castle Kinfauns, (01738) 620777. Despite the unashamed magnificence of this country house hotel, set in extensive grounds, service in the imposing Library restaurant is friendly and welcoming. Fine ingredients are cooked with care, but not always with much in the way of seasoning. Cider and onion soup, or saddle of rabbit on a beetroot sauce, might precede main dishes of basil-stuffed chicken breast, or a mixed grill of west coast fish with saffron risotto. Desserts favour fruit, although steamed ginger pudding might appear. House wines are £13.95. Open all week.

• **Melrose** (Borders)
Burt's Hotel The Square, (01896) 822285. This eighteenth-century hotel in the Scottish Borders has been run by the Henderson family for 30 years. They are strong on personal hospitality, local produce, and imaginative yet classically inclined restaurant and bar menus, the latter perhaps taking in calves' liver on a tropical fruit salsa with tarragon and garlic dressing. The restaurant might offer a brandade of smoked salmon, cod and trout mixed with avocado, chilli and asparagus, followed by lamb chops with redcurrant jelly and mint sauce. Peach Melba with clotted cream might round off a meal. Open all week.

• **Moffat** (Dumfries & Galloway)
Beechwood Country House Harthope Place, (01683) 220210. Set in 12 acres of grounds populated with beech trees, this handsome house overlooks the Annan valley and the town of Moffat. A traditional and uncomplicated style of cooking characterises the five-course set-price menus, with four options per course. Start with mouclade, seafood patties with raspberry dressing, or terrine of chicken and coriander, then choose between soup or sorbet before a main course of beef stroganoff, or grilled halibut with tomato and lovage. For dessert try that old Scottish favourite raspberry cranachan, or perhaps Amaretto-poached pear with cinnamon syrup, and finish with cheese. Closed Mon to Thur L.

• **Oban** (Argyll & Bute)
Knipoch Hotel Knipoch, (01852) 316251. A pleasantly situated country house hotel, with views of nearby Loch Feochan, Knipoch offers both a full restaurant menu at dinner and a new, more flexible, bistro-style menu in the bar. The daily-changing, no-choice restaurant menu comes in three or five courses, typically starting with soup. Main course might be prune and walnut stuffed pork with port sauce, with perhaps whisky crêpes to finish (fish and cheese make up the five-course menu). The bistro turns out soups, sandwiches, pâté and salads, as well as perhaps salmon or scallops smoked on the premises, and

maybe rhubarb crumble to finish. Bistro open all week L and D, restaurant open all week D only.

• **Plockton** (Highland)
Plockton Inn Innes Street, (01599) 544222. A buzzy pub with a large garden, located only 100 yards from the harbour and, not surprisingly, specialising in seafood. The dinner menu offers starters of haggis, or fish soup, followed by venison bangers and mash, seafood platters, or Plockton prawns (langoustines) with mayonnaise. Daily blackboard specials also advertise deep-fried sprats with chilli dip, Vietnamese-style duck, whole sea bass with lime and coriander butter, or swordfish steak with salsa verde. Puddings vary from sticky toffee to brown sugar meringues with fruit. Lighter dishes on the lunch menu come in starter or main course sizes. Open all week.

• **Shieldaig** (Highland)
Tigh an Eilean Shieldaig, (01520) 755251. Food is a strong point at this small, unassuming hotel on the shore of Loch Torridon. Plenty of fish appears on the daily-changing menu offered in the smart dining room, the high-quality raw materials generally receiving simple treatment: local spiny lobster may be served with Charentais melon to start, while Kinlochbervie lemon sole Mornay might be among main courses. Non-fish options take in guinea fowl with port sauce, and mushroom and asparagus feuilleté. Finish with Scottish cheeses or perhaps banana fritters with ginger, lime and butterscotch sauce. Open all week; bar food all day, restaurant D only (booking advisable).

• **Stromness** (Orkney)
Hamnavoe 35 Graham Place, (01856) 850606. A small restaurant with a homely ambience is a useful find on this far-flung island, but it is only open for dinner. From the short carte reporters have enjoyed fresh white crabmeat wrapped in smoked salmon, followed by roast salmon on a bed of sweet potato, or there may be a seafood platter. Orkney steaks and a vegetarian option are also available. Finish with a champagne sorbet with fruit, or clootie dumpling with brandy and cream. Open D Tue to Sun.

• **Turnberry** (South Ayrshire)
Turnberry Hotel Turnberry, (01655) 331000. An imposing hotel favoured by the golfing fraternity, Turnberry enjoys lovely views across the Firth of Clyde. Eating options include the Mediterranean-style Terrace brasserie and the Clubhouse, where golfers can enjoy simple, wholesome cooking, as well as the expensive main restaurant, open all week for dinner and Sunday for lunch. Stewart Cameron's traditional French cooking makes room for a few Scottish classics, and a typical dinner menu features seafood, game, Scottish beef and locally grown produce. Start perhaps with terrine of foie gras, duck and chicken, before a main course of pithiviers of scallops, salmon, halibut and red mullet, and finish with baked fig tarte Tatin with butterscotch ice cream.

• **West Linton** (Borders)
Old Bakehouse Main Street, (01968) 660830. The range of smørrebrød (Danish open sandwiches), a long-standing feature of this pleasantly chintzy wood-panelled restaurant, has been retained by Jens and Anita Steffens who took over early in 1999, having previously been in the Guide at Cuilmore Cottage. Toppings for the sandwiches include smoked mackerel with horseradish cream, and peppered pastrami with dill pickle; otherwise the varied menu runs from starters of black pudding with spiced apple sauce, to main courses of roast local lamb loin on spicy couscous, or simple baked cod in cream and parsley sauce with a sun-dried tomato crust. House wine is £10.35. Open Wed to Sun L, Wed to Sat D.

Wales

• **Cardiff** (Cardiff)

Buffs 8 Mount Stuart Square, (029) 2046 4628. This handsome wine bar, hard by the old docks, caters for weekday lunch and early supper trade, opening from 11am to 7pm. It offers keenly priced blackboard specials in the wine bar – seafood risotto, or spicy lamb pancakes – along with salt beef salad and fishcakes. In the restaurant, start with baked laverbread with bacon, or crab cakes with tomato and chilli dressing, follow with calves' liver, or beef in oyster sauce, and finish with lemon tart. Open Mon to Fri.

De Courcey's Tyla Morris Ave, (029) 2089 2232. A smart restaurant set in three acres of grounds, off the beaten track but not far from the city centre. Menus include an à la carte 'gourmet' option plus a set-price 'house' alternative. Head chef David Leeworthy aims for modest innovation within a somewhat traditional framework, producing starters of pan-fried red mullet on fennel risotto, or pea and broad bean soup with coriander, perhaps followed by mildly curried monkfish with pasta, or loin of lamb with leek mousse and a red wine and thyme sauce. Conclude with hot apricot soufflé with caraway ice cream, or goats' cheese and almond cheesecake. Open Sun L and Tue to Sat D.

Metropolis 60 Charles Street, (029) 2034 4300. The multiple personalities of this ground-floor bar and first-floor restaurant are evident in the varying influences of its décor: anything goes. A broadly Mediterranean menu embraces squid with tapénade mash and pesto, and a niçoise salad with feta parcels, followed by calf's liver with polenta and swede Tatin, or sea bass with salmon brandade and Pernod butter sauce. Closed Sun.

Le Monde 60 St Mary Street, (029) 2038 7376. The rules of engagement are to queue (bookings are taken only for large parties), then jostle to choose fish and seafood (or steak) from large display cabinets, and wine from blackboards, then go to your table, stopping off at the salad bar on the way. Chargrilling and baking in sea salt are the two favoured cooking methods for the splendidly fresh fish (priced by weight). For starters, maybe opt for a pint of shrimps, deep-fried squid, or fish pâté. To finish, crêpes suzette is the only option. Closed Sun. Under the same roof, and run along similar lines, are La Brasserie (closed Sun, tel (029) 2037 2164) and Champers (closed Sun L, tel (029) 2037 3363); another branch of the expanding empire is Caesar's Arms in Creigiau (see Round-up entry).

• **Chepstow** (Monmouthshire)

Wye Knot 18A The Back, (01291) 622929. A spacious, airy restaurant on the riverbank with friendly efficient service of ambitious modern dishes from a blackboard menu. High-quality ingredients are put to good use, producing smooth, strongly flavoured chicken liver parfait, perhaps followed by tender pork loin on creamy mash with crisp black pudding and smoked bacon. Finish with crisp charlotte of rhubarb and pears with honey and saffron ice cream. Breads come on a trolley, coffee with tiny chocolates and minuscule Danish pastries. Wines include several by the glass; most bottles are below £20. Closed Sat L and Sun D.

• **Church Bay** (Isle of Anglesey)

Lobster Pot Church Bay, (01407) 730588. Lindy Wood took over this family business from her parents in the 1980s and makes weekly treks around the Lleyn Peninsula to buy lobsters and crabs from local fishermen. The fruits of her travels turn up in many forms: grilled with garlic butter, thermidor, or as part of a seafood platter. Starters are kept simple – sweet-cured herring, potted shrimps – and steak, chicken or duck are the non-seafood options. Finish with pavlova or fruit pie. Open Easter to Oct Tue to Sat (also Sun in Aug and bank hols).

• **Creigiau** (Cardiff)

Caesar's Arms Cardiff Road, (029) 2089 0486. Just outside Cardiff, down a winding country lane, Caesar's Arms is more country restaurant than pub, though you enter through a bar where drinks are served. Food is listed on boards behind the bar, but the best bet is just to point out what you want from the meats, fish and game on display in chiller cabinets. These are simply grilled and served with a sauce of choice, plus chips or boiled potatoes and salad from the self-service counter. Starters, also on display, might include wild mushroom risotto, or provençale fish soup. Wines, also listed on blackboards, are wide ranging and reasonably priced. Closed Sun D.

• **GLANWYDDEN** (Conwy)
Queen's Head Glanwydden, (01492) 546570. Sally and Robert Cureton have been running this attractive country pub-restaurant for 20 years. Food is ordered at the bar from a lengthy menu of hot and cold appetisers, pasta and salad dishes, steaks and at least half a dozen fish 'specialities'. The latter have included Conwy crab salad, and baked plaice fillet with shrimp and fennel butter, while among meat specials have been Glanwydden lamb cutlets with plum and port sauce, and steak and mushroom pie. Finish with pecan pie or tiramisù. At lunchtime, open rolls might be filled with rare beef and gherkins or grilled cheese and smoked bacon. Open all week, food served all day Sun. Reports, please.

• **LAUGHARNE** (Carmarthenshire)
Cors Restaurant Laugharne, (01994) 427219. This country house restaurant, close to the river Corran, boasts beautiful landscaped gardens, pleasant staff and an attractive weekly-changing menu that makes good use of fish and local products. Typical starters have included seared scallops with chives, and potato and dill pancake with smoked salmon, while mains run to roast rack of Carmarthenshire salt marsh lamb, and grilled turbot fillets with truffle oil, asparagus and lemon. House wines start at £9.50. Open Thur to Sat D.

• **LLANABER** (Gwynedd)
Llwyndu Farmhouse Llanaber, (01341) 280144. The ancient doorway of this sixteenth-century farmhouse with rooms – in an enviable position overlooking Cardigan Bay – leads to oak beams, inglenook fireplaces and a stone-walled dining room. A modern daily-changing menu based on local produce may offer smoked haddock rarebit with laverbread, roast shoulder of Welsh lamb, or vegetarian Glamorgan cutlet. Local fish and their own organic salads, vegetables and herbs also feature strongly. Finish with butterscotch banana pancakes. Open Mon to Sat D only.

• **LLANFYLLIN** (Powys)
Seeds 5 Penybryn Cottages, High Street, (01691) 648604. Chef-proprietor Mark Seager has been producing his traditional style of food in this rural location for a decade now. Perhaps smoked salmon and hot asparagus to start, followed by rack of Welsh lamb with a herb crust or chicken with port and cream sauce as main courses. Puddings have included rich chocolate terrine and lemon posset. The restaurant is non-smoking. Closed Mon.

• **LLANGOLLEN** (Denbighshire)
Gales 18 Bridge Street, (01978) 860089. Set in the historic town of Llangollen, close to the River Dee, this small hotel has a Georgian exterior that gives little indication of the modish Continental bistro to be found within. The diverse daily-changing menu typically takes in pepper and onion quiche, monkfish in a creamy coconut, piri-piri and soy sauce, and chicken korma with pineapple. Finish with banana crème fraîche and mascarpone brûlée, or Amaretto cheesecake. Closed Sun.

• **LLANWDDYN** (Powys)
Lake Vyrnwy Hotel Lake Vyrnwy, (01691) 870692. The hotel is inextricably linked to the body of water whose name it bears; man-made at the end of the nineteenth century the lake provides a magnificent panorama for those diners lucky enough to get a window table. The hotel specialises in outdoor pursuits, including fishing (on the lake, of course),

orienteering, bird-watching and falconry. The dining room, including a conservatory, is the setting for fixed-price menus that have typically provided warm aromatic confit duck leg on beetroot mash with a sweet onion jus, followed by poached fillet of Cornish sea bass on Vichy carrots, saffron potatoes and shellfish cream, with iced pistachio parfait on a warm fudge sauce to finish. Open all week.

• **PENMAENPOOL** (Gwynedd)
Penmaenuchaf Hall Penmaenpool, (01341) 422129. Fresh flowers from the garden contribute to the elegance of the dining room, but there are also charming views of rhododendrons and azaleas in their own habitat. Menu descriptions, also somewhat flowery, are sometimes hard to reconcile with the food on the plate, provided by yet another new chef this year, but successful dishes have included a 'mille-feuille' tower of aubergine wafers sandwiching layers of plaice fillet, aubergine purée and mushy peas with a good shellfish sauce. While subtlety and bananas are not often closely connected, banana tarte Tatin with a subtle butterscotch sauce was considered the best dish of one meal. Open all week.

• **SOLVA** (Pembrokeshire)
The Old Pharmacy 5 Main Street, (01437) 720005. The well-travelled Lawton brothers run a bright and homely café-restaurant, open all day from 10 until 9.30 every day except Tuesday. In the dining room at the rear, overlooking the riverside garden, options take in morning coffee and afternoon tea (try a cappuccino with home-made bara brith) and light lunches (maybe Solva crab sandwich, or fish and chips with tartare sauce). More ambitious evening meals might feature local lobster bisque, herb-crusted rack of Welsh lamb, or Gressingham duck with plum sauce. Finish with tiramisù or baked Alaska. Thirty or so reasonably priced wines. Closed Tue.

• **SWANSEA** (Swansea)
L'Amuse 93 Newton Road, (01792) 366006. Kate Cole is the francophile chef-proprietor of this small restaurant, assisted front-of-house by the 'efficient, unflappable' Emmanuele. Among recommended dishes has been the house speciality croustillant de pied de cochon with sauce gribiche. Otherwise the set-price menu typically goes in for starters of scallops with peas and red wine sauce, or a salad of duck gizzards with sauté potatoes and bacon, perhaps followed by modern main courses of seared tuna with ratatouille, roast lamb rump with pesto mash, or duck magret with strawberry sauce. High standards continue with Alpine cheeses and desserts such as white chocolate mousse with nectarines. Open Tue to Sat.

P.A.'s 95 Newton Road, (01792) 367723. Menus change frequently in this compact wine and food bar, where fish is a big draw. At lunch, cream of fennel soup, or crab pâté, might be followed by salmon with tomato and chilli salsa, or fried plaice with tartare sauce. A daily specials board might offer marinated chargrilled red snapper, or baked fillet of sewin with cockle and tarragon sauce, while the carte typically goes in for duck liver and orange pâté with onion marmalade, followed by Welsh lamb with rosemary roast potatoes, and caramelised oranges in Grand Marnier. Closed Sun D.

• **TENBY** (Pembrokeshire)
Mews Bistro The Mews, Upper Frog Street, (01834) 844068. Sit outside at lunchtime (July and August only) on the flower-clad terrace, or in the bustling dining room. Fish, not surprisingly, dominates: global influences (Creole, Thai and Mediterranean) appear in mussels with green pepper, garlic and black bean sauce, or Tenby sea bass with gazpacho. The large menu includes plenty of choice for vegetarians and carnivores. Passion fruit crème brûlée is a typical dessert. Closed Sun D Nov to May, Mon D Nov to March.

• **TREDUNNOCK** (Monmouthshire)
The Newbridge Tredunnock, (01633) 451000. An oasis in rural Welsh

borderlands, this warm, welcoming and attractively refurbished country pub and restaurant (stripped wooden floors, terracotta walls, exposed beams) overlooks the River Usk. Its modern menu includes foie gras and chicken liver parfait, and crispy duck confit, while main courses are mostly grills and roasts: chargrilled beef with béarnaise, or roast fillet of cod, for example. Finish with caramelised lemon tart with blackcurrant ice cream. Open all week.

• **Usk** (Monmouthshire)
Bush House 15 Bridge Street, (01291) 672929. This pleasant French bistro-style restaurant, run by self-taught chef Steven Rogers, has dark green paintwork, Toulouse-Lautrec posters, lots of pot plants, and tables set with candles and large glasses on green and white clothed tables. The menu calls on Mediterranean and Middle Eastern ideas to spice up dishes that use ingredients as local as medallions of Brecon venison, which might come with tasty gnocchi and tangy red cabbage. Beef and lamb are also Welsh, and adventurous fish dishes might include chargrilled grey mullet with oriental bubble and squeak. Interesting modestly priced, short wine list. Closed Sun D; also closed Mon to Fri L in winter.

• **Welsh Hook** (Pembrokeshire)
Stone Hall Welsh Hook, (01348) 840212. Martine Watson offers 'genuine French cuisine' at her 600-year-old manor house, where inglenook fireplaces, wood panelling and ten acres of gardens and woodland add to the atmosphere. Scallops with garlic, snails in cream, cassoulet and sole meunière confirm the credentials of the bilingual carte and set dinner menu, while seasonal local produce is the other driving force. Profiteroles or crème brûlée are typical desserts. Open D Tue to Sun.

Channel Islands

• **St Peter Port** (Guernsey)
La Frégate St Peter Port, (01481) 724624. The restaurant and cocktail bar have been refurbished, but wonderful views of the harbour and the mostly classical French style of cooking remain unchanged. On a generous carte, starters might include hot cheese beignets with herb sauce, or cold peppered smoked chicken with avocado salad, while typical main courses have been rack of lamb carved at table, and steamed chicken breast stuffed with crab in a cream sauce. Finish perhaps with profiteroles or cheese. A 'gourmand' menu is available, and lunches are generally lighter and simpler. Al fresco dining on the terrace is an option in fine weather. Wines are pricey. Open all week.

Le Nautique Quay Steps, (01481) 721714. One of Guernsey's oldest-established seafood restaurants, located on the front overlooking the harbour, is under new ownership. Chef-proprietor Günter Botzenhardt, formerly of La Frégate, takes a traditional approach, while right-hand man Kevin Gauvain adds some modern ideas. Thus, menus offer smoked salmon with horseradish cream, lobster thermidor, and Dover sole meunière, alongside gazpacho of crab with ginger and coriander, or sea bass with chilli and pineapple. Besides fish, there are also plenty of meat (mainly chargrills) and vegetarian options. To finish, an Austrian nut pudding with walnut ice cream may tempt. Closed Sat L and Sun.

Northern Ireland

• **Londonderry** (Co Londonderry)
Ardmore Restaurant 32 Ardmore Road, (028) 7134 9279. Set in acres of parkland, with a conservatory overlooking the lake, waterfall and gardens, this elegant eighteenth-century house offers a fairly formal country house dining experience. The cooking is predominantly classical French in style, though wider influences are apparent. Starters of red onion tartlet with goats' cheese, or home-made salmon and crab cakes, might be followed by baked turbot or roast fillet of venison,

with perhaps lemon tart with orange ice cream to finish; vegetarian and gastronomic menus are also available. The extensive global wine list includes six half-bottles and six by the glass. Another change of chef, so more reports please. Open all week.

The Good Food Club 2000

Many thanks to all the following people who contributed to this year's *Guide* . . .

Dr K.R. Aberdour
Dr A.H. Abrahams
Dr Sidney Abrahams
Mr A.D. Abrams
Ann Adams
Robert Adams
Peter Adcock
Dr Clive Addis-Jones
Jacqueline Ah-Fong
Maggie Ainsley
Mr and Mrs John Aird
Mrs P.M. Albers
Mr and Mrs Edward Album
Richard and Jo Alderson
R.C. Aldridge
Mr and Mrs M.S. Alexander
V. Alexander
Harry Allen
Mrs P. Allison
Catherine Allwood
J.C.P. Amos
Mark Andrew
Gwen and Peter Andrews
Philip Andrews
Catherine Angell
Mr and Mrs Kurt Angelrath
Major A.J. Anspach
Mrs M.S. Antoncini
Mr T. Appleton
Cynthia Archer
Mr P.F. Arden
W.M.J. Armstrong
William Arrowsmith
Mrs H.G. Ashburn
G. Ashworth
V. Ashworth
Brian Atkinson
Gail Atkinson
Ian Atlee
Jack and Mireille Attas
Martin Attewell
H.L.K. Avis
Jean Avis
Ann Bagnall
Mrs J. Bailey
Jane and Martin Bailey
Mr R. Bailey
Iain Baillie
Mr W.H. Baily
Mr A. Baker
Alan and Margot Baker
Graham Balfry
Mr and Mrs C. Ballard
Katrina Balmforth
Bryan Barker
John Barker
Glenice Barnard
Mr and Mrs Barnes
Mr K.J. Barnes
Mike Barnes
Richard Barnes
J.M. Barney
Mrs C.A. Baron
Mr and Mrs R.S. Barratt
G.J. Barrett
Victoria Barrett
Sarah Barrington
Ian Barron
Janet Barron
Tony Barrow
Mr B.J. Barry
Jane Barry
Mr M.D. Bartlett
David and Vivien Barton
John Baster
David Bate
Penny Bateman
E.A. Baxter
Stephen Baxter
N. Baybutt
Conrad Bayliss
B. and H. Beaumont
Tim Beaumont
Harvey Beaver
Anthony Beck
Mr F.R. Beckett
R.S. Beddoe
Prof and Mrs John Belchem
C.J. Bell
Jeffrey Bell
Mr P. Bell
Helen Bellis
David Ben-Aryeah
Mr A. Benda
Mr T. Bendhem
J. Bennett
Mr and Mrs R.G. Bennett
Mr and Mrs M. Benton
W.M. Bentsen
Stephen Beresford
Michael Berger
P. Berman
Mr and Mrs Edward Bernard
Gabriele Berneck
B.A. Bernstein
Miss C. Berry
Mr and Mrs E. Berry
Mr W.J. Best
Dr Delia Bickerton
Jeff Bidwell
Dr C. Bielawski
Mr and Mrs P. Billinghurst
Mark Billington
Betty and Chris Birch
Sir Roger Birch CBE
Michael Bird
Mr R.G. Birt
Rhian Bishop
Andrzej Bisztyga
Anne Blackburn
C.T. Blackburn
Roger Blackburn
Diana Blake
Edward Blincoe
Mr and Mrs S. Bliss
Edgar and Anita Blum
P.M. Bolton
Julia Bolwell
Alison Bond
Peter Bontoft
Norman Bookbinder
Dr Ben Booth
Martin Booth
Mr and Mrs W.H. Booth
Robin Bourne
Mr A.J. Bowen
Gill Bracey
Anthony Bradbury
Julian Bradley
Pierce Bradley
Mr M. Brady
Aimee Brame
H. Bramwell
Mr and Mrs Frank Branney
Mr B. Brears
Mr and Mrs Edwin Brew
W.G. Brewer
Mrs J. Bridge
Jonica Bridge
Tom Briody
B.J. Britton
David Britton
Mr Roy Bromell
Douglas Brooks
Gillian Brooks
Grahame Brooks
Miss D. Brown
Dr and Mrs D.G. Brown
Graham Brown
Heather and Andrew Brown
Ian Brown
Mrs J. Brown
Eric Bruce
Neil Bruce
David Brundrett
Mr and Mrs S.G. Brunning
Dr John Brunton
William Bruton
R.A. Bryan
Mr and Mrs Edgar Bryant
Mr and Mrs J.H. Bryant
Mary Bryne
Percival Buchanan
Mr and Mrs H.G. Buck
Mrs J.S. Buckingham
Paula Buckland
R.W. Buckle
Mrs J. Bull

Daphne Bullock
Prof and Mrs R.G.H. Bunce
A.E. Bundy
Carol Bunker
Mr and Mrs Stephen Bunn
Mr and Mrs A.G.M. Burge
Daphne Burgess
J.S. Burn
Mr G.H. Burns
Mr M.H. Burr
Robert and Dorothy Burrows
A.W. Burton
Ms S. Burton
David Busby
Richard Bush
Mr and Mrs Butler
Jane Butler
Peter Byworth
Prof Robert Cahn
Gordon Cain
Mrs J. Cameron
Greg Campbell
Mrs R.A. Campbell-Gibson
Mr and Mrs P.H. Carlisle
L. Carne
Jason Carpenter
Mr R. Carpenter
Dr John Carroll
Mr A.E. Carter
A.J. Carter
Mr N. Carter
Paul Carter
David Cartwright
Mr J.A.H. Cartwright
Mike Carwithen
Michael Casey
Dr R.E. Catlow
Judith Cawert
Jacky Ceeney
George Cernoch
Ian Chalmers
M.A. Chamberlain
M.S. Chance
Mr A.W.T. Chapman
P. and H. Chapman
Mr and Mrs R.S. Charles
S. Charles
Roger Chater
Lt.Col and Mrs G. Chatham
Mrs E. Chatten
H. Chaytor
Peter Cheetham
Judith Chegwidden
Mr W.J. Chesneau
Mrs S. Chester
Meryl and Mike Chetwood
Marie Chevallier
Grace Ciappara
Lesley Clare
Mr and Mrs Beverley Clark
Celia Clark
Gordon Clark
Mary Clark
Sandra Clark
C. Clarke
John and Pamela Clarke
Neil and Gilly Clarke
Dr D.F.G. Clegg
K. Cleveland
Fiona and Mark Clifton
Clive Coates
Peter Cobb
Roger Cockbill
A. Cohen
Ann Cohen
Mr and Mrs Cole
K.J. Coleman
L. Coleman
Robby and Jenny Coleman
N.P. Coley
Anna Collard
Janet Collett
David Collier
Nicholas Collingwood
J.H. Collins
Michael Colquitt
Hannah Colton
Geoffrey Colvile
Sara Colville
Sheila Colvin
Mr R.T. Combe
Mr M. Comninos
Richard Comyn
Mrs M. Conlin
Peggy Connor
Mr A.S. Cook
John Cook
Dr and Mrs R.C. Cooke
Prof R.C. Cookson FRS.
G.V. Coombs
Dr and Mrs A.L. Cooper
Mr and Mrs A.M. Cooper
Dr and Mrs J.C.W. Cope
Ron and Sheila Corbett
Mr and Mrs Corin
T. Cornish
D.W. Costain
Sean Coughlan
Stephen Court
Simon Couzens
Hilary Cowan
Mr S. Cowan
Andrea Cox
Dr David Cox
Diane Cox
Gail Cox
Sally Cox
Mrs C. Cramb
David and Christina Cramb
Mr and Mrs Peter Crane
Bernard Crean
Hugh Creighton
Mr and Mrs Crisp
S.M. Croft
Richard Crosby
Mr A. Cross
Rodney Cross
Diana Culshaw
Dr and Mrs P.N. Cunliffe
Richard Curry
Dr Stan da Prato
W.J.A. Dacombe
M.E. Dakin
Michael Dallas
Mr G.W. Dalton
Mrs S.T. Daly
Mr and Mrs Dalzell
Valerie Daniel
Patricia Darby
Chris and Rachael Daubney
David Davey
Helen Davey
Tony Davey
Mr and Mrs D.W.M. Davidson
Mr W.H. Davidson
Beatrix Davies
Duncan Davies
Dr Gareth Davies
Naomi Davies
Peter and Valerie Davies
Mrs S. Davies
Gwilym Davies-Jones
D.S. Davis
Miss M.L. Davis
G. Davison
Dr and Mrs R.P.R. Dawber
Roger Dawe
Mr and Mrs Keith Dawson
Paul Dawson
C.J. Day
Mr M.J. Day
Sarah Day
Mr and Mrs F.C. de Paula
M.H. de Silva
Mrs M. Deacon
Sue and Nigel Deacon
Mr and Mrs R. Dean
Ms N.C. Dee
Mrs L. Deeks
Mr and Mrs Jonathan Denby
Mr and Mrs Dewar
K.H Dinsley
Simon Dixon
Mr D.J. Dobbert
Mr G.M. Dobbie
B.M. Dobble
M.L. Dodd
Mr Dodman
Mrs B. Doherty
Maggi Doohan
Brian Doris
Mr and Mrs James Douglas
P. Douglas
Susy Dowse
Robin Drummond
Mr and Mrs S. Drury
Laleh Dubash
John Ducker
Sally Duckham
Ian Duckworth
James Dumville
Simon Dunning
Paul Dwyer
Paul Dyer
Dr R.J. Eaglen
Dr and Mrs Lindsay Easton
Mr and Mrs K. Eckett
Dr S. Eden
Mr A. Edwards
Aileen Edwards
Bryan Edwards
Guy Edwards
Malcolm Edwards
Paul Edwards
John Elder
Steven Elief
Mr and Mrs Denis Elliott
Mr I.R. Elliott
James Elliott
Mr L.C. Elliott
Lynn Elliott

Roy Elliott
J.M. Ellis
Jean Embleton
Pauline J. Emerick
Prof and Mrs C.E. Engel
Manfred Engel
D.G. Esaias
Robin and Glenna Etheridge
C. Evans
Mr and Mrs G.H. Evans
J.L.D. Evans
Peter Evans
Mrs V. Evans
Angus Ewart
Trevor Faber
P.T.A. Fagan
John Fahy
I. Fair
Mrs J. Fairbrother
John Fairley
Mr E. Farrar
Malcolm Farrer-Brown
Ann Farrow
Sally Fawcett
Mr G.A. Fenn
John Fenwick
Mrs Fereday
C.G. Ferguson
Alan Field
G.A. Field
Mr A.E.M. Fine
Dr F. Fisher
Linda Fisher
Sir Richard Fitzherbert
T.C. Flanagan
Mrs S. Fleming
G.E Fletcher
Mr G.R.K. Fletcher
Mrs M. Fletcher
Mrs M. Fone
D.E. Ford
Mrs P.L. Forrest
Marie Forsyth
Mr A. Foster
G. Foster
P.R.N. Fowler
Mr R.J.N. Fowler
Sherry Fowler
Paul Fox
Mr H.M. Foy
Linda Frain
Dr M.L. Franks
Mr C. Fraser
Mr R. Freeman
Allen Freer
M. French
Mr and Mrs P.J. Frogley
Dr D.J. Frost
G.E. Frost
Mr and Mrs G.W. Frost
Mrs M. Frost
Claire Fuller
Mr A. Furness
Mr S. Futter
Christine Fyffe
Mr D.A Gamble
Mr and Mrs Tony Gamble
R.A. Gamblin
David and Elsie Garland
R.J. Garlick
Amanda Garrett
A.B. Garrioch
Dr Ian Gavin
Janet Gayler
Geoffrey Gee
Helen Gell
Rosemary George
A. Georgiades
R. Getvoldsen
Mr A. Gibbon
Richard Gibson
Kathryn and Ben Gilbert
Michael Gilchrist
Michael Gillette-Browning
R.C. Glossop
Angela Goddard
Jason Goddard
Hilary and Alan Godfrey
Mr and Mrs Jim Godfrey
Dr Lawrence Goldie
Mr D.C. Goldrei
Linda and Susie Goldschmidt
Lord and Lady Goodhart
L.D. Goodman
P. Goodman
Katherine Goodrich
Larry and Pauline Goodson
C.A. Goodwin
Ashley Gordon
Mr M. Gordon-Russell
Paul Gordon-Saker
M. Gore
Mr and Mrs David Gostyn
G.K. Gouldman
Robert Gower
Mr M.B. Gowers
Mr D. Graham
Dr A. Grant
Pat and Ken Gray
Mr and Mrs C.J. Green
David Green
Kate Green
Mr and Mrs Greenhow
F.C. Greenop
Alan Greenwood
Jim Greenwood
Mr W.N. Greenwood
Conal Gregory
T. Gribbin
Mr R.F. Grieve
Mr J. Griffiths
T.J. Griffiths
Mr R.F.B. Grimble
William Grime
Mr N.M. Grimwood
John Grist
Lt K.R. Groves
T. Grumley-Grennan
John Guest
Sally Gugen
Mrs P.A. Gunther
Michelle and Spencer Hagard
Alan and Karen Haig
Mrs A.L. Haines
Dr C.I. Haines
Amanda Haley
Dr Bryan Hall
Mr I. Hall
John and Joan Hall
Nick Hall
Richard Hall
Dr J. Ham
Dr B. Hamilton
Ms D. Hammett
John Hammond
Gordon Hands
Mr F.G. Hankins
Philip Hanna
David Hansen
Maurice Hanssen
David Harcus
David and Vicki Harding
Mr R. Harding
Anne Hardy
Felice Hardy
Mrs J.E. Hardy
Christopher Harlowe
Alice Harper
Tim Harper
G. Harris
James Harris
Paul Harrison
Mrs S. Harrison
Elfine Hartley
Mr J.D. Hartley
Brian Harvey
J.C. Harvey
Dr Peter Harvey
Dr David Haslam
Mrs M. Haste
Mr and Mrs P.R. Hawksworth
Norma Hayes
J. Hayter
Sheila Hazelden
Canon N. Heavisides
A.E. Henderson
L.G. Henry
Mr N.F. Henshaw
G.A. Hepworth
Philip Herlihy
Dr Andrew Herxheimer
D.W. Heskett
M.I. Hesselberg
Gad Heuman
Janet and David Hewer
Alistair Hewitson
Judy Hiam
Jennifer Hicks
John Hicks
J.E. Hilditch
Joan Hilditch
Rupert and Nicola Hill
Wendy Hillary
L. Hillman
Barbara Hindley
Mr E. Hinds
Roger Hird
Dr Peter Hitt
Leslie Hoare
Mr and Mrs P.A. Hoare
Kate Hobson
Mr and Mrs R. Hodges
Colin Hodson
Roger Hole
Nick Hollis
Mr J.F. Holman
N.E. Holmes
P.B. Homer
Chris Honnor
Chris Hook
Dr and Mrs David Hooker
Mrs D. Hooley
Mrs J. Hope
Gillian Hopkinson
Mr Hopper
M.R. Hornsey
Andrew Horsler

Dr Keith Hotten
Mrs C.E. Housley
Mr D.P. Howell
Mark Howells
Mr P. Howkins
Melvyn Hoyle
G. Huckle
Kathryn Hugh
A.F. Hughes
Mr C. Hughes
J.M. Hughes
Dr L. Hughes
Andrew Humble
Gary Hunt
Sheila Hunt
Dr Tim Hunt
D. Hunter
Colin Huntley
Mr C.J. Hurd
Mary Hutchinson
Dr James Hutton
Mr T.J. Hypher
Rosemary Inge
Mr A.H. Ingram
K.G. Isaacson
R.J. Ivory
Mrs B.W. Jack
Dr H.R.S. Jack
Louise Jack
James McG. Jackson
Peter Jackson
Mr A.L. Jacobs
Dr P. Jacques
E.M. James
G.S. James
Peter James
Mrs M. Jameson
Bruce Jamieson
Alan and Christine Jeffery
A.B. Jenkins
Valerie Jenkins
Paul Jerome
Elspeth Jervie
David Jervois
Stephen Jessel
Mrs E.M. Jewell
Peter Johncock
Brian Johnson
Brian and Margaret Johnson
Russell L. Johnson
Miss K. Johnston
Alexander Johnstone
Dr Jacqueline Jolleys
David Jones
Ian Jones
Mel Jones
Oliver Jones
Paul Joslin
Paulo Karat
Mr R. Karpinski
Dr Leon Kaufman
J.G. Kavanagh
J.R. Kay
Alexander Keeling
Sheila Keene
John Kelcey
Geoffrey Kemp
Mr P.G. Kemp
R. Kendall
Julia Kendrick
A.W. Kenny
Mr R.B. Kenyon
T.G. Keown
Doris Ker
Peter Kershaw
Rev Peter Kettle
Elizabeth Key
Mr and Mrs D. Khan
Mr J.H. Kilby
Parker Kincaid
Michael King
Mr S. King
J. Kirby
Mr and Mrs Michael Kirk
Ronald Kirkby
Ruth Kitching
Charles Kleimunt
R. Knight
C.F. Kongh
Ms H. Kroll
Bill and Helen Kronfeld
Mr I. Laidlaw-Dickson
Mr and Mrs G. Lakmaker
A.J. Lambert
R. Lambert
Karen Lancaster
M.D. Lane
Mr P. Lane
Peter Lashmar
Mr A. Laurence
John Lawrence
Peter Lawrence
Mr A. Lawson
Marcia Layton
Dr Susan Lea
A.J.N. Lee
Geoffrey Lee
R.J.A. Lee
Mrs J.M. Lefeaux
J. Legge
Mrs K. Leonard
Michael Leonard
Mr P.L. Leonard
Andrew Leslie
Mr D.J. Lethem
Michael Levene
Lionel Leventhal
Mr and Mrs M. Lever
Peter Lewars
Alan Lewis
Benjamin Lewis
Mrs C. Lewis
Carole Lewis
Mrs D.F. Lewis
David Lewis
Graham and Angela Lewis
Paul Lewis
Mr and Mrs R.G. Lightwood
Jillian Lindon
Keith and Katherine Lindop
D.R. Linnell
Mr and Mrs Noel Livesey
Dr David Lloyd
Andrew Lobbenberg
Mrs Janet Lockett
Victoria Logue
Ian Long
Sheila M. Longbottom
L.F. Lord
Jacqui and Richard Lote
Mr G.M. Lough
Deborah Loveluck
Martin Lovett
Andrew Low
Mr and Mrs P.A. Lowater
Mrs G. Lowes
Mr and Mrs B. Lox
Jeremy Lucas
Mr M. Lucas
Mr J.N. Lunn
Mrs J.F. Lyons
Mr and Mrs A. Lysandrides
Michael Mabbs
C.J. Mabley
Col T.C.H. Macafee
Bruce MacEacharn
Mr R.B. MacGeachy
Mr J.B. MacGill
Andy Macgowan
Mr A.J. Macintosh
Michael Mackenzie
Mrs S.A. Mackenzie
Mr R.H. Mackett
Mrs A. Mackinnon
Sharon Maclaren
Helen Maclennan
Dr and Mrs B. Macnamara
Jean Macpherson
Michael Madden
Glyn Maddocks
Prof Margaret Maden
H.T. Madoc-Jones
Peter Mair
Mr C. Makin
Geoffrey Makin
Mrs J.W. Makinson
Adrian Mann
Lynn Manning
Janet Mansfield
Susan Mansfield
Dr Howard Manvel
Mrs R. Marcus
Judge Bernard Marder
Mr and Mrs David Margetts
David Mariano
Andrew Marks
Dr C. Markus
Philippa Marnham
Pamela Marriott
June Marsden
Mr and Mrs J.R. Marsh
R.O. Marshall
Sophie Marshall
Mr and Mrs T.F. Marshall
Mr and Mrs St John Marston
Ali Martin
Fiona Martin
Mr and Mrs G.D. Martin
Roger and Joan Martin
Charles Mason
David Massey
Don Massey
Michael Masters
Douglas Matheson
Bernard D. Mathews
Dr R.H. Mathews
Ray Mathews
Michael Matthews
Ian May
Mrs R.J. McArdle
Andrew McAlpine
Bruce McAlpine
Mr and Mrs Nick McAndrew
Mark McCance
Ronald McCellar
Louise McCormick
Walter McCrindle
Colin and Lilian McGhee
Mike McKechnie
C. McKeown

Colin McKerrow
David McLeod
Mr D.C. McQueen
Alan McViety
Mrs A. Mead
Dr A. Melinkoff
Sally Melling
Claire Mendez
Mr and Mrs Malcolm Menzies
David Metcalfe
Michael Meyer
Jane Miller
Janet Miller
Mr and Mrs J. Mills
Mr K.S. Mingle
Mrs J. Minter
G.J. Mist
Mr and Mrs R.E. Mitchell
Wilson Mitchell
A.J. Mole
Mrs P.I. Monk
David Monks
Linda Montague
Wendy Montague
Dr V. Montegriffo
Prof Eric Moonman
Jane Moor
Mr and Mrs Moore
E.A. Moore
F.R. Moore
David and Trish Morgan
John Morgan
Veronica Morgan
Chris Morrell
Mrs B. Morris
Brian Moss
Mrs G. Mumby
Mr S. Munby
George Murphy
Mr G.R. Murray
Rev A.G. Mursell
Edward Myatt
Mrs N.E. Myring
Cheryl Naclerio
Mr and Mrs Natton
Mr C.H. Naylor
Zan Nelson
Iain Nesbitt
Jenny Newby
Paul and Susan Newby
Mr and Mrs Adrian Newell
Neil Newman
Dr Paul Nicholas
Tim Nicholas
Dr and Mrs J.W. Nicholls
B.S. Nichols
Jane Nicholson
John Nisbet
David Nobbs
Peter Noble
Mr and Mrs Max Nocton
Dr J.R. Norman
Mr J.G. Norris
Graham Norwood
David Nutt
Mr G.H. Nuttall
D.A O'Bryen
Michael and Lisa O'Hare
Lucy O'Leary
Mr W.B. O'Neill
Greg O'Reilly
Charles Oatwig-Thain
John Oddey
Anthony Ogden
J. Oglanby
R.R. Ogle
John Oldale
B.P. Oliver
John and Jean Orchard
Anne Orton
Patricia Orwell
Mr and Mrs R.E. Osborne
D.M. Owen
Lt Col D.L.H. Owen
Mrs Meriel Packman
Aidan Paddick
Dianne Page
Mrs J.E. Pailthorpe
Ms Painter
James Palmer
M. Palmer
Michael Panter
Lawrence Parish
Sefton Parke
Mr J.J. Parker
Mr and Mrs R. Parker
Richard and Andrea Parker
Mrs V.A. Parker
Chris Parkin
Trevor Parkinson
David Parnell
Alan and Janet Parry
Pamela Parry
Dr C.J. Parsons
M. Partridge
Janette Paterson
R.C Patrick
David Patten
Michael Pattison
Iain Patton
Ms L. Pavincich
Mr and Mrs Tony Peace
Henry Peach
Christopher Peeke
Mr and Mrs C.S. Perkins
Emma Perry
Lisa and David Perry
B. Perryman
Mrs E.M. Petrusewicz
Drs Anne and Andrew Phellas
D.E. Phillips
Laura Phillips
C.N. Phipps
B.J. Pickering
David Pilling
Harry Piper
Michael Pitel
Hugh Pitt
S.C.W. Pitt
Prof Peter Plesch
A.G.S. Pollock
Dr and Mrs A.F. Polmear
David Poole
Mr and Mrs R.J.M Pope
Lucy Portch
Judy Potts
John Poulter
Mr and Mrs S.G. Pratt
Mr and Mrs M.J. Price
Edwin Prince
Mrs A. Proudfoot
Barbara and Allan Prys-Williams
Mrs J. Pugh
Lt Col R.G.L. Pugh
Howard Pursey
Mr M.J. Radcliffe
Lynn Raeburn
Alvin Rakoff
Dr and Mrs D.G.S. Randall
Colin Randell
Dr A.M. Rankin
Dr M.S. Raschid
Susan Rasmussen
Gordon Ratcliffe
Mr S. Ratcliffe
Dr and Mrs Len Ratoff
Gerald Ratzin
Marie-Stella Ray
H.R. Raymond
Mary Rayner
Wendy Rea
Mrs M.A. Read
Susan Reed
Prof L. Rees
Lawrence Reid
Maureen Rennie
John Reuter
G. Rhodes
John Rhodes
J.N. Richards
Mr C.J. Richardson
M. Rickman
Carol Riddick
Celia Ridley
Gordon Ringrose
Dr B. Ritson
Alan Roberts
Franklyn Roberts
Lynne Roberts
Mark Roberts
David and Susie Robertson
Capt N. Robertson
Ronald and Rosemary Robertson
C.J. Robinson
Mr D.R. Robinson
Harry Robinson
Mr and Mrs Ivor Robinson
John Robotham
Mr and Mrs M. Roche
J. Rochelle
Lord Rodgers
David Rodgers
Anne Rogers
Sir Frank Rogers
James Rogers
Larry Rolland
Sylvia Rondel
Peter Rooke
Mr and Mrs Jeffery Rose
Rebecca Rosner
Mr J. Ross
H.H. Rosser
Dieter Rossi
Virginia Routh
Prof David Rowley
Jill Rowley
Dr R. Rowsell
Mr and Mrs Ian Royle
H. Rubinstein
J.E.M. Ruffer
Mrs L. Rushton
Mr D. Russell
Mr G. Russell
Gianna Russian
Mr J.S. Rutter
Michael Ryan
Ilse Ryder

George and Maggie Rylance
Mrs C. Rymer
K. Saalson
Lady Sachs
Mr L. Saffron
Jackie Sandford
Jeff Sargant
Jane Sargent
Timothy Saunt
Jane Savage
Paul Saxon
Alan Sayer
Chrisopher Scarles
Tony Schneider
Michael Schofield
Mr R.T. Scholes
Alexander Schouvaloff
Howard Schuman
K.H. Scollay
Esme Scott
Dr G.L. Scott
D.G. Scotter
D.N. Sedgman
Derek Seel
David Sefton
Denis Selby
R.A. Seligman
Paul Sellers
John Sergeant
Chris Sexton
John T.L. Share
Cliff and Ann-Marie Sharp
Craig Sharp
Mr and Mrs P.J. Shaw
Peter Shaw
Dennis Shead
Miss M.H. Shepley
Louise Sheppard
P.R. Shilson
Basil Short
Robin Shuckburgh
J. Shute
Michael and Marjorie Siddall
Dr G. Silverstone
G.K. Simons
Audrey and David Simpson
Mr J.A. Simpson
Dr J.R. Simpson
S.M. Sims
Peter Skinnard
Mrs J. Skinner
Duncan Slater
Fred Slegg
K.R Slingo
Malcolm Slocombe
Simon Small
Mr N.S.L. Smart
Carole Smith
Eddie Smith
Elaine Smith
F. Smith
Irene Smith
J.C. Smith
Jonathan Smith
Katherine Smith
Kenneth Smith
Marjorie Smith
Prof Lord Smith of Clifton
Mr and Mrs G.H. Snell
R.J. Snow
G. Spalton
Wg Cdr R.M. Sparkes
Alan Spedding
John Spencer Gilks
Mr and Mrs Jeffrey Stackhouse
Susan Stanley
Mr J. Stanley-Smith
Sarah Stanton-Nadin
P.A. Staples
John Steadman
Mr and Mrs M. Steadman
Anne Stein
Mrs G.M. Stein
Mrs Stephens
Alastair Stevenson
Dr Andrew Stevenson
Capt and Mrs J.S. Stewart
Dr and Mrs James Stewart
R.A. Stewart
Judy Stober
F.M. Stockdale
Victor Stone
Mrs C.M.R. Stoneham
Mr and Mrs A.N. Storey
Hilary and Malcolm Strong
Mr Julian Struthers Danskin
Ray and Douglas Stuart
B.D Sullivan
David Suratgar
Heather Sutton
Mrs A.J.G. Swainson
Michael Swallow
Keith Sykes
Brenda Symes
Mr and Mrs E.J.J. Syrett
Stephen Tarr
John Tarrant
Mr and Mrs Tate
Dr D.M. Taub
Lady Tavistock
A.C. Taylor
Carole Taylor
Elizabeth Taylor
George Taylor
Mrs J.L. Taylor
Mrs Jean Taylor
Paul Taylor
Mr and Mrs A.G. Tennent
Mrs M.E. Thacker
Russell Thersby
Alan Thomas
Gethyn Thomas
Ian Thomas
Brenda and Chris Thomason
Val Thomasson
Mr C.J. Thompson
E.J. Thompson
N.J. Thompson
Mr and Mrs Gavin Thomson
Irene Thomson
Mrs R. Thorburn
Mrs Thorne
Mr and Mrs G.N. Thornton
Jo Thornton
Mr and Mrs T. Thorpe
Elizabeth Thring
Mr and Mrs Thurlow
Michael Thursfield
Graham Thwaites
Caroline Tidbury
Mary Tigue
C. Tilson
Julian Tobin
C. and D. Tomlinson
John Tomlinson
Michael Tomlinson
M.J. Toomey
Dr C. Torrance
M. Tosh
Brian Towers
David Treadwell
Sylvia Trench
Ross Trotter
Mr and Mrs J.C.M. Troughton
John Trumper
Mr B.W.B. Turner
Barbara Turner
David Turner
Prof and Mrs J.J. Turner
John and Mary Turner
Keith Turner
R.L. Turner
Stuart Turner
Peter Turpie
Mrs Curzon Tussaud
J.G. Tyror
Ian Tysh
Mr and Mrs R. Umbers
Adrian Underwood
Mr A.R. Underwood
Mr P.G. Urben
John Urquhart
Mr S. Valente
Mrs J. Van Rijn
Mr and Mrs Ian Vance
Mr J. Vanderbilt-Sloane
P. Varney
Suzanne Vazquez
Sue Velamail
Dr Vanessa Venning
Mr J. Vernon
Georgina Vestey
Mrs A. Vicars-Mills
Michael Wace
Prof D.J. Waddington
Lilian Wakefield
Mrs A.M. Walden
Mary Waldron
Dr David Walker
Maureen Walker
Mrs Val Walker-Dendle
Pauline and Eric Wall
Millie Wallace
G. Waller
Dr Graham Wallis
Francine Walsh
Patricia Walsh
Mrs P.R. Walters
Ann Ward
Mrs O.M. Ward
Mr A.J. Wardrop
Mrs G.M. Warren
Mr R.A. Wartnaby
A. Washbourn
William and Jeannie Waterman
Anne Waters
Mr and Mrs J.S. Waters
Robert N. Waterson
Barbara Watkins
Mrs E. Watkins

A.R. Watson
H. Watson
Philip Watson
Richard Watson
Mr I.R. Watts
Anthony Webb
John Webb
Dr M Webb
Mr and Mrs M.P. Webb
R.A. Webb
Richard Webb
Mr and Mrs Henry Webber
Dr I. Webster
John Wedge
Harry Weinberger
Joanna Weldon
Keith Wells
A.R. Welton
I.E. West
Mr J.F.M. West
M.J. West
Charles Weston
Mr T.J.M. Weston
Stacey Whatling
Mr and Mrs John Wheeler
Jane White
N.H. White
Sandra Whitham
John Whiting
Mrs B. Whitley
Paul Whittaker
Mr and Mrs S. Whittle
D.A. Whitworth
Mr D.N. Whyte
Miss J. Wiblin
D.T. Wiggins
Joanne Wight-Croftend
Hon Giles Wigoder
R.N. Wilby
R.C. Wiles
David Wilkins
Prof Wilks
Mr P. Willer
Dr and Mrs D.J. Williams
Donald Williams
Dr E. Williams
Mary Williams
Robert Williams
Drs A. and C. Wilson
C.H. Wilson
Mr and Mrs Ian Wilson
Prof P.N. Wilson
Ralph Wilson
Wendy and Richard Wilson
John Window
Mr and Mrs Winning
G.M. Wisenfeld
R. Witham-Parkins
Mr and Mrs T. Withers
Mr W.J. Woodage
Paula Woodgate
James and Lis Woods
Barbara Wooldridge
Mr and Mrs P. Wraight
Dr D.G. Wray
Geraldine Wright
Mrs S. Wright
Sue Wright
D.J. Wyatt
Mr and Mrs John Wyatt
R.A. Wyld
Suzanne Wynn
Jon Wynne-Tyson
R.J. Yates
Mr S.J. Yates
Michael York-Palmer
George Yorke
Prof J.S. Yudkin

Index of entries

Index of entries

Names in bold are main entries. Names in italics are Round-ups.

Abbotsbury Seafood Bar, Weymouth 691
A Bit on the Side, Penrith 687
Acorn Inn, Evershot 674
Adams Café, London W12 39
Adare Manor, Adare 641
Adlard's, Norwich 420
Admiral Codrington, London SW3 39
Admiralty, London WC2 40
After Eight Restaurant, Rochdale 450
Airds Hotel, Port Appin 582
Air Organic, Glasgow 695
a.k.a., London WC1 41
Alastair Little, London W1 41
Alastair Little Lancaster Road, London W11 42
The Albannach, Lochinver 576
Al Bustan, London SW1 42
Al Duca, London SW1 43
Alfonso's, Cookham 290
Alfresco, St Ives 454
Al Hamra, London W1 43
Al San Vincenzo, London W2 44
Al-Shami, Oxford 426
Altnaharrie Inn, Ullapool 590
Amandier, London W2 44
Amberley Castle, Queen's Room, Amberley 220
Amerdale House, Arncliffe 223
L'Amuse, Swansea 700
Anchor Inn, Sutton Gault 481
Ancient Camp Inn, Eaton Bishop 305
Angel, Lavenham 359
Angel Hotel, Midhurst 407
Angel Inn, Hetton 335
Angel Inn, Long Crendon 375
Anglesea Arms, London W6 45
Annie's, Ballydehob 642
Annie's, Moreton-in-Marsh 410
Apprentice, London SE1 197
The Aquarium, Norwich 685
Arancia, London SE16 46
Archiestown Hotel, Archiestown 533
Ardmore Restaurant, Londonderry 701
Arisaig House, Arisaig 534
Ark, Erpingham 309
Armless Dragon, Cardiff 597
Armstrongs, Barnsley 228
Aroma II, London W1 46
Arthouse Hotel, Arthouse Grill, Glasgow 562
Arundell Arms, Lifton 367
Asakusa, London NW1 47
Assaggi, London W2 47
Assolas Country House, Kanturk 655
Atlantic Bar and Grill, London W1 48
Atrium, Edinburgh 547
Auberge du Lac, Welwyn Garden City 502
Aubergine, London SW10 48
Auchterarder House, Auchterarder 535
Auctioneer, Clitheroe 287
Aurora, London W1 197
L'Aventure, London NW8 197
Avenue, London SW1 49
Aynsome Manor, Cartmel 276
Azou, London W6 50
Babur Brasserie, London SE23 50
Back to Basics, London W1 51
Baile-na-Cille, Uig 589
Balgonie Country House, Ballater 537
Bali Sugar, London W11 51
Ballathie House, Kinclaven 573
Ballinalacken Castle, Lisdoonvarna 658
Ballylickey Manor, Le Rendez-Vous, Ballylickey 643

Ballymaloe House, Shanagarry 662
Balmoral, Number One, Edinburgh 548
Balzac Bistro, London W12 197
Bank, Birmingham 239
Bank, London WC2 52
Bank Restaurant, Crieff 694
Bank Square, Wilmslow 509
Barnard's, Denmead 297
Barton Cross, Huxham 346
Bath Priory, Bath 230
Baumann's Brasserie, Coggeshall 673
Bay Horse Hotel, Ulverston 493
Bay Horse Inn, Forton 675
Beadles, Birkenhead 239
Bear Hotel, Crickhowell 603
Beaujolais, Cheltenham 671
Becher's Brook, Liverpool 370
Beeches, Waldley 496
Beechwood Country House, Moffat 696
Beetle & Wedge, Moulsford 412
Belair House, London SE21 52
Belgo Centraal, London WC2 198
Belgo Noord, London NW1 53
La Belle Epoque, Belfast 634
Belle Epoque, Knutsford 680
Belle Epoque, London SW3 198
Bell Inn, Horndon on the Hill 340
Bell's Diner, Bristol 257
Belvedere, London W8 53
Bentley's, Shelf 464
Beotys, London WC2 198
Berlioz, Birmingham 668
Bertie's Supper Rooms, Elland 306
Bertorelli's, London WC2 198
Bettys, Harrogate 678
Bettys, Ilkley 679
Bettys, Northallerton 685
Bettys, York 693
Bibendum, London SW3 54
Bibis, Leeds 681
Bindon Country House, Wellesley Restaurant, Langford Budville 357
Birdcage, London W1 55
Bishopstrow House, Warminster 498
Y Bistro, Llanberis 608
Bistro 21, Durham 301
Blackaller Hotel, North Bovey 685
Black Bull Inn, Moulton 412
Black Chapati, Brighton & Hove 252
Black Horse Inn, Grimsthorpe 677
Blagraves House, Barnard Castle 666
Blairs Cove House, Durrus 653
Bleeding Heart, London EC1 55
Blewbury Inn, Blewbury 668
Blostin's, Shepton Mallet 688
Blue Bar Café, Edinburgh 549
Blue Bicycle, York 693
Bluebird, London SW3 56
Blue Elephant, London SW6 57
Blue Goose, Bristol 669
Blue Lion, East Witton 304
Blue Print Café, London SE1 57
Boar's Head, Ardington 665
Boar's Head, Ripley 448
Boath House, Auldearn 536
Boathouse, Stratford-upon-Avon 475
Bodysgallen Hall, Llandudno 612
Boisdale, London SW1 198
The Bonham, Edinburgh 549
Books for Cooks, London W11 199
Borrowdale Gates Hotel, Grange in Borrowdale 322
Les Bouviers, Merley 684
Bowlish House, Shepton Mallet 464
Box Tree, Ilkley 347
Brackenbury, London W6 58
Bradley's, Huddersfield 342
Bradleys, London NW3 58
Brady's, London SW18 59
Braidwoods, Dalry 545
La Braseria, Swansea 624
The Brasserie, Hawarden 607
Brasserie Forty Four, Leeds 360
Brasserie Four Seven, Sudbury 478
Brasserie St Quentin, London SW3 59
Brazz, Exeter 310
Brazz, Taunton 485
Bridge House, Beaminster 235
Bridgewater Hall, Charles Hallé Restaurant, Manchester 390
Brilliant, Southall 468
Brio, Leeds 681
Brockencote Hall, Chaddesley Corbett 278
Brock's, Padstow 429
Brookdale House, North Huish 685

Brook's, Brighouse 669
Brown's, Worcester 520
Bruce Arms, West Tanfield 504
Bruerne's Lock, Stoke Bruerne 473
Brula, Twickenham 691
Bryan's, Leeds 681
Buckland Manor, Buckland 267
Buffs, Cardiff 698
Burnt Chair, Richmond 445
Burrastow House, Walls 591
Burt's Hotel, Melrose 696
Bu-San, London N7 199
Bushby's Brasserie, Brighton 669
Bush House, Usk 701
Butlers Wharf Chop House, London SE1 199
Butley-Orford Oysterage, Orford 686
But 'n' Ben, Auchmithie 534
Buttery, Glasgow 562
By Appointment, Norwich 686
Cactus Blue, London SW3 60
Le Cadre, London N8 199
Caesar's Arms, Creigiau 698
Café at All Saints, Hereford 679
Café Bleu, Newark 684
Café du Jardin, London WC2 60
Café du Marché, London EC1 199
Café Exchange, Manchester 683
Café Gandolfi, Glasgow 563
Café Ikon, Birmingham 668
Café Japan, London NW11 61
Café Niçoise, Colwyn Bay 601
Café 152, Aldeburgh 665
Café Portugal, London SW8 199
Café Spice Namaste, London E1 and SW11 61
Café St-Honoré, Edinburgh 550
Café 21, Ponteland 438
Café 21, Sunderland 479
Calcot Manor, Tetbury 690
Callow Hall, Ashbourne 224
Cambio de Tercio, London SW5 62
Cameron House, Georgian Room, Alexandria 531
Cantaloupe, London EC2 63
Cantina Vinopolis, London SE1 63
Canyon, Richmond 446
The Capital, London SW3 64
Le Caprice, London SW1 65
Captain's Table, Woodbridge 519
Carlton House, Llanwrtyd Wells 617
Carluccio's Caffè, London W1 200
Carters Knox Manor, Low Laithe 682
Carved Angel, Dartmouth 294
Carved Angel Café, Dartmouth 295
Cassia Oriental, London W1 200
Le Cassoulet, Cardiff 598
Castle, Hurst 345
Castle Cottage, Harlech 606
Castle Hotel, Taunton 486
Castle House, Hereford 334
Castleman Hotel, Chettle 672
Cauldron Bistro, Swanage 689
Le Caveau, Skipton 468
Cavendish Hotel, Baslow 666
Cawdor Arms, Llandeilo 609
Cayenne, Belfast 635
Cellar, Anstruther 532
Cellar, Warwick 498
Chadwick's, Yarm 523
Champany Inn, Linlithgow 575
Le Champignon Sauvage, Cheltenham 281
Chandlers, Lichfield 681
Chapel, London NW1 200
Chapter One, Farnborough 312
Chapters, Stokesley 473
Chapter Two, London SE3 200
Le Chardon, London SE22 65
Charles' Bistro, Thirsk 690
Charlton House, Mulberry Restaurant, Shepton Mallet 465
Chavignol, Chipping Norton 285
Che, London SW1 200
Cheng-du, London NW1 66
Chequers, Gedney Dyke 676
Cherwell Boathouse, Oxford 426
Chester Grosvenor Hotel, Arkle, Chester 283
Chewton Glen, New Milton 418
Chez Bruce, London SW17 66
Chez Gérard, London W1 201
Chez Hans, Cashel 645
Chez Liline, London N4 67
Chez Lindsay, Richmond 446
Chezmax, London SW10 68
Chez Moi, London W11 68
cheznico, London W1 69
Chez Nous, Plymouth 437
Chiang Rai, Manchester 391

China House, Orient, London W1 70
Chinon, London W14 70
Chiswick, London W4 71
Chor Bizarre, London W1 71
La Chouette, Dinton 298
Christopher's, London WC2 72
Chuen Cheng Ku, London W1 201
Chung Ying, Birmingham 240
Churchill Arms, Paxford 434
Chutney Mary, London SW10 72
Cider Press, Drybrook 300
Circus, London W1 73
City Rhodes, London EC4 74
Clarence, Tea Room, Dublin 648
Clarke's, London W8 74
Clifton House, Nairn 578
Cliveden, Waldo's, Taplow 484
Clock, London W7 75
Clos du Roy, Bath 231
Club Gascon, London EC1 75
Clytha Arms, Clytha 601
Cnapan, Newport 619
Cole's, Southwater 469
Le Colombier, London SW3 76
Columbine, Buxton 670
Combe House, Gittisham 319
Comme Ça, Chichester 672
Commons, Dublin 648
Como Lario, London SW1 201
Congham Hall, Grimston 677
The Connaught, London W1 76
Cookhouse, Bromfield 670
Coppull Moor, Coppull Moor 673
Coq d'Argent, London EC2 77
Le Coq Hardi, Dublin 649
Corney & Barrow, London WC2 201
Cornish Range, Mousehole 684
Corse Lawn House, Corse Lawn 291
Cors Restaurant, Laugharne 699
Cotswold House, Chipping Campden 672
Cotto, London W14 78
Country Friends, Dorrington 300
Courtyard, Ludlow 379
Cow Dining Room, London W2 78
Crab & Lobster, Asenby 224
Crannog, Fort William 560
Crawford Gallery Café, Cork 646
The Creel, St Margaret's Hope 584
Creelers, London SW3 79
Creelers Seafood Bistro, Broadford 693
Crinan Hotel, Crinan 694
Cringletie House, Peebles 580
Critchards, Porthleven 439
Criterion Brasserie MPW, London W1 79
Croft's, Frome 676
Cromleach Lodge, Castlebaldwin 645
Cromwellian, Kirkham 356
Crooked Billet, Newton Longville 419
Croque-en-Bouche, Malvern Wells 389
The Cross, Kingussie 574
Crossways, Wilmington 509
Crown and Castle, Trinity, Orford 425
Crown at Whitebrook, Whitebrook 626
Crowne Plaza Midland, French Restaurant, Manchester 391
Crown Hotel, Southwold 470
Crowthers, London SW14 80
Cucina, London NW3 81
Culloden House, Inverness 571
Culter Mill, Biggar 693
Currarevagh House, Oughterard 661
Daffodil, Cheltenham 671
Dakota, London W11 81
Daneswood House, Shipham 467
Daphne, London NW1 201
Daphne's, London SW3 201
Daquise, London SW7 202
Darleys, Derby 298
Darroch Learg, Ballater 538
Dartmoor Inn, Lydford 383
De Courcey's, Cardiff 698
De La Pole Arms, Wingfield 692
Del Buongustaio, London SW15 82
Delfina Studio Café, London SE1 82
Depot, London SW14 83
Design House, Halifax 327
Desport's, Stratford-upon-Avon 476
Devonshire Arms, Burlington Restaurant, Bolton Abbey 245
Devonshire Fell, Burnsall 270
Dew Pond, Old Burghclere 423
Dexter's, Deddington 296
Dicken's, Wethersfield 505

Dining Room, Reigate 444
Ditto, London SW18 83
Diwana Bhel Poori, London NW1 202
Dormy House, Broadway 264
Dove, Dargate 293
The Dower House, Muir of Ord 577
Drewe Arms, Broadhembury 263
Drimcong House, Moycullen 660
Druidstone, Broad Haven 596
Druimard Country House, Dervaig 545
Drum and Monkey, Harrogate 330
Drumnacree House, Alyth 532
Dunain Park, Inverness 571
Dundas Arms, Kintbury 680
Dusty Miller, Low Laithe 378
Dwyers, Waterford 662
Dylanwad Da, Dolgellau 604
Eagle, London EC1 84
East End Arms, East End 303
Eastern Promise, Grampound 677
Eastwell Manor, Boughton Lees 247
Ebury Wine Bar, London SW1 202
L'Ecrivain, Dublin 649
Edenwater House, Ednam 558
Edgwarebury Hotel, Beaufort Restaurant, Elstree 306
Ees Wyke, Near Sawrey 414
Efes Kebab House, London W1 202
Elio's, Barton-upon-Humber 666
El Nido, Forton 676
Endeavour, Staithes 471
English Garden, London SW3 84
Epworth Tap, Epworth 309
L'Escargot, London W1 85
Eslington Villa, Gateshead 318
Esseborne Manor, Hurstbourne Tarrant 346
L'Estaminet, London WC2 86
Euphorium, London N1 86
Eurasia, Glasgow 563
Fairyhill, Reynoldston 623
Faisan Doré (and Pheasants Too), Ross-on-Wye 452
Falcon Inn, Fotheringhay 676
Faraday's, Aberdeen 527
Far East, Liverpool 371
Farlam Hall, Brampton 250
Farleyer House, Aberfeldy 528
Farmgate, Midleton 660
Farsyde, Ilkley 348
Fat Duck, Bray 250
Feathers Hotel, Woodstock 519
Fifth Floor, London SW1 87
Fina Estampa, London SE1 87
Findons, Warwick 499
Fins, Fairlie 560
Firehouse Rôtisserie, Bath 667
Firenze, Kibworth Beauchamp 680
First Floor, London W11 88
Fischer's Baslow Hall, Baslow 229
Fish!, London SE1 88
Fish Central, London EC1 202
Fisherman's Lodge, Newcastle upon Tyne 417
Fishers, Edinburgh 550
Fishers, Oxford 686
Fishes', Burnham Market 268
Fitz Henry, Edinburgh 694
Fleur de Sel, Storrington 474
Floodlite, Masham 403
Fontana, Holywood 637
Food for Thought, Fowey 316
Foresters Arms, Carlton-in-Coverdale 275
Formula Veneta, London SW10 203
La Fourchette, Brighton & Hove 253
Four Seasons, London W2 89
Four Seasons, Nantgaredig 618
Fourth Floor, Leeds 361
Fouters Bistro, Ayr 536
Fox and Goose, Fressingfield 676
Fox and Hounds, Sinnington 688
Fox Inn, Corscombe 291
Fox Inn, Lower Oddington 682
Frederick's, London N1 203
La Frégate, St Peter Port 701
French House Dining Room, London W1 90
French Partridge, Horton 341
Les Frères Jacques, Dublin 650
Frogg Manor, Broxton 670
Froize Inn, Chillesford 672
Fung Shing, London WC2 90
Gales, Llangollen 699
Galley, Exeter 675
Galley, Swanage 482
Le Gallois, Cardiff 598
Gamba, Glasgow 695
The Gamp, Foulsham 316
Garden Café, Haddington 696
Gasche's, Weybourne 691
The Gate, Guildford 678

Gate, London W6 203
Gaudí, London EC1 91
Le Gavroche, London W1 92
Gay Hussar, London W1 92
Gemini, Tadworth 484
General Havelock Inn, Haydon Bridge 333
General Tarleton, Ferrensby 314
George & Dragon, Rowde 452
George Hotel, Yarmouth 523
Georgian House, Kendal 350
Gidleigh Park, Chagford 279
Gifto's Lahore Karahi, Southall 688
Gilbey's, Amersham 665
Gilbeys, London W5 203
Gilby's, Cardiff 599
Gilpin Lodge, Windermere 513
Gingerman, Brighton & Hove 253
Ginger Tree, Ballyclare 633
Glass Boat, Bristol 258
Glass House, Ambleside 220
The Glasshouse, Kew 352
Globe Restaurant, London SE1 93
Golden Dragon, London W1 93
Golden Palace, Harrow 678
The Goose, Britwell Salome 262
Gordon Ramsay, London SW3 94
Gordon's, Inverkeilor 570
Le Gothique, London SW18 203
Gourmet Garden, London NW4 95
Grafton Manor, Bromsgrove 266
Grand Hotel, Mirabelle, Eastbourne 301
Granita, London N1 95
Grapevine, Odiham 686
Gravetye Manor, East Grinstead 303
Great Eastern Dining Room, London EC2 96
Great Eastern Hotel, Aurora, London EC2 96
Great House, Lavenham 360
Great Nepalese, London NW1 203
Greek Valley, London NW8 204
Greenhead House, Sheffield 688
Greenhouse, London W1 97
Green Inn, Ballater 539
Green Man, Gosfield 677
Green Olive, London W9 98
Greens, Manchester 392
Green Street Seafood Café, Bath 231
Gregans Castle, Ballyvaughan 643
Gresslin's, London NW3 98
Greywalls, Gullane 569
Griffin Inn, Fletching 315
Griffin Inn, Llyswen 618
Grosvenor Arms, Hindon 337
Gunfield, Dartmouth 295
Haldanes, Edinburgh 551
Half Door, Dingle 646
Halkin Hotel, London SW1 99
Hallidays, Funtington 317
Hambleton Hall, Hambleton 328
Hamilton's, Doncaster 299
Hamnavoe, Stromness 697
Hanni's, Sale 459
Hanson's, Swansea 625
Harbour Inn, Bowmore 541
Harbour Lights, Porthgain 621
Hare and Hounds, Foss Cross 315
Harveys, Bristol 258
Harris's, Penzance 435
Harrow Inn, Little Bedwyn 682
Harrow Inn, West Ilsley 504
Harry's Place, Great Gonerby 324
Hart's, Nottingham 422
Hartwell House, Aylesbury 226
Harvey's Point, Donegal 647
Hazlewood Castle, Restaurant 1086, Tadcaster 483
Hedgehogs, Kelsale 679
Helter Skelter, London SW9 100
Hexham Royal Hotel, Hexham 336
Hibiscus, Ludlow 379
Highbullen, Chittlehamholt 672
High Moor, Wrightington 692
Hilaire, London SW7 100
Hoebridge Inn, Gattonside 694
Holbeck Ghyll, Windermere 514
Hole in the Wall, Bath 667
Holly, London SE15 101
Homewood Park, Hinton Charterhouse 337
Horn of Plenty, Tavistock 487
Horton Grange, Seaton Burn 462
Hoste Arms, Burnham Market 269
Hotel du Vin & Bistro, Bristol 259
Hotel du Vin & Bistro, Tunbridge Wells 490
Hotel du Vin & Bistro, Winchester 511
Hotel Portmeirion, Portmeirion 621
House, London E14 204

House, London SW3 101
Howard's House, Teffont Evias 488
Howie's, Edinburgh 694
Hundred House Hotel, Norton 420
Hungry Monk, Jevington 350
Hunstrete House, Hunstrete 344
Hunters, New Alresford 416
Hunters, Winchester 511
Hyatt Regency, Number 282, Birmingham 240
Ibla, London W1 102
ICA Café, London SW1 204
Ichi-Riki, London SW1 204
Idaho, London N6 204
Il Forno, London W1 89
Inaho, London W2 205
Incognico, London WC2 103
Inter-Continental, Le Soufflé, London W1 103
Inverlochy Castle, Fort William 561
Island Hotel, Tresco 690
Isle of Eriska, Eriska 559
Isola, London SW1 104
Istanbul Iskembecisi, London N16 105
Itsu, London SW3 105
Ivy, London WC2 106
Ivy House, Braithwaite 249
Iznik, London N5 106
Jack in the Green, Rockbeare 687
Jacob's Ladder, Dublin 650
JaK's, London SW1 107
Jeremy's at Borde Hill, Haywards Heath 333
Jerichos, Windermere 514
Jersey Pottery Restaurant, Gorey 629
Jew's House, Lincoln 367
Joe Allen, London WC2 205
John Burton-Race at the Landmark, London NW1 107
Jolly Sportsman, East Chiltington 302
Junction 28, Bassaleg 594
Juniper, Altrincham 218
Justin de Blank, London SW1 108
K10, London EC2 111
Kalpna, Edinburgh 552
Kastoori, London SW17 109
Kennel Holt Hotel, Cranbrook 292
Kennington Lane, London SE11 109
Kensington Place, London W8 110
Kiku, London W1 110
Kilcamb Lodge, Strontian 587
Killermont Polo Club, Glasgow 695
Killiecrankie Hotel, Killiecrankie 573
Kinfauns Castle, Kinfauns 696
Kinghams, Shere 466
Kings Arms, Amersham 222
Kings Arms, Fernhurst 313
Kings Arms Inn, Stockland 688
King's Cliffe House, King's Cliffe 354
King Sitric, Howth 654
Kinloch House, Blairgowrie 541
Kinnaird, Dunkeld 547
Kirroughtree Hotel, Newton Stewart 579
Knife & Cleaver, Houghton Conquest 679
Knipoch Hotel, Oban 696
Konditor & Cook, London SE1 205
Koreana, Manchester 392
Kosmos Taverna, Manchester 393
Kulu Kulu Sushi, London W1 111
Kwizeen, Blackpool 668
Lacken House, Kilkenny 657
Lahore Kebab House, London E1 205
Lake Country House, Llangammarch Wells 615
Lake Vyrnwy Hotel, Llanwddyn 699
Lamb at Buckland, Buckland 268
L'Amuse, Swansea 700
Landgate Bistro, Rye 453
Lanesborough, The Conservatory, London SW1 112
Langan's Brasserie, London W1 112
Langar Hall, Langar 356
Langley House Hotel, Langley Marsh 359
Langs, Burton on the Wolds 271
Lansdowne, London NW1 113
Lanterna, Scarborough 461
Larchwood House, Bantry 644
Laughing Monk, Strete 476
Launceston Place, London W8 113
Laurent, London NW2 114
Lavender, London SW11 114

L'Aventure, London NW8 197
Leaping Hare Vineyard Restaurant, Stanton 471
Leatherne Bottel, Goring 321
L'Ecrivain, Dublin 649
Leela's, Newcastle upon Tyne 684
Left Bank, Pembroke 620
Leftbank, Birmingham 241
Leith's at Dartmouth House, London W1 206
Lemonia, London NW1 206
The Lemon Tree, Bishop's Stortford 668
Lemon Tree, Oxford 427
Leodis, Leeds 362
L'Escargot, London W1 85
L'Estaminet, London WC2 86
Let's Eat/Let's Eat Again, Perth 581
Lettonie, Bath 232
Lewtrenchard Manor, Lewdown 365
Lighthouse, Aldeburgh 217
Light House, London SW19 115
The Lime Tree, Limavady 638
Lime Tree, Manchester 393
Lincoln, Manchester 394
L'Incontro, London SW1 205
Lindsay House, London W1 116
Linthwaite House, Bowness-on-Windermere 248
Little Barwick House, Barwick 228
Little Georgia, London E8 117
Little Yang Sing, Manchester 394
Livebait, London SE1 117
Livebait's Café Fish, London W1 118
Llwyndu Farmhouse, Llanaber 699
Lobster Pot, Church Bay 698
Lobster Pot, London SE11 118
Lochbay, Stein 585
Loch Fyne, Buxton 671
Loch Fyne Oyster Bar, Cairndow 542
Loch Fyne Oyster Bar, Elton 674
Loch Fyne Restaurant, Twickenham 691
Lochgreen House, Troon 588
Loch Torridon Hotel, Achnasheen 530
L'Odéon, London W1 139
Lodge Hotel, Huddersfield 342
Loft, Blair Atholl 540
Lola's, London N1 119
Lomo, London SW10 119
London Hilton, Windows Rooftop Restaurant, London W1 206
London Marriott, County Hall Restaurant, London SE1 120
Longueville House, Mallow 659
Longueville Manor, St Saviour 631
L'Oranger, London SW1 143
Lords of the Manor, Upper Slaughter 494
Lou Pescadou, London SW5 120
Love Café, London W1 206
Lovetts, Douglas 647
Lower Slaughter Manor, Lower Slaughter 377
Luca, Surbiton 480
Lucknam Park, Colerne 288
Lundum's, London SW7 121
Lux, Glasgow 695
Lygon Arms, Broadway 264
Lynwood House, Barnstaple 666
MacCallums' Oyster Bar, Troon 589
MacNean Bistro, Blacklion 644
Maes-y-Neuadd, Talsarnau 625
Magenta's, Carlisle 274
Magno's, London WC2 206
Magpie Café, Whitby 505
Magpies, Horncastle 340
Maharaja, Birmingham 668
Maison Bleue at Mortimer's, Bury St Edmunds 271
Maison Novelli, London EC1 121
Mallards, Saint Michael's On Wyre 458
Mandalay, London W2 206
Mandarin Kitchen, London W2 122
Mandarin Oriental Hyde Park, Foliage, London SW1 123
Le Manoir aux Quat' Saisons, Great Milton 325
Manor House, Walkington 496
Manor House, Bybrook Restaurant, Castle Combe 277
Manor House Inn, Carterway Heads 276
Mansion House, Poole 438
Mantanah, London SE25 124
Manzi's, London WC2 207

Marco's, Norwich 421
Margot's, Padstow 430
Market Restaurant, Manchester 683
Markwicks, Bristol 260
Marlfield House, Gorey 654
Marquis, London W1 207
Marsh Goose, Moreton-in-Marsh 410
Martins, Edinburgh 552
Martins, Llandudno 612
Mash, London W1 124
Mash, Manchester 395
Matfen Hall, Matfen 404
Matsuri, London SW1 125
Maxine's, Midhurst 408
Mayflower, Cheltenham 282
McClements, Twickenham 491
McCoy's Bistro, Staddlebridge 470
Mediterranean, Sheffield 688
Mela, London WC2 125
Melton's, York 524
Mem Saheb, London E14 126
Merchant House, Ludlow 380
Merchants, Nottingham 422
Mermaid Café, Dublin 651
Mesclun, London N16 126
Metro, Belfast 635
Metrogusto, London SW8 127
Metropolis, Cardiff 698
Metropolitan, Newcastle upon Tyne 418
Mews Bistro, Tenby 700
Mezzanine, London SE1 207
Mezzo, London W1 127
Michael Caines at Royal Clarence, Exeter 311
Michael's Nook, Grasmere 322
Michels, Ripley 448
Middlethorpe Hall, York 525
Midsummer House, Cambridge 273
Mill, Alvechurch 219
Mill at Harvington, Harvington 678
Miller Howe, Windermere 515
Mims, Barnet 227
Mirabelle, London W1 128
Mirch Masala, London SW16 207
Mitchells/Mitchells West End, Glasgow 695
Mitsukoshi, London SW1 207
Miyama, London W1 129
Momo, London W1 208
Monachyle Mhor, Balquhidder 539
Le Monde, Cardiff 698
Mon Plaisir, London WC2 130
Monsieur Max, Hampton Hill 329
Montana, London SW6 130
Montcalm Hotel, Crescent, London W1 131
Moody Goose, Bath 232
Morgan's Brasserie, St David's 624
Moro, London EC1 131
Morston Hall, Morston 411
Mortimer's Seafood Restaurant, Ipswich 349
Moshi Moshi Sushi, London EC2, EC4 and E14 132
Moss Nook, Manchester 396
Moxon's, London SW4 208
Mr Kong, London WC2 129
Mr Underhill's, Ludlow 381
Mulberry House, Torquay 690
Mulberry Tree, Wrightington 693
Mustard and Punch, Honley 339
Nairns, Glasgow 564
Nansloe Manor, Helston 678
Nantyffin Cider Mill Inn, Crickhowell 603
National Gallery, Crivelli's Garden, London WC2 133
National Portrait Gallery, Portrait, London WC2 133
Le Nautique, St Peter Port 701
Neal Street Restaurant, London WC2 134
Neil's, Tavistock 690
The Newbridge, Tredunnock 700
Newbury Manor, Sharlands, Newbury 416
New Emperor, Manchester 396
New End, London NW3 135
New Inn, Coln St Aldwyns 289
Newport House, Newport 661
New Tayyabs, London E1 135
New World, London W1 208
Nick's Warehouse, Belfast 636
Nico Central, London W1 136
Nico Central, Manchester 397
Nicole's, London W1 136
No. 6 Art & Seafood Café, Padstow 430
Noble Rot, London W1 137
Nobody Inn, Doddiscombsleigh 674
Nobu, London W1 137

No 7 Fish Bistro, Torquay 690
Northcote Manor, Burrington 270
Northcote Manor, Langho 358
North Garden, Liverpool 682
North Hill Exchange Brasserie, Colchester 673
Nosh Brothers, London W11 208
Number Sixteen, Glasgow 564
Nutters, Cheesden 280
Oak Room Marco Pierre White, London W1 138
Ocean Treasure, Manchester 397
Odette's, London NW1 139
Offshore, London W11 140
Old Bakehouse, West Linton 697
Old Bank House, Lymington 683
Old Barn, Leverton 365
Old Beams, Waterhouses 500
Old Bell, Malmesbury 388
Old Bridge Hotel, Huntingdon 344
Old Chesil Rectory, Winchester 512
Old Coach House, Barham 666
Old Delhi, London W2 140
Ye Olde Bulls Head, Beaumaris 595
Old Fire Engine House, Ely 307
Old Forge, Storrington 475
Old Hall, Todmorden 490
Old Hoops, Saffron Walden 687
Old House, Wickham 507
Old Manor House, Romsey 451
Old Parsonage Hotel, Parsonage Restaurant & Bar, Oxford 428
The Old Pharmacy, Solva 700
Old Pines, Spean Bridge 585
Old Rectory, Campsea Ashe 274
Old Rectory Country House, Llansanffraid Glan Conwy 616
Old Steam Bakery, Beer 236
Old Trout, Thame 488
Old Vicarage, Ridgeway 447
Old Vicarage, Witherslack 518
Old Vicarage Hotel, Worfield 521
Old Woolhouse, Northleach 685
Olive Branch, Marsden 402
Oliver's 24, Harrogate 678
Olive Tree, Leeds 681
Olivo, London SW1 141
One Devonshire Gardens, Glasgow 565
1 Lombard Street, London EC3 141
192, London W11 142
One-O-One, London SW1 143
One Paston Place, Brighton & Hove 254
On The Edge, Newmillerdam 685
Orestone Manor, Maidencombe 386
Orrery, London W1 144
Orsino, London W11 208
Osteria Antica Bologna, London SW11 145
Ostlers Close, Cupar 544
Overton Grange, Ludlow 382
Oxo Tower, London SE1 145
Oysters, Barton on Sea 666
Ozer, London W1 146
Pacific, Manchester 398
Painswick Hotel, Painswick 433
Palais du Jardin, London WC2 147
Parade, London W5 147
Paris, Leeds 681
Paris House, Woburn 692
Park Hotel Kenmare, Kenmare 656
La Parmigiana, Glasgow 566
P.A.'s, Swansea 700
Passione, London W1 148
Patio, London W12 209
Patrick Guilbaud, Dublin 651
Paul Heathcote's, Longridge 376
Pauls, Folkestone 675
Peacock Alley, Dublin 652
Pearl City, Manchester 683
Peat Inn, Peat Inn 579
Penhelig Arms Hotel, Aberdovey 593
Penmaenuchaf Hall, Penmaenpool 700
Penrhos Court, Kington 355
Peppers, Nantwich 413
Percy's at Coombeshead, Virginstow 495
Perkins, Plumtree 437
Perry's, Weymouth 692
Peter Tavy Inn, Peter Tavy 435
Le Petit Blanc, Birmingham 242
Le Petit Blanc, Cheltenham 282
Le Petit Blanc, Oxford 428
Le Petit Canard, Maiden Newton 683
La Petite Auberge, Great Missenden 326
Le Petit Pierrot, Claygate 287

Pétrus, London SW1 149
Pharmacy Restaurant and Bar, London W11 149
Pheasant Inn, Keyston 353
Philpotts Mezzaluna, London NW2 209
Phoenix, London SW15 150
Pied-à-Terre, London W1 151
The Pier at Harwich, Harwich 330
Pierhouse, Port Appin 583
Pink Geranium, Melbourn 405
Pizzeria Castello, London SE1 209
Planters, Malvern Wells 390
Plas Bodegroes, Pwllheli 622
Plas Dolmelynllyn, Ganllwyd 606
Plockton Inn, Plockton 697
Plough Inn, Saxton 461
Plumber Manor, Sturminster Newton 478
The Poet, London EC3 209
Pomegranates, London SW1 209
Le Pont de la Tour, London SE1 152
Pool Court at 42, Leeds 362
Poons, London W2 210
Poons, London WC2 209
Poons, London WC2 210
Popeseye, London W14 152
Pophams, Winkleigh 516
Porte des Indes, London W1 153
Porthminster Beach Café, St Ives 454
Porthole Eating House, Bowness-on-Windermere 248
Porth Tocyn Hotel, Abersoch 594
Le Poussin at Parkhill, Lyndhurst 385
Priory Bay Hotel, Seaview 687
Priory Hotel, Wareham 497
Prism, London EC3 153
Prospect Grill, London WC2 154
Punch Bowl Inn, Crosthwaite 293
Puppet Theatre, Glasgow 566
Purple Onion, Middlesbrough 406
Purple Sage, London W1 154
Putney Bridge, London SW15 155
Quaglino's, London SW1 210
Quails, Chobham 286
Quality Chop House, London EC1 156
Quartier Vert, Bristol 260
Queensberry Hotel, Olive Tree, Bath 233
Queen's Head, Glanwydden 699
Queens Head, Great Whittington 677
Quentin's, Brighton & Hove 254
Quince & Medlar, Cockermouth 288
Quo Vadis, London W1 156
Radha Krishna Bhavan, London SW17 157
Rafters, Sheffield 463
Ragam, London W1 210
Ramore, Portrush 638
Rampsbeck Hotel, Watermillock 500
Ramsons Restaurant and Café Bar, Ramsbottom 443
Randall & Aubin, London W1 210
Rani, London N3 157
Ransome's Dock, London SW11 158
Rasa/Rasa W1, London N16 and W1 159
Rascasse, Leeds 363
Ravenwood Hall, Bury St Edmunds 670
Read's, Faversham 312
Real Greek, London N1 159
Red House, Marsh Benham 403
Red House, Whitchurch 506
Red Lion Inn, Llanfihangel Nant Melan 614
The Red Lion Inn, Longdon Green 682
Redmond's, London SW14 160
Red Onion Bistro, Sudbury 479
Red Pepper, London W9 161
Regatta, Aldeburgh 218
Renaissance, Bakewell 226
Rendez Vous Provençal, Bath 667
Restaurant Bosquet, Kenilworth 351
Restaurant Elizabeth, Oxford 686
Restaurant Gilmore, Birmingham 242
Restaurant Martel, Gateforth 317
Restaurant Martin Wishart, Edinburgh 553
Restaurant Michael Deane, Belfast 637
Rhodes & Co, Edinburgh 554
Rhodes & Co, Manchester 399
Rhodes in the Square, London SW1 161
Richard's, Llandudno 613

Richmond Arms, Bath 234
Rick's Just for Starters, Harrogate 678
Rick Stein's Café, Padstow 431
Rising Sun, St Mawes 457
Riso, London W4 162
Ritcher's, Wells 502
Ritz, London W1 163
Riva, London SW13 163
River Café, London W6 164
River House, Lympstone 384
River House, Poulton-le-Fylde 441
Riverside, Evershot 675
Riverside, King's Lynn 680
Riverside House, Ashford 225
Riverside Inn, Aymestrey 665
Riverside Inn, Canonbie 693
Riverside Restaurant, West Bay 503
River Station, Bristol 261
R.K. Stanleys, London W1 211
Roade House, Roade 449
Rockingham Arms, Lockington 374
Rococo, Glasgow 695
Rococo, King's Lynn 354
Roebuck, Brimfield 256
Rogano, Glasgow 567
Roly's Bistro, Dublin 652
Rookery Hall, Worleston 521
Rose & Crown, Romaldkirk 450
Röser's, Hastings 331
Rose Street, Wokingham 518
Rosleague Manor, Letterfrack 657
Rosmarino, London NW8 165
Rothay Manor, Ambleside 221
Rouille, Milford On Sea 408
Roussillon, London SW1 165
Royal China, London W1 and W2 166
Royal Crescent, Pimpernel's, Bath 234
Royal Oak, Yattendon 693
Royal Opera House, Amphitheatre Restaurant, London WC2 211
RSJ, London SE1 166
Rules, London WC2 167
Russons, Stratford-upon-Avon 689
Saagar, Nottingham 686
Sabras, London NW10 168
Saga, London W1 211
Saigon Thuy, London SW18 168
St David's Hotel & Spa, Cardiff 600
St James, Bushey 272
St John, London EC1 169
St Martin's on the Isle, St Martin's 456
St Petroc's, Padstow 431
St Tudno Hotel, Llandudno 614
Sala Thong, Buxton 671
Salisbury Tavern, London SW6 169
Salloos, London SW1 170
Salt House, London NW8 171
Salusbury, London NW6 171
Salvo's, Leeds 364
Sanam, Manchester 683
San Carlo, Birmingham 668
Sandgate Hotel, Sandgate 459
Sankey's, Tunbridge Wells 691
Sarkhel's, London SW18 172
Sartoria, London W1 172
Schnecke, London W1 173
Scoretulloch House, Darvel 694
Scott's Brasserie, Ipswich 679
Scutchers Bistro, Long Melford 375
Sea Crest, St Brelade 630
Seafood Restaurant, Padstow 432
Searcy's, London EC2 173
Seaview Hotel, Seaview 687
Sebastians, Oswestry 425
Seeds, Llanfyllin 699
Selasih, London W1 211
September Brasserie, Blackpool 244
78 St Vincent, Glasgow 567
Severnshed, Bristol 262
Shangri La, Liverpool 371
Shanks, Bangor 634
Sharrow Bay, Ullswater 492
Sheedys, Lisdoonvarna 658
Sheekey's, London WC2 174
Sheene Mill, Melbourn 405
Sheen Falls Lodge, La Cascade, Kenmare 656
Shiro, Ahakista 642
Shore, Edinburgh 554
Silver Darling, Aberdeen 527
Simply Heathcotes, Manchester 399
Simply Heathcotes, Preston 442
Simply Nico, London SW1 211
Simply Poussin, Brockenhurst 265
Simpson's, Kenilworth 352

Singapore Garden, London NW6 175
Singers, Tadcaster 483
Sir Charles Napier, Chinnor 284
60 Hope Street, Liverpool 372
62 Restaurant & Theatre Bar, London SE1 212
Skippers, Edinburgh 555
Smith's of Sheffield, Sheffield 463
The Smithy, Little Eccleston 682
Snows on the Green, London W6 175
Soanes Restaurant, Petworth 436
Sofra, London WC2 212
Soho Soho, London W1 176
Soho Spice, London W1 176
Sol, Shrewsbury 467
Sonny's, London SW13 177
Sonny's, Nottingham 423
Sotheby's Café, London W1 212
Soufflé, Maidstone 387
Sous le Nez en Ville, Leeds 364
Soviet Canteen, London SW10 177
Spencers, Emsworth 307
Spice Box, Boston Spa 246
Spiga, London W1 178
La Spighetta, London W1 212
Splinters, Christchurch 286
Sportsman's Arms, Wath-in-Nidderdale 501
Spread Eagle, London SE10 178
Spread Eagle, Sawley 460
The Square, London W1 179
Sri Siam Soho, London W1 180
Stafford Hotel, London SW1 212
Stagg Inn, Titley 489
Star Inn, Harome 329
Star Inn, Lidgate 366
Star of India, London SW5 213
Stephen Bull, London W1 180
Steven Saunders at the Lowry, Manchester 400
Stile, Willington 692
Stock, Manchester 684
Stock Hill House, Gillingham 319
Stone Hall, Welsh Hook 701
Stour Bay Café, Manningtree 402
Strattons, Swaffham 481
Stravaigin, Glasgow 568
Strawberry Tree, Milton Ernest 409
Sugar Club, London W1 181
Suma's, Gorey 629
Summer Isles Hotel, Achiltibuie 529
Summer Lodge, Evershot 310
Sundial, Herstmonceux 335
Sushi-Say, London NW2 182
Swallow Hotel, Sir Edward Elgar, Birmingham 243
The Swan, Lavenham 680
Sycamore House, Little Shelford 369
Symposium, Bradford 669
Tabb's, Portreath 440
Tai Pan, Liverpool 372
Tai Pan, Manchester 400
Tajine, London W1 182
Le Talbooth, Dedham 296
The Talbot, Knightwick 680
Tamarind, London W1 183
La Tante Claire, London SW1 183
Tan-y-Foel, Capel Garmon 597
Tas, London SE1 184
Tate Gallery Restaurant, London SW1 185
Tate Modern, London SE1 213
Tatsuso, London EC2 213
Taychreggan, Kilchrenan 572
Tbilisi, London N7 213
Teatro, London W1 185
Teca, London W1 186
Ten, London EC2 213
Tentazioni, London SE1 187
Terrace, London W8 187
Terre à Terre, Brighton & Hove 255
Thai Bistro, London W4 214
Thai Garden, London E2 188
Thatched Cottage, Brockenhurst 670
Theobalds, Ixworth 349
36 on the Quay, Emsworth 308
Thornton's, Dublin 653
Thorpe Grange Manor, Huddersfield 343
Three Acres Inn, Roydhouse 687
Three Chimneys, Colbost 543
Three Choirs Restaurant, Newent 684
Three Crowns, Brinkworth 669
Three Hares, Bilbrough 667
Three Horseshoes, Madingley 386
Three Lions, Stuckton 477
Three Main Street, Fishguard 605
3 Monkeys, London SE24 214
Tico Tico, Bristol 669

Tigh an Eilean, Shieldaig 697
Time, London SE10 188
Tir-a-Môr, Criccieth 602
Titanic, London W1 189
Tokyo Diner, London WC2 214
Tolbooth, Stonehaven 586
Tollgate Inn, Holt 338
La Toque, Beeston 236
Tot Hill House, Stowmarket 689
Tower Restaurant, Edinburgh 555
Trawlers, Looe 377
Tregain, Portloe 440
Tregildry Hotel, Gillan 676
Tregynon Farmhouse, Pontfaen 620
Trengilly Wartha Inn, Constantine 673
Tresanton Hotel, St Mawes 458
Trout, Tadpole Bridge 689
Truffles, Bruton 266
Turnberry Hotel, Turnberry 697
Turner's, London SW3 189
Tuscan Square, Edinburgh 556
Two Brothers, London N3 190
Two Fat Ladies, Glasgow 695
TW1, Twickenham 491
2 Quail, Dornoch 546
22 Chesterton Road, Cambridge 273
22 Mill Street, Chagford 280
Tyddyn Llan, Llandrillo 611
Ty'n Rhos, Llanddeiniolen 609
Ubiquitous Chip, Glasgow 568
Underscar Manor, Applethwaite 222
Uplands, Cartmel 277
Utah, London SW19 191
The Vale, London W9 214
Valvona & Crolla Caffè Bar, Edinburgh 556
Vama – The Indian Room, London SW10 214
Vasco & Piero's Pavilion, London W1 214
Venture In, Ombersley 424
Village Bakery, Melmerby 684
Village Bistro, London N6 215
Villandry, London W1 191
Vine House, Paulerspury 434
Vineyard at Stockcross, Stockcross 472
Vintners Rooms, Edinburgh 557
Vrisaki, London N22 215
Wagamama, London WC1 192
Wallett's Court, St Margaret's At Cliffe 456
Walnut Tree Inn, Llandewi Skirrid 610
Waltzing Weasel, Birch Vale 238
Warehouse Brasserie, Colchester 673
Waterdine, Llanfair Waterdine 373
Waterford House, Middleham 406
Waterloo Bar and Kitchen, London SE1 192
Waterside Inn, Bray 251
Weavers, Haworth 332
Weavers Shed, Golcar 320
Weaver's Wine Bar, Diss 674
Wednesdays, Beverley 237
Welcome to Town, Llanrhidian 616
Well House, St Keyne 455
Wellington Inn, Lund 382
Well View, Moffat 576
Wesley House, Winchcombe 510
West Arms, Llanarmon Dyffryn Ceiriog 608
West House, Biddenden 237
West Port, St Andrews 583
Wheatsheaf, Beetham 667
Wheatsheaf, Swinton 587
White Cottage, Aboyne 529
White Hart, Great Yeldham 326
White Hart, Lydgate 384
White Hart, Nayland 414
White Horse Hotel, Blakeney 245
White House, Oxford 429
White House, Prestbury 441
White House, Williton 508
White Moss House, Grasmere 323
White Onion, London N1 193
Whitstable Oyster Fishery Co, Whitstable 507
Whytes, Brighton & Hove 256
Wife of Bath, Wye 522
Wig & Mitre, Lincoln 368
Wildebeest Arms, Stoke Holy Cross 689
Wild Mushroom, Westfield 691
William IV, London NW10 194
Willowburn Hotel, Clachan-seil 543
Wilsons, London W14 194
Wiltons, London SW1 195
Windmill, Burgh Le Marsh 670
Wine Bar, Bishop's Waltham 244

Winter Glen, Edinburgh 557
Winteringham Fields, Winteringham 516
Wiz, London W11 215
The Wizard, Nether Alderley 415
Wodka, London W8 215
The Wolfe, Wolf's Castle 627
Wood Hall, Linton 369
Woodhayes, Whimple 692
Woodhouse Inn, Corby Glen 674
Woods, Bath 667
Woods Brasserie, Cardiff 600
Worsley Arms, Hovingham 679
Wye Knot, Chepstow 698
Wykeham Arms, Winchester 512
Yang Sing, Manchester 401
Y Bistro, Llanberis 608
Ye Olde Bulls Head, Beaumaris 595
Yetman's, Holt 338
Yew Tree Inn, Clifford's Mesne 672
Ynyshir Hall, Eglwysfach 604
Yorke Arms, Ramsgill 443
Yoshino, London W1 215
Zafferano, London SW1 195
Zaika, London SW3 196
Zen Central, London W1 216
Zen Chelsea, London SW3 216
Ziba, Liverpool 373
Zinc Bar & Grill, London W1 216

Report Form 2001

To the Editor *The Good Food Guide*
FREEPOST, 2 Marylebone Road, London NW1 4DF

Or send your report by electronic mail to: *guidereports@which.co.uk*

From my personal experience the following establishment should/should not be included in the *Guide* (please print in BLOCK CAPITALS):

____

____

Telephone__________________

I had lunch/dinner/stayed there on (date) ______________ 00___

I would rate this establishment ____ out of ten.

please continue overleaf

My meal for ____ people cost £ ______________ *attach bill where possible*

☐ Please tick if you would like more report forms

Reports received up to the end of **May 2001** will be used in the research of the 2002 edition.

I am not connected in any way with management or proprietors, and have not been asked by them to write to the *Guide*.
Name and address (BLOCK CAPITALS, please)

____

____

Signed ______________________________________

As a result of your sending us this report form, we may send you information on **The Good Food Guide** and **The Which? Hotel Guide** in the future. If you would prefer not to receive such information, please tick this box [ ].

Report Form 2001

To the Editor *The Good Food Guide*
FREEPOST, 2 Marylebone Road, London NW1 4DF

Or send your report by electronic mail to: *guidereports@which.co.uk*

From my personal experience the following establishment should/should not be included in the *Guide* (please print in BLOCK CAPITALS):

____

____

Telephone________________

I had lunch/dinner/stayed there on (date) ____________ 00___

I would rate this establishment _____ out of ten.

please continue overleaf

My meal for ____ people cost £ ______________ *attach bill where possible*

☐ Please tick if you would like more report forms

Reports received up to the end of **May 2001** will be used in the research of the 2002 edition.

I am not connected in any way with management or proprietors, and have not been asked by them to write to the *Guide*.
Name and address (BLOCK CAPITALS, please)

____

____

Signed ____

As a result of your sending us this report form, we may send you information on **The Good Food Guide** and **The Which? Hotel Guide** in the future. If you would prefer not to receive such information, please tick this box [ ].

Report Form 2001

To the Editor *The Good Food Guide*
FREEPOST, 2 Marylebone Road, London NW1 4DF

Or send your report by electronic mail to: *guidereports@which.co.uk*

From my personal experience the following establishment should/should not be included in the *Guide* (please print in BLOCK CAPITALS):

____

____

Telephone__________________

I had lunch/dinner/stayed there on (date) _______________ 00___

I would rate this establishment _____ out of ten.

please continue overleaf

My meal for ____ people cost £ ______________ *attach bill where possible*

☐ Please tick if you would like more report forms

Reports received up to the end of **May 2001** will be used in the research of the 2002 edition.

I am not connected in any way with management or proprietors, and have not been asked by them to write to the *Guide*.
Name and address (BLOCK CAPITALS, please)

____

____

Signed ______________________________________

As a result of your sending us this report form, we may send you information on **The Good Food Guide** and **The Which? Hotel Guide** in the future. If you would prefer not to receive such information, please tick this box [ ].